ECONOMICS

Eighteenth Edition

PAUL A. SAMUELSON

Institute Professor Emeritus
Massachusetts Institute of Technology

WILLIAM D. NORDHAUS

Sterling Professor of Economics
Yale University

Tata McGraw-Hill Publishing Company Limited

NEW DELHI

McGraw-Hill Offices

New Delhi New York St Louis San Francisco Auckland Bogotá Caracas
Kuala Lumpur Lisbon London Madrid Mexico City Milan Montreal
San Juan Santiago Singapore Sydney Tokyo Toronto

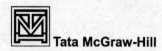
Tata McGraw-Hill

ECONOMICS

Tata McGraw-Hill Edition

Tenth reprint 2008
RYZDRRAXDRLLL

Reprinted in India by arrangement with The McGraw-Hill Companies, Inc., New York

Sales territories: India, Pakistan, Nepal, Bangladesh, Sri Lanka and Bhutan

Library of Congress Cataloging-in-Publication Data

Samuelson, Paul Anthony, 1915-
  Economics / Paul A Samuelson, William D. Nordhaus.—18th ed.
      p.   cm.
  Includes index.
  ISBN 0-07-287205-5 (alk. paper)
  1. Economics. I. Nordhaus, William D.   II. Title.
HB171.5.S25 2005
330—dc22   2004048113

ISBN-13: 978-0-07-059855-3
ISBN-10: 0-07-059855-X

Published by Tata McGraw-Hill Publishing Company Limited,
7 West Patel Nagar, New Delhi 110 008, and printed at
Pashupati Printers Pvt. Ltd., Delhi 110 095

PAUL A. SAMUELSON, founder of the renowned MIT graduate department of economics, was trained at the University of Chicago and Harvard. His many scientific writings brought him world fame at a young age, and in 1970 he was the first American to receive a Nobel Prize in economics. One of those rare scientists who can communicate with the lay public, Professor Samuelson wrote an economics column for *Newsweek* for many years and was economic adviser to President John F. Kennedy. He testifies often before Congress and serves as academic consultant to the Federal Reserve, the U.S. Treasury, and various private, nonprofit organizations. Professor Samuelson, between researches at MIT and tennis games, is a visiting professor at New York University. His six children (including triplet boys) have contributed 15 grandchildren.

WILLIAM D. NORDHAUS is one of America's eminent economists. Born in Albuquerque, New Mexico, he was an undergraduate at Yale, received his Ph.D. in economics at MIT, and is now Sterling Professor of Economics at Yale University and on the staff of the Cowles Foundation for Research in Economics and the National Bureau of Economic Research. His economic research has spanned a wide variety of topics—including the environment, price measurement, energy, technological change, economic growth, and trends in profits and productivity. In addition, Professor Nordhaus takes a keen interest in economic policy. He served as a member of President Carter's Council of Economic Advisers from 1977 to 1979, serves on many government advisory boards and committees, and writes occasionally for *The New York Times* and other periodicals. He regularly teaches the Principles of Economics course at Yale. Professor Nordhaus lives in New Haven, Connecticut, with his wife, Barbara, and his golden retriever, Pandora. Two of them share enthusiasms for music, hiking, travel, and skiing.

To Franco Modigliani and James Tobin,
colleagues and dear friends,
economic pioneers,
champions of equity

Contents in Brief

Preface   xvii
Economics and the Internet   xxiii

Contents

PART TWO
MICROECONOMICS: SUPPLY, DEMAND, AND PRODUCT MARKETS
63

PART FOUR
**APPLIED MICROECONOMICS:
INTERNATIONAL TRADE, GOVERNMENT,
AND THE ENVIRONMENT**
291

PART SIX
GROWTH, DEVELOPMENT, AND
THE GLOBAL ECONOMY
553

PART SEVEN
UNEMPLOYMENT, INFLATION, AND
ECONOMIC POLICY
643

Preface

The twentieth century witnessed a spectacular change in the living standards of most of the world, particularly those in the affluent countries of North America, Western Europe, and East Asia. People are asking, Will the twenty-first century repeat the successes of the last century? Will the affluence of the few spread to the many in poor countries? Or will the horsemen of the apocalypse—famine, war, and disease—continue to grip Africa and perhaps even spread more widely? To a large extent, the answers to these questions depend mainly on the economic successes of countries—in education, in investment, in foreign trade, and in health care.

The Growing Role of Markets

Over the past quarter-century, both attitudes and economic institutions have changed dramatically. Dozens of countries have rejected socialist and collectivist approaches and adopted market systems. Strong economic growth has been experienced in countries as diverse as Ireland, Botswana, and the Philippines. At no time in recorded history have so many enjoyed such a sustained period of economic growth as they have during the past half-century.

You might think that prosperity would lead to a declining interest in economic affairs, but paradoxically an understanding of the enduring truths of economics has become even more vital in the affairs of people and nations. The United States grappled with slow growth in living standards; yet over the last decade productivity growth has rebounded so sharply that the nation has combined rapid output growth with declining employment.

In the larger scene, the world has become increasingly interconnected as computers and communications create an ever-more-competitive global marketplace. Developing countries like China, India, and Russia—three giants that relied heavily on central planning until recently—need a firm understanding of the institutions of a market economy if they are to attain the living standards of the affluent. At the same time, there is growing concern about international environmental problems and the need to forge agreements to preserve our precious natural heritage. All these fascinating changes are part of the modern drama that we call economics.

ECONOMICS Reborn

For more than half a century, this book has served as the standard-bearer for the teaching of introductory economics in classrooms in America and throughout the world. Each new edition distills the best thinking of economists about how markets function and about what society can do to improve people's living standards. But economics has changed profoundly since the first edition of this text appeared in 1948. And because economics is above all a living and evolving organism, *Economics* is born anew each edition as the authors have the exciting opportunity to present the latest thinking of modern economists and to show how the subject can contribute to a more prosperous world.

Our task then is this: We want to present a clear, accurate, and interesting introduction to the principles of modern economics and to the institutions of the American and world economies. Our primary goal is to survey economics, and in doing this we emphasize the basic economic principles that will endure beyond today's headlines.

THE EIGHTEENTH EDITION

Economics is a dynamic science—changing to reflect the shifting trends in economic affairs, in the environment, in the world economy, and in society at large. As economics and the world around it evolve, so does this book. These seven features differentiate this edition from other books:

1. The Core Truths of Economics. Often, economics appears to be an endless procession of new puzzles, problems, and dilemmas. But as experienced teachers have learned, there are a few basic concepts that underpin all of economics. Once these basic concepts have been mastered, learning is much quicker and more enjoyable. *We have therefore chosen to focus on the central core of economics—on those enduring truths that will be just as important in the twenty-first century as they were in the twentieth.* Microeconomic concepts such as scarcity, efficiency, the gains from specialization, and the principle of comparative advantage will be crucial concepts as long as scarcity itself exists. Moreover, students of macroeconomics must receive a firm grounding in the concepts of aggregate supply and demand and must understand the role of national and international monies. Students will learn the widely accepted theory of economic growth, but they should also understand the controversial theories of the business cycle.

2. Innovation in Economics. Economics has made many advances in understanding the role of innovation. We are accustomed to the dizzying speed of invention in computers, where new products and software appear monthly. The Internet is revolutionizing communications and making inroads into commerce.

In addition, we emphasize innovations in economics itself. Economists are tinkerers, innovators, and inventors in their own way. History shows that economic ideas can produce tidal waves when they are applied to real-world problems. Among the important innovations we survey is the application of economics to our environmental problems through "emissions trading" plans. Other important economic innovations discussed are improved regulatory mechanisms and the radical new step of European monetary unification. One of the most influential economic innovations of the last few years involves the measurement of consumer prices. We explain how behavioral economics has changed views of consumer theory. Network economics is explained, and we describe how it affects economic efficiency and market power and how it has entered into the debate about how to deal with Microsoft's monopolistic behavior. One of the most important innovations for our common future is dealing with global public goods like climate change, and we analyze new ways to deal with international environmental problems, including approaches such as the Kyoto Protocol.

3. Small Is Beautiful. Economics has increased its scope greatly over the past half-century. The flag of economics flies over its traditional territory of the marketplace, but it also covers the environment, legal studies, statistical and historical methods, art, gender and racial discrimination, and even family life. But at its core, economics is the science of choice, which means that we, as authors, must choose the most important and enduring issues for this text. In a survey, as in a meal, small is beautiful because it is digestible.

Choosing the subjects for this text required many hard choices. To select these topics, we continually survey teachers and leading scholars to determine the issues most crucial for an informed citizenry and a new generation of economists. We drew up a list of key ideas and bid adieu to material we judged inessential or dated. *At every stage, we asked whether the material was, as best we could judge, necessary for a student's understanding of the economics of the twenty-first century.* Only when a subject passed this test was it included. The result of this campaign is a book that has lost more than one-quarter of its weight in the last few editions. Farm economics, labor unions, Marxian economics, the lump-of-labor fallacy, and health economics have been trimmed to make room for environmental economics, network economics, real business cycles, and financial economics.

4. Policy Issues for the New Century. For many students, the lure of economics is its relevance to public policy. The eighteenth edition emphasizes policy in both microeconomics and macroeconomics. As human societies grow, they begin to overwhelm the environment and ecosystems of the natural world. Environmental economics, presented in Chapter 18, helps students understand the externalities associated with economic activity and then analyzes different approaches to making human economies compatible with natural systems. New examples—such as dividend tax reform, the minimum wage, international outsourcing, the value of a brand, as well as problems of financial finagling—bring the core principles of microeconomics to life.

A second area of central importance is financial and monetary economics. We have completely reorganized our treatment of monetary economics by introducing a new chapter, "Financial Markets and the Special Case of Money." This chapter places monetary economics in the larger context of finance and, along with the chapter on central banking, explores the critical role that money plays in the business cycle.

Drawing upon history, economic chronicles, and the authors' experience, the eighteenth edition continues the use of case studies and empirical evidence to illustrate economic theories. The dilemmas involved in combating poverty hit home when we understand the 1996 welfare reforms. The need for economic approaches to the environment is illustrated by the dilemma of global warming. Our appreciation of macroeconomic analysis increases when we see how government deficits lower national saving.

5. Debates about Globalization. The last decade has witnessed pitched battles over the role of international trade in our economies. Some argue that the decline in American manufacturing employment comes because jobs are exported to Mexico and China, although a careful analysis of job trends questions this assessment. Whatever the causes, the United States was definitely faced with the puzzle of rapid output growth and a decline in employment in the early 2000s.

One of the major debates of recent years has been over "globalization," which concerns the increasing economic integration of different countries. Americans have learned that no country is an economic island. Immigration and international trade have profound effects on the goods that are available, the prices we pay, and the wages we earn. Terrorism can wreck havoc on the economy at home, while war causes famines and reduces living standards in Africa. No one can fully understand the impact of growing trade and capital flows without a careful study of the theory of comparative advantage. The eighteenth edition continues to increase the material devoted to international economics and the interaction between international trade and domestic economic events.

6. The Contending Schools of Macroeconomics. One of the major obstacles to understanding modern economics is the proliferation of contesting schools of macroeconomics. Teachers often wonder how students can understand the subject when macroeconomists themselves are so divided. While many people fret about the divisiveness of modern macroeconomics, we think it is a sign of health and prefer lively debate to complacent consensus.

The eighteenth edition analyzes all major schools of modern macroeconomics within the clear organizing synthesis of aggregate supply and demand. We show how macroeconomics of the Keynesian, old and new classical, real-business cycle, and monetarist varieties can be understood as emphasizing different aspects of expectations, market clearing, and aggregate demand. Each school is clearly presented and compared with its competitors in a balanced and evenhanded way. For each, the empirical evidence is

presented and evaluated. The major schools are discussed in Chapter 33, "The Warring Schools of Macroeconomics." We also emphasize the importance of the *policy implications* of the different approaches.

Economists are increasingly examining the determinants of long-run economic growth, the recent rebound in productivity growth, and the generation of innovation and new technological knowledge. Putting economic growth front and center is necessary if students are to understand modern debates about the role of government debt and deficits. The eighteenth edition reflects this revival by synthesizing growth theories and findings into the central section on macroeconomics.

7. Clarity. Although there are many new features in the eighteenth edition, the pole star for our pilgrimage in preparing this edition has been to present economics clearly and simply. Students enter the classroom with a wide range of backgrounds and with many preconceptions about how the world works. Our task is not to change students' values. Rather, we strive to help students understand enduring economic principles so that they may better be able to apply them—to make the world a better place for themselves, their families, and their communities. Nothing aids understanding better than clear, simple exposition. We have labored over every page to improve this survey of introductory economics. We have received thousands of comments and suggestions from teachers and students and have incorporated their counsel in the eighteenth edition.

Optional Matter

Economics courses range from one-quarter surveys to year-long intensive honors courses. This textbook has been carefully designed to meet all situations. The more advanced materials have been put in separate sections and chapters. These will appeal to curious students and to students in demanding courses that survey the entire discipline thoroughly. We have included advanced questions for discussion to test the mettle of the most dedicated student.

If yours is a fast-paced course, you will appreciate the careful layering of the more advanced material. Hard-pressed courses can skip the advanced sections, covering the core of economic analysis without losing the thread of the economic reasoning. This book will challenge the most advanced young scholar. Indeed, many of today's leading economists have written to say they've relied upon *Economics* all along their pilgrimage to the Ph.D.

Format

The eighteenth edition employs an expanded set of in-text logos, and material to help illustrate the central topics. You will find three distinctive logos, indicating warnings for the fledgling economist, examples of economics in action, and biographical material on the great economists of the past and present. But these central topics are not drifting off by themselves in unattached boxes. Rather, they are integrated right into the chapter so that students can read them without breaking their train of thought. Keep these logos in mind as you read through the text:

 is a warning that students should pause to ensure that they understand a difficult or subtle point.

 is an interesting example or application of the analysis, and often it represents one of the major innovations of modern economics.

 presents biographies of important economic figures. Sometimes these are famous economists like Adam Smith, while at other times they are people who introduced economics into public policy.

New features in this edition include fresh end-of-chapter questions, with a special accent upon short problems that reinforce the major concepts surveyed in the chapter.

Terms printed in **bold type** in the text mark the first occurrence and definition of the most important words that constitute the language of economics.

But these many changes have not altered one bit the central stylistic beacon that has guided *Economics* since the first edition: to use simple sentences, clear explanations, and concise tables and graphs.

For Those Who Prefer Macro First

Although, like the previous edition, this new edition has been designed to cover microeconomics first, many teachers continue to prefer beginning with macroeconomics. Many believe that the beginning student finds macro more approachable and will more quickly develop a keen interest in economics when the issues of macroeconomics are encountered first. We have taught economics in both sequences and find both sequences work well.

Whatever your philosophy, this text has been carefully designed for it. Instructors who deal with microeconomics first can move straight through the chapters. Those who wish to tackle macroeconomics first should skip from Part One directly to Part Five, knowing that the exposition and cross-references have been tailored with their needs in mind.

In addition, for those courses that do not cover the entire subject, the eighteenth edition is available in two paperback volumes, *Microeconomics* (Chapters 1 to 19 of the full text) and *Macroeconomics* (Chapters 1 to 3 and 20 to 34 of the full text).

Auxiliary Teaching and Study Aids

Students of this edition will benefit greatly from the *Study Guide*. This carefully designed supplement was prepared by Gary Lemon of Depauw University, who worked in close collaboration with us in our revision. When used alongside classroom discussions and when employed independently for self-study, the *Study Guide* has proved to be an impressive success. There is a full-text *Study Guide*, as well as micro and macro versions. The *Study Guides* are available electronically for online purchase or packaged with the text via code-card access.

In addition, instructors will find both the *Instructor's Resource Manual* and the *Test Bank* useful for planning their courses and preparing multiple sets of test questions in both print and computerized formats. Moreover, McGraw-Hill/Irwin has designed a beautiful set of two-color overhead transparencies for presenting the tabular and graphical material in the classroom. The graphs and figures in this edition can also be viewed electronically as PowerPoint slides. The slides can be downloaded from our website (www. mhhe.com/economics/samuelson18). The website also contains chapter summaries, self-grading practice quizzes, Web questions, and links to the websites suggested for further research at the end of each chapter.

Economics in the Computer Age

The electronic age has revolutionized the way that scholars and students can access information. In economics, the information revolution allows us quick access to economic statistics and research. An important feature of the eighteenth edition is the section "Economics and the Internet," which appears just before Chapter 1. This little section provides a road map for the state of economics on the Information Superhighway.

In addition, each chapter has an updated section at the end with suggestions for further reading and addresses of websites that can be used to deepen student understanding or find data and case studies.

Students can also purchase *The Power of Macroeconomics* and *The Power of Microeconomics*, which contain lessons directly tied to this text. These programs are lively combinations of PowerPoints with audio and are designed to reinforce economics concepts. They allow students to move at their own pace, and they engage students with questions during the presentation. *The Power of Macroeconomics* and *The Power of Microeconomics* were developed by Peter Navarro at the University of California at Irvine, Graduate School of Management. A complete description of this supplement can be found at www.powerofeconomics.com.

Acknowledgments

This book has two authors but a multitude of collaborators. We are profoundly grateful to colleagues, reviewers, students, and McGraw-Hill's staff for contributing to the timely completion of the eighteenth edition of *Economics*. Colleagues at MIT, Yale, and elsewhere who graciously contributed their comments and suggestions include William C. Brainard, E. Cary Brown, John Geanakoplos, Robert J. Gordon, Lyle Gramely, Paul Joskow, Alfred Kahn, Richard Levin, Robert Litan, Barry Nalebuff, Merton J. Peck, Gustav Ranis, Herbert Scarf, Robert M. Solow, James Tobin, Janet Yellen, and Gary Yohe.

In addition, we have benefited from the tireless devotion of those whose experience in teaching elementary economics is embodied in this edition. We are particularly grateful to the reviewers of the eighteenth edition. They include:

Mohammad Akacem, *University of Colorado, Denver*
Mohua Das, *Centre College*
George Euskirchen, *Thomas More College*
Adam Forest, *Seattle University*
Satyajit Ghosh, *University of Scranton*
Aroop Mahanty, *University of Maryland*
Donald Milley, *Youngstown State University*
Ibrahim Oweiss, *Georgetown University*
Dennis Petruska, *Youngstown State University*
Edward Scahill, *University of Scranton*

Students at MIT, Yale, and other colleges and universities have served as an "invisible college." They constantly challenge and test us, helping to make this edition less imperfect than its predecessor. Although they are too numerous to enumerate, their influence is woven through every chapter. Nancy King helped in logistics at the New Haven end of the operation.

This project would have been impossible without the skilled team from McGraw-Hill who nurtured the book at every stage. We particularly would like to thank, in chronological order to their appearance on the scene, Executive Editor Lucille Sutton, Developmental Editor Karen Minnich, Editorial Assistant Becca Hicks, Project Manager Susanne Riedell, Production Manager Becky Szura, and Marketing Manager Marty Quinn. This group of skilled professionals turned a pile of diskettes and a mountain of paper into a finely polished work of art.

A WORD TO THE SOVEREIGN STUDENT

You have read in the history books of revolutions that shake civilizations to their roots—religious conflicts, wars for political liberation, struggles against colonialism and imperialism. A decade ago, economic revolutions in Eastern Europe, in the former Soviet Union, in China, and elsewhere tore those societies apart. Young people battered down walls, overthrew established authority, and agitated for democracy and a market economy because of discontent with their centralized socialist governments.

Students like yourselves are marching, and even going to jail, to win the right to study radical ideas and learn from Western textbooks like this one in the hope that they may enjoy the freedom and economic prosperity of democratic market economies.

The Intellectual Marketplace

Just what is the market that students in repressed societies are agitating for? In the pages that follow, you will learn about the markets for stocks and bonds, Mexican pesos and European Euros, unskilled labor and highly trained neurosurgeons. You have probably read in the newspaper about the gross domestic product, the consumer price index, the stock market, and the unemployment rate. After you have completed a thorough study of the chapters in this textbook, you will know precisely what these words mean. Even more important, you will also understand the economic forces that influence and determine them.

There is also a marketplace of ideas, where contending schools of economists fashion their theories and try to persuade their scientific peers. You will find in the chapters that follow a fair and impartial review of the thinking of the intellectual giants of our profession—from the early economists like Adam Smith, David Ricardo, and Karl Marx to modern-day titans like John Maynard Keynes, Milton Friedman, and James Tobin.

Skoal!

As you begin your journey into the land of markets, it would be understandable if you are anxious. But take heart. The fact is that we envy you, the beginning student, as you set out to explore the exciting world of economics for the first time. This is a thrill that, alas, you can experience only once in a lifetime. So, as you embark, we wish you bon voyage!

Paul A. Samuelson
William D. Nordhaus

For the Student: Economics and the Internet

The Information Age is revolutionizing our lives. Its impact on scholars and students has been particularly profound because it allows inexpensive and rapid access to vast quantities of information. The Internet, which is a huge and growing public network of linked computers and information, is changing the way we study, shop, share our culture, and communicate with our friends and family.

In economics, the Internet allows us quick access to economics statistics and research. With just a few clicks of a mouse, we can find out about the most recent unemployment rate, track down information on poverty and incomes, or investigate the intricacies of our banking system. A few years ago, it might have taken weeks to dig out the data necessary to analyze an economic problem. Today, with a computer and a little practice, that same task can be done in a few minutes.

This book is not a manual for driving on the Information Superhighway. That skill can be learned in classes on the subject or from informal tutorials. Rather, we want to provide a road map that shows the locations of major sources of economic data and research. With this map and some rudimentary navigational skills, you can explore the various sites and find a rich array of data, information, studies, and chat rooms. Additionally, at the end of each chapter there is a list of useful websites that can be used to follow up the major themes of that chapter.

Note that some of these sites may be free, some may require a registration or be available through your college or university, and others may require paying a fee. Pricing practices change rapidly, so while we have attempted to include primarily free sites, we have not excluded high-quality sites that may charge a fee.

Data and Institutions

The Internet is an indispensable source of useful data and other information. Since most economic data are provided by governments, the first place to look is the Web pages of government agencies and international organizations. The starting point for U.S. government statistics, www.fedstats.gov, provides one-stop shopping for federal statistics with links to over 70 government agencies that produce statistical information. Sources are organized by subject or by agency, and the contents are fully searchable. Another good launching site into the federal statistical system is the Economic Statistics Briefing Room at www.whitehouse.gov/fsbr/esbr.html. Additionally, the Commerce Department operates a huge database at www.stat-usa.gov, but use of parts of this database requires a subscription (which may be available at your college or university).

The best single statistical source for data on the United States is the *Statistical Abstract of the United States*, published annually. It is available online at www.census.gov/statab/www. If you want an overview of the U.S. economy, you can read the *Economic Report of the President* at www.gpoaccess.gov/eop/index.html.

Most of the major economic data are produced by specialized agencies. One place to find general data is the Department of Commerce, which encompasses the Bureau of Economic Analysis (BEA) (www.bea.gov) and the Census Bureau (www.census.gov). The BEA site includes all data and articles published in the *Survey of Current Business*, including the national income and product accounts, international trade and investment flows, output by industry, economic growth, personal income and labor series, and regional data.

The Census Bureau site goes well beyond a nose count of the population. It also includes the economic census as well as information on housing, income and poverty, government finance, agriculture, foreign trade, construction, manufacturing, transportation, and retail and wholesale trade. In addition to making Census Bureau publications available, the site allows users to create custom extracts of popular microdata sources including the Survey of Income and Program Participation, Consumer Expenditure Survey, Current Population Survey, American Housing Survey, and, of course, the most recent census.

The Bureau of Labor Statistics (at www.bls.gov) provides easy access to commonly requested labor data, including employment and unemployment, prices and living conditions, compensation, productivity, and technology. Also available are labor-force data from the Current Population Survey and payroll statistics from the Current Employment Statistics Survey.

A useful source for financial data is the website of the Federal Reserve Board at www.federalreserve.gov. This site provides historical U.S. economic and financial data, including daily interest rates, monetary and business indicators, exchange rates, balance-of-payments data, and price indexes. In addition, the Office of Management and Budget at www.gpo.gov/usbudget/index.html makes available the federal budget and related documents.

International statistics are often harder to find. The World Bank at www.worldbank.org has information on its programs and publications at its site, as does the International Monetary Fund, or IMF, at www.imf.org. The United Nations website (www. unsystem.org) is slow and confusing but has links to most international institutions and their databases. A good source of information about high-income countries is the Organisation for Economic Cooperation and Development, or OECD, at www.oecd.org. The OECD's website contains an array of data on economics, education, health, science and technology, agriculture, energy, public management, and other topics.

Economic Research and Journalism

The Internet is rapidly becoming the world's library. Newspapers, magazines, and scholarly publications are increasingly posting their writing in electronic form. Most of these present what is already available in the paper publications. Some interesting sources can be found at the *Economist* at www.economist.com and the *Financial Times* (www.ft.com). The *Wall Street Journal* at www.wsj.com is currently expensive and not a cost-effective resource. Current policy issues are discussed at www.policy.com. The online magazine *Slate* at www.slate.com occasionally contains excellent essays on economics.

For scholarly writings, many journals are making their contents available online. WebEc at www.helsinki.fi/WebEc/ contains a listing of websites for many economic journals. The archives of many journals are available at www.jstor.org.

There are now a few websites that bring many resources together at one location. One place to start is

Resources for Economists on the Internet, sponsored by the American Economic Association and edited by Bill Goffe, at www.rfe.org. Also see *WWW Resources in Economics*, which has links to many different branches of economics at netec.wustl.edu/WebEc/WebEc.html. For working papers, the National Bureau of Economic Research (NBER) website at www.nber.org contains current economic research. The NBER site also contains general resources, including links to data sources and the official U.S. business-cycle dates.

An excellent site that archives and serves as a depository for working papers is located at econwpa.wustl.edu/wpawelcome.html. This site is particularly useful for finding background material for research papers.

Did someone tell you that economics is the dismal science? You can chuckle over economist jokes (mostly at the expense of economists) at netec.mcc.ac.uk/JokEc.html.

A Word of Warning

Note that, because of rapid technological change, this list will soon be out of date. New sites with valuable information and data are appearing every day . . . and others are disappearing almost as rapidly.

Before you set off into the wonderful world of the Web, we would pass on to you some wisdom from experts. Remember the old adage: You only get what you pay for:

Warning: Be careful to determine that your sources and data are reliable. The Internet and other electronic media are easy to use and equally easy to abuse.

The Web is the closest thing in economics to a free lunch. But you must select your items carefully to ensure that they are palatable and digestible.

Basic Concepts

CHAPTER

1

The Fundamentals of Economics

The Age of Chivalry is gone; that of sophisters, economists, and calculators has succeeded.

Edmund Burke

As you begin your studies, you are probably wondering, Why study economics? In fact, people do it for a number of reasons.

Many study economics because they hope to make money.

Some people worry that they will be considered illiterate if they cannot understand the laws of supply and demand.

Others are interested in learning about how computers and the information revolution are shaping our society or why inequality in the distribution of income in the United States has risen so sharply in recent years.

For Whom the Bell Tolls

All these reasons, and many more, make good sense. Still, as we have come to realize, there is one overriding reason for learning the basic lessons of economics: All your life—from cradle to grave and beyond—you will run up against the brutal truths of economics. As a voter, you will make decisions on issues that cannot be understood until you have mastered the rudiments of this subject. Without studying economics, you cannot be fully informed about international trade, the economic impact of the Internet, or the tradeoff between inflation and unemployment.

Choosing your life's occupation is the most important economic decision you will make. Your future depends not only on your own abilities but also on how economic forces beyond your control affect your wages. Also, your knowledge of economics may help you invest the nest egg you save from your earnings. Of course, studying economics cannot make you a genius. But without economics the dice of life are loaded against you.

There is no need to belabor the point. We hope you will find that, in addition to being useful, economics is a fascinating field in its own right. Generations of students, often to their surprise, have discovered how stimulating economics can be.

SCARCITY AND EFFICIENCY: THE TWIN THEMES OF ECONOMICS

What is economics? Over the last half-century, the study of economics has expanded to include a vast range of topics. What are the major definitions of

3

these growing subjects?[1] The important ones are that economics:

- Explores the behavior of the financial markets, including interest rates and stock prices.
- Examines the reasons why some people or countries have high incomes while others are poor and suggests ways that incomes of the poor can be raised without harming the economy.
- Studies business cycles—the ups and downs of unemployment and inflation—along with policies to moderate them.
- Studies international trade and finance and the impacts of globalization.
- Looks at growth in developing countries and proposes ways to encourage the efficient use of resources.
- Asks how government policies can be used to pursue important goals such as rapid economic growth, efficient use of resources, full employment, price stability, and a fair distribution of income.

This list is a good one, yet you could extend it many times over. But if we boil down all these definitions, we find one common theme:

Economics is the study of how societies use scarce resources to produce valuable commodities and distribute them among different people.

Behind this definition are two key ideas in economics: that goods are scarce and that society must use its resources efficiently. Indeed, economics is an important subject because of the fact of scarcity and the desire for efficiency.

Consider a world without scarcity. If infinite quantities of every good could be produced or if human desires were fully satisfied, what would be the consequences? People would not worry about stretching out their limited incomes because they could have everything they wanted; businesses would not need to fret over the cost of labor or health care;

---

[1] This list contains several specialized terms from economics. To master the subject, you will need to understand its vocabulary. If you are not familiar with a particular word or phrase, you should consult the Glossary at the back of this book. The Glossary contains most of the major technical economic terms used in this book. All terms printed in boldface are defined in the Glossary.

governments would not need to struggle over taxes or spending or pollution because nobody would care. Moreover, since all of us could have as much as we pleased, no one would be concerned about the distribution of incomes among different people or classes.

In such an Eden of affluence, all goods would be free, like sand in the desert or seawater at the beach. All prices would be zero, and markets would be unnecessary. Indeed, economics would no longer be a useful subject.

But no society has reached a utopia of limitless possibilities. Ours is a world of **scarcity,** full of **economic goods.** A situation of scarcity is one in which goods are limited relative to desires. An objective observer would have to agree that, even after two centuries of rapid economic growth, production in the United States is simply not high enough to meet everyone's desires. If you add up all the wants, you quickly find that there are simply not enough goods and services to satisfy even a small fraction of everyone's consumption desires. Our national output would have to be many times larger before the average American could live at the level of the average doctor or major-league baseball player. Moreover, outside the United States, particularly in Africa, hundreds of millions of people suffer from hunger and material deprivation.

Given unlimited wants, it is important that an economy make the best use of its limited resources. That brings us to the critical notion of efficiency. **Efficiency** denotes the most effective use of a society's resources in satisfying people's wants and needs. By contrast, consider an economy with unchecked monopolies or unhealthy pollution or government corruption. Such an economy may produce less than would be possible without these factors, or it may produce a distorted bundle of goods that leaves consumers worse off than they otherwise could be—either situation is an inefficient allocation of resources.

In economics, we say that an economy is producing efficiently when it cannot make anyone economically better off without making someone else worse off.

The essence of economics is to acknowledge the reality of scarcity and then figure out how to organize society in a way which produces the most efficient use of resources. That is where economics makes its unique contribution.

Microeconomics and Macroeconomics

Adam Smith is usually considered the founder of the field of **microeconomics,** the branch of economics which today is concerned with the behavior of individual entities such as markets, firms, and households. In *The Wealth of Nations* (1776), Smith considered how individual prices are set, studied the determination of prices of land, labor, and capital, and inquired into the strengths and weaknesses of the market mechanism. Most important, he identified the remarkable efficiency properties of markets and saw that economic benefit comes from the self-interested actions of individuals. These remain important issues today, and while the study of microeconomics has surely advanced greatly since Smith's day, he is still cited by politicians and economists alike.

The other major branch of our subject is **macroeconomics,** which is concerned with the overall performance of the economy. Macroeconomics did not even exist in its modern form until 1936, when John Maynard Keynes published his revolutionary *General Theory of Employment, Interest and Money*. At the time, England and the United States were still stuck in the Great Depression of the 1930s, with over one-quarter of the American labor force unemployed. In his new theory Keynes developed an analysis of what causes business cycles, with alternating spells of high unemployment and high inflation. Today, macroeconomics examines a wide variety of areas, such as how total investment and consumption are determined, how central banks manage money and interest rates, what causes international financial crises, and why some nations grow rapidly while others stagnate. Although macroeconomics has progressed far since his first insights, the issues addressed by Keynes still define the study of macroeconomics today.

The two branches—microeconomics and macroeconomics—converge to form the core of modern economics.

THE LOGIC OF ECONOMICS

Economic life is an enormously complicated hive of activity, with people buying, selling, bargaining, investing, and persuading. The ultimate purpose of economic science and of this text is to understand this complex undertaking. How do economists go about their task?

Economists use the *scientific approach* to understand economic life. This involves observing economic affairs and drawing upon statistics and the historical record. For complex phenomena like the impacts of budget deficits or the causes of inflation, historical research has provided a rich mine of insights.

Often, economics relies upon analyses and theories. Theoretical approaches allow economists to make broad generalizations, such as those concerning the advantages of international trade and specialization or the disadvantages of tariffs and quotas.

In addition, economists have developed a specialized technique known as *econometrics*, which applies the tools of statistics to economic problems. Using econometrics, economists can sift through mountains of data to extract simple relationships.

Budding economists must also be alert to common fallacies in economic reasoning. Because economic relationships are often complex, involving many different variables, it is easy to become confused about the exact reason behind events or the impact of policies on the economy. The following are some of the common fallacies encountered in economic reasoning:

- *The post hoc fallacy*. The first fallacy involves the inference of causality. *The post hoc fallacy occurs when we assume that, because one event occurred before another event, the first event caused the second event.*[2] An example of this syndrome occurred in the Great Depression of the 1930s in the United States. Some people had observed that periods of business expansion were preceded or accompanied by rising prices. From this, they concluded that the appropriate remedy for depression was to raise wages and prices. This idea led to a host of legislation and regulations to prop up wages and prices in an inefficient manner. Did these measures promote economic recovery? Almost surely not. Indeed, they probably slowed recovery, which did not occur until total spending began to

---

[2] "Post hoc" is shorthand for *post hoc, ergo propter hoc*. Translated from the Latin, the full expression means "after this, therefore necessarily because of this."

rise as the government increased military spending in preparation for World War II.

• *Failure to hold other things constant.* A second pitfall is failure to hold other things constant when thinking about an issue. For example, we might want to know whether raising tax rates will raise or lower tax revenues. Some people have put forth the seductive argument that we can eat our fiscal cake and have it too. They argue that cutting tax rates will at the same time raise government revenues and lower the budget deficit. They point to the Kennedy-Johnson tax cuts of 1964, which lowered tax rates sharply and were followed by an increase in government revenues in 1965. Hence, they argue, lower tax rates produce higher revenues.

What is wrong with this reasoning? This argument overlooks the fact that the economy grew from 1964 to 1965. Because people's incomes grew during that period, government revenues also grew, even though tax rates were lower. Careful studies indicate that revenues would have been even higher in 1965 had tax rates not been lowered in 1964. Hence, this analysis fails to hold other things (namely, total incomes) constant.

Remember to hold other things constant when you are analyzing the impact of a variable on the economic system.

• *The fallacy of composition.* Sometimes we assume that what holds true for part of a system also holds true for the whole. In economics, however, we often find that the whole is different from the sum of the parts. *When you assume that what is true for the part is also true for the whole, you are committing the fallacy of composition.*

Here are some true statements that might surprise you if you ignored the fallacy of composition: (1) If one farmer has a bumper crop, she has a higher income; if all farmers produce a record crop, farm incomes will fall. (2) If one person receives a great deal more money, that person will be better off; if everyone receives a great deal more money, the society is likely to be worse off. (3) If a high tariff is put on the product of a particular industry, the producers in that industry are likely to profit; if high tariffs are put on all industries, most producers and consumers will be worse off.

These examples contain no tricks or magic. Rather, they are the results of systems of interacting individuals. Often the behavior of the aggregate looks very different from the behavior of individual people.

We mention these fallacies only briefly in this introduction. Later, as we introduce the tools of economics, we will provide examples of how inattention to the logic of economics can lead to false and sometimes costly errors. When you reach the end of this book, you can look back to see why each of these paradoxical examples is true.

COOL HEADS AT THE SERVICE OF WARM HEARTS

Economics has, over the last century, grown from a tiny acorn into a mighty oak. Under its spreading branches we find explanations of the gains from international trade, advice on how to reduce unemployment and inflation, formulas for investing your retirement funds, and even proposals for selling the rights to pollute. Throughout the world, economists are laboring to collect data and improve our understanding of economic trends.

You might well ask, What is the purpose of this army of economists measuring, analyzing, and calculating? *The ultimate goal of economic science is to improve the living conditions of people in their everyday lives.* Increasing the gross domestic product is not just a numbers game. Higher incomes mean good food, warm houses, and hot water. They mean safe drinking water and inoculations against the perennial plagues of humanity.

Higher incomes produce more than food and shelter. High-income countries have the resources to build schools so that young people can learn to read and develop the skills necessary to use modern machinery and computers. As incomes rise further, nations can afford scientific research to determine agricultural techniques appropriate for a country's climate and soils or to develop vaccines against local diseases. With the resources freed up by economic growth, people have free time for artistic pursuits, such as poetry and music, and the population has the leisure time to read, to listen, and to perform. Although there is no single pattern of economic development, and cultures differ around the world, freedom from hunger, disease, and the elements is a universal human goal.

But centuries of human history also show that warm hearts alone will not feed the hungry or heal the sick. A free and efficient market will not necessarily produce a distribution of income that is socially acceptable. Determining the best route to economic progress or an equitable distribution of society's output requires cool heads, ones that objectively weigh the costs and benefits of different approaches, trying as hard as humanly possible to keep the analysis free from the taint of wishful thinking. Sometimes, economic progress will require shutting down an outmoded factory. Sometimes, as when the formerly socialist countries adopted market principles, things get worse before they get better. Choices are particularly difficult in the field of health care, where limited resources literally involve life and death.

You may have heard the saying, "From each according to his ability, to each according to his need." Governments have learned that no society can long operate solely on this utopian principle. To maintain a healthy economy, governments must preserve incentives for people to work and to save. Societies can support the unemployed for a while, but when unemployment insurance covers too much for too long, people come to depend upon the government and stop looking for work. If they begin to believe that the government owes them a living, this may dull the sharp edge of enterprise. Just because government programs derive from lofty purposes does not mean that they should be pursued without care and efficiency.

Society must find the right balance between the discipline of the market and the compassion of government social programs. By using cool heads to inform our warm hearts, economic science can do its part in ensuring a prosperous and just society.

B. THE THREE PROBLEMS OF ECONOMIC ORGANIZATION

Every human society—whether it is an advanced industrial nation, a centrally planned economy, or an isolated tribal nation—must confront and resolve three fundamental economic problems. Every society must have a way of determining *what* commodities are produced, *how* these goods are made, and *for whom* they are produced.

Indeed, these three fundamental questions of economic organization—*what, how,* and *for whom*—are as crucial today as they were at the dawn of human civilization. Let's look more closely at them:

- *What* commodities are produced and in what quantities? A society must determine how much of each of the many possible goods and services it will make and when they will be produced. Will we produce pizzas or shirts today? A few high-quality shirts or many cheap shirts? Will we use scarce resources to produce many consumption goods (like pizzas)? Or will we produce fewer consumption goods and more investment goods (like pizza-making machines), which will boost production and consumption tomorrow?
- *How* are goods produced? A society must determine who will do the production, with what resources, and what production techniques they will use. Who farms and who teaches? Is electricity generated from oil, from coal, or from the sun? Will factories be run by people or robots?
- *For whom* are goods produced? Who gets to eat the fruit of economic activity? Is the distribution of income and wealth fair and equitable? How is the national product divided among different households? Are many people poor and a few rich? Do high incomes go to teachers or athletes or autoworkers or venture capitalists? Will society provide minimal consumption to the poor, or must people work if they are to eat?

Positive Economics versus Normative Economics

In thinking about economic questions, we must distinguish questions of fact from questions of fairness. Positive economics describes the facts of an economy, while normative economics involves value judgments.

Positive economics deals with questions such as: Why do doctors earn more than janitors? Does free trade raise or lower the wages of most Americans? What is the impact of computers on productivity? Although these are difficult questions to answer, they can all be resolved by reference to analysis and empirical evidence. That puts them in the realm of positive economics.

Normative economics involves ethical precepts and norms of fairness. Should poor people be required to work if they are to get government assistance? Should unemployment be raised to ensure that price inflation does not become too rapid? Should the United States break up Microsoft because it has violated the antitrust laws? There are no right or wrong answers to these questions because they involve ethics and values rather than facts. They can be resolved only by political debate and decisions, not by economic analysis alone.

MARKET, COMMAND, AND MIXED ECONOMIES

What are the different ways that a society can answer the questions of *what, how,* and *for whom?* Different societies are organized through *alternative economic systems,* and economics studies the various mechanisms that a society can use to allocate its scarce resources.

We generally distinguish two fundamentally different ways of organizing an economy. At one extreme, government makes most economic decisions, with those on top of the hierarchy giving economic commands to those further down the ladder. At the other extreme, decisions are made in markets, where individuals or enterprises voluntarily agree to exchange goods and services, usually through payments of money. Let's briefly examine each of these two forms of economic organization.

In the United States, and increasingly around the world, most economic questions are settled by the market mechanism. Hence their economic systems are called market economies. A **market economy** is one in which individuals and private firms make the major decisions about production and consumption. A system of prices, of markets, of profits and losses, of incentives and rewards determines *what, how,* and *for whom.* Firms produce the commodities that yield the highest profits (the *what*) by the techniques of production that are least costly (the *how*). Consumption is determined by individuals' decisions about how to spend the wages and property incomes generated by their labor and property ownership (the *for whom*). The extreme case of a market economy, in which the

government keeps its hands off economic decisions, is called a **laissez-faire** economy.

By contrast, a **command economy** is one in which the government makes all important decisions about production and distribution. In a command economy, such as the one which operated in the Soviet Union during most of the twentieth century, the government owns most of the means of production (land and capital); it also owns and directs the operations of enterprises in most industries; it is the employer of most workers and tells them how to do their jobs; and it decides how the output of the society is to be divided among different goods and services. In short, in a command economy, the government answers the major economic questions through its ownership of resources and its power to enforce decisions.

No contemporary society falls completely into either of these polar categories. Rather, all societies are **mixed economies,** with elements of market and command. There has never been a 100 percent market economy (although nineteenth-century England came close).

Today most decisions in the United States are made in the marketplace. But the government plays an important role in overseeing the functioning of the market; governments pass laws that regulate economic life, produce educational and police services, and control pollution. Most societies today operate mixed economies.

C. SOCIETY'S TECHNOLOGICAL POSSIBILITIES

Every gun that is made, every warship launched, every rocket fired signifies, in the final sense, a theft from those who hunger and are not fed.

President Dwight D. Eisenhower

Each economy has a stock of limited resources—labor, technical knowledge, factories and tools, land, energy. In deciding *what* and *how* things should be produced, the economy is in reality deciding how to allocate its resources among the thousands of different possible commodities and services. How much land will go into growing wheat? Or into housing the population? How many factories will produce computers? How many will make pizzas? How many children will grow up to play professional sports or to be professional economists or to program computers?

Faced with the undeniable fact that goods are scarce relative to wants, an economy must decide how to cope with limited resources. It must choose among different potential bundles of goods (the *what*), select from different techniques of production (the *how*), and decide in the end who will consume the goods (the *for whom*).

INPUTS AND OUTPUTS

To answer these three questions, every society must make choices about the economy's inputs and outputs. **Inputs** are commodities or services that are used to produce goods and services. An economy uses its existing *technology* to combine inputs to produce outputs. **Outputs** are the various useful goods or services that result from the production process and are either consumed or employed in further production. Consider the "production" of pizza. We say that the eggs, flour, heat, pizza oven, and chef's skilled labor are the inputs. The tasty pizza is the output. In education, the inputs are the time of the faculty, the laboratories and classrooms, the textbooks, and so on, while the outputs are informed, productive, and well-paid citizens.

Another term for inputs is **factors of production.** These can be classified into three broad categories: land, labor, and capital.

- *Land*—or, more generally, natural resources—represents the gift of nature to our productive processes. It consists of the land used for farming or for underpinning houses, factories, and roads; the energy resources that fuel our cars and heat our homes; and the nonenergy resources like copper and iron ore and sand. In today's congested world, we must broaden the scope of natural resources to include our environmental resources, such as clean air and drinkable water.

- *Labor* consists of the human time spent in production—working in automobile factories, tilling the land, teaching school, or baking pizzas. Thousands of occupations and tasks, at all skill levels, are performed by labor. It is at once the

most familiar and the most crucial input for an advanced industrial economy.

- *Capital* resources form the durable goods of an economy, produced in order to produce yet other goods. Capital goods include machines, roads, computers, hammers, trucks, steel mills, automobiles, washing machines, and buildings. As we will see later, the accumulation of specialized capital goods is essential to the task of economic development.

Restating the three economic problems in terms of inputs and outputs, a society must decide (1) *what* outputs to produce, and in what quantity; (2) *how* to produce them—that is, by what techniques inputs should be combined to produce the desired outputs; and (3) *for whom* the outputs should be produced and distributed.

THE PRODUCTION-POSSIBILITY FRONTIER

Countries cannot have unlimited amounts of all goods. They are limited by the resources and the technologies available to them. The need to choose among limited opportunities is dramatized during wartime. In debating whether the United States should go to war in Iraq, people wanted to know how much the war would cost. Would the war effort divert $50 billion, or $100 billion, or even more from the civilian economy to occupying and rebuilding Iraq? And, as the numbers began to climb, people naturally asked, Why are we policing Baghdad rather than New York, or repairing the electrical system in the Middle East rather than in the U.S. Midwest? As the quotation above from President Eisenhower indicates, the more output that goes for military tasks, the less there is available for civilian consumption and investment.

Let us dramatize this choice by considering an economy which produces only two economic goods, guns and butter. The guns, of course, represent military spending, and the butter stands for civilian spending. Suppose that our economy decides to throw all its energy into producing the civilian good, butter. There is a maximum amount of butter that can be produced per year. The maximal amount of butter depends on the quantity and quality of the economy's resources and the productive efficiency with which they are used. Suppose 5 million pounds

Alternative Production Possibilities		
Possibilities	Butter (millions of pounds)	Guns (thousands)
A	0	15
B	1	14
C	2	12
D	3	9
E	4	5
F	5	0

TABLE 1-1. Limitation of Scarce Resources Implies the Guns-Butter Tradeoff

Scarce inputs and technology imply that the production of guns and butter is limited. As we go from A to B . . . to F, we are transferring labor, machines, and land from the gun industry to butter and can thereby increase butter production.

These are two extreme possibilities. In between are many others. If we are willing to give up some butter, we can have some guns. If we are willing to give up still more butter, we can have still more guns.

A schedule of possibilities is given in Table 1-1. Combination F shows the extreme, where all butter and no guns are produced, while A depicts the opposite extreme, where all resources go into guns. In between—at E, D, C, and B—increasing amounts of butter are given up in return for more guns.

How, you might well ask, can a nation turn butter into guns? Butter is transformed into guns not physically but by the alchemy of diverting the economy's resources from one use to the other.

We can represent our economy's production possibilities more vividly in the diagram shown in Figure 1-1. This diagram measures butter along the horizontal axis and guns along the vertical one. (If

FIGURE 1-1. The Production Possibilities in a Graph

This figure displays the alternative combinations of production pairs from Table 1-1.

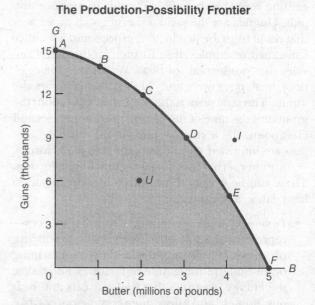

FIGURE 1-2. A Smooth Curve Connects the Plotted Points of the Numerical Production Possibilities

This frontier shows the schedule along which society can choose to substitute guns for butter. It assumes a given state of technology and a given quantity of inputs. Points outside the frontier (such as point *I*) are infeasible or unattainable. Any point inside the curve, such as *U*, indicates that the economy has not attained productive efficiency, as is the case, for instance, when unemployment is high during severe business cycles.

of butter is the maximum amount that can be produced with the existing technology and resources.

At the other extreme, imagine that all resources are instead devoted to the production of guns. Again, because of resource limitations, the economy can produce only a limited quantity of guns. For this example, assume that the economy can produce 15,000 guns of a certain kind if no butter is produced.

you are unsure about the different kinds of graphs or about how to turn a table into a graph, consult the appendix to this chapter.) We plot point *F* in Figure 1-1 from the data in Table 1-1 by counting over 5 butter units to the right on the horizontal axis and going up 0 gun units on the vertical axis; similarly, *E* is obtained by going 4 butter units to the right and going up 5 gun units; and finally, we get *A* by going over 0 butter units and up 15 gun units.

If we fill in all intermediate positions with new rust-colored points representing all the different combinations of guns and butter, we have the continuous rust curve shown as the *production-possibility frontier,* or *PPF,* in Figure 1-2.

The **production-possibility frontier** (or *PPF*) shows the maximum amounts of production that can be obtained by an economy, given its technological knowledge and quantity of inputs available. The *PPF* represents the menu of goods and services available to society.

Putting the PPF to Work

The *PPF* in Figure 1-2 was drawn for guns and butter, but this concept can be applied to a broad range of situations. Thus the more resources the government uses to build public goods like highways, the less will be left to produce private goods like houses; the more we choose to consume of food, the less we can consume of clothing; the more society decides to consume today, the less can be its production of capital goods to turn out more consumption goods in the future.

The graphs in Figures 1-3 to 1-5 present some important applications of *PPF*s. Figure 1-3 shows the effect of economic growth on a country's production possibilities. An increase in inputs, or improved technological knowledge, enables a country to produce more of all goods and services, thus shifting out the *PPF.* The figure also illustrates that poor countries must devote most of their resources to food production while rich countries can afford more luxuries as productive potential increases.

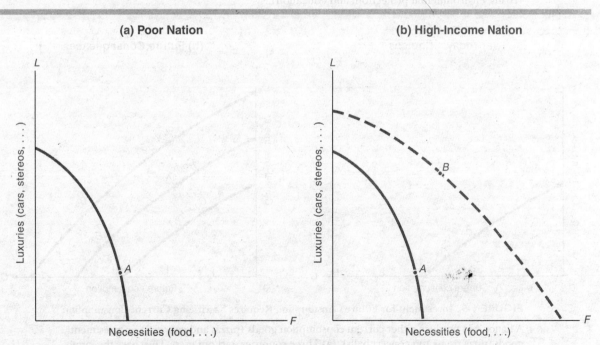

(a) Poor Nation **(b) High-Income Nation**

FIGURE 1-3. Economic Growth Shifts the *PPF* Outward

(a) Before development, the nation is poor. It must devote almost all its resources to food and enjoys few comforts. **(b)** Growth of inputs and technological change shift out the *PPF.* With economic growth, a nation moves from *A* to *B,* expanding its food consumption little compared with its increased consumption of luxuries. It can increase its consumption of both goods if it desires.

FIGURE 1-4. Economies Must Choose between Public Goods and Private Goods

(a) A poor frontier society lives from hand to mouth, with little left over for public goods like highways or public health. **(b)** A modern urbanized economy is more prosperous and chooses to spend more of its higher income on public goods and government services (roads, environmental protection, and education).

FIGURE 1-5. Investment for Future Consumption Requires Sacrificing Current Consumption

A nation can produce either current-consumption goods (pizzas and concerts) or investment goods (pizza ovens and concert halls). **(a)** Three countries start out even. They have the same *PPF*, shown in the panel on the left, but they have different investment rates. Country 1 does not invest for the future and remains at A_1 (merely replacing machines). Country 2 abstains modestly from consumption and invests at A_2. Country 3 sacrifices a great deal of current consumption and invests heavily. **(b)** In the following years, countries that invest more heavily forge ahead. Thus thrifty Country 3 has shifted its *PPF* far out, while Country 1's *PPF* has not moved at all. Countries that invest heavily have higher investment and consumption in the future.

Figure 1-4 depicts the choice between private goods (bought at a price) and public goods (paid for by taxes). Poor countries can afford little of public goods like public health and higher education. But with economic growth, public goods as well as environmental quality take a larger share of output.

Figure 1-5 portrays an economy's choice between (*a*) current-consumption goods and (*b*) investment or capital goods (machines, factories, etc.). By sacrificing current consumption and producing more capital goods, a nation's economy can grow more rapidly, making possible more of *both* goods (consumption and capital) in the future.

The Tradeoff of Time

The production-possibility frontier can also illustrate nonmarket tradeoffs that we meet in daily life. One of the most important decisions that people confront is how to use their time. People have limited time available to pursue different activities. For example, as a student, you might have 10 hours to study for upcoming tests in both economics and history. If you study only history, you will get a high grade there and do poorly in economics, and vice versa. Treating the grades on the two tests as the "output" of your studying, sketch out the *PPF* for grades, given your limited time resources. Alternatively, if the two student commodities are "grades" and "fun," how would you draw this *PPF*? Where are you on this frontier? Where are your lazy friends?

Opportunity Costs

Life is full of choices. Because resources are scarce, we must always consider how to spend our limited incomes or time. When you decide whether to study economics, buy a car, or go to college, in each case you must consider how much the decision will cost in terms of forgone opportunities. The cost of the forgone alternative is the *opportunity cost* of the decision.

The concept of opportunity cost can be illustrated using the *PPF*. Examine the frontier in Figure 1-2, which shows the tradeoff between guns and butter. Suppose the country decides to increase its

gun purchases from 9000 guns at *D* to 12,000 units at *C*. What is the opportunity cost of this decision? You might calculate the cost in dollar terms. But in economics we always need to "pierce the veil" of money to examine the *real* impacts of alternative decisions. On the most fundamental level, the opportunity cost of moving from *D* to *C* is the butter that must be given up to produce the extra guns. In this example, the opportunity cost of the 3000 extra guns is 1 million pounds of butter forgone.

Or consider the real-world example of the cost of opening a gold mine near Yellowstone National Park. The developer argues that the mine will have but a small cost because Yellowstone's revenues will hardly be affected. But an economist would answer that the dollar receipts are too narrow a measure of cost. We should ask whether the unique and precious qualities of Yellowstone might be degraded if a gold mine were to operate, with the accompanying noise, water and air pollution, and decline in amenity values for visitors. While the dollar cost might be small, the opportunity cost in lost wilderness values might be large indeed.

In a world of scarcity, choosing one thing means giving up something else. The **opportunity cost** of a decision is the value of the good or service forgone.

Efficiency

All of our explanations up to now have implicitly assumed that the economy is producing efficiently—that is, it is on, rather than inside, the production-possibility frontier. Remember that efficiency means that the economy's resources are being used as effectively as possible to satisfy people's needs and desires. One important aspect of overall economic efficiency is productive efficiency.

Productive efficiency occurs when an economy cannot produce more of one good without producing less of another good; this implies that the economy is on its production-possibility frontier.

Let's see why productive efficiency requires being on the *PPF*. Start in the situation shown by point *D* in Figure 1-2. Say the market calls for another million pounds of butter. If we ignored the constraint shown by the *PPF*, we might think it possible to produce more butter without reducing gun production, say, by moving to point *I*, to the right of point *D*. But point *I* is outside the frontier, in the "infeasible" region. Starting from *D*, we cannot get more butter without giving up some guns. Hence point *D* displays productive efficiency, while point *I* is infeasible.

One further point about productive efficiency can be illustrated using the *PPF*: Being on the *PPF* means that producing more of one good inevitably requires sacrificing other goods. When we produce more guns, we are substituting guns for butter. *Substitution* is the law of life in a full-employment economy, and the production-possibility frontier depicts the menu of society's choices.

Unemployed Resources and Inefficiency. Even casual observers of modern life know that society has unemployed resources in the form of idle workers, idle factories, and idled land. When there are unemployed resources, the economy is not on its production-possibility frontier at all but, rather, somewhere *inside* it. In Figure 1-2, point *U* represents a point inside the *PPF*; at *U*, society is producing only 2 units of butter and 6 units of guns. Some resources are unemployed, and by putting them to work, we can increase our output of all goods; the economy can move from *U* to *D*, producing more butter and more guns, thus improving the economy's efficiency. We can have our guns and eat more butter too.

One source of inefficiency occurs during business cycles. From 1929 to 1933, in the Great Depression, the total output produced in the United States declined by almost 25 percent. This occurred not because the *PPF* shifted in but because various shocks reduced spending and pushed the economy inside its *PPF*. Then the buildup for World War II expanded demand, and output grew rapidly as the economy pushed back to the *PPF*. Similar situations arise during business-cycle recessions. When total output in the U.S. economy declined in 1982 or in 1991—or when the Japanese economy stagnated in the 1990s—the economy's underlying productivity had not suddenly declined during those years. Rather, frictions and declining overall spending pushed the economy temporarily inside its *PPF* for those periods.

Business-cycle depressions are not the only reason why an economy might be inside its *PPF*. One of the most dramatic declines in production occurred during the early 1990s after countries threw off their socialist planning systems and adopted free markets. Because of the disruptions to organizations and production patterns, output fell and unemployment rose as firms responded to changing markets and the new rules of capitalism. No period of peacetime history saw such sustained declines in output as the "real business cycles" of the postsocialist economies.

However painful this transition was to the market, for most postsocialist economies the downturn was but a temporary setback. Those economies that began their reforms early and made the most thorough reforms—such as Poland and Slovenia—turned the corner earliest and have surpassed their pretransition levels of real output. Their *PPF*s are once again shifting outward. Reluctant reformers like Ukraine or war-torn countries like Serbia have seen continued declines in their real output and living standards.

As we close this introductory chapter, let us return briefly to our opening theme, Why study economics? Perhaps the best answer to the question is a famous one given by Keynes in the final lines of *The General Theory of Employment, Interest and Money*:

> The ideas of economists and political philosophers, both when they are right and when they are wrong, are more powerful than is commonly understood. Indeed the world is ruled by little else. Practical men, who believe themselves to be quite exempt from any intellectual influences, are usually the slaves of some defunct economist. Madmen in authority, who hear voices in the air, are distilling their frenzy from some academic scribbler of a few years back. I am sure that the power of vested interests is vastly exaggerated compared with the gradual encroachment of ideas. Not, indeed, immediately, but after a certain interval; for in the field of economic and political philosophy there are not many who are influenced by new theories after they are twenty-five or thirty years of age, so that the ideas which civil servants and politicians and even agitators apply to current events are not likely to be the newest. But, soon or late, it is ideas, not vested interests, which are dangerous for good or evil.

To understand how the powerful ideas of economics apply to the central issues of human societies—ultimately, this is why we study economics.

SUMMARY

A. Introduction

1. What is economics? Economics is the study of how societies choose to use scarce productive resources that have alternative uses, to produce commodities of various kinds, and to distribute them among different groups. We study economics to understand not only the world we live in but also the many potential worlds that reformers are constantly proposing to us.

2. Goods are scarce because people desire much more than the economy can produce. Economic goods are scarce, not free, and society must choose among the limited goods that can be produced with its available resources.

3. Microeconomics is concerned with the behavior of individual entities such as markets, firms, and households. Macroeconomics views the performance of the economy as a whole. Through all economics, beware of the fallacy of composition and the post hoc fallacy, and remember to keep other things constant.

B. The Three Problems of Economic Organization

4. Every society must answer three fundamental questions: *what, how,* and *for whom? What* kinds and quantities are produced among the wide range of all possible goods and services? *How* are resources used in producing these goods? And *for whom* are the goods produced (that is, what is the distribution of income and consumption among different individuals and classes)?

5. Societies answer these questions in different ways. The most important forms of economic organization today are *command* and *market*. The command economy is directed by centralized government control; a market economy is guided by an informal system of prices and profits in which most decisions are made by private individuals and firms. All societies have different combinations of command and market; all societies are mixed economies.

C. Society's Technological Possibilities

6. With given resources and technology, the production choices between two goods such as butter and guns can be summarized in the *production-possibility frontier* (*PPF*). The *PPF* shows how the production of one good (such as guns) is traded off against the production of another good (such as butter). In a world of scarcity, choosing one thing means giving up something else. The value of the good or service forgone is its opportunity cost.

7. Productive efficiency occurs when production of one good cannot be increased without curtailing production of another good. This is illustrated by the *PPF*. When an economy is on its *PPF*, it can produce more of one good only by producing less of another good.

8. Production-possibility frontiers illustrate many basic economic processes: how economic growth pushes out the frontier, how a nation chooses relatively less food and other necessities as it develops, how a country chooses between private goods and public goods, and how societies choose between consumption goods and capital goods that enhance future consumption.

9. Societies are sometimes inside their production-possibility frontier. When unemployment is high or when revolution or inefficient government regulations hamper economic activity, the economy is inefficient and operates inside its *PPF*.

CONCEPTS FOR REVIEW

Fundamental Concepts

scarcity and efficiency
free goods vs. economic goods
macroeconomics and microeconomics
normative vs. positive economics
fallacy of composition, post hoc fallacy
"keep other things constant"
cool heads, warm hearts

Key Problems of Economic Organization

what, how, and *for whom*
alternative economic systems: command vs. market
laissez-faire
mixed economies

Choice among Production Possibilities

inputs and outputs
production-possibility frontier (*PPF*)
productive efficiency and inefficiency
opportunity cost

FURTHER READING AND INTERNET WEBSITES

Further Reading

Robert Heilbroner, *The Worldly Philosophers*, 7th ed., (Touchstone Books, 1999), provides a lively biography of the great economists along with their ideas and impact. The authoritative work on the history of economic analysis is Joseph Schumpeter, *History of Economic Analysis* (McGraw-Hill, New York, 1954).

Websites

One of the greatest books of all economics is Adam Smith, *The Wealth of Nations* (many publishers, 1776). Every economics student should read a few pages to get the flavor of his writing. *The Wealth of Nations* can be found at www.bibliomania.com/NonFiction/Smith/Wealth/index.html.

Log onto one of the Internet reference sites for economics such as *Resources for Economists on the Internet* (www.rfe.org or rfe.wustl.edu/EconFAQ.html). Browse through some of the sections to familiarize yourself with the site. You might want to look up your college or university, look at recent news in a newspaper or magazine, or check some economic data.

Two sites for excellent analyses of public policy issues in economics are those of the Brookings Institution (www.brook.edu) and of the American Enterprise Institute (www.aei.org). Each of these publishes books and has policy briefs on line.

QUESTIONS FOR DISCUSSION

1. The great English economist Alfred Marshall (1842–1924) invented many of the tools of modern economics, but he was most concerned with the application of these tools to the problems of society. In his inaugural lecture, Marshall wrote:

   > It will be my most cherished ambition to increase the numbers who Cambridge University sends out into the world with cool heads but warm hearts, willing to give some of their best powers to grappling with the social suffering around them; resolved not to rest content till they have opened up to all the material means of a refined and noble life. [*Memorials of Alfred Marshall*, A. C. Pigou, ed. (MacMillan and Co., London, 1925), p. 174, with minor edits.]

   Explain how the cool head might provide the essential positive economic analysis to implement the normative value judgments of the warm heart. Do you agree with Marshall's view of the role of the teacher? Do you accept his challenge?

2. The late George Stigler, an eminent conservative Chicago economist, wrote as follows:

   > No thoroughly egalitarian society has ever been able to construct or maintain an efficient and progressive economic system. It has been universal experience that some system of differential rewards is necessary to stimulate workers. [*The Theory of Price*, 3d ed. (Macmillan, New York, 1966), p. 19.]

   Are these statements positive or normative economics? Discuss Stigler's view in light of Alfred Marshall's quote in question 1. Is there a conflict?

3. Define each of the following terms carefully and give examples: *PPF*, scarcity, productive efficiency, inputs, outputs.

4. As people become wealthier, time becomes their major scarce resource. Suppose that you are very rich but have only a few hours a week of spare time. Give some examples of steps you can take to economize on your use of time. Compare time use of a wealthy person with that of a poor person.

5. Assume that Econoland produces haircuts and shirts with inputs of labor. Econoland has 1000 hours of labor available. A haircut requires ½ hour of labor, while a shirt requires 5 hours of labor. Construct Econoland's production-possibility frontier.

6. Assume that scientific inventions have doubled the productivity of society's resources in butter production without altering the productivity of gun manufacture. Redraw society's production-possibility frontier in Figure 1-2 to illustrate the new tradeoff.

7. Some scientists believe that we are rapidly depleting our natural resources. Assume that there are only two inputs (labor and natural resources) producing two goods (concerts and gasoline) with no improvement in society's technology over time. Show what would

happen to the *PPF* over time as natural resources are exhausted. How would invention and technological improvement modify your answer? On the basis of this example, explain why it is said that "economic growth is a race between depletion and invention."

8. Say that Diligent has 10 hours to study for upcoming tests in economics and history. Draw a *PPF* for grades,

given Diligent's limited time resources. If Diligent studies inefficiently by listening to loud music and chatting with friends, where will Diligent's grade "output" be relative to the *PPF*? What will happen to the grade *PPF* if Diligent increases study inputs from 10 hours to 15 hours?

Appendix 1

HOW TO READ GRAPHS

> *A picture is worth a thousand words.*
>
> **Chinese Proverb**

Before you can master economics, you must have a working knowledge of graphs. They are as indispensable to the economist as a hammer is to a carpenter. So if you are not familiar with the use of diagrams, invest some time in learning how to read them—it will be time well spent.

What is a *graph*? It is a diagram showing how two or more sets of data or variables are related to one another. Graphs are essential in economics because, among other reasons, they allow us to analyze economic concepts and examine historical trends.

You will encounter many different kinds of graphs in this book. Some graphs show how variables change over time (see, for example, the inside of the front cover); other graphs show the relationship between different variables (such as the example we will turn to in a moment). Each graph in the book will help you understand an important economic relationship or trend.

THE PRODUCTION-POSSIBILITY FRONTIER

The first graph that you encountered in this text was the production-possibility frontier. As we showed in the body of this chapter, the production-possibility frontier, or *PPF*, represents the maximum amounts of a pair of goods or services that can both be produced with an economy's given resources, assuming that all resources are fully employed.

Let's follow up an important application, that of choosing between food and machines. The essential data for the *PPF* are shown in Table 1A-1, which is very much like the example in Table 1-1. Recall that each of the possibilities gives one level of food production and one level of machine production. As the quantity of food produced increases, the production of machines falls. Thus, if the economy produced 10 units of food, it could produce a maximum of 140 machines, but when the output of food is 20 units, only 120 machines can be manufactured.

Production-Possibility Graph

The data shown in Table 1A-1 can also be presented as a graph. To construct the graph, we represent each of the table's pairs of data by a single point on a two-dimensional plane. Figure 1A-1 displays

Alternative Production Possibilities		
Possibilities	**Food**	**Machines**
A	0	150
B	10	140
C	20	120
D	30	90
E	40	50
F	50	0

TABLE 1A-1. The Pairs of Possible Outputs of Food and Machines

The table shows six potential pairs of outputs that can be produced with the given resources of a country. The country can choose one of the six possible combinations.

FIGURE 1A-1. Six Possible Pairs of Food-Machine Production Levels

This figure shows the data of Table 1A-1 in graphical form. The data are exactly the same, but the visual display presents the data more vividly.

in a graph the relationship between the food and machine outputs shown in Table 1A-1. Each pair of numbers is represented by a single point in the graph. Thus the row labeled "A" in Table 1A-1 is graphed as point *A* in Figure 1A-1, and similarly for points *B*, *C*, and so on.

In Figure 1A-1, the vertical line at left and the horizontal line at the bottom correspond to the two variables—food and machines. A **variable** is an item of interest that can be defined and measured and that takes on different values at different times or places. Important variables studied in economics are prices, quantities, hours of work, acres of land, dollars of income, and so forth.

The horizontal line on a graph is referred to as the *horizontal axis,* or sometimes the *X axis.* In Figure 1A-1, food output is measured on the black horizontal axis. The vertical line is known as the *vertical axis,* or *Y axis.* In Figure 1A-1, it measures the number of machines produced. Point *A* on the vertical axis stands for 150 machines. The lower left-hand corner, where the two axes meet, is called the *origin.* It signifies 0 food and 0 machines in Figure 1A-1.

A Smooth Curve

In most economic relationships, variables can change by small amounts as well as by the large increments shown in Figure 1A-1. We therefore generally draw economic relationships as continuous curves. Figure 1A-2 shows the *PPF* as a smooth curve in which the points from *A* to *F* have been connected.

By comparing Table 1A-1 and Figure 1A-2, we can see why graphs are so often used in economics. The smooth *PPF* reflects the menu of choice for the economy. It is a visual device for showing what types of goods are available in what quantities. Your eye can see at a glance the relationship between machine and food production.

Slopes and Lines

Figure 1A-2 depicts the relationship between maximum food and machine production. One important way to describe the relationship between two variables is by the slope of the graph line.

The **slope** of a line represents the change in one variable that occurs when another variable changes. More precisely, it is the change in the variable *Y* on the vertical axis per unit change in the variable *X* on the horizontal axis. For example, in Figure 1A-2, say that food production rose from 25 to 26 units. The

The Production-Possibility Frontier

FIGURE 1A-2. A Production-Possibility Frontier

A smooth curve fills in between the plotted pairs of points, creating the production-possibility frontier.

slope of the curve in Figure 1A-2 tells us the precise change in machinery production that would take place. *Slope is an exact numerical measure of the relationship between the change in* Y *and the change in* X.

We can use Figure 1A-3 to show how to measure the slope of a straight line, say, the slope of the line between points *B* and *D.* Think of the movement from *B* to *D* as occurring in two stages. First comes a horizontal movement from *B* to *C* indicating a 1-unit increase in the *X* value (with no change in *Y*). Second comes a compensating vertical movement up or down, shown as *s* in Figure 1A-3. (The movement of 1 horizontal unit is purely for convenience. The formula holds for movements of any size.) The two-step movement brings us from one point to another on the straight line.

Because the *BC* movement is a 1-unit increase in *X,* the length of *CD* (shown as *s* in Figure 1A-3) indicates the change in *Y* per unit change in *X.* On a graph, this change is called the *slope* of the line *ABDE.*

Often slope is defined as "the rise over the run." The *rise* is the vertical distance; in Figure 1A-3, the rise is the distance from *C* to *D.* The run is the horizontal distance; it is *BC* in Figure 1A-3. The rise over the run in this instance would be *CD* over *BC.* Thus

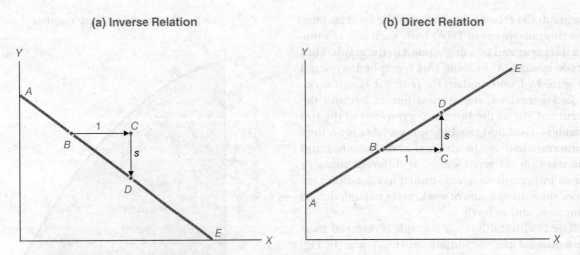

FIGURE 1A-3. Calculation of Slope for Straight Lines

It is easy to calculate slopes for straight lines as "rise over run." Thus in both **(a)** and **(b)**, the numerical value of the slope is rise/run = $CD/BC = s/1 = s$. Note that in **(a)**, CD is negative, indicating a negative slope, or an inverse relationship between X and Y.

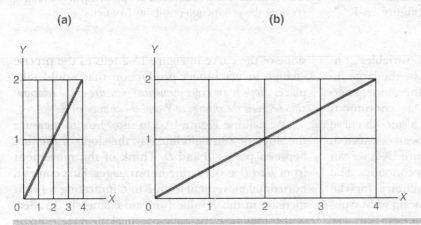

FIGURE 1A-4. Steepness Is Not the Same as Slope

Note that even though **(a)** looks steeper than **(b)**, they display the same relationship. Both have a slope of ½, but the X axis has been stretched out in **(b)**.

the slope of BD is CD/BC. (For those who have studied calculus, question 7 at the end of this appendix relates slopes to derivatives.)

The key points to understand about slopes are the following:

1. The slope can be expressed as a number. It measures the change in Y per unit change in X, or "the rise over the run."
2. If the line is straight, its slope is constant everywhere.
3. The slope of the line indicates whether the relationship between X and Y is direct or inverse.

Direct relationships occur when variables move in the same direction (that is, they increase or decrease together); *inverse relationships* occur when the variables move in opposite directions (that is, one increases as the other decreases).

Thus a negative slope indicates the X-Y relation is inverse, as it is in Figure 1A-3(*a*). Why? Because an increase in X calls for a decrease in Y.

People sometimes confuse slope with the appearance of steepness. This conclusion is often but not always valid. The steepness depends on the scale of the graph. Panels (*a*) and (*b*) in Figure 1A-4 both portray exactly the same relationship. But in (*b*), the horizontal scale has been stretched out compared with (*a*). If you calculate carefully, you will see that the slopes are exactly the same (and are equal to ½).

Slope of a Curved Line

A curved or nonlinear line is one whose slope changes. Sometimes we want to know the slope at *a given point*, such as point *B* in Figure 1A-5. We see that the slope at point *B* is positive, but it is not obvious exactly how to calculate the slope.

To find the slope of a smooth curved line at a point, we calculate the slope of the straight line that just touches, but does not cross, the curved line at the point in question. Such a straight line is called a *tangent* to the curved line. Put differently, the slope of a curved line at a point is given by the slope of the straight line that is tangent to the curve at the given point. Once we draw the tangent line, we find the slope of the tangent line with the usual right-angle measuring technique discussed earlier.

To find the slope at point *B* in Figure 1A-5, we simply construct straight line *FBJ* as a tangent to the curved line at point *B*. We then calculate the slope of the tangent as *NJ/MN*. Similarly, the tangent line *GH* gives the slope of the curved line at point *D*.

Another example of the slope of a nonlinear line is shown in Figure 1A-6. This shows a typical microeconomics curve, which is dome-shaped and has a maximum at point *C*. We can use our method of slopes as tangents to see that the slope of the curve is always positive in the region where the curve is rising and negative in the falling region. At the peak or maximum of the curve, the slope is exactly zero. A zero slope signifies that a tiny movement in the *X* variable around the maximum has no effect on the value of the *Y* variable.[1]

---

[1] For those who enjoy algebra, the slope of a line can be remembered as follows: A straight line (or linear relationship) is written as $Y = a + bX$. For this line, the slope of the curve is *b*, which measures the change in *Y* per unit change in *X*.

A curved line or nonlinear relationship is one involving terms other than constants and the *X* term. An example of a nonlinear relationship is the quadratic equation $Y = (X - 2)^2$. You can verify that the slope of this equation is negative for $X < 2$ and positive for $X > 2$. What is its slope for $X = 2$?

For those who know calculus: A zero slope comes where the derivative of a smooth curve is equal to zero. For example, plot and use calculus to find the zero-slope point of a curve defined by the function $Y = (X - 2)^2$.

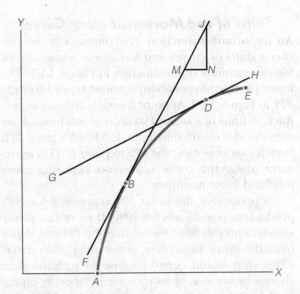

FIGURE 1A-5. Tangent as Slope of Curved Line

By constructing a tangent line, we can calculate the slope of a curved line at a given point. Thus the line *FBMJ* is tangent to smooth curve *ABDE* at point *B*. The slope at *B* is calculated as the slope of the tangent line, that is, as *NJ/MN*.

FIGURE 1A-6. Different Slopes of Nonlinear Curves

Many curves in economics first rise, then reach a maximum, then fall. In the rising region from *A* to *C* the slope is positive (see point *B*). In the falling region from *C* to *E* the slope is negative (see point *D*). At the curve's maximum, point *C*, the slope is zero. (What about a U-shaped curve? What is the slope at its minimum?)

Shifts of and Movement along Curves

An important distinction in economics is that between shifts of curves and movement along curves. We can examine this distinction in Figure 1A-7. The inner production-possibility frontier reproduces the *PPF* in Figure 1A-2. At point *D* society chooses to produce 30 units of food and 90 units of machines. If society decides to consume more food with a given *PPF*, then it can *move along* the *PPF* to point *E*. This movement along the curve represents choosing more food and fewer machines.

Suppose that the inner *PPF* represents society's production possibilities for 1990. If we return to the same country in 2000, we see that the *PPF* has *shifted* from the inner 1990 curve to the outer 2000 curve. (This shift would occur because of technological change or because of an increase in labor or capital available.) In the later year, society might choose to be at point *G*, with more food and machines than at either *D* or *E*.

The point of this example is that in the first case (moving from *D* to *E*) we see movement along the curve, while in the second case (from *D* to *G*) we see a shift of the curve.

Some Special Graphs

The *PPF* is one of the most important graphs of economics, one depicting the relationship between two economic variables (such as food and machines or guns and butter). You will encounter other types of graphs in the pages that follow.

Time Series. Some graphs show how a particular variable has changed over time. Look, for example, at the graphs on the inside front cover of this text. The left-hand graph shows a time series, since the American Revolution, of a significant macroeconomic variable, the ratio of the federal government debt to total gross domestic product, or *GDP*—this ratio is the *debt-GDP ratio*. Time-series graphs have time on the horizontal axis and variables of interest (in this case, the debt-GDP ratio) on the vertical axis.

FIGURE 1A-7. Shift of Curves versus Movement along Curves

In using graphs, it is essential to distinguish *movement along* a curve (such as from high-investment *D* to low-investment *E*) from a *shift* of a curve (as from *D* in an early year to *G* in a later year).

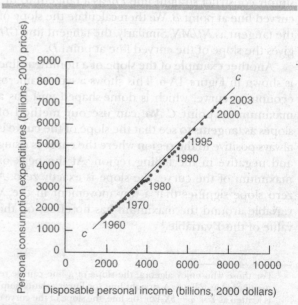

FIGURE 1A-8. Scatter Diagram of Consumption Function Shows Important Macroeconomic Law

Observed points of consumption spending fall near the *CC* line, which displays average behavior over time. Thus, the rust-colored point for 2003 is so near the *CC* line that it could have been quite accurately predicted from that line even before the year was over. Scatter diagrams allow us to see how close the relationship is between two variables.

This graph shows that the debt-GDP ratio has risen sharply during every major war.

Scatter Diagrams. Sometimes individual pairs of points will be plotted, as in Figure 1A-1. Often, combinations of variables for different years will be plotted. An important example of a scatter diagram from macroeconomics is the *consumption function,* shown in Figure 1A-8. This scatter diagram shows the nation's total disposable income on the horizontal axis and total consumption (spending by households on goods like food, clothing, and housing) on the vertical axis. Note that consumption is very closely linked to income, a vital clue for understanding changes in national income and output.

Diagrams with More than One Curve. Often it is useful to put two curves in the same graph, thus obtaining a "multicurve diagram." The most important example is the *supply-and-demand diagram,* shown in Chapter 3 (see page 55). Such graphs can show two different relationships simultaneously, such as how consumer purchases respond to price (demand) and how business production responds to price (supply). By graphing the two relationships together, we can determine the price and quantity that will hold in a market.

This concludes our brief excursion into graphs. Once you have mastered these basic principles, the graphs in this book, and in other areas, can be both fun and instructive.

SUMMARY TO APPENDIX

1. Graphs are an essential tool of modern economics. They provide a convenient presentation of data or of the relationships among variables.
2. The important points to understand about a graph are: What is on each of the two axes (horizontal and vertical)? What are the units on each axis? What kind of relationship is depicted in the curve or curves shown in the graph?
3. The relationship between the two variables in a curve is given by its slope. The slope is defined as "the rise over the run," or the increase in Y per unit increase in X. If it is upward- (or positively) sloping, the two variables are directly related; they move upward or downward together. If the curve has a downward (or negative) slope, the two variables are inversely related.
4. In addition, we sometimes see special types of graphs: time series, which show how a particular variable moves over time; scatter diagrams, which show observations on a pair of variables; and multicurve diagrams, which show two or more relationships in a single graph.

CONCEPTS FOR REVIEW

Elements of Graphs

horizontal, or X, axis
vertical, or Y, axis
slope as "rise over run"
slope (negative, positive, zero)
tangent as slope of curved line

Examples of Graphs

time-series graphs
scatter diagrams
multicurve graphs

QUESTIONS FOR DISCUSSION

1. Consider the following problem: After your 8 hours a day of sleep, you have 16 hours a day to divide between leisure and study. Let leisure hours be the X variable and study hours be the Y variable. Plot the straight-line relationship between all combinations of X and Y on a blank piece of graph paper. Be careful to label the axes and mark the origin.

2. In question 1, what is the slope of the line showing the relationship between study and leisure hours? Is it a straight line?

3. Let us say that you absolutely need 6 hours of leisure per day, no more, no less. On the graph, mark the point that corresponds to 6 hours of leisure. Now consider a *movement along the curve:* Assume that you decide that you need only 4 hours of leisure a day. Plot the new point.

4. Next show a *shift of the curve:* You find that you need less sleep, so you have 18 hours a day to devote to leisure and study. Draw the new (shifted) curve.

5. Keep a record of your leisure and study for a week. Plot a time-series graph of the hours of leisure and study each day. Next plot a scatter diagram of hours of leisure and hours of study. Do you see any relationship between the two variables?

6. Go to the website of the Bureau of Economic Analysis at www.bea.gov. Then click on "Gross Domestic Product." On the next page, click on "Interactive NIPA data." Then click on "Frequently Requested NIPA Tables." Click on "Table 1.2 (Real Gross Domestic Product)," which is the total output of the economy. This will probably come up with the quarterly data.

   a. Construct a graph that shows the time series for real GDP for the last six quarters. Is the general trend upward or downward? (In macroeconomics, we will learn that the slope is downward is recessions.)

   b. Construct a scatter plot showing "Imports" on the vertical axis and "Gross domestic product" on the horizontal axis. Describe the relationship between the numbers. (In macroeconomics, this will be the marginal propensity to import.)

7. *For those who have studied calculus:* The slope of a smooth line or curve is its derivative. The following are the equations for two inverse demand curves (where price is a function of output). For each curve, assume that the function holds only when $P \geq 0$ and $X \geq 0$.

   a. $P = 100 - 5X$

   b. $P = 100 - 20X + 1X^2$

   For each demand curve, determine its slope when $X = 0$ and when $X = 1$. For linear demand curves such as **a**, what is the condition under which the law of downward-sloping demand holds? Is curve **b** concave (like a dome) or convex (like a cup)?

CHAPTER

2

Markets and Government in a Modern Economy

Every individual endeavors to employ his capital so that its produce may be of greatest value. He generally neither intends to promote the public interest, nor knows how much he is promoting it. He intends only his own security, only his own gain. And he is in this led by an invisible hand to promote an end which was no part of his intention. By pursuing his own interest he frequently promotes that of society more effectually than when he really intends to promote it.

Adam Smith
The Wealth of Nations (1776)

The Mixed Economy

This textbook focuses primarily on the market economy of modern industrialized nations. Before the rise of the market economy, going back to medieval times, aristocracies and town guilds directed much of the economic activity in Europe and Asia. However, about two centuries ago, governments began to exercise less and less power over prices and production methods. Feudalism gradually gave way to markets, or what we call the "market mechanism" or "competitive capitalism."

In most of Europe and North America, the nineteenth century became the age of **laissez-faire.** This doctrine, which translates as "leave us alone," holds that government should interfere as little as possible in economic affairs and leave economic decisions to the private decision making of buyers and sellers. Many governments espoused this economic philosophy in the middle of the nineteenth century.

Nevertheless, a century ago, with the experience of many excesses of capitalism—including corruption, dangerous products, and poverty—most industrialized countries began to retreat from unbridled laissez-faire. Government's role expanded steadily as it regulated monopolies, levied income taxes, and began to provide a social safety net for the elderly, unemployed, and impoverished.

This new system, called the **welfare state,** is one in which markets direct the detailed activities of day-to-day economic life while government regulates social conditions and provides pensions, health care, and other necessities for poor families.

In the late twentieth century, the tide shifted again as conservative governments in many countries began to reduce taxes and deregulate government's control over the economy. Many government-owned industries were "privatized," income-tax rates were lowered, and the generosity of many welfare programs was trimmed so that governments could stem the rapid growth of expenditures.

The most dramatic turn toward the market came in Russia and the socialist countries of Eastern Europe. After decades of extolling the advantages of a government-run command economy, beginning around 1990, these countries scrapped central planning and made the difficult transition to a decentralized, market economy. China, while still run by the dictatorship of the Communist party, has enjoyed an economic boom in the last three decades by allowing private enterprises and foreign firms to operate within its borders. Previously poor regions like Taiwan, Hong Kong, and Chile have enjoyed rapid income growth by embracing capitalism and reducing the role of government in their economies.

This capsule history of the shifting boundary between government and market raises many questions. What exactly is a market economy, and what makes it such a powerful engine of growth? What is the "capital" in "capitalism"? What government controls are needed to make markets function effectively? The time has come to understand the principles that lie behind the market economy and to review government's role in economic life.

A. WHAT IS A MARKET?

In a country like the United States, most economic decisions are resolved through the market, so we begin our systematic study there. Who solves the three fundamental questions—*what, how,* and *for whom*—in a market economy? You may be surprised to learn that *no one individual or organization or government is responsible for solving the economic problems in a market economy.* Instead, millions of businesses and consumers engage in voluntary trade, intending to improve their own economic situations, and their actions are invisibly coordinated by a system of prices and markets.

To see how remarkable this is, consider the city of New York. Without a constant flow of goods into and out of the city, New Yorkers would be on the verge of starvation within a week. For New York to thrive, many kinds of goods must be provided. From the surrounding counties, from 50 states, and from the far corners of the world, goods travel for days and weeks with New York as their destination.

How is it that 10 million people can sleep easily at night, without living in mortal terror of a breakdown in the elaborate economic processes upon which they rely? The surprising answer is that, without coercion or centralized direction by anyone, these economic activities are coordinated through the market.

Everyone in the United States notices how much the government does to control economic activity: it places tolls on bridges, polices the streets, regulates drugs, levies taxes, sends armies around the world, and so forth. But we seldom think about how much of our ordinary economic life proceeds without government intervention. Thousands of commodities are produced by millions of people every day, willingly, without central direction or master plan.

Not Chaos, but Economic Order

The market looks like a jumble of sellers and buyers. It seems almost a miracle that food is produced in suitable amounts, gets transported to the right place, and arrives in a palatable form at the dinner table. But a close look at New York or other economies is convincing proof that a market system is neither chaos nor miracle. It is a system with its own internal logic. And it works.

A market economy is an elaborate mechanism for coordinating people, activities, and businesses through a system of prices and markets. It is a communication device for pooling the knowledge and actions of billions of diverse individuals. Without central intelligence or computation, it solves problems of production and distribution involving billions of unknown variables and relations, problems that are far beyond the reach of even today's fastest supercomputer. Nobody designed the market, yet it functions remarkably well. In a market economy, no single individual or organization is responsible for production, consumption, distribution, or pricing.

How do markets determine prices, wages, and outputs? Originally, a market was an actual place where buyers and sellers could engage in face-to-face bargaining. The *marketplace*—filled with slabs of butter, pyramids of cheese, layers of wet fish, and heaps of vegetables—used to be a familiar sight in many villages and towns, where farmers brought their goods to sell. In the United States today there are still important markets where many traders gather together to do business. For example, wheat and corn are traded at the Chicago Board of Trade, oil and platinum are traded at the New York Mercantile Exchange, and gems are traded at the Diamond District in New York City.

In a general sense, markets are places where buyers and sellers interact, exchange goods and services, and determine prices. There are markets for almost everything. You can buy artwork by old masters at auction houses in New York, or pollution permits at the Chicago Board of Trade, or illegal drugs from delivery services in many large cities. A market may be centralized, like the stock market. It may be decentralized, as in the case of labor. Or it may exist only electronically, as is increasingly the case with "e-commerce" on the Internet.

A **market** is a mechanism through which buyers and sellers interact to determine prices and exchange goods and services.

In a market system, everything has a **price,** which is the value of the good in terms of money (the role of money will be discussed in Section B of this chapter). Prices represent the terms on which people and firms voluntarily exchange different commodities. When I agree to buy a used Ford from a dealer for $8050, this agreement indicates that the Ford is worth at least $8050 to me and that the $8050 is worth at least as much as the Ford to the dealer. The used-car market has determined the price of a used Ford and, through voluntary trading, has allocated this good to the person for whom it has the highest value.

In addition, prices serve as *signals* to producers and consumers. If consumers want more of any good, the price will rise, sending a signal to producers that more supply is needed. When a terrible disease reduces beef production, the supply of beef decreases and raises the price of hamburgers. The higher price encourages farmers to increase their production of beef and, at the same time, encourages consumers to substitute other foods for hamburgers and beef products.

What is true of the markets for consumer goods is also true of markets for factors of production, such as land or labor. If more computer programmers are needed to run Internet businesses, the price of computer programmers (their hourly wage) will tend to rise. The rise in relative wages will attract workers into the growing occupation.

Prices coordinate the decisions of producers and consumers in a market. Higher prices tend to reduce consumer purchases and encourage production. Lower prices encourage consumption and discourage production. Prices are the balance wheel of the market mechanism.

Market Equilibrium. At every moment, some people are buying while others are selling; firms are inventing new products while governments are passing laws to regulate old ones; foreign companies are opening plants in America while American firms are selling their products abroad. Yet in the midst of all this turmoil, markets are constantly solving the *what, how,* and *for whom.* As they balance all the forces operating on the economy, markets are finding a **market equilibrium of supply and demand.**

A market equilibrium represents a balance among all the different buyers and sellers. Depending upon the price, households and firms all want to buy or sell different quantities. The market finds the equilibrium price that simultaneously meets the desires of buyers and sellers. Too high a price would mean a glut of goods with too much output; too low a price would produce long lines in stores and a deficiency of goods. Those prices for which buyers desire to buy exactly the quantity that sellers desire to sell yield an equilibrium of supply and demand.

How Markets Solve the Three Economic Problems

We have just described how prices help balance consumption and production (or demand and supply) in an individual market. What happens when we put all the different markets together—beef, cars, land, labor, capital, and everything else? These markets work simultaneously to determine a general equilibrium of prices and production.

By matching sellers and buyers (supply and demand) in each market, a market economy simultaneously solves the three problems of *what, how,* and *for whom.* Here is an outline of a market equilibrium:

1. *What* goods and services will be produced is determined by the dollar votes of consumers—not every 2 or 4 years at the polls, but in their daily purchase decisions. The money that they pay into businesses' cash registers ultimately provides the payrolls, rents, and dividends that households receive as income.

   Firms, in turn, are motivated by the desire to maximize profits. **Profits** are net revenues, or the difference between total sales and total costs. Firms abandon areas where they are losing profits; by the same token, firms are lured by high profits into production of goods in high demand. Some of the most profitable activities today are producing and marketing drugs—drugs for depression, anxiety, impotence, and all other manner of human frailty. Lured by the high profits, companies are investing billions in research to come up with yet more new and improved medicines.

2. *How* things are produced is determined by the competition among different producers. The best way for producers to meet price competition and maximize profits is to keep costs at a minimum by adopting the most efficient methods of production. Sometimes change is incremental and consists of little more than tinkering with the

machinery or adjusting the input mix to gain a cost advantage, which can be very important in a competitive market. At other times there are drastic shifts in technology, as with steam engines displacing horses because steam was cheaper per unit of useful work, or airplanes replacing railroads as the most efficient mode for long-distance travel. Right now we are in the midst of just such a transition to a radically different technology, with computers revolutionizing many tasks in the workplace, from the checkout counter to the lecture room.

3. *For whom* things are produced—who is consuming and how much—depends, in large part, on the supply and demand in the markets for factors of production. Factor markets (i.e., markets for factors of production) determine wage rates, land rents, interest rates, and profits. Such prices are called *factor prices*. The same person may receive wages from a job, dividends from stocks, interest on a bond, and rent from a piece of property. By adding up all the revenues from factors, we can calculate the person's market income. The distribution of income among the population is thus determined by the quantity of factor services (person-hours, acres, etc.) and the prices of the factors (wage rates, land rents, etc.).

Be warned, however, that incomes reflect more than the rewards for sweaty labor or frugal living. High incomes can come from large inheritances, good luck, and skills highly prized in the marketplace. Those with low incomes are often pictured as lazy, but the truth is that low incomes are generally the result of poor education, discrimination, or living where jobs are few and wages are low. When we see someone on the unemployment line, we should remember, "There, but for the grace of supply and demand, go I."

Monarchs of the Marketplace

Who rules a market economy? Do giant companies like Microsoft and General Motors call the tune? Or perhaps Congress and the president? Or advertising moguls from Madison Avenue? All these people and institutions affect us, but in the end the major forces affecting the shape of the economy are the dual monarchs of *tastes* and *technology*.

One fundamental determinant is the tastes of the population. These innate and acquired tastes—as expressed in the dollar votes of consumer demands—

direct the uses of society's resources. They pick the point on the production-possibility frontier (*PPF*).

The other major factor is the resources and technology available to a society. The economy cannot go outside its *PPF*. You can fly to Hong Kong, but there are no flights yet to Mars. Therefore, the economy's resources limit the candidates for the dollar votes of consumers. *Consumer demand has to dovetail with business supply of goods and services to determine what is ultimately produced.*

You will find it helpful to recall the dual monarchy when you wonder why some technologies fail in the marketplace. From the Stanley Steamer—a car that ran on steam—to the Premiere smokeless cigarette, which was smokeless but also tasteless, history is full of products that found no markets. How do useless products die off? Is there a government agency that pronounces upon the value of new products? No such agency is necessary. Rather, they become extinct because there is no consumer demand for the products at the going market price. These products make losses rather than profits. This reminds us that profits serve as the rewards and penalties for businesses and guide the market mechanism.

Like a farmer using a carrot and a stick to coax a donkey forward, the market system deals out profits and losses to induce firms to produce desired goods efficiently.

A Picture of Prices and Markets

We can picture the circular flow of economic life in Figure 2-1 on page 29. The diagram provides an overview of how consumers and producers interact to determine prices and quantities for both inputs and outputs. Note the two different kinds of markets in the circular flow. At the top are the product markets, or the flow of outputs like pizza and shoes; at the bottom are the markets for inputs or factors of production like land and labor. Further, see how decisions are made by two different entities, consumers and businesses.

Consumers buy goods and sell factors of production; businesses sell goods and buy factors of production. Consumers use their income from the sale of labor and other inputs to buy goods from businesses; businesses base their prices of goods on the costs of labor and property. Prices in goods markets are set to balance consumer demand with

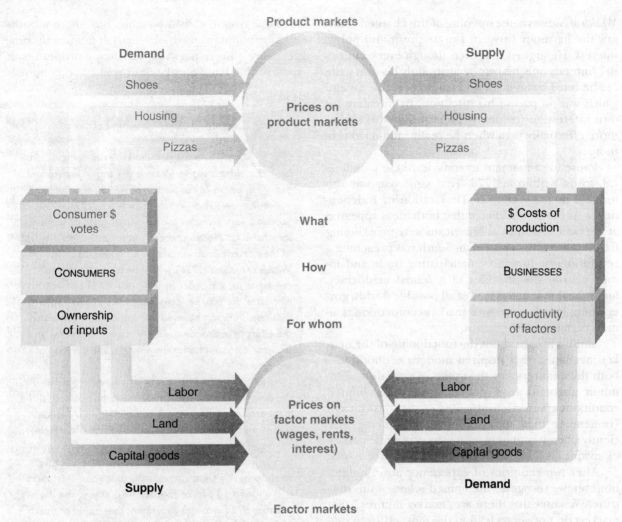

FIGURE 2-1. The Market System Relies on Supply and Demand to Solve the Trio of Economic Problems

We see here the circular flow of a market economy. Dollar votes of consumers (households, governments, and foreigners) interact with business supply in the product markets at top, helping to determine *what* is produced. Business demand for inputs meets the supply of labor and other inputs in the factor markets below, determining wage, rent, and interest payments; incomes thus influence *for whom* goods are delivered. Business competition to buy factor inputs and sell goods most cheaply determines *how* goods are produced.

business supply; prices in factor markets are set to balance household supply with business demand.

All this sounds complicated. But it is simply the total picture of the intricate web of interdependent supplies and demands, interconnected through a market mechanism to solve the economic problems of *what, how,* and *for whom.* Look at Figure 2-1 carefully.

A few minutes spent studying it will surely help you understand the workings of a market economy.

The Invisible Hand

The order contained in a market economy was first recognized by Adam Smith. In one of the most famous passages of all economics, quoted from *The*

Wealth of Nations at the opening of this chapter, Smith saw the harmony between private profit and public interest. He argued that even though every individual "intends only his own security, only his own gain, . . . he is led by an invisible hand to promote an end which was no part of his intention. By pursuing his own interest he frequently promotes that of society more effectually than when he really intends to promote it."

Pause for a moment to consider these paradoxical words, written in 1776. That same year was also marked by the American Declaration of Independence. It is no coincidence that both ideas appeared at the same time. Just as Americans were proclaiming freedom from tyranny, Adam Smith was preaching a revolutionary doctrine emancipating trade and industry from the shackles of a feudal aristocracy. Smith held that in this best of all possible worlds, government interference with market competition is almost certain to be injurious.

Smith's insight about the functioning of the market mechanism has inspired modern economists—both the admirers and the critics of capitalism. Economic theorists have proved that under limited conditions a perfectly competitive economy is efficient (remember that an economy is producing efficiently when it cannot increase the economic welfare of anyone without making someone else worse off).

After two centuries of experience and thought, however, we recognize the limited scope of this doctrine. We know that there are "market failures," that markets do not always lead to the most efficient outcome. One set of market failures concerns monopolies and other forms of imperfect competition. A second failure of the "invisible hand" comes when there are spillovers or externalities outside the marketplace—positive externalities such as scientific discoveries and negative spillovers such as pollution.

A final reservation comes when the income distribution is politically or ethically unacceptable. When any of these elements occur, Adam Smith's invisible-hand doctrine breaks down and government may want to step in to mend the flawed invisible hand.

In summary:

Adam Smith discovered a remarkable property of a competitive market economy. Under perfect competition and with no market failures, markets will squeeze as many useful goods and services out of the available resources as is possible. But where monopolies or pollution or similar market failures become pervasive, the remarkable efficiency properties of the invisible hand may be destroyed.

Adam Smith: Founding Father of Economics

"For what purpose is all the toil and bustle of this world? What is the end of avarice and ambition, of the pursuit of wealth, of power, and pre-eminence?" Thus wrote Adam Smith (1723–1790), of Scotland, who glimpsed for the social world of economics what Isaac Newton recognized for the physical world of the heavens. Smith answered his questions in *The Wealth of Nations* (1776), where he explained the self-regulating natural order by which the oil of self-interest lubricates the economic machinery in an almost miraculous fashion. Smith believed that the toil and bustle had the effect of improving the lot of the common man and woman. "Consumption is the sole end and purpose of all production."

Smith was the first apostle of economic growth. At the dawn of the Industrial Revolution, he pointed to the great strides in productivity brought about by specialization and the division of labor. In a famous example, he described the specialized manufacturing of a pin factory in which "one man draws out the wire, another straightens it, a third cuts it," and so it goes. This operation allowed 10 people to make 48,000 pins in a day, whereas if "all wrought separately, they could not each of them make twenty, perhaps not one pin a day." Smith saw the result of this division of labor as "universal opulence which extends itself to the lowest ranks of the people." Imagine what he would think if he returned today to see what two more centuries of economic growth have produced!

Smith wrote hundreds of pages railing against countless cases of government folly and interference. Consider the seventeenth-century guild master who was attempting to improve his weaving. The town guild decided, "If a cloth weaver intends to process a piece according to his own invention, he should obtain permission from the judges of the town to employ the number and length of threads that he desires after the question has been considered by four of the oldest merchants and four of the oldest weavers of the guild." Smith argued that such restrictions—whether imposed by government or by monopolies, whether on production or on foreign trade—limit the proper workings of the market system and ultimately hurt both workers and consumers.

None of this should suggest that Smith was an apologist for the establishment. He had a distrust of all entrenched power, private monopolies as much as public monarchies. He was for the common people. But, like many of the great economists, he had learned from his research that the road to waste is paved with good intentions.

Above all, it is Adam Smith's vision of the self-regulating "invisible hand" that is his enduring contribution to modern economics.

B. TRADE, MONEY, AND CAPITAL

Since the time of Adam Smith, market economies have evolved enormously. Advanced capitalist economies, such as the United States, Western Europe, and Japan, have three distinguishing features: trade and specialization, money, and capital.

- An advanced economy is characterized by an elaborate network of *trade*, among individuals and countries, that depends on great *specialization* and an intricate division of labor.
- Modern economies today make extensive use of *money*, or the means of payment. The flow of money is the lifeblood of our system. Money provides the yardstick for measuring the economic value of things and for financing trade.
- Modern industrial technologies rest on the use of vast amounts of *capital:* precision machinery, large-scale factories, and stocks of inventories. Capital goods leverage human labor power into a much more efficient factor of production and allow productivity many times greater than that possible in an earlier age.

TRADE, SPECIALIZATION, AND DIVISION OF LABOR

As compared to the economies of the 1700s, today's economies depend heavily on the specialization of individuals and firms, connected by an extensive network of trade. Western economies have enjoyed rapid economic growth as increasing specialization has allowed workers to become highly productive in particular occupations and to trade their output for the commodities they need.

Specialization occurs when people and countries concentrate their efforts on a particular set of tasks—it permits each person and country to use to best advantage the specific skills and resources that are available. One of the facts of economic life is that, rather than have everyone do everything in a mediocre way, it is better to establish a *division of labor*—dividing production into a number of small specialized steps or tasks. A division of labor permits tall people to play basketball, numerate people to teach, and persuasive people to sell cars. It sometimes takes many years to receive the training for particular careers—it usually takes 14 postgraduate years to become a certified neurosurgeon.

Capital and land are also highly specialized. In the case of land, some lands form the precious sandy strips of beach between populous cities and warm oceans; others are valuable vineyard lands of France or California; still other lands border on deepwater ports and serve as centers of trade for the world.

Capital also is highly specialized. The computer software that went along with the labor to write this textbook took over a decade to be developed, but it is useless at managing an oil refinery or solving large numerical problems. One of the most impressive examples of specialization is the computer chip that manages automobiles, increases their efficiency, and can even serve as a "black box" to record accident data.

The enormous efficiency of specialization allows the intricate network of trade among people and nations that we see today. Very few of us produce a single finished good; we make but the tiniest fraction of what we consume. We might teach a small part of one college's curriculum, or empty coins from parking meters, or separate the genetic material of fruit flies. In exchange for this specialized labor, we will receive an income adequate to buy goods from all over the world.

The idea of *gains from trade* forms one of the central insights of economics. Different people or countries tend to specialize in certain areas; they then engage in the voluntary exchange of what they produce for what they need. Japan has grown enormously productive by specializing in manufacturing goods such as automobiles and consumer electronics; it exports much of its manufacturing output to pay for imports of raw materials. By contrast, countries which have tried the strategy of becoming self-sufficient—attempting to produce most of what they consume—have discovered that this is the road to stagnation. Trade can enrich all nations and increase *everyone's* living standards.

To summarize:

Advanced economies engage in specialization and division of labor, which increase the productivity of their resources. Individuals and countries then voluntarily trade goods in which they specialize for others' products, vastly increasing the range and quantity of consumption and having the potential to raise everyone's living standards.

Globalization

You can hardly open a newspaper today without reading about the most recent trends in "globalization." What exactly does this term mean? How can economics contribute to understanding the issues?

Globalization is a popular term that is used to denote an increase in *economic integration among nations*. Increasing integration is seen today in the dramatic growth in the flows of goods, services, and capital across national borders.

One major component of globalization is the spectacular increase in the share of national output devoted to imports and exports. With a continuous drop in transportation and communication costs, along with declining tariffs and other barriers to trade, the share of trade in U.S. national output has more than doubled over the last half-century. Domestic producers now compete with producers from around the world in their prices and design decisions.

The increased share of trade has been accompanied by increased specialization in the production process itself as different stages of production are "outsourced" to different countries. A typical example is the production of Barbie dolls:

The plastic and hair come from Taiwan and Japan. Assembly used to be done in those countries but has now migrated to lower-cost locations in Indonesia, Malaysia, and China. The molds themselves come from the United States, as do the paints used in decorating. China supplies labor and the cotton cloth used for dresses. The dolls sell for $10, of which 35 cents covers Chinese labor, 65 cents covers foreign materials, $1 covers Hong Kong profits and transportation, and the rest is Mattel profit, marketing, and transportation expenses in the United States.[1]

Evidence indicates that this process of slicing up the productive process is typical of manufacturing activities in the United States and other high-income countries.

A second component of globalization is the increasing integration of financial markets. Financial integration is seen in the accelerated pace of lending and borrowing among nations as well as in the convergence of interest rates among different countries. The major causes of financial market integration have been the dismantling of restrictions on capital flows among nations, cost reductions, and innovations in financial markets, particularly the use of new kinds of financial instruments.

Financial integration among nations has undoubtedly led to gains from trade, as nations with productive uses for capital can borrow from countries with excess savings. In the last two decades, Japan has served as the world's major lending country. Surprisingly, the United States has been the world's largest borrower—partly because of its low national saving rate and partly because of the technological dynamism of its computer and biotechnology industries.

Integration of goods and financial markets has produced impressive gains from trade in the form of lower prices, increased innovation, and more rapid economic growth. But these gains have been accompanied by painful side effects.

One consequence of economic integration is the unemployment and lost profits that occur when low-cost foreign producers displace domestic production. The unemployed textile worker and the bankrupt soybean farmer find little solace in the fact that consumers are enjoying lower prices for clothing and food. Those who lose from increased international trade are the tireless advocates of "protectionism" in the form of tariffs and quotas on international trade.

---

[1] See Feenstra in the Further Reading section at the end of this chapter.

A second consequence comes when financial integration triggers international financial crises. Over the last decade, economic problems in Russia, Brazil, and Argentina spilled over into stock and bond markets around the world. The contagion arising from small disturbances is a direct result of closely linked markets. American investors put their funds into Thailand, seeking higher returns. But these same investors are likely to pull out their funds quickly when they smell trouble, and that can lead to a financial crisis as countries attempt to prop up exchange rates or financial institutions in the face of a massive speculative attack.

Globalization raises many new issues for policymakers. Are the gains from trade worth the domestic costs in terms of social disruption and dislocation? Should countries prevent investors from moving funds in and out so rapidly that domestic financial markets are threatened? Does integration lead to greater inequality? Should international institutions become lenders of last resort for countries in financial difficulties? These questions are on the minds of policymakers around the world who are attempting to deal with globalization.

MONEY: THE LUBRICANT OF EXCHANGE

If specialization permits people to concentrate on particular tasks, money then allows people to trade their specialized outputs for the vast array of goods and services produced by others.

Money is the means of payment in the form of currency and checks used to buy things. Money is a lubricant that facilitates exchange. When everyone trusts and accepts money as payment for goods and debts, trade is facilitated. Just imagine how complicated economic life would be if you had to barter goods for goods every time you wanted to buy a pizza or go to a concert. What services could you offer Sal's Pizza? What could you barter with your college to cover your tuition? Money acts as a ubiquitous matchmaker between buyers and sellers, effortlessly effecting little marriages of mutual self-interest billions of times every day.

Governments control the money supply through their central banks. But like other lubricants, money can get overheated and damage the economic engine. It can grow out of control and cause a hyperin-

flation, in which prices increase very rapidly. When that happens, people concentrate on spending their money quickly, before it loses its value, rather than investing it for the future. That's what happened to several Latin American countries in the 1980s, and many former socialist economies in the 1990s, when they had inflation rates exceeding 1000 percent or even 10,000 percent per year. Imagine getting your paycheck and having it lose 20 percent of its value by the end of the week!

Money is the medium of exchange. Proper management of the money supply is one of the major issues for government macroeconomic policy in all countries.

CAPITAL

An advanced industrial economy like the United States employs a vast array of buildings, machines, computers, software, and so on. These are the factors of production called **capital**—a produced factor of production, a durable input which is itself an output of the economy.

Most of us do not realize how much our daily activities depend upon capital, including our houses, the highways on which we drive, and the wires that bring electricity and cable TV to our homes. The total net capital stock in the U.S. economy is over $30 trillion, including government-owned, business, and residential capital. This amounts to more than $110,000 per person.

As we have seen, capital is one of the three major factors of production. The other two, land and labor, are often called *primary factors of production*. That means their supply is mostly determined by noneconomic factors, such as the fertility rate and the country's geography. Capital, by contrast, has to be produced before you can use it. For example, some companies build textile machinery, which is then used to make shirts; some companies build farm tractors, which are then used to help produce corn.

Use of capital involves time-consuming, roundabout methods of production. People learned long ago that indirect and roundabout production techniques often are more efficient than direct methods of production. For example, the most direct method of catching fish is to wade into a stream and grab fish with your hands, but this yields more frustration than fish. By using a fishing rod (which is capital equipment), fishing time becomes more productive in terms of fish caught per day. By using even more capital, in the form of nets and fishing boats, fishing becomes productive enough to feed many people and provide a good living to those who operate the specialized nets and equipment.

Growth from the Sacrifice of Current Consumption. If people are willing to save—to abstain from present consumption and wait for future consumption—society can devote resources to new capital goods. A larger stock of capital helps the economy grow faster by pushing out the *PPF.* Look back at Figure 1-5 to see how forgoing current consumption in favor of investment adds to future production possibilities. High rates of saving and investment help explain how Taiwan, China, and other Asian countries have grown so fast over the last three decades. By comparison, many poor countries save and invest little—they start the economic race at the back and fall further behind because they cannot accumulate productive capital.

We summarize as follows:

Economic activity involves forgoing current consumption to increase our capital. Every time we invest—building a new factory or road, increasing the years or quality of education, or increasing the stock of useful technical knowledge—we are enhancing the future productivity of our economy and increasing future consumption.

Capital and Private Property

In a market economy, capital typically is privately owned, and the income from capital goes to individuals. Every patch of land has a deed, or title of ownership; almost every machine and building belongs to an individual or corporation. *Property rights* bestow on their owners the ability to use, exchange, paint, dig, drill, or exploit their capital goods. These capital goods also have market values, and people can buy and sell the capital goods for whatever price the goods will fetch. *The ability of individuals to own and profit from capital is what gives capitalism its name.*

However, while our society is one built on private property, property rights are limited. Society determines how much of "your" property you may bequeath

to your heirs and how much must go in inheritance taxes to the government. Society determines how much your factory can pollute and where you can park your car. Even your home is not your castle: you must obey zoning laws and, if necessary, make way for a road.

Interestingly enough, the most valuable economic resource, labor, cannot be turned into a commodity that is bought and sold as private property. Since the abolition of slavery, it has been illegal to treat human earning power like other capital assets. You are not free to sell yourself; you must rent yourself at a wage.

Property Rights for Capital and Pollution

Property rights define the ability of individuals or firms to own, buy, sell, and use the capital goods and other property in a market economy. These rights are enforced through the legal framework, which constitutes the set of laws within which an economy operates. An efficient and acceptable legal framework for a market economy includes the definition of property rights, the laws of contract, and a system for adjudicating disputes.

As the ex-communist countries are discovering, it is very difficult to have a market economy when there are no laws enforcing contracts or guaranteeing that a company can keep its own profits. And when the legal framework breaks down, as in the former Yugoslavia or in drug-producing countries like Colombia, people begin to fear for their lives and have little time or inclination to make long-term investments for the future. Production falls and the quality of life deteriorates. Indeed, many of the most horrifying African famines were caused by civil war and the breakdown in the legal order, not by bad weather.

The environment is another example where poorly designed property rights harm the economy. Water and air are generally open-access resources, meaning that no one owns or controls them. As the saying goes, "Everyone's business is nobody's business." In this area, people do not weigh all the costs of their actions. Someone might throw trash into the water or emit smoke into the air because the costs of dirty water or foul air are borne by other people. By contrast, people are less likely to throw trash on their own lawn or burn coal in their own living room because they themselves will bear the costs.

In recent years, economists have proposed extending property rights to environmental commodities by selling or auctioning permits to pollute and allowing them to be traded on markets. Preliminary evidence suggests that this extension of property rights has given much more powerful incentives to reduce pollution efficiently.

A modern economy depends upon special features to become highly productive. Division of labor and specialized capital goods allow individuals to become highly skilled in particular areas. But specialized entities can survive only because monetized trade allows different people and countries easily to sell their products and buy things for everyday life. Specialization creates enormous efficiencies; increased production makes trade possible; money allows trade to take place quickly and efficiently; and a sophisticated financial system is crucial for transforming some people's savings into other people's capital.

C. THE ECONOMIC ROLE OF GOVERNMENT

An ideal market economy is one in which all goods and services are voluntarily exchanged for money at market prices. Such a system squeezes the maximum benefits out of a society's available resources without government intervention. In the real world, however, no economy actually conforms totally to the idealized world of the smoothly functioning invisible hand. Rather, every market economy suffers from imperfections which lead to such ills as excessive pollution, unemployment, and extremes of wealth and poverty.

For that reason, no government anywhere in the world, no matter how conservative, keeps its hands off the economy. In modern economies, governments take on many tasks in response to the flaws in the market mechanism. The military, the police, the national weather service, and highway construction are all typical areas of government activity. Socially useful ventures such as space exploration and scientific research benefit from government funding. Governments may regulate some businesses (such as banking and drugs) while subsidizing others (such as education and health care). Governments also tax their citizens and redistribute some of the proceeds to the elderly and needy.

How do governments perform their functions? Governments operate by requiring people to pay taxes, obey regulations, and consume certain collective goods and services. Because of its coercive powers, the government can perform functions that would not be possible under voluntary exchange. Government coercion increases the freedoms and consumption of those who benefit while reducing the incomes and opportunities of those who are taxed or regulated.

Governments have three main economic functions in a market economy. These functions are increasing efficiency, promoting equity, and fostering macroeconomic stability and growth.

1. Governments increase *efficiency* by promoting competition, curbing externalities like pollution, and providing public goods.
2. Governments promote *equity* by using tax and expenditure programs to redistribute income toward particular groups.
3. Governments foster *macroeconomic stability and growth*—reducing unemployment and inflation while encouraging economic growth—through fiscal policy and monetary regulation.

We will examine briefly each function.

EFFICIENCY

Adam Smith recognized that the virtues of the market mechanism are fully realized only when the checks and balances of perfect competition are present. What is meant by **perfect competition?** This technical term refers to a market in which no firm or consumer is large enough to affect the market price. For example, the wheat market is perfectly competitive because the largest wheat farm, producing only a minuscule fraction of the world's wheat, can have no appreciable effect upon the price of wheat.

The invisible-hand doctrine applies to economies in which all markets are perfectly competitive. Perfectly competitive markets will produce an efficient allocation of resources, so the economy is on its production-possibility frontier. When all industries are subject to the checks and balances of perfect competition, as we will see later in this book, markets will produce the bundle of outputs most desired by consumers using the most efficient techniques and the minimum amount of inputs.

Alas, there are many ways that markets can fall short of efficient perfect competition. The three most important ones involve imperfect competition, such as monopolies; externalities, such as pollution; and public goods, such as national defense and light-houses. In each case, market failure leads to inefficient production or consumption, and government can play a useful role in curing the disease.

Imperfect Competition

One serious deviation from an efficient market comes from *imperfect competition* or *monopoly* elements. Whereas under perfect competition no firm or consumer can affect prices, **imperfect competition** occurs when a buyer or seller can affect a good's price. For example, if the telephone company or a labor union is large enough to influence the price of phone service or labor, respectively, some degree of imperfect competition has set in. When imperfect competition arises, society may move inside its *PPF*. This would occur, for example, if a single seller (a monopolist) raised the price to earn extra profits. The output of that good would be reduced below the most efficient level, and the efficiency of the economy would thereby suffer. In such a situation, the invisible-hand property of markets may be violated.

What is the effect of imperfect competition? Imperfect competition leads to prices that rise above cost and to consumer purchases that are reduced below efficient levels. The pattern of too high price and too low output is the hallmark of the inefficiencies associated with imperfect competition.

In reality, almost all industries possess some measure of imperfect competition. Airlines, for example, may have no competition on some of their routes but face several rivals on others. The extreme case of imperfect competition is the *monopolist*—a single supplier who alone determines the price of a particular good or service. For example, Microsoft has been a monopolist in the production of Windows operating systems.

Over the last century, most governments have taken steps to curb the most extreme forms of imperfect competition. Governments sometimes regulate the price and profits of monopolies such as local water, telephone, and electric utilities. In addition, government antitrust laws prohibit actions such as price fixing and agreeing to divide up markets. The most important check to imperfect competition, however, is the opening of markets to competitors, whether they be domestic or foreign. Few monopolies can long withstand the attack of competitors unless governments protect them through tariffs or regulations.

Externalities

A second type of inefficiency arises when there are spillovers or externalities, which involve involuntary imposition of costs or benefits. Market transactions involve voluntary exchange in which people exchange goods or services for money. When a firm buys a chicken to make frozen drumsticks, it buys the chicken from its owner in the chicken market, and the seller receives the full value of the hen. When you buy a haircut, the barber receives the full value for time, skills, and rent.

But many interactions take place outside markets. While airports produce a lot of noise, they generally do not compensate the people living around the airport for disturbing their peace. On the other hand, some companies which spend heavily on research and development have positive spillover effects for the rest of society. For example, researchers at AT&T invented the transistor and launched the electronic revolution, but AT&T's profits increased by only a small fraction of the global social gains. In each case, an activity has helped or hurt people outside the marketplace; that is, there was an economic transaction without an economic payment.

Externalities (or spillover effects) occur when firms or people impose costs or benefits on others outside the marketplace.

Governments are generally more concerned with negative externalities than positive ones. As our society has become more densely populated and as the production of energy, chemicals, and other materials increases, negative externalities or spillover effects have grown from little nuisances into major threats. This is where governments come in. Government *regulations* are designed to control externalities like air and water pollution, damage from strip mining, hazardous wastes, unsafe drugs and foods, and radioactive materials.

In many ways, governments are like parents, always saying no: Thou shalt not expose thy workers to dangerous conditions. Thou shalt not pour out poisonous smoke from thy factory chimney. Thou shalt not sell mind-altering drugs. Thou shalt not drive without wearing thy seat belt. And so forth. Finding the correct balance between free markets and government regulation is a difficult task that requires careful analysis of the costs and benefits of each approach. But few people today would argue for returning to the unregulated economic jungle where firms would be allowed to dump pollutants like plutonium wherever they wanted.

Public Goods

While negative externalities like pollution or global warming command most of the headlines, positive externalities may well be economically more significant. Important examples of positive externalities are construction of a highway network, operation of a national weather service, support of basic science, and provision of measures to enhance public health. These are not goods which can be bought and sold in markets. Adequate private production of these public goods will not occur because the benefits are so widely dispersed across the population that no single firm or consumer has an economic incentive to provide the service and capture the returns.

The polar case of a positive externality is a public good. **Public goods** are commodities which can be enjoyed by everyone and from which no one can be excluded. A classic example of a public good is the military. When a nation goes to war—to root out terrorists, to look for weapons of mass destruction, to grab land or oil, or to stir up patriotic sentiments—all must pay the piper and all will suffer the consequences, whether they want to or not.

Because private provision of public goods is generally insufficient, the government must step in to encourage the production of public goods. In buying public goods like national defense or lighthouses, the government is behaving exactly like any other large spender. By casting sufficient dollar votes in certain directions, it causes resources to flow there. Once the dollar votes are cast, the market mechanism then takes over and channels resources to firms so that the lighthouses or tanks get produced.

Are Lighthouses Public Goods?

For many years, lighthouses were used to illustrate the notion of public goods. They save lives and cargoes. But lighthouse keepers cannot reach out to collect fees from ships; nor, if they could, would it serve an efficient social purpose for them to exact an economic penalty on ships who use their services. The light can be provided most efficiently free of charge, for it costs no more to warn 100 ships than to warn a single ship of the nearby rocks.

This view became controversial when Nobel Prize–winning economist Ronald Coase reviewed the history of lighthouses in England and Wales and determined that these had been *privately* operated. Coase found that English lighthouses operated profitably under licenses purchased from the Crown and were financed by government-authorized "light duties" levied on ships which used nearby ports. From this history, Coase concluded that "contrary to the belief of many economists, a lighthouse service can be provided by private enterprise." Some have even concluded that lighthouses are not public goods.

But let's look carefully here. The two key attributes of a public good are that the cost of extending the service to an additional person is zero ("nonrivalry") and that it is impossible to exclude individuals from enjoying it ("nonexcludability"). Both these characteristics are applicable to lighthouses.

But a "public" good is not necessarily publicly provided. Often, it is provided by no one. Moreover, just because it is privately provided does not indicate that it is efficiently provided or that a market mechanism can pay for the lighthouse. The English example shows the interesting case where, *if* provision of the public good can be tied to another good or service (in this case, vessel tonnage), and *if* the government gives private persons the right to collect what are essentially taxes, then an alternative mechanism for *financing* the public good can be found. Such an approach would work poorly where the fees could not be easily tied to tonnage (such as in international waterways). And it would not work at all if the government refused to privatize the right to collect light duties on shipping.

America shows quite a different experience. From its earliest days, the United States believed that navigational aids should be government-provided. Indeed, one of the first acts of the first Congress, and America's first public-works law, provided that "the necessary support, maintenance, and repairs of all lighthouses, beacons, [and] buoys ... shall be defrayed out of the Treasury of the United States."

But, like many public goods, lighthouses were provided meager funding, and it is interesting to note what happened in the absence of navigational aids. A fascinating case lies off the east coast of Florida, which is a treacherous waterway with a 200-mile reef lying submerged a few feet below the surface in the most active hurricane track of the Atlantic Ocean. This heavily used channel was prime territory for storm, shipwreck, and piracy.

There were no lighthouses in Florida until 1825, and no private-sector lighthouses were ever built in this area. The market responded vigorously to the perils, however. What arose from the private sector was a thriving "wrecking" industry. Wreckers were ships that lurked near the dangerous reefs waiting for an unfortunate boat to become disabled. The wreckers would then appear, offer their help in saving lives and cargo, tow the boat into the appropriate port, and then claim a substantial part of the value of the cargo. Wrecking was the major industry of south Florida in the mid-nineteenth century and made Key West the richest town in America at that time.

While wreckers probably had positive value added, they provided none of the public-good attributes of lighthouses. Indeed, because many cargoes were insured, there was significant "moral hazard" involved in navigation. Connivance between wreckers and captains often enriched both at the expense of owners and insurance companies. It was only when the U.S. Lighthouse Service, financed by government revenues, began to build lighthouses through the Florida channel that the number of shipwrecks began to decrease—and the wreckers were gradually driven out of business.

Lighthouses are no longer a central issue of public policy today and are mainly of interest to tourists. They have been largely replaced by the satellite-based Global Positioning System (GPS), which is also a public good provided free by the government. But the history of lighthouses reminds us of the problems that can arise when public goods are inefficiently provided.

Taxes. The government must find the revenues to pay for its public goods and for its income-redistribution programs. Such revenues come from taxes levied on personal and corporate incomes, on wages, on sales of consumer goods, and on other items. All levels of government—city, state, and federal—collect taxes to pay for their spending.

Taxes sound like another "price"—in this case the price we pay for public goods. But taxes differ from prices in one crucial respect: taxes are not voluntary. Everyone is subject to the tax laws; we are all obligated to pay for our share of the cost of public goods. Of course, through our democratic process, we as citizens choose both the public goods and the taxes to pay for them. However, the close connection between spending and consumption that we see for private goods does not hold for taxes and public goods. I pay for a hamburger only if I want one, but I must pay my share of the taxes used to finance defense and public education even if I don't care a bit for these activities.

EQUITY

Our discussion of market failures like monopoly or externalities focused on defects in the allocative role of markets—imperfections that can be corrected by careful intervention. But assume for the moment that the economy functioned with complete efficiency—always on the production-possibility frontier and never inside it, always choosing the right amount of public versus private goods, and so forth. Even if the market system worked perfectly, it might still lead to a flawed outcome.

Markets do not necessarily produce a fair distribution of income. A market economy may produce inequalities in income and consumption that are not acceptable to the electorate.

Why might the market mechanism produce an unacceptable solution to the question *for whom?* The reason is that incomes are determined by a wide variety of factors, including effort, education, inheritance, factor prices, and luck. The resulting income distribution may not correspond to a fair outcome. Moreover, recall that goods follow dollar votes and not the greatest need. A rich man's cat may drink the milk that a poor boy needs to remain healthy. Does this happen because the market is failing? Not at all, for the market mechanism is doing its job—putting goods in the hands of those who have the dollar votes. Even the most efficient market system may generate great inequality.

Often the income distribution in a market system is the result of accidents of birth. Every year *Forbes* magazine lists the 400 richest Americans, and it's impressive how many of them either received their wealth by inheritance or used inherited wealth as a springboard to even greater wealth. Would everyone regard that as necessarily right or ideal? Should someone be allowed to become a billionaire simply by inheriting 5000 square miles of rangeland or the family's holding of oil wells? That's the way the cookie crumbles under laissez-faire capitalism.

For most of American history, economic growth was a rising tide that lifted all boats, raising the incomes of the poor as well as those of the rich. But over the last two decades, changes in family structure and declining wages of the less skilled and less educated have reversed the trend. With a return to greater emphasis on the market has come greater homelessness, more children living in poverty, and deterioration of many of America's central cities.

Income inequalities may be politically or ethically unacceptable. A nation does not need to accept the outcome of competitive markets as predetermined and immutable; people may examine the distribution of income and decide it is unfair. If a democratic society does not like the distribution of dollar votes under a laissez-faire market system, it can take steps to change the distribution of income.

Let's say that voters decide to reduce income inequality. What tools could the government use to implement that decision? First, it can engage in *progressive taxation,* taxing large incomes at a higher rate than small incomes. It might impose heavy taxes on wealth or on large inheritances to break the chain of privilege. The federal income and inheritance taxes are examples of such redistributive progressive taxation.

Second, because low tax rates cannot help those who have no income at all, governments can make *transfer payments,* which are money payments to people. Such transfers today include aid for the elderly, blind, and disabled and for those with dependent children, as well as unemployment insurance for the jobless. This system of transfer payments provides a "safety net" to protect the unfortunate from privation. And, finally, governments sometimes subsidize consumption of low-income groups by providing food stamps, subsidized medical care, and low-cost housing—though in the United States, such spending comprises a relatively small share of total spending.

These programs have become increasingly unpopular in the last two decades. As the real wages of the middle class have stagnated, people naturally ask why they should support the homeless or able-bodied people who do not work. What can economics contribute to debates about equality? Economics as a science cannot answer such normative questions as how much of our market incomes—if any—should be transferred to poor families. This is a political question that can be answered only at the ballot box.

Economics can, however, analyze the costs and benefits of different redistributive systems. Economists have devoted much time to analyzing whether different income-redistribution devices (such as taxes and food stamps) lead to social waste (e.g., people working less or buying drugs rather than food). They have also studied whether giving poor people cash rather than goods is likely to be a more efficient way of reducing poverty. Economics cannot answer questions of how much poverty is acceptable and fair, but it can help design more effective programs to increase the incomes of the poor.

MACROECONOMIC GROWTH AND STABILITY

Since its origins, capitalism has been plagued by periodic bouts of inflation (rising prices) and recession (high unemployment). Since World War II, for example, there have been 10 recessions in the United States, some putting millions of people out of work. These fluctuations are known as the *business cycle.*

Today, thanks to the intellectual contribution of John Maynard Keynes and his followers, we know how to control the worst excesses of the business cycle. By careful use of fiscal and monetary policies, governments can affect output, employment, and inflation. The *fiscal policies* of government involve the power to tax and the power to spend. *Monetary policy* involves determining the supply of money and interest rates; these affect investment in capital goods and other interest-rate-sensitive spending. Using these two fundamental tools of macroeconomic policy, governments can influence the level of total spending, the rate of growth and level of output, the levels of employment and unemployment, and the price level and rate of inflation in an economy.

Governments in advanced industrial countries have successfully applied the lessons of the Keynesian

Failure of market economy	Government intervention	Current examples of government policy
Inefficiency:		
Monopoly	Encourage competition	Antitrust laws, deregulation
Externalities	Intervene in markets	Antipollution laws, antismoking ordinances
Public goods	Encourage beneficial activities	Build guidance systems, provide public education
Inequality:		
Unacceptable inequalities of income and wealth	Redistribute income	Progressive taxation of income and wealth
		Income-support or transfer programs (e.g., food stamps)
Macroeconomic problems:		
Business cycles (high inflation and unemployment)	Stabilize through macroeconomic policies	Monetary policies (e.g., changes in money supply and interest rates)
		Fiscal policies (e.g., taxes and spending programs)
Slow economic growth	Stimulate growth	Improve efficiency of tax system
		Raise national savings rate by reducing budget deficit or increasing budget surplus

TABLE 2-1. Government Can Remedy the Shortcomings of the Market

revolution over the last half-century. Spurred on by active monetary and fiscal policies, the market economies witnessed a period of unprecedented economic growth in the three decades after World War II.

In the 1980s, governments became more concerned with designing macroeconomic policies to promote long-term objectives, such as economic growth and productivity. (*Economic growth* denotes the growth in a nation's total output, while *productivity* represents the output per unit input or the efficiency with which resources are used.) For example, tax rates were lowered in most industrial countries in order to improve incentives for saving and production. Many economists emphasize the importance of public saving through smaller budget deficits as a way to increase national saving and investment.

Macroeconomic policies for stabilization and economic growth include fiscal policies (of taxing and spending) along with monetary policies (which affect interest rates and credit conditions). Since the development of macroeconomics in the 1930s, governments have succeeded in curbing the worst excesses of inflation and unemployment.

Table 2-1 summarizes the economic role played by government today. It shows the important governmental functions of promoting efficiency, achieving a fairer distribution of income, and pursuing the macroeconomic objectives of economic growth and stability. In all advanced industrial societies we find some variant of a **mixed economy,** in which the market determines output and prices in most individual sectors while government steers the overall economy with programs of taxation, spending, and monetary regulation.

TWILIGHT OF THE WELFARE STATE?

In 1942, the great Austria-born Harvard economist Joseph Schumpeter argued that the United States was "capitalism living in an oxygen tent" on its march to socialism. Capitalism's success would breed alienation and self-doubt, sapping its efficiency and innovation. But he was wrong. The next half-century saw sustained growth in government's involvement in the economies of North America and Western Europe along with the most impressive economic performance ever recorded.

Rapid economic growth has been accompanied by increased skepticism about government's role. Critics of government say that the state is overly intrusive; governments create monopoly; government failures are just as pervasive as market failures; high taxes distort the allocation of resources; social security threatens to overload workers in the decades ahead; environmental regulation dulls the spirit of enterprise; government attempts to stabilize the economy must fail at best and increase inflation at worst. In short, for some, government is the problem rather than the solution.

Guardians of Economic Freedom: Friedrich Hayek and Milton Friedman

Economists, being human, are subject to fluctuations in opinions and ideology. Because government policies seemed so successful in mobilizing the U.S. and U.K. war economies for military victory over Germany and Japan during World War II, and because active macroeconomic policies seemed to succeed in conquering the Great Depression, conservative laissez-faire ideologies came to represent only minority opinion among most free-world professional economists.

Two eminent scholars never wavered in their skepticism about the merits of heavy government intervention in the economy. Friedrich Hayek (1899–1992), of Vienna, London, and Chicago, and Milton Friedman (1912–), of the University of Chicago and Stanford, received Nobel Prizes in economics for their scientific innovations. Their work is today highly regarded by conservative and "libertarian" economic thinkers.

Hayek's most influential work examined the efficiency of different forms of economic organization. The 1920s and 1930s witnessed a great debate as to whether resources could be efficiently organized under socialism. Oskar Lange and Abba Lerner argued that a socialist firm could use capitalist-style pricing and thereby emulate a market economy without the monopolistic tendencies of capitalism. Hayek provided an important rebuttal. He pointed out that costs and production possibilities are not known. Only with the incentives of a private, free-enterprise system could the information dispersed among the millions of economic agents be effectively mobilized and used. No system can generate innovations without the carrot of profits and the stick of bankruptcy. Modern economics, with its emphasis on dispersed and asymmetrical information, owes much to the brilliant insights of Hayek.

Hayek's best-seller, and the book that most captured the attention of the broader public, was *The Road to Serfdom*. In this work he warned that the road to the hell of totalitarian tyranny and economic inefficiency was paved by the good intentions of modest interferences with free markets and private enterprise.

Friedman's statistical and analytic researches have ranged widely. He documented how small the differences are between the saving rates of rich and poor in the long run after adjusting saving for temporary ups and downs in income. This led to the permanent-income theory of consumption (which is discussed in the macroeconomic sections of this text). Together with Anna Schwartz, Friedman authored the definitive *Monetary History of the United States, 1876–1960* (1963). This book launched the monetarist revolution and led to an appreciation among macroeconomists of how the money supply can affect aggregate spending, prices, and output. Friedman helped convince economists that monetary policy definitely matters for overall economic activity.

During the last half of the twentieth century, everywhere—in the United States, Western Europe, and Asia, as well as in the former Soviet Union and China—there has been a significant swing back toward the competitive-market pole and away from the centralized-command pole. No one within the economist guild has been more important, both as an architect and as an expositor of this shift, than Milton Friedman. His classic book, *Capitalism and Freedom* (1962), argues why a rational thinker might, along with advocating free international trade and maximal deregulation, deplore the minimum wage, state licensing of surgeons, and prohibition of drugs like heroin and cocaine. All thoughtful economists should study his arguments carefully.

The Mixed Economy Today

In weighing the relative merits of state and market, public debate often oversimplifies the complex choices that societies face. Markets have worked miracles in some countries. But without the right kind of legal and political structure, and without the social overhead capital that promotes trade and private investment, markets have also produced corrupt capitalism with great inequality, pervasive poverty, and declining living standards.

In economic affairs, success has many parents, while failure is an orphan. The success of market economies may lead people to overlook the many successes of collective action over the last century. Government programs have helped reduce poverty and malnutrition and have reduced the scourge of terrible diseases like tuberculosis and smallpox. Public expenditures have increased literacy and life expectancy. Military and diplomatic actions have brought down many of the worst tyrants. Macroeconomic successes have reduced the sting of inflation and unemployment. State-supported science has penetrated the atom, discovered the DNA molecule, and explored space.

Of course, these successes do not belong to governments alone. Governments harnessed private ingenuity through the market mechanism to help achieve these social aims. And, in some cases, governments were like orators who didn't know when enough was enough.

The debate about government's successes and failures demonstrates again that drawing the boundary between market and government is an enduring problem. The tools of economics are indispensable to help societies find the golden mean between laissez-faire market mechanisms and democratic rules of the road. The good mixed economy is, perforce, the limited mixed economy. But those who would reduce government to the constable plus a few lighthouses are living in a dream world. An efficient and humane society requires both halves of the mixed system—market and government. Operating a modern economy without both is like trying to clap with one hand.

SUMMARY

A. What Is a Market?

1. In an economy like the United States, most economic decisions are made in markets, which are mechanisms through which buyers and sellers meet to trade and to determine prices and quantities for goods and services. Adam Smith proclaimed that the *invisible hand* of markets would lead to the optimal economic outcome as individuals pursue their own self-interest. And while markets are far from perfect, they have proved remarkably effective at solving the problems of *how, what*, and *for whom.*

2. The market mechanism works as follows to determine the *what* and the *how:* The dollar votes of people affect prices of goods; these prices serve as guides for the amounts of the different goods to be produced. When people demand more of a good, its price will increase and businesses can profit by expanding production of that good. Under perfect competition, a business must find the cheapest method of production, efficiently using labor, land, and other factors; otherwise, it will incur losses and be eliminated from the market.

3. At the same time that the *what* and *how* problems are being resolved by prices, so is the problem of *for whom.* The distribution of income is determined by the ownership of factors of production (land, labor, and capital) and by factor prices. People possessing fertile land or the ability to hit home runs will earn many dollar votes to buy consumer goods. Those without property or with skills, color, or sex that the market undervalues will receive low incomes.

B. Trade, Money, and Capital

4. As economies develop, they become more specialized. Division of labor allows a task to be broken into a number of smaller chores that can each be mastered and performed more quickly by a single worker. Specialization arises from the increasing tendency to use roundabout methods of production that require many specialized skills. As individuals and countries become increasingly specialized, they tend to concentrate on particular commodities and trade their surplus output for goods produced by others. Voluntary trade, based on specialization, benefits all.

5. Trade in specialized goods and services today relies on money to lubricate its wheels. Money is the universally acceptable medium of exchange—including primarily currency and checking deposits. It is used to pay for everything from apple tarts to zebra skins. By accepting money, people and nations can specialize in producing a few goods and can then trade them for others; without money, we would waste much time negotiating and bartering.

6. Capital goods—produced inputs such as machinery, structures, and inventories of goods in process—permit roundabout methods of production that add much to a nation's output. These roundabout methods take time

and resources to get started and therefore require a temporary sacrifice of present consumption in order to increase future consumption. The rules that define how capital and other assets can be bought, sold, and used are the system of property rights. In no economic system are private-property rights unlimited.

C. The Economic Role of Government

7. Although the market mechanism is an admirable way of producing and allocating goods, sometimes market failures lead to deficiencies in the economic outcomes. The government may step in to correct these failures. Its role in a modern economy is to ensure efficiency, to correct an unfair distribution of income, and to promote economic growth and stability.

8. Markets fail to provide an efficient allocation of resources in the presence of imperfect competition or externalities. Imperfect competition, such as monopoly, produces high prices and low levels of output. To combat these conditions, governments regulate businesses or put legal antitrust constraints on business behavior. Externalities arise when activities impose costs or bestow benefits that are not paid for in the marketplace. Governments may decide to step in and regulate these spillovers (as it does with air pollution) or provide for *public goods* (as in the case of public health).

9. Markets do not necessarily produce a fair distribution of income; they may spin off unacceptably high inequality of income and consumption. In response, governments can alter the pattern of incomes (the *for whom*) generated by market wages, rents, interest, and dividends. Modern governments use taxation to raise revenues for transfers or income-support programs that place a financial safety net under the needy.

10. Since the development of macroeconomics in the 1930s, the government has undertaken a third role: using fiscal powers (of taxing and spending) and monetary policy (affecting credit and interest rates) to promote long-run economic growth and productivity and to tame the business cycle's excesses of inflation and unemployment. Since 1980, the blend of the mixed economy called the welfare state has been on the defensive in the enduring struggle over the boundary between state and market.

CONCEPTS FOR REVIEW

The Market Mechanism

market, market mechanism
markets for goods and for factors
   of production
prices as signals
market equilibrium
perfect and imperfect competition
Adam Smith's invisible-hand doctrine

Features of a Modern Economy

specialization and division of labor
money
factors of production (land, labor,
   capital)
capital, private property, and property
   rights

Government's Economic Role

efficiency, equity, stability
inefficiencies: monopoly and
   externalities
inequity of incomes under markets
macroeconomic policies:
   fiscal and monetary policies
   stabilization and growth

FURTHER READING AND INTERNET WEBSITES

Further Reading

A useful discussion of globalization is contained in "Symposium on Globalization in Perspective," *Journal of Economic Perspectives,* Fall 1998.

For examples of the writings of libertarian economists, see Milton Friedman, *Capitalism and Freedom* (University of Chicago Press, 1963), and Friedrich Hayek, *The Road to Serfdom* (University of Chicago Press, 1994).

A strong defense of government interventions is found in a history of the 1990s by Nobel Prize winner and Clinton adviser Joseph E. Stiglitz, *The Roaring Nineties: A New History of the World's Most Prosperous Decade* (Norton, New York, 2003). Paul Krugman's columns in *The New York Times* are a guide to current economic issues from the perspective of one of America's most distinguished economists; his most recent book, *The Great Unraveling: Losing Our Way in the New Century*

(Norton, New York, 2003), collects his columns from the early 2000s.

A fascinating example of how a small economy is organized without money is found in R. A. Radford, "The Economic Organization of a P.O.W. Camp," *Economica*, vol. 12, November 1945, pp. 189–201.

Websites

You can explore recent analyses of the economy along with a discussion of major economic policy issues in the

Economic Report of the President at w3.access.gpo.gov/eop/. See www.whitehouse.gov for federal budget information and as an entry point into the useful Economic Statistics Briefing Room.

Major issues are presented from a conservative or libertarian economic perspective at the website of the Cato Institute, www.cato.org/.

QUESTIONS FOR DISCUSSION

1. What determines the composition of national output? In some cases, we say that there is "consumer sovereignty," meaning that consumers decide how to spend their incomes on the basis of their tastes and market prices. In other cases, decisions are made by political choices of legislatures. Consider the following examples: transportation, education, police, energy efficiency of appliances, health-care coverage, television advertising. For each, describe whether the allocation is by consumer sovereignty or by political decision. Would you change the method of allocation for any of these goods?

2. When a good is limited, some means must be found to ration the scarce commodity. Some examples of rationing devices are auctions, ration coupons, and first-come, first-served systems. What are the strengths and weaknesses of each? Explain carefully in what sense a market mechanism "rations" scarce goods and services.

3. This chapter discusses many "market failures," areas in which the invisible hand guides the economy poorly, and describes the role of government. Is it possible that there are, as well, "government failures," government attempts to curb market failures that are worse than the original market failures? Think of some examples of government failures. Give some examples in which government failures are so bad that it is better to live with the market failures than to try to correct them.

4. Consider the following cases of government intervention: regulations to limit air pollution, income support for the poor, and price regulation of a telephone monopoly. For each case, (*a*) explain the market failure, (*b*) describe a government intervention to treat the problem, and (*c*) explain how "government failure" (see the definition in question 3) might arise because of the intervention.

5. The circular flow of goods and inputs illustrated in Figure 2-1 has a corresponding flow of dollar incomes and spending. Draw a circular-flow diagram for the

dollar flows in the economy, and compare it with the circular flow of goods and inputs. What is the role of money in the dollar circular flow?

6. Give three examples of specialization and division of labor. In what areas are you and your friends thinking of specializing? What might be the perils of overspecialization?

7. "Lincoln freed the slaves. With one pen stroke he destroyed much of the capital the South had accumulated over the years." Comment.

8. The table below shows some of the major expenditures of the federal government. Explain how each one relates to the economic role of government.

9. Why does the saying "No taxation without representation" make sense for public goods but not private goods? Explain the mechanisms by which individuals can "protest" against (*a*) taxes that are thought excessive to pay for defense spending, (*b*) tolls that are thought excessive to pay for a bridge, and (*c*) prices that are thought excessive for an airline flight from New York to Miami.

Major Expenditure Categories for Federal Government	
Budget category	**Federal spending, 2005 ($, billion)**
Health care and Medicare	547
Social security	515
National defense	451
Income security	348
Interest on public debt	178
Natural resources and environment	31
International affairs	38

Source: Office of Management and Budget, *Budget of the United States Government*, Fiscal Year 2005.

CHAPTER

3

Basic Elements of Supply and Demand

What is a cynic? A man who knows the price of everything and the value of nothing.

Oscar Wilde

Like the weather, markets are dynamic, subject to periods of storm and calm, and constantly evolving. Yet, as with weather forecasting, a careful study of markets will reveal certain forces underlying the apparently random movements. To forecast prices and outputs in individual markets, you must first master the analysis of supply and demand.

Take the example of gasoline prices, illustrated in Figure 3-1 on page 46. (This graph shows the "real gasoline price," or the price corrected for movements in the general price level.) Demand for gasoline and other oil products rose sharply after World War II as people fell in love with the automobile and moved increasingly to the suburbs. Next, in the 1970s, supply restrictions, wars among producers, and political revolutions reduced production, with the consequent price spikes seen after 1973 and 1979. In the years that followed, a combination of energy conservation, smaller cars, the growth of the information economy, and expanded production around the world led to falling oil prices. War in Iraq in 2003 produced yet further turmoil in oil markets. As Figure 3-1 shows, the real price of gasoline (in 2003 prices) fell from around $2.80 per gallon in 1980 to around $1.60 per gallon in early 2004. Most of the volatility of oil prices has been associated with supply interruptions during wars or revolutions.

What lay behind these dramatic shifts? Economics has a very powerful tool for explaining such changes in the economic environment. It is called the *theory of supply and demand.* This theory shows how consumer preferences determine consumer demand for commodities, while business costs are the foundation of the supply of commodities. The increases in the price of gasoline occurred either because the demand for gasoline had increased or because the supply of oil had decreased. The same is true for every market, from Internet stocks to diamonds to land: changes in supply and demand drive changes in output and prices. If you understand how supply and demand work, you have gone a long way toward understanding a market economy.

This chapter introduces the notions of supply and demand and shows how they operate in competitive markets for *individual commodities.* We begin with demand curves and then discuss supply curves. Using these basic tools, we will see how the market price is determined where these two curves intersect—where the forces of demand and supply are just in balance. It is the movement of prices—the price mechanism—which brings supply and demand into balance or

45

FIGURE 3-1. Gasoline Prices Move with Demand and Supply Changes

Gasoline prices have fluctuated sharply over the last four decades. Supply reductions in the 1970s produced two dramatic "oil shocks," which provoked social unrest and calls for increased regulation. Reductions in demand from new energy-saving technologies led to the long decline in price after 1980. Wars against Iraq led to price spikes in 1990 and 2003. The tools of supply and demand are crucial for understanding these trends.

Source: U.S. Departments of Energy and Labor. The price of gasoline has been converted into 2003 prices using the consumer price index.

equilibrium. This chapter closes with some examples of how supply-and-demand analysis can be applied.

A. THE DEMAND SCHEDULE

Both common sense and careful scientific observation show that the amount of a commodity people buy depends on its price. The higher the price of an article, other things held constant,[1] the fewer units

consumers are willing to buy. The lower its market price, the more units of it are bought.

There exists a definite relationship between the market price of a good and the quantity demanded of that good, other things held constant. This relationship between price and quantity bought is called the **demand schedule**, or the **demand curve**.

Let's look at a simple example. Table 3-1 presents a hypothetical demand schedule for cornflakes. At each price, we can determine the quantity of cornflakes that consumers purchase. For example, at $5 per box, consumers will buy 9 million boxes per year.

At a lower price, more cornflakes are bought. Thus, at a price of $4, the quantity bought is 10 million boxes. At yet a lower price (*P*) equal to $3, the quantity demanded (*Q*) is still greater, at 12 million. And so forth. We can determine the quantity demanded at each listed price in Table 3-1.

---

[1] Later in this chapter we discuss the other factors that influence demand, including income and tastes. The term "other things held constant" simply means we are varying the price without changing any of these other determinants of demand.

Demand Schedule for Cornflakes		
	(1) Price ($ per box) *P*	**(2)** Quantity demanded (millions of boxes per year) *Q*
A	5	9
B	4	10
C	3	12
D	2	15
E	1	20

TABLE 3-1. The Demand Schedule Relates Quantity Demanded to Price

At each market price, consumers will want to buy a certain quantity of cornflakes. As the price of cornflakes falls, the quantity of cornflakes demanded will rise.

FIGURE 3-2. A Downward-Sloping Demand Curve Relates Quantity Demanded to Price

In the demand curve for cornflakes, price (*P*) is measured on the vertical axis while quantity demanded (*Q*) is measured on the horizontal axis. Each pair of (*P*, *Q*) numbers from Table 3-1 is plotted as a point, and then a smooth curve is passed through the points to give us a demand curve, DD. The negative slope of the demand curve illustrates the law of downward-sloping demand.

THE DEMAND CURVE

The graphical representation of the demand schedule is the *demand curve*. We show the demand curve in Figure 3-2, which graphs the quantity of cornflakes demanded on the horizontal axis and the price of cornflakes on the vertical axis. Note that quantity and price are inversely related; that is, *Q* goes up when *P* goes down. The curve slopes downward, going from northwest to southeast. This important property is called the *law of downward-sloping demand*. It is based on common sense as well as economic theory and has been empirically tested and verified for practically all commodities—cornflakes, gasoline, college education, and illegal drugs being a few examples.

Law of downward-sloping demand: When the price of a commodity is raised (and other things are held constant), buyers tend to buy less of the commodity. Similarly, when the price is lowered, other things being constant, quantity demanded increases.

Quantity demanded tends to fall as price rises for two reasons. First is the **substitution effect.** When the price of a good rises, I will substitute other similar goods for it (as the price of beef rises, I eat more chicken). A second reason why a higher price reduces quantity demanded is the **income effect.** This comes into play because when a price goes up, I find myself somewhat poorer than I was before. If

gasoline prices double, I have in effect less real income, so I will naturally curb my consumption of gasoline and other goods.

Market Demand

Our discussion of demand has so far referred to "the" demand curve. But whose demand is it? Mine? Yours? Everybody's? The fundamental building block for demand is individual preferences. However, in this chapter we will always focus on the *market demand,* which represents the sum total of all individual demands. The market demand is what is observable in the real world.

The market demand curve is found by adding together the quantities demanded by all individuals at each price.

Does the market demand curve obey the law of downward-sloping demand? It certainly does. If prices drop, for example, the lower prices attract new customers through the substitution effect. In addition, a price reduction will induce extra purchases of goods by existing consumers through both the income and the substitution effects. Conversely, a rise in the price of a good will cause some of us to buy less.

The Explosive Growth in Computer Demand

We can illustrate the law of downward-sloping demand for the case of personal computers (PCs). The prices of the first PCs were high, and their computing power was relatively modest. They were found in few businesses and even fewer homes. It is hard to believe that just 20 years ago students wrote most of their papers in longhand and did most calculations by hand or with simple calculators.

But the prices of computing power fell sharply over the last two decades. As the prices fell, new buyers were enticed to buy their first computers. PCs came to be widely used for work, for school, and for fun. In the early 2000s, as the value of computers increased with the development of the Internet, yet more people jumped on the computer bandwagon. Worldwide, PC sales totaled about 100 million in 2002.

Figure 3-3 shows the prices and quantities of computers and peripheral equipment in the United States as calculated by government statisticians. The prices reflect the cost of purchasing computers with constant quality—that is, they take into account the rapid quality change of the average computer purchased. You can see how falling prices along with improved software, increased utility of the Internet and e-mail, and other factors have led to an explosive growth in computer output.

Forces behind the Demand Curve

What determines the market demand curve for cornflakes or gasoline or computers? A whole array of factors influences how much will be demanded at a given price: average levels of income, the size of the population, the prices and availability of related goods, individual and social tastes, and special influences.

- The *average income* of consumers is a key determinant of demand. As people's incomes rise, individuals tend to buy more of almost everything, even if prices don't change. Automobile purchases tend to rise sharply with higher levels of income.

- The *size of the market*—measured, say, by the population—clearly affects the market demand curve. California's 35 million people tend to buy 35 times more apples and cars than do Rhode Island's 1 million people.

- The prices and availability of *related goods* influence the demand for a commodity. A particularly important connection exists among substitute goods—ones that tend to perform the same function, such as cornflakes and oatmeal, pens and pencils, small cars and large cars, or oil and natural gas. Demand for good A tends to be low if the price of substitute product B is low. (For example, if the price of computers falls, will that increase or decrease the demand for typewriters?)

- In addition to these objective elements, there is a set of subjective elements called *tastes* or *preferences*. Tastes represent a variety of cultural and historical influences. They may reflect genuine psychological or physiological needs (for liquids, love, or excitement). And they may include artificially contrived cravings (for cigarettes, drugs, or fancy sports cars). They may also contain a large element of tradition or religion (eating beef is popular in America but taboo in India, while curried jellyfish is a delicacy in Japan but would make many Americans gag).

- Finally, *special influences* will affect the demand for particular goods. The demand for umbrellas is high in rainy Seattle but low in sunny Phoenix; the demand for air conditioners will rise in hot weather; the demand for automobiles will be low in New York, where public transportation is plentiful and parking is a nightmare. In addition, expectations about future economic conditions, particularly prices, may have an important impact on demand.

The determinants of demand are summarized in Table 3-2, which uses automobiles as an example.

Shifts in Demand

As economic life evolves, demand changes incessantly. Demand curves sit still only in textbooks.

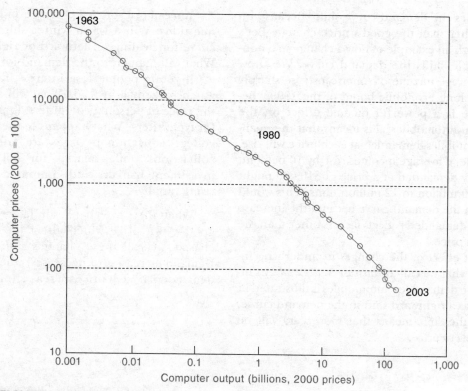

FIGURE 3-3. Declining Computer Prices Have Fueled an Explosive Growth in Computer Power

The prices of computers and peripheral devices such as printers are measured in terms of the cost of purchasing a given bundle of characteristics (such as memory or speed of calculations). The price of computer power has fallen more than a thousandfold since 1963. Falling prices along with higher incomes and a growing variety of uses have led to a 150,000-fold growth in the quantity of computers produced.

Source: Department of Commerce estimates of real output and prices. Note that the data are plotted on ratio scales.

Factors affecting the demand curve	Example for automobiles
1. **Average income**	As incomes rise, people increase car purchases.
2. **Population**	A growth in population increases car purchases.
3. **Prices of related goods**	Lower gasoline prices raise the demand for cars.
4. **Tastes**	Having a new car becomes a status symbol.
5. **Special influences**	Special influences include availability of alternative forms of transportation, safety of automobiles, expectations of future price increases, etc.

TABLE 3-2. Many Factors Affect the Demand Curve

Why does the demand curve shift? Because influences other than the good's price change. Let's work through an example of how a change in a nonprice variable shifts the demand curve. We know that the average income of Americans rose sharply during the long economic boom of the 1990s. Because there is a powerful income effect on the demand for automobiles, this means that the quantity of automobiles demanded at each price will rise. For example, if average incomes rose by 10 percent, the quantity demanded at a price of $10,000 might rise from 10 million to 12 million units. This would be a shift in the demand curve because the increase in quantity demanded reflects factors other than the good's own price.

The net effect of the changes in underlying influences is what we call an *increase in demand*. An increase in the demand for automobiles is illustrated in Figure 3-4 as a rightward shift in the demand curve. Note that the shift means that more cars will be bought at every price.

You can test yourself by answering the following questions: Will a warm winter shift the demand curve for heating oil leftward or rightward? Why? What will happen to the demand for baseball tickets if young people lose interest in baseball and watch basketball instead? What will a sharp fall in the price of personal computers do to the demand for typewriters? What happens to the demand for a college education if wages are falling for blue-collar jobs while salaries for college-educated investment bankers and computer scientists are rising rapidly?

When there are changes in factors other than a good's own price which affect the quantity purchased, we call these changes shifts in demand. Demand increases (or decreases) when the quantity demanded at each price increases (or decreases).

FIGURE 3-4. Increase in Demand for Automobiles

As elements underlying demand change, the demand for automobiles is affected. Here we see the effect of rising average income, increased population, and lower gasoline prices on the demand for automobiles. We call this shift of the demand curve an increase in demand.

> ### Movements along Curves versus Shifts of Curves
>
> Do not confuse movements along curves with shifts of curves. Great care must be taken not to confuse a change in demand (which denotes a shift of the demand curve) with a change in the quantity demanded (which means moving to a different point on the same demand curve after a price change).
>
> A change in demand occurs when one of the elements underlying the demand curve shifts. Take the case of pizzas. As incomes increase, consumers will want to buy more pizzas even if pizza prices do not change. In other words, higher incomes will increase demand and shift the demand curve for pizzas out and to the right. This is a shift in the demand for pizzas.
>
> Distinguish this from a change in quantity demanded that occurs because consumers tend to buy more pizzas as pizza prices fall, all other things remaining constant. Here, the increased purchases result not from an increase in demand but from the price decrease. This change represents a *movement along* the demand curve, not a *shift of* the demand curve. A movement along the demand curve means that other things were held constant when price changed.

B. THE SUPPLY SCHEDULE

Let us now turn from demand to supply. The supply side of a market typically involves the terms on which businesses produce and sell their products. The supply of tomatoes tells us the quantity of tomatoes that will be sold at each tomato price. More precisely, the supply schedule relates the quantity supplied of a good to its market price, other things constant. In considering supply, the other things that are held constant include input prices, prices of related goods, and government policies.

The **supply schedule** (or **supply curve**) for a commodity shows the relationship between its market price and the amount of that commodity that producers are willing to produce and sell, other things held constant.

THE SUPPLY CURVE

Table 3-3 shows a hypothetical supply schedule for cornflakes, and Figure 3-5 plots the data from the table in the form of a supply curve. These data show that at a cornflakes price of $1 per box, no cornflakes at all will be produced. At such a low price, breakfast cereal manufacturers might want to devote their factories to producing other types of cereal, like bran flakes, that earn them more profit than cornflakes. As the price of cornflakes increases, ever more cornflakes will be produced. At ever-higher cornflakes prices, cereal makers will find it profitable to add more workers and to buy more automated cornflakes-stuffing machines and even more cornflakes factories. All these will increase the output of cornflakes at the higher market prices.

Figure 3-5 shows the typical case of an upward-sloping supply curve for an individual commodity. One important reason for the upward slope is "the law of diminishing returns" (a concept we will learn more about later). Wine will illustrate this important law. If society wants more wine, then additional labor will have to be added to the limited land sites suitable for producing wine grapes. Each new worker will be adding less and less extra product. The price needed to coax out additional wine output is therefore higher. By raising the price of wine, society can persuade wine producers to

Supply Schedule for Cornflakes		
	(1) Price ($ per box) P	(2) Quantity supplied (millions of boxes per year) Q
A	5	18
B	4	16
C	3	12
D	2	7
E	1	0

TABLE 3-3. Supply Schedule Relates Quantity Supplied to Price

The table shows, for each price, the quantity of cornflakes that cereal makers want to produce and sell. Note the positive relation between price and quantity supplied.

FIGURE 3-5. Supply Curve Relates Quantity Supplied to Price

The supply curve plots the price and quantity pairs from Table 3-3. A smooth curve is passed through these points to give the upward-sloping supply curve, *SS*.

produce and sell more wine; the supply curve for wine is therefore upward-sloping. Similar reasoning applies to many other goods as well.

Forces behind the Supply Curve

In examining the forces determining the supply curve, the fundamental point to grasp is that producers supply commodities for profit and not for fun or charity. One major element underlying the supply curve is the *cost of production*. When production costs for a good are low relative to the market price, it is profitable for producers to supply a great deal. When production costs are high relative to price, firms produce little, switch to the production of other products, or may simply go out of business.

Production costs are primarily determined by the *prices of inputs* and *technological advances*. The prices of inputs such as labor, energy, or machinery obviously have a very important influence on the cost of producing a given level of output. For example, when oil prices rose sharply in the 1970s, the increase raised the price of energy for manufacturers, increased their production costs, and lowered their supply. By contrast, as computer prices fell over the last three decades, businesses increasingly substituted computerized processes for other inputs, as for example in payroll or accounting operations; this increased supply.

An equally important determinant of production costs is *technological advances,* which consist of changes that lower the quantity of inputs needed to produce the same quantity of output. Such advances include everything from scientific breakthroughs to better application of existing technology or simply reorganization of the flow of work. For example, manufacturers have become much more efficient over the last decade or so. It takes far fewer hours of labor to produce an automobile today than it did just 10 years ago. This advance enables car makers to produce more automobiles at the same cost. To give another example, if Internet commerce allows purchasers to compare more easily the prices of necessary inputs, that will lower the cost of production.

But production costs are not the only ingredient that goes into the supply curve. Supply is also influenced by the *prices of related goods,* particularly goods that are alternative outputs of the production process. If the price of one production substitute rises, the supply of another substitute will decrease. For example, auto companies typically make several different car models in the same factory. If there's more demand for one model, and its price rises, they will switch more of their assembly lines to making that model, and the supply of the other models will fall. Or if the demand and price for trucks rise, the entire factory can be converted to making trucks, and the supply of cars will fall.

Government policy also has an important impact on the supply curve. Environmental and health considerations determine what technologies can be used, while taxes and minimum-wage laws can significantly raise input prices. In the local electricity market, government regulations influence both the number of firms that can compete and the prices they charge. Government trade policies have a major impact upon supply. For instance, when a free-trade agreement opens up the U.S. market to Mexican footwear, the total supply of footwear in the United States increases.

Factors affecting the supply curve	Example for automobiles
1. **Technology**	Computerized manufacturing lowers production costs and increases supply.
2. **Input prices**	A reduction in the wage paid to autoworkers lowers production costs and increases supply.
3. **Prices of related goods**	If truck prices fall, the supply of cars rises.
4. **Government policy**	Removing quotas and tariffs on imported automobiles increases total automobile supply.
5. **Special influences**	Internet shopping and auctions allow consumers to compare the prices of different dealers more easily and drives high-cost sellers out of business.

TABLE 3-4. Supply Is Affected by Production Costs and Other Factors

Finally, *special influences* affect the supply curve. The weather exerts an important influence on farming and on the ski industry. The computer industry has been marked by a keen spirit of innovation, which has led to a continuous flow of new products. Market structure will affect supply, and expectations about future prices often have an important impact upon supply decisions.

Table 3-4 highlights the important determinants of supply, using automobiles as an example.

Shifts in Supply

Businesses are constantly changing the mix of products and services they provide. What lies behind these changes in supply behavior?

When changes in factors other than a good's own price affect the quantity supplied, we call these changes shifts in supply. Supply increases (or decreases) when the amount supplied increases (or decreases) at each market price.

When automobile prices change, producers change their production and quantity supplied, but the supply and the supply curve do not shift. By contrast, when other influences affecting supply change, supply changes and the supply curve shifts.

We can illustrate a shift in supply for the automobile market. Supply would increase if the introduction of cost-saving computerized design and manufacturing reduced the labor required to produce cars, if autoworkers took a pay cut, if there were lower production costs in Japan, or if the government repealed environmental regulations on the industry. Any of these elements would increase the supply of automobiles in the United States at each price. Figure 3-6 illustrates an increase in the supply of automobiles.

To test your understanding of supply shifts, think about the following: What would happen to the world supply curve for oil if a revolution in Saudi Arabia led to declining oil production? What would happen to the supply curve for clothing if tariffs were slapped on Chinese imports into the United States? What happens to the supply curve for computers if Intel introduces a new computer chip that dramatically increases computing speeds?

FIGURE 3-6. Increased Supply of Automobiles

As production costs fall, the supply of automobiles increases. At each price, producers will supply more automobiles, and the supply curve therefore shifts to the right. (What would happen to the supply curve if Congress were to put a restrictive quota on automobile imports?)

> **Reminder on Shifts of Curves versus Movements along Curves**
>
> As you answer the questions above, make sure to keep in mind the difference between moving along a curve and a shift of the curve. Look back at the gasoline-price curve in Figure 3-1 on page 46. When the price of oil rose and the production of oil declined because of political disturbances in the 1970s, these changes resulted from an inward shift of the supply curve. When sales of gasoline declined in response to the higher price, that was a movement along the demand curve.
>
> Does the history of computer prices and quantities shown in Figure 3-3 on page 49 look more like shifting supply or shifting demand? (Question 8 at the end of this chapter explores this issue further.)
>
> How would you describe a rise in chicken production that was induced by a rise in chicken prices? What about the case of a rise in chicken production because of a fall in the price of chicken feed?

C. EQUILIBRIUM OF SUPPLY AND DEMAND

Up to this point we have been considering demand and supply in isolation. We know the amounts that are willingly bought and sold at each price. We have seen that consumers demand different amounts of cornflakes, cars, and computers as a function of these goods' prices. Similarly, producers willingly supply different amounts of these and other goods depending on their prices. But how can we put both sides of the market together?

The answer is that supply and demand interact to produce an equilibrium price and quantity, or a market equilibrium. The **market equilibrium** comes at that price and quantity where the forces of supply and demand are in balance. At the equilibrium price, the amount that buyers want to buy is just equal to the amount that sellers want to sell. The reason we call this an equilibrium is that, when the forces of supply and demand are in balance, there is no reason for price to rise or fall, as long as other things remain unchanged.

Let us work through the cornflakes example in Table 3-5 to see how supply and demand determine a market equilibrium; the numbers in this table come from Tables 3-1 and 3-3. To find the market price and quantity, we find a price at which the amounts desired to be bought and sold just match. If we try a price of

$5 per box, will it prevail for long? Clearly not. As row A in Table 3-5 shows, at $5 producers would like to sell 18 million boxes per year while demanders want to buy only 9. The amount supplied at $5 exceeds the amount demanded, and stocks of cornflakes pile up in supermarkets. Because too few consumers are chasing too many cornflakes, the price of cornflakes will tend to fall, as shown in column (5) of Table 3-5.

Say we try $2. Does that price clear the market? A quick look at row D shows that at $2 consumption exceeds production. Cornflakes begin to disappear from the stores at that price. As people scramble around to find their desired cornflakes, they will tend to bid up the price of cornflakes, as shown in column (5) of Table 3-5.

We could try other prices, but we can easily see that the equilibrium price is $3, or row C in Table 3-5. At $3, consumers' desired demand exactly equals producers' desired production, each of which is 12 units. Only at $3 will consumers and suppliers both be making consistent decisions.

A **market equilibrium** comes at the price at which quantity demanded equals quantity supplied. At that equilibrium, there is no tendency for the price to rise or fall. The equilibrium price is also called the **market-clearing price.** This denotes that all supply and demand orders are filled, the books are "cleared" of orders, and demanders and suppliers are satisfied.

	(1) Possible price ($ per box)	(2) Quantity demanded (millions of boxes per year)	(3) Quantity supplied (millions of boxes per year)	(4) State of market	(5) Pressure on price
Combining Demand and Supply for Cornflakes					
A	5	9	18	Surplus	↓ Downward
B	4	10	16	Surplus	↓ Downward
C	3	12	12	Equilibrium	Neutral
D	2	15	7	Shortage	↑ Upward
E	1	20	0	Shortage	↑ Upward

TABLE 3-5. Equilibrium Price Comes Where Quantity Demanded Equals Quantity Supplied

The table shows the quantities supplied and demanded at different prices. Only at the equilibrium price of $3 per box does amount supplied equal amount demanded. At too low a price there is a shortage and price tends to rise. Too high a price produces a surplus, which will depress the price.

EQUILIBRIUM WITH SUPPLY AND DEMAND CURVES

We often show the market equilibrium through a supply-and-demand diagram like the one in Figure 3-7; this figure combines the supply curve from Figure 3-5 with the demand curve from Figure 3-2. Combining the two graphs is possible because they are drawn with exactly the same units on each axis.

We find the market equilibrium by looking for the price at which quantity demanded equals quantity supplied. *The equilibrium price comes at the intersection of the supply and demand curves, at point* C.

How do we know that the intersection of the supply and demand curves is the market equilibrium? Let us repeat our earlier experiment. Start with the initial high price of $5 per box, shown at the top of the price axis in Figure 3-7. At that price, suppliers

want to sell more than demanders want to buy. The result is a *surplus,* or excess of quantity supplied over quantity demanded, shown in the figure by the black line labeled "Surplus." The arrows along the curves show the direction that price tends to move when a market is in surplus.

At a low price of $2 per box, the market shows a *shortage,* or excess of quantity demanded over quantity supplied, here shown by the black line labeled "Shortage." Under conditions of shortage, the competition among buyers for limited goods causes the price to rise, as shown in the figure by the arrows pointing upward.

We now see that the balance or equilibrium of supply and demand comes at point C, where the supply and demand curves intersect. At point C, where the price is $3 per box and the quantity is 12 units, the quantities demanded and supplied are equal: there are no shortages or surpluses; there is no tendency for price to rise or fall. At point C and only at point C, the forces of supply and demand are in balance and the price has settled at a sustainable level.

The equilibrium price and quantity come where the amount willingly supplied equals the amount willingly demanded. In a competitive market, this equilibrium is found at the intersection of the supply and demand curves. There are no shortages or surpluses at the equilibrium price.

Effect of a Shift in Supply or Demand

The analysis of the supply-and-demand apparatus can do much more than tell us about the equilibrium price and quantity. It can also be used to predict the impact of changes in economic conditions on prices and quantities. Let's change our example to the staff of life, bread. Suppose that a spell of bad weather raises the price of wheat, a key ingredient of bread. That shifts the supply curve for bread to the left. This is illustrated in Figure 3-8(*a*), where the bread supply curve has shifted from SS to S'S'. In contrast, the demand curve has not shifted because people's sandwich demand is largely unaffected by farming weather.

What happens in the bread market? The bad harvest causes bakers to produce less bread at the old price, so quantity demanded exceeds quantity supplied. The price of bread therefore rises, encouraging production and thereby raising quantity supplied,

FIGURE 3-7. Market Equilibrium Comes at the Intersection of Supply and Demand Curves

The market equilibrium price and quantity come at the intersection of the supply and demand curves. At a price of $3, at point C, firms willingly supply what consumers willingly demand. When the price is too low (say, at $2), quantity demanded exceeds quantity supplied, shortages occur, and the price is driven up to equilibrium. What occurs at a price of $4?

FIGURE 3-8. Shifts in Supply or Demand Change Equilibrium Price and Quantity

(a) If supply shifts leftward, a shortage will develop at the original price. Price will be bid up until quantities willingly bought and sold are equal, at new equilibrium E'. (b) A shift in the demand curve leads to excess demand. Price will be bid up as equilibrium price and quantity move upward to E''.

---

while simultaneously discouraging consumption and lowering quantity demanded. The price continues to rise until, at the new equilibrium price, the amounts demanded and supplied are once again equal.

As Figure 3-8(a) shows, the new equilibrium is found at E', the intersection of the new supply curve $S'S'$ and the original demand curve. Thus a bad harvest (or any leftward shift of the supply curve) raises prices and, by the law of downward-sloping demand, lowers quantity demanded.

Suppose that new baking technologies lower costs and therefore increase supply. That means the supply curve shifts down and to the right. Draw in a new $S''S''$ curve, along with the new equilibrium E'''. Why is the equilibrium price lower? Why is the equilibrium quantity higher?

We can also use our supply-and-demand apparatus to examine how changes in demand affect the market equilibrium. Suppose that there is a sharp increase in family incomes, so everyone wants to eat more bread. This is represented in Figure 3-8(b) as a "demand shift" in which, at every price, consumers demand a higher quantity of bread. The demand curve thus shifts *rightward* from DD to $D'D'$.

The demand shift produces a shortage of bread at the old price. A scramble for bread ensues, with long lines in the bakeries. Prices are bid upward until supply and demand come back into balance at a higher price. Graphically, the increase in demand has changed the market equilibrium from E to E'' in Figure 3-8(b).

For both examples of shifts—a shift in supply and a shift in demand—a variable underlying the demand or supply curve has changed. In the case of supply, there might have been a change in technology or input prices. For the demand shift, one of the influences affecting consumer demand—incomes, population, the prices of related goods, or tastes—changed and thereby shifted the demand schedule (see Table 3-6).

	Demand and supply shifts	Effect on price and quantity
If demand rises . . .	The demand curve shifts to the right, and . . .	Price ↑ Quantity ↑
If demand falls . . .	The demand curve shifts to the left, and . . .	Price ↓ Quantity ↓
If supply rises . . .	The supply curve shifts to the right, and . . .	Price ↓ Quantity ↑
If supply falls . . .	The supply curve shifts to the left, and . . .	Price ↑ Quantity ↓

TABLE 3-6. The Effect on Price and Quantity of Different Demand and Supply Shifts

When the elements underlying demand or supply change, this leads to shifts in demand or supply and to changes in the market equilibrium of price and quantity.

Interpreting Changes in Price and Quantity

Let's go back to our bread example. Suppose that you go to the store and see that the price of bread has doubled. Does the increase in price mean that the demand for bread has risen, or does it mean that bread has become more expensive to produce? The correct answer is that without more information, you don't know—it could be either one, or even both. Let's look at another example. If fewer airline tickets are sold, is the cause that airline fares have gone up or that demand for air travel has gone down? Airlines will be most interested in the answer to this question.

Economists deal with these sorts of questions all the time: When prices or quantities change in a market, does the situation reflect a change on the supply side or the demand side? Sometimes, in simple situations, looking at price and quantity simultaneously gives you a clue about whether it's the supply curve that's shifted or the demand curve. For example, a rise in the price of bread accompanied by a *decrease* in quantity suggests that the supply curve has shifted to the left (a decrease in supply). A rise in price accompanied by an *increase* in quantity indicates that the demand curve for bread has probably shifted to the right (an increase in demand).

This point is illustrated in Figure 3-9. In both panel (a) and panel (b), quantity goes up. But in (a) the price rises, and in (b) the price falls. Figure 3-9(a)

shows the case of an increase in demand, or a shift in the demand curve. As a result of the shift, the equilibrium quantity demanded increases from 10 to 15 units. The case of a movement along the demand curve is shown in Figure 3-9(b). In this case, a supply shift changes the market equilibrium from point E to point E″. As a result, the quantity demanded changes from 10 to 15 units. But demand does not change in this case; rather, quantity demanded increases as consumers move along their demand curve from E to E″ in response to a price change.

The Elusive Concept of Equilibrium

The notion of equilibrium is one of the most elusive concepts of economics. We are familiar with equilibrium in our everyday lives from seeing, for example, an orange sitting at the bottom of a bowl or a pendulum at rest. In economics, equilibrium means that the different forces operating on a market are in balance, so the resulting price and quantity reconcile the desires of purchasers and suppliers. Too low a price means that the forces are not in balance, that the forces attracting demand are greater than the forces attracting supply, so there is excess demand, or a shortage. We also know that a competitive market is a mechanism for producing equilibrium. If the price is too low, demanders will bid up the price to the equilibrium level.

The notion of equilibrium is tricky, however, as is seen by the statement of a leading pundit: "Don't lecture me about supply and demand equilibrium. The supply of oil is always equal to the demand for oil. You simply can't tell the difference." The pundit is right in an accounting sense. Clearly the oil sales recorded by the oil producers should be exactly equal to the oil purchases recorded by the oil consumers. But this bit of arithmetic cannot repeal the laws of supply and demand. More important, if we fail to understand the nature of economic equilibrium, we cannot hope to understand the way that different forces affect the marketplace.

In economics, we are interested in knowing the quantity of sales that will clear the market, that is, the equilibrium quantity. We also want to know the price at which consumers willingly buy what producers willingly sell. Only at this price will both buyers and sellers be satisfied with their decisions. Only at this price and quantity will there be no tendency for price and quantity to change. Only by looking at the equilibrium of supply and demand can we hope to understand such paradoxes as the fact

that immigration may not lower wages in the affected cities, that land taxes do not raise rents, and that bad harvests raise (yes, raise!) the incomes of farmers.

Supply, Demand, and Immigration

A fascinating and important example of supply and demand, full of complexities, is the role of immigration in determining wages. If you ask people, they are likely to tell you that immigration into California or Florida surely lowers the wages of people in those regions. It's just supply and demand. They might point to Figure 3-10(*a*), which shows a supply-and-demand analysis of immigration. According to this analysis, immigration into a region shifts the supply curve for labor to the right and pushes down wages.

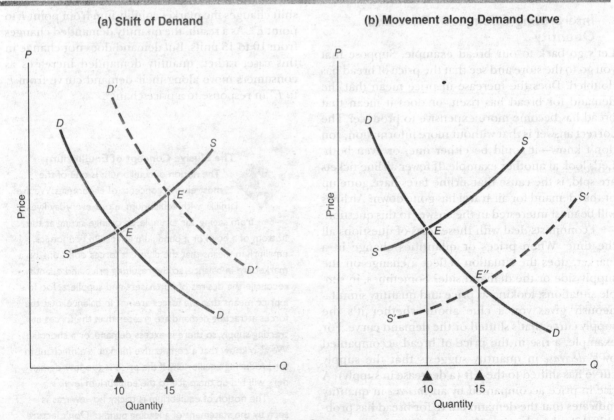

FIGURE 3-9. Shifts of and Movements along Curves

Start out with initial equilibrium at *E* and a quantity of 10 units. In (**a**), an increase in demand (i.e., a shift of the demand curve) produces a new equilibrium of 15 units at *E'*. In (**b**), a shift in supply results in a movement along the demand curve from *E* to *E''*.

FIGURE 3-10. Impact of Immigration on Wages

In (**a**), new immigrants cause the supply curve for labor to shift from SS to $S'S'$, lowering equilibrium wages. But more often, immigrants go to cities with growing labor markets. Then, as shown in (**b**), the wage changes are small if the supply increase comes in labor markets with growing demand.

Careful economic studies cast doubt on this simple reasoning. A recent survey of the evidence concludes:

> [The] effect of immigration on the labor market outcomes of natives is small. There is no evidence of economically significant reductions in native employment. Most empirical analysis . . . finds that a 10 percent increase in the fraction of immigrants in the population reduces native wages by at most 1 percent.[2]

How can we explain the small impact of immigration on wages? Labor economists emphasize the high geographic mobility of the American population. This means that new immigrants will quickly spread around the entire country. Once they arrive, immigrants may move to cities where they can get jobs—workers tend to move to those cities where the demand for labor is already rising because of a strong local economy.

This point is illustrated in Figure 3-10(*b*), where a shift in labor supply to S' is associated with a higher demand curve, D'. The new equilibrium wage at E'' is the same as the original wage at E. Another factor is that native-born residents may move out when immigrants move in, so the total supply of labor is unchanged. This would leave the supply curve for labor in its original position and leave the wage unchanged.

Immigration is a good example for demonstrating the power of the simple tools of supply and demand.

RATIONING BY PRICES

Let us now take stock of what the market mechanism accomplishes. By determining the equilibrium prices and quantities, the market allocates or rations out the scarce goods of the society among the possible uses. Who does the rationing? A planning board? Congress? The president? No. The marketplace, through the interaction of supply and demand, does the rationing. This is *rationing by the purse.*

---

[2] Rachel M. Friedberg and Jennifer Hunt, "The Impact of Immigrants on Host Country Wages, Employment, and Growth," *Journal of Economic Perspectives*, Spring 1995, pp. 23–44.

What goods are produced? This is answered by the signals of the market prices. High oil prices stimulate oil production, whereas low food prices drive productive resources out of agriculture. Those who have the most dollar votes have the greatest influence on what goods are produced.

For whom are goods produced? The power of the purse dictates the distribution of income and consumption. Those with higher incomes end up with larger houses, more clothing, and longer vacations. When backed up by cash, the most urgently felt needs get fulfilled through the demand curve.

Even the *how* question is decided by supply and demand. When corn prices are low, it is not profitable for farmers to use expensive tractors and irrigation systems. When oil prices are high, oil companies drill in deep offshore waters and employ novel seismic techniques to find oil.

With this introduction to supply and demand, we begin to see how desires for goods, as expressed through demands, interact with costs of goods, as reflected in supplies. Further study will deepen our understanding of these concepts and will show how these tools can be applied to other important areas. But even this first survey will serve as an indispensable tool for interpreting the economic world in which we live.

SUMMARY

1. The analysis of supply and demand shows how a market mechanism solves the three problems of *what, how,* and *for whom.* A market blends together demands and supplies. Demand comes from consumers who are spreading their dollar votes among available goods and services, while businesses supply the goods and services with the goal of maximizing their profits.

A. The Demand Schedule

2. A demand schedule shows the relationship between the quantity demanded and the price of a commodity, other things held constant. Such a demand schedule, depicted graphically by a demand curve, holds constant other things like family incomes, tastes, and the prices of other goods. Almost all commodities obey the *law of downward-sloping demand,* which holds that quantity demanded falls as a good's price rises. This law is represented by a downward-sloping demand curve.

3. Many influences lie behind the demand schedule for the market as a whole: average family incomes, population, the prices of related goods, tastes, and special influences. When these influences change, the demand curve will shift.

B. The Supply Schedule

4. The supply schedule (or supply curve) gives the relationship between the quantity of a good that producers desire to sell—other things constant—and that good's price. Quantity supplied generally responds positively to price, so the supply curve is upward-sloping.

5. Elements other than the good's price affect its supply. The most important influence is the commodity's production cost, determined by the state of technology and by input prices. Other elements in supply include the prices of related goods, government policies, and special influences.

C. Equilibrium of Supply and Demand

6. The equilibrium of supply and demand in a competitive market occurs when the forces of supply and demand are in balance. The equilibrium price is the price at which the quantity demanded just equals the quantity supplied. Graphically, we find the equilibrium at the intersection of the supply and demand curves. At a price above the equilibrium, producers want to supply more than consumers want to buy, which results in a surplus of goods and exerts downward pressure on price. Similarly, too low a price generates a shortage, and buyers will therefore tend to bid price upward to the equilibrium.

7. Shifts in the supply and demand curves change the equilibrium price and quantity. An increase in demand, which shifts the demand curve to the right, will increase both equilibrium price and quantity. An increase in supply, which shifts the supply curve to the right, will decrease price and increase quantity demanded.

8. To use supply-and-demand analysis correctly, we must (*a*) distinguish a change in demand or supply (which produces a shift of a curve) from a change in the quantity demanded or supplied (which represents a movement along a curve); (*b*) hold other things constant, which requires distinguishing the impact of a change in a commodity's price from the impact of changes in other influences; and (*c*) look always for the supply-and-demand equilibrium, which comes at the point where forces acting on price and quantity are in balance.

9. Competitively determined prices ration the limited supply of goods among those who demand them.

CONCEPTS FOR REVIEW

supply-and-demand analysis
demand schedule or curve, *DD*
law of downward-sloping demand
influences affecting demand curve

supply schedule or curve, *SS*
influences affecting supply curve
equilibrium price and quantity

shifts of supply and demand curves
all other things held constant
rationing by prices

FURTHER READING AND INTERNET WEBSITES

Further Reading

Supply-and-demand analysis is the single most important and useful tool in microeconomics. Supply-and-demand analysis was developed by the great British economist Alfred Marshall in *Principles of Economics,* 9th ed. (New York, Macmillan, [1890] 1961). To reinforce your understanding, you might look in textbooks on intermediate microeconomics. Two good references are Hal R. Varian, *Intermediate Microeconomics: A Modern Approach,* 6th ed. (Norton, New York, 2002), and Edwin Mansfield and Gary Yohe, *Microeconomics: Theory and Applications,* 10th ed. (Norton, New York, 2000).

A recent survey of the economic issues in immigration is in George Borjas, *Heaven's Door: Immigration Policy and the American Economy* (Princeton University Press, Princeton, N.J., 1999).

Websites

Websites in economics are proliferating rapidly, and it is hard to keep up with all the useful sites. A good place to start is always rfe.org/. A good starting point for multiple sites in economics is rfe.org/OtherInt/MultSub/index.html, and the Google search engine has its own economics site at directory.google.com/Top/Science/Social_Sciences/Economics/. Another useful starting point for Internet resources in economics can be found at www.oswego.edu/~economic/econweb.htm.

You can examine a recent study of the impact of immigration on American society from the National Academy of Sciences, *The New Americans* (1997), at www.nap.edu. This site provides free access to over 1000 studies from economics and the other social and natural sciences.

QUESTIONS FOR DISCUSSION

1. a. Define carefully what is meant by a demand schedule or curve. State the law of downward-sloping demand. Illustrate the law of downward-sloping demand with two cases from your own experience.
   b. Define the concept of a supply schedule or curve. Show that an increase in supply means a rightward and downward shift of the supply curve. Contrast this with the rightward and upward shift of the demand curve implied by an increase in demand.

2. What might increase the demand for hamburgers? What would increase the supply? What would inexpensive frozen pizzas do to the market equilibrium for hamburgers? To the wages of teenagers who work at McDonald's?

3. Explain why the price in competitive markets settles down at the equilibrium intersection of supply and demand. Explain what happens if the market price starts out too high or too low.

4. Explain why each of the following is *false:*
   a. A freeze in Brazil's coffee-growing region will lower the price of coffee.
   b. "Protecting" American textile manufacturers from Chinese clothing imports will lower clothing prices in the United States.
   c. The rapid increase in college tuitions will lower the demand for college.
   d. The war against drugs, with increased interdiction of imported cocaine, will lower the price of domestically produced marijuana.

5. The following are four laws of supply and demand. Fill in the blanks. Demonstrate each law with a supply-and-demand diagram.
   a. An increase in demand generally raises price and raises quantity demanded.
   b. A decrease in demand generally _____ price and _____ quantity demanded.

c. An increase in supply generally lowers price and raises quantity demanded.

d. A decrease in supply generally _____ price and _____ quantity demanded.

6. For each of the following, explain whether quantity demanded changes because of a demand shift or a price change, and draw a diagram to illustrate your answer:

a. As a result of decreased military spending, the price of Army boots falls.

b. Fish prices fall after the pope allows Catholics to eat meat on Friday.

c. An increase in gasoline taxes lowers the consumption of gasoline.

d. After the Black Death struck Europe in the fourteenth century, wages rose.

7. Examine the graph for the price of gasoline in Figure 3-1, page 46. Then, using a supply-and-demand diagram, illustrate the impact of each of the following on price and quantity demanded:

a. Improvements in transportation lower the costs of importing oil into the United States in the 1960s.

b. After the 1973 war, oil producers cut oil production sharply.

c. After 1980, smaller automobiles get more miles per gallon.

d. A record-breaking cold winter in 1995–1996 unexpectedly raises the demand for heating oil.

e. A global economic recovery in 1999–2000 leads to a sharp upturn in oil prices.

8. Examine Figure 3-3 on page 49. Does the price-quantity relationship look more like a supply curve or a demand curve. Assuming that the demand curve was unchanged over this period, trace supply curves for 1972 and 2000 that would have generated the (P, Q) pairs for those years. Explain what forces might have led to the shift in the supply curve.

9. From the following data, plot the supply and demand curves and determine the equilibrium price and quantity:

Supply and Demand for Pizzas		
Price ($ per pizza)	Quantity demanded (pizzas per semester)	Quantity supplied (pizzas per semester)
10	0	40
8	10	30
6	20	20
4	30	10
2	40	0
0	125	0

What would happen if the demand for pizzas tripled at each price? What would occur if the price were initially set at $4 per pizza?

Microeconomics: Supply, Demand, and Product Markets

4

Applications of Supply and Demand

You cannot teach a parrot to be an economist simply by teaching it to say "supply" and "demand."

Anonymous

We now move from our introductory survey to a detailed study of microeconomics—of the behavior of individual firms, consumers, and markets. Individual markets contain much of the grand sweep and drama of economic history and the controversies of economic policy. Within the confines of microeconomics we will study the reasons for the vast disparities in earnings between neurosurgeons and textile workers. Microeconomics is crucial to understanding why computer prices have fallen so rapidly and why the use of computers has expanded exponentially. We cannot hope to understand the bitter debates about health care or the minimum wage without applying the tools of supply and demand to these sectors. Even topics such as illegal drugs or crime and punishment are usefully illuminated by considering the way the demand for addictive substances differs from that for other commodities.

But understanding supply and demand requires more than simply parroting the words. A full mastery of microeconomic analysis means understanding the derivation of demand curves and supply curves, learning about different concepts of costs, and understanding how perfect competition differs from monopoly. All these and other key topics will be our subjects as we tour through the fascinating world of microeconomics.

Our survey of microeconomics begins with an analysis of *product markets*—the markets for goods and services. We will examine where consumer demand comes from, how businesses make decisions, and how prices and profits coordinate the allocation of resources in a competitive market. We will also examine the market failures that arise when monopolies or other forms of imperfect competitors dominate industry. In subsequent parts, we will examine *factor markets* and *the role of government* in a modern mixed economy.

A. PRICE ELASTICITY OF DEMAND AND SUPPLY

The theory of supply and demand can be used to answer a wide range of practical questions. When war or revolution breaks out in the Middle East and the price of crude oil rises, how much of the increase is passed on in the price of gasoline? Does raising the minimum wage help low-income workers, or does it hurt them? When a financially troubled airline lowers its ticket prices, will ticket sales increase so much that total revenue actually rises?

In order to turn supply and demand into a truly useful tool, we need to know *how much* supply and demand respond to changes in price. Some purchases, like those for vacation travel, are very sensitive to price changes. Others, like food or electricity, are necessities for which consumer purchases respond very little to price changes. The quantitative relationship between price and quantity purchased is analyzed using the crucial concept of *elasticity*. The payoff to this new concept will come in the second half of the chapter, when we examine the microeconomic impacts of taxes and other types of government intervention.

PRICE ELASTICITY OF DEMAND

Let's look first at the response of consumer demand to price changes:

The **price elasticity of demand** (sometimes simply called **price elasticity**) measures how much the quantity demanded of a good changes when its price changes. The precise definition of price elasticity is the percentage change in quantity demanded divided by the percentage change in price.

Goods vary enormously in their price elasticity, or sensitivity to price changes. When the price elasticity of a good is high, we say that the good has "elastic" demand, which means that its quantity demanded responds greatly to price changes. When the price elasticity of a good is low, it is "inelastic" and its quantity demanded responds little to price changes.

For necessities like food, fuel, shoes, and prescription drugs demand tends to be inelastic. Such items are the staff of life and cannot easily be forgone when their prices rise. By contrast, you can easily substitute other goods when luxuries like European holidays, 17-year-old Scotch whiskey, and Italian designer clothing rise in price.

Goods that have ready substitutes tend to have more elastic demand than those that have no substitutes. If all food or footwear prices were to rise 20 percent tomorrow, you would hardly expect people to stop eating or to go around barefoot, so food and footwear demands are price-inelastic. On the other hand, if mad-cow disease drives up the price of British beef, people can turn to beef from other countries or to lamb or poultry for their meat

needs. Therefore, British beef shows a high price elasticity.

The length of time that people have to respond to price changes also plays a role. A good example is that of gasoline. Suppose you are driving across the country when the price of gasoline suddenly increases. Is it likely that you will sell your car and abandon your vacation? Not really. So in the short run, the demand for gasoline may be very inelastic.

In the long run, however, you can adjust your behavior to the higher price of gasoline. You can buy a smaller and more fuel-efficient car, ride a bicycle, take the train, move closer to work, or carpool with other people. The ability to adjust consumption patterns implies that demand elasticities are generally higher in the long run than in the short run.

Economic factors determine the size of price elasticities for individual goods: elasticities tend to be higher when the goods are luxuries, when substitutes are available, and when consumers have more time to adjust their behavior.

Calculating Elasticities

If we can observe how much quantity demanded changes when price changes, we can calculate the elasticity. The precise definition of price elasticity, E_D, is the percentage change in quantity demanded divided by the percentage change in price. For convenience, we drop the minus signs, so elasticities are all positive.

We can calculate the coefficient of price elasticity numerically according to the following formula:

Price elasticity of demand = E_D

$$= \frac{\text{percentage change in quantity demanded}}{\text{percentage change in price}}$$

Now we can be more precise about the different categories of price elasticity:

- When a 1 percent change in price calls forth more than a 1 percent change in quantity demanded, the good has **price-elastic demand.** For example, if a 1 percent increase in price yields a 5 percent decrease in quantity demanded, the commodity has a highly price-elastic demand.

- When a 1 percent change in price produces less than a 1 percent change in quantity demanded, the good has **price-inelastic demand.** This case occurs, for instance, when a 1 percent increase in price yields only a 0.2 percent decrease in demand.

- One important special case is **unit-elastic demand,** which occurs when the percentage change in quantity is exactly the same as the percentage change in price. In this case, a 1 percent increase in price yields a 1 percent decrease in demand. We will see later that this condition implies that total expenditures on the commodity (which equal $P \times Q$) stay the same even when the price changes.

To illustrate the calculation of elasticities, let us examine the simple case of the response of purchases to the price increase which is shown in Figure 4-1. In the original situation, price was 90 and quantity demanded was 240 units. A price increase to 110 led consumers to reduce their purchases to 160 units. In Figure 4-1, consumers were originally at point A but moved along their demand schedule to point B when the price rose.

Table 4-1 shows how we calculate price elasticity. The price increase is 20 percent, with the resulting quantity decrease being 40 percent. The price elasticity of demand is evidently $E_D = 40/20 = 2$. The price elasticity is greater than 1, and this good therefore has price-elastic demand in the region from A to B.

FIGURE 4-1. Elastic Demand Shows Large Quantity Response to Price Change

Market equilibrium is originally at point A. In response to a 20 percent price increase, quantity demanded declines 40 percent, to point B. Price elasticity is $E_D = 40/20 = 2$. Demand is therefore elastic in the region from A to B.

Case A: Price = 90 and quantity = 240

Case B: Price = 110 and quantity = 160

Percentage price change = $\Delta P/P = 20/100 = 20\%$

Percentage quantity change = $\Delta Q/Q = -80/200$
$$= -40\%$$

Price elasticity = $E_D = 40/20 = 2$

TABLE 4-1. Example of Good with Elastic Demand

Consider the situation where price is raised from 90 to 110. According to the demand curve, quantity demanded falls from 240 to 160. Price elasticity is the ratio of percentage change in quantity divided by percentage change in price. We drop the minus signs from the numbers so that all elasticities are positive.

In practice, calculating elasticities is somewhat tricky, and we emphasize three key steps where you have to be especially careful:

1. Recall that we drop the minus signs from the numbers, thereby treating all percentage changes as *positive*. That means all elasticities are written as positive numbers, even though prices and quantities demanded move in opposite directions for downward-sloping demand curves.

2. Note that the definition of elasticity uses *percentage changes* in price and demand rather than absolute changes. This has the neat effect that a change in the units of measurement does not affect the elasticity. So whether we measure price in pennies or dollars, the price elasticity stays the same.

3. Note the use of *averaging* to calculate percentage changes in price and quantity. The formula for a percentage change is $\Delta P/P$. The value of ΔP in Table 4-1 is clearly $20 = 110 - 90$. But it's not immediately clear what value we should use for P in the denominator. Is it the original value of 90, the final value of 110, or something in between?

   For very small percentage changes, such as from 100 to 99, it does not much matter whether we use 99 or 100 as the denominator. But for larger changes, the difference is significant. To avoid ambiguity, we will take the average price to be the base price for calculating price changes. In Table 4-1, we used the average of the two prices $[P = (90 + 110)/2 = 100]$ as the base or denominator in the elasticity formula. Similarly, we used

FIGURE 4-2. Price Elasticity of Demand Falls into Three Categories

the average quantity $[Q = (160 + 240)/2 = 200]$ as the base for measuring the percentage change in quantity. The exact formula for calculating elasticity is therefore

$$E_D = \frac{\Delta Q}{(Q_1 + Q_2)/2} \div \frac{\Delta P}{(P_1 + P_2)/2}$$

where P_1 and Q_1 represent the original price and quantity and P_2 and Q_2 stand for the new price and quantity.

Price Elasticity in Diagrams

It's possible to determine price elasticities in diagrams as well. Figure 4-2 illustrates the three cases of elasticities. In each case, price is cut in half and consumers change their quantity demanded from A to B.

In Figure 4-2(a), a halving of price has tripled quantity demanded. Like the example in Figure 4-1, this case shows price-elastic demand. In Figure 4-2(c), cutting price in half led to only a 50 percent increase in quantity demanded, so this is the case of price-inelastic demand. The borderline case of unit-elastic demand is shown in Figure 4-2(b); in this example, the doubling of quantity demanded exactly matches the halving of price.

Figure 4-3 displays the important polar extremes where the price elasticities are infinite and zero, or completely elastic and completely inelastic. Completely inelastic demands, or ones with zero elasticity,

are ones where the quantity demanded responds **not** at all to price changes; such demand is seen to **be a** vertical demand curve. By contrast, when demand is infinitely elastic, a tiny change in price will lead to an indefinitely large change in quantity demanded, as in the horizontal demand curve in Figure 4-3.

FIGURE 4-3. Perfectly Elastic and Inelastic Demands

Polar extremes of demand are vertical demand curves, which represent perfectly inelastic demand ($E_D = 0$), and horizontal demand curves, which show perfectly elastic demand ($E_D = \infty$).

Elasticity Is Not the Same as Slope

We must always remember not to confuse the elasticity of a curve with its slope. This distinction is easily seen when we examine the straight-line demand curves that are often found in illustrative examples. We often depict demand curves as linear, or straight lines, because they are easy to draw. So it's only natural to ask, What is the price elasticity of a straight-line demand curve?

That question turns out to have a surprising answer. Along a straight-line demand curve, the price elasticity varies from zero to infinity! Table 4-2 gives a detailed set of elasticity calculations using the same technique as that in Table 4-1. This table shows that linear demand curves start out with high price elasticity, where price is high and quantity is low, and end up with low elasticity, where price is low and quantity high.

This illustrates an important point. When you see a demand curve in a diagram, it is in general not true that a steep slope for the demand curve means inelastic demand and a flat slope signifies elastic demand. The slope is not the same as the elasticity because the demand curve's slope depends upon the changes in P and Q, whereas the elasticity depends upon the percentage changes in P and Q. The only exceptions are the polar cases of completely elastic and inelastic demands.

One way to see this point is to examine Figure 4-2(b). This demand curve is clearly not a straight line with constant slope. Yet it has a constant demand elasticity of $E_D = 1$ because the percentage change in price is equal everywhere to the percentage change in quantity. So remember: Elasticity is definitely different from slope.

Figure 4-4 illustrates the pitfall of confusing slope and elasticity. This figure plots a linear or straight-line demand curve. Because it is linear, it has the same slope everywhere. But the top of the line, near A, has a very small percentage price change and a very large percentage quantity change, and the elasticity is extremely large. Therefore, price elasticity is relatively large when we are high on the linear DD curve. Conversely, when we are in the bottom part of the linear demand curve, the price elasticity is less than unity. Near the horizontal axis, price elasticity is close to zero.

				Numerical Calculation of Elasticity Coefficient			
Q	ΔQ	P	ΔP	$\dfrac{Q_1 + Q_2}{2}$	$\dfrac{P_1 + P_2}{2}$	$E_D = \dfrac{\Delta Q}{(Q_1 + Q_2)/2} \div \dfrac{\Delta P}{(P_1 + P_2)/2}$	
0		6					
	10		2	5	5	$\dfrac{10}{5} \div \dfrac{2}{5} = 5$	(elastic)
10		4					
	10		2	15	3	$\dfrac{10}{15} \div \dfrac{2}{3} = 1$	(unit-elastic)
20		2					
	10		2	25	1	$\dfrac{10}{25} \div \dfrac{2}{1} = 0.2$	(inelastic)
30		0					

TABLE 4-2. Calculation of Price Elasticity along a Linear Demand Curve

ΔP denotes the change in price, i.e., $\Delta P = P_2 - P_1$, while $\Delta Q = Q_2 - Q_1$. To calculate numerical elasticity, the percentage change of price equals price change, ΔP, divided by average price $[(P_2 + P_1)/2]$; the percentage change in output is calculated as ΔQ divided by average quantity, $[(Q_2 + Q_1)/2]$. Treating all figures as positive numbers, the resulting ratio gives numerical price elasticity of demand, E_D. Note that for a straight line, elasticity is high at the top, low at the bottom, and exactly 1 in the middle.

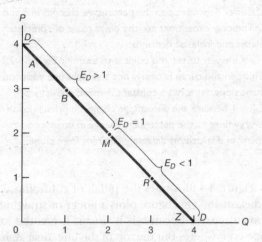

FIGURE 4-4. Slope and Elasticity Are Not the Same Thing

All points on the straight-line demand curve have the same slope. But above the midpoint, demand is elastic; below it, demand is inelastic; at the midpoint, demand is unit-elastic. Only in the case of vertical or horizontal curves, shown in Fig. 4-3, can you infer the price elasticity from slope alone.

Above the midpoint M of any straight line, demand is elastic, with $E_D > 1$. At the midpoint, demand is unit-elastic, with $E_D = 1$. Below the midpoint, demand is inelastic, with $E_D < 1$.

In summary, while the extreme cases of completely elastic and completely inelastic demand can be determined from the slopes of the demand curves alone, for the in-between cases, which correspond to virtually all goods, elasticities cannot be inferred by slope alone. (See Figure 4-5 for one way to calculate elasticity from a diagram.)

A Shortcut for Calculating Elasticities. A simple rule will allow you to calculate the price elasticity of a demand curve: *The elasticity of a straight line at a point is given by the ratio of the length of the line segment below the point to the length of the line segment above the point.*

To see this, first examine Figure 4-4. Note that at midpoint M the length of the segment above (AM) and that of the segment below (MZ) are exactly equal; hence the elasticity is $MZ/AM = 1$. At point B, this formula yields $E_D = BZ/AB = 3/1 = 3$; at R, $E_D = 1/3$.

FIGURE 4-5. A Simple Rule for Calculating the Demand Elasticity

To calculate the demand elasticity, take the ratio of the length of the straight-line segment below the point to the length of the line segment above the point. Hence, at point B the elasticity can be calculated to be 3. For nonlinear demand curves, simply draw the tangent line and calculate its elasticity.

Knowing how to calculate E_D for a straight line enables you to calculate it for any point along a curved demand curve, as shown in Figure 4-5. (1) Draw the straight line tangent to the curve at your point (e.g., at B in Figure 4-5), and then (2) calculate E_D for the straight line at that point (e.g., E_D at $B = 3$). The result will be the correct elasticity for the curve at point B.

ELASTICITY AND REVENUE

Many businesses want to know whether raising prices will raise or lower revenues. This question is of strategic importance for businesses like airlines, baseball teams, and magazines, which must decide whether it is worthwhile to raise prices and whether the higher prices make up for lower demand. Let's look at the relationship between price elasticity and total revenue.

Total revenue is by definition equal to price times quantity (or $P \times Q$). If consumers buy 5 units at $3 each, total revenue is $15. If you know the price elasticity of demand, you know what will happen to total revenue when price changes:

1. When demand is price-inelastic, a price decrease reduces total revenue.
2. When demand is price-elastic, a price decrease increases total revenue.
3. In the borderline case of unit-elastic demand, a price decrease leads to no change in total revenue.

The concept of price elasticity is widely used today as businesses attempt to separate customers into groups with different elasticities. This technique has been extensively pioneered by the airlines (see the box that follows). Another example is software companies, which have a wide range of different prices for their products in an attempt to exploit different elasticities. For example, if you are desperate about buying a new operating system immediately, your elasticity is low and the seller will profit from charging you a relatively high price. On the other hand, if you are not in a hurry for an upgrade, you can search around for the best price and your elasticity is high. In this case, the seller will try to find a way to make the sale by charging a relatively low price.

Fly the Financial Skies of "Elasticity Air"

Understanding demand elasticities is worth billions of dollars each year to U.S. airlines. Ideally, airlines would like to charge a relatively high price to business travelers, while charging leisure passengers a low-enough price to fill up all their empty seats. That is a strategy for raising revenues and maximizing profits.

But if they charge low-elasticity business travelers one price and high-elasticity leisure passengers a lower price, the airlines have a big problem—keeping the two classes of passengers separate. How can they stop the low-elasticity business travelers from buying up the cheap tickets meant for the leisure travelers and not let high-elasticity leisure flyers take up seats that business passengers would have been willing to buy?

The airlines have solved their problem by engaging in "price discrimination" among their different customers in a way that exploits different price elasticities. **Price discrimination** is the practice of charging different prices for the same service to different customers. Airlines offer discount fares for travelers who plan ahead and who tend to stay longer. One way of separating the two groups is to offer discounted fares to people who stay over a Saturday night—a rule that discourages business travelers who want to get home for the weekend. Also, discounts are often unavailable at the last minute because many business trips are unplanned expeditions to handle an unforeseen crisis—another case of price-inelastic demand. Airlines have devised extremely sophisticated computer programs to manage their seat availability as a way of ensuring that their low-elasticity passengers cannot benefit from discount fares.

The Paradox of the Bumper Harvest

We can use elasticities to illustrate one of the most famous paradoxes of all economics: the paradox of the bumper harvest. Imagine that in a particular year nature smiles on farming. A cold winter kills off the pests; spring comes early for planting; there are no killing frosts; rains nurture the growing shoots; and a sunny October allows a record crop to come to market. At the end of the year, family Jones happily settles down to calculate its income for the year. The Joneses are in for a major surprise: *The good weather and bumper crop have lowered their and other farmers' incomes.*

How can this be? The answer lies in the elasticity of demand for foodstuffs. The demands for basic food products such as wheat and corn tend to be inelastic; for these necessities, consumption changes very little in response to price. But this means farmers as a whole receive less total revenue when the harvest is good than when it is bad. The increase in supply arising from an abundant harvest tends to lower the price. But the lower price doesn't increase quantity demanded very much. The implication is that a low price elasticity of food means that large harvests (high Q) tend to be associated with low revenue (low $P \times Q$).

These ideas can be illustrated by referring back to Figure 4-2. We begin by showing how to measure revenue in the diagram itself. Total revenue is the product of price times quantity, $P \times Q$. Further, the area of a rectangle is always equal to the product of its base times its height. Therefore, total revenue at any point on a demand curve can be found by examining the area of the rectangle determined by the P and Q at that point.

Next, we can check the relationship between elasticity and revenue for the unit-elastic case in Figure 4-2(b). Note that the shaded revenue region ($P \times Q$) is $1000 million for both points A and B. The shaded areas representing total revenue are the same because of offsetting changes in the Q base and the P height. This is what we would expect for the borderline case of unit-elastic demand.

We can also see that Figure 4-2(a) corresponds to elastic demand. In this figure, the revenue rectangle expands from $1000 million to $1500 million when price is halved. Since total revenue goes up when price is cut, demand is elastic.

Value of demand elasticity	Description	Definition	Impact on revenues
Greater than one ($E_D > 1$)	Elastic demand	Percentage change in quantity demanded *greater* than percentage change in price	Revenues *increase* when price decreases
Equal to one ($E_D = 1$)	Unit-elastic demand	Percentage change in quantity demanded *equal* to percentage change in price	Revenues *unchanged* when price decreases
Less than one ($E_D < 1$)	Inelastic demand	Percentage change in quantity demanded *less* than percentage change in price	Revenues *decrease* when price decreases

TABLE 4-3. Elasticities: Summary of Crucial Concepts

In Figure 4-2(*c*) the revenue rectangle falls from $40 million to $30 million when price is halved, so demand is inelastic.

Which diagram illustrates the case of agriculture, where a bumper harvest means lower total revenues for farmers? Clearly it is Figure 4-2(*c*). Which represents the case of vacation travel, where a lower price could mean higher revenues? Surely Figure 4-2(*a*).

Table 4-3 shows the major points to remember about price elasticities.

Cigarette Taxes and Smoking

What is the impact of cigarette taxes on smoking? Some people say, "It's so addictive that people will pay anything for their daily weeds." Economists look to the price elasticity of demand to answer this question.

An interesting experiment took place in New Jersey, which doubled its cigarette tax from 40 cents to 80 cents per pack in 1998. This tax increase pushed the average price of cigarettes from $2.40 to $2.80 per pack. Economists estimate that, after correcting for trends in consumption and sales from neighboring states, cigarette consumption decreased from 52 million to 47.5 million packs.

Using the elasticity formula, you can calculate that the short-run elasticity is 0.59. (Make sure you can get the same number.) Similar estimates come from more detailed statistical studies. The evidence indicates, therefore, that the demand for cigarettes is inelastic in the short run but definitely responds to cigarette prices.

PRICE ELASTICITY OF SUPPLY

Of course, consumption is not the only thing that changes when prices go up or down. Businesses also respond to price in their decisions about how much to produce. Economists define the price elasticity of supply as the responsiveness of the quantity supplied of a good to its market price.

More precisely, the **price elasticity of supply** is the percentage change in quantity supplied divided by the percentage change in price.

As with demand elasticities, there are polar extremes of high and low elasticities of supply. Suppose the amount supplied is completely fixed, as in the case of perishable fish brought to market to be sold at whatever price they will fetch. This is the limiting case of zero elasticity, or completely inelastic supply, which is a vertical supply curve.

At the other extreme, say that a tiny cut in price will cause the amount supplied to fall to zero, while the slightest rise in price will coax out an indefinitely large supply. Here, the ratio of the percentage change in quantity supplied to percentage change in price is extremely large and gives rise to a horizontal supply curve. This is the polar case of infinitely elastic supply.

Between these extremes, we call supply elastic or inelastic depending upon whether the percentage change in quantity is larger or smaller than the percentage change in price. In the borderline unit-elastic case, where price elasticity of supply equals 1, the percentage increase of quantity supplied is exactly equal to the percentage increase in price.

You can readily see that the definitions of price elasticities of supply are exactly the same as those for price elasticities of demand. The only difference is that for supply the quantity response to price is positive, while for demand the response is negative.

The exact definition of the price elasticity of supply, E_S, is as follows:

$$E_S = \frac{\text{percentage change in quantity supplied}}{\text{percentage change in price}}$$

Figure 4-6 displays three important cases of supply elasticity: (a) the vertical supply curve, showing completely inelastic supply; (c), the horizontal supply curve, displaying completely elastic supply; and (b), an intermediate case of a straight line, going through the origin, illustrating the borderline case of unit elasticity.[1]

What factors determine supply elasticity? The major factor influencing supply elasticity is the ease with which production in the industry can be increased. If all inputs can be readily found at going market prices, as is the case for the textile industry, then output can be greatly increased with little increase in price. This would indicate that supply elasticity is relatively large. On the other hand, if production capacity is severely limited, as is the case for gold mining, then even sharp increases in the price of gold will call forth but a small response in gold production; this would be inelastic supply.

Another important factor in supply elasticities is the time period under consideration. A given change in price tends to have a larger effect on amount supplied as the time for suppliers to respond increases. For very brief periods after a price increase, firms may be unable to increase their inputs of labor, materials, and capital, so supply may be very price-inelastic. However, as time passes and businesses can hire more labor, build new factories, and expand capacity, supply elasticities will become larger.

We can use Figure 4-6 to illustrate how supply may change over time for the fishing case. Supply curve (a) might hold for fish on the day they are brought to market, where they are simply auctioned off for whatever they will bring. Curve (b) might hold for the intermediate run of a year or so, with

Supply Elasticities

FIGURE 4-6. Supply Elasticity Depends upon Producer Response to Price

When supply is fixed, supply elasticity is zero, as in curve (a). Curve (c) displays an indefinitely large quantity response to price changes. Intermediate case (b) arises when the percentage quantity and price changes are equal.

the given stock of fishing boats and before new labor is attracted to the industry. Over the very long run, as new fishing boats are built, new labor is attracted, and new fish farms are constructed, the supply of fish might be very price-elastic, as in case (c) in Figure 4-6.

B. APPLICATIONS TO MAJOR ECONOMIC ISSUES

Having laid the groundwork with our study of elasticities, we now show how these tools can assist our understanding of many of the basic economic trends and policy issues. We begin with one of the major transformations since the Industrial Revolution, the decline of agriculture. Next, we examine the implications of taxes on an industry, using the example of a gasoline tax. We then analyze the consequences of various types of government intervention in markets.

---

[1] You can determine the elasticity of a supply curve that is not a straight line as follows: (*a*) Draw the straight line that lies tangent to the curve at a point, and (*b*) then measure the elasticity of that tangential straight line.

FIGURE 4-7. **Prices of Basic Farm Products Have Declined Sharply**

One of the major forces affecting the United States has been the steady decline in the prices of basic farm products—wheat, corn, soybeans, and the like. Over the second half of the twentieth century, farm prices have declined 2 percent per year relative to the general price level. Note the temporary reversal during the commodity shortages of the 1970s. (Source: Bureau of Labor Statistics.)

THE ECONOMICS OF AGRICULTURE

Our first application of supply-and-demand analysis comes from agriculture. The first part of this section lays out some of the economic fundamentals of the farm sector. Then we will use the theory of supply and demand to study the effects of government intervention in agricultural markets.

Long-Run Relative Decline of Farming

Farming was once our largest single industry. A hundred years ago, half the American population lived and worked on farms, but that number has declined to less than 3 percent of the workforce today. At the same time, prices for farm products have fallen relative to incomes and other prices in the economy. Figure 4-7 shows the steady decline of farm prices over the last half-century. While median family income has more than doubled, farm incomes have stagnated. Farm-state senators fret about the decline of the family farm.

A single diagram can explain the cause of the sagging trend in farm prices better than libraries of books and editorials. Figure 4-8 shows an initial equilibrium with high prices at point *E*. Observe what happens to agriculture as the years go by. Demand for food increases slowly because most foods are

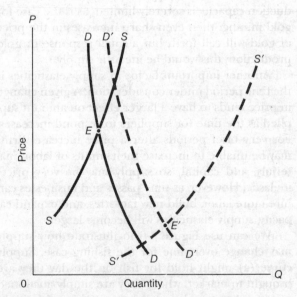

FIGURE 4-8. **Agricultural Distress Results from Expanding Supply and Price-Inelastic Demand**

Equilibrium at *E* represents conditions in the farm sector decades ago. Demand for farm products tends to grow more slowly than the impressive increase in supply generated by technological progress. Hence, competitive farm prices tend to fall. Moreover, with price-inelastic demand, farm incomes decline with increases in supply.

necessities; the demand shift is consequently modest in comparison to growing average incomes.

What about supply? Although many people mistakenly think that farming is a backward business, statistical studies show that productivity (output per unit of input) has grown more rapidly in agriculture than in most other industries. Important advances include mechanization through tractors, combines, and cotton pickers; fertilization and irrigation; selective breeding; and development of genetically modified crops. All these innovations have vastly increased the productivity of agricultural inputs. Rapid productivity growth has increased supply greatly, as shown by the supply curve's shift from *SS* to *S'S'* in Figure 4-8.

What must happen at the new competitive equilibrium? Sharp increases in supply outpaced modest increases in demand, producing a downward trend in farm prices relative to other prices in the economy. And this is precisely what has happened in recent decades, as is seen in Figure 4-7.

Crop Restrictions. In response to falling incomes, farmers have often lobbied the federal government for economic assistance. Over the years, governments at home and abroad have taken many steps to help farmers. They have raised prices through price supports; they have curbed imports through tariffs and quotas; and they sometimes simply sent checks to farmers who agreed *not* to produce on their land.

The paradox of the bumper harvest has an interesting application here. *Many governments attempt to help farmers by reducing their production.* How could this be in the interests of farmers? Figure 4-9 shows the economics of this policy. If the Department of Agriculture requires every farmer to reduce the amount of production, the effect is a shifting of the supply curve up and to the left. Because food demands are inelastic, crop restrictions not only raise the price of crops but also tend to raise farmers' total revenues and earnings. Just as bumper harvests hurt farmers, crop restrictions tend to raise farm incomes. Of course, consumers are hurt by the crop restrictions and higher prices—just as they would be if a flood or drought created a scarcity of food.

Production restrictions are typical of government market interferences that raise the incomes of one group at the expense of others. We will see in later chapters that this kind of policy is inefficient: the gain to farmers is less than the harm to consumers.

FIGURE 4-9. Crop-Restriction Programs Raise Both Price and Farm Income

Before the crop restriction, the competitive market produces an equilibrium with low price at *E*. When government restricts production, the supply curve is shifted leftward to *S'S'*, moving the equilibrium to *E'* and raising price to *B*. Confirm that new revenue rectangle *0BE'S'* is larger than original revenue rectangle *0AEX*—higher revenue being the result of inelastic demand.

IMPACT OF A TAX ON PRICE AND QUANTITY

Governments levy taxes on a wide variety of commodities—on cigarettes and alcohol, on payrolls and profits. Supply-and-demand analysis can help us predict who will bear the true burden of a tax and how a tax will affect output.

As an example, we will look at the case of a gasoline tax to illustrate the way that taxes affect market output and price. Although American politicians periodically make a fuss about them, gasoline taxes are far lower in the United States than in most European countries, where gas taxes are $2 to $5 per gallon—as compared to around 50 cents on average in the United States. Many economists and environmentalists advocate much higher gasoline taxes for the United States. They point out that higher taxes would curb consumption, and thereby reduce pollution and our dependence on insecure foreign sources of oil.

For concreteness, suppose that the government decides to discourage oil consumption by levying a gasoline tax of $1 per gallon. Prudent legislators would of course be reluctant to raise gas taxes so sharply without a firm understanding of the consequences of such a move. They would want to know the incidence of the tax. *By incidence we mean the ultimate economic effect of a tax on the real incomes of producers or consumers.* Just because businesses write a check for the taxes does not mean that the taxes in fact reduce their profits. By using supply and demand, we can analyze who actually bears the burden, or what the incidence is, of the tax.

It could be that the burden of the tax is shifted forward to the consumers, if the retail price of gasoline goes up by the full $1 of the tax. Or perhaps consumers cut back so sharply on gasoline purchases that the burden of the tax is shifted back completely onto the oil companies. Where the actual impact lies between these extremes can be determined only from supply-and-demand analysis.

Figure 4-10 provides the answer. It shows the original pretax equilibrium at *E*, the intersection of the original *SS* and *DD* curves, at a gasoline price of $1 a gallon and total consumption of 100 billion gallons per year. We portray the imposition of a $1 tax in the retail market for gasoline as an upward shift of the supply curve, with the demand curve remaining unchanged. The demand curve does not shift because the quantity demanded at each retail price is unchanged after the gasoline-tax increase. Note that the demand curve for gasoline is relatively inelastic.

By contrast, the supply curve definitely does shift upward by $1. The reason is that producers are willing to sell a given quantity (say, 100 billion gallons) only if they receive the same *net* price as before. That is, at each quantity supplied, the market price must rise by exactly the amount of the tax. If producers had originally been willing to sell 80 billion gallons at $0.90 per gallon, they would still be willing to sell the same amount at a retail price of $1.90 (which, after subtracting the tax, yields the producers the same $0.90 per gallon).

What will be the new equilibrium price? The answer is found at the intersection of the new supply and demand curves, or at *E'*, where *S'S'* and *DD* meet. Because of the supply shift, the price is higher. Also, the quantity supplied and demanded is reduced. If we read the graph carefully, we find that the new equilibrium price has risen from $1 to about $1.90. The new equilibrium output, at which supply and demand are in equilibrium, has fallen from 100 billion to about 80 billion gallons.

Who ultimately pays the tax? What is its incidence? Clearly the oil industry pays a small fraction, for it receives only 90 cents ($1.90 less the $1 tax) rather than $1. But the consumer bears most of the burden, with the retail price rising 90 cents, because supply is relatively price-elastic whereas demand is relatively price-inelastic.

FIGURE 4-10. **Gasoline Tax Falls on Both Consumer and Producer**

What is the incidence of a tax? A $1 tax on gasoline shifts the supply curve up $1 everywhere, giving a new supply curve, *S'S'*, parallel to the original supply curve, *SS*. This new supply curve intersects *DD* at the new equilibrium, *E'*, where price to consumers has risen 90 cents and producers' price has fallen 10 cents. The rust arrows show changes in *P* and *Q*. Note that consumers bear most of the burden of the tax.

Subsidies. If taxes are used to discourage consumption of a commodity, subsidies are used to encourage production. One pervasive example of subsidies comes in agriculture. You can examine the impact of a subsidy in a market by shifting *down* the supply curve. The general rules for subsidies are exactly parallel to those for taxes.

General Rules on Tax Shifting. Gasoline is just a single example of how to analyze tax shifting. Using this apparatus, we can understand how cigarette taxes affect both the prices and the consumption of cigarettes; how taxes or tariffs on imports affect foreign trade; and how property taxes, social security taxes, and corporate-profit taxes affect land prices, wages, and interest rates.

The key issue in determining the incidence of a tax is the relative elasticities of supply and demand. If demand is inelastic relative to supply, as in the case of gasoline, most of the cost is shifted to consumers. By contrast, if supply is inelastic relative to demand, as is the case for land, then most of the tax is shifted to the suppliers. Here is the general rule for determining the incidence of a tax:

The incidence of a tax denotes the impact of the tax on the incomes of producers and consumers. In general, the incidence depends upon the relative elasticities of demand and supply. A tax is shifted forward to consumers if the demand is inelastic relative to supply; a tax is shifted backward to producers if supply is relatively more inelastic than demand.

MINIMUM FLOORS AND MAXIMUM CEILINGS

Sometimes, rather than taxing or subsidizing a commodity, the government legislates maximum or minimum prices. History is full of examples. From biblical days, governments have limited the interest rates that lenders can charge (so-called usury laws). In wartime, governments often impose wage and price controls to prevent spiraling inflation. During the energy crisis of the 1970s, there were controls on gasoline prices. Today, there are increasingly stringent limitations on the prices that doctors or hospitals can charge, and a few large cities, including New York, have rent controls on apartments.[2] Proposals to increase the minimum wage are among the most controversial issues of economic policy.

These kinds of interferences with the laws of supply and demand are genuinely different from those in which the government imposes a tax and then lets the market act through supply and demand. Although political pressures always exist to keep prices down

and wages up, experience has taught that sector-by-sector price and wage controls tend to create major economic distortions. Nevertheless, as Adam Smith well knew when he protested against mercantilist policies of an earlier age, most economic systems are plagued by inefficiencies stemming from well-meaning but inexpert interferences with the mechanisms of supply and demand. Setting maximum or minimum prices in a market tends to produce surprising and sometimes perverse economic effects. Let's see why.

Two important examples of government intervention are the minimum wage and price controls on gasoline. These will illustrate the surprising side effects that can arise when governments interfere with market determination of price and quantity.

The Minimum-Wage Controversy

The minimum wage sets a minimum hourly rate that employers are allowed to pay workers. In the United States, the federal minimum wage began in 1938 when the government required that covered workers be paid at least 25 cents an hour. By 1947, the minimum wage was fully 65 percent of the average rate paid to manufacturing workers (see Figure 4-11). Although it was occasionally raised, the minimum wage eroded relative to average wages and, at $5.15 per hour, amounted to only 34 percent of manufacturing wages at the end of 2003.

This is an issue that divides even the most eminent economists. For example, Nobel laureate Gary Becker stated flatly, "Hike the minimum wage, and you put people out of work." Another group of Nobel Prize winners countered, "We believe that the federal minimum wage can be increased by a moderate amount without significantly jeopardizing employment opportunities." Yet another leading economist, Alan Blinder of Princeton, an economic adviser to President Clinton, wrote as follows:

The folks who earn the lowest wages have been suffering for years. They need all the help they can get, and they need it in a hurry. About 40 percent of all minimum-wage employees are the sole wage earner in their households, and about two-thirds of the teenagers earning the minimum wage live in households with below-average incomes. Frankly, I do not know whether a modest minimum-wage increase would decrease employment or not. If it does, the effect will likely be very small. (*New York Times*, May 23, 1996)

---

[2] See question 9 at the end of this chapter for an examination of rent controls.

FIGURE 4-11. The Minimum Wage and Teenage Unemployment, 1947–2002

The solid line shows the level of the minimum wage relative to average hourly earnings in manufacturing. Note how the minimum wage declined slowly relative to other wages over the last half-century. Additionally, the dashed black line shows the ratio of teenage unemployment to overall unemployment. Do you see any relationship between the two lines? What does this tell you about the minimum-wage controversy?

Source: Data are from the U.S. Department of Labor. Background on the minimum wage can be found at the Labor Department's website at www.dol.gov/esa/minwage/q-a.htm.

How can nonspecialists sort through the issues when the experts are so divided? How can we resolve these apparently contradictory statements? To begin with, we should recognize that statements on the desirability of raising the minimum wage contain personal value judgments. Such statements might be informed by the best positive economics and still make different recommendations on important policy issues.

A cool-headed analysis indicates that the minimum-wage debate centers primarily on issues of interpretation rather than fundamental disagreements on empirical findings. Begin by looking at Figure 4-12, which depicts the market for unskilled workers. The

figure shows how a minimum wage rate sets a floor for most jobs. As the minimum wage rises above the market-clearing equilibrium at M, the total number of jobs moves up the demand curve to E, so employment falls. The gap between labor supplied and labor demanded is shown as U. This represents the amount of unemployment.

Using supply and demand, we see that there is likely to be a rise in unemployment and a decrease in employment of low-skilled workers. But how large will these magnitudes be? And what will be the impact on the wage income of low-income workers? On these questions, we can look at the empirical evidence.

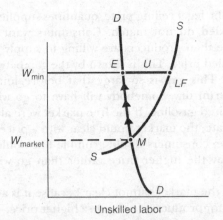

FIGURE 4-12. Effects of a Minimum Wage

Setting the minimum-wage floor at W_{min}, high above the free-market equilibrium rate at W_{market}, results in employment at E. Employment is reduced, as the arrows show, from M to E. Additionally, unemployment is U, which is the difference between labor supplied at LF and employment at E. If the demand curve is inelastic, increasing the minimum wage will increase the income of low-wage workers. To see this, shade in the rectangle of total wages before and after the minimum-wage increase.

Most studies indicate that a 10 percent increase in the minimum wage would reduce employment of teenagers by between 1 and 3 percent. The impact on adult employment is even smaller. Some recent studies put the employment effects very close to zero, and one set of studies suggests that employment might even increase. So a careful reading of the quotations from the eminent economists indicates that some economists consider small to be "insignificant" while others emphasize the existence of at least some job losses. Our example in Figure 4-12 shows a case where the *employment* decline (shown as the difference between M and E) is very small while the *unemployment* caused by the minimum wage (shown by the U line) is relatively large.

Figure 4-11 on page 78 shows the history of the minimum wage and teenage unemployment over the last half-century. With the declining power of the labor movement, the ratio of the minimum wage to the manufacturing wage declined from 65 percent in 1947 to around one-third in 2003. There was a slight upward trend in the unemployment rate of teenagers over this period. It is worth examining the pattern of changes to see whether you can detect

an impact of the minimum wage on teenage unemployment.

Another factor in the debate relates to the impact of the minimum wage on incomes. Virtually every study concludes that the demand for low-wage workers is price-inelastic. The results we just cited indicate that the price elasticity is between 0.1 and 0.3. This leads to the surprising conclusion that *raising the minimum wage would increase the incomes of low-income workers as a whole.* Given the elasticities just cited, a 10 percent increase in the minimum wage will increase the incomes of the affected groups by 7 to 9 percent. Figure 4-12 shows how the *incomes* of low-income workers rise despite the decline in their *total employment.* This can be seen by comparing the income rectangles under the equilibrium points E and M. (See question 8e at the end of this chapter.)

The impact on incomes is yet another reason why people may disagree about the minimum wage. Those who are particularly concerned about the welfare of low-income groups may feel that modest inefficiencies are a small price to pay for higher incomes. Others—who worry more about the cumulative costs of market interferences or about the impact of higher costs upon prices, profits, and international competitiveness—may hold that the inefficiencies are too high a price. Still others might believe that the minimum wage is an inefficient way to transfer buying power to low-income groups; they would prefer using direct income transfers or government wage subsidies rather than gumming up the wage system. How important are each of these three concerns to you? Depending upon your priorities, you might reach quite different conclusions on the advisability of increasing the minimum wage.

Energy Price Controls

Another example of government interference comes when the government legislates a maximum price ceiling. This occurred in the United States in the 1970s, and the results were sobering. We return to our analysis of the gasoline market to see how price ceilings function.

Let's set the scene. Suppose there is suddenly a sharp rise in oil prices. This has occurred because of reduced cartel supply and booming demand, but it might also come about because of political disturbances in the Middle East due to war or revolution. Figure 3-1 on p. 46 showed the results of the interaction of supply and demand in oil markets, with wars and revolutions producing oil price increases in 1973, 1979, 1990, and 2003.

Politicians, seeing the sudden jump in prices, rise to denounce the situation. They claim that consumers are being "gouged" by profiteering oil companies. They worry that the rising prices threaten to ignite an inflationary spiral in the cost of living. They fret about the impact of rising prices on the poor and elderly. They call upon the government to "do something." In the face of rising prices, the U.S. government might be inclined to listen to these arguments and place a ceiling on oil prices, as it did from 1973 to 1981.

What are the effects of such a ceiling? Suppose the initial price of gasoline is $1 a gallon. Then, because of a drastic cut in oil supply, the market price of gasoline rises to $2 a gallon. Now consider the gasoline market after the supply shock. In Figure 4-13, the postshock equilibrium is given at point E. Enter the government, which passes a law setting the maximum price for gasoline at the old level of $1 a gallon. We can picture this legal maximum price as the ceiling-price line CJK in Figure 4-13.

At the legal ceiling price, quantities supplied and demanded do not match. Consumers want more gasoline than producers are willing to supply at the controlled price. This is shown by the gap between J and K. This gap is so large that before long the pumps run dry. Somebody will have to go without the desired gasoline. If the free market were allowed to operate, the market would clear with a price of $2 or more; consumers would grumble but would willingly pay the higher price rather than go without fuel.

But the market cannot clear because it is against the law for producers to charge a higher price. There follows a period of frustration and shortage—a game of musical cars in which somebody is left without gasoline when the pump runs dry. The inadequate supply of gasoline must somehow be rationed. Initially, this may be done through a "first-come, first-served" approach, with or without limiting sales to each customer. Lines form, and much time has to be spent foraging for fuel.

Eventually, some kind of nonprice rationing mechanism evolves. For gasoline and other storable goods, the shortage is often managed by making people wait in line—rationing by the "queue." Sometimes people who have privileged access to the good engage in black-market sales, which are illegal transactions above the regulated price. There is great waste as people spend valuable time trying to secure their needs. Sometimes, governments design a more efficient system of nonprice rationing based on formal allocation or coupon rationing.

Under coupon rationing, each customer must have a coupon as well as money to buy the goods—in effect, there are two kinds of money. When rationing is adopted and coupons are meted out according to "need," shortages disappear because demand is limited by the allocation of the coupons. Just how do ration coupons change the supply-and-demand picture? Clearly, the government must issue just enough of them to lower the demand curve to $D'D'$ in Figure 4-13, where supply and the new demand balance at the ceiling price.

Price controls on goods like energy, with or without formal rationing, have fallen out of favor in most market economies. History has shown that legal and illegal evasions of price controls grow over time, and the inefficiencies eventually overwhelm whatever favorable impacts the controls might have on

FIGURE 4-13. Price Controls Produce Shortages

Without a legal price ceiling, price would rise to E. At the ceiling price of $1, supply and demand do not balance, and shortages break out. Some method of rationing, formal or informal, is needed to allocate the short supply and bring the actual demand down to $D'D'$.

consumers. Particularly when there is room for ample substitution (i.e., when elasticities of supply or demand are high), price controls are costly, difficult to administer, and ineffective. While price controls are rarely seen in most industries, they are today becoming more pervasive in medical care. We will see in Part 4 that price controls in medicine are leading to the same kinds of inefficiencies that were seen for gasoline a few decades ago.

There is an important and profound lesson here: Goods are always scarce. Society can never fulfill everyone's wishes. In normal times, price itself rations the scarce supplies. When governments step in to interfere with supply and demand, prices no longer fill the role of rationers. Waste, inefficiency, and aggravation are certain companions of such interferences.

SUMMARY

A. Elasticity of Demand and Supply

1. Price elasticity of demand measures the quantitative response of demand to a change in price. Price elasticity of demand (E_D) is defined as the percentage change in quantity demanded divided by the percentage change in price. That is,

   Price elasticity of demand = E_D

   $$= \frac{\text{percentage change in quantity demanded}}{\text{percentage change in price}}$$

   In this calculation, the sign is taken to be positive, and P and Q are averages of old and new values.
2. We divide price elasticities into three categories: (*a*) Demand is elastic when the percentage change in quantity demanded exceeds the percentage change in price; that is, $E_D > 1$. (*b*) Demand is inelastic when the percentage change in quantity demanded is less than the percentage change in price; here, $E_D < 1$. (*c*) When the percentage change in quantity demanded exactly equals the percentage change in price, we have the borderline case of unit-elastic demand, where $E_D = 1$.
3. Price elasticity is a pure number, involving percentages; it should not be confused with slope.
4. The demand elasticity tells us about the impact of a price change on total revenue. A price reduction increases total revenue if demand is elastic; a price reduction decreases total revenue if demand is inelastic; in the unit-elastic case, a price change has no effect on total revenue.
5. Price elasticity of demand tends to be low for necessities like food and shelter and high for luxuries like snowmobiles and vacation air travel. Other factors affecting price elasticity are the extent to which a good has ready substitutes and the length of time that consumers have to adjust to price changes.
6. Price elasticity of supply measures the percentage change of output supplied by producers when the market price changes by a given percentage.

B. Applications to Major Economic Issues

7. One of the most fruitful arenas for application of supply-and-demand analysis is agriculture. Improvements in agricultural technology mean that supply increases greatly, while demand for food rises less than proportionately with income. Hence free-market prices for foodstuffs tend to fall. No wonder governments have adopted a variety of programs, like crop restrictions, to prop up farm incomes.
8. A commodity tax shifts the supply-and-demand equilibrium. The tax's incidence (or impact on incomes) will fall more heavily on consumers than on producers to the degree that the demand is inelastic relative to supply.
9. Governments occasionally interfere with the workings of competitive markets by setting maximum ceilings or minimum floors on prices. In such situations, quantity supplied need no longer equal quantity demanded; ceilings lead to excess demand, while floors lead to excess supply. Sometimes, the interference may raise the incomes of a particular group, as in the case of farmers or low-skilled workers. Often, distortions and inefficiencies result.

CONCEPTS FOR REVIEW

Elasticity Concepts

price elasticity of demand, supply
elastic, inelastic, unit-elastic demand
E_D = % change in Q/% change in P
determinants of elasticity

total revenue = $P \times Q$
relationship of elasticity and revenue
   change

Applications of Supply and Demand

incidence of a tax
distortions from price controls
rationing by price vs. rationing by
   the queue

FURTHER READING AND INTERNET WEBSITES

Further Reading

If you have a particular concept you want to review, such as
elasticity, you can often look in an encyclopedia of economics, such as John Black, *Oxford Dictionary of Economics,*
2nd ed. (Oxford, New York, 2002), or David W. Pearce,
ed., *The MIT Dictionary of Modern Economics* (MIT Press,
Cambridge, Mass., 1992). The most comprehensive encyclopedia, covering many advanced topics in four volumes, is John Eatwell, Murray Milgate, and Peter Newman,
The New Palgrave: A Dictionary of Economics (Macmillan,
London, 1987).

The minimum wage has generated a fierce debate among
economists. A recent book by two labor economists presents evidence that the minimum wage has little effect on
employment: David Card and Alan Krueger, *Myth and Measurement: The New Economics of the Minimum Wage* (Princeton
University Press, Princeton, N.J., 1997).

Websites

There are currently no reliable online dictionaries
for terms in economics. There are few good websites
for understanding fundamental economic concepts like
supply and demand or elasticities. There is a concise
online encyclopedia of economics at www.econlib.org/
library/CEE.html, which is generally reliable but covers
only a small number of topics. Sometimes, the free site of
the *Encyclopedia Britannica* at www.britannica.com will provide background or historical material. When all else fails,
you can go to the omnibus economics site on the Web,
www.hkkk.fi/EconVLib.html, which is expanding rapidly
and has online materials from many areas.

Current issues such as the minimum wage are often discussed in policy papers at the website of the Economic
Policy Institute, a think tank focusing on economic issues
of workers, at www.epinet.org.

QUESTIONS FOR DISCUSSION

1. "A good harvest will generally lower the income of
   farmers." Illustrate this proposition using a supply-and-
   demand diagram.
2. For each pair of commodities, state which you think is
   the more price-elastic and give your reasons: perfume
   and salt; penicillin and ice cream; automobiles and automobile tires; ice cream and chocolate ice cream.
3. "The price drops by 1 percent, causing the quantity
   demanded to rise by 2 percent. Demand is therefore
   elastic, with $E_D > 1$." If you change 2 to $\frac{1}{2}$ in the first
   sentence, what two other changes will be required in
   the quotation?
4. Consider a competitive market for apartments. What
   would be the effect on the equilibrium output and

price after the following changes (other things held
equal)? In each case, explain your answer using supply
and demand.
   a. A rise in the income of consumers
   b. A $10-per-month tax on apartment rentals
   c. A government edict saying apartments cannot rent
      for more than $200 per month
   d. A new construction technique allowing apart-
      ments to be built at half the cost
   e. A 20 percent increase in the wages of construction
      workers
5. Consider a proposal to raise the minimum wage by
   10 percent. After reviewing the arguments in the chapter, estimate the impact upon employment and upon

the incomes of affected workers. Using the numbers you have derived, write a short essay explaining how *you* would decide if you had to make a recommendation on the minimum wage.

6. A conservative critic of government programs has written, "Governments know how to do one thing well. They know how to create shortages and surpluses." Explain this quotation using examples like the minimum wage or interest-rate ceilings. Show graphically that if the demand for unskilled workers is price-elastic, a minimum wage will decrease the total earnings (wage times quantity demanded of labor) of unskilled workers.

7. Consider what would happen if a tariff of $2000 were imposed on imported automobiles. Show the impact of this tariff on the supply and the demand, and on the equilibrium price and quantity, of American automobiles. Explain why American auto companies and autoworkers often support import restraints on automobiles.

8. Elasticity problems:

   a. The world demand for crude oil is estimated to have a short-run price elasticity of 0.05. If the initial price of oil were $30 per barrel, what would be the effect on oil price and quantity of an embargo that curbed world oil supply by 5 percent? (For this problem, assume that the oil-supply curve is completely inelastic.)

   b. To show that elasticities are independent of units, refer to Table 3-1. Calculate the elasticities between each demand pair. Change the price units from dollars to pennies; change the quantity units from millions of boxes to tons, using the conversion factor of 10,000 boxes to 1 ton. Then recalculate the elasticities in the first two rows. Explain why you get the same answer.

   c. Demand studies find that the price elasticity of demand for cocaine is 0.5. Suppose that half the cocaine users in New York City support their habit by predatory criminal activities. Using supply-and-demand analysis, show the impact on crime in New York City of an interdiction program that decreases the supply of crack into the New York market by 50 percent. (Assume that supply is completely inelastic for this exercise.) What would be the effect of reducing supply constraints on criminal activity and on drug use if the government reduced its interdiction efforts and this lowered the price of cocaine by 50 percent? Discuss the impact on price and addiction of a program that successfully rehabilitated half of the cocaine users.

   d. Can you explain why farmers during a depression might approve of a government program requiring that pigs be killed and buried under the ground?

   e. Look at the impact of the minimum wage shown in Figure 4-12. Draw in the rectangles of total income with and without the minimum wage. Which is larger? Relate the impact of the minimum wage to the price elasticity of demand for unskilled workers.

9. No one likes to pay rent. Yet scarcities of land and urban housing often cause rents to soar in cities. In response to rising rents and hostility toward landlords, governments sometimes impose *rent controls*. These generally limit the increases on rent to a small year-to-year increase and can leave controlled rents far below free-market rents.

   a. Redraw Figure 4-13 to illustrate the impact of rent controls for apartments.

   b. What will be the effect of rent controls on the vacancy rate of apartments?

   c. What nonrent options might arise as a substitute for the higher rents?

   d. Explain the words of a European critic of rent controls: "Except for bombing, nothing is as efficient at destroying a city as rent controls." (*Hint:* What would happen to maintenance?)

10. Review the example of the New Jersey cigarette tax (p. 72). Using graph paper or a computer, draw supply and demand curves that will yield the prices and quantities before and after the tax. (Figure 4-10 shows the example for a gasoline tax.) For this example, assume that the supply curve is perfectly elastic. [*Extra credit:* A demand curve with constant price elasticity takes the form $Y = AP^{-e}$, where Y is quantity demanded, P is price, A is a scaling constant, and e is the (absolute value) of the price elasticity. Solve for the values of A and e which will give the correct demand curve for the prices and quantities in the New Jersey example.]

CHAPTER

5

Demand and Consumer Behavior

*O, reason not the need:
our basest beggars
Are in the poorest thing
superfluous.*

King Lear

Each day involves endless decisions about how to allocate our scarce money and time. Should we eat breakfast or sleep late? Spend our evenings reading or visit with friends? Buy a new car or fix our old one? Spend our income today or save for the future? As we balance competing demands and desires, we make the choices that define our lives.

The results of these individual choices are what underlie the demand curves and price elasticities that we saw in earlier chapters. In this chapter we explore the basic principles of consumer choice and behavior. We shall see how observed patterns of market demand can be explained by the process of individuals' pursuing their most preferred bundle of consumption goods. We also will learn how to measure the benefits that each of us receives from participating in a market economy.

CHOICE AND UTILITY THEORY

In explaining consumer behavior, economics relies on the fundamental premise that people choose those goods and services they value most highly. To describe the way consumers choose among different consumption possibilities, economists a century ago developed the notion of *utility*. From the notion of utility, they were able to derive the demand curve and explain its properties.

What do we mean by "utility"? In a word, **utility** denotes satisfaction. More precisely, it refers to how consumers rank different goods and services. If basket A has higher utility than basket B for Smith, this ranking indicates that Smith prefers A over B. Often, it is convenient to think of utility as the subjective pleasure or usefulness that a person derives from consuming a good or service. But you should definitely resist the idea that utility is a psychological function or feeling that can be observed or measured. *Rather, utility is a scientific construct that economists use to understand how rational consumers divide their limited resources among the commodities that provide them with satisfaction.*

In the theory of demand, we say that people maximize their utility, which means that they choose the bundle of consumption goods that they most prefer.

Marginal Utility and the Law of Diminishing Marginal Utility

How does utility apply to the theory of demand? Say that consuming the first unit of ice cream gives you a certain level of satisfaction or utility. Now imagine consuming a second unit. Your total utility goes up

84

because the second unit of the good gives you some additional utility. What about adding a third and fourth unit of the same good? Eventually, if you eat enough ice cream, instead of adding to your satisfaction or utility, it makes you sick!

This leads us to the fundamental economic concept of marginal utility. When you eat an additional unit of ice cream, you will get some additional satisfaction or utility. The increment to your utility is called **marginal utility.**

The expression "marginal" is a key term in economics and always means "additional" or "extra." Marginal utility denotes the additional utility you get from the consumption of an additional unit of a commodity.

A century ago, when economists thought about utility, they enunciated the **law of diminishing marginal utility.** This law states that the amount of extra or marginal utility declines as a person consumes more and more of a good.

What is the reason for this law? Utility tends to increase as you consume more of a good. However, according to the law of diminishing marginal utility, as you consume more and more, your total utility will grow at a slower and slower rate. Growth in total utility slows because your marginal utility (the extra utility added by the last unit consumed of a good) diminishes as more of the good is consumed. The diminishing marginal utility results from the fact that your enjoyment of the good drops off as more and more of it is consumed.

The law of diminishing marginal utility states that, as the amount of a good consumed increases, the marginal utility of that good tends to diminish.

A Numerical Example

We can illustrate utility numerically as in Table 5-1. The table shows in column (2) that total utility (U) enjoyed increases as consumption (Q) grows, but it increases at a decreasing rate. Column (3) measures marginal utility as the extra utility gained when 1 extra unit of the good is consumed. Thus when the individual consumes 2 units, the marginal utility is $7 - 4 = 3$ units of utility (call these units "utils").

Focus next on column (3). The fact that marginal utility declines with higher consumption illustrates the law of diminishing marginal utility.

(1) Quantity of a good consumed Q	(2) Total utility U	(3) Marginal utility MU
0	0	
		4
1	4	
		3
2	7	
		2
3	9	
		1
4	10	
		0
5	10	

TABLE 5-1. Utility Rises with Consumption

As we consume more of a good or service like pizza or concerts, total utility increases. The increment of utility from one unit to the next is the "marginal utility"—the extra utility added by the last extra unit consumed. By the law of diminishing marginal utility, the marginal utility falls with increasing levels of consumption.

Figure 5-1 on page 86 shows graphically the data on total utility and marginal utility from Table 5-1. In part (a), the gray blocks add up to the total utility at each level of consumption. In addition, the smooth gray curve shows the smoothed utility level for fractional units of consumption. It shows utility increasing, but at a decreasing rate. Figure 5-1(b) depicts marginal utilities. Each of the gray blocks of marginal utility is the same size as the corresponding block of total utility in (a). The straight black line in (b) is the smoothed curve of marginal utility.

The law of diminishing marginal utility implies that the marginal utility (MU) curve in Figure 5-1(b) must slope downward. This is exactly equivalent to saying that the total utility curve in Figure 5-1(a) must look concave, like a dome.

Relationship of Total and Marginal Utility. Using Figure 5-1, we can easily see that the total utility of consuming a certain amount is equal to the sum of the marginal utilities up to that point. For example, assume that 3 units are consumed. Column (2) of Table 5-1 shows that the total utility is 9 units. In

FIGURE 5-1. The Law of Diminishing Marginal Utility

Total utility in **(a)** rises with consumption, but it rises at a decreasing rate, showing diminishing marginal utility. This observation led early economists to formulate the law of downward-sloping demand.

The gray blocks show the extra utility added by each new unit. The fact that total utility increases at a decreasing rate is shown in **(b)** by the declining steps of marginal utility. If we make our units smaller, the steps in total utility are smoothed out and total utility becomes the smooth gray curve in **(a)**. Moreover, smoothed marginal utility, shown in **(b)** by the black downward-sloping smooth curve, becomes indistinguishable from the slope of the smooth curve in **(a)**.

column (3) we see that the sum of the marginal utilities of the first 3 units is also $4 + 3 + 2 = 9$ units.

Examining Figure 5-1(b), we see that the total area under the marginal utility curve at a particular level of consumption—as measured either by blocks or by the area under the smooth MU curve—must equal the height of the total utility curve shown for the same number of units in Figure 5-1(a).

Whether we examine this relationship using tables or graphs, we see that total utility is the sum of all the marginal utilities that were added from the beginning.

History of Utility Theory

Modern utility theory stems from *utilitarianism*, which has been one of the major currents of Western intellectual thought of the last two centuries. The notion of utility arose soon after 1700, as the basic ideas of mathematical probability were being developed. Thus Daniel Bernoulli, a member of a brilliant Swiss family of mathematicians, observed in 1738 that people act as if the dollar they stand to gain in a fair bet is worth less to them than the dollar they stand to lose. This means that they are averse to risk and that successive new dollars of wealth bring them smaller and smaller increments of true utility.[1]

An early introduction of the utility notion into the social sciences was accomplished by the English philosopher Jeremy Bentham (1748–1832). After studying legal theory, and under the influence of Adam Smith's doctrines, Bentham turned to the study of the principles necessary for drawing up social legislation. He proposed that society should be organized on the "principle of utility," which he defined as the "property in any object . . . to produce pleasure, good or happiness or to prevent . . . pain, evil or unhappiness."[2] All legislation, according to Bentham, should be designed on utilitarian principles, to promote "the greatest happiness of the greatest number." Among his other legislative proposals were quite modern-sounding ideas about crime and punishment in which he suggested that raising the "pain" to criminals by harsh punishments would deter crimes.

Bentham's views about utility seem familiar to many people today. But they were revolutionary 200 years ago because they emphasized that social and economic policies should be designed to achieve certain practical results, whereas legitimacy at that time was usually based on tradition, the divine right of kings, or religious doctrines. Today, many political thinkers defend their legislative proposals with utilitarian notions of what will make the largest number of people best off.

The next step in the development of utility theory came when the neoclassical economists—such as William Stanley Jevons (1835–1882)—extended Bentham's utility concept to explain consumer behavior. Jevons thought economic theory was a "calculus of pleasure and pain," and he developed the theory that rational people would base their consumption decisions on the extra or marginal utility of each good. Many utilitarians of the nineteenth century believed that utility was a psychological reality—directly and cardinally measurable, like length or temperature. They looked to their own sentiments for affirmation of the law of diminishing marginal utility.

Ordinal Utility. Economists today generally reject the notion of a cardinal (or measurable) utility that people feel or experience when consuming goods and services. Utility does not ring up like numbers on a gasoline pump. Rather, what counts for modern demand theory is the principle of **ordinal utility.** Under this approach, consumers need to determine only their preference ranking of bundles of commodities. Ordinal utility asks, "Is bundle A preferred to bundle B?" Or, "Do I prefer a pastrami sandwich to a chocolate milk shake?" Using only such ordinal preference rankings, we can establish firmly the general properties of market demand curves described in this chapter and in its appendix.[3]

EQUIMARGINAL PRINCIPLE: EQUAL MARGINAL UTILITIES PER DOLLAR FOR EVERY GOOD

We now want to use utility theory to explain consumer demand and to understand the nature of demand curves. We assume that each consumer maximizes his or her utility, which means that the consumer chooses the most preferred bundle of goods from what is available.

What are the implications of utility maximization? Certainly I would not expect that the last egg I am buying brings exactly the same marginal utility as the last pair of shoes I am buying, for shoes cost much more per unit than eggs. A more sensible rule would be: If good A costs twice as much as good B, then buy good A only when its marginal utility is at least twice as great as good B's marginal utility.

This leads to the *equimarginal principle* that I should arrange my consumption so that the last dollar spent on each good is bringing me the same

---

[1] The economics of risk, uncertainty, and gambling are examined in Chapter 11.

[2] See Bentham in the Further Reading section at the end of this chapter. Note that the term *utility* was used by Bentham in quite a different way from today's usage, in which utility is something that is useful.

[3] A statement such as "Situation A is preferred to situation B"—which does not require that we know how much A is preferred to B—is called *ordinal*, or dimensionless. Ordinal variables are ones that we can rank in order, but for which there is no measure of the quantitative difference between the situations. We might rank pictures in an exhibition by order of beauty without having a quantitative measure of beauty.

For certain special situations the concept of *cardinal*, or dimensional, utility is useful. An example of a cardinal measure comes when we say that a substance at 100 K (kelvin) is twice as hot as one at 50 K. People's behavior under conditions of uncertainty is today often analyzed using a cardinal concept of utility. This topic will be examined further in Chapter 11.

marginal utility. In such a situation, I am attaining maximum satisfaction or utility from my purchases.

Equimarginal principle: The fundamental condition of maximum satisfaction or utility is the equimarginal principle. It states that a consumer having a fixed income and facing given market prices of goods will achieve maximum satisfaction or utility when the marginal utility of the last dollar spent on each good is exactly the same as the marginal utility of the last dollar spent on any other good.

Why must this condition hold? If any one good gave more marginal utility per dollar, I would increase my utility by taking money away from other goods and spending more on that good—until the law of diminishing marginal utility drove its marginal utility per dollar down to equality with that of other goods. If any good gave less marginal utility per dollar than the common level, I would buy less of it until the marginal utility of the last dollar spent on it had risen back to the common level.[4] The common marginal utility per dollar of all commodities in consumer equilibrium is called the *marginal utility of income.* It measures the additional utility that would be gained if the consumer could enjoy an extra dollar's worth of consumption.

This fundamental condition of consumer equilibrium can be written in terms of the marginal utilities (MUs) and prices (Ps) of the different goods in the following compact way:[5]

$$\frac{MU_{\text{good 1}}}{P_1} = \frac{MU_{\text{good 2}}}{P_2}$$

$$= \frac{MU_{\text{good 3}}}{P_3} = \cdots$$

$$= MU \text{ per \$ of income}$$

Why Demand Curves Slope Downward

Using the fundamental rule for consumer behavior, we can easily see why demand curves slope downward. For simplicity, hold the common marginal utility per dollar of income constant. Then increase the price of good 1. With no change in quantity consumed, the first ratio (i.e., $MU_{\text{good 1}}/P_1$) will be below the MU per dollar of all other goods. The consumer will therefore have to readjust the consumption of good 1. The consumer will do this by (*a*) lowering the consumption of good 1, thereby (*b*) raising the MU of good 1, until (*c*) at the new, reduced level of consumption of good 1, the new marginal utility per dollar spent on good 1 is again equal to the MU per dollar spent on other goods.

A higher price for a good reduces the consumer's desired consumption of that commodity; this shows why demand curves slope downward.

Leisure and the Optimal Allocation of Time

A Spanish toast to a friend wishes "health, wealth, and the time to enjoy them." This saying captures the idea that we must allocate our time budgets in much the same way as we do our dollar budgets. Time is the great equalizer, for even the richest person has but 24 hours a day to "spend." Let's see how our earlier analysis of allocating scarce dollars applies to time.

Consider leisure, often defined as "time which one can spend as one pleases." Leisure brings out our personal eccentricities. The seventeenth-century philosopher Francis Bacon held that the purest of human pleasures was gardening. The modern British statesman Winston Churchill wrote of his holiday: "I have had a delightful month building a cottage and dictating a book: 200 bricks and 2000 words a day."

Whatever *your* tastes, the principles of utility theory can apply well. Suppose that, after satisfying all your obligations, you have 3 hours a day of free time and can devote it to gardening, laying bricks, or

---

[4] At a few places in economics the indivisibility of units is important and cannot be glossed over. Thus, Hondas cannot be divided into arbitrarily small portions the way juice can. Suppose I buy one Honda, but definitely not two. Then the marginal utility of the first car is enough larger than the marginal utility of the same number of dollars spent elsewhere to induce me to buy this first unit. The marginal utility that the second Honda would bring is enough less to ensure I do not buy it. When indivisibility matters, our equality rule for equilibrium can be restated as an inequality rule.

[5] The discerning reader will wonder whether the following mathematical condition seems to imply cardinal, or dimensional, utility (see footnote 3). In fact it does not. An ordinal utility measure is one that we can stretch while always maintaining the same greater-than or less-than relationship (like measuring with a rubber band). If the utility scale is stretched (say, by doubling or multiplying times 3.1415), then you can see that all the numerators in the condition are changed by the same amount, so the consumer equilibrium condition still holds. This is shown in the appendix to this chapter by the use of indifference curves.

writing history. What is the best way to allocate your time? Let's ignore the possibility that time spent on some of these activities might be an investment that will enhance your earning power in the future. Rather, assume that these are all pure consumption or utility-yielding pursuits. The principles of consumer choice suggest that you will make the best use of your time when you equalize the marginal utilities of the last minute spent on each activity.

To take another example, suppose you want to maximize your knowledge in your courses but you have only a limited amount of time available. Should you study each subject for the same amount of time? Surely not. You may find that an equal study time for economics, history, and chemistry will not yield the same amount of knowledge in the last minute. If the last minute produces a greater marginal knowledge in chemistry than in history, you would raise your total knowledge by shifting additional minutes from history to chemistry, and so on, until the last minute yields the same incremental knowledge in each subject.

The same rule of maximum utility per hour can be applied to many different areas of life, including engaging in charitable activities, improving the environment, or losing weight. It is not merely a law of economics. It is a law of rational choice.

Are Consumers Wizards?

All of this discussion makes it sound as if consumers are mathematical wizards who routinely make calculations of marginal utility to the tenth decimal place and solve complicated systems of equations in their everyday lives.

This unrealistic view is definitely not what we assume in economics. We know that most decisions are made in a routine way and that people sometimes buy "lemons" or are bilked by unscrupulous sales pitches. What is usually assumed is that consumers are reasonably consistent in their tastes and actions—that they do not flail around in unpredictable ways and do not make themselves miserable by persistent errors. If most people act consistently most of the time, avoiding erratic changes in buying behavior and generally choosing their most preferred bundles, our scientific theory will provide a reasonably good approximation to the facts.

As always, however, we must be alert to situations where irrational or inconsistent behavior crops up. A new area of research is *behavioral economics*, which recognizes that people have limited time and memory and that patterns of irrational-looking behavior are prevalent. This approach attempts to explain why households save too little for retirement, why stock market bubbles occur, or how used-car markets behave when people's information is limited. Nobel Prizes in 2001 and 2002 were awarded to George Akerlof of the University of California at Berkeley for developing a better understanding of the role of asymmetric information and the market for "lemons" and to Daniel Kahneman of Princeton University and Vernon L. Smith of George Mason University for "the analysis of human judgment and decision-making . . . and the empirical testing of predictions from economic theory by experimental economists."

AN ALTERNATIVE APPROACH: SUBSTITUTION EFFECT AND INCOME EFFECT

The concept of marginal utility has helped explain the fundamental law of downward-sloping demand. But over the last few decades, economists have developed an alternative approach to the analysis of demand—one that makes no mention of marginal utility. This alternative approach uses "indifference curves," which are explained in the appendix to this chapter, to rigorously and consistently produce the major propositions about consumer behavior. This approach also helps explain the factors that tend to make the responsiveness of quantity demanded to price—the price elasticity of demand—large or small.

Indifference analysis asks about the substitution effect and the income effect of a change in price. By looking at these, we can see why the quantity demanded of a good declines as its price rises.

Substitution Effect

The substitution effect is the most obvious factor for explaining downward-sloping demand curves. If the price of coffee goes up while other prices do not, then coffee has become relatively more expensive. When coffee becomes a more expensive beverage, less coffee and more tea or cola will be bought. Similarly, because sending electronic mail is cheaper and quicker than sending letters through the regular mail, people are increasingly relying on electronic mail for correspondence. More generally, the **substitution effect** says that when the price of a good rises, consumers will tend to substitute other goods for the more expensive good in order to satisfy their desires more inexpensively.

Consumers, then, behave the way businesses do when the rise in price of an input causes firms to substitute low-priced inputs for high-priced inputs. By this process of substitution, businesses can produce a given amount of output at the least total cost. Similarly, when consumers substitute less expensive goods for more expensive ones, they are buying a given amount of satisfaction at less cost.

Income Effect

In addition, when your money income is fixed, a price increase is just like a reduction in your "real income." (*Real income* means the actual amount of goods and services that your money income can buy.) When a price rises and money incomes are fixed, consumers' real incomes fall because they cannot afford to buy the same quantity of goods as before. This produces the **income effect,** which denotes the impact of a price change on a good's quantity demanded due to the effect of the price change on real incomes. Because a lower real income generally leads to lower consumption, the income effect will normally reinforce the substitution effect in making the demand curve downward-sloping.

To obtain a quantitative measure of the income effect, we examine a good's **income elasticity.** This term denotes the percentage change in quantity demanded divided by the percentage change in income, holding other things, such as prices, constant. High income elasticities, such as those for airline travel or yachts, indicate that the demand for these goods rises rapidly as income increases. Low income elasticities, such as for food or cigarettes, denote a weak response of demand as income rises.

Calculation of Income Elasticity

Suppose you are a city planner for Santa Fe, New Mexico, and you are concerned about the growth in the demand for water consumption by households in that arid region. You make inquiries and find the following data for 2000:

The population is 62,000; the projected growth rate of the population is 20 percent per decade; per capita annual water consumption in 2000 was 1000 gallons; per capita incomes are projected to grow by 25 percent over the next decade; and the income elasticity of water use per capita is 0.50. You then estimate the water needs for 2010 (with unchanged prices) as

Water consumption in 2010 = population in 2000 ×
  population growth factor × per capita water use ×
      [1 + (income growth × income elasticity)]

  = 62,000 × 1.2 × 1000 × (1 + 0.25 × 0.50)

  = 83,700,000

From these data, you project a growth in total household water use of 35 percent from 2000 to 2010.

Income and substitution effects combine to determine the major characteristics of demand curves of different commodities. Under some circumstances the resulting demand curve is very price-elastic, as where the consumer has been spending a good deal on the commodity and ready substitutes are available. In this case both the income and the substitution effects are strong and the quantity demanded responds strongly to a price increase.

But consider a commodity like salt, which requires only a small fraction of the consumer's budget. Salt is not easily replaceable by other items and is needed in small amounts to complement more important items. For salt, both income and substitution effects are small, and demand will tend to be price-inelastic.

FROM INDIVIDUAL TO MARKET DEMAND

Having analyzed the principles underlying a single individual's demand for coffee or electronic mail, we next examine how the entire market demand derives from the individual demand. *The demand curve for a good for the entire market is obtained by summing up the quantities demanded by all the consumers.* Each consumer has a demand curve along which the quantity demanded can be plotted against the price; it generally slopes downward and to the right. If all consumers were exactly alike in their demands and if

FIGURE 5-2. Market Demand Derived from Individual Demands

We add all individual consumers' demand curves to get the market demand curve. At each price, such as $5, we add quantities demanded by each person to get the market quantity demanded. The figure shows how, at a price of $5, we add horizontally Smith's 1 unit demanded to Brown's 2 units to get the market demand of 3 units.

there were 1 million consumers, we could think of the market demand curve as a millionfold enlargement of each consumer's demand curve.

But people are not all exactly alike. Some have high incomes, some low. Some greatly desire coffee; others prefer cola. To obtain the total market curve, all we have to do is calculate the sum total of what all the different consumers will consume at any given price. We then plot that total amount as a point on the market demand curve. Or, if we like, we might construct a numerical demand table by summing the quantities demanded by all individuals at each market price.[6]

The market demand curve is the sum of individual demands at each price. Figure 5-2 shows how to add individual *dd* demand curves horizontally to get the market *DD* demand curve.

---

[6] Here and in other chapters, we label *individual* demand and supply curves with lowercase letters (*dd* and *ss*), while using uppercase letters (*DD* and *SS*) for the *market* demand and supply curves.

Demand Shifts

We know that changes in the price of coffee affect the quantity of coffee demanded. We know this from budget studies, from historical experience, and from examining our own behavior. We discussed briefly in Chapter 3 some of the important nonprice determinants of demand. We now review the earlier discussion in light of our analysis of consumer behavior.

An increase in income tends to increase the amount we are willing to buy of most goods. Necessities tend to be less responsive than most goods to income changes, while luxuries tend to be more responsive to income. And there are a few anomalous goods, known as inferior goods, for which purchases may shrink as incomes increase because people can afford to replace them with other, more desirable goods. Soup bones, intercity bus travel, and black-and-white TVs are examples of inferior goods for many Americans today.

What does all this mean in terms of the demand curve? The demand curve shows how the quantity of a good demanded responds to a change in its own price. But the demand is also affected by the prices of other goods, by consumer incomes, and by special influences. The demand curve was drawn on the assumption that these other things were held constant. But what if these other things change? Then the whole demand curve will shift to the right or to the left.

Figure 5-3 illustrates changes in factors affecting demand. Given people's incomes and the prices for other goods, we can draw the demand curve for coffee as *DD*. Assume that price and quantity are at point *A*. Suppose that incomes rise while the prices of coffee and other goods are unchanged. Because coffee is a normal good with a positive income elasticity, people will increase their purchases of coffee. Hence the demand curve for coffee will shift to the right, say, to *D'D'*, with *A'* indicating the new quantity demanded of coffee. If incomes should fall, then we would expect a reduction in demand and in quantity bought. This downward shift we illustrate by *D''D''* and by *A''*.

FIGURE 5-3. Demand Curve Shifts with Changes in Income or in Other Goods' Prices

As incomes increase, consumers generally want more of a good, thus increasing demand or shifting demand outward (explain why higher incomes shift *DD* to *D'D'*). Similarly, a rise in the price of a substitute good increases or shifts out the demand curve (e.g., from *DD* to *D'D'*). Explain why a decrease in income would generally shift demand to *D''D''*. Why would a decrease in chicken prices shift hamburger demand to *D''D''*?

Substitutes and Complements

Everyone knows that raising the price of beef will decrease the amount of beef demanded. We have seen that it will also affect the demand for other commodities. For example, a higher price for beef will increase the demand for substitutes like chicken. A higher beef price may lower the demand for goods like hamburger buns and ketchup that are used along with beef hamburgers. It will probably have little effect on the demand for economics textbooks.

We say, therefore, that beef and chicken are substitute products. Goods A and B are **substitutes** if an increase in the price of good A will increase the demand for substitute good B. Hamburgers and hamburger buns, or cars and gasoline, on the other hand, are complementary products; they are called **complements** because an increase in the price of good A causes a decrease in the demand for its complementary good B. In between are **independent goods,** such as beef and textbooks, for which a price change for one has no effect on the demand for the other. Try classifying the pairs turkey and cranberry sauce, oil and coal, college and textbooks, shoes and shoelaces, salt and shoelaces.

Say Figure 5-3 represented the demand for beef. A fall in the price of chickens may well cause consumers to buy less beef; the beef demand curve would therefore shift to the left, say, to *D''D''*. But what if the price of hamburger buns were to fall? The resulting change on *DD*, if there is one, will be in the direction of increased beef purchases, a rightward shift of the demand curve. Why do we see this difference in response? Because chicken is a rival or substitute product for beef, while hamburger buns are complements to beef.

Review of key concepts:

- The **substitution effect** occurs when a higher price leads to substitution of other goods for the good whose price has risen.
- The **income effect** is the change in the quantity demanded of a good because the change in its price has the effect of changing a consumer's real income.
- **Income elasticity** is the percentage change in quantity demanded of a good divided by the percentage change in income.
- Goods are **substitutes** if an increase in the price of one increases the demand for the other.

- Goods are **complements** if an increase in the price of one decreases the demand for the other.
- Goods are **independent** if a price change for one has no effect on the demand for the other.

Empirical Estimates of Price and Income Elasticities

For many economic applications, it is essential to have numerical estimates of price elasticities. For example, an automobile manufacturer will want to know the impact on sales of the higher car prices that result from installation of costly pollution-control equipment; a college needs to know the impact of higher tuition rates on student applications; and a publisher will calculate the impact of higher textbook prices on its sales. All these applications require a numerical estimate of price elasticity.

Similar decisions depend on income elasticities. A government planning its road or rail network will estimate the impact of rising incomes on automobile travel; the federal government must calculate the effect of higher incomes on energy consumption in designing policies for air pollution or global warming; in determining the necessary investments for generating capacity, electrical utilities require income elasticities for estimating electricity consumption.

Economists have developed useful statistical techniques for estimating price and income elasticities. The quantitative estimates are derived from market data on quantities demanded, prices, incomes, and other variables. Tables 5-2 and 5-3 show selected estimates of elasticities.

THE ECONOMICS OF ADDICTION

In a free-market economy, the government generally lets people decide what to buy with their money. If some want to buy expensive cars while others want to buy expensive houses, we assume that they know what is best for them and that in the interests of personal freedom the government should respect their preferences.

In some cases, but sparingly and with great hesitation, the government decides to overrule private adult decisions. These are cases of *merit goods,* whose consumption is thought intrinsically worthwhile, and the opposite, which are *demerit goods,* whose consumption is deemed harmful. For these goods, we recognize that some consumption activities have

Commodity	Price elasticity
Tomatoes	4.60
Green peas	2.80
Legal gambling	1.90
Taxi service	1.24
Furniture	1.00
Movies	0.87
Shoes	0.70
Legal services	0.61
Medical insurance	0.31
Bus travel	0.20
Residential electricity	0.13

TABLE 5-2. Selected Estimates of Price Elasticities of Demand

Estimates of price elasticities of demand show a wide range of variation. Elasticities are generally high for goods for which ready substitutes are available, like tomatoes or peas. Low price elasticities exist for those goods like electricity which are essential to daily life and which have no close substitutes.

Source: Heinz Kohler, *Microeconomics: Theory and Applications* (Heath, Lexington, Mass., 1992).

Commodity	Income elasticity
Automobiles	2.46
Owner-occupied housing	1.49
Furniture	1.48
Books	1.44
Restaurant meals	1.40
Clothing	1.02
Physicians' services	0.75
Tobacco	0.64
Eggs	0.37
Margarine	−0.20
Pig products	−0.20
Flour	−0.36

TABLE 5-3. Income Elasticities for Selected Products

Income elasticities are high for luxuries, whose consumption grows rapidly relative to income. Negative income elasticities are found for "inferior goods," whose demand falls as income rises. Demand for many staple commodities, like clothing, grows proportionally with income.

Source: Heinz Kohler, *Microeconomics: Theory and Applications* (Heath, Lexington, Mass., 1992).

such serious effects that overriding individuals' private decisions may be desirable. Today, most societies provide for free public education and emergency health care; on the other hand, society also penalizes or forbids consumption of such harmful substances as cigarettes, alcohol, and heroin.

One of the most controversial cases of demerit goods concerns addiction. An addictive substance is one for which the desire to consume depends significantly on past consumption. The heavy smoker and the addicted heroin user may bitterly regret the acquired habit; but, such is the nature of addiction, it is difficult to kick the habit after it has become established. A regular user of cigarettes or heroin is much more likely to desire these substances than is a nonuser. Moreover, for highly addictive goods, demands are likely to be quite price-inelastic. By contrast, for conventional goods, demands today are not likely to depend so directly on consumption patterns yesterday.

The markets for addictive substances are big business. Consumer expenditures on tobacco products in 2002 were $76 billion, while total expenditures on alcoholic products were $126 billion. Numbers for illegal drugs involve guesswork, but recent estimates of spending on illegal drugs place the total at around $65 billion annually.

Consumption of these substances raises major public policy issues because addictive substances may injure users and often impose costs and harms on society. The harms to users include around 450,000 premature deaths annually, along with a wide variety of medical problems attributable to smoking; 10,000 highway fatalities a year attributed to alcohol; and failures in school, job, and family, along with high levels of AIDS, from intravenous heroin use. Harms to society include the predatory crime that addicts of high-price drugs engage in; the costs of providing subsidized medical care to those who consume drugs, cigarettes, or tobacco; the rapid spread of communicable diseases, especially AIDS and pneumonia; and the tendency of existing users to recruit new users.

One policy approach, often followed in the United States, is to prohibit the sale and use of addictive substances and to enforce prohibition with criminal sanctions. Economically, prohibition can be interpreted as a sharp upward shift in the supply curve. After the upward shift, the price of the addictive substance is much higher. During Prohibition (1920–1933), alcohol prices were approximately 3 times higher than before. Estimates are that cocaine currently sells for at least 20 times its free-market price.

What is the effect of supply restrictions on the consumption of addictive substances? And how does the prohibition affect the injuries to self and to society? To answer these questions, we need to consider the nature of the demand for addictive substances. The evidence indicates that casual consumers of illegal drugs have cheap substitutes like alcohol and tobacco and thus will have relatively high price elasticity of demand. By contrast, hard-core users are often addicted to particular substances and have price-inelastic demands.

One possible outcome is shown in Figure 5-4. This illustrates the impact of moving from legalized or decriminalized drugs to drug prohibition by tightening supply from SS to $S'S'$ for the hard-core users

FIGURE 5-4. Demand for Addictive Substances by Hard-Core Users

Demand for addictive substances is price-inelastic for hard-core users of drugs like heroin. As a result, if prohibition shifts supply from SS to $S'S'$, total spending on drugs will rise from $0HCG$ to $0ABF$. For drugs that are highly price-inelastic, this implies that spending on drugs will rise when supply is restrained. What will happen to criminal activity after prohibition if a substantial fraction of the income of addicts is obtained by theft? Can you see why some people would argue for reduced drug enforcement or even legalization in this case?

FIGURE 5-5. Demand for Addictive Substances by Casual Users

Demand may be quite elastic for casual users (those who are not addicted or for whom substitute products are readily available). In this case, restrictions or price increases will have a significant impact on use. Moreover, because demand is price-elastic, total spending on drugs with restrictions falls from $0HCG$ to $0ABF$. This depicts the argument of those who would severely limit the availability of addictive substances.

of a highly addictive substance like heroin. In this case, demand is highly price-inelastic. As a result of the shift in supply and rise in price, total spending on drugs increases sharply. For such drugs, the outlays may be so great that the user engages in predatory crime. The results, in the view of two economists who have studied the subject, are that "the market in illegal drugs promotes crime, destroys inner cities, spreads AIDS, corrupts law enforcement officials and politicians, produces and exacerbates poverty, and erodes the moral fabric of society."[7]

Others argue that drug use is highly price-sensitive, especially for casual users, as is shown in Figure 5-5. For example, a teenager might experiment with an addictive substance if it is affordable, while a high price (accompanied by low availability) would be unlikely to tempt that person down the road to addiction. In this case, supply restraints are likely to both lower use sharply and reduce spending on addictive substances.

One of the major difficulties with regulating addictive substances comes because of the patterns of substitution among them. Many drugs appear to be close substitutes rather than complements. As a result, experts caution, raising the price of one substance may drive users to other harmful substances. For example, states that have criminal penalties for marijuana use tend to have higher teenage consumption of alcohol and tobacco.

Clearly, social policy toward addictive substances raises extremely complex issues. But the economic theory of demand provides some important insights into the impacts of alternative approaches. First, it suggests that raising the prices of harmful addictive substances can reduce the number of casual users who will be attracted into the market. Second, it cautions us that many of the negative consequences of illegal drugs result from the prohibition of addictive substances rather than from their consumption per se. Many thoughtful observers conclude with the paradoxical observation that the overall costs of addictive substances—to users, to other people, and to the ravaged inner cities in which the drug trade thrives—would be lower if government prohibitions were relaxed and the resources currently devoted to supply restrictions were instead put into treatment and counseling.

THE PARADOX OF VALUE

More than two centuries ago, in *The Wealth of Nations*, Adam Smith posed the paradox of value:

> Nothing is more useful than water; but it will scarce purchase anything. A diamond, on the contrary, has scarce any value in use; but a very great quantity of other goods may frequently be had in exchange for it.

In other words, how is it that water, which is essential to life, has little value, while diamonds, which are generally used for conspicuous consumption, command an exalted price?

Although this paradox troubled Adam Smith 200 years ago, we can imagine a dialogue between a probing student and a modern-day Adam Smith as follows:

Student: How can we resolve the paradox of value?

Modern Smith: The simplest answer is that the supply and demand curves for water intersect at a very

---

[7] See Miron and Zwiebel in the Further Reading section at the end of this chapter.

low price, while the supply and demand for diamonds yield a very high equilibrium price.

Student: But you have always taught me to go behind the curves. Why do supply and demand for water intersect at such a low price and for diamonds at a high price?

Modern Smith: The answer is that diamonds are very scarce and the cost of getting extra ones is high, while water is relatively abundant and costs little in many areas of the world.

Student: But where is utility in this picture?

Modern Smith: You are right that this answer still does not reconcile the cost information with the equally valid fact that the world's water is vastly more critical than the world's supply of diamonds. So, we need to add a second truth: The total utility from water consumption does not determine its price or demand. Rather, water's price is determined by its *marginal* utility, by the usefulness of the *last* glass of water. Because there is so much water, the last glass sells for very little. Even though the first few drops are worth life itself, the last few are needed only for watering the lawn or washing the car.

Student: Now I get it. The theory of economic value is easy to understand if you just remember that in economics the tail wags the dog. It is the tail of marginal utility that wags the dog of prices and quantities.

Modern Smith: Precisely! An immensely valuable commodity like water sells for next to nothing because its last drop is worth next to nothing.

We can restate this dialogue as follows: The more there is of a commodity, the less is the relative desirability of its last little unit. It is therefore clear why water has a low price and why an absolute necessity like air can become a free good. In both cases, it is the large quantities that pull the marginal utilities so far down and thus reduce the prices of these vital commodities.

CONSUMER SURPLUS

The paradox of value emphasizes that the recorded monetary value of a good (measured by price times quantity) may be a misleading indicator of the total economic value of that good. The measured economic

value of the air we breathe is zero, yet air's contribution to welfare is immeasurably large.

The gap between the total utility of a good and its total market value is called **consumer surplus.** The surplus arises because we "receive more than we pay for" as a result of the law of diminishing marginal utility.

We have consumer surplus basically because we pay the same amount for each unit of a commodity that we buy, from the first to the last. We pay the same price for each egg or glass of water. Thus we pay for *each* unit what the *last* unit is worth. But by our fundamental law of diminishing marginal utility, the earlier units are worth more to us than the last. Thus, we enjoy a surplus of utility on each of these earlier units.

Figure 5-6 illustrates the concept of consumer surplus in the case where money provides a firm

Consumer Surplus for an Individual

FIGURE 5-6. Because of Diminishing Marginal Utility, Consumer's Satisfaction Exceeds What Is Paid

The downward-sloping demand for water reflects the diminishing marginal utility of water. Note how much excess or surplus satisfaction occurs from the earlier units. Adding up all the gray surpluses ($8 of surplus on unit 1 + $7 of surplus on unit 2 + ⋯ + $1 of surplus on unit 8), we obtain the total consumer surplus of $36 on water purchases.

In the simplified case seen here, the area between the demand curve and the price line is the total consumer surplus.

measuring rod for utility. Here, an individual consumes water, which has a price of $1 per gallon. This is shown by the horizontal rust line at $1 in Figure 5-6. The consumer considers how many gallon jugs to buy at that price. The first gallon is highly valuable, slaking extreme thirst, and the consumer is willing to pay $9 for it. But this first gallon costs only the market price of $1, so the consumer has gained a surplus of $8.

Consider the second gallon. This is worth $8 to the consumer, but again costs only $1, so the surplus is $7. And so on down to the ninth gallon, which is worth only 50 cents to the consumer, and so it is not bought. The consumer equilibrium comes at point E, where 8 gallons of water are bought at a price of $1 each.

But here we make an important discovery: Even though the consumer has paid only $8, the total value of the water is $44. This is obtained by adding up each of the marginal utility columns (= $9 + $8 + ⋯ + $2). Thus the consumer has gained a surplus of $36 over the amount paid.

Figure 5-6 examines the case of a single consumer purchasing water. We can also apply the concept of consumer surplus to a market as a whole. The market demand curve in Figure 5-7 is the horizontal summation of the individual demand curves. The logic of the individual consumer surplus carries over to the market as a whole. The area of the market demand curve above the price line, shown as *NER* in Figure 5-7, represents the total consumer surplus.

Because consumers pay the price of the last unit for all units consumed, they enjoy a surplus of utility over cost. Consumer surplus measures the extra value that consumers receive above what they pay for a commodity.

Applications of Consumer Surplus

The concept of consumer surplus is useful in helping evaluate many government decisions. For example, how can the government decide on the value of building a new highway or of preserving a recreation site? Suppose a new highway has been proposed. Being free to all, it will bring in no revenue. The value to users will be found in time saved or in safer trips and can be measured by the individual consumer surplus. To avoid difficult

Consumer Surplus for a Market

FIGURE 5-7. Total Consumer Surplus Is the Area under the Demand Curve and above the Price Line

The demand curve measures the amount consumers would pay for each unit consumed. Thus the total area under the demand curve (0*REM*) shows the total utility attached to the consumption of water. By subtracting the market cost of water to consumers (equal to 0*NEM*), we obtain the consumer surplus from water consumption as the gray triangle *NER*. This device is useful for measuring the benefits of public goods and the losses from monopolies and import tariffs.

issues of interpersonal utility comparisons, we assume that there are 10,000 users, all identical in every respect.

Suppose that each individual's consumer surplus is $350 for the highway. The highway will raise consumer economic welfare if its total cost is less than $3.5 million (10,000 × $350). Economists use consumer surplus when they are performing a *cost-benefit analysis*, which attempts to determine the costs and benefits of a government program. Generally, an economist would recommend that a free road should be built if its total consumer surplus exceeds its costs. Similar analyses have been used for environmental questions such as whether to preserve wilderness areas for recreation or whether to require new pollution-abatement equipment.

The concept of consumer surplus also points to the enormous privilege enjoyed by citizens of modern societies. Each of us enjoys a vast array of enormously valuable goods that can be bought at low prices. This is a humbling thought. If you know someone who is bragging about his economic productivity, or explaining how high her real wages are, suggest a moment of reflection. If such people were transported with their specialized skills to an uninhabited desert island, how much would their wages buy? Indeed, without capital machinery, without the cooperation of others, and without the technological knowledge which each generation inherits from the past, how much could any of us produce? It is only too clear that all of us reap the benefits of an economic world

we never made. As the great British sociologist L. T. Hobhouse said:

> The organizer of industry who thinks that he has "made" himself and his business has found a whole social system ready to his hand in skilled workers, machinery, a market, peace and order—a vast apparatus and a pervasive atmosphere, the joint creation of millions of men and scores of generations. Take away the whole social factor and we [are] but . . . savages living on roots, berries, and vermin.

Now that we have surveyed the essentials of demand, we move on to costs and supply.

SUMMARY

1. Market demands or demand curves are explained as stemming from the process of individuals' choosing their most preferred bundle of consumption goods and services.

2. Economists explain consumer demand by the concept of utility, which denotes the relative satisfaction that a consumer obtains from using different commodities. The additional satisfaction obtained from consuming an additional unit of a good is given the name *marginal utility*, where "marginal" means the extra or incremental utility. The law of diminishing marginal utility states that as the amount of a commodity consumed increases, the marginal utility of the last unit consumed tends to decrease.

3. Economists assume that consumers allocate their limited incomes so as to obtain the greatest satisfaction or utility. To maximize utility, a consumer must satisfy the *equimarginal principle* that the marginal utilities of the last dollar spent on each and every good must be equal.

   Only when the marginal utility per dollar is equal for apples, bacon, coffee, and everything else will the consumer attain the greatest satisfaction from a limited dollar income. But be careful to note that the marginal utility of a $50-per-ounce bottle of perfume is not equal to the marginal utility of a 50-cent glass of cola. Rather, their marginal utilities divided by price per unit are all equal in the consumer's optimal allocation. That is, their marginal utilities per last dollar, MU/P, are equalized.

4. Equal marginal utility or benefit per unit of resource is a fundamental rule of choice. Take any scarce resource,

such as time. If you want to maximize the value or utility of that resource, make sure that the marginal benefit per unit of the resource is equalized in all uses.

5. The market demand curve for all consumers is derived by adding horizontally the separate demand curves of each consumer. A demand curve can shift for many reasons. For example, a rise in income will normally shift DD rightward, thus increasing demand; a rise in the price of a substitute good (e.g., chicken for beef) will also create a similar upward shift in demand; a rise in the price of a complementary good (e.g., hamburger buns for beef) will in turn cause the DD curve to shift downward and leftward. Still other factors—changing tastes, population, or expectations—can affect demand.

6. We can gain added insight into the factors that cause downward-sloping demand by separating the effect of a price rise into substitution and income effects. (a) The substitution effect occurs when a higher price leads to substitution of other goods to meet satisfactions; (b) the income effect means that a price increase lowers real income and thereby reduces the desired consumption of most commodities. For most goods, substitution and income effects of a price increase reinforce one another and lead to the law of downward-sloping demand. We measure the quantitative responsiveness of demand to income by the income elasticity, which is the percentage change in quantity demanded divided by the percentage change in income.

7. Remember that it is the tail of marginal utility that wags the market dog of prices and quantities. This

point is emphasized by the concept of *consumer surplus*. We pay the same price for the last quart of milk as for the first. But, because of the law of diminishing marginal utility, marginal utilities of earlier units are greater than that of the last unit. This means that we would have been willing to pay more than the market price for each of the earlier units. The excess of total value over market value is called consumer surplus.

Consumer surplus reflects the benefit we gain from being able to buy all units at the same low price. In simplified cases, we can measure consumer surplus as the area between the demand curve and the price line. It is a concept relevant for many public decisions—such as deciding when the community should incur the heavy expenses of a road or bridge or set aside land for a wilderness area.

CONCEPTS FOR REVIEW

utility, marginal utility
utilitarianism
law of diminishing marginal utility
demand shifts from income and
    other sources
ordinal utility

equimarginal principle of equal MU
    of last dollar spent on each good:
    $MU_1/P_1 = MU_2/P_2 = \cdots = MU$
    per \$ of income
market demand vs. individual demand
income elasticity

substitutes, complements, independent goods
substitution effect and income effect
merit goods, demerit goods
paradox of value
consumer surplus

FURTHER READING AND INTERNET WEBSITES

Further Reading

An advanced treatment of consumer theory can be found in intermediate textbooks; see the Further Reading section in Chapter 3 for some good sources.

Consumers often need help in judging the utility of different products. Look at *Consumer Reports* for articles that attempt to rate products. They sometimes rank products as "Best Buys," which might mean the most utility per dollar of expenditure.

Jeffrey A. Miron and Jeffrey Zwiebel, "The Economic Case against Drug Prohibition," *Journal of Economic Perspectives*, Fall 1995, pp. 175–192, is an excellent nontechnical survey of the economics of drug prohibition.

Utilitarianism was introduced in Jeremy Bentham, *An Introduction to the Principles of Morals* (1789).

Websites

Data on total personal consumption expenditures for the United States are provided at the website of the Bureau of

Economic Analysis, www.bea.doc.gov. Data on family budgets are contained in the Bureau of Labor Statistics, *Consumer Expenditures*, available at www.bls.gov.

Practical guides for consumers are provided at a government site, www.consumer.gov. The organization Public Citizen lobbies in Washington "for safer drugs and medical devices, cleaner and safer energy sources, a cleaner environment, fair trade, and a more open and democratic government." Its website at www.citizen.org contains articles on many consumer, labor, and environmental issues.

There are a number of new sites on behavioral economics, for example, www.business2.com/webguide/ 0,1660,65005,00.html. You can read the Nobel lectures of laureates Akerlof, Kahneman, and Smith, with their views on behavioral economics, at www.nobel.se/ economics/laureates/.

QUESTIONS FOR DISCUSSION

1. Explain the meaning of utility. What is the difference between total utility and marginal utility? Explain the law of diminishing marginal utility and give a numerical example.

2. Each week, Tom Wu buys two hamburgers at $2 each, eight cokes at $0.50 each, and eight slices of pizza at $1 each, but he buys no hot dogs at $1.50 each. What can you deduce about Tom's marginal utility for each of the four goods?

3. Which pairs of the following goods would you classify as complementary, substitute, or independent goods: beef, ketchup, lamb, cigarettes, gum, pork, radio, television, air travel, bus travel, taxis, and paperbacks? Illustrate the resulting shift in the demand curve for one good when the price of another good goes up. How would a change in income affect the demand curve for air travel? The demand curve for bus travel?

4. Why is it wrong to say, "Utility is maximized when the marginal utilities of all goods are exactly equal"? Correct the statement and explain.

5. Here is a way to think about consumer surplus as it applies to movies:
   a. How many movies did you watch last year?
   b. How much in total did you pay to watch movies last year?
   c. What is the *maximum* you would pay to see the movies you watched last year?
   d. Calculate **c** minus **b**. That is your consumer surplus from movies.

6. Consider the following table showing the utility of different numbers of days skied each year:

Number of days skied	Total utility ($)
0	0
1	70
2	110
3	146
4	176
5	196
6	196

Construct a table showing the marginal utility for each day of skiing. Assuming that there are 1 million people with preferences shown in the table, draw the market demand curve for ski days. If lift tickets cost $40 per day, what are the equilibrium price and quantity of days skied?

7. For each of the commodities in Table 5-2, calculate the impact of a doubling of price on quantity demanded. Similarly, for the goods in Table 5-3, what would be the impact of a 50 percent increase in consumer incomes?

8. As you add together the identical demand curves of more and more people (in a way similar to the procedure in Figure 5-2), the market demand curve becomes flatter and flatter on the same scale. Does this fact indicate that the elasticity of demand is becoming larger and larger? Explain your answer carefully.

9. An interesting application of supply and demand to addictive substances compares alternative techniques for supply restriction. For this problem, assume that the demand for addictive substances is inelastic.
   a. One approach (used today for heroin and cocaine and for alcohol during Prohibition) is to reduce supply at the nation's borders. Show how this raises price and increases the total income of the suppliers in the drug industry.
   b. An alternative approach (followed today for tobacco and alcohol) is to tax the goods heavily. Using the tax apparatus developed in Chapter 4, show how this reduces the total income of the suppliers in the drug industry.
   c. Comment on the difference between the two approaches.

10. Suppose you are very rich and very fat. Your doctor has advised you to limit your food intake to 2000 calories per day. What is your consumer equilibrium for food consumption?

11. *Numerical problem on consumer surplus:* Assume that the demand for travel over a bridge takes the form $Y = 1,000,000 - 50,000P$, where Y is the number of trips over the bridge and P is the bridge toll (in dollars).
    a. Calculate the consumer surplus if the bridge toll is $0, $1, and $20.
    b. Assume that the cost of the bridge is $1,800,000. Calculate the toll at which the bridge owner breaks even. What is the consumer surplus at the break-even toll?
    c. Assume that the cost of the bridge is $8 million. Explain why the bridge should be built even though there is no toll that will cover the cost.

Appendix 5

GEOMETRICAL ANALYSIS OF CONSUMER EQUILIBRIUM

A century ago, the economist Vilfredo Pareto (1848–1923) discovered that all the important elements of demand theory could be analyzed without the utility concept. Pareto developed what are today called indifference curves. This appendix presents the modern theory of indifference analysis and then derives the major conclusions of consumer behavior with that new tool.

THE INDIFFERENCE CURVE

Start by assuming that you are a consumer who buys different combinations of two commodities, say, food and clothing, at a given set of prices. For each combination of the two goods, assume that you prefer one to the other or are indifferent between the pair. For example, when asked to choose between combination A of 1 unit of food and 6 units of clothing and combination B of 2 units of food and 3 of clothing, you might (1) prefer A to B, (2) prefer B to A, or (3) be indifferent between A and B.

Now suppose that A and B are equally good in your eyes—that you are indifferent as to which of them you receive. Let us consider some other combinations of goods about which you are likewise indifferent, as listed in the table for Figure 5A-1.

Figure 5A-1 shows these combinations diagrammatically. We measure units of clothing on one axis and units of food on the other. Each of our four combinations of goods is represented by its point, A, B, C, D. But these four are by no means the only combinations among which you are indifferent. Another batch, such as $1\frac{1}{2}$ units of food and 4 of clothing, might be ranked as equal to A, B, C, or D, and there are many others not shown. The curved contour of Figure 5A-1, linking up the four points, is an **indifference curve.** The points on the curve represent consumption bundles among which the consumer is indifferent; all are equally desirable.

Law of Substitution

Indifference curves are drawn as bowl-shaped, or convex to the origin. Hence, as you move downward and to the right along the curve—a movement that implies increasing the quantity of food and reducing the units of clothing—the curve becomes flatter. The

curve is drawn in this way to illustrate a property that seems most often to hold true in reality and which we call the law of substitution:

The scarcer a good, the greater its relative substitution value; its marginal utility rises relative to the marginal utility of the good that has become plentiful.

Thus, in going from A to B in Figure 5A-1, you would swap 3 of your 6 clothing units for 1 extra food unit. But from B to C, you would sacrifice only 1 unit of your remaining clothing supply to obtain a third food unit—a 1-for-1 swap. For a fourth unit of food, you would sacrifice only ½ unit from your dwindling supply of clothing.

If we join the points A and B of Figure 5A-1, we find that the slope of the resulting line (neglecting its negative sign) has a value of 3. Join B and C, and the slope is 1; join C and D, and the slope is ½. These figures—3, 1, ½—are the *substitution ratios* (sometimes called the *marginal rates of substitution*) between the two goods. As the size of the movement along the curve becomes very small, the closer the substitution ratio comes to the actual slope of the indifference curve.

The slope of the indifference curve is the measure of the goods' relative marginal utilities, or of the substitution terms on which—for very small changes—the consumer would be willing to exchange a little less of one good in return for a little more of the other.

An indifference curve that is convex in the manner of Figure 5A-1 conforms to the law of substitution. As the amount of food you consume goes up—and the quantity of clothing goes down—food must become relatively cheaper in order for you to be persuaded to take a little extra food in exchange for a little sacrifice of clothing. The precise shape and slope of an indifference curve will, of course, vary from one consumer to the next, but the typical shape will take the form shown in Figures 5A-1 and 5A-2.

The Indifference Map

The table in Figure 5A-1 is one of an infinite number of possible tables. We could start with a more preferred consumption situation and list some of the

A Consumer's Indifference Curve

FIGURE 5A-1. **Indifference Curves for a Pair of Goods**

Getting more of one good compensates for giving up some of the other. The consumer likes situation A exactly as much as B, C, or D. The food-clothing combinations that yield equal satisfaction are plotted as a smooth indifference curve. This is convex from below in accord with the law of substitution, which says that as you get more of a good, its substitution ratio, or the indifference curve's slope, diminishes.

Indifference Combinations

	Food	Clothing
A	1	6
B	2	3
C	3	2
D	4	1½

different combinations that would bring the consumer this higher level of satisfaction. One such table might have begun with 2 food units and 7 clothing units; another with 3 food units, 8 clothing units. Each table could be portrayed graphically, each with a corresponding indifference curve.

Figure 5A-2 shows four such curves; the curve from Figure 5A-1 is labeled U_3. This diagram is analogous to a geographic contour map. A person who walks along the path indicated by a particular height contour on such a map is neither climbing nor descending; similarly, the consumer who moves from one position to another along a single indifference curve enjoys neither increasing nor decreasing satisfaction from the change in consumption. Only a few of the possible indifference curves are shown in Figure 5A-2.

Note that as we increase both goods and thus move in a northeasterly direction across this map, we are crossing successive indifference curves; hence, we are reaching higher and higher levels of satisfaction (assuming that the consumer gets

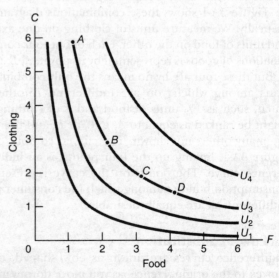

FIGURE 5A-2. **A Family of Indifference Curves**

The curves labeled U_1, U_2, U_3, and U_4 represent indifference curves. Which indifference curve is most preferred by the consumer?

A Consumer's Budget Line

Alternative Consumption Possibilities

	Food	Clothing
M	4	0
	3	1$\frac{1}{2}$
	2	3
	1	4$\frac{1}{2}$
N	0	6

FIGURE 5A-3. Income Constrains Consumer Spending

The budget limit on expenditures can be seen in a numerical table. The total cost of each budget (reckoned as $1.50F + $1C) adds up to exactly $6 of income. We can plot the budget constraint as a straight line whose absolute slope equals the P_F/P_C ratio. NM is the consumer's budget line. When income is $6, with food and clothing prices $1.50 and $1, the consumer can choose any point on this budget line. (Why is its slope $1.50/$1 = $\frac{3}{2}$?)

greater satisfaction from receiving increased quantities of both goods). Curve U_3 stands for a higher level of satisfaction than U_2; U_4, for a higher level of satisfaction than U_3; and so forth.

BUDGET LINE OR BUDGET CONSTRAINT

Now let us set a particular consumer's indifference map aside for a moment and give the consumer a fixed income. He has, say, $6 per day to spend, and he is confronted with fixed prices for each food and clothing unit—$1.50 for food, $1 for clothing. It is clear that he could spend his money on any one of a variety of alternative combinations of food and clothing. At one extreme, he could buy 4 food units and no clothing; at the other, 6 clothing units and no food. The table with Figure 5A-3 illustrates some of the possible ways in which he could allocate his $6.

Figure 5A-3 plots five of these possibilities. Note that all the points lie on a straight line, labeled NM.

Moreover, any other attainable point, such as 3$\frac{1}{3}$ food units and 1 clothing unit, lies on NM. The straight budget line NM sums up all the possible combinations of the two goods that would just exhaust the consumer's income.[1] The slope of NM (neglecting its sign) is $\frac{3}{2}$, which is the ratio of the food price to the clothing price. The meaning of the slope is that, given these prices, every time our consumer gives up 3 clothing units (thereby dropping down 3 vertical units on the diagram), he can gain 2 units of food (i.e., move right 2 horizontal units).

We call NM the consumer's **budget line** or **budget constraint.**

---

[1] This is so because, if we designate quantities of food and clothing bought as F and C, respectively, total expenditure on food must be $1.50F and total expenditure on clothing, $1C. If daily income and expenditure are $6, the following equation must hold: $6 = $1.50F + $1C. This is a linear equation, the equation of the budget line NM. Note:

Arithmetic slope of NM = $1.50 ÷ $1

= price of food ÷ price of clothing

THE EQUILIBRIUM POSITION OF TANGENCY

Now we are ready to put our two parts together. The axes of Figure 5A-3 are the same as those of Figures 5A-1 and 5A-2. We can superimpose the gray budget line NM upon this rust consumer indifference map, as shown in Figure 5A-4. The consumer is free to move anywhere along NM. Positions to the right and above NM are not allowed because they require more than $6 of income; positions to the left and below NM are irrelevant because the consumer is assumed to spend the full $6.

Where will the consumer move? Obviously, to that point which yields the greatest satisfaction—that is, to the highest possible indifference curve—which

in this case must be at the rust point B. At B, the budget line just touches, but does not cross, the indifference curve U_3. At this point of tangency, where the budget line just kisses but does not cross an indifference contour, is found the highest utility contour the consumer can reach.

Geometrically, the consumer is at equilibrium where the slope of the budget line (which is equal to the ratio of food to clothing prices) is exactly equal to the slope of the indifference curve (which is equal to the ratio of the marginal utilities of the two goods).

Consumer equilibrium is attained at the point where the budget line is tangent to the highest indifference curve. At that point, the consumer's substitution ratio is just equal to the slope of the budget line.

Put differently, the substitution ratio, or the slope of the indifference curve, is the ratio of the marginal utility of food to the marginal utility of clothing. So our tangency condition is just another way of stating that the ratio of prices must be equal to the ratio of marginal utilities; in equilibrium, the consumer is getting the same marginal utility from the last penny spent on food as from the last penny spent on clothing. Therefore, we can derive the following equilibrium condition:

$$\frac{P_F}{P_C} = \text{substitution ratio} = \frac{MU_F}{MU_C}$$

This is exactly the same condition as we derived for utility theory in the main part of this chapter.

CHANGES IN INCOME AND PRICE

Two important applications of indifference curves are frequently used to consider the effects of (a) a change in money income and (b) a change in the price of one of the two goods.

Income Change

Assume, first, that the consumer's daily income is halved while the two prices remain unchanged. We could prepare another table, similar to the table for Figure 5A-3, showing the new consumption possibilities. Plotting these points on a diagram such as Figure 5A-5, we should find that the new budget line occupies the position $N'M'$ in Figure 5A-5. The line

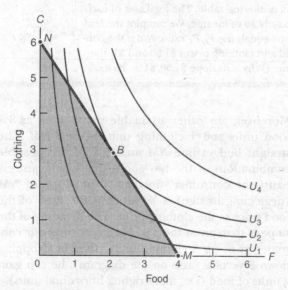

Consumer's Equilibrium

FIGURE 5A-4. Consumer's Most Preferred and Feasible Consumption Bundle Is Attained at B

We now combine the budget line and indifference contours in one diagram. The consumer reaches the highest indifference curve attainable with fixed income at point B, which is the tangency of the budget line with the highest indifference curve. At tangency point B, substitution ratio equals price ratio P_F/P_C. This means that all goods' marginal utilities are proportional to their prices, with the marginal utility of the last dollar spent on every good being equalized.

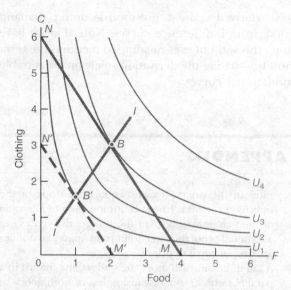

FIGURE 5A-5. Effect of Income Change on Equilibrium

An income change shifts the budget line in a parallel way. Thus, halving income to $3 shifts NM to N'M', moving equilibrium to B'. (Show what raising income to $8 would do to equilibrium. Estimate where the new tangency point would come.)

FIGURE 5A-6. Effect of Price Change on Equilibrium

A rise in the price of food makes the budget line pivot on N, rotating from NM to NM''. The new tangency equilibrium is at B'', where there is definitely less food consumed but clothing consumption may either go up or down.

has made a parallel shift inward.[2] The consumer is now free to move only along this new (and lower) budget line; to maximize satisfaction, he will move to the highest attainable indifference curve, or to point B'. A tangency condition for consumer equilibrium applies here as before.

Single Price Change

Now return our consumer to his previous daily income of $6, but assume that the price of food rises from $1.50 to $3 while the price of clothing is unchanged. Again we must examine the change in the budget line. This time we find that it has pivoted on point N and is now NM'', as illustrated in Figure 5A-6.[3]

The common sense of such a shift is clear. Since the price of clothing is unchanged, point N is just as available as it was before. But since the price of food has risen, point M (which represents 4 food units) is

---

[2] The equation of the new N'M' budget line is now $3 = $1.50F + $1C.

[3] The budget equation of NM'' is now $6 = $3F + $1C.

no longer attainable. With food costing $3 per unit, only 2 units can now be bought with a daily income of $6. So the new budget line still passes through N, but it must pivot at N and pass through M'', which is to the left of M.

Equilibrium is now at B'', and we have a new tangency point. Higher food price has definitely reduced food consumption, but clothing consumption may move in either direction. To clinch your understanding, work out the cases of an increase in income and a fall in the price of clothing or food.

DERIVING THE DEMAND CURVE

We are now in a position to derive the demand curve. Look carefully at Figure 5A-6. Note that as we increased the price of food from $1.50 per unit to $3 per unit, we kept other things constant. Tastes as represented by the indifference curves did not change, and money income and the price of clothing stayed constant. Therefore, we are in the ideal position to trace the demand curve for food. At a price of $1.50, the consumer buys 2 units of food, shown as equilibrium point B. When the price rises to $3 per unit, the food purchased is 1 unit, at equilibrium point B''.

If you draw in the budget line corresponding to a price of $6 per unit of food, the equilibrium occurs at point B''', and food purchases are 0.45 unit.

Now plot the price of food against the purchases of food, again holding other things constant. You will have derived a neat downward-sloping demand curve from indifference curves. Note that we have done this without ever needing to mention the term "utility"—basing the derivation solely on measurable indifference curves.

SUMMARY TO APPENDIX

1. An indifference curve depicts the points of equally desirable consumption bundles. The indifference contour is usually drawn convex (or bowl-shaped) in accordance with the law of diminishing relative marginal utilities.

2. When a consumer has a fixed money income, all of which she spends, and is confronted with market prices of two goods, she is constrained to move along a straight line called the budget line or budget constraint. The line's slope will depend on the ratio of the two market prices; how far out it lies will depend on the size of her income.

3. The consumer will move along this budget line until reaching the highest attainable indifference curve. At this point, the budget line will touch, but not cross, an indifference curve. Hence, equilibrium is at the point of tangency, where the slope of the budget line (the ratio of the prices) exactly equals the slope of the indifference curve (the substitution ratio or the ratio of the marginal utilities of the two goods). This gives additional proof that, in equilibrium, marginal utilities are proportional to prices.

4. A fall in income will move the budget line inward in a parallel fashion, usually causing less of both goods to be bought. A change in the price of one good alone will, other things being constant, cause the budget line to pivot so as to change its slope. After a price or income change, the consumer will again attain a new tangency point of highest satisfaction. At every point of tangency, the marginal utility per dollar is equal for every good. By comparing the new and old equilibrium points, we trace the usual downward-sloping demand curve.

CONCEPTS FOR REVIEW

indifference curves
slope or substitution ratio
budget line or budget constraint

convexity of indifference curves and
  law of diminishing relative
  marginal utilities

optimal tangency condition: $P_F/P_C =$
  substitution ratio $= MU_F/MU_C$

QUESTIONS FOR DISCUSSION

1. Draw the indifference curves (*a*) between complementary goods like left shoes and right shoes and (*b*) between perfect substitutes like two bottles of cola sitting next to each other in a store.

2. Consider pig products and yachts. Draw a set of indifference curves and budget lines like those in Figure 5A-5 which show pig products as an inferior good and yachts as a "luxury" with an income elasticity greater than 1.

CHAPTER

6

Production and Business Organization

The business of America is business.

Calvin Coolidge

Before we can eat our daily bread, someone must bake it. Similarly, the economy's ability to build cars, generate electricity, write computer programs, and deliver the multitude of goods and services that are in our gross domestic product depends upon our productive capacity. Productive capacity is determined by the size and quality of the labor force, by the quantity and quality of the capital stock, by the nation's technical knowledge along with the ability to use that knowledge, and by the nature of public and private institutions. Why are living standards high in North America? Low in tropical Africa? For answers, we should look to how well the machine of production is running.

Our goal is to understand how market forces determine the supply of goods and services. Over the next three chapters we will lay out the essential concepts of production, cost, and supply and show how they are linked. We first explore the fundamentals of production theory, showing how firms transform inputs into desirable outputs. Production theory also helps us understand why productivity and living standards have risen over time and how firms manage their internal activities.

Building on our knowledge of production, Chapter 7 then develops the essential concepts of business cost. Businesses decide what inputs to employ in production on the basis of the costs and productivities of various inputs. Finally, we use the theory of production and cost to show how businesses decide how much output to produce. This is the basis for the supply curve we first saw in our basic analysis of supply and demand.

A. THEORY OF PRODUCTION AND MARGINAL PRODUCTS

BASIC CONCEPTS

A modern economy has an enormously varied set of productive activities. A farm takes fertilizer, seed, land, and labor and turns them into wheat or corn. Modern factories take inputs such as energy, raw materials, computerized machinery, and labor and use them to produce tractors, TVs, or tubes of toothpaste. An airline takes airplanes, fuel, labor, and computerized reservation systems and provides passengers with the ability to travel quickly through its network of routes. An accounting firm takes pencils, computers, paper, office space, and labor and produces audits or tax returns for its clients.

Our discussion assumes that the farm, factory, airline, and accounting firm always strive to produce efficiently, that is, at lowest cost. In other words, they always attempt to produce the maximum level of output for a given dose of inputs, avoiding waste whenever possible. Later on, in deciding what goods or services to produce and sell, firms are assumed to maximize economic profits as well.

The Production Function

We have spoken of inputs like land and labor and outputs like wheat and toothpaste. But if you have a fixed amount of inputs, how much output can you get? In practice, the answer depends on the state of technology and engineering knowledge. On any day, given the available technical knowledge, land, machinery, and so on, only a certain quantity of tractors or toothpaste can be obtained from a given amount of labor. The relationship between the amount of input required and the amount of output that can be obtained is called the *production function*.

The **production function** specifies the maximum output that can be produced with a given quantity of inputs. It is defined for a given state of engineering and technical knowledge.

For example, we can imagine a book of technical specifications that shows the production function for generating electricity. On one page there are specifications for different-size gas turbines, showing their inputs (initial capital cost, fuel consumption, and the amount of labor needed to run the turbine) and their outputs (amount of electricity generated). The next page includes descriptions of several sizes of coal-fired generating plants, showing inputs and outputs. Yet other pages describe nuclear power plants, solar power stations, and so forth. Together they constitute the production function for electricity generation.

Or consider the humble task of ditchdigging. Outside our windows in America, we see a large and expensive tractor, driven by one person with another to supervise. This team can easily dig a trench 5 feet deep and 50 feet long in 2 hours. When we visit Vietnam, we see 50 laborers armed only with picks. The same trench might take an entire day. These two techniques—one capital-intensive and the other labor-intensive—are part of the production function for ditchdigging.

There are literally millions of different production functions—one for each and every product or service. Most of them are not written down but are in people's minds. In areas of the economy where technology is changing rapidly, like computer software and biotechnology, production functions may become obsolete soon after they are used. And some, like the blueprints of a medical laboratory or cliff house, are specially designed for a specific location and purpose and would be useless anywhere else. Nevertheless, the concept of a production function is a useful way of describing the productive capabilities of a firm.

Total, Average, and Marginal Product

Starting with a firm's production function, we can calculate three important production concepts: total, average, and marginal product. We begin by computing the total physical product, or **total product,** which designates the total amount of output produced, in physical units such as bushels of wheat or number of sneakers. Figure 6-1(*a*) on page 109 and column (2) of Table 6-1 on page 110 illustrate the concept of total product. For this example, they show how total product responds as the amount of labor applied is increased. The total product starts at zero for zero labor and then increases as additional units of labor are applied, reaching a maximum of 3900 units when 5 units of labor are used.[1]

Once we know the total product, it is easy to derive an equally important concept, the marginal product. Recall that the term "marginal" means "extra."

The **marginal product** of an input is the extra output produced by 1 additional unit of that input while other inputs are held constant.

For example, assume that we are holding land, machinery, and all other inputs constant. Then labor's marginal product is the extra output obtained by adding 1 unit of labor. The third column of Table 6-1 calculates the marginal product. The marginal product of labor starts at 2000 for the first unit of

---

[1] In this chapter we talk of "units of labor" as being one input into the production process. It is customary to measure labor in terms of hours of work (person-hours) to reflect the fact that people work different numbers of hours per week. For simplicity, however, we simply refer to numbers of workers and assume that each person works the same number of hours.

FIGURE 6-1. Marginal Product Is Derived from Total Product

Diagram (a) shows the total product curve rising as additional inputs of labor are added, holding other things constant. However, total product rises by smaller and smaller increments as additional units of labor are added (compare the increments of the first and the fifth worker). By smoothing between points, we get the rust-colored total product curve.

Diagram (b) shows the declining steps of marginal product. Make sure you understand why each dark rectangle in (b) is equal to the equivalent dark rectangle in (a). The area in (b) under the rust-colored marginal product curve (or the sum of the dark rectangles) adds up to the total product in (a).

labor and then falls to only 100 units for the fifth unit. Marginal product calculations such as this are crucial for understanding how wages and other factor prices are determined.

The final concept is the **average product,** which equals total output divided by total units of input. The fourth column of Table 6-1 shows the average product of labor as 2000 units per worker with one worker, 1500 units per worker with two workers, and so forth. In this example, average product falls through the entire range of increasing labor input.

Figure 6-1 plots the total and marginal products from Table 6-1. Study this figure to make sure you understand that the blocks of marginal products in (b) are related to the changes in the total product curve in (a).

The Law of Diminishing Returns

Using production functions, we can understand one of the most famous laws in all economics, the law of diminishing returns:

The **law of diminishing returns** holds that we will get less and less extra output when we add additional doses of an input while holding other inputs fixed. In other words, the marginal product of each unit of input will decline as the amount of that input increases, holding all other inputs constant.

The law of diminishing returns expresses a very basic relationship. As more of an input such as labor is added to a fixed amount of land, machinery, and other inputs, the labor has less and less of the other factors to work with. The land gets more crowded,

(1) Units of labor input	(2) Total product	(3) Marginal product	(4) Average product
0	0		
		2,000	
1	2,000		2,000
		1,000	
2	3,000		1,500
		500	
3	3,500		1,167
		300	
4	3,800		950
		100	
5	3,900		780

TABLE 6-1. Total, Marginal, and Average Product

The table shows the total product that can be produced for different inputs of labor when other inputs (capital, land, etc.) and the state of technical knowledge are unchanged. From total product, we can derive important concepts of marginal and average products.

the machinery is overworked, and the marginal product of labor declines.

The law of diminishing returns can be fleshed out by putting ourselves in the boots of a farmer performing an agricultural experiment illustrated by Table 6-1. Given a fixed amount of land and other inputs, assume that we use no labor inputs at all. With zero labor input there is no corn output. Hence, Table 6-1 records zero product when labor is zero.

Now add 1 unit of labor to the same fixed amount of land. We observe that 2000 bushels of corn are produced. In the next stage of our controlled experiment, we continue to hold other inputs fixed and go from 1 unit of labor to 2 units of labor. The second unit of labor adds only 1000 bushels of additional output, which is less than what the first unit of labor added. The third unit of labor has an even lower marginal product than does the second, and the fourth unit adds yet a bit less. The experiment reported in Table 6-1 thus illustrates the law of diminishing returns.

Figure 6-1 also illustrates the law of diminishing returns for labor, holding land and other inputs constant. Here we see that the marginal product curve

declines as labor inputs increase, which is the precise meaning of diminishing returns. In Figure 6-1(a), diminishing returns are seen as a concave or dome-shaped total product curve.

What is true for labor is also true for land and any other input. We can interchange land and labor, now holding labor constant and varying land. Land's marginal product is the change in total output that results from 1 additional unit of land, with all other inputs held constant. We can calculate the marginal product of each input (labor, land, machinery, water, fertilizer, etc.), and the marginal product would apply to any output (wheat, corn, steel, soybeans, and so forth). We would find that other inputs also tend to show the law of diminishing returns.

Diminishing Returns in Farm Experiments

The law of diminishing returns is often observed in agriculture. As Farmer Tilly adds more labor, the fields will be more thoroughly seeded and weeded, irrigation ditches will be neater, and scarecrows better oiled. At some point, however, the additional labor becomes less and less productive. The third hoeing of the field or the fourth oiling of the machinery adds little to output. Eventually, output grows very little as more people crowd onto the farm; too many tillers spoil the crop.

Researchers often conduct experiments to determine the impact of different combinations of inputs on output. Figure 6-2 shows the results of an experiment in which different doses of phosphorus (P_2O_5) were applied on two different plots, holding constant land area, nitrogen fertilizer, labor, and other inputs. Real-world experiments are complicated by "random errors"—in this case, due primarily to differences in soils. You can see that diminishing returns set in quickly after about 100 pounds of phosphorus per acre. Indeed, beyond an input level of around 300 pounds per acre, the marginal product of additional phosphate fertilizer is negative.

Diminishing returns are a key factor in explaining why many countries in Asia are so poor. Living standards in crowded India or Bangladesh are low because there are so many workers per acre of land

FIGURE 6-2. Diminishing Returns in Corn Production

Agricultural researchers experimented with different doses of phosphorus fertilizer on two different plots to estimate the production function for corn in western Iowa. In conducting the experiment, they were careful to hold constant other things such as nitrogen fertilizer, water, and labor inputs. Because of variations in soils and microclimate, even the most careful scientist cannot prevent some random variation, which accounts for the jagged nature of the lines. If you fit a smooth curve to the data, you will see that the relationship displays diminishing returns for every dose and that marginal product becomes negative for a phosphate input of around 300.

Source: Earl O. Heady, John T. Pesek, and William G. Brown, *Crop Response Surfaces and Economic Optima in Fertilizer Use* (Agricultural Experiment Station, Iowa State College, Ames, Iowa, 1955), table A-15.

and not because farmers are ignorant or fail to respond to economic incentives.

We can also use the example of studying to illustrate the law of diminishing returns. You might find that the first hour of studying economics on a given day is productive—you learn new laws and facts, insights and history. The second hour might find your attention wandering a bit, with less learned. The third hour might show that diminishing returns have set in with a vengeance, and by the next day the third hour is a blank in your memory. Does the law

of diminishing returns suggest why the hours devoted to studying should be spread out rather than crammed into the day before exams?

The law of diminishing returns is a widely observed empirical regularity rather than a universal truth like the law of gravity. It has been found in numerous empirical studies, but exceptions have also been uncovered. Moreover, diminishing returns might not hold for all levels of production. The very first inputs of labor might actually show increasing marginal products, since a minimum amount of labor may be needed just to walk to the field and pick up a shovel. Notwithstanding these reservations, diminishing returns will prevail in most situations.

RETURNS TO SCALE

Diminishing returns and marginal products refer to the response of output to an increase of a *single* input when all other inputs are held constant. We saw that increasing labor while holding land constant would increase food output by ever-smaller increments.

But sometimes we are interested in the effect of increasing *all* inputs. For example, what would happen to wheat production if land, labor, water, and other inputs were increased by the same proportion? Or what would happen to the production of tractors if the quantities of labor, computers, robots, steel, and factory space were all doubled? These questions refer to the *returns to scale*, or the effects of scale increases of inputs on the quantity produced. Three important cases should be distinguished:

- **Constant returns to scale** denote a case where a change in all inputs leads to a proportional change in output. For example, if labor, land, capital, and other inputs are doubled, then under constant returns to scale output would also double. Many handicraft industries (such as haircutting in America or handloom operation in a developing country) show constant returns.

- **Increasing returns to scale** (also called **economies of scale**) arise when an increase in all inputs leads to a more-than-proportional increase in the level of output. For example, an engineer planning a small-scale chemical plant will generally find that increasing the inputs of labor, capital, and materials by 10 percent will increase the total output by more than 10 percent. Engineering studies have determined that many manufacturing processes enjoy modestly increasing returns to scale for plants up to the largest size used today.

- **Decreasing returns to scale** occur when a balanced increase of all inputs leads to a less-than-proportional increase in total output. In many processes, scaling up may eventually reach a point beyond which inefficiencies set in. These might arise because the costs of management or control become large. One case has occurred in electricity generation, where firms found that when plants grew too large, risks of plant failure grew too large. Many productive activities involving natural resources, such as growing wine grapes or providing clean drinking water to a city, show decreasing returns to scale.

Production shows increasing, decreasing, or constant returns to scale when a balanced increase in all inputs leads to a more-than-proportional, less-than-proportional, or just-proportional increase in output.

One of the common findings of engineers is that modern mass-production techniques require that factories be a certain minimum size. Chapter 2 explained that as output increases, firms may divide production into smaller steps, taking advantage of specialization and division of labor. In addition, large-scale production allows intensive use of specialized capital equipment, automation, and computerized design and manufacturing to perform simple and repetitive tasks quickly.

Information technologies often display strong economies of scale. A good example is Microsoft Windows 98. Developing this program required more than $1 billion in research, development, beta-testing, and promotion. Yet the cost of adding Windows 98 to a new computer is very close to zero because doing so simply requires a few seconds of computer time. We will see that strong economies of scale often lead to firms with significant market power and sometimes pose major problems of public policy.

SHORT RUN AND LONG RUN

Production requires not only labor and land but also time. Pipelines cannot be built overnight, and once built they last for decades. Farmers cannot change

crops in midseason. It often takes a decade to plan, construct, test, and commission a large power plant. Moreover, once capital equipment has been put in the concrete form of a giant automobile assembly plant, the capital cannot be economically dismantled and moved to another location or transferred to another use.

To account for the role of time in production and costs, we distinguish between two different time periods. We define the **short run** as a period in which firms can adjust production by changing variable factors such as materials and labor but cannot change fixed factors such as capital. The **long run** is a period sufficiently long that all factors including capital can be adjusted.

To understand these concepts more clearly, consider the way the production of steel might respond to changes in demand. Say that Nippon Steel is operating its furnaces at 70 percent of capacity when an unexpected increase in the demand for steel occurs because of the need to rebuild from an earthquake in Japan or California. To adjust to the higher demand for steel, the firm can increase production by increasing worker overtime, hiring more workers, and operating its plants and machinery more intensively. The factors which are increased in the short run are called *variable* factors.

Suppose that the increase in steel demand persisted for an extended period of time, say, several years. Nippon Steel would examine its capital needs and decide that it should increase its productive capacity. More generally, it might examine all its *fixed* factors, those that cannot be changed in the short run because of physical conditions or legal contracts. The period of time over which all inputs, fixed and variable, can be adjusted is called the long run. In the long run, Nippon might add new and more efficient production processes, install a rail link or new computerized control system, or build a plant in Mexico. When all factors can be adjusted, the total amount of steel will be higher and the level of efficiency can increase.

Efficient production requires time as well as conventional inputs like labor. We therefore distinguish between two different time periods in production and cost analysis. The **short run** is the period of time in which only some inputs, the variable inputs, can be adjusted. In the short run, fixed factors, such as plant and equipment, cannot be fully modified or adjusted. The **long run** is the period in which all factors employed by the firm, including capital, can be changed.

That Smells So Good!

The production processes of a modern market economy are extraordinarily complex. We can illustrate this with the lowly hamburger.

As Americans spend more time in the workplace and less in the kitchen, their demand for prepared food has risen dramatically. TV dinners have replaced store-bought carrots and peas, while hamburgers bought at McDonald's now number in the billions. The move to processed foods has the undesirable property that the food—after being washed, sorted, sliced, blanched, frozen, thawed, and re-heated—often loses most of its flavor. You want a hamburger to smell and taste like a hamburger, not like cooked cardboard.

This is where the "production of tastes and smells" enters. Companies like International Flavors and Fragrances (IFF) synthesize the flavor of potato chips, breakfast cereals, ice cream, cookies, and just about every other kind of processed food, along with the fragrance of many fine perfumes, soaps, and shampoos. If you read most food labels, you will discover that the food contains "natural ingredients" or "artificial ingredients"—such compounds as amyl acetate (banana flavor) or benzaldehyde (almond flavor).

But these unfamiliar chemicals can do amazing things. A food researcher recounts the following experience in the laboratories of IFF:

[After dipping a paper fragrance-testing filter into each bottle from the lab,] I closed my eyes. Then I inhaled deeply, and one food after another was conjured from the glass bottles. I smelled fresh cherries, black olives, sautéed onions, and shrimp. [The] most remarkable creation took me by surprise. After closing my eyes, I suddenly smelled a grilled hamburger. The aroma was uncanny, almost miraculous. It smelled like someone in the room was flipping burgers on a hot grill. But when I opened my eyes, there was just a narrow strip of white paper.[2]

---

[2] Eric Schlosser, *Fast Food Nation* (Perennial Press, New York, 2002), p. 129.

This story reminds us that "production" in a modern economy is much more than planting potatoes and casting steel. It sometimes involves disassembling things like chickens and potatoes into their tiny constituents, and then reconstituting them along with new synthesized tastes halfway around the world. Such complex production processes can be found in every sector, from pharmaceuticals that change our mood or help our blood flow more smoothly to financial instruments that take apart, repackage, and sell the streams of mortgage payments. And most of the time, we don't even know what exotic substances lie between the simple (recycled) paper that wraps our $2 hamburger.

TECHNOLOGICAL CHANGE

Economic history records that total output in the United States has grown more than tenfold over the last century. Part of that gain has come from increased inputs, such as labor and machinery. But much of the increase in output has come from technological change, which improves productivity and raises living standards.

Some examples of technological change are dramatic: wide-body jets that increased the number of passenger-miles per unit of input by almost 50 percent; fiber optics that have lowered cost and improved reliability in telecommunications; and improvements in computer technologies that have increased computational power by more than 1000 times in three decades. Other forms of technological change are more subtle, as is the case when a firm adjusts its production process to reduce waste and increase output.

We distinguish *process innovation,* which occurs when new engineering knowledge improves production techniques for existing products, from *product innovation,* whereby new or improved products are introduced in the marketplace. For example, a process innovation allows firms to produce more output with the same inputs or to produce the same output with fewer inputs. In other words, a process innovation is equivalent to a shift in the production function.

Figure 6-3 illustrates how technological change, in the form of a process innovation, would shift the total product curve. The lower line represents the

FIGURE 6-3. Technological Change Shifts Production Function Upward

The solid line represents maximum producible output for each level of inputs given the state of technical knowledge in 1995. As a result of improvements in computer technology and management practices, technological change shifts the production function upward, allowing much more output to be produced in 2005 for each level of inputs.

feasible output, or production function, for a particular industry in the year 1995. Suppose that productivity, or output per unit of input, in this industry is rising at 4 percent per year. If we return to the same industry a decade later, we would likely see that changes in technical and engineering knowledge have led to a 48 percent improvement in output per unit of input $[(1 + .04)^{10} = 1.48]$.

Next consider product innovations, which involve new or improved products. It is much more difficult to quantify the importance of product innovations, but they may be even more important in raising living standards than process innovations. Today's array of goods and services is clearly far different from what prevailed just 50 years ago. In producing this textbook, the authors used computer software, microprocessors, Internet sites, and databases that were not available when the previous edition was written. Medicine, communications, and entertainment are other areas where product innovations have been critical. The whole area of the Internet, from e-commerce to e-mail, was not found even in science fiction literature 20 years ago. For fun, and to see this point, try to find any commodity or production process that has not changed since your grandparents were your age!

Figure 6-3 shows the happy case of a technological advance. Is the opposite case—technological regress—possible? For a well-functioning market economy, the answer is no. Indeed, that is one of the key advantages of a market economy over an economy ruled by government dictates. Inferior technologies tend to be discarded in a market economy, while more productive technologies are introduced because they will increase the profits of the innovating firms. If, for example, someone invented an expensive new mousetrap that never caught a mouse, no profit-oriented firm would produce such a device; and if a poorly managed firm decided to produce it, rational consumers who lived in mouse-infested houses would surely decline to buy it. Well-functioning markets innovate with better, not inferior, mousetraps and other goods and services.

When there are market failures, however, technological regress might occur even in a market economy. An unregulated company might introduce a socially wasteful process, say, dumping toxic wastes into a stream, because the wasteful process is cheaper to operate. *But the economic advantage of inferior technologies comes only because the social costs of pollution are not included in the firm's calculations of the costs of production.* If pollution costs were included in a firm's decisions, by, for instance, strict liability rules or pollution taxes, the retrogressive process would no longer be profitable. In competitive markets, inferior products follow Neanderthals into extinction.

Networks

Many products have little use by themselves and generate value only when they are used in combination with other products. Such products are strongly complementary. An important case is a *network*, where different people are linked together through a particular medium. Types of networks include both those defined by physical linkages, such as telecommunication systems, electricity transmission networks, computer clusters, pipelines, and roads, and the indirect networks that occur when people use compatible systems (such as Windows operating systems) or speak the same language (such as English).

To understand the nature of networks, consider how far you could drive your car without a network of gas stations or how valuable your telephone or e-mail would be if no one else had telephones or computers. Similarly, credit cards and ATM cards have value because they can be used in many locations.

Network markets are special because consumers derive benefits not simply from their own use of a good but also from the number of other consumers who adopt the good. This is known as an *adoption externality*. When I get a phone, everyone else with a phone can now communicate with me. Therefore, my joining this network leads to positive external effects for others. The network externality is the reason why many colleges provide universal e-mail for all their students and faculty—the value of e-mail is much higher when everyone participates. Figure 6-4 on page 116 illustrates how one individual's joining a network has an external benefit to others.

Economists have discovered many important features of network markets. First, network markets are "tippy," meaning that the equilibrium tips toward one or only a few products. Because consumers dislike buying products that may turn out to be incompatible with dominant technologies, the equilibrium tends to gravitate to a single product which wins out over its rivals. One of the best-known examples is computer operating systems, where Microsoft Windows became the dominant system in part because consumers wanted to make sure that their computers could operate all the available software. (The important antitrust case involving Microsoft is discussed in Chapter 17.)

A second interesting feature is that "history matters" in network markets. A famous example is the QWERTY keyboard used with your computer. You might wonder why this particular configuration of keys, with its awkward placement of the letters, became the standard. The design of the QWERTY keyboard in the nineteenth century was based on the concept of keeping frequently used keys (like "e" and "o") physically separated in order to prevent manual typewriters from jamming. By the time the technology for electronic typing evolved, tens of millions of people had already learned to type on millions of

typewriters. Replacing the QWERTY keyboard with a more efficient design would have been both expensive and difficult to coordinate. Thus, the placement of the letters remains unchanged on today's keyboards.

This example shows how an embedded network technology can be extremely stable. A similar example that worries many environmentalists is America's "wasteful" automobile culture, where the existing network of cars, roads, gasoline stations, and residential locations will be difficult to dislodge in favor of more environmentally friendly alternatives, like improved mass transit.

Third, because networks involve a complicated interplay of economies of scale, expectations, dynamics, and tipping, they lead to a fascinating array of business strategies. The tippy nature of networks means that they tend to be "winner-take-all" markets with intense rivalry in the early stages and but a few competitors once the winning technology has emerged. In addition, network markets are often inertial, so once a product has a substantial lead, it may be very difficult for other products to catch up. These characteristics mean that companies often want to get an early lead on their rivals.

Suppose you are producing a network product. In order to build on your early lead, you might persuade users that you are number one by puffing up your sales; use "penetration pricing" by offering very low prices to early adopters; bundle your product with another popular product; or raise questions about your competitors' quality or staying power. Above all, you would probably invest heavily in advertising to shift out the demand curve for the product. If you are the fortunate winner, you will benefit from the economies of scale in the network and enjoy your monopoly profits. But don't take your dominant position for granted. Once your commanding lead is questioned, the virtuous cycle of market dominance can easily turn into the vicious cycle of decline.

Networks raise important issues for public policy. Should government set standards to ensure competition? Should government regulate network industries? How should government antitrust policy treat monopolists like Microsoft that have been the fortunate winners in the network race but use anticompetitive tactics? These questions are on the minds of many public policy-makers today.[3]

---

[3] See the Further Reading section at the end of this chapter.

FIGURE 6-4. Value of Networking Increases as Membership Rises

Assume that each person derives a value of $1 for each additional person who is connected to a telephone or e-mail network. If Ed decides to join, he will get $4 of value from being connected to Adam, Beth, Carlos, and Dorothy. But there is an "adoption externality" because each of the four people already in the network gets $1 of additional value when Ed joins, for a total of $4 of external additional value.

These network effects make it difficult for networks to get started. (To see this, note the low value of joining for the first and second person.) But the equilibrium "tips" toward full adoption when many people are in the network. (What is the value to the tenth person who joins the network?)

PRODUCTIVITY AND THE AGGREGATE PRODUCTION FUNCTION

Productivity

One of the most important measures of economic performance is productivity. **Productivity** is a concept measuring the ratio of total output to a weighted average of inputs. Two important variants are **labor productivity,** which calculates the amount of output per unit of labor, and **total factor productivity,** which measures output per unit of total inputs (typically of capital and labor).

During the economic expansion of the late 1990s, the U.S. economy showed robust growth in output and productivity. From 1995 to 2000, output in the U.S. business sector grew on average by 4.7 percent per year. During that period, labor hours worked grew by 2.0 percent per year. The difference was the growth of labor productivity, which averaged 2.7 percent over this period.

Productivity Growth from Economies of Scale

Productivity grows because of economies of scale and because of technological change. Economies of scale and mass production have been important elements of productivity growth over the last century. Most production processes are many times larger than they were during the nineteenth century. A large ship in the mid-nineteenth century could carry 2000 tons of goods, while the largest supertankers today carry over 1 million tons of oil.

What would be the effect of a general increase in the scale of economic activity? If increasing returns prevailed, the larger scale of inputs and production would lead to greater productivity. Suppose that, with no change in technology, the typical firm's inputs increased by 10 percent and that because of economies of scale, output increased by 11 percent. Economies of scale would be responsible for a growth in total factor productivity of 1 percent.

While increasing returns to scale are potentially large in many sectors, at some point decreasing returns to scale may take hold. As firms become larger and larger, the problems of management and coordination become increasingly difficult. In relentless pursuit of greater profits, a firm may find itself expanding into more geographic markets or product lines than it can effectively manage. A firm can have only one chief executive officer, one chief financial officer, one board of directors. With less time to study each market and spend on each decision, top managers may become insulated from day-to-day production and begin to make mistakes.

Like empires that have been stretched too thin, such firms find themselves exposed to invasion by smaller and more agile rivals. Those who study management report that the world's largest automobile manufacturer, General Motors, became increasingly isolated from the outside world and from competitive pressures. As a result, it was slow to respond to changes in the automobile market when oil prices rose in the 1970s, and it lost much market share to smaller and nimbler firms. Hence, while technology might ideally allow constant or increasing returns to scale, the need for management and supervision may eventually lead to decreasing returns to scale in giant firms.

Empirical Estimates of the Aggregate Production Function

Now that we have examined the principles of production theory, we can apply these theories to measure how well the whole U.S. economy has been performing. To do this, we need to look at the *aggregate production functions*, which relate total output to the quantity of inputs (like labor, capital, and land) and to total productivity. What have economic studies found? Here are a few of the important results:

- Total factor productivity has been increasing throughout the twentieth century because of technological progress and higher levels of worker education and skill. The average rate of total productivity growth was slightly under 1½ percent per year during the twentieth century.
- The capital stock has been growing faster than the number of worker-hours. As a result, labor has a growing quantity of capital goods to work with; hence labor productivity and wages have tended to rise even faster than the 1½ percent per year attributable to total factor productivity growth alone.
- The rate of return on capital (the rate of profit) might have been expected to encounter diminishing returns because each capital unit now has less labor to cooperate with it. In fact, capital's rate of return has remained about the same.
- Over the twentieth century, labor productivity grew at an average rate of slightly more than 2 percent per year. From the early 1970s to the mid-1990s, however, all measures of productivity showed a marked growth slowdown, and real wages and living standards consequently stagnated over this period. Since the mid-1990s, fueled largely by the computer revolution, there has been a marked upturn in productivity growth, with rates close to the historical norm.

We end with a final word on the difficulties of measuring productivity growth accurately. Recent empirical studies suggest that we have seriously underestimated productivity growth. Studies of medical care, capital goods, consumer electronics, computers and computer software, and lighting indicate that our measuring rod for productivity may be badly flawed. One particularly important shortcoming is the failure to account for the economic value of new and improved products. For example, when compact discs replaced long-playing records, our measures of productivity did not include the improvement in durability and sound quality. One study found that productivity in treatment of heart attacks was 5 percent per year more rapid than the conventional measures. Some experts believe that the true rate of productivity growth might be twice as large as official estimates.

B. BUSINESS ORGANIZATIONS

THE NATURE OF THE FIRM

So far we have talked about production functions as if they were machines that could be operated by anyone: put a pig in one end and a sausage comes out the other. In reality, almost all production is done by specialized organizations—the small, medium, and large businesses that dominate the landscape of modern economies. Why does production generally take place in firms rather than in our basements?

Firms or business enterprises exist for many reasons, but the most important is that *business firms are specialized organizations devoted to managing the process of production.* Among their important functions are exploiting economies of mass production, raising funds, and organizing factors of production.

The most compelling factor leading to the organization of production in firms arises from *economies of mass production.* Efficient production requires specialized machinery and factories, assembly lines, and the division of labor into many small operations. Studies indicate that efficient production of automobiles requires production rates of at least 300,000 units per year.

We could hardly expect that workers would gather spontaneously to perform each task correctly and in the right sequence. Or, for the example of baseball, how likely is it that 25 people would organize themselves into just the right combination of pitchers, catchers, and hitters, all in the right order and using the best strategy? In fact, we need firms to coordinate the production process, purchasing or renting land, capital, labor, and materials. If there were no need for specialization and division of labor,

we could each produce our own electricity, digital watch, and compact disc in our own backyard. We obviously cannot perform such feats; efficiency generally requires large-scale production in businesses.

A second function of firms is *raising resources* for large-scale production. Developing a new commercial aircraft costs well over $1 billion; the research and development expenses for a new computer microprocessor, like Intel's Pentium chip, are just as high. Where are such funds to come from? In the nineteenth century, businesses could often be financed by wealthy, risk-taking individuals. But the days of such fabulously wealthy captains of industry are past. Today, in a private-enterprise economy, most funds for production must come from company profits or from money borrowed in financial markets. Indeed, efficient production by private enterprise would be virtually unthinkable if corporations could not raise billions of dollars each year for new projects.

A third reason for the existence of firms is to *manage the production process.* The manager is the person who organizes production, introduces new ideas or products or processes, makes the business decisions, and is held accountable for success or failure. Production cannot, after all, organize itself. Someone has to supervise the construction of a new factory, negotiate with labor unions, and purchase materials and supplies.

If you were to purchase the franchise for a baseball team, you would have to rent a stadium, hire baseball players, negotiate with people for concessions, hire ushers, deal with unions, and sell tickets. Once all these factors of production are engaged, someone has to monitor their daily activities to ensure that the job is being done effectively and honestly.

Business firms are specialized organizations devoted to managing the process of production. Production is organized in firms because efficiency generally requires large-scale production, the raising of significant financial resources, and careful management and monitoring of ongoing activities.

BIG, SMALL, AND INFINITESIMAL BUSINESSES

Production in a market economy takes place in a wide variety of business organizations—from the tiniest individual proprietorships to the giant corporations that dominate economic life in a capitalist economy. There are currently more than 18 million different businesses in America. The majority of these are tiny units owned by a single person—the individual proprietorship. Others are partnerships, owned by two or perhaps two hundred partners. The largest businesses tend to be corporations.

Tiny businesses predominate in numbers. But in sales and assets, in political and economic power, and in size of payroll and employment, the few hundred largest corporations dominate the economy.

The Individual Proprietorship

At one end of the spectrum are the individual proprietorships, the classic small businesses often called "mom-and-pop" stores. A small store might do a few hundred dollars of business per day and barely provide a minimum wage for the owners' efforts.

These businesses are large in number but small in total sales. For most small businesses, a tremendous amount of personal effort is required. The self-employed often work 50 or 60 hours per week and take no vacations, yet the average lifetime of a small business is only a year. Still, some people will always want to start out on their own. Theirs may be the successful venture that gets bought out for millions of dollars.

The Partnership

Often a business requires a combination of talents— say, lawyers or doctors specializing in different areas. Any two or more people can get together and form a partnership. Each agrees to provide some fraction of the work and capital, to share some percentage of the profits, and of course to share the losses or debts.

Today, partnerships account for only a small fraction of total economic activity. The reason is that partnerships pose certain disadvantages that make them impractical for large businesses. The major disadvantage is *unlimited liability*. General partners are liable without limit for all debts contracted by the partnership. If you own 1 percent of the partnership and the business fails, you will be called upon to pay 1 percent of the bills and the other partners will be assessed their 99 percent. But if your partners cannot pay, you may be called upon to pay all the debts even if you must sell off your prize possessions to do so.

The peril of unlimited liability and the difficulty of raising funds explain why partnerships tend to be confined to small, personal enterprises such as agriculture and retail trade. Partnerships are simply too risky for most situations.

The Corporation

The bulk of economic activity in an advanced market economy takes place in private corporations. Centuries ago, corporate charters were awarded by special acts of the monarch or legislature. The British East India Company was a privileged corporation and as such it practically ruled India for more than a century. In the nineteenth century, railroads often had to spend as much money on getting a charter through the legislature as on preparing their roadbeds. Over the past century, laws have been passed that allow almost anyone the privilege of forming a corporation for almost any purpose.

Today, a **corporation** is a form of business organization chartered in one of the fifty states or abroad and owned by a number of individual stockholders. The corporation has a separate legal identity, and indeed is a legal "person" that may on its own behalf buy, sell, borrow money, produce goods and services, and enter into contracts. In addition, the corporation enjoys the right of *limited liability*, whereby each owner's investment and financial exposure in the corporation is strictly limited to a specified amount.

The central features of a modern corporation are the following:

- The ownership of a corporation is determined by the ownership of the company's common stock. If you own 10 percent of a corporation's shares, you have 10 percent of the ownership. Publicly owned corporations are valued on stock exchanges, like the New York Stock Exchange. It is in such stock markets that the titles to the largest corporations are traded and that much of the nation's risk capital is raised and invested.
- In principle, the shareholders control the companies they own. They collect dividends in proportion to the fraction of the shares they own, and they elect directors and vote on many important issues. But don't think that the shareholders have a significant role in running giant corporations. In practice, shareholders of giant corporations exercise virtually no control because they are too dispersed to overrule the entrenched managers.

- The corporation's managers and directors have the legal power to make decisions for the corporation. They decide what to produce and how to produce it. They negotiate with labor unions and decide whether to sell the firm if another firm wishes to take it over. When the newspaper announces that a firm has laid off 20,000 workers, this decision was made by the managers. The shareholders own the corporation, but the managers run it.

Advantages and Disadvantages of Corporations. Why are corporations so predominant in a market economy? Simply because it is an extremely efficient way to engage in business. A corporation is a legal person that can conduct business. Also, the corporation may have perpetual succession or existence, regardless of how many times the shares of stock change hands. Corporations are hardly little democracies, so their managers can make decisions quickly, and often ruthlessly, which is in stark contrast to the way economic decisions are made by legislatures.

In addition, corporate stockholders enjoy limited liability, which protects them from incurring the debts or losses of the corporation beyond their initial contribution. If we buy $1000 of stock, we cannot lose more than our original investment.

Corporations face one major disadvantage: The government levies an extra tax on corporate profits. For an unincorporated business, any income after expenses is taxed as ordinary personal income. The large corporation is treated differently in that some of its income is doubly taxed—first as corporate profits and then as individual income on dividends.

The Bush administration proposed in 2003 to eliminate the individual tax on dividends in order to eliminate the double taxation of dividends. Congress considered the president's proposal and went halfway . . . for a few years. It reduced the maximum individual tax on dividends to 15 percent, eliminated the tax completely for a single year (2008), and then reinstated it for 2009. (This bizarre outcome was the result of limitations imposed on the total revenue loss from the 2003 tax cut.)

Sometimes, corporations undertake actions that provoke public outrage and government actions. In the late nineteenth century, corporations engaged in fraud, price fixing, and bribery, which led to enactment of antitrust and securities-fraud legislation. In the last few years, corporate scandals erupted when it was discovered that some companies engaged in massive accounting fraud and many corporate executives feathered their nests with huge bonuses and stock options. In private as in public life, power sometimes corrupts.

Efficient production often requires large-scale enterprises, which need billions of dollars of invested capital. Corporations, with limited liability and a convenient management structure, can attract large supplies of private capital, produce a variety of related products, and pool investor risks.

Production in the Firm or the Market?

If markets are such a powerful mechanism for efficiency, why does so much production take place within large organizations? A related question is, Why do some firms decide on an integrated production structure while others contract out a large fraction of their sales? For example, before 1982 AT&T was vertically and horizontally integrated, doing its own research and development, designing and producing its own equipment, installing and renting telephones, and providing telephone service. By contrast, most personal computers are "produced" by assemblers who purchase the hard drives, circuits, monitors, and keyboards from outside vendors and package and sell them.

These central issues of industrial organization were first raised by Ronald Coase in a pathbreaking study for which he was awarded the 1991 Nobel Prize.[4] This exciting area analyzes the comparative advantage of organizing production through the hierarchical control of firms as compared to the contractual relationships of the market.

Why might organizing through large firms be efficient? Perhaps the most important reason is the difficulty of designing "complete contracts" that cover all contingencies. For example, suppose Snoozer Inc. thinks it has discovered a hot new drug to cure laziness. Should it do the research in its own laboratories or contract out to another company, WilyLabs, Inc.? The problem with contracting out is that there are all kinds of unforeseen contingencies that could affect the profitability of the drug. What would happen if the drug proves useful for other conditions? What if the patent, tax, or international-trade laws change? What if there is a patent-infringement suit?

Because of the contractual incompleteness, the company runs the risk of the *holdup problem*. Suppose that

---

[4] See the Further Reading section at the end of this chapter for examples of Coase's and related writings.

WilyLabs discovers that the antilaziness drug works only when taken with another drug that WilyLabs owns. WilyLabs goes to Snoozer and says, "Sorry, pal, but to get both drugs will cost you another $100 million." This is holdup with a vengeance. Fear of being held up in situations which involve relationship-specific investments and contractual incompleteness will lead Snoozer to do the research internally so that it can control the outcomes of its research.

The recent trend in many industries has been to move away from highly integrated firms by "outsourcing" or contracting out production. This has definitely been the trend in the computer industry since the days when IBM was almost as integrated as AT&T. Contracting out can function well in situations where, as in the PC industry, the components are standardized or "commoditized." Another example is Nike, which contracts out much of its production because the production process is standard and Nike's real value is tied to its design and trademark. In addition, new contractual forms, such as long-term contracts based on reputations, attempt to minimize holdup problems.

Those who study organizations point to the vital importance of large firms in promoting innovation and increasing productivity. In the nineteenth century, railroads not only brought wheat from farm to market but also introduced time zones. Indeed, the very notion of being "on time" first became crucial when being off schedule produced train wrecks. As the tragic story of centrally planned economies so clearly shows, without the organizational genius of the modern private-enterprise firm, all the land, labor, and capital can work for naught.

SUMMARY

A. Theory of Production and Marginal Products

1. The relationship between the quantity of output (such as wheat, steel, or automobiles) and the quantities of inputs (of labor, land, and capital) is called the production function. Total product is the total output produced. Average product equals total output divided by the total quantity of inputs. We can calculate the marginal product of a factor as the extra output added for each additional unit of input while holding all other inputs constant.

2. According to the law of diminishing returns, the marginal product of each input will generally decline as the amount of that input increases, when all other inputs are held constant.

3. The returns to scale reflect the impact on output of a balanced increase in all inputs. A technology in which doubling all inputs leads to an exact doubling of outputs displays constant returns to scale. When doubling inputs leads to less than double (more than double) the quantity of output, the situation is one of decreasing (increasing) returns to scale.

4. Because decisions take time to implement, and because capital and other factors are often very long-lived, the reaction of production may change over different time periods. The short run is a period in which variable factors, such as labor or material inputs, can be easily changed but fixed factors cannot. In the long run, the capital stock (a firm's machinery and factories) can depreciate and be replaced. In the long run, all inputs, fixed and variable, can be adjusted.

5. Technological change refers to a change in the underlying techniques of production, as occurs when a new product or process of production is invented or an old product or process is improved. In such situations, the same output is produced with fewer inputs or more output is produced with the same inputs. Technological change shifts the production function upward.

6. Attempts to measure an aggregate production function for the American economy tend to corroborate theories of production and marginal products. In the twentieth century, technological change increased the productivity of both labor and capital. Total factor productivity (measuring the ratio of total output to total inputs) grew at around 1½ percent per year over the twentieth century, although from the 1970s to the mid-1990s the rate of productivity growth slowed markedly and real wages stopped growing. But underestimating the importance of new and improved products may lead to a significant underestimate of productivity growth.

B. Business Organizations

7. Business firms are specialized organizations devoted to managing the process of production.

8. Firms come in many shapes and sizes—with some economic activity in tiny one-person proprietorships, some in partnerships, and the bulk in corporations. Each kind of enterprise has advantages and disadvantages. Small businesses are flexible, can market new products, and can disappear quickly. But they suffer from the fundamental disadvantage of being unable to

accumulate large amounts of capital from a dispersed group of investors. Today's large corporation, granted limited liability by the state, is able to amass billions of dollars of capital by borrowing from banks, bondholders, and stock markets.

9. In a modern economy, business corporations produce most goods and services because economies of mass production necessitate that output be produced at high volumes, the technology of production requires much more capital than a single individual would willingly put at risk, and efficient production requires careful management and coordination of tasks by a centrally directed entity.

CONCEPTS FOR REVIEW

inputs, outputs, production function
total, average, and marginal product
diminishing marginal product and
   the law of diminishing returns
constant, increasing, and decreasing
   returns to scale
short run vs. long run
technological change: process
   innovation, product innovation

productivity
network industries: adoption
   externalities, tipping, history
   matters, winner-take-all market
aggregate production function
reasons for firms: scale economies,
   financial needs, management

major business forms: individual
   proprietorship, partnership,
   corporation
unlimited and limited liability
firm vs. market and the holdup
   problem

FURTHER READING AND INTERNET WEBSITES

Further Reading

Ronald Coase's classic work is "The Nature of the Firm," *Economica*, November 1937. Students may enjoy a recent nontechnical survey of the field in the symposium "The Firm and Its Boundaries," *Journal of Economic Perspectives*, Fall 1998. For a thoughtful analysis of network effects, see the symposium in *Journal of Economic Perspectives*, Spring 1994. A fascinating study of networks and the new economy is contained in Chapter 7 in Carl Shapiro and Hal R. Varian, *Information Rules: A Strategic Guide to the Network Economy* (Harvard Business School Press, Cambridge, Mass., 1997).

The story of how General Motors misunderstood the energy revolution in the 1970s is told in Daniel Yergin, *The*

Epic Quest for Oil, Money, and Power (Simon and Schuster, New York, 1992). The comic side of GM is told in Michael Moore's film, *Roger and Me*.

Websites

One of the most interesting websites about networks is compiled by Hal R. Varian, dean of the School of Information Management and Systems at the University of California at Berkeley. This site, called "The Economics of the Internet, Information Goods, Intellectual Property and Related Issues," is at www.sims.berkeley.edu/resources/infoecon.

A specialized site on network economics maintained by Nicholas Economides of New York University is found at raven.stern.nyu.edu/networks/site.html.

QUESTIONS FOR DISCUSSION

1. Explain the concept of a production function. Describe the production function for hamburgers, computers, concerts, haircuts, and a college education.

2. Consider a production function of the following form: $X = 100L^{1/2}$, where $X =$ output and $L =$ input of labor (assuming other inputs are fixed).

a. Construct a figure like Figure 6-1 and a table like Table 6-1 for inputs of $L = 0, 1, 2, 3,$ and 4.

b. Explain whether this production function shows diminishing returns to labor. What values would the exponent need to take for this production function to exhibit increasing returns to labor?

3. The following table describes the actual production function for oil pipelines. Fill in the missing values for marginal products and average products:

(1)	(2)	(3)	(4)
	18-Inch Pipe		
Pumping horsepower	Total product (barrels per day)	Marginal product (barrels per day per hp)	Average product (barrels per day per hp)
10,000	86,000		
20,000	114,000		
30,000	134,000		
40,000	150,000		
50,000	164,000		

4. Using the data in question 3, plot the production function of output against horsepower. On the same graph, plot the curves for average product and marginal product.

5. Suppose you are running the food concession at the athletic events for your college. You sell hot dogs, colas, and potato chips. What are your inputs of capital, labor, and materials? If the demand for hot dogs declines, what steps could you take to reduce output in the short run? In the long run?

6. An important distinction in economics is between shifts of the production function and movements along the production function. For the food concession in question 5, give an example of both a shift of and a movement along the hot-dog production function. Illustrate each with a graph of the relation between hot-dog production and labor employed.

7. Substitution occurs when firms replace one input for another, as when a farmer uses tractors rather than labor when wages rise. Consider the following changes in a firm's behavior. Which represent substitution of one factor for another with an unchanged technology, and which represent technological change? Illustrate each with a graphical production function.

a. When the price of oil increases, a firm replaces an oil-fired plant with a gas-fired plant.

b. A bookseller reduces its sales staff by 60 percent after it sets up an Internet outlet.

c. Over the period 1970–2000, a typesetting firm decreases its employment of typesetters by 200 workers and increases its employment of computer operators by 100 workers.

d. After a successful unionization drive for clerical workers, a college buys personal computers for its faculty and reduces its secretarial workforce.

8. Consider a firm that produces pizzas with capital and labor inputs. Define and contrast diminishing returns and decreasing returns to scale. Explain why it is possible to have diminishing returns for one input and constant returns to scale for both inputs.

9. Show that if the marginal product is always decreasing, the average product is always above the marginal product.

10. Review the example of a network shown in Figure 6-4. Assume that only one person can join the network each month, starting with Adam and proceeding clockwise.

a. Construct a table showing the value to the joining person as well as the external value to others (i.e., the value to all others in the network) when an additional person joins. (*Hint:* The entries for Ed are $4 and $4.) Then calculate the total social value for each level of membership. Graph the relationship between the size of the network and the total social value. Explain why this shows increasing returns rather than diminishing returns.

b. Assume that the cost of joining is $4.50. Draw a graph which shows how membership changes over time if six people are in the network to begin with. Draw another one which shows what happens if there are initially three people in the network. What is the point at which the equilibrium "tips" toward universal membership?

c. Suppose you are the sponsor of the network shown in Figure 6-4. What kind of pricing could you use to get the network started when there are only one or two members?

7

Analysis of Costs

*Costs merely register
competing attractions.*

Frank Knight
Risk, Uncertainty, and Profit
(1921)

Everywhere that production goes, costs follow close behind like a shadow. Firms must pay for their inputs: screws, solvents, software, sponges, secretaries, and statisticians. Profitable businesses are acutely aware of this simple fact as they determine their production strategies, since every dollar of unnecessary costs reduces the firm's profits by that same dollar.

But the role of costs goes far beyond influencing production and profits. Costs affect input choices, investment decisions, and even the decision of whether to stay in business. Is it cheaper to hire a new worker or to pay overtime? To open a new factory or expand an old one? To invest in new machinery domestically or relocate production abroad? Businesses want to choose those methods of production that are most efficient and produce output at the lowest cost.

This chapter is devoted to a thorough analysis of cost. First we consider the full array of economic costs, including the central notion of marginal costs. Then we examine how business accountants measure cost in practice. Finally, we look at the notion of opportunity cost, a broad concept that can be applied to a wide range of decisions. This comprehensive study of cost will lay the foundation for understanding the supply decisions of business firms.

A. ECONOMIC ANALYSIS OF COSTS

TOTAL COST: FIXED AND VARIABLE

Consider a firm that produces a quantity of output (denoted by q) using inputs of capital, labor, and materials. The firm buys these inputs in the factor markets. The firm's accountants have the task of calculating the total dollar costs incurred to produce output level q.

Table 7-1 on page 125 shows the total cost (TC) for each different level of output q. Looking at columns (1) and (4), we see that TC goes up as q goes up. This makes sense because it takes more labor and other inputs to produce more of a good; extra factors involve an extra money cost. It costs $110 in all to produce 2 units, $130 to produce 3 units, and so forth. In our discussion, we assume that the firm always produces output at the lowest possible cost.

(1) Quantity q	(2) Fixed cost FC ($)	(3) Variable cost VC ($)	(4) Total cost TC ($)
0	55	0	55
1	55	30	85
2	55	55	110
3	55	75	130
4	55	105	160
5	55	155	210
6	55	225	280

TABLE 7-1. Fixed, Variable, and Total Costs

The major elements of a firm's costs are its fixed costs (which do not vary at all when output changes) and its variable costs (which increase as output increases). Total costs are equal to fixed plus variable costs: $TC = FC + VC$.

Fixed Cost

Columns (2) and (3) of Table 7-1 break total cost into two components: total fixed cost (FC) and total variable cost (VC).

What are a firm's **fixed costs?** Sometimes called "overhead" or "sunk costs," they consist of items such as rent for factory or office space, contractual payments for equipment, interest payments on debts, salaries of tenured faculty, and so forth. These must be paid even if the firm produces no output, and they do not change if output changes. For example, a law firm might have an office lease which runs 10 years and remains an obligation even if the firm shrinks to half its previous size. Because FC is the amount that must be paid regardless of the level of output, it remains constant at $55 in column (2).

Variable Cost

Column (3) of Table 7-1 shows variable cost (VC). **Variable costs** are those which vary as output changes. Examples include materials required to produce output (such as steel to produce automobiles), production workers to staff the assembly lines, power to operate factories, and so on. In a supermarket, checkout clerks are a variable cost, since managers can adjust the clerks' hours worked to match the number of shoppers coming through the store.

By definition, VC begins at zero when q is zero. VC is the part of TC that grows with output; indeed,

the jump in TC between any two outputs is the same as the jump in VC. Why? Because FC stays constant at $55 throughout and cancels out in the comparison of costs between different output levels.

Let us summarize these cost concepts:

Total cost represents the lowest total dollar expense needed to produce each level of output q. TC rises as q rises.

Fixed cost represents the total dollar expense that is paid out even when no output is produced; fixed cost is unaffected by any variation in the quantity of output.

Variable cost represents expenses that vary with the level of output—such as raw materials, wages, and fuel—and includes all costs that are not fixed.

Always, by definition,

$$TC = FC + VC$$

Minimum Attainable Costs

Anyone who has managed a business knows that when we write down a cost schedule like the one in Table 7-1, we make the firm's job look altogether too simple. Why is this so? Because much hard work lies behind Table 7-1. To attain the lowest level of costs, the firm's managers have to make sure that they are paying the least possible amount for necessary materials, that the lowest-cost engineering techniques are incorporated into the factory layout, that employees are being honest, and that countless other decisions are made in the most economical fashion.

For example, suppose you are the owner of a baseball team. You have to negotiate salaries with players, choose managers, bargain with vendors, worry about electricity and other utility bills, consider how much insurance to buy, and deal with the 1001 other issues that are involved in running the team with minimum cost.

The fixed and variable costs shown in Table 7-1 are the minimum costs that result from all these hours of managerial work.

DEFINITION OF MARGINAL COST

Marginal cost is one of the most important concepts in all of economics. **Marginal cost** (MC) denotes the extra or additional cost of producing 1 extra unit of output. Say a firm is producing 1000 compact discs for a total cost of $10,000. If the total cost of producing 1001 discs is $10,006, then the marginal cost of production is $6 for the 1001st disc.

Sometimes, the marginal cost of producing an extra unit of output can be quite low. For an airline flying planes with empty seats, the added cost of another passenger is literally peanuts; no additional capital (planes) or labor (pilots and flight attendants) is necessary. In other cases, the marginal cost of another unit of output can be quite high. Consider an electric utility. Under normal circumstances, it can generate enough power using only its lowest-cost, most efficient plants. But on a hot summer day, when everyone's air conditioners are running and demand for electricity is high, the utility may be forced to turn on its old, high-cost, inefficient generators. This added electric power comes at a high marginal cost to the utility.

Table 7-2 uses the data from Table 7-1 to illustrate how we calculate marginal costs. The rust-colored MC numbers in column (3) of Table 7-2 come from subtracting the TC in column (2) from the TC of the

subsequent quantity. Thus the MC of the first unit is $30(= \$85 - \$55)$; the marginal cost of the second unit is $25(= \$110 - \$85)$; and so on.

Instead of getting MC from the TC column, we could get the MC figures by subtracting each VC number in column (3) of Table 7-1 from the VC in the row below it. Why? Because variable cost always grows exactly like total cost, the only difference being that VC must (by definition) start out from 0 rather than from the constant FC level. (Check that $30 - 0 = 85 - 55$, and $55 - 30 = 110 - 85$, and so on.)

The marginal cost of production is the additional cost incurred in producing 1 extra unit of output.

Marginal Cost in Diagrams. Figure 7-1 illustrates total cost and marginal cost. It shows that TC is related to MC in the same way that total product is related to marginal product or that total utility is related to marginal utility.

What kind of shape would we expect actual MC curves to have? Empirical studies have found that for most production activities in the short run (i.e., when the capital stock is fixed), marginal cost curves are U-shaped like the one shown in Figure 7-1(b). This U-shaped curve falls in the initial phase, reaches a minimum point, and finally begins to rise.

(1) Output q	(2) Total cost TC ($)	(3) Marginal cost MC ($)
0	55	
		30
1	85	
		25
2	110	
		20
3	130	
		—
4	160	
		50
5	210	

TABLE 7-2. Calculation of Marginal Cost

Once we know total cost, it is easy to calculate marginal cost. To calculate the MC of the fifth unit, we subtract the total cost of the four units from the total cost of the five units, i.e., $MC = \$210 - \$160 = \$50$. Fill in the blank for the marginal cost of the fourth unit.

The Marginal Cost of Distributing Software

When the giant software company Microsoft attempted to invade the market for Internet browsers, it did this by giving away its Internet Explorer (IE) browser, either as a stand-alone product or in combination with the Windows operating system. Its competitors complained that Microsoft was engaged in "predatory behavior." How could it give the browser away and not lose money.

The answer is that, while it cost Microsoft a great deal to develop Internet Explorer, the marginal cost of distributing an extra unit of the product was close to zero. That is, the cost to Microsoft of delivering 1,000,001 units was no more than the cost of 1,000,000 units. As long as the marginal cost of IE was zero, Microsoft was not losing money by giving it away.

(a) Total Cost

(b) Marginal Cost

FIGURE 7-1. The Relationship between Total Cost and Marginal Cost

These graphs show the data from Table 7-2. Marginal cost in **(b)** is found by calculating the extra cost added in **(a)** for each unit increase in output. Thus to find the *MC* of producing the fifth unit, we subtract $160 from $210 to get *MC* of $50. A smooth black curve has been drawn through the points of *TC* in **(a),** and the smooth black *MC* curve in **(b)** links the discrete steps of *MC*.

AVERAGE COST

We complete our catalog of the cost concepts with a discussion of different kinds of average or unit cost. Table 7-3 expands the data of Tables 7-1 and 7-2 to include three new measures: average cost, average fixed cost, and average variable cost.

Average or Unit Cost

Like marginal cost, average cost (*AC*) is a concept widely used in business; by comparing average cost with price or average revenue, businesses can determine whether or not they are making a profit. **Average cost** is the total cost divided by the total number of units produced, as shown in column (6) of Table 7-3. That is,

$$\text{Average cost} = \frac{\text{total cost}}{\text{output}} = \frac{TC}{q} = AC$$

In column (6), when only 1 unit is produced, average cost has to be the same as total cost, or $85/1 = $85. But for $q = 2$, $AC = TC/2 = $110/2 = 55, as shown.

Note that average cost falls lower and lower at first. (We shall see why in a moment.) *AC* reaches a minimum of $40 at $q = 4$, and then slowly rises.

Figure 7-2 plots the cost data shown in Table 7-3. Figure 7-2(*a*) depicts the total, fixed, and variable costs at different levels of output. Figure 7-2(*b*) shows the different average cost concepts, along with a smoothed marginal cost curve. Graph (*a*) shows how total cost moves with variable cost while fixed cost remains unchanged.

Now turn to graph (*b*). This plots the U-shaped *AC* curve and aligns *AC* right below the *TC* curve from which it is derived.

Finally, Figure 7-3 shows how marginal cost is related to the slope of the total cost curve.

Average Fixed and Variable Cost

Just as we separated total cost into fixed and variable costs, we can also break average cost into fixed and variable components. **Average fixed cost** (*AFC*) is defined as FC/q. Since total fixed cost is a

(1)	(2)	(3)	(4)	(5)	(6)	(7)	(8)
Quantity q	Fixed cost FC ($)	Variable cost VC ($)	Total cost $TC = FC + VC$ ($)	Marginal cost per unit MC ($)	Average cost per unit $AC = TC/q$ ($)	Average fixed cost per unit $AFC = FC/q$ ($)	Average variable cost per unit $AVC = VC/q$ ($)
0	55	0	55		Infinity	Infinity	Undefined
				30			
1	55	30	85		85	55	30
				25			
2	55	55	110		55	27½	27½
				20			
3	55	75	130		43⅓	18⅓	25
				30			
4*	55	105	160	40*	40*	13¾	26¼
				50			
5	55	155	210		42	11	___
				___			
6	55	225	280		46⅔	9⅙	37½
				90			
7	55	___	370		52⁵⁄₇	7⁶⁄₇	45
				110			
8	55	___	480		60	6⅞	53⅛

*Minimum level of average cost.

TABLE 7-3. All Cost Concepts Derive from Total Cost Schedule

We can derive all the different cost concepts from the TC in column (4). Columns (5) and (6) are the important ones to concentrate on: marginal cost is calculated by subtraction of adjacent rows of TC and is shown in rust. The starred MC of 40 at an output of 4 is the smoothed MC from Fig. 7-2(b). In column (6), note the point of minimum cost of $40 on the U-shaped AC curve in Fig. 7-2(b). (Can you see why the starred MC equals the starred AC at the minimum? Also, calculate and fill in all the missing numbers.)

constant, dividing it by an increasing output gives a steadily falling average fixed cost curve [see column (7) of Table 7-3]. In other words, as a firm sells more output, it can spread its overhead cost over more and more units. For example, a software firm may have a large staff of programmers to develop a new graphics program. The number of copies sold does not directly affect how many programmers are necessary, thus making them a fixed cost. So if the program is a best-seller, the AFC of the programmers is low; if the program is a failure, their AFC is high.

The dashed gray AFC curve in Figure 7-2(b) is a hyperbola, approaching both axes: it drops lower and lower, approaching the horizontal axis as the constant FC gets spread over more and more units. If we allow fractional units of q, AFC starts infinitely high as finite FC is spread over ever tinier q.

Average variable cost (AVC) equals variable cost divided by output, or $AVC = VC/q$. As you can see in both Table 7-3 and Figure 7-2(b), for this example AVC first falls and then rises.

Minimum Average Cost

Do not confuse average cost with marginal cost—it's an easy mistake to make. Indeed, average cost can be much higher or lower than marginal cost, as Figure 7-2(b) shows.

(a) Total, Fixed, and Variable Cost

(b) Average Cost, Marginal Cost

FIGURE 7-2. All Cost Curves Can Be Derived from the Total Cost Curve

(a) Total cost is made up of fixed cost and variable cost. (b) The rust-colored curve of marginal cost falls and then rises, as indicated by the MC figures given in column (5) of Table 7-3. Note how MC intersects AC at its minimum.

But Figure 7-2(b) also shows that there is an important link between MC and AC: When the MC of an added unit of output is below its AC, its AC is declining. And when MC is above AC, AC is increasing. At the point where MC equals AC, the AC curve is flat. For the typical U-shaped AC curve, the point where MC equals AC is also the point where AC hits its minimum level. Check this for yourself on the graph.

FIGURE 7-3. Relation of Slope and Marginal Cost

Focus a microscope on the total cost curve to examine the cost of going from an output of 3999 to 4000. The figure clarifies the distinction between (1) MC as the incremental cost for a finite-step change in output and (2) MC as the cost for an infinitesimal change in output measured by the tangent. The distance from a to b represents 1 extra unit of output. The b to d distance represents the resulting increase in total cost. Hence $MC = (d - b)/(b - a)$, which is the first and simplest definition of marginal cost.

The second definition of marginal cost is as the slope of the total cost curve. The slope of the curve at point a is given by the slope of the tangent at point a, which is given by the distance from b to c divided by the distance from a to b. In the limit for a smooth curve, as the size of the output increment becomes smaller and smaller and we recalculate the ratios in the new, smaller triangle, the discrepancy between the two definitions becomes negligible. That is, bd/bc approaches 1 as b approaches a.

Remember these important rules:

- When marginal cost is below average cost, it is pulling average cost down.
- When MC is above AC, it is pulling AC up.
- When MC just equals AC, AC is neither rising nor falling and is at its minimum. Hence, at the bottom of a U-shaped AC, MC = AC = minimum AC.

This is a critical relationship. It means that a firm searching for the lowest average cost of production should look for the level of output at which marginal costs equal average costs.

Why is this so? If MC is below AC, the last unit produced costs less than the average cost of all the previous units produced. If the last unit costs less than the previous ones, the new *AC* (i.e., the *AC* including the last unit) must be less than the old *AC*, so *AC* must be falling. By contrast, if *MC* is above *AC*, the last unit costs more than the average cost of the previous units. Hence the new average cost (the *AC* including the last unit) must be higher than the old *AC*. Finally, when *MC* is just equal to *AC*, the last unit costs exactly the same as the average cost of all previous units. Hence the new *AC*, the one including the last unit, is equal to the old *AC*; the *AC* curve is flat when *AC* equals *MC*.

To better understand the relationship between *MC* and *AC*, study the curves in Figure 7-2(*b*) and the numbers in Table 7-3. Note that for the first 3 units, *MC* is below *AC*, and *AC* is therefore declining. At exactly 4 units, *AC* equals *MC*. Over 4 units, *MC* is above *AC* and pulling *AC* up steadily. Graphically, that means the rising *MC* curve will intersect the *AC* curve precisely at the point where it turns upward: *the* AC *curve is always pierced at its minimum point by the rising* MC *curve*. In terms of our cost curves, if the *MC* curve is below the *AC* curve, the *AC* curve must be falling.

Batting Averages to Illustrate MC and AC Rules

We can illustrate the *MC AC* relationship using batting averages. Let *AB* be your lifetime batting average up to this year (your average) and *MB* be your batting average for this year (your marginal). For simplicity, we also assume that there are 100 "at bats" each year.

When your *MB* is below *AB*, it will pull the new *AB* down. For example, suppose that your lifetime batting average for your first 3 years was .300 and your batting average for your fourth year was .100. Your new lifetime average or *AB* at the end of your fourth year is .250. Similarly, if your *MB* in your fourth year is higher than your lifetime average for your first 3 years, your lifetime average will be pulled up. If your batting average in the fourth year is the same as your lifetime average for the first 3 years, your lifetime average will not change (i.e., if *MB* = *AB*, then the new *AB* is equal to the old *AB*).

THE LINK BETWEEN PRODUCTION AND COSTS

What determines a firm's cost curve? Clearly the prices of inputs like labor and land are important factors influencing costs. Higher rents and wages mean higher costs, as any business manager will tell you.

But the cost curve for a firm also depends very closely on the firm's production function. To see this, note that if technological improvements allow the firm to produce the same output with fewer inputs, the firm's costs will fall, and the cost curve will shift down.

Indeed, if you know factor prices and the production function, you can calculate the cost curve. Suppose a firm is aiming to produce a particular level of output. The production function (plus factor prices) will tell us which is the least costly combination of inputs the firm can select that can yield that output. When we calculate the total cost of the least-cost bundle of inputs for every possible level of output, we have the total cost shown in Tables 7-1 through 7-3.

We can see the derivation of cost from production data in the simple numerical example shown in Table 7-4. Suppose Farmer Smith rents 10 acres of land and can hire farm labor to produce wheat. Per period, land costs $5.5 per acre and labor costs $5 per worker. Using up-to-date farming methods, Smith can produce according to the production function shown in the first three columns of Table 7-4. In this example, land is a fixed cost (because Farmer Smith operates under a 10-year lease), while labor is a variable cost (because farmworkers, unlike tenured faculty members, can easily be hired and fired).

Using the production data and the input-cost data, for each level of output we calculate the total cost of production shown in column (6) of Table 7-4. As an example, consider the total cost of production for 3 tons of wheat. Using the given production function, Smith can produce this quantity with 10 acres of land and 15 farmhands. The total cost of producing 3 tons of wheat is (10 acres × $5.5 per acre) + (15 workers × $5 per worker) = $130. Similar calculations will give all the other total cost figures in column (6) of Table 7-4.

Note that these total costs are identical to the ones shown in Tables 7-1 through 7-3, so the other cost concepts shown in the tables (i.e., *MC, FC, VC, AC, AFC*, and *AVC*) are also applicable to the production-cost example of Farmer Smith.

Diminishing Returns and U-Shaped Cost Curves

The relationship between cost and production helps us explain why average cost curves tend to be U-shaped. Recall that Chapter 6's analysis of production distinguished two different time periods, the

(1) Output (tons of wheat)	(2) Land inputs (acres)	(3) Labor inputs (workers)	(4) Land rent ($ per acre)	(5) Labor wage ($ per worker)	(6) Total cost ($)
0	10	0	5.5	5	55
1	10	6	5.5	5	85
2	10	11	5.5	5	110
3	10	15	5.5	5	130
4	10	21	5.5	5	160
5	10	31	5.5	5	210
6	10	45	5.5	5	280
7	10	63	5.5	5	370
8	10	85	5.5	5	480

TABLE 7-4. Costs are Derived from Production Data and Input Costs

Farmer Smith rents 10 acres of wheatland and employs variable labor. According to the farming production function, careful use of labor and land allows the inputs and yields shown in columns (1) to (3) of the table. At input prices of $5.5 per acre and $5 per worker, we obtain Smith's cost of production shown in column (6). All other cost concepts (such as those shown in Table 7-3) can be calculated from the total cost data.

short run and the long run. The same concepts apply to costs as well:

- The *short run* is the period of time that is long enough to adjust variable inputs, such as materials and production labor, but too short to allow all inputs to be changed. In the short run, fixed or overhead factors such as plant and equipment cannot be fully modified or adjusted. Therefore, in the short run, labor and materials costs are typically variable costs, while capital costs are fixed.
- In the *long run,* all inputs can be adjusted— including labor, materials, and capital. Hence, in the long run, all costs are variable and none are fixed.[1]

Note that whether a particular cost is fixed or variable depends on the length of time we are considering. In the short run, for example, the number of planes that an airline owns is a fixed cost. But over the longer run, the airline can clearly control the size of its fleet by buying or selling planes. Indeed, there is an active market in used planes, making it relatively easy to dispose of unwanted planes. Typically, in the short run, we will consider capital to be the fixed cost and labor to be the variable cost. That is not always true (think of your

college's tenured faculty), but generally labor inputs can be adjusted more easily than can capital.

Why is the cost curve U-shaped? Consider the short run in which capital is fixed but labor is variable. In such a situation, there are diminishing returns to the variable factor (labor) because each additional unit of labor has less capital to work with. As a result, the marginal cost of output will rise because the extra output produced by each extra labor unit is going down. In other words, diminishing returns to the variable factor will imply an increasing short-run marginal cost. This shows why diminishing returns lead to rising marginal costs after some point.

Figure 7-4, which contains exactly the same data as Table 7-4, illustrates the point. It shows that the region of increasing marginal product corresponds to falling marginal costs, while the region of diminishing returns implies rising marginal costs.

We can summarize the relationship between the productivity laws and the cost curves as follows:

In the short run, when factors such as capital are fixed, variable factors tend to show an initial phase of increasing marginal product followed by diminishing marginal product. The corresponding cost curves show an initial phase of declining marginal costs, followed by increasing *MC* after diminishing returns have set in.

---

[1] For a more complete discussion of the long and short runs, see Chapter 6.

(a) Diminishing Returns . . .

(b) . . . Produce Upward-Sloping *MC*

FIGURE 7-4. Diminishing Returns and U-Shaped Cost Curves

The U-shaped marginal cost curve in (**b**) arises from the shape of the marginal product curve in (**a**). With fixed land and variable labor, the marginal product of labor in (**a**) first rises to the left of *B*, peaks at *B*, and then falls at *D* as diminishing returns to labor set in.

The marginal cost curve derives from production data. In the region to the left of *B* in (**b**)—such as at point *A*—rising marginal product means that marginal cost is falling; at *B*, peak marginal product occurs at minimum marginal cost; to the right of *B* (e.g., at *D*), the marginal cost of producing output increases as the marginal product of labor falls.

Overall, increasing and then diminishing marginal product to the variable factor gives a U-shaped marginal cost curve.

CHOICE OF INPUTS BY THE FIRM

Marginal Products and the Least-Cost Rule

Every firm must decide *how* to produce its output. Should electricity be produced with oil or coal? Should cars be assembled in the United States or Mexico? Should classes be taught by faculty or graduate students? We now complete the link between production and cost by using the marginal product concept to illustrate how firms select the least-cost combinations of inputs.

In our analysis, we will rely on the fundamental assumption that *firms minimize their costs of production.* This cost-minimization assumption actually makes good sense not only for perfectly competitive firms but for monopolists or even nonprofit organizations like colleges or hospitals. It simply states that the firm should strive to produce its output at the lowest possible cost and thereby have the maximum amount of revenue left over for profits or for other objectives.

A simple example will illustrate how a firm might decide between different input combinations. Say a firm's engineers have calculated that the desired output level of 9 units could be produced with two possible options. In both cases, energy (E) costs \$2 per unit, while labor (L) costs \$5 per hour. Under option 1, the input mix is $E = 10$ and $L = 2$. Option 2 has $E = 4$ and $L = 5$. Which is the preferred option? At the market prices for inputs, total production costs for option 1 are (\$2 × 10) + (\$5 × 2) = \$30, while total costs for option 2 are (\$2 × 4) + (\$5 × 5) = \$33. Therefore, option 1 would be the preferred least-cost combination of inputs.

More generally, there are usually many possible input combinations, not just two. But we don't have to calculate the cost of every different combination of inputs in order to find the one which costs the least. Here's a simple way to find the least-cost combination: Start by calculating the marginal product of each input, as we did in Chapter 6. Then divide the marginal product of each input by its factor price. *This gives you the marginal product per dollar of input.* The cost-minimizing combination of inputs comes when the marginal product per dollar of input is equal for all inputs. That is, the marginal contribution to output of each dollar's worth of labor, of land, of oil, and so forth, must be just the same.

Following this reasoning, a firm will minimize its total cost of production when the marginal product per dollar of input is equalized for each factor of production. This is called the least-cost rule.

Least-cost rule: To produce a given level of output at least cost, a firm should buy inputs until it has equalized the marginal product per dollar spent on each input. This implies that

$$\frac{\text{Marginal product of } L}{\text{Price of } L} = \frac{\text{marginal product of } A}{\text{price of } A} = \cdots$$

This rule for firms is exactly analogous to what consumers do when they maximize utilities, as we saw in Chapter 5. In analyzing consumer choice, we saw that to maximize utility, consumers should buy goods so that the marginal utility per dollar spent on each consumer good is equalized for all commodities.

One way of understanding the least-cost rule is the following: Break each factor into packages worth $1 each. (In our earlier energy-labor example, $1 of labor would be one-fifth of an hour, while $1 of energy would be ½ unit.) Then the least-cost rule states that the marginal product of each dollar-unit of input must be equalized. If the marginal products per $1 of inputs were not equal, you could reduce the low-MP-per-dollar input and increase the high-MP-per-dollar input and produce the same output at lower cost.

A corollary of the least-cost rule is the substitution rule.

Substitution rule: If the price of one factor falls while all other factor prices remain the same, firms will profit by substituting the now-cheaper factor for the other factors until the marginal products per dollar are equal for all inputs.

Let's take the case of labor (L). A fall in the price of labor will raise the ratio MP_L/P_L above the MP/P ratio for other inputs. Raising the employment of L lowers MP_L by the law of diminishing returns and therefore lowers MP_L/P_L. Lower price and MP of labor then bring the marginal product per dollar for labor back into equality with that ratio for other factors.

B. ECONOMIC COSTS AND BUSINESS ACCOUNTING

From General Motors down to the corner deli, businesses use more or less elaborate systems to keep track of their costs. Many of the cost categories in business accounting look very similar to the concepts of economic cost we learned above. But there are some important differences between how businesses measure costs and how economists would do it. In this section we will lay out the rudiments of business accounting and point out the differences and similarities with economic costs.

THE INCOME STATEMENT, OR STATEMENT OF PROFIT AND LOSS

Let us start with a small company, called Hot Dog Ventures, Inc. As the name suggests, this company sells gourmet frankfurters in a small store. The operation consists of buying the materials (hot dogs, top-flight buns, expensive mustard, espresso coffee beans) and hiring people to prepare and sell the food. In addition, the company has taken out a loan of $100,000 for its cooking equipment and other restaurant furnishings, and it must pay rent on its store. The founders of Hot Dog Ventures have big aspirations, so they incorporated the business and issued common stock (see Chapter 6 on forms of business organization).

To determine whether Hot Dog Ventures is earning a profit, we must turn to the **income statement,** or—as many companies prefer to call it—the *statement of profit and loss,* shown in Table 7-5. This statement reports the following: (1) Hot Dog Venture's revenues from sales in 2004, (2) the expenses to be charged against those sales, and (3) the net income, or profits remaining after expenses have been deducted. This gives the fundamental identity of the income statement:

Net income (or profit) = total revenue − total expenses

This definition gives the famous "bottom line" of profits that firms want to maximize. And in many ways, business profits are close to an economist's definition of economic profits. Let's next examine

Income Statement of Hot Dog Ventures, Inc. (January 1, 2004, to December 31, 2004)			
(1)	Net sales (after all discounts and rebates)		$250,000
	Less cost of goods sold:		
(2)	Materials	$ 50,000	
(3)	Labor cost	90,000	
(4)	Miscellaneous operating costs (utilities, etc.)	10,000	
(5)	Less overhead costs:		
(6)	Selling and administrative costs	15,000	
(7)	Rent for building	5,000	
(8)	Depreciation	15,000	
(9)	Operating expenses	$185,000	185,000
(10)	Net operating income		$ 65,000
	Less:		
(11)	Interest charges on equipment loan		6,000
(12)	State and local taxes		4,000
(13)	Net income (or profit) before income taxes		$ 55,000
(14)	Less: Corporation income taxes		18,000
(15)	Net income (or profit) after taxes		$ 37,000
(16)	Less: Dividends paid on common stock		15,000
(17)	Addition to retained earnings		$ 22,000

TABLE 7-5. The Income Statement Shows Total Sales and Expenses for a Period of Time

the profit-and-loss statement in more detail, starting from the top. The first line gives the revenues, which were $250,000. Lines 2 through 9 represent the cost of different inputs into the production process. For example, the labor cost is the annual cost of employing labor, while rent is the annual cost of using the building. The selling and administrative costs include the costs of advertising the product and running the back office, while miscellaneous operating costs include the cost of electricity.

The first three cost categories—materials, labor cost, and miscellaneous operating costs—basically correspond to the variable costs of the firm, or its *cost of goods sold*. The next three categories, lines 6 through 8, correspond to the firm's fixed costs, since in the short run they cannot be changed.

Line 8 shows a term we haven't seen before, *depreciation*, which relates to the cost of capital goods. Firms can either rent capital or own their capital goods. In the case of the building, which Hot Dog

Ventures rented, we deducted the rent in item (7) of the income statement.

When the firm owns the capital good, the treatment is more complicated. Suppose the cooking equipment has an estimated useful lifetime of 10 years, at the end of which it is useless and worthless. In effect, some portion of the cooking equipment is "used up" in the productive process each year. We call the amount used up "depreciation," and calculate that amount as the cost of the capital input for that year. **Depreciation** measures the annual cost of a capital input that a company actually owns itself.

The same reasoning would apply to any capital goods that a company owns. Trucks wear out, computers become obsolete, and buildings eventually begin to fall apart. For each of these, the company would take a depreciation charge. There are a number of different formulas for calculating each year's depreciation, but each follows two major principles: (*a*) The total amount of depreciation over the asset's lifetime must equal the capital good's historical cost or purchase price; (*b*) the depreciation is taken in annual accounting charges over the asset's accounting lifetime, which is usually related to the actual economic lifetime of the asset.

We can now understand how depreciation would be charged for Hot Dog Ventures. The equipment is depreciated according to a 10-year lifetime, so the $150,000 of equipment has a depreciation charge of $15,000 per year (using the simplest "straight-line" method of depreciation). If Hot Dog Ventures owned its store, it would have to take a depreciation charge for the building as well.

Adding up all the costs so far gives us the operating expenses (line 9). The net operating income is net revenues minus operating expenses (line 1 minus line 9). Have we accounted for all the costs of production yet? Not quite. Line 11 includes the annual cost of interest on the $100,000 loan. This should be thought of as the cost of borrowing the financial capital. While this is a fixed cost, it is typically kept separate from the other fixed costs. State and local taxes, such as property taxes, are treated as another expense. Deducting lines 11 and 12 gives a total of $55,000 in profits before income taxes. How are these profits divided? Approximately $18,000 goes to the federal government in the form of corporate income taxes. That leaves a profit of $37,000 after taxes. Dividends of $15,000 on the common stock are paid, leaving $22,000 to be plowed back as retained earnings in the business. Again, note that profits are a residual of sales minus costs.

THE BALANCE SHEET

Business accounting is concerned with more than the profits and losses that are the economic driving force. Business accounts also include the **balance sheet**, which is a picture of financial conditions on a given date. This statement records what a firm, person, or nation is worth at a given point in time. On one side of the balance sheet are the **assets** (valuable properties or rights owned by the firm). On the other side are two items, the **liabilities** (money or obligations owed by the firm) and **net worth** (or net value, equal to total assets minus total liabilities).

One important distinction between the income statement and the balance sheet is that between stocks and flows. A **stock** represents the level of a variable, such as the amount of water in a lake or, in this case, the dollar value of a firm. A **flow** variable represents the change per unit of time, like the flow of water in a river or the flow of revenue and expenses into and out of a firm. *The income statement measures the flows into and out of the firm, while the balance sheet measures the stocks of assets and liabilities at the end of the accounting year.*

The fundamental identity or balancing relationship of the balance sheet is that total assets are balanced by total liabilities plus the net worth of the firm to its owners:

$$\text{Total assets} = \text{total liabilities} + \text{net worth}$$

We can rearrange this relationship to find

$$\text{Net worth} = \text{assets} - \text{liabilities}$$

Let us illustrate this by considering Table 7-6, which shows a simple balance sheet for Hot Dog Ventures, Inc. On the left are assets, and on the right are liabilities and net worth. A blank space has been deliberately left next to the net worth entry because the only correct entry compatible with our fundamental balance sheet identity is $200,000. *A balance sheet must always balance because net worth is a residual defined as assets minus liabilities.* Suppose one item on a balance sheet changes (such as an increase in assets); then there must be a corresponding change on the balance sheet to maintain balance (a decrease in assets, an increase in liabilities, or an increase in net worth).

To illustrate how net worth always balances, suppose that hot dogs valued at $40,000 have spoiled. Your accountant reports to you: "Total assets are down $40,000; liabilities remain unchanged. This means total net worth has decreased by $40,000, and I have no choice but to write net worth down from the previous $200,000 to only $160,000." That's how accountants keep score.

We summarize our analysis of accounting concepts as follows:

1. The income statement shows the flow of sales, cost, and revenue over the year or accounting period. It measures the flow of dollars into and out of the firm over a specified period of time.
2. The balance sheet indicates an instantaneous financial picture or snapshot. It is like a measure of the stock of water in a lake. The major items are assets, liabilities, and net worth.

Balance Sheet of Hot Dog Ventures, Inc. (December 31, 2004)			
Assets		**Liabilities and net worth**	
		Liabilities	
Current assets:		Current liabilities:	
Cash	$ 20,000	Accounts payable	$ 20,000
Inventory	80,000	Notes payable	30,000
Fixed assets:		Long-term liabilities:	
Equipment	150,000	Bonds payable	100,000
Buildings	100,000		
		Net worth	
		Stockholders' equity:	
		Common stock	....
Total	$350,000	Total	$350,000

TABLE 7-6. The Balance Sheet Records the Stock of Assets and Liabilities, plus Net Worth, of a Firm at a Given Point in Time

Accounting Conventions

In examining the balance sheet in Table 7-6 you might well ask, How are the values of the different items measured? How do the accountants know that the equipment is worth $150,000?

The answer is that accountants use a set of agreed-upon rules or accounting conventions to answer most questions. The most important assumption used in a balance sheet is that the value placed on almost every item reflects its *historical cost.* This differs from the economist's concept of "value," as we will see in the next section. For example, the inventory of hot-dog buns is valued at the price that was paid for them. A newly purchased fixed asset—a piece of equipment or a building—is valued at its purchase price (this being the historical-cost convention). Older capital is valued at its purchase price minus accumulated depreciation, thus accounting for the gradual decline in usefulness of capital goods. Accountants use historical cost because it reflects an objective evaluation and is easily verified.

In Table 7-6 current assets are convertible into cash within a year, while fixed assets represent capital goods and land. Most of the specific items listed are self-explanatory. Cash consists of coins, currency, and money on deposit in the bank. Cash is the only asset whose value is exact rather than an estimate.

On the liabilities side, accounts payable and notes payable are sums owed to others for goods bought or for borrowed funds. Bonds payable are long-term loans floated in the market. The last item on the balance sheet is net worth, or stockholders' equity. This is the net value of the firm's assets less liabilities, when valued at historical cost. The net worth must equal $200,000.

Financial Finagling

Now that we have reviewed the principles of accounting, we see that there is considerable judgment involved in determining the exact treatment of certain items. In the late 1990s, under pressure to produce rapidly growing earnings, many companies manipulated their accounts to show glowing results or to paper over losses. Some of the most egregious examples included pretending capital assets that were traded were revenues (Enron, Global Crossing); capitalizing the outflow while recognizing the inflow as current revenues (Enron, Qwest); increasing the salvage value of trucks over time (Waste Management); increasing the value of the unused capacity of landfills even as they fill up (Waste Management); and reporting happy proforma numbers when the reality was unpleasant (Amazon.com, Yahoo, and Qualcomm, among a crowd of other dot-coms dead or alive). In the wake of disclosures of accounting frauds, WorldCom and Enron actually went bankrupt.

The Rise and Fall of Enron

To see how an accounting fraud works, let's take the example of Enron. Enron started off as a (genuinely) profitable business which owned the largest interstate network of natural-gas pipelines. To continue its rapid growth, it turned to trading natural-gas futures, and then it leveraged its "business model" into other markets.

Along the way, however, its profits began to decline and it hid the declines from investors. You might well ask, How could a large, publicly owned company like Enron have fooled virtually all of the people most of the time until 2001?

To begin with, some of Enron's activities were genuinely novel, so investors could reasonably have believed for a while that Enron was a sound business. Its success in hiding its failures rested on four complementary factors. First, when troubles arose, Enron began to exploit ambiguities in accounting principles, such as the ones described above. One example was a deal called "Project Braveheart" with Blockbuster Video. This deal projected revenues over the next 20 years with a present value of $111 million, and Enron accounted for these as current revenues even though the projections were based on highly dubious assumptions.

Second, the firm elected not to report the details of many financial transactions—for example, it hid hundreds of partnerships from its stockholders. Third, the board of directors and outside auditors were passive and did not challenge or in some cases even inquire into some details of Enron's accounts. Finally, the investment community, such as the large mutual funds, exercised little deep independent analysis of Enron's numbers even though at the peak Enron absorbed $70 billion of investors' funds.[2]

The Enron case is a reminder that financial markets, accounting firms, and investment managers can be fooled into investing billions and billions of dollars when firm insiders engage in aggressive accounting and fraudulent practices. The history of such accounting frauds is a reminder of the importance of sound accounting practices and the need for vigilant oversight by government and nongovernment bodies.

C. OPPORTUNITY COSTS

In this section we look at costs from yet another angle. Remember that one of the cardinal tenets of economics is that resources are scarce. That means every time we choose to use a resource one way, we've given up the opportunity to utilize it another way. That's easy to see in our own lives, where we must constantly decide what to do with our limited time and income. Should we go to a movie or study for next week's test? Should we travel to Mexico or buy a car? Should we get postgraduate or professional training or begin work right after college?

In each of these cases, making a choice in effect costs us the opportunity to do something else. The best alternative forgone is called the opportunity cost, which we met briefly in Chapter 1 and develop more thoroughly here. The immediate dollar cost of going to a movie instead of studying is the price of a ticket, but the opportunity cost also includes the possibility of getting a higher grade on the exam. The opportunity costs of a decision include all its consequences, whether they reflect monetary transactions or not.

Decisions have opportunity costs because choosing one thing in a world of scarcity means giving up something else. The **opportunity cost** is the value of the most valuable good or service forgone.

One important example of opportunity cost is the cost of going to college. If you went to a public university in 2003, the total costs of tuition, books, and travel averaged about $6000. Does this mean that $6000 was your opportunity cost of going to school? Definitely not! You must include as well the *opportunity cost of the time* spent studying and going to classes. A full-time

---

[2] See this chapter's Further Reading section for an additional analysis.

job for a college-age high school graduate paid $22,000 in 2003. If we add up both the actual expenses and the earnings forgone, we would find that the opportunity cost of college was $28,000 (equal to $6000 + $22,000) rather than $6000 per year.

Business decisions have opportunity costs, too. Do all opportunity costs show up on the profit-and-loss statement? Not necessarily. In general, business accounts include only transactions in which money actually changes hands. By contrast, the economist always tries to "pierce the veil of money" to uncover the real consequences that lie behind the dollar flows and to measure the true *resource costs* of an activity. Economists therefore include all costs—whether they reflect monetary transactions or not.

There are several important opportunity costs that do not show up on income statements. For example, in many small businesses, the family may put in many unpaid hours, which are not included as accounting costs. Nor do business accounts include a capital charge for the owner's financial contributions. Nor do they include the cost of the environmental damage that occurs when a business dumps toxic wastes into a stream. But from an economic point of view, each of these is a genuine cost to the economy.

Let's illustrate the concept of opportunity cost by considering the owner of Hot Dog Ventures. The owner puts in 60 hours a week but earns no "wages." At the end of the year, as Table 7-5 showed, the firm earns a profit of $37,000—pretty good for a neophyte firm.

Or is it? The economist would insist that we should consider the value of a factor of production regardless of how the factor happens to be owned. We should count the owner's own labor as a cost even though the owner does not get paid directly but instead receives compensation in the form of profits. Because the owner has alternative opportunities for work, we must value the owner's labor in terms of the lost opportunities.

A careful examination might show that Hot Dog Venture's owner could find a similar and equally interesting job working for someone else and earning $60,000. This represents the opportunity cost or earnings forgone because the owner decided to become the unpaid owner of a small business rather than the paid employee of another firm.

Therefore, the economist continues, let us calculate the true economic profits of the hot-dog firm. If we take the measured profits of $37,000 and subtract the $60,000 opportunity cost of the owner's labor, we find a net *loss* of $23,000. Hence, although the accountant might conclude that Hot Dog Ventures is economically viable, the economist would pronounce that the firm is an unprofitable loser.

OPPORTUNITY COST AND MARKETS

At this point, however, you might well say: "Now I'm totally confused. First I learned that price is a good measure of true social cost in the marketplace. Now you tell me that opportunity cost is the right concept. Can't you economists make up your minds?"

Actually, there is a simple explanation: *In well-functioning markets, when all costs are included, price equals opportunity cost.* Assume that a commodity like wheat is bought and sold in a competitive market. If I bring my wheat to market, I will receive a number of bids from prospective buyers: $2.502, $2.498, and $2.501 per bushel. These represent the values of my wheat to, say, three different flour mills. I pick the highest—$2.502. The opportunity cost of this sale is the value of the best available alternative—that is, the second-highest bid, at $2.501—which is almost identical to the price that is accepted. As the market approaches perfect competition, the bids get closer and closer until, at the limit, the second-highest bid (which is our definition of opportunity cost) exactly equals the highest bid (which is the price). In competitive markets, numerous buyers compete for resources to the point where price is bid up to the best available alternative and is therefore equal to the opportunity cost.

Opportunity Cost outside Markets. The concept of opportunity cost is particularly crucial when you are analyzing transactions that take place outside markets. How do you measure the value of a road or a park? Of a health or safety regulation? Even the allocation of student time can be explained using opportunity cost.

• The notion of opportunity cost explains why students watch more TV the week after exams than the week before exams. Watching TV right before an exam has a high opportunity cost, for the alternative use of time (studying) has high value in improving grade performance and getting a good job. After exams, time has a lower opportunity cost.

- Say the federal government wants to drill for oil off the California coast. A storm of complaints is heard. A defender of the program states, "What's all the ruckus about? There's valuable oil out there, and there is plenty of seawater to go around. This is very low-cost oil for the nation." In fact, the opportunity cost might be very high. If drilling leads to oil spills that spoil the beaches, it might reduce the recreational value of the ocean. That opportunity cost might not be easily measured, but it's every bit as real as the value of oil under the waters.

The Road Not Traveled. Opportunity cost, then, is a measure of what has been given up when we make a decision. Consider what Robert Frost had in mind when he wrote,

> Two roads diverged in a wood, and I—
> I took the one less traveled by,
> And that has made all the difference.

What other road did Frost have in mind? An urban life? An avocation where he would not be able to write of roads and walls and birches? Imagine the immeasurable opportunity cost to all of us if Robert Frost had taken the road more traveled by.

But let us return from the poetic to the practical. The crucial point to grasp is this:

Economic costs include, in addition to explicit money outlays, those opportunity costs incurred because resources can be used in alternative ways.

SUMMARY

A. Economic Analysis of Costs

1. Total cost (TC) can be broken down into fixed cost (FC) and variable cost (VC). Fixed costs are unaffected by any production decisions, while variable costs are incurred on items like labor or materials which increase as production levels rise.

2. Marginal cost (MC) is the extra total cost resulting from 1 extra unit of output. Average total cost (AC) is the sum of ever-declining average fixed cost (AFC) and average variable cost (AVC). Short-run average cost is generally represented by a U-shaped curve that is always intersected at its minimum point by the rising MC curve.

3. Useful rules to remember are

$$TC = FC + VC \quad AC = TC/q \quad AC = AFC + AVC$$

At the bottom of U-shaped AC, $MC = AC =$ minimum AC.

4. Costs and productivity are like mirror images. When the law of diminishing returns holds, the marginal product falls and the MC curve rises. When there is an initial stage of increasing returns, MC initially falls.

5. We can apply cost and production concepts to a firm's choice of the best combination of factors of production. Firms that desire to maximize profits will want to minimize the cost of producing a given level of output. In this case, the firm will follow the least-cost rule: different factors will be chosen so that the marginal

product per dollar of input is equalized for all inputs. This implies that $MP_L/P_L = MP_A/P_A = \cdots$.

B. Economic Costs and Business Accounting

6. To understand accounting, the most important relationships are:
   a. The character of the income statement (or profit-and-loss statement); the residual nature of profits; depreciation on fixed assets
   b. The fundamental balance sheet relationship between assets, liabilities, and net worth; the breakdown of each of these into financial and fixed assets; and the residual nature of net worth

C. Opportunity Costs

7. The economist's definition of costs is broader than the accountant's. Economic cost includes not only the obvious out-of-pocket purchases or monetary transactions but also more subtle opportunity costs, such as the return to labor supplied by the owner of a firm. These opportunity costs are tightly constrained by the bids and offers in competitive markets, so price is close to opportunity cost for marketed goods and services.

8. The most important application of opportunity cost arises for nonmarket goods—those like clean air or health or recreation—which may be highly valuable even though they are not bought and sold in markets.

CONCEPTS FOR REVIEW

Analysis of Costs

total costs: fixed and variable
marginal cost
least-cost rule:

$$\frac{MP_L}{P_L} = \frac{MP_A}{P_A} = \frac{MP_{any\ factor}}{P_{any\ factor}}$$

$TC = FC + VC$
$AC = TC/q = AFC + AVC$

Accounting Concepts

income statement (profit-and-loss
    statement): sales, cost, profits
depreciation

fundamental balance sheet identity
assets, liabilities, and net worth
stocks vs. flows
opportunity cost
cost concepts in economics and
    accounting

FURTHER READING AND INTERNET WEBSITES

Further Reading

Advanced treatment of cost and production theory can be found in intermediate textbooks. See the list provided in Chapter 3.

You can find interesting articles on business cost, production, and decision problems in magazines such as *Business Week, Fortune, Forbes,* and *The Economist.* An excellent nontechnical analysis of the Enron fraud is contained in Paul M. Healy and Krishna G. Palepu, "The Fall of Enron," *Journal of Economic Perspectives,* Spring 2003, pp. 3–26.

Websites

Good case studies on costs and production can be found in the business press. See the websites of the business magazines listed above, www.businessweek.com, www.fortune.com, www.forbes.com, and www.economist.com. Some of these sites require a fee or subscription.

Information about individual firms is filed with the Securities and Exchange Commission and can be found at www.sec.gov/edgarhp.htm.

QUESTIONS FOR DISCUSSION

1. During his major-league career from 1936 to 1960, Ted Williams had 7706 at bats and 2654 hits.
   a. What was his lifetime batting average?
   b. In his last year, 1960, Williams had 310 at bats and 98 hits. What was his lifetime batting average at the end of 1959? What was his batting average for 1960?
   c. Explain the relationship between his average for 1959 and the change of his lifetime average from 1959 to 1960. State how this illustrates the relationship between *MC* and *AC*.
2. To the $55 of fixed cost in Table 7-3, add $90 of additional *FC*. Now calculate a whole new table, with the same *VC* as before but new *FC* = $145. What happens to *MC, AVC*? To *TC, AC, AFC*? Can you verify that minimum *AC* is now at $q^* = 5$ with *AC* = $60 = *MC*?
3. Explain why *MC* cuts *AC* and *AVC* at their minimum values (i.e., the bottom of their U-shaped cost curves).

4. "Compulsory military service allows the government to fool itself and the people about the true cost of a big army." Compare the budget cost and the opportunity cost of a voluntary army (where army pay is high) with those of compulsory service (where pay is low). What does the concept of opportunity cost contribute to analyzing the quotation?
5. Consider the data in Table 7-7, which contains a situation similar to that in Table 7-4.
   a. Calculate the *TC, VC, FC, AC, AVC,* and *MC*. On a piece of graph paper, plot the *AC* and *MC* curves.
   b. Assume that the price of labor doubles. Calculate a new *AC* and *MC*. Plot the new curves and compare them with those in **a**.
   c. Now assume that total factor productivity doubles (i.e., that the level of output doubles for each input combination). Repeat the exercise in **b**. Can you see two major factors that tend to affect a firm's cost curves?

(1) Output (tons of wheat)	(2) Land inputs (acres)	(3) Labor inputs (workers)	(4) Land rent ($ per acre)	(5) Labor wage ($ per worker)
0	15	0	12	5
1	15	6	12	5
2	15	11	12	5
3	15	15	12	5
4	15	21	12	5
5	15	31	12	5
6	15	45	12	5
7	15	63	12	5

TABLE 7-7.

6. Explain the fallacies in each of the following:
   a. Average costs are minimized when marginal costs are at their lowest point.
   b. Because fixed costs never change, average fixed cost is a constant for each level of output.
   c. Average cost is rising whenever marginal cost is rising.
   d. The opportunity cost of drilling for oil in Yosemite Park is zero because no firm produces anything there.
   e. A firm minimizes costs when it spends the same amount on each input.

Appendix 7

PRODUCTION, COST THEORY, AND DECISIONS OF THE FIRM

The production theory described in Chapter 6 and the cost analysis of this chapter are among the fundamental building blocks of microeconomics. A thorough understanding of production and cost is necessary for an appreciation of how economic scarcity gets translated into prices in the marketplace. This appendix develops these concepts further and introduces the concept of an equal-product curve, or isoquant.

A NUMERICAL PRODUCTION FUNCTION

Production theory and cost analysis have their roots in the concept of a production function, which shows the maximum amount of output that can be produced with various combinations of inputs. Table 7A-1 starts with a numerical example of a constant-returns-to-scale production function, showing the amount of inputs along the axes and the amount of output at the grid points of the table.

Along the left-hand side are listed the varying amounts of land, going from 1 unit to 6 units. Along the bottom are listed amounts of labor, which also go from 1 to 6. Output corresponding to each land row and labor column is listed inside the table.

If we are interested in knowing exactly how much output there will be when 3 units of land and 2 units of labor are available, we count up 3 units of land and then go over 2 units of labor. The answer is seen to be 346 units of product. (Can you identify some other input combinations that will produce $q = 346$?) Similarly, we find that 3 units of land and 6 of labor produce 600 units of q. Remember that the production function shows the maximum output available given engineering skills and technical knowledge available at a particular time.

Land \ Labor	1	2	3	4	5	6
6	346	490	600	692	775	846
5	316	448	548	632	705	775
4	282	400	490	564	632	692
3	245	346	423	490	548	600
2	200	282	346	400	448	490
1	141	200	245	282	316	346

TABLE 7A-1. A Tabular Picture of a Production Function Relating Amount of Output to Varying Combinations of Labor and Land Inputs

When you have 3 land units and 2 labor units available, the engineer tells you the maximum obtainable output is 346 units. Note the different ways to produce 346. Do the same for 490. (The production function shown in the table is a special case of the Cobb-Douglas production function, one given by the formula $Q = 100\sqrt{2LA}$.)

THE LAW OF DIMINISHING MARGINAL PRODUCT

Table 7A-1 can nicely illustrate the law of diminishing returns. First, recall that the marginal product of labor is the extra production resulting from 1 additional unit of labor when land and other inputs are held constant. At any point in Table 7A-1, we can find the marginal product of labor by subtracting the output from the number on its right in the same row. Thus, when there are 2 units of land and 4 units of labor, the marginal product of an additional laborer would be 48, or 448 minus 400 in the second row.

By the "marginal product of land" we mean, of course, the extra product resulting from 1 additional unit of land when labor is held constant. It is calculated by comparing adjacent items in a given column. Thus, when there are 2 units of land and 4 units of labor, the marginal product of land is shown in the fourth column as $490 - 400$, or 90.

We can easily find the marginal product of each of our two factors by comparing adjacent entries in the vertical columns or horizontal rows of Table 7A-1.

Having defined the concept of marginal product of an input, we now can easily define the law of diminishing returns: *The law of diminishing returns states* that as we increase one input and hold other inputs constant, the marginal product of the varying input will, at least after some point, decline.

To illustrate this, hold land constant in Table 7A-1 by sticking to a given row—say, the row corresponding to land equal to 2 units. Now let labor increase from 1 to 2 units, from 2 to 3 units, and so forth. What happens to q at each step?

As labor goes from 1 to 2 units, the level of output increases from 200 to 282 units, or by 82 units. But the next dose of labor adds only 64 units, or $346 - 282$. Diminishing returns have set in. Still further additions of a single unit of labor give us, respectively, only 54 extra units of output, 48 units, and finally 42 units. You can easily verify that the law holds for other rows and that the law holds when land is varied and labor held constant.

We can use this example to verify our intuitive justification of the law of diminishing returns—the assertion that the law holds because the fixed factor decreases relative to the variable factor. According to this explanation, each unit of the variable factor has less and less of the fixed factor to work with. So it is natural that extra product should drop off.

If this explanation is to hold water, output should increase proportionately when both factors are increased together. When labor increases from 1 to 2 and land simultaneously increases from 1 to 2, we should get the same increase in product as when both increase *simultaneously* from 2 to 3. This can be verified in Table 7A-1. In the first move we go from 141 to 282, and in the second move the product increases from 282 to 423, an equal jump of 141 units.

LEAST-COST FACTOR COMBINATION FOR A GIVEN OUTPUT

The numerical production function shows us the different ways to produce a given level of output. But which of the many possibilities should the firm use? If the desired level of output is $q = 346$, there are no less than four different combinations of land and labor, shown as A, B, C, and D in Table 7A-2.

As far as the engineer is concerned, each of these combinations is equally good at producing an output of 346 units. But the manager, interested in minimizing cost, wants to find the combination that costs the least.

(1) Input Combinations		(3) Total cost when $P_L = \$2$ $P_A = \$3$ ($\$$)	(4) Total cost when $P_L = \$2$ $P_A = \$1$ ($\$$)
Labor L	Land A		
A	1	6	20	
B	2	3	13	7
C	3	2	12	
D	6	1	15	

TABLE 7A-2. Inputs and Costs of Producing a Given Level of Output

Assume that the firm has chosen 346 units of output. Then it can use any of the four choices of input combinations shown as A, B, C, and D. As the firm moves down the list, production becomes more labor-intensive and less land-intensive. Fill in the missing numbers.

The firm's choice among the different techniques will depend on input prices. When $P_L = \$2$ and $P_A = \$3$, verify that the cost-minimizing combination is C. Show that lowering the price of land from $\$3$ to $\$1$ leads the firm to choose a more land-intensive combination at B.

Let us suppose that the price of labor is $\$2$ and the price of land $\$3$. The total costs when input prices are at this level are shown in the third column of Table 7A-2. For combination A, the total labor and land cost will be $\$20$, equal to $(1 \times \$2) + (6 \times \$3)$. Costs at B, C, and D will be, respectively, $\$13$, $\$12$, and $\$15$. At the assumed input prices, C is the least costly way to produce the given output.

If either of the input prices changes, the equilibrium proportion of the inputs will also change so as to use less of the input that has gone up most in price. (This is just like the substitution effect in Chapter 5's discussion of consumer demand.) As soon as input prices are known, the least-cost method of production can be found by calculating the costs of different input combinations.

Equal-Product Curves

The commonsense numerical analysis of the way in which a firm will combine inputs to minimize costs can be made more vivid by the use of diagrams. We will take the diagrammatic approach by putting together two new curves, the equal-product curve and the equal-cost line.

Let's turn Table 7A-1 into a continuous curve by drawing a smooth curve through all the points that yield $q = 346$. This smooth curve, shown in Figure 7A-1, indicates all the different combinations of labor and land that yield an output of 346 units. This is called an **equal-product curve** or **isoquant** and is analogous to the consumer's indifference curve discussed in the appendix to Chapter 5. You should be able to draw on Figure 7A-1 the corresponding equal-product curve for output equal to 490 by getting the data from Table 7A-1. Indeed, an infinite number of such equal-product contour lines could be drawn in.

Equal-Cost Lines

Given the price of labor and land, the firm can evaluate the total cost for points A, B, C, and D or for any other point on the equal-product curve. The firm will minimize its costs when it selects that point on its equal-product curve that has the lowest total cost.

An easy technique for finding the least-cost method of production is to construct **equal-cost lines.** This is done in Figure 7A-2, where the family of parallel straight lines represents a number of equal-cost curves when the price of labor is $2 and the price of land $3.

FIGURE 7A-2. Equal-Cost Lines

Every point on a given equal-cost line represents the same total cost. The lines are straight because factor prices are constant, and they all have a negative slope equal to the ratio of labor price to land price, $2/$3, and hence are parallel.

To find the total cost for any point, we simply read off the number appended to the equal-cost line going through that point. The lines are all straight and parallel because the firm is assumed to be able to buy all it wishes of either input at constant prices. The lines are somewhat flatter than 45° because the price of labor P_L is somewhat less than the price of land P_A. More precisely, we can always say that the arithmetic value of the slope of each equal-cost line must equal the ratio of the price of labor to that of land—in this case $P_L/P_A = \frac{2}{3}$.

Equal-Product and Equal-Cost Contours: Least-Cost Tangency

Combining the equal-product and equal-cost lines, we can determine the optimal, or cost-minimizing, position of the firm. Recall that the optimal input combination comes at that point where the given output of $q = 346$ can be produced at least cost. To find such a point, simply superimpose the single rust equal-product curve upon the family of gray equal-cost lines, as shown in Figure 7A-3. The firm will always keep moving along the rust convex curve of Figure 7A-3 as long as it is able to cross over to lower cost lines. Its equilibrium will therefore be at C, where the equal-product curve touches (but does not cross) the lowest equal-cost line. This is a point of

FIGURE 7A-1. Equal-Product Curve

All the points on the equal-product curve represent the different combinations of land and labor that can be used to produce the same 346 units of output.

Substituting Inputs to Minimize Cost of Production

FIGURE 7A-3. Least-Cost Input Combination Comes at C

The firm desires to minimize its costs of producing a given output of 346. It thus seeks out the least expensive input combination along its rust equal-product curve. It looks for the input combination that is on the lowest of the equal-cost lines. Where the equal-product curve touches (but does not cross) the lowest equal-cost line is the least-cost position. This tangency means that factor prices and marginal products are proportional, with equalized marginal products per dollar.

tangency, where the slope of the equal-product curve just matches the slope of an equal-cost line and the curves are just kissing.

We already know that the slope of the equal-cost curves is P_L/P_A. But what is the slope of the equal-product curve? Recall from Chapter 1's appendix that the slope at a point of a curved line is the slope of the straight line tangent to the curve at the point in question. For the equal-product curve, this slope is

a "substitution ratio" between the two factors. It depends upon the relative marginal products of the two factors of production, namely, MP_L/MP_A—just as the rate of substitution between two goods along a consumer's indifference curve was earlier shown to equal the ratio of the marginal utilities of the two goods (see the appendix to Chapter 5).

Least-Cost Conditions

Using our graphical apparatus, we have therefore derived the conditions under which a firm will minimize its costs of production:

1. The ratio of marginal products of any two inputs must equal the ratio of their factor prices:

$$\text{Substitution ratio} = \frac{\text{marginal product of labor}}{\text{marginal product of land}}$$

$$= \begin{array}{c} \text{slope of} \\ \text{equal-product} \\ \text{curve} \end{array} = \frac{\text{price of labor}}{\text{price of land}}$$

2. We can also rewrite condition 1 in a different and illuminating way. From the last equation it follows that the marginal product per dollar received from the (last) dollar of expenditure must be the same for every productive input:

$$\frac{\text{Marginal product of } L}{\text{Price of } L} =$$
$$\frac{\text{marginal product of } A}{\text{price of } A} = \cdots$$

But you should not be satisfied with abstract explanations. Always remember the commonsense economic explanation which shows how a firm will distribute its expenditure among inputs to equalize the marginal product per dollar of spending.

SUMMARY TO APPENDIX

1. A production-function table lists the output that can be produced for each labor column and each land row. Diminishing returns to one variable factor, when other factors are held fixed or constant, can be shown by calculating the decline of marginal products in any row or column.

2. An equal-product curve or isoquant depicts the alternative input combinations that produce the same level of output. The slope, or substitution ratio, along such an equal-product curve equals relative marginal products (e.g., MP_L/MP_A). Curves of equal total cost are parallel lines with slopes equal to factor-price ratios

(P_L/P_A). Least-cost equilibrium comes at the tangency point, where an equal-product curve touches but does not cross the lowest TC curve. In least-cost equilib-rium, marginal products are proportional to factor prices, with equalized marginal product per dollar spent on all factors (i.e., equalized MP_i/P_i).

CONCEPTS FOR REVIEW

equal-product curves, isoquants
parallel lines of equal TC
substitution ratio $= MP_L/MP_A$

P_L/P_A as the slope of parallel equal-TC lines

least-cost tangency condition:
$MP_L/MP_A = P_L/P_A$ or $MP_L/P_L = MP_A/P_A$

QUESTIONS FOR DISCUSSION

1. Show that raising labor's wage while holding land's rent constant will steepen the gray equal-cost lines and move tangency point C in Figure 7A-3 northwest toward B, with the now-cheaper input substituted for the input which is now more expensive. If we substitute capital for labor, restate the result. Should union leaders recognize this relationship?

2. What is the least-cost combination of inputs if the production function is given by Table 7A-1 and input prices are as shown in Figure 7A-3, where $q = 346$? What would be the least-cost ratio for the same input prices if output doubled to $q = 692$? What has happened to the "factor intensity," or land-labor ratio? Can you see why this result would hold for any output change under constant returns to scale?

CHAPTER

8

Analysis of Perfectly Competitive Markets

*Cost of production
would have no effect
on competitive price if
it could have none on
supply.*

John Stuart Mill

There are two sides to every market: supply and demand. Having examined each in detail, we now put the two components together to examine how the market as a whole behaves. This first chapter on industrial organization analyzes the behavior of perfectly competitive markets; these are idealized markets in which all firms and consumers are too small to affect the price. We begin with an investigation of the supply decisions of competitive firms. We then examine some special cases of competitive markets. We conclude this chapter by showing that a perfectly competitive industry will be efficient. After we have mastered the central case of perfect competition, we move on in the following chapters to monopoly and other forms of imperfect competition.

A. SUPPLY BEHAVIOR OF THE COMPETITIVE FIRM

BEHAVIOR OF A COMPETITIVE FIRM

We begin with an analysis of perfectly competitive firms. If you own such a firm, how much should you produce? How much wheat should Farmer Smith produce if wheat sells at $3 per bushel?

In analyzing the supply behavior of perfectly competitive firms, we make two observations. First, we will assume that our competitive firm *maximizes profits.* Second, we observe that perfect competition is a world of *atomistic firms who are price-takers.*

Profit Maximization

Why would a firm want to maximize profits? Recall that profits equal total revenues minus total costs. Profits are like the net earnings or take-home pay of a business. They represent the amount a firm can pay in dividends to the owners, reinvest in new plant and equipment, or employ to make financial investments. All these activities increase the value of the firm to its owners.

Profit maximization requires the firm to manage its internal operations efficiently (prevent waste, encourage worker morale, choose efficient production processes, and so forth) and to make sound decisions in the marketplace (buy the correct quantity of inputs at least cost and choose the optimal level of output).

Because profits involve both costs and revenues, the firm must have a good grasp of its cost structure. Turn back to Table 7-3 in the previous chapter to make sure you are clear on the important concepts of total cost, average cost, and marginal cost.

Perfect Competition

Perfect competition is the world of *price-takers*. A perfectly competitive firm sells a homogeneous product (one identical to the product sold by others in the industry). It is so small relative to its market that it cannot affect the market price; it simply takes the price as given. When Farmer Smith sells a homogeneous product like wheat, she sells to a large pool of buyers at the market price of $3 per bushel. Just as consumers must generally accept the prices that are charged by Internet access providers or movie theaters, so must competitive firms accept the market prices of the wheat or oil that they produce.

We can depict a price-taking perfect competitor by examining the way demand looks to a perfectly competitive firm. Figure 8-1 shows the contrast between the industry demand curve (the *DD* curve) and the demand curve facing a single competitive firm (the *dd* curve). Because a competitive industry is populated by firms that are small relative to the market, the firm's segment of the demand curve is only a tiny segment of the industry's curve. Graphically, the competitive firm's portion of the demand curve is so small that, to the lilliputian eye of the perfect competitor, the firm's *dd* demand curve looks completely horizontal or infinitely elastic. Figure 8-1 illustrates how the elasticity of demand for a single competitor appears very much greater than that for the entire market.

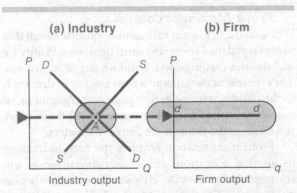

(a) Industry   (b) Firm

FIGURE 8-1. Demand Curve Is Completely Elastic for a Perfectly Competitive Firm

The industry demand curve on the left has inelastic demand at the market equilibrium at *A*. However, the demand curve for the perfectly competitive firm on the right is horizontal (i.e., completely elastic). The demand curve on the right is horizontal because a perfect competitor has such a small fraction of the market that it can sell all it wants at the market price.

Because competitive firms cannot affect the price, the price for each unit sold is the extra revenue that the firm will earn. For example, at a market price of $40 per unit, the competitive firm can sell all it wants at $40. If it decides to sell 101 units rather than 100 units, its revenue goes up by exactly $40.

Implant these key points in your long-term memory:

1. Under **perfect competition,** there are many small firms, each producing an identical product and each too small to affect the market price.
2. The perfect competitor faces a completely horizontal demand (or *dd*) curve.
3. The extra revenue gained from each extra unit sold is therefore the market price.

Competitive Supply Where Marginal Cost Equals Price

Given its costs, demand, and desire to maximize profits, how does a competitive firm decide on the amount that it will supply? Say *you* are managing Billy Bob Tucker's oil operations and must set the profit-maximizing output. Examine the data in Table 8-1, which contains the same cost data in thousands as Table 7-3 in the previous chapter. For this example, assume that the market price for oil is $40 per unit. Say Billy Bob starts out by selling 3000 units. This yields total revenue of $40 × 3000 = $120,000, with total cost of $130,000, so the firm incurs a loss of $10,000.

Now you analyze your operations and see that if you sell more oil, the revenue from each unit is $40 while the marginal cost is only $21. Additional units bring in more revenue than they cost. So you raise production to 4000 units. At this output, the firm has revenues of $40 × 4000 = $160,000 and costs of $160,000, so profits are zero.

Flush with your success, you decide to boost output some more, to 5000 units. At this output, the firm has revenues of $40 × 5000 = $200,000 and costs of $210,000. Now you're losing $10,000 again. What went wrong?

When you go back to your accounts, you see that at the output level of 5000, the marginal cost is $60, which is more than the market price of $40, so you are losing $20 (equal to price minus *MC*) on the last unit produced. Now you see the light: *The maximum-profit output comes at that output where marginal cost equals price.*

(1)	(2)	(3)	(4)	(5)	(6)	(7)
		Supply Decision of Competitive Firm				
Quantity *q*	Total cost *TC* ($)	Marginal cost per unit *MC* ($)	Average cost *AC* ($)	Price *P* ($)	Total revenue *TR* ($)	Profit π ($)
0	55,000					
1,000	85,000	27	85	40	40,000	−45,000
2,000	110,000	22	55	40	80,000	−30,000
3,000	130,000	21	43.33	40	120,000	−10,000
3,999	159,960.01	38.98	40.000+	40	159,960	−0.01
		39.99				
4,000	160,000	40	40	40	160,000	0
		40.01				
4,001	160,040.01	40.02	40.000+	40	160,040	−0.01
5,000	210,000	60	42	40	200,000	−10,000

TABLE 8-1. Profit Is Maximized at Production Level Where Marginal Cost Equals Price

This table uses the same cost data as that analyzed in Table 7-3 of the previous chapter. The dark rust marginal-cost figures in column (3) are calculated by making a tiny adjustment in output around each output level. You can see the actual *MC* of going from 3999 to 4000 units and from 4000 to 4001 units; averaging those two gives *MC* of 40 at the point of minimum average cost of 4000 units. Alternatively, the dark *MC* numbers can be read off the smooth *MC* curve.

Next, examine the profit level in column (7) associated with each output level. Note that the maximum profit comes at that output where price equals *MC*. If output is raised above that level, the additional revenue of $40 per unit is less than the additional cost, so profit is lowered. What happens if output is set below a *q* of 4000?

The reason underlying this proposition is that the competitive firm can always make additional profit as long as the price is greater than the marginal cost of the last unit. Total profit reaches its peak—is maximized—when there is no longer any extra profit to be earned by selling extra output. At the maximum-profit point, the last unit produced brings in an amount of revenue exactly equal to that unit's cost. What is that extra revenue? It is the price per unit. What is that extra cost? It is the marginal cost.

Let's test this rule by looking at Table 8-1. Starting at the profit-maximizing output of 4000 units, if Billy Bob sells 1 more unit, that unit would bring a price of $40 while the marginal cost of that unit is $40.01. So the firm would lose money on the 4001st unit. Similarly, the firm would lose $0.01 if it produced 1 less unit. This shows that the firm's

maximum-profit output comes at exactly *q* = 4000, where price equals marginal cost.

Rule for a firm's supply under perfect competition: A firm will maximize profits when it produces at that level where marginal cost equals price:

Marginal cost = price   or   *MC* = *P*

Figure 8-2 on page 150 illustrates a firm's supply decision diagrammatically. When the market price of output is $40, the firm consults its cost data in Table 8-1 and finds that the production level corresponding to a marginal cost of $40 is 4000 units. Hence, at a market price of $40, the firm will wish to produce and sell 4000 units. We can find that profit-maximizing amount in Figure 8-2 at the intersection of the price line at $40 and the *MC* curve at point *B*.

Firm's Supply and Marginal Cost

FIGURE 8-2. Firm's Supply Curve Is Its Rising Marginal Cost Curve

For a profit-maximizing competitive firm, the upward-sloping marginal cost (MC) curve is the firm's supply curve. For market price at $d'd'$, the firm will supply output at the intersection point at A. Explain why intersection points at B and C represent equilibria for prices at d and d'' respectively. The shaded gray region represents the loss from producing at A when price is \$40.

In general, then, the firm's marginal cost curve can be used to find its optimal production schedule: the profit-maximizing output will come where the price intersects the marginal cost curve.

We designed this example so that at the profit-maximizing output the firm has zero profits, with total revenues equal to total costs. (Recall that these are *economic profits* and include all opportunity costs, including the owner's labor and capital.) Point B is the **zero-profit point,** the production level at which the firm makes zero economic profits; at the zero-profit point, price equals average cost, so revenues just cover costs.

What if the firm chooses the wrong output? Suppose the firm chooses output level A in Figure 8-2 when the market price is \$40. It would be losing money because the last units have marginal cost above price. We can calculate the loss of profit if the firm mistakenly produces at A by the shaded gray triangle in Figure 8-2. This depicts the surplus of MC over price for production between B and A.

The general rule then is:

A profit-maximizing firm will set its output at that level where marginal cost equals price. Diagrammatically, this means that a firm's marginal cost curve is also its supply curve.

Total Cost and the Shutdown Condition

Our general rule for firm supply leaves open one possibility—that the price will be so low that the firm will want to shut down. Isn't it possible that at the $P = MC$ equilibrium, Billy Bob may be losing a truckful of money and would want to shut down? In general, a firm will want to shut down in the short run when it can no longer cover its variable costs.

For example, suppose the firm were faced with a market price of \$35, shown by the horizontal $d''d''$ line in Figure 8-2. At that price, MC equals price at point C, a point at which the price is actually less than the average cost of production. Would the firm want to keep producing even though it was incurring a loss?

Surprisingly, the correct answer is yes. The firm should *minimize its losses,* which is the same thing as maximizing profits. Producing at point *C* would result in a loss of only $20,000, whereas shutting down would involve losing $55,000 (which is the fixed cost). The firm should therefore continue to produce.

To understand this point, remember that a firm must still cover its contractual commitments even when it produces nothing. In the short run, the firm must pay fixed costs such as interest to the bank, rentals on the oil rigs, and directors' salaries. The balance of the firm's costs are variable costs, such as those for materials, production workers, and fuel, which would have zero cost at zero production. It will be advantageous to continue operations, with *P* at least as high as *MC,* as long as revenue covers variable costs.

The critically low market price at which revenues just equal variable costs (or, equivalently, at which losses exactly equal fixed costs) is called the **shutdown point.** For prices above the shutdown point, the firm will produce along its marginal cost curve because, even though the firm might be losing money, it would lose more money by shutting down. For prices below the shutdown point, the firm will produce nothing at all because by shutting down the firm will lose only its fixed costs. This gives the shutdown rule:

Shutdown rule: The shutdown point comes where revenues just cover variable costs or where losses are equal to fixed costs. When the price falls below average variable costs, the firm will maximize profits (minimize its losses) by shutting down.

Figure 8-3 shows the shutdown and zero-profit points for a firm. The zero-profit point comes where price is equal to *AC,* while the shutdown point comes where price is equal to *AVC.* Therefore, the firm's supply curve is the solid rust line in Figure 8-3. It first goes up the vertical axis to the price corresponding to the shutdown point; next jumps to the shutdown point at *M',* where *P* equals the level of *AVC* and then continues up the *MC* curve for prices above the shutdown price.

The analysis of shutdown conditions leads to the surprising conclusion that profit-maximizing firms may in the short run continue to operate even though they are losing money. This condition will hold particularly for firms that are heavily indebted and therefore have high fixed costs (the airlines being a good example). For these firms, as long as

Zero-Profit and Shutdown Prices

FIGURE 8-3. Firm's Supply Curve Travels Down the *MC* Curve to the Shutdown Point

The firm's supply curve corresponds to its *MC* curve as long as revenues exceed variable costs. Once price falls below P_s, the shutdown point, losses are greater than fixed costs, and the firm shuts down. Hence the solid rust curve is the firm's supply curve.

losses are less than fixed costs, profits are maximized and losses are minimized when they pay the fixed costs and still continue to operate.

Unemployed Rigs in the Drilling Industry

A striking example of the shutdown rule at work was seen in the oil industry. In 1985, when the price of crude oil was $27 a barrel, there were about 35,000 oil wells drilled in the United States. But by the next year, the number of wells being drilled had fallen by 50 percent to under 19,000. Had the oil fields run dry? Not at all. Rather, production was discouraged because the price of oil fell by almost half, to only $14 a barrel. it was the profits, not the wells, that dried up. As a result, companies just shut down many drilling rigs. This works in reverse, as well. During the Persian Gulf war in 1990, the price of oil skyrocketed and drilling activity increased as drilling became more profitable.

B. SUPPLY BEHAVIOR IN COMPETITIVE INDUSTRIES

Our discussion up to now has concerned only the individual firm. But a competitive market comprises many firms, and we are interested in the behavior of all firms together, not just a single firm. How can we move from the one to the many? From Billy Bob's operation to the entire oil industry?

SUMMING ALL FIRMS' SUPPLY CURVES TO GET MARKET SUPPLY

Suppose we are dealing with a competitive market for oil. At a given price, firm A will bring a given quantity of oil to market, firm B will bring another quantity, as will firms C, D, and so on. In each case, the quantity supplied will be determined by each firm's marginal costs. The *total* quantity brought to market at a given price will be the *sum* of the individual quantities that all firms supply at that price.[1]

This reasoning leads to the following relationship between individual and market supplies:

---

[1] Recall that the *DD* market demand curve is similarly obtained by horizontal summation of individual *dd* demand curves.

The market supply curve for a good is obtained by adding horizontally the supply curves of all the individual producers of that good.

Figure 8-4 illustrates this for two firms. To get the industry's supply curve *SS*, add horizontally, at the same price, all firms' supply curves *ss*. At a price of $40, firm A will supply 4000 units while firm B will supply 11,000 units. Therefore, the industry supply curve, shown in Figure 8-4(c), adds the two supplies together and finds total industry supply of 15,000 units at a price of $40. If there are 2 million rather than 2 firms, we would still derive industry output by adding all the 2 million individual-firm quantities at the going price. Horizontal addition of output at each price gives us the industry supply curve.

SHORT-RUN AND LONG-RUN EQUILIBRIUM

Almost a century ago, Cambridge University's great economist Alfred Marshall helped forge the supply-and-demand tools we use today. He noticed that in the short run, demand shifts produce greater price adjustments and smaller quantity adjustments than they do in the long run. We can understand this observation by distinguishing two time periods for

FIGURE 8-4. Add All Firms' Supply Curves to Derive Market Supply

The diagrams show how the market supply curve (*SS*) is composed of two individual supply curves (*ss*). We horizontally add quantities supplied by each firm at $40 to get total market supply at $40. This applies at each price and to any number of firms. If there are 1000 firms identical to firm A, the market supply curve would look like firm A's supply curve with a thousandfold change of horizontal scale.

market equilibrium that correspond to different cost categories: (1) *short-run equilibrium,* when any change in output must use the same fixed amount of capital, and (2) *long-run equilibrium,* when capital and all other factors are variable and there is free entry and exit of firms from the industry.

Entry and Exit of Firms

The long run involves "free entry and exit of firms." The birth (entry) and death (exit) of firms are important factors that affect the evolution of a market economy. Firms *enter* an industry either when they are newly formed or when an existing firm decides to move into a new sector. Firms *exit* when they stop producing; they might leave voluntarily because a line of production is unprofitable, or they might go bankrupt if the entire firm cannot pay its bills. We say that there is *free entry and exit* when there are no barriers to entry or exit, such as government regulations or intellectual property rights (e.g., patents or software).

The magnitude of births and deaths of firms in a dynamic economy like the United States is surprising. For example, there were 5½ million firms at the beginning of 1996.

In that year, 512,000 firms went out of business and 598,000 businesses were born. Most firms exit quietly, but sometimes large firms have a noisy exit, as occurred when the telecommunications giant WorldCom, with $104 billion of assets, went under because of a massive accounting fraud. In 2001–2003, the airline industry was struggling to reduce costs and capacity in the wake of terrorist threats, and several major airlines went bankrupt. Although the smooth cost curves do not always capture the drama of entry and exit, the underlying logic of *P, MC,* and *AC* is a powerful force driving the growth and decline of major industries.

Let's illustrate the distinction between short-run and long-run equilibriums with an example. Consider the market for fresh fish supplied by a local fishing fleet. Suppose the demand for fish increases; this case is shown in Figure 8-5(*a*) below as a shift from *DD* to *D'D'*. With higher prices, fishing captains will want to increase their catch. In the short run, they cannot build new boats, but they can hire extra crews and work longer hours. Increased inputs of variable factors will produce a greater quantity of fish along the *short-run supply curve* $S_S S_S$, shown in Figure 8-5(*a*).

FIGURE 8-5. Effect of Increase in Demand on Price Varies in Different Time Periods

We distinguish between periods in which firms have time to make (**a**) adjustments in variable factors such as labor (short-run equilibrium) and (**b**) full adjustment of all factors, fixed as well as varying (long-run equilibrium). The longer the time for adjustments, the greater the elasticity of supply response and the smaller the rise in price.

The short-run supply curve intersects the new demand curve at E', the point of short-run equilibrium.

The high prices lead to high profits, which in the long run coax out more shipbuilding and attract more sailors into the industry. Additionally, new firms may start up or enter the industry. This gives us the *long-run supply curve $S_L S_L$* in Figure 8-5(b) and the long-run equilibrium at E''. The intersection of the long-run supply curve with the new demand curve yields the long-run equilibrium attained when all economic conditions (including the number of ships, shipyards, and firms) have adjusted to the new level of demand.

Long-Run Industry Supply. What is the shape of the long-run supply curve for an industry? Suppose that an industry has free entry of identical firms. If the identical firms use general inputs, such as unskilled labor, that can be attracted from the vast ocean of other uses without affecting the prices of those general inputs, we get the case of constant costs shown by the horizontal $S_L S_L$ supply curve in Figure 8-6.

FIGURE 8-6. Long-Run Industry Supply Depends on Cost Conditions

With entry and exit free and any number of firms able to produce on identical, unchanged cost curves, the long-run $S_L S_L$ curve will be horizontal at each firm's minimum average cost or zero-profit price. If the industry uses a specific factor, such as scarce beachfront property, the long-run supply curve must slope upward like $S_L S_L'$ as higher production employs less well-suited inputs.

By contrast, suppose some of the inputs used in the industry are in relatively short supply—for example, fertile vineyard land for the wine industry or scarce beachfront properties for summer vacations. Then the supply curve for the wine or vacation industry must be upward-sloping, as shown by $S_L S_L'$ in Figure 8-6.

Why must the long-run supply curve of industries using scarce factors be rising? We must invoke the law of diminishing returns. For the case of the rare vineyard land, when firms apply increasing inputs of labor to fixed land, they receive smaller and smaller increments of wine-grape output; but each dose of labor costs the same in wages, so the MC of wine rises. This long-run rising MC means that the long-run supply curve must be rising.

The Long Run for a Competitive Industry

Our analysis of zero-profit conditions showed that firms might stay in business for a time even though they are unprofitable. This situation is possible particularly for firms with high fixed capital costs. With this analysis we can understand why in business downturns many of America's largest companies, such as General Motors, stayed in business even though they were losing billions of dollars.

Such losses raise a troubling question: Is it possible that capitalism is heading toward "euthanasia of the capitalists," a situation where increased competition produces chronic losses? For this question, we need to analyze the long-run shutdown conditions. We showed that firms shut down when they can no longer cover their variable costs. But in the long run, *all* costs are variable. A firm that is losing money can pay off its bonds, release its managers, and let its leases expire. In the long run, all commitments are once again options. Hence, in the long run firms will produce only when price is at or above the zero-profit condition where price equals average cost.

There is, then, a critical zero-profit point below which long-run price cannot remain if firms are to stay in business. In other words, long-run price must cover out-of-pocket costs such as labor, materials, equipment, taxes, and other expenses, along with opportunity costs such as competitive return on the owner's invested capital. That means long-run price must be equal to or above total long-run average cost.

What happens if the long-run price falls below this critical zero-profit level? Firms, not making a profit, will start leaving the industry. Since fewer firms are producing, the short-run market supply curve will shift to the left, and the price will rise (draw the graph for yourself). Eventually, the price will rise enough so that the industry is no longer unprofitable.

But the process works in the other direction as well. Suppose that the long-run price is above total long-run average cost, so firms are making positive economic profits. Now suppose entry into the industry is absolutely free in the long run, so any number of identical firms can come into the industry and produce at exactly the same costs as those firms already in the industry. In this situation, new firms will be attracted by prospective profits, the short-run supply curve shifts to the right, and price falls. Eventually it falls to the zero-profit level, so it is no longer profitable for other firms to enter the industry.

The conclusion is that in the long run, the price in a competitive industry will tend toward the critical point where identical firms just cover their full competitive costs. Below this critical long-run price, firms would leave the industry until price returns to long-run average cost. Above this long-run price, new firms would enter the industry, thereby forcing market price back down to the long-run equilibrium price where all competitive costs are just covered.

Zero-profit long-run equilibrium: In a competitive industry populated by identical firms with free entry and exit, the long-run equilibrium condition is that price equals marginal cost equals the minimum long-run average cost for each identical firm:

$P = MC$ = minimum long-run AC = zero-profit price

This is the long-run **zero-economic-profit** condition.

We have reached a surprising conclusion about the long-run profitability of competitive capitalism. The forces of competition tend to push firms and industries toward a zero-profit long-run state. In the long run, competitive firms will earn the normal return on their investment, but no more. Profitable industries tend to attract entry of new firms, thereby driving down prices and reducing profits toward zero. By contrast, firms in unprofitable industries leave to seek better profit opportunities; prices and profits then tend to rise. *The long-run equilibrium in a perfectly competitive industry is therefore one with no economic profits.*

C. SPECIAL CASES OF COMPETITIVE MARKETS

We have now developed the basic apparatus of supply and demand. This section probes more deeply into supply-and-demand analysis. We first consider certain general propositions about competitive markets and then continue with some special cases.

GENERAL RULES

We analyzed above the impact of demand and supply shifts in competitive markets. These findings apply to virtually any competitive market, whether it is for codfish, brown coal, Douglas fir, Japanese yen, IBM stock, or petroleum. Are there any general rules? The propositions that follow investigate the impact of shifts in supply or demand upon the price and quantity bought and sold. Remember always that by a shift in demand or supply we mean a shift of the demand or supply curve or schedule, not a movement along the curve.

Demand rule: (*a*) Generally, an increase in demand for a commodity (the supply curve being unchanged) will raise the price of the commodity. (*b*) For most commodities, an increase in demand will also increase the quantity demanded. A decrease in demand will have the opposite effects.

Supply rule: An increase in supply of a commodity (the demand curve being constant) will generally lower the price and increase the quantity bought and sold. A decrease in supply has the opposite effects.

These two rules of supply and demand summarize the qualitative effects of shifts in supply and demand. But the quantitative effects on price and quantity depend upon the exact shapes of the supply and demand curves. In the cases that follow, we will see the response for a number of important cost and supply situations.

Constant Cost

Production of many manufacturing items, such as textiles, can be expanded by merely duplicating factories, machinery, and labor. Producing 200,000 shirts per day simply requires that we do the same thing as we did when we were manufacturing 100,000 per day but on a doubled scale. In addition, assume that the textile industry uses land, labor, and other inputs in the same proportions as the rest of the economy.

In this case the long-run supply curve *SS* in Figure 8-7 is a horizontal line at the constant level of unit costs. A rise in demand from *DD* to *D'D'* will shift the new intersection point to *E'*, raising *Q* but leaving *P* the same.

Increasing Costs and Diminishing Returns

The last section discussed industries, such as for wine or beach properties, where a product uses an input in limited supply. In the case of wine vineyards, good sites are limited in number. The annual output of wine can be increased to some extent by adding more labor to each acre of land. But the law of diminishing returns will eventually operate if variable factors of production, such as labor, are added to fixed amounts of a factor such as land.

As a result of diminishing returns, the marginal cost of producing wine increases as wine production rises. Figure 8-8 shows the rising supply curve *SS*. How will price be affected by an increase in demand? The figure shows that higher demand will increase

FIGURE 8-8. Increasing-Cost Case

the price of this good even in the long run with identical firms and free entry and exit.

Fixed Supply and Economic Rent

Some goods or productive factors are completely fixed in amount, regardless of price. There is only one *Mona Lisa* by da Vinci. Nature's original endowment of land can be taken as fixed in amount. Raising the price offered for land cannot create an additional corner at 57th Street and Fifth Avenue in New York City. Raising the pay of star athletes is unlikely to change their effort. When the quantity supplied is constant at every price, the payment for the use of such a factor of production is called **rent** or **pure economic rent.**

When supply is independent of price, the supply curve is vertical in the relevant region. Land will continue to contribute to production no matter what its price. Figure 8-9 shows the case of land, for which a higher price cannot coax out any increase in output.

An increase in the demand for a fixed factor will affect only the price. Quantity supplied is unchanged. And the rise in price exactly equals the upward shift in demand.

When a tax is placed upon the fixed commodity, the tax is completely paid by (or "shifted" back to)

FIGURE 8-7. Constant-Cost Case

FIGURE 8-9. Factors with Fixed Supply Earn Rent

FIGURE 8-10. Backward-Bending Supply Curve

the supplier (say, the landowner). The supplier absorbs the entire tax out of economic rent. The consumer buys exactly as much of the good or service as before and at no higher price.

Backward-Bending Supply Curve

Firms in poor countries noted that when they raised wages, the local workers often worked fewer hours. When the wage was doubled, instead of continuing to work 6 days a week, the workers might work 3 days and go fishing for the other 3 days. The same has been observed in high-income countries. As improved technology raises real wages, people feel that they want to take part of their higher earnings in the form of more leisure and early retirement. Chapter 5 described income and substitution effects, which explain why a supply curve might *bend backward*.

Figure 8-10 shows what a supply curve for labor might look like. At first the labor supplied rises as higher wages coax out more labor. But beyond point *T*, higher wages lead people to work fewer hours and to take more leisure. An increase in demand raises the price of labor, as was stated in the demand rule at the beginning of this section. But note why we were cautious to add "for most commodities" to

demand rule (*b*), for now the increase in demand decreases the quantity of labor supplied.

Verification of backward-bending supply can be found in many areas. One of the most interesting examples came when oil-rich countries curbed their production of oil after the price of oil quadrupled in the early 1970s.

Shifts in Supply

All the above discussions dealt with a shift in demand and no shift in supply. To analyze the supply rule, we must now shift supply, keeping demand constant. If the law of downward-sloping demand is valid, increased supply must decrease price and increase quantity demanded. You should draw your own supply and demand curves and verify the following quantitative corollaries of the supply rule:

(*c*) An increased supply will decrease *P* most when demand is inelastic.
(*d*) An increased supply will increase *Q* least when demand is inelastic.

What are commonsense reasons for these rules? Illustrate with cases of elastic demand for autos and of inelastic demand for electricity.

D. EFFICIENCY AND EQUITY OF COMPETITIVE MARKETS

EVALUATING THE MARKET MECHANISM

One of the remarkable features of the last decade has been the "rediscovery of the market." Many countries have abandoned the heavy-handed interventionism of government command and regulation for the subtle coordination of the invisible hand. Having reviewed the basic operation of competitive markets, let's ask how well they perform. Do they deserve high grades for satisfying people's economic needs? Is society getting many guns and much butter for a given amount of inputs? Or does the butter melt on the way to the store, while the guns have crooked barrels? We will provide an overview of the efficiency of competitive markets in this chapter. Further analysis is presented in later chapters after we have discussed factor markets and the role of government.

The Concept of Efficiency

In analyzing an economy, we are centrally concerned with the concept of *allocative efficiency* or *efficiency* (sometimes called *Pareto efficiency* or *Pareto optimality*). An economy is efficient when it provides its consumers with the most desired set of goods and services, given the resources and technology of the economy.

Allocative efficiency (or **efficiency**) occurs when no possible reorganization of production can make anyone better off without making someone else worse off. Under conditions of allocative efficiency, one person's satisfaction or utility can be increased only by lowering someone else's utility.

We can think of the concept of efficiency intuitively in terms of the production-possibility frontier. An economy is clearly inefficient if it is inside the *PPF*. If we move out to the *PPF*, no one need suffer a decline in utility. At a minimum, an efficient economy is on its *PPF*. But efficiency goes further and requires not only that the right mix of goods be produced but also that these goods be allocated among consumers to maximize consumer satisfactions.

Efficiency of Competitive Equilibrium

One of the most profound results in all economics is that the allocation of resources by perfectly competitive markets is efficient. This important result assumes that all markets are perfectly competitive and that there are no externalities like pollution or imperfect information. However, even if the economy is efficient, this says nothing about the fairness of the distribution of income in competitive markets. In this section, we use a simplified example to illustrate the general principles underlying the efficiency of competitive markets.

Consider an idealized situation where all individuals are identical. Further assume: (*a*) Each person works at growing food. As people increase their work and cut back on their leisure hours, each additional hour of sweaty labor becomes increasingly tiresome. (*b*) Each extra unit of food consumed brings diminished marginal utility (*MU*).[2] (*c*) Because food production takes place on fixed plots of land, by the law of diminishing returns each extra minute of work brings less and less extra food.

Figure 8-11 shows supply and demand for our simplified competitive economy. When we sum horizontally the identical supply curves of our identical farmers, we get the upward-stepping *MC* curve. As we saw earlier in this chapter, the *MC* curve is also the industry's supply curve, so the figure shows *MC = SS*. Also, the demand curve is the horizontal summation of the identical individuals' marginal utility (or demand-for-food) curves; it is represented by the downward-stepping *MU = DD* curve for food in Figure 8-11.

The intersection of the *SS* and *DD* curves shows the competitive equilibrium for food. At point *E*, farmers supply exactly what consumers want to purchase at the equilibrium market price. Each person will be working up to the critical point where the declining marginal-utility-of-consuming-food curve intersects the rising marginal-cost-of-growing-food curve. Figure 8-11 shows a new concept, **economic surplus,** which is the rust area between the supply

---

[2] To keep matters at their simplest, we measure welfare in fixed "utils" of leisure time (or "disutils" of sweaty labor time). We further assume that each hour of forgone leisure has a constant marginal utility, so all utilities and costs are reckoned in these leisure-labor units.

FIGURE 8-11. At Competitive Equilibrium Point *E*, the Marginal Costs and Utilities of Food Are Exactly Balanced

Many identical farmer-consumers bring their food to market. The upward-stepping *MC* = *SS* curve adds together the individual marginal cost curves, while the downward-stepping *MU* = *DD* curve represents the horizontal sum of consumer valuations of food. At competitive market equilibrium *E*, the marginal gain from the last unit of food equals the marginal cost (in terms of forgone leisure) required to produce the last unit of food at *E*.

The cost of producing food is shown by the dark gray slices. The light rust slices above the *SS* curve and below the price line add up to the "producer surplus." The dark rust slices under *DD* and above the price line are the "consumer surplus." The sum of the consumer and producer surpluses is "economic surplus," or the total gain from production in this industry. Economic efficiency means that economic surplus (the total rust area) is maximized. Any other output level would reduce the economic surplus. For example, the light gray area to the right of *E* shows the economic loss from producing too much food at *FF*.

and demand curves at the equilibrium. The economic surplus is the sum of the consumer surplus that we met in Chapter 5, which is the area between the demand curve and the price line, and the **producer surplus,** which is the area between the price line and the *SS* curve. The producer surplus includes the rent and profits to firms and owners of specialized inputs in the industry and indicates the excess of revenues over cost of production.

The economic surplus is the welfare or net utility gain from production and consumption of a good; it is equal to the consumer surplus plus the producer surplus.

A careful analysis of the competitive equilibrium will show that it maximizes the economic surplus available in that industry. For this reason, it is economically efficient. At the competitive equilibrium at point *E* in Figure 8-11, the representative consumer will have higher utility or economic surplus than would be possible with any other feasible allocation of resources.

Another way of seeing the efficiency of the competitive equilibrium is by comparing the economic effect of a small change from the equilibrium at *E*. As the following three-step process shows, if *MU* = *P* = *MC*, then the allocation is efficient.

1. *P* = *MU*. Consumers choose food purchases up to the amount where *P* = *MU*. As a result, every person is gaining *P* utils of satisfaction from the last unit of food consumed. (Utils of satisfaction are measured in terms of the constant marginal utility of leisure, as discussed in footnote 2.)
2. *P* = *MC*. As producers, each person is supplying food up to the point where the price of food exactly equals the *MC* of the last unit of food supplied (the *MC* here being the cost in terms of the forgone leisure needed to produce the last unit of food). The price then is the utils of leisure-time satisfaction lost because of working to grow that last unit of food.
3. Putting these two equations together, we see that *MU* = *MC*. This means that the utils gained from the last unit of food consumed exactly equal the leisure utils lost from the time needed to produce that last unit of food. *It is exactly this condition—that the marginal gain to society from the last unit consumed equals the marginal cost to society of that last unit produced—which guarantees that a competitive equilibrium is efficient.*

Equilibrium with Many Consumers and Markets

Let us now turn from our simple parable about identical farmer-consumers to an economy populated by millions of different firms, hundreds of millions of people, and countless commodities. Can a perfectly competitive economy still be efficient in this more complex world?

The answer is "yes," or better yet, "yes, if . . ." Efficiency requires some stringent conditions that are addressed in later chapters. These include having reasonably well-informed consumers, perfectly competitive producers, and no externalities like pollution or incomplete knowledge. For such economies, a system of perfectly competitive markets will earn the economist's gold star of allocational efficiency.

Figure 8-12 illustrates how a competitive system brings about a balance between utility and cost for a single commodity with nonidentical firms and consumers. On the left, we add horizontally the demand curves for all consumers to get the market curve DD in the middle. On the right, we add all the different firms' MC curves to get the industry SS curve in the middle.

At the competitive equilibrium at point E, consumers on the left get the quantity they are willing to purchase of the good at the price reflecting efficient social MC. On the right, the equilibrium market price also allocates production efficiently among firms. The gray area under SS in the middle represents the minimized sum of the gray cost areas on the right. Each firm is setting its output so that $MC = P$. Production efficiency is achieved because there is no reorganization of production that would allow the same level of industry output to be produced at lower cost.

Many Goods. Our economy produces not only food but also clothing, movies, vacations, and many other commodities. How does our analysis apply when consumers must choose among many products?

The principles are exactly the same, but now we recall one further condition: Utility-maximizing consumers spread their dollars among different goods until the marginal utility of the last dollar is equalized for each good consumed. In this case, as long as the ideal conditions are met, a competitive economy is efficient with a multitude of goods and factors of production.

In other words, a perfectly competitive economy is efficient when marginal private cost equals marginal social costs and when both equal marginal utility. Each industry must balance MC and MU. For example, if movies have 2 times the MC of

FIGURE 8-12. Competitive Market Integrates Consumers' Demands and Producers' Costs

(a) Individual demands are shown on the left. We add the consumers' dd curves horizontally to obtain the market demand DD curve in the middle.

(b) The market brings together all consumer demands and firm supplies to reach market equilibrium at E. The horizontal price-of-food line shows where each consumer on the left and each producer on the right reach equilibrium. At P^*, see how each consumer's MU is equated to each firm's MC, leading to allocative efficiency.

(c) For each competitive firm, profits are maximized when the supply curve is given by the rising MC curve. The gray area depicts each firm's cost of producing the amount at E. At prices equal to marginal cost, the industry produces output at the least total cost.

hamburgers, the P and the MU of movies must also be twice those of hamburgers. Only then will the MUs, which are equal to the Ps, be equal to the MCs. By equating price and marginal cost, competition guarantees that an economy can attain allocative efficiency.

The perfectly competitive market is a device for synthesizing (*a*) the willingness of consumers possessing dollar votes to pay for goods with (*b*) the marginal costs of those goods as represented by firms' supply. Under certain conditions, competition guarantees efficiency, in which no consumer's utility can be raised without lowering another consumer's utility. This is true even in a world of many factors and products.

The Central Role of Marginal-Cost Pricing

This chapter has stressed the importance of competition and marginal cost in attaining an efficient allocation of resources. But the importance of marginal cost extends far beyond perfect competition. Using marginal cost to achieve production efficiency holds for any society or organization trying to make the most effective use of its resources—whether that entity is a capitalist or socialist economy, a profit-maximizing or nonprofit organization, a university or a church, or even a family.

The essential role of marginal cost in a market economy is this: Only when prices are equal to marginal costs is the economy squeezing the maximum output and satisfaction from its scarce resources of land, labor, and capital.

Only when each firm has its own marginal cost equal to each other firm's MC—as will be the case when each MC has been set equal to a common price—will the industry be producing its total output at minimum total cost. Only when price is equal to marginal cost for all firms will society be on its production-possibility frontier.

> **Marginal Cost as a Benchmark for Efficiency**
> The use of marginal cost as a benchmark for efficient resource allocation is applicable not just to profit-maximizing firms but to all economic problems, indeed to all problems involving scarcity. Suppose that you are convinced that "market socialism" should replace central planning in China. You insist that the socialist firms must produce wheat efficiently. Efficiency requires that the marginal cost of wheat and all other goods be set by equating some kind of price with the marginal cost of production for each and every farm and firm.
>
> Or suppose that you have been charged with solving a critical environmental problem, such as global warming or acid rain. You will soon find that marginal cost will be crucial to attaining your environmental objectives most efficiently. By ensuring that the marginal costs of reducing emissions or of cleaning the environment are equalized in every sector, you can guarantee that your environmental objectives are being reached at the lowest possible costs. We quickly learn that even worthy goals should be efficiently attained in a world of scarcity.

QUALIFICATIONS

We have now seen the essence of the invisible hand—the remarkable efficiency properties of competitive markets. But we must quickly qualify the analysis by pointing to shortcomings of the market.

There are two important areas where markets fail to achieve a social optimum. First, markets may be inefficient in situations where pollution or other externalities are present or when there is imperfect competition or information. Second, the distribution of incomes under competitive markets, even when it is efficient, may not be socially desirable or acceptable. We will review both of these points in later chapters, but it will be useful to describe each of these shortcomings briefly here.

Market Failures

What are the market failures which spoil the idyllic picture assumed in our discussion of efficient markets? The important ones are imperfect competition, externalities, and imperfect information.

Imperfect Competition. When a firm has market power in a particular market (say it has a monopoly because of a patented drug or a local electricity franchise), the firm can raise the price of its product above its marginal cost. Consumers buy less of such goods than they would under competition, and consumer satisfaction is reduced. This kind of reduction of consumer satisfaction is typical of the inefficiencies created by imperfect competition.

Externalities. Externalities are another important market failure. Recall that externalities arise when some of the side effects of production or consumption are not included in market prices. For example, a power company might pump sulfurous fumes into the air, causing damage to neighboring homes and to people's health. If the power company does not pay for the harmful impacts, pollution will be inefficiently high and consumer welfare will suffer.

Not all externalities are harmful. Some are beneficial, such as the externalities that come from knowledge-generating activities. For example, when Chester Carlson invented xerography, he became a millionaire; but he still received only a tiny fraction of the benefits when the world's secretaries and students were relieved of billions of hours of drudgery. Another positive externality arises from public-health programs, such as inoculation against smallpox, cholera, or typhoid; an inoculation protects not only the inoculated person but also others whom that person might otherwise have infected.

Imperfect Information. A third important market failure is imperfect information. The invisible-hand theory assumes that buyers and sellers have complete information about the goods and services they buy and sell. Firms are assumed to know about all the production functions for operating in their industry. Consumers are presumed to know about the quality and prices of goods—such as which cars are lemons or the safety and efficacy of pharmaceuticals and angioplasty.

Clearly, reality is far from this idealized world. The critical question is, How damaging are departures from perfect information? In some cases, the loss of efficiency is slight. I will hardly be greatly disadvantaged if I buy a chocolate ice cream that is slightly too sweet or if I don't know the exact temperature of the beer that flows from the tap. In other cases, the loss is severe. Take the case of steel mogul Eben Byers, who a century ago took Radithor, sold as an aphrodisiac and cure-all, to relieve his ailments. Later analysis showed that Radithor was actually distilled water laced with radium. Byers died a hideous death when his jaw and other bones disintegrated. This kind of invisible hand we don't need.

One of the important tasks of the government is to identify those areas where informational deficiencies are economically significant—such as drugs—and then to find appropriate remedies.

The Role of Government Intervention

In light of the potential inefficiencies and inequities of market capitalism, should governments intervene by regulation, corrective taxation, and income supplementation for the poor? Is society satisfied with outcomes where the maximal amount of bread is produced? Or will modern democracies take loaves from the wealthy and pass them out to the poor?

There are no scientifically correct answers here. These are normative questions appropriately answered at the ballot box. Positive economics cannot say what steps governments should take to correct the inequalities and inefficiencies of the marketplace. But economics can offer valuable insights into the potential inefficiencies and harmful side effects of alternative interventions and remedies so that the goals of a modern society can be achieved in the most effective manner.

SUMMARY

A. Supply Behavior of the Competitive Firm

1. A perfectly competitive firm sells a homogeneous product and is too small to affect the market price. Competitive firms are assumed to maximize their profits. To maximize profits, the competitive firm will choose that output level at which price equals the marginal cost of production, that is, $P = MC$. Diagrammatically, the competitive firm's equilibrium will come where the rising MC supply curve intersects its horizontal demand curve.

2. Variable costs must be taken into consideration in determining a firm's short-run shutdown point. Below

the shutdown point, the firm loses more than its fixed costs. It will therefore produce nothing when price falls below the shutdown price.

3. A competitive industry's long-run supply curve, $S_L S_L$, must take into account the entry of new firms and the exodus of old ones. In the long run, all of a firm's commitments expire. It will stay in business only if price is at least as high as long-run average costs. These costs include out-of-pocket payments to labor, lenders, material suppliers, or landlords and opportunity costs, such as returns on the property assets owned by the firm.

B. Supply Behavior in Competitive Industries

4. Each firm's rising MC curve is its supply curve. To obtain the supply curve of a group of competitive firms, we add horizontally their separate supply curves. The supply curve of the industry hence represents the marginal cost curve for the competitive industry as a whole.

5. Because firms can adjust production over time, we distinguish two different time periods: (*a*) short-run equilibrium, when variable factors like labor can change but fixed factors like capital and the number of firms cannot, and (*b*) long-run equilibrium, when the numbers of firms and plants, and all other conditions, adjust completely to the new demand conditions.

6. In the long run, when firms are free to enter and leave the industry and no one firm has any particular advantage of skill or location, competition will eliminate any excess profits earned by existing firms in the industry. So, just as free exit implies that price cannot fall below the zero-profit point, free entry implies that price cannot exceed long-run average cost in long-run equilibrium.

7. When an industry can expand its production without pushing up the prices of its factors of production, the resulting long-run supply curve will be horizontal. When an industry uses factors specific to it, such as scarce beachfront property, its long-run supply curve will slope upward.

C. Special Cases of Competitive Markets

8. Recall the general rules that apply to competitive supply and demand: Under the demand rule, an increase in the demand for a commodity (the supply curve being unchanged) will generally raise the price of the commodity and also increase the quantity demanded. A decrease in demand will have the opposite effects.

Under the supply rule, an increase in the supply of a commodity (the demand curve being constant) will generally lower the price and increase the quantity sold. A decrease in supply has the opposite effects.

9. Important special cases include constant and increasing costs, completely inelastic supply (which produces economic rents), and backward-bending supply. These special cases will explain many important phenomena found in markets.

D. Efficiency and Equity of Competitive Markets

10. The analysis of competitive markets sheds light on the efficient organization of a society. Allocative efficiency occurs when there is no way of reorganizing production and distribution such that everyone's satisfaction can be improved. Put differently, an economy is efficient when no individual can be made better off without making another individual worse off.

11. Under ideal conditions, a competitive economy attains allocative efficiency. Efficiency requires that all firms are perfect competitors and that there are no externalities like pollution or improved information. Efficiency implies that economic surplus is maximized, where economic surplus equals consumer surplus plus producer surplus.

12. Efficiency comes because (*a*) when consumers maximize satisfaction, the marginal utility (in terms of leisure) just equals the price; (*b*) when competitive producers supply goods, they choose output so that marginal cost just equals price; (*c*) since $MU = P$ and $MC = P$, it follows that $MU = MC$. Thus the marginal social cost of producing a good under perfect competition just equals its marginal utility valuation in terms of goods or leisure forgone. It is exactly this condition—that the marginal gain to society from the last unit consumed equals the marginal cost to society of that last unit produced—which guarantees that a competitive equilibrium is efficient.

13. There are exacting limits on the conditions under which an efficient competitive equilibrium can be attained: There can be no externalities and no imperfect competition, and consumers and producers must have complete information. The presence of imperfections leads to a breakdown of the *price ratio = marginal cost ratio = marginal utility ratio* conditions, and hence to inefficiency.

14. The outcome of competitive markets, even when efficient, may not be socially desirable. Competitive markets by themselves will not necessarily ensure outcomes that correspond to the society's ideals about the fair distribution of income and consumption. Societies may modify the laissez-faire equilibrium to change the income distribution to correct for a perceived unfairness of dollar votes of demand.

CONCEPTS FOR REVIEW

Competitive Supply

$P = MC$ as maximum-profit condition
firm's *ss* supply curve and its *MC*
   curve
zero-profit condition, where
   $P = MC = AC$
shutdown point, where
   $P = MC = AVC$

summing individual *ss* curves to get
   industry *SS*
short-run and long-run equilibrium
long-run zero-profit condition
producer surplus + consumer
   surplus = economic surplus
efficiency = maximizing economic
   surplus

Efficiency and Equity

allocative efficiency, Pareto efficiency
conditions for allocative efficiency:
   $MU = P = MC$
efficiency of competitive markets
efficiency vs. equity

FURTHER READING AND INTERNET WEBSITES

Further Reading

The efficiency of perfect competition is one of the major findings of microeconomics. Advanced books in microeconomics, such as those listed in Chapter 4, can give insights into the basic findings.

Nobel prizes in economics were awarded to Kenneth Arrow, John Hicks, and Gerard Debreu for their contributions to developing the theory of perfect competition and its relationship to economic efficiency. Their essays surveying the field are highly useful and are contained in Assar Lindbeck,

Nobel Lectures in Economics (University of Stockholm, 1992). See also the Nobel website listed below for the Nobel citations for these economists.

Websites

For the citations of Arrow, Hicks, and Debreu, look at the website www.nobel.se/economics/index.html to read about the importance of their contributions and how they relate to economics.

QUESTIONS FOR DISCUSSION

1. Explain why each of the following statements about profit-maximizing competitive firms is incorrect. Restate each one correctly.
   a. A competitive firm will produce output up to the point where price equals average variable cost.
   b. A firm's shutdown point comes where price is less than minimum average cost.
   c. A firm's supply curve depends only on its marginal cost. Any other cost concept is irrelevant for supply decisions.
   d. The $P = MC$ rule for competitive industries holds for upward-sloping, horizontal, and downward-sloping *MC* curves.
   e. The competitive firm sets price equal to marginal cost.

2. Suppose you are a perfectly competitive firm producing computer memory chips. Your production capacity is 1000 units per year. Your marginal cost is $10 per chip up to capacity. You have a fixed cost of $10,000 if production is positive and $0 if you shut down. What are your profit-maximizing levels of production and profit if the market price is (*a*) $5 per chip, (*b*) $15 per chip, and (*c*) $25 per chip? For case (*b*), explain why production is positive even though profits are negative.

3. One of the most important rules of economics, business, and life is the *sunk-cost principle*, "Let bygones be bygones." This means that sunk costs (which are bygone in the sense that they are unrecoverably lost) should be ignored when decisions are being made. Only future costs, involving marginal and variable costs, should count in making rational decisions.

   To see this, consider the following: We can calculate fixed costs in Table 8-1 as the cost level when output is 0. What are fixed costs? What is the profit-maximizing level of output for the firm in Table 8-1 if price is $40 while fixed costs are $0? $55,000? $100,000? $1,000,000,000? Minus $30,000? Explain the implication for a firm trying to decide whether to shut down.

4. Examine the cost data shown in Table 8-1. Calculate the supply decision of a profit-maximizing competitive firm when price is $21, $40, and $60. What would the level of total profit be for each of the three prices? What would happen to the exit or entry of identical firms in the long run at each of the three prices?

5. Using the cost data shown in Table 8-1, calculate the price elasticity of supply between $P = 40$ and $P = 40.02$ for the individual firm. Assume that there are 2000 identical firms, and construct a table showing the industry supply schedule. What is the industry price elasticity of supply between $P = 40$ and $P = 40.02$?

6. Examine Figure 8-12 to see that competitive firm C is not producing at all. Explain the reason why the profit-maximizing output level for firm C is at $q_c = 0$. What would happen to total industry cost of production if firm C produced 1 unit while firm B produced 1 less unit than the competitive output level?

Say that firm C is a mom-and-pop grocery store. Why would chain grocery stores A and B drive C out of business? How do you feel about keeping C in business? What would be the economic impact of legislation that divided the market into three equal parts between the mom-and-pop store and chain stores A and B?

7. Often, consumer demand for a commodity will depend upon the use of durable goods, such as housing or transportation. In such a case, demand will show a time-varying pattern of response similar to that of supply. A good example is gasoline. In the short run the stock of automobiles is fixed, while in the long run consumers can buy new automobiles or bicycles.

What is the relationship between the time period and the price elasticity of demand for gasoline? Sketch the short-run and long-run demand curves for gasoline. Show the impact of a decline in the supply of gasoline in both periods. Describe the impact of an oil shortage on the price of gasoline and the quantity demanded in both the long run and the short run. State two new rules of demand, (c) and (d), parallel to the rules of supply (c) and (d) discussed in the General Rules portion of Section C above, that relate the impact of a shift in supply on price and quantity in the long run and the short run.

8. Interpret this dialogue:

A: "How can competitive profits be zero in the long run? Who will work for nothing?"

B: "It is only *excess* profits that are wiped out by competition. Managers get paid for their work; owners get a normal return on capital in competitive long-run equilibrium—no more, no less."

9. Consider three firms which are emitting sulfur into the California air. We will call supply the units of pollution control or reduction. Each firm has a cost-of-reduction schedule, and we will say that these schedules are given by the MC curves of firms A, B, and C in Figure 8-12.

a. Interpret the "market" supply or MC schedule for reducing sulfur emissions, shown in the middle of Figure 8-12.

b. Say that the pollution-control authority decides to seek 10 units of pollution control. What is the efficient allocation of pollution control across the three firms?

c. Say that the pollution-control authority decides to have the first two firms produce 5 units each of pollution control. What is the additional cost?

d. Say that the pollution-control authority decides upon a "pollution charge" to reduce pollution to 10 units. Can you identify what the appropriate charge would be using Figure 8-12? Can you say how each firm would respond? Would the pollution reduction be efficient?

e. Explain the importance of marginal cost in the efficient reduction of pollution in this case.

10. In any competitive market, such as illustrated in Figure 8-11, the area above the market price line and below the *DD* curve is consumer surplus (see the discussion in Chapter 5). The area above the *SS* curve and below the price line is producer surplus and equals profits plus rent to the firms in the industry or owners of specialized inputs to the industry. The sum of the producer and consumer surpluses is economic surplus and measures the net contribution of that good to utility above the cost of production.

Can you find any reorganization of production that would increase the economic surplus in Figure 8-11 as compared to the competitive equilibrium at point *E*? If the answer is no, then the equilibrium is allocationally efficient (or Pareto-efficient). Define allocational efficiency; then answer the question and explain your answer.

Imperfect Competition and Monopoly

The best of all monopoly profits is a quiet life.

J. R. Hicks

Perfect competition is an idealized market of atomistic firms who are price-takers. In fact, while they are easily analyzed, such firms are hard to find. When you buy your car from Ford or Toyota, your hamburgers from McDonald's or Wendy's, or your computer from Dell or Apple, you are dealing with firms large enough to affect the market price. Indeed, most markets in the economy are dominated by a handful of large firms, often only two or three. Welcome to the world you live in, the world of imperfect competition.

A. PATTERNS OF IMPERFECT COMPETITION

The major kinds of imperfect competition are monopoly, oligopoly, and monopolistic competition. We shall see that for a given technology, prices are higher and outputs are lower under imperfect competition than under perfect competition. But imperfect competitors have virtues along with these vices. Large firms exploit economies of large-scale production and are responsible for much of the innovation that propels long-term economic growth. If you understand how imperfectly competitive markets work, you will have a much deeper understanding of modern industrial economies.

What exactly is perfect competition? Recall that a perfectly competitive market is one in which no firm is large enough to affect the market price. By this strict definition, few markets in the U.S. economy are perfectly competitive. Think of the following: aircraft, aluminum, automobiles, computer software, breakfast cereals, chewing gum, cigarettes, electricity distribution, refrigerators, and wheat. How many of these are sold in perfectly competitive markets? Certainly not aircraft, aluminum, or automobiles. Until World War II there was only one aluminum company, Alcoa. Even today, the four largest U.S. firms produce three-quarters of U.S. aluminum output. The world commercial-aircraft market is dominated by only two firms, Boeing and Airbus. In the automotive industry, too, the top five automakers (including Toyota and Honda) have almost 80 percent of the U.S. car and light-truck market. In the software industry, there is tremendous innovation, yet most software applications, from tax accounting to word processing, are ones in which a few firms dominate the market.

What about breakfast cereals, chewing gum, cigarettes, and refrigerators? These markets are dominated even more completely by a relatively small number of companies. Nor does the retail market in electricity meet the definition of perfect competition. In most localities, a single company distributes all the electricity used by the population. Very few of us will find it economical to build a windmill to generate our own power!

Looking at the list above, you will find that only wheat falls within our strict definition of perfect competition. All the other goods, from autos to cigarettes, fail the competitive test for a simple reason: Some of the firms in the industry can affect the market price by changing the quantity they sell. To put it another way, they have *some* control over the price of their output.

Definition of Imperfect Competition

If a firm can appreciably affect the market price of its output, the firm is classified as an "imperfect competitor."

Imperfect competition prevails in an industry whenever individual sellers have some measure of control over the price of their output.

Imperfect competition does not imply that a firm has absolute control over the price of its product. Take the cola market, where Coca-Cola and Pepsi

together have the major share of the market, and imperfect competition clearly prevails. If the average price of other producers' sodas in the market is 75 cents, Pepsi may be able to set the price of a can at 70 or 80 cents and still remain a viable firm. The firm could hardly set the price at $40 or 5 cents a can because at those prices it would go out of business. We see, then, that an imperfect competitor has some but not complete discretion over its prices.

Moreover, the amount of discretion over price will differ from industry to industry. In some imperfectly competitive industries, the degree of monopoly power is very small. In the retail computer business, for example, more than a few percent difference in price will usually have a significant effect upon a firm's sales. In the market for operating systems, by contrast, Microsoft has a virtual monopoly and has great discretion about the price of its Windows software.

Graphical Depiction. Figure 9-1 shows graphically the difference between the demand curves faced by perfectly and imperfectly competitive firms. Figure 9-1(*a*) reminds us that a perfect competitor faces a horizontal demand curve, indicating that it can sell all it wants at the going market price. An imperfect

(a) Firm Demand under Perfect Competition

(b) Firm Demand under Imperfect Competition

FIGURE 9-1. Acid Test for Imperfect Competition Is Downward Tilt of Firm's Demand Curve

(**a**) The perfectly competitive firm can sell all it wants along its horizontal *dd* curve without depressing the market price. (**b**) But the imperfect competitor will find that its demand curve slopes downward as higher price drives sales down. And unless it is a sheltered monopolist, a cut in its rivals' prices will appreciably shift its own demand curve leftward to *d'd'*.

competitor, in contrast, faces a downward-sloping demand curve. Figure 9-1(*b*) shows that if an imperfectly competitive firm increases its sales, it will definitely depress the market price of its output as it moves down its *dd* demand curve.

We can also see the difference between perfect and imperfect competition in terms of price elasticity. *For a perfect competitor, demand is perfectly elastic; for an imperfect competitor, demand has a finite elasticity.* A careful measurement will show that the price elasticity is around 2 at point *B* in Figure 9-1(*b*).

VARIETIES OF IMPERFECT COMPETITORS

A modern industrial economy like the United States is a jungle populated with many species of imperfect competition. The dynamics of the personal computer industry, driven by rapid improvements in technology, are different from the patterns of competition in the not-so-lively funeral industry. Nevertheless, much can be learned about an industry by paying careful attention to its market structure, particularly the number and size of sellers and how much of the market the largest sellers control. Economists classify imperfectly competitive markets into three different market structures.

Monopoly

How imperfect can imperfect competition get? The most extreme case is **monopoly:** a single seller with complete control over an industry. (It is called a "monopolist," from the Greek words *mono* for "one" and *polist* for "seller.") It is the only firm producing in its industry, and there is no industry producing a close substitute.

True monopolies are rare today. Most monopolies persist because of some form of government regulation or protection. For example, a pharmaceutical company that discovers a new wonder drug may be granted a patent, which gives it monopoly control over that drug for a number of years. Another important example of monopoly is a franchised local utility, such as the firm that provides your household water. In such cases there is truly a single seller of a service with no close substitutes. One of the few examples of a monopoly without government license is Microsoft Windows, which has succeeded in maintaining its monopoly through network economies along with rough (and sometimes illegal) tactics against its competitors.

But even monopolists must always be looking over their shoulders for potential competitors. The pharmaceutical company will find that a rival will produce a similar drug; telephone companies that were monopolists a decade ago now must reckon with cellular telephones; Bill Gates worries that some small firm is waiting in the wings to unseat Microsoft's monopolistic position. *In the long run, no monopoly is completely secure from attack by competitors.*

Oligopoly

The term **oligopoly** means "few sellers." Few, in this context, can be a number as small as 2 or as large as 10 or 15 firms. The important feature of oligopoly is that each individual firm can affect the market price. In the airline industry, the decision of a single airline to lower fares can set off a price war which brings down the fares charged by all its competitors.

Oligopolistic industries are relatively common in the U.S. economy, especially in the manufacturing, transportation, and communications sectors. For example, there are only a few car makers, even though the automobile industry sells many different models. The same is true in the market for household appliances: stores are filled with many different models of refrigerators and dishwashers, all made by a handful of companies. You might be surprised to know that the breakfast cereal industry is an oligopoly dominated by a few firms even though there seem to be endless varieties of cereals.

Monopolistic Competition

The last category of imperfect competition is **monopolistic competition;** this occurs when a large number of sellers produce differentiated products. This market structure resembles perfect competition in that there are many sellers, none of whom have a large share of the market. It differs from perfect competition in that the products sold by different firms are not identical. **Differentiated products** are ones whose important characteristics vary. Personal computers, for example, have differing characteristics such as speed, memory, hard disk, modem, size, and weight. Because computers are differentiated, they can sell at slightly different prices.

The classic case of monopolistic competition is the retail gasoline market. You may go to the local Shell station, even though it charges slightly more, because it is on your way to work. But if the price at Shell rises more than a few pennies above the competition, you might switch to the Merit station a short distance away.

This example illustrates the importance of location in product differentiation. It takes time to go to the bank or the grocery store, and the amount of time needed to reach different stores will affect our shopping choices. The *whole price* of a good includes not just its dollar price but also the opportunity cost of search, travel time, and other non-dollar costs. Because the whole prices of local goods are lower than those in faraway places, people generally tend to shop close to home or to work. This consideration also explains why large shopping complexes are so popular: they allow people to buy a wide variety of goods while economizing on shopping time. Today, shopping on the Internet is increasingly important because, even when shipping costs are added, the time required to buy the good online can be very low compared to getting in your car or walking to a shop.

Product quality is an increasingly important part of product differentiation today. Goods differ in their characteristics as well as their prices. Most personal computers can run the same software, and there are many manufacturers. Yet the personal computer industry is a monopolistically competitive industry, because computers differ in speed, size, memory, repair services, and ancillaries like CDs, DVDs, Internet connections, and sound systems. Indeed, a whole batch of monopolistically competitive computer magazines is devoted to explaining the differences among the computers produced by the monopolistically competitive computer manufacturers!

Competition vs. Rivalry

When studying oligopolies, it is important to recognize that imperfect competition is not the same as no competition. Indeed, some of the most vigorous rivalries in the economy occur in markets where there are but a few firms. Just look at the cutthroat competition in the airline industry, where

Types of Market Structures				
Structure	Number of producers and degree of product differentiation	Part of economy where prevalent	Firm's degree of control over price	Methods of marketing
Perfect competition	Many producers; identical products	Financial markets and agricultural products	None	Market exchange or auction
Imperfect competition				
Monopolistic competition	Many producers; many real or perceived differences in product	Retail trade (pizzas, beer, . . .), personal computers	Some	Advertising and quality rivalry; administered prices
Oligopoly	Few producers; little or no difference in product	Steel, chemicals, . . .		
	Few producers; products are differentiated	Cars, word-processing software, . . .		
Monopoly	Single producer; product without close substitutes	Franchise monopolies (electricity, water); Microsoft Windows; patented drugs	Considerable	Advertising

TABLE 9-1. Alternative Market Structures

Most industries are imperfectly competitive. Here are the major features of different market structures.

two or three airlines may fly a particular route but still engage in periodic fare wars.

How can we distinguish the rivalry of oligopolists from perfect competition? Rivalry encompasses a wide variety of behavior to increase profits and market share. It includes advertising to shift out the demand curve, price cuts to attract business, and research to improve product quality or develop new products. Perfect competition says nothing about rivalry but simply means that no single firm in the industry can affect the market price.

Table 9-1 on page 169 gives a picture of the various possible categories of imperfect and perfect competition. This table is an important summary of the different kinds of market structure and warrants careful study.

SOURCES OF MARKET IMPERFECTIONS

Why do certain industries display near-perfect competition while others are dominated by a handful of large firms? Most cases of imperfect competition can be traced to two principal causes. First, industries tend to have fewer sellers when there are significant economies of large-scale production and decreasing costs. Under these conditions, large firms can simply produce more cheaply and then undersell small firms, which cannot survive.

Second, markets tend toward imperfect competition when there are "barriers to entry" that make it difficult for new competitors to enter an industry. In some cases, the barriers may arise from government laws or regulations which limit the number of competitors. In other cases, there may be economic factors that make it expensive for a new competitor to break into a market. We will examine both sources of imperfect competition.

Costs and Market Imperfection

The technology and cost structure of an industry help determine how many firms that industry can support and how big they will be. The key is whether there are economies of scale in an industry. If there are economies of scale, a firm can decrease its average costs by expanding its output, at least up to a point. That means bigger firms will have a cost advantage over smaller firms.

When economies of scale prevail, one or a few firms will expand their outputs to the point where they produce most of the industry's total output. The industry then becomes imperfectly competitive. Perhaps a single monopolist will dominate the industry; a more likely outcome is that a few large sellers will control most of the industry's output; or there might be a large number of firms, each with slightly different products. Whatever the outcome, we must inevitably find some kind of imperfect competition instead of the atomistic perfect competition of price-taking firms.

Many industries enjoy increasing returns to scale. Numerous detailed econometric and engineering studies confirm that many nonagricultural industries show declining average long-run costs. For example, Table 9-2 shows the results of one study of six U.S. industries. It suggests that in many industries the point of minimum average cost occurs at a large fraction of industry output—10 or 20 or even 50 percent. These industries will tend to be oligopolistic, since they can support only a few large producers.

To understand further how costs may determine market structure, let's look at a case which is favorable for perfect competition. Figure 9-2(a) shows an industry where the point of minimum average cost is reached at a relatively low level of output. Any firm which tries to expand its output beyond this point will find its costs rapidly rising. As a result, this industry can support the large number of efficiently operating firms that are needed for perfect competition. Figure 9-2(a) illustrates the cost curves in the perfectly competitive farm industry.

Now consider Figure 9-2(b), which shows an industry where firms enjoy increasing returns to scale up to a point, above which the scale economies are exhausted and average costs begin to increase. However, the AC curve is relatively flat and does not turn up soon enough to avoid the breakdown of perfect competition; that is, the limited demand curve of the industry allows only a small number of firms to coexist at the point of minimum average cost. Such a cost structure will tend to lead to oligopoly. Most manufacturing industries in the United States—including steel, automobiles, cement, and oil—have a demand and cost structure similar to the one in Figure 9-2(b).

A final important case is natural monopoly. A **natural monopoly** is a market in which the industry's

Industry	(1) Share of U.S. output needed by a single firm to exploit economies of scale (%)	(2) Actual average market share of top three firms (%)	(3) Reasons for economies of large-scale operations
Beer brewing	10–14	13	Need to create a national brand image and to coordinate investment
Cigarettes	6–12	23	Advertising and image differentiation
Glass bottles	4–6	22	Need for central engineering and design staff
Cement	2	7	Need to spread risk and raise capital
Refrigerators	14–20	21	Marketing requirements and length of production runs
Petroleum	4–6	8	Need to spread risk on crude-oil ventures and coordinate investment

TABLE 9-2. Industrial Competition Is Based on Cost Conditions

This study examined the impact of cost conditions on concentration patterns. Column (1) shows the estimate of the point where the long-run average cost curve begins to turn up, as a share of industry output. Compare this with the average market share of each of the top three firms in column (2).

Source: F. M. Scherer and David Ross, *Industrial Market Structure and Economic Performance*, 3d ed. (Houghton Mifflin, Boston, 1990).

FIGURE 9-2. Market Structure Depends on Relative Cost and Demand Factors

Cost and demand conditions affect market structures. In perfectly competitive (**a**), total industry demand *DD* is so vast relative to the efficient scale of a single seller that the market allows viable coexistence of numerous perfect competitors. In (**b**), costs turn up at a higher level of output relative to total industry demand *DD*. Coexistence of numerous perfect competitors is impossible, and oligopoly will emerge. When costs fall rapidly and indefinitely, as in the case of natural monopoly in (**c**), one firm can expand to monopolize the industry.

output can be efficiently produced only by a single firm. This occurs when the technology exhibits economies of scale over a range of output that is as large as the entire demand. Figure 9-2(c) shows the cost curves of a natural monopolist. The technology has perpetual increasing returns to scale, and average and marginal costs therefore fall forever. As output grows, the firm can charge lower and lower prices and still make a profit, since its average cost is falling. So peaceful competitive coexistence of thousands of perfect competitors will be quite impossible because one large firm is so much more efficient than a collection of small firms.

Some important examples of natural monopolies are the local distribution in telephone, electricity, gas, and water as well as long-distance links in railroads, highways, and electrical transmission. Many of the most important natural monopolies are "network industries" (see the discussion in Chapter 6). Technological advances, however, can undermine natural monopolies. Most of the U.S. population is now served by two cellular telephone networks, which use radio waves instead of wires and are undermining the demand for landline telephone services. Similar trends in other markets, such as cable TV, are occurring as competitors invade these natural monopolies and are turning them into hotly contested oligopolies.

Barriers to Entry

Although cost differences are the most important factor behind market structures, barriers to entry can also prevent effective competition. **Barriers to entry** are factors that make it hard for new firms to enter an industry. When barriers are high, an industry may have few firms and limited pressure to compete. Economies of scale act as one common type of barrier to entry, but there are others, including legal restrictions, high cost of entry, advertising, and product differentiation.

Legal Restrictions. Governments sometimes restrict competition in certain industries. Important legal restrictions include patents, entry restrictions, and foreign-trade tariffs and quotas. A *patent* is granted to an inventor to allow temporary exclusive use (or monopoly) of the product or process that is patented. For example, pharmaceutical companies are often granted valuable patents on new drugs in which they have invested hundreds of millions of

research-and-development dollars. Patents are one of the few forms of government-granted monopolies that are generally approved of by economists. Governments grant patent monopolies to encourage inventive activity. Without the prospect of monopoly patent protection, a company or a sole inventor might be unwilling to devote time and resources to research and development. The temporarily high monopoly price and the resulting inefficiency is the price society pays for the invention.

Governments also impose *entry restrictions* on many industries. Typically, utilities, such as telephone, electricity distribution, and water, are given *franchise monopolies* to serve an area. In these cases, the firm gets an exclusive right to provide a service, and in return the firm agrees to limit its profits and provide universal service in its region even when some customers might be unprofitable.

Historians who study the tariff have written, "The tariff is the mother of trusts." (See question 10 at the end of this chapter for an analysis of this subject.) This is because government-imposed *import restrictions* have the effect of keeping out foreign competitors. It could very well be that a single country's market for a product is only big enough to support two or three firms in an industry, while the world market is big enough to support a large number of firms. Then a protectionist policy might change the industry structure from Figure 9-2(a) to (b) or even to (c). When markets are broadened by abolishing tariffs in a large free-trade area, vigorous and effective competition is encouraged and monopolies tend to lose their power. One of the most dramatic examples of increased competition has come in the European Union, which has lowered tariffs among member countries steadily over the last three decades and has benefited from larger markets for firms and lower concentration of industry.

High Cost of Entry. In addition to legally imposed barriers to entry, there are economic barriers as well. In some industries the price of entry simply may be very high. Take the commercial-aircraft industry, for example. The high cost of designing and testing new airplanes serves to discourage potential entrants into the market. It is likely that only two companies—Boeing and Airbus—can afford the $10 to $15 billion that the next generation of aircraft will cost to develop.

In addition, companies build up intangible forms of investment, and such investments might be very expensive for any potential new entrant to match. Consider the software industry. Once a spreadsheet program (like Excel) or a word-processing program (like Microsoft Word) has achieved wide acceptability, potential competitors find it difficult to make inroads into the market. Users, having learned one program, are reluctant to switch to another. Consequently, in order to get people to try a new program, any potential entrant will need to run a big promotional campaign, which would be expensive and may still result in failure to produce a profitable product. (Recall our discussion of network effects in Chapter 6.)

Advertising and Product Differentiation. Sometimes it is possible for companies to create barriers to entry for potential rivals by using advertising and product differentiation. Advertising can create product awareness and loyalty to well-known brands. For example, Pepsi and Coca-Cola spend hundreds of millions of dollars per year advertising their brands, which makes it very expensive for any potential rivals to enter the cola market.

In addition, product differentiation can impose a barrier to entry and increase the market power of producers. In many industries—such as breakfast cereals, automobiles, household appliances, and cigarettes—it is common for a small number of manufacturers to produce a vast array of different brands, models, and products. In part, the variety appeals to the widest range of consumers. But the enormous number of differentiated products also serves to discourage potential competitors. The demands for each of the individual differentiated products will be so small that they will not be able to support a large number of firms operating at the bottom of their U-shaped cost curves. The result is that perfect competition's *DD* curve in Figure 9-2(*a*) contracts so far to the left that it becomes like the demand curves of oligopoly or monopoly shown in Figure 9-2(*b*) and (*c*). Hence, differentiation, like tariffs, produces greater concentration and more imperfect competition.

What Is the Value of a Brand?

In a world of differentiated products, some firms earn fancy profits because of the value of their brands. Brand value is established when a firm has a product that is seen as better, more reliable, or tastier than other products, branded or non-branded. According to estimates by *Business Week* magazine, the brands with the highest values in 2003 were the following:[1]

Rank	Brand	Brand value, 2003 ($, billion)
1	Coca-Cola	70.5
2	Microsoft	65.2
3	IBM	51.8
4	GE	42.3
5	Intel	31.1
6	Nokia	29.4
7	Disney	28.0
8	McDonald's	24.7
9	Marlboro	22.2
10	Mercedes	21.4

Thus, for Coca-Cola, the market value of the firm was $70 billion more than would be justified by its plant, equipment, and other assets. How do firms establish and maintain brand value? First, they usually have an innovative product, such as a new drink or operating system, a cute cartoon figure, or a high-quality automobile. Second, they maintain their brand value by heavy advertising, often associating a product like Marlboro cigarettes with a good-looking character in a romantic setting. Third, they protect their brands using intellectual property rights such as patents and copyrights. In one sense, brand value is the residue of past innovative activity.

B. MARGINAL REVENUE AND MONOPOLY

In this section we will consider the most extreme form of imperfect competition, monopoly. Our analysis will illustrate the major drawbacks of imperfect competition, which are that it restricts output and raises prices. As an essential part of this analysis, we will define a new concept, marginal revenue, which will turn out to have important applications for oligopolists and perfect competitors as well.

[1] *Business Week*, August 4, 2003, available on the Internet at bwnt.businessweek.com/brand/2003/index.asp.

THE CONCEPT OF MARGINAL REVENUE

Price, Quantity, and Total Revenue

Suppose that a firm finds itself in possession of a complete monopoly in its industry. The firm might be the fortunate owner of a patent for a new anticancer drug, or it might own the operating code to a valuable computer program. If the monopolist wishes to maximize its profits, what price should it charge and what output level should it produce?

To answer these questions, we need a new concept, *marginal revenue* (or *MR*). From the firm's demand curve, we know the relationship between price (P) and quantity sold (q). These are shown in columns (1) and (2) of Table 9-3 and as the black demand curve (dd) for the monopolist in Figure 9-3(a).

We next calculate the total revenue at each sales level by multiplying price times quantity. Column (3) of Table 9-3 shows how to calculate the **total revenue** (*TR*), which is simply $P \times q$. Thus 0 units bring in *TR* of 0; 1 unit brings in $TR = \$180 \times 1 = \$180$; 2 units bring in $\$160 \times 2 = \$320$; and so forth.

In this example of a straight-line or linear demand curve, total revenue at first rises with output, since the reduction in P needed to sell the extra q is moderate in this upper, elastic range of the demand curve. But when we reach the midpoint of

		Total and Marginal Revenue	
(1) Quantity q	**(2)** Price $P = AR = TR/q$ ($)	**(3)** Total revenue $TR = P \times q$ ($)	**(4)** Marginal revenue *MR* ($)
0	200	0	
			+180
1	180	180	
			+140
2	160	320	
			+100
3	140	420	
			+60
4	120	480	+40
			+20
5	100	500	
6	80	480	—
			−60
7	60	—	
			−100
8	40	320	
			−140
9	—	180	
			−180
10	0	0	

TABLE 9-3. Marginal Revenue Is Derived from Demand Schedule

Total revenue (*TR*) in column (3) comes from multiplying P by q. To get marginal revenue (*MR*), we increase q by a unit and calculate the change in total revenue. *MR* is less than P because of the lost revenue from lowering the price on previous units to sell another unit of q. Note that *MR* is positive when demand is elastic. But after demand turns inelastic, *MR* becomes negative even though price is still positive.

(a) Marginal Revenue

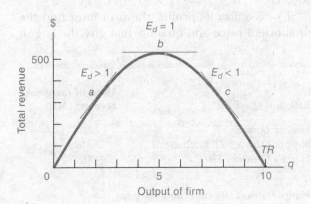

(b) Total Revenue

the straight-line demand curve, *TR* reaches its maximum. This comes at $q = 5$, $P = \$100$, with $TR = \$500$. Increasing q beyond this point brings the firm into the inelastic demand region. For inelastic demand, reducing price increases sales less than proportionally, so total revenue falls. Figure 9-3(*b*) shows *TR* to be dome-shaped, rising from zero at a very high price to a maximum of $500 and then falling to zero as price approaches zero.

How could you find the price at which revenues are maximized? You would see in Table 9-3 that *TR* is maximized when $q = 5$ and $P = 100$. This is the point where the demand elasticity is exactly 1.

Note that the price per unit can be called *average revenue* (*AR*) to distinguish it from total revenue. Hence, we get $P = AR$ by dividing *TR* by q (just as we earlier got *AC* by dividing *TC* by q). Verify that if column (3) had been written down before column (2), we could have filled in column (2) by division.

Marginal Revenue and Price

The final new concept is marginal revenue.

Marginal revenue (*MR*) is the change in revenue that is generated by an additional unit of sales. *MR* can be either positive or negative.

Table 9-3 shows marginal revenue in column (4). *MR* is calculated by subtracting the total revenues of adjacent outputs. When we subtract the *TR* we get by selling q units from the *TR* we get by selling $q + 1$ units, the difference is extra revenue or *MR*. Thus, from $q = 0$ to $q = 1$, we get $MR = \$180 - \$0$. From $q = 1$ to $q = 2$, *MR* is $\$320 - \$180 = \$140$.

FIGURE 9-3. Marginal Revenue Curve Comes from Demand Curve

(a) The rust steps show the increments of total revenue from each extra unit of output. *MR* falls below *P* from the beginning. *MR* becomes negative when *dd* turns inelastic. Smoothing the incremental steps of *MR* gives the smooth, thin rust *MR* curve, which in the case of straight line *dd* will always have twice as steep a slope as *dd*.

(b) Total revenue is dome-shaped—rising from zero where $q = 0$ to a maximum (where *dd* has unitary elasticity) and then falling back to zero where $P = 0$. *TR*'s slope gives smoothed *MR* just as jumps in *TR* give steps of incremental *MR*.

Source: Table 9-3.

MR is positive until we arrive at $q = 5$ and negative from then on. What does the strange notion of negative marginal revenue mean? That the firm is paying people to take its goods? Not at all. *Negative* MR *means that in order to sell additional units, the firm must decrease its price on earlier units so much that its total revenues decline.*

For example, when the firm sells 5 units, it gets

$$TR\,(5 \text{ units}) = 5 \times \$100 = \$500$$

Now say the firm wishes to sell an additional unit of output. Because it is an imperfect competitor, it can increase sales only by lowering price. So to sell 6 units, it lowers the price from \$100 to \$80. It gets \$80 of revenue from the sixth unit, but it gets only $5 \times \$80$ on the first 5 units, yielding

$$TR\,(6 \text{ units}) = (5 \times \$80) + (1 \times \$80)$$
$$= \$400 + \$80 = \$480$$

Marginal revenue between 5 and 6 units is $\$480 - \$500 = -\$20$. The necessary price reduction on the first 5 units was so large that, even after adding in the sale of the sixth unit, total revenue fell. This is what happens when *MR* is negative. To test your understanding, fill in the blanks in columns (2) to (4) of Table 9-3.

Note that even though *MR* is negative, *AR*, or price, is still positive. Do not confuse marginal revenue with average revenue or price. Table 9-3 shows that they are different. In addition, Figure 9-3(*a*) plots the demand (*AR*) curve and the marginal revenue (*MR*) curve. Scrutinize Figure 9-3(*a*) to see that the plotted rust steps of *MR* definitely lie below the black *dd* curve of *AR*. In fact, *MR* turns negative when *AR* is halfway down toward zero.

To summarize:

With demand sloping downward,

$P > MR\,(= P -$ reduced revenue on all previous $q)$

Elasticity and Marginal Revenue

What is the relationship between the price elasticity of demand and marginal revenue?

Marginal revenue is positive when demand is elastic, zero when demand is unit-elastic, and negative when demand is inelastic.

This result is an important implication of the definition of elasticity that we used in Chapter 4. Recall that demand is elastic when a price decrease leads to a revenue increase. In such a situation, a price decrease raises output demanded so much that revenues rise, so marginal revenue is positive. For example, in Table 9-3, as price falls in the elastic region from $P = \$180$ to $P = \$160$, output demanded rises sufficiently to raise total revenue, and marginal revenue is positive.

What happens when demand is unit-elastic? A percentage price cut then just matches the percentage output increase, and marginal revenue is therefore zero. Can you see why marginal revenue is always negative in the inelastic range? Why is the marginal revenue for the perfect competitor's infinitely elastic demand curve always positive?

Table 9-4 shows the important elasticity relationships. Make sure you understand them and can apply them.

PROFIT-MAXIMIZING CONDITIONS

We are now ready to find the maximum-profit equilibrium of the monopolist. If a monopolist faces a given demand curve and wishes to maximize total profit (*TP*), what should it do? By definition, total profit equals total revenue minus total costs; in symbols, $TP = TR - TC = (P \times q) - TC$.

To maximize its profits, the firm must find the equilibrium price and quantity that give the largest

If demand is	Relation of Q and P	Effect of Q on *TR*	Value of marginal revenue (*MR*)
Elastic ($E_D > 1$)	% change Q > % change P	Higher Q raises *TR*	$MR > 0$
Unit-elastic ($E_D = 1$)	% change Q = % change P	Higher Q leaves *TR* unchanged	$MR = 0$
Inelastic ($E_D < 1$)	% change Q < % change P	Higher Q lowers *TR*	$MR < 0$

TABLE 9-4. Relationships of Demand Elasticity, Output, Price, Revenue, and Marginal Revenue

profit, or the largest difference between *TR* and *TC*. The major finding is that *maximum profit will occur when output is at that level where the firm's marginal revenue is equal to its marginal cost.*

One way to determine this maximum-profit condition is by using a table of costs and revenues, such as Table 9-5. To find the profit-maximizing quantity and price, compute total profit in column (5). This column tells us that the monopolist's best quantity, which is 4 units, requires a price of $120 per unit. This produces a total revenue of $480, and, after subtracting total costs of $250, we calculate total profit to be $230. A glance shows that no other price-output combination has as high a level of total profit.

A second and equivalent way of arriving at the same answer is to compare marginal revenue, column (6), and marginal cost, column (7). As long as each additional unit of output provides more revenue than it costs—that is to say, as long as *MR* is greater than *MC*—the firm's profit will increase. So the firm should continue to increase its output as long as *MR* is greater than *MC*. By contrast, suppose that at a given level of output *MR* is less than *MC*. This means that increasing output would lead to a lower level of profits, so the profit-maximizing firm should at that point cut back on output. Clearly, the best-profit point comes at the point where marginal revenue exactly equals marginal cost, as is shown by the data in Table 9-5. The rule for finding maximum profit is therefore:

			Summary of Firm's Maximum Profit				
(1)	(2)	(3)	(4)	(5)	(6)	(7)	
		Total	Total	Total	Marginal	Marginal	
	Price	revenue	cost	profit	revenue	cost	
Quantity	*P*	*TR*	*TC*	*TP*	*MR*	*MC*	
q	($)	($)	($)	($)	($)	($)	
0	200	0	145	−145			
					+180	30	*MR > MC*
1	180	180	175	+5			
					+140	25	
2	160	320	200	+120			
					+100	20	
3	140	420	220	+200			
					+60	30	
4*	120*	480	250	+230	+40	40	*MR = MC*
					+20	50	
5	100	500	300	+200			
					−20	70	
6	80	480	370	+110			
					−60	90	
7	60	420	460	−40			
					−100	110	*MR < MC*
8	40	320	570	−250			

*Maximum-profit equilibrium.

TABLE 9-5. Equating Marginal Cost to Marginal Revenue Gives Firm's Maximum-Profit *q* and *P*

Total and marginal costs of production are now brought together with total and marginal revenues. The maximum-profit condition is where *MR* = *MC*, with *q** = 4, *P** = $120, and maximum *TP* = $230 = ($120 × 4) − $250.

The maximum-profit price (P^*) and quantity (q^*) of a monopolist come where the firm's marginal revenue equals its marginal cost:

$MR = MC$, at the maximum-profit P^* and q^*

These examples show the logic of the $MC = MR$ rule for maximizing profits, but we always want to understand the intuition behind the rules. Look for a moment at Table 9-5 and suppose that the monopolist is producing $q = 2$. At that point, its MR for producing 1 full additional unit is +$100, while its MC is $20. Thus, if it produced 1 additional unit, the firm would make additional profits of $MR - MC = \$100 - \$20 = \$80$. Indeed, column (5) of Table 9-5 shows that the extra profit gained by moving from 2 to 3 units is exactly $80.

Thus, when MR exceeds MC, additional profits can be made by increasing output; when MC exceeds MR, additional profits can be made by decreasing q. Only when $MR = MC$ can the firm maximize profits, because there are no additional profits to be made by changing its output level.

Monopoly Equilibrium in Graphs

Figure 9-4 shows the monopoly equilibrium. Part (*a*) combines the firm's cost and revenue curves. The maximum-profit point comes at that output where

---

FIGURE 9-4. Profit-Maximizing Equilibrium Can Be Shown Using Either Total or Marginal Curves

(a) At E, where MC intersects MR, the equilibrium position of maximum profit is found. Any move from E will lose some profit. Price is on the demand curve at G, above E; and since P is above AC, the maximized profit is a positive profit. (Can you explain why the rust-shaded rectangle measures total profit? And why the gray triangles of shading on either side of E show the reduction in total profit that would come from a departure from $MR = MC$?)

Panel (**b**) tells the same story of maximizing profit as does (**a**), but it uses total concepts rather than marginal concepts. The TR curve shows the total revenue, while the TC curve shows total cost. (Why is TR equal to 0 at $q = 0$ and at $q = 10$?) Total profit (TP) is equal to TR minus TC, or geometrically as the vertical distance from TC up to TR. At the maximum-profit point, the difference between the total revenue and total cost curves is at its maximum. The slope of each curve is that curve's marginal value (e.g., the slope of TR is the MR). At the maximum profit, TR and TC are parallel and therefore have equal slopes, $MR = MC$.

(a) Profit Maximization

(b) Total Cost, Revenue, and Profit

MC equals *MR*, which is given at their intersection at *E*. The monopoly equilibrium, or maximum-profit point, is at an output of $q^* = 4$. To find the profit-maximizing price, we run vertically up from *E* to the *dd* curve at *G*, where $P^* = \$120$. The fact that average revenue at *G* lies above average cost at *F* guarantees a positive profit. The actual amount of profit is given by the rust area in Figure 9-4(*a*).

The same story is told in part (*b*) with curves of total revenue, cost, and profit. Total revenue is dome-shaped. Total cost is ever rising. The vertical difference between them is total profit, which begins negative and ends negative. In between, *TP* is positive, reaching its maximum of \$230 at $q^* = 4$. At the maximum-profit output, the black slopes of *TR* and *TC* (which are *MR* and *MC* at those points) are parallel and therefore equal. If the slopes were pointing outward in a non-parallel fashion (as at $q = 2$), the firm would gain extra profit by expanding *q*. At $q^* = 4$, marginal cost and marginal revenue are balanced. At that point total profit (*TP*) reaches its maximum, as an additional unit adds exactly equal amounts to costs and revenues.

A monopolist will maximize its profits by setting output at the level where $MC = MR$. Because the monopolist has a downward-sloping demand curve, this means that $P > MR$. Because price is above marginal cost for a profit-maximizing monopolist, the monopolist reduces output below the level that would be found in a perfectly competitive industry.

Perfect Competition as a Polar Case of Imperfect Competition

Although we have applied the *MC* and *MR* rule to monopolists that desire to maximize profits, this rule is actually applicable far beyond the present analysis. A little thought shows that the $MC = MR$ rule applies with equal validity to a profit-maximizing perfect competitor. We can see this in two steps:

1. MR *for a perfect competitor.* The first question is, What is *MR* for a perfect competitor? For a perfect competitor, the sale of extra units will never depress price, and the "lost revenue on all previous *q*" is therefore equal to zero. Price and marginal revenue are identical for perfect competitors.

   Under perfect competition, price equals average revenue equals marginal revenue ($P = AR = MR$). A perfect competitor's *dd* curve and its *MR* curve coincide as horizontal lines.

2. $MR = P = MC$ *for a perfect competitor.* In addition, we can see that the logic of profit maximization for monopolists applies equally well to perfect competitors, but the result is a little different. Economic logic shows that profits are maximized at that output level where *MC* equals *MR*. But by step 1 above, for a perfect competitor, *MR* equals *P*. Therefore, the $MR = MC$ profit-maximization condition becomes the special case of $P = MC$ that we derived in the last chapter for a perfect competitor:

   Because a perfect competitor can sell all it wants at the market price, $MR = P = MC$ at the maximum-profit level of output.

You can see this result visually by redrawing Figure 9-4(*a*). If the graph applied to a perfect competitor, the *dd* curve would be horizontal at the market price, and it would coincide with the *MR* curve. The profit-maximizing $MR = MC$ intersection would also come at $P = MC$. We see then how the general rule for profit maximization applies to perfect as well as imperfect competitors.

THE MARGINAL PRINCIPLE: LET BYGONES BE BYGONES

We close this chapter with a more general point about the use of marginal analysis in economics. While economic theory will not necessarily make you fabulously wealthy, it does introduce you to some new ways of thinking about costs and benefits. *One of the most important lessons of economics is that you should look at the marginal costs and marginal benefits of decisions and ignore past or sunk costs.* We might put this as follows:

Let bygones be bygones. Don't look backward. Don't cry over spilt milk or moan about yesterday's losses. Make a hard-headed calculation of the extra costs you'll incur by any decision, and weigh these against its extra advantages. Make a decision based on marginal costs and marginal benefits.

This is the **marginal principle,** which means that people will maximize their incomes or profits or satisfactions by counting only the marginal costs and marginal benefits of a decision. There are countless situations in which the marginal principle applies. We have just seen that the marginal principle of equating marginal cost and marginal revenue is the rule for profit maximization by firms. Another example is investment decisions. When deciding about whether to invest in a company or sell a house, forget about past gains or losses and decide only on the basis of marginal returns and costs. The marginal principle is one of the central lessons of economics.

Monopolists of the Gilded Age

Economic abstractions sometimes hide the human drama of monopoly, so we close this section by recounting one of the most colorful periods of American business history. Because of changing laws and customs, monopolists in today's America bear little resemblance to the brilliant, unscrupulous, and often dishonest robber barons of the Gilded Age (1870–1914). Legendary figures like Rockefeller, Gould, Vanderbilt, Frick, Carnegie, Rothschild, and Morgan were driven to create entire industries like railroads or oil, provide their finance, develop the western frontier, destroy their competitors, and pass on fabulous fortunes to their heirs.

The last three decades of nineteenth-century America experienced robust economic growth lubricated by tremendous graft and corruption. Daniel Drew was a cattle rustler, horse trader, and railroader who mastered the trick of "watering the stock." This practice involved depriving his cattle of water until they reached the slaughterhouse; he then induced a great thirst with salt and allowed the beasts to engorge themselves on water just before being weighed. Later, tycoons would "water their stock" by inflating the value of their securities.

The railroaders of the American frontier west were among the most unscrupulous entrepreneurs on record. The transcontinental railroads were funded with vast federal land grants, aided by bribes and stock gifts to numerous members of Congress and the cabinet. Shortly after the Civil War, the wily railroader Jay Gould attempted to corner the entire gold supply of the United States, and with it the nation's money supply. Gould later promoted his railroad by describing the route of his northern line—snowbound much of the year—as a tropical paradise, filled with orange groves, banana plantations, and monkeys. By century's end, all the bribes, land grants, watered stock, and fantastic promises had led to the greatest rail system in the world.

The story of John D. Rockefeller epitomizes the nineteenth-century monopolist. Rockefeller saw visions of riches in the fledgling oil industry and began to organize oil refineries. He was a meticulous manager and sought to bring "order" to the quarrelsome wildcatters. He bought up competitors and consolidated his hold on the industry by persuading the railroads to give him deep and secret rebates and supply information about his competitors. When competitors stepped out of line, Rockefeller's railroads refused to ship their oil and even dumped it on the ground. By 1878, John D. controlled 95 percent of the pipelines and oil refineries in the United States. Prices were raised and stabilized, ruinous competition was ended, and monopoly was achieved.

Rockefeller devised an ingenious new device to ensure control over his alliance. This was the "trust," in which the stockholders turned their shares over to "trustees" who would then manage the industry to maximize its profits. Other industries imitated the Standard Oil Trust, and soon trusts were set up in kerosene, sugar, whiskey, lead, salt, and steel.

These practices so upset agrarians and populists that the nation soon passed antitrust laws (see Chapter 17). In 1910, the Standard Oil Corporation was dissolved in the first great victory by the Progressives against "Big Business." Ironically, Rockefeller actually profited from the breakup because the price of Standard Oil shares soared when they were offered to the public.

Great monopolies produced great wealth. Whereas the United States had three millionaires in 1861, there were 4000 of them by 1900 ($1 million at the turn of the century is equivalent to about $100 million in today's dollars).

Great wealth in turn begot conspicuous consumption (a term introduced into economics by Thorstein Veblen in *The Theory of the Leisure Class,* 1899). Like European popes and aristocrats of an earlier era, American tycoons wanted to transform their fortunes into lasting monuments. The wealth was spent in constructing princely palaces such as the "Marble House," which can still be seen in Newport, Rhode Island; in buying vast art collections, which form the core of the great American museums like New York's Metropolitan Museum of Art; and in launching foundations and universities such as those named after Stanford, Carnegie, Mellon, and Rockefeller. Long after their private monopolies were broken up by the government or overtaken by competitors, and long after their wealth was largely dissipated by heirs and overtaken by later generations of entrepreneurs, the philanthropic legacy of the robber barons continues to shape American arts, science, and education.[2]

---

[2] See the Further Reading section for books on this topic.

SUMMARY

A. Patterns of Imperfect Competition

1. Most market structures today fall somewhere on a spectrum between perfect competition and pure monopoly. Under imperfect competition, a firm has some control over its price, a fact seen as a downward-sloping demand curve for the firm's output.

2. Important kinds of market structure are (a) monopoly, where a single firm produces all the output in a given industry; (b) oligopoly, where a few sellers of a similar or differentiated product supply the industry; (c) monopolistic competition, where a large number of small firms supply related but somewhat differentiated products; and (d) perfect competition, where a large number of small firms supply an identical product. In the first three cases, firms in the industry face downward-sloping demand curves.

3. Economies of scale, or decreasing average costs, are the major source of imperfect competition. When firms can lower costs by expanding their output, perfect competition is destroyed because a few companies can produce the industry's output most efficiently. When the minimum efficient size of plant is large relative to the national or regional market, cost conditions produce imperfect competition.

4. In addition to declining costs, other forces leading to imperfect competition are barriers to entry in the form of legal restrictions (such as patents or government regulation), high entry costs, advertising, and product differentiation.

B. Marginal Revenue and Monopoly

5. We can easily derive a firm's total revenue curve from its demand curve. From the schedule or curve of total revenue, we can then derive marginal revenue, which denotes the change in revenue resulting from an additional unit of sales. For the imperfect competitor, marginal revenue is less than price because of the lost revenue on all previous units of output that will result when the firm is forced to drop its price in order to sell an extra unit of output. That is, with demand sloping downward,

$$P = AR > MR = P - \text{lost revenue on all previous } q$$

6. Recall Table 9-4's rules relating demand elasticity, price and quantity, total revenue, and marginal revenue.

7. A monopolist will find its maximum-profit position where $MR = MC$, that is, where the last unit it sells brings in extra revenue just equal to its extra cost. This same $MR = MC$ result can be shown graphically by the intersection of the MR and MC curves or by the equality of the slopes of the total revenue and total cost curves. In any case, *marginal revenue = marginal cost* must always hold at the equilibrium position of maximum profit.

8. For perfect competitors, marginal revenue equals price. Therefore, the profit-maximizing output for a competitor comes where $MC = P$.

9. Economic reasoning leads to the important *marginal principle*. In making decisions, count marginal future advantages and disadvantages, and disregard sunk costs that have already been paid.

CONCEPTS FOR REVIEW

Patterns of Imperfect Competition	Marginal Revenue and Monopoly	$MR = P$, $P = MC$, for perfect
perfect vs. imperfect competition	marginal (or extra) revenue, MR	competitor
monopoly, oligopoly, monopolistic competition	$MR = MC$ as the condition for maximizing profits	natural monopoly
product differentiation		the marginal principle
barriers to entry (government and economic)		

FURTHER READING AND INTERNET WEBSITES

Further Reading

The theory of monopoly was developed by Alfred Marshall around 1890; see his *Principles of Economics,* 9th ed. (Macmillan, New York, 1961).

An excellent review of monopoly and industrial organization is F. M. Scherer and David Ross, *Industrial Market Structure and Economic Performance,* 3d ed. (Houghton Mifflin, Boston, 1990).

The Gilded Age period gave birth to "yellow journalism" in the United States and fostered many muckraking histories, such as Matthew Josephson, *The Robber Barons* (New York,

Harcourt Brace, 1934). A more balanced recent account is Ron Chernow, *Titan: The Life of John D. Rockefeller, Sr.* (Random House, New York, 1998).

Websites

An important legal case over the last decade has concerned whether Microsoft had a monopoly on PC operating systems. This is thoroughly discussed in the "Findings of Fact" of the Microsoft antitrust case by Judge Thomas Penfield Jackson (November 5, 1999). His opinion and further developments can be found at www.microsoft.com/presspass/legalnews.asp.

QUESTIONS FOR DISCUSSION

1. List the distinguishing features of perfect and imperfect competition. What are the main varieties of imperfect competition? In which category would you place General Motors? Your local pizza restaurant? Microsoft? Your college or university?

2. Explain why each of the following statements is false. For each, write the correct statement.
   a. A monopolist maximizes profits when $MC = P$.
   b. The higher the price elasticity, the higher is a monopolist's price above its MC.
   c. Monopolists ignore the marginal principle.
   d. Monopolists will maximize sales. They will therefore produce more than perfect competitors and their price will be lower.

3. What is MR's numerical value when dd has unitary elasticity? Explain.

4. In his opinion in the Microsoft antitrust case, Judge Jackson wrote: "[T]hree main facts indicate that Microsoft enjoys monopoly power. First, Microsoft's share of the market for Intel-compatible PC operating systems is extremely large and stable. Second, Microsoft's dominant market share is protected by a high barrier to entry. Third, and largely as a result of that barrier, Microsoft's customers lack a commercially viable alternative to Windows." (See the website reference, section 34, in this chapter's Further Readings.) Why are these elements related to monopoly? Are all three necessary? If not, which ones are crucial? Explain your reasoning.

5. Figure 9-4 shows the maximum-profit equilibrium position. Explain in detail how it really shows two different ways of describing exactly the same fact: namely, that a firm will stop expanding its production where the extra cost of further output just balances its extra revenue.

6. Redraw Figure 9-4(*a*) for a perfect competitor. Why is *dd* horizontal? Explain why the horizontal *dd* curve coincides with *MR*. Then proceed to find the profit-maximizing *MR* and *MC* intersection. Why does this yield the competitive condition $MC = P$? Now redraw Figure 9-4(*b*) for a perfect competitor. Show that the slopes of *TR* and *TC* must still match at the maximum-profit equilibrium point for a perfect competitor.

7. Banana Computer Company has fixed costs of production of $100,000, while each unit costs $600 of labor and $400 of materials and fuel. At a price of $3000, consumers would buy no Banana computers, but for each $10 reduction in price, sales of Banana computers increase by 1000 units. Calculate marginal cost and marginal revenue for Banana Computer, and determine its monopoly price and quantity.

8. Show that a profit-maximizing monopolist will never operate in the price-inelastic region of its demand curve.

9. Explain the error in the following statement: "A firm out to maximize its profits will always charge the highest price that the traffic will bear." State the correct result, and use the concept of marginal revenue to

explain the difference between the correct and the erroneous statements.

10. Recall from page 180 how trusts were organized to monopolize industries like oil and steel. Explain the saying, "The tariff is the mother of trusts." Use Figure 9-2 to illustrate your analysis. Use the same diagram to explain why lowering tariffs and other trade barriers reduces monopoly power.

11. *For students who like calculus:* You can show the condition for profit maximization easily using calculus. Define

$TP(q)$ = total profits, $TC(q)$ = total costs, and $TR(q)$ = total revenues. Marginal this-or-that is the derivative of this-or-that with respect to output, so $dTR/dq = TR'(q) = MR$ = marginal revenue.

a. Explain why $TP = TR - TC$.

b. Show that a maximum of the profit function comes where $TC'(q) = TR'(q)$. Interpret this finding.

Oligopoly and Monopolistic Competition

Putnam (Braniff Airlines): *Do you have a suggestion for me?*

Crandall (American Airlines): *Yes. I have a suggestion for you. Raise your . . . fares 20% and I'll raise mine the next morning. . . . You'll make more money and I will too.*

Putnam: *We can't talk about pricing.*

Crandall: *Oh . . ., Howard. We can talk about any . . . thing we want to talk about.*

A tape-recorded conversation between Howard Putnam, head of Braniff Airlines, and Robert Crandall, head of American Airlines

Earlier chapters analyzed the market structures of perfect competition and complete monopoly. If you look out the window at the American economy, however, you'll find that such polar cases are rare; you are more likely to see varieties of imperfect competition between these two extremes. Most industries are populated by a small number of firms competing with each other.

What are the key features of these intermediate types of imperfect competitors? How do they set their prices? To answer this question, we look closely at what happens under oligopoly and monopolistic competition, paying special attention to the role of concentration and strategic interaction. The next section then focuses on large corporations, since these are the predominant form of economic organization in the modern capitalist economy. We end the chapter with a comparison of the economic costs and benefits of imperfect competition.

A. BEHAVIOR OF IMPERFECT COMPETITORS

Look back at Table 9-1, which shows the following kinds of market structures: (1) *Perfect competition* is found when a large number of firms produce an identical product. (2) *Monopolistic competition* occurs when a large number of firms produce slightly differentiated products, while (3) *oligopoly* is an intermediate form of imperfect competition in which an industry is dominated by a few firms. The most concentrated market structure is (4) *monopoly,* in which a single firm produces the entire output of an industry.

In many situations—such as deciding whether government should intervene in a market or whether a firm has abused its monopoly position—economists need a quantitative measure of the extent of market power. **Market power** signifies the degree of control that a single firm or a small number of firms have over the price and production decisions in an industry.

Measures of Market Power

The most common measure of market power is the *concentration ratio* for an industry, illustrated in Figure 10-1. The **four-firm concentration ratio** is defined as the percent of total industry production (or shipments) that is accounted for by the largest four firms. Similarly, the eight-firm concentration ratio is the percent of output shipped by the top eight firms.

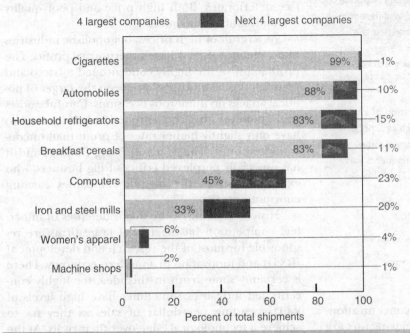

Concentration Measured by Value of Shipments in Manufacturing Industries, 1997

■ 4 largest companies   ■ Next 4 largest companies

Industry	4 largest	Next 4 largest
Cigarettes	99%	1%
Automobiles	88%	10%
Household refrigerators	83%	15%
Breakfast cereals	83%	11%
Computers	45%	23%
Iron and steel mills	33%	20%
Women's apparel	6%	4%
Machine shops	2%	1%

Percent of total shipments

FIGURE 10-1. Concentration Ratios Are Quantitative Measures of Market Power

For refrigerators, automobiles, and many other industries, a few firms produce most of the domestic output. Compare this with the ideal of perfect competition, in which each firm is too small to affect the market price.

Source: U.S. Bureau of the Census, 1997 data.

In a pure monopoly, the four- and eight-firm concentration ratios would be 100 percent because one firm produces 100 percent of the output, while for perfect competition, both ratios would be close to zero because even the largest firms produce a tiny fraction of industry output.

Many economists believe that traditional concentration ratios do not adequately measure market power. An alternative, which better captures the role of dominant firms, is the **Herfindahl-Hirschman Index (HHI).** This is calculated by summing the squares of the percentage market shares of all participants in a market. Perfect competition would have an HHI of near zero, while complete monopoly has an HHI of 10,000. (For the formula and an example, see question 2 at the end of this chapter.)

To illustrate the difference between these two measures, the four-firm concentration ratios in the beer and airline industries are not far apart (85 and 71 percent, respectively). Yet the beer industry is dominated by Anheuser-Busch, while the market share of the leading airline is much smaller. So when we calculate the alternative index, the beer industry has an HHI of 2757 while the airline industry's is only 1434.

Warning on Concentration Measures

Although concentration measures are widely used in economics and in law, they are often misleading because of international competition and structural change. Conventional concentration measures include only domestic production and exclude imports. Because foreign competition has risen sharply over the last three decades, the actual market power of domestic firms is much less than is indicated by conventional measures. As a result, in industries which are exposed to international competition, concentration ratios will overstate the extent of market power. For example, the conventional concentration measure shown in Figure 10-1 indicates that the top four automotive firms had 88 percent of the market. But if imports are included in sales, these same four firms had only 60 percent of the market.

In addition, concentration measures ignore the impact of competition from other industries. For example, concentration ratios have historically been calculated for a narrow industry definition, such as paired-wire telephone services. Sometimes, however, strong competition comes from other quarters. Cellular telephones provide a major threat to conventional paired-wire local telephone service even though the two are produced by different industries. To reflect this technological convergence, the Federal Communications Commission now reviews mergers among telecommunications firms by using market shares that aggregate different segments such as cable TV, cellular, and paired-wired telephony.

In the end, some measure of concentration of a market is essential for many legal purposes, such as aspects of antitrust law examined in Chapter 17. A careful delineation of the market which includes all competitors can be helpful in determining whether monopolistic abuses are a real threat.

THE NATURE OF IMPERFECT COMPETITION

In analyzing the determinants of concentration, economists have found that three major factors are at work in imperfectly competitive markets. These factors are economies of scale, barriers to entry, and strategic interaction (the first two were analyzed in the previous chapter, and the third is the subject of detailed examination in the next chapter):

- *Costs.* When the minimum efficient size of operation for a firm occurs at a sizable fraction of industry output, only a few firms can profitably survive and oligopoly is likely to result.
- *Barriers to competition.* When there are large economies of scale or government restrictions to entry, they will limit the number of competitors in an industry.
- *Strategic interaction.* When only a few firms operate in a market, they will soon recognize their interdependence. **Strategic interaction,** which is a genuinely new feature of oligopoly that has inspired the field of game theory, occurs when each firm's business depends upon the behavior of its rivals.

Why are economists particularly concerned about industries characterized by imperfect competition? The answer is that such industries behave in certain ways that are inimical to the public interest. For example, imperfect competition generally leads to prices that are above marginal costs. Sometimes,

without the spur of competition, the quality of service deteriorates. Both high price and poor quality are undesirable outcomes.

As a result of high prices, oligopolistic industries often (but not always) have supernormal profits. The profitability of the highly concentrated tobacco and pharmaceutical industries has been the target of political attacks on numerous occasions. Careful studies show, however, that concentrated industries tend to have only slightly higher rates of profit than unconcentrated ones. This is a surprising finding, and it has especially perplexed critics of big business, who expected to find the biggest companies earning enormous profits.

Historically, one of the major defenses of imperfect competition has been that large firms are responsible for most of the research and development (R&D) and innovation in a modern economy. There is certainly some truth in this idea, for highly concentrated industries sometimes have high levels of R&D spending per dollar of sales as they try to achieve a technological edge over their rivals. At the same time, individuals and small firms have produced many of the greatest technological breakthroughs. We will review this important question in detail later in this chapter.

THEORIES OF IMPERFECT COMPETITION

While the concentration of an industry is important, it does not tell the whole story. Indeed, to explain the behavior of imperfect competitors, economists have developed a field called *industrial organization*. We cannot cover this vast area here. Instead, we will focus on three of the most important cases of imperfect competition—collusive oligopoly, monopolistic competition, and small-number oligopoly.

Collusive Oligopoly

The degree of imperfect competition in a market is influenced not just by the number and size of firms but by their behavior. When only a few firms operate in a market, they see what their rivals are doing and react. For example, if there are two airlines operating along the same route and one raises its fare, the other must decide whether to match the increase or to stay with the lower fare, undercutting its rival.

Strategic interaction is a term that describes how each firm's business strategy depends upon its rivals' business behavior.

When there are only a small number of firms in a market, they have a choice between *cooperative* and *noncooperative* behavior. Firms act noncooperatively when they act on their own without any explicit or implicit agreement with other firms. That's what produces price wars. Firms operate in a cooperative mode when they try to minimize competition. When firms in an oligopoly actively cooperate with each other, they engage in **collusion.** This term denotes a situation in which two or more firms jointly set their prices or outputs, divide the market among themselves, or make other business decisions jointly.

During the early years of American capitalism, before the passage of effective antitrust laws, oligopolists often merged or formed a trust or cartel (recall Chapter 9's discussion of trusts, page 180). A **cartel** is an organization of independent firms, producing similar products, that work together to raise prices and restrict output. Today, with only a few exceptions, it is strictly illegal in the United States and most other market economies for companies to collude by jointly setting prices or dividing markets. (The antitrust laws pertaining to such behavior are discussed in Chapter 17.)

Nonetheless, firms are often tempted to engage in tacit collusion, which occurs when they refrain from competition without explicit agreements. When firms tacitly collude, they often quote identical high prices, pushing up profits and decreasing the risk of doing business. A recent examination found that about 9 percent of major corporations have admitted to or been convicted of illegal price fixing. In recent years, makers of infant formula, scouring pads, and kosher Passover products have been investigated for price fixing, while private universities, art dealers, the airlines, and the telephone industry have been accused of collusive behavior.

The rewards of successful collusion can be great. Imagine a four-firm industry—call the firms A, B, C, and D—where all the rivals have tired of ruinous price wars. They tacitly agree to charge the same price and not undercut each other. The firms hope to form a **collusive oligopoly** by finding the price which maximizes their joint profits. Figure 10-2 illustrates oligopolist A's situation. A's demand curve, $D_A D_A$, is drawn assuming that the other firms all

FIGURE 10-2. Collusive Oligopoly Looks Much Like Monopoly

After experience with disastrous price wars, firms will surely recognize that each price cut is canceled by competitors' price cuts. So oligopolist A may estimate its demand curve $D_A D_A$ by assuming that others will be charging similar prices. When firms collude to set a jointly profit-maximizing price, the price will be very close to that of a single monopolist. Can you see why profits are equal to the gray rectangle?

follow A's pricing policy and charge the same prices; each firm's demand curve will have the same elasticity as the industry's *DD* curve. Firm A will get one-fourth of the shared market as long as all firms charge the same price.

The maximum-profit equilibrium for the collusive oligopolist is shown in Figure 10-2 at point *E*, the intersection of the firm's *MC* and *MR* curves. Here, the appropriate demand curve is $D_A D_A$, which recognizes that the other firms will charge the same price as A. The optimal price for the collusive oligopolist is shown at point *G* on $D_A D_A$, just above point *E*. This price is identical to the monopoly price: it is well above marginal cost and earns the colluding oligopolists a handsome monopoly profit.

When oligopolists can collude to maximize their joint profits, taking into account their mutual interdependence, they will produce the monopoly output and price and earn the monopoly profit.

Although many oligopolists would be delighted to earn such high profits, in reality many obstacles hinder effective collusion. First, collusion is illegal. Second, firms may "cheat" on the agreement by cutting their price to selected customers, thereby increasing their market share. Clandestine price cutting is particularly likely in markets where prices are secret, where goods are differentiated, where there is more than a handful of firms, or where the technology is changing rapidly. Third, the growth of international trade means that many companies face intensive competition from foreign firms as well as domestic companies.

Indeed, experience shows that running a successful cartel is a difficult business, whether the collusion is explicit or tacit.

A long-running thriller in this area is the story of the international oil cartel known as the Organization of Petroleum Exporting Countries, or OPEC. OPEC is an international organization which sets production quotas for its members, which include Saudi Arabia, Iran, and Algeria. Its stated goal is "to secure fair and stable prices for petroleum producers; an efficient, economic and regular supply of petroleum to consuming nations; and a fair return on capital to those investing in the industry." Its critics claim it is really a collusive monopolist attempting to maximize the profits of producing countries.

OPEC became a household name in 1973, when it reduced production sharply and oil prices skyrocketed. But a successful cartel requires that members set a low production quota and maintain discipline. Every few years, price competition breaks out when some OPEC countries ignore their quotas. This happened in a spectacular way in 1986, when Saudi Arabia drove oil prices from $28 per barrel down to below $10. It is particularly hard to enforce a cartel among parties that hate each other or even—as with Iraq, Iran, and Kuwait—are fighting real wars as well as price wars.

Another problem faced by OPEC is that it must negotiate production quotas rather than prices. This may lead to high levels of price volatility because demand is unpredictable and highly price-inelastic. Oil prices are frequently volatile when political events heat up in the Middle East—most recently in the run-up to the Iraq invasion in early 2003.

The airline industry is another example of a market with a history of repeated—and failed—attempts at collusion. It would seem a natural candidate for collusion. There are only a few major airlines, and on many routes there are only one or two rivals. But just look back to the quote at the beginning of the chapter, where an airline executive proposed a collusive price-fixing arrangement. Since then, Braniff has gone bankrupt twice. Two major airlines, United and US Airways, went bankrupt in the wake of the terrorist attacks of September 11, 2001. If collusion among the airlines existed, it clearly did not make the industry profitable. Indeed, the evidence shows that the only time an airline can charge supernormal fares is when it has a near-monopoly on all flights to a city.

Monopolistic Competition

At the other end of the spectrum from collusive oligopolies is **monopolistic competition.** Monopolistic competition resembles perfect competition in three ways: there are many buyers and sellers, entry and exit are easy, and firms take other firms' prices as given. The distinction is that products are identical under perfect competition, while under monopolistic competition they are differentiated.

Monopolistic competition is very common—just scan the shelves at any supermarket and you'll see a dizzying array of different brands of breakfast cereals, shampoos, and frozen foods. Within each product group, products or services are different, but close enough to compete with each other. Here are some other examples of monopolistic competition: There may be several grocery stores in a neighborhood, each carrying the same goods but at different locations. Gas stations, too, all sell the same product, but they compete on the basis of location and brand name. The several hundred magazines on a newsstand rack are monopolistic competitors, as are the 50 or so competing brands of personal computers. The list is endless.

For our analysis, the important point is that product differentiation means each seller has some freedom to raise or lower prices, more so than in a perfectly competitive market. *Product differentiation leads to a downward slope in each seller's demand curve.* Figure 10-3 might represent a monopolistically competitive fishing magazine which is in short-run equilibrium at G. The firm's dd demand curve shows the relationship between sales and its price when other magazine prices are unchanged; its demand

Monopolistic Competition before Entry

FIGURE 10-3. Monopolistic Competitors Produce Many Similar Goods

Under monopolistic competition, numerous small firms sell differentiated products and therefore have downward-sloping demand. Each firm takes its competitors' prices as given. Equilibrium has $MR = MC$ at E, and price is at G. Because price is above AC, the firm is earning a profit, area $ABGC$.

Monopolistic Competition after Entry

FIGURE 10-4. Free Entry of Numerous Monopolistic Competitors Wipes Out Profit

The typical seller's original profitable dd curve in Fig. 10-3 will be shifted downward and leftward to $d'd'$ by the entry of new rivals. Entry ceases only when each seller has been forced into a long-run, no-profit tangency such as at G'. At long-run equilibrium, price remains above MC, and each producer is on the left-hand declining branch of its long-run AC curve.

curve slopes downward since this magazine is a little different from everyone else's because of its special focus. The profit-maximizing price is at G. Because price at G is above average cost, the firm is making a handsome profit represented by area $ABGC$.

But our magazine has no monopoly on writers or newsprint or insights on fishing. Firms can enter the industry by hiring an editor, having a bright new idea and logo, locating a printer, and hiring workers. Since the fishing magazine industry is profitable, entrepreneurs bring new fishing magazines into the market. With their introduction, the demand curve for the products of existing monopolistically competitive fishing magazines shifts leftward as the new magazines nibble away at our magazine's market.

The ultimate outcome is that fishing magazines will continue to enter the market until all economic profits (including the appropriate opportunity costs for owners' time, talent, and contributed capital) have been beaten down to zero. Figure 10-4 shows

the final long-run equilibrium for the typical seller. In equilibrium, the demand is reduced or shifted to the left until the new $d'd'$ demand curve just touches (but never goes above) the firm's AC curve. Point G' is a long-run equilibrium for the industry because profits are zero and no one is tempted to enter or forced to exit the industry.

This analysis is well illustrated by the personal computer industry. Originally, such computer manufacturers as Apple and Compaq made big profits. But the personal computer industry turned out to have low barriers to entry, and numerous small firms entered the market. Today, there are dozens of firms, each with a small share of the computer market but no economic profits to show for its efforts.

The monopolistic competition model provides an important insight into American capitalism: The rate of profit will in the long run be zero in this kind of imperfectly competitive industry as firms enter with new differentiated products.

In the long-run equilibrium for monopolistic competition, prices are above marginal costs but economic profits have been driven down to zero.

Some critics believe that monopolistic competition is inherently inefficient, even though profits are zero in the long run. They argue that monopolistic competition breeds an excessive number of new products and that eliminating unnecessary product differentiation could really cut costs and lower prices. To understand their reasoning, look back at the long-run equilibrium price at G' in Figure 10-4. At that point, price is above marginal cost; hence, output is reduced below the ideal competitive level.

This economic critique of monopolistic competition has considerable appeal. It takes real ingenuity to demonstrate the gains to human welfare from adding Apple Cinnamon Cheerios to Honey Nut Cheerios and Whole Grain Cheerios. It is sometimes hard to see the reason for gasoline stations on every corner of an intersection. But there is logic to the great variety of goods and services produced by a modern market economy. Reducing the number of monopolistic competitors, while cutting costs, might well end up lowering consumer welfare because it would reduce the diversity of available products. Centrally planned socialist countries tried to standardize output to a small number of goods—a standard uniform of gray shirts, so to speak—but their consumers became highly dissatisfied when they looked at the variety available in market economies. People will pay a premium to be free to choose.

Rivalry among the Few

For our third example of imperfect competition, we turn back to markets in which only a few firms compete. This time, instead of focusing on collusion, we consider the fascinating case where firms have a strategic interaction with each other. Strategic interaction is found in any market which has relatively few competitors. Like a tennis player trying to outguess her opponent, each business must ask how its rivals will react to changes in key business decisions. If GE introduces a new model of refrigerator, what will Whirlpool, its principal rival, do? If American Airlines lowers its transcontinental fares, how will United react?

Consider as an example the market for air shuttle services between New York and Washington, currently served by Delta and US Airways. This market is called a **duopoly** because it is served by two firms. Suppose that Delta has determined that if it cuts fares 10 percent, its profits will rise as long as US Airways does not match its cut but its profits will fall if US Airways does match its price cut. If they cannot collude, Delta must make an educated guess as to how US Airways will respond to its price moves. Its best approach would be to estimate how US Airways would react to each of its actions and then to maximize profits *with strategic interaction recognized*. This analysis is the province of game theory, to which we turn shortly.

Similar strategic interactions are found in many large industries: in television, in automobiles, even in economics textbooks. Unlike the simple approaches of monopoly and perfect competition, it turns out that there is no simple theory to explain how oligopolists behave. Different cost and demand structures, different industries, even different temperaments on the part of the firms' managers will lead to different strategic interactions and to different pricing strategies. Sometimes, the best behavior is to introduce some randomness into the response simply to keep the opposition off balance.

Competition among the few introduces a completely new feature into economic life: It forces firms to take into account competitors' reactions to price and output deviations and brings strategic considerations into their markets.

Game Theory

To analyze strategic interactions more carefully, economists rely upon a fascinating area of economic theory known as *game theory*. This is the analysis of situations involving two or more interacting decision makers who have conflicting objectives. Consider the following findings of game theorists in the area of imperfect competition:

- As the number of noncooperative oligopolists becomes large, industry price and quantity tend toward the perfectly competitive outcome.
- If firms decide to collude rather than compete, the market price and quantity will be close to those generated by a monopoly. But experiments suggest that as the number of firms increases,

collusive agreements become more difficult to police and the frequency of cheating and non-cooperative behavior increases.

- In many situations, there is no stable equilibrium for oligopoly. Strategic interplay may lead to unstable outcomes as firms threaten, bluff, start price wars, capitulate to stronger firms, punish weak opponents, signal their intentions, or simply exit from the market.

The next chapter explores the theory of games in greater depth.

PRICE DISCRIMINATION

When firms have market power, they can sometimes increase their profits through price discrimination. **Price discrimination** occurs when the same product is sold to different consumers for different prices.

Consider the following example. You run a company selling a successful personal-finance program called MyMoney. Your marketing manager comes in and says:

Look, boss. Our market research shows that our buyers fall into two categories: (1) our current customers, who are locked into MyMoney because they keep their financial records using our program, and (2) potential new buyers who have been using other programs. Why don't we raise our price, but give a rebate to new customers who are willing to switch from our competitors? I've run the numbers. If we raise our price from $20 to $30 but give a $15 rebate for people who have been using other financial programs, we will make a bundle.

You are intrigued by the suggestion. Your house economist constructs the demand curves in Figure 10-5. Her research indicates that your old customers have more price-inelastic demand than your potential new customers because new customers must pay substantial switching costs. If your rebate program works and you succeed in segmenting the market, the numbers show that your profits will rise from $1200 to $1350. (To make sure you understand the analysis, use the data shown in Figure 10-5 to estimate the monopoly price and profits if you set a single monopoly price and if you price-discriminate between the two markets.)

FIGURE 10-5. Firms Can Increase Their Profits through Price Discrimination

You are a profit-maximizing monopoly seller of computer software with zero marginal cost. Your market contains established customers in **(a)** and new customers in **(b)**. Old customers have more inelastic demand because of the high costs of switching to other programs.

If you must set a single price, you will maximize profits at a price of $20 and earn profits of $1200. But suppose you can segment your market between locked-in current users and reluctant new buyers. This would increase your profits to ($30 × 30) + ($15 × 30) = $1350.

Price discrimination is widely used today, particularly with goods that are not easily transferred from the low-priced market to the high-priced market. Here are some examples:

- Identical textbooks are sold at lower prices in Europe than in the United States. What prevents wholesalers from purchasing large quantities abroad and undercutting the domestic market? A protectionist import quota prohibits the practice. However, as an individual, you might well reduce the costs of your books by buying them abroad through online bookstores.

- Airlines are the masters of price discrimination (review our discussion of "Elasticity Air" in Chapter 4). They segment the market by pricing tickets differently for those who travel in peak or off-peak times, for those who are business or pleasure travelers, and for those who are willing to stand by. This allows them to fill their planes without eroding revenues.

- Local utilities often use "two-part prices" (sometimes called nonlinear prices) to recover some of their overhead costs. If you look at your telephone or electricity bill, it will generally have a "connection" price and a "per-unit" price of service. Because connection is much more price-inelastic than the per-unit price, such two-part pricing allows sellers to lower their per-unit prices and increase the total quantity sold.

- Firms engaged in international trade often find that foreign demand is more elastic than domestic demand. They will therefore sell at lower prices abroad than at home. This practice is called "dumping" and is sometimes banned under international-trade agreements.

- Sometimes a company will actually *degrade* its top-of-the-line product to make a less capable product, which it will then sell at a discounted price to capture a low-price market. For example, IBM inserted special commands to slow down its laser printer from 10 pages per minute to 5 pages per minute so that it could sell the slow model at a lower price without cutting into sales of its top model.

What are the economic effects of price discrimination? Surprisingly, they often improve economic welfare. To understand this point, recall that monopolies raise their price and lower their sales to increase profits. In doing so, they may capture the market for eager buyers but lose the market for reluctant buyers. By charging different prices for those willing to pay high prices (who get charged high prices) and those willing to pay only lower prices (who may sit in the middle seats or get a degraded product, but at a lower price), the monopolist can increase both its profits and consumer satisfactions.[1]

B. INNOVATION AND INFORMATION

The world of imperfect competition contains many different species, from huge corporations to tiny e-commerce vendors on the Internet. Much of the output of a modern economy is produced by the largest corporations, like General Electric, General Motors, and Wal-Mart. Almost one-third of our total output is produced by the largest 500 firms. These organizations are qualitatively different from competitive firms. They possess enormous resources, and they operate globally in many markets simultaneously. Their survival depends not just on pricing but also on developing new commodities, new technologies, and new markets that can pay off for years to come.

In this section we examine the behavior of large firms and the issues raised by the increasing importance of information as an economic commodity. We begin by examining the role of control and bounded rationality. We next look at the significance of large firms in innovation and then discuss the novel issues raised by the Internet and the growing problem of intellectual property rights.

BEHAVIOR OF LARGE CORPORATIONS

Divorce of Ownership and Control

The first step in understanding the behavior of large corporations is to realize that they are mostly "publicly owned." Corporate shares can be bought by

---

[1] For an example of how perfect price discrimination improves efficiency, see question 3 at the end of this chapter.

anyone, and ownership is spread among many investors. Take a company like AT&T. In 1999, more than 5 million people owned its shares, which were worth almost $147 billion. But no single person owned even 1 percent of the total. Although some of the large software and Internet companies are exceptions, such dispersed ownership is typical of our large publicly owned corporations.

Because the stock of large companies is so widely dispersed, *ownership is typically divorced from control.* Individual owners cannot easily affect the actions of large corporations. And while the stockholders of a company elect its board of directors—a group of insiders and knowledgeable outsiders—it is the salaried management which makes the major decisions about corporate strategy and day-to-day operations. The managers have acquired special training and management skills, and they are much more intimately acquainted with the details of the company.

In some situations, there is no conflict of interest between management and stockholders. Higher profits benefit everyone. But there are two important potential conflicts between managers and stockholders. First, top managers may vote themselves large salaries, stock options, expense accounts, bonuses, free apartments, expensive artwork, and generous retirement pensions at the stockholders' expense. Nobody is arguing that managers should work for the minimum wage, but executive pay in U.S. corporations has risen very rapidly in recent years. Some top executives at poorly performing companies—or even at companies like WorldCom or Enron which later went bankrupt—received salaries and bonuses totaling $100 million or more. Why, economists ask, are American executives often paid 10 or 20 times more than are executives in comparable firms of other countries?

A second conflict of interest may arise in connection with retaining earnings. The managers of a company have a tendency to hold on to profits and use them to expand the size of the company instead of paying them out as dividends or buying back shares. But there may be situations where the profits that are reinvested could be more profitable invested outside the company. In some cases, shareholders would benefit if the company would agree to be taken over by another corporation or to simply liquidate itself and pay out the proceeds. But few are the occasions when management gladly votes itself out of jobs and the firm out of business.

Rationality and Rules of Thumb

Economists often write of optimizing behavior in which consumers maximize utility and firms maximize profits. But in the real world, people have limited resources and are forced to make decisions on the basis of incomplete information or analysis. Searching for the absolute maximum of profits or utility would take too much time. Consumers cannot spend all day looking for the lowest-priced head of lettuce; a firm cannot spend millions of dollars hiring econometricians to study the price elasticity for each one of its thousand products. Instead, as Nobel Prize–winning economist Herbert Simon has emphasized, firms and consumers often exhibit *bounded rationality.* This means that they usually strive to make a "pretty good" decision, rather than waste resources hunting for the "absolutely best" decision.

In some situations the use of a *rule of thumb*—or simplified decision rule—is an economical way of making choices. For example, it is common practice for companies—especially ones in imperfectly competitive markets—to set prices on a "cost-plus-markup" basis. This is how it works: Instead of setting prices by an *MR* and *MC* comparison, companies take the calculated average cost of a product and mark it up by adding a fixed percentage—say, 20 percent of the average cost. This cost-plus-markup figure then becomes the selling price. Note that if all goes as planned, the price will cover all direct and overhead costs and earn the firm a solid profit.

Does markup pricing indicate that firms do not maximize profits? To some extent, yes. But a better explanation would be that markup pricing is a useful rule of thumb that economizes on scarce managerial resources in a world of bounded rationality. Managers have many tasks other than setting prices. So while markup pricing does not maximize profits to the last decimal point, it may come reasonably close to maximum profits given the other demands on management time.

INFORMATION, INNOVATION, AND SCHUMPETERIAN ECONOMICS

Economic theory tends to glorify perfect competition as the most efficient market structure. Imperfect competitors, by contrast, set prices too high, earn supernormal profits, and neglect product quality. This dismal view of monopoly was challenged by one of the great economists of the last century, Joseph Schumpeter. He argued that the essence of economic development is innovation and that monopolists in fact are the wellsprings of innovation in a capitalist economy.

Joseph Schumpeter: Economist as Romantic

Born in the Austrian Empire, Joseph Schumpeter (1883–1950), a legendary scholar whose research ranged widely in the social sciences, led a flamboyant private life.

He began studying law, economics, and politics at the University of Vienna—then one of the world centers of economics and home of the "Austrian School" that today reveres laissez-faire capitalism. He became the youngest professor in the Austrian Empire and was both the bane and the champion of his students. Six months into his teaching career at the University of Czernowitz (on the Russian border of the waning Austrian Empire), he charged into the library and scolded the librarian for not allowing his students to have free use of the books. After trading insults, the librarian challenged Schumpeter to a duel, which, thanks to his aristocratic training, Schumpeter won by nicking the librarian on the shoulder. After that, his students had unlimited access to the needed books.

In between dueling, insulting the stodgy faculty by showing up at faculty meetings in riding pants, and carousing, Schumpeter devoted himself to introducing economic theory to the European continent, founding the Econometric Society, and traveling to England and America. At the end of World War I, he had a disastrously short career as Austrian state secretary of finance. He later moved to Harvard, where he eventually became embittered as the theories of his great rival, John Maynard Keynes, swept the profession and the war ravaged his homeland.

Schumpeter's writings covered much of economics, sociology, and history, but his first love was economic theory. His magisterial *History of Economic Analysis* (published posthumously in 1954) has never been surpassed as a survey of the emergence of modern economics. His "popular" book, *Capitalism, Socialism, and Democracy* (1942), laid out the Schumpeterian hypothesis on the technological superiority of monopoly and developed the theory of competitive democracy which later grew into public-choice theory. He ominously predicted that capitalism would wither away because of disenchantment among the elites. Were he alive today, he might well join in the conservative complaint that the welfare state drains the economic vitality of the market economy.

The Economics of Information

Schumpeter's early classic, *The Theory of Economic Development* (1911), broke with the traditional static analysis of its time by emphasizing the importance of the entrepreneur or innovator, the person who introduces "new combinations" in the form of new products or methods of organization. Innovations result in temporary supernormal innovational profits, which are eventually eroded away by imitators. Ever the romantic, Schumpeter saw in the entrepreneur the hero of capitalism, the person of "superior qualities of intellect and will," motivated by the will to conquer and the joy of creation.

This vision of capitalism as a dynamic process has inspired a new generation of growth theorists, such as Stanford's Paul Romer, who have developed a Schumpeterian theory of induced innovation to supplement the more traditional neoclassical growth theory. Modern interpretations of the Schumpeterian vision emphasize the special economic problems involved in the **economics of information.** Information is a fundamentally different commodity from normal goods. *Because information is costly to produce but cheap to reproduce, markets in information are subject to severe market failures.*

Consider the production of a software program, such as Windows XP. Developing this program took several years and cost Microsoft over $1 billion. Yet you can purchase a legal copy for about $199 or buy an illegal pirated copy for $5. The same phenomenon is at work in publishing, pharmaceuticals, entertainment, and other areas where goods have high information content. In each of these areas, the research and development on the product may be a laborious process that takes years. But once the work is recorded on paper, in a computer, or on a compact disc, it can be reproduced and used by a second person essentially for free.

The inability of firms to capture the full monetary value of their inventions is called **inappropriability.** Case studies have found that the social return to invention (the value of inventions to all consumers and producers) is many times the appropriable private return to the inventor (the monetary value of the invention to the inventor).

Information is expensive to produce but cheap to reproduce. To the extent that the rewards to invention are inappropriable, we would expect private research and development to be underfunded, with the most significant underinvestment in basic research. The inappropriability and high social returns on research lead most governments to subsidize basic research in health and science and to promise special incentives for creative activities.

Intellectual Property Rights

Governments have long recognized that creative activities need special support because the rewards for producing valuable information like inventions are reduced by imitation. The U.S. Constitution therefore authorizes Congress "to promote the Progress of Science and useful Arts, by securing, for limited Times, to Authors and Inventors, the exclusive Right to their respective Writings and Discoveries." Thus special laws governing patents, copyrights, business and trade secrets, and electronic media create **intellectual property rights.** The purpose is to give the owner special protection against the material's being copied and used by others without compensation to the owner or original creator.

The earliest intellectual property right was the **patent,** under which the U.S. government creates a monopoly over a "novel, nonobvious, and useful" invention for a limited period, currently 20 years. Similarly, copyright laws provide legal protection against unauthorized copying of original works in different media such as text, music, video, software, art, and information goods.

Why would governments actually *encourage* monopolies? In effect, patents and copyrights create property rights in books, music, and ideas. By creating property rights, governments encourage artists and inventors to invest time, effort, and money in the creative process. Put differently, by allowing inventors to have monopolies on their intellectual property, the government increases the degree of appropriability

and thereby increases the incentives for people to invent useful new products, write books, compose songs, and write computer software. A patent also requires disclosure of the technological details of the invention, which encourages further invention and imitation. Examples of successful patents include those on the cotton gin, the telephone, the Xerox machine, and many best-selling pharmaceutical drugs.

The Dilemma of the Internet

Inventions that improve communications are hardly limited to the modern age. But the rapid growth of electronic storage, access, and transmission of information highlights the dilemma of providing incentives for creating new information. Many new information technologies have large up-front or sunk costs and virtually zero marginal costs. With the low cost of electronic information systems like the Internet, it is technologically possible to make most information available to everyone, everywhere, at essentially zero marginal cost. Note that perfect competition cannot survive here because a price equal to zero marginal cost will yield zero revenues and therefore no viable firms.

The economics of the new information economy highlights the conflict between efficiency and incentives. On the one hand, all information might be provided free—databases, economics textbooks, movies, concerts. Free provision of information looks economically efficient because the price would be equal to the marginal cost, which is zero. But a zero price on intellectual property would reduce or destroy the profit incentives to produce new data, books, and concerts because creators would reap no return or profits from their creative activity. Society has struggled with this dilemma in the past. But with costs of reproduction and transmission so much cheaper for electronic information than for traditional information, finding sensible public policies and enforcing intellectual property rights is becoming ever more difficult.

Experts emphasize that intellectual property laws are often hard to enforce, especially when they apply across national borders. Recently, the United States got into a trade dispute with China because that country was condoning the illegal copying of American movies, musical recordings, and software. A DVD movie that sells for $25 in the United States can be picked up for 50 cents in China.

Industrial R&D Performance by Size of Company			
Size of company (employees)	R&D-Sales Ratio (percent)		Total company R&D ($, billions)
	1983	1999	1999
Fewer than 500	2.2	8.9	31.3
500 to 999	na	4.0	6.4
1,000 to 4,999	2.0	3.1	23.9
5,000 to 9,999	1.3	2.2	14.2
10,000 to 24,999	2.3	2.8	24.5
25,000 or more	3.4	2.0	59.9

TABLE 10-1. Research and Development by Size of Firm

Two decades ago, large firms did most of the research and development (R&D). In the last decade, with the increasing importance of Internet and other new-economy firms, small firms forged ahead in the invention business, and they now have larger R&D-sales ratios than the largest industrial corporations.

Source: National Science Foundation, *Research and Development in Industry, 1999,* available at www.nsf.gov/sbe/srs/.

Why might countries fight such piracy? Appropriability is increased by strengthening intellectual property rights. It is also increased when the innovating firm has a large share of the product market. If Microsoft sells 95 percent of the operating systems for personal computers, it will naturally benefit substantially from research in that area. By contrast, small firms have less ability to appropriate the value of their inventions, particularly if intellectual property rights are weak. If I invent a new game and cannot protect it with a patent or other means, I have such a small share of the computer market that I will probably not benefit at all.

The Schumpeterian Hypothesis

It was just this dilemma that led Joseph Schumpeter to advance his bold hypothesis in support of monopolies:

> The modern standard of life of the masses evolved during the period of relatively unfettered "big business." If we list the items that enter the modern workman's budget and, from 1899 on, observe the course of their prices, . . . we cannot fail to be struck by the rate of the advance which, considering the spectacular improvement in qualities, seems to have been greater and not smaller than it ever was before. . . .
>
> Nor is this all. As soon as we . . . inquire into the individual items in which progress was most conspicuous,

the trail leads not to the doors of those firms that work under conditions of comparatively free competition but precisely to the doors of the large concerns—which, as in the case of agricultural machinery, also account for much of the progress in the competitive sector—and a shocking suspicion dawns upon us that big business may have had more to do with creating that standard of life than keeping it down.[2]

How well has the bold Schumpeterian hypothesis survived the scrutiny of scholars? The facts are much more complex than this simple hypothesis would suggest. To begin with, this view might have had greater validity a century ago, when large firms were tiny by today's standards and most firms had great difficulty raising capital to promote their innovations. Moreover, it is surely true that our corner grocery store today does little R&D.

But careful studies indicate that individuals and small firms play an increasingly vital role in the inventive process. Table 10-1 above shows the amount of R&D performed by different firm classes as well as the ratio of R&D to sales for each. In earlier years, most R&D was indeed undertaken by large firms. But in the last decade, particularly with the

---

[2] J. A. Schumpeter, *Capitalism, Socialism, and Democracy* (Harper, New York, 1942), p. 81.

increasing importance of the "new economy" and Internet firms, research by small firms has grown rapidly. Small firms, with less than 500 employees, now do one-fifth of all research and development, and the largest firms do less than two-fifths

Moreover, studies indicate that small firms are responsible for a disproportionate share of major inventions and innovations. When John Jewkes and his colleagues traced the history of the most important inventions of this century, they found that less than half came from the laboratories of large corporations. The importance of small inventors has been confirmed in recent years as major new products seem to arise from nowhere—every day we seem to receive an advertisement for a new software package developed by some unheard-of start-up firm. One business investor put this in a striking way, saying, "If I want really great ideas, I look for a firm with three people under 25 in sandals."

The relationship between innovation and market power is complex. Because large firms have made a major contribution to research and innovation, we should be cautious about claims that bigness is unmitigated badness. At the same time, we must recognize that small businesses and individuals have made some of the most revolutionary technological breakthroughs and are performing an ever-larger share of industry-financed R&D. To promote rapid innovation, a nation must preserve a variety of approaches and organizations.

C. A BALANCE SHEET ON IMPERFECT COMPETITION

Politicians like to extol "small business" and the "family farm" while disparaging "big businesses" with their "obscene profits." Does economic analysis justify this romantic picture? In this section we assess the economic impact of imperfect competition on today's economy. We begin by showing how imperfect competition distorts resource allocation. Then we provide quantitative estimates of the waste due to imperfect competition. We conclude by examining the policy measures that governments can use to control the damage from imperfect competition.

ECONOMIC COSTS OF IMPERFECT COMPETITION

The Cost of Inflated Prices and Insufficient Output

Our analysis has shown how imperfect competitors reduce output and raise price, thereby producing less than would be forthcoming in a perfectly competitive industry. This can be seen most clearly for monopoly, which is the most extreme version of imperfect competition. To see how and why monopoly keeps output too low, imagine that all dollar votes are distributed properly and that all industries other than one are perfectly competitive, with MC equal to P and no externalities. In this world, price is the correct economic standard or measure of scarcity: price measures both the marginal utility of consumption to households and the marginal cost of producing goods by firms.

Now Monopoly Inc. enters the picture. A monopolist is not a wicked firm—it doesn't rob people or force its goods down consumers' throats. Rather, Monopoly Inc. exploits the fact that it is the sole seller of a good or service. By keeping its output a little scarce, Monopoly Inc. raises its price above marginal cost. Since $P = MC$ is necessary for economic efficiency, the monopolist's output will be less than the efficient output; the marginal value of the good to consumers is therefore above its marginal cost. The same is true for oligopoly and monopolistic competition, as long as companies can hold prices above marginal cost.

The Quiet Life of a Monopolist

The eminent British economist J. R. Hicks wrote, "The best of all monopoly profits is the quiet life." This saying captures the notion that market power allows managers to pursue goals other than maximizing profits. Sometimes, non-profit-maximizing behavior can be as damaging as profit maximizing. We discussed some of these tendencies—such as giving valuable stock options—earlier in this chapter.

History records many occasions where monopolists produced shoddy products or uncivil service. Consumers often complain about the sleepy local-franchise monopolist who won't introduce new products and insists on the same old service year after year. When AT&T had a monopoly on telephone equipment, consumers had to be satisfied with plain black phones for many years. Once competitors entered, there was a sharp increase in the variety of colors, styles, and ancillary equipment (such as answering or fax machines).

Measuring the Waste from Imperfect Competition

We can depict the efficiency losses from imperfect competition by using a simplified version of our monopoly diagram, here shown in Figure 10-6. If the industry could be competitive, then the equilibrium would be reached at the point where $MC = P$, at point E. Under universal perfect competition, this industry's quantity would be 6 with a price of 100.

FIGURE 10-6. Monopolists Cause Economic Waste by Restricting Output

Monopolists make their output scarce and thereby drive up price and increase profits. If industry were competitive, equilibrium would be at point E, where economic surplus is maximized.

At the monopolist's output at point B (with $Q = 3$ and $P = 150$), price is above MC, and consumer surplus is lost. Adding together all the consumer-surplus losses between $Q = 3$ and $Q = 6$ leads to economic waste from monopoly equal to the gray shaded area ABE. In addition, the monopolist has monopoly profits (that would have been consumer surplus) given by the rust shaded region $GBAF$.

Now consider the impact of monopoly—perhaps one gained by a tariff, perhaps by a foreign-trade quota, or perhaps because government prevented entry by regulation or allowed a labor union to monopolize the labor in the industry. Whatever the source, the monopolist would set its MC equal to MR (not to industry P), displacing the equilibrium to $Q = 3$ and $P = 150$ in Figure 10-6. The rust area $GBAF$ is the monopolist's profit, which compares with a zero-profit competitive equilibrium.

The inefficiency loss from monopoly is sometimes called **deadweight loss.** This term refers to the loss of economic welfare arising from distortions in prices and output such as those due to monopoly, taxation, tariffs, or quotas. Consumers might enjoy a great deal of consumer surplus if a new antipain drug is sold at marginal cost; however, if a firm monopolizes the product, say because of a patent, and raises prices to the monopoly level, consumers will lose more than the monopolist will gain. That net loss in economic welfare is called deadweight loss.

We can picture the deadweight loss from a monopoly diagrammatically in Figure 10-6. Point E is the efficient level of production at which $MC = P$. For each unit that the monopolist reduces output below E, the efficiency loss is the vertical distance between the demand curve and the MC curve. The total deadweight loss from the monopolist's output restriction is the sum of all such losses, represented by the gray triangle ABE.

To see this, recall that the DD curve represents the good's marginal value to consumers at each level of output, while the MC curve represents the opportunity cost of devoting production to this good rather than to other industries. For example, at $Q = 3$, the vertical difference between B and A represents the difference between the value and the cost of a small increase in the output of Q. Adding up all these differences from $Q = 3$ to $Q = 6$ gives the shaded region ABE.

The technique of measuring the costs of market imperfections by "little triangles" of deadweight loss, such as the one in Figure 10-6, can be extended to other areas. Similar analysis applies to foreign-trade tariffs and quotas, taxes and subsidies, and externalities.

INTERVENTION STRATEGIES

In discussing the problem of imperfect competition, the great market-oriented economist Milton Friedman wrote: "There is only a choice among three evils:

private unregulated monopoly, private monopoly regulated by the state, and government operation." We close this chapter by examining the major approaches that governments use to deal with the abuses of market power. The first three policy measures form the core of modern policies toward big business:

1. The major method for combating market power is the use of *antitrust policy*. Antitrust policies are laws that prohibit certain kinds of behavior (such as firms' joining together to fix prices) or curb certain market structures (such as pure monopolies and highly concentrated oligopolies). This important policy approach will be explored in detail in Chapter 17.

2. More generally, anticompetitive abuses can be avoided by *encouraging competition* whenever possible. There are many government policies that can promote vigorous rivalry even among large firms. It is particularly crucial to reduce barriers to entry into all lines of business. That means encouraging small businesses and not walling off domestic markets from foreign competition.

3. Over the last 100 years, American government has evolved a new tool for government control of industry: *regulation*. Economic regulation allows specialized regulatory agencies to oversee the prices, outputs, entry, and exit of firms in regulated industries such as public utilities and transportation. Unlike antitrust policies, which tell businesses what not to do, regulation tells businesses what to do and how to price products. It is, in effect, government control without government ownership. In an earlier era, this approach was taken for sectors that were thought to be "natural monopolies," such as electric power and telephone service. Today, the major area of government regulation is health care, as we will see in Part Four.

The next three strategies have been tried from time to time but are seldom used in modern market economies like the United States:

4. *Government ownership* of monopolies has been an approach widely used outside the United States. For some natural monopolies such as water, gas, and electricity distribution, it is thought that efficient production requires a single seller. In such cases, the real dilemma is whether to impose gov-

ernment ownership or government regulation on the industries. Most market economies have chosen the regulatory route, and in recent years many governments have "privatized" (or sold off to private owners) industries such as telephone companies that were formerly government enterprises.

5. *Price controls* on most goods and services have been used in wartime, partly as a way of containing inflation, partly as a way of keeping down prices in concentrated industries. Studies indicate that these controls are a very blunt instrument: they lead to numerous distortions and subterfuges that undermine the economy's efficiency. During the most recent experience with economy-wide price controls in the United States, in the 1970s, there were long lines for gasoline when its price was set too low, and shortages also cropped up for beef, natural gas, and even toilet paper. Placing the entire economy under price controls to curtail a few monopolists is like poisoning the entire garden to kill a few chinch bugs. Today, outside of the health-care sector, price controls are seldom used.

6. *Taxes* have sometimes been used to alleviate the income-distribution effects. By taxing monopolies, a government can reduce monopoly profits, thereby softening some of the socially unacceptable effects of monopoly. But if taxation overcomes the objections to monopoly based on equity, it does little to reduce the distortion of output. A nondistorting tax drains profits but has no effect on output. If the tax increases marginal cost, it is likely to push the monopolist even further from the efficient level of output—raising price and lowering output even more.

The Bottom Line

What is the bottom line on the advantages and disadvantages of imperfect competition? To begin with, the question of "monopoly versus competition" is too simple to be useful—it is much like asking whether big animals are better than small animals. As the survey above emphasizes, there is a vast array of species of imperfect competition. Most have evolved to handle the special characteristics of the market they deal with—automobile firms are large publicly owned companies because they need to raise capital to gain the efficiencies of mass production; lawyers are organized in partnerships because of the need to pool skills and enhance trust among clients; colleges are nonprofit organizations because profits and teaching are hard to mix; farms are operated by families because of the need to perform a wide variety of activities in sparsely populated regions.

In virtually all cases, as Milton Friedman states in his quote on page 198, governments are choosing among different evils when they curb excessive market power. After two centuries of observing different market structures, many economists have concluded that *promoting vigorous competition among unregulated firms is almost always the*

least of these evils. Removing barriers to entry and exit and ensuring strong prohibitions against collusion are the surest formula for preventing monopoly pricing and encouraging rapid innovation. The keys to this strategy might be summarized in the following rules:

- Remove government constraints to competition.
- Remember that "the tariff is the mother of trusts."
- Promote vigorous competition from foreign firms.
- Use auctions and competitive bidding whenever possible.
- Don't try to second-guess future technological trends.
- Encourage small businesses to challenge established firms.

SUMMARY

A. Behavior of Imperfect Competitors

1. Recall the four major market structures: (*a*) *Perfect competition* is found when no firm is large enough to affect the market price. (*b*) *Monopolistic competition* occurs when a large number of firms produce slightly differentiated products. (*c*) *Oligopoly* is an intermediate form of imperfect competition in which an industry is dominated by a few firms. (*d*) *Monopoly* comes when a single firm produces the entire output of an industry.

2. Measures of concentration are designed to indicate the degree of market power in an imperfectly competitive industry. Industries which are more concentrated tend to have higher levels of R&D expenditures, but their profitability is not higher on average.

3. High barriers to entry and complete collusion can lead to collusive oligopoly. This market structure produces a price and quantity relation similar to that under monopoly.

4. Another common structure is the monopolistic competition that characterizes many retail industries. Here we see many small firms, with slight differences in the quality of products (such as different locations of gasoline stations). The existence of product differentiation leads each firm to face a downward-sloping *dd* demand curve. In the long run, free entry extinguishes profits as these industries show an equilibrium in which firms' *AC* curves are tangent to their *dd* demand curves. In this tangency equilibrium, prices are above marginal costs but the industry exhibits greater diversity of

quality and service than would occur under perfect competition.

5. A final situation recognizes the strategic interplay when an industry has but a handful of firms. Where a small number of firms compete in a market, they must recognize their strategic interactions. Competition among the few introduces a completely new feature into economic life: It forces firms to take into account competitors' reactions to price and output deviations and brings strategic considerations into these markets.

6. Price discrimination occurs when the same product is sold to different consumers for different prices. This practice often occurs when sellers can segment their market into different groups.

B. Innovation and Information

7. A careful study of the actual behavior of oligopolists shows certain kinds of behavior at variance with standard economic assumptions about profit maximization. One limit on profit maximization is bounded rationality. This principle recognizes that it may take time and effort to make perfectly informed decisions, so managers may make less-than-perfect decisions, often employing rules of thumb, to economize on search and decision time. An important example of rule-of-thumb behavior is markup pricing—where prices are set by adding a percentage increase on top of costs of production. Also, remember that market power can allow firms to lead the easy life.

8. Schumpeter emphasized the importance of the innovator, who introduces "new combinations" in the form of new products or methods of organization and is rewarded by temporary entrepreneurial profits. The Schumpeterian hypothesis holds that traditional monopoly theory ignores the dynamics of technological change. According to this view, monopolies and oligopolies are the chief source of innovation and growth in living standards—to turn large firms into perfect competitors would risk raising prices in the long run as the fragmentation of industry slows technological progress.

9. Today, the economics of information emphasizes the difficulties involved in efficient production and distribution of new and improved knowledge. Information is different from normal goods because it is expensive to produce but cheap to reproduce. The inability of firms to capture the full monetary value of their inventions is called inappropriability. To increase appropriability, governments create intellectual property rights governing patents, copyrights, trade secrets, and electronic media. The growth of electronic information systems like the Internet raises, in heightened form, the dilemma of the efficient pricing of information services.

C. A Balance Sheet on Imperfect Competition

10. Monopoly power often leads to economic inefficiency when price rises above marginal cost, costs are bloated by lack of competitive pressure, and product quality deteriorates.

11. To curb the abuses of imperfect competition, governments in an earlier age sometimes used taxation, price controls, and nationalization. These are little used today in most market economies. The three major tools in American industrial policy today are regulation, antitrust laws, and the encouragement of competition. Of these, the most important is to ensure vigorous rivalry by lowering the barriers to competition whenever possible.

CONCEPTS FOR REVIEW

Models of Imperfect Competition	**Aspects of Imperfect Competition**	deadweight losses
concentration: concentration ratios, HHI	separation of ownership from control	older approaches:
	limits on profit maximization:	taxation
market power	bounded rationality	price controls
strategic interaction	markup pricing	government ownership
tacit and explicit collusion	Schumpeterian hypothesis	current approaches:
imperfect competition:	economics of information:	regulation
collusive oligopoly	inappropriability	antitrust policy
monopolistic competition	protection of intellectual property	pro-competitive policies
small-number oligopoly	rights	
no-profit equilibrium in monopolistic competition	dilemma of efficient production of knowledge	
inefficiency of $P > MC$		

FURTHER READING AND INTERNET WEBSITES

Further Reading

An excellent review of oligopoly theory is F. M. Scherer and David Ross, *Industrial Market Structure and Economic Performance*, 3d ed. (Houghton Mifflin, Boston, 1990).

The Schumpeterian hypothesis was developed in Joseph Schumpeter, *Capitalism, Socialism, and Democracy*, (Harper & Row, New York, 1942). Evidence on this hypothesis is developed in Scherer and Ross, cited above.

Many of the economic, business, and policy issues involved in the new information economy are covered in a nontechnical book by two eminent economists, Carl Shapiro and Hal R. Varian: *Information Rules* (Harvard Business

School Press, Cambridge, Mass., 1998). A discussion of the economics of the Internet is contained in Jeffrey K. MacKie-Mason and Hal Varian, "Economic FAQs about the Internet," *Journal of Economic Perspectives*, Summer 1994, p. 92.

Websites

One of the most interesting websites about the Internet and intellectual property rights is compiled by Hal R. Varian, dean of the School of Information Management and Systems at the University of California at Berkeley. This site, called "The Economics of the Internet, Information Goods, Intellectual Property and Related Issues," is at www.sims.berkeley.edu/resources/infoecon. Also see the Web page of the Program for Research on the Information Economy, directed by Jeffrey MacKie-Mason at the University of Michigan, at www.si.umich.edu/~prie.

OPEC has its site at www.opec.org. This site makes interesting reading from the point of view of oil producers, many of which are Arab countries.

Data and methods pertaining to concentration ratios can be found in a Bureau of the Census publication at www.census.gov/prod/ec97/m31s-cr.pdf.

QUESTIONS FOR DISCUSSION

1. Review collusive oligopoly and monopolistic competition, which are two theories of imperfect competition discussed in this chapter. Draw up a table that compares perfect competition, monopoly, and the two theories with respect to the following characteristics: (*a*) number of firms; (*b*) extent of collusion; (*c*) price vs. marginal cost; (*d*) price vs. long-run average cost; (*e*) efficiency.

2. Consider an industry whose firms have the following sales:

Firm	Sales	Firm	Sales
Appel Computer	1000	Fettucini Computer	200
Banana Computer	800	Grapefruit Computer	150
Cumquat Computer	600	Hamburger Computer	100
Dellta Computer	400	InstantCoffee Computer	50
Endive Computer	300	Jasmine Computer	1

The Herfindahl-Hirschman Index (HHI) is defined as

$$HHI = (\text{market share of firm 1 in } \%)^2$$
$$+ (\text{market share of firm 2 in } \%)^2 + \cdots$$
$$+ (\text{market share of last firm in } \%)^2$$

   a. Calculate the four-firm and six-firm concentration ratios for the computer industry.
   b. Calculate the HHI for the industry.

   c. Suppose that Appel Computer and Banana Computer were to merge with no change in the sales of any of the different computers. Calculate the new HHI.

3. "Perfect price discrimination" occurs when each consumer is charged his or her maximum price for the product. When this happens, the monopolist is able to capture the entire consumer surplus. Draw a demand curve for each of six consumers and compare (*a*) the situation in which all consumers face a single price with (*b*) a market under perfect price discrimination. Explain the paradoxical result that perfect price discrimination removes the inefficiency of monopoly.

4. "It is naive to try to break up monopolies into even a few effectively competing units, because the basic cause of monopoly is the law of decreasing cost with mass production. Moreover, if there are even a few firms, the price is likely to be close to marginal cost." Discuss both parts of this statement.

5. A recent interesting study of the Internet by two economists states:

   Traditional pricing schemes are not appropriate [for information services]. If you buy a table we like, we generally have to go to the manufacturer to buy one for ourselves; we can't simply copy yours. With information goods, the pricing-by-replication breaks down. Once the sunk costs of software are invested, replication costs are essentially zero. This is a much greater problem [with electronic information] than that which publishers face from unauthorized photocopying, since the cost of replication is essentially zero.[3]

[3] Condensed from MacKie-Mason and Varian, cited in the Further Reading section.

Analyze this quotation in terms of the issues concerning the economics of information. Explain why appropriability is an issue for a book or page on the Internet but not for a chair or gallon of gasoline. Why might high charges for photocopying material or for access to the Internet impede efficiency? Relate this question to the Schumpeterian hypothesis.

6. Explain the following statements:
   a. In the retail drugstore business, each store has a little market power but fails to earn any economic profit on its activities.
   b. According to the theory of bounded rationality, it is truly efficient for GE not to adjust the price of its refrigerators so that $MC = MR$ each and every day.

7. The government decides to tax a monopolist at a constant rate of $\$x$ per unit. Show the impact upon output and price. Is the posttax equilibrium closer to or further from the ideal equilibrium of $P = MC$?

8. Firms often lobby for tariffs or quotas to provide relief from import competition.
   a. Suppose that the monopolist shown in Figure 10-6 has a foreign competitor that will supply output perfectly elastically at a price slightly above the monopolist's $AC = MC$. Show the impact of the foreign competitor's entry into the market.
   b. What would be the effect on the price and quantity if a prohibitive tariff were levied on the foreign good? (A prohibitive tariff is one that is so high as to effectively wall out all imports.) What would be the effect of a small tariff? Use your analysis to explain the statement, "The tariff is the mother of monopoly."

9. Explain in words and with the use of diagrams why a monopolistic equilibrium leads to economic inefficiency relative to a perfect competitor. Why is the condition $MC = P = MU$ of Chapter 8 critical for this analysis?

FIGURE 10-7. Perfect Competition

10. In long-run equilibrium, both perfectly competitive and monopolistically competitive markets achieve a tangency between the firm's dd demand curve and its AC average cost curve. Figure 10-4 shows the tangency for a monopolistic competitor, while Figure 10-7 displays the tangency for the perfect competitor. Discuss the similarities or differences in the two situations with respect to:
    a. The elasticity of the demand curve for the firm's product
    b. The extent of divergence between price and marginal cost
    c. Profits
    d. Economic efficiency

11. Reread the history of OPEC. Draw a set of supply and demand curves in which supply is completely price-inelastic. Show that a cartel that sets a quantity target (the inelastic supply curve) will experience more volatile prices if demand is price-inelastic than if demand is price-elastic when (*a*) the demand curve shifts horizontally by a certain quantity (a forecasting error) or (*b*) there is a shift in the supply curve (say, due to cheating by a cartel member).

CHAPTER

11

Uncertainty and Game Theory

*Strategic thinking is
the art of outdoing an
adversary, knowing
that the adversary is
trying to do the same
to you.*

Avinash Dixit and Barry Nalebuff
Thinking Strategically (1991)

Life is full of uncertainty and strategic behavior. A capsule history of exploring for oil in Russia will illustrate this point. During the turmoil of the 1990s, oil production in Russia declined sharply, and Russia fell from being the world's largest oil producer to number three. Western oil companies were invited to participate in investing in and modernizing the Russian oil fields.

Suppose that you are in charge of a Texaco joint venture in Siberia. What obstacles would you face? You would of course face the normal risks that plague oil producers everywhere—the risks of a price plunge, of embargoes, or of an attack on your tankers by some hostile regime. Added to these are the uncertainties of operating in a new area: you are unfamiliar with the geological formations, with the terrain for getting the oil to the market, with the success rate on drilling wells, and with the skills of the workforce.

In addition to these uncertainties is a set of political risks involved in dealing with a divided central government in Moscow, with autonomous regions, with localities, and with the Russian "mafia" in a country where property rights, bribes, and taxation are subject to haggling and the rule of bureaucracy rather than the rule of law.

The dilemmas of the Texaco joint venture show that economic activity often raises complexities that are not captured in our elementary theories. One topic, called the *economics of uncertainty*, analyzes the impact of the many uncertainties involved in economic life. Our oil company must deal with the uncertainties of drilling, of volatile prices, and of shifting markets. Households must contend with uncertainty about future wages or employment and about the return on their investments in education or in financial assets. Occasionally, people suffer from misfortunes such as devastating hurricanes, earthquakes, or illness.

A second topic, known as *game theory*, analyzes those aspects of economic life which involve haggling, bargaining, and strategizing. In perfectly competitive markets, all parties take prices as given and need not worry about others' reactions to their actions. In most circumstances, however, strategic considerations are of the essence. Our oil company must worry about whether a big oil find will simply be expropriated by the Russians. An oligopolistic firm must worry about how other firms will react to its price or output decisions. Will a price cut lead to a price war? Will the price war lead to bankruptcy? Many large firms engage in collective bargaining with a union to determine wages and conditions of work. Will too tough a position lead to a crippling strike?

We often see elements of bargaining in economic policymaking. When governments make decisions about taxes and expenditures, these often result from intricate bargaining between political parties, or between the president and Congress, or among the many power brokers in Congress. Even family life involves subtle elements of strategy and bargaining about the allocation of chores or the division of the family's income.

No study of the realities of economic life is complete without a thorough study of the fascinating interplay of uncertainty and game theory.

A. ECONOMICS OF RISK AND UNCERTAINTY

Our analysis of markets presumed that costs and demands were known for certain and that each firm could predict how other firms would behave. In reality, business life is teeming with risk and uncertainty. Let's see how risk clouds the picture if you are in the oil business and decide to drill a well. To begin with, you might plan on costs of $100 million for the well, but this is just a guess because you don't know how deep you need to drill to find oil, or whether your equipment will break down and need to be replaced, or how long your crew will need to be on the job. In addition, you cannot know about the revenues from the well because of price and output uncertainty. Price uncertainty comes because oil prices fluctuate widely—they have been as low as $10 a barrel and as high as $38 a barrel over the last 20 years. Output uncertainty is undoubtedly the major worry, for your well may be dry, or it may yield too little to be worth operating, or it may be a lucrative gusher.

These problems are not confined to the oil business. Virtually all firms find that output prices will fluctuate from month to month; input prices are often highly volatile; the behavior of competitors cannot be forecast in advance. The essence of business is to invest now in order to make profits in the future, in effect putting fortunes up as hostage to future uncertainties. Economic life is a risky business.

Modern economics has developed useful tools to incorporate uncertainty into the analysis of business and household behavior and of financial markets. This section examines the role of markets in spreading risks over space and time, presents the theory of individual behavior under uncertainty, and provides the essential theory underlying insurance markets. These topics are but a brief glimpse into the fascinating world of risk and economic life.

SPECULATION: SHIPPING ASSETS OR GOODS ACROSS SPACE AND TIME

We begin by considering the role of speculative markets. **Speculation** involves buying and selling in order to make profits from fluctuations in prices. A speculator wants to buy low and sell high. The item might be grain, oil, eggs, stocks, or foreign currencies. Speculators do not buy these items for their own sake. The last thing they want is to see the egg truck show up at their door. Rather, they make a profit from price changes.

Many people think of speculation as a slightly sinister activity, particularly when it arises from accounting frauds and inside information. But speculation can be beneficial to society. The economic function of speculators is to "move" goods from periods of abundance to periods of scarcity. Even though speculators may never see a barrel of oil or a truckload of eggs, they can help even out the price differences of these commodities among regions or over time. They do this by buying when goods are abundant and prices are low and selling when goods are scarce and prices are high, and this indeed can improve a market's efficiency.

Arbitrage and Geographic Price Patterns

The simplest case is one in which speculative activity reduces or eliminates regional price differences by buying and selling the same commodity. This activity is called **arbitrage,** which is the purchase of a good or asset in one market for immediate resale in another market in order to profit from a price discrepancy.

Let's say that the price of wheat is 50 cents per bushel higher in Chicago than in Kansas City. Further, suppose that the costs of insurance and transportation are 10 cents per bushel. An *arbitrager* (someone engaged in arbitrage) can purchase wheat in Kansas City, ship it to Chicago, and make a profit of 40 cents per bushel. As a result of market arbitrage, the differential will be reduced so that the price differential between Chicago and Kansas City can never exceed 10 cents per bushel. *More generally, as a result of arbitrage, the price difference between markets will generally be less than the cost of moving the good from one market to the other.*

The frenzied activities of arbitragers—talking on the phone simultaneously to several brokers in several markets, searching out price differentials, trying to eke out a tiny profit every time they can buy low and sell high—tend to align the prices of identical products in different markets. Once again, we see the invisible hand at work—the lure of profit acts to smooth out price differentials across markets and make markets function more efficiently.

Speculation and Price Behavior over Time

Forces of speculation will tend to establish definite patterns of prices over time as well as over space. But the difficulties of predicting the future make this pattern less perfect: we have an equilibrium that is constantly being disturbed but is always in the process of reforming itself—rather like a lake's surface under the play of the winds.

Consider the simplest case of a crop like corn that is harvested once a year and can be stored for future use. To avoid shortages, the crop must last for the entire year. Since no one passes a law regulating the storage of corn, how does the market bring about an efficient pattern of pricing and use over the year? The equilibrium is set by the activities of speculators trying to make a profit.

A well-informed corn speculator realizes that if all the corn is thrown on the market after the autumn harvest, it will fetch a very low price because there will be a glut on the market. Several months later, when corn is running short, the price will tend to skyrocket. In this case, speculators can make a profit by (1) purchasing some of the autumn crop while it is cheap, (2) putting it into storage, and (3) selling it later when the price has risen.

As a result of the speculative activities, the autumn price increases, the spring supply of corn increases, and the spring price declines. The process of speculative buying and selling tends to even out the supply, and therefore the price, over the year.

Moreover, if there is brisk competition among well-informed speculators, none of them will make excess profits. The returns to speculators will include the interest on invested capital, the appropriate earnings for their time, plus a risk premium to compensate them for whatever risks they incur with their funds.

There is one and only one monthly price pattern that will result in zero profits for competitive speculators. A little thought will show that it will not be a pattern of constant prices. Rather, the competitive speculative price pattern will produce the lowest prices after the autumn harvest, followed by a gradual price rise until the peak is reached just before the new corn is harvested. The price would normally rise from month to month to compensate for the storage and interest costs of carrying the crop. Figure 11-1 below shows the behavior of prices over an idealized yearly cycle.

Speculation reveals the invisible-hand principle at work. By evening out supplies and prices, speculation actually increases economic efficiency. By moving goods over time from periods of abundance to periods of scarcity, the speculator is buying where the price and marginal utility of the good are low and selling where the price and marginal utility are high. By pursuing their private interests (profits), speculators are at the same time increasing the public interest (total utility).

FIGURE II-I. Speculators Even Out the Price of a Commodity over Time

When a good is stored, the expected price rise must match holding costs. In equilibrium, price is lowest at harvest time, rising gently with accumulated storage, insurance, and interest costs until the next harvest. This flexible pattern tends to even out consumption over the seasons. Otherwise, a harvest glut would cause very low autumn price and sky-high spring price.

Shedding Risks through Hedging

One important function of speculative markets is to allow people to shed risks through hedging. **Hedging** consists of reducing the risk involved in owning an asset or commodity by making a counteracting sale of that asset. Let's see how it works. Consider someone who owns a corn warehouse. She buys 2 million bushels of Kansas corn in the fall, stores it for 6 months, and sells it in the spring at a 10-cents-per-bushel profit, just covering her costs.

The problem is that corn prices tend to fluctuate. If the price of corn rises, she makes a large windfall gain. But if the price falls sharply, the decrease could completely wipe out her profits or even drive her into bankruptcy. If the warehouse owner wants to earn her living by storing corn and wants to avoid speculating on the price of corn, what can she do?

The answer is that she can avoid all the corn-price risk by hedging her investments. The owner hedges by selling the corn the moment it is bought from the farmers rather than waiting until it is shipped 6 months later. Upon buying 2 million bushels of corn in September, she sells the corn immediately for delivery in the future at an agreed-upon price that will just yield a 10-cents-per-bushel storage cost. She thereby protects herself against all corn-price risk. *Hedging allows businesses to insulate themselves from the risk of price changes.*

The Economic Impacts of Speculation

But who buys the corn, and why? Here is where the speculator and the speculative market enter: The speculator agrees to buy the warehouse owner's corn now for future delivery. This transfers the risks from the original owner to the speculator. You might wonder exactly why the speculator agreed to take on the corn-price risk. Perhaps the speculator believed that corn prices would rise and that he would make a super-normal return on the investment; perhaps he sold a "futures contract" (one which promises future delivery) to buyers who wished to lock in the price of corn before it rose; perhaps he sold it to investors who wished to put a small corn position in their portfolios. The point is that someone, somewhere, had an economic incentive to take on the risk of corn-price fluctuations.

Speculative markets serve to improve the price and allocation patterns across space and time as well as to help transfer risks. These tasks are performed by speculators who, spurred on by the desire to profit from price changes, in fact show the invisible hand at work. If we look behind the veil of money, we see that ideal speculation reallocates goods from times of feast (when prices are low) to times of famine (when prices are high).

Our discussion has suggested that ideal speculative markets can increase economic efficiency. Let's see how. Say that identical consumers have utility schedules in which satisfaction in one year is independent of that in every other year. Now suppose that in the first of 2 years there is a big crop—say, 3 units per person—while the second year has a small crop of only 1 unit per person. If this crop deficiency could be foreseen perfectly, how should the consumption of the 2-year, 4-unit total be spread over the 2 years? Neglecting storage, interest, and insurance costs, *total utility and economic efficiency for the 2 years together will be maximized only when consumption is equal in each year.*

Why is uniform consumption better than any other division of the available total? Because of the law of diminishing marginal utility. This is how we might reason: "Suppose I consume more in the first year than in the second. My marginal utility (MU) in the first year will be low, while it will be high in the second year. So if I carry some crop over from the first to the second year, I will be moving consumption from low-MU times to high-MU times. When consumption levels are equalized, MUs will be equal and I will be maximizing my total utility."

A graph can illuminate this argument. If we measure utility in dollars, with each dollar always denoting the same marginal utility, the demand curves for the risky commodity would look just like the marginal utility schedule of Figure 5-1 on page 86. The two curves of Figure 11-2(a) on page 208 show what would happen with no carryover and with unequal consumption. Here, price is determined first at A_1, where higher S_1S_1 intersects DD, and second at A_2, where the lower supply S_2S_2 intersects DD. Total utility of the gray shaded areas would add up to only $(4 + 3 + 2) + 4$, or \$13.

But with optimal carryover of 1 unit to the second year, as shown in Figure 11-2(b), Ps and Qs will be equalized at E_1 and E_2, and the total utility of the shaded areas will add up to $(4 + 3) + (4 + 3)$, or \$14 per person. A little analysis can show that the gain in utility of \$1 is measured by Figure 11-2(b)'s dark rust

(a) Without Carryover	(b) With Carryover

FIGURE 11-2. Speculative Storage Can Improve Efficiency

The gray areas measure total utility enjoyed each year. Carrying 1 unit to the second year equalizes Q and also P and MU and increases total utility by the amount of the dark rust block.

This diagram will apply equally well to a number of situations. It could be labeled "(a) Without Arbitrage across Regional Markets" and "(b) With Arbitrage across Markets." We can also use this diagram to illustrate risk aversion if we label it "(a) With a Risky Gamble" and "(b) Without a Risky Gamble." Insurance then serves to move people from (a) to (b) by spreading the risks across many independent potential gambles.

block, which represents the excess of the second unit's marginal utility over that of the third. This shows why the equality of marginal utilities, which is achieved by ideal speculation, is optimal.

Our discussion has focused on one kind of speculation and arbitrage—that involving commodities. Even more important today are activities involving financial assets such as stocks, bonds, mortgages, and foreign exchange. Every day, literally trillions of dollars of assets change hands as people speculate, hedge, and invest their funds. The general principles underlying financial speculation, hedging, and arbitrage are exactly the same as those outlined here, although the stakes are even higher.

Ideal speculation serves the important function of reducing undesired variations in consumption. In a world with individuals who display diminishing marginal utility, speculation can increase total utility and allocational efficiency.

RISK AND UNCERTAINTY

What are people's attitudes toward risk? Why do people try to insulate themselves from many important risks? What market institutions help individuals avoid

major risks? Why do markets fail to provide insurance in some circumstances? We turn now to these issues.

Whenever you drive a car, own a house, or invest in the stock market, you are risking life, limb, or fortune. How do people behave when faced by risk? People generally want to avoid major risks to their income and consumption. When people avoid risks, they are "risk-averse."

A person is **risk-averse** when the displeasure from losing a given amount of income is greater than the pleasure from gaining the same amount of income.

For example, suppose that we are offered a risky coin flip in which we will win $1000 if the coin comes up heads and lose $1000 if the coin comes up tails. This bet has an *expected value* of 0 (equal to a probability of ½ times $1000 and a probability of ½ times − $1000). A bet which has a zero expected value is called a fair bet. If we turn down all fair bets, we are risk-averse.

In terms of the utility concept that we analyzed in Chapter 5, risk aversion is the same as *diminishing marginal utility of income*. Being risk-averse implies that the gain in utility achieved by getting an extra amount of income is less than the loss in utility from losing the same amount of income. For a fair bet (such as flipping a coin for $1000), the expected dollar value is zero. But in terms of utility, the expected utility value is negative because the utility you stand to win is less than the utility you stand to lose.

We can use Figure 11-2 to illustrate the concept of risk aversion. Say that situation (*b*) is the initial position, in which you have equal amounts of consumption in states 1 and 2, consuming 2 units in both states. A "risk lover" comes to you and says, "Let's flip a coin for 1 unit." The risk lover is in effect offering you the chance to move to situation (*a*), where you would have 3 units of consumption if the coin came up heads and 1 unit if tails. By careful calculation, you see that if you refuse the bet and stay in situation (*b*), the expected value of utility is 7 utils ($= \frac{1}{2} \times 7$ utils $+ \frac{1}{2} \times 7$ utils), whereas if you accept the bet, the expected value of utility is $6\frac{1}{2}$ utils ($= \frac{1}{2} \times 9$ utils $+ \frac{1}{2} \times 4$ utils). This example shows that if you are risk-averse, with diminishing marginal utility, you will avoid actions that increase uncertainty without some expectation of gain.

Say that I am a corn farmer. While I clearly must contend with the natural hazards of farming, I do not also want to bear corn-price risks. Suppose that the expected value of the corn price is $4 per bushel, where this expectation arises from two equally likely outcomes with prices of $3 and $5 per bushel. Unless I can shed the price risk, I am forced into a lottery where I must sell my 10,000-bushel crop for either $30,000 or $50,000 depending upon the flip of the corn-price coin.

But by the principle of risk aversion and diminishing marginal utility, I would prefer a sure thing. That is, I would prefer to hedge my price risk by selling my corn for the expected-value price of $4, yielding a total of $40,000. Why? Because the prospect of losing $10,000 is more painful than the prospect of gaining $10,000 is pleasant. If my income is cut to $30,000, I will have to cut back on important spending, such as college tuition or a new roof. On the other hand, the extra $10,000 might be less critical, going toward luxuries like a winter vacation or a new 100-horsepower, air-conditioned lawn mower.

People are generally risk-averse, preferring a sure thing to uncertain levels of consumption: people prefer outcomes with less uncertainty and the same average values. For this reason, activities that reduce the uncertainties of consumption lead to improvements in economic welfare.

The Troubling Rise in Gambling

Gambling has historically been a "vice" that was—along with illegal drugs, commercial sex, alcohol, and tobacco—discouraged by the state. Attitudes about such activities ebb and flow. Over the last two decades, attitudes toward gambling became permissive as those toward drugs and tobacco hardened. Only one state permitted casino gambling in 1978, but the number had risen to 27 by the late 1990s. This spread was accompanied by the rapid growth of state lotteries. Overall, gambling has been one of the fastest-growing sectors of the (legal) economy in the last two decades.

Gambling is a different animal from speculation. While ideal speculative activity increases economic welfare, gambling raises serious economic issues. To begin with, aside from recreational value, gambling does not create goods and services. In the language of game theory described in the second half of this chapter, gambling is a "negative-sum game" for the players—the customers are (almost) sure to lose in the long run because the house takes a cut of all bets. In addition, by its very nature, gambling increases income inequality. People who sit down to the gambling table with the same amount of money go away with widely different amounts. A gambler's family must expect to be on top of the world one week only to be living on crumbs and remorse when luck changes. Some observers also believe that gambling has adverse social impacts. These include addiction to gambling, neighborhood crime, political corruption, and infiltration of gambling by organized crime.

Given the substantial economic case against gambling, how can we understand the recent trend to legalize gambling and operate government lotteries? One reason is that when states are starved for tax revenues, they look under every tree for new sources; they rationalize lotteries and casinos as a way to channel private vices to the public interest by skimming off some of the revenues to finance public projects. In addition, legal gambling may drive out illegal numbers rackets and take some of the profitability out of organized crime. Notwithstanding these rationales, many observers raise questions about an activity in which the state profits by promoting irrational behavior among those who can least afford it.

INSURANCE AND RISK SPREADING

Risk-averse individuals want to avoid risks. But risks cannot simply be buried. When a house burns down, when someone is killed in an automobile accident, or when a hurricane tears through Florida—someone, somewhere, must bear the cost.

Markets handle risks by **risk spreading.** This process takes risks that would be large for one person and spreads them around so that they are but small risks for a large number of people. The major form of risk spreading is **insurance,** which is a kind of gambling in reverse.

For example, in buying fire insurance on a house, homeowners seem to be betting with the insurance company that the house will burn down. If it does not, the owners forfeit the small premium charge. If it does burn down, the company must reimburse the owners for the loss at an agreed-upon rate. What is true of fire insurance is equally true of life, accident, automobile, or any other kind of insurance.

The insurance company is spreading risks by pooling many different risks: it may insure millions of houses or lives or cars. The advantage for the insurance company is that what is unpredictable for one individual is highly predictable for a population. Say that the Inland Fire Insurance Company insures 1 million homes, each worth $100,000. The chance that a house will burn down is 1 in 1000 per year. The expected value of losses to Inland is then .001 × $100,000 = $100 per house per year. It charges each homeowner $100 plus another $100 for administration and for reserves.

Each homeowner is faced with the choice between the *certain* loss of $200 for each year or the *possible* 1-in-1000 catastrophic loss of $100,000. Because of risk aversion, the household will choose to buy insurance that costs more than the expected value of the household's loss in order to avoid the small chance of a catastrophic loss. Insurance companies can set a premium that will earn the company a profit and at the same time produce a gain in expected utility of individuals. Where does the economic gain come from? It arises from the law of diminishing marginal utility.

Insurance transfers risks from those who are more risk-averse or who are exposed to disproportionately heavy risks to those who are less risk-averse or those who can more easily bear risks. Although insurance appears to be just another form of gambling, it actually has exactly the opposite effect. Whereas nature deals us risks, insurance helps reduce individual risks by spreading them out.

Capital Markets and Risk Sharing

Another form of risk sharing takes place in the capital markets because the financial ownership of *physical* capital can be spread among many owners through the vehicle of corporate ownership.

Take the example of investment to develop a new commercial aircraft. A completely new design, including research and development, might require $2 billion of investment spread over 10 years. Yet there is no guarantee that the plane will find a large-enough commercial market to repay the invested funds. Few people have the wealth or inclination to undertake such a risky venture.

Market economies accomplish this task through publicly owned corporations. A company like Boeing is owned by millions of people, none of whom owns a major portion of the shares. In a hypothetical case, divide Boeing's ownership equally among 10 million individuals. Then the $2 billion investment becomes $200 per person, which is a risk that many would be willing to bear if the returns on Boeing stock appear attractive.

One of the most exciting and rapidly growing areas of economics is *financial economics*. This topic examines how investors can allocate their funds to maximize return for a given level of risk and how the prices of stocks and other financial assets behave. Financial markets have brought economics into the home and dormitory for millions of people who invest online, save for a college education, or manage their pension funds. Financial economics is covered in depth in the macroeconomics chapters of this text.

By spreading the ownership of risky investments among a multitude of owners, capital markets can spread risks and encourage much larger investments and risks than would be tolerable for individual owners.

MARKET FAILURES IN INFORMATION

Our analysis up to now has assumed that investors and consumers are well informed about the risks they face and that speculative and insurance markets function efficiently. In reality, markets involving risk and uncertainty are plagued by market failures. Two of the major failures are adverse selection and moral hazard. When these are present, markets may give the wrong signals, incentives may get distorted, and sometimes markets may simply not exist. Because of market failures, governments may decide to step in and offer social insurance.

Moral Hazard and Adverse Selection

While insurance is a useful device for reducing risks, sometimes insurance is not available. The reason is that efficient insurance markets can thrive only under limited conditions.

What are the conditions for efficient insurance markets? First, there must be a large number of insurable events. Only then will companies be able to spread the risks so that what is a large risk to an individual will become a small risk to many people. Moreover, the events must be statistically independent. No prudent insurance company would sell all its fire-insurance policies in the same building or sell only hurricane insurance in Miami. Insurance companies try to diversify their coverage among many independent risks.

Additionally, there must be sufficient experience regarding such events so that insurance companies can reliably estimate the losses. For example, after the September 11 terrorist attacks, private terrorism insurance was canceled because insurance companies could not get reliable estimates of the chances of future attacks (see question 3 at the end of this chapter).

Finally, the insurance must be relatively free of moral hazard. **Moral hazard** is at work when insurance increases risky behavior and thereby changes the probability of loss. In many situations moral hazard is unimportant. Few people will risk death because they have a generous life-insurance policy. In some areas, moral hazard is severe. Studies indicate that the presence of insurance increases the amount of cosmetic surgery undertaken and the utilization of long-term care such as nursing homes, and most medical-insurance policies consequently exclude these services.

When these ideal conditions are met—when there are many outcomes, all more or less independent, and when the probabilities can be accurately gauged and are not contaminated by moral hazard—private insurance markets can function efficiently.

Adverse Selection. Sometimes, private insurance is unavailable because of adverse selection. **Adverse selection** arises when the people with the highest risk are also the most likely to buy the insurance.

For example, assume that the population is equally divided between healthy people and sick people. The healthy people average $2000 of medical care each year; the sick people—perhaps with AIDS or cancer—have costs averaging $8000. If everybody is insured, the average cost would be $5000 per year.

Now suppose that Blue Cross sets a uniform price for all insured. This might be the case because government required *nondiscrimination* among insured people. Or it might occur because of *asymmetric information,* where people know about their health status but the insurance company does not. In either case, the sick people would gladly buy the Blue Cross policy, while the healthy might remain uninsured rather than pay the high premiums. Since the healthy people are uninsured, the insurance covers only the high-cost, sick people. The price of insurance rises to $8000 to cover the costs.

We see that uniform market pricing of medical insurance has led to adverse selection—raising the cost, limiting the coverage, and producing an incomplete market. Similar market failures are particularly important factors in disability insurance and in long-term-care insurance.

Grade Insurance?

Consider the following fantastic scheme: You are surfing the Web and hit on a new company called G-Insure.com, which offers "grade insurance" for students. In return for a modest premium, the company promises to compensate students for the income loss from poor grades. This seems like a good idea because the income risks are high for most workers.

On reflection, can you see why G-Insure.com is almost sure to be a fraud? Why no honest insurance company would offer such coverage? The reason is that grades depend too much on individual effort and that the market would be infected with moral hazard and adverse selection. These problems lead to a "missing market" in the sense that supply and demand intersect at a zero level of insurance.

Social Insurance

When market failures are so severe that the private market cannot provide adequate coverage, there may be a role for **social insurance,** which is mandatory insurance provided by the government. In these circumstances, the government may choose to step in and provide broad and universal coverage. The taxing and regulatory powers of government, plus the ability to prevent adverse selection through universal coverage, can make government insurance a welfare-improving measure.

One important example of social insurance is unemployment insurance. This is an example of a private market that cannot function because so many of the requirements for private insurance are violated. Insurance companies do not provide unemployment insurance because the moral hazard is so high (people may decide to become unemployed if benefits are generous), because of severe adverse selection (those who often lose jobs are more likely to participate), and because spells of unemployment are not independent (they tend to occur together during business-cycle recessions). At the same time, some countries feel that people should have a safety net under them should they lose their job. As a result, governments often step in to provide unemployment insurance. The government cannot remove the problem of moral hazard, but adverse selection is avoided by universal coverage.

Another important example of cases where governments step in is health insurance for the elderly. We noted above the problems of adverse selection that arise when healthy people decline coverage and leave insurers to cover only high-cost individuals. Adverse selection is particularly serious for the aged because medical costs in the last year of life are almost 20 percent of all health-care costs. Today, to avoid adverse selection, the U.S. government offers Medicare, universal health coverage for the elderly, which is paid for through premiums and through taxes on active workers.

B. GAME THEORY

Economic life is full of situations in which people or firms or countries compete for dominance. The oligopolies that we analyzed in the previous chapter sometimes break out into economic warfare. Such rivalry was seen in the last century when Vanderbilt and Drew repeatedly cut shipping rates on their parallel railroads. In recent years, Southwest Airlines tried to lure customers from its bigger rivals by offering fares far below prevailing levels. When larger airlines such as American and United were deciding how to react, they also had to take into account how Southwest would react when they reacted, and so forth. These situations typify an area of economic analysis known as "game theory."

Game theory analyzes the way that two or more players choose strategies that jointly affect each other. This theory, which sounds frivolous in its terminology, is in fact fraught with significance and was largely developed by John von Neumann (1903–1957), a Hungarian-born mathematical genius. Game theory has been used by economists to study the interaction of oligopolists, union-management disputes, countries' trade policies, international environmental agreements, reputations, and a host of other situations.

Game theory offers insights for politics, warfare, and everyday life as well. For example, it suggests that in some circumstances a carefully chosen random pattern of behavior may be the best strategy. A security guard should make rounds at random, not in a fixed routine. And you should occasionally bluff at poker, not simply to win a pot with a weak hand but also to ensure that other players do not drop out when you bet high on a good hand.

Thinking about Price Setting

Let's begin by analyzing the dynamics of price cutting. You are the head of an established firm, Amazing.com, whose motto is "We will not be undersold." You open your browser and discover that nEwBooks, an upstart Internet bookseller, has an advertisement that says, "We sell for 10 percent less." Figure 11-3 shows the dynamics. The vertical rust arrows show nEwBooks' price cuts; the horizontal rust arrows show Amazing's responding strategy of matching each price cut.

By tracing through the pattern of reaction and counterreaction, you can see that this kind of rivalry will end in mutual ruin at a zero price. Why? Because the only price compatible with both strategies is a price of zero: 90 percent of zero is zero.

Finally, it dawns on the two firms: When one firm cuts its price, the other firm will match the price cut.

FIGURE 11-3. What Happens When Two Firms Insist on Undercutting Each Other?

Trace through the steps by which dynamic price cutting leads to ever-lower prices for two rivals.

Only if the firms are shortsighted will they think that they can undercut each other for long. Soon each begins to ask, What will my rival do if I cut my price, or raise my price, or leave it alone? *Once you begin to consider how others will react to your actions, you have entered the realm of game theory.*

BASIC CONCEPTS

We will illustrate the basic concepts of game theory by analyzing a **duopoly price game.** A duopoly is a market which is served by only two firms. For simplicity, we assume that each firm has the same cost and demand structure. Further, each firm can choose whether to charge its normal price or lower its price below marginal costs and try to drive its rival into bankruptcy and then capture the entire market. The novel element in the duopoly game is that the firm's profits will depend on its rival's strategy as well as on its own.

A useful tool for representing the interaction between two firms or people is a two-way **payoff table.** A payoff table is a means of showing the strategies and the payoffs of a game between two players. Figure 11-4 shows the payoffs in the duopoly price game for our two companies. In the payoff table, a firm can choose between the strategies listed in its rows or columns.

For example, nEwBooks can choose between its two columns and Amazing can choose between its two rows. In this example, each firm decides whether to charge its normal price or to start a price war by choosing a lower price.

Combining the two decisions of each duopolist gives four possible outcomes, which are shown in the four cells of the table. Cell A, at the upper left, shows the outcome when both firms choose the normal price; D is the outcome when both choose to conduct a price war; and B and C result when one firm has a normal price and one a war price.

The numbers inside the cells show the **payoffs** of the two firms, that is, the profits earned by each firm for each of the four outcomes. The rust number in the lower left shows the payoff to the player on the left (Amazing); the black entry in the upper right shows the payoff to the player at the top (nEwBooks). Because the firms are identical, the payoffs are mirror images.

Alternative Strategies

Now that we have described the basic structure of a game, we next consider the behavior of the players. The new element in game theory is analyzing not only your own actions but also the interaction between your goals and moves and those of your opponent. But in trying to outwit your opponent, you must always remember that your opponent is trying to outwit you.

The guiding philosophy in game theory is the following: Pick your strategy by asking what makes most sense for you assuming that your opponents are analyzing your strategy and doing what is best for them.

Let's apply this maxim to the duopoly example. First, note that our two firms have the highest joint profits in outcome A. Each firm earns $10 when both follow a normal-price strategy. At the other extreme is the price war, where each cuts its price and runs a big loss.

In between are two interesting strategies where only one firm engages in the price war. In outcome C, for example, nEwBooks follows a normal-price strategy while Amazing engages in a price war. Amazing takes most of the market but loses a great deal of money because it is selling below cost; nEwBooks is actually better off selling at a normal price rather than responding.

FIGURE 11-4. A Payoff Table for a Price War

The payoff table shows the payoffs associated with different strategies. Amazing.com has a choice between two strategies, shown as its two rows; nEwBooks can choose between its two strategies, shown as two columns. The entries in the cells show the profits for the two players. For example, in cell C, Amazing plays "price war" and nEwBooks plays "normal price." The result is that Amazing has rust profit of −$100 while nEwBooks has black profit of −$10. Thinking through the best strategies for each player leads to the dominant equilibrium in cell A.

Dominant Strategy. In considering possible strategies, the simplest case is that of a **dominant strategy.** This situation arises when one player has a single best strategy *no matter what strategy the other player follows.*

In our price-war game, for example, consider the options open to Amazing. If nEwBooks conducts business as usual with a normal price, Amazing will get $10 of profit if it plays the normal price and will lose $100 if it declares economic war. On the other hand, if nEwBooks starts a war, Amazing will lose $10 if it follows the normal price but will lose even more if it also engages in economic warfare. You can see that the same reasoning holds for nEwBooks. Therefore, no matter what strategy the other firm follows, each firm's best strategy is to have the normal price. *Charging the normal price is a dominant strategy for both firms in this particular price-war game.*

When both (or all) players have a dominant strategy, we say that the outcome is a **dominant equilibrium.** We can see that in Figure 11-4, outcome A is a dominant equilibrium because it arises from a situation where both firms are playing their dominant strategies.

Nash Equilibrium. Most interesting situations do not have a dominant equilibrium, and we must therefore

look further. We can use our duopoly example to explore this case. In this example, which we call the *rivalry game,* each firm considers whether to charge its normal price or to raise its price toward the monopoly price and try to earn monopoly profits.

The rivalry game is shown in Figure 11-5. The firms can stay at their normal-price equilibrium, which we found in the price-war game. Or they can raise their price in the hopes of earning monopoly profits. Our two firms have the highest *joint* profits in cell A; here they earn a total of $300 when each follows a high-price strategy. Situation A would surely come about if the firms could collude and set the monopoly price. At the other extreme is the competitive-style strategy of the normal price, where each rival has profits of $10.

In between are two interesting strategies where one firm chooses a normal-price and one a high-price strategy. In cell C, for example, nEwBooks follows a high-price strategy but Amazing undercuts. Amazing takes most of the market and has the highest profit of any situation, while nEwBooks actually loses money. In cell B, Amazing gambles on high price, but nEwBooks' normal price means a loss for Amazing.

The Rivalry Game

* Nash equilibrium

FIGURE 11-5. Should a Duopolist Try the Monopoly Price?

In the rivalry game, each firm can earn $10 by staying at its normal price. If both raise price to the high monopoly level, their joint profits will be maximized. However, each firm's temptation to "cheat" and raise its profits by lowering price ensures that the normal-price Nash equilibrium will prevail in the absence of collusion.

In this example of the rivalry game, Amazing has a dominant strategy; it will profit more by choosing a normal price no matter what nEwBooks does. On the other hand, nEwBooks does not have a dominant strategy, because nEwBooks would want to play normal if Amazing plays normal and would want to play high if Amazing plays high.

This leaves nEwBooks with an intriguing dilemma. Should it play high and hope that Amazing will follow suit? Or play safe by playing normal? By thinking through the payoffs, it becomes clear that nEwBooks should play normal price. The reason is simple— nEwBooks should start by putting itself in Amazing's shoes. You can see that Amazing will play normal price no matter what nEwBooks does because that is Amazing's dominant strategy. Therefore, nEwBooks should find its best action by assuming that Amazing will follow Amazing's best strategy, which immediately leads to nEwBooks' playing normal. This illustrates the basic rule of game theory: You should set your strategy on the assumption that your opponent will act in his or her best interest.

We have in fact described a deep concept known as the Nash equilibrium, named after mathematician John Nash, who won a Nobel Prize for his discovery. A **Nash equilibrium** is a solution in which no player can improve his or her payoff given the other player's

strategy. In other words, each player's strategy is a best response against the other player's strategy.[1]

The Nash equilibrium is also sometimes called the **noncooperative equilibrium,** because each party chooses that strategy which is best for itself—without collusion or cooperation and without regard for the welfare of society or any other party.

We can verify that the starred strategies in Figure 11-5 are Nash equilibria. That is, neither nEwBooks nor Amazing can improve its payoffs from the (normal, normal) equilibrium as long as the other doesn't change its strategy. If Amazing moves to its high-price strategy, its profits go from $10 to −$20, while if nEwBooks raises its price from the normal-price Nash equilibrium, its profits go from $10 to −$30. (Verify that the dominant equilibrium shown in Figure 11-4 is also a Nash equilibrium.)

---

[1] More precisely, suppose that firm A picks strategy S_A while firm B picks strategy S_B. The pair of strategies $(S_A{}^*, S_B{}^*)$ is a Nash equilibrium if neither player can find a better strategy to play under the assumption that the other player sticks to his or her original strategy. That is, as long as A plays strategy $S_A{}^*$, B cannot do better than to play strategy $S_B{}^*$, and the analogous rule holds for A. This discussion focuses on two-person games, but the analysis (and particularly the important Nash equilibrium) can be usefully extended to many-person ("n-person") games.

SOME IMPORTANT EXAMPLES OF GAME THEORY

To Collude or Not to Collude

Is the noncooperative Nash equilibrium an efficient one that is in the best interests of the two players? One of the important lessons of game theory is that the noncooperative equilibrium can be inefficient for the players. Figure 11-5 highlights this point. The starred Nash equilibrium in cell D brings in less total profit for the duopolists than *any* of the other outcomes. The best joint solution is A, with each duopolist charging the high price and earning total profits of $300. The worst is the noncooperative Nash equilibrium with total profits of $20.

How can the Nash equilibrium survive when both oligopolists together are earning less than they would with any other outcome? Remember Adam Smith's maxim: "People of the same trade seldom meet together . . . but the conversation ends . . . in some contrivance to raise prices." Why don't the firms just collude and choose the monopoly price?

Let's consider the **cooperative equilibrium,** which occurs when the players act in unison and set strategies that will maximize their joint payoffs. They may decide to form a cartel, setting a high price and dividing all profits equally between the firms. Clearly, this will help the duopolists at the expense of the consumers.

But it is not always so easy to reach and sustain the cooperative monopoly solution. To begin with, cartels and collusion in restraint of trade are illegal in most market economies. But the highest hurdle is self-interest. Say that the price has been collusively set at (high, high) in cell A of Figure 11-5. Then Amazing secretly decides to sell a little output at a lower price, in effect moving to cell C. Amazing might be able to do this undetected for a while. During this time, Amazing would earn higher profits, $150 instead of $100.

Eventually, nEwBooks would notice that its profits had fallen. It would then reassess its strategy and, perhaps concluding that the cartel had come unglued, would also cut its price to the normal level. If the cooperative equilibrium (high, high) was not enforceable, the firms would quickly gravitate to the noncooperative or Nash equilibrium in outcome D (normal, normal).

We can apply this reasoning to perfectly competitive markets as well. *A perfectly competitive equilibrium is a Nash or noncooperative equilibrium in which each firm and consumer makes decisions by taking the prices of everyone else as given.* In this equilibrium, each firm maximizes profits and each consumer maximizes utility, leading to a zero-profit outcome in which price equals marginal cost.

Recall Adam Smith's doctrine of the invisible hand: "By pursuing [an individual's] own interest, he frequently promotes that of society more effectually than when he really intends to promote it." The paradox of the invisible hand is that, even though each person is behaving in a noncooperative manner, the economic outcome is socially efficient. Moreover, the competitive equilibrium is a Nash equilibrium in the sense that no individual would be better off by changing strategies as long as all other individuals continue with their strategies.

In the perfectly competitive world, noncooperative behavior produces the socially desirable state of economic efficiency.

By contrast, if some parties (such as our two duopolists) were to *cooperate* and decide to move to the monopoly price in cell A, the efficiency of the economy would suffer. This suggests why governments want to enforce antitrust laws that contain harsh penalties for those who collude to fix prices or divide up the markets.

The Prisoner's Dilemma

In our price-cutting game in Figure 11-5, we saw that competition among firms led to the competitive outcome with low prices. We also saw that, by an almost miraculous coincidence of economic life, Adam Smith's invisible hand produces in perfectly competitive markets an efficient allocation of resources.

But the beneficial outcome of the invisible hand does not arise in all circumstances. This is illustrated in the **prisoner's dilemma,** one of the most famous of all games. Figure 11-6 is like Figure 11-5; here it refers to prisoners Molly and Knuckles, who are partners in crime. The district attorney interviews each separately, saying, "I have enough on both of you to send you to jail for a year. But I'll make a deal with you: If you *alone* confess, you'll get off with a 3-month sentence, while your partner will

The Prisoner's Dilemma

FIGURE 11-6. To Confess or Not to Confess, That Is the Prisoner's Dilemma

No matter what the other does, when faced with these terms, it is always better for each prisoner to confess and act noncooperatively (selfishly). Only through cooperation or altruism can the pair move to cell D and avoid long prison terms.

serve 10 years. If you *both* confess, you'll both get 5 years."

What should Molly do? Should she confess and hope to get a short sentence? Three months are preferable to the year she would get if she remains silent. But wait. There is an even better reason for confessing. Suppose Molly doesn't confess and, unbeknownst to her, Knuckles does confess. Molly stands to get 10 years! It's clearly better in this situation for Molly to confess and get 5 years rather than 10 years.

Knuckles is in the same dilemma: if only he knew what Molly was thinking, or what Molly thought Knuckles was thinking Molly was thinking, or . . .

The significant result here is that when both prisoners act selfishly by confessing, they both end up with long prison terms. Only when they *both* act collusively or altruistically will they end up with short prison terms.

The Pollution Game

An important example, similar in structure to the prisoner's dilemma, is the *pollution game* shown in Figure 11-7. Consider an economy with externalities such as pollution. In a world of unregulated firms, each profit-maximizing firm would prefer to pollute rather than install expensive pollution-control equipment. Moreover, any firm which behaves altruistically

and cleans up its wastes will have higher production costs, higher prices, and fewer customers. If its costs are high enough, the firm may even go bankrupt. The pressures of Darwinian competition will drive all firms to the starred Nash equilibrium in cell D in Figure 11-7; here neither firm can improve its profits by lowering pollution.

The pollution game is an example of a situation in which the invisible-hand mechanism of efficient perfect competition breaks down. *This is a situation in which the noncooperative or Nash equilibrium is inefficient.*

When the Nash equilibria become dangerously inefficient, governments may step in. By setting efficient regulations or emissions charges, or perhaps by establishing efficient property rights, government can induce firms to move to outcome A, the "low-pollute, low-pollute" world. In that equilibrium, the firms make the same profit as in the high-pollution world, and the earth is a healthier place to live in.

Deadly Arms Races

Game theory has wide applications in political science, military strategy, and evolutionary biology. A particularly dangerous game with an inefficient noncooperative equilibrium, seen many times in history, is the *arms race*. Say you are superpower A

FIGURE 11-7. Noncooperative Behavior Leads to More Pollution

In the deadly pollution game, each unregulated profit-maximizing firm emits pollution into streams and air. If a single firm cleans up its production, it raises prices to cover cleanup costs, loses business, and suffers a decline in profits. The noncooperative Nash equilibrium in D leads to the high-pollution solution at bottom right. Government can overcome this by enforcing the cooperative equilibrium in A, where profits are the same and the environment has been cleaned up.

facing hostile superpower R, or anticipating the rise of superpower C. You want to make sure that you have sufficient nuclear weapons to deter aggression. Because you are uncertain about your opponent's intentions, you play it safe by having a modest weapons superiority over your opponent. Your generals tell you that this is just prudent military policy.

Now put yourself in the shoes of R, which is watching you engage in a military buildup. R does not know your intentions. Its generals also counsel a strategy of prudent superiority. So A wants 10 percent more bombs than R, and R wants 10 percent more bombs than A. This triggers an explosive arms race.

Do not think for a moment that this is a fanciful example. The noncooperative arms race between the United States and the Soviet Union over the 1945–1991 period led to massive military spending and an arsenal of almost 100,000 nuclear warheads.

These situations call for cooperative solutions in which the parties get together to reduce the armaments. Arms-control agreements move the outcome from an inefficient noncooperative equilibrium to a less inefficient cooperative outcome. In doing so, they can increase the security and welfare of all participants.

Winner-take-all Society?

Is it possible that economic life is increasingly becoming a giant tournament—the civilian equivalent of an arms race?

Ask yourself what all the following have in common: best-sellers, patents, Olympic gold medalists, supermodels, victorious lawsuits, Nobel Prize winners, and presidents of the United States. They are all outcomes of **winner-take-all games,** situations in which the payoffs are determined primarily by *relative* merit rather than absolute merit. There is only one gold medalist in the 400-meter dash, only one winner to a lawsuit, and only one book at the top of the best-seller list. Compare such situations with factory workers, whose earnings are determined by *absolute* marginal productivity rather than relative marginal productivity.

One common feature of such contests is that the rewards are heavily concentrated at the very top. Supermodel Claudia Schiffer is reported to have earned $10.5 million in 1998, while most models make very little or nothing. Best-selling authors like Stephen King or Danielle Steel are paid up to $60 million for the rights to their books, while surveys indicate that the average writer makes not much more than the minimum wage. Comedian Jerry Seinfeld is reported to have earned almost $300 million in 1998. By contrast, in a recent year, only one-tenth of the members of the Actors' Guild were actually paid for appearing in films, while hopefuls kept the wolf from the door with activities such as driving taxis and waiting on tables.

Figure 11-8 shows the winner-take-all game. Lucky or talented Winner has a powerful incentive to participate in the winner-take-all tournament; she ultimately prevails and gets an income of $300,000. Runner-Up has the choice of working in an absolute-return industry like manufacturing or joining the tournament in entertainment, athletics, or law. If Runner-Up thinks he has an even chance of prevailing, he enters the race because he estimates that his expected earnings are $100,000 in winner-take-all industries and $50,000 in conventional occupations.

The outcome is the "overcrowded" equilibrium at the lower right, where both people enter the tournament. National income is higher here than in the dull equilibrium, where there are no exciting contests, but lower than in the efficient outcome, where Runner-Up does not enter the contest. An inefficient winner-take-all equilibrium generates the highest inequality of earnings of all outcomes.

A fascinating study by Robert Frank and Philip Cook explores the consequences of what they call a "winner-take-all society." The following quote suggests how game theory has illuminated this important part of economic life:

> Whereas free marketeers maintain that market incentives lead to socially efficient results, our claim is that winner-take-all markets attract too many contestants, result in inefficient patterns of consumption and investment, and often degrade our culture. . . . The explosion of top salaries has stemmed largely from the growing prevalence of winner-take-all markets.[2]

Frank and Cook argue the need for "positional arms control" (such as reforming the legal system) and progressive taxes on consumption as a way of reducing the waste from excessive competition for large prizes in entertainment, athletics, and business.

_____

[2] See Frank and Cook, pp. 6 and 19, in the Further Reading section.

The Winner-Take-All Game

		Winner	
		Work in standard industry	**Work in winner-take-all industry**
Runner-Up	Work in standard industry	A* $50 $50 NI = $100	B† $300 $50 NI = $350
	Work in winner-take-all industry	C $50 $200 NI = $250	D‡ $300 $0 NI = $300

Note: Earnings in thousands.
* Dull
† Efficient
‡ Overcrowded

FIGURE 11-8. When Too Many People Enter Contests, National Income Can Fall

In the winner-take-all game, Winner gets high rewards in professional sports or high-stakes lawsuits. Runner-Up at left is lured into the winner-take-all market by the possibility of a large gain. Like too many fishing boats chasing the same fish, winner-take-all markets are overcrowded with many people ultimately getting low earnings. Total incomes would rise if Runner-Up stayed in a standard, absolute-reward industry.

Games, Games, Everywhere ...

The insights of game theory pervade economics, the social sciences, business, and everyday life. In economics, for example, game theory can explain trade wars as well as price wars (some illuminating examples are provided in the questions at the end of this chapter).

Game theory can also suggest why foreign competition may lead to greater price competition. What happens when Japanese firms enter a U.S. market where firms had tacitly colluded on a price strategy that led to a high oligopolistic price? The foreign firms may "refuse to play the game." They did not agree to the rules, so they may cut prices to gain market shares. Collusion may break down.

A key feature in many games is the attempt of players to build *credibility*. You are credible if you are expected to keep your promises and carry out your threats. But you cannot gain credibility with simple promises. Credibility must be consistent with the incentives of the game.

How can you get credibility? Here are some examples: Central banks earn reputations for being tough on inflation by adopting politically unpopular policies. Even greater credibility comes when the central bank's rules are written into law or the nation's constitution. Businesses make credible promises by writing contracts that inflict penalties if they do not perform as promised. A more perilous strategy is for an army to burn its bridges behind it. Because there is no retreat, the threat to fight to the death is a credible one.

These few examples provide a small taste from the vast harvest produced by game theorists over the last half-century. This area has been enormously useful in helping economists and other social scientists think about situations where small numbers of people are well informed and try to outwit each other in markets, politics, or military affairs.

SUMMARY

A. Economics of Risk and Uncertainty

1. Economic life is full of uncertainty. Consumers face uncertain incomes and employment patterns as well as the threat of catastrophic losses; businesses have uncertain costs, and their revenues contain uncertainties about price and production.

2. In well-functioning markets, arbitrage, speculation, and insurance help smooth out the unavoidable risks. Speculators are people who buy and sell assets or commodities with an eye to making profits on price differentials across markets. They move goods across regions from low-price to high-price markets, across time from periods of abundance to periods of scarcity, and even across uncertain states of nature to periods when chance makes goods scarce.

3. The profit-seeking action of speculators and arbitragers tends to create certain equilibrium patterns of price over space and time. These market equilibria are zero-profit outcomes where the marginal costs and marginal utilities in different regions, times, or uncertain states of nature are in balance. To the extent that speculators moderate price and consumption instability, they are part of the invisible-hand mechanism that performs the socially useful function of reallocating goods from feast times (when prices are low) to famine times (when prices are high).

4. Speculative markets allow individuals to hedge against unwelcome risks. The economic principle of risk aversion, which derives from diminishing marginal utility, implies that individuals will not accept risky situations with zero expected value. Risk aversion implies that people will buy insurance to reduce the disastrous declines in utility from fire, death, or other calamities.

5. Insurance and risk spreading tend to stabilize consumption in different states of nature. Insurance takes large individual risks and spreads them so broadly that they become acceptable to a large number of individuals. Insurance is beneficial because, by helping to equalize consumption across different uncertain states, it raises the expected level of utility.

6. The conditions for operation of efficient insurance markets are stringent: there must be large numbers of independent events, with little chance of moral hazard or adverse selection. When market failures such as adverse selection arise, prices can become distorted or markets may simply not exist. If private insurance markets fail, the government may step in to provide social insurance. Even in the most laissez-faire of advanced market economies today, governments insure against unemployment and health risks in old age.

B. Game Theory

7. Economic life contains many situations of strategic interaction among firms, households, governments, or others. Game theory analyzes the way that two or more parties, who interact in an arena such as a market, choose actions or strategies that jointly affect each participant.

8. The basic structure of a game includes the players, who have different actions or strategies, and the payoffs, which describe the profits or other benefits that the players obtain in each outcome. The key new concept is the payoff table of a game, which shows the strategies and the payoffs or profits of the different players.

9. The key to choosing strategies in game theory is for players to think through both their own and their opponent's goals, never forgetting that the other side is doing the same. When playing a game in economics or any other field, assume that your opponent will choose his or her best option. Then pick your strategy so as to maximize your benefit, always assuming that your opponent is similarly analyzing your options.

10. Sometimes a dominant strategy is available, one that is best no matter what the opposition does. More often, we find the Nash equilibrium (or noncooperative equilibrium) a useful equilibrium concept. A Nash equilibrium is one in which no player can improve his or her payoff given the other player's strategy. Sometimes, parties can collude or cooperate, which produces the cooperative equilibrium.

11. A Nash equilibrium produces an efficient outcome in Adam Smith's invisible-hand game. Here, noncollusive firms produce at prices equal to marginal costs, and the noncooperative equilibrium is efficient. In such situations, cooperation leads to inefficient production.

12. Sometimes, however, noncooperative behavior leads to social ruin, as when competitors pollute the planet or engage in dangerous arms races. Winner-take-all games, such as lawsuits or athletic contests, can induce the entry of too many contestants and increase the inequality of fame and incomes.

CONCEPTS FOR REVIEW

Risk and Uncertainty

arbitrage leading to regional
    equalization of prices
ideal seasonal price pattern
speculation, arbitrage, hedging
risk aversion and diminishing
    marginal utility
consumption stability vs.
    instability

insurance and risk spreading
market failure in information
moral hazard, adverse selection
social insurance

Game Theory

players, strategies, payoffs
payoff table
dominant strategy and equilibrium

Nash or noncooperative equilibrium
cooperative or collusive equilibrium
important games:
    collusion
    prisoner's dilemma
    pollution
    winner-take-all
credibility

FURTHER READING AND INTERNET WEBSITES

Further Reading

Game theory was developed in 1944 by John von Neumann and Oscar Morgenstern and published in *Theory of Games and Economic Behavior* (Princeton University Press, Princeton, N.J., 1980). An entertaining review of game theory by two leading microeconomists is Avinash K. Dixit and Barry J. Nalebuff, *Thinking Strategically: The Competitive Edge in Business, Politics, and Everyday* (Norton, New York, 1993). A nontechnical biography of John Nash by journalist Silvia Nasar, *A Beautiful Mind: A Biography of John Forbes Nash Jr.* (Touchstone Books, 1999), is a vivid history of game theory and of one of its most brilliant theorists.

For an analysis of gambling, see William R. Eadington, "The Economics of Casino Gambling," *Journal of Economic Perspectives*, Summer 1999.

See Robert H. Frank and Philip J. Cook, *The Winner-Take-All Society* (Free Press, New York, 1995) for an interesting analysis of winner-take-all games.

Websites

Game theorists have set up a number of sites. See particularly those by David Levine of UCLA at levine.sscnet.ucla. edu and Al Roth of Harvard at www.economics.harvard. edu/~aroth/alroth.html.

QUESTIONS FOR DISCUSSION

1. Suppose a friend offers to flip a fair coin, with you paying your friend $100 if it comes up heads and your friend paying you $100 if it comes up tails. Explain why the expected dollar value is $0. Then explain why the expected utility value is negative if you are risk-averse.

2. Consider the example of grade insurance (see page 211). Suppose that under grade insurance, students would be compensated $5000 a year for each point that their grade point average fell below the top grade (this figure might be an estimate of the impact of grades on future earnings). Explain why the presence of grade insurance would produce moral hazard and adverse selection. Why would moral hazard and adverse selection make insurance companies reluctant to sell grade insurance? Are you surprised that you cannot buy grade insurance?

3. After the terrorist attacks of September 11, 2001, most insurance companies canceled their insurance coverage for terrorism. According to President Bush, "More than $15 billion in real estate transactions have been canceled or put on hold because owners and investors could not obtain the insurance protection they need."
As a result, the federal government stepped in to provide coverage for up to $90 billion in claims. Using the principles of insurance, explain why insurance companies might decline to insure property against terrorist attacks. Explain whether or not you think that the federal program is an appropriate form of social insurance.

4. In the early nineteenth century, little of the nation's agricultural output was sold in markets, and transportation costs were very high. What would you expect to have been the degree of variation of prices across regions compared with today?

5. Assume that a firm is making a risky investment (say, spending $2 billion developing a competitor to Windows). Can you see how the widely diversified ownership of this firm could allow near-perfect risk spreading on the software investment?

6. In the late 1980s, "arbs" (arbitragers) who became rich on the illegal use of inside information gave a bad name to speculation and arbitrage. Suppose that speculation and arbitrage are made a criminal offense (as was the case until recently in Russia). Explain the economic damage that could result.

7. Consider the dilemma of maintaining free trade shown in the payoff table in Figure 11-9, which gives total real national incomes (in billions) for two countries as a function of foreign-trade policies. Each country can have a policy either of free trade with no tariffs or quotas or of protectionism with high tariffs on imported goods and services. The payoffs are the real incomes in each country.

   a. List the four outcomes, and calculate each region's national income and world income.

   b. Show how countries acting noncooperatively (without agreements and in their own selfish national interest) will be led to a trade war at the Nash equilibrium in cell D. What is the effect of the trade war on total world income?

   c. What is the impact on incomes of a trade agreement that abolishes all trade restrictions and produces free trade?

   d. Is there an incentive for each country to "cheat" on the trade agreement? What happens if the cheating leads to retaliation and to the high-tariff outcome?

Free Trade vs. Protection

United States

		Free trade[†]	Protection*
Japan	Free trade[†]	A[†] $6,000 $3,000	B $6,100 $1,900
	Protection*	C $4,800 $3,200	D* $5,000 $2,000

*Nash equilibrium
[†]Cooperative equilibrium

FIGURE 11-9. Countries Gain from Trade but Lose from Trade War

Japan and the United States can agree to the cooperative equilibrium at A in which they reduce all tariffs and quotas and enjoy the benefits of free trade. Each is tempted to "cheat" by putting trade restrictions on imports, thus gaining income at home while hurting total world income, moving to B or C. Retaliation would lead to the worst of all worlds, at D.

Factor Markets: Labor, Land, and Capital

How Markets Determine Incomes

You know, Ernest, the rich are different from us.

F. Scott Fitzgerald

Yes, I know. They have more money than we do.

Ernest Hemingway

A. INCOME AND WEALTH

Earlier chapters have surveyed the output and prices of goods and services produced by tiny farms and giant corporations. But the vast array of products that we enjoy do not simply gush from the earth—they are produced by workers who are equipped with machines, which are housed in factories, which are sitting on land. These inputs into the productive process earn factor incomes—wages, profits, interest, and rents. The time has come to understand the determination of factor prices along with the forces that affect the distribution of income among the population.

America is a land of extremes of income and wealth. If you are one of the 400 richest Americans, you are probably a 60-year-old white male with a degree from a top university and a net worth of about $3 billion. This tiny sliver of American society owns about 5 percent of the total wealth of the country. In the past, you made your fortune in manufacturing or real estate, but recent billionaires come largely from the information economy in software and communications. Your voyage to the top was as much the product of birth as of brains, for your family probably gave you a head start with a substantial investment in the family business, but there are more self-made men and women today than there were a decade ago.

At the other extreme are forgotten people who never make the cover of *Forbes* or *People* magazine. Listen to the story of Robert Clark, homeless and unemployed. A roofer and Vietnam veteran, he came to Miami from Detroit looking for work. He slept on the city streets on a piece of cardboard covered by a stolen sheet. Every day he and other homeless men crept out of the culverts into the daylight to work for temporary-employment firms. These firms charged clients $8 to $10 an hour, paid the men the minimum wage, and then took most of the money back for transportation and tools. Clark's pay stub showed earnings of $31.28 for 31 hours of work.

How can we understand these extremes of income and wealth? Why are some people paid $10 million a year, while others net only $1 an hour? Why is real estate in Tokyo or Manhattan worth thousands of dollars a square foot, while land in the desert may sell for but a few dollars an acre? And what is the source of the billions of dollars of profits earned by giant enterprises like Microsoft and General Electric?

225

Questions about the distribution of income are among the most controversial in all economics. Some people argue that high incomes are the unfair result of past inheritance and luck while poverty stems from discrimination and lack of opportunity. Others believe that people get what they deserve and that interfering with the market distribution of income would injure an economy's efficiency and make everyone worse off. Government programs in America today reflect an uneasy consensus that incomes should be largely determined by market earnings but the government should provide a social "safety net" to catch the deserving poor who fall below some minimum standard of living.

INCOME

In measuring the economic status of a person or a nation, the two yardsticks most often used are income and wealth. **Income** refers to the flow of wages, interest payments, dividends, and other things of value accruing during a period of time (usually a year). The aggregate of all incomes is *national income,* the components of which are shown in Table 12-1.

The biggest share of national income goes to labor, either as wages or salaries or as fringe benefits. The remainder goes to the different types of *property income:* rent, net interest, corporate profits, and proprietors' income. This last category basically includes the returns to the owners of small businesses.[1]

The earnings in a market economy are distributed to the owners of the economy's factors of production in the form of wages, profits, rent, and interest.

Factor Incomes vs. Personal Incomes

It is important to understand the distinction between factor incomes and personal incomes. Table 12-1 reports the distribution of factor incomes—the division between labor and property incomes. But the same person may own many different factors of production. For example, someone might receive a salary, earn interest on money in a savings account, get dividends from shares in a mutual fund, and

---

[1] Economists and accountants often measure "income" in different ways. We studied accounting measures of income and wealth in Chapter 7.

Type of income	Amount ($, billion)	Share of total (%)	Examples
Labor income:			
Wages and salaries	5003.7	59.9	Autoworker's wages; teacher's salary
Benefits and other labor income	973.7	11.7	Company contribution to pension fund
Property income:			
Proprietors' income	756.5	9.1	Barber's earnings; lawyer's share of partnership net income
Rental income	142.4	1.7	Landlord's rent from apartments after expenses and depreciation
Corporate profits	787.4	9.4	Microsoft's profits
Net interest	684.2	8.2	Interest paid on savings account
Total	**8347.9**	**100.0**	

TABLE 12-1. Division of National Income, 2002

National income includes all the incomes paid to factors of production. Almost three-quarters consists of wages and other kinds of compensation of labor, while the rest is divided among rents, corporate profits, and the incomes of proprietors.

Source: U.S. Department of Commerce, Bureau of Economic Analysis, at the Web page www.bea.gov.

collect rent on a real-estate investment. In economic language, we observe that a person's market income is simply the quantities of factors of production sold by that person times the wage or price of each factor.

Almost three-quarters of national income goes to labor, while the rest is distributed as some form of returns to capital. The last quarter-century has been a turbulent one. What has been the impact of oil-price shocks, the computer revolution, globalization, corporate downsizing, and the long economic boom on labor's share of the total income pie? Looking at Figure 12-1, we can see that the share of national income going to labor has changed very little since 1970. This is one of the remarkable features of the income distribution in the United States.

Role of Government

How does government fit into this picture? Governments at every level form the largest source of wages, rents, and interest payments. The results of government purchases are included in the payments to factors of production shown in Table 12-1.

Yet government also has a direct role in incomes that does not show up in Table 12-1. To begin with,

the government collects a sizable share of national income through taxation and other levies. In 2003 about 30 percent of gross domestic product was collected by federal, state, and local governments as various types of taxes, including personal income taxes, corporate-profit taxes, and social security taxes.

But what governments tax, they also spend or give away. Governments at all levels provide incomes in the form of **transfer payments,** which are payments by governments to individuals that are not made in return for current goods or services. The biggest single category of transfer payments is social security for older Americans, but transfer payments also include unemployment insurance, farm subsidies, and welfare payments. Whereas Americans derived almost none of their incomes from governments in 1929, fully 13 percent of personal incomes in 2003 came from government transfer payments.

Personal income equals market income plus transfer payments. Most market income comes from wages and salaries; a small, affluent minority derives its market income from earnings on property. The major component of government transfers is social security payments to the elderly.

FIGURE 12-1. The Share of Labor in National Income

The share of labor income increased gradually from World War II until 1970. Since then, it has been remarkably stable at around 72 percent of national income. The remainder of income is distributed among rents, interest, corporate profits, and proprietors' income. The share of property-type income is 100 minus the labor share.

Source: U.S. Department of Commerce.

WEALTH

We see that some income comes from interest or dividends on holdings of bonds or stocks. This brings us to the second important economic concept: **Wealth** consists of the net dollar value of assets owned at a given point in time. Note that wealth is a *stock* (like the volume of a lake) while income is a *flow* per unit of time (like the flow of a stream). A household's wealth includes its tangible items (houses, cars and other consumer durable goods, and land) and its financial holdings (such as cash, savings accounts, bonds, and stocks). All items that are of value are called *assets,* while those that are owed are called *liabilities.* The difference between total assets and total liabilities is called wealth or *net worth.*

Table 12-2 presents a breakdown of the asset holdings of Americans from 1989 to 2001. The single most important asset of most households is the family home: 68 percent of families own houses, as compared with 55 percent a generation ago. Most households own a modest amount of financial wealth in savings accounts, and about one-fifth directly own corporate stocks. But it turns out that a large proportion of the nation's financial wealth is concentrated in the hands of a small fraction of the population. About one-third of all wealth is owned by the richest 1 percent of American households.

Distribution of Assets of All Families as Percentage of All Assets, 1989–2001					
	Percentage of Total Assets				
Type of Asset	**1989**	**1992**	**1995**	**1998**	**2001**
Financial:					
Bank deposits and similar	9.4	8.4	7.7	6.7	6.4
Bonds	3.1	2.7	2.3	1.7	1.9
Stocks	6.2	7.6	10.4	14.3	14.2
Retirement accounts	6.6	8.1	10.3	11.2	11.9
Other	5.3	4.8	6.0	6.8	7.5
Tangible and other assets:					
Own home	31.9	32.2	30.0	27.9	27.2
Other real estate and property	13.4	13.3	10.0	9.6	9.4
Vehicles	3.9	3.9	4.5	3.8	3.5
Business equity	18.6	18.0	17.2	16.9	17.0
Other	1.7	1.1	1.5	1.0	1.0
Family net worth (2001 dollars, thousands):					
Median	64.6	61.3	66.4	78.0	86.1
Average	255.4	230.5	244.8	307.4	395.5

TABLE 12-2. Trends in Assets Owned by American Families

Households own tangible assets (such as houses and cars) as well as financial assets (such as savings accounts and stocks). Financial assets grew as a share of total assets, but the largest single asset for most Americans continues to be the family home. Note how the share of stocks in portfolios grew sharply. Also, note that the median wealth is much smaller than the average, reflecting the great inequality of wealth holding.

Source: Federal Reserve Board, Survey of Consumer Finances, available in *Federal Reserve Bulletin* or at www.federalreserve. gov/pubs/oss/oss2/2001/scf2001home.html.

B. INPUT PRICING BY MARGINAL PRODUCTIVITY

The **theory of income distribution** (or **distribution theory**) studies how incomes are determined in a market economy. People are often puzzled by the vast differences in incomes of different families. Are they caused by differences in talents? By monopoly power? By government intervention? Why is Bill Gates worth $60 billion while half of American black families have zero or negative net worth? Why are land prices so much higher in the city than in the desert?

Our first answer to these questions is that the distribution theory is a special case of the theory of prices. Wages are the price of labor; rents are the price for using land; and so forth. Moreover, the prices of factors of production are primarily set by the interaction between supply and demand for different factors—just as the prices of goods are largely determined by the supply and demand for goods.

But pointing to supply and demand is just the first step on the road to understanding income distribution in a competitive market economy. We will see that the key to incomes lies in the *marginal products* of different factors of production. In this section, we will see that wages are determined by the value of the *marginal product of labor,* or what is known as the marginal revenue product of labor. The same holds for other factors of production as well. We first discuss this new concept and then show how it solves the puzzle of how incomes are determined.

THE NATURE OF FACTOR DEMANDS

The demand for factors differs from that for consumption goods in two important respects: (1) Factor demands are derived demands, and (2) factor demands are interdependent demands.

Demands for Factors Are Derived Demands

Let's consider the demand for office space by a firm which produces computer software. A software company will rent office space for its programmers, customer service representatives, and other workers.

Similarly, other companies like pizza shops or banks will need space for their activities. In each region, there will be a downward-sloping demand curve for office space linking the rent being charged by landlords to the amount of office space desired by companies—the lower the price, the more space companies will want to rent.

But there is an essential difference between ordinary demands by consumers and the demand by firms for inputs. Consumers demand final goods like computer games or pizzas because of the direct enjoyment or utility these consumption goods provide. By contrast, a business does not pay for inputs like office space because they yield direct satisfaction. Rather, it buys inputs because of the production and revenue that it can gain from employment of those factors.

Satisfactions are in the picture for inputs—but at one stage removed. The satisfaction that consumers get from playing computer games determines how many games the software company can sell, how many order takers it needs, and how much office space it must rent. The more successful its software, the greater its demand for office space. An accurate analysis of the demand for inputs must, therefore, recognize that consumer demands do *ultimately* determine business demands for office space.

This analysis is not limited to office space. Consumer demands determine the demand for all inputs, including farmland, oil, and pizza ovens. Can you see how the demand for professors of economics is ultimately determined by the demand for economics courses by students?

The firm's demand for inputs is derived indirectly from the consumer demand for its final product.

Economists therefore speak of the demand for productive factors as a **derived demand.** This means that when firms demand an input, they do so because that input permits them to produce a good which consumers desire now or in the future. Figure 12-2 on page 230 shows how the demand for a given input, such as fertile cornland, must be regarded as being derived from the consumer demand curve for corn. In the same way, the demand for office space is derived from the consumer demand for software and all the other products and services provided by the companies that rent office space.

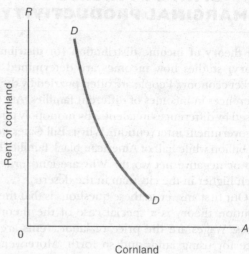

(a) Commodity Demand

Price of corn

Corn

(b) Derived Factor Demand

Rent of cornland

Cornland

FIGURE 12-2. Demand for Factors Is Derived from Demand for Goods They Produce

The rust curve of derived demand for cornland comes from the black curve of commodity demand for corn. Shift the black curve out, and out goes the rust curve. If the black commodity curve becomes more inelastic, the same tends to happen to the rust input demand curve.

Demands for Factors Are Interdependent

Production is a team effort. A chain saw by itself is useless for cutting down a tree. A worker with empty hands is equally worthless. Together, the worker and the saw can cut the tree very nicely. In other words, the productivity of one factor, such as labor, depends upon the amount of other factors available to work with.

Therefore, it is generally impossible to say how much output has been created by a single input taken by itself. Asking which factor is more important is like asking whether a mother or a father is more essential in producing a baby.

It is the *interdependence* of productivities of land, labor, and capital that makes the distribution of income a complex topic. Suppose you were charged with distributing the entire output of a nation. If land had by itself produced so much, and labor had by itself produced so much, and machinery had by itself produced the rest, distribution would be easy. Moreover, under supply and demand, if each factor produced a certain amount by itself, it could enjoy the undivided fruits of its own work.

But reread the above paragraph and underline such words as "by itself." They refer to a fantasy world of independent productivities which simply does not exist in reality. When an omelette is produced by chef's labor and chicken's eggs and cow's butter and land's natural gas, how can you unscramble the separate contributions of each input?

To find the answer, we must look to the interaction of marginal productivities and factor supplies—both of which determine the competitive price and quantity.

> **Review of Production Theory**
> Before showing the relationship between factor prices and marginal products, we will review the essentials of Chapter 6's production theory.
> The theory of production begins with the notion of the *production function*. The production function indicates the maximum amount of output that can be produced, with a given state of technical knowledge, for each combination

		Marginal Revenue Product		
(1) Unit of labor (workers)	(2) Total product (bushels)	(3) Marginal product of labor (bushels per worker)	(4) Price of output ($ per bushel)	(5) Marginal revenue product of labor ($ per worker)
0	0			
		20,000	3	60,000
1	20,000			
		10,000	3	30,000
2	30,000			
		5,000	3	15,000
3	35,000			
		3,000	3	9,000
4	38,000			
		1,000	3	3,000
5	39,000			

TABLE 12-3. Calculation of Marginal Revenue Product for Perfectly Competitive Firm

The marginal product of labor is shown in column (3). Marginal revenue product of labor shows how much additional revenue the firm receives when an additional unit of labor is employed. It equals the marginal product in column (3) times the competitive output price in column (4).

of factor inputs. The production-function concept provides a rigorous definition of marginal product. Recall that the *marginal product* of an input is the extra product or output added by 1 extra unit of that input while other inputs are held constant.[2] The first three columns of Table 12-3 provide a review of the way marginal products are calculated.

As a final element of review, recall the *law of diminishing returns*. Column (3) of Table 12-3 shows that each successive unit of labor has a declining marginal product. "Declining marginal product" is another name for diminishing returns. Moreover, we can interchange land for labor, varying the amount of land while holding constant labor and other inputs, and we would generally observe the law of diminishing returns at work for land as well as for labor.

---

[2] Note that the marginal product of a factor is expressed in *physical* units of product per unit of additional input. So economists sometimes use the term "marginal physical product" rather than "marginal product," particularly when they want to avoid any possible confusion with a concept we will soon encounter called "marginal revenue product." For brevity, we will skip the word "physical" and abbreviate marginal product as *MP*.

DISTRIBUTION THEORY AND MARGINAL REVENUE PRODUCT

The fundamental point about distribution theory is that *the demands for the various factors of production are derived from the revenues that each factor yields on its marginal product.* Before showing this result, we begin by defining some new terms.

Marginal Revenue Product

We can use the tools of production theory to devise a key concept, *marginal revenue product (MRP)*. Suppose we are operating a giant shirt factory. We know how many shirts each additional worker produces. But the firm wants to maximize profits measured in dollars, for it pays salaries and dividends with money, not with shirts. We therefore need a concept that measures the additional *dollars* each additional unit of input produces. Economists give the name "marginal revenue product" to the money value of the additional output generated by an extra unit of input.

The **marginal revenue product** of input A is the additional revenue produced by an additional unit of input A.

Perfectly Competitive Case. It is easy to calculate marginal revenue product when product markets are perfectly competitive. In this case, each unit of the worker's marginal product (MP_L) can be sold at the competitive output price (P). Moreover, since we are considering perfect competition, the output price is unaffected by the firm's output, and price therefore equals marginal revenue (MR). If we have an MP_L of 10,000 bushels and a price and MR of \$3, the dollar value of the output produced by the last worker—the marginal revenue product of labor (MRP_L)—is \$30,000 (equal to 10,000 × \$3). This is shown in column (5) of Table 12-3. Hence, under perfect competition, each worker is worth to the firm the dollar value of the last worker's marginal product; the value of each acre of land is the marginal product of land times the output price; and so forth for each factor.

Table 12-3 provides an essential linkage between production theory and factor demand theory; it should be studied carefully. The first three columns show the inputs, output, and marginal product of labor. Taking the marginal product in column (4), we can calculate the marginal revenue product of labor (in dollars per worker) in column (5). It is this last column which is critical for determining the demand for labor, as we will see later in this chapter. Once we know the wage rate, we can calculate the demand for labor from column (5).

Imperfect Competition. What happens in the case of imperfect competition, where the individual firm's demand curve is downward-sloping? Here, the marginal revenue received from each extra unit of output sold is less than the price because the firm must lower its price on previous units to sell an additional unit. Each unit of marginal product will be worth $MR < P$ to the firm.

To continue our previous example, say that the MR is \$2 while the price is \$3. Then the MRP of the second worker in Table 12-3 would be \$20,000 (equal to the MP_L of 10,000 × the MR of \$2), rather than the \$30,000 of the competitive case.
To summarize:

Marginal revenue product represents the additional revenue a firm earns from using an additional unit of an input, with other inputs held constant. It is calculated as the marginal product of the input multiplied by the marginal revenue obtained from selling an extra unit of output. This holds for labor (L), land (A), and other inputs. In symbols:

$$\text{Marginal revenue product of labor}$$
$$(MRP_L) = MR \times MP_L$$

$$\text{Marginal revenue product of land}$$
$$(MRP_A) = MR \times MP_A$$

and so forth.

Under conditions of perfect competition, because $P = MR$,

$$\text{Marginal revenue product}$$
$$(MRP_i) = P \times MP_i$$

for each input.

THE DEMAND FOR FACTORS OF PRODUCTION

Having analyzed the underlying concepts, we now show how profit-maximizing firms decide upon the optimal combination of inputs, which allows us to derive the demand for inputs.

Factor Demands for Profit-Maximizing Firms

What determines the demand for any factor of production? We can answer this question by analyzing how a profit-oriented firm chooses its optimal combination of inputs.

Imagine that you are a profit-maximizing farmer. In your area, you can hire all the farmhands you want at \$20,000 per worker. Your accountant hands you a spreadsheet with the data in Table 12-3. How would you proceed?

You could try out different possibilities. If you hire one worker, the additional revenue (the MRP) is \$60,000 while the marginal cost of the worker is \$20,000, so your extra profit is \$40,000. A second worker gives you an MRP of \$30,000 for an additional profit of \$10,000. The third worker produces extra output yielding revenue of only \$15,000 but costs \$20,000; hence, it is not profitable to hire the third worker. Table 12-3 shows that the maximum profit is earned by hiring two workers.

By using this reasoning, we can derive the rule for choosing the optimal combination of inputs:

To maximize profits, firms should add inputs up to the point where the marginal revenue product of the input equals the marginal cost or price of the input.

For perfectly competitive factor markets, the rule is even simpler. Recall that under perfect competition the marginal revenue product equals price times marginal product ($MRP = P \times MP$).

The profit-maximizing combination of inputs for a perfectly competitive firm comes when the marginal product times the output price equals the price of the input:

Marginal product of labor $\times$ output price
= price of labor = wage rate

Marginal product of land $\times$ output price
= price of land = rent

and so forth.

We can understand this rule by the following reasoning: Say that each kind of input is bundled into little packages each worth $1—packages of $1 worth of labor, $1 worth of land, and so forth. To maximize profits, firms will purchase inputs up to that point where each little $1 package produces output which is worth just $1. In other words, each $1 input package will produce MP units of corn so that the $MP \times P$ just equals $1. The MRP of the $1 units is then exactly $1 under profit maximization.

Least-Cost Rule. We can restate the condition much more generally in a way that applies to both perfect and imperfect competition in product markets (as long as factor markets are competitive). Reorganizing the basic conditions shown above, profit maximization implies:

$$\frac{\text{Marginal product of labor}}{\text{Price of labor}} = \frac{\text{Marginal product of land}}{\text{price of land}} = \cdots$$

$$= \frac{1}{\text{marginal revenue}}$$

Suppose that you own a cable television monopoly in Denver. If you want to maximize profits, you will want to choose the best combination of workers, land easements for your cables, trucks, and testing equipment to minimize costs. If a month's truck rental costs $8000 while monthly labor costs per worker are $800, costs are minimized when the marginal products *per dollar of input* are the same. Since trucks cost 10 times as much as labor, truck MP must be 10 times labor MP.

Least-cost rule: Costs are minimized when the marginal product per dollar of input is equalized for each input. This holds for both perfect and imperfect competitors in product markets.

Marginal Revenue Product and the Demand for Factors

Having derived the MRP for different factors, we can now understand the demand for factors of production. We just saw that a profit-maximizing firm would choose input quantities such that the price of each input equaled the MRP of that input. This means that from the MRP schedule for an input, we can immediately determine the relationship between the price of the input and the quantity demanded of that input. This relationship is what we call the demand curve.

Glance back at Table 12-3 on page 231. This table shows in the last column the MRP of labor for our corn farm. By the profit-maximizing condition, we know that at a wage of $60,000 the firm would choose 1 unit of labor; at a $30,000 wage, 2 units of labor would be sought; and so forth.

The MRP schedule for each input gives the demand schedule of the firm for that input.

We have used this result in Figure 12-3 to draw a labor demand curve for our corn farm using the data shown in Table 12-3. We have in addition drawn a

FIGURE 12-3. Demand for Inputs Derived through Marginal Revenue Products

The demand for labor is derived from the marginal revenue product of labor. This figure uses the data for the competitive firm displayed in Table 12-3.

smooth curve through the individual points to show how the demand curve would appear if fractional units of labor could be purchased.

From Firm to Market Demand. The final step in determining the demand for labor and other factors is the aggregation of the demand curves for different firms. As with all demand curves, the competitive-market demand curve is the *horizontal summation of the demand curves of all the firms.* Hence, if there were 1000 identical firms, then the market demand for labor would be exactly like that in Figure 12-3 except the horizontal axis would have each entry multiplied by 1000. We see, then, that the competitive demand for factors of production is determined by the sum of the demands of all the firms at each marginal revenue product.

Substitution Rule. A corollary of the least-cost rule is the **substitution rule:** If the price of one factor rises while other factor prices remain fixed, the firm will profit from substituting more of the other inputs for the more expensive factor. A rise in labor's price, P_L, will reduce MP_L/P_L. Firms will respond by reducing employment and increasing land use until equality of marginal products per dollar of input is restored—thus lowering the amount of needed L and increasing the demand for land acres. A rise in land's price, P_A, alone will, by the same logic, cause labor to be substituted for more expensive land. Like the least-cost rule, the substitution rule and the derived demand for factors apply to both perfect and imperfect competition in product markets.

SUPPLY OF FACTORS OF PRODUCTION

A complete analysis of the determination of factor prices and of incomes must combine both the demand for inputs just described and the supplies of different factors. The general principles of supply vary from input to input, and this topic will be explored in depth in the next two chapters. At this point we provide a few introductory comments.

In a market economy, most factors of production are privately owned. People "own" their labor in the sense that they control its use; but this crucial "human capital" can today only be rented, not sold. Capital and land are generally privately owned by households and by businesses.

Decisions about *labor* supply are determined by many economic and noneconomic factors. The important determinants of labor supply are the price of labor (i.e., the wage rate) and demographic factors, such as age, gender, education, and family structure. The quantity of *land* and other natural resources is determined by geology and cannot be significantly changed, although the quality of land is affected by conservation, settlement patterns, and improvements. The supply of *capital* depends upon past investments made by businesses, households, and governments. In the short run, the stock of capital is fixed like land, but in the long run the supply of capital reacts to economic factors such as risks, taxes, and rates of return.

Can we say anything about the elasticity of supply of inputs? Actually, the supply curve may slope positively or be vertical and might even have a negative slope. For most factors, we would expect that the supply responds positively to the factor's price in the

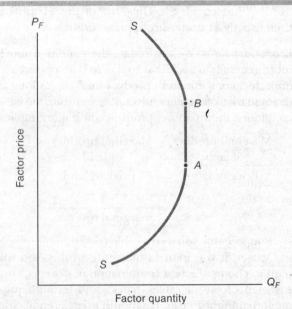

FIGURE 12-4. Supply Curve for Factors of Production

Supplies of factors of production depend upon characteristics of the factors and the preferences of their owners. Generally, supplies will respond positively to price, as in the region below *A*. For factors that are fixed in supply, like land, the supply curve will be perfectly inelastic, as from *A* to *B*. In special cases where a higher price of the factor increases the income of its owner greatly, as with labor or oil, the supply curve may bend backward, as in the region above *B*.

long run; in this case, the supply curve would slope upward and to the right. The *total* supply of land is usually thought to be unaffected by price, and in this case the *total* supply of land will be perfectly inelastic, with a vertical supply curve. In some special cases, when the return to the factor increases, owners may supply less of the factor to the market. For example, if people feel they can afford to work fewer hours when wages rise, the supply curve for labor might bend backward at high wage rates, rather than slope upward.

The different possible elasticities for the supply of factors are illustrated by the *SS* supply curve shown in Figure 12-4.

DETERMINATION OF FACTOR PRICES BY SUPPLY AND DEMAND

A full analysis of the distribution of income must combine the supply of and demand for factors of production. Earlier parts of this section provided the underpinnings for analysis of demand and gave a brief description of supply. We showed that, for given factor prices, profit-maximizing firms would choose input combinations according to their marginal revenue products. As the price of land falls, each farmer would substitute land for other inputs such as labor, machinery, and fertilizer. Each farmer therefore would show a demand for cornland inputs like that in Figure 12-2(*b*).

How do we obtain the *market demand* for inputs (whether cornland, unskilled labor, or computers)? We add together the individual demands of each of the firms. Thus at a given price of land, we add together all the demands for land of all the firms at that price; and we do the same at every price of land. In other words, *we add horizontally the demand curves for land of all the individual firms to obtain the market demand curve for land.* We follow the same procedure for any input, summing up all the derived demands of all the businesses to get the market demand for each input. And in each case, the derived demand for the input is based on the marginal revenue product of the input under consideration.[3] Figure 12-5 shows a general demand curve for a factor of production as the *DD* curve.

How do we find the overall market equilibrium? *The equilibrium price of the input in a competitive market*

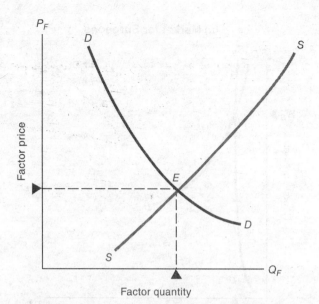

FIGURE 12-5. Factor Supply and Derived Demand Interact to Determine Factor Prices and Income Distribution

Factor prices and quantities are determined by the interaction of factor supply and demand.

comes at that level where the quantities supplied and demanded are equal. This is illustrated in Figure 12-5, where the derived demand curve for a factor intersects its supply curve at point *E*. Only at this price will the amount that owners of the factor willingly supply just balance the amount that the buyers willingly purchase.

Of Slicers and Flippers

We can apply these concepts to two factor markets to see why disparities in incomes are so high. Figure 12-6 on the next page shows the markets for two kinds of labor—surgeons and fast-food workers. The supply of surgeons is severely limited by the need for medical licensing and the length and cost of education and training; as a result, there are but 50,000 practicing surgeons in the United States. Demand for surgery is growing rapidly along with other health-care services. The result is that surgeons earn $240,000 a year on average. Moreover, an increase in demand will result in a sharp increase in earnings with little increase in output.

At the other end of the earnings scale are fast-food workers. These jobs have no skill or educational

---

[3] Note that this process of adding factor demand curves horizontally is exactly the same procedure that we followed in obtaining market demand curves for goods in Chapter 5.

(a) Market for Surgeons

(b) Market for Fast-Food Workers

FIGURE 12-6. The Markets for Surgeons and Fast-Food Workers

In (**a**), we see the impact of a limited supply of surgeons: small output and high earnings per surgeon. What would be the effect on total earnings of surgeons and on the price of an operation if an aging population increased the demand for surgeons?

In (**b**), open entry and low skill requirements imply a highly elastic supply of fast-food workers. Wages are beaten down and employment is high. What would be the effect on wages and employment if more teenagers looked for jobs?

requirements and are open to virtually everyone. The supply is highly elastic, and employment grew by almost 2 million workers from 1991 to 2001. Wages are close to the minimum wage because of the ease of entry into this market, and the average full-time fast-food employee makes $9500 a year. What is the reason for the vast difference in earning power of surgeons and hamburger flippers? It is mainly the quality of labor, not the quantity of hours.

The Rich and the Rest

If you are one of the richest Americans, you might have $50 million of interest, dividends, and other property income, while the median household earns less than $1000 a year on its financial wealth. Figure 12-7 explains this difference. The rate of return on stocks or bonds is not that much higher for the richest than for the middle class.

Rather, the rich have a much bigger wealth base on which to earn. The shaded rectangles in Figure 12-7 show

the capital earnings of the two groups. Make sure you understand that it is the amount of wealth rather than the rate of return that makes the rectangle of the top wealth holders so large.

These two examples show how factor prices and individual incomes are determined by underlying market forces. Supply and demand operate to create high returns to factors that have either limited supply or high demand as reflected in high marginal revenue product. If a factor such as surgeons becomes scarcer—say, because training requirements are tightened—the price of this factor will rise and surgeons will enjoy higher incomes. However, if demand decreases in some field like psychiatry—perhaps because insurance companies decide to cut back on psychiatric coverage, or because close substitutes like social workers and psychologists lure away patients, or because people rely more heavily on medications than on therapy—the lower demand will produce a fall in psychiatrists' incomes. Competition giveth, but competition also taketh away.

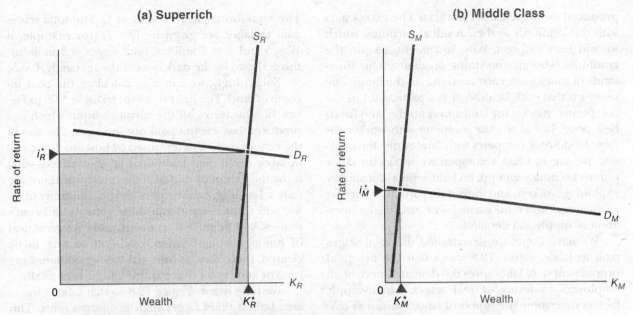

FIGURE 12-7. Differences in Total Returns to Wealth

This figure shows the demand and supply for wealth held by the superrich and the middle class. The horizontal axis shows the total wealth, while the vertical axis shows the rate of return on wealth. The shaded region is $r \times W$, or total income earned on wealth. Why is the shaded rectangle of the rich so much larger than that of the middle class? The reason is primarily that the wealth of the rich (K_R) is so much larger than that of the middle class (K_M).

THE DISTRIBUTION OF NATIONAL INCOME

With our new understanding of marginal-productivity theory, we can now come back to the question raised at the beginning of the chapter. In a world of intense competition, how do markets allocate national income among the many factors of production?

A simplified theory of factor-income distribution was first proposed around 1900 by John Bates Clark, a distinguished economist at Columbia University. It can be applied to competitive markets for any number of final products and factor inputs. But it is most easily grasped if we consider a simplified world with only one product in which all accounts are kept in "real" units, that is, in terms of goods. The goods could be corn or a basket of different goods and services, but we will call it Q. Moreover, by setting the price equal to 1, we can conduct the entire discussion in real terms, with the value of output being Q and with the wage rate being the real wage in terms of goods or Q. In this

situation, a production function tells how much Q is produced for each quantity of labor-hours, L, and for each quantity of acres of homogeneous land, A. Note that because $P = 1$, under perfect competition $MRP = MP \times P = MP \times 1 = MP$. The wage is therefore equal to MP_L.

Clark reasoned as follows: A first worker has a large marginal product because there is so much land to work with. Worker 2 has a slightly smaller marginal product. But the two workers are alike, so they must get exactly the same wage. The puzzle is, which wage? The MP of worker 1, or that of worker 2, or the average of the two?

Under perfect competition, the answer is clear: Landlords will not hire a worker if the market wage exceeds that worker's marginal product. So competition will ensure that *all* the workers receive a wage rate equal to the marginal product of the last worker.

But now there is a surplus of total output over the wage bill because earlier workers had higher MPs than the last worker. What happens to the excess MPs produced by all the earlier workers? The excess stays with the landlords as their residual earnings, which we will later call *rent*. Why, you might ask, do the landlords, who may be sitting on their yachts thousands of miles away, earn anything on the land? The reason is that each landowner is a participant in the competitive market for land and rents the land for its best price. Just as worker competes with worker for jobs, landowner competes with landowner for workers. We see in Clark's competitive world no labor unions keeping wages up, no landowners' conspiracy exploiting workers, and indeed no particular fairness in the wages and rents earned—we just see the operation of supply and demand.

We have therefore determined the total wages paid to labor. Figure 12-8 shows that the marginal product curve of labor gives the demand curve of all employers in terms of real wages. Labor-supply factors determine the supply of labor (shown as *SS*).

FIGURE 12-8. Marginal Product Principles Determine Factor Distribution of Income

Each vertical slice represents the marginal product of that unit of labor. Total national output 0*DES* is found by adding all the vertical slices of *MP* up to the total supply of labor at *S*.

The distribution of output is determined by marginal product principles. Total wages are the lower rectangle (equal to the wage rate 0*N* times the quantity of labor 0*S*). Land rents get the residual upper triangle *NDE*.

The equilibrium wage comes at *E*. The total wages paid to labor are given by $W \times L$ (for example, if $W = 5$ and $L = 1$ million, total wages = 5 million); this is shown by the dark area of the rectangle, 0*SEN*.

Surprisingly, we can also calculate the rent income of land. The light rust rent triangle *NDE* in Figure 12-8 measures all the surplus output which was produced but was not paid out in wages. The size of the rent triangle is determined by how much the *MP* of labor declines as additional labor is added—that is, by the extent of diminishing returns. If there are only a few high-quality acres, additional units of labor will show sharp diminishing returns and rent's share will be large. If, by contrast, there is a great deal of homogeneous frontier land just waiting to be cleared, there may be little tendency to diminishing returns and land's rent triangle will be very small.

We have drawn Figure 12-8 so that labor's wages are about 3 times larger than property's rents. This 3-to-1 relationship reflects the fact that labor earnings constitute about three-quarters of national income.

Marginal-Productivity Theory with Many Inputs

The marginal-productivity theory is a great step forward in understanding the pricing of different inputs. Note additionally that the positions of land and labor could be reversed to get a complete theory of distribution. To switch the roles of labor and land, hold labor constant and add successive units of variable land to fixed labor. Calculate each successive acre's marginal product.

Then draw a demand curve showing how many acres labor owners will demand of land at each rent rate. In the new version of Figure 12-8 that you draw, find a new *E'* point of equilibrium. Identify land's rectangle of rent as determined by rent times quantity of land. Identify labor's residual wage triangle. Finally, note the complete symmetry of the factors. This new graph shows that we should think of the distributive shares of each and every factor of production as being simultaneously determined by their interdependent marginal products.

That is not all. Instead of labor and land, suppose the only two factors were labor and some versatile capital goods. Suppose a smooth production function relates *Q* to labor and capital with the same general properties as in Figure 12-8. In this case, you can redraw Figure 12-8 and get an identical picture of income distribution between labor and capital. Indeed, we can perform the same operation for three, four, or any number of factors.

In competitive markets, the demand for inputs is determined by the marginal products of factors. In the simplified case where factors are paid in terms of the single output, we get

Wage = marginal product of labor

Rent = marginal product of land

and so forth for any factor. This distributes 100 percent of output, no more and no less, among all the factors of production.

We see, then, that the aggregate theory of the distribution of income is compatible with the competitive pricing of any number of goods produced by any number of factors. This simple but powerful theory shows how the distribution of income is related to productivity in a competitive market economy.

Now that we are armed with the general principles underlying the pricing of factors of production and the determination of the distribution of income, we can turn to a detailed discussion of the special features in the three major factor markets—land, labor, and capital.

AN INVISIBLE HAND FOR INCOMES?

We have now sketched how a perfectly competitive economy distributes national product among the different inputs in a simplified world.

People naturally ask, Are incomes under market capitalism fair and just? In one sense, this is like asking whether animals get their fair shares of food in the jungle. Just as the battles of the jungle distribute food without regard to right or wrong, so does a competitive market distribute wages and profits according to productivity rather than ethics.

Is there an invisible hand in the marketplace that ensures that the most deserving people will obtain their just rewards? Or that those who toil long hours or nights and weekends or in tedious or dangerous work will receive a decent standard of living? Or that those who toil long hours in developing countries will get a comfortable living standard?

In reality, competitive markets do not guarantee that income and consumption will necessarily go to the neediest or most deserving. Laissez-faire competition might lead to great inequality, to malnourished children who grow up to raise more malnourished children, and to the perpetuation of inequality of incomes and wealth for generations. There is no economic law that ensures that the poor countries of Africa will catch up to rich countries of North America. The rich may get healthier and richer as the poor get sicker and poorer. In a market economy, the distribution of income and consumption reflects not only hard work, ingenuity, and cunning but also factors such as race, gender, location, health, and luck.

While the market can work wonders in producing a growing array of goods and services in an efficient manner, there is no invisible hand which ensures that a laissez-faire economy will produce a fair and equitable distribution of income and property.

SUMMARY

A. Income and Wealth

1. Distribution theory is concerned with the basic question of *for whom* economic goods are to be produced. In examining how the different factors of production—land, labor, and capital—get priced in the market, distribution theory considers how supplies and demands for these factors are linked and how they determine all kinds of wages, rents, interest rates, and profits.

2. Income refers to the total receipts or cash earned by a person or household during a given time period (usually a year). Income consists of labor earnings, property income, and government transfer payments.

3. National income consists of the labor earnings and property income generated by the economy in a year. Government takes a share of that national income in the form of taxes and gives back part of what it collects as transfer payments. The posttax personal income of

an individual includes the returns on all the factors of production—labor and property—that the individual owns, plus transfer payments from the government, less taxes.

4. Wealth consists of the net dollar value of assets owned at a given point in time. Wealth is a stock, while income is a flow per unit of time. A household's wealth includes its tangible items such as houses and its financial holdings such as bonds. Items that are of value are called assets, while those that are owed are called liabilities. The difference between total assets and total liabilities is called wealth or net worth.

B. Input Pricing by Marginal Productivity

5. To understand the pricing of different factors of production, we must analyze the theory of production and the derived demand for factors. The demand for inputs is a derived demand: we demand pizza ovens not for their own sake but for the pizzas that they can produce for consumers. Factor demand curves are derived from demand curves for final products. An upward shift in the final demand curve causes a similar upward shift in the derived factor demand curve; greater inelasticity in commodity demand produces greater inelasticity of derived factor demand.

6. We met in earlier chapters the concepts of the production function and marginal products. The demand for a factor is drawn from its marginal revenue product (*MRP*), which is defined as the extra revenue earned from employing an extra unit of a factor. In any market, *MRP* of a factor equals the marginal revenue earned by the sale of an additional unit of the product times the marginal product of the factor ($MRP = MR \times MP$). For competitive firms, because price equals marginal revenue, this simplifies to $MRP = P \times MP$.

7. A firm maximizes profits (and minimizes costs) when it sets the *MRP* of each factor equal to that factor's marginal cost, which is the factor's price. This can be stated equivalently as a condition in which the *MRP* per dollar of input is equalized for each input. This must hold in equilibrium because a profit-maximizing employer will hire any factor up to the point where the factor's marginal product will return in dollars of marginal revenue just what the factor costs.

8. To obtain the market demand for a factor, we add horizontally all firms' demand curves. This, along with the particular factor's own supply curve, determines the supply-and-demand equilibrium. At the market price for the factor of production, the amounts demanded and supplied will be exactly equal—only at equilibrium will the factor price have no tendency to change.

9. The marginal-productivity theory of income distribution analyzes the way total national income gets distributed among the different factors. Competition of numerous landowners and laborers drives factor prices to equal their marginal products. That process will allocate exactly 100 percent of the product. Any factor, not just labor alone, can be the varying factor. Because each unit of the factor gets paid only the *MP* of the last unit hired, there is a residual surplus of output left over from the *MP*s of early inputs. This residual is exactly equal to the incomes of the other factors under marginal productivity pricing. Hence, the marginal-productivity theory of distribution, though simplified, is a logically complete picture of the distribution of income under perfect competition.

10. Even though a competitive economy may squeeze the maximum amount of bread out of its available resources, one major reservation about a market economy remains. We have no reason to think that incomes will be fairly distributed under laissez-faire capitalism. Market incomes might produce acceptable differences or enormous disparities in income and wealth that persist for generations.

CONCEPTS FOR REVIEW

income distribution
income (flow), wealth (stock)
national income
transfer payments
personal income
marginal product, marginal revenue
   product, derived demand

marginal revenue product of input i
   $= MRP_i = MR \times MP_i = P \times MP_i$
   for competitive firm
distribution theory
MP rectangle, residual rent triangle

factor demands under competition:
   $MP_i \times P =$ factor price$_i$, which
   gives least-cost rule:
$$\frac{MP_L}{P_L} = \frac{MP_A}{P_A} = \cdots$$
$$= \frac{1}{\text{marginal revenue}}$$
fairness of market incomes

FURTHER READING AND INTERNET WEBSITES

Further Reading

Bradley R. Schiller, *The Economics of Poverty and Discrimination* (Prentice-Hall, New York, 1998), provides a comprehensive review of income distribution and poverty.

Websites

Information on the distribution of income is gathered by the Census Bureau at www.census.gov/hhes/www/income.html.

The most comprehensive data on the population is gathered in the decennial census, available at www.census.gov.

If you want to examine data on income dynamics, an exemplary site for data is that on the Panel Study on Income Dynamics at www.isr.umich.edu/src/psid.

QUESTIONS FOR DISCUSSION

1. For each of the following factors, name the final output for which the item is a derived demand: wheatland, gasoline, barber, machine tool for basketballs, wine press, economics textbook.
2. Table 12-4 shows the basic numbers for production of pizzas, holding other factors constant.
   a. Fill in the blanks in columns (3) and (5).
   b. Construct a diagram like that in Figure 12-3 which shows the marginal revenue product of pizza workers and labor inputs.

   c. If the wage of pizza workers is $30 per worker, how many workers will be employed?
   d. Assume that the price of pizzas doubles. Draw the new *MRP* curve. Estimate the impact on the employment of pizza workers, assuming no other changes.
3. Over the last century, hours of work per lifetime have declined about 50 percent while real earnings have increased by a factor of 8. Assuming that the main change was an increase in the marginal-productivity-of-labor

		Marginal Revenue Product		
(1)	**(2)**	**(3)**	**(4)**	**(5)**
Unit of labor (workers)	**Total product (pizzas)**	**Marginal product of labor (pizzas per worker)**	**Price of output ($ per pizza)**	**Marginal revenue product of labor ($ per worker)**
0	0		5	
1	30	___	5	___
2	50	___	5	___
3	60	___	5	___
4	65	___	5	___
5	68	___	5	___
6	68	___		

TABLE 12-4.

schedule, draw supply-and-demand diagrams for labor in 1900 and 2000 that will explain this trend. In your diagrams, put the number of hours worked per lifetime on the horizontal axis and the real wage rate on the vertical axis. What key factor about the supply of labor must you invoke to explain this historical trend?

4. Why is each of the following incorrect? State the correct proposition.
   a. Marginal revenue product is calculated as total revenue earned per worker.
   b. Distribution theory is simple. You simply figure out how much each factor produces and then give the factor its share of output.
   c. Under competition, workers get paid the total output produced minus the costs of raw materials.

5. Figure 12-1 shows that the share of labor in national income changed little from 1948 to 2003 even though total real GDP rose by 600 percent. Draw a set of economywide curves like those in Figure 12-8 which can explain these two facts.

6. Labor leaders used to say, "Without any labor there is no product. Hence labor deserves *all* the product." Apologists for capital would reply, "Take away all capital goods, and labor scratches a bare pittance from the earth; practically all the product belongs to capital."

Analyze the flaws in these arguments. If you were to accept the arguments, show that they would allocate 200 or 300 percent of output to two or three factors, whereas only 100 percent can be allocated. How does Clark's marginal-productivity theory resolve this dispute?

7. Draw the supply and demand curves for the oil market. Now suppose that a workable electric car shifts demand away from oil. Draw the new demand curve and the new equilibrium. Describe the outcome in terms of the price of oil, the quantity consumed, and the total income of the oil producers.

8. Consider the marginal product distribution theory illustrated in Figure 12-8. If immigration increases labor supply, the economy moves down the labor demand curve. Will labor's wage fall? (Show that the answer is yes.) Will the residual earnings of land, capital, and other factors rise? (Again, show that the answer is yes.) Can you tell what will happen to the absolute total of labor's rectangle as well as to the share of labor income in the total? (Show that the answers are both no.)

9. In the marginal-productivity theory shown in Figure 12-8, let land rather than labor be the varying input. Draw a new figure and explain the theory with this new diagram. What is the residual factor?

CHAPTER

13

The Labor Market

*Work is the curse of the
drinking class.*

Oscar Wilde

Labor is more than an abstract factor of production. Workers are people who want good jobs with high wages so that they can buy the things they need and want. Laborers need to eat, but they also have feelings, so workers naturally worry about both the quantity and the quality of jobs.

This chapter explores how wages are set in a market economy. The first section reviews the supply of labor and the determination of wages under competitive conditions. This is followed by a discussion of some of the noncompetitive elements of labor markets, including labor unions and the thorny problem of labor market discrimination.

A. FUNDAMENTALS OF WAGE DETERMINATION

THE GENERAL WAGE LEVEL

In analyzing labor earnings, economists tend to look at the average **real wage,** which represents the purchasing power of an hour's work, or the money wages divided by the cost of living.[1] By that measure, American workers today are far better off than they were 100 years ago. Figure 13-1 on page 244 shows the real average hourly wage, or the dollar wage adjusted for inflation, along with the average hours of work.

The same powerful gains for workers are found in every industrial country. Across Western Europe, Japan, and the rapidly industrializing countries of East Asia, there has definitely been a steady, long-term improvement in the average worker's ability to buy food, clothing, and housing, as well as in the health and longevity of the population. In Europe and the United States, these gains began in earnest in the early 1800s, with the advent of the technological and social changes associated with the Industrial Revolution. Before that time real wages meandered up and down, with few long-term gains.

That is not to say that the Industrial Revolution was an unmitigated benefit to workers, especially in the laissez-faire days of the 1800s. In point of fact, a Dickens novel could hardly do justice to the dismal

---

[1] In this chapter, we will generally use the term "wages" as a shorthand expression for wages, salaries, and other forms of compensation.

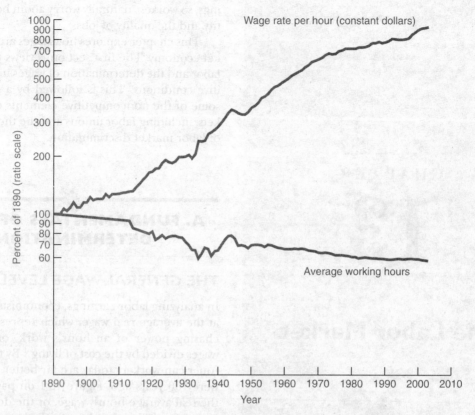

FIGURE 13-1. Wages Have Improved as Hours of Work Have Declined

With advancing technology and improved capital goods, American workers enjoy higher wages while working fewer hours. Slower growth in productivity in the last two decades has led to slower growth in real wages.

conditions of child labor, workplace dangers, and poor sanitation in early-nineteenth-century factories. A workweek of 84 hours was the prevailing rule, with time out for breakfast and sometimes supper. A good deal of work could be squeezed out of a 6-year-old child, and if a woman lost two fingers in a loom, she still had eight left.

Was it a mistake for people to leave the farms for the rigors of the factory? Probably not. Modern historians emphasize that even with the demanding conditions in the factories, living standards were nevertheless greatly improved over those in the earlier centuries of agrarian feudalism. The Industrial Revolution was a giant step forward for the working class, not a step back. The idyllic picture of the healthful, jolly countryside peopled by stout yeomen and happy peasantry is a historical myth unsupported by statistical research.

DEMAND FOR LABOR

Marginal Productivity Differences

We begin our examination of the general wage level by examining the factors underlying the demand for labor. The basic tools were provided in the last chapter, where we saw that the demand for a factor of production reflects the marginal productivity of that input.

Figure 13-2 illustrates the marginal-productivity theory. At a given time and with a given state of technology, there exists a relationship between the quantity of labor inputs and the amount of output. By the law of diminishing returns, each additional unit of labor input will add a smaller and smaller slab of output. In the example shown in Figure 13-2, at 10 units of labor, the competitively determined general wage level will be $20 per unit.

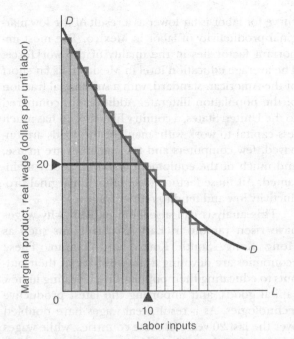

FIGURE 13-2. Demand for Labor Reflects Marginal Productivity

The demand for labor is determined by its marginal productivity in producing national output. The light gray vertical slices represent the extra output produced by the first, second, . . . unit of labor. The competitively determined general wage level at 10 units of labor is $20 per unit, equal to the marginal productivity of the tenth unit. The labor demand curve shifts up and out over time with capital accumulation, technological advance, and improvements in labor quality.

But probe deeper and ask what lies behind the marginal product. To begin with, the marginal productivity of labor will rise if workers have more or better capital goods to work with. Compare the productivity of a ditchdigger using a bulldozer with that of a similar digger using a hand shovel, or the communications capabilities of medieval messengers with modern e-mail. Second, marginal productivity of better-trained or better-educated workers will generally be higher than that of workers with less "human capital."

These reasons explain why wages and living standards rose so much during the twentieth century. Wages are high in the United States and other industrial countries because these nations have accumulated substantial capital stocks: dense networks of roads, rails, and communications; substantial amounts of plant and equipment for each worker; and adequate inventories

of spare parts. Even more important are the vast improvements in technologies compared to those of an earlier era. We have seen lightbulbs replace oil lamps, airplanes replace horses, xerography replace quill and ink, computers replace abacuses, and Internet commerce invade traditional ways of doing business. Just imagine how productive the average American would be today with the technologies of 1900.

The quality of labor inputs is another factor determining the general wage level. By any measure—literacy, education, or training—the U.S. labor force of 2000 was vastly superior to the one of 1900. Years of education are necessary to produce an engineer capable of designing precision equipment. A decade of training must precede the ability to perform successful brain surgery. Overall, the proportion of all adults who have completed college rose from 6 percent in 1950 to 25 percent in 2002. Such accumulations of human capital provide a substantial boost to the productivity of labor.

International Comparisons

The same reasoning explains why wage levels differ so dramatically across the world. Look at Table 13-1 below, which shows average wages plus benefits in

Region	Wages and fringe benefits in manufacturing, 2001 ($ per hour)
Germany	23.84
United States	20.32
Japan	19.59
Italy	13.76
United Kingdom	16.14
South Korea	8.09
Mexico	2.34
Sri Lanka	0.48

TABLE 13-1. General Wage Levels Vary Enormously across Countries

Western European nations, Japan, and the United States are high-wage countries, while Sri Lanka's hourly wages are a tiny fraction of American levels. General wage levels are determined by supply and demand for labor, but other factors such as capital, education levels, technology levels, and civil strife have a major impact on supply and demand curves.

Source: U.S. Bureau of Labor Statistics at ftp://ftp.bls.gov/pub/special. requests/ForeignLabor/supptab.txt.

manufacturing industries for eight countries. Wages are 9 times higher in the United States than in Mexico, 2½ times higher in Japan than in South Korea, and 50 times higher in Germany than in Sri Lanka.

What accounts for the enormous differences? It's not that governments in Sri Lanka and Mexico are suppressing wage increases, though government policies do have some impact on the minimum wage and other aspects of the labor market. Rather, real wages differ among countries primarily because of the operation of the supply and demand for labor. Look at Figure 13-3. Suppose that Figure 13-3(*a*) represents the state of affairs in the United States while Figure 13-3(*b*) describes Mexico. In Figure 13-3(*a*), the supply of U.S. workers is shown by the supply curve, $S_{US}S_{US}$, while the demand for workers is represented by $D_{US}D_{US}$. The equilibrium wage will settle at the level shown at E_{US}. If the wage were lower than E_{US}, shortages of labor would occur and employers would bid up wages to E_{US}, restoring the equilibrium. Similar forces determine E_M, the Mexican wage.

We see that the Mexican wage is lower than the U.S. wage principally because the Mexican demand

curve for labor is far lower as a result of the low marginal productivity of labor in Mexico. The most important factor lies in the quality of the workforce. The average education level in Mexico falls far short of the American standard, with a substantial fraction of the population illiterate. Additionally, compared to the United States, a country like Mexico has much less capital to work with: many of the roads are unpaved, few computers and fax machines are in use, and much of the equipment is old or poorly maintained. All these factors make labor's marginal productivity low and tend to reduce wages.

This analysis can also help explain why wages have risen rapidly in East Asian regions such as Hong Kong, South Korea, and Taiwan. These economies are devoting a sizable share of their outputs to educating their populations, investing in new capital goods, and importing the latest productive technologies. As a result, real wages have doubled over the last 20 years in these countries, while wages have stagnated in relatively closed countries which invest less in education, public health, and tangible capital.

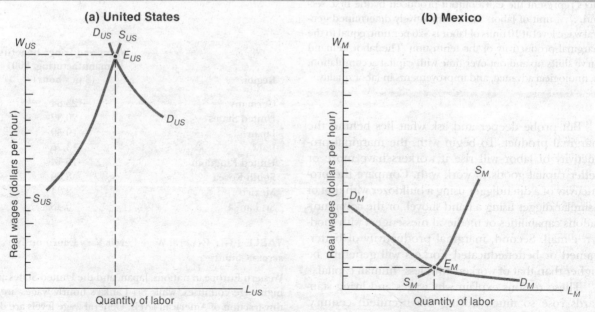

FIGURE 13-3. Favorable Resources, Skills, Management, Capital, and Technology Explain High U.S. Wages

Supply and demand determine a higher competitive wage in the United States than in Mexico. The major forces leading to high U.S. wages are a better-educated and more skilled workforce, a larger stock of capital per worker, and modern technologies.

THE SUPPLY OF LABOR

Determinants of Supply

So far we have focused on the demand side of the labor market. Now we turn to the supply side. *Labor supply* refers to the number of hours that the population desires to work in gainful activities. The three key elements for labor supply are hours per worker, labor-force participation, and immigration.

Hours Worked. While some people have jobs with flexible hours, most Americans work between 35 and 40 hours a week, without much leeway to increase or cut back their weekly hours. However, most people have a lot of control over how many hours they work over the course of their lifetimes. They may decide to go to college, to retire early, or to work part-time rather than full-time—all of these can reduce the number of total lifetime hours worked. On the other hand, the decision to moonlight and take on a second job will increase the lifetime hours worked.

Suppose that wages rise. Will that increase or decrease the lifetime hours of work? Look at the supply curve of labor in Figure 13-4. Note how the supply curve rises at first in a northeasterly direction; then at the critical point *C*, it begins to bend back in a northwesterly direction. How can we explain why higher wages may first increase and then decrease the quantity of labor supplied?

Put yourself in the shoes of a worker who has just been offered higher hourly rates and is free to choose the number of hours to be worked. You are tugged in two different directions. On one side is the *substitution effect*. (Chapter 5 explained that the substitution effect operates when people consume more of, or substitute in favor of, a good whose relative price falls and consume less of a good whose relative price increases.) Because each hour of work is now better paid, each hour of leisure has become more expensive; you thus have an incentive to substitute extra work for leisure.

But acting against the substitution effect is the *income effect*. With the higher wage, your income is higher. With a higher income, you will want to buy more goods and services, and, in addition, you will want more leisure time. You can afford to take longer vacations or to retire earlier than you otherwise would.

Which will be more powerful, the substitution effect or the income effect? There is no single correct answer; it depends upon the individual. In the case

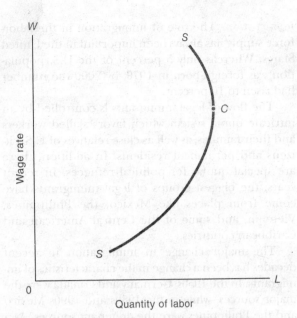

FIGURE 13-4. As Wages Rise, Workers May Work Fewer Hours

Above the critical point *C*, raising the wage rate reduces the amount of labor supplied as the income effect outweighs the substitution effect. Why? Because at higher wages workers can afford more leisure even though each extra hour of leisure costs more in wages forgone.

shown in Figure 13-4, for all wage rates below point *C*, labor supplied increases with a higher wage: the substitution effect outweighs the income effect. But from point *C* upward, the income effect outweighs the substitution effect, and labor supplied declines as wage rates climb higher.

Labor-Force Participation. One of the most dramatic developments in recent decades has been the sharp influx of women into the workforce. The labor-force participation rate of women (i.e., the fraction of women over 15 employed or actively looking for jobs) has jumped from 34 percent in 1950 to 60 percent today. In part this can be explained by rising real wages, which have made working more attractive for women. However, a change of this magnitude cannot be explained by economic factors alone. To understand such a significant alteration in working patterns, one must look outside economics to changing social attitudes toward the role of women as mothers, homemakers, and workers.

Immigration. The role of immigration in the labor-force supply has always been important in the United States. Whereas only 5 percent of the U.S. population was foreign-born in 1970, by 2000 the number had risen to 10 percent.

The flow of legal immigrants is controlled by an intricate quota system which favors skilled workers and their families, as well as close relatives of U.S. citizens and permanent residents. In addition, there are special quotas for political refugees. In recent years, the biggest groups of legal immigrants have come from places like Mexico, the Philippines, Vietnam, and some of the Central American and Caribbean countries.

The major change in immigration in recent decades has been a change in the characteristics of immigrants. In the 1950s, Germany and Canada were the major sources, while in the 1980s and 1990s Mexico and the Philippines were the dominant sources. As a result, recent immigrants have been relatively much less skilled and educated than those of an earlier age.

From the point of view of labor supply, the overall effect of recent immigration has been an increase in the supply of low-skilled workers in the United States relative to high-skilled workers. Studies have estimated that this change in supply has contributed to the decline in the wages of less educated groups relative to the college-educated.

Empirical Findings

Theory does not tell us whether the labor supply of a group will react positively or negatively to a wage change. Will an income-tax increase on high-income workers—which reduces their after-tax wages—cause them to reduce their work effort? Will subsidizing the wages of the working poor reduce or increase their hours worked? These vital questions must be considered by the president and legislators as they weigh issues of equity and efficiency. We often need to know the exact shape or elasticity of the labor supply curve.

Table 13-2 presents a summary of numerous studies of the subject. This survey shows that the

Labor-Supply Patterns			
Group of workers	**Labor-Force Participation Rate (% of population)**		**Response of labor supply to increase in real wages**
	1960	**2002**	
Adult males	86	77	Supply curve found to be backward-bending in most studies. Thus income effect dominates substitution effect. Supply elasticity is relatively small, in the order of -0.1 to -0.2; this implies that a 10% increase in real wages would lead to a 1 to 2% reduction in labor supplied.
Adult females	36	60	Most studies find positive effect of labor supplied in response to higher real wages.
Teenagers	48	48	Highly variable response.
Entire population 16 years and over	59	67	Elasticity of total labor supply is close to zero, with income effects just balancing out substitution effects. Estimated labor-supply elasticity for entire population is in the range from 0 to 0.2.

TABLE 13-2. Empirical Estimates of Labor-Supply Responses

Economists have devoted careful study to the response of labor supply to real wages. For males, the supply curve is backward-bending (that is, the elasticity is negative), while teenagers and adult females generally respond positively to wages. For the economy as a whole, the labor supply curve is close to completely inelastic or vertical.

Source of data: U.S. Department of Labor, *Employment and Earnings*, March 2003.

labor supply curve for adult males appears to be slightly backward-bending, while the responses of other demographic groups look more like a conventional upward-sloping supply curve. For the population as a whole, labor supply appears to respond very little to a change in real wages.

WAGE DIFFERENTIALS

While analysis of the general wage level is important for comparing different countries and times, we often want to understand *wage differentials*. In practice, wage rates differ enormously. The average wage is as hard to define as the average person. An auto executive may earn $40 million a year at the same time that a clerk earns $15,000 and a farmhand $12,000. A doctor may earn 15 or 20 times more than a lifeguard even though both are saving lives. In the same factory, a skilled machinist may earn $500 a week, while an unskilled janitor gets $200. Women may be paid $400 a week at the same time that equally qualified men earn $500.

In addition, wages vary significantly among broad industry groups. Table 13-3 on this page shows that smaller, nonunionized sectors such as farming, retail trade, or private households tend to pay low wages, while the larger firms in manufacturing pay twice as much. But within major sectors there are large variations that depend on worker skills and market conditions—fast-food workers make much less than doctors even though they all provide services.

How can we explain these wage differentials? Let's consider first a *perfectly competitive labor market*, one in which there are large numbers of workers and employers, none of which has the power to affect wage rates appreciably.[2] If all jobs and all people are identical in a perfectly competitive labor market, competition will cause the hourly wage rates to be exactly equal. No employer would pay more for the work of one person than for that person's identical twin or for another person who possessed identical skills.

---

[2] Few labor markets are perfectly competitive in reality, but some (such as a large city's market for inexperienced teenage workers or clerical workers) approach the competitive concept reasonably closely.

Compensation by Industry	
Industry	Average earnings per full-time employee, 2001* ($ per year)
All industries	**39,667**
Farms	24,657
Mining	60,871
Manufacturing	45,580
Retail trade	23,009
Finance, insurance, and real estate	63,738
Security and commodity brokers	161,879
Services	37,647
Private households	14,975
Government	41,700

* Total compensation per full-time equivalent worker.

TABLE 13-3. Earnings Vary by Industry

Average annual wages and salaries by broad industry groups range from a high of $60,871 in mining to a low of $24,657 in farming. Among narrow industry groups, we see that average hourly earnings vary enormously between security analysts and those who work in private households.

Source: U.S. Bureau of Economic Analysis at www.bea.gov. Table 6.6C in the complete NIPA tables.

This means that to explain the pervasive wage differences across industries or individuals, we must look to either differences in jobs, differences in people, or imperfect competition in labor markets.

Differences in Jobs: Compensating Wage Differentials

Some of the tremendous wage differentials observed in everyday life arise because of differences in the quality of jobs. Jobs differ in their attractiveness; hence wages may have to be raised to coax people into the less attractive jobs.

Wage differentials that serve to compensate for the relative attractiveness, or nonmonetary differences, among jobs are called **compensating differentials.**

Window washers must be paid more than janitors because of the risks of climbing skyscrapers. Workers often receive 5 percent extra pay on the

4 P.M. to 12 P.M. "swing shift" and 10 percent extra pay for the 12 midnight to 8 A.M. "graveyard shift." For hours beyond 40 per week or for holiday and weekend work, 1½ to 2 times the base hourly pay is customary. Jobs that involve hard physical labor, tedium, low social prestige, irregular employment, seasonal layoff, or physical risk all tend to be less attractive. No wonder, then, that companies must pay $50,000 to $80,000 a year to recruit people to work at dangerous and lonely jobs on offshore oil platforms or in northern Alaska. Similarly, for jobs that are especially pleasant or psychologically rewarding, such as those of park rangers and lifeguards, pay levels tend to be modest.

To test whether a given difference in pay between two jobs is a compensating differential, ask people who are well qualified for both jobs: "Would you take the higher-paying job in preference to the lower?" If they are not eager to take the higher-paying job, the pay difference is probably a compensating differential that reflects the nonmonetary differences between the jobs.

Differences in People: Labor Quality

We have just seen that some wage differentials serve to compensate for the differing degrees of attractiveness of different jobs. But look around you. Garbage collectors make much less than lawyers, yet surely the legal life has higher prestige and much more pleasant working conditions. We see countless examples of high-paying jobs that are more pleasant rather than less pleasant than low-paying work. We must look to factors beyond compensating differentials to explain the reason for most wage differences.

One key to wage disparities lies in the tremendous qualitative differences among people, differences traceable to variations in innate mental and physical abilities, upbringing, education and training, and experience. A biologist might classify all of us as members of the species *Homo sapiens*, but a personnel officer would insist that people differ enormously in their abilities to contribute to a firm's output.

While many of the differences in labor quality are determined by noneconomic factors, the decision to accumulate **human capital** can be evaluated economically. The term "human capital" refers to the stock of useful and valuable skills and knowledge accumulated by people in the process of their education and training. Doctors, lawyers, and engineers invest many years in their formal education and on-the-job training. They spend large sums on tuition and wages forgone, investing $100,000 to $200,000 in college and graduate training, and often work long hours. Part of the high salaries of these professionals should be viewed as a return on their investment in human capital—a return on the education that makes these highly trained workers a very special kind of labor.

Economic studies of incomes and education show that human capital is a good investment on average. Figure 13-5 shows the income profiles for different groups as a function of their education and experience. Groups with higher education start out with higher incomes and enjoy more rapid growth in incomes than do less educated groups.

FIGURE 13-5. Earnings Benefit from Education and Experience

Earnings profiles of men show that earnings rise with both education and years of experience.

Adapted from Kevin M. Murphy and Finis Welch, "The Structure of Wages," *Quarterly Journal of Economics,* February 1992.

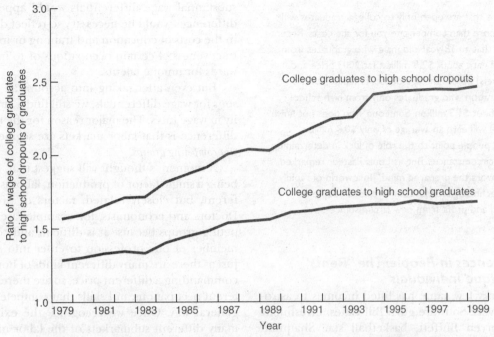

FIGURE 13-6. Relative Income Gains Have Been Dramatic for College Graduates

Income profiles changed dramatically in the last two decades. With rising skill requirements, incomes of college graduates rose sharply relative to those of persons with only a high school education, particularly for young workers.

Source: *Economic Report of the President, 2000.* Data apply to full-time, year-round male workers.

Figure 13-6 shows the ratio of the hourly earnings of college graduates to those of high school graduates. Relative earnings rose sharply after 1980 as the "price of skill" rose. Studies by labor economists have shown that individuals who have high quantitative abilities or computer skills have an economic advantage in today's labor market.

Should You Invest in "Human Capital"?

Students may be surprised to learn that every day in college is an investment in human capital. When a student goes to college, each year he or she might pay $10,000 in tuition and $20,000 in opportunity costs of earnings forgone. That would mean a 4-year outlay of $120,000. This cost is just as much an investment as buying a bond or speculating on the stock of Internet companies.

Does college actually pay off? The evidence suggests that it does. In 1999, the average annual earnings of a 30 year-old male high school graduate working full-time were $35,000. A similar person with a bachelor's degree or more earned $68,000. Moreover, the returns to a college education have soared dramatically over the last 20 years. Whereas a college graduate earned 25 percent more than a high school graduate with the same background in 1979, two decades later the earnings differential had widened to 55 percent (see Figure 13-6). More and more, in today's service economy, companies are processing information rather than raw materials. In the information economy, the skills learned in college are a prerequisite for a high-paying job. A high school dropout is generally at a severe disadvantage in the job market.

Even if you have to borrow for your education, put off years of gainful employment, live away from home, and pay for food and books, your lifetime earnings in the occupations that are open only to college graduates will probably more than compensate you for the costs. Recent data show that an 18-year-old male who graduates from college will earn about $2.5 million (at 2003 price and income levels) before the age of 65. A member of the same generation who graduates only from high school will earn about $1.3 million. Someone who does not finish high school will earn an average of only $0.8 million.

Often, people point to the role of luck in determining economic circumstances. But, as Louis Pasteur remarked, "Chance favors the prepared mind." In a world of rapidly changing technologies, education prepares people to understand and profit from new circumstances.

Differences in People: The "Rents" of Unique Individuals

For the lucky few, fame has lifted incomes to astronomical levels. Software guru Bill Gates, investment wizard Warren Buffett, basketball star Shaquille O'Neal, and even economists who consult for business can earn fabulous sums for their services.

These extremely talented people have a particular skill that is highly valued in today's economy. Outside their special field, they might earn but a small fraction of their high incomes. Moreover, their labor supply is unlikely to respond perceptibly to wages that are 20 or even 50 percent higher or lower. Economists refer to the excess of these wages above those of the next-best available occupation as a pure economic rent; these earnings are logically equivalent to the rents earned by fixed land.

Some economists have suggested that technological changes are making it easier for a small number of top individuals to serve a larger share of the market (recall our discussion of winner-take-all markets in Chapter 11). Top entertainers or athletes can now give a single performance that reaches a billion people via television and recordings—something that was not possible just a few years ago. If this trend continues, and labor rents rise further, the income gap between the winners and the runners-up may widen even further in the years ahead.

Segmented Markets and Noncompeting Groups

Even in a perfectly competitive world where people could move easily from one occupation to another, substantial wage differentials would appear. These differences would be necessary to reflect differences in the costs of education and training or in the unattractiveness of certain occupations or to indicate rewards for unique talents.

But even after taking into account all these reasons for wage differentials, we still find a large disparity in wage rates. The major reason for the remaining difference is that labor markets are segmented into *noncompeting groups*.

A moment's thought will suggest that, instead of being a single factor of production, labor is many different, but closely related, factors of production. Doctors and economists, for example, are noncompeting groups because it is difficult and costly for a member of one profession to enter into the other. Just as there are many different kinds of houses, each commanding a different price, so are there many different occupations and skills that compete only in a general way. Once we recognize the existence of many different submarkets of the labor market, we can see why wages may differ greatly among groups.

Why is the labor market divided into so many noncompeting groups? The major reason is that, for professions and skilled trades, it takes a large investment of time and money to become proficient. If coal mining declines because of environmental restrictions, the miners can hardly hope to land jobs teaching environmental economics overnight. Once people specialize in a particular occupation, they become part of a particular labor submarket. They are thereby subject to the supply and demand for that skill and will find that their own labor earnings rise and fall depending upon events in that occupation and industry. Because of this segmentation, the wages for one occupation can diverge substantially from the wages in other areas.

The job choice of new immigrants is a classic case of noncompeting groups. Rather than just answering random classified ads, new immigrants from a particular country tend to cluster in certain occupations. For example, in many cities, such as Los Angeles and New York, a large number of grocery stores tend to be owned by Koreans. The reason is that the Koreans can get advice and support from friends and relatives who also own grocery stores. As immigrants get more experience and education in the United States and become more fluent in English, their job choice widens and they become part of the overall labor supply.

Summary of Competitive Wage Determination	
Labor situation	Wage result
1. People are all alike—jobs are all alike.	No wage differentials
2. People are all alike—jobs differ in attractiveness.	Compensating wage differentials
3. People differ, but each type of labor is in unchangeable supply (noncompeting groups).	Wage differentials that reflect supply and demand for segmented markets
4. People differ, but there is some mobility among groups (partially competing groups).	General-equilibrium pattern of wage differentials as determined by general demand and supply (includes 1 through 3 as special cases)

TABLE 13-4. Market Wage Structure Shows Great Variety of Patterns under Competition

In addition, the theory of noncompeting groups helps us understand labor market discrimination. We will see in the next section of this chapter that much discrimination arises because workers are separated by gender, race, or other personal characteristics into noncompeting groups as a result of custom, law, or prejudice.

While the theory of noncompeting groups highlights an important aspect of labor markets, we must recognize that in the longer run entry and exit will reduce differentials. It is true that copper miners are unlikely to become computer programmers when computers and fiber optics displace rotary dials and copper wires. Consequently, we may see wage differentials arise between the two kinds of labor. But in the longer run, as more young people study computer science rather than go to work in copper mines, competition will tend to reduce some of the differentials of these noncompeting groups.

Table 13-4 summarizes the different forces at work in determining wage rates in competitive conditions.

B. LABOR MARKET ISSUES AND POLICIES

Our survey has up to now examined the case of competitive labor markets. In reality, distortions prevent the operation of perfect competition in labor markets. One source of imperfect competition is labor unions. Unions represent a significant, although shrinking, fraction of workers. A second facet of

labor markets is discrimination—also less important than in earlier decades, but still an important issue to consider. Yet another factor acting on labor markets is government policies. By setting minimum wages (discussed in Chapter 4), encouraging or discouraging unions, or outlawing discrimination, governments have a powerful effect on labor markets.

HISTORY AND PRACTICE OF LABOR UNIONS

Sixteen million Americans, or 13 percent of wage and salary workers, belonged to labor unions in 2002. Unions definitely have market power and sometimes serve as monopoly suppliers of labor. Unions negotiate collective-bargaining agreements which specify who can fill different jobs, what they will be paid, and what the work rules are. Furthermore, in negotiating collective-bargaining contracts, unions raise issues which are important to all workers, such as pensions, health-care benefits, and working hours. And unions can decide to go on strike—withdraw their labor supply completely and even cause a factory to shut down—in order to win a better deal from an employer. The study of unions is an important part of understanding the dynamics of labor markets.

How did American labor unions begin? In 1881, the present-day labor movement began to take shape with the founding of the American Federation of Labor (AFL). For almost half a century, until his death in 1924, Samuel Gompers dominated this organization and gave the movement its characteristic pattern.

Gompers's strategy was simple: Because he believed that no movement opposed to capitalism would flourish on American soil, he insisted on *business unionism*. Under this principle, American unions were engaged primarily in improving the economic status of workers—the struggle for higher wages, shorter hours, more vacations, better working conditions, and improved fringe benefits. American unions were the opposite of the labor movements in many European countries; abroad, unions have sometimes dominated major political parties and waged a class struggle to alter the form of government or to promote socialism.

At the beginning, labor was organized as *craft unions*, in which workers were grouped on the basis of a particular skill, such as carpentry or bricklaying. This strategy prevented the organization of huge mass-production industries into a single union. By the 1930s, astute union advocates began to see the handwriting on the wall: *industrial unions* (those organizing an entire industry, such as steel or coal) were the wave of the future. Industrial unions were introduced in 1935 with the formation of the Congress of Industrial Organizations (CIO). Today, American labor unions are organized into the AFL-CIO, which is the major national labor organization in the United States.

The wages and fringe benefits of unionized workers are determined by **collective bargaining.** This is the process of negotiation between representatives of firms and of workers for the purpose of establishing mutually agreeable conditions of employment. The centerpiece is the *economic package*. This includes the basic wage rates for different job categories, along with the rules for holidays and coffee breaks. In addition, the agreement contains provisions for fringe benefits such as a pension plan, coverage for health care, and similar items.

A second important and often controversial subject is *work rules*. These concern work assignments and tasks, job security, and workloads. Particularly in declining industries, the staffing requirements are a major issue because the demand for labor is falling. In the railroad industry, for example, there were decades of disputes about the number of people needed to run a train.

Collective bargaining is a complicated business, a matter of give-and-take. Much effort is spent negotiating purely economic issues, dividing the pie between wages and profits. Sometimes agreements get hung up on issues of management prerogatives, such as the ability to reassign workers or change work rules. In the end, both workers and management have a large stake in ensuring that workers are satisfied and productive on their jobs.

Government and Collective Bargaining

The history of labor unions reminds us that the legal framework is an important determinant of economic organization. Two hundred years ago, when labor first tried to organize in England and America, common-law doctrines against "conspiracy in restraint of trade" were used to block unions. In the early 1900s, unions and their members were convicted by courts, fined, jailed, and harassed by various injunctive procedures. The Supreme Court repeatedly struck down acts designed to improve working conditions for women and children and other reform legislation on hours and wages.

It was only after the pendulum swung toward support of unions and collective bargaining that the explosive growth of unions began. A major landmark was the Clayton Act (1914), hailed as "labor's Magna Carta" and designed to remove labor from antitrust prosecution. The Fair Labor Standards Act (1938) barred child labor, called for time-and-a-half pay for weekly hours over 40, and set a federal minimum wage for most nonfarm workers.

The most important labor legislation of all was the National Labor Relations (or Wagner) Act of 1935. This law stated: "Employees shall have the right to . . . join . . . labor organizations, to bargain collectively . . . , and to engage in concerted activities." Spurred by pro-labor legislation, union membership rose from less than one-tenth of the labor force in the 1920s to one-quarter of the workforce by the end of World War II. The decline of American unions began in the early 1970s. In essence, the monopoly power of unions was eroded by the deregulation of many industries, increased international competition, and a less favorable government attitude toward unions.

HOW UNIONS RAISE WAGES

How can labor unions raise the wages and improve the working conditions of their members? *Unions gain market power by obtaining a legal monopoly on the provision of labor services to a particular firm or industry.* Using this monopoly, they compel firms to provide wages, benefits, and working conditions that are above the competitive level. For example, if nonunion plumbers earn $20 per hour in Alabama, a union might bargain with a large construction firm to set the wage at $30 per hour for that firm's plumbers.

Such an agreement is, however, valuable to the union only if the firm's access to alternative labor supplies can be restricted. Hence, under a typical collective-bargaining agreement, firms agree not to hire nonunion plumbers, not to contract out plumbing services, and not to subcontract to nonunion firms. Each of these provisions helps prevent erosion of the union's monopoly lock on the supply of plumbers to the firm. In some industries, like steel and autos, unions will try to unionize the entire industry so that firm A's unionized workers need not compete with firm B's nonunion workers. All these steps are necessary to protect high union wage rates.

Figure 13-7 shows the impact of agreed-upon high standard wages, where the union forces employers to pay wages at the standard rate shown by the horizontal line rr. The equilibrium is at E', where rr intersects the employers' demand curve. Note that the union has not directly reduced supply when it sets high standard wage rates. How does the market operate when wages are set above the market-clearing level? At the high wage rates, employment is limited by the firms' demand for labor. The number of workers who seek employment exceeds the demand by the segment $E'F$. These excess workers might be unemployed and waiting for vacancies in the high-paying union sector, or they might become discouraged and look for jobs in other sectors. The workers from E' to F are as effectively excluded from jobs as they would be if the union had directly limited entry.

The need to prevent nonunion competition also explains many of the political goals of the national labor movement. It explains why unions want to limit immigration; why unions support protectionist legislation to limit imports of foreign goods, which are goods made by workers who are not members of American unions; why quasi unions like medical associations fight to restrict the practice of medicine by other groups; and why unions sometimes oppose deregulation in industries such as trucking, communications, and airlines.

Theoretical Indeterminacy of Collective Bargaining

In most collective-bargaining negotiations, the workers press for higher wages while management holds out

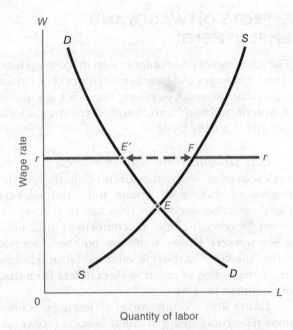

FIGURE 13-7. Unions Set High Standard Wage and Limit Employment

Raising the standard wage to rr increases wages and decreases the employment in the unionized labor market. Because of supply and demand imbalance, workers from E' to F cannot find employment in this market.

If unions push real wages too high for an entire economy, firms will demand E' while workers will supply F. Thus the black arrow from E' to F represents the amount of classical unemployment. This source of unemployment is particularly important when a country cannot affect its price level or exchange rate, and it differs from the unemployment caused by insufficient aggregate demand.

for lower compensation costs. This is a situation known as *bilateral monopoly*—where there is but one buyer and one seller. The outcome of bilateral monopoly cannot be predicted by economic forces of costs and demands alone; it depends as well on psychology, politics, and countless other intangible factors.[3]

---

[3] Situations like labor-management bargains are the subject of game theory, analyzed in Chapter 11. The theoretical indeterminacy of collective bargaining stems from the following result from game theory: A two-person noncooperative game does not generally have a unique outcome. Rather, as with wars or strikes, the outcome depends on many factors, such as bargaining power, prestige, bluffing ability, and even each side's perception of the strength of its opponent.

EFFECTS ON WAGES AND EMPLOYMENT

The advocates of labor unions claim that unions have raised real wages and have benefited workers. Critics argue that the result of raising wages is high unemployment, inflation, and distorted resource allocation. What are the facts?

Has Unionization Raised Wages?

Let's start by reviewing the effects of unions on relative wages. Taking all private industrial workers together, union workers in 1995 had total compensation 38 percent above the compensation of nonunion workers. However, this raw number does not reflect the fact that the skill, educational, and industrial composition of union workers differs from that of nonunion workers.

Taking into account worker differences, economists have concluded that union workers receive on average a 10 to 15 percent wage differential over nonunion workers. The differential ranges from a negligible amount for hotel workers and barbers to 25 to 30 percent higher earnings for skilled construction workers or coal miners. The pattern of results suggests that where unions can effectively monopolize labor supply and control entry, they will be most effective in raising wages. There is some evidence that the impact of unions on wages has eroded in recent years.

Overall Impacts. Granted that unions raise the wages of union members, we might ask whether unions bootstrap the entire economy to a higher real wage. Most economists now believe that unions redistribute income not from capital to labor but from nonunion labor to union labor. Put differently, if unions succeed in raising their wages above competitive levels, their gains come at the expense of the wages of nonunion workers.

This analysis is supported by empirical evidence showing that the share of national income going to labor has changed little over the last six decades. Once cyclical influences on labor's share are removed, we can see no appreciable impact of unionization on the share of wages in the United States (see Figure 12-1 on page 227). Moreover, the evidence from heavily unionized European countries suggests that when unions succeed in raising money wage rates, they sometimes trigger an inflationary wage-price spiral with little or no permanent effect upon real wages.

Effects on Employment

If unions do not affect overall real wage levels, this suggests that their impact lies primarily upon relative wages. That is, wages in unionized industries would rise relative to those in nonunionized industries. Moreover, employment would tend to be reduced in unionized and expanded in nonunionized industries.

When powerful unions raise real wages to artificially high levels, the result is an excess supply of labor that is called *classical unemployment*. This case is also illustrated by Figure 13-7. Assume that unions raise wages above the market-clearing wage at E to a higher real wage at rr. Then, if the supply of and demand for labor in general are unchanged, the arrow between E' and F will represent the number of workers who want to work at wage rr but cannot find work. This is called classical unemployment because it results from real wages that are above competitive levels.

Economists often contrast classical unemployment with the unemployment that occurs in business cycles, often called Keynesian unemployment, which results from insufficient aggregate demand. The effects of too high real wages were seen after the economic unification of Germany in 1990. The economic union fixed East German wages at a level estimated to be at least twice as high as could be justified by labor's marginal revenue product. The result was a sharp decline in employment in eastern Germany after unification.

This analysis suggests that when an economy gets locked into real wages that are too high, high levels of unemployment may result. The unemployment will not respond to the traditional macroeconomic policy of increasing aggregate spending but, rather, will require remedies that lower real wages.

Declining Unionism in the United States

One of the major trends in American labor markets has been the gradual erosion of labor unions since World War II. Whereas unions had organized one-quarter of the labor force in 1955, the fraction has fallen sharply since 1980. The share of unionized workers in manufacturing has shrunk dramatically in the last two decades; only in the public sector are unions still a powerful force.

One of the reasons for the decline in unions is the waning power of the strike, which is the ultimate threat in collective bargaining. In the 1970s U.S. labor unions used that weapon regularly, averaging almost 300 strikes per year. More recently, though, strikes have become relatively uncommon; in fact, they have virtually disappeared from the American labor market. The reason for the decline is that strikes have often backfired on workers. In 1981, the striking air-traffic controllers were all fired by President Reagan. When the professional football players went on strike in 1987, they were forced back to work when the football owners put on the games with replacement players. In 1992, workers striking at Caterpillar Inc., a huge maker of heavy equipment, had to end their 6-month strike when Caterpillar threatened to fill their jobs with permanent replacements. The inability to hurt firms through strikes has led to a significant weakening in the overall power of labor unions in the last two decades.

You might wonder if the declining power of unions will reduce labor compensation. Economists generally hold that a decline in union power will lower the relative wages of union workers rather than lower the overall share of labor. Look back at Figure 12-1 to examine the share of labor in national income. Can you determine any effect of the declining power of unions after 1980 on labor's share? Most economists believe not.

DISCRIMINATION

Racial, ethnic, and gender discrimination has been a pervasive feature of human societies since the beginning of recorded history. At one extreme, seen before the Civil War in the United States, black slaves were considered property, had virtually no rights, and were often treated harshly. In other times or places, such as in the United States during the segregation period or under apartheid in South Africa until the 1990s, blacks were segregated in housing, consumption, and transportation and faced prohibitions against interracial marriage and the most desirable forms of employment. Even today, in an era when discrimination is illegal, subtle forms of informal, premarket, criminal-justice, and statistical discrimination continue to lead to disparate outcomes between men and women and particularly among different racial and ethnic groups.

Those who study or experience discrimination know that it extends far beyond the marketplace. Our discussion is limited to economic discrimination, focusing primarily on employment. We want to know why group differences persist decades after discrimination became illegal. We need to understand the

sources of the differences between the wages of white males and those of other groups. Why do African-American and Hispanic citizens in the United States continue to have a measurably lower level of income and wealth than other groups? Why are women excluded from many of the best jobs in business? These are troubling questions that need answers.

ECONOMIC EXPLANATIONS OF DISCRIMINATION

Definition of Discrimination

When economic differences arise because of irrelevant personal characteristics such as race, gender, sexual orientation, or religion, we call this **discrimination**. Discrimination typically involves either (*a*) disparate treatment of people on the basis of personal characteristics or (*b*) practices (such as tests) that have an adverse impact on certain groups.

Economists who first began to study discrimination, like the University of Chicago's Gary Becker, realized that a fundamental puzzle arises: If two groups of workers have equivalent productivity, but one has lower wages, why don't competitive profit-maximizing firms hire the low-wage workers and increase their profits? For example, suppose that a group of managers in a competitive market decides to pay blue-eyed workers more than equally productive brown-eyed workers. Nondiscriminating firms could enter the market, undercut the costs and prices of the discriminating firms by hiring mainly brown-eyed workers, and drive the discriminating firms out of business. Thus, even if some employers are biased against a group of workers, their bias should not be sufficient to reduce that group's income. Becker's analysis suggests, therefore, that forces other than pure discriminating attitudes are necessary to produce income disparities between equivalent groups.

Discrimination by Exclusion

The most pervasive form of discrimination is to exclude certain groups from employment or housing. The history of black Americans illustrates how social processes depressed their wages and social status. After slavery was abolished, the black population of the American south fell into a caste system of peonage under "Jim Crow" legislation. Even though legally free and subject to the laws of supply and demand, black workers had earnings far below those of whites. Why? Because they had inferior schooling and were excluded from the best jobs by trade unions, local laws, and customs. They were consequently shunted into menial, low-skilled occupations that were effectively noncompeting groups. Employment segregation allowed discrimination to persist for decades.

Supply and demand can illustrate how exclusion lowers the incomes of groups that are targets of discrimination. Under discrimination, certain jobs are reserved for the privileged group, as is depicted in Figure 13-8(a). In this labor market, the supply of privileged workers is shown by S_pS_p, while the demand for such labor is depicted as D_pD_p. Equilibrium wages occur at the high level shown at E_p.

Meanwhile, Figure 13-8(b) shows what is happening for minority workers, who, because they live in areas with poor schools and cannot afford private education, do not receive training for the high-paying jobs. With low levels of skills, they take low-skilled jobs and have low marginal revenue products, so their wages are depressed to the low-wage equilibrium at E_m.

Note the difference between the two markets. Because minorities are excluded from good jobs, market forces have decreed that they earn much lower wages than the privileged workers. Someone might even argue that minorities "deserve" lower wages because their competitive marginal revenue products are lower. But this rationalization overlooks the root of the wage differential, which is that wage differences arose because certain groups were excluded from the good jobs by their inability to obtain education and training and by the force of custom, law, or collusion.

Taste for Discrimination

The exclusion example still raises the issue of why some profit-maximizing firms do not evade the laws or customs to undercut their competitors. One solution proposed by Becker was that either firms or their customers have a "taste for discrimination." Perhaps some managers do not like hiring black workers; maybe salespersons are prejudiced and don't want to sell to Hispanic customers. Critics complain that this approach is tautological, in essence saying, "Things are the way they are because people like them that way."

Statistical Discrimination

One of the most interesting variants of discrimination occurs because of the interplay between incomplete information and perverse incentives. This is known as **statistical discrimination,** in which individuals are treated on the basis of the average behavior of members of the group to which they belong rather than on the basis of their personal characteristics.

One common example arises when an employer screens employees on the basis of their college. The

(a) Market for the Privileged   **(b) Market for Minorities**

FIGURE 13-8. Discrimination by Exclusion Lowers the Wage Rates of Excluded Minorities

Discrimination is often enforced by excluding certain groups from privileged jobs. If minorities are excluded from good jobs in market **(a)**, they must work in inferior jobs in **(b)**. The privileged group enjoys high wage rates at E_p, while minorities earn low wage rates at E_m in market **(b)**.

employer may have observed that people who graduate from better schools are *on average* more productive; in addition, grade point averages are often difficult to compare because of differences in grading standards. Employers therefore often hire people on the basis of their college rather than of their grades. A more careful screening process would show that there are many highly qualified workers from the less well-known schools. We see here a common form of statistical discrimination based on average quality of schooling.

Statistical discrimination leads to economic inefficiencies because it reinforces stereotypes and reduces the incentives of individual members of a group to develop skills and experience. Consider someone who goes to a little-known school. She knows that she will be largely judged by the quality of her schooling credentials. The grade point average, the difficulty of the courses taken, her actual knowledge, and her on-the-job experience may be ignored. The result is that, when subject to statistical discrimination, individuals have greatly reduced incentives to invest in activities that will improve their skills and make them better workers.

Statistical discrimination is particularly pernicious when it involves race, gender, or ethnic groups. If employers treat all black youths as "unproductive" because of average experience with hiring black youths, then gifted individuals not only will be treated as the average worker but will have little incentive to upgrade their skills.

Statistical discrimination is seen in many areas of society. Life insurance and automobile insurance generally average the risks of people who are careful with those who live dangerously; this tends to reduce the incentive to behave cautiously and leads to a decrease in the average amount of caution in the population. Women were traditionally excluded from quantitatively oriented professions like engineering; as a result, women were more likely to choose humanities and social sciences for their majors and their careers, thereby reinforcing the stereotype that women were uninterested in engineering.

Statistical discrimination not only stereotypes individuals on the basis of group characteristics; it also reduces the incentives of individuals to make investments in education and training and thereby tends to reinforce the original stereotype.

ECONOMIC DISCRIMINATION AGAINST WOMEN

The largest group to suffer from economic discrimination is women. A generation ago, women earned about 70 percent of the wages of men. Part of this was due to differences in education, job experience, and other factors. Today, the gender gap has shrunk sharply. Most of the remaining difference is the "family gap"—a wage penalty against women with children.

What lay behind the income differentials between men and women? The causes are complex, grounded in social customs and expectations, statistical discrimination, and economic factors such as education and work experience. In general, women are not paid less than men for the same job. Rather, the lower pay of women arose because women were excluded from certain high-paying professions, such as engineering, construction, and coal mining. In addition, women tended to interrupt their careers to have children and perform household duties, and this continues to persist in the family gap. Also, economic inequality of the sexes was maintained because, until recently, few women were elected to the boards of directors of large corporations, to senior partnerships in major law firms, or to tenured professorships in top universities.

EMPIRICAL EVIDENCE

Having analyzed the mechanisms by which discrimination is enforced, let us next examine empirical evidence on earnings differentials. On average, women and minorities earn less than do white men. For example, women who worked full-time had earnings equal to 60 percent of men's earnings in 1967. By 1998, that number had risen to 73 percent.

Labor economists emphasize that earnings differentials are not the same as discrimination. Wage differentials often reflect differences in skill and productivity. Many Hispanic workers, particularly immigrants, have historically received less education than have native whites; women customarily spend more time out of the labor force than do men. Since both education and continuing work experience are linked to higher pay, it is not surprising that some earnings differentials exist.

How much of the earnings differentials is due to discrimination rather than productivity? Here are some recent findings:

- For women, the extent of discrimination has shrunk markedly in recent years. Aside from the family gap—which refers to the fact that women with children have an earnings penalty of 10 to 15 percent—women appear to have approximately the same earnings as equally qualified men have.
- The gap between African-Americans and whites was extremely large in the early twentieth century. African-American workers made major progress in the first seven decades of the twentieth century. Data from the 1980s and 1990s indicate that black men suffer a 12 to 15 percent loss in earnings due to labor market discrimination. Black women, by contrast, appear to have earnings roughly comparable to those of equally qualified white women.
- One of the major encouraging trends is the crumbling of barriers to employment of women and minorities in highly paid professions. In the period from 1950 to 2000, the fraction of women employed as physicians, engineers, lawyers, and economists has grown sharply—for example, from 4 to 29 percent of lawyers. Similar trends are found in other areas that were traditionally tied to gender or race.

REDUCING LABOR MARKET DISCRIMINATION

Over the last half-century, government has taken numerous measures to end discriminatory practices. The major steps were legal landmarks, such as the Civil Rights Act of 1964 (which outlaws employment discrimination based on race, color, religion, sex, or national origin) and the Equal Pay Act of 1963 (which requires that employers pay men and women equally for the same work).

Such laws helped dismantle the most blatant discriminatory practices, but more subtle barriers remain. To counter them, more aggressive and controversial policies have been introduced, including measures such as *affirmative action*. This requires that employers show they are taking extra steps to locate and hire underrepresented groups. Studies indicate that this approach has had a positive effect on the hiring and wages of women and minorities. Affirmative action has, however, been widely criticized in recent years as representing "reverse discrimination," and some states have banned its use in employment and education.

Uneven Progress

Discrimination is a complex social and economic process. It was enforced by laws that denied disadvantaged groups equal access to jobs, housing, and education. Even after equality under law was established, separation of races and sexes perpetuated social and economic stratification.

The progress in narrowing the earnings gaps among different groups slowed over the last two decades. The disintegration of the traditional nuclear family, cuts in government social programs, harsh drug laws and imprisonment rates, a backlash against many antidiscrimination programs, and the declining relative wages of the unskilled have led to declining living standards for many minority groups. Progress is uneven, and substantial differences in incomes, wealth, and jobs persist.

SUMMARY

A. Fundamentals of Wage Determination

1. The demand for labor, as for any factor of production, is determined by labor's marginal product. Therefore, a country's general wage level tends to be higher when its workers are better trained and educated, when it has more and better capital to work with, and when it uses more advanced production techniques.

2. For a given population, the supply of labor depends on three key factors: population size, average number of hours worked, and labor-force participation. For the United States, immigration has been a major source of new workers in recent years, increasing the proportion of relatively unskilled workers.

3. As wages rise, there are two opposite effects on the supply of labor. The substitution effect tempts each

worker to work longer because of the higher pay for each hour of work. The income effect operates in the opposite direction because higher wages mean that workers can now afford more leisure time along with other good things of life. At some critical wage, the supply curve may bend backward. The labor supply of very gifted, unique people is quite inelastic: their wages are largely pure economic rent.

4. Under perfect competition, if all people and jobs were exactly alike, there would be no wage differentials. The equilibrium wage rates determined by supply and demand would all be equal. But once we drop unrealistic assumptions concerning the uniformity of people and jobs, we find substantial wage differentials even in a perfectly competitive labor market. Compensating wage differentials, which compensate for nonmonetary differences in the quality of jobs, explain some of the differentials. Differences in the quality of labor explain many of the other differentials. In addition, the labor market is made up of innumerable categories of noncompeting and partially competing groups.

B. Labor Market Issues and Policies

5. Labor unions occupy an important but diminishing role in the American economy, in terms of both membership and influence. Management and labor representatives meet together in collective bargaining to negotiate a contract. Such agreements typically contain provisions for wages, fringe benefits, and work rules. Unions affect wages by bargaining for standard rates. However, in order to raise real wages above prevailing market-determined levels, unions generally must prevent entry or competition from nonunion workers.

6. According to economic theory, there is no unique outcome of a collective-bargaining session. Bilateral monopoly or management-union bargaining (like war or two-person games) has a theoretically indeterminate solution. Empirical studies find that unions have raised the wages of their members 10 to 30 percent relative to those of nonunionized workers with the same characteristics. This union differential may have eroded in the last decade's period of competition from nonunion and foreign labor.

7. While unions may raise the wages of their members, they probably do not increase a country's real wages or labor's share of national income. They are likely to increase unemployment among union members who would prefer to wait for recall from layoff of their high-paid jobs rather than move or take low-paying jobs in other industries. And in a nation with inflexible prices, real wages that are too high may induce classical unemployment.

8. By an accident of history, a tiny minority of white males in the world has enjoyed the greatest affluence. Even more than a century after the abolition of slavery, inequality of opportunity and economic, racial, and gender discrimination continue to lead to loss of income by underprivileged groups.

9. There are many sources of discrimination. One important mechanism is the establishment and maintenance of noncompeting groups. By segmenting labor markets, reserving managerial and professional positions for white men while relegating women and minorities to menial, dead-end jobs, an economy can allow inequality of earnings to persist for decades. In addition, statistical discrimination occurs when individuals are treated on the basis of the average behavior of members of the group to which they belong. This subtle form of discrimination stereotypes individuals on the basis of group characteristics, reduces the incentives of individuals to engage in self-improvement, and thereby reinforces the original stereotype.

10. Steps to reduce labor market discrimination have been taken in many directions. Early approaches focused on outlawing discriminatory practices, while later steps mandated policies such as affirmative action.

CONCEPTS FOR REVIEW

Wage Determination under Perfect Competition

elements in demand for labor:
  labor quality
  technology
  quality of other inputs
elements in supply of labor:
  hours
  labor-force participation
  immigration

income effect vs. substitution effect
compensating differentials in wages
rent element in wages
segmented markets and non-
    competing groups

Labor Market Issues

collective bargaining
unions as monopolies
control of entry by unions

effect of unions on real wages
classical unemployment
discrimination
earnings differentials: quality
    differences vs. discrimination
statistical discrimination
antidiscrimination policies

FURTHER READING AND INTERNET WEBSITES

Further Reading

The elements of the theory of human capital are given in Gary S. Becker, *Human Capital: A Theoretical and Empirical Analysis, with Special Reference to Education*, 3d ed. (University of Chicago Press, 1993).

Labor economics is an active area. Many important topics are covered in advanced surveys, such as Ronald G. Ehrenberg and Robert S. Smith, *Modern Labor Economics: Theory and Public Policy*, 8th ed. (Addison Wesley Longman, New York, 2002).

An excellent overview of the economics of discrimination is contained in the symposium on discrimination in product, credit, and labor markets in *Journal of Economic Perspectives*, Spring 1998.

Websites

Analysis of the labor market data for the United States comes from the Bureau of Labor Statistics, at www.bls.gov.

This site also has an online version of *The Monthly Labor Review*, which is an excellent source for studies about wages and employment. For example, to find out about trends in relative wages, see "Earnings of College Graduates: Women Compared with Men," *Monthly Labor Review*, March 1998, online at www.bls.gov/opub/mlr/mlrhome.htm.

An excellent review of trends in labor markets with special reference to new technologies and discrimination is in *Economic Report of the President, 2000*, chap. 4, "Work and Learning in the 21st Century," available online at w3.access.gpo.gov/eop/.

For an international perspective, visit the site of the International Labour Organization at www.ilo.org.

QUESTIONS FOR DISCUSSION

1. What steps could be taken to break down the segmented markets shown in Figure 13-8?
2. Explain, both in words and with a supply-and-demand diagram, the impact of each of the following upon the wages and employment in the affected labor market:
   a. *Upon union bricklayers:* The bricklayers' union negotiated a lower standard work rule, from 60 bricks per hour to 50 bricks per hour.
   b. *Upon airline pilots:* After the deregulation of the airlines, nonunion airlines like Continental increased their market share by 20 percent.
   c. *Upon M.D.s:* Many states began to allow nurses to be given more of physicians' responsibilities.
   d. *Upon American autoworkers:* Japan agreed to limit its exports of automobiles to the United States.
3. Explain what would happen to wage differentials as a result of each of the following:
   a. An increase in the cost of going to college
   b. Free migration among the nations of Europe
   c. Introduction of free public education into a country where education had previously been private and expensive

   d. Through technological change, a large increase in the number of people reached by popular sports and entertainment programs
4. Discrimination occurs when disadvantaged groups like women or African-Americans are segmented into low-wage markets. Explain how each of the following practices, which prevailed in some cases until recently, helped perpetuate discriminatory labor market segmentation:
   a. Many state schools would not allow women to major in engineering.
   b. Many top colleges would not admit women.
   c. Nonwhites and whites received schooling in separate school systems.
   d. Elite social clubs would not admit women, African-Americans, or Catholics.
   e. Employers refused to hire workers who had attended inner-city schools because the average productivities of workers from those schools were low.
5. Recent immigration has increased the number of low-skilled workers with little impact upon the supply of highly trained workers. A recent study by George Borjas,

Richard Freeman, and Lawrence Katz estimated that the wages of high school dropouts declined by 4 percent relative to the wages of college graduates in the 1980s as a result of immigration and trade.

a. To see the impact of *immigration,* turn back to Figure 12-6 in the previous chapter. Redraw the diagrams, labeling part (*a*) "Market for Skilled Workers" and part (*b*) "Market for Unskilled Workers." Then let immigration increase the supply of unskilled labor down and to the right while leaving the supply of skilled workers unchanged. What would happen to the relative wages of the skilled and unskilled and to the relative levels of employment as a result of immigration?

b. Next analyze the impact of *international trade* on wages and employment. Suppose that lower trade barriers increased the demand for skilled workers

in (*a*) while reducing the demand for domestic unskilled workers in (*b*). Show that this would tend to increase the inequality between skilled and unskilled workers.

6. People often worry that high tax rates would reduce the supply of labor. Consider the impact of higher taxes with a backward-bending supply curve as follows: Define the before-tax wage as W, the posttax wage as W_p, and the tax rate as t. Explain the relationship $W_p = (1 - t)W$. Draw up a table showing the before-tax and posttax wages when the before-tax wage is \$20 per hour for tax rates of 0, 15, 25, and 40 percent.

Now turn to Figure 13-4. For the regions above and below point *C*, show the impact of a lower tax rate upon the supply curve. In your table, show the relationship between the tax rate and the government's tax revenues.

CHAPTER

14

Land and Capital

*Land is a good
investment: they ain't
making it no more.*

Will Rogers

The United States is a "capitalist" economy. By this, we mean that most of the country's capital and other assets are privately owned. In 2003, the net stock of capital in the United States was more than $100,000 per capita, of which 68 percent was owned by private corporations, 14 percent by private persons, and 19 percent by governments. Moreover, the ownership of the nation's wealth was highly concentrated in the portfolios of the richest Americans.

By contrast, in socialist countries, like Russia before 1991 or China today, most of the land and capital is owned by government, and there are no super-rich individuals like J. P. Morgan or Bill Gates. Under capitalism, individuals and private firms do most of the saving, own most of the wealth, and get most of the profits on these investments.

The difference between poor and rich countries comes in large measure from the ability to generate large flows of savings and invest those savings in high-return capital. But a nation's nonhuman assets include much beyond its plant and equipment. We would also want to count its agricultural land, natural resources like oil and minerals, and environmental assets like clean air, national parks, or sandy beaches.

In this chapter we will study the workings of the factor markets for land and capital. We will start by looking at the market for land, which is a nonproduced factor. Then we will turn to the crucial questions of the supply and demand for capital, which is an output of the economy as well as an input. This will give us a much deeper understanding of some key features of a capitalist economy. The appendix to this chapter reviews the behavior of the totality of markets, known as general-equilibrium theory.

A. LAND AND RENT

Rent as Return to Fixed Factors

Unless you are planning to run your company from a balloon, land is an essential factor of production for any business. The unusual feature of land is that its quantity is fixed and completely unresponsive to price.[1]

The price of using land or other inputs in fixed supply is called its **rent** (or **pure economic rent**).

---

[1] Sometimes natural resources are included along with land. We postpone our analysis of the economics of natural resources until Chapter 18.

Rent is calculated as dollars per unit of time per unit of the fixed factor. The rent on land in the Arizona desert might be 50 cents per acre per year, while that in midtown New York or Tokyo might be $1 million per acre per year. Economists apply the term "rent" not only to land but also to any factor that is fixed in supply. If you decided to pay $1 million for Jennifer Lopez to perform at your birthday party, you would be paying rent for the use of that unique factor.[2]

Rent (or pure economic rent) is the payment for the use of factors of production that are fixed in supply.

Market Equilibrium. The supply curve for land is completely inelastic—that is, vertical—because the supply of land is fixed. In Figure 14-1, the demand and supply curves intersect at the equilibrium point *E*. It is toward this factor price that the rent of land must tend. Why?

If rent were above the equilibrium, the amount of land demanded by all firms would be less than the fixed supply. Some landowners would be unable to rent their land and would have to offer their land for less and thus bid down its rent. By similar reasoning, the rent could not long remain below the equilibrium. If it did, the bidding of unsatisfied firms would force rents back up toward the equilibrium level. Only at a competitive price where the total amount of land demanded exactly equals the fixed supply will the market be in equilibrium.

Suppose the land can be used only to grow corn. If the demand for corn rises, the demand curve for corn-land will shift up and to the right, and the rent will rise. This leads to an important point about land: The price of land is high because the price of corn is high. This is a fine example of *derived demand*—which signifies that the demand for the factor is derived from the demand for the product produced by the factor.

Because the supply of land is inelastic, land will always work for whatever it can earn. Thus the value of the land derives entirely from the value of the product, and not vice versa.

---

[2] Always remember that "rent" is used in a special and specific way in economics to reflect the payments to factors in fixed supply. Everyday usage of the word includes other meanings, such as the payment for use of an apartment or building.

FIGURE 14-1. Fixed Land Must Work for Whatever It Can Earn

Perfectly inelastic supply characterizes the case of rent, sometimes also called pure economic rent. We run up the *SS* curve to the factor demand curve to determine rent. Aside from land, we can apply rent considerations to gold mines, 7-foot-tall basketball players, and anything else in fixed supply.

Taxing Land

The fact that the supply of land is fixed has a very important consequence. Consider the land market in Figure 14-2 on page 266. Suppose the government introduces a 50 percent tax on all land rents, taking care to ensure that there is no tax on buildings or improvements, because that certainly would affect the volume of construction activity. All that is being taxed is the rent on the fixed supply of agricultural and urban land sites.

After the tax, the total demand for the land's services will not have changed. At a price (*including* tax) of $200 in Figure 14-2, people will continue to demand the entire fixed supply of land. Hence, with land fixed in supply, the market rent on land services (including the tax) will be unchanged and must be at the original market equilibrium at point *E*.

What will happen to the rent received by the landowners? Demand and quantity supplied are unchanged, so the market price will be unaffected by

FIGURE 14-2. Tax on Fixed Land Is Shifted Back to Landowners, with Government Skimming Off Pure Economic Rent

A tax on fixed land leaves prices paid by users unchanged at *E* but reduces rent retained by landowners to *E'*. What can the landowners do but accept a lower return? This provides the rationale for Henry George's single-tax movement, which aimed to capture for society the increased land values without distorting the allocation of resources.

the tax. Therefore, the tax must have been completely paid out of the landowner's income.

The situation can be visualized in Figure 14-2. What the farmer pays and what the landlord receives are now two quite different things. As far as the landlords are concerned, once the government steps in to take its 50 percent share, the effect is just the same as it would be if the net demand to the owners had shifted down from *DD* to *D'D'*. Landowners' equilibrium return after taxes is now only *E'*, or half as much as *E*. *The whole of the tax has been shifted backward onto the owners of the factor in perfectly inelastic supply.*

Landowners will surely complain. But under perfect competition there is nothing they can do about it, since they cannot alter the total supply and the land must work for whatever it can get. Half a loaf is better than none.

You might at this point wonder about the effects of such a tax on economic efficiency. The striking result is that *a tax on rent will lead to no distortions or*

economic inefficiencies. This surprising result comes because a tax on pure economic rent does not change anyone's economic behavior. Demanders are unaffected because their price is unchanged. The behavior of suppliers is unaffected because the supply of land is fixed and cannot react. Hence, the economy operates after the tax exactly as it did before the tax—with no distortions or inefficiencies arising as a result of the land tax.

A tax on pure economic rent will lead to no distortions or inefficiencies.

Henry George's Single-Tax Movement

The theory of pure economic rent was the basis for the single-tax movement of the late 1800s. At the time, America's population was expanding rapidly as people migrated here from all over the world. With the growth in population and the expansion of railroads into the American west, land rents soared, creating handsome profits for those who were lucky or farsighted enough to buy land early.

Why, some people asked, should lucky landowners be permitted to receive these "unearned land increments"? Henry George (1839–1897), a journalist who thought a great deal about economics, crystallized these sentiments in his best-selling book *Progress and Poverty* (1879). He called for financing government principally through property taxes on land, while cutting or eliminating all other taxes on capital, labor, and the improvements on the land. George believed that such a "single tax" could improve the distribution of income without harming the productivity of the economy.

While the U.S. economy obviously never went very far toward the single-tax ideal, many of George's ideas were picked up by subsequent generations of economists. In the 1920s, the English economist Frank Ramsey extended George's approach by analyzing the efficiency of different kinds of taxes. This led to the development of efficient or Ramsey tax theory. This analysis shows that taxes are least distortionary if levied on sectors whose supplies or demands are highly price-inelastic.

The reasoning behind Ramsey taxes is essentially the same as that shown in Figure 14-2. If a commodity is highly inelastic in supply or demand, a tax on that sector will have very little impact on production and consumption, and the distortion will be relatively small.

B. CAPITAL AND INTEREST

You can have your cake and eat it too:
Lend it out at interest.

Anonymous

BASIC CONCEPTS

Economic analysis traditionally divides factors of production into three categories: land, labor, and capital. The first two of these are called *primary* or *original factors* of production, whose supplies are determined largely outside the marketplace. To them we add a *produced factor* of production, capital.

Capital (or capital goods) consists of those durable produced goods that are in turn used as productive inputs for further production. Some capital goods might last a few years, while others might last for a century or more. But the essential property of a capital good is that it is both an input and an output.

There are three major categories of capital goods: structures (such as factories and homes), equipment (consumer durable goods like automobiles and producer durable equipment like machine tools and computers), and inventories of inputs and outputs (such as cars in dealers' lots).

Prices and Rentals on Capital Goods

Capital goods are bought and sold in capital-goods markets. For example, Dell sells computers to businesses; these computers are used by firms to help improve the efficiency of their payroll systems or production management. When sales occur, we observe the *prices of capital goods.*

Most capital goods are owned by the firm that uses them. Some capital goods, however, are rented out by their owners. Payments for the temporary use of capital goods are called *rentals.* An apartment that is owned by Ms. Landlord might be rented out for a year to a student—the monthly payment of $600 constitutes a rental. We distinguish rent on fixed factors like land from rentals on durable factors like capital.[3]

Rate of Return on Capital Goods

One of the most important tasks of any economy, business, or household is to allocate its capital across different possible investments. Should a country devote its investment resources to heavy manufacturing like steel or to information technologies like the Internet? Should Intel build a $4 billion factory to produce the next generation of microprocessors? Should Farmer Jones, hoping to improve his record keeping, buy a customized accounting program or go with one of the popular varieties available for around $100? All these questions involve costly investments—laying out money today to obtain a return in the future.

In deciding upon the best investment, we need a measure for that yield or return on capital. One important measure is the **rate of return on capital,** which denotes the net dollar return per year for every dollar of invested capital.

Let's consider the example of a rental car company. Ugly Duckling Rental Company buys a used Ford for $10,000 and rents it out for $2500 per year. After calculating all expenses (maintenance, insurance, depreciation,[4] etc.), and ignoring any change in car prices, Ugly Duckling earns a net rental of $1200 each year. We say, then, that the rate of return on the Ford is 12 percent per year ($= \$1200 \div \$10,000$). Note also that the rate of return is a pure number per unit of time. That is, it has the dimensions of (dollars per period)/(dollars) and is usually calculated as percent per year.

You might be considering different investments: rental cars, oil wells, apartments, education, and so forth. Your financial advisers tell you that you do not have sufficient cash to invest in everything, so how can you decide which investments to make?

One useful approach is to compare the rates of return on capital of the different investments. For each one, you first calculate the dollar cost of the capital good. Then estimate the net annual dollar receipts or rentals yielded by the asset. The ratio of the annual net rental to the dollar cost is the rate of return on capital: it tells you the amount of money you get back for every dollar invested, measured as dollars per year per dollar of investment.

---

[3] Remember the warning in footnote 2, above, about the special meaning of the term "rent" in economics. A similar warning applies to "rental."

[4] *Depreciation* is an estimate of the loss in dollar value of a capital good due to obsolescence or wear and tear during a period of time.

The rate of return on capital is the annual net return (rentals less expenses) per dollar of invested capital. It is a pure number—percent per year.

Of Wine, Trees, and Drills. Here are some examples of rates of return on investments:

- I buy grape juice for $10 and sell it a year later as wine for $11. If there are no other expenses, the rate of return on this investment is $1/$10, or 10 percent per year.
- I plant a pine tree with labor cost of $100. At the end of 25 years the grown tree sells for $430. The rate of return on this capital project is then 330 percent per quarter-century, which, a calculator will show, is equivalent to a return of 6 percent per year. That is, $100 × (1.06)^{25} = 430.
- I buy a $20,000 piece of oil-drilling equipment. For 10 years it earns annual rentals of $30,000, but I incur annual expenses of $26,000 for fuel, insurance, and maintenance. The $4000 net return covers interest and repays the principal of $20,000 over 10 years. What is the rate of return on the drill? Statistical tables show that the rate of return is 15 percent per year.

Financial Assets vs. Tangible Assets

If we examine the balance sheet of a firm or individual, it will contain a mixture of financial assets and tangible assets. **Tangible assets** consist of land and capital goods like computers, buildings, and automobiles that are used to produce further goods and services. But we must distinguish these from financial assets, which are essentially pieces of paper. More precisely, **financial assets** are monetary claims by one party against another party. An important example is a mortgage, which is a claim by a bank against a homeowner for monthly payments of interest and principal; these payments will repay the original loan that helped finance the house purchase.

Often, as in the case of a mortgage, a tangible asset will lie behind (or serve as collateral for) a financial asset. In other cases, such as student loans, a financial asset may derive from a promise to pay based on the future earning power of a person.

It is clear that tangible assets are essential parts of an economy because they increase the productivity

of other factors. What is the function of financial assets? They are crucial because of a mismatch between savers and investors. Students need money to pay for college, but they do not have the current earnings or savings to pay the bills. Older people, who are working and saving for retirement, may have income in excess of their expenditures and can provide the savings. A vast financial system of banks, mutual funds, insurance companies, and pension funds—often supplemented by government loans and guarantees—serves to channel the funds of those who are saving to those who are investing. Without this financial system, it would not be possible for firms to make the huge investments needed to develop new products, for people to buy houses before they have saved the entire housing price, or for students to go to college without first saving the large sums necessary. The major elements of our financial system are analyzed in the chapters on macroeconomics.

Financial Assets and Interest Rates

When people save, they expect a return. This is the **interest rate,** or the financial return on funds, or the annual return on borrowed funds. The yield you get when you put your money in a time deposit at a commercial bank is an example of an interest rate. Say that the interest rate for 2005 is 5 percent per year. If you deposit $1000 on January 1, 2005, you will end up with $1050 on January 1, 2006.

You will usually see interest rates quoted as *x* percent per year. This is the interest that would be paid if the sum were borrowed for an entire year; for shorter or longer periods, the interest payment is adjusted proportionately.

There are many varieties of interest rates. There are long-term and short-term interest rates, depending on the duration of the loan or the bond; there are fixed-interest-rate loans and variable-interest-rate loans; there are interest rates on supersafe bonds (like U.S. government securities); and there are interest rates on highly risky "junk bonds."

To summarize:

Households and other savers provide financial resources or funds to those who want to invest in tangible or intangible capital. The rate of interest represents the price that a borrower pays to a lender for the use of the money for a period of time; interest rates are quoted as a certain percent yield per year.

Real vs. Nominal Interest Rates

The interest rates just discussed are measured in dollar or *nominal* terms and not in terms of trees or wine or cars. Interest is the yield on an investment measured in dollars per year per dollar of investment. But dollars can become distorted yardsticks. The prices of fish, trees, wine, and other goods change from year to year as the general price level rises due to inflation.[5] We therefore need to find a real return on capital, one that measures the quantity of goods we get tomorrow for goods forgone today.

As an example, say that you invested 1000 rubles in a Russian bond in 1995. Because you were offered a 70 percent interest rate, you might have looked forward to getting a hefty return, ending up with 1700 rubles at the end of the year. But when you later took your money out to buy some consumer goods, you found that prices had risen 65 percent during 1995. In terms of the real quantity of goods, you could actually buy only 3 percent more (1.030 = 1.70/1.65) than you could have bought at the start of the year. In other words, if you had loaned 1000 market baskets of goods at the beginning of 1995, you could have obtained only 1030 market baskets of goods the following year. The difference between real and nominal interest rates is particularly dramatic during periods of high inflation.

We call the real yield on funds the **real interest rate**, as opposed to the **nominal interest rate**, which is the dollar return on dollars invested. For low rates of interest and inflation, the real interest rate is very close to the nominal interest rate minus the rate of inflation.[6]

The real interest rate is the return on funds in terms of goods and services; we generally calculate

U.S. financial instrument	Nominal rate of return, 1976–2003 (% per year)
Tax-free state and local bonds	7.3
Federal government bonds:	
Short term	6.5
Long term	8.3
Corporate bonds:	
Safe (Aaa)	9.2
Risky (Baa)	10.3
Consumer loans:	
Mortgages	9.9
Credit cards	16.2
New-car loans	11.2

TABLE 14-1. Interest Rates on Selected Financial Instruments

Nominal interest rates depend upon risk, inflation, and tax treatment. The lowest interest rates are on tax-free and safe state and local securities, followed by taxable federal government obligations. Credit cards are expensive sources of credit but easy to obtain. Foreign debt from risky countries with high sovereign risk and high inflation can be many times higher.

Source: Federal Reserve Board.

the real interest rate as the nominal interest rate minus the rate of inflation.

Table 14-1 shows nominal interest rates on different instruments over the last three decades. (Using the formula, you can obtain real interest rates by taking into account that inflation averaged 4 percent per year over this period.)

PRESENT VALUE OF ASSETS

Capital goods are durable assets that produce a stream of rentals or receipts over time. If you own an apartment building, you will collect rental payments over the life of the building, much as the owner of a fruit orchard will pick fruit from the trees each season.

Suppose you become weary of tending the building and decide to sell it. To set a fair price for the building, you would need to determine the value today of the entire stream of future income. The value of that stream is called the present value of the capital asset.

---

[5] The *rate of inflation* is defined as the rate of change of prices from one period to the next. If the general price level is 100 in 2000 and 103.5 in 2001, the rate of inflation is 3.5 percent per year.

[6] In other words, let π be the inflation rate, i the nominal interest rate, and r the real interest rate. The exact calculation of the real interest rate is $1 + r = (1 + i)/(1 + \pi)$. For small values of i and π, however, $r = i - \pi$.

The **present value** is the dollar value today of a stream of income over time. It is measured by calculating how much money invested today would be needed, at the going interest rate, to generate the asset's future stream of receipts.

Let's start with a very simple example. Let's say somebody offers to sell you a bottle of wine that matures in exactly 1 year and can then be sold for exactly $11. Assuming the market interest rate is 10 percent per year, what is the present value of the wine—that is, how much should you pay for the wine today? Pay exactly $10, because $10 invested today at the market interest rate of 10 percent will be worth $11 in 1 year. So the present value of next year's $11 wine is today $10.

Present Value for Perpetuities

We present the first way of calculating present value by examining the case of a *perpetuity*, which is an asset like land that lasts forever and pays $N each year from now to eternity. We are seeking the present value (V) if the interest rate is i percent per year, where the present value is the amount of money invested today that would yield exactly $N each year. This is simply

$$V = \frac{\$N}{i}$$

where V = present value of the land ($)
          N = perpetual annual receipts
               ($ per year)
          i = interest rate in decimal terms (e.g.,
               0.05, or $\frac{5}{100}$ per year)

This says that if the interest rate is always 5 percent per year, an asset yielding a constant stream of income will sell for exactly 20 (= 1 ÷ $\frac{5}{100}$) times its annual income. In this case, what would be the present value of a perpetuity yielding $100 every year? At a 5 percent interest rate its present value would be $2000 (= $100 ÷ 0.05).

The formula for perpetuities can also be used to value stocks. Suppose that a share of Spring Water Co. is expected to pay a dividend of $1 every year into the indefinite future and that the discount rate on stocks is 5 percent per year. Then the stock price should be $P = \$1/0.05 = \$20$ per share. (These numbers are corrected for inflation, so the numerator is

"real dividends" and the denominator is a "real interest rate" or a "real discount rate.")

General Formula for Present Value

Having seen the simple case of the perpetuity, we move to the general case of the present value of an asset with an income stream that varies over time. The main thing to remember about present value is that future payments are worth less than current payments and they are therefore *discounted* relative to the present. Future payments are worth less than current payments just as distant objects look smaller than nearby ones. The interest rate produces a similar shrinking of time perspective.

Let's take a fantastic example.[7] Say that someone proposes to pay $100 billion to your heirs in 999 years. How much should you pay for this today? According to the general rule for present value, to figure out the value today of $P payable t years from now, ask yourself how much must be invested today to grow into $P at the end of t years. Say the interest rate is 6 percent per annum. Applying this each year to the growing amount, a principal amount of $P grows in t years to $\$P \times (1 + 0.06)^t$. Hence, we need only invert this expression to find present value: the present value of $P payable t years from now is only $\$P/(1 + 0.06)^t$. Using this formula, we determine that the present value of $100 billion paid in 999 years is $0.0000000000000052.

In most cases, there are several terms in an asset's stream of income. In present-value calculations, each dollar must stand on its own feet. First, evaluate the present value of each part of the stream of future receipts, giving due allowance for the discounting required by its payment date. Then simply add together all these separate present values. This summation will give you the asset's present value.

The exact formula for present value (V) is the following:

$$V = \frac{N_1}{1 + i} + \frac{N_2}{(1 + i)^2} + \cdots + \frac{N_t}{(1 + i)^t} + \cdots$$

In this equation, i is the one-period market interest rate (assumed constant). Further, N_1 is the net receipts

---

[7] Question 9 at the end of this chapter asks about the present value of the real estate of Manhattan when it was purchased by the Dutch.

(positive or negative) in period 1, N_2 the net receipts in period 2, N_t the net receipts in period t, and so forth. Then the stream of payments $(N_1, N_2, \ldots, N_b, \ldots)$ will have the present value, V, given by the formula.

For example, assume that the interest rate is 10 percent per year and that I am to receive $1100 next year and $2662 in 3 years. The present value of this stream is

$$V = \frac{1100}{(1.10)^1} + \frac{2662}{(1.10)^3} = 3000$$

Figure 14-3 shows graphically the calculation of present value for a machine that earns steady net annual rentals of $100 over a 20-year period and has no scrap value at the end. Its present value is not $2000 but only $1157. Note how much the later dollar earnings are scaled down or discounted because of our time perspective. The total area remaining after discounting (the rust shaded area) represents the machine's total present value—the value today of the stream of all future incomes.

Acting to Maximize Present Value

The present-value formula tells us how to calculate the value of any asset once we know the earnings. But note that an asset's future receipts usually depend on business decisions: Shall we use a truck 8 or 9 years? Overhaul it once a month or once a year? Replace it with a cheap, nondurable truck or an expensive, durable one?

FIGURE 14-3. Present Value of an Asset

The lower, rust area shows the present value of a machine giving net annual rentals of $100 for 20 years with an interest rate of 6 percent per year. The upper, gray area has been discounted away. Explain why raising the interest rate increases the gray area and therefore depresses the market price of an asset.

There is one rule that gives correct answers to all investment decisions: Calculate the present value resulting from each possible decision. Then always act so as to maximize present value. In this way you will have more wealth to spend whenever and however you like.

PROFITS

In addition to wages, interest, and rent, economists often talk about a fourth category of income called *profits*. What are profits? How do they differ from interest and the returns on capital more generally?

Reported Profit Statistics

Accountants define **profits** as the difference between total revenues and total costs. To calculate profits, start with total revenues from sales. Subtract all expenses (wages, salaries, rents, materials, interest, excise taxes, and the rest). What is left over is the residual called profits.[8]

Determinants of Profits

What determines the rate of corporate profits in a market economy? Profits are in fact a combination of different elements, including the implicit returns on owners' capital, reward for risk bearing, and innovational profits.

Profits as Implicit Returns. To the economist, business profits are a hodgepodge of different elements. Much of reported business profits is primarily the return to the owners of the firm for the capital and labor provided by the owners, that is, for factors of production supplied by them.

For example, some profits are the return on the personal work provided by the owners of the firm—such as the doctor or lawyer who works in a small professional corporation. Part is the rent return on land owned by the firm. In large corporations, most

---

[8] In analyzing profits, it is important to distinguish *business profits* from *economic profits.* Business profits (also called business income or business earnings) are the residual income measured by accountants; they equal sales less costs. Business profits include an implicit return on the capital owned by firms. Economic profits are the earnings after all costs—both money and implicit or opportunity costs—are subtracted. In large corporations, therefore, economic profits would equal business profits less an implicit return on the capital owned by the firm along with any other costs (such as unpaid management time) not fully compensated at market prices.

profits are the opportunity costs of invested capital. These returns are called *implicit returns* (or costs), which is the name given to the opportunity costs of factors owned by firms.

Thus some of what is ordinarily called profit is really nothing but rentals, rents, and wages under a different name. "Implicit rentals," "implicit rent," and "implicit wages" are the names economists give to the earnings on factors that the firm itself owns.

Profits as Reward for Risk Bearing. Profits also include a reward for the riskiness of the investments. Most businesses must incur a *risk of default,* which occurs when a loan or investment cannot be paid, say because the borrower went bankrupt. In addition, there are many *insurable risks,* such as those for fires or hurricanes, analyzed in Chapter 11, which can be covered through purchase of insurance.

A third kind of risk is the *uninsurable* or *systematic risk* of investments. A company may have a high degree of sensitivity to business cycles, which means that its earnings fluctuate a great deal when aggregate output goes up or down. Yet a fourth category is *sovereign risk,* which occurs when a nation defaults on its obligations and (because the government is "sovereign" and exercises ultimate legal authority) there is no recourse in the legal system.

Because they contain elements of these four kinds of risk, corporate profits are the most volatile component of national income. The rights to earn corporate profits — corporate stocks or equities — must therefore provide a significant premium to attract risk-averse investors. This excess return on equities above that on risk-free investments is called the *equity premium.*

Empirical studies suggest that the equity premium averaged around 6 percent per year over the twentieth century. However, during the stock market bubble of the late 1990s, the equity premium declined to around zero. This implied that the future return on stocks might be relatively low. The poor performance of stock market investments since 2000 is a reminder that equities are indeed a risky investment.

Profits as Reward for Innovation. A third kind of profits consists of the returns to innovation and invention. A growing economy is constantly producing new products—from telephones in the nineteenth century to automobiles early in the twentieth century to the computer-related goods and services in the present era. These new products are the result of research, development, and marketing. We call the person who brings a new product or process to market an *innovator* or *entrepreneur.*

What do we mean by "innovators"? Innovators are people who have the vision, originality, and daring to introduce new ideas in business. Our economy has been revolutionized by the discoveries of great inventors like Alexander Graham Bell (the telephone), Jack Kilby (integrated circuit), and Kary Mullis (polymerase chain reaction). Some inventors amass great fortunes from their entrepreneurship. A recent compilation of the world's richest people found three of the top four people were among the founders of Microsoft.

Every successful innovation creates a temporary pool of monopoly. We can identify *innovational profits* (sometimes called *Schumpeterian profits*) as the temporary excess return to innovators or entrepreneurs. For a short time, innovational profits are earned. These profit earnings are temporary and are soon competed away by rivals and imitators. But just as one source of innovational profits is disappearing, another is being born. An economy will generate innovational profits as long as it produces new products and processes.

Review

Let's review the terms we have learned before turning to apply them:

- A modern industrial economy has accumulated large stocks of *capital,* or capital goods. These are the machines, buildings, and inventories that are so vital to an economy's productivity.
- The annual dollar earnings on capital are called *rentals.* When we divide the net earnings (rentals less costs) by the dollar value of the capital generating the rentals, we obtain the *rate of return on capital* (measured in percent per year).
- Capital is financed by savers who lend funds and hold financial assets. The dollar yield on these financial assets is the *interest rate,* measured in percent per year.

- Capital goods and financial assets generate a stream of income over time. This stream can be converted into a *present value*, that is, the value that the stream of income would be worth today. This conversion is made by asking what quantity of dollars today would be just sufficient to generate the asset's stream of income at going market interest rates.

- *Profits* are a residual income item, equal to total revenues minus total costs. Profits contain elements of implicit returns (such as return on owners' capital), return for risk bearing, and innovational profits.

THE THEORY OF CAPITAL AND INTEREST

Now that we have surveyed the major concepts, we turn to an analysis of the *classical theory of capital*. This approach was developed independently by the Austrian E. V. Bohm-Bawerk, the Swede Knut Wicksell, and Irving Fisher of the United States.

Roundaboutness

In Chapter 2, we noted that investment in capital goods involves indirect or *roundabout* production. Instead of catching fish with our hands, we find it ultimately more worthwhile first to build boats and make nets—and then to use the boats and nets to catch many more fish than we could by hand.

Put differently, investment in capital goods involves forgoing present consumption to increase future consumption. Consuming less today frees labor for making nets to catch many more fish tomorrow. In the most general sense, capital is productive because by forgoing consumption today we get more consumption in the future.

To see this, imagine two islands that are exactly alike. Each has the same amount of labor and natural resources. Island A uses these primary factors directly to produce consumption goods like food and clothing; it uses no produced capital goods at all. By contrast, thrifty Island B sacrifices current consumption and uses its resources and labor to produce capital goods, such as plows, shovels, and looms. After this temporary sacrifice of current consumption, B ends up with a large stock of capital goods.

FIGURE 14-4. Investments Today Yield Consumption Tomorrow

Two islands begin with equal endowments of labor and natural resources. Lazy Island A invests nothing and shows a modest growth in per capita consumption. Thrifty Island B devotes an initial period to investment, forgoing consumption, and then enjoys the harvest of much higher consumption in the future.

Figure 14-4 shows the way that Island B forges ahead of A. For each island, measure the amount of consumption per person that can be enjoyed while maintaining the existing capital stock. Because of its thrift, Island B, using roundabout, capital-intensive methods of production, will enjoy more future consumption than Island A. Island B gets more than 100 units of future-consumption goods for its initial sacrifice of 100 units of present consumption.

By sacrificing current consumption and building capital goods today, societies can increase their consumption in the future.

Diminishing Returns and the Demand for Capital

What happens when a nation sacrifices more and more of its consumption for capital accumulation and as production becomes more and more roundabout or indirect? We would expect the law of diminishing returns to set in. Let's take the example of computers. The first computers were expensive and used intensively. Three decades ago, scientists would eke every last hour of time from an expensive mainframe computer that had less power than today's personal computer. By 2004, the nation's stock of computers had millions of times more computational and storage capacity. But the marginal product of computer power—the value of the last calculation or the last byte of storage—had diminished greatly as computer inputs increased relative to labor, land, and other capital. More generally, as capital accumulates, diminishing returns set in and the rate of return on the investments tends to fall.

Surprisingly, the rate of return on capital has not fallen markedly over the course of the last two centuries, even though our capital stocks have grown manyfold. Rates of return have remained high because innovation and technological change have created profitable new opportunities as rapidly as past investment has annihilated them. Even though computers are thousands of times more powerful than they were three decades ago, new applications in every corner of society from medical diagnostics to Internet commerce continue to make investments in computers profitable.

Irving Fisher: Economist as Crusader

Irving Fisher (1867–1947) was a multifaceted genius and crusader. His pioneering economic research ranged from fundamental theoretical studies on utility and capital theory to practical investigations into business cycles, index numbers, and monetary reform.

Among his fundamental contributions was the development of a complete theory of capital and interest in *The Nature of Capital and Income* (1906) and *The Theory of Interest* (1907). Fisher described the interplay between the interest rate and innumerable other elements of the economy. Yet the basic determinants of the interest rate, Fisher showed, were two fundamental pillars: impatience as reflected in "time discounting" and investment opportunity as reflected in the "marginal rate of return over cost." It was Fisher who uncovered the deep relationship between interest and capital and the economy, as described in this summary from *The Theory of Interest*:

> The truth is that the rate of interest is not a narrow phenomenon applying only to a few business contracts, but permeates all economic relations. It is the link which binds man to the future and by which he makes all his far-reaching decisions. It enters into the price of securities, land, and capital goods generally, as well as into rent, wages, and the value of all "interactions." It affects profoundly the distribution of wealth.

In short, upon its accurate adjustment depend the equitable terms of all exchange and distribution.

Fisher always aimed at research that could be empirically applied. His philosophy is embodied in the Econometric Society, which he helped found, whose constitution trumpeted a science which would lead to "the advancement of economic theory in its relation to statistics and mathematics [and] the unification of the theoretical-quantitative and the empirical-quantitative approach."

In addition to research on pure economics, Fisher was a habitual crusader. He lobbied for a "compensated dollar" as a substitute for the gold standard. After he contracted tuberculosis, he became an impassioned advocate for improved health and developed 15 rules of personal hygiene. These included a strong advocacy of Prohibition and idiosyncracies such as chewing 100 times before swallowing. It is said that with no alcohol and much chewing, dinner parties at the Fishers were not the liveliest gatherings in New Haven.

Fisher's most famous forecast came in 1929 when he argued that the stock market had achieved a "permanent plateau of prosperity." He put his money behind his forecast, and his substantial wealth was wiped out in the Great Depression.

Even though Fisher's financial acumen has been questioned, his legacy in economics has grown steadily, and he is generally regarded as the greatest American economist of all time.

Determination of Interest and the Return on Capital

We can use the classical theory of capital to understand the determination of the rate of interest. Households *supply* funds for investment by abstaining from consumption and accumulating savings over time. At the same time, businesses *demand* capital goods to combine with labor, land, and other inputs. In the end, a firm's demand for capital is driven by its desire to make profits by producing goods.

Or, as Irving Fisher put the matter a century ago:

> The quantity of capital and the rate of return on capital are determined by the interaction between (1) people's *impatience* to consume now rather than accumulate more capital goods for future consumption (perhaps for old-age retirement or for that proverbial rainy day); and (2) *investment opportunities* that yield higher or lower returns to such accumulated capital.

To understand interest rates and the return on capital, consider an idealized case of a closed economy with perfect competition and without risk or inflation. In deciding whether to invest, a profit-maximizing firm will always compare its cost of borrowing funds with the rate of return on capital. If the rate of return is higher than the market interest rate at which the firm can borrow funds, it will undertake the investment. If the interest rate is higher than the rate of return on investment, the firm will not invest.

Where will this process end? Eventually, firms will undertake all investments whose rates of return are higher than the market interest rate. Equilibrium is then reached when the amount of investment that firms are willing to undertake at a given interest rate just equals the savings which that interest rate calls forth.

In a competitive economy without risk or inflation, the competitive rate of return on capital would be equal to the market interest rate. The market interest rate serves two functions: It rations out society's scarce supply of capital goods for the uses that have the highest rates of return, and it induces people to sacrifice current consumption in order to increase the stock of capital.

Graphical Analysis of the Return on Capital

We can illustrate capital theory by concentrating on a simple case in which all physical capital goods are alike. In addition, assume that the economy is in a steady state with no population growth or technological change.

In Figure 14-5, *DD* shows the demand curve for the stock of capital; it plots the relationship between the quantity of capital demanded and the rate of return on capital. Recall from Chapter 12 that the demand for a factor like capital is a derived demand—the demand comes from the *marginal product of capital,* which is the extra output yielded by additions to the capital stock.

The law of diminishing returns can be seen in the fact that the demand-for-capital curve in Figure 14-5 is downward-sloping. When capital is very scarce, the most profitable roundabout projects have a very high rate of return. Gradually, as the community exploits all the high-yield projects by accumulating capital, with total labor and land fixed, diminishing returns

FIGURE 14-5. Short-Run Determination of Interest and Returns

In the short run, the economy has inherited a given stock of capital from the past, shown as the vertical *SS* supply-of-capital schedule. Intersection of the short-run supply curve with the demand-for-capital schedule determines the short-run return on capital, and the short-run real interest rate, at 10 percent per year.

to capital set in. The community must then invest in lower-yield projects as it moves down the demand-for-capital curve.

Short-Run Equilibrium. We can now see how supply and demand interact. In Figure 14-5, past investments have produced a given stock of capital, shown as the vertical short-run supply curve, *SS.* Firms will demand capital goods in a manner shown by the downward-sloping demand curve, *DD.*

At the intersection of supply and demand, at point *E,* the amount of capital is just rationed out to the demanding firms. At this short-run equilibrium, firms are willing to pay 10 percent a year to borrow funds to buy capital goods. At that point, the lenders of funds are satisfied to receive exactly 10 percent a year on their supplies of capital.

Thus, in our simple, riskless world, the rate of return on capital exactly equals the market interest rate. Any higher interest rate would find firms un-willing to borrow for their investments; any lower in-terest rate would find firms clamoring for the too scarce capital. Only at the equilibrium interest rate of 10 percent are supply and demand equilibrated. (Recall that these are *real* interest rates because there is no inflation.)

But the equilibrium at E is sustained only for the short run: At this high interest rate, people desire to accumulate more wealth, that is, to continue saving. This means that the capital stock increases. However, because of the law of diminishing returns, the rate of return and the interest rate move downward. As cap-ital increases—while other things such as labor, land, and technical knowledge remain unchanged—the rate of return on the increased stock of capital goods falls to ever-lower levels.

This process is shown graphically in Figure 14-6. Note that capital formation is taking place at point E.

So each year, the capital stock is a little higher as net investment occurs. As time passes, the community moves slowly down the DD curve as shown by the black arrows in Figure 14-6. You can actually see a se-ries of very thin short-run supply-of-capital curves in the figure—S, S', S'', S''', ... These curves show how the short-run supply of capital increases with capital accumulation.

Long-Run Equilibrium. What are the long-run equilib-rium stock and return on capital? The eventual equi-librium is shown at E' in Figure 14-6; this is where the long-run supply of capital (shown as $S_L S_L$) intersects with the demand for capital. In long-run equilibrium, the interest rate is at that level where the desired capi-tal stock held by firms just matches the desired wealth that people want to own. At the long-run equilibrium, net saving stops, net capital accumulation is zero, and the capital stock is no longer growing.

FIGURE 14-6. Long-Run Equilibration of the Supply and Demand for Capital

In the long run, society accumulates capital, so the supply curve is no longer vertical. As pic-tured here, the supply of capital and wealth is responsive to higher interest rates. At the original short-run equilibrium at E there is net investment, so the economy moves down the DD demand curve as shown by the black arrows. Long-run equilibrium comes at E', where net saving ceases.

The long-run equilibrium stock of capital comes at that real interest rate where the value of assets that people want to hold exactly matches the amount of capital that firms want for production.

APPLICATIONS OF CLASSICAL CAPITAL THEORY

We have completed our survey of the classical theory of interest and capital. But capital theory needs some amplifications and qualifications to account for important realistic features of economic life.

Taxes and Inflation

Investors always keep a sharp eye out for inflation and taxes. Recall that inflation tends to reduce the quantity of goods you can buy with your dollars. Therefore, we want to calculate the real interest rate or the real return to our investments, removing the effect of the changing yardstick of money. Another important feature is taxes. Part of our incomes goes to the government to pay for public goods and other government programs. Therefore, investors will want to focus on the posttax return on investments.

Technological Disturbances

A deeper complexity involves technological change. Historical studies show that inventions and discoveries raise the return on capital and thereby affect equilibrium interest rates. Indeed, the tendency toward falling interest rates via diminishing returns has been just about canceled out by inventions and technological progress.

Some economists (such as Joseph Schumpeter) have likened the investment process to a plucked violin string: In a world of unchanging technology, the string gradually comes to rest as capital accumulation drives down returns on capital. But before the economy has settled into a steady state, an outside event or invention comes along to pluck the string and set the forces of investment in motion again.

Uncertainty and Expectations

The final qualification concerns the risks that exist in investment decisions. In real life no one has a crystal ball to read the future. All investments, resting as they do on estimates of future earnings, must necessarily involve guesses about future costs and payoffs. Our discussion assumed that there were no risks. But in fact almost any loan or investment has an element of risk. Machines break down; an oil well may turn out to be a dry hole; your favorite Internet company may go belly up. Investments differ in their degree of risk, but no investment is completely risk-free.

Investors are generally averse to holding risky assets. They would rather hold an asset that is sure to yield them 10 percent than an asset that is equally likely to yield 0 or 20 percent. Investors must therefore receive an extra return, or *risk premium*, to induce them to hold investments with high systematic or uninsurable risk.

EMPIRICAL FINDINGS

Returns to Labor and Capital

A final comparison, in Figure 14-7, shows the trends in the return to labor and capital in the United States over the last four decades. Real wages (which are dollar wages corrected for movements in the price of consumption goods) grew steadily until the late 1970s and then stagnated for two decades. The pretax rate of profit on capital declined from its peak in the mid-1960s and has averaged around 8 percent per year for the last three decades.

Note as well that the rate of profit actually declined in the late 1990s—even as the rate of innovation and productivity growth rebounded. This most recent trend suggests that the entrepreneurs of the new economy were largely unsuccessful in their attempts to appropriate the social returns from their innovative activity.

VALEDICTORY THOUGHTS ON FACTOR PRICES, EFFICIENCY, AND DISTRIBUTION

Economists emphasize that a free market in capital and land will promote high rates of saving and investment, rapid economic growth, and healthy

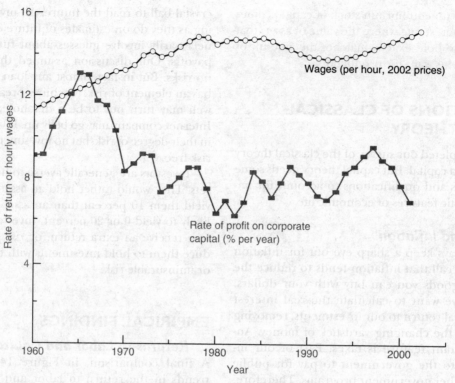

FIGURE 14-7. Trends in Wages and Profits in the United States

How have the returns to labor and capital varied in recent years? Real wages grew sharply in the period after World War II, stagnated in the mid-1970s, and then resumed growth in the mid-1990s. After peaking in the mid-1960s, the pretax rate of profit on American business capital fell sharply and then meandered around 8 percent per year over the last 3 decades.

Source: U.S. Departments of Commerce and Labor.

productivity growth. At the same time, many people worry that this same free market will lead the rich to become richer while the poor fall behind. We would offer three final thoughts on these debates:

1. *Competitive factor markets promote efficiency.* People's market incomes are determined by rents, interest, and wages. We may or may not like the competitive distribution of income, but we must recognize that competitive pricing helps solve the question of *how* goods are to be produced in an efficient manner. Getting the prices right is crucial to ensuring efficient selection of inputs in the production process.

    Consider, for example, how different relative proportions of land and labor are reflected in

different countries. Compare the United States, with plentiful land and scarce labor, with Hong Kong, where land is precious and labor abundant. As a result of supply and demand, wages are high relative to rents in America while the opposite is true in Hong Kong. Because these relative scarcities are transmitted by factor prices, markets help ensure that efficient land-labor combinations are used. Americans have huge farms and use labor sparingly, while land in Hong Kong is reserved for industry and housing rather than for land-intensive agriculture.

2. *Capital markets balance saving and investment.* When people look at profits, they usually think about the dollars that corporations are paying to

management and stockholders. These perceptions overlook the basic point about the role of capital in a market economy. The accumulation of capital and its return are driven by two fundamental forces. On the one hand, the demand for capital results from the fact that indirect or roundabout production processes are productive; by abstaining from consumption today, society can raise consumption in the future. On the other hand, people must be willing to abstain from consumption in order to accumulate financial assets, lending funds to firms that will make the productive investments in roundabout productive processes. These two forces of technology and impatience are brought into balance by the interest rate, which ensures that society's accumulation of capital just matches the amount that people are willing to hold back from consumption in the form of savings.

3. *Governments can reduce inequality without impairing efficiency.* Finally, we must remember that incomes are not carved in granite. Factor prices are affected by government policies, and incomes can be modified by transfer payments. If society dislikes the inequality brought about by high land rents or fabulous wages of unique individuals, taxes on these factors can reduce inequality without inducing great inefficiencies. Well-designed taxes on high incomes and inheritances, efficient wage subsidies to low-wage workers, and transfer programs to help the truly needy can reduce the worst inequalities of a market economy—without impairing the ability of factor prices to guide markets to efficient allocations.

With well-designed tax and transfer programs, a country can have its cake of growing productivity and share the cake more equally among its citizens.

Our basic survey of the economics of labor, land, and capital concludes the essential analytical core of microeconomics. The appendix to this chapter pushes out the frontier of our understanding by examining the behavior of the totality of markets, known as general equilibrium, and examining the efficiency properties of markets. Armed with our new tools from the previous chapters, we are prepared for the concluding chapters on microeconomics in Part Four; these examine important applications of the basic tools, including the structure of international trade, the role of government, and policies to combat inequality and environmental degradation.

SUMMARY

A. Land and Rent

1. The return to fixed factors like land is called pure economic rent, or rent, for short. Since the supply curve for land is vertical and totally inelastic, the rent will be price-determined rather than price-determining.

2. A factor like land that is inelastically supplied will continue to work the same amount even though its factor reward is reduced. For this reason, Henry George pointed out that rent is in the nature of a surplus rather than a reward necessary to coax out the factor's effort. This provides the basis for his single-tax proposal to tax the unearned increment of land value, without shifting the tax forward to consumers or distorting production. Modern tax theory extends this proposition by showing that inefficiencies are minimized by taxing goods that are relatively inelastic in supply or demand.

B. Capital and Interest

3. A third factor of production is capital, a produced durable good that is used in further production. In the most general sense, investing in capital represents deferred consumption. By postponing consumption today and producing buildings or equipment, society increases consumption in the future. It is a technological fact that roundabout production yields a positive rate of return.

4. Recall the definitions:
   Capital goods: durable produced goods used for further production
   Rentals: net annual dollar returns on capital goods
   Rate of return on capital: net annual receipts on capital divided by dollar value of capital (measured as percent per year)

Interest rate: yield on funds, measured as percent per year

Real interest rate: yield on funds corrected for inflation, also measured as percent per year

Present value: value today of a stream of future returns generated by an asset

Profits: a residual income item equal to revenues minus costs

5. Assets generate streams of income in future periods. By calculating the present value, we can convert the stream of returns into a single value today. This is done by asking what amount of dollars today will generate the stream of future returns when invested at the market interest rate.

6. The exact present-value formula is as follows: Each dollar payable t years from now has a present value (V) of $\$1/(1 + i)^t$. So for any net-receipt stream $(N_1, N_2, \ldots, N_t, \ldots)$ where N_t is the dollar value of receipts t years in the future, we have

$$V = \frac{N_1}{1 + i} + \frac{N_2}{(1 + i)^2} + \cdots + \frac{N_t}{(1 + i)^t} + \cdots$$

7. Interest is a device that serves two functions in the economy. As a motivating device, it provides an incentive for people to save and accumulate wealth. As a rationing device, interest allows society to select only those investment projects with the highest rates of return. However, as more and more capital is accumulated, and as the law of diminishing returns sets in, the rate of return on capital and the interest rate will be beaten down by competition. Falling interest rates are a signal to society to adopt more capital-intensive projects with lower rates of return.

8. Saving and investment involve waiting for future consumption rather than consuming today. Such thrift interacts with the net productivity of capital to determine interest rates, the rate of return on capital, and the capital stock. The funds or financial assets needed to purchase capital are provided by households that are willing to sacrifice consumption today in return for larger consumption tomorrow. The demand for capital comes from firms that have a variety of roundabout investment projects. In long-run equilibrium, the interest rate is thus determined by the interaction between the net productivity of capital and the willingness of households to sacrifice consumption today for consumption tomorrow.

9. Important qualifications of classical capital theory include the following: Technological change shifts the productivity of capital; imperfect foresight means that capital's return is highly volatile; and investors must consider the impact of taxes and inflation.

10. Profits are revenues less costs. Reported business profits are chiefly corporate earnings. Economically, we distinguish three categories of profits: (*a*) An important source is profits as implicit returns. Firms generally own many of their own nonlabor factors of production—capital, natural resources, and patents. In these cases, the implicit return on unpaid or owned inputs is part of profits. (*b*) Another source of profits is uninsurable risk, particularly that associated with the business cycle or sovereign risk. (*c*) Finally, innovational profits will be earned by entrepreneurs who introduce new products or innovations.

CONCEPTS FOR REVIEW

Land

rent
inelastic supply of land
taxation of fixed factors
Henry George's "single tax"

Capital and Interest

capital, capital goods
tangible assets vs. financial assets

rentals, rate of return on capital,
  interest rate, profits
investment as abstaining from
  consumption
real vs. nominal interest rate
present value
twin elements in interest determination: returns to roundaboutness
  and impatience

source of profits:
  implicit returns
  uninsurable risks
  innovation

FURTHER READING AND INTERNET WEBSITES

Further Reading

The foundations of capital theory were laid by Irving Fisher, *The Theory of Interest* (Macmillan, New York, 1930). The theory of rent was developed by David Ricardo in *Principles of Political Economy and Taxation* (1819, various publishers).

Modern capital and finance theories are very popular subjects, often covered in the macroeconomics part of an introductory course or in special courses. Good books on the subject are Burton Malkiel, *A Random Walk Down Wall Street* (Norton, New York, 2000), and Lawrence S. Ritter, William L. Silber, and Gregory F. Udell, *Principles of Money, Banking, and Financial Markets,* 10th ed. (Addison Wesley Longman, New York, 1999). Jeremy Siegel and Peter Bernstein, *Stocks for the Long Run* (McGraw-Hill, New York, 2002) has lots of interesting tables and graphs.

A recent book surveying financial history and theory is Robert Shiller, *Irrational Exuberance* (Princeton University Press, Princeton, N.J., 2000).

Websites

Data on financial markets are plentiful. See finance.yahoo.com for an entry point into stock and bond markets as well as information on individual companies. Also see www.bloomberg.com for up-to-date financial information.

Data on financial markets are also produced by the Federal Reserve System at www.federalreserve.gov. The lives and patents of great inventors can be found at www.invent.org/index.asp.

QUESTIONS FOR DISCUSSION

1. Define "pure economic rent."
   a. Show that an increase in supply of the rent-earning factor will depress its rent and lower the prices of goods that use much of it.
   b. Explain the following statement from rent theory: "It is not true that the price of corn is high because the price of land is high. Rather, the reverse is closer to the truth: the price of cornland is high because the price of corn is high." Illustrate with a diagram.
   c. Consider the quotation in **b**. Why is this correct for the market as a whole but incorrect for the individual farmer? Explain the fallacy of composition that is at work here.
2. Calculate the present value of each of the following income streams, where I_t = the income t years in the future and i is the constant interest rate in percent per year. Round to two decimal points where the numbers are not integers.
   a. $I_0 = 10$, $I_1 = 110$, $I_3 = 133.1$; $i = 10$.
   b. $I_0 = 17$, $I_1 = 21$, $I_2 = 33.08$, $I_3 = 23.15$; $i = 5$.
   c. $I_0 = 0$, $I_1 = 12$, $I_2 = 12$, $I_3 = 12, \ldots$; $i = 5$.
3. Calculate the real interest rates for each financial instrument in Table 14-1 with an inflation rate of 4 percent per year.

4. Contrast the following four returns on durable assets: (*a*) rent on land, (*b*) rental of a capital good, (*c*) rate of return on a capital good, and (*d*) real interest rate. Give an example of each.
5. Using the supply-and-demand analysis of interest, explain how each of the following would affect interest rates in capital theory:
   a. An innovation that increased the marginal product of capital at each level of capital
   b. A decrease in the desired wealth holdings of households
   c. A 50 percent tax on the return on capital (in the short run and the long run)
6. Looking back to Figures 14-5 and 14-6, review how the economy moved from the short-run equilibrium interest rate at 10 percent per year to the long-run equilibrium. Now explain what would occur in both the long run and the short run if innovations shift up the demand-for-capital curve. What would happen if the government debt became very large and a large part of people's supply of capital was siphoned off to holdings of government debt?
7. Explain the rule for calculating the present discounted value of a perpetual income stream. At 5 percent, what is the worth of a perpetuity paying $100 per year?

Paying $200 per year? Paying $N per year? At 10 or 8 percent, what is the worth of a perpetuity paying $100 per year? What does doubling the interest rate do to the capitalized value of a perpetuity—say, a perpetual bond?

8. Recall the algebraic formula for a convergent geometric progression:

$$1 + K + K^2 + \cdots = \frac{1}{1 - K}$$

for any fraction K less than 1. If you set $K = 1/(1 + i)$, can you verify the present-value formula for a permanent income stream, $V = \$N/i$? Provide an alternative proof using common sense. What would be the value of a lottery that paid you and your heirs $5000 per year forever, assuming an interest rate of 6 percent per year?

9. The value of land in Manhattan was around $80 billion in 2003. Imagine that it is 1626 and you are the economic adviser to the Dutch when they are considering whether to buy Manhattan. Further, assume that the relevant interest rate for calculating the present value is 4 percent per year. Would you advise the Dutch that a purchase price of $24 is a good deal or not? How would your answer change if the interest rate were 6 percent? 8 percent? (*Hint:* For each interest rate, calculate the present value in 1626 of the land value as of 2003. Then compare that with the purchase price in 1626.)

10. An increase in interest rates will generally lower the prices of assets. To see this, calculate the present value of the following two assets at interest rates of 5 percent, 10 percent, and 20 percent per year:

a. A perpetuity yielding $100 per year

b. A Christmas tree that will sell for $50 one year from now

Explain why the price of the long-lived asset is more sensitive to interest-rate changes than the price of the short-lived asset.

Appendix 14

MARKETS AND ECONOMIC EFFICIENCY

Having completed our analysis of the way that product and factor markets operate, we naturally want to analyze the ensemble of markets. The whole often behaves differently from the sum of the parts. In economics, the whole is called the "general equilibrium of all markets." Analysis of general equilibrium is one of the most important topics of modern economics, but it is also quite technical. We have therefore reserved the essentials of general-equilibrium theory for this appendix.

THE EFFICIENCY OF PERFECT COMPETITION

Two centuries ago, Adam Smith proclaimed that, through the workings of the invisible hand, those who pursue their own self-interest in a competitive economy will most effectively promote the public interest. This concept—that the rough-and-tumble of market competition is a potent force for raising output and living standards—is one of the most profound and powerful ideas in history.

One of the great achievements of modern economics has been to understand the exact meaning of Adam Smith's argument. Over the last two centuries, economists have refined the notion of "public interest" and today understand its logic and limitations. Efficiency, as economists define it, is a process by which society squeezes the maximum amount of consumer satisfaction out of the available resources. More precisely, **allocative efficiency** (sometimes called **Pareto efficiency**,[1] or just *efficiency* for short) occurs when there is no way to reorganize production or consumption so that it will increase the satisfaction of one person without reducing the satisfaction of another person. Or, to put it another way, an efficient situation is one where no one can be made better off without making someone else worse off.

Today, we know the following:

Under limited conditions, including perfect competition, a market economy will display allocative efficiency. In such a system, the economy as a whole is efficient, and no one can be made better off without making someone else worse off.

This is truly an astounding statement about the power of competition to produce beneficial results. It means that, given the resources and technology of the society, even the most skilled planner cannot come along with a computer or an ingenious reorganization scheme and find a solution superior to the competitive marketplace; no reorganization can make everyone better off. And this result is true whether the economy has one or two or two million competitive markets for goods and factors.

A GENERAL EQUILIBRIUM OF ALL MARKETS

Having stated the fundamental proposition about competitive markets, we will explore the reasons behind this remarkable result. Let's review first what we have learned in earlier chapters about the behavior of individual markets:

1. Competitive supply and demand operate to determine prices and quantities in individual markets.
2. Market demand curves are derived from the marginal utilities of different goods.
3. The marginal costs of different commodities lie behind their competitive supply curves.
4. Firms calculate marginal costs of products and marginal revenue products of factors and then choose inputs and outputs so as to maximize profits.
5. These marginal revenue products, summed for all firms, provide the derived demands for the factors of production.
6. These derived demands for land, labor, or capital goods interact with their market supplies to determine factor prices such as rent, wages, and interest rates.
7. The factor prices and quantities determine incomes, which then close the circle back to steps 1 and 2 by helping to determine the demand for different commodities.

---

[1] It is so-called after Vilfredo Pareto (1848–1923), the Italian economist who first proposed the concept.

Each of these statements is the result of **partial-equilibrium analysis,** which examines the behavior of a single market, household, or firm, taking the behavior of all other markets and the rest of the economy as given. In this appendix, we are concerned with **general-equilibrium analysis,** which examines how (and how successfully) all the households, firms, and markets interact simultaneously to solve the questions of *how, what,* and *for whom.*

Interaction of All Markets in General Equilibrium

It is the interconnectedness of economic life that makes it so intricate and complex. How was it that a revolution in Iran in 1979 led to a worldwide oil-price increase, lowering the demand for automobiles and causing thousands of steelworkers to lose their jobs? How did a default on a few billion dollars' worth of Russian junk bonds shake the world market in 1997 and produce a massive realignment of trillions of dollars in stock and bond markets in the United States and other countries? These and countless other economic impacts take place through the general-equilibrium interactions of the seven steps outlined above.

Notice how our list of steps follows a logical progression from step to step. The textbook chapters follow in almost the same order. But in real life, which comes first? Is there an orderly sequence that determines prices in single markets on Monday, evaluates consumer preferences on Tuesday, and reckons business costs on Wednesday and marginal products on Thursday? Obviously not. *All these partial-equilibrium processes are going on simultaneously.*

That is not all. These different activities do not go on independently, each in its own little groove, careful not to get in the way of the others. All the processes of supply and demand, of cost and preference, of factor productivity and demand are really different aspects of one vast, simultaneous, interdependent process.

A Circular Flow. Like an invisible web, the markets for inputs and outputs are connected in an interdependent system that we call a general equilibrium. Figure 14A-1 on page 285 depicts the basic structure of a general equilibrium. The outer loop shows the demands and supplies of all goods and factors. We speak here not of a single good or factor but of *all*

different products (corn, medical care, air travel, etc.), which are made by a vast array of factors of production (cornland, surgeons, aircraft, etc.).

Each good or factor is exchanged in a market, and the equilibrium of supply and demand determines the price and quantity of the item. That marriage of supply and demand is occurring millions of times every day, for all kinds of commodities from abacuses to zwieback. Note in Figure 14A-1 that the upper section of the loop carries the supplies and demands for products, while the lower section shows the supplies and demands for factors of production. See how consumers demand products and supply factors; indeed, households buy their consumption goods with the incomes they earn from the factors they supply. Similarly, businesses buy factors and supply products, paying out factor incomes and profits with the revenues from the products that they sell.

The economy's general equilibrium contains a logical structure behind the millions of markets determining prices and outputs: (1) Households, which want to maximize their satisfactions, supply factors and buy products while (2) firms, guided by the lure of profits, transform factors bought from households into products sold to households. The logical structure of a general-equilibrium system is complete.

PROPERTIES OF A COMPETITIVE GENERAL EQUILIBRIUM

Not surprisingly, analyzing a general-equilibrium system is more complicated than using partial-equilibrium analysis, which deals with only a single market. A general-equilibrium system represents a whole economy, rather than just part of one. It may contain many different kinds of labor, machines, and land, all of which are serving as inputs to produce dozens of different kinds of computers, hundreds of different specifications of automobiles, thousands of different items of clothing, and so on. It contains services like cellular connections, college courses, and vacations at Disneyland, as well as goods like heavy-construction equipment, pizzas, and cellular telephones.

How can we possibly know that a competitive market economy is efficient? In answering this question, we proceed as follows: (1) We first describe the

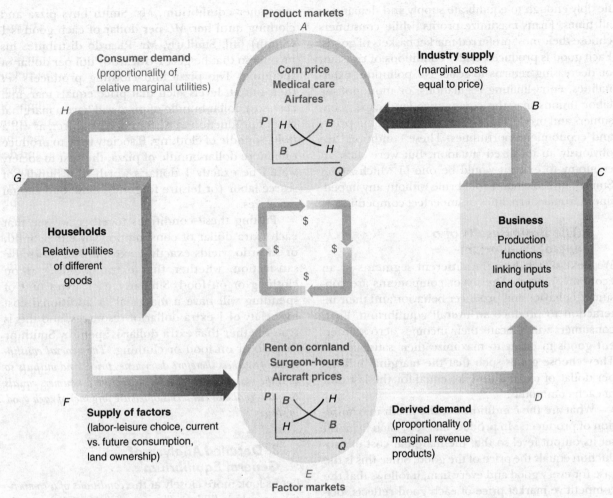

FIGURE 14A-1. Inputs, Production, Outputs, and Consumption Form the Circular Flow of Economic Life

The general equilibrium of an economy links together the supplies and demands of a vast number of factors and products. Observe how profit-maximizing firms and utility-maximizing households interact in product markets at *A* and in factor markets at *E*. Also, note that the flow of money inside the circular flow moves in the opposite direction from the flow of goods and factors.

---

assumptions of our general economic equilibrium. (2) We then describe in a summary fashion the properties of a general equilibrium. (3) Next, in a more technical discussion, we sketch the properties of a general equilibrium in more detail. (4) Finally, we show why a perfectly competitive general equilibrium will be efficient.

I. The Basic Principles of a General Equilibrium

What assumptions do we make in analyzing a competitive economy? We assume that all markets are perfectly competitive—that is, they are subject to the relentless competition of many buyers and sellers. Each price, whether for an input or an output, moves flexibly enough to equilibrate supply and demand at all times. Firms maximize profits, while consumers choose their most preferred market baskets of goods. Each good is produced under conditions of constant or decreasing returns to scale. No pollution, externalities, entry-limiting regulations, or monopolistic labor unions mar the competitive landscape. Consumers and producers are well informed about prices and economic opportunities. These conditions are obviously an idealized situation. But were such an economy to exist, it would be one in which Adam Smith's invisible hand could rule without any impediment from externalities or imperfect competition.

2. The Basic Results of a General Equilibrium

We next sketch how the different segments of an economy interact. The major components are consumer behavior and producer behavior and their interaction to produce an overall equilibrium. First, consumers will allocate their incomes across different goods in order to maximize their satisfactions. They choose goods such that the marginal utilities per dollar of expenditure are equal for the last unit of each commodity.

What are the conditions for the profit maximization of producers? In product markets, each firm will set its output level so that the marginal cost of production equals the price of the good. Since this is the case for every good and every firm, it follows that the competitive market price of each good reflects society's marginal cost of that good.

Putting together these two statements yields the conditions for a competitive equilibrium. For each consumer, the marginal utility of consumption for each good is proportional to that good's marginal cost. Hence, the marginal utility per last dollar spent on each good is equalized for every good.

An example will clarify this result. Say that we have two individuals, Ms. Smith and Mr. Ricardo, and two kinds of goods, pizza and clothing. Set the utility scale so that 1 util equals $1.[2] In the

consumer equilibrium, Ms. Smith buys pizza and clothing until her *MU* per dollar of each good is 1 (Smith) util. Similarly, Mr. Ricardo distributes his income so that he gets 1 (Ricardo) util per dollar of spending. The pizza and clothing producers set their output levels such that price equals marginal cost, so a dollar-bundle of pizza will have a marginal cost of production of $1 for each producer, as will a dollar-bundle of clothing. If society were to produce one more dollar-bundle of pizza, the cost to society would be exactly 1 dollar's worth of a bundle of scarce labor (or leisure forgone), land, and capital resources.

Putting these conditions together, we see that each extra dollar of consumption, by either Smith or Ricardo, yields exactly 1 extra util of subjective satisfaction, whether that extra spending is on clothing or on food. Similarly, each extra unit of spending will have a marginal or additional cost to society of 1 extra dollar of resources, and this is true whether that extra dollar is spent by Smith or Ricardo or on food or clothing. *The general equilibrium of markets therefore determines prices and outputs so that the marginal utility of each good to consumers equals the marginal cost (in terms of leisure forgone) of each good to society.*

3. Detailed Analysis of General Equilibrium

Let us look more closely at the *conditions of a competitive general equilibrium.* These conditions fall naturally into two categories; the first, relating to consumers, corresponds to the upper section of the loop of Figure 14A-1, while the second, concerning production, corresponds to the lower section.

a. Consumer Equilibrium. Our analysis of consumer behavior in Chapter 5 showed that, when choosing among goods, consumers would maximize their utility by equalizing the marginal utility per dollar of spending. This rule implies the following condition:

$$\frac{MU_1}{MU_2} = \frac{P_1}{P_2}$$

In words, the ratio of the marginal utilities of two goods is equal to the ratio of their prices. This condition must hold for any individual consumer who buys the two goods in question.

---

[2] To simplify the analysis, we have adopted a special "money-leisure metric" for utility. This means that we adjust our utility yardstick so that the marginal utility of an additional hour of leisure is always constant and has a value of $1. We can then express all prices in these dollar-units of leisure, so a "util" is a unit of utility in this money-leisure metric.

b. Producer Equilibrium. The behavior of profit-maximizing firms leads to an analogous but somewhat more complex set of conditions, covered in Chapters 6 through 8. In those chapters we found that competitive firms choose input and output levels as follows:

i. The *output condition* for producers is that the level of output is set so that the price of each good equals the marginal cost of that good. By rearranging terms in this equation, we then find

$$\frac{MC_1}{MC_2} = \frac{P_1}{P_2}$$

This equation says that, in a competitive economy, the ratio of the marginal costs of two final products is equal to their price ratio. The equality holds for all goods that are produced and for all firms that produce these goods. We can also interpret the ratio of marginal costs as the slope of the production-possibility frontier, which gives the rate at which society can transform one good into another. If a pizza's MC is $1 and a haircut's MC is $10, then, by transferring resources from barbers to farmers, society can transform one haircut into 10 units of pizza.

The fundamental point to understand about a competitive economy is that the competitive prices reflect social costs or scarcities. We just noted that the ratio of marginal costs tells us the rate at which society can transform one good into another. But because the ratio of marginal costs equals the price ratio, it follows that relative prices reflect the rate at which society can transform one good into another. It is just this essential result—that competitive prices provide an accurate signal of the relative scarcity of different goods—which shows how perfectly competitive markets contribute to allocative efficiency.

ii. Competition also leads to certain *input conditions* for producers. We have seen that profit-maximizing firms choose the amount of each input so that the value of its marginal product is equal to its price. Hence:

> Marginal product of land in good 1
> × price of good 1 = rent on land
>
> Marginal product of land in good 2
> × price of good 2 = rent on land

Marginal product of labor in good 1
× price of good 1 = wage of labor

and so forth.

These relationships have several important implications. First, because each firm in a given industry faces the same prices for inputs and outputs, the marginal product of input A is the same for each firm in that industry.

By rearranging the terms in the above equations, we can see that the ratio of marginal revenue products of inputs is equal to the ratio of their prices:

$$\frac{\text{Marginal revenue product of land in good 1}}{\text{Marginal revenue product of labor in good 1}} = \frac{\text{price of land}}{\text{price of labor}}$$

This relationship holds for all firms that use land and labor to produce good 1. Moreover, it holds for all factors of production (capital, oil, unskilled labor, etc.) and for all produced goods.

The input conditions are important because they imply that the ratios of marginal products of factors are the same for all inputs and all firms in all uses. If labor is scarce relative to land in the American southwest, land rents will be low relative to labor wages. The low rent-wage ratio will signal farmers to spread their labor thinly across large farms and will lead to large houses, wide roads, and shorter commuting times. In Manhattan, with much higher ratios of land prices to labor wages, we see more high-rise apartments and longer commuting times, and farms are found only in dreams of rural life.

To summarize:

In competitive general equilibrium, with utility-maximizing consumers and profit-maximizing firms:

- The ratios of marginal utilities of goods for all consumers are equal to the relative prices of those goods.
- The ratios of marginal costs of goods produced by firms are equal to the relative prices of those goods.
- The relative marginal revenue products of all inputs are equal for all firms and all goods and are equal to those inputs' relative prices.

4. The Efficiency of Competitive Markets

Now that we have seen the way a competitive economy allocates resources, we can understand why a competitive economy is efficient.

A general-equilibrium market system will display allocative efficiency when there is perfect competition, with well-informed producers and consumers and no external effects. In such a system, each good's price is equal to its marginal costs and each factor's price is equal to the value of its marginal product. When each producer maximizes profits and each consumer maximizes utility, the economy as a whole is efficient. No one can be made better off without making someone else worse off.

What is the reason for this surprising coincidence between public welfare and private interest? We can easily see the logic by using an example. Suppose some economic wizard comes forth and says, "I have found a way of reorganizing the perfectly competitive economy to make everyone better off. We are producing too few pizzas. Simply give everyone more pizzas and fewer shirts, and everyone will be better off."

But the self-proclaimed wizard is mistaken. Suppose the current price of shirts is $15, while the price of pizzas is $5. On the consumer's side, each individual has allocated his or her budget so that the marginal utility of the last pizza is just one-third of the marginal utility of the last shirt. So consumers would certainly not want to have more pizzas and fewer shirts unless they could get more than three pizzas for each shirt given up.

Can the economy squeeze out more than three pizzas for each forgone shirt? Not if it is competitively organized. Under perfect competition, the ratio of the price of shirts to the price of pizzas is the ratio of the marginal costs of the two goods. Hence, if their price ratio is $15/$5 = 3, producers can squeeze out only three more pizzas for each shirt not produced. Indeed, if the production-possibility frontier is bowed out, producers will actually get somewhat less than three pizzas for every shirt forgone.

We see why our wizard is wrong. Consumers are willing to eat more pizzas and have fewer shirts only if they can improve their satisfactions, which means that they must get more than three pizzas for every shirt forgone. But this is not possible because profit-maximizing producers cannot get more than three pizzas by producing one less shirt. Therefore the proposed reorganization will not improve everybody's economic satisfaction.

The reasoning, of course, extends far beyond pizzas and shirts. With a little thought, you can see that it works as well for all consumer goods. With a little more work, you can even see how it will extend to include reorganizations of inputs and production across firms. And it is easy to see that it would apply to trade among nations as well as trade within a nation.

The basic point to see is that, because prices serve as signals of economic scarcity for producers and social utility for consumers, a competitive price mechanism allows the best mix of goods and services to be produced from a society's resources and technology.

A Graphical Demonstration

These points can be shown neatly using a device known as the *utility-possibility frontier* (or the *UPF*). This curve shows the outer limit of utilities or satisfactions that an economy can attain. Such a concept is very similar in spirit to the production-possibility frontier. The major difference is that the *UPF* places utilities or levels of satisfaction on the two axes, as is shown in Figure 14A-2 on page 289. The *UPF* slopes downward to indicate that, on the frontier, as one person's satisfaction increases, the other person's must decrease.

Note that the *UPF* is drawn somewhat wavy. This shape indicates that the scale of the individual utility measure is arbitrary; however, the inability to measure and compare individual utilities is completely unimportant for analyzing efficiency. All that matters here is that a person's level of satisfaction rises as the utility index increases. Because of this positive relation between utility and desired levels of consumption, we are guaranteed that each person will want to move out as far as possible on his or her utility axis.

Now comes the important point: An efficient economy is one that is on the frontier of its utility-possibility curve. One such efficient (or Pareto-efficient) point is shown at *A* in Figure 14A-2. Why is point *A* Pareto-efficient? Because there is no feasible

FIGURE 14A-2. Efficient Allocations Are on the Utility-Possibility Frontier

Economic efficiency occurs when no one's satisfaction can be improved without hurting someone else. This means that efficient outcomes are on society's utility-possibility frontier (*UPF*). Moving from outcome *A* to outcome *C* improves Smith's welfare only by hurting Jones; both are efficient allocations. Point *B* is inside the *UPF* and is inefficient because Jones, Smith, or both can be made better off without hurting anyone else.

economic reorganization that makes anyone better off without making someone else worse off. We can, of course, move to point *C*. Such a move would certainly delight Smith, whose consumption and satisfaction are increased. But Smith's gain comes only at Jones's expense. When all possible gains to Smith must come at Jones's expense, the economy is on its *UPF* and is operating efficiently.

An economy is efficient when it is on the utility-possibility frontier.

This concludes our analysis of the behavior of a market economy. Knowing the efficiency properties of competitive markets is one of the central lessons of microeconomics. Recall as well, however, the shortcomings of markets and possible public-policy remedies for market failures and income inequalities. These important topics are the subject of the chapters that follow.

SUMMARY TO APPENDIX

1. Under certain conditions, including perfect competition, a market economy will display allocative efficiency. Allocative efficiency (sometimes called Pareto efficiency) signifies that no one person can be made better off without making someone else worse off.

2. The general equilibrium of all markets is interrelated in a circular flow by a web of price connections. Households supply factors of production and demand final goods; businesses buy factors of production, transform them, and sell them as final goods.

3. The central result of general-equilibrium analysis is this: Because prices serve as signals of economic scarcity for producers and social utility for consumers, a competitive price mechanism allows the maximum output and satisfaction to be produced from a society's resources and technology. Under idealized perfect competition, the economy is on both its production-possibility frontier and its utility-possibility frontier.

CONCEPTS FOR REVIEW

partial equilibrium vs. general equilibrium
allocative (or Pareto) efficiency
utility-possibility frontier (*UPF*)

key conditions in efficient general equilibrium:
 *MU*s proportional to *P*s
 *MC*s proportional to *P*s
 ∴ *MU*s proportional to input *MC*s

QUESTIONS FOR DISCUSSION

1. State carefully the two theorems about competitive economies. How would they apply to the following quotations?
   a. "Perfect competition affords the ideal condition for the distribution of wealth." (Francis Walker, 1892)
   b. "The invisible hand, if it is to be found anywhere, is likely to be found picking the pockets of the poor." (Edward Nell, 1982)
   c. Adam Smith's quotation on the invisible hand (see Chapter 2, page 25).
   d. "Pareto . . . suggested that competition brought about a state in comparison to which no consumer's satisfaction can be made higher, within the limitations of available resources and techno-

logical know-how, without at the same time lowering at least one other consumer's satisfaction level." (Tjalling Koopmans, 1957)

2. The analysis of the efficiency of competitive economies assumes that there is no technological advance. Recall the Schumpeterian hypothesis from Chapter 10. How does this elaboration qualify the view of economic efficiency of the competitive mechanism? What kind of market failure is exemplified by invention? In a world of rapid potential technological advance, use production-possibility curves to illustrate how in the long run an innovative economy with imperfect competition might produce higher consumption than an efficient but technologically stagnant competitive economy.

Applied Microeconomics: International Trade, Government, and the Environment

Comparative Advantage and Protectionism

TO THE CHAMBER OF DEPUTIES: We are subject to the intolerable competition of a foreign rival, who enjoys such superior facilities for the production of light that he can inundate our national market at reduced price. This rival is no other than the sun. Our petition is to pass a law shutting up all windows, openings, and fissures through which the light of the sun is used to penetrate our dwellings, to the prejudice of the profitable manufacture we have been enabled to bestow on the country.
Signed: The Candle Makers

F. Bastiat

A. THE NATURE OF INTERNATIONAL TRADE

As we go about our daily lives, it is easy to overlook the importance of international trade. America ships enormous volumes of food, airplanes, computers, and machinery to other countries; and in return we get vast quantities of oil, footwear, cars, coffee, and other goods and services. While Americans pride themselves on their ingenuity, it is sobering to reflect how many of our products—including gunpowder, classical music, clocks, railroads, penicillin, and radar—arose from the ingenuity of long-forgotten people in faraway places.

What are the economic forces that lie behind international trade? Simply put, trade promotes specialization, and specialization increases productivity. Over the long run, increased trade and higher productivity raise living standards for all nations. Gradually, countries have realized that opening up their economies to the global trading system is the most secure road to prosperity.

In this chapter, we extend our analysis by examining the principles governing *international trade*, which is the system by which nations export and import goods, services, and capital. International economics involves many of the most controversial questions of the day: Why does the United States benefit from importing almost one-quarter of its automobiles and half of its petroleum? What are the advantages of free trade? How should the principles governing trade be extended to intellectual property rights, such as patents and copyrights? The economic stakes are high in finding wise answers to these questions.

International vs. Domestic Trade

At the deepest level, trade is trade, whether it involves people within the same nation or people in different countries. There are, however, three important differences between domestic and international trade, and these have important practical and economic consequences:

1. *Expanded trading opportunities.* The major advantage of international trade is that it expands trading horizons. If people were forced to consume only what they produced at home, the world would be poorer on both the material and the spiritual planes. Canadians could drink no wine, Americans could eat no bananas, and most of the world would be without jazz and Hollywood movies.

2. *Sovereign nations.* Trading across frontiers involves people and firms living in different nations. Each nation is a sovereign entity which regulates the flow of people, goods, and finance crossing its borders. This contrasts with domestic trade, where there is a single currency, where trade and money flow freely within the borders, and where people can migrate easily to seek new opportunities. In international trade, political barriers to trade are sometimes erected when affected groups object to foreign trade and nations impose tariffs or quotas. This practice, called protectionism, is analyzed at the end of this chapter.

3. *Exchange rates.* Most nations have their own currencies. I want to pay for a Japanese car in dollars, while Toyota wants to be paid in Japanese yen. Dollars are bought and sold for yen according to the exchange rate, which is the relative price of different currencies (such as the price of Japanese yen in terms of U.S. dollars). The international financial system must ensure a smooth flow and exchange of dollars, yen, and other currencies—or else risk a breakdown in trade. The financial aspects of international trade are analyzed in the chapters on macroeconomics.

Trends in Foreign Trade

What are the major components of international trade for the United States? Table 15-1 shows the composition of U.S. foreign trade for 2002. The bulk of trade is in goods, particularly manufactured goods, although service trade has increased rapidly. The data reveal that despite being an advanced industrial economy, the United States exports surprisingly large amounts of primary commodities (such as food) and imports large quantities of sophisticated, capital-intensive manufactured goods (like automobiles and computer parts). Moreover, we find a great deal of two-way, or intraindustry, trade. Within a particular industry, the United States exports and imports at the same time because a high degree of product differentiation means that different countries tend to have niches in different parts of a market.

THE SOURCES OF INTERNATIONAL TRADE IN GOODS AND SERVICES

What are the economic factors that lie behind the patterns of international trade? Nations find it beneficial to participate in international trade for several

U.S. Merchandise Trade, 2002 (billions of dollars)	Exports	Imports
Goods	**693.3**	**1,163.6**
Foods and beverages	49.5	49.7
Industrial supplies	156.9	269.0
Capital goods	290.6	283.8
Motor vehicles	78.4	203.9
Consumer goods	84.4	307.8
Other goods	33.5	49.3
Services	**279.3**	**210.4**
Travel	73.1	60.1
Passenger fares	18.0	22.4
Other transportation	28.3	38.8
Royalties and license fees	38.7	16.4
Other private services	108.1	54.6
Military sales and government	13.1	18.1
Total goods and services	**972.6**	**1,373.9**

TABLE 15-1. International Trade in Goods and Services

The United States exports a wide array of goods and services from food to intellectual property. In 2002, U.S. imports exceeded exports by $401 billion, reflecting large increases in borrowing from abroad. The United States exports a large volume of primary commodities, especially food and coal, mainly because of its ample natural resources. At the same time, it imports many manufactured goods, like cars and cameras, because other countries specialize in different market niches and enjoy economies of scale.

Source: U.S. Department of Commerce.

reasons: diversity in the conditions of production, differences in tastes among nations, and decreasing costs of large-scale production.

Diversity in Natural Resources

Trade may take place because of the diversity in productive possibilities among countries. In part, these differences reflect endowments of natural resources. One country may be blessed with a supply of petroleum, while another may have a large amount of fertile land. Or a mountainous country may generate large amounts of hydroelectric power which it sells to its neighbors, while a country with deep-water harbors may become a shipping center.

Differences in Tastes

A second reason for trade lies in preferences. Even if the conditions of production were identical in all regions, countries might engage in trade if their tastes for goods were different.

For example, suppose that Norway and Sweden both produce fish from the sea and meat from the land in about the same amounts but the Swedes have a great fondness for meat while the Norwegians are partial to fish. A mutually beneficial export of meat from Norway and fish from Sweden would take place. Both countries would gain from this trade; the sum of human happiness is increased, just as when Jack Sprat trades fat meat for his wife's lean.

Differences in Costs

Perhaps the most important reason for trade is differences among countries in production costs. For example, manufacturing processes enjoy economies of scale; that is, they tend to have lower average costs of production as the volume of output expands. So when a particular country gets a head start in producing a particular product, it can become the high-volume, low-cost producer. The economies of scale give it a significant cost and technological advantage over other countries, which find it cheaper to buy from the leading producer than to make the product themselves.

Large scale is often an important advantage in industries with large research-and-development expenses. As the leading aircraft maker in the world, Boeing can spread the enormous cost of designing, developing, and testing a new plane over a large sales volume. That means it can sell planes at a lower price than competitors with a smaller volume. Boeing's only real competitor, Airbus, got off the ground through large subsidies from several European countries to cover its research-and-development costs.

The example of decreasing cost helps explain the important phenomenon of extensive intraindustry trade shown in Table 15-1. Why is it that the United States both imports and exports computers and related equipment? Consider a company such as Intel, which produces high-end semiconductors. Intel has facilities in the United States as well as in China, Malaysia, and the Philippines, and the company often ships products manufactured in one country to be assembled and tested in another country. Another example is Dell Computers, which is the world's largest vendor of personal computers. Dell basically assembles parts that are produced by other companies, but Dell chooses the

components from around the world depending upon prices and the reliability of the manufacturer. Similar patterns of intraindustry specialization are seen with cars, steel, textiles, and many other manufactured products.

B. COMPARATIVE ADVANTAGE AMONG NATIONS

THE PRINCIPLE OF COMPARATIVE ADVANTAGE

It is only common sense that countries will produce and export goods for which they are uniquely qualified. But there is a deeper principle underlying *all* trade—in a family, within a nation, and among nations—that goes beyond common sense. The *principle of comparative advantage* holds that a country can benefit from trade even if it is absolutely more efficient (or absolutely less efficient) than other countries in the production of every good. Indeed, trade according to comparative advantage provides mutual benefits to all countries.

Uncommon Sense

Take a world in which there are only two goods, computers and clothing. Suppose that the United States has higher output per worker (or per unit of input) than the rest of the world in making both computers and clothing. But suppose the United States is relatively more efficient in the production of computers than it is in clothing. For example, it might be 50 percent more productive in computers and 10 percent more productive in clothing than other countries. In this case, it would benefit the United States to export that good in which it is relatively more efficient (computers) and import that good in which it is relatively less efficient (clothing).

Or consider a poor country like Mali. How could impoverished Mali, whose workers use handlooms and have productivity that is only a fraction of that of workers in industrialized countries, hope to export any of its textiles? Surprisingly, according to the principle of comparative advantage, Mali can benefit by exporting the goods in which it is *relatively* more efficient (like textiles) and importing those goods which it produces *relatively* less efficiently (like turbines and automobiles).

The principle of **comparative advantage** holds that each country will benefit if it specializes in the production and export of those goods that it can produce at relatively low cost. Conversely, each country will benefit if it imports those goods which it produces at relatively high cost.

This simple principle provides the unshakable basis for international trade.

Ricardo's Analysis of Comparative Advantage

Let us illustrate the fundamental principles of international trade by considering America and Europe of a century ago. If labor (or resources, more generally) is absolutely more productive in America than in Europe, does this mean that America will import nothing? And is it economically wise for Europe to "protect" its markets with tariffs or quotas?

These questions were first answered in 1817 by the English economist David Ricardo, who showed that international specialization benefits a nation. He called this result the law of comparative advantage.

For simplicity, Ricardo worked with only two regions and only two goods, and he chose to measure all production costs in terms of labor-hours. We will follow his lead here, analyzing food and clothing for Europe and America.[1]

Table 15-2 shows the illustrative data. In America, it takes 1 hour of labor to produce a unit of food, while a unit of clothing requires 2 hours of labor. In Europe the cost is 3 hours of labor for food and 4 hours of labor for clothing. We see that America has *absolute advantage* in both goods, for it can produce them with greater absolute efficiency than can Europe. However, America has *comparative advantage* in food, while Europe has comparative advantage in clothing, because food is relatively inexpensive in America while clothing is relatively less expensive in Europe.

From these facts, Ricardo proved that both regions will benefit if they specialize in their areas of comparative advantage—that is, if America specializes in the production of food while Europe specializes in the production of clothing. In this situation, America will export food to pay for European clothing, while Europe will export clothing to pay for American food.

---

[1] An analysis of comparative advantage with many countries and many commodities is presented later in this chapter.

American and European Labor Requirements for Production		
	Necessary Labor for Production (labor-hours)	
Product	**In America**	**In Europe**
1 unit of food	1	3
1 unit of clothing	2	4

TABLE 15-2. Comparative Advantage Depends Only on Relative Costs

In a hypothetical example, America has lower labor costs in both food and clothing. American labor productivity is between 2 and 3 times Europe's (twice in clothing, thrice in food).

To analyze the effects of trade, we must measure the amounts of food and clothing that can be produced and consumed in each region (1) if there is no international trade and (2) if there is free trade with each region specializing in its area of comparative advantage.

Before Trade. Start by examining what occurs in the absence of any international trade, say, because all trade is illegal or because of a prohibitive tariff. Table 15-2 shows the real wage of the American worker for an hour's work as 1 unit of food or ½ unit of clothing. The European worker earns only ⅓ unit of food or ¼ unit of clothing per hour of work.

Clearly, if perfect competition prevails in each isolated region, the prices of food and clothing will be different in the two places because of the difference in production costs. In America, clothing will be 2 times as expensive as food because it takes twice as much labor to produce a unit of clothing as it does to produce a unit of food. In Europe, clothing will be only ⅓ as expensive as food.

After Trade. Now suppose that all tariffs are repealed and free trade is allowed. For simplicity, further assume that there are no transportation costs. What is the flow of goods when trade is opened up? Clothing is relatively more expensive in America (with a price ratio of 2 as compared to ⅓), and food is relatively more expensive in Europe (with a price ratio of ¾ as compared to ½). Given these relative prices, and with no tariffs or transportation costs, food will soon be shipped from America to Europe and clothing from Europe to America.

As European clothing penetrates the American market, American clothiers will find prices falling and profits shrinking, and they will begin to shut down their factories. By contrast, European farmers will find that the prices of foodstuffs begin to fall when American products hit the European markets; they will suffer losses, some will go bankrupt, and resources will be withdrawn from farming.

After all the adjustments to international trade have taken place, the prices of clothing and food must be equalized in Europe and America (just as the water in two connecting pipes must come to a common level once you remove the barrier between them). Without further knowledge about the exact supplies and demands, we cannot know the exact level to which prices will move. But we do know that the relative prices of food and clothing must lie somewhere between the European price ratio (which is ¾ for the ratio of food to clothing prices) and the American price ratio (which is ½). Let us say that the final ratio is ⅔, so 2 units of clothing trade for 3 units of food. For simplicity, we measure prices in American dollars and assume that the free-trade price of food is $2 per unit, which means that the free-trade price of clothing is $3 per unit.

With free trade, the regions have shifted their productive activities. America has withdrawn resources from clothing and produces food, while Europe has contracted its farm sector and expanded its clothing manufacture. *Under free trade, countries shift production toward their areas of comparative advantage.*

The Economic Gains from Trade

What are the economic effects of opening up the two regions to international trade? America as a whole benefits from the fact that imported clothing costs less than clothing produced at home. Likewise, Europe benefits by specializing in clothing and consuming food that is less expensive than domestically produced food.

We can most easily reckon the gains from trade by calculating the effect of trade upon the real wages of workers. Real wages are measured by the quantity of goods that a worker can buy with an hour's pay. Using Table 15-2, we can see that the real wages after trade will be greater than the real wages before trade

for workers in both Europe *and* America. For simplicity, assume that each worker buys 1 unit of clothing and 1 unit of food. Before trade, this bundle of goods costs an American worker 3 hours of work and a European worker 7 hours of work.

After trade has opened up, as we found, the price of clothing is $3 per unit while the price of food is $2 per unit. An American worker must still work 1 hour to buy a unit of food, because food is domestically produced; but at the price ratio of 2 to 3, the American worker need work only 1½ hours to produce enough to buy 1 unit of European clothing. Therefore the bundle of goods costs the American worker 2½ hours of work when trade is allowed—this represents an increase of 20 percent in the real wage of the American worker.

For European workers, a unit of clothing will still cost 4 hours of labor in a free-trade situation. To obtain a unit of food, however, the European worker need produce only ⅔ of a unit of clothing (which requires ⅔ × 4 hours of labor) and then trade that ⅔ clothing unit for 1 unit of American food. The total European labor needed to obtain the bundle of consumption is then 4 + 2⅔ = 6⅔, which represents an increase in real wages of about 5 percent over the no-trade situation.

When countries concentrate on their areas of comparative advantage under free trade, each country is better off. Compared to a no-trade situation, workers in each region can obtain a larger quantity of consumer goods for the same amount of work when they specialize in their areas of comparative advantage and trade their own production for goods in which they have a relative disadvantage.

GRAPHICAL ANALYSIS OF COMPARATIVE ADVANTAGE

We can use the production-possibility frontier (*PPF*) to expand our analysis of comparative advantage. We will continue the numerical example based upon labor costs, but the theory is equally valid in a competitive world with many different inputs.

America without Trade

Chapter 1 introduced the *PPF*, which shows the combinations of commodities that can be produced with a society's given resources and technology. Using the production data shown in Table 15-2, and assuming that both Europe and America have 600 units of labor, we can easily derive each region's *PPF*. The table that accompanies Figure 15-1 shows the possible levels of food and clothing that America can produce with its inputs and technology. Figure 15-1 plots the production possibilities; the rust line *DA* shows America's *PPF*. The *PPF* has a slope of −½, for this represents the terms on which food and clothing can be substituted in production. In competitive markets with no international trade, the price ratio of food to clothing will also be one-half.

So far we have concentrated on production and ignored consumption. Note that if America is isolated from all international trade, it can consume only what it produces. Say that, for the incomes and demands in the marketplace, point *B* in Figure 15-1 marks America's production and consumption in the absence of trade. Without trade, America produces

and consumes 400 units of food and 100 units of clothing.

We can do exactly the same thing for Europe. But Europe's *PPF* will look different from America's because Europe has different efficiencies in producing food and clothing. Europe's price ratio is ¾, reflecting Europe's relative productivity in food and clothing.

Opening Up to Trade

Now allow trade between the two regions. Food can be exchanged for clothing at some price ratio. We call the ratio of export prices to import prices the **terms of trade.** To indicate the trading possibilities, we put the two *PPF*s together in Figure 15-2. America's rust *PPF* shows its domestic production possibilities, while Europe's gray *PPF* shows the terms on which it can domestically substitute food and clothing. Note that Europe's *PPF* is drawn closer to the origin than America's because Europe has lower productivities in both industries; it has an absolute disadvantage in the production of both food and clothing.

Europe need not be discouraged by its absolute disadvantage, however, for it is the difference in relative productivities or *comparative* advantage that makes trade beneficial. The gains from trade are illustrated by the outer lines in Figure 15-2. If America could trade at Europe's relative prices, it could produce 600 units of food and move northwest along the outer gray line in Figure 15-2(*a*)—where the gray line represents the price ratio or terms of trade that are generated by Europe's *PPF*. Similarly, if Europe could trade at America's prices, Europe could specialize in clothing and move southeast along the rust line in Figure 15-2(*b*)—where the rust line is America's pretrade price ratio.

This leads to an important and surprising conclusion: Small countries have the most to gain from international trade. Small countries affect world prices the least and therefore can trade at world prices that are very different from domestic prices. Additionally, countries that are very different from other countries gain most, much while large countries have the least to gain. (These points are raised in question 3 at the end of this chapter.)

Equilibrium Price Ratio. Once trade opens up, some set of prices must hold in the world marketplace depending upon the overall market supplies and demands. Without further information we cannot

America's production-possibility schedule
(1-to-2 constant-cost ratio)

Possibilities	Food (units)	Clothing (units)
A	600	0
B	400	100
C	200	200
D	0	300

FIGURE 15-1. American Production Data

The constant-cost line *DA* represents America's domestic production-possibility frontier. America will produce and consume at *B* in the absence of trade.

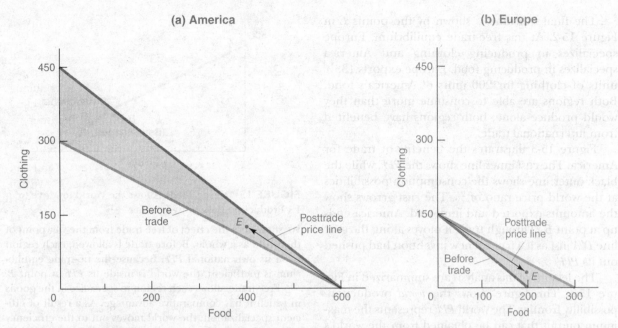

FIGURE 15-2. Comparative Advantage Illustrated

Through trade, both Europe and America improve their available consumption. If no trade
is allowed, each region must be satisfied with its own production. It is therefore limited to
its production-possibility curve, shown for each region as the line marked "Before trade."
After borders are opened and competition equalizes the relative prices of the two goods,
the relative-price line will be as shown by the arrows. If each region is faced with prices
given by the arrows, can you see why its consumption possibilities must improve?

specify the exact price ratio, but we can determine
what the price range will be. The prices must lie somewhere between the prices of the two regions. That is,
we know that the relative price of food to clothing
must lie somewhere in the range between ½ and ¾.

The final price ratio will depend upon the relative demands for food and clothing. If food were very
much in demand, the food price would be relatively
high. If food demand were so high that Europe produced food as well as clothing, the price ratio would
be at Europe's relative prices, or ¾. On the other
hand, if clothing demand were so strong that America produced clothing as well as food, the terms of
trade would equal America's price ratio of ½. If each
region specializes completely in the area of its comparative advantage, with Europe producing only
clothing and America producing only food, the price
ratio will lie somewhere between ½ and ¾. The exact
ratio will depend on the strength of demand.

Assume now that the demands are such that the
final price ratio is ⅔, with 3 units of food selling for
2 units of clothing. With this price ratio, each region
will then specialize—America in food and Europe in
clothing—and export some of its production to pay
for imports at the world price ratio of ⅔.

Figure 15-2 illustrates how trade will take place.
Each region will face a consumption-possibility
curve according to which it can produce, trade, and
consume. *The consumption-possibility curve begins at
the region's point of complete specialization and then runs
out at the world price ratio of ⅔.* Figure 15-2(*a*) shows
America's consumption possibilities as a thin black
arrow with a slope of −⅔ coming out of its complete-
specialization point at 600 units of food and no
clothing. Similarly, Europe's posttrade consumption possibilities are shown in Figure 15-2(*b*) by the
black arrow running southeast from its point of
complete specialization with a slope of −⅔.

The final outcome is shown by the points E in Figure 15-2. At this free-trade equilibrium, Europe specializes in producing clothing and America specializes in producing food. Europe exports $133\frac{1}{3}$ units of clothing for 200 units of America's food. Both regions are able to consume more than they would produce alone; both regions have benefited from international trade.

Figure 15-3 illustrates the benefits of trade for America. The rust inner line shows the *PPF*, while the black outer line shows the consumption possibilities at the world price ratio of $\frac{2}{3}$. The rust arrows show the amounts exported and imported. America ends up at point B'. Through trade it moves along the gray line $D'A$ just as if a fruitful new invention had pushed out its *PPF*.

The lessons of this analysis are summarized in Figure 15-4. This figure shows the *world* production-possibility frontier. The world *PPF* represents the maximum output that can be obtained from the world's resources when goods are produced in the most efficient manner—that is, with the most efficient division of labor and regional specialization.

FIGURE 15-4. Free Trade Allows the World to Move to Its Production-Possibility Frontier

We show here the effect of free trade from the viewpoint of the world as a whole. Before trade is allowed, each region is on its own national *PPF*. Because the no-trade equilibrium is inefficient, the world is inside its *PPF* at point B.

Free trade allows each region to specialize in the goods in which it has comparative advantage. As a result of efficient specialization, the world moves out to the efficiency frontier at point E.

FIGURE 15-3. America before and after Trade

Free trade expands the consumption options of America. The rust line DA represents America's production-possibility curve; the gray line $D'A$ is the new consumption possibility curve when America is able to trade freely at the price ratio of $\frac{2}{3}$ and, in consequence, to specialize completely in the production of food (at A). The rust arrows from S to B' and A to S show the amounts exported (+) and imported (−) by America. As a result of free trade, America ends up at B', with more of both goods available than would be the case if it consumed what it produced along DA.

The world *PPF* is built up from the two regional *PPF*s in Figure 15-2 by determining the maximum level of world output that can be obtained from the individual regional *PPF*s. For example, the maximum quantity of food that can be produced (with no clothing production) is seen in Figure 15-2 to be 600 units in America and 200 units in Europe, for a world maximum of 800 units. This same point (800 food, 0 clothing) is then plotted in the world *PPF* in Figure 15-4. Additionally, we can plot the point (0 food, 450 clothing) in the world *PPF* by inspection of the regional *PPF*s. All the individual points in between can be constructed by a careful calculation of the maximum world outputs that can be produced if the two regions are efficiently specializing in the two goods.

Before opening up borders to trade, the world is at point B. This is an inefficient point—inside the world *PPF*—because regions have different levels of relative efficiency in different goods. After opening the borders to trade, the world moves to the free-trade equilibrium at E, where countries are specializing in their areas of comparative advantage.

Free trade in competitive markets allows the world to move to the frontier of its production-possibility curve.

America's
comparative
advantage ←————•——————•——————•——————•——————•——————•————→ comparative
advantage Microprocessors Computers Aircraft Automobiles Wine Croissants advantage

FIGURE 15-5. With Many Commodities, There Is a Spectrum of Comparative Advantages

EXTENSIONS TO MANY COMMODITIES AND COUNTRIES

The world of international trade consists of more than two regions and two commodities. However, the principles we explained above are essentially unchanged in more realistic situations.

Many Commodities

When two regions or countries produce many commodities at constant costs, the goods can be arranged in order according to the comparative advantage or cost of each. For example, the commodities might be microprocessors, computers, aircraft, automobiles, wine, and croissants—all arranged in the comparative-advantage sequence shown in Figure 15-5. As you can see from the figure, of all the commodities, microprocessors are least expensive in America relative to the costs in Europe. Europe has its greatest comparative advantage in croissants. Two decades ago, America was dominant in the commercial-aircraft market, but Europe has now gained a substantial market share, so aircraft have been moving right on the line.

We can be virtually certain that the introduction of trade will cause America to produce and export microprocessors, while Europe will produce and export croissants. But where will the dividing line fall? Between aircraft and automobiles? Or wine and croissants? Or will the dividing line fall on one of the commodities rather than between them—perhaps automobiles will be produced in both places.

You will not be surprised to find that the answer depends upon the demands and supplies of the different goods. We can think of the commodities as beads arranged on a string according to their comparative advantage; the strength of supply and demand will determine where the dividing line between American and European production will fall. An increased demand for microprocessors and computers, for example, would tend to shift prices in the direction of American goods. The shift might lead America to specialize so much more in areas of its comparative advantage that it would no longer be

profitable to produce in areas of comparative disadvantage, like automobiles.

Many Countries

What about the case of many countries? Introducing many countries need not change our analysis. As far as a single country is concerned, all the other nations can be lumped together into one group as "the rest of the world." The advantages of trade have no special relationship to national boundaries. The principles already developed apply between groups of countries and, indeed, between regions within the same country. In fact, they are just as applicable to trade between our northern and southern states as to trade between the United States and Canada.

Triangular and Multilateral Trade

With many countries brought into the picture, it will generally be beneficial to engage in *triangular* or *multilateral trade* with many other countries. Bilateral trade between two countries is generally unbalanced.

Consider the simple example of triangular trade flows presented in Figure 15-6, where the arrows show the direction of exports. America buys consumer electronics from Japan, Japan buys oil and primary commodities from developing countries, and developing countries buy computers from America. In reality, trade patterns are more complex than this triangular example.

FIGURE 15-6. Triangular Trade Benefits All

In reality, international trade, like domestic trade, is many-sided.

QUALIFICATIONS AND CONCLUSIONS

We have now completed our look at the elegant theory of comparative advantage. Its conclusions apply for any number of countries and commodities. Moreover, it can be generalized to handle many inputs, changing factor proportions, and diminishing returns. But we cannot conclude without noting two important qualifications to this elegant theory:

1. *Classical assumptions.* From a theoretical point of view, the major defect of comparative-advantage theory lies in its classical assumptions. This theory assumes a smoothly working competitive economy. Trade might lead to worsening environmental problems if there are local or global public goods (see Chapter 17 for a further discussion). Moreover, inefficiencies might arise in the presence of inflexible prices and wages, business cycles, and involuntary unemployment. When there are macroeconomic or microeconomic market failures, trade might well push a nation *inside* its *PPF*. When the economy is in depression or the price system malfunctions because of environmental or other reasons, we cannot be sure that countries will gain from trade.

   Given these reservations, there can be little wonder that the theory of comparative advantage sells at a big discount during business downturns. In the Great Depression of the 1930s, as unemployment soared and real outputs fell, nations built high tariff walls at their borders and the volume of foreign trade shrank sharply. Additionally, during the prosperous 1990s, free trade was increasingly attacked by environmental advocates, who saw it as a means of allowing companies to dump pollutants in oceans or in countries with lax regulations. Labor unions and environmentalists were among the leading critics of the latest attempts to promote freer trade (see the section "Negotiating Free Trade" at the end of this chapter).

2. *Income distribution.* A second proviso concerns the impact on particular people, sectors, or factors of production. We showed above that opening a country to trade will raise a country's national income. The country can consume more of all goods and services than would be possible if the borders were sealed to trade.

But this does not mean that every individual, firm, sector, or factor of production will benefit from trade. If, through imports, free trade increases the supply of goods that are produced by particular factors of production or in particular regions, those factors or regions may end up with lower incomes than they had under restricted trade. Suppose that free trade increases the supply of cheap cotton shirts in the United States. We would not be surprised to learn that textile firms suffered losses and bankruptcies. Recent studies indicate that unskilled workers in high-income countries have suffered reductions in real wages in the last three decades because of the increased imports of goods from low-wage developing countries. Wage losses occurred because imports are produced by developing-country factors that are close substitutes for the unskilled labor in high-income countries.

The theory of comparative advantage shows that other sectors will gain more than the injured sectors will lose. Moreover, over long periods of time, those displaced from low-wage sectors eventually gravitate to higher-wage jobs. But those who are temporarily injured by international trade are genuinely harmed and are vocal advocates for protection and trade barriers.

Notwithstanding its limitations, the theory of comparative advantage is one of the deepest truths in all of economics. Nations that disregard comparative advantage pay a heavy price in terms of their living standards and economic growth.

C. PROTECTIONISM

Go back to the beginning of this chapter and reread the "Petition of the Candle Makers," written by the French economist Frederic Bastiat to satirize solemn proposals to protect domestic goods from imports. Today, people often regard foreign competition with suspicion, and campaigns to "Buy American" sound patriotic.

Yet economists since the time of Adam Smith have marched to a different drummer. Economists generally believe that free trade promotes a mutually beneficial division of labor among nations; free and open trade allows *each* nation to expand its production and consumption possibilities, raising the world's living standard. Protectionism prevents the forces of comparative advantage from working to maximum advantage.

This section reviews the economic arguments about protectionism.

SUPPLY-AND-DEMAND ANALYSIS OF TRADE AND TARIFFS

Free Trade vs. No Trade

The theory of comparative advantage can be illuminated through the analysis of supply and demand for goods in foreign trade. Consider the clothing market in America. Assume, for simplicity, that America is a small part of the market and therefore cannot affect the world price of clothing. (This assumption

will allow us to analyze supply and demand very easily; the more realistic case in which a country can affect world prices will be considered later in this chapter.)

Figure 15-7 shows the supply and demand curves for clothing in America. The demand curve of American consumers is drawn as *DD* and the domestic supply curve of American firms as *SS*. We assume that the price of clothing is determined in the world market and is equal to $4 per unit. Although transactions in international trade are carried out in different currencies, for now we can simplify by converting the foreign supply schedule into a dollar supply curve by using the current exchange rate.

No-Trade Equilibrium. Suppose that transportation costs or tariffs for clothing were prohibitive (say,

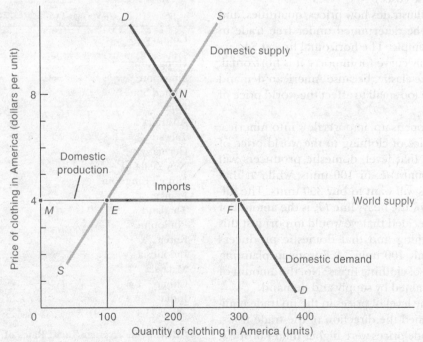

FIGURE 15-7. American Production, Imports, and Consumption with Free Trade

We see here the free-trade equilibrium in the market for clothing. America has a comparative disadvantage in clothing. Therefore, at the no-trade equilibrium at *N*, America's price would be $8, while the world price is $4.

Assuming that American demand does not affect the world price of $4 per unit, the free-trade equilibrium comes when America produces *ME* (100 units) and imports the difference between domestic demand and domestic supply, shown as *EF* (or 200 units).

$100 per unit of clothing). Where would the no-trade equilibrium lie? In this case, the American market for clothing would be at the intersection of *domestic* supply and demand, shown at point *N* in Figure 15-7. At this no-trade point, prices would be relatively high at $8 per unit, and domestic producers would be meeting all the demand.

Free Trade. Next, open up trade in clothing. In the absence of transport costs, tariffs, and quotas, the price in America must be equal to the world price. Why? Because if the American price were above the European price, sharp-eyed entrepreneurs would buy where clothing was cheap (Europe) and sell where clothing was expensive (America); Europe would therefore export clothing to America. Once trade flows fully adjusted to supplies and demands, the price in America would equal the world price level. (In a world with transportation and tariff costs, the price in America would equal the world price adjusted for these costs.)

Figure 15-7 illustrates how prices, quantities, and trade flows will be determined under free trade in our clothing example. The horizontal line at $4 represents the supply curve for imports; it is horizontal, or perfectly price-elastic, because American demand is assumed to be too small to affect the world price of clothing.

Once trade opens up, imports flow into America, lowering the price of clothing to the world price of $4 per unit. At that level, domestic producers will supply the amount *ME*, or 100 units, while at that price consumers will want to buy 300 units. The difference, shown by the heavy line *EF*, is the amount of imports. Who decided that we would import just this amount of clothing and that domestic producers would supply only 100 units? A European planning agency? A cartel of clothing firms? No, the amount of trade was determined by supply and demand.

Moreover, the level of prices in the no-trade equilibrium determined the direction of the trade flows. America's no-trade prices were higher than Europe's, so goods flowed into America. Remember this rule: *Under free trade, indeed in markets generally, goods flow uphill from low-price regions to high-price regions.* When markets are opened to free trade, clothing flows uphill from the lower-price European market to the higher-price American market until the price levels are equalized.

Trade Barriers

For centuries, governments have used tariffs and quotas to raise revenues and influence the development of individual industries. Since the eighteenth century—when the British Parliament attempted to impose tariffs on tea, sugar, and other commodities on its American colonies—tariff policy has proved fertile soil for revolution and political struggle.

We can use supply-and-demand analysis to understand the economic effects of tariffs and quotas. To begin with, note that a **tariff** is a tax levied on imports. A **quota** is a limit on the quantity of imports. The United States has quotas on many products, including peanuts, textiles, and beef.

Table 15-3 shows the average tariff rates for major countries for 2001. Note that tariffs vary widely for different goods in most countries. It would take deep study to understand why tariffs on imports of

Average Tariff Rates, 2001	
Country	**Rate (%)**
Hong Kong	0.0
Singapore	1.0
United States	2.0
Japan	2.2
Australia	3.0
Taiwan	3.1
Germany	3.5
New Zealand	3.5
United Kingdom	3.5
France	3.5
Thailand	3.7
Philippines	8.3
Korea	8.6
Indonesia	8.9
Malaysia	9.5
China	17.0
India	27.2

TABLE 15-3. Average Tariff Rates of Countries, 2001

Tariff rates vary widely among countries. The United States and regions like Singapore and Hong Kong have low tariff rates today, although there are exceptions such as for textiles and steel. Countries like India and China continue to maintain protectionist trade barriers, although China's are scheduled to fall as China joins the World Trade Organization.

Source: World Trade Organization and government organizations.

horses are zero while those on asses are 6.8 percent of value in the United States. On the other hand, it does not take much study to understand why textiles and steel have tight quotas or high tariffs, because these are industries with political clout in Congress or the White House.

Prohibitive Tariff. The easiest case to analyze is a *prohibitive tariff*—one that is so high that it chokes off all imports. Looking back at Figure 15-7, what would happen if the tariff on clothing were more than $4 per unit (that is, more than the difference between America's no-trade price of $8 and the world price of $4)? This would be a prohibitive tariff, shutting off all clothing trade. Any importer who buys clothing at the world price of $4 would sell it in America at the no-trade price of $8. But this price would not cover the cost of the good plus the tariff. Prohibitive tariffs thus kill off all trade.

Nonprohibitive Tariff. Lower tariffs (less than $4 per unit of clothing) would injure but not kill off trade. Figure 15-8 shows the equilibrium in the clothing market with a $2 tariff. Again assuming no transportation costs, a $2 tariff means that foreign clothing will sell in America for $6 per unit (equal to the $4 world price plus the $2 tariff).

The equilibrium result of a $2 tariff is that domestic consumption (or quantity demanded) is lowered from 300 units in the free-trade equilibrium to 250 units after the tariff is imposed, the amount of domestic production is raised by 50 units, and the quantity of imports is lowered by 100 units. This example summarizes the economic impact of tariffs:

A tariff will tend to raise price, lower the amounts consumed and imported, and raise domestic production.

FIGURE 15-8. Effect of a Tariff

A tariff lowers imports and consumption and raises domestic production and price. Starting from the free-trade equilibrium in Fig. 15-7, America now puts a $2 tariff on clothing imports. The price of European clothing imports rises to $6 (including the tariff).

The market price rises from $4 to $6, so the total amount demanded falls. Imports shrink from 200 to 100 units, while domestic production rises from 100 to 150 units.

Quotas. Quotas have the same qualitative effect as tariffs. A prohibitive quota (one that prevents all imports) is equivalent to a prohibitive tariff. The price and quantity would move back to the no-trade equilibrium at *N* in Figure 15-8. A less stringent quota might limit imports to 100 clothing units; this quota would equal the heavy line *HJ* in Figure 15-8. A quota of 100 units would lead to the same equilibrium price and output as did the $2 tariff.

Although there is no essential difference between tariffs and quotas, some subtle differences do exist. A tariff gives revenue to the government, perhaps allowing other taxes to be reduced and thereby offsetting some of the harm done to consumers in the importing country. A quota, on the other hand, puts the profit from the resulting price difference into the pocket of the importers or exporters lucky enough to get a permit or import license. They can afford to use the proceeds to wine, dine, or even bribe the officials who give out import licenses.

Because of these differences, economists generally regard tariffs as the lesser evil. However, if a government is determined to impose quotas, it should auction off the scarce import-quota licenses. An auction will ensure that the government rather than the importer gets the revenue from the scarce right to import; in addition, the bureaucracy will not be tempted to allocate quota rights by bribery, friendship, or nepotism.

Transportation Costs. What of transportation costs? The cost of moving bulky and perishable goods has the same effect as tariffs, reducing the extent of beneficial regional specialization. For example, if it costs $2 per unit to transport clothing from Europe to the United States, the supply-and-demand equilibrium would look just like Figure 15-8, with the American price $2 above the European price.

But there is one difference between protection and transportation costs: Transport costs are imposed by nature—by oceans, mountains, and rivers—whereas restrictive tariffs are squarely the responsibility of nations. Indeed, one economist called tariffs "negative railroads." Imposing a tariff has the same economic impact as throwing sand in the engines of vessels that transport goods to our shores from other lands.

The Economic Costs of Tariffs

What happens when America puts a tariff on clothing, such as the $2 tariff shown in Figure 15-8? There are three effects: (1) The domestic producers, operating under a price umbrella provided by the tariff, can expand production; (2) consumers are faced with higher prices and therefore reduce their consumption; and (3) the government gains tariff revenue.

Tariffs create economic inefficiency. When tariffs are imposed, the economic loss to consumers exceeds the revenue gained by the government plus the extra profits earned by producers.

Diagrammatic Analysis. Figure 15-9 shows the economic cost of a tariff. The supply and demand curves are identical to those in Figure 15-8, but three areas are highlighted. (1) Area *B* is the tariff revenue collected by the government. It is equal to the amount of the tariff times the units of imports and totals $200. (2) The tariff raises the price in domestic markets from $4 to $6, and producers increase their output to 150. Hence total profits rise by $250, shown by area *LEHM* and equal to $200 on old units and an additional $50 on the 50 new units. (3) Finally, note that a tariff imposes a heavy cost on consumers. The total consumer-surplus loss is given by area *LMJF* and is equal to $550.

The overall social impact is, then, a gain to producers of $250, a gain to the government of $200, and a loss to consumers of $550. The net social cost (counting each of these dollars equally) is therefore $100. We can reckon this as equal to areas *A* and *C*. The interpretation of these areas is important:

- Area *A* is the net loss that comes because domestic production is more costly than foreign production. When the domestic price rises, businesses are thereby induced to increase the use of relatively costly domestic capacity. They produce output up to the point where the marginal cost is $6 per unit instead of up to $4 per unit under free trade. Firms reopen inefficient old factories or work existing factories extra shifts. From an economic point of view, these plants have a comparative disadvantage because the new clothing produced by these factories could be produced more cheaply abroad. The new social cost of this inefficient production is area *A*, equal to $50.

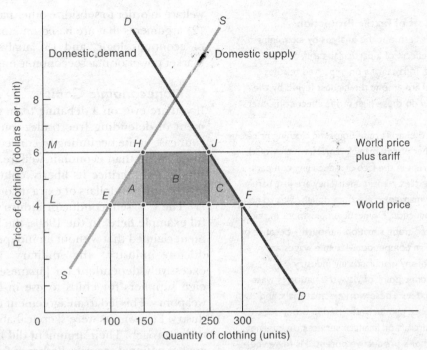

FIGURE 15-9. Economic Cost of a Tariff

Imposing a tariff raises revenues and leads to inefficiency. We see the impact of the tariff as three effects. Rectangle *B* is the tariff revenue gained by the government. Triangle *A* is the excess cost of production by firms producing under the umbrella of the tariff. Triangle *C* is the net loss in consumer surplus from the inefficiently high price. Areas *A* and *C* are the irreducible inefficiencies caused by the tariff.

- In addition, there is a net loss to the country from the higher price, shown by area *C*. This is the loss in consumer surplus that cannot be offset by business profits or tariff revenue. This area represents the economic cost incurred when consumers shift their purchases from low-cost imports to high-cost domestic goods. This area is also equal to $50.

Hence, the total social loss from the tariff is $100, calculated either way.

Figure 15-9 illustrates one feature that is important in understanding the politics and history of tariffs. When a tariff is imposed, part of the economic impact comes because tariffs redistribute income from consumers to the protected domestic producers and workers. In the example shown in Figure 15-9, areas *A* and *C* represent efficiency losses from inefficiently high domestic production

and inefficiently low consumption, respectively. Under the simplifying assumptions used above, the efficiency losses sum up to $100. The redistribution involved is much larger, however, equaling $200 raised in tariff revenues levied upon consumers of the commodity plus $250 in higher profits. Consumers will be unhappy about the higher product cost, while domestic producers and workers in those firms will benefit. We can see why battles over import restrictions generally center more on the redistributive gains and losses than on the issues of economic efficiency.

Imposing a tariff has three effects: It encourages inefficient domestic production; it raises prices, thus inducing consumers to reduce their purchases of the tariffed good below efficient levels; and it raises revenues for the government. Only the first two of these necessarily impose efficiency costs on the economy.

The Cost of Textile Protection

Let's flesh out this analysis by examining the effects of a particular tariff, one on clothing. Today, tariffs on imported textiles and apparel are among the highest levied by the United States. How do these high tariffs affect consumers and producers?

To begin with, the tariffs raise domestic clothing prices. Because of the higher prices, many factories, which would otherwise be bankrupt in the face of a declining comparative advantage in textiles, remain open. They are just barely profitable, but they manage to eke out enough sales to continue domestic production. Domestic employment in textiles exceeds the free-trade situation, although—because of pressure from foreign competition—textile wages are among the lowest of any manufacturing industry.

From an economic point of view, the nation is wasting resources in textiles. These workers, materials, and capital would be more productively used in other sectors—perhaps in aircraft or financial services or Internet commerce. The nation's productive potential is lower because it keeps factors of production working in an industry in which it has lost its comparative advantage.

Consumers, of course, pay for this protection of the textile industry with higher prices. They get less satisfaction from their incomes than they would if they could buy textiles from Korea, China, or Indonesia at prices that exclude the high tariffs. Consumers are induced to cut back on their clothing purchases, channeling funds into food, transportation, and recreation, whose relative prices are lowered by the tariffs.

Finally, the government gets revenues from tariffs on textiles. These revenues can be used to buy public goods or to reduce other taxes, so (unlike the consumer loss or the productive inefficiency) this effect is not a real social burden.

THE ECONOMICS OF PROTECTIONISM

Having examined the impact of tariffs on prices and quantities, we now turn to an analysis of the arguments for and against protectionism. The arguments for tariff or quota protection against the competition of foreign imports take many different forms. Here are the main categories: (1) noneconomic arguments that suggest it is desirable to sacrifice economic welfare in order to subsidize other national objectives, (2) arguments that are based on a misunderstanding of economic logic, and (3) analyses that rely on market power or macroeconomic imperfections.

Noneconomic Goals

If you are ever on a debating team given the assignment of defending free trade, you will strengthen your case at the beginning by conceding that there is more to life than economic welfare. A nation surely should not sacrifice its liberty, culture, and human rights for a few dollars of extra income.

The U.S. semiconductor industry provides a useful example here. In the 1980s, the Defense Department claimed that without an independent semiconductor industry, the military would become excessively dependent on Japanese and other foreign suppliers for chips to use in high-technology weaponry. This led to an agreement to protect the industry. Economists were skeptical about the value of this approach. Their argument did not question the goal of national security. Rather, it focused on the efficiency of the means of achieving the desired result. They thought that protection was more expensive than a policy targeting the domestic industry, perhaps a program to buy a minimum number of high-quality chips.

National security is not the only noneconomic goal in trade policy. Countries may desire to preserve their cultural traditions or environmental conditions. France recently has argued that its citizens need to be protected from "uncivilized" American movies. The fear is that the French film industry could be drowned by the new wave of stunt-filled, high-budget Hollywood thrillers. As a result, France has maintained strict quotas on the number of U.S. movies and television shows that can be imported. In another example, the Swiss government chose to ban trucks passing through Switzerland in an effort to preserve the tranquility and clean air of its mountain valleys.

Unsound Grounds for Tariffs

Mercantilism. To Abraham Lincoln has been attributed the remark, "I don't know much about the tariff. I do know that when I buy a coat from England, I have the coat and England has the money. But when I buy a coat in America, I have the coat and America has the money."

This reasoning represents an age-old fallacy typical of the so-called mercantilist writers of the seventeenth and eighteenth centuries. They considered a country fortunate which sold more goods than it bought, because such a "favorable" balance of trade meant that gold would flow into the country to pay for its export surplus.

The mercantilist argument confuses means and ends. Accumulating gold or other monies will not improve a country's living standard. Money is worthwhile not for its own sake but for what it will buy from other countries. Most economists today therefore reject the idea that raising tariffs to run a trade surplus will improve a country's economic welfare.

Tariffs for Special Interests. The single most important source of pressure for protective tariffs is powerful special-interest groups. Firms and workers know very well that a tariff on their particular products will help *them* even if it imposes costs on others. Adam Smith understood this point well when he wrote:

> To expect freedom of trade is as absurd as to expect Utopia. Not only the prejudices of the public, but what is much more unconquerable, the private interests of many individuals, irresistibly oppose it.

If free trade is so beneficial to the nation as a whole, why do the proponents of protectionism continue to wield such a disproportionate influence in legislatures? The few who benefit gain much from specific protection and therefore devote large sums to lobbying politicians. By contrast, individual consumers are only slightly affected by the tariff on one product; because losses are small and widespread, individuals have little incentive to spend resources expressing an opinion on every tariff case. A century ago, outright bribery was used to buy the votes necessary to pass tariff legislation. Today, powerful political action committees (PACs), financed by labor or business, round up lawyers and drum up support for tariffs or quotas on textiles, lumber, steel, sugar, and other goods.

If political votes were cast in proportion to total economic benefit, nations would legislate most tariffs out of existence. But all dollars of economic interests do not always get proportional representation. It is much harder to organize the masses of consumers and producers to agitate for the benefits

of free trade than it is to organize a few companies or labor unions to argue against "cheap Chinese labor" or "unfair Japanese competition." In every country, the tireless enemies of free trade are the special interests of protected firms and workers.

A dramatic case is the U.S. quota on sugar, which benefits a few producers while costing American consumers over $1 billion a year. The average consumer is probably unaware that the sugar quota costs 1½ cents a day per person, so there is little incentive to lobby for free trade.

Competition from Cheap Foreign Labor. Of all the arguments for protection, the most persistent is that free trade exposes U.S. workers to competition from low-wage foreign labor. The only way to preserve high U.S. wages, so the argument goes, is to protect domestic workers by keeping out or putting high tariffs on goods produced in low-wage countries. An extreme version of this contention is that under free trade U.S. wages would converge to the low foreign wages. This point was trumpeted by presidential candidate Ross Perot during the debates over the North American Free Trade Agreement (NAFTA) when he argued:

> Philosophically, [NAFTA] is wonderful, but realistically it will be bad for our country. That thing is going to create a giant sucking sound in the United States at a time when we need jobs coming in, not jobs going out. Mexican wages will come up to $7½ an hour and our wages will come down to $7½ an hour.

This argument sounds plausible, but it is all wrong because it ignores the principle of comparative advantage. The reason American workers have higher wages is that they are on average more productive. If America's wage is 5 times that in Mexico, it is because the marginal product of American workers is on average 5 times that of Mexican workers. Trade flows according to comparative advantage, not wage rates or absolute advantage.

Having shown that the nation gains from importing the goods produced by "cheap foreign labor" in which it has a comparative disadvantage, we should not ignore the costs that this strategy may temporarily impose on the affected workers and firms. If plants in a particular locality are unexpectedly shut down because production moves overseas, the local labor market may be inundated with job seekers. Older workers with outdated job skills may have trouble finding attractive jobs and will suffer a decline in their real incomes. The difficulties of displaced workers will be greater when the overall economy is depressed or when the local labor markets have high unemployment. Over the long run, labor markets will reallocate workers from declining to advancing industries, but the transition may be costly for many people.

In summary:

> The cheap-foreign-labor argument is flawed because it ignores the theory of comparative advantage. A country will benefit from trade even though its wages are far above those of its trading partners. High wages come from high efficiency, not from tariff protection.

Retaliatory Tariffs. While many people would agree that a world of free trade would be the best of all possible worlds, they note that this is not the world we live in. They reason, "As long as other countries impose import restrictions or otherwise discriminate against our products, we have no choice but to play the protection game in self-defense. We'll go along with free trade only as long as it is fair trade. But we insist on a level playing field." On several occasions in the 1990s, the United States went to the brink of trade wars with Japan and China, threatening high tariffs if the other country did not stop some objectionable trade practice.

Those who advocate this approach argue that it can beat down the walls of protection in other countries. This rationale was described in an analysis of protection in the *Economic Report of the President:*

> Intervention in international trade . . . , even though costly to the U.S. economy in the short run, may, however, be justified if it serves the strategic purpose of increasing the cost of interventionist policies by foreign governments. Thus, there is a potential role for carefully targeted measures . . . aimed at convincing other countries to reduce their trade distortions.

While potentially valid, this argument should be used with great caution. Just as threatening war leads to armed conflict as often as to arms control, protectionist bluffs may end up hurting the bluffer as well

as the opponent. Historical studies show that retaliatory tariffs usually lead other nations to raise their tariffs still higher and are rarely an effective bargaining chip for multilateral tariff reduction.

Import Relief. In the United States and other countries, firms and workers that are injured by foreign competition attempt to get protection in the form of tariffs or quotas. Today, relatively little direct tariff business is conducted on the floor of Congress. Congress realized that tariff politics was too hot to handle and has set up specialized agencies to investigate and rule on complaints. Generally, a petition for relief is analyzed by the U.S. Department of Commerce and the U.S. International Trade Commission. Relief measures include the following actions:

- The *escape clause* was popular in earlier periods. It allows temporary import relief (tariffs, quotas, or export quotas negotiated with other countries) when an industry has been "injured" by imports. Injury occurs when the output, employment, and profits in a domestic industry have fallen while imports have risen.
- *Antidumping tariffs* are levied when foreign countries sell in the United States at prices below average costs or at prices lower than those in the home market. When dumping is found, a "dumping duty" is placed on the imported good.
- *Countervailing duties* are imposed when foreigners subsidize exports to the United States. They have become the most popular form of import relief and have been pursued in hundreds of cases.

What is the justification for such measures? Import relief sounds reasonable, but it actually is completely counter to the theory of comparative advantage. That theory says that an industry which cannot compete with foreign firms ought to be injured by imports. *From an economic vantage point, less productive industries are actually being killed off by the competition of more productive domestic industries.*

This sounds ruthless indeed. No industry willingly dies. No region gladly undergoes conversion to new industries. Often the shift from old to new industries involves considerable unemployment and hardship. The weak industry and region feel they are being singled out to carry the burden of progress.

Potentially Valid Arguments for Protection

Finally, we can consider three arguments for protection that may have true economic merit:

- Tariffs may shift the terms of trade in a country's favor.
- Temporary tariff protection for an "infant industry" with growth potential may be efficient in the long run.
- A tariff may under certain conditions help reduce unemployment.

The Terms-of-Trade or Optimal-Tariff Argument.

One valid argument for imposing tariffs is that doing so will shift the terms of trade in a country's favor and against foreign countries. The phrase *terms of trade* refers to the ratio of export prices to import prices. The idea is that when a large country levies tariffs on its imports, the reduced demand for the good in world markets will lower the equilibrium price and thereby reduce the pretariff cost of the good to the country. Such a change will improve the country's terms of trade and increase domestic real income. The set of tariffs that maximizes domestic real income is called the *optimal tariff*.

The terms-of-trade argument goes back 150 years to the free-trade proponent John Stuart Mill. It is the only argument for tariffs that is valid under conditions of full employment and perfect competition. Suppose that the U.S. imposes an "optimal" tariff on imported oil. The tariff will increase the price of domestic oil and will reduce the world demand for oil. The world market price of oil will therefore be bid down. So part of the tariff actually falls on the oil producer. (We can see that a very small country could not use this argument, since it cannot affect world prices.)

Have we not therefore found a theoretically secure argument for tariffs? The answer would be yes if we could forget that this is a "begger-thy-neighbor" policy and could ignore the reactions of other countries. But other countries are likely to react. After all, if the United States were to impose an optimal tariff of 30 percent on its imports, why should the European Union and Japan not put 30 or 40 percent tariffs on their imports? In the end, as every country calculated and imposed its own nationalistic optimal tariff, the overall level of tariffs might spiral upward in the tariff version of an arms race.

Ultimately, such a situation would surely not represent an improvement of either world or individual economic welfare. When all countries impose optimal tariffs, it is likely that *everyone's* economic welfare will decline as the impediments to free trade become great. All countries are likely to benefit if all countries abolish trade barriers.

Tariffs for Infant Industries.

In his famous *Report on Manufactures* (1791), Alexander Hamilton proposed to encourage the growth of manufacturing by protecting "infant industries" from foreign competition. According to this doctrine, which received the cautious support of free-trade economists like John Stuart Mill and Alfred Marshall, there are lines of production in which a country could have a comparative advantage if only they could get started.

Such infant industries would not be able to survive the rough treatment by larger bullies in the global marketplace. With some temporary nurturing, however, they might grow up to enjoy economies of mass production, a pool of skilled labor, inventions well adapted to the local economy, and the technological efficiency typical of many mature industries. Although protection will raise prices to the consumer at first, the mature industry would become so efficient that cost and price would actually fall. A tariff is justified if the benefit to consumers at that later date would be more than enough to make up for the higher prices during the period of protection.

This argument must be weighed cautiously. Historical studies have turned up some genuine cases of protected infant industries that grew up to stand on their own feet. And studies of successful newly industrialized countries (such as Singapore and Taiwan) show that they have often protected their manufacturing industries from imports during the early stages of industrialization. But subsidies will be a more efficient and transparent way of nurturing young industries. In fact, the history of tariffs reveals many cases like steel, sugar, and textiles in which perpetually protected infants have not shed their diapers after these many years.

Brazil's Tragic Protection of Its Computer Industry

Brazil offers a striking example of the pitfalls of protectionism. In 1984, Brazil passed a law actually banning most foreign computers. The idea was to provide a protected environment in which Brazil's own infant computer industry could develop. The law was vigorously enforced by special "computer police" who would search corporate offices and classrooms looking for illegal imported computers.

The results were startling. Technologically, Brazilian-made computers were years behind the fast-moving world market, and consumers paid 2 or 3 times the world price — when they could get them at all. By one estimate, the law cost Brazilian consumers about $900 million each year. At the same time, because Brazilian computers were so expensive, they could not compete on the world market, so Brazilian computer companies could not take advantage of economies of scale by selling to other countries. The high price of computers hurt competitiveness in the rest of the economy as well. "We are effectively very backward because of this senseless nationalism," said Zelia Cardoso de Mello, Brazil's economy minister in 1990. "The computer problem effectively blocked Brazilian industry from modernizing."

The combination of pressure from Brazilian consumers and businesses and U.S. demands for open markets forced Brazil to drop the ban on imported computers in 1992. Within a year, electronics stores in São Paulo and Rio de Janeiro were filled with imported laptop computers, laser printers, and cellular telephones, and Brazilian companies could begin to exploit the computer revolution. Each country and each generation learns anew the lessons of comparative advantage.

Tariffs and Unemployment. Historically, a powerful motive for protection has been the desire to increase employment during a period of recession or stagnation. Protection creates jobs by raising the price of imports and diverting demand toward domestic production; Figure 15-8 demonstrates this effect. As domestic demand increases, firms will hire more workers and unemployment will fall.[2] This too is a

---

[2] Those who have studied the chapters on macroeconomics can understand the mechanism by which tariffs increase employment in the short run. Protectionist measures increase spending on domestic production and thereby increase aggregate demand. This expenditure switch will have multiplier effects in the short run much like those of investment or government spending on goods and services.

beggar-thy-neighbor policy, for it raises domestic demand at the expense of output and employment in other countries.

However, while economic protection may raise employment, it does not constitute an effective program to pursue high employment, efficiency, and stable prices. Macroeconomic analysis shows that there are better ways of reducing unemployment than by imposing import protection. By the appropriate use of monetary and fiscal policy, a country can increase output and lower unemployment. Moreover, the use of general macroeconomic policies will allow workers displaced from low-productivity jobs in industries losing their comparative advantage to move to high-productivity jobs in industries enjoying a comparative advantage.

This lesson was amply demonstrated in the 1990s. From 1991 to 1999, the United States created 16 million net new jobs while maintaining open markets and low tariffs; its trade deficit increased sharply during this period. By contrast, the countries of Europe created virtually no new jobs while moving toward a position of trade surpluses, while Japan had rising unemployment with a growing trade surplus.

Tariffs and import protection are an inefficient way to create jobs or to lower unemployment. A more effective way to increase productive employment is through domestic monetary and fiscal policy.

Other Barriers to Trade

While this chapter has mainly spoken of tariffs, most points apply equally well to any other impediments to trade. Quotas have much the same effects as tariffs, for they prevent the comparative advantages of different countries from determining prices and outputs in the marketplace. In recent years, countries have negotiated quotas with other countries. The United States, for example, forced Japan to put "voluntary" export quotas on automobiles and negotiated similar export quotas on televisions, shoes, and steel.

We should also mention the so-called nontariff barriers (or NTBs). These consist of informal restrictions or regulations that make it difficult for countries to sell their goods in foreign markets. For example, American firms complained that Japanese regulations shut them out of the telecommunications, tobacco, and construction industries.

How important are the nontariff barriers relative to tariffs? Economic studies indicate that nontariff barriers were actually more important than tariffs during the 1960s because of a quota on oil imports; in recent years, they have effectively doubled the protection found in the tariff codes. In a sense, nontariff barriers have been substitutes for more conventional tariffs as the latter have been reduced.

MULTILATERAL TRADE NEGOTIATIONS

Given the tug-of-war between the economic benefits of free trade and the political appeal of protection, which force has prevailed? The history of U.S. tariffs, shown in Figure 15-10, has been bumpy. For most of American history, the United States was a high-tariff

nation. The pinnacle of protectionism came after the infamous Smoot-Hawley tariff of 1930, which was opposed by virtually every American economist yet sailed through Congress.

The trade barriers erected during the Great Depression helped raise prices and exacerbated economic distress. In the trade wars of the 1930s, countries attempted to raise employment and output by raising trade barriers at the expense of their neighbors. Nations soon learned that at the end of the tariff-retaliation game, all were losers.

Negotiating Free Trade

At the end of World War II, the international community established a number of institutions to promote peace and economic prosperity through cooperative policies.

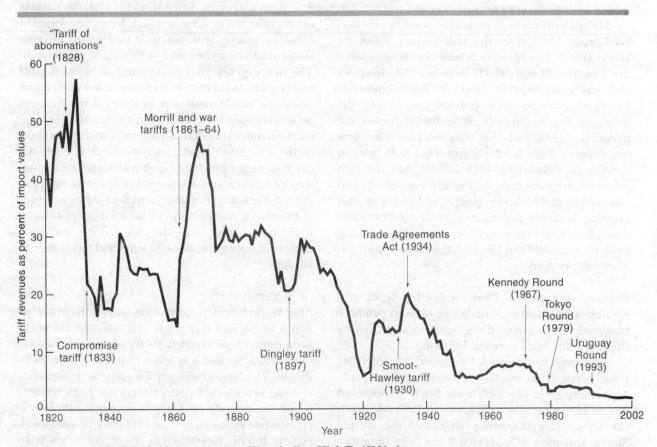

FIGURE 15-10. America Was Historically a High-Tariff Nation

Tariffs were high for most of our nation's history, but trade negotiations since the 1930s have lowered tariffs significantly.

Multilateral Agreements. One of the most successful multilateral agreements was the General Agreement on Tariffs and Trade (GATT), which became the World Trade Organization (WTO) at the beginning of 1995. Their charters speak of raising living standards through "substantial reduction of tariffs and other barriers to trade and the elimination of discriminatory treatment in international commerce." As of 2003, the WTO had 146 member countries, which accounted for 90 percent of international trade.

Among the principles underlying the WTO are (1) countries should work to lower trade barriers; (2) all trade barriers should be applied on a nondiscriminatory basis across nations (i.e., all nations should enjoy "most-favored-nation" status); (3) when a country increases its tariffs above agreed-upon levels, it must compensate its trading partners for the economic injury; and (4) trade conflicts should be settled by consultations and arbitration.

Multilateral trade negotiations successfully lowered trade barriers in the half-century following World War II. The latest successful negotiations were the Uruguay Round, which included 123 countries and was completed in 1994. In 2001, countries launched a new round in Doha, Qatar. Among the items on the agenda are agriculture, intellectual property rights, and the environment. The new negotiations have been controversial both among developing countries, which believe that the rich countries are protecting agriculture too heavily, and among antiglobalization groups, which argue that growing trade is hurting the environment while doing little to aid poor countries. In the face of rising protests in Seattle and Cancun, the Doha round has made no progress.

Regional Approaches. Over the last few years, governments have taken a number of steps to promote free trade or to broaden regional markets. Among the most important were the following.

The most controversial proposal for lowering trade barriers was the North American Free Trade Agreement (NAFTA), which was hotly debated and passed by Congress by a close vote in 1993. Mexico is the second-largest trading partner of the United States, and most U.S.-Mexico trade is in manufactured goods. NAFTA not only allows goods to pass tariff-free across the borders but also liberalizes regulations on investments by the United States and Canada in Mexico. Proponents of the plan argued that it would allow a more efficient pattern of specialization and would enable U.S. firms to compete more effectively against firms in other countries; opponents, particularly labor groups, argued that it would increase the supply of goods produced by low-skilled labor and thereby depress the wages of workers in the affected industries. Economists caution, however, that regional trading agreements like NAFTA can cause inefficiency if they exclude potential trading countries. They point to the stagnation in the Caribbean countries, which were excluded from the free-trade provisions of NAFTA, as a cautionary example of the dangers of the regional approach.

The most far-reaching trade accord has been the movement toward a single market among the major European countries. Since World War II, the nations of the European Union (EU) have developed a common market with minimal barriers to international trade or movement of factors of production. The first step involved eliminating all internal tariff and regulatory barriers to trade and labor and capital flows. The most recent step, analyzed in the chapters on macroeconomics, was the introduction of a common currency (the "Euro") for most of the members of the EU. Additionally, in 2002–2003, the EU decided to expand its membership to include 12 countries of Eastern and Southern Europe, among them Poland, the Czech Republic, and Romania. European unification is one of history's most eloquent tributes to the power of an idea—the idea that free and open trade promotes economic efficiency and technological advance.

Appraisal

After World War II, policymakers around the world believed firmly that free trade was essential for world prosperity. These convictions translated into several successful agreements to lower tariffs, as Figure 15-10 shows. The free-trade philosophy of economists and market-oriented policymakers has been severely tested by periods of high unemployment, by exchange-rate disturbances, and recently by antiglobalization forces. Nevertheless, most countries have continued the trend toward increased openness and outward orientation.

Economic studies generally show that countries have benefited from lower trade barriers as trade flows and living standards have grown. But the struggle to preserve open markets is constantly tested as the political and economic environment changes. One of the severest challenges to free trade was the terrorist attack of September 11, 2001. That event was a reminder that dangerous as well as beneficial things and people cross national borders, and many economists were concerned that tightened security would tighten borders and slow trade flows. The few years of experience after the September 11 attacks indicate that, outside of tourism, international trade was little affected by the attacks and the public policies undertaken to heighten surveillance.

SUMMARY

A. The Nature of International Trade

1. Specialization, division of labor, and trade increase productivity and consumption possibilities. The gains from trade hold among nations as well as within a nation. Engaging in international exchange is more efficient than relying only on domestic production. International trade differs from domestic trade because it broadens the market, because trade takes place among sovereign nations, and because countries usually have their own monies which must be converted using foreign exchange rates.

2. Diversity is the fundamental reason that nations engage in international trade. Within this general principle, we see that trade occurs (*a*) because of differences in the conditions of production, (*b*) because of decreasing costs (or economies of scale), and (*c*) because of diversity in tastes.

B. Comparative Advantage among Nations

3. Recall that trade occurs because of differences in the conditions of production or diversity in tastes. The foundation of international trade is the Ricardian principle of comparative advantage. The principle of comparative advantage holds that each country will benefit if it specializes in the production and export of those goods that it can produce at relatively low cost. Conversely, each country will also benefit if it imports those goods which it produces at relatively high cost. This principle holds even if one region is absolutely more or less productive than another in all commodities. As long as there are differences in *relative* or *comparative* efficiencies among countries, every country must enjoy a comparative advantage or a comparative disadvantage in the production of some goods.

4. The law of comparative advantage predicts more than just the geographic pattern of specialization and the direction of trade. It also demonstrates that countries are made better off and that real wages (or, more generally, total national income) are improved by trade and the resulting enlarged world production. Quotas and tariffs, designed to "protect" workers or industries, will lower a nation's total income and consumption possibilities.

5. Even with many goods or many countries, the same principles of comparative advantage apply. With many commodities, we can arrange products along a continuum of comparative advantage, from relatively more efficient to relatively less efficient. With many countries, trade may be triangular or multilateral, with countries having large bilateral (or two-sided) surpluses or deficits with other individual countries.

C. Protectionism

6. Completely free trade equalizes prices of tradeable goods at home with those in world markets. Under trade, goods flow uphill from low-price to high-price markets.

7. A tariff raises the domestic prices of imported goods, leading to a decline in consumption and imports along with an increase in domestic production. Quotas have very similar effects and may, in addition, lower government revenues.

8. A tariff causes economic waste. The economy suffers losses from decreased domestic consumption and from the wasting of resources on goods lacking comparative advantage. The losses generally exceed government revenues from the tariff.

9. Most arguments for tariffs simply rationalize special benefits to particular pressure groups and cannot withstand economic analysis. Three arguments that can stand up to careful scrutiny are the following: (*a*) The terms-of-trade or optimal tariff can in principle raise the real income of a large country at the expense of its trading partners. (*b*) In a situation of less-than-full employment, tariffs might push an economy toward fuller

employment, but monetary or fiscal policies could attain the same employment goal with fewer inefficiencies than this beggar-thy-neighbor policy. (*c*) Sometimes, infant industries may need temporary protection in order to realize their true long-run comparative advantages.

10. The principle of comparative advantage must be qualified if markets malfunction because of unemployment or exchange-market disturbances. Moreover, individual sectors or factors may be injured by trade if imports lower their returns.

CONCEPTS FOR REVIEW

Principles of International Trade

absolute and comparative advantage
(or disadvantage)
principle of comparative advantage
economic gains from trade
triangular and multilateral trade
world vs. national *PPF*s

consumption vs. production
possibilities with trade

Economics of Protectionism

price equilibrium with and without
trade
tariff, quota, nontariff barriers

effects of tariffs on price, imports,
and domestic production
mercantilist, cheap-foreign-labor, and
retaliatory arguments
the optimal tariff, unemployment,
and infant-industry exceptions
WTO and trade negotiations

FURTHER READING AND INTERNET WEBSITES

Further Reading

The theory of comparative advantage was discovered and discussed by David Ricardo in *Principles of Political Economy and Taxation* (1819, various publishers).

This is online at several sites, including www.econlib.org/library/Ricardo/ricP.html. A classic review of the debate about free trade is Jagdish Bhagwati, *Protectionism* (MIT Press, Cambridge, Mass., 1990). An interesting survey of the pros and cons of globalization, generally favorable to increased trade, is Gary Burtless, Robert Z. Lawrence, Robert E. Litan, and Robert J. Shapiro, *Globaphobia: Confronting Fears about Trade,* (Brookings Institution Press, Washington, D.C., 1998). Some of the best popular writing on international economics is found in *The Economist,* which is also available at www.economist.com.

Websites

The World Bank (www.worldbank.org) has information on its programs and publications at its site, as does the International Monetary Fund, or IMF (www.imf.org). The United Nations website has links to most international institutions and their databases (www.unsystem.org). Another good source of information about high-income countries is the Organisation for Economic Cooperation and Development, or OECD (www.oecd.org). U.S. trade data are available at www.census.gov.

You can find information on many countries through their statistical offices. A compendium of national agencies is available at www.census.gov/main/www/stat_int.html.

One of the best sources for policy writing on international economics is www.iie.com/homepage.htm, the website of the Institute for International Economics.

QUESTIONS FOR DISCUSSION

1. State whether or not each of the following is correct and explain your reasoning. If the quotation is incorrect, provide a corrected statement.
   a. "We Mexicans can never compete profitably with the Northern colossus. Her factories are too efficient, she has too many computers and

   machine tools, and her engineering skills are too advanced. We need tariffs, or we can export nothing!"
   b. "If American workers are subjected to the unbridled competition of cheap Mexican labor, our real wages must necessarily fall drastically."

c. "The principle of comparative advantage applies equally well to families, cities, and states as it does to nations and continents."

d. The quotation from Ross Perot on page 309.

2. Reconstruct Figure 15-1 and its accompanying table to show the production data for Europe; assume that Europe has 600 units of labor and that labor productivities are those given in Table 15-2.

3. What if the data in Table 15-2 changed from (1, 2; 3, 4) to (1, 2; 2, 4)? Show that all trade is killed off. Use this to explain the adage *"Vive la différence!"* (freely translated as "Let diversity thrive!"). Why do the largest gains in trade flow to small countries whose pretrade prices are very different from prevailing world prices?

4. *Follow-up to question 3:* Suppose that the data in Table 15-2 pertain to a newly industrialized country (NIC) and America. What are the gains from trade between the two countries? Now suppose that NIC adopts American technology and has production possibilities identical to those in the American column of Table 15-2. What will happen to international trade? What will happen to NIC's living standards and real wages? What will happen to America's living standards? Is there a lesson here for the impact of converging economies on trade and welfare?

5. A U.S. senator wrote the following: "Trade is supposed to raise the incomes of all nations involved—or at least that is what Adam Smith and David Ricardo taught us. If our economic decline has been caused by the economic growth of our competitors, then these philosophers—and the entire discipline of economics they founded—have been taking us on a 200-year ride."

Explain why the first sentence is correct. Also explain why the second sentence does not follow from the first. Can you give an example of how economic growth of Country J could lower the standard of living in Country A? (*Hint:* The answer to question 4 will help uncover the fallacy in the quotation.)

6. Modern protectionists have used the following arguments for protecting domestic industries against foreign competition:

a. In some situations, a country can improve its standard of living by imposing protection if no one else retaliates.

b. Wages in Korea are but one-tenth of those in the United States. Unless we limit the imports of Korean manufactures, we face a future in which our trade deficit continues to rise under the onslaught of competition from low-wage East Asian workers.

c. A country might be willing to accept a small drop in its living standard to preserve certain industries that it deems necessary for national security, such as supercomputers or oil, by protecting them from foreign competition.

d. *For those who have studied macroeconomics:* If inflexible wages and prices or an inappropriate exchange rate leads to recession and high unemployment, tariffs might increase output and lower the unemployment rate.

In each case, relate the argument to one of the traditional defenses of protectionism. State the conditions under which it is valid, and decide whether you agree with it.

7. The United States has had quotas on steel, shipping, automobiles, textiles, and many other products. Economists estimate that by auctioning off the quota rights, the Treasury would gain at least $10 billion annually. Use Figure 15-9 to analyze the economics of quotas as follows: Assume that the government imposes a quota of 100 on imports, allocating the quota rights to importing countries on the basis of last year's imports. What would be the equilibrium price and quantity of clothing? What would be the efficiency losses from quotas? Who would get revenue rectangle *B*? What would be the effect of auctioning off the quota rights?

16

Government Taxation and Expenditure

*The spirit of a people,
its cultural level,
its social structure,
the deeds its policy may prepare,
all this and more is written
in its fiscal history. . . .
He who knows
how to listen to its messenger
here discerns the thunder
of world history more clearly
than anywhere else.*

Joseph Schumpeter

When we look at a market economy—providing all sorts of products from apples and boats to X-ray machines and zithers—it would be tempting to think that markets require little more than skilled workers and lots of capital. But history has shown that markets cannot work effectively alone. At a minimum, an effective market economy needs police to ensure physical security, an independent judicial system to enforce contracts, regulatory mechanisms to prevent monopolistic abuses and lethal pollution, schools to educate the young, and a public health system to ward off communicable diseases. Exactly where to draw the line between government and private activities is a difficult and controversial question, and people today debate the appropriate role of government in education, health care, and income support.

As economists, we want to go beyond the partisan debates and analyze the functions of government— government's comparative advantage in the mixed economy. The present chapter examines the role of government in an advanced industrialized economy. What are the appropriate goals for economic policy in a market economy, and what instruments are available to carry them out? The chapter then takes a close look at government taxation and spending. Subsequent chapters survey the tools that government has to promote vigorous competition, issues involved in protecting the environment, and finally issues involved in combating poverty. These topics are among the most important applications of microeconomics and allow us to use our economic tools to analyze many of the major economic problems facing a modern society.

A. GOVERNMENT CONTROL OF THE ECONOMY

Debates about the role of government often take place on bumper stickers, with rallying cries such as "No new taxes" or "Balance the budget." These simplistic phrases cannot capture the serious business of government economic policy. Say the populace decides that it wants to devote more resources to improving public health; or that the country needs to mobilize its air force to combat ethnic cleansing in Kosovo; or that protecting our precious environment for future generations is a key national priority; or that more resources should be devoted to educating the young; or that unemployment in a deep recession should be reduced. A market economy cannot automatically solve these problems. Each of these objectives can be met if and only if the government changes its taxes, spending, or regulations. The thunder of world history is heard in fiscal policy because taxing and spending are such powerful instruments for social change.

THE TOOLS OF GOVERNMENT POLICY

In a modern industrial economy, no sphere of economic life is untouched by the government. We can identify three major instruments or tools that government uses to influence private economic activity:

1. *Taxes* on incomes and goods and services. These reduce private income, thereby reducing private expenditures (on automobiles or restaurant food) and providing resources for public expenditures (on missiles and school lunches). The tax system also serves to discourage certain activities by taxing them more heavily (such as smoking cigarettes) while encouraging other activities by taxing them lightly or even subsidizing them (such as owner-occupied housing).

2. *Expenditures* on certain goods or services (such as roads, education, or police protection), along with *transfer payments* (like social security and health-care subsidies) that provide resources to individuals.

3. *Regulations* or controls that direct people to perform or refrain from certain economic activities. Examples include rules that limit the amount firms can pollute, or that divide up the radio spectrum, or that mandate testing the safety of new drugs.

Trends in the Size of Government

When Schumpeter wrote of the thunder of fiscal history, he was referring to the drama over government budgets and their impacts on the economy. For more than a century, national income and production have been rising in all industrial economies. At the same time, in most countries, government expenditures have been rising even faster than the overall economy. Each period of emergency—depression, war, or concern over social problems such as poverty or pollution—expanded the activity of government. After the crisis passed, government controls and spending never returned to their previous levels.

Before World War I, the combined federal, state, and local government expenditures or taxation amounted to little more than one-tenth of the entire U.S. national income. The war effort during World War II compelled government to consume about half the nation's greatly expanded total output. By 2002, expenditures of all levels of government in the United States ran around 30 percent of GDP.

Figure 16-1 on page 320 shows the trend in taxes and expenditures for all levels of government in the United States. The rising curves indicate that the shares of government taxes and spending have grown steadily upward over the last century.

Government's expansion has not occurred without opposition; each new spending and tax program provoked a fierce reaction. For example, when social security was first introduced in 1935, opponents denounced it as an ominous sign of socialism. But with the passage of time, political attitudes evolve. The "socialistic" social security system is today defended by politicians of all stripes as an essential part of the "social contract" between the generations. The radical doctrines of one era become accepted gospel of the next.

Figure 16-2 on page 321 shows how government spending as a percentage of GDP varies among countries. High-income countries tend to tax and spend a larger fraction of GDP than do poor countries. Can we discern a pattern among wealthy countries? Within the high-income countries, no simple law relating tax burdens and the citizenry's well-being can do justice to the true diversity of the fiscal facts of nations.[1] For example, financing for education and health care, two of the largest components of government spending, is organized very differently across countries.

The Growth of Government Controls and Regulation

In addition to the growth in spending and taxing, there has also been a vast expansion in the laws and regulations governing economic affairs.

---

[1] Figs. 16-1 and 16-2 show the total expenditures of governments. Such expenditures include purchases of goods and services (like missiles and education) as well as transfer payments (like social security payments and interest on the government debt). Purchases of goods and services are called "exhaustive" because they make a direct claim upon the production of a country; transfer payments, by contrast, increase people's income and allow individuals to purchase goods and services but do not directly reduce the quantity of goods and services available for private consumption and investment.

FIGURE 16-1. Government's Share of the Economy Has Grown Sharply

Government expenditures include spending on goods, services, and transfers at the federal, state, and local levels. Note how spending grew rapidly during wartime but did not return to prewar levels afterward. The difference between spending and taxes is the government deficit or surplus.

Source: U.S. Department of Commerce.

Nineteenth-century America came as close as any economy has come to being a pure laissez-faire society—the system that the British historian Thomas Carlyle labeled "anarchy plus the constable." This philosophy permitted people great personal freedom to pursue their economic ambitions and produced a century of rapid material progress. But critics saw many flaws in this laissez-faire idyll. Historians record periodic business crises, extremes of poverty and inequality, deep-seated racial discrimination, and poisoning of water, land, and air by pollution. Muckrakers and progressives called for a bridle on capitalism so that the people could steer this wayward beast in more humane directions.

Beginning in the 1890s, the United States gradually turned away from the belief that "government governs best which governs least." Presidents Theodore Roosevelt, Woodrow Wilson, Franklin Roosevelt, and Lyndon Johnson—in the face of strenuous opposition—pushed out the boundaries of federal control over the economy, devising new regulatory and fiscal tools to combat the economic ailments of their time.

Constitutional powers of government were interpreted broadly and used to "secure the public interest" and to "police" the economic system. In 1887, the federal Interstate Commerce Commission (ICC) was established to regulate rail traffic across state boundaries. Soon afterward, the Sherman Antitrust Act and other laws were aimed against monopolistic combinations in "restraint of trade."

During the 1930s, a whole set of industries came under *economic regulation*, in which government sets the prices, conditions of exit and entry, and safety standards. Regulated industries since that time have included the airlines, trucking, and barge and water traffic; electric, gas, and telephone utilities; financial markets; and oil and natural gas, as well as pipelines.

In addition to regulating the prices and standards of business, the nation attempted to protect health and safety through increasingly stringent *social regulation*. Following the revelations of the muckraking era

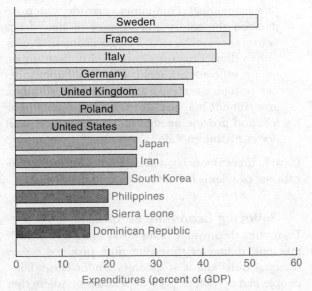

FIGURE 16-2. Government Spending Is Highest in High-Income Lands, 1999

Governments of poor countries tax and spend relatively little of national income. With affluence come greater demands for public goods and redistributional taxation to aid low-income families.

Source: OECD.

of the early 1900s, pure food and drug acts were passed. During the 1960s and 1970s, Congress passed a series of acts that regulated mine safety and then worker safety more generally; regulated air and water pollution; authorized safety standards for automobiles and consumer products; and regulated strip mining, nuclear power, and toxic wastes.

Over the last two decades, the tide of government economic regulation has ebbed. Economists argued persuasively that many economic regulations were impeding competition and keeping prices up rather than down. Indeed, the first major federal regulatory agency, the Interstate Commerce Commission, was abolished shortly after its hundredth birthday. In the area of social regulations, economists have emphasized the need to ensure that the benefits of regulations outweigh their costs.

Still, there is no likelihood of a return to the laissez-faire era. Government programs have changed the very nature of capitalism. Private property is less and less wholly private. Free enterprise has become progressively less free. Irreversible evolution is part of history.

THE FUNCTIONS OF GOVERNMENT

We are beginning to get a picture of how government directs and interacts with the economy. What are the appropriate economic goals for government action in a modern mixed economy? Let's examine the four major functions:

1. Improving economic efficiency
2. Reducing economic inequality
3. Stabilizing the economy through macroeconomic policies
4. Conducting international economic policy

Improving Economic Efficiency

A central economic purpose of government is to assist in the socially desirable allocation of resources. This is the *microeconomic* side of government policy; it concentrates on the *what* and *how* of economic life. Microeconomic policies differ among countries according to customs and political philosophies. Some countries emphasize a hands-off, laissez-faire approach, leaving most decisions to the market. Other countries lean toward heavy government regulation, or even public ownership of businesses, in which production decisions are made by government planners.

The United States is fundamentally a market economy. On any microeconomic issue, most people presume that the market will solve the economic problem at hand. But sometimes there is good reason for government to override the allocational decisions of market supply and demand.

The Limits of the Invisible Hand. Earlier chapters have explained how the invisible hand of perfect competition would lead to an efficient allocation of resources. But this invisible-hand result holds only under very limited conditions. All goods must be produced efficiently by perfectly competitive firms. All goods must be private goods like loaves of bread, the total of which can be cut up into separate slices of consumption for different individuals, so that the more I consume out of the total, the less you consume. There can be no externalities like air pollution. Consumers and firms must be fully informed about the prices and characteristics of the goods they buy and sell.

If all these idealized conditions were met, the invisible hand could provide perfectly efficient production and distribution of national output, and there would be no need for government intervention to promote efficiency.

Yet even in this ideal case, if there were to be a division of labor among people and regions, and if a price mechanism were to work, government would have an important role. Courts and police forces would be needed to ensure fulfillment of contracts, nonfraudulent and nonviolent behavior, freedom from theft and external aggression, and the legislated rights of property.

Inescapable Interdependencies. Laissez-faire with minimal government intervention might be a good system if the idealized conditions listed above were truly present. In reality, each and every one of the idealized conditions enumerated above is violated to some extent in all human societies. Most production takes place in units too large for truly perfect competition. Unregulated factories do tend to pollute the air, water, and land. When contagious diseases threaten to break out, private markets have little incentive to develop effective public-health programs. Consumers are sometimes poorly informed about the characteristics of the goods they buy. The market is not ideal. There are market failures.

In other words, government often deploys its weapons to correct significant market failures, of which the most important are the following:

- *The breakdown of perfect competition.* When monopolies or oligopolies collude to reduce rivalry or drive firms out of business, government may apply antitrust policies or regulation.
- *Externalities and public goods.* The unregulated market may produce too much air pollution and too little investment in public health or knowledge. Government can use its influence to control harmful externalities or to fund programs in science and public health. Government can levy taxes on activities which impose external public costs (such as cigarette smoking), or it can subsidize activities which are socially beneficial (such as education or prenatal health care).
- *Imperfect information.* Unregulated markets tend to provide too little information for consumers to make well-informed decisions. In an earlier era, hucksters hawked snake oil remedies that would just as easily kill you as cure you. This led to food and drug regulations requiring that

pharmaceutical companies provide extensive data on the safety and efficacy of new drugs before they can be sold. The government also requires that companies provide information on energy efficiency of major household appliances like refrigerators and water heaters. In addition, government may use its spending power to collect and provide needed information itself, as it does with automobile crash-and-safety data.

Clearly, there is much on the agenda of possible allocational problems for government to handle.

Reducing Economic Inequality

Even when the invisible hand works and is marvelously efficient, it may at the same time produce a very unequal distribution of income. Under laissez-faire, people end up rich or poor depending on where they were born, on their inherited wealth, on their talents and efforts, on their luck in finding oil, and on their gender or the color of their skin. To some people, the distribution of income arising from unregulated competition looks as arbitrary as the Darwinian distribution of food and plunder in the jungle.

In the poorest societies, there is little excess income to take from the better-off and provide to the unfortunate. But as societies become more affluent, they can devote more resources to providing services for poor people; this activity—income redistribution—is the second major economic function of government. The welfare states of North America and Western Europe now devote a significant share of their revenues to maintaining minimum standards of health, nutrition, and income.

Income redistribution is usually accomplished through taxation and spending policies, though regulation sometimes plays a role as well. Most wealthy countries now rule that children shall not go hungry because of the economic circumstances of their parents; that the poor shall not die because of insufficient money for needed medical care; that the young shall receive free public education; and that the old shall be able to live out their years with a minimum level of income. In the United States, these government activities are provided primarily by transfer programs, such as food stamps, Medicaid, and social security.

But attitudes about redistribution evolve as well. With rising tax burdens and government budget deficits, along with rising costs of income-support programs, taxpayers increasingly resist redistributive programs and progressive taxation. Sweden, which took the welfare state to its extreme and collects 63 percent of national income as taxes, is today struggling to trim spending while maintaining the most important redistributive programs.

Stabilizing the Economy through Macroeconomic Policies

Early capitalism was prone to financial panics and bouts of inflation and depression, and the traumatic memory of the Great Depression of the 1930s is still vivid among older Americans. Today government has the responsibility of preventing such calamitous business depressions by the proper use of monetary and fiscal policy, as well as close regulation of the financial system. In addition, government tries to smooth out the ups and downs of the business cycle, in order to avoid either large-scale unemployment at the bottom of the cycle or raging price inflation at the top of the cycle. More recently, government has become concerned with finding economic policies which boost long-term economic growth. These questions are considered at length in the chapters on macroeconomics.

Conducting International Economic Policy

As we saw in the last chapter's review of international trade, the United States has become increasingly linked to the global economy in recent years. Government now plays a critical role representing the interests of the nation on the international stage and negotiating beneficial agreements with other countries on a wide range of issues. We can group the international issues of economic policy into four main areas:

- *Reducing trade barriers.* An important part of economic policy involves harmonizing laws and reducing trade barriers so as to encourage fruitful international specialization and division of labor. In recent years, nations have negotiated a series of trade agreements to lower tariffs and other trade barriers on agricultural products, manufactured goods, and services.

  Such agreements are often contentious. They sometimes harm certain groups, as when removing textile tariffs reduces employment in that

industry. In addition, international agreements may require giving up national sovereignty as the price of raising incomes. Suppose that one country's laws protect intellectual property rights, such as patents and copyrights, while another country's laws allow free copying of books, videos, and software. Whose laws shall prevail?

- *Conducting assistance programs.* Rich nations have numerous programs designed to improve the lot of the poor in other countries. These involve direct foreign aid, disaster and technical assistance, the establishment of institutions like the World Bank to give low-interest-rate loans to poor countries, and concessionary terms on exports to poor nations.

- *Coordinating macroeconomic policies.* Nations have seen that fiscal and monetary policies of other nations affect inflation, unemployment, and financial conditions at home. The international monetary system cannot manage itself; establishing a smoothly functioning exchange-rate system is a prerequisite for efficient international trade. When the East Asian economic "flu" broke out in 1997, the impacts on trade and finance threatened to slow economic growth in Japan, Europe, and the United States. Particularly in tightly integrated regions, like Western Europe, countries work to coordinate their fiscal, monetary, and exchange-rate policies, or even adopt a common currency, so that inflation or unemployment in one country does not spill over to hurt the entire area.

- *Protecting the global environment.* The most recent facet of international economic policy is to work with other nations to protect the global environment in cases where several countries contribute to or are affected by spillovers. The most active areas historically have been protecting fisheries and water quality in rivers. More recently, as scientists have raised concerns about ozone depletion, deforestation, global warming, and species extinction, nations have begun to consider ways to protect our global resources. Clearly, international environmental problems can be resolved only through the cooperation of many nations.

Even the staunchest conservatives agree that government has a major role to play in representing the national interest in the anarchy of nations.

PUBLIC-CHOICE THEORY

For the most part, our analysis has concentrated on the *normative* theory of government—on the appropriate policies that the government *should follow* to increase the welfare of the population. But economists are not starry-eyed about the government any more than they are about the market. Governments can make bad decisions or carry out good ideas badly. Indeed, just as there are market failures such as monopoly and pollution, so are there "government failures" in which government interventions lead to waste or redistribute income in an undesirable fashion.

These issues are the domain of **public-choice theory,** which is the branch of economics and political science that studies the way that governments make decisions. Public-choice theory examines the way different voting mechanisms can function and shows that there are no ideal mechanisms to sum up individual preferences into social choices. This approach also analyzes government failures, which arise when state actions fail to improve economic efficiency or when the government redistributes income unfairly. Public-choice theory points to issues such as the short time horizons of elected representatives, the lack of a hard budget constraint, and the role of money in financing elections as sources of government failures. A careful study of government failures is crucial for understanding the limitations of government and ensuring that government programs are not excessively intrusive or wasteful.

The Economics of Politics

Since the time of Adam Smith, economists have focused most of their energy on understanding the workings of the marketplace. But serious economists have also pondered the government's role in society. Joseph Schumpeter pioneered public-choice theory in *Capitalism, Socialism, and Democracy* (1942), and Kenneth Arrow's Nobel Prize–winning study on social choice brought mathematical rigor to this field. The landmark study by Anthony Downs, *An Economic Theory of Democracy* (1957), sketched a powerful new theory which held that politicians set economic policies in order to be reelected. Downs showed how parties tend to move toward the center of the political spectrum, and he posed the "voting paradox," which holds that it is irrational for people to vote given the small likelihood of any individual affecting the outcome.

Further studies by James Buchanan and Gordon Tullock in *The Calculus of Consent* (1959) defended checks and balances and advocated the use of unanimity in political decisions, arguing that unanimous decisions do not coerce anyone and therefore impose no costs. For this and other works, Buchanan received the Nobel Prize for Economics in 1986. Public-choice economics received careful study by conservative politicians during the early 1980s. It was applied to such areas as farm policy, regulation, and the courts, and it formed the theoretical basis for a proposed constitutional amendment to balance the budget.

B. GOVERNMENT EXPENDITURES

Nowhere can the changes in government's role be seen more clearly than in the area of government spending. Look back at Figure 16-1 on page 320. It shows the share of national output going to government spending, which includes things like purchases of goods, salaries of government workers, social security and other transfers, and interest on the government debt. You can see that government's share rose for most of the twentieth century, with temporary bulges during wartime, but it has leveled off in recent years.

FISCAL FEDERALISM

While we have been referring to government as if it were a single entity, in fact Americans face three levels of government: federal, state, and local. This reflects a division of fiscal responsibilities among the different levels of government—a system known as *fiscal federalism.* The boundaries are not always clear-cut, but in general the federal government directs activities that concern the entire nation—paying for defense, space exploration, and foreign affairs. Local governments educate children, police streets, and remove garbage. States build highways, run university systems, and administer welfare programs.

The total U.S. spending and its distribution by major function at the different levels of government are

Share of Total Government Expenditures 2001 ($, billion)*			
Government function	Federal	State	Local
National defense	100%	0%	0%
Income security and unemployment	100	0	0
Retirement and disability	97	3	0
Health	52	44	4
Prisons	6	63	31
Education	5	18	77
Total	56%	20%	24%
Total current expenditures	1,936.4	585.1	707.5

*Figures exclude investment and denote spending, not financing, of major items.

TABLE 16-1. Federal, State, and Local Government Current Expenditures by Major Function, 2001

In the early days of the Republic, most spending was at the state and local levels. Today, more than half of total government outlays are federal. But note how the different levels of government divide functions.

Source: U.S. Bureau of Economic Analysis.

shown in Table 16-1. The dominance of the federal role is a comparatively recent phenomenon. Before the twentieth century, local government was by far the most important of the three levels. The federal government did little more than support the military, pay interest on the national debt, and finance a few public works. Most of its tax collection came from liquor and tobacco excises and import tariffs. But the combination of two hot world wars and one cold war—along with the rise of transfer programs such as social security and Medicare—boosted spending, while the advent of the national income tax in 1913 provided a source of funds that no state or locality could match.

To understand fiscal federalism, economists emphasize that spending decisions should be allocated among the levels of government according to the spillovers from government programs. In general, localities are responsible for *local public goods*, activities whose benefits are largely confined to local residents. Since libraries are used by townspeople and streetlights illuminate city roads, decisions about these goods are appropriately made by local residents. Many federal functions involve *national public goods*, which provide benefits to all the nation's citizens. For example, an AIDS vaccine would benefit people from every state, not just those living near the laboratory where it is

discovered; similarly, when the U.S. Army waged war in the Persian Gulf, oil supplies were protected for the entire country. What about global public goods like protecting the ozone layer or slowing global warming? These are *international public goods* because they transcend the boundaries of individual countries.

An efficient system of fiscal federalism takes into account the way the benefits of public programs spill over political boundaries. The most efficient arrangement is to locate the tax and spending decisions so that the beneficiaries of programs pay the taxes and can weigh the tradeoffs.

Federal Expenditures

Let's look now at the different levels of government. The U.S. government is the world's biggest enterprise. It buys more automobiles and steel, meets a bigger payroll, and handles more money than any other organization anywhere. The numbers involved in federal finance are astronomical—in the billions and trillions of dollars. The federal budget expenditures for 2005 are projected to be $2400 billion or $2.4 trillion; this enormous number amounts to roughly $8200 for each American, or approximately

Federal Expenditures, Fiscal Year 2005		
Description	Expenditures ($, billion)	Percent of total
Total outlays or expenditures	**2400**	**100.0%**
1. Social security	515	21.5%
2. National defense	451	18.8%
3. Income security	348	14.5%
4. Medicare	294	12.3%
5. Net interest	178	7.4%
6. Health	253	10.5%
7. Education, training, employment, and social services	89	3.7%
8. Transportation	70	2.9%
9. Veterans benefits and services	57	2.4%
10. Administration of justice	19	0.8%
11. Natural resources and environment	31	1.3%
12. Agriculture	43	1.8%
13. General science, space, and technology	38	1.6%
14. International affairs	38	1.6%
15. General government	17	0.7%

TABLE 16-2. Federal Spending Is Dominated by Defense and Entitlement Programs

About one-fifth of federal spending is for defense or pensions due to past wars. More than half of spending today is for rapidly growing entitlement programs—income security, social security, and health. Note how small is item 15, the traditional cost of government.

Source: Office of Management and Budget, *Budget of the U.S. Government, Fiscal Year 2005.*

20 percent of total national output (gross domestic product, or GDP).

Table 16-2 above lists the major categories of federal expenditure for fiscal year 2005. (The federal fiscal year 2005 covers October 1, 2004, through September 30, 2005.)

The most rapidly expanding items in the last two decades have been entitlement programs, which provide benefits or payments to any persons who meet certain eligibility requirements set down by law. The major entitlements are social security (old-age, survivors, and disability insurance), health programs (including Medicare for those over 65 and Medicaid for indigent families), and income-security programs (including subsidies for food and unemployment insurance). In fact, virtually the entire growth in federal spending in recent years can be accounted for by entitlement programs, which increased from 28 percent of the budget in 1960 to 60 percent in 2005.

State and Local Expenditures

Although the battles over the federal budget command the headlines, state and local units provide many of the essential functions in today's economy. Figure 16-3 illustrates the way states and localities spend their money. By far the largest item is education because most of the nation's children are educated in schools financed primarily by local governments. By attempting to equalize the educational resources available to every child, public education helps level out the otherwise great disparities in economic opportunity.

In recent years, the fastest-growing categories of spending for states and localities have been health care and prisons. In the last two decades, the number of prisoners in state prisons tripled, as the United States fought a war on crime partly by using longer prison sentences, especially for drug offenders. At the same time, state and local governments were forced to absorb their share of rising health-care costs.

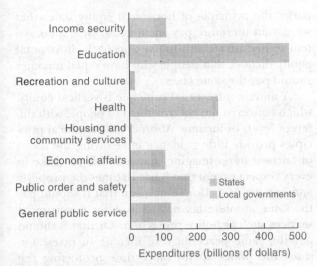

FIGURE 16-3. Distribution of Spending by State and Local Governments, 2001

State and local programs include providing education, financing hospitals, and maintaining the streets. Education and health take an increasing fraction of state and local spending.

Source: Bureau of Economic Analysis, *Survey of Current Business,* June 2003.

CULTURAL AND TECHNOLOGICAL IMPACTS

Government programs have subtle impacts on the country beyond the dollar spending. The federal government has changed the landscape through the interstate highway system. By making automotive travel much faster, this vast network lowered transportation costs, displaced the railroads, and brought goods to every corner of the country. It also helped accelerate urban sprawl and the growth of the suburban culture.

The government has put the United States on the map in many areas of science and technology. Government support gave a powerful start to the electronics industries. The development of the transistor by Bell Labs, for example, was partially funded by the U.S. military, anxious for better radar and communications. Today's computer and airplane industries were boosted in their early years by strong government support. The Internet was developed by the Department of Defense to create a network that would continue to function in the event of nuclear war.

Because of the weight of its spending power, the government has an enormous voice in the development of science and technology. Throughout the 1980s and early 1990s, federal funds supported about half of all research and development. In recent years, federal funding for health-care research has more than doubled, helping spawn the booming biotechnology industry. Often, if you follow a successful invention upstream to its source, you will find that government subsidized the inventor's education, supported basic university research in biology or physics, and purchased prototype versions for defense. Economic studies indicate that these funds were well spent, moreover, for the rates of return to education and research are estimated to compare favorably with those in other areas.

C. ECONOMIC ASPECTS OF TAXATION

Taxes are what we pay for a civilized society.

Justice Oliver Wendell Holmes

Governments must pay for their programs. The funds come mainly from taxes, and any shortfall is a deficit that is borrowed from the public.

But in economics we always need to pierce the veil of monetary flows to understand the flow of real resources. Behind the dollar flows of taxes, what the government really needs is the economy's scarce land, labor, and capital. When the nation fights a war in the Balkans, Congress argues about how to finance the war; but what really happens is that people are diverted from their civilian jobs, airplanes transport troops rather than tourists, and oil goes to airplanes rather than cars. When the government gives out a grant for biotechnology research, its decision really means that a piece of land that might have been used for an office building is now being used for a laboratory.

In taxing, government is in reality deciding how to draw the required resources from the nation's households and businesses for public purposes. The money raised through taxation is the vehicle by which real resources are transferred from private goods to collective goods.

PRINCIPLES OF TAXATION

Benefit vs. Ability-to-Pay Principles

Once the government has decided to collect some amount of taxes, it has a bewildering array of possible taxes available to it. It can tax income, tax profits, or tax sales. It can tax the rich or tax the poor, tax the old or tax the young. Are there any guidelines that can help construct a fair and efficient tax system?

Indeed there are. Economists and political philosophers have proposed two major principles for organizing a tax system:

- The **benefit principle,** which holds that individuals should be taxed in proportion to the benefit they receive from government programs. Just as people pay private dollars in proportion to their consumption of private bread, a person's taxes should be related to his or her use of collective goods like public roads or parks.

- The **ability-to-pay principle,** which states that the amount of taxes people pay should relate to their income or wealth. The higher the wealth or income, the higher the taxes. Usually tax systems organized along the ability-to-pay principle are also *redistributive,* meaning that they raise funds from higher-income people to increase the incomes and consumption of poorer groups.

For instance, if the construction of a new bridge is funded by tolls on the bridge, that's a reflection of the benefit principle, since you pay for the bridge only if you use it. But if the bridge were funded out of income-tax collections, that would be an example of the ability-to-pay principle.

Horizontal and Vertical Equity

Whether they are organized along benefit or ability-to-pay lines, most modern tax systems attempt to incorporate modern views about fairness or equity. One important principle is that of **horizontal equity,** which states that those who are essentially equal should be taxed equally.

The notion of equal treatment of equals has deep roots in Western political philosophy. If you and I are alike in every way except the color of our eyes, all principles of taxation would hold that we should pay equal taxes. In the case of benefit taxation, if we receive exactly the same services from the highways or parks, the principle of horizontal equity states that we should therefore pay equal taxes. Or if a tax system follows the ability-to-pay approach, horizontal equity dictates that people who have equal incomes should pay the same taxes.

A more controversial principle is **vertical equity,** which concerns the tax treatment of people with different levels of income. Abstract philosophical principles provide little guidance in resolving the issues of fairness here. Imagine that A and B are alike in every respect except that B has 10 times the property and income of A. Does that mean that B should pay the same absolute tax dollars as A for government services such as police protection? Or that B should pay the same percentage of income in taxes? Or, since the police spend more time protecting the property of well-to-do B, is it perhaps fair for B to pay a larger fraction of income in taxes?

Be warned that general and abstract principles cannot determine the tax structure for a nation. When Ronald Reagan campaigned for lower taxes, he did so because he thought high taxes were unfair to those who had worked hard and saved for the future. A decade later, Bill Clinton said, "We now have real fairness in the tax code with over 80 percent of the new tax burden being borne by those who make over $200,000 a year." What looks fair to the goose seems foul to the gander.

Horizontal equity is the principle that equals should be treated equally. Vertical equity holds that people in unequal circumstances should be treated unequally and fairly, but there is no consensus on exactly how vertical equity should be applied.

Pragmatic Compromises in Taxation

How have societies resolved these thorny philosophical questions? Governments have generally adopted pragmatic solutions that are only partially based on benefit and ability-to-pay approaches. Political representatives know that taxes are highly unpopular. After all, the cry of "taxation without representation" helped launch the American Revolution. Modern tax systems are an uneasy compromise between lofty principles and political pragmatism. As the canny French finance minister Colbert wrote three centuries ago, "Raising taxes is like plucking a goose: you want to get the maximum number of feathers with the minimum amount of hiss."

What practices have emerged? Often, public services primarily benefit recognizable groups, and those groups have no claim for special treatment by virtue of their average incomes or other characteristics. In such cases, modern governments generally rely on benefit taxes.

Thus, local roads are usually paid for by local residents. "User fees" are charged for water and sewage treatment, which are treated like private goods. Taxes collected on gasoline may be devoted (or "earmarked") to roads.

Progressive and Regressive Taxes. Benefit taxes are a declining fraction of government revenues. Today, advanced countries rely heavily on **progressive income taxes.** With progressive taxes, a family with $50,000 of income is taxed more than one with $20,000 of income. Not only does the higher-income family pay a larger income tax, but it in fact pays a higher fraction of its income.

This progressive tax is in contrast to a strictly **proportional tax,** in which all taxpayers pay exactly the same proportion of income. A **regressive tax** takes a larger fraction of income in taxes from poor families than it does from rich families.

A tax is called *proportional, progressive,* or *regressive* depending on whether it takes from high-income people the same fraction of income, a larger fraction of income, or a smaller fraction of income than it takes from low-income people.[2]

The different kinds of taxes are illustrated in Figure 16-4. What are some examples? A personal income tax that is graduated to take more and more out of each extra dollar of income is progressive. Economists have found, for example, that the cigarette tax is regressive. The reason is that the number of cigarettes purchased rises less rapidly than income. For example, some studies have determined that the income elasticity of cigarette use is around 0.6. This means that a 10 percent increase in income leads to expenditures on cigarettes, and cigarette taxes, of 6 percent. Thus high-income groups pay a smaller fraction in cigarette taxes than do low-income groups.

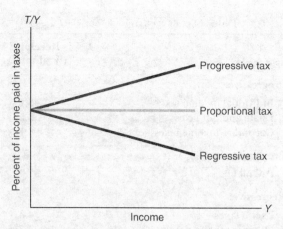

FIGURE 16-4. Progressive, Proportional, and Regressive Taxes

Taxes are progressive if they take a larger fraction of income as income rises; proportional if they are a constant fraction of income; and regressive if they place a larger relative burden on low-income families than on high-income families.

Direct and Indirect Taxes. Taxes are classified as direct or indirect. **Indirect taxes** are ones that are levied on goods and services and thus only "indirectly" on individuals. Examples are excise and sales taxes, cigarette and gasoline taxes, tariffs on imports, and property taxes. By contrast, **direct taxes** are levied directly upon individuals or firms. Examples of direct taxes are personal income taxes, social security or other payroll taxes, and inheritance and gift taxes. Direct taxes have the advantage of being easier to tailor to fit personal circumstances, such as size of family, income, age, and more generally the ability to pay. By contrast, indirect taxes have the advantage of being cheaper and easier to collect, since they can be levied at the retail or wholesale level.

FEDERAL TAXATION

Let us now try to understand the principles by which the federal system of taxation is organized. Table 16-3 provides an overview of the major taxes collected by the federal government and shows whether they are progressive, proportional, or regressive.

---

[2] It should be noted that the words "progressive" and "regressive" are technical economic terms relating to the proportions that taxes bear to different incomes.

Federal Tax Receipts, Fiscal Year 2002	
	Receipts (% of total)
Progressive:	
Individual income taxes	43.1
Estate and gift taxes	3.6
Corporate income taxes	8.1
Proportional:	
Payroll taxes	37.9
Regressive:	
Excise taxes	4.6
Other taxes and receipts	2.7
Total	**100.0%**

TABLE 16-3. Income and Payroll Taxes Are the Main Federal Revenue Sources

Progressive taxes are still the leading source of federal revenues, but proportional payroll taxes are closing fast. Regressive consumption taxes have declined sharply at the federal level.

Source: Office of Management and Budget, *Budget of the U.S. Government, Fiscal Year 2005.*

The Individual Income Tax

Our discussion will concentrate on the individual income tax, which is the most complex and controversial part of the tax system. The income tax is a direct tax, and it is the tax which most clearly reflects the ability-to-pay principle.

The individual income tax arrived late in our nation's history. The Constitution forbade any direct tax that was not apportioned among the states according to population. This was changed in 1913, when the Sixteenth Amendment to the Constitution provided that "Congress shall have power to lay and collect taxes on income, from whatever source derived."

How does the federal income tax work? The principle is simple, although the forms are complicated. You start by calculating your income; you next subtract certain expenses, deductions, and exemptions to obtain taxable income. You then calculate your taxes on the basis of your taxable income.

Table 16-4 shows a calculation of individual taxes for a family of four at different levels of income. Column (1) shows different levels of *adjusted gross income*—that is, wages, interest, dividends, and other income earned by the household.

[1] Adjusted gross income (before exemptions and deductions) ($)	[2] Individual income tax ($)	[3] Average tax rate (%) (3) = [(2) ÷ (1)] × 100	[4] Marginal tax rate (= tax on extra dollar) (%)	[5] Disposable income ($) (5) = (1) − (2)
5,000	−2,010	−40	−40	7,010
10,000	−4,010	−40	−40	14,010
20,000	−2,878	−14	21	22,878
50,000	3,184	6	15	45,646
100,000	12,097	12	27	85,700
200,000	34,909	17	30	122,700
500,000	123,006	25	39	189,100
1,000,000	278,084	28	39	699,663
10,000,000	3,057,284	31	39	6,741,543

TABLE 16-4. Federal Income Tax for a Family of Four, 2002

The table shows incomes, taxes, and tax rates for a representative family of four in 2002. Because of the earned-income tax credit, low-income workers get a tax rebate—this is a "negative income tax" on wages. Marginal tax rates are initially negative, are zero at around $11,000 of income, and then rise to almost 40 percent of income for top taxpayers. Average or effective rates are always less than marginal rates because the income tax is progressive.

Source: Derived from *TurboTax* computerized tax program. Table assumes that deductions are the greater of the standard deduction or 20 percent of income.

Assuming that our household has four people and takes certain deductions, column (2) shows the tax due. Note that the tax is negative for those with wage incomes of $5000, $10,000, and $20,000 because of the *earned-income tax credit;* in this income range, the government is actually transferring income to low-income families.

Column (3) shows the **effective** or **average tax rate,** which is equal to total taxes divided by total income. From this calculation, we see just how progressive the personal-income-tax code really is. A $50,000-a-year family is made to bear a relatively heavier burden than a $20,000-a-year family—the former pays 9 percent of income in taxes, while the latter has a negative rate of minus 2 percent. Someone earning $1 million each year is made to bear a still heavier relative burden.

Column (4) introduces an important new concept. The **marginal tax rate** is the extra tax that is paid per dollar of additional income. We have met the term "marginal" before, and it always means "extra." If you must pay $30 of additional taxes for every $100 of extra income, your marginal tax rate is 30 percent. Under current law, the marginal tax rate is minus 40 percent for poor families and rises to 15 percent for those just entering the positive tax system. The marginal tax rate is a critical tool for tax analysis because people and companies tend to respond to their marginal tax rates, not their average tax rates. Moreover, when marginal tax rates are extremely high, incentives are dulled and effort may significantly decrease.

The marginal tax rate is a central concept of tax analysis. It refers to the extra tax paid per dollar of extra income and is particularly important for understanding the incentive effects of taxation.

For incomes above $250,000, the marginal tax rate from the federal income tax is about 39 percent. If you live in New York City, you would add 8 percent for New York state and city taxes and 2.9 percent for health insurance for a total marginal tax rate on labor earnings of close to 50 percent. This may seem like a high rate, but the top rate today is far below the top rate of 94 percent during World War II. Figure 16-5 shows the history of the highest marginal tax rate in the United States.

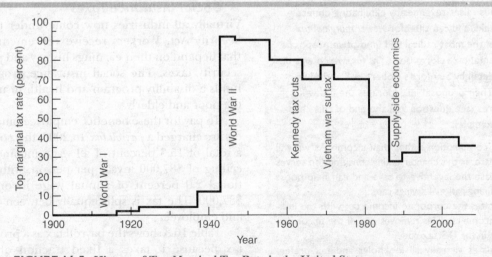

FIGURE 16-5. History of Top Marginal Tax Rate in the United States

The marginal tax rate is the extra tax that is paid per dollar of additional income. The top marginal tax rate on individual incomes reached 94 percent during World War II, was reduced in steps to a low of 28 percent during the Reagan years, was raised to 39 percent in the Clinton years, and was lowered to 35 percent in the 2003 Bush economic package.

Source: U.S. Department of the Treasury.

The notion of marginal tax rates is extremely important in modern economics. Remember the "marginal principle": People should be concerned only with the extra costs or benefits that occur; they should "let bygones be bygones." Under this principle, the major effect of any tax on incentives comes from the marginal tax rate. This notion has formed the intellectual core of supply-side economics.

Column (5) shows the amount of *disposable income after taxes.* Note that it always pays to get more income: even when a rock star makes another million dollars, she still has $610,000 of disposable income left over [= $1,000,000 − (39% × $1,000,000)].

Radical Tax Reform: The Flat Tax

The individual income tax is a powerful engine for raising revenues. But it has become enormously complex over the century since its introduction. Moreover, it is full of loopholes or "tax preferences" that provide benefits to particular forms of income or expenditure and even to individual groups of taxpayers. For example, expenditures on mortgage interest and medical care are deductible from income—they are, in effect, subsidized spending.

Economists have campaigned tirelessly for a more streamlined tax system—one that *broadens* the tax base, and thus raises revenues by eliminating unnecessary tax breaks, and can therefore *lower marginal tax rates*. One of the most radical and innovative proposals for fundamental tax reform is the *flat tax,* which was developed in detail by Stanford's Robert Hall and Alvin Rabushka.[3] Their proposal incorporates the following major features (see question 9 at the end of this chapter for an example):

- It taxes consumption rather than income. As we will discuss later in this chapter, taxing consumption serves to increase the incentive to save and can help boost the declining national savings rate.
- It integrates the corporate income tax with the individual income tax. This removes one of the major distortions in the U.S. tax code.
- It eliminates virtually all loopholes and tax preferences. Gone are subsidies for medical care, owner-occupied homes, and charitable contributions.
- It provides a basic exemption of around $20,000 per family and then imposes a constant marginal tax rate of 19 percent above that level.

The economic effects of a flat tax would be far-reaching. Most tax lawyers would be out of business. Heavily taxed entities such as corporations would find their taxes lowered and would experience a major capital gain. High-income wage earners would find their taxes cut in half. At the same time, the amount of owner-occupied housing and medical expenditures would shrink and charitable giving would drop sharply. Hall and Rabushka estimate that their plan would increase per capita output by almost $3000 in a decade.

The plan's critics point out that it would lead to a major redistribution of income to high-income people at the expense of low- and middle-income households. The losers will question whether the rich, who have already enjoyed massive increases in their wealth during the 1980s and 1990s, deserve yet another big windfall. We see here yet another example of the tradeoff between fairness and efficiency that runs through many of the most controversial economic policy issues.

Social Insurance Taxes

Virtually all industries now come under the Social Security Act. Workers receive retirement benefits that depend on their earnings history and past social security taxes. The social insurance program also funds a disability program and health insurance for the poor and elderly.

To pay for these benefits, employees and employers are charged a *payroll tax.* In 2003, this consisted of a total of 15.3 percent of all wage income below a ceiling of $87,000 a year per person, with an additional 2.9 percent of annual wage income above $87,000. The tax is split equally between employer and employee.

Table 16-3 shows the payroll tax as a proportional tax because it taxes a fixed fraction of employment earnings. It does have some regressive features, however, because it exempts property income and is higher on low wages than on high wages.

The payroll tax is the fastest-growing source of federal revenues, rising from zero in 1929, to 18 percent of revenues in 1960, to 38 percent in 2003.

---

[3] *The Flat Tax,* 2d ed. Hoover Institute Press, Palo Alto, Calif., 1995).

Corporation Taxes

The federal government collects a wide variety of other taxes, some of which are shown in Table 16-3. The *corporate income tax* is a tax on the profits of corporations. The top federal corporation tax rate in 2003 was set at 35 percent of corporate profits.

The corporation income tax has been heavily criticized by some economists. Opponents oppose the tax, arguing that corporations are but legal fictions and should not be taxed. By taxing first corporate profits and then the dividends paid by corporations and received by individuals, the government subjects corporations to double taxation. This argument was endorsed by the administration of George W. Bush, which recommended in 2003 abolishing the tax on dividends at the individual level. Congress went halfway by reducing the maximum tax on dividends to 15 percent (as compared to a maximum of 35 percent on ordinary income in 2003).

Consumption Taxes

While the United States relies heavily on income taxes, a radically different approach is consumption taxes, which are taxes on purchases of goods and services rather than on income. The rationale is that people should be penalized for what they *use* rather than what they *produce*. Sales taxes are the most familiar example of consumption tax. The United States has no national sales tax, although there are a number of *federal excise taxes* on specific commodities such as cigarettes, alcohol, and gasoline. Sales and excise taxes are generally regressive because they consume a larger fraction of the income of poor families than of high-income families.

Many have argued that the United States should rely more heavily on sales or consumption taxes. One tax, widely used outside the United States, is the *value-added tax,* or VAT. The VAT is like a sales tax, but it collects taxes at each stage of production. Thus, if a VAT were levied on bread, it would be collected from the farmer for wheat production, from the miller for flour production, from the baker at the dough stage, and from the grocer at the delivered-loaf stage.

The advocates of consumption taxes argue that the country is currently saving and investing less than is necessary for future needs and that by substituting consumption taxes for income taxes, the national savings rate would increase. Critics of consumption taxes respond that such a change is undesirable because sales taxes are more regressive than today's income tax. The *flat tax,* discussed earlier, is actually equivalent to a highly simplified system of personal consumption taxation. This approach would set all marginal-tax rates at a uniform low rate (around 20 percent) and eliminate most deductions and tax-exempt fringe benefits, such as for health care and mortgage interest (see question 9).

STATE AND LOCAL TAXES

Under the U.S. system of fiscal federalism, state and local governments rely on a very different set of taxes than does the federal government. Figure 16-6 illustrates the main sources of funds that finance state and local expenditures.

Property Tax

The *property tax* is levied primarily on real estate—land and buildings. Each locality sets an annual tax rate which is levied on the assessed value of the land and structures. In many localities, the assessed value may be much smaller than the true market value. The property tax accounts for about 30 percent of the total revenues of state and local finance. Figure 16-6 shows that localities are the main recipient of property taxes.

FIGURE 16-6. States and Localities Rely on Transfers and Indirect Taxes

Cities rely heavily on property taxes because houses and land cannot easily flee to the next town to avoid a city's tax. States get most revenues from sales and income taxes.

Source: Bureau of Economic Analysis, *Survey of Current Business,* June 2003.

Because about one-fourth of property values are from land, the property tax has elements of a capital tax and elements of a Henry George–type land tax. Economists believe that the land component of the property tax has little distortion, while the capital component will drive investment from high-tax central cities out to the low-tax suburbs.

Whatever the views of economists, the property tax became controversial during the housing boom of the 1970s, when housing valuations and taxes skyrocketed. Across the country, taxpayers revolted. In Massachusetts, voters passed "Proposition 2½," limiting tax payments to 2½ percent of market value. Today, almost half the states have limitations on property or other taxes; these limits prevent state and local taxes from rising as rapidly as they did in the 1970s. During recessions, the tax limits sometimes push cities and states into fiscal crises as the governments run out of tax funds and are forced to cut services.

Other Taxes

Most other state taxes are closely related to the analogous federal taxes. States get most of their revenues from *general sales taxes* on goods and services. Each purchase at the department store or restaurant incurs a percentage tax (food and other necessities are exempt in some states). States tax the net income of corporations. Forty-five states imitate the federal government, on a much smaller scale, by taxing individuals according to the size of their incomes.

There are other miscellaneous revenues. Many states levy "highway user taxes" on gasoline. A growing source of revenue is lotteries and legalized gambling, in which the states benefit from encouraging people to impoverish themselves.

TAXES AND EFFICIENCY

Taxes affect both economic efficiency and the distribution of income. In recent years, the impacts on efficiency have become a principal concern of tax policy as economists and policymakers study the effect of incentives upon individual and business behavior. In tax policy, this involves primarily the question of how people respond to different levels of marginal tax rates.

An important political movement was the rise of *supply-side economics* in the 1980s. This program, championed by Republican President Ronald Reagan, pursued a macroeconomic policy directed toward long-run economic growth rather than business-cycle management; followed a budget policy that bolstered defense, cut civilian programs, and gave little weight to fiscal deficits; launched a program to reduce the burden of federal regulations, especially those pertaining to health, safety, and the environment; and, most important, lowered tax rates and tax burdens.

The major legacy of this period was the tax reforms of 1981 and 1986. These acts lowered marginal tax rates dramatically, broadened the tax base, and completely overhauled the individual income tax. The fiscal programs of these periods also led to a major increase in the federal budget deficit and to a government debt that grew sharply relative to national output.

How do high tax rates affect economic behavior? In the area of labor supply, the impacts are mixed. As we saw in Chapter 13, the impact of tax rates on hours worked is unclear because the income and substitution effects of wage changes work in opposite directions. As a result of progressive taxes, some people may choose more leisure over more work. Other people may work harder in order to make their millions. Many high-income doctors, artists, celebrities, and business executives, who enjoy their jobs and the sense of power or accomplishment that they bring, will work as hard for $800,000 after tax as for $1,000,000 after tax. Moreover, high taxes on winner-take-all activities may reduce the supply of talent to those overcrowded areas. Figure 16-7 shows how an increase in the tax rate on labor will affect labor supply; note the paradox that work effort may actually decline after a tax-rate cut if the labor supply curve is backward-bending.

In the area of saving and investment, taxes clearly have major impacts upon economic activity. When taxes are high in one sector, resources will flow into more lightly taxed areas. For example, because corporate capital is double-taxed, people's savings will flow out of the corporate sector and into lightly taxed sectors like oil and gas or into vacation homes financed by tax-deductible interest payments. If risky investments are taxed unfavorably, investors may prefer safer investments. The inefficiency comes as much from the divergence of taxes across sectors as from the existence of high taxes.[4]

---

[4] One interesting example of the interaction of efficiency and taxes is the Laffer curve, which is discussed in question 8 at the end of this chapter.

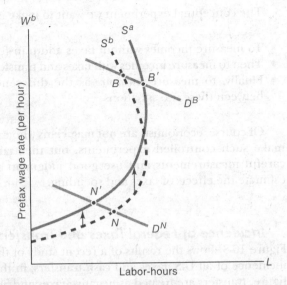

FIGURE 16-7. Response of Work to Taxes Depends on Shape of Supply Curve

Supply and demand plots labor supplied against pretax wage. Before-tax supply curve of labor (S^b) shifts vertically upward to after-tax supply (S^a) after imposition of a 25 percent income tax on labor earnings. If demand for labor intersects supply in the normal region at bottom, we see an expected decline in labor supplied from N to N'. If the labor supply is backward-bending, as at top, the labor supplied actually rises with the tax increase, going from B to B'.

Efficiency vs. Fairness

Economists have long been concerned with the impact of taxes on economic efficiency. Recall from Chapter 14 that Henry George argued that a tax on land will have little impact on efficiency because the supply of land is completely inelastic. The modern theory of efficient taxation puts forth the *Ramsey tax rule,* which states that the government should levy the heaviest taxes on those inputs and outputs that are most price-inelastic in supply or demand.[5] The rationale for the Ramsey tax rule is that if a commodity is very price-inelastic in supply or demand, a tax on the commodity will have little impact upon consumption and production. In some circumstances, Ramsey taxes may constitute a way of raising revenues with a minimum loss of economic efficiency.

---

[5] Recall Chapter 14's discussion of Henry George's single tax and the extension to efficient or Ramsey taxes.

But economies and politics do not run on efficiency alone. While stiff taxation of land rents or food might be efficient, many would think them unfair. A sober reminder of the dilemma was the proposal to introduce a poll tax in Britain in 1990. A *poll tax* is a *lump-sum tax,* or a fixed tax per person. The advantage of this tax is that, like a land tax, it would induce no inefficiencies. After all, people are unlikely to decamp to Russia or commit hari-kari to avoid the tax, so the economic distortions would arguably be minimal.

Alas, the British government underestimated the extent to which the populace felt this tax to be unfair. The poll tax is highly regressive because it places a much higher proportional burden on low-income people than on high-income people. Criticism of the poll tax played a key role in bringing down the Thatcher government after 11 years in power. This illustrates clearly the difficult choice between efficiency and fairness in taxes and other areas of economic policy.

Taxing "Bads" rather than "Goods": Green Taxes

While economists have rarely advocated poll taxes, they have favored an approach wherein the tax system would weigh more heavily on "bads" than on "goods." The main source of inefficiency is that taxes generally tax "goods"—economic activities like working, investing in capital, saving, or risk taking—and thereby discourage these activities. An alternative approach is to tax "bads." Traditional taxes on bads include "sin taxes": taxes on alcohol, cigarettes, and other substances that have harmful health effects.

A new approach to taxation is to tax pollution and other undesirable externalities; such taxes are called *green taxes* because they are designed to help the environment as well as to raise revenues. Say that the nation decides to help slow global warming by levying a "carbon tax," which is a tax on carbon-dioxide emissions from power plants and other sources. By standard economic reasoning we know that the tax will lead firms to lower their carbon-dioxide emissions, thereby improving the environment. In addition, of course, this green tax will provide revenues, which the government can use either to finance its activities or to reduce tax rates on beneficial activities like working or saving. So green taxes are doubly effective: the state gets revenue, and the environment is improved because the taxes discourage harmful externalities.

THE THORNY PROBLEM OF TAX INCIDENCE

Who actually ends up paying all these taxes that governments levy? We should not assume that the people or firms that send the tax revenues to the government will end up paying that tax. Just because the oil company sends the gasoline-tax receipts to the Treasury does not mean that the taxes come out of the profits of the oil company. Businesses may be able to shift the tax "forward" onto their customers by raising their price by the amount of the tax. Or they may shift the tax "backward" onto their suppliers (owners of labor, land, and other factors), who find themselves with lower wages, rents, and other factor prices than they would have enjoyed had there been no tax.

The question of shifting of taxes concerns **tax incidence.** This concept involves the way the tax burden ultimately is borne and its total effects on prices, quantities, and the composition of production and consumption.

Tax-incidence questions include these: When Congress raises the gasoline tax, what is the impact? Is it passed forward to consumers? Does it lower the price of crude oil, so the incidence is on the oil producers? Or is the incidence somewhere in between? Does it change coal prices? And will it kill off oil production, so it has incidence effects beyond those which show up in money prices and wages and even beyond the burdens that you can allocate among the different citizens?

Microeconomics provides some important tools for analyzing tax incidence. In earlier chapters, we saw the incidence of a gasoline tax. In such simple cases, involving only supply of and demand for a single commodity, incidence analysis is straightforward. In other cases, the effects cascade through the economy, making analysis extremely complex and sometimes requiring general-equilibrium approaches.

We might want to know the *fiscal incidence* of the government tax and transfer system as a whole. Fiscal incidence examines the impact of both tax and expenditure programs on the incomes of the population. Fiscal incidence concerns the overall degree of progressivity or regressivity of government programs. It is estimated by allocating all taxes and transfer payments to different groups. Such a study is only approximate, since no one is sure how much the corporation tax or the property tax gets shifted.

The conceptual experiment we want to make is

- To measure incomes without taxes and transfers
- Then to measure incomes with taxes and transfers
- Finally, to measure *incidence* as the difference between these two situations

Of course, economists are not magicians who can make such controlled experiments, but they take careful measurements and use good judgment to estimate the effects of taxes and spending.

Incidence of Federal Taxes and Transfers

Figure 16-8 shows the results of a recent study of the incidence of all U.S. taxes and cash transfers; in this figure, transfers are treated as negative taxes and are measured in the negative direction. The interesting contribution of this approach is that it examines *lifetime income and taxes* rather than looking at only a single year. Thus it takes into account important changes that occur over a lifetime (e.g., people go in and out of the labor market, and they pay social security taxes when young and then receive the taxes as benefits when retired). The study also takes into account the incredible complexity of our tax system, as described above.

The results indicate that the tax system is generally progressive from the top to the bottom, with the lowest group receiving net transfers while the top group has the highest average tax rate. A closer look at the structure of the tax and transfer system indicates that its progressive structure, particularly at the bottom, comes primarily from transfers rather than from taxes.

This pattern of fiscal impact is similar to that found in other countries. Studies of the fiscal systems of high-income countries have determined that the tax system has almost no effect on the distribution of income. This surprising result comes because the effects of progressive income taxes are generally offset by regressive taxes, notably social security contributions and sales or value-added taxes. The major progressive elements of public programs (that is, the major elements which redistribute income to low-income households) are income-support programs such as cash grants, food stamps, public pensions, and subsidized health care.

FIGURE 16-8. Who Pays the Taxes and Who Benefits from Transfers?

How does the modern welfare state affect the income of its citizens over their entire life cycle? Fullerton and Rogers estimated the impact on a household's lifetime income of all federal, state, and local taxes and cash transfers that were in place in 1984. The tax and transfer system is progressive at almost every income category. Note that the system actually transfers income to the lowest group while the highest group has a net tax rate of 15 percent.

Source: Don Fullerton and Diane Lim Rogers, *Who Bears the Lifetime Tax Burden?* (Brookings Institution, Washington, D.C., 1993), p. 123. The data have been updated to 2003 incomes, and the lifetime incomes were converted into annualized incomes using a 5 percent real interest rate.

FINAL WORD

Our introductory survey of government's role in the economy is a sobering reminder of the responsibilities and shortcomings of collective action. On the one hand, governments must defend their borders, stabilize their economies, protect the public health, and regulate pollution. On the other hand, policies often reflect primarily the attempt to redistribute income from consumers to politically powerful interest groups.

Does this mean we should abandon the visible hand of government for the invisible hand of markets? Economics cannot answer such deep political questions; all it can do is examine the strengths and weaknesses of both collective and market choices, and point to mechanisms (such as green taxes or subsidies to research and development) by which a mended invisible hand may be more efficient than the extremes of either pure laissez-faire or unbridled bureaucratic rule making.

SUMMARY

A. Government Control of the Economy

1. The economic role of government has increased sharply over the last century. The government influences and controls private economic activity by using taxes, expenditures, and direct regulation.
2. A modern welfare state performs four economic functions: (*a*) It remedies market failures; (*b*) it

redistributes income and resources; (*c*) it establishes macroeconomic stabilization policy to stabilize the business cycle and promote long-term economic growth; and (*d*) it manages international economic affairs.
3. Public-choice theory analyzes how governments actually behave. Just as the invisible hand can break down,

so there are government failures, in which government interventions lead to waste or redistribute income in an undesirable fashion.

B. Government Expenditures

4. The American system of public finance is one of fiscal federalism. The federal government concentrates its spending on issues of national concern—on national public goods like defense and space exploration. States and localities generally focus on local public goods—those whose benefits are largely confined within state or city boundaries.

5. Government spending and taxation today take approximately one-third of total national output. Of this total, about 60 percent is spent at the federal level, and the balance is divided between state and local governments. Only a small fraction of government outlays is devoted to traditional functions like police and the courts.

C. Economic Aspects of Taxation

6. Notions of "benefits" and "ability to pay" are two principal theories of taxation. A tax is progressive, proportional, or regressive as it takes a larger, equal, or smaller fraction of income from rich families than it does from poor families. Direct and progressive taxes on incomes are in contrast to indirect and regressive sales and excise taxes.

7. More than half of federal revenues come from personal and corporate income taxes. The rest comes from taxes on payrolls or consumption goods. Local governments raise most of their revenue from property taxes, while sales taxes are most important for states.

8. The individual income tax is levied on "income from whatever source derived," less certain exemptions and deductions. The marginal tax rate, denoting the fraction paid in taxes for every dollar of additional income, is the key to determining the impact of taxes on incentives to work and save. Marginal tax rates were lowered sharply during the 1980s, but top rates were raised in the Clinton years and then lowered in the Bush fiscal package of 2003.

9. The fastest-growing federal tax is the payroll tax, used to finance social security. This is an "earmarked" levy, with funds going to provide public pensions and health and disability benefits. Because there are visible benefits at the end of the stream of payments, the payroll tax has elements of a benefit tax.

10. Economists point to the Ramsey tax rule, which emphasizes that efficiency will be promoted when taxes are levied more heavily on those activities that are relatively price-inelastic. A new approach is green taxes, which levy fees on environmental externalities, reducing harmful activities while raising revenues that would otherwise be imposed on goods or productive inputs. But in all taxes, equity and political acceptability are severe constraints.

11. The incidence of a tax refers to its ultimate economic burden and to its total effect on prices, outputs, and other economic magnitudes. Those who pay a tax can often pass its burden forward to consumers or backward to factors of production. The current U.S. tax and transfer system is moderately progressive.

CONCEPTS FOR REVIEW

Functions of Government

three tools of government economic control:
 taxes
 expenditures
 regulation
market failures vs. government failures
public-choice theory

four functions of government:
 efficiency
 distribution
 stabilization
 international representation

Government Expenditures and Fiscal Incidence

fiscal federalism and local vs. national public goods

economic impact of government spending
benefit and ability-to-pay principles
horizontal and vertical equity
direct and indirect taxes
progressive, proportional, and regressive taxes
tax and transfer incidence and shifting
Ramsey and green taxes

FURTHER READING AND INTERNET WEBSITES

Further Reading

An excellent review of tax issues is contained in the symposium on tax reform in *Journal of Economic Perspectives,* Summer 1987.

Current issues in public policy are surveyed annually by scholars from the Brookings Institution in *Setting National Priorities* (Brookings Institution, Washington, D.C., various years).

Websites

Data on government budget and tax trends can be found at government sites. For example, overall trends are presented by the Bureau of Economic Analysis at www.bea.gov. Budget information for the federal government comes from the Office of Management and Budget at www.whitehouse.gov/OMB.

The Internal Revenue Service (IRS) has a lively site with a plethora of tax statistics at www.irs.gov and www.irs.gov/tax stats/index.html.

Two organizations which study taxation and have good websites are the National Tax Association at www.ntanet.org and the Brookings Institution at www.brookings.org. Policy papers by a British research institute that focuses on social security and taxation can be found at www.ifs.org.uk.

QUESTIONS FOR DISCUSSION

1. Recall Justice Oliver Wendell Holmes's statement, "Taxes are what we pay for a civilized society." Interpret this statement, remembering that in economics we always need to pierce the veil of monetary flows to understand the flow of real resources.

2. In considering whether you want a pure laissez-faire economy or government regulation, discuss whether there should be government controls over prostitution, addictive drugs, heart transplants, assault weapons, and alcohol. Discuss the relative advantages of high taxes and prohibition for such goods (recall the discussion of drug prohibition in Chapter 5).

3. Critics of the U.S. tax system argue that it harms incentives to work, save, and innovate and therefore reduces long-run economic growth. Can you see why "green taxes" might promote economic efficiency and economic growth? Consider, for example, taxes on sulfur or carbon-dioxide emissions or on leaky oil tankers. Construct a list of taxes that you think would increase efficiency, and compare their effects with the effects of taxes on labor or capital income.

4. Tax economists often speak of lump-sum taxes, which are levied on individuals without regard to their economic activity. Lump-sum taxes are efficient because they impose zero marginal tax rates on all inputs and outputs.

   Assume that the government imposes a lump-sum tax of $200 on each individual. Show the effect of this on the supply and demand for labor in a graph. Does the marginal revenue product of labor still equal the wage in equilibrium?

   In a lifetime framework, the dynamic equivalent of a lump-sum tax is an "endowment tax," which would tax individuals on the basis of their potential labor incomes. Fullerton and Rogers (op. cit., page 337) find that a perfectly efficient proportional endowment tax would increase average lifetime incomes by 1.3 percent. Would you favor such a change? Describe some of the difficulties in implementing an endowment tax.

5. Make a list of different federal taxes in order of their progressiveness. If the federal government were to trade in income taxes for consumption or sales taxes, what would be the effect in terms of overall progressiveness of the tax system?

6. Some public goods are local, spilling out to residents of small areas; others are national, benefiting an entire nation; some are global, affecting all nations. A private good is one whose spillover is negligible. Give some examples of purely private goods and of local, national, and global public goods or externalities. For each, indicate the level of government that could design relevant policies most efficiently, and suggest one or two appropriate government actions that could solve the externality.

7. Below are some incidence questions that can be answered using supply and demand. Use graphs to explain your answers.

a. In the 1993 Budget Act, Congress raised federal gasoline taxes by 4.3 cents a gallon. Assuming the wholesale price of gasoline is determined in world markets, what is the relative impact of the tax on American producers and consumers?

b. Social insurance taxes are generally levied on labor earnings. What is their incidence if labor supply is perfectly inelastic? If labor supply is backward-bending?

c. If firms must earn a posttax rate of return on investment determined in world capital markets, what is the incidence of a tax on corporate income in a small open economy?

8. An interesting question involves the *Laffer curve,* named for California economist and sometime senatorial candidate Arthur Laffer. In Figure 16-9, the Laffer curve shows how revenues rise as *tax rates* are increased, reach a maximum at point *L*, and then decline to zero at a 100 percent tax rate as activity is completely discouraged. The exact shape of the Laffer curve for different taxes is highly controversial.

A common mistake in discussing taxes is the post hoc fallacy (see Chapter 1's discussion of this). Proponents of lower taxes often invoke the Laffer curve in their arguments. They point to tax cuts of the 1960s to suggest that the economy is to the right of the peak of Mt. Laffer, say at *B*. They say, in effect, "After the Kennedy-Johnson tax cuts of 1964, federal revenues actually rose from $110 billion in 1963 to $133 billion in 1966. Therefore, cutting taxes raises revenues." Explain why this does not prove that the economy was to the right of *L*. Further explain why this is an example of the post hoc fallacy. Give a correct analysis.

9. Under the flat tax, all personal and corporate income is taxed only once at a low fixed rate. Table 16-5 shows how such a flat tax might work. Compare the average and marginal tax rates of the flat tax with the tax schedule shown in Table 16-4 in the text. List advantages and disadvantages of both. Which is more progressive?

FIGURE 16-9. The Laffer Curve

(1) Adjusted gross income ($)	(2) Deductions and exemptions ($)	(3) Taxable income ($)	(4) Individual income tax ($)
5,000	20,000	0	0
10,000	20,000	0	0
20,000	20,000	0	0
50,000	20,000	30,000	6,000
100,000	20,000	80,000	16,000
1,000,000	20,000	980,000	196,000

TABLE 16-5.

CHAPTER

17

Promoting More Efficient Markets

Markets are a great way to organize economic activity, but they need adult supervision.

David Wessel

Before studying economics, many people think that the government needs to be a watchdog guarding consumers against monopolistic abuses and price gouging. Once encountering the invisible-hand theory, we might be more reluctant to intervene, however, because economics teaches us that competitive markets can lead to efficient production and pricing. For the most part, governments in market economies today rely on the force of rivalry and competition—the carrot of profits and the stick of bankruptcy—to stimulate the private sector to behave efficiently.

But the forces of competition cannot work effectively when competitors are absent or feeble. When there is excessive market power, government can take steps to promote competition. There are other market failures that may call for government intervention. Sometimes people may not have adequate information to judge product quality. So the government requires that drug companies demonstrate the safety and efficacy of new drugs. The government also regulates industries like banking and electricity, tries to protect consumers from false advertising and financial misrepresentation, and engages in zoning decisions which control the economic use of land.

How can governments best promote efficient markets? How best to control market failures without hindering the powerful efficiency gains of unfettered market competition and rivalry? Sometimes, the public interest compels regulation in a limited domain; at other times, economic regulation creates more problems than it solves, and governments are well advised to deregulate a sector. Public policy in this area—focusing on regulation and antitrust—is surveyed in this chapter.

A. BUSINESS REGULATION: THEORY AND PRACTICE

Federal regulation of American industry goes back more than a century to the founding of the Interstate Commerce Commission (ICC) in 1887. The ICC was designed as much to prevent price wars and to guarantee service to small towns as it was to control monopoly. Later, federal regulation spread to banks in 1913, to electric power in 1920, and to communications, securities markets, labor, trucking, and air travel during the 1930s. In recent years, as we will see, the federal government has changed its course by deregulating many industries.

341

In attempting to control economic activity, governments can use commands or market incentives. Historically the main form of regulation has been a direct approach, where governments issue *command-and-control orders*. In this approach, governments command people to undertake or desist from certain activities through government regulation. For example, the government might require that businesses locate only in commercial areas or that they do not pour chemicals in rivers. Government commands today cover a wide variety of areas, including not only pollution and zoning but also informational reporting, labor standards on wages and hours, and many regulations specific to particular industries such as those using pesticides or producing new drugs.

Recently, economists have been instrumental in convincing government to try a brand new form of regulation: reliance on *market incentives*. The best example of the use of market incentives is the 1990 Clean Air Act, discussed in the next chapter. This bill set up markets for buying and selling "tradeable emissions permits"—in essence, licenses to pollute. Such harnessing of market forces has the possibility of achieving regulatory goals much more efficiently than command-and-control methods.

> **Regulation** consists of government rules or market incentives designed to control the price, sale, or production decisions of firms.

TWO BRANDS OF REGULATION

It is customary to distinguish between two forms of regulation. **Economic regulation** involves the control of prices, entry and exit conditions, and standards of service. It is most important in industries that are natural monopolies. (Recall that a natural monopoly is a market in which the industry's output can be efficiently produced only by a single firm.) Prominent examples are regulation of public utilities (telephone, electricity, natural gas, and water) as well as regulations in other industries (transportation, radio, and TV). The financial industry has been heavily regulated since the 1930s, with strict rules specifying what banks, brokerage firms, and insurance companies can and cannot do.

In addition, there is a newer form of regulation, known as **social regulation,** which is used to protect the environment along with the health and safety of workers and consumers. Its rules are aimed at correcting a wide variety of side effects or externalities that result from economic activity. Programs to clean our air and water, to ensure the safety of nuclear power, or to curb international environmental problems such as ozone depletion or climate change are the most prominent examples of social regulation. Because of its importance, we will study environmental regulation in detail in the next chapter.

WHY REGULATE INDUSTRY?

Regulation restrains the unfettered market power of firms. What are the legitimate reasons why governments might choose to override the decisions made in free markets? There are three major *public-interest justifications* of regulation. The first is to regulate firm behavior to prevent abuses of market power by monopolies or oligopolies. A second major reason is to remedy informational failures, such as those which occur when consumers have inadequate information about the characteristics of important products like drugs or energy-using appliances. A third reason is to correct externalities like pollution—this is the subject of social regulation, studied in the next chapter.

Containing Market Power

The traditional public-interest view of economic regulation is normative: that regulatory measures should be taken to reduce excessive market power. More specifically, government should regulate industries where there are too few firms to ensure vigorous rivalry. Government should regulate industries particularly in the extreme case of natural monopoly.

An important example of a natural monopoly is local water distribution. The cost of gathering water, building a water-distribution system, and piping water into every home is sufficiently great that it would not pay to have more than one firm provide local water service, so this is a natural monopoly. Sometimes water service is provided by the government; more often, it is provided by a regulated privately owned water company.

Another type of natural monopoly can occur when there are *economies of scope*, which arise when a number of different products can be produced more efficiently together than apart. A prominent example of economies of scope is computer software. Many software programs incorporate additional features as they evolve. For example, when consumers buy software to prepare their federal income taxes, the CD-ROM usually contains several other modules, including a link to a Web page, government documents, and a tax preparation manual. This shows economies of scope because the different modules can be more inexpensively produced, packaged, and used together than separately.

A final component of natural monopoly, particularly prevalent in network industries, is the requirement for standardization and coordination through the system for efficient operation. Railroads need standard track gauges, electrical transmission requires load balancing, and communications require standard codes so that different parts can "talk" to each other.

We know from our discussion of declining costs in earlier chapters that pervasive economies of scale are inconsistent with perfect competition; we will see oligopoly or monopoly in such cases. But the point here is even more extreme: *When there are such powerful economies of scale or scope that only one firm can survive, we have a natural monopoly.*

Why do governments sometimes regulate natural monopolies? They do so because a natural monopolist, enjoying a large cost advantage over its potential competitors and facing price-inelastic demand, can jack up its price sharply, obtain enormous monopoly profits, and create major economic inefficiencies. In the early 1990s, cable television companies exploited their local monopolies in providing multiple channels with high-quality pictures by raising prices sharply. This provoked Congress and several states to enact legislation regulating the prices set by these companies. Studies indicated that this price regulation was ineffective and may actually have raised prices in some categories. Consequently, in the 1996 Communications Act, Congress changed its mind and lifted price and entry controls, with the idea that greater competition would be more beneficial for consumers than price controls.

In earlier times, regulation was justified on the dubious grounds that it was needed to prevent cutthroat or destructive competition. This was one argument for continued control over railroads, trucks, airlines, and buses, as well as for regulation of the level of agricultural production. Economists today have little sympathy for this argument. After all, competition with increased efficiency and low prices is exactly what an efficient market system is designed to ensure.

Remedying Information Failures

Another reason for regulation is that consumers have inadequate information about products. For example, testing pharmaceutical drugs is expensive and scientifically complex. The government regulates drugs by allowing the sale of only those drugs which are proved "safe and efficacious." Government also prohibits false and misleading advertising. In both cases, the government is attempting to correct for the market's failure to provide information efficiently.

One area where regulating the provision of information is particularly critical is financial markets. When people buy stocks or bonds of private companies, they are placing their fortunes in the hands of people about whom they know next to nothing. Before buying shares of IBM or ZYX.com, I will examine their financial statements to determine what their sales, earnings, and dividends have been. But can I know exactly how they measure earnings? How can I be sure that they are reporting honestly?

This is where government regulation of financial markets steps in. Most regulations of the financial industry serve the purpose of improving the quantity and quality of information so that markets can work better. When a company sells stocks or bonds in the United States, it is required to issue copious documentation of its current financial condition and future prospects. Companies' books must be certified by independent auditors. Government requirements are sometimes reinforced by the private sector: companies listed on the New York Stock Exchange must comply with an even tougher set of accounting regulations.

Occasionally, particularly in times of speculative frenzies, companies will bend or even break the rules. This happened on a large scale in the late 1990s and early 2000s, particularly in communications and many new-economy firms. When these illegal practices were made public, Congress passed a new law in 2002; this law made it illegal to lie to an auditor, established an independent board to oversee accountants, and provided new oversight powers to the Securities and Exchange Commission (SEC). Some argue that this kind of law should be welcomed by honest businesses: tough reporting standards are beneficial to financial markets because they reduce informational asymmetries between buyers and sellers, promote trust, and encourage financial investment.

Dealing with Externalities

Government regulation can also be justified when there are externalities. The classic example of regulation of this type, which we analyze in the next chapter, is antipollution measures. But there are other interesting cases. One pervasive example is local zoning regulation, which limits how landowners can use their land. Most zoning regulations specify whether a plot of land can be used for residences, stores, or industry and how big the buildings can be.

What is the justification for zoning regulation? Allowing a junkyard in a quiet residential area, for instance, would generate externalities that might harm everyone in the neighborhood. Similarly, a 50-story office building in a neighborhood of 2-story homes might overwhelm the local transportation system and other neighborhood services.

The economic impact of zoning can be huge. Being able to build a 50-story building on a plot of land, as opposed to a 2-story one, can dramatically affect the value of the land. That's why zoning is perhaps the most important type of regulation undertaken at the local level of government.

INTEREST-GROUP THEORIES OF REGULATION

So far we have been looking at the normative public-interest justifications for government regulation. We should recognize, however, that regulation creates profits and thereby produces interest groups which have vested interests in the regulatory outcomes. Sometimes, because of the interaction between regulation and politics, regulation has the perverse result of restricting entry into the regulated industry, and thus actually *raising prices and profits* for established companies.[1] Hence, a regulated industry may lobby in favor of continued regulation, in order to keep out competitors and keep profits high.

Economists who emphasize the anticompetitive aspect of regulation make the following argument:

You say that regulation is in the interest of consumers and workers. Don't believe it. Rather, regulation is designed to boost the incomes of producers by limiting entry and preventing competition in the regulated industry. Any gains to consumers or workers are purely incidental.

The historical record shows that there is much truth to this view. For example, numerous economic studies have shown that regulation often keeps prices *high*. For many years, trucking companies and airlines had to get permission before lowering prices or entering new markets. Other types of regulation also have the effect of limiting competition. For example, high standards for new drugs mean that the process of getting regulatory approval is lengthy and expensive. That keeps out many smaller companies which cannot afford the years of testing that a new drug requires.

An example of a regulatory program benefiting the industry at the expense of taxpayers came in the savings and loan industry. The federal program of deposit insurance was established in the 1930s to help restore confidence and prevent bank panics. By the early 1980s, however, it became clear that the program was poorly designed. It provided a government guarantee on bank deposits without ensuring that banks behaved prudently with the insured deposits. Deregulation of industry here meant less intensive bank examination. Banks often would pay high interest rates to attract deposits and then use the money to make risky loans and investments and to pay high salaries to their executives. When the banks began going bankrupt, the government had to pick up the tab; losses mounted to the hundreds of billions of dollars. Because of intense lobbying and generous campaign contributions, appropriate government action to stop the wasteful practices was delayed for years until Congress acted to curb the worst abuses in 1989. Who were the major beneficiaries of the corrupt regulatory regime in the banking industry? Primarily bankers, banks, and bank stockholders. Who were the losers? The taxpayers.

PUBLIC-UTILITY REGULATION OF NATURAL MONOPOLY

A traditional economic argument for regulation is to prevent monopoly pricing by natural monopolists. Let us see exactly how regulators control excessive price increases of monopolists. Recall that a natural monopoly is an industry in which the most efficient way of organizing production is through a single firm. Figure 17-1 shows the way the *AC, MC,* and industry demand curve might look for a natural

---

[1] The germinal work in this area was by George Stigler of the University of Chicago, who won a Nobel Prize for this and other contributions. The Chicago School has been highly influential in its view that government intervention in the economy often does more harm than good.

FIGURE 17-1. Cost Curves for a Natural Monopolist

For a natural monopolist, the *AC* curve is still falling at the point where it cuts the industry's *DD* curve. Thus efficiency requires that output be produced by a single firm. (Can you estimate from the diagram how much more expensive it would be if Q^* were to be produced by two firms, each producing $\frac{1}{2}Q^*$?)

monopoly. Note that the industry demand curve (*DD*) intersects the firm's *MC* curve where *AC* is falling. If two similar firms were to produce the industry output, the average cost for the two firms would be well above that of a single firm.

Suppose that the legislature decides to impose *public-utility regulation* on a particular industry. How would it proceed? It would first set up a public-utility commission to oversee prices, service, and entry into and exit from the industry. The most important decision would be to determine the pricing of the monopoly firm.

Traditionally, regulation imposes *average cost pricing* on regulated firms. For example, an electric utility would take all its costs (fixed as well as variable) and allocate or "distribute" them to each product sold (say, electricity and steam). Then each class of customer would be charged the *fully distributed average cost* of that type of service.

Figure 17-2 illustrates public-utility regulation. Point *M* (associated with output Q_M) is the unregulated profit-maximizing output of the monopolist we examined in Chapter 9. Here we find high price, reduced quantity, and handsome profits (as shown by the shaded region in Figure 17-2).

In traditional regulation, the monopolist is allowed to charge a price only high enough to cover average cost. In this case, the firm will set its price where the demand curve *DD* intersects the *AC* curve. Hence, the equilibrium is at point *R*, with output Q_R.

How good is the solution? Economically speaking, it might represent an improvement over unregulated monopoly. First, the owners of the monopoly are presumably no more deserving than the consumers. So there is no reason to allow them to extract monopoly profits from consumers.

Second, in making the monopolist cut its price from P_M to P_R, the regulators have reduced the discrepancy between price and marginal cost. This change improves economic efficiency because the additional output is worth more to consumers in marginal utility than it costs society in terms of the marginal cost. Only when price is equal to marginal cost in all sectors is society using its resources most efficiently.

Ideally Regulated Pricing. If $P = MC$ is such a good thing, why shouldn't the regulators force the monopolist to lower price until it equals marginal cost at the intersection point of the *DD* and *MC* curves (at *I*)?

Actually, *marginal-cost pricing* where $P = MC$ is the ideal target for economic efficiency. But it presents a serious practical obstacle: If a firm with declining average cost sets price equal to marginal cost, it will incur a chronic loss. The reason is that if *AC* is falling, then $MC < AC$, so setting $P = MC$ implies having $P < AC$. When price (or average revenue) is less than average cost, the firm is losing money. To see this point visually, examine the ideal regulatory solution at point *I* in Figure 17-2. At that point, price equals marginal cost, but *MC* is less than average cost. When average cost is greater than price, the firm is losing money. Since firms will not operate at a loss for long, and governments are reluctant to subsidize monopolists, the ideal regulatory solution is rarely pursued.

In an alternative approach, pricing is based on *two-part tariffs.* The firm charges a fixed fee (say, a few dollars a month) to cover the overhead costs and then adds a variable cost (per phone call, unit of electricity, or whatever the commodity is) to cover the marginal cost. This approach can come even closer to the ideal marginal-cost pricing than does traditional average cost pricing.

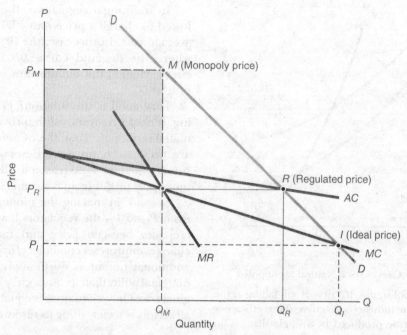

FIGURE 17-2. Ideal and Practical Regulation of Monopolists

Maximum-profit equilibrium for the unregulated monopolist is at *M*, directly above the intersection of *MR* and long-run *MC*, with price above *MC*.

Public-utility commissions customarily require that prices be equal to average cost at *R*, where the demand curve intersects the long-run average cost curve. This wipes out excess profit and brings price down closer to marginal cost. Ideally, price should be forced all the way down to *I*, where price = *MC* and hence marginal social costs and marginal benefits are appropriately balanced. At point *I*, there is no efficiency loss from price being above marginal cost.

Economic Innovations: Performance-Based Regulation

As we saw above, under traditional rate-of-return regulation, prices are determined to be the cost of production plus an authorized rate of return on invested capital. This approach offers very weak incentives to economize and is biased toward capital-intensive production techniques. The incentives are actually perverse because if price equals average cost, firms can actually increase profits by raising costs. As one economist noted, this is the only market where you can profit by putting a fancy Oriental carpet in your office!

A radical new approach that can improve incentives is *performance-based regulation*. Under this approach, firms are regulated on performance rather than on inputs, usually by use of a *price cap*. One formula is that regulated prices should move with "inflation minus *X*." Under this approach,

the maximum price that the regulated firm could charge would be raised each year by an amount equal to the inflation rate ("inflation") less a normative annual efficiency improvement ("*X*"). The attractiveness of this approach is that it mimics a competitive market. Firms become price-takers, and any cost reduction flows directly into profits. The perverse incentives of conventional regulation are removed. Well-designed price-cap regulation encourages utilities to reduce costs, allows the introduction of competition, and reduces uneconomical cross subsidization.

This novel technique has been employed in several industries in the United States and abroad over the last decade. While price caps provide superior incentives for efficiency, they are not without flaws. The major disadvantage of this approach is uncertainty about the appropriate *X* rate. *X* should represent the target rate of cost reduction relative to the economy as a whole. If *X* is set incorrectly for too long, the firm will either go bankrupt or earn large windfall monopoly profits. For this reason, all agencies which use price caps review the X factor periodically.

THE COSTS OF REGULATION

Economists have studied the impact of regulation to weigh its costs and benefits. The results of the latest comprehensive survey are shown in Table 17-1. The

	The Impact of Regulation, U.S., 1988*			
	Efficiency Gains or Losses			Income redistribution ($, billion)
	Benefits ($, billion)	Costs ($, billion)	Net benefits ($, billion)	
Economic regulation:				
Telecommunications	0.0	14.1	−14.1	42.3
Agriculture	0.0	6.7	−6.7	18.4
Airline	0.0	3.8	−3.8	7.7
Rail	0.0	2.3	−2.3	6.8
Milk	0.0	0.7	−0.7	2.2
Natural gas	0.0	0.3	−0.3	5.0
Credit	0.0	0.3	−0.3	0.8
Barge	0.0	0.3	−0.3	0.8
Davis-Bacon Act	0.0	0.2	−0.2	0.5
Ocean	0.0	0.1	−0.1	0.2
Postal rates	0.0	na	0.0	8.0
Social regulation:				
Environment	58.4	66.5	−8.1	na
Nuclear power	na	6.5	na	na
Occupational safety	0.0	8.8	−8.8	na
Highway safety	35.6	7.7	27.9	na
Pharmaceuticals	na	2.3	na	na
Equal opportunity	na	0.9	na	na
Consumer products	na	0.03	na	na
Other:				
International trade	0.0	17.3	−17.3	98.1
Total, all regulations and trade:†				
Billions of dollars	94	139	−35	191
As percent of gross domestic product	2.1	3.2	−0.8	4.4

*All estimates are in 1988 dollars; na = not available.

†Note that the na's are set at zero. This is likely to understate benefits slightly and to understimate the total amount of redistribution.

TABLE 17-1. Regulation Affects Efficiency and Redistributes Income

Studies of the impact of economic and social regulation show that economic regulations have few benefits, cause substantial efficiency losses, and redistribute much income. Social regulations have benefits, although these benefits are often extremely difficult to measure.

Source: Robert W. Hahn and John A. Hird, "The Costs and Benefits of Regulation: Review and Synthesis," *Yale Journal on Regulation*, vol. 8, 1991, pp. 233–287. Where a range of estimates is given, the midpoint is taken.

effects of regulation include both efficiency gains or losses (such as those that come when inefficiently high levels of pollution are curbed) and income redistribution (as occurs when high trucking prices redistribute income from consumers to truckers). Most studies suggest that the main effects of economic regulation are losses in efficiency and large amounts of income redistribution. The record of social regulation is mixed, with some cases showing significant benefits and others having large costs with few benefits. The costs of both social and economic regulation (including the restrictions on international trade) are estimated to have been around 3.2 percent of net domestic product as of 1988. While no studies comparable to that in Table 17-1 are currently available, it is likely that the overall burden of regulation is today lower with the declining barriers to trade, further deregulation of industry, and fewer major social regulations over the last decade.

Decline of Economic Regulation

For the last two decades, many economists have argued that most economic regulation was actually creating monopoly power rather than curbing it. This idea is partially based on the interest-group view of regulation analyzed above. In addition, observers noted that economic regulation had spread far beyond the local natural monopolies. By the mid-1970s, regulators were issuing their orders to railroads and trucks, airlines and buses, radio and TV broadcasting, oil and natural gas, pecans and milk, and virtually all financial markets. Many of these regulated industries were closer to the pole of perfect competition than to natural monopoly, as Figure 17-3 suggests.

Pioneering Deregulation in the Airline Industry

Since 1975, the federal government has partially or completely deregulated many industries, including petroleum, airlines, trucking, railroad, stockbroking, long-distance telephone service, banking, communications, the financial sector, and natural gas. Each of these industries has structural characteristics that are favorable to competition because their markets are large relative to the efficient size of individual firms.

The airline industry provides a dramatic example of the dilemmas of deregulation. Since its creation in the 1930s, the Civil Aeronautics Board (CAB) viewed its role as deterring competition. No major new air

FIGURE 17-3. Degree of Natural Monopoly in Different Industries

This figure displays several regulated and unregulated industries by their degree of natural monopoly or of perfect competition. In perfectly competitive industries, the efficient level of output for an individual firm is tiny relative to the market, while the average cost for a natural monopoly continues to decline even when the firm produces total industry output. Agriculture and mining are inherently quite competitive, while highways and local network utilities such as for water are close to polar natural monopolies. The asterisk (*) indicates industries that have historically been heavily regulated or even operated by governments.

carriers were allowed to enter the interstate market from 1938 to 1978. When innovative low-cost and no-frills airfares were proposed, the CAB slapped these proposals down. The CAB was (as the interest-group view of regulation predicted) devoted to keeping airfares up, not down.

In 1977, President Carter appointed Alfred Kahn chairman of the CAB. A distinguished economist and critic of regulation, Kahn set out to allow more competition through entry and fare flexibility. Shortly thereafter, Congress passed legislation allowing free entry and exit on all domestic air routes. Airlines were free to set whatever fares the traffic would bear.

Many people worried that there would be massive layoffs and loss of service without regulation. However, after more than two decades of experience with deregulation, the airline industry employs 65 percent more people and logs 70 percent more domestic passenger-miles. Studies indicate that (after correcting for inflation) average fares fell sharply over the years after deregulation; that utilization of aircraft has increased; and that airlines have become extraordinarily innovative in their pricing strategies. The competition has been so intense that the airline industry has shown very low profitability over the last decade, and bankruptcies are quite common. New airlines like Southwest Airlines have started up to replace bankrupt old ones. By most measures, the industry has operated more efficiently since deregulation.

The success of airline deregulation encouraged economists and noneconomists around the world to trust an unregulated market to make allocational decisions even in industries where firms have the potential for significant market power.

Economics in Action: Deregulating Electric Power

One of the most active areas for deregulation in the last decade has been the electric-power industry. This industry consists of four stages of production—generation, high-voltage transmission, physical distribution to retail customers, and retail sales to customers. Until recently, the entire electric-power industry was considered to be a natural monopoly and was therefore heavily regulated. Many countries have controlled monopoly through government ownership of major facilities, while others have used traditional rate-of-return public-utility regulation to control the prices and markets of electric utilities. Until the 1990s, electricity in the United States was produced predominantly by regulated, vertically integrated monopolies supplying large areas.

Over the last two decades, a new view emerged to challenge the traditional view of the electric-power industry. The new view held that, while the generation segment is technically complex, the optimal scale of plant is sufficiently small so that reasonably competitive markets can emerge among alternative generators. Retail distribution is a standard natural monopoly (like water and local telephone service) which requires regulatory scrutiny, such as through cost-of-service pricing.

The most complex area of electric power is long-distance transmission. Transmission of power is not like a roadway in which electrons are moved from point A to point B. Rather, it is a highly interrelated network which requires centralized management and has significant economies of scale.

The United States moved cautiously to break up and deregulate the vertically integrated monopolists that dominated the electric-power industry. In part, deregulation looked attractive after the successful experience of the airline industry. Additionally, the successful breakup of the Bell telecommunications monopoly along with an application of the Bell Doctrine (both discussed later in this chapter) suggested that deregulation of the electricity industry would bring significant economic benefits.

The package of reforms to deregulate the electricity industry contained the following elements:

- Privatize public enterprises when electricity is produced by the government. This will provide "hard budget constraints" for managers—giving them a strong incentive to minimize costs—and remove the tendency for governments to subsidize politically sensitive consumption.
- Deregulate the generation stage by allowing free entry and removing price controls. This will weed out the high-cost producers and promote the introduction of new technologies. Freeing prices has led to establishing "spot markets" for electricity, with prices that vary sharply with supply and demand and help manage severe shortages that sometimes occur during emergencies or heat waves.[2]
- Establish an independent long-distance transmission agency that is either regulated or operated by a quasi-governmental organization. This is the most difficult part of the package because the transmission agency must encourage entry in generation and supply, manage the network, and provide adequate revenues for building new capacity.

This package was applied in many countries, including Britain, Sweden, and Chile, and has been followed in the United States by several states. In some cases, the deregulation worked smoothly and brought considerable

---

[2] How does a spot market work? A typical case is that each generator declares its offers of quantities and prices of supply for each half-hour of the following day. The transmission agency then ranks these offers on the basis of costs and, combining them with estimates of demand, sets up a plan for least-cost operations for the coming day. The plan also yields a series of spot (or short-term) prices. The spot prices have proved highly variable, as is appropriate for an industry in which the marginal cost varies so greatly depending upon the load. You can look up the spot prices in *The Wall Street Journal* to see how they move from day to day. Spot markets exist for many commodities.

benefits to consumers in the form of lower electricity prices.

But when it was poorly executed, as in California, electricity deregulation was sometimes a fiasco. One problem in California was that the state imposed price controls on the retail sale of electricity but not on the wholesale purchase. Another problem came in the design of the auction, which allowed companies like Enron to manipulate purchases and sales and drive up prices. When wholesale prices in California soared, the largest public utility in California went bankrupt, the state took over the program and bought massive amounts of power at sky-high prices, and the auction system was disbanded. The high prices paid by the state led to a major budget crisis. This entire episode gave a black eye to deregulation and set off investigations and lawsuits to sift through the rubble.

Electricity deregulation made the headlines in 2003 when most of the northeast of the United States suffered a massive blackout. In this case, the problem arose because the different parts of the transmission system were poorly coordinated in the new, deregulated environment. Transmission systems operate as a kind of "weakest-link" technology, where one wayward part of the system can bring the entire grid down. A weakest-link technology in networks particularly needs the "adult supervision" of regulators.

Deregulation: An Unfinished Story

The deregulation movement of the last three decades has produced both successes and failures. The experience shows how difficult it is to design regulatory mechanisms that allow market forces to provide appropriate incentives while ensuring that monopoly power or informational deficiencies are held to a minimum. Some economists believe that the United States moved from careful decontrol in the 1970s to mindless deregulation in the 1990s. They point to a series of market failures that surfaced in the late 1990s and early 2000s that indicated the need for greater government scrutiny:

- The government had progressively moved to deregulate many aspects of electricity production. The great blackout of 2003 suggested the need for greater federal regulation of standards for transmission to ensure greater reliability. (See the discussion of electricity deregulation above.)

- The accounting scandals involving Enron, WorldCom, and many other companies indicated the need for tighter accounting standards and enhanced fiduciary requirements for corporate boards of directors. Congress enacted legislation in 2002 to increase the policing powers of the Securities and Exchange Commission.

- When Congress deregulated financial markets in 1997, this allowed banks to engage in investment banking and stock-brokerage services. Many economists believe that this created incentives for research analysts in the brokerage branch to tout stocks of companies for which the investment banking branch marketed bonds or in which the bank had bad loans.

Stanford's John McMillan uses an interesting analogy to describe the role of government regulation. Sports are contests in which individuals and teams strive to defeat opponents with all their strength and talent. But the participants must adhere to a set of extremely detailed rules; moreover, referees keep an eagle eye on players to make sure they obey the rules, with appropriately scaled penalties for infractions. Without carefully crafted rules, a game would turn into a bloody brawl. Similarly, government regulations along with a strong legal system are necessary in a modern economy to ensure that healthy competition does not monopolize, pollute, defraud, mislead, maim, and otherwise mistreat workers and consumers. This sports analogy reminds us that government still has an important role to play in monitoring the economy and setting the rules of the road.

B. ANTITRUST POLICY

Now we will examine in detail one of the oldest and most important forms of government oversight of business, antitrust policy. This branch of microeconomic policy is designed to promote vigorous competition and rivalry in markets and to prevent monopolistic abuses.

Review of Imperfect Competition

Chapters 9 and 10 discussed the way that imperfect competitors set their prices and quantities. Let's begin by reviewing the major elements of the economic theory that relate to government antimonopoly policies:

- Imperfect competitors are inefficient because they set prices above marginal cost. The consumers in the monopolistic or oligopolistic industry are consuming less of its goods than would be the case if the goods were efficiently supplied.

- Many industries have technologies that exhibit significant economies of scale and scope. It would be unrealistic to try to produce the output of such industries with perfectly competitive firms, for that would require that firms be inefficiently small. In rare cases, the technology in an industry can be efficiently produced only by a single firm; we call this a "natural monopoly."

- In the long run, most economic progress comes from technological change. According to the Schumpeterian hypothesis, large firms with considerable market power are responsible for much invention and technological change. Government policies should be especially careful not to harm the incentives for innovation.

- The major abuses in markets—either too high a price or poor product quality—come when an industry is effectively monopolized. A good rule of thumb is that an industry behaves like a monopolist when a single firm or colluding group of firms produces more than three-quarters of the output in an industry.

- The government has taken on the responsibility of preventing monopolization from occurring and of regulating monopolies when they are inevitable. Antitrust policies attempt to prevent monopolization or anticompetitive abuses; economic regulation is used to control the exercise of monopoly power in natural monopolies.

With the decline of economic regulation as a major tool for preventing monopolistic abuses, governments increasingly focus on the promotion of competition and on the application of antitrust policy as the major weapons for encouraging economic efficiency in markets. In this section we discuss antitrust policies, which attack anticompetitive abuses in two different ways. First, they prohibit certain kinds of *business conduct*, such as price fixing, that restrain competitive forces. Second, they restrict some market structures, such as monopolies, that are

thought most likely to restrain trade and abuse their economic power in other ways.

The framework for antitrust policy was set by a few key legislative statutes and by a century of court decisions. In recent years, under the prodding of economists, antitrust policy has been evolving away from the "big is bad" philosophy and toward the *economic approach to antitrust*. Emphasizing the intrinsic rivalry of oligopolists, the economic approach holds that the most powerful incentives for large business to reduce prices and improve product quality occur in a deregulated world in which barriers to entry are low and markets are open to domestic and foreign competition. In this view, antitrust policy should be reserved for the worst abuses of market power.

THE FRAMEWORK STATUTES

Antitrust law is like a huge forest that has grown from a handful of seeds. The statutes on which the law is based are so concise and straightforward that they can be quoted in Table 17-2; it is astounding how much law has grown from so few words.

Sherman Act (1890)

Monopolies had long been illegal under the common law, based on custom and past judicial decisions. But the body of laws proved ineffective against the mergers, cartels, and trusts that swept through the American economy in the 1880s.[3]

In 1890, populist sentiments led to passage of the Sherman Act, which is the cornerstone of American antitrust law. Section 1 of the Sherman Act prohibits contracts, combinations, and conspiracies "in restraint of trade." Section 2 prohibits "monopolizing" and conspiracies to monopolize. Neither the statute nor the accompanying discussion contains any clear notion about the exact meaning of monopoly or actions which were prohibited. The meaning was fleshed out in later case law.

---

[3] A *trust* is a group of firms, usually in the same industry, that combine together by a legal agreement to regulate production, prices, or other industrial conditions. To get the flavor of the times, review the section "Monopolists of the Gilded Age" in Chapter 9.

The Antitrust Laws

Sherman Antitrust Act (1890, as amended)

§1. Every contract, combination in the form of trust or otherwise, or conspiracy, in restraint of trade or commerce among the several States, or with foreign nations, is declared to be illegal.

§2. Every person who shall monopolize, or attempt to monopolize, or combine or conspire with any other person or persons, to monopolize any part of the trade or commerce among the several States, or with foreign nations, shall be deemed guilty of a felony. . . .

Clayton Antitrust Act (1914, as amended)

§2. It shall be unlawful . . . to discriminate in price between different purchasers of commodities of like grade and quality . . . where the effect of such discrimination may be substantially to lessen competition or tend to create a monopoly in any line of commerce. . . . *Provided,*
That nothing herein contained shall prevent differentials which make only due allowance for differences in the cost. . . .

§3. That it shall be unlawful for any person . . . to lease or make a sale or contract . . . on the condition, agreement, or understanding that the lessee or purchaser thereof shall not use or deal in the . . . commodities of a competitor . . . where the effect . . . may be to substantially lessen competition or tend to create a monopoly in any line of commerce.

§7. No [corporation] . . . shall acquire . . . the whole or any part . . . of another [corporation] . . . where . . . the effect of such an acquisition may be substantially to lessen competition, or to tend to create a monopoly.

Federal Trade Commission Act (1914, as amended)

§5. Unfair methods of competition . . . and unfair or deceptive acts or practices . . . are declared unlawful.

TABLE 17-2. American Antitrust Law Is Based on a Handful of Statutes

The Sherman, Clayton, and Federal Trade Commission acts laid the foundation for American antitrust law. Interpretation of these acts has fleshed out modern antitrust doctrines.

Clayton Act (1914)

The Clayton Act was passed to clarify and strengthen the Sherman Act. It outlawed *tying contracts* (in which a customer is forced to buy product B if she wants product A); it ruled *price discrimination* and exclusive dealings illegal; it banned *interlocking directorates* (in which some people would be directors of more than one firm in the same industry) and *mergers* formed by acquiring common stock of competitors. These practices were not illegal per se (meaning "in themselves") but only when they might substantially lessen competition. The Clayton Act emphasized prevention as well as punishment.

Another important element of the Clayton Act was that it specifically provided antitrust immunity to labor unions.

Federal Trade Commission

In 1914 the Federal Trade Commission (FTC) was established to prohibit "unfair methods of competition" and to warn against anticompetitive mergers. In 1938, the FTC was also empowered to ban false and deceptive advertising. To enforce its powers, the FTC can investigate, hold hearings, and issue cease-and-desist orders.

BASIC ISSUES IN ANTITRUST: CONDUCT AND STRUCTURE

While the basic antitrust statutes are straightforward, it is not easy in practice to decide how to apply them to specific situations of market structure or conduct. Actual law has evolved through an interaction of economic theory and case law.

Illegal Conduct

Some of the earliest antitrust decisions concerned illegal behavior. The courts have ruled that certain kinds of collusive behavior are illegal per se; there is simply no defense that will justify these actions. The offenders cannot defend themselves by pointing to some worthy objective (such as product quality) or mitigating circumstance (such as low profits).

The most important class of per se illegal conduct is agreements among competing firms to fix prices, restrict output, or divide markets. Such actions have the effect of raising prices and lowering output. Even the severest critics of antitrust policy can find no redeeming virtue in price fixing.

Other forms of conduct are also limited by antitrust laws. These include:

- *Predatory pricing*, in which a firm sells its goods for less than production costs (usually interpreted as marginal cost or average variable cost). The argument against predatory pricing is that a big company can use its financial resources to cut prices and drive smaller rivals out of business, and then it can jack up prices. In recent years, some giant discount chains have been accused of predatory pricing by smaller local competitors.
- *Tying contracts* or arrangements, whereby a firm will sell product A only if the purchaser buys product B.
- *Price discrimination*, in which a firm sells the same product to different customers at different prices for reasons not related to cost or competition. (Recall the discussion of price discrimination in Chapter 10.)

Note that the practices on this list relate to a firm's *conduct*. It is the acts themselves that are illegal, not the structure of the industry in which the acts take place. Perhaps the most celebrated example is the great electric-equipment conspiracy. In 1961, the electric-equipment industry was found guilty of collusive price agreements. Executives of the largest companies—such as GE and Westinghouse—conspired to raise prices and covered their tracks like characters in a spy novel by meeting in hunting lodges, using code names, and making telephone calls from phone booths. Although the top executives in these companies were apparently unaware of what the vice presidents just below them were doing, they had put much pressure on their vice presidents for increased sales. The companies agreed to pay extensive damages to their customers for overcharges, and some executives were jailed for their antitrust violations.

Recent Price-Fixing Cases. An interesting academic case involved an investigation by the Justice Department of the way that colleges and universities set tuition and scholarship aid. The government claimed that a small group of educational institutions conspired to reduce scholarship competition for top students by agreeing to award scholarships only on the basis of financial need and by comparing prospective aid awards to commonly admitted applicants. One of the defendants, the Massachusetts Institute of Technology (MIT), fought the government in the courts, arguing that nonprofit institutions should meet a different standard than profit-maximizing businesses. MIT prevailed on appeal in court, but this case raised novel issues about the manner in which antitrust law and regulations will be applied to activities of educational and other nonprofit institutions.

New Tools for Antitrust Policy

Most economists today agree that antitrust policy should promote low prices and high product quality. Few kind words can be heard about monopolies. But true monopoly is extremely rare, and policymakers must analyze the behavior of a wide variety of different oligopolistic market structures.

In the past, trustbusters have focused primarily on market shares as well as on particular forms of anticompetitive behavior. But today, with the advent of better data and powerful computers, economists can look at the actual behavior of prices when weighing the advisability of mergers.

A recent example shows how the tools of economics can be used to weigh antitrust decisions. In 1997, there was a proposed merger between Staples and Office Depot, two office-supply retail chains. Because the industry was relatively unconcentrated, the standard guidelines would have given the merger a green light.

But government economists gathered and analyzed actual scanner price and quantity data for every item sold by the two stores in different cities. Using the tools of industrial organization and econometrics, they discovered an important pattern: Staples' prices were significantly lower in cities where Office Depot also had a store than in cities where only Staples was present. This was strong evidence that the merger would allow Staples to raise prices. The merger was therefore disallowed.

Some economists believe that data on actual behavior will replace market-share data in analyzing business behavior. Given the weakness of market-share data in predicting economic behavior and performance, many will welcome this change.

Structure: Is Bigness Badness?

While price fixing and other illegal activities are important, the most visible antitrust cases concern the structure of industries rather than the conduct of companies. They consist of attempts to *break up* large firms as well as preventive *antimerger* proceedings against proposed mergers of large firms.

The first surge of antitrust activity under the Sherman Act focused on dismantling existing monopolies. In 1911, the Supreme Court ordered that the American Tobacco Company and Standard Oil be broken up into many separate companies. In condemning these flagrant monopolies, the Supreme Court enunciated the important "rule of reason": Only *unreasonable* restraints of trade (mergers, agreements, and the like) came within the scope of the Sherman Act and were considered illegal.

The rule-of-reason doctrine virtually nullified the antitrust laws' attack on monopolistic mergers, as shown by the U.S. Steel case (1920). J. P. Morgan had put this giant together by merger, and at its peak it controlled 60 percent of the market. But the Supreme Court held that pure size or monopoly by itself was no offense. In that period, as today, courts focused more on anticompetitive conduct than on pure monopoly *structure*.

Recent Structural Cases

The most important antitrust cases of recent years involved three giant firms in two vitally important industries—telecommunications and computers. A review of the three cases reveals the flavor of modern thinking about antitrust policy.

The AT&T case and the Bell Doctrine. Until the early 1980s, AT&T was a vertically and horizontally integrated monopolist in the telecommunications market. It handled more than 95 percent of all long-distance calls, provided 85 percent of all local lines, and sold most of the nation's telephone equipment. The complex of companies owned by AT&T—often

called the Bell System—included Bell Telephone Labs, Western Electric Company, and 23 Bell operating companies.

In 1974, the Department of Justice filed a far-reaching suit. It contended that AT&T had (1) monopolized the regulated long-distance market by anticompetitive means, such as preventing MCI and other carriers from connecting to the local markets, and (2) monopolized the telecommunications-equipment market by refusing to purchase equipment from non-Bell suppliers.

The fundamental theory underlying the case was called the "Bell Doctrine" by William Baxter, legal scholar and former head of the federal Antitrust Division. This holds that regulated monopolists have the incentive and the opportunity to monopolize related markets (such as ones they buy from or sell to) and that the most effective solution is to "quarantine" the monopoly segment by separating its ownership and control from the ownership and control of potentially competitive segments of the industry. In short, regulated monopoly and competition should not be mixed.

The economic theory behind the Bell Doctrine is that a monopolist, particularly a regulated monopolist, can increase its profits by integrating horizontally or vertically. For example, higher profits can be attained by disadvantaging potential competitors in the related industry or by charging excessive costs for its own unregulated products (such as telephone equipment) to the regulated entity which are then passed on through the cost-plus formula (for telephone service). This behavior is particularly likely when regulators have imperfect information about the firm's costs and behavior.

Faced with the prospect of losing the antitrust suit, the company settled in a "consent decree" that almost fully conformed to the Bell Doctrine. The local Bell operating companies were divested (or legally separated) from AT&T and were regrouped into seven large regional telephone holding companies. AT&T retained its long-distance operations as well as Bell Labs (the research organization) and Western Electric (the equipment manufacturer). The net effect was an 80 percent reduction in the size and sales of the Bell System. The regulated monopolists were no longer allowed to operate in related competitive markets.

The dismantling of the Bell System set off a breathtaking revolution in the telecommunications industry. New technologies are changing the landscape as cellular phone systems are eating away at the natural monopoly of Alexander Graham Bell's wire-based system; telephone companies are joining forces to bring television signals into homes; fiber-optic lines are beginning to function as data superhighways, carrying massive amounts of data around the country and the world. The Internet is linking people and places together in ways that were unimagined a decade ago. The one clear lesson of the breakup of the Bell System is that monopoly is not necessary for rapid technological change.

The IBM case. A second set of antitrust cases in recent years involved computer companies. The first case was an attempt by the government to dismember IBM. Filed in 1969, the suit charged that IBM "has attempted to monopolize and has monopolized . . . general purpose digital computers." The government charged that IBM had a dominant market share, with 76 percent of the market in 1967. Moreover, the government claimed that IBM had used many devices to prevent others from competing; the alleged anticompetitive steps included tie-in pricing, excessively low prices to discourage entry, and introduction of new products that tended to reduce the attractiveness of the products of other companies.

IBM contested the government case with tenacity and vigor. IBM's major defense was that the government was penalizing success rather than anticompetitive behavior. The fundamental dilemma in such cases had been crisply stated in the Alcoa case: "The successful competitor having been urged to compete must not be turned on when he wins." IBM claimed that the government was punishing the firm that had accurately foreseen the enormous potential in the computer revolution and had dominated the industry through its "superior skill, foresight, and industry."

The case dragged along inconclusively until the Reagan administration's antitrust chief, William Baxter, decided in 1982 to dismiss the case as "without merit." The government's reasoning was that, unlike the telecommunications industry, the computer industry was unregulated and subject to the full force of market competition. Baxter held that this industry was intrinsically competitive and that government attempts to restructure the computer market were more likely to harm than promote economic efficiency.

Antitrust in the New Economy: The Microsoft Case

The most recent major antitrust case involved the giant software company Microsoft. In 1998, the federal government and 19 states lodged a far-reaching suit alleging that Microsoft had illegally maintained its dominant position in the market for operating systems and used that dominance to leverage itself into other markets, such as the Internet browser market. The government claimed that "Microsoft has engaged in a broad pattern of unlawful conduct with the purpose and effect of thwarting emerging threats to its powerful and well-entrenched operating system monopoly."

The complaint argued that Microsoft had engaged in a wide variety of anticompetitive practices such as predatory conduct and pricing, illegal tying, and exclusionary agreements in violation of the Sherman Act. Although a monopoly acquired by fair means is legal, acting to stifle competition is illegal.

Microsoft's bare-knuckles approach to Netscape in the "browser wars" was particularly singled out in the complaint. One anticompetitive practice, according to the government, was distributing its Internet Explorer browser for free and tying it to Windows 98. This constituted predatory pricing under which Microsoft used its market power in operating systems to undercut Netscape. Microsoft often used colorful language in describing its conduct, as when Paul Maritz, Microsoft's group vice president, described its strategy regarding Netscape, "We are going to cut off their air supply. Everything they're selling, we're going to give away for free." Microsoft used the "good monopoly" defense, arguing that its Internet Explorer was popular with consumers "for the simple reason that it offers superior technology and has won virtually all of the recent independent reviews against Netscape's Navigator browser."

The government also alleged that Microsoft leveraged its monopoly by forcing companies to enter exclusionary agreements to distribute Microsoft software and products at the expense of its competitors. For example, an IBM executive testified that IBM's OS/2 operating system was unable to compete with Windows because Microsoft had locked up independent software companies with restrictive license agreements. Consequently, software developers were discouraged from writing programs for the OS/2 platform, which reduced the viability and popularity of OS/2 while cementing Microsoft's dominance. In addition, Microsoft allegedly coerced computer makers to install Microsoft's Internet Explorer, not Netscape's Navigator, by threatening to withdraw their Windows licenses if they refused. Microsoft defended itself by claiming that such licensing and cooperative agreements are common in the software industry. (All these relate to the "network" characteristics of operating systems.)

In his "Findings of Fact," Judge Jackson declared that Microsoft was a monopoly that had controlled more than 90 percent of the market share for PC operating systems since 1990 and that Microsoft had abused its market power and caused "consumer harm by distorting competition." His opinion contained a stinging indictment:

> Three main facts indicate that Microsoft enjoys monopoly power. First, Microsoft's share of the market for Intel-compatible PC operating systems is extremely large and stable. Second, Microsoft's dominant market share is protected by a high barrier to entry. Third, and largely as a result of that barrier, Microsoft's customers lack a commercially viable alternative to Windows....
>
> Most harmful of all is the message that Microsoft's actions have conveyed to every enterprise with the potential to innovate in the computer industry. Through its conduct toward Netscape, IBM, Compaq, Intel, and others, Microsoft has demonstrated that it will use its prodigious market power and immense profits to harm any firm that insists on pursuing initiatives that could intensify competition against one of Microsoft's core products. Microsoft's past success in hurting such companies and stifling innovation deters investment in technologies and businesses that exhibit the potential to threaten Microsoft. The ultimate result is that some innovations that would truly benefit consumers never occur for the sole reason that they do not coincide with Microsoft's self-interest.

In asserting that consumers have been harmed by Microsoft's monopoly status, the judge cited a Microsoft study that suggested Microsoft could have charged $49 instead of $89 for the retail upgrade to Windows 98 but chose to charge $89 because it was the "revenue-maximizing" price (see question 10 at the end of this chapter for a discussion).

In his "Findings of Law," Judge Jackson found that Microsoft had violated sections 1 and 2 of the Sherman Act. He found that "Microsoft maintained its monopoly power by anticompetitive means [,] attempted to monopolize the Web browser market, . . . and violated . . . the Sherman Act by unlawfully tying its Web browser to its operating system."

The final stage of the case was the "remedy" phase, which involved taking steps to end the illegal monopolistic practices. The Department of Justice proposed the radical step of separating Microsoft along functional lines. This "divestiture" would require a separation of Microsoft into two separate, independent companies. One company ("WinCo") would own Microsoft's Windows and other operating-system businesses, and the other ("AppCo") would own the applications and other businesses.

In 2000, Judge Jackson accepted Justice's remedy recommendation with no modifications. But then the case took a bizarre twist when it turned out that Judge Jackson had been holding private heart-to-heart discussions with journalists even as he was trying the case. He was chastised for his unethical conduct and removed from the case. Shortly thereafter, the new Bush administration decided it would not seek to separate Microsoft but would settle for "conduct" remedies. These measures would restrict Microsoft's conduct so as to protect competition—steps such as prohibiting contractual tying and discriminatory pricing as well as ensuring interoperability of Windows with non-Windows software. After extensive further hearings, the case was settled in November 2002 with Microsoft intact but under the court's watchful eye for a 5-year period.

Mergers: Law and Practice

Companies can gain market power through growth (plowing back earnings and building new plants). But a much easier way to gain market share, or simply to get bigger, is to merge with another company. The 1980s saw a tremendous growth in merger activity.

Horizontal mergers—in which companies in the same industry combine—are forbidden under the Clayton Act when the merger is likely to reduce competition in the industry substantially. Case law and government merger guidelines clarified the meaning of the vague statutory language. The government uses the Herfindahl-Hirschman Index (HHI) to evaluate mergers.[4] Under these guidelines, industries are divided into three groups: unconcentrated (HHI below 1000), moderately concentrated (HHI 1000 to 1800), and highly concentrated (HHI above 1800). Mergers in the latter two types of industries will be challenged even in cases where the merging firms involved have small market shares.

---

[4] The HHI is equal to the sum of the squares of the percentage market shares of firms in the industry. See Chapter 10 for a discussion of the HHI.

Vertical mergers occur when two firms at different stages of the production process come together. In the early years, the courts took a hard line toward vertical mergers. They worried about the potential restriction of competition through exclusive dealings if two independent firms merged. Courts tended to pay relatively little heed to the potential efficiencies of joint operations in vertical mergers.

A third kind of combination, called **conglomerate mergers,** joins together unrelated businesses. In a conglomerate merger, a chemical or steel company might buy an oil company. The critics of conglomerates make two points. First, they note that the absolute size of the largest corporations is awesome. The largest 200 corporations control more than $2.5 trillion of assets. The largest corporations therefore have great economic and political power. Increasingly, many observers worry more about the way that large organizations can buy favors in the political process than about how they abuse their market power.

The second point made by the critics of conglomerates is that many of these combinations serve no economic purpose. They are, it is argued, simply a brand of "boardroom poker" to entertain managers bored with supervising their tiresome steel or chemical operations. And, indeed, there is a point here: What does the airplane business have in common with meatpacking? Or typewriters with birth-control pills? Or computer leasing with passenger-bus operations?

Conglomerates are not without defenders. Some economists argue that these mergers bring good modern management to backward firms and that takeovers, like bankruptcy, represent the economy's way of eliminating deadwood in the economic struggle for survival. But there is no consensus on the merits or demerits of conglomerate mergers, and they are largely tolerated as long as they do not increase concentration in particular industries.

ANTITRUST LAWS AND EFFICIENCY

Economic and legal views toward regulation and antitrust have changed dramatically over the last three decades. During the period, industries were deregulated, and antitrust law abandoned its mission "to put an end to great aggregations of capital because of the helplessness of the individual before them" (to quote from the 1945 Alcoa decision).

Increasingly, regulation and antitrust are aimed toward the goal of improving economic efficiency.

What has prompted the changing attitude toward antitrust policy? First, economists found that concentrated industries sometimes had outstanding performance. Consider firms like Intel, Microsoft, and Boeing. They have had substantial market shares, but they have also been highly innovative and commercially successful. Whereas economic theory held that monopoly keeps prices high, historical experience indicates that highly concentrated industries often had rapidly declining prices relative to less concentrated industries. At the same time, some unconcentrated industries, such as agriculture and financial services, exhibited outstanding performance. No iron law has been found to link structure and performance.

How can we explain this paradox? Some economists invoke the Schumpeterian hypothesis. Firms in concentrated industries collect monopoly profits, to be sure. But the size of the market also means that large firms can appropriate much of the return on research-and-development (R&D) investments, which explains the high levels of R&D and the rapid technological change in concentrated industries. If, as Schumpeter claimed, technological change originates in large firms, it would be foolish to slay these giant geese who lay such golden eggs.

A second thrust of the new approach to regulation and antitrust arose from revised views of the nature of competition. Considering both experimental evidence and observation, many economists have come to believe that intense rivalry will spring up even in oligopolistic markets as long as collusion is strictly prohibited. Indeed, in the words of Richard Posner, formerly a law professor and currently a federal judge,

> The only truly unilateral acts by which firms can get or keep monopoly power are practices like committing fraud on the Patent Office or blowing up a competitor's plant, and fraud and force are in general adequately punished under other statutes.[5]

In this view, the only valid purpose of the antitrust laws should be to replace existing statutes with a simple prohibition against *agreements*—explicit or tacit—that unreasonably restrict competition.

---

[5] See Posner in the Further Reading section at the end of this chapter.

Third, the swing of the pendulum against strict antitrust enforcement came from the increasing emphasis on market forces and market-based incentives. This position was inspired by proponents of the Chicago School, which held that most monopoly power derives from government interventions. According to this view, the major pools of monopoly power lie in areas protected by government fiat. Important examples include economic regulations and rules (see Table 17-1) in such diverse areas as foreign trade, the exemption of labor unions from antitrust laws, monopoly protection conveyed by the patent laws, barriers to entry into the professions, and restrictions in medical care. Advocates of the laissez-faire view argue that reducing government regulation would enhance competition.

A final reason for the reduced activism in antitrust has been the increase in import competition. As more foreign firms gain a foothold in the American economy, they tend to compete vigorously for market share and often upset established sales patterns and pricing practices. For example, when the sales of Japanese automakers increased, the cozy coexistence of the Big Three American auto firms dissolved. Many economists believe that the threat of foreign competition is a much more powerful tool for enforcing market discipline than are antitrust laws.

SUMMARY

A. Business Regulation: Theory and Practice

1. Regulation consists of government rules commanding firms to alter their business conduct. Economic regulation involves the control of prices, production, entry and exit conditions, and standards of service in a particular industry; social regulation consists of rules aimed at correcting information failures and externalities, particularly those that impinge on health and safety and the environment.

2. The normative view of regulation is that government intervention is appropriate when there are major market failures. These include excess market power in an industry, inadequate supply of information to consumers and workers, and externalities such as pollution. Economists have developed a positive theory of regulation in which regulation often serves the purpose of actually benefiting regulated firms, whose interests are furthered by exclusion of potential rivals.

3. The strongest case for economic regulation comes in regard to natural monopolies. Natural monopoly occurs when average costs are falling for every level of output, so the most efficient organization of the industry requires production by a single firm. Few industries come close to this condition today—perhaps only local utilities like water and electricity.

4. In conditions of natural monopoly, governments regulate the price and service of private companies. Traditionally, government regulation of monopoly has required that price be set at the average cost of production. The ideal regulation would require price to be set equal to marginal cost, but this approach is impractical because it requires that government subsidize the monopolist. A new approach is performance-based regulation, such as price caps, which provides superior incentives to regulated firms to reduce costs and improve productivity.

5. Given the strength of competitive forces, particularly from the global marketplace, the case for economic regulation holds for few industries today. The deregulation movement of the 1970s reduced the extent of economic regulation markedly, producing gains in industries such as the airlines.

B. Antitrust Policy

6. Antitrust policy, prohibiting anticompetitive conduct and preventing monopolistic structures, is the primary way that public policy limits abuses of market power by large firms. This policy grew out of legislation like the Sherman Act (1890) and the Clayton Act (1914). The primary purposes of antitrust policy are (*a*) to prohibit anticompetitive activities (which include agreements to fix prices or divide up territories, price discrimination, and tie-in agreements) and (*b*) to break up monopoly structures. In today's legal theory, such structures are those that have excessive market power (a large share of the market) and also engage in anticompetitive acts.

7. In addition to limiting the behavior of existing firms, antitrust law prevents mergers that would lessen

competition. Today, horizontal mergers (between firms in the same industry) are the main source of concern, while vertical and conglomerate mergers tend to be tolerated.

8. Antitrust policy has been significantly influenced by economic thinking during the last three decades. As a result, antitrust policy now focuses almost exclusively on improving efficiency and ignores earlier populist concerns with bigness itself. Moreover, in today's economy—with intense competition from foreign producers and deregulated rivals—many believe that antitrust policy should concentrate primarily on preventing collusive agreements like price fixing.

CONCEPTS FOR REVIEW

Regulation
two kinds of regulation: economic vs. social regulation
old-style (command-and-control) vs. new (economic-incentive) regulation
natural monopoly

reasons for regulation:
    market power
    externalities
    information failures

Antitrust Policy
Sherman, Clayton, and FTC acts

per se prohibitions vs. the "rule of reason"
mergers:
    vertical
    horizontal
    conglomerate
efficiency-oriented antitrust policy

FURTHER READING AND INTERNET WEBSITES

Further Reading

Law and economics advanced greatly under the influence of scholars like Richard Posner, now a circuit court judge. His book, *Antitrust Law: An Economic Perspective* (University of Chicago Press, 1976), is a classic.

Websites

An excellent website with links to many issues on antitrust is www.antitrust.org. The homepage for the Antitrust Division of the Department of Justice, at www.usdoj.gov/atr/overview.html, contains excellent source material on

antitrust issues. You can also keep up to date by looking for recent articles from *The Economist* at www.economist.com.

Innovative studies of the economics of regulation are undertaken by the AEI-Brookings Joint Center on Regulatory Studies at www.aei.brookings.org. See Kenneth J. Arrow et al., *Benefit-Cost Analysis in Environmental, Health, and Safety Regulation* (1996), at that site for a review of the major issues involved in cost-benefit analysis and for a Supreme Court brief filed in 2000 by 40 economists arguing for increased use of cost-benefit analysis in environmental regulation.

QUESTIONS FOR DISCUSSION

1. What are the major weapons that government has to restrain monopoly power? Describe the strengths and weaknesses of each policy.
2. Review the three pricing outcomes in Figure 17-2. Can you think of the difficulties of implementing the ideal regulated price? (*Hint:* Where does the country get the revenues? Is MC easy to measure?) Similarly, can you think of reasons why many economists would

prefer the unregulated to the regulated outcome? (*Hint:* What if P_M is not much above P_R? What if you worried about the interest-group theory of regulation?)
3. Explain why price-cap or inflation-minus-X price regulation has better incentives than average cost price regulation. Explain why the latter is better able to prevent monopoly profits.

4. "Microsoft, the large software company, is not bad just because it is big." Discuss, particularly with reference to the application of antitrust laws to large companies.

5. Examine the cost and demand curves in Figure 17-1. Using those curves, draw in the monopoly price and output. Compare these with the ideal regulated output and price. Describe the difference.

6. Two important approaches to antitrust are *structure* and *conduct.* The former looks only at the structure of the industry (such as the concentration of firms); the latter, at firm conduct (e.g., price fixing).

   a. Review the various statutes and cases to see which are related to conduct and which to structure. What about the government merger guidelines?

   b. What are the advantages and disadvantages of each approach?

7. Make a list of the industries that you feel are candidates for the title "natural monopoly." Then review the different strategies for intervention to prevent exercise of monopoly power. What would you do about each industry on your list?

8. Show that a profit-maximizing, unregulated monopolist will never operate in the price-inelastic region of its demand curve. Show how regulation can force the monopolist onto the inelastic portion of its demand curve. What will be the impact of an increase in the regulated price of a monopolist upon revenues and profits when it is operating on (a) the elastic portion of the demand curve, (b) the inelastic portion of the demand curve, and (c) the unit-elastic portion of the demand curve?

9. Review the merger guidelines in this chapter, the definition of the HHI from Chapter 10, and the table and discussion in question 2 of Chapter 10. Into which class does the airline industry fall? If the government decided that the code-sharing agreements were equivalent to mergers, would any of the agreements pass the merger guidelines?

10. In his Findings of Fact, Judge Jackson wrote: "It is indicative of monopoly power that Microsoft felt that it had substantial discretion in setting the price of its Windows 98 upgrade product (the operating system product it sells to existing users of Windows 95). A Microsoft study from November 1997 reveals that the company could have charged $49 for an upgrade to Windows 98—there is no reason to believe that the $49 price would have been unprofitable—but the study identifies $89 as the revenue-maximizing price. Microsoft thus opted for the higher price." Explain why these facts would indicate that Microsoft is not a perfect competitor. What further information would be needed to prove Microsoft was a monopoly?

CHAPTER 18

Protecting the Environment

Growth for the sake of growth is the ideology of the cancer cell.

Edward Abbey

Clean air, clean water, unspoiled land—all of us would agree that these are desirable goals. But how much are we willing to pay to achieve them? And what is the threat to humanity if we do not respect the limits of our natural environment?

At one pole is an environmentalist philosophy of confines and perils. In this view, human activities threaten to disrupt the intricate web of natural ecosystems, unintended consequences threaten to overwhelm human ingenuity, and we must be ever vigilant lest the dikes break and we are inundated by the angry seas. The environmentalist point of view is well expressed in the bleak warning from the distinguished Harvard biologist E. O. Wilson:

> Environmentalism . . . sees humanity as a biological species tightly dependent on the natural world. . . . Many of Earth's vital resources are about to be exhausted, its atmospheric chemistry is deteriorating, and human populations have already grown dangerously large. Natural ecosystems, the wellsprings of a healthful environment, are being irreversibly degraded. . . . I am radical enough to take seriously the question heard with increasing frequency: Is humanity suicidal?[1]

Believers in this dismal picture argue that humans must practice "sustainable" economic growth and learn to live within the limitations of our scarce natural resources or we will suffer dire and irreparable consequences.

At the other pole are "cornucopians," who believe that we are far from exhausting either natural resources or the capabilities of technology. In this optimistic view, we can look forward to limitless economic growth and rising living standards, with human ingenuity well able to cope with any environmental problems. If oil runs out, there is plenty of coal. If that doesn't pan out, then rising energy prices will induce innovation on solar or nuclear power. Cornucopians view technology, economic growth, and market forces as the saviors, not the villains.

Generally, mainstream economists tend to lie between the environmentalist and the cornucopian extremes. They recognize that humans have been encroaching on the environment for ages. Historically, the major interventions occurred when humans moved into settlements, converted forests into farms, and began to domesticate plants and animals. But this qualitative transformation pales beside today's massive bioengineering, deforestation, and extraction of mineral and plant resources from the earth. In this

---

[1] For the Wilson article, see the Further Reading section at the end of this chapter.

chapter, we will see how the tools of economics can be used to understand our environmental problems and to design policies that make our world more habitable.

A. POPULATION AND RESOURCE LIMITATIONS

MALTHUS AND THE DISMAL SCIENCE

Fear of the voracious appetite of a fast-growing human population lies at the heart of many worries about the environment, as the quotation from Wilson at the start of this chapter suggests. Consider the following editorial from the world's leading scientific journal:

> First of all, it is important to identify the main villain as overpopulation. In the good old days, . . . in truth there were famine, starvation, horses and buggies that contributed to pollution, fireplaces that spewed forth soot from burning soft coal, and water contaminated with microorganisms. The humans were so few, and the land so vast, that these insults to nature could be absorbed without serious consequences. This is no longer true.[2]

Half of this proposition concerns the behavior of human populations, which we take up here. The other half involves the sources of pollution and other environmental problems, a topic which is taken up in Section C.

Economic analysis of population dates back to the Reverend T. R. Malthus. He first developed his views while arguing at breakfast against his father's perfectionist opinion that the human race was always improving. Finally the son became so agitated that he wrote *An Essay on the Principle of Population* (1798), which was a best-seller and has since influenced the thinking of people all over the world about population and economic growth.

Malthus began with the observation of Benjamin Franklin that in the American colonies, where resources were abundant, population tended to double every 25 years or so. He then postulated a universal tendency for population—unless checked by limited food supply—to grow exponentially, or by a geometric progression. Eventually, a population which doubles

every generation—1, 2, 4, 8, 16, 32, 64, 128, 256, 512, 1024, . . .—becomes so large that there is not enough space in the world for all the people to stand.

Economics at Work: Compound Interest and Exponential Growth

Exponential growth and compound interest are important tools in economics. Exponential (or geometric) growth occurs when a variable increases at a constant proportional rate from period to period. Thus, if a population of 200 is growing at 3 percent per year, it would equal 200 in year 0, 200×1.03 in year 1, $200 \times 1.03 \times 1.03$ in year 2, . . . , $200 \times (1.03)^{10}$ in year 10, and so on.

When money is invested continuously, it earns compound interest, meaning that interest is earned on past interest. Money earning compound interest grows geometrically. An intriguing calculation is to determine how much the $24 received by the Indians for Manhattan Island would, if deposited at compound interest, be worth today. Say that this fund was placed in an endowment that earned 6 percent each year from 1626. It would be worth $90 billion in 2005.

A useful rule about compound interest is the **rule of 70**, which states that a magnitude growing at a rate of g per year will double in $(70/g)$ years. For example, a human population growing at 2 percent a year will double in 35 years, whereas if you invest your funds at 7 percent per year, the funds will double in value every 10 years.

After invoking compound interest, Malthus had one further card to play. At this point he unleashed the devil of diminishing returns. He argued that because land is fixed while labor inputs keep growing, the supply of food would tend to grow by an arithmetic progression and not by a geometric progression. (Compare 1, 2, 3, 4, . . . , with 1, 2, 4, 8, ...) Malthus concluded gloomily:

> As population doubles and redoubles, it is as if the globe were halving and halving again in size—until finally it has shrunk so much that food production has shrunk below the level necessary to support the population.

When the law of diminishing returns is applied to a fixed supply of land, food production tends not to keep up with a population's geometric-progression rate of growth.

---

[2] *Science*, Sept. 10, 1993, p. 1371.

Actually, Malthus did not say that population would necessarily increase at a geometric rate. This was only its tendency if unchecked. He described the checks that operate, in all times and places, to hold population down. In his first edition, he stressed the "positive" checks that increase the death rate: pestilence, famine, and war. Later, he held out hope that population growth could be slowed by "moral restraint" such as abstinence and postponed marriages.

This important application of diminishing returns illustrates the profound effects a simple theory can have. Malthus's ideas had wide repercussions. His book was used to support a stern revision of the English poor laws. Under the influence of Malthus's writings, people argued that poverty should be made as uncomfortable as possible. In this view, government cannot improve the welfare of the poor population since any increase in the incomes of the poor would only cause workers to reproduce until all were reduced to a bare subsistence.

Even today, the ghost of Malthus reappears in "doomsday" economics, such as a famous computer study called *The Limits to Growth* and its 1992 sequel *Beyond the Limits*. The predictions of this modern-day Malthusianism were even more dismal than the original gospel:

> If present growth trends in world population, industrialization, pollution, food problems, and resource depletion continue unchanged, the limits to growth on this planet will be reached within the next one hundred years. The most probable results will be a rather sudden and uncontrollable decline in both population and industrial capacity.[3]

Flawed Prophecies of Malthus. Despite Malthus's careful statistical studies, demographers today think that his views were oversimplified. In his discussion of diminishing returns, Malthus did not anticipate the technological miracle of the Industrial Revolution; nor did he understand that the birth-control movement and new technologies would provide families with the capability to reduce the birth rate. In fact, population growth in most Western nations began to decline after 1870 just as living standards and real wages grew most rapidly.

In the century following Malthus, technological advance shifted out the production-possibility frontiers of countries in Europe and North America. Indeed, technological change occurred so quickly that output far outpaced population, resulting in a rapid rise in real wages. Nevertheless, the germs of truth in Malthus's doctrines are still important for understanding population trends in poor countries where the race between population and food supply continues today.

WEALTHIER IS HEALTHIER

There is no doubt that as humans spread around the globe, they tend to displace trees, wolves, and marsh weeds to make way for farms, cities, and human settlements. But is it also true, as modern-day Malthusians suggest, that economic growth and industrialization are the road to environmental ruin?

No such simple conclusion can be read from the historical record. One important finding is that pollution trends tend to follow an inverse U-shaped curve across different stages of economic development (see Figure 18-1). The rising part of the curve

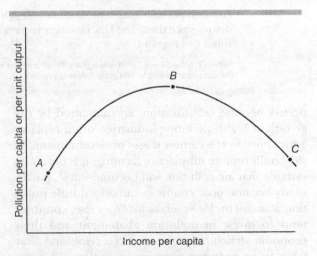

FIGURE 18-1. Pollution and Economic Growth

Does pollution increase with economic growth? Empirical studies indicate that pollution tends to follow an inverse U-shaped curve as incomes rise. At low levels of income at *A*, subsistence agriculture produces little pollution. Then, with initial stages of development, the growth of heavy industries without pollution controls leads to higher per capita pollution at *B*. Finally, with pollution abatement and the trend away from industry and toward services in advanced countries, pollution declines at *C*.

---

[3] See *The Limits to Growth*, p. 23, in this chapter's Further Reading section.

Pollution per Unit Output

FIGURE 18-2. Trends in Pollution in the United States, 1900–2000

Pollution per unit output peaked in the first half of the twentieth century and has declined sharply since then. The U.S. economy is currently in the downward-sloping region between B and C of Fig. 18-1.

Source: Environmental Protection Agency, Department of Energy, and Department of Commerce. For each pollutant, the quantity is divided by real gross domestic product.

occurs because urbanization, accompanied by the growth of highly polluting industries, often replaces agriculture in the earliest stages of development. As steel mills replace subsistence farming, it is nearly inevitable that air pollution will become worse, particularly because poor countries can afford little pollution abatement. However, as incomes rise, countries tend to invest in pollution abatement and their economic structures evolve toward services and away from heavy industry, reducing pollution. This can explain the inverse U-shaped pollution curve in Figure 18-1.

The longer-term trends in pollution in the United States bear out these theories. Figure 18-2 shows the amount of pollution per unit output over the last century for five major pollutants. For each, the ratio has declined sharply during the twentieth century.

What is the relationship between economic development and human health? Here, studies clearly indicate that human health is positively associated with per capita income and education—environmental degradation, such as poor sanitation and unsafe drinking water, is worst in the poorest countries. One of the most thoughtful students of the relationship among population, economic development, and pollution is Oxford's Wilfred Beckerman, who summarized his findings as follows:

> The important environmental problems for the 75% of the world's population that live in developing countries are local problems of access to safe drinking water or decent sanitation, and urban degradation. Furthermore, there is clear evidence that . . . in the end the best—and probably the only—way to attain a decent environment in most countries is to become rich.[4]

---

[4] See this chapter's Further Reading section for the Beckerman article.

B. NATURAL-RESOURCE ECONOMICS

RESOURCE CATEGORIES

What are the important natural resources? They include land, water, and the atmosphere. The land gives us food and wine from fertile soils, as well as oil and other minerals from the earth's mantle. Our waters give us fish, recreation, and a remarkably efficient medium for transportation. The precious atmosphere yields breathable air, beautiful sunsets, and flying space for airplanes. Natural resources and the environment are in one sense just another set of factors of production, like labor and capital. They serve humans because we derive output or satisfaction from their services.

Appropriable vs. Inappropriable Resources

In analyzing natural resources, economists make two key distinctions. The most important is whether the resources are appropriable or inappropriable. Recall that a commodity is called **appropriable** when firms or consumers can capture its full economic value. Appropriable natural resources include land (whose fertility can be captured by the farmer who sells wheat or wine produced on the land), mineral resources like oil and gas (where the owner can sell the value of the mineral deposit on markets), and trees (where the owner can sell the land or the trees to the highest bidder). In a well-functioning competitive market, we would expect that appropriable natural resources would be efficiently priced and allocated.

But a second category, known as **inappropriable** resources, can definitely cause economic problems. An inappropriable resource is one whose costs and benefits do not accrue to its owner. In other words, inappropriable resources are ones involving externalities. (Recall that *externalities* are those situations in which production or consumption imposes uncompensated costs or benefits on other parties.)

Examples of inappropriable resources are found in every corner of the globe. Consider, for instance, the depletion of stocks of many important fish, such as whales, tuna, herring, and sturgeon. A school of tuna can provide not only food for the dinner table but also stock for breeding future generations of tuna. Yet the breeding potential is not reflected in the market price of fish. No market buys or sells the mating behavior of yellowtail tuna. Consequently, when a fishing company pulls out a tuna, it does not compensate society for the depletion of future breeding potential. This is why unregulated fisheries often tend to be overfished.

This leads to one of the fundamental results of the economics of resources and the environment:

When markets do not capture all the costs and benefits of using natural resources, and there are important externalities, markets give the wrong signals and prices are distorted. Markets generally produce too much of goods that generate negative externalities and too little of goods that produce positive externalities.

Renewable vs. Nonrenewable Resources

Techniques used for managing resources depend on whether the resources are renewable or nonrenewable. A **nonrenewable resource** is one whose services are essentially fixed in supply or which does not regenerate quickly. Important examples are the fossil fuels, which were laid down millions of years ago and can be treated as fixed for human civilizations, and nonfuel mineral resources, such as copper, silver, gold, stone, and sand.

A second category is **renewable resources,** whose services are replenished regularly and which, if properly managed, can yield useful services indefinitely. Solar energy, agricultural land, river water, forests, and fisheries are among the most important categories of renewable resources.

The principles of efficient management of these two classes of resources present quite different challenges, as we will see below. Efficient use of a nonrenewable resource entails the distribution of a finite quantity of the resource over time: Should we use our low-cost natural gas for this generation or save it for the future? By contrast, prudent use of renewable resources involves ensuring that the flow of services is efficiently maintained, say, through appropriate forest management, protection of breeding grounds of fish, or regulation of pollution into rivers and lakes.

Table 18-1 shows this fundamental division of resources along with major examples of each.

	Renewable	Nonrenewable
Appropriable	Timber, agricultural land, solar energy	Oil, natural gas, copper
Inappropriable	Fisheries, air quality, mountain views	Climate, radioactive wastes

TABLE 18-1. Resource Classification

Resources are classified as appropriable or inappropriable according to whether there are significant externalities involved in their production or consumption. In addition, for nonrenewable resources, like oil and natural gas, the economic question is how to allocate the finite resource over space and time. For renewable resources, like timber or fisheries, the key issue is prudent management so that the yield maximizes the value of the resource.

ALLOCATION OF APPROPRIABLE NATURAL RESOURCES

Our survey begins with appropriable natural resources—those which are privately owned and whose costs and benefits are largely captured in the marketplace. What are the most important appropriable natural-resource industries? Table 18-2 shows the value added in each of the major industries as measured in the national income and product accounts. The total of all marketed natural-resource industries constituted 2.6 percent of total output in 2001; two industries, farming and oil and gas, accounted for two-thirds of the economic output of the marketed natural resources.

Even though the share of resources in total income is low, it would be foolish to be complacent and assume that resources are unimportant for economic

Sector	Value added, 2001* ($, billion)	Percentage of gross domestic product, 2001
Renewable-resource industries		1.1
Farming	80.6	
Forestry and fisheries	17.2	
Renewable power generation	10.4	
Nonrenewable-resource industries		1.5
Oil and natural gas	110.3	
Coal	10.5	
Other nonfuel minerals:		
Geologically scarce[†]	8.8	
Geologically superabundant[‡]	2.9	
Stone, clay, sand, etc.	16.8	

*Total sales less purchases of materials; includes profit, wages, interest, rent, depreciation, and taxes.

[†]Includes 17 minerals such as copper, gold, silver, and vanadium.

[‡]Includes minerals such as iron and aluminum.

TABLE 18-2. Production from Different Resources, 2001

Many important goods and services are produced from renewable and nonrenewable resources. Estimates of total output or sales include not only the economic value of the natural resource but also the returns to capital and labor.

Source: "Benchmark Input-Output for 1997," available at www.bea.gov, and Robert Gordon et al., *Toward a New Iron Age?* (Yale University Press, New Haven, 1989).

growth. Might we not someday exhaust some essential natural resource, like energy, and find ourselves devoting much effort to finding replacement power? Nothing would plunge a modern industrial economy into chaos and poverty more quickly than exhausting the fuels for computers, cars, hospitals, and electric motors. This is worrisome because 90 percent of American energy consumption today comes from finite, nonrenewable sources like oil, gas, and coal. Should we be taking steps to limit the use of these most precious stocks of society's capital so that they will still be available for our grandchildren?

Economists answer this question in two ways. First, they point out that fossil fuels like oil and gas are limited but not "essential." An *essential* resource is one, like oxygen, for which there are no substitutes. Substitutes exist for all the energy resources. We can substitute coal for oil and gas in most uses; we can liquefy or gasify coal where liquid or gas fuels are needed; when coal runs out, we can use higher-cost solar energy, nuclear fission, and perhaps someday even nuclear fusion. These last three are superabundant in the sense that when we run out of solar energy, the earth will already be uninhabitable.

A second point concerns the relative productivity of different assets. Many environmentalists argue that energy and other natural resources like wilderness areas and old-growth forests are very special kinds of capital that need to be preserved so that we can maintain "sustainable" economic growth.

Economists have a different point of view. They tend to regard natural resources as a special category of productive assets—along with fast computers, human capital in an educated workforce, and technological knowledge in its software, scientists, and engineers. Both economists and environmentalists agree that this generation should leave an adequate stock of capital assets for future generations; but economists focus less on the exact form of capital than on its productivity. Economists ask, Would future generations benefit more from larger stocks of natural capital such as oil, gas, and coal or from more produced capital such as additional scientists, better laboratories, and libraries linked together by information superhighways?

The substitutability of natural capital and other kinds of capital is shown by the production indifference curve or "isoquant" in Figure 18-3. We show

FIGURE 18-3. Natural Capital and Produced Capital Are Substitutes in Production

Output can be produced with either natural capital (K_N) or human capital (K_H). This equal-product curve shows the combination of inputs that will yield a given amount of output in the future (Q^*). Environmentalists urge conserving natural capital so that future stocks are large, as at *C*. Economists emphasize the need to ensure that scarce capital goes to sectors with the highest yield. If natural capital is abundant, it would be more efficient to go to point *B*, where we consume stocks of natural capital today while building up stocks of human capital and improving technology through research and development.

there the amounts of the two kinds of capital that would be required to attain a certain level of output in the future (Q^*), holding other inputs constant. That output can be produced at point *C* with a conservationist policy that emphasizes reducing energy use today, leaving much oil and gas and relatively little human capital for the future. Or it might be produced with a low-energy-price and high-education strategy at *B*. Either of these is feasible, and the more desirable one is the one that has a higher consumption both now and in the future.

Note as well that the isoquant hits the vertical axis at point *A*, indicating that we can produce future output level Q^* *with no oil and gas*. How is this possible? With the greater scientific and technical knowledge represented by point *A*, society can develop and introduce substitute technologies like clean coal or solar energy to replace the exhausted oil and gas. The curve hits the axis to indicate that in the long run, oil and gas are not essential.

Resource Price Trends

In 1973, following a war and an embargo in the Mideast, the price of oil skyrocketed, and many other resource prices also moved sharply upward. Many people feared that the world was on the verge of running out of its key nonrenewable resources. Even experts in the oil industry forecast oil prices to be $100 to $200 per barrel by the year 2000 in today's dollars.

Three decades later, the price of oil was far below the forecasts. Adjusting for overall inflation, the price of oil is barely higher now than it was before the oil-price shocks of the 1970s occurred. Surprisingly, the same is true for almost every natural resource—prices

have been falling rather than rising in the long run. Figure 18-4 shows the price trends of a number of resources compared to the price of labor over the last half-century. All have become less scarce relative to labor, although periods of shortages, such as the 1970s, have reversed the trends temporarily.

Looking at this issue from another vantage point, if the resource pessimists were correct, we would expect that an ever-growing fraction of our economy would be devoted to producing natural resources. In fact, the share of resource industries in the total economy has been declining for two centuries. Figure 18-5 shows the percentage of total national output in agriculture, forestry, fisheries, mining, and resource utilities. These industries formed about 13 percent of the economy in the late 1940s but declined to 5 percent of the economy by 2001. Most of the decline came in agriculture, for reasons that were described in

FIGURE 18-4. Prices of Most Resources Have Fallen Relative to Labor's Wage

For most natural resources, productivity and new discoveries have offset depletion, so their market prices have fallen relative to the price of labor, or the wage rate. This is illustrated for four important natural resources. The long-term decline was reversed in the 1970s during the period of resource scarcity, but the trend then continued in the last quarter-century.

Source: Bureau of Labor Statistics and Department of Energy.

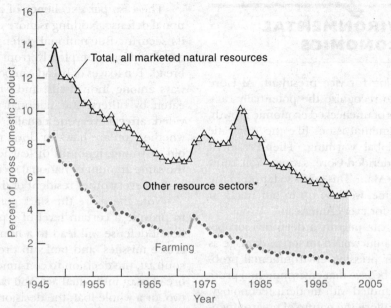

*Other resource sectors include forestry, fisheries, mining, electric, gas, and water utilities.

FIGURE 18-5. Appropriable Natural Resources Are Declining Relative to Economy

Over the last half-century, the share of natural-resource activities has shrunk dramatically. The downward trend is primarily due to the declining importance of farming, while other marketed natural resources have kept pace with the rest of the economy.

Source: Data show the shares of industrial gross product originating in total GDP from U.S. Commerce Department.

Chapter 4. The impact of the oil crises of the 1970s is shown as bumps in Figure 18-5, as oil and gas prices and their share of the national economy spiked upward, but the downward trend resumed in the beginning of the 1980s.

What lies behind these trends? The answer parallels our discussion of Malthus, above. In reality, the price-reducing influence of technological change and new discoveries has offset the price-increasing effect of depletion. For example, copper telephone wires are being replaced by fiber-optic cables, which use much cheaper and more plentiful raw materials. This same phenomenon is occurring in most of the natural-resource sectors.

The Resource Wager

In 1980 Julian Simon, an economist and a leading advocate of the cornucopian school, issued a challenge to the environmental pessimists. Offering to let them pick any natural resources they wanted, Simon, who believed that technology could find substitutes for any depleted resources, was willing to bet that the prices of the chosen resources would fall, and not rise.

Simon's challenge was taken up by Paul Ehrlich, a noted biologist and environmentalist. Ehrlich first came to fame in 1968 as author of *The Population Bomb*, in which he predicted imminent famines across the world. In a later book, he forecast shortages of key raw materials by 1985. Not surprisingly, Ehrlich found Simon's offer irresistible. Ehrlich bet $1000 that the prices of five metals—chrome, copper, nickel, tin, and tungsten—would rise by 1990, after adjustment for inflation.

Simon won hands down. After adjusting for inflation, the prices of all five metals dropped sharply over the decade (see Figure 18-4 for the general trend). Ehrlich had not only overlooked the long-term relative trend in resource prices but had the bad fortune to pick a decade in which the business cycle reinforced longer-term forces.

C. ENVIRONMENTAL ECONOMICS

When he was running for vice president, Al Gore spoke of the need to recognize the potentially catastrophic implications of unchecked economic growth, pointing to environmental issues like the Antarctic ozone hole and global warming. Then-President George H. W. Bush derided Gore, saying, "You know why I call him Ozone Man? This guy is so far off in the environmental extreme, we'll be up to our necks in owls and out of work for every American."

This political debate mirrors a deep division between those who see injury piled on top of damage as nations neglect their pressing environmental problems and others who believe that environmental problems can be easily handled with modern technology. In this section, we explore the nature of environmental externalities, describe why they produce economic inefficiencies, and analyze potential remedies.

EXTERNALITIES

We have already met the concept of an *externality*, which is an activity that imposes involuntary costs or benefits on others, or an activity whose effects are not completely reflected in prices and market transactions.

Externalities come in many guises. Some are positive, while others are negative. Thus when a firm dumps toxic wastes into a stream, it may kill fish and plants and reduce the stream's value for recreation. This is a negative or harmful externality because the firm does not compensate people for the damages. When you discover a better way to clean up oil spills, the benefit will extend to many people who do not pay you for it. This is a positive or beneficial externality.

Some externalities are pervasive, while others have only small spillover components. When a carrier of bubonic plague entered a town during the Middle Ages, the entire population could be felled by the Black Death. On the other hand, when you eat an onion at a football stadium on a windy day, the external impacts are hardly noticeable.

Public vs. Private Goods

A polar case of an externality is a *public good*, which is a commodity that can be provided to everyone as easily as it can be provided to one person.

The case par excellence of a public good is national defense. Nothing is more vital to a society than its security. But national defense, as an economic good, differs completely from a *private good* like bread. Ten loaves of bread can be divided up in many ways among individuals, and what I eat cannot be eaten by others. But national defense, once provided, affects everyone equally. It matters not at all whether you are hawk or dove, pacifist or militarist, old or young, ignorant or learned—you will receive the same amount of national security from the Army as does every other resident of the country.

Note therefore the stark contrast: The decision to provide a certain level of a public good like national defense will lead to a number of submarines, cruise missiles, and tanks to protect each of us. By contrast, the decision to consume a private good like bread is an individual act. You can eat four slices, or two, or a whole loaf; the decision is purely your own and does not commit anyone else to a particular amount of bread consumption.

The example of national defense is a dramatic and extreme case of a public good. But when you think of a smallpox vaccine, a park concert, a dam upstream on a river that prevents flood damage downstream, or many similar government projects, you generally find elements of public goods involved. In summary:

Public goods are ones whose benefits are indivisibly spread among the entire community, whether or not individuals desire to purchase the public good. **Private goods,** by contrast, are ones that can be divided up and provided separately to different individuals, with no external benefits or costs to others. Efficient provision of public goods often requires government action, while private goods can be efficiently allocated by markets.

Global Public Goods

Perhaps the thorniest of all market failures are global public goods. These are externalities whose impacts are indivisibly spread across the entire globe. Important examples are actions to slow global warming (considered later in this chapter), measures to prevent ozone depletion, or the discovery of new products (like a malaria vaccine).

Global public goods pose particular problems because there are no effective market or political mechanisms available to allocate them efficiently. Markets here routinely fail because individuals do not have appropriate incentives to produce them, while national governments cannot capture all the benefits of investments in global public goods.

Why do global public goods differ from other goods? If a terrible storm destroys much of America's corn crop, the price system will guide farmers and consumers to equilibrate needs and availabilities. If America's public road system needs modernization, voters will lobby the government to develop an efficient transportation system. But if problems arise concerning global public goods, such as global warming or antibiotic resistance, neither market participants nor national governments have appropriate incentives to find an efficient outcome. The marginal cost of investments to any individual or nation is much less than the global marginal benefits, and underinvestment is the certain outcome.

MARKET INEFFICIENCY WITH EXTERNALITIES

Abraham Lincoln said that government is "to do for the people what needs to be done, but which they cannot, by individual effort, do at all, or do so well, for themselves." Pollution control satisfies this guideline since the market mechanism does not provide an adequate check on polluters. Firms will not voluntarily restrict emissions of noxious chemicals, nor will they always abstain from dumping toxic wastes in landfills. Pollution control is therefore generally held to be a legitimate government function.

Analysis of Inefficiency

Why do externalities like pollution lead to economic inefficiency? Take a hypothetical coal-burning electric utility. Dirty Light & Power generates an externality by spewing out tons of noxious sulfur dioxide fumes. Some of the sulfur harms the utility, requiring more frequent repainting and raising the firm's medical bills. But most of the damage is "external" to the firm, settling throughout the region, harming vegetation and buildings and causing various kinds of respiratory ailments and even premature death in people.

Being a sound profit-maximizing enterprise, Dirty Light & Power must decide how much pollution it should emit. With no pollution cleanup, its workers and plant will suffer. Cleaning up every molecule, on the other hand, will require heavy expenses for low-sulfur, cleaner fuels, recycling systems, scrubbing equipment, and so forth. A complete cleanup would cost so much that Dirty Light & Power could not hope to survive in the marketplace.

The managers therefore decide to clean up just to the point where the benefits to the firm from additional *abatement* or pollution removal (marginal private benefits) are equal to the extra cost of cleanup (marginal cost of abatement). The firm's accountants estimate that the marginal private benefits are $10 per ton of sulfur dioxide removed. Further, the firm's engineers tell management that removing the fiftieth of the 400 tons normally emitted will have a marginal cost of $10 per ton. The firm has found its private optimal level of pollution abatement of 50 tons, at which the marginal private benefit to the firm just equals the marginal private cost of abatement. Put differently, when Dirty Light & Power produces electricity in a least-cost manner, weighing only private costs and benefits, it will set its pollution at 350 tons and remove 50 tons.

Suppose, however, that a team of environmental scientists and economists is asked to examine the overall impacts on society rather than the impacts affecting only Dirty Light & Power. In examining the total impacts, the auditors find that the marginal social benefits of pollution control—including improved health and increased property values in neighboring regions—are 10 times the marginal private benefits. The impact from each extra ton on Dirty Light & Power is $10, but the rest of society suffers an additional impact of $90 per ton of external costs. Why doesn't Dirty Light & Power include the $90 of additional social benefits in its calculations? The $90 is excluded because these benefits are external to the firm and have no effect on its profits.

We now see how pollution and other externalities lead to inefficient economic outcomes: In an unregulated environment, firms will determine their most profitable pollution levels by equating the marginal private benefit from abatement with the marginal private cost of abatement. When the pollution spillovers are significant, the private equilibrium will produce inefficiently high levels of pollution and too little cleanup activity.

Socially Efficient Pollution. Given that private decisions on pollution control are inefficient, is there a better solution? Should pollution be completely prohibited? Should we require the damaged parties to negotiate with the polluters or allow them to sue for damages? Is there an engineering solution?

In general, economists look to determine the socially efficient level of pollution by balancing social costs and benefits. More precisely, *efficiency requires that the marginal social benefits from abatement equal the marginal social costs of abatement.* This equality occurs when the marginal benefits to the nation's health and property of reducing pollution by 1 unit just equal the marginal costs of that reduction.

How might an efficient level of pollution be determined? Economists recommend an approach known as *cost-benefit analysis,* in which efficient standards are set by balancing the marginal costs of an action against the marginal benefits of that action. In the case of Dirty Light & Power, suppose that experts study the cost data for abatement and environmental damage. They determine that marginal social costs and marginal social benefits are equalized when the amount of abatement is increased from 50 tons to 250 tons. At the efficient pollution rate, they find that the marginal costs of abatement are $40 per ton, while the marginal social benefits from the last unit removed are also $40 per ton.

Why is it efficient for the firm to emit 150 tons (abate 250 tons) rather than emit 400 tons (abate 0 tons)? Because at this emissions rate the net social value of production is maximized. If Dirty Light & Power were to emit more than 150 tons of pollution, the extra environmental damage would outweigh the cost savings from lower abatement. On the other hand, if pollution were to be cut below 150 tons, the marginal costs of pollution cleanup would be greater than the marginal benefits from cleaner air. Here again, as in many areas, we find the most efficient outcome by equating marginal cost and marginal benefit of an activity.

Cost-benefit analysis will show why extreme "no-risk" or "zero-discharge" policies are generally wasteful. Reducing pollution to zero would generally impose astronomically high cleanup costs, while the marginal benefits of reducing the last few grams of pollution may be quite modest. In some cases, it may even be impossible to continue to produce with zero emissions, so a no-risk philosophy might require closing down the computer industry or banning all vehicular traffic. Generally, economic efficiency calls for a compromise, balancing the extra value of the industry's output against the extra damage from pollution.

An unregulated market economy will generate levels of pollution (or other externalities) at which the marginal private benefit of abatement equals the marginal private cost of abatement. Efficiency requires that marginal social benefit equal marginal social abatement cost. In an unregulated economy, there will be too little abatement and too much pollution.

Valuing Damages

One of the major difficulties involved in setting efficient environmental policies arises because of the need to estimate the benefits of pollution control and other policies. As we described above, efficient management of the environment requires balancing the impacts and costs on the margin of additional pollution. For example, if emissions fees are equal to the marginal damages, we need to calculate damages from pollution.

In cases where pollution affects only marketed goods and services, the measurement is relatively straightforward. If a warmer climate reduces wheat yields, we can measure the damage by the change in the net value of the wheat. Similarly, if a new road requires tearing down someone's house, we can calculate the market value of a replacement dwelling.

Unfortunately, many types of environmental damage, particularly in nonmarket sectors, are much harder to value. For example, environmentalists recently called for a ban on logging across much of the Pacific northwest in order to preserve the habitat of the spotted owl. That would cost thousands of logging jobs and raise lumber prices. How should we value the benefits in terms of the continued existence of the spotted owl? Or, to take another example, the *Exxon Valdez* oil spill in Prince William Sound, Alaska, damaged beaches and killed wildlife. How much is the life of a sea otter worth?

Economists have developed several approaches for estimating impacts, such as those on owls and otters, that do not show up directly in market prices. The most reliable techniques examine the impact of environmental damage on different activities and then put market-derived values on those activities. For example, in estimating the impact of emissions of sulfur dioxide, environmental economists first estimate the impact of higher emissions on health, and they then place a dollar value on health changes using either survey techniques or estimates that are revealed by people's actual behavior.

Some of the most difficult cases occur in situations that involve ecosystems and the survival of different species. How much should society pay to ensure that the spotted owl survives? Most people will never see a spotted owl, just as they will never see a whooping crane or actually visit Prince William Sound. They may nevertheless place a value on these natural resources. Some environmental economists use a technique called *contingent valuation,* which involves asking people how much they would be willing to pay in a hypothetical situation, say, to keep some natural resource undamaged. This technique will yield answers, but they have not always proved to be reliable.

Few would doubt that a healthy and clean environment has a high value, but placing reliable values on the environment, particularly on the nonmarket components, has proved a difficult business.

Graphical Analysis of Pollution

We can illustrate these points with the help of Figure 18-6. The upward-sloping market *MC* curve is the marginal cost of abatement. The downward-sloping curves are the marginal benefits of reducing pollution, with the upper solid *MSB* line being the marginal social benefit from less pollution while the lower *MPB* line is the marginal private benefit of abatement to the polluter.

FIGURE 18-6. Inefficiency from Externalities

When marginal social benefit (*MSB*) diverges from marginal private benefit (*MPB*), markets will generate unregulated equilibrium at *I*, with too little abatement or pollution cleanup. Efficient cleanup comes at *E*, where *MSB* equals *MC*.

> **Warning on Graphing Pollution**
>
> In analyzing pollution, it is useful to think of pollution control or abatement as a "good." In the graphs, we therefore measure marginal costs and benefits on the vertical axis and the abatement or pollution removed on the horizontal axis. The trick here is to remember that because pollution removal is a good, it is measured positively on the horizontal axis. You can also think of pollution as measured negatively from the far-right point of 400. So abatement of zero is pollution of 400, while abatement of 400 means zero pollution.

The unregulated market solution comes at point *I*, where the marginal private costs and benefits are equated. At this point, only 50 tons are removed, and the marginal private costs and benefits are $10 per ton. But the unregulated market solution is inefficient. We can see this by performing an experiment that increases abatement by 10 tons; this is represented by the thin slice to the right of point *I*. For this additional removal, the marginal benefits are given by the total area of the slice under the *MSB* curve, while the marginal costs are given by the area of the slice under the *MC* curve. The net benefits are that part of the slice shown by the shaded area between the two curves.

The efficient level of pollution comes at point *E*, where marginal social benefits are equated to marginal costs of abatement. At that point, both *MSB* and *MC* are equal to $40 per ton. Also, because *MSB* and *MC* are equal, the experiment of increasing abatement by a tiny amount will find that there is no difference between the curves, so there is no net benefit from additional pollution control. We can also measure the net benefits of the efficient solution relative to the unregulated market by taking all the little slices of net benefit from the shaded slice to point *E*. This calculation shows that the area *ISE* represents the gains from efficient removal of pollutants.

As a final experiment, consider a zero-risk philosophy which desired to remove every last particle of pollution—here, abatement would be 400 units. In Figure 18-6, the marginal social benefits are zero with no pollution at point *B* because the last particle does no harm. By contrast, the marginal costs are relatively high at point *Z*. (We also show a special

case, illustrated by the dashed *MC′* line, where the marginal costs become astronomical with zero pollution. For example, it would be enormously expensive to reduce *all* the pollution from energy use.)

By adding up all the little slices to the right of the efficient point, we can calculate that the excess costs of a zero-risk approach are given by the area *EZB*. This example shows why economists are skeptical of approaches that advocate reducing pollution to zero—they would probably bankrupt the economy.

POLICIES TO CORRECT EXTERNALITIES

What are the weapons that can be used to combat inefficiencies arising from externalities? The most visible activities are government antipollution programs that use either direct controls or financial incentives to induce firms to correct externalities. More subtle approaches use enhanced property rights to give the private sector the instruments for negotiating efficient solutions. We survey these approaches in this section.

Government Programs

Direct Controls. For almost all pollution, as well as other health and safety externalities, governments rely on direct regulatory controls; these are often called *social regulations* (see Chapter 17). For example, the 1970 Clean Air Act reduced allowable emissions of three major pollutants by 90 percent. In 1977, utilities were told to reduce sulfur emissions at new plants by 90 percent. In a series of regulations over the last decades, firms were told they must phase out ozone-depleting chemicals. And so it goes with regulation.

How does the government enforce a pollution regulation? To continue our example of Dirty Light & Power, the state Department of Environmental Protection might tell Dirty Light & Power to increase its abatement to 250 tons of particulate matter. Under *command-and-control regulations,* the regulator would simply order the firm to comply, giving detailed instructions on what pollution-control technology to use and where to apply it. There would be little scope for novel approaches or tradeoffs within the firm or across firms. *If* standards are appropriately set—a very big "if"—the outcome might approach the efficient pollution level described in the previous part of this section.

While it is possible that the regulator might choose a combination of pollution-control edicts that guarantees economic efficiency, in practice that is not very likely. Indeed, much pollution control suffers from extensive government failures. For example, pollution regulations are often set without comparisons of marginal costs and marginal benefits, and without such comparisons there is no way to determine the most efficient level of pollution control. Indeed, for some regulatory programs, the law specifically prohibits cost-benefit comparison as a way of setting standards.

In addition, standards are inherently a very blunt tool. Efficient pollution reduction requires that the marginal cost of pollution be equalized across all sources of pollution. Command-and-control regulations generally do not allow differentiation across firms, regions, or industries. Hence, regulations are usually the same for large firms and small firms, for cities and rural areas, and for high-polluting and low-polluting industries. Even though firm A might be able to reduce a ton of pollution at a tiny fraction of the cost to firm B, both firms will be required to meet the same standard; nor will there be any incentives for the low-cost firm to reduce pollution more than the standard even though it would be economical to do just that. Study after study has confirmed that our environmental goals have proved unnecessarily costly because we have used command-and-control regulation.

Market Solution: Emissions Fees. In order to avoid some of the pitfalls of direct controls, many economists have suggested that environmental policy rely more on economic incentives than on government commands. One approach is the use of *emissions fees,* which would require that firms pay a tax on their pollution equal to the amount of external damage it causes. If Dirty Light & Power were imposing external marginal costs of $35 per ton on the surrounding community, the appropriate emissions charge would be $35 per ton. This is in effect *internalizing* the externality by making the firm face the social costs of its activities. In calculating its private costs, Dirty Light & Power would find that, at point *E* in Figure 18-6, an additional ton of pollution would cost it $5 of internal costs to the firm plus $35 in emissions fees, for an overall marginal cost of $40 per ton of pollution. By equating the new marginal *private* benefit (private benefit plus emissions fee) with the marginal abatement cost,

the firm would curb its pollution back to the efficient level. *If* the emissions fee were correctly calculated—another big "if"—profit-minded firms would be led as if by a mended invisible hand to the efficient point where marginal social costs and marginal social benefits of pollution are equal.

The alternative approaches are shown graphically in Figure 18-7, which is similar to Figure 18-6 except we have simplified it by removing the marginal private-benefit curve. With the direct-control approach, the government simply instructs the firm to remove 250 tons of pollutants (or to emit no more than 150 tons). This would in effect place the standard at the heavy vertical line. If the standard were set at the right level, the firm would undertake the socially efficient level of abatement. Hence, with efficient regulation, the firm will choose point *E*, with *MSB* equal to *MC*.

What about the case of emissions fees? Say that the government charges the firm $35 per ton of pollutant emitted. In effect, this means that the marginal private benefit of abatement would go from $5 to $40 per ton. Faced with this incentive, the firm would again choose efficient point *E* in Figure 18-7.

FIGURE 18-7. Pollution Standards and Emissions Fees

When government sets the pollution limitation at 150 tons, or requires removal of 250 tons, this standard will lead to efficient pollution at point *E*. The same result can be achieved with pollution fees of $35 per ton: at a $35-per-ton fee plus $5 per ton of marginal private damage, the sum will equal marginal cost and lead to efficient abatement at point *E*.

Market Solution: Tradeable Emissions Permits. A new approach that does not require the government to legislate taxes is the use of tradeable emissions permits. With this approach, instead of telling firms that they must pay $x per unit of pollution and then allowing firms to choose the level of pollution, the government chooses the level of pollution and allocates the appropriate number of permits. The price of permits, which represents the level of the emissions fee, is then set by supply and demand in the market for permits. Assuming that firms know their costs of production and abatement, the tradeable-permits approach has the same outcome as the emissions-fee approach. One major difference between the two approaches is that the government often allocates emissions permits to firms to win their political support. This means that industry gets the revenues from the permits, while the government gets the revenues from emissions fees.

Economic Innovations: Trading Pollution Permits

Most environmental regulations use a command-and-control approach that limits the emissions from individual sources, such as power plants or automobiles. This approach cannot cap overall emissions. More importantly, it virtually guarantees that the overall program is extremely inefficient because it does not satisfy the condition that emissions from all sources must have equal marginal costs of abatement.

In 1990, the United States introduced a radical new approach to environmental control in its program on control of sulfur dioxide, which is one of the most harmful environmental pollutants. Under the 1990 Clean Air Act amendments, the government issues a certain number of permits to emit sulfur dioxide each year for the entire country. By 2000, emissions were required to be reduced by 50 percent relative to 1990 levels. The innovative aspect of the plan is that the permits are freely tradeable. Electric utilities receive pollution permits and are allowed to buy and sell them with each other just like pork bellies or wheat. Those firms which can reduce their sulfur emissions most cheaply do so and sell their permits to pollute; other firms which need additional permits for new plants or have no leeway to reduce emissions find it economical to buy permits rather than install expensive antipollution equipment or shut down.

Environmental economists believe that the enhanced incentives allow the ambitious targets to be met at a much lower cost than would be paid under traditional command-and-control regulation. Studies by economist Tom Tietenberg of Colby College in Maine have determined that the traditional approaches cost 2 to 10 times as much as would cost-effective regulations like emissions trading.

The behavior of this market has produced a big surprise. Originally, the government projected that permits in the early years would sell for around $300 per ton of sulfur dioxide. But in practice, the market price in the early years fell to below $100 per ton. One reason for the success was that the program gave strong incentives for firms to innovate, and firms found that low-sulfur coal could be used much more easily and cheaply than had earlier been anticipated. This important experiment has given powerful support to economists who argue for market-based approaches to environmental policy.

Private Approaches

It is generally thought that some form of government intervention in the market is necessary to overcome the market failures associated with pollution and other externalities. In some cases, however, strong property rights and liability laws can substitute for government regulations or taxes.

One private-sector approach relies upon *liability laws* rather than upon direct government regulations. Under this approach, the legal system makes the generator of externalities legally liable for any damages caused to other persons. In effect, by imposing an appropriate liability system, the externality is internalized.

In some areas, this doctrine is well established. For example, in most states, if you are injured by a negligent driver, you can sue for damages. Or if you are injured or become ill from a defective product, the company can be sued for product liability.

While liability rules are in principle an attractive means of internalizing the nonmarket costs of production, they are quite limited in practice. They usually involve high litigation costs, which add an additional cost to the original externality. In addition, many damages cannot be litigated because of incomplete property rights (such as those involving clean air) or because of the large number of companies that contribute to the externality (as in the case of chemicals flowing into a stream).

A second private approach relies upon strong property rights and *negotiations among parties*. This approach was developed by the University of Chicago's Ronald Coase, who showed that voluntary negotiations among the affected parties can sometimes lead to an efficient outcome.

For example, suppose that I am a farmer using fertilizers that flow downstream and kill many of the fish in your ponds. Further, suppose that you cannot sue me for killing your fish. If your fish business is sufficiently profitable, you may try to get me to reduce my fertilizer use *even if you cannot sue me*. In other words, if there is a net profit to be made from reorganizing our joint operations, we have a powerful incentive to get together and agree on the efficient level of fertilizer runoff. Moreover, this incentive would exist without any government antipollution program or liability system.

Where property rights are well defined and transaction costs are low, particularly when there are few affected parties, strong liability laws or negotiation can sometimes operate to produce an efficient resolution in the presence of externalities.

CLIMATE CHANGE: TO SLOW OR NOT TO SLOW

Of all the environmental issues, none is so worrisome to scientists as the threat of global warming from the greenhouse effect. Climatologists and other scientists warn that the accumulation of gases like carbon dioxide (CO_2) largely produced by the combustion of fossil fuels, is likely to lead to global warming and other significant climatic changes over the next century. On the basis of climate models, scientists project that if current trends continue, the earth may warm 4 to 8° Fahrenheit over the next century. This would take the earth's climate out of the range experienced during the entire period of human civilization.

The greenhouse effect is the granddaddy of public-good problems; actions today will affect the climate for all people in all countries for centuries to come. The costs of reducing CO_2 emissions come in the near term as countries cut back their use of fossil fuels by conserving energy and using alternative energy sources (solar energy or perhaps nuclear power), plant trees,

and take other measures. In the short run, that means we will have to accept more expensive energy, lower living standards, and lower consumption levels. The benefits of emissions reductions will come many years in the future, when lower emissions reduce future climate-induced damages—with less disruption to agriculture, seacoasts, and ecosystems.

Economists have begun to study the economic impacts of climate change in order to understand how nations might undertake sensible strategies. Economic studies indicate that the market economies in advanced countries like the United States are likely to be relatively insulated from climate change in the coming decades. The major impacts are likely to be in agriculture and on unmanaged ecosystems such as forests, fisheries, and coral reefs. Many scientists are concerned about the potential for abrupt climate changes, which might shift weather patterns dramatically in a few years. Such prospects are genuinely frightening, but there are currently no reliable ways of assessing their likelihood.

An efficient strategy for containing climate change requires weighing the marginal costs of reducing CO_2 emissions against the marginal benefits. Figure 18-8 shows schematically the marginal costs of reductions as *MC* and the marginal social benefits as

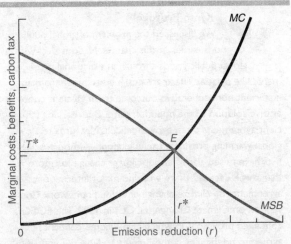

FIGURE 18-8. Carbon Taxes Can Slow Harmful Climate Change

Slowing climate change efficiently requires setting carbon taxes at T^* or limiting carbon dioxide emissions to r^* to balance marginal costs of reductions with marginal benefits of reducing damages from climate change.

MSB. The vertical axis measures costs and benefits in dollars, while the horizontal axis measures emissions reductions in percent reduction of carbon dioxide. Point *E* in the graph represents the efficient point at which marginal abatement costs equal marginal benefits from slowing climate change. This is the point which maximizes the present value of future human consumption. By contrast, the pure-market solution comes with emissions reductions at 0, where *MSB* is far above the zero *MC.* An extreme environmentalist solution, which attempts to avoid any disruption to natural ecosystems, comes at the right-hand edge of the graph, where *MC* far exceeds *MSB.*

How can point *E*, the efficient level of CO_2 reduction, be achieved? Since CO_2 emissions come from burning carbon-containing fuels, some have suggested a "carbon tax" on the carbon content of fuels. Fuels which contain more carbon, like coal, would be taxed more heavily than low-carbon fuels like natural gas. Economists have developed models that estimate efficient paths for carbon taxes—ones that balance the costs of higher taxes with the benefits of reduced damages from global warming. These models can serve as a guide to policymakers as they design policies to combat global warming.

Global Public Goods and the Kyoto Protocol

We discussed the problem of global public goods earlier in this chapter. Nations deal with global public goods through international agreements like treaties. These are designed to move from an inefficient noncooperative outcome to an efficient cooperative solution to the pollution game. But reaching efficient agreements often proves difficult. Measures to slow global warming provide a useful example. Although scientists have raised alarms about climate change for more than three decades, there were no major international agreements on climate change until the Framework Convention on Climate Change (FCCC) in 1992. The FCCC contained provisions in which high-income countries agreed to nonbinding commitments to limit the emissions of greenhouse gases like CO_2.

When voluntary measures were ineffective, countries negotiated the 1997 Kyoto Protocol on climate change. Under the protocol, high-income countries along with formerly socialist countries agreed to *binding commitments* to reduce by 2010 their total emissions of greenhouse gases by 5 percent (relative to 1990 levels). Each country was allocated a specific target. Based on both economic theory and the experience of the U.S. sulfur dioxide trading program (discussed above), the Kyoto Protocol included a provision for emissions trading among countries.

Economists have undertaken detailed analyses of the Kyoto Protocol. The major conclusions are, first, that limiting greenhouse-gas emissions is likely to be an expensive undertaking. Economic models estimate that the present value of the global abatement costs of an extended Kyoto Protocol would be about $1 trillion in 2000 prices. A second conclusion is that limiting the Kyoto Protocol to high-income and formerly socialist countries significantly reduces its cost-effectiveness. By excluding energy-intensive developing countries like China, the cost of meeting the global emissions goal is raised by a factor of between two and four relative to a cost-effective global agreement.

Many studies indicated that the United States would carry the major economic burden of implementing the Kyoto Protocol. Because of its rapid economic growth and falling energy prices, emissions of carbon dioxide in the United States were growing much more rapidly than in the other participating countries. Partly because of the costs and partly because of its political distaste for international agreements, the Bush administration withdrew the United States from the Kyoto Protocol in 2001. The other participating countries are moving ahead with implementation on schedule. The future role of the United States in global-warming policies will remain a contentious issue in the years ahead.

Quarrel and Pollute, or Reason and Compute?

We began this chapter with gloomy questions about the future of humanity. Having surveyed the field, how should we conclude? Depending on one's perspective, it is easy to become either optimistic or pessimistic about our ability to understand and cope with threats to our environment. On the one hand, it is true that we are moving into uncharted waters, depleting many resources while altering others in an irreversible manner, and gambling with our world in more ways than we know. Humans seem just as quarrelsome as they were at the dawn of recorded history, and they have devised weapons that are awesomely effective at avenging their quarrels. At the same time, our powers of observation and analysis are also orders of magnitude more formidable. The capability to monitor, analyze, and compute is growing even faster than our ability to emit wastes, cut trees, and produce yet more people.

What will prevail in this race between our tendencies to quarrel and pollute and our powers to reason and compute? Are there enough resources to allow the poor to enjoy the consumption standards of today's high-income countries, or will today's rich pull the ladder up behind them? There are no final answers to these deep questions, but many economists believe that if we manage our environmental resources wisely, *Homo sapiens* can not only survive but also thrive for a long time to come.

SUMMARY

A. Population and Resource Limitations

1. Malthus's theory of population rests on the law of diminishing returns. He contended that population, if unchecked, would tend to grow at a geometric (or exponential) rate, doubling every generation or so. But each member of the growing population would have less land and natural resources to work with. Because of diminishing returns, income could grow at an arithmetic rate at best; output per person would tend to fall so low as to stabilize population at a subsistence level of near-starvation.

2. Over the last century and a half, Malthus and his followers have been criticized on several grounds. Among the major criticisms are that Malthusians ignored the possibility of technological advance and overlooked the significance of birth control as a force in lowering population growth.

3. Studies of the relationship between pollution, population, and income have determined that the demand for environmental quality rises rapidly with per capita income, so for most indicators environmental quality improves rather than deteriorates as per capita income rises.

B. Natural-Resource Economics

4. Natural resources are nonrenewable when they are essentially fixed in supply and cannot regenerate quickly. Renewable resources are ones whose services are replenished regularly and which, if properly managed, can yield useful services indefinitely.

5. From an economic point of view, the crucial distinction is between appropriable and inappropriable resources. Natural resources are appropriable when firms or consumers can capture the full benefits of their services; examples include vineyards or oil fields. Natural resources are inappropriable when their costs or benefits do not accrue to the owners; in other words, they involve externalities. Examples include air quality and climate, which have externalities that are affected by such activities as the burning of fossil fuels.

6. Important examples of appropriable, nonrenewable natural resources are fossil fuels such as oil, gas, and coal. Economists argue that because private markets can efficiently price and allocate their services, such natural resources should be treated the same as any other capital asset.

C. Environmental Economics

7. A major market failure that is increasing in importance is externalities. These occur when the costs (or benefits) of an activity spill over to other people, without those other people being paid (or paying) for the costs (or benefits) incurred (or received).

8. The most clear-cut example of an externality is the case of public goods, like defense, where all consumers in a group share equally in the consumption and cannot be excluded. Less obvious examples like public health, inventions, parks, and dams also possess public-good properties. These contrast with private goods, like bread, which can be divided and provided to a single individual.

9. Environmental problems arise because of externalities that stem from production or consumption. An unregulated market economy will produce too much pollution and too little pollution abatement. Unregulated firms decide on abatement (and other public goods) by comparing the marginal private benefits with the marginal private costs. Efficiency requires that marginal social benefits equal marginal social abatement costs.

10. There are numerous steps by which governments can internalize or correct the inefficiencies arising from externalities. Alternatives include decentralized solutions (such as negotiations or legal liability rules) and government-imposed approaches (such as pollution-emission standards or emissions taxes). Experience indicates that no approach is ideal in all circumstances, but many economists believe that greater use of

market-oriented approaches would improve the efficiency of regulatory systems.

11. Global public goods, like slowing climate change, present the thorniest problems, which often cannot be solved by either markets or national governments. Nations must devise new tools to forge international agreements when global environmental trends threaten our living standards or ecosystems.

CONCEPTS FOR REVIEW

Population and Natural Resources

Malthusian population theory
renewable vs. nonrenewable resources
appropriable vs. inappropriable
   resources

Environmental Economics

externalities and public goods
private vs. public goods
inefficiency of externalities
internal vs. external costs, social vs.
   private costs

remedies for externalities:
   standards
   taxes
   liability
   bargaining and the Coase theorem
tradeable emissions permits
global public goods

FURTHER READING AND INTERNET WEBSITES

Further Reading

Environmental economics is a rapidly growing field. You can explore advanced topics in a textbook, such as Thomas H. Tietenberg, *Environmental Economics and Policy*, 3d ed. (Addison-Wesley, 2000). An excellent book of readings is Robert Stavins, ed., *Economics of the Environment: Selected Readings* (Norton, New York, 2000).

One of the most influential books of all times is T. R. Malthus, *Essay on Population* (1798, many publishers). An online version can be found at www.ac.wwu.edu/~stephan/malthus/malthus.0.html. The influential books by the new Malthusians Donella H. Meadows, Dennis L. Meadows, and Jørgen Randers are *The Limits to Growth* (Potomac, Washington, D.C., 1972) and *Beyond the Limits* (Chelsea Green, Post Mills, Vt., 1992). The quote from Wilson is from Edward O. Wilson, "Is Humanity Suicidal?" *New York Times Magazine*, May 30, 1993, p. 27. See Wilfred Beckerman, "Economic Growth and the Environment," *World Developement*, vol. 20, no. 4, 1992, p. 482, for the positive slant.

Websites

One of the best websites on resources and the environment is maintained by the nonprofit organization Resources for the Future at www.rff.org/. You can consult this site for a wide range of issues.

Population data are available from the United Nations at www.un.org/popin/. Energy data are available at the comprehensive site of the Energy Information Agency at www.eia.doe.gov.

You can learn more about environmental policy at the website of the U.S. Environmental Protection Agency at www.epa.gov. International environmental policy is found at the site of the United Nations Environmental Programme at www.unep.org. Information on the Kyoto Protocol and other programs to address climate change can be found at www.ipcc.ch and www.unfccc.de.

QUESTIONS FOR DISCUSSION

1. What is the difference between renewable and nonrenewable resources? Give examples of each.

2. What is meant by an inappropriable natural resource? Provide an example, and explain why the market allocation of this resource is inefficient. What would be your preferred way to improve the market outcome?

3. A *geometric progression* is a sequence of terms $(g_1, g_2, \ldots, g_t, g_{t+1}, \ldots)$ in which each term is the same multiple of

its predecessor: $g_2/g_1 = g_3/g_2 = \cdots = g_{t+1}/g_t = \beta$. If $\beta = 1 + i > 1$, the terms grow exponentially like compound interest, where i is the interest rate. An arithmetic progression is a sequence $(a_1, a_2, a_3, \ldots, a_t, a_{t+1}, \ldots)$ in which the difference between each term and its predecessor is the same constant: $a_2 - a_1 = a_3 - a_2 = \cdots = a_{t+1} - a_t = \cdots = \alpha$. Give examples of each. Satisfy yourself that any geometric progression with $\beta > 1$ must eventually surpass any arithmetic progression. Relate this to Malthus's theory.

4. Recall that Malthus asserted that unchecked population would grow geometrically, while food supply—constrained by diminishing returns—would grow only arithmetically. Use a numerical example to show why per capita food production must decline if population is unchecked while diminishing returns lead food production to grow more slowly than labor inputs.

5. "Local public goods" are ones that mainly benefit the residents of a town or state—such as beaches or schools open only to town residents. Is there any reason to think that towns might act competitively to provide the correct amount of local public goods to their residents? If so, does this suggest an economic theory of "fiscal federalism" whereby local public goods should be locally supplied?

6. Decide whether each of the following externalities is serious enough to warrant collective action. If so, which of the four remedies considered in this chapter would be most efficient?
   a. Steel mills emitting sulfur oxides into the Birmingham air
   b. Smoking by people in restaurants
   c. Smoking by students without roommates in their own rooms
   d. Driving by persons under the influence of alcohol, involving 25,000 fatalities per year
   e. Driving by persons under 21 under the influence of alcohol

7. Get your classmates together to do a contingent-valuation analysis on the value of the following: Keeping Prince William Sound pristine; preventing the extinction of spotted owls for another 10,000 years; ensuring that there are at least 1 million spotted owls in existence for another 10,000 years; reducing the chance of dying in an automobile accident from 1 in 1000 to 1 in 2000 each year. How reliable do you think this technique is for gathering information about people's preferences?

8. Don Fullerton and Robert Stavins argue that the following are myths about how economists think about the environment (see Chapter 1 in the Stavins book in the Further Reading section). For each, explain why it is a myth and what the correct approach is:
   a. Economists believe that the market solves all environmental problems.
   b. Economists always recommend market solutions to environmental problems.
   c. Economists always use market prices to evaluate environmental issues.
   d. Economists are concerned only with efficiency and never with income distribution.

9. **Advanced problem:** Global public goods pose special problems because no single nation can capture the benefits of its pollution-control efforts. To see this, redraw Figure 18-8, labeling it "Emissions Reduction for the United States." Label all the curves with "U.S." to indicate that they refer to costs and benefits for the United States alone. Next, draw a new *MSB* curve which is everywhere 3 times higher than the MSB_{US} to indicate that the benefits to the world are 3 times those to the United States. Consider the "nationalistic" equilibrium at E in which the United States maximizes its own net benefits. Can you see why this is inefficient from the point of view of the entire globe? (*Hint:* The reasoning is exactly analogous to Figure 18-6.)

   Consider this issue from the point of view of game theory. The Nash equilibrium would occur when each country chose the nationalistic equilibrium you have just analyzed. Describe why this is exactly analogous to the inefficient Nash equilibrium in the pollution game of Chapter 11—only here the players are nations rather than firms. Now consider the cooperative game where nations get together to find the efficient equilibrium. Describe the efficient equilibrium in terms of global *MC* and *MSB* curves. Can you see why the efficient equilibrium would require a uniform carbon tax in each country?

CHAPTER
19

Efficiency vs. Equality: The Big Tradeoff

[The conflict] between equality and efficiency [is] our biggest socioeconomic tradeoff, and it plagues us in dozens of dimensions of social policy. We can't have our cake of market efficiency and share it equally.

Arthur Okun (1975)

About a century ago, many Western governments began to intervene in the marketplace and introduce a social safety net as a bulwark against socialist pressures—this new conception of society was called the "welfare state." Attitudes toward the welfare state evolved gradually into the mixed market economy found today in the democracies of Europe and North America. In these countries, the market is responsible for production and pricing of most goods and services, while governments manage the economy and provide a safety net for the poor, unemployed, and aged.

One of the most controversial aspects of government policy involves policies toward the poor. Should families have guaranteed incomes? Or perhaps just minimum levels of food, shelter, and health care? Should taxation be progressive, redistributing incomes from the rich to the poor? Or should taxation be aimed primarily at promoting economic growth and efficiency?

Surprisingly, these questions have been just as contentious as societies have become richer. You might think that as a country becomes more prosperous, it would devote a larger share of its incomes to programs helping the needy at home and abroad. This has not always proved to be the case. As tax burdens have risen over the last half-century, tax revolts have sparked reductions in tax rates. People are also increasingly aware that attempts to equalize incomes can harm incentives and efficiency. Today, people ask: How much of the economic pie must be sacrificed in order to divide it more equally? How should we redesign income-support programs to retain the objective of reducing want and inequality without bankrupting the nation?

The purpose of this chapter is to examine the distribution of income along with the dilemmas of policies designed to reduce inequality. These issues are among the most controversial economic questions of today. It is here that cool-headed economic analysis of the trends in incomes and of the strengths and weaknesses of different programs will have a large payoff in promoting both a sense of fairness and continued rapid growth of the mixed economy.

A. THE SOURCES OF INEQUALITY

To measure the inequality of control over economic resources, we need to concern ourselves with both income and wealth differences. Recall that by **personal income** we mean the total receipts or cash earned by a person or household during a given time period (usually a year). The major components of personal income are labor earnings, property income (such as rents, interest, and dividends), and government transfer payments. **Disposable personal income** consists of personal income less any taxes paid. **Wealth** or "net worth" consists of the dollar value of financial and tangible assets minus the amount of money owed to banks and other creditors. You can refresh your memory about the major sources of income and wealth by reviewing Tables 12-1 and 12-2 (below and on page 384).

THE DISTRIBUTION OF INCOME AND WEALTH

Statistics show that in 2001 the median income of American families was $42,228—this means that half of all families received less than this figure while half received more. This number concerns the *distribution of income,* which shows the variability or dispersion of incomes. To understand the income distribution, consider the following experiment: Suppose one person from each household writes down the yearly income of his or her household on an index card. We can then sort these cards into *income classes.* Some of the cards go into the lowest 20 percent, the group with under $17,970 of income. Some go into the next class. A few go into the top 5 percent of households, those with incomes of $150,500 and above.

The actual income distribution of American households in 2001 is shown in Table 19-1. Column (1) shows the different income-class fifths, or quintiles, plus the top 5 percent of households. Column (2) shows the range of household incomes in each income class. Column (3) shows the percentage of the households in each income class, while column (4) shows the percentage of total national income that goes to the households in an income class.

Table 19-1 enables us to see at a glance the wide range of incomes in the U.S. economy. The poorest fifth of U.S. households have incomes less than $17,970, while households in the top fifth have incomes of more than $83,500. About 5 percent of households have incomes over $150,500. Some people earn much more than that, but as you move further up the income pyramid, the numbers get smaller and smaller. If we made an income pyramid out of building blocks, with each layer portraying $500 of income, the peak would be far higher than Mount Everest, but most people would be within a few feet of the ground.

How to Measure Inequality among Income Classes

How can we measure the degree of income inequality? At one pole, if incomes were absolutely equally distributed, there would be no difference between the lowest 20 percent and the highest 20 percent of the population: each quintile would receive exactly

(1) Income class of households	(2) Income range	(3) Percentage of all households in this class	(4) Percentage of total income received by households in this class
Lowest fifth	Under $17,970	20	3.5
Second fifth	$17,971 to $33,314	20	8.7
Third fifth	$33,315 to $53,000	20	14.6
Fourth fifth	$53,001 to $83,500	20	23.0
Highest fifth	$83,501 and over	20	50.1
Top 5 percent	$150,500 and over	5	22.4

TABLE 19-1. Distribution of Money Incomes of American Households, 2001

How was total income distributed among households in 2001? We group households into the fifth (or quintile) with the lowest income, the fifth with the second-lowest income, and so on.

Source: U.S. Bureau of the Census, *Money Income of Households, Families, and Persons in the United States: 2001,* Current Population Report, Series P-60, no. 218, September 2002, available on the Internet at www.census.gov/hhes/www/.

20 percent of the nation's income. That's what absolute equality means.

The reality is far different. The lowest fifth, with 20 percent of the households, garners less than 4 percent of the total income. Meanwhile the situation is reversed for the top 5 percent of households, which get 22 percent of the income.

We can show the degree of inequality in a diagram known as the **Lorenz curve,** a widely used device for analyzing income and wealth inequality. Figure 19-1 is a Lorenz curve showing the amount of inequality listed in the columns of Table 19-2; that is, it contrasts the patterns of (1) absolute equality, (2) absolute inequality, and (3) actual 2001 American inequality.

Absolute equality is depicted by the numbers in column (4) of Table 19-2. When they are plotted, these become the diagonal 45° dashed rust line of Figure 19-1's Lorenz diagram.

At the other extreme, we have the hypothetical case of absolute inequality, where one person has all the income. Absolute inequality is shown in column (5) of Table 19-2 and by the lowest curve on the Lorenz diagram—the dashed, right-angled black line.

Any actual income distribution, such as that for 2001, will fall between the extremes of absolute equality and absolute inequality. The rust-colored column (6) in Table 19-2 presents the data derived from the first two columns in a form suitable for plotting as an actual Lorenz curve. This actual Lorenz curve appears in Figure 19-1 as the solid rust intermediate

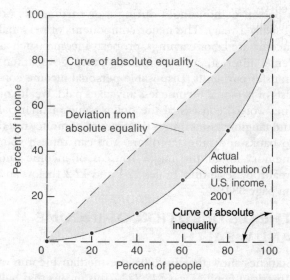

FIGURE 19-1. Lorenz Curve Shows Income Inequality

By plotting the figures from Table 19-2's column (6), we see that the solid rust actual-distribution-of-income curve lies between the two extremes of absolute equality and absolute inequality. The shaded area of this Lorenz curve (as a percentage of the triangle's area) measures the relative inequality of income. (How would the curve have looked back in the roaring 1920s when inequality was greater? In an egalitarian Utopia where all have equal inheritances and opportunities?)

(1)	(2)	(3)	(4)	(5)	(6)
	Percentage of total income received by households in this class	Percentage of households in this class and lower ones	Percentage of Income Received by This Class and Lower Ones		
Income class of households			Absolute equality	Absolute inequality	Actual distribution
Lowest fifth	3.5	0	0	0	3.5
Second fifth	8.7	20	20	0	12.2
Third fifth	14.6	40	40	0	26.8
Fourth fifth	23.0	80	80	0	49.8
Highest fifth	50.1	100	100	100	100.0

TABLE 19-2. Actual and Polar Cases of Inequality

By cumulating the income shares of each quintile shown in column (2), we can compare in column (6) the actual distribution with polar extremes of complete inequality and equality.

Source: Table 19-1.

curve. The shaded area indicates the deviation from absolute equality, hence giving us a measure of the degree of inequality of income distribution.

The Gini Coefficient

Economists often need to calculate quantitative measures of inequality. One useful measure is the *Gini coefficient.* This is measured by calculating the shaded area in the Lorenz curve of Figure 19-1 and multiplying it by 2. The Gini coefficient is equal to 1 under complete inequality and 0 under complete equality. To see this, recall that a society with equal incomes would have the Lorenz curve run along the 45° line, so the area would be zero. Conversely, when the Lorenz curve runs along the axes, the area is one-half, which, when multiplied by 2, gives a Gini coefficient of 1.

Using the Gini coefficient approach, the Census Bureau calculates that inequality was little changed from 1967 to 1980 (the Gini coefficient rose from .399 to .403) but then rose steadily from 1980 to 2001 (from .403 to .466).

Distribution of Wealth

One major source of the inequality of income is inequality of ownership of *wealth*, which is the net ownership of financial claims and tangible property. Those who are fabulously wealthy—whether because of inheritance, skill, or luck—enjoy incomes far above the amount earned by the average household. Those without wealth begin with an income handicap.

In market economies, wealth is much more unequally distributed than is income, as Figure 19-2(*b*) shows. In the United States, the top 10 percent of

(a) Income Inequalities

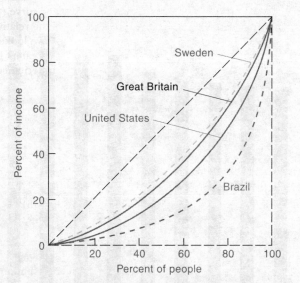

(b) Inequality of Wealth

FIGURE 19-2. Inequality Differs in Different Societies and Is Greater for Wealth Than for Income

(a) Advanced economies show less inequality of income distribution than do middle-income economies.
(b) Holdings of wealth tend to be more concentrated than do annual incomes. The United States and Great Britain have similar income distributions, but British wealth is somewhat more concentrated than America's. Socialist countries like China show much less concentration of private wealth.

Source: Ana M. Aizcorbe, Arthur B. Kennickell, and Kevin B. Moore, "Recent Changes in U.S. Family Finances: Evidence from the 1998 and 2001 Survey of Consumer Finances," *Federal Reserve Bulletin,* vol. 89 (January 2003), pp. 1–32 (available online), and World Bank, *World Development Report,* various issues.

households in 2001 owned 70 percent of wealth, and the top 1 percent of the households owned around 40 percent of all wealth. Studies by New York University's Edward Wolff show that the distribution of wealth has become much more unequal over time.

Societies are ambivalent about large wealth holdings. A century ago, President T. Roosevelt criticized "malefactors of great wealth" and proposed sharply progressive income and inheritance taxes. A century later, however, legislation was passed in the United States that would abolish all inheritance and gift taxes after 2010, labeling them as "death taxes." If the abolition withstands legislative repeal, it may provide yet another boost to wealth inequality in the years ahead.

Inequality across Countries

Countries show quite different income distributions depending upon their economic and social structure. Figure 19-3 shows the inequality of different countries as measured by the Gini coefficient. (Recall the Gini coefficient from the box on page 385.) Market-oriented countries like the United States tend to have the most unequal income distributions among the high-income countries. The welfare states of northern Europe tend to have the least inequality. The sources of high inequality in the United States are discussed later in this chapter.

The experience of developing countries shows an interesting relationship. Inequality begins to rise as

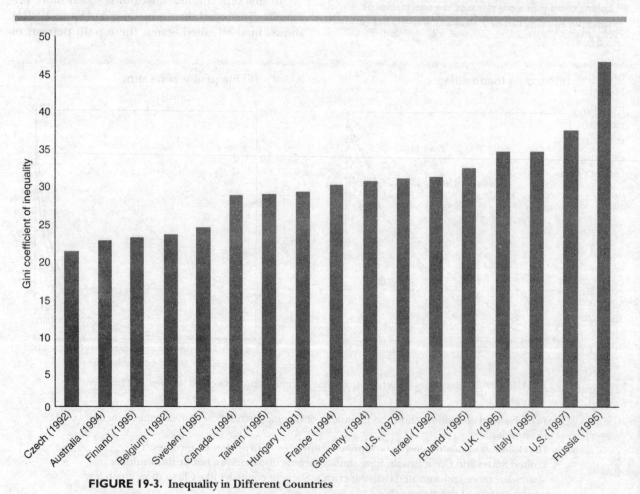

FIGURE 19-3. Inequality in Different Countries

Inequality differs greatly across major countries. Russia and today's United States have the greatest income inequality, while northern European countries generally have the least inequality. This graph shows the Gini coefficient as defined in the text.

Source: Koen Vleminckx, Luxembourg Income Study, August 1998, available online.

countries begin to industrialize, after which inequality then declines. The greatest extremes of inequality—with conspicuous opulence appearing alongside the most abject poverty—occur in middle-income countries, particularly Latin American countries like Peru, Brazil, and Venezuela.

INEQUALITY IN LABOR INCOME

What are the sources of inequality? The first place we would look for an answer is labor incomes, which account for about 75 percent of factor incomes. Even if property incomes were distributed equally, much inequality would remain. The forces that produce inequalities in earnings are differences in abilities and skills of labor, in intensities of work, in occupations, and in other factors.

Abilities and Skills

People vary enormously in their abilities—in physical, mental, and temperamental dimensions. However, these personal differences are of little help in explaining the puzzle of income dispersion. Physical traits (such as strength or height or girth) and measured mental traits (such as intelligence quotient or tone perception) explain relatively little of the difference among the earnings of people.

This is not to say that individual abilities matter little. The ability to hit a home run or charm an audience greatly enhances a person's earning potential. But the skills valued in the marketplace are varied and often difficult to measure. Markets tend to reward willingness to take risks, ambition, luck, strokes of engineering genius, good judgment, and hard work—none of which is easily measured in standardized tests. As Mark Twain might have said, "You don't have to be smart to make money. But you *do* have to know how to make money."

Intensities of Work

The intensity of work varies enormously among individuals. The workaholic may log 70 hours a week on the job, never take a vacation, and postpone retirement indefinitely. An ascetic might work just enough to pay for life's necessities. Differences in income might be great simply because of differences in work effort, yet no one would say that economic opportunity was therefore genuinely unequal.

Occupations

One important source of income inequality is people's occupations. At the low end of the scale we find domestic servants, fast-food personnel, and unskilled service workers. A full-time, year-round employee at McDonald's or at a car wash might earn $10,000 a year today.

At the other extreme are the high-earning professionals. What single profession seems to make the most money? In recent years it has without question been medical doctors. Physicians had average earnings after expenses of $160,000 in 1998, up almost 70 percent since 1986.

What is the source of such vast differences among occupations? Part of the disparity comes from investments in human capital, such as the years of training needed to become a doctor. Abilities also play a role, for example, in limiting engineering jobs to those who have some quantitative skills. Some jobs pay more because they are dangerous or unpleasant (recall the discussion of compensating differentials in Chapter 13). And when the supply of labor is limited in an occupation, say, because of union restrictions or professional licensing rules, the supply restrictions drive up the wages and salaries of that occupation.

Other Factors

In addition to ability, intensity of work, and occupation, other factors affect the inequality of wage earnings. We saw in Chapter 13 that discrimination and exclusion from certain occupations have played an important role in keeping down the incomes of women and many minority groups.

In addition, the home life and community experience of children have a major impact on later earnings. Children of the affluent benefit from their environment at every stage. A child of poverty often experiences crowding, poor nutrition, run-down schools, and overworked teachers. The scales are tipped against many inner-city children before they are 10 years old.

Some economists believe that changing technology, immigration, international trade, and the increasing prevalence of winner-take-all markets are creating greater inequality. To take the first of these, recall Chapter 11's discussion of how technology is leveraging individual performance so that it reaches many more people. As a result, while talented athletes made little more than the average factory worker three decades ago, signing bonuses for basketball's free agents today are approaching $100 million. Similar trends are seen in other sports, in entertainment, and in salaries of corporate officers.

INEQUALITY IN PROPERTY INCOME

The greatest disparities in income arise from differences in *property income,* which consists of income on assets like stocks, bonds, and real estate. With few exceptions, the people at the very top of the income pyramid derive most of their money from property income. By contrast, the poor own few financial assets and therefore earn no income on their nonexistent wealth. Let's examine the sources of differences in wealth—saving, entrepreneurship, and inheritance—and thus of inequalities in property income.

Life-Cycle Saving as a Source of Wealth

While most people scrimp and save to put away a few dollars for their retirement, such thrift is probably not the major source of wealth in the United States. The difficulty of accumulating a large fortune by saving out of normal labor earnings can be illustrated using a realistic example. Suppose that the average middle-class family saved about $2000 annually (5 percent of its income) for 20 years. Further

suppose that through prudent investments it managed to obtain a real return after taxes of 5 percent each year. At the end of the period, total accumulated wealth would be $73,200—a sum equal to only one-sixth of average family net worth.

Entrepreneurship

Compared to thrift, entrepreneurship is a much more important road to riches. Table 19-3 displays the experience of the top 100 wealth holders in 2003. These data suggest that most of the richest people in America got that way by taking risks and creating profitable new businesses, such as computer software companies, television networks, and retail chains. The people who invented new products or services or organized the companies that brought them to market got rich on the "Schumpeterian profits" from these innovations. This group of wealthy individuals includes folk heroes like Bill Gates (head of software giant Microsoft), the Waltons (founders of Wal-Mart), and Warren Buffett (investment guru).

America's 100 Richest People			
		Amount of Net Worth	
Source of wealth	**Number of persons**	**Billions of dollars**	**Percent**
Inheritance	8	18.8	3
Finance	16	99.4	16
Entrepreneurship	76	506.7	81
Communications	12	70.4	11
Entertainment	3	9.5	2
Industry	13	72.7	12
New economy	12	152.7	24
Oil	6	19.8	3
Real estate	9	28.4	5
Retailing	21	153.2	25
Total	**100**	**624.9**	**100**

TABLE 19-3. How Did the Richest Americans Reach the Summit?

In 2003, 100 Americans had net worth of at least $2 billion, according to *Forbes* magazine. Most gained their wealth by entrepreneurship (like Bill Gates or the Waltons). A small fraction gained wealth by inheritance or finance.

Source: *Forbes,* October 2003, available at www.forbes.com/richlist2003/rich400land.html.

Inheritance

What about inheritance? About one-quarter of the 100 wealthiest individuals in 1999 got there by inheriting wealth rather than creating it, but that number may understate the importance of inheritance in determining the distribution of income. According to surveys, two-thirds of the top 1 percent of wealth holders in America inherited a substantial fraction of their property. It is this concentration of inherited wealth in a small number of hands which draws the most strenuous objections from people who are worried about the unequal distribution of wealth.

POVERTY IN AMERICA

Societies tend to define and concentrate on particular groups or problems. In the 1960s, the United States declared "war on poverty" and launched ambitious health and nutrition programs to eradicate economic privation. Before we can analyze antipoverty programs, we must examine the definition of poverty, a surprisingly elusive concept.

The Illusive Concept of Poverty

The word "poverty" means different things to different people. Clearly poverty is a condition in which people have inadequate incomes, but it is hard to draw an exact line between the poor and the nonpoor. Economists have therefore devised certain techniques which provide the official definition of poverty.

Poverty was officially defined in the 1960s in the United States as an income insufficient to buy basic food, clothing, shelter, and other necessities. This was calculated from family budgets and double-checked by examining the fraction of incomes that was spent on food. Since that time, the poverty budget has been updated by the government's consumer price index to reflect changes in the cost of living. According to the standard definition, the subsistence cost of living for a family of four was $18,850 in 2004. This figure represents the "poverty line" or demarcation between poor and nonpoor families. The poverty line also varies by family size.

While an exact figure for measuring poverty is helpful, scholars recognize that "poverty" is a relative term. The notion of a subsistence budget includes subjective questions of taste and social convention. Housing that is today considered substandard often includes household appliances and plumbing that were unavailable to the millionaires and robber barons of an earlier age.

Because of shortcomings in the current definition, a panel of experts of the National Academy of Sciences recommended in 1995 that the definition of poverty be changed to reflect *relative-income status*. The panel recommended that a family be considered poor if its consumption is less than 50 percent of the median family's consumption of food, clothing, and housing. Poverty in the relative-income sense would decline when inequality decreased; poverty would be unchanged if the economy prospered with no change in the distribution of income and consumption. In this new world, a rising tide would lift all boats but not change the fraction of the population considered poor. This radical new approach is being weighed carefully by the government.

Who Are the Poor?

Poverty hits some groups harder than others. Table 19-4 shows the incidence of poverty in different groups for 2001. While 11.7 percent of the total population was counted as falling below the 2001 poverty line, the rate among black and Hispanic families was almost triple that of non-Hispanic whites.

Perhaps the most ominous trend is that single-parent families headed by women are an increasingly large share of the poor population. In 1959, about 18 percent of poor families were headed by women raising children alone. By 2001, the poverty rate of that group was 26 percent. Social scientists worry that the children in these families will receive inadequate nutrition and education and will find it difficult to escape from poverty when they are adults.

No discussion of poverty would be accurate without an analysis of the position of minorities. Almost one-third of African-American, Hispanic, and Native American families have below-standard incomes.

Why are so many female-headed and minority families poor? What is the role of discrimination?[1] Experienced observers insist that blatant racial or gender discrimination in which firms simply pay minorities or women less is vanishing today. Yet the relative poverty of women and blacks is increasing.

---

[1] The economics of discrimination in the workplace is analyzed in Chapter 13.

Poverty in Major Groups, 2001	
Population group	**Percentage of group in poverty**
Total population	11.7
By racial and ethnic group:	
White (non-Hispanic)	7.8
Black	22.7
Hispanic	21.8
By age:	
Under 18 years	16.3
18 to 64 years	10.1
65 years and over	10.1
By type of family:	
Married couple	4.9
Female householder, no husband present	26.4
Male householder, no wife present	13.1

TABLE 19-4. Incidence of Poverty in Different Groups, 2001

Whites and married couples have lower-than-average poverty rates. Blacks, Hispanics, and female-headed households have above-average poverty rates.

Source: U.S. Bureau of the Census, *Poverty in the United States: 2001*, Current Population Report, Series P-60, no. 219, September 2002, available at www.census.gov.

How can we reconcile these two apparently contradictory trends? The major factor at work is the increasing gap between earnings of highly educated and skilled workers and those of unskilled and less educated workers. Over the last 25 years, the wage differential between these two groups has grown sharply, as we will see in the next section. The growing wage gap has hit minority groups particularly hard.

Trends in Inequality

The history of inequality in the United States is shown in Figure 19-4 on page 391. This shows the ratio of the incomes received by the top fifth of families to those received by the bottom fifth. We can see three distinct periods: falling inequality until World War II, stable shares until 1980, and then rising inequality over the last two decades. Since 1980, the ratio of upper- to lower-group incomes has increased by almost 50 percent.

Diminishing Inequality: 1929–1975. By any measure, in this period the poor enjoyed the fruits of economic growth along with more affluent groups. According to historical studies, the real income of the bottom fifth of the population rose steadily from the 1920s to the mid-1970s, growing slightly faster than the overall U.S. economy. As a result, the share of total income going to the poorest fifth of families rose from 3.8 percent to about 5 percent between 1929 and 1975. Over the same stretch, the poverty rate dropped so far that some people hoped that poverty could be eliminated completely.

Why did inequality narrow over this period? Inequality declined in part because of the narrowing of wage inequality. With increasing education of poorer groups and unionization of the workforce, the gap declined. Government policies like social security made a big difference for the elderly population, while programs like cash assistance and food stamps for the indigent and unemployment insurance boosted the incomes of other groups. Moreover, our progressive income-tax system, which taxed high incomes more heavily than low incomes, tended to reduce the degree of inequality.

Widening Gaps: 1975–2001. In the last quarter-century, several of these trends have reversed themselves. The share of total income going to the bottom quintile declined sharply in the 1980s, sinking from 5.4 percent in 1975 to 3.5 percent in 2001.

FIGURE 19-4. Trends in Inequality in the United States, 1929–2001.

A useful measure of inequality is the ratio of the incomes of the top fifth of the population to those of the bottom fifth. The share of top incomes declined after 1929 with the stock market collapse of the 1930s, the low unemployment and reduced barriers to women and minorities during World War II, and the migration from the farm to the city. Since 1980, income inequality has grown sharply with higher immigration and decline of wages of the unskilled.

Source: U.S. Bureau of the Census, with historical series spliced together by authors.

Average real incomes for families in the bottom fifth are well below their peak. However, the poverty rate did begin to decline during the long economic expansion of the 1990s, reaching a low of 11.3 percent in 2000.

Although the incomes of the poor stagnated during the last quarter-century, the share of income going to the richest Americans soared. From 1975 to 2001, the share of total income going to the top 5 percent of households rose from 16 to 22.4 percent. Indeed, a recent study of high-income households indicates that most of the gains at the top were actually at the tip of the income pyramid, going to the top 0.1 percent of taxpayers.

Why did inequality rise in recent decades? After intensely debating this question for years, economists have identified several causes of rising inequality. For one, government policies changed in the early 1980s: transfer programs to poor families were cut, while the richest groups were helped by the supply-side tax cuts of the 1980s. But government actions are only part of the story. The last two decades saw sharp increases in the compensation of top executives and professionals, while the rising share of births going to single mothers sharply increased the number of female-headed

households, which tend to have much higher rates of poverty.

Perhaps the most important cause of rising inequality is the fact that well-educated workers fared far better after 1980 than their less educated counterparts. Economists have closely studied the *college-high school wage premium*, which is the pay differential between a worker with a college degree and a similar worker with only a high school diploma. Over the last decade the college-high school wage premium has grown sharply. According to the 1994 *Economic Report of the President*, in 1981 college graduates earned about 45 percent more than high school graduates. But by 1997, full-time college graduates earned 103 percent more than high school graduates. This increasing wage premium widened the gap between the top and bottom of the income distribution.[2]

Why did the 1980s see increasing returns to education? One reason was a surge of immigration and competition from foreign imports. Both of these trends tend to hit hardest at less educated workers, who in earlier decades had been able to earn a good living working in factories making automobiles, steel,

---

[2] Recall the discussion of rising wage gaps in Chapter 13.

and other goods. In the 1980s these high-paying manufacturing jobs for workers without college educations began to dry up. In addition, increasing deregulation and foreign competition tended to erode the market power of labor unions, lowering the relative wages of highly paid union workers. At the same time, many of the new jobs that were being created called for relatively high levels of skills and education. The increasing prevalence of computers in the workplace places a high premium on literacy and analytical skills. All together, these trends have raised the degree of income inequality in the United States and most high-income countries.

We can point to at least one factor that did not lead to greater inequality: There was no decline in labor's share of national income. The fraction of total incomes coming from wages, salaries, and supplements in 1999 was virtually identical to what it had been a quarter-century earlier. This dog, at least, did not bite.

This concludes our description of the measurement and sources of inequality. In the next section, we turn to an analysis of government programs to combat poverty and reduce inequality. High-income democracies everywhere are rethinking these programs as they redefine the role of the state.

B. ANTIPOVERTY POLICIES

All societies take steps to provide for their poor citizens. But what is given to the poor must come from other groups, and that is undoubtedly the major point of resistance to redistributive programs. In addition, economists worry about the impact of redistribution upon the efficiency and morale of a country. These issues assume greater importance as resistance to tax increases has stiffened. In this section, we review the rise of the welfare state, consider the costs of income redistribution, and survey the current system of income maintenance.

The Rise of the Welfare State

The early classical economists believed the distribution of income was unalterable. They argued that attempts to alleviate poverty by government interventions in the economy were foolish endeavors that would simply end up reducing total national income. This view was contested by the English economist

and philosopher John Stuart Mill. While cautioning against interferences with the market mechanism, he argued eloquently that government policies could reduce inequality.

A half-century later, at the end of the nineteenth century, political leaders in Western Europe took steps that marked a historic turning point in the economic role of government. Bismarck in Germany, Gladstone and Disraeli in Britain, followed by Franklin Roosevelt in the United States introduced a new concept of government responsibility for the welfare of the populace.

This marked the rise of the **welfare state**, in which government overrides market forces to protect individuals against specified contingencies and to guarantee people a minimum standard of living.

Important welfare-state policies include public pensions, accident and sickness insurance, unemployment insurance, health insurance, food and housing programs, family allowances, and income supplements for certain groups of people. These policies were introduced gradually from 1880 through to the modern era. The welfare state came late to the United States, being introduced in the New Deal of the 1930s with unemployment insurance and social security. Medical care for the aged and the poor was added in the 1960s. Most high-income countries provide universal health care for their citizens, but after a fierce debate in 1994, the U.S. Congress decided not to pass universal health benefits. In 1996 the federal government turned back the clock by removing the guarantee of a minimum income. The debate over redistribution never ends.

THE COSTS OF REDISTRIBUTION

One of the goals of a modern mixed economy is to provide a safety net for those who are temporarily or permanently unable to provide adequate incomes for themselves. One reason for these policies is to promote greater equality.

What are the different concepts of equality? To begin with, democratic societies affirm the principle of equality of *political rights*—generally including the right to vote, the right to trial by jury, and the right to free speech and association. In the 1960s, liberal philosophers espoused the view that people should also have equal *economic opportunity*. In other words, all people should play by the same rules on a level playing field. All should have equal access to the best schools, training, and jobs. Then discrimination on the basis of race or gender or religion would disappear. Many steps were taken to promote greater equality, but inequalities of opportunity have proved very stubborn, and even America at the dawn of the new millennium falls far short of the goal of equal economic opportunity.

A third, and the most far-reaching, ideal is equality of *economic outcome*. In this utopia, people would have the same consumption whether they were smart or dull, eager or lazy, lucky or unfortunate. Wages would be the same for doctor and nurse, lawyer and secretary. "From each according to his abilities, to each according to his needs" was Karl Marx's formulation of this philosophy.

Today, even the most radical socialist recognizes that some differences in economic outcome are necessary if the economy is to function efficiently. Without some differential reward for different kinds of work, how can we ensure that people will do the unpleasant as well as the pleasant work, that they will work on dangerous offshore oil derricks as well as in pleasant parks? Insisting on equality of outcomes would severely hamper the functioning of the economy.

The Leaky Bucket

In taking steps to redistribute income from the rich to the poor, governments may harm economic efficiency and reduce the amount of national income available to distribute. On the other hand, if equality is a social good, it is one worth paying for.

The question of how much we are willing to pay in reduced efficiency for greater equity was addressed by Arthur Okun in his "leaky bucket" experiment. He noted that if we value equality, we would approve when a dollar is taken in a bucket from the very rich and given to the very poor. But, he continued, suppose the bucket of redistribution has a leak in it. Suppose only a fraction—maybe one-half—of each dollar in taxes paid by the rich actually reaches the poor. Then redistribution in the name of equity has been at the expense of economic efficiency.[3]

Okun presented a fundamental dilemma. Redistributional measures like the progressive income tax, analyzed

---

[3] Arthur M. Okun, *Equality and Efficiency: The Big Tradeoff* (Brookings Institution, Washington, D.C., 1975).

in Chapter 16, will reduce real output by reducing incentives to work and save. As a nation considers its income-distribution policies, it will want to weigh the benefit of greater equality against the impact of these policies on total national income.

Redistribution Costs in Diagrams

We can illustrate Okun's point by using the income-possibility curve of Figure 19-5. This graph shows the incomes available to different groups when government programs redistribute income.

We begin by dividing the population in half; the real income of the low-income group is measured on the vertical axis of Figure 19-5, while the income of the upper half is measured on the horizontal axis. At point A, which is the pre-redistribution point, no taxes are levied and no transfers are given, so people simply live with their market incomes. In a competitive economy, point A will be efficient and the no-redistribution policy maximizes total national income.

Unfortunately, at laissez-faire point A, the upper-income group receives substantially more income

FIGURE 19-5. Redistributing Income May Harm Economic Efficiency

Point A marks the most efficient outcome, with maximal national output. If society could redistribute with no loss of efficiency, the economy would move toward point E. Because redistributive programs generally create distortions and efficiency losses, the path of redistribution might move along the rust line *ABZ*. Society must decide how much efficiency to sacrifice to gain greater equality. Why would everyone want to avoid inefficient redistributional programs that take the economy from point B to point C?

than the lower half. People might strive for greater equality by tax and transfer programs, hoping to move toward the point of equal incomes at E. If such steps could be taken without reducing national output, the economy would move along the black line from A toward E. The slope of the AE line is $-45°$, reflecting the assumption about efficiency that the redistributive bucket has no leaks, so every dollar taken from the upper half increases the income of the lower half by exactly $1. Along the $-45°$ line, total national income is constant, indicating that redistributional programs have no impact upon the total national income.

Most redistributive programs do affect efficiency. If a country redistributes income by imposing high tax rates on the wealthiest people, their saving and work effort may be reduced or misdirected, with a resulting lower total national output. They may spend more money on tax lawyers, save less for retirement, or invest less in high-yielding but risky innovations. Also, if society puts a guaranteed floor beneath the incomes of the poor, the sting of poverty will be reduced and the poor may work less. All these reactions to redistributive programs reduce the total size of real national income.

In terms of Okun's experiment, we might find that for every $100 of taxation on the rich, the income of the poor increased by only $50, with the rest dissipated because of reduced effort or administrative costs. The bucket of redistribution has developed a large leak. Costly redistribution is shown by the ABZ curve in Figure 19-5. Here, the hypothetical frontier of real incomes bends away from the $-45°$ line because taxes and transfers produce inefficiencies.

The experience of socialist countries exemplifies how attempts to equalize incomes by expropriating property from the rich can end up hurting everyone. By prohibiting private ownership of businesses, socialist governments reduced the inequalities that arise from large property incomes. But the reduced incentives for work, investment, and innovation crippled this radical experiment of "to each according to his needs" and impoverished entire countries. By 1990, comparisons of living standards in East and West had convinced many socialist countries that private ownership of business would benefit the living standards of workers as well as capitalists.

How Big Are the Leaks?

Okun characterized our redistributive system of taxes and transfers as a leaky bucket. But just how big are the leaks in the American economy? Is the country closer to Figure 19-5's point A, where the leaks are negligible? Or to B, where they are substantial? Or to Z, where the redistributive bucket is in fact a sieve? To find the answer, we must examine the major inefficiencies induced by high tax rates and by generous income-support programs: administrative costs, damage to work and saving incentives, and socioeconomic costs.

- The government must hire tax collectors to raise revenues and social security accountants to disburse them. These are clear inefficiencies or regrettable necessities, but they are small: the Internal Revenue Service spends only half a penny on administrative costs for each dollar of collected revenues.

- As the tax collector's bite grows larger and larger, might I not become discouraged and end up working less? Tax rates might conceivably be so high that total revenues are actually lower than they would be at more modest tax rates. Empirical evidence, however, suggests that the damage of taxes on work effort is limited. For a few groups, the labor supply curve may actually be backward-bending, indicating that a tax on wages might increase rather than decrease work effort. Most studies find a small impact of taxes on labor effort for middle-income and high-income workers. However, there may well be substantial impacts of the tax and transfer system on the behavior of poor people.

- Perhaps the most important potential leakage from the revenue bucket is the savings component. Some believe that current government programs discourage saving and investment. Some economic studies indicate that by taxing income rather than consumption, total saving is discouraged. Additionally, economists worry that the nation's saving rate has declined sharply because of generous social programs—especially social security and Medicare—that reduce the need for people to save for old age and health contingencies.

- Some claim that the leaks cannot be found in the cost statistics of the economist; instead, the costs of equality are seen in attitudes rather than in dollars. Is the business ethic downplayed? Are people so turned off by the prospect of high taxes that they turn on to drugs and idleness? Is the welfare system leading to a permanent underclass, a society of people who are trapped in a culture of dependency?

- Some people criticize the entire notion of costly redistribution, arguing as follows: Poverty is rooted in malnourishment in the early years, broken families, illiteracy at home, poor education, and lack of job training. Poverty begets poverty; the vicious cycle of malnutrition, poor education, drug dependency, low productivity, and low incomes leads to yet another generation of poor families. These analysts contend that enhanced programs to provide health care and adequate food for poor families will increase productivity and efficiency rather than decrease output. By breaking the vicious cycle of poverty today, we will be raising the skills, human capital, and productivity of the children of poverty tomorrow. Programs to break the cycle of poverty are investments that require resources today to increase productivity tomorrow.

Adding Up the Leaks

When all the leaks are added up, how big are they? Okun argued that the leaks are small, particularly when funds for redistributive programs are drawn from the tap of a broad-based income tax. Others disagree strenuously, pointing to high marginal tax rates and overly generous transfer programs as confusing and destructive of economic efficiency.

What is the reality? While much research has been undertaken on the cost of redistribution, the truth has proved elusive. A cautious verdict is that there are but modest losses to economic efficiency from redistributional programs of the kind used in the United States today. For many people, the efficiency costs of redistribution are a reasonable price to pay for reducing the economic and human costs of poverty in malnutrition, poor health, lost job skills, and human misery. But countries whose welfare-state policies have gone far beyond those in the United States see major inefficiencies. Egalitarian countries like Sweden and the Netherlands, which provide cradle-to-grave protection for their citizens, found declining labor-force participation, growing unemployment, and rising budget deficits. These countries have taken steps to reduce the burden of the welfare state.

Countries need to design their policies carefully to avoid the extremes of unacceptable inequality or great inefficiency.

ANTIPOVERTY POLICIES: PROGRAMS AND CRITICISMS

All societies provide for their aged, their young, and their sick. Sometimes, the support comes from families or religious organizations. Over the last century, nations have increasingly moved the source of income support for the needy to central governments. Yet, as governments have assumed larger responsibilities for more people, the fiscal burdens of transfer programs have grown steadily. Today, most high-income countries face the prospect of rising tax burdens to finance public-health and retirement programs as well as income-support programs for poor families. This rising tax burden has provoked a sharp backlash against "welfare programs," particularly in the United States. Let's review the major antipoverty programs and recent reforms.

Income-Security Programs

What are the major income-security programs today? Let's look briefly at a few of the programs that have been established in the United States.

Most income-security programs are targeted at the elderly rather than the poor, as is shown in Table 19-5. The major programs are social security, which is a contributory federal retirement program, and Medicare, which is a subsidized health program for those over 65 years old. These two programs are the largest transfer programs in the United States and in most other high-income countries, and they are projected to be a source of continued spending growth over the coming decades.

Programs specifically targeted to poor households are a patchwork quilt of federal, state, and local programs. Some of these are cash assistance; some subsidize particular spending (such as the food-stamps program, which provides poor families with coupons that allow them to purchase food at a small fraction of its market cost); and others are transfers "in kind," such as Medicaid, which provides poor families with free health care. Most of the programs targeted to poor families have shrunk sharply over the last two decades.

The most controversial program was cash assistance to poor parents with small children. This program was drastically reformed in 1996, and we will discuss the reform below.

How much do all federal programs add up to in terms of budget expenditures? Table 19-5 shows the level of federal spending for income-security programs

Federal Entitlement Programs, 2003		
Program	Amount ($, billion)	Percentage of total federal spending
General programs	**779**	**36.4**
Social security	478	22.4
Medicare	245	11.4
Unemployment insurance	56	2.6
Programs for low-income households	**456**	**21.3**
Medicaid	196	9.2
Other income security	147	6.9
Food and nutrition	43	2.0
Housing assistance	34	1.6
Earned-income tax credit	36	1.7
All income-security programs	**1,235***	**57.7**

*Includes both outlays and reduced tax revenues.

TABLE 19-5. Most Federal Income-Security Dollars Go for General Programs like Social Security

Federal programs for income security are largely concentrated on the population as a whole, rather than on the poor. Note as well the high cost of health programs for both the poor and the nonpoor.

Source: *Budget of the United States Government, 2004.*

for both the general population and poor households. All federal poverty programs today amount to 21 percent of the total federal budget.

Incentive Problems of the Poor

One of the major obstacles faced by poor families is that the rules in most welfare programs severely reduce the incentives of low-income adults to seek work. If a poor person on welfare gets a job, the government will trim back food stamps, income-support payments, and rent subsidies, and the person might even lose medical benefits. We might say that poor people face high marginal "tax rates" (or, more accurately, "benefit-reduction rates") because welfare benefits are sharply reduced as earnings rise.

THE BATTLE OVER WELFARE REFORM

The traditional welfare system has few defenders. Some want to dismantle it; others, to strengthen it. Some wish to devolve responsibility for income

support to states, localities, or families; others, to strengthen the federal role. These disparate approaches reflect disparate views of poverty and lead to strikingly different policy proposals.

Two Views of Poverty

Social scientists put forth a wide variety of proposals to cure or alleviate poverty. The different approaches often reflect differing views of the roots of poverty. Proponents of strong government action see poverty as the result of social and economic conditions over which the poor have little control. They stress malnutrition, poor schools, broken families, discrimination, lack of job opportunities, and a dangerous environment as central determinants of the fate of the poor. If you hold this view, you might well believe that government bears a responsibility to alleviate poverty—either by providing income to the poor or by correcting the conditions that produce poverty.

A second view holds that poverty grows out of maladaptive individual behavior—behavior that is the responsibility of individuals and is properly cured by the poor themselves. In earlier centuries, laissez-faire apologists held that the poor were shiftless, lazy, or drunk; as a charity worker wrote almost a century ago, "Want of employment . . . is, as often as not, [caused by] drink." Sometimes the government itself is blamed for breeding dependency upon a patchwork of government programs that squelch individual initiative. Critics who hold these views advocate that the government should cut back on welfare programs so that people will develop their own resources.

The poverty debate was succinctly summarized by the eminent social scientist William Wilson:

> Liberals have traditionally emphasized how the plight of disadvantaged groups can be related to the problems of the broader society, including problems of discrimination and social class subordination. . . . Conservatives, in contrast, have traditionally stressed the importance of different group values and competitive resources in accounting for the experiences of the disadvantaged.[4]

Much of today's debate can be better understood if these two views and their implications are factored into the political equation.

----

[4] William Julius Wilson, "Cycles of Deprivation and the Underclass Debate," *Social Service Review*, December 1985, pp. 541–559.

Income Supplemental Programs in the United States Today

Most high-income countries provide guaranteed income supplements for poor families with children, and that model was followed by the United States until 1996. At that time, the country took a radically different approach to increasing incomes of the poor. First, it augmented a program to supplement wages of working families. Second, it fundamentally altered cash assistance programs, abolishing a federal entitlement for poor families.

The Earned-Income Tax Credit

The wage supplement program is called the *earned-income tax credit* or *EITC*. This credit applies to labor incomes and is in effect a wage supplement. In 2002, it amounted to a supplement to earned income of as much as 40 percent up to a maximum of $4140; working families receive some credit for incomes up to about $34,000. It is known as a "refundable" credit because it is actually paid to an individual when the individual owes no taxes.

Table 19-6 shows the impact of the earned-income tax credit for a family at different income levels. What is the difference between a traditional cash-assistance program and the earned-income tax

Current Structure of Earned-Income Tax Credit, 2002		
Market earnings ($)	Algebraic tax (+ if tax; − if benefits received) ($)	Income after tax and credit ($)
0	0	0
4,000	−1,610	5,610
8,000	−3,210	11,210
12,000	−4,140	16,140
24,000	−2,138	26,138
28,000	−1,296	29,296
32,000	−453	32,453

TABLE 19-6. Earned-Income Tax Credit Increases Reward for Work but Does Not Touch the Very Poorest

Under the current earned-income tax credit, labor earnings are increased by a supplement of up to 40 percent up to a maximum of $4140 and then phased out. This provides "negative taxes" for the very low-income wage earners.

Source: U.S. Department of the Treasury. This example assumes two parents and two children.

credit? Cash assistance provides a minimum benefit for poor families and then reduces the benefit as market income increases. The earned-income tax credit, by contrast, gives nothing to those who do not work and supplements the earnings of those who do work. The philosophy of the EITC in essence is, "Those who do not work shall not get government dollars."

The 1996 U.S. Welfare Reform

From the 1930s until 1996, poor families could also benefit from a federal cash-assistance program known as Aid to Families with Dependent Children. This was a federal-state *entitlement program,* meaning that anyone who met certain qualifications could receive the benefits as a matter of law.

President Clinton had run on a platform of "reforming welfare as we know it." In 1996, he teamed up with a Republican Congress and completely changed the rules for cash assistance. The old program was replaced by the Temporary Assistance for Needy Families (TANF) program, which removed the federal entitlement to cash benefits and turned the program over to the 50 states.

The major provisions of the new program were the following:

- A "block grant," a fixed amount of federal funding, was given to the states to fund the federal part of cash benefits. This replaced an earlier system in which the federal government picked up 50 percent or more of state spending.
- The entitlement for federal cash assistance under TANF was removed.
- Each family is subject to a lifetime limit of 5 years of benefits under the federally supported program. After 5 years, TANF funds can no longer be used to support the family, even if it moves to a new state or has been off the welfare rolls for a number of years.
- Adults in the program must engage in work activities after 2 years of benefits.
- Legal immigrants may be excluded from TANF benefits.
- Other major low-income-support programs were largely unchanged.

Appraisal. The 1996 welfare reform was a radical experiment in social policy. One aspect is the effect on *labor markets.* To the extent that the loss of benefits forces people to seek work, this will increase the supply of relatively uneducated and unskilled labor. This increased supply will tend to lower wages of the lowest-paid workers and increase income inequality. (This effect operates much the same way that the sharp increase in immigration has contributed to lowering of wages of the unskilled in the last two decades.) If the equilibrium wages of some workers are driven down below the minimum wage, this may also lead to an increase in the unemployment rate of these groups.

One important feature of the new law is the *devolution of responsibility* for cash assistance to the states. This provision is one of the sharpest contrasts with the philosophy behind centralized income-support programs. Some economists believe that giving states "block grants" or lump-sum dollar amounts and placing decision-making responsibility in the states for benefits of a mobile population will give strong incentives for states to trim welfare benefits to reduce the costs and the fiscal burden of the low-income population. This has been called a "race to the bottom" in which the equilibrium is for states to have the lowest-possible benefits and drive low-income households elsewhere. Evidence through 2000 indicates that states have, indeed, reduced the benefits paid to nonworking poor families.

The *impacts* of the expanded EITC and 1996 welfare reform have surprised most analysts. Among the major impacts have been the following:

- The fall in welfare caseloads has been unprecedented, widespread, and continuous (see Figure 19-6). From 1995 to 2001, the number of households on welfare has fallen by more than 60 percent. While a decline was expected, its size and duration were surprising. Even when employment was falling after 2000, caseloads continued to decline.
- There was a large increase in the labor-force participation rate of single women with young children. The combination of economic incentives and a strong labor market was successful in pushing women off welfare and into jobs.
- The predicted impact on the economic well-being of low-income households is ambiguous because, even if employment increases, the higher labor earnings may be more than offset by lower government benefits. As of 2000, the overall effect of a strong economy and welfare reform was lower poverty rates and higher average incomes of former welfare recipients. Only the lowest quintile of female-headed households, and particularly

FIGURE 19-6. Welfare Cases, 1970–2000

Welfare participation tends to track the business cycle. However, since the EITC expansion and the 1996 welfare reform, caseloads have dropped sharply.

Source: Rebecca Blank, based on data from the U.S. Department of Health and Human Services.

recent immigrants, showed a decline in incomes in the late 1990s.

The successes of the combination of EITC and welfare reform in the late 1990s took place in the context of an economy with very low unemployment and strong state support of employment programs. The next major test of the system is whether the gains will continue in the 2001–2004 period of employment decline and state budget crises.

ECONOMIC POLICY AT CENTURY'S DAWN

As we enter the new century, how should government's role in the economy be redefined? We close with three final reflections:

1. We have examined the key economic functions of the government. The government combats market failures, redistributes income, stabilizes

the economy, and promotes long-term economic growth. Each of these is essential. No serious person today proposes shutting down the government. No one today proposes to allow nuclear dumping, to let poor orphans starve in the streets, to privatize the central bank, or to open the borders to all flows of people, goods, and drugs. The question is not whether government should regulate the economy but how and where it should intervene.

2. While government plays a central role in a civilized society, we must constantly reassess the mission and instruments of government policy. Governments have a monopoly on political power, and this imposes a special responsibility for government to operate efficiently. Every public dollar spent on wasteful programs could be used for promoting scientific research or alleviating hunger. Every inefficient tax reduces people's consumption opportunities, whether for food or education or housing. The central premise of economics is

that resources are scarce—and this applies to the government as well as to the private sector.

3. While economics can analyze the major public-policy controversies, it cannot have the final word. For underlying all public-policy debates are normative assumptions and value judgments about what is just and fair. What an economist does, therefore, is try very hard to keep positive science cleanly separated from normative judgments—to draw a line between the economic calculations of the head and the human feelings of the heart. But keeping description separate from prescription does not mean that the professional economist is a bloodless computer. Economists are as divided in their political philosophies as is the rest of the population. Conservative economists argue strenuously for reducing the scope of government and ending programs to redistribute income. Liberal economists are just as passionate in advocating reducing poverty or using macroeconomic policies to combat unemployment. Economic science cannot say which political point of view is right or wrong. But it can arm us for the great debate.

SUMMARY

A. The Sources of Inequality

1. In the last century, the classical economists believed that inequality was a universal constant, unchangeable by public policy. This view does not stand up to scrutiny. Poverty made a glacial retreat over the early part of this century, and absolute incomes for those in the bottom part of the income distribution rose sharply. Since around 1980, this trend has reversed, and inequality has increased.

2. The Lorenz curve is a convenient device for measuring the spreads or inequalities of income distribution. It shows what percentage of total income goes to the poorest 1 percent of the population, to the poorest 10 percent, to the poorest 95 percent, and so forth. The Gini coefficient is a quantitative measure of inequality.

3. Poverty is essentially a relative notion. In the United States, poverty was defined in terms of the adequacy of incomes in the early 1960s. By this standard of measured income, little progress in reducing inequality has been made in the last decade.

4. The distribution of American income today appears to be less unequal than in the early part of this century or than in less developed countries now. But it still shows a considerable measure of inequality, which has been increasing over the last quarter-century. Wealth is even more unequally distributed than is income, both in the United States and in other capitalist economies.

5. To explain the inequality in income distribution, we can look separately at labor income and property income. Labor earnings vary because of differences in abilities and in intensities of work (both hours and effort) and because occupational earnings differ, due to divergent amounts of human capital, among other factors.

6. Property incomes are more unevenly distributed than labor earnings, largely because of the great disparities in wealth. Inheritance helps the children of the wealthy begin ahead of the average person; only a small fraction of America's wealth can be accounted for by life-cycle savings.

B. Antipoverty Policies

7. Political philosophers write of three types of equality: (a) equality of political rights, such as the right to vote; (b) equality of opportunity, providing equal access to jobs, education, and other social systems; and (c) equality of outcome, whereby people are guaranteed equal incomes or consumptions. Whereas the first two types of equality are increasingly accepted in most advanced democracies like the United States, equality of outcome is generally rejected as impractical and too harmful to economic efficiency.

8. Equality has costs as well as benefits; the costs show up as drains from Okun's "leaky bucket." That is, attempts to reduce income inequality by progressive taxation or transfer payments may harm economic incentives to work or save and may thereby reduce the size of national output. Potential leakages are administrative costs and reduced hours of work or saving rates.

9. Major programs to alleviate poverty are welfare payments, food stamps, Medicaid, and a group of smaller or less targeted programs. As a whole, these programs are criticized because they impose high benefit-reduction rates (or marginal "tax" rates) on low-income families when families begin to earn wages or other income.

CONCEPTS FOR REVIEW

trends of income distribution
Lorenz curve of income and wealth
Gini coefficient
labor and property income
relative roles of luck, life-cycle savings,
    risk taking, inheritance

college–high school wage premium
poverty
welfare state
Okun's "leaky bucket"
equality: political, of opportunity, of
    outcome

equality vs. efficiency
income-support programs
income-possibility curve: ideal and
    realistic cases

FURTHER READING AND INTERNET WEBSITES

Further Reading

An influential book on equality versus efficiency is Arthur Okun, *Equality and Efficiency: The Big Tradeoff* (Brookings Institution, Washington, D.C., 1975).

For a nontechnical review of issues in health-care reform, see the symposium in *Journal of Economic Perspectives*, Summer 1994.

Websites

The Census Department collects poverty data. See www.census.gov/hhes/www/poverty.html. For information on welfare and poverty, see www.welfareinfo.org. The site www.doleta.gov describes the results of welfare reform from the perspective of individuals. International comparisons are available from the Luxembourg Income Study at lissy.ceps.lu/IncStat.htm.

The Urban Institute (www.urban.org) and the Joint Center for Poverty Research (www.jcpr.org) are organizations devoted to analyzing trends in poverty and income distribution.

QUESTIONS FOR DISCUSSION

1. Let each member of the class anonymously write down on a card an estimate of his or her family's annual income. From these, draw up a frequency table showing the distribution of incomes. What is the median income? The mean income?

2. What effect would the following have on the Lorenz curve of after-tax incomes? (Assume that the taxes are spent by the government on a representative slice of GDP.)
   a. A proportional income tax (i.e., one taxing all incomes at the same rate)
   b. A progressive income tax (i.e., one taxing high incomes more heavily than low incomes)
   c. A sharp increase in taxes on cigarettes and food
   Draw four Lorenz curves to illustrate the original income distribution and the income distribution after each action, **a** to **c**.

3. Review Okun's leaky bucket experiment. Get a group together and have each member of the group write down on a piece of paper how large a leak should be tolerated when government transfers $100 from the top income quintile to the bottom income quintile. Is it 99 percent? Or 50 percent? Or zero? Each person should write a short justification of the maximum number. Tabulate the results and then discuss the differences.

4. Consider two ways of supplementing the income of the poor: (*a*) cash assistance (say, $500 per month) and (*b*) categorical benefits such as subsidized food or medical care. List the pros and cons of using each strategy. Can you explain why the United States tends to use mainly strategy (*b*)? Do you agree?

5. In a country called Econoland, there are 10 people. Their incomes (in thousands) are $3, $6, $2, $8, $4, $9, $1, $5, $7, and $5. Construct a table of income

quintiles like Table 19-2. Plot a Lorenz curve. Calculate the Gini coefficient defined in Section A.

6. People continue to argue about what form assistance for the poor should take. One school says, "Give people money and let them buy health services and the foods they need." The other school says, "If you give money to the poor, they may spend it on beer and drugs. Your dollar goes further in alleviating malnourishment and disease if you provide the services in kind. The dollar that you earn may be yours to spend, but society's income-support dollar is a dollar that society has the right to channel directly to its targets."

The argument of the first school might rest on demand theory: Let each household decide how to maximize its utility on a limited budget. Chapter 5 shows why this argument might be right. But what if the parents' utility includes mainly beer and lottery tickets and no milk or clothing for the children? Might you agree with the second view? From your own personal experience and reading, which of these two arguments would you endorse? Explain your reasoning.

Macroeconomics: Economic Growth and Business Cycles

20

Overview of Macroeconomics

*The whole purpose of the economy is
production of goods or services for
consumption now or in the future.
I think the burden of proof should
always be on those who would
produce less rather than more, on
those who would leave idle people or
machines or land that could be used.
It is amazing how many reasons can
be found to justify such waste: fear
of inflation, balance-of-payments
deficits, unbalanced budgets,
excessive national debt, loss of
confidence in the dollar.*

James Tobin,
National Economic Policy

Are jobs plentiful or hard to find? Are real wages and living standards growing rapidly, or is the economy stagnating? Is the central bank raising interest rates to slow price increases, or easing monetary conditions to pull the economy out of a recession? What are the impacts of globalization and foreign trade on domestic employment and output? These questions are central to macroeconomics, which is the subject of the following chapters.

Macroeconomics is the study of the behavior of the economy as a whole. It examines the forces that affect many firms, consumers, and workers at the same time. It contrasts with **microeconomics,** which studies individual prices, quantities, and markets.

Two central themes will run through our survey of macroeconomics: (1) the short-term fluctuations in output, employment, and prices that we call the *business cycle* and (2) the longer-term trends in output and living standards known as *economic growth.*

The development of macroeconomics was one of the major breakthroughs of twentieth-century economics, leading to a much better understanding of how to combat periodic economic crises and how to stimulate long-term economic growth. In response to the Great Depression, John Maynard Keynes developed his revolutionary theory, which helped explain the forces producing economic fluctuations and suggested how governments can control the worst excesses of the business cycle. At the same time, economists have endeavored to understand the mechanics of long-term economic growth. Thanks to Keynes, his critics, and his modern successors, we know that in its choice of macroeconomic policies—those affecting the money supply, taxes, and government spending—a nation can speed or slow its economic growth, trim the excesses of price inflation or unemployment from business cycles, or take measures to deal with imbalances that arise in foreign trade or international finance.

Macroeconomic issues dominated the U.S. political and economic agenda for much of the last century. In the 1930s, when production, employment, and prices collapsed in the United States and across much of the industrial world, economists and political leaders wrestled with the calamity of the Great Depression. During the Vietnam war in the 1960s and the energy crises of the 1970s, the burning issue was "stagflation," a combination of slow growth and rising prices that left Americans feeling miserable. The 1990s witnessed a period of rapid growth, falling unemployment, and stable prices—years when everything went right, labeled by some as "the fabulous decade." The bubble burst in the early 2000s, however, as the economy was rocked by a sharp stock market decline, terrorism, and war in Iraq.

Sometimes, macroeconomic failures raise life-and-death questions for countries and even for ideologies. The communist leaders of the former Soviet Union proclaimed that they would overtake the West economically. History proved that to be a hollow promise, as Russia, a country teeming with natural resources and military might, was unable to produce adequate butter for its citizens along with the guns for its imperial armies. Eventually, macroeconomic failures brought down the communist regimes of the Soviet Union and Eastern Europe and convinced people of the economic superiority of private markets as the best approach to encouraging rapid economic growth.

This chapter will serve as an introduction to macroeconomics. It presents the major concepts and shows how they apply to key historical and policy questions of recent years. But this introduction is only a first course to whet the appetite. Not until you have mastered all the chapters in Parts Five and Six can you fully enjoy the rich macroeconomic banquet that has been a source of both inspiration for economic policy and continued controversy among macroeconomists.

A. KEY CONCEPTS OF MACROECONOMICS

THE BIRTH OF MACROECONOMICS

The 1930s marked the first stirrings of the science of macroeconomics, founded by John Maynard Keynes as he tried to understand the economic mechanism that produced the Great Depression. After World War II, reflecting both the increasing influence of Keynesian views and the fear of another depression, the U.S. Congress formally proclaimed federal responsibility for macroeconomic performance. It enacted the landmark Employment Act of 1946, which stated:

> The Congress hereby declares that it is the continuing policy and responsibility of the federal government to use all practicable means consistent with its needs and obligations . . . to promote maximum employment, production, and purchasing power.

For the first time, Congress affirmed the government's role in promoting output growth, fostering employment, and maintaining price stability.

Since the 1946 Employment Act, the nation's priorities among these three goals have shifted; but in the United States, as in all market economies, these goals still frame the central macroeconomic questions:

1. *Why do output and employment sometimes fall, and how can unemployment be reduced?* All market economies show patterns of expansion and contraction known as *business cycles*. The last major business-cycle downturn in the United States came in 2001, when production of goods and services fell and millions of people lost their jobs. For much of the postwar period, one key goal of macroeconomic policy has been to use monetary and fiscal policy to reduce the severity of business-cycle downturns and unemployment.

From time to time countries experience high unemployment that persists for long periods, sometimes as long as a decade. Such a period occurred in the United States during the Great Depression, which began in 1929. In the next few years, unemployment rose to almost one-quarter of the workforce, while industrial production fell by one-half. European countries in the 1990s had a mild depression, with persistent unemployment of over 10 percent in many countries.

Macroeconomics examines the sources of persistent unemployment. Having considered the possible diagnoses, macroeconomics also suggests possible remedies, such as increasing aggregate demand or reforming labor market institutions. The lives and fortunes of millions of people depend upon whether macroeconomists can find the right answers to these questions.

2. *What are the sources of price inflation, and how can it be kept under control?* A market economy uses prices as a yardstick to measure economic values and conduct business. During periods of rapidly rising prices, called *price inflation*, the price yardstick loses its value. When prices are rising rapidly—a phenomenon we call *inflation*—the price yardstick loses its value. During periods of high inflation, people get confused about relative prices and make mistakes in their spending and investment decisions. Tax burdens may rise.

People spend much of their time worrying that inflation is eating away at their incomes.

Macroeconomic policy has increasingly emphasized price stability as a key goal. In the United States the overall rate of inflation has fallen from more than 10 percent per year in the late 1970s to around 3 percent per year in the 1990s and early 2000s. Some countries today have not succeeded in containing inflation, however. Formerly socialist countries like Russia and many Latin American and developing countries experienced inflation rates of 50, 100, or 1000 percent per year in the last two decades. Why was the United States able to keep the inflationary tiger in the cage, while Russia failed to do so? Macroeconomics can suggest the proper role of monetary and fiscal policies, of exchange-rate systems, and of an independent central bank in containing inflation.

3. *How can a nation increase its rate of economic growth?* Above all, macroeconomics is concerned with economic growth, which refers to the growth in the productive potential of an economy. An economy's productive potential is the central factor in determining the growth in its real wages and living standards. After World War II, rapid economic growth in Asian countries such as Japan, South Korea, and Taiwan produced dramatic gains in living standards for their peoples. A few countries, particularly those of sub-Saharan Africa, have suffered declining per capita output and living standards over the last two decades. Nations want to know the ingredients in a successful growth recipe. Among the key factors in rapid economic growth are the predominance of free markets, high rates of saving and investment, low trade barriers, and an honest government with strong property rights.

All economies face inevitable tradeoffs among these goals. Increasing the rate of growth of output over the long run may require greater investment in education and capital, but higher investment requires lower current consumption of items like food, clothing, and recreation. Additionally, policymakers are sometimes forced to rein in the economy through macroeconomic policies when it grows too fast, or when unemployment falls too low, in order to prevent rising inflation.

There are no simple formulas for resolving these dilemmas, and macroeconomists often differ on the proper approach to take when confronted with high inflation, rising unemployment, or slow growth. But sound macroeconomic policies can help achieve a country's economic objectives in the most effective manner.

The Patron Saint of Macroeconomics

Every discussion of macroeconomic policy must begin with John Maynard Keynes. Keynes (1883–1946) was a many-sided genius who won eminence in the fields of mathematics, philosophy, and literature. In addition, he found time to run a large insurance company, advise the British treasury, help govern the Bank of England, edit a world-famous economics journal, collect modern art and rare books, start a repertory theater, and marry a leading Russian ballerina. He was also an investor who knew how to make money by shrewd speculation, both for himself and for his college, King's College, Cambridge.

His principal contribution, however, was his invention of a new way of looking at macroeconomics and macroeconomic policy. Before Keynes, most economists and policymakers accepted the highs and lows of business cycles as being as inevitable as the tides. These long-held views left them helpless in the face of the Great Depression of the 1930s. But Keynes took an enormous intellectual leap in his 1936 book, *The General Theory of Employment, Interest, and Money*. He made a twofold argument: First, he argued that it is possible for high unemployment and underutilized capacity to persist in market economies. In addition, he argued that government fiscal and monetary policies can affect output and thereby reduce unemployment and shorten economic downturns.

These propositions had an explosive impact when Keynes first introduced them, engendering much controversy and dispute. In the postwar period, Keynesian economics came to dominate macroeconomics and government policy. During the 1960s, virtually every analysis of macroeconomic policy was grounded in the Keynesian view of the world. Since then, new developments incorporating supply factors, expectations, and alternative views of wage and price dynamics have undermined the earlier Keynesian consensus. While few economists now believe that government action can eliminate business cycles, as Keynesian economics once seemed to promise, neither economics nor economic policy has been the same since Keynes's great discovery.

OBJECTIVES AND INSTRUMENTS OF MACROECONOMICS

Having surveyed the principal issues of macroeconomics, we now turn to a discussion of the major goals and instruments of macroeconomic policy. How do economists evaluate the success of an economy's overall performance? What are the tools that governments can use to pursue their economic goals? Table 20-1 lists the major objectives and instruments of macroeconomic policy.

Measuring Economic Success

The major macroeconomic goals are a high level and rapid growth of output, low unemployment, and stable prices. We will use this section both to define the major

Objectives
Output:
High level and rapid growth of output
Employment:
High level of employment with low involuntary unemployment
Price-level stability

Instruments
Monetary policy:
Controlling the money supply to determine interest rates
Fiscal policy:
Government expenditures   Taxation

TABLE 20-1. Goals and Instruments of Macroeconomic Policy

The top part of the table displays the major goals of macroeconomic policy. The lower half shows the major instruments or policy measures available to modern economies. Policymakers change the instruments of policy to affect the pace and direction of economic activity.

macroeconomic terms and to discuss their importance. A more detailed treatment of the data of macroeconomics is postponed to the next chapter. Some key data are provided in the appendix to this chapter.

Output. The ultimate objective of economic activity is to provide the goods and services that the population desires. What could be more important for an economy than to produce ample shelter, food, education, and recreation for its people?

The most comprehensive measure of the total output in an economy is the **gross domestic product** (GDP). GDP is the measure of the market value of all final goods and services—beer, cars, rock concerts, donkey rides, and so on—produced in a country during a year. There are two ways to measure GDP. *Nominal GDP* is measured in actual market prices. *Real GDP* is calculated in constant or invariant prices (where we measure the number of cars times the prices of cars in a given year such as 2000).

Real GDP is the most closely watched measure of output; it serves as the carefully monitored pulse of a nation's economy. Figure 20-1 shows the history of real GDP in the United States since 1929. Note the economic decline during the Great Depression of the 1930s, the boom during World War II, the steep recessions in 1975 and 1982, the rapid growth period from 1982 to 2001, and then the slow growth between 2001 and 2004.

Despite the short-term fluctuations seen in business cycles, advanced economies generally exhibit a steady long-term growth in real GDP and an improvement in living standards; this process is known as *economic growth.* The American economy has proved itself a powerful engine of progress over a period of more than a century, as shown by the growth in potential output.

Potential GDP represents the maximum sustainable level of output that the economy can produce. When an economy is operating at its potential, there are high levels of utilization of the labor force and the capital stock. When output rises above potential output, price inflation tends to rise, while a below-potential level of output leads to high unemployment.

Potential output is determined by the economy's productive capacity, which depends upon the inputs available (capital, labor, land, etc.) and the economy's technological efficiency. Potential GDP tends

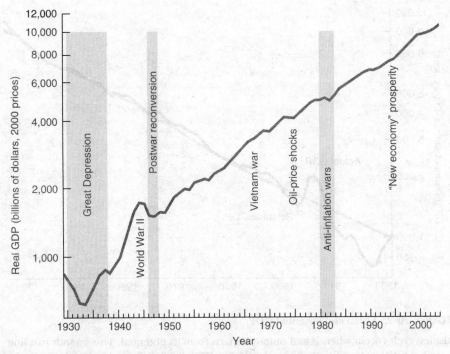

FIGURE 20-1. U.S. Real Gross Domestic Product, 1929–2003

Real GDP is the most comprehensive measure of an economy's output. Note how sharply output fell in the Great Depression of the 1930s. Except for the turmoil of the oil-price shocks of the 1970s and the anti-inflation policies of the early 1980s, economic growth has been steadier since World War II.

Source: U.S. Department of Commerce. Shaded regions are major economic downturns.

to grow steadily because inputs like labor and capital and the level of technology change quite slowly over time. By contrast, actual GDP is subject to large business-cycle swings if spending patterns change sharply.

During business downturns, actual GDP falls below its potential and unemployment rises. In 1982, for example, the U.S. economy produced more than $400 billion less than potential output. This represented $6000 lost per family during a single year. A *recession* is a period of significant decline in total output, income, and employment, usually lasting from 6 months to a year and marked by widespread contractions in many sectors of the economy. A severe and protracted downturn is called a *depression*. Output can be temporarily above potential output during booms and wartime as capacity limits are strained, but the high utilization rates bring rising inflation and are usually brought to an end by monetary or fiscal policy.

Figure 20-2 on page 410 shows the estimated potential and actual output for the period 1930–2003. Note how large the gap between actual and potential output was during the Great Depression of the 1930s.

High Employment, Low Unemployment. Of all the macroeconomic indicators, employment and unemployment are most directly felt by individuals. People want to be able to get high-paying jobs without searching or waiting too long, and they want to have job security and good benefits. In macroeconomic terms, these are the objectives of *high employment,* which is the counterpart of *low unemployment.* Figure 20-3 on page 411 shows trends in unemployment over the last six decades. The **unemployment rate** on the vertical axis is the percentage of the labor force that is unemployed. The labor force includes all employed persons and those unemployed

FIGURE 20-2. Actual and Potential GDP

Business cycles occur when actual output departs from its potential. The smooth rust line shows potential or trend output over the period 1929–2003. Potential output has grown about 3.4 percent annually. Note the large gap between actual and potential output during the Great Depression of the 1930s.

Source: U.S. Department of Commerce and authors' estimates. Note that actual GDP is directly estimated from underlying data while potential output is an analytical concept derived from actual GDP and unemployment data.

individuals who are seeking jobs. It excludes those without work who are not looking for jobs.

The unemployment rate tends to reflect the state of the business cycle: when output is falling, the demand for labor falls and the unemployment rate rises. Unemployment reached epidemic proportions in the Great Depression of the 1930s, when as much as one-quarter of the workforce was idled. Since World War II, unemployment in the United States has fluctuated but has avoided the high rates associated with depressions and the low levels that would trigger great inflations.

Price Stability. The third macroeconomic objective is to maintain *price stability.* This term means that the overall price level is either unchanged or rising very slowly.

To track prices, government statisticians construct **price indexes,** or measures of the overall price level. An important example is the **consumer price index** (CPI), which measures the average price of goods and services bought by consumers. We will generally denote the overall price level by the letter *P.*

Economists measure price stability by looking at the **inflation rate,** or **rate of inflation.** The inflation rate is the percentage change in the overall level of prices from one year to the next. For example, the CPI was 177.1 in 2001 and 179.9 in 2002 (where 1983 = 100). We thus calculate the inflation rate for 2002 as

$$\text{Inflation } 2002 = [P(2002) - P(2001)]/P(2001)$$
$$\times 100\%$$
$$= [(179.9 - 177.1)/177.1] \times 100\%$$
$$= 1.6\%$$

Figure 20-4 on page 412 illustrates the rate of inflation for the CPI from 1930 to 2003. Over this entire period, inflation averaged 3.3 percent per year. Note that price changes fluctuated greatly over the years,

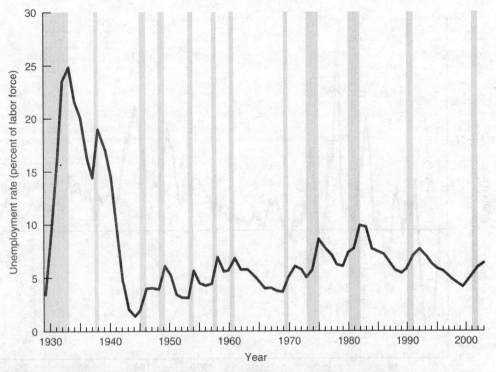

FIGURE 20-3. Unemployment Rises in Recessions, Falls during Expansions

The unemployment rate measures the fraction of the labor force that is looking for work but cannot find work. Unemployment reached tragic proportions during the 1930s, peaking at 25 percent in 1933. Unemployment rises in business-cycle downturns and falls during expansions. Shaded regions are NBER recessions.

Source: U.S. Department of Labor.

varying from minus 10 percent in 1932 to 14 percent in 1947.

A *deflation* occurs when prices decline (which means that the rate of inflation is negative). At the other extreme is a *hyperinflation,* a rise in the price level of a thousand or a million percent a year. In such situations, as in Weimar Germany in the 1920s, Brazil in the 1980s, or Russia in the 1990s, prices are virtually meaningless and the price system breaks down.

Price stability is important because a smoothly functioning market system requires that prices accurately and easily convey information about relative scarcities. History has shown that high inflation imposes many costs—some visible and some hidden—on an economy. With high inflation, taxes become highly variable, the real values of people's pensions are eroded, and people spend real resources to avoid depreciating rubles or pesos. But declining prices or deflation is also costly. Hence, most nations seek the golden mean of stable or slowly rising prices as the best way of encouraging the price system to function efficiently.

To summarize:

The goals of macroeconomic policy are:

1. A high and growing level of national output
2. High employment with low unemployment
3. A stable or gently rising price level

The Tools of Macroeconomic Policy

Put yourself in the shoes of the chief economist advising the government. Unemployment is rising and GDP is falling. Or perhaps productivity growth has declined, and you wish to increase potential output growth. Or your country has a balance-of-payments crisis, with a large trade deficit and an attack on the

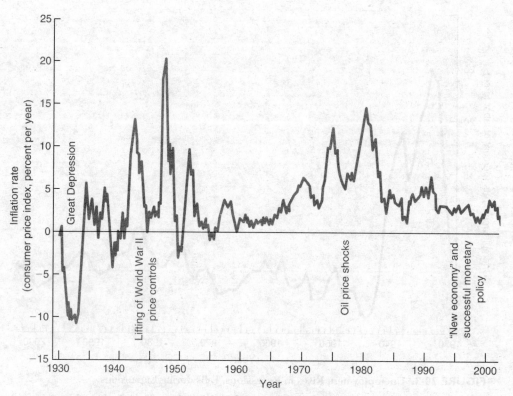

FIGURE 20-4. Consumer Price Inflation, 1929–2003

The rate of inflation measures the rate of change of prices from one year to the next; here we see the rate of inflation as measured by the consumer price index (CPI). Since World War II, prices have mainly moved upward, particularly after the oil shocks of 1973 and 1979. Since 1984, the United States has enjoyed low inflation.

Source: U.S. Department of Labor. Data show rate of inflation from 12 months earlier.

currency. What policies will help reduce inflation or unemployment, speed economic growth, or correct a trade imbalance?

Governments have certain instruments that they can use to affect macroeconomic activity. A *policy instrument* is an economic variable under the control of government that can affect one or more of the macroeconomic goals. By changing monetary, fiscal, and other policies, governments can avoid the worst excesses of the business cycle or increase the growth rate of potential output. The major instruments of macroeconomic policy are listed in the bottom half of Table 20-1.

Fiscal Policy. **Fiscal policy** denotes the use of taxes and government expenditures. *Government expenditures* come in two distinct forms. First there are

government purchases. These comprise spending on goods and services—purchases of tanks, construction of roads, salaries for judges, and so forth. In addition, there are government transfer payments, which boost the incomes of targeted groups such as the elderly or the unemployed. Government spending determines the relative size of the public and private sectors, that is, how much of our GDP is consumed collectively rather than privately. From a macroeconomic perspective, government expenditures also affect the overall level of spending in the economy and thereby influence the level of GDP.

The other part of fiscal policy, *taxation*, affects the overall economy in two ways. To begin with, taxes affect people's incomes. By leaving households with more or less disposable or spendable income, **taxes** tend to affect the amount people spend on goods and services as well as the amount of private savings. Private consumption and saving have important effects on investment and output in the short and long run.

In addition, taxes affect the prices of goods and factors of production and thereby affect incentives and behavior. For example, from 1962 until 1986, the United States employed an investment tax credit, which was a rebate to businesses that bought capital goods, as a way of stimulating investment and boosting economic growth. Many provisions of the tax code have an important impact on economic activity through their effect on the incentives to work and to save.

Monetary Policy. The second major instrument of macroeconomic policy is **monetary policy,** which the government conducts through managing the nation's money, credit, and banking system. You may have read how our central bank, the Federal Reserve System, operates to regulate the money supply. But what exactly is the money supply? **Money** consists of the means of exchange or method of payment. Today, people use currency and checking accounts to pay their bills. By engaging in central-bank operations, the Federal Reserve can regulate the amount of money available to the economy.

How does such a minor thing as the money supply have such a large impact on macroeconomic activity? By changing the money supply, the Federal Reserve can influence many financial and economic variables, such as interest rates, stock prices, housing prices, and foreign exchange rates. Restricting the money supply leads to higher interest rates and reduced investment, which, in turn, causes a decline in GDP and lower inflation. If the central bank is faced with a business downturn, it can increase the money supply and lower interest rates to stimulate economic activity.

The exact nature of monetary policy is one of the most important areas of macroeconomics. A policy of "tight money" in the United States raised interest rates, slowed economic growth, and raised unemployment in the period 1979–1982. Then, from 1982 until 2000, careful monetary management by the Federal Reserve supported the longest economic expansion in American history. Over the last decade, monetary policy has become the major weapon used by the U.S. government to fight the business cycle. Exactly how a central bank can control economic activity will be thoroughly analyzed in the chapters on monetary policy.

Other Times, Other Policies

Countries often seek new ways to solve old economic problems. One problem that has produced many innovative ideas is controlling inflation. The standard approach to slowing inflation, as we will see, has been for governments to take monetary and fiscal steps to reduce output and raise unemployment. Because this is such unpleasant medicine, governments have often searched for other methods of controlling inflation. One experimental approach is called *incomes policies* and involves direct control over prices and wages. This approach is widely applied during wartime and sometimes in peacetime emergencies. Incomes policies have ranged from wage and price controls, used primarily in wartime, to less drastic measures like voluntary wage and price guidelines used in peacetime. A generation ago, many economists thought incomes policies might be an inexpensive way to reduce inflation. For example, the Nixon administration in 1971 imposed a draconian set of mandatory wage and price controls in the hope that they would slow inflation without producing a recession.

A review of incomes policies during the Nixon regime and similar periods generally finds that they had little durable impact in reducing inflation. Those experiences, along with a more conservative attitude toward government intervention, have led to a general disenchantment with direct wage-price policies. Many economists now believe that incomes policies are simply ineffective. Others think they are pernicious—interfering with free markets, gumming up relative price movements, and failing to reduce inflation. Most high-income countries no longer use incomes policies, but they are often employed by developing countries and countries making the transition to a market economy.

Summary:

A nation has two major kinds of policies that can be used to pursue its macroeconomic goals—fiscal policy and monetary policy.

1. Fiscal policy consists of government expenditure and taxation. Government expenditure influences the relative size of collective spending and private consumption. Taxation subtracts from incomes, reduces private spending, and affects private saving. In addition, it affects investment and potential output. Fiscal policy is primarily

employed today to affect long-term economic growth through its impact on national saving and on incentives to work and save.

2. Monetary policy, conducted by the central bank, determines the money supply and financial conditions. Changes in the money supply move interest rates up or down and affect spending in sectors such as business investment, housing, and foreign trade. Monetary policy has an important effect on both actual GDP and potential GDP.

INTERNATIONAL LINKAGES

No nation is an island unto itself. All nations participate in the world economy and are linked together through trade and finance. The trade linkages of imports and exports of goods and services are seen when the United States imports cars from Japan or exports computers to Mexico. Financial linkages come when the United States lends funds to Mexico to stabilize the Mexican peso or when British pension funds diversify their portfolios by investing in the booming U.S. stock market.

Nations keep a close watch on their foreign-trade flows. One particularly important index is net exports, which is the numerical difference between the value of exports and the value of imports. When exports exceed imports, the difference is a surplus, while a negative net-export balance is a deficit. Hence when its exports totaled $1062 billion in 2003 while imports were $1555 billion, the United States had a foreign-trade deficit of $494 billion, or 4.4 percent of GDP.

As the costs of transportation and communication have declined, international linkages have become tighter than they were a generation ago. International trade has replaced empire building and military conquest as the surest road to national wealth and influence. Some economies today trade over half their output.

For most of the twentieth century, the United States had a surplus in its foreign trade, exporting more than it imported. But trading patterns changed dramatically in the last quarter-century. Because of a decline in the national saving rate and booming investment, the U.S. net-export position turned sharply toward deficit, surpassing 4 percent of GDP in the early 2000s. As the deficits piled up, the United States by 2003 owed on balance almost $3 trillion to foreigners. Some economists worry

that the large foreign debt poses major risks for the United States—risks that we will analyze in later chapters.

As economies become more closely linked, policymakers devote increasing attention to international economic policy. International trade is not an end in itself. Rather, nations are properly concerned about international trade because trade serves the ultimate goal of improving living standards. The major areas of concern are trade policies and international financial management.

Trade policies consist of tariffs, quotas, and other regulations that restrict or encourage imports and exports. Most trade policies have little effect on macroeconomic performance, but from time to time, as was the case in the 1930s, restrictions on international trade are so severe that they cause major economic dislocations, inflations, or recessions.

A second set of policies is *international financial management.* A country's international trade is influenced by its foreign exchange rate, which represents the price of its own currency in terms of the currencies of other nations. As part of their monetary policies, nations adopt different systems to regulate their foreign exchange markets. Particularly in small open economies, managing the exchange rate is the single most important macroeconomic policy.

The international economy is an intricate web of trading and financial connections among countries. When the international economic system runs smoothly, it contributes to rapid economic growth; when trading systems break down, production and incomes suffer throughout the world. Countries therefore consider the impacts of trade policies and international financial policies on their domestic objectives of output, employment, and price stability.

B. AGGREGATE SUPPLY AND DEMAND

The economic history of nations can be seen in their macroeconomic performance. Economists have developed aggregate supply-and-demand analysis to help explain the major trends in output and prices. We begin by explaining this important tool of macroeconomics and then use it to understand some important historical events.

INSIDE THE MACROECONOMY: AGGREGATE SUPPLY AND DEMAND

Definitions of Aggregate Supply and Demand

How do different forces interact to determine overall economic activity? Figure 20-5 shows the relationships among the different variables inside the macroeconomy. It separates variables into two categories: those affecting aggregate supply and those affecting aggregate demand. Dividing variables into these two categories helps us understand what determines the levels of output, prices, and unemployment.

The lower part of Figure 20-5 shows the forces affecting aggregate supply. **Aggregate supply** refers to the total quantity of goods and services that the nation's businesses willingly produce and sell in a given period. Aggregate supply (often written *AS*) depends

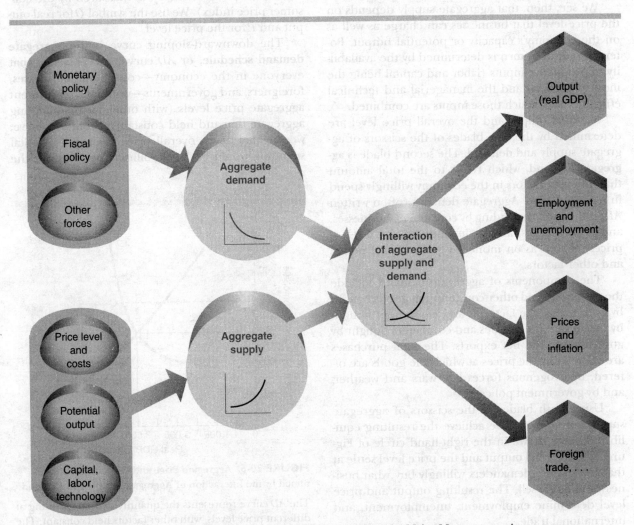

FIGURE 20-5. Aggregate Supply and Demand Determine the Major Macroeconomic Variables

This key diagram shows the major factors affecting overall economic activity. On the left are the major variables determining aggregate supply and demand; these include policy variables, like monetary and fiscal policies, along with stocks of capital and labor. In the center, aggregate supply and demand interact as the level of demand beats upon the available resources. The chief outcomes are shown on the right in hexagons: output, employment, the price level, and international trade.

upon the price level, the productive capacity of the economy, and the level of costs.

In general, businesses would like to sell everything they can produce at high prices. Under some circumstances, prices and spending levels may be depressed, so businesses might find they have excess capacity. Under other conditions, such as during a wartime boom, factories may be operating at capacity as businesses scramble to produce enough to meet all their orders.

We see, then, that aggregate supply depends on the price level that businesses can charge as well as on the economy's capacity or potential output. Potential output in turn is determined by the availability of productive inputs (labor and capital being the most important) and the managerial and technical efficiency with which those inputs are combined.

National output and the overall price level are determined by the twin blades of the scissors of aggregate supply and demand. The second blade is **aggregate demand,** which refers to the total amount that different sectors in the economy willingly spend in a given period. Aggregate demand (often written *AD*) is the sum of spending by consumers, businesses, and governments, and it depends on the level of prices, as well as on monetary policy, fiscal policy, and other factors.

The components of aggregate demand include the cars, food, and other consumption goods bought by consumers; the factories and equipment bought by businesses; the missiles and computers bought by government; and net exports. The total purchases are affected by the prices at which the goods are offered, by exogenous forces like wars and weather, and by government policies.

Using both blades of the scissors of aggregate supply and demand, we achieve the resulting equilibrium, as is shown in the right-hand circle of Figure 20-5. National output and the price level settle at that level where demanders willingly buy what businesses willingly sell. The resulting output and price level determine employment, unemployment, and international trade.

Aggregate Supply and Demand Curves

Aggregate supply and demand curves are often used to help analyze macroeconomic conditions. Recall that in Chapter 3 we used market supply and demand curves to analyze the prices and quantities of individual products. An analogous graphical apparatus can help us understand how monetary policy or technological change acts through aggregate supply and demand to determine national output and the price level.

Figure 20-6 shows the aggregate supply and demand schedules for the output of an entire economy. On the horizontal, or quantity, axis is the total output (real GDP) of the economy. On the vertical axis is the overall price level (say, as measured by the consumer price index). We use the symbol Q for real output and P for the price level.

The downward-sloping curve is the **aggregate demand schedule,** or *AD* curve. It represents what everyone in the economy—consumers, businesses, foreigners, and governments—would buy at different aggregate price levels (with other factors affecting aggregate demand held constant). From the curve, we see that at an overall price level of 150, total spending would be $3000 billion (per year). If the

FIGURE 20-6. Aggregate Price and Output Are Determined by the Interaction of Aggregate Supply and Demand

The *AD* curve represents the quantity of total spending at different price levels, with other factors held constant. The *AS* curve shows what firms will produce and sell at different price levels, other things equal.

National output and the overall price level are determined at the intersection of the aggregate demand and supply curves, at point *E*. This equilibrium occurs at an overall price level where firms willingly produce and sell what consumers and other demanders willingly buy.

price level rises to 200, total spending would fall to $2300 billion.

The upward-sloping curve is the **aggregate supply schedule,** or *AS* curve. This curve represents the quantity of goods and services that businesses are willing to produce and sell at each price level (with other determinants of aggregate supply held constant). According to the curve, businesses will want to sell $3000 billion at a price level of 150; they will want to sell a higher quantity, $3300 billion, if prices rise to 200. As the level of total output demanded rises, businesses will want to sell more goods and services at a higher price level.

(We have drawn the *AS* curve as upward-sloping and the *AD* curve as downward-sloping, but at this point we have not explained the reasons for the slopes. A more detailed discussion of the curves and their slopes will be provided in later chapters.)

> ### Warning on AS and AD Curves
> Before proceeding, here is one important word of caution: Do not confuse the macroeconomic *AD* and *AS* curves with the microeconomic *DD* and *SS* curves. The microeconomic supply and demand curves show the quantities and prices of individual commodities, with such things as national income and other goods' prices held as given. By contrast, the aggregate supply and demand curves show the determination of total output and the overall price level, with such things as the money supply, fiscal policy, and the capital stock held constant. Aggregate supply and demand explain how taxes affect national output and the movement of all prices; microeconomic supply and demand might consider the way increases in gasoline taxes affect purchases of automobiles. The two sets of curves have a superficial resemblance, but they explain very different phenomena.

Macroeconomic Equilibrium. We now see how aggregate output and the price level adjust or equilibrate to bring aggregate supply and aggregate demand into balance. That is, we use the *AS* and *AD* concepts to see how *equilibrium values of price and quantity* are determined or to find the *P* and *Q* that satisfy the buyers and sellers all taken together. For the *AS* and *AD* curves shown in Figure 20-6, the overall economy is in equilibrium at point *E*. Only at that point, where the level of output is $Q = 3000$ and $P = 150$, are spenders and sellers satisfied. Only at point *E* are demanders willing to buy exactly the amount that businesses are willing to produce and sell.

How does the economy reach its equilibrium? Indeed, what do we mean by equilibrium? A **macroeconomic equilibrium** is a combination of overall price and quantity at which all buyers and sellers are satisfied with their purchases, sales, and prices. Figure 20-6 illustrates the concept. If the price level were higher than equilibrium, say, at $P = 200$, businesses would want to sell more than purchasers would want to buy; businesses would desire to sell quantity *C*, while buyers would want to purchase only amount *B*. Goods would pile up on the shelves as firms produced more than consumers bought. Eventually, firms would cut production and begin to shave their prices. As the price level declined from its original too high level of 200, the gap between desired spending and desired sales would narrow until the equilibrium at $P = 150$ and $Q = 3000$ was reached. Once the equilibrium is reached, neither buyers nor sellers wish to change their quantities demanded or supplied, and there is no pressure on the price level to change.

MACROECONOMIC HISTORY: 1900–2003

We can use the aggregate supply-and-demand apparatus to analyze some of the major macroeconomic events of twentieth-century American history. We focus on the economic expansion during the Vietnam war, the deep recession caused by the monetary contraction of the early 1980s, and the phenomenal record of economic growth for that century. For recent data on major macroeconomic variables, see this chapter's appendix.

Wartime Boom. The American economy entered the 1960s having experienced numerous recessions. John Kennedy took over the presidency hoping to resuscitate the economy. This was the era when the "New Economics," as the Keynesian approach was called, came to Washington. Economic advisers to Presidents Kennedy and Johnson recommended expansionary policies, and Congress enacted measures to stimulate the economy, including sharp cuts in personal and corporate taxes in 1963 and 1964. GDP grew 4 percent annually during the early 1960s, unemployment declined, and prices were stable. By 1965, the economy was at its potential output.

Unfortunately, the government underestimated the magnitude of the buildup for the Vietnam war; defense spending grew by 55 percent from 1965 to 1968. Even when it became clear that a major inflationary boom was under way, President Johnson postponed painful fiscal steps to slow the economy. Tax increases and civilian expenditure cuts came only in 1968, which was too late to prevent inflationary pressures from overheating the economy. The Federal Reserve accommodated the expansion with rapid money growth and low interest rates. As a result, the economy grew very rapidly over the period 1966–1970. Under the pressure of low unemployment and high factory utilization, inflation began to rise, inaugurating the "age of inflation" that lasted from 1966 through 1981.

Figure 20-7 illustrates the events of this period. The tax cuts and defense expenditures increased aggregate demand, shifting the aggregate demand curve to the right from *AD* to *AD′*, with the equilibrium shifting from *E* to *E′*. Output and employment rose sharply, and prices began to accelerate as output exceeded capacity limits. Economists learned that it was easier to stimulate the economy than to persuade policymakers to raise taxes to slow the economy when inflation threatened. This lesson led many to question the wisdom of using fiscal policies to stabilize the economy.

Tight Money, 1979–1982. The 1970s were a period of turmoil in which oil prices rose by a factor of 10, wages accelerated, and price inflation became embedded in the U.S. and many other economies. As Figure 20-4, on page 412 shows, inflation rose to double-digit levels over the 1978–1980 period, and interest rates rose to nearly 20 percent per year.

Double-digit inflation was unacceptable. In response, the Federal Reserve, under the leadership of economist Paul Volcker, prescribed the strong medicine of tight money to slow the inflation. Interest rates rose sharply in 1979 and 1980, the stock market fell, and credit was hard to find. The Fed's tight-money policy slowed spending by consumers and businesses. Particularly hard-hit were interest-sensitive components of aggregate demand. After 1979, housing construction, automobile purchases, business investment, and net exports declined sharply.

We can picture how tight money raised interest rates and reduced aggregate demand in Figure 20-7 simply by reversing the arrow. That is, tight monetary policy reduced spending and produced a leftward and downward shift of the aggregate demand curve—exactly the opposite of the effect of the defense buildup during the 1960s. The decrease in aggregate demand reduced output almost 10 percent below its potential by the end of 1982, and the unemployment rate rose from below 6 percent in 1979 to more than 10 percent at the end of 1982.

The reward for these austere measures was a dramatic decline in inflation, from an average of 12 percent per year in the 1978–1980 period to 4 percent during the period from 1983 to 1988. Tight monetary policies succeeded in bringing to an end the age of inflation, but the nation paid for this achievement through higher unemployment and lower output during the period of tight money.

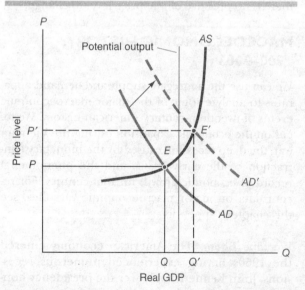

FIGURE 20-7. Wartime Boom Is Propelled by Increasing Aggregate Demand

During wartime, increased military spending increases aggregate spending, moving aggregate demand from *AD* to *AD′*, with equilibrium output increasing from *E* to *E′*. When output rises far above potential output, the price level moves up sharply from *P* to *P′*, and wartime inflation ensues.

The tough monetary policies of the 1980s set the stage for the long economic expansion from 1982 through 2000. This period, marked by a single mild recession in 1990–1991, proved to be the period of the greatest macroeconomic stability in American history. Real GDP grew at an average rate of 3 percent annually, with price inflation averaging slightly above 3½ percent. By the late 1990s, many of those in the workforce had never experienced a severe business cycle or inflationary episode, and some were proclaiming naively that the business cycle was abolished in this "new era" economy.

The Growth Century. The final act in our macroeconomic drama concerns the growth of output and prices over the entire period since 1900. Output has grown by a factor of almost 20 since the beginning of the twentieth century. How can we explain this phenomenal increase?

A careful look at American economic growth reveals that the growth rate during the twentieth century averaged 3½ percent per year. Part of this growth was due to growth in the scale of production as inputs of capital, labor, and even land grew sharply over this period. Just as important were improvements in efficiency due to new products (such as automobiles) and new processes (such as electronic computing). Other, less visible factors also contributed to economic growth, such as improved management techniques and improved services (including such innovations as the assembly line and overnight delivery). Many economists believe that the measured growth understates true growth because our official statistics tend to miss the contribution to living standards from new products and improvements in product quality. For example, with the introduction of the indoor toilet, millions of people no longer had to struggle through the winter snows to relieve themselves in outhouses, yet this increased comfort never showed up in measured gross domestic product.

How can we picture the tremendous rise in output in our *AS-AD* apparatus? Figure 20-8 shows the way. The increase in inputs and improvements in efficiency led to a massive rightward shift of the *AS* curve from AS_{1900} to AS_{2000}. There was also a sharp increase in the cost of production, as average hourly earnings rose from $0.10 per hour to $13.20 per

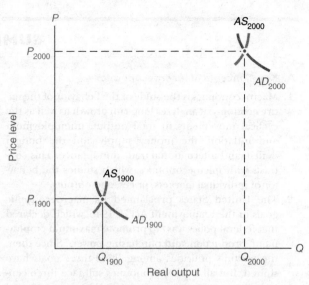

FIGURE 20-8. Growth in Potential Output Determines Long-Run Economic Performance

Over the twentieth century, increases in labor, capital, and efficiency led to a vast increase in the economy's productive potential, shifting aggregate supply far to the right. In the long run, aggregate supply is the primary determinant of output growth.

hour, so the *AS* curve also shifted upward. The overall effect, then, was the increase in both output and prices shown in Figure 20-8.

The Role of Economic Policy

What was the role of macroeconomic policy in the growth century? The striking change over the twentieth century was the discovery and application of macroeconomics, along with a good appreciation of the role and limitations of monetary and fiscal policy. The second half of the century saw rapid growth and much-attenuated business cycles as compared to the first five decades of the century. The application of fiscal policy, and especially monetary policy, helped lower unemployment and provided largely stable prices over the last two decades. This was no miracle cure, however. Recessions have not been banished from the land, and the application of sound macroeconomic policies has not spread throughout the world. But the fundamental knowledge is available to reduce the risk of galloping inflation and deep depressions.

SUMMARY

A. Key Concepts of Macroeconomics

1. Macroeconomics is the study of the behavior of the entire economy: it analyzes long-run growth as well as the cyclical movements in total output, unemployment and inflation, the money supply and the budget deficit, and international trade and finance. This contrasts with microeconomics, which studies the behavior of individual markets, prices, and outputs.

2. The United States proclaimed its macroeconomic goals in the Employment Act of 1946, which declared that federal policy was "to promote maximum employment, production, and purchasing power." Since then, the nation's priorities among these three goals have shifted. But all market economies still face three central macroeconomic questions: (a) Why do output and employment sometimes fall, and how can unemployment be reduced? (b) What are the sources of price inflation, and how can it be kept under control? (c) How can a nation increase its rate of economic growth?

3. In addition to these perplexing questions is the hard fact that there are inevitable conflicts or tradeoffs among these goals: rapid growth in future living standards may mean reducing consumption today, and curbing inflation may involve a temporary period of high unemployment.

4. Economists evaluate the success of an economy's overall performance by how well it attains these objectives: (a) high levels and rapid growth of output and consumption [output is usually measured by the gross domestic product (GDP), which is the total value of all final goods and services produced in a given year; also, GDP should be close to potential GDP, the maximum sustainable or high-employment level of output]; (b) low unemployment rate and high employment, with an ample supply of good jobs; (c) price-level stability (or low inflation).

5. Before the science of macroeconomics was developed, countries tended to drift around in the shifting macroeconomic currents without a rudder. Today, there are numerous instruments with which governments can steer the economy: (a) Fiscal policy (government spending and taxation) helps determine the allocation of resources between private and collective goods, affects people's incomes and consumption, and provides incentives for investment and other economic decisions. (b) Monetary policy (particularly central-bank regulation of the money supply to influence interest rates and credit conditions) affects sectors in the economy that are interest-sensitive. The most affected sectors are housing, business investment, and net exports.

6. The nation is but a small part of an increasingly integrated global economy in which countries are linked together through trade of goods and services and through financial flows. A smoothly running international economic system contributes to rapid economic growth, but the international economy can throw sand in the engine of growth when trade flows are interrupted or the international financial mechanism breaks down. Dealing with international trade and finance is high on the agenda of all countries.

B. Aggregate Supply and Demand

7. The central concepts for understanding the determination of national output and the price level are aggregate supply (AS) and aggregate demand (AD). Aggregate demand consists of the total spending in an economy by households, businesses, governments, and foreigners. It represents the total output that would be willingly bought at each price level, given the monetary and fiscal policies and other factors affecting demand. Aggregate supply describes how much output businesses would willingly produce and sell given prices, costs, and market conditions.

8. AS and AD curves have the same shapes as the familiar supply and demand curves analyzed in microeconomics. The downward-sloping AD curve shows the amount that consumers, firms, and other purchasers would buy at each level of prices, with other factors held constant. The AS curve depicts the amount that businesses would willingly produce and sell at each price level, other things held constant. (But beware of potential confusions of microeconomic and aggregate supply and demand.)

9. The overall macroeconomic equilibrium, determining both aggregate price and output, comes where the AS and AD curves intersect. At the equilibrium price level, purchasers willingly buy what businesses willingly sell. Equilibrium output can depart from full employment or potential output.

10. Recent American history shows an irregular cycle of aggregate demand and supply shocks and policy reactions. In the mid-1960s, war-bloated deficits plus easy money led to a rapid increase in aggregate demand. The result was a sharp upturn in prices and inflation. At the end of the 1970s, economic policymakers reacted to the rising inflation by tightening monetary policy and raising interest rates. The result lowered

spending on interest-sensitive demands such as housing, investment, and net exports. The period of austerity in the early 1980s ushered in a long period of macroeconomic stability.

11. Over the long run of the twentieth century, the growth of potential output increased aggregate supply enormously and led to continual growth in output and living standards.

CONCEPTS FOR REVIEW

Major Macroeconomic Concepts

macroeconomics vs. microeconomics
gross domestic product (GDP),
    actual and potential
employment, unemployment,
    unemployment rate

inflation, deflation
consumer price index (CPI)
net exports
fiscal policy (government
    expenditures, taxation)
money, monetary policy

Aggregate Supply and Demand

aggregate supply, aggregate demand
AS curve, *AD* curve
equilibrium of *AS* and *AD*
sources of long-run economic growth

FURTHER READING AND INTERNET WEBSITES

Further Reading

The great classic of macroeconomics is John Maynard Keynes, *The General Theory of Employment, Interest, and Money* (Harcourt, New York, first published in 1935). Keynes was one of the most graceful writers among economists.

There are many good intermediate textbooks on macroeconomics. You may consult these when you want to dig more deeply into specific topics.

Websites

Macroeconomic issues are a central theme of analysis in *Economic Report of the President*. Various years are available online at w3.access.gpo.gov/eop/. Another good source on macroeconomic issues is the Congressional Budget Office, which issues periodic reports on the economy and the state of the budget at www.cbo.gov.

Research organizations often contain excellent online discussions of current macroeconomic issues. See especially the websites of the Brookings Institution www.brookings.org and the American Enterprise Institute www.aei.org/.

QUESTIONS FOR DISCUSSION

1. What are the major objectives of macroeconomics? Write a brief definition of each of these objectives. Explain carefully why each objective is important.
2. Using the data from the appendix to this chapter, calculate the following:
   a. The inflation rate in 1981 and 1999
   b. The growth rate of real GDP in 1982 and 1984
   c. The average inflation rate from 1970 to 1980 and from 1990 to 1999
   d. The average growth rate of real GDP from 1970 to 1999

3. What would be the effect of each of the following on aggregate demand or on aggregate supply, as indicated (always holding other things constant)?
   a. A large cut in personal and business taxes (on *AD*).
   b. An arms-reduction agreement reducing defense spending (on *AD*)
   c. An increase in potential output (on *AS*)
   d. A monetary loosening that lowers interest rates (on *AD*)

4. For each of the events listed in question 3, use the *AS-AD* apparatus to show the effect on output and on the overall price level.

5. Put yourself in the shoes of an economic policymaker. The economy is in equilibrium with $P = 100$ and $Q = 3000$ = potential GDP. You refuse to "accommodate" inflation; that is, you want to keep prices absolutely stable at $P = 100$, no matter what happens to output. You can use monetary and fiscal policies to affect aggregate demand, but you cannot affect aggregate supply in the short run. How would you respond to:
   a. A surprise increase in investment spending
   b. A sharp food-price increase following catastrophic floods of the Mississippi River
   c. A productivity decline that reduces potential output
   d. A sharp decrease in net exports that followed a deep depression in East Asia

6. In 1981–1983, the Reagan administration implemented a fiscal policy that reduced taxes and increased government spending.
   a. Explain why this policy would tend to increase aggregate demand. Show the impact on output and prices assuming only an *AD* shift.
   b. The supply-side school holds that tax cuts would affect aggregate supply mainly by increasing potential output. Assuming that the Reagan fiscal measures affected *AS* as well as *AD*, show the impact on output and the price level. Explain why the impact of the Reagan fiscal policies on output is unambiguous while the impact on prices is unclear.

7. The Clinton economic package as passed by Congress in 1993 had the effect of tightening fiscal policy by raising taxes and lowering spending. Show the effect of this policy (*a*) assuming that there is no counteracting monetary policy and (*b*) assuming that monetary policy completely neutralized the impact on GDP and that the lower deficit leads to higher investment and higher growth of potential output.

8. The last major business downturn in the United States occurred in the early 1980s. Consider the data on real GDP and the price level in Table 20-2.
   a. For the years 1981 to 1985, calculate the rate of growth of real GDP and the rate of inflation. Can you determine in which year there was a steep business downturn or recession?
   b. In an *AS-AD* diagram like Figure 20-6 (page 416), draw a set of *AS* and *AD* curves that trace out the price and output equilibria shown in the table. How would you explain the recession that you have identified?

Year	Real GDP ($, billion, 2000 prices)	Price level* (2000 = 100)
1980	5161.7	54.1
1981	5291.7	59.1
1982	5189.3	62.7
1983	5423.8	65.2
1984	5813.6	67.7
1985	6053.7	69.7

*Note that the price index shown is the price index for GDP, which measures the price trend for all components of GDP.

TABLE 20-2.

Appendix 20

MACROECONOMIC DATA FOR THE UNITED STATES

Year	Nominal GDP ($, billion)	Real GDP, 2000 prices ($, billion)	Unemployment rate (%)	CPI 1982–84 = 100	Inflation rate (CPI) (% per year)	Federal budget surplus (+) or deficit (−) ($, billion)	Net exports ($, billion)
1929	103.6	865.2	3.2	17.1	0.0	1.1	0.4
1933	56.4	635.5	24.9	13.0	−5.1	−1.3	0.1
1939	92.2	950.7	17.2	13.9	−1.4	−2.6	0.8
1945	223.1	1786.3	1.9	18.0	2.3	−43.0	−0.8
1948	269.2	1643.2	3.8	24.1	8.1	8.8	5.5
1950	293.8	1777.3	5.2	24.1	1.3	7.6	0.7
1960	526.4	2501.8	5.5	29.6	1.7	2.1	4.2
1970	1038.5	3771.9	5.0	38.8	5.7	−15.2	4.0
1971	1127.1	3898.6	6.0	40.5	4.4	−24.5	0.6
1972	1238.3	4105.0	5.6	41.8	3.2	−19.7	−3.4
1973	1382.7	4341.5	4.9	44.4	6.2	−5.5	4.1
1974	1500.0	4319.6	5.6	49.3	11.0	−9.6	−0.8
1975	1638.3	4311.2	8.5	53.8	9.1	−73.1	16.0
1976	1825.3	4540.9	7.7	56.9	5.8	−55.5	−1.6
1977	2030.9	4750.5	7.1	60.6	6.5	−48.3	−23.1
1978	2294.7	5015.0	6.1	65.2	7.6	−35.1	−25.4
1979	2563.3	5173.4	5.9	72.6	11.3	−22.0	−22.5
1980	2789.5	5161.7	7.2	82.4	13.5	−65.9	−13.1
1981	3128.4	5291.7	7.6	90.9	10.3	−64.6	−12.5
1982	3255.0	5189.3	9.7	96.5	6.2	−145.1	−20.0
1983	3536.7	5423.8	9.6	99.6	3.2	−193.5	−51.7
1984	3933.2	5813.6	7.5	103.9	4.3	−195.6	−102.7
1985	4220.3	6053.7	7.2	107.6	3.6	−213.2	−115.2
1986	4462.8	6263.6	7.0	109.6	1.9	−229.6	−132.7
1987	4739.5	6475.1	6.2	113.6	3.6	−186.9	−145.2
1988	5103.8	6742.7	5.5	118.3	4.1	−166.9	−110.4
1989	5484.4	6981.4	5.3	124.0	4.8	−160.1	−88.2
1990	5803.1	7112.5	5.6	130.7	5.4	−208.3	−78.0
1991	5995.9	7100.5	6.9	136.2	4.2	−245.3	−27.5
1992	6337.7	7336.6	7.5	140.3	3.0	−322.9	−33.2
1993	6657.4	7532.7	6.9	144.5	3.0	−290.7	−65.0
1994	7072.2	7835.5	6.1	148.2	2.6	−221.4	−93.6
1995	7397.7	8031.7	5.6	152.4	2.8	−199.2	−91.4
1996	7816.9	8328.9	5.4	156.9	3.0	−147.8	−96.2
1997	8304.3	8703.5	4.9	160.5	2.3	−47.4	−101.6
1998	8747.0	9066.9	4.5	163.0	1.6	47.8	−159.9
1999	9268.4	9470.3	4.2	166.6	2.2	101.3	−260.5
2000	9817.0	9817.0	4.0	172.2	3.4	189.4	−379.5
2001	10100.8	9866.6	4.8	177.1	2.8	45.4	−366.5
2002	10480.8	10083.0	5.8	179.9	1.6	−258.6	−426.3
2003	10990.8	10397.0	6.0	184.0	2.3	−467.7	−498.5

TABLE 20A-1.

Table 20A-1 contains some of the major macroeconomic data discussed in this chapter.
Major data can be obtained through government websites at www.fedstats.gov, www.bea.gov,
or www.bls.gov.

CHAPTER

21

Measuring Economic Activity

When you can measure what you are speaking about, and express it in numbers, you know something about it; when you cannot measure it, when you cannot express it in numbers, your knowledge is of a meager and unsatisfactory kind; it may be the beginning of knowledge, but you have scarcely, in your thoughts, advanced to the stage of science.

Lord Kelvin

Of all the concepts in macroeconomics, the single most important one is the gross domestic product (GDP), which measures the total value of goods and services produced in a country. GDP is part of the *national income and product accounts* (or *national accounts*), which are a body of statistics that enable policymakers to determine whether the economy is contracting or expanding and whether a severe recession or inflation threatens. When economists want to determine the level of economic development of a country, they look at its GDP per capita.

While the GDP and the rest of the national accounts may seem to be arcane concepts, they are truly among the great inventions of the twentieth century. Much as a satellite in space can survey the weather across an entire continent, so can the GDP give an overall picture of the state of the economy. In this chapter, we explain how economists measure GDP and other major macroeconomic concepts.

GROSS DOMESTIC PRODUCT: THE YARDSTICK OF AN ECONOMY'S PERFORMANCE

What is the *gross domestic product*? GDP is the name we give to the total market value of the final goods and services produced within a nation during a given year. It is the figure you get when you apply the measuring rod of money to the diverse goods and services—from apples to zithers—that a country produces with its land, labor, and capital resources. GDP equals the total production of consumption and investment goods, government purchases, and net exports to other lands.

The gross domestic product (GDP) is the most comprehensive measure of a nation's total output of goods and services. It is the sum of the dollar values of consumption (C), gross investment (I), government purchases of goods and services (G), and net exports (X) produced within a nation during a given year.

In symbols:

$$\text{GDP} = C + I + G + X$$

GDP is used for many purposes, but the most important one is to measure the overall performance of an economy. If you were to ask an economic historian what happened during the Great Depression, the best short answer would be:

Between 1929 and 1933, GDP fell from $104 billion to $56 billion. This sharp decline in the dollar value of goods and services produced by the American economy caused high unemployment, hardship, a steep stock market decline, bankruptcies, bank failures, riots, and political turmoil.

Similarly, if you were to ask what was unusual about the 1990s, a macroeconomist might reply:

The 1990s were the longest economic expansion in the nation's history. From 1992 to 2000, real GDP grew steadily, increasing by 34 percent with falling unemployment, stable inflation, and rising stock market prices.

We now discuss the elements of the national income and product accounts. We start by showing different ways of measuring GDP and distinguishing real from nominal GDP. We then analyze the major components of GDP. We conclude with a discussion of the measurement of the general price level and the rate of inflation.

Two Measures of National Product: Goods Flow and Earnings Flow

How do economists actually measure GDP? One of the major surprises is that we can measure GDP in two entirely independent ways. As Figure 21-1 shows, GDP can be measured either as a flow of products or as a sum of earnings.

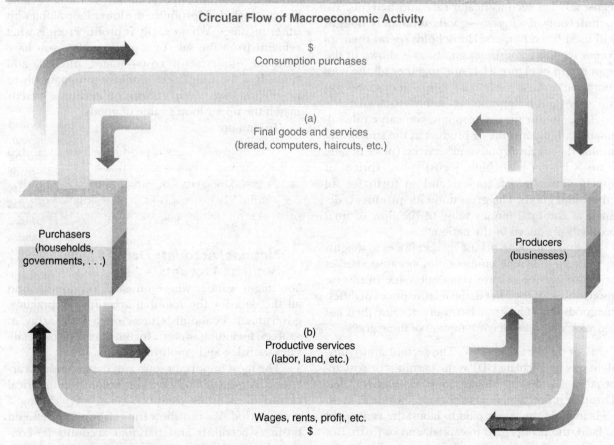

Circular Flow of Macroeconomic Activity

FIGURE 21-1. Gross Domestic Product Can Be Measured Either as (a) a Flow of Final Products or, Equivalently, as (b) a Flow of Costs

In the upper loop, purchasers buy final goods and services. The total dollar flow of their spending each year is one measure of gross domestic product. The lower loop measures the annual flow of costs of output: the earnings that businesses pay out in wages, rent, interest, dividends, and profits.

The two measures of GDP must always be identical. Note that this figure is the macroeconomic counterpart of Fig. 2-1, which presented the circular flow of supply and demand.

To demonstrate the different ways of measuring GDP, we begin by considering an oversimplified world in which there is no government, foreign trade, or investment. For the moment, our little economy produces only *consumption goods,* which are items that are purchased by households to satisfy their wants. (Important note: Our first example is oversimplified to show the basic ideas. In the realistic examples that follow, we will add investment, government, and the foreign sector.)

Flow-of-Product Approach. Each year the public consumes a wide variety of final goods and services: goods such as apples, computer software, and blue jeans; services such as health care and haircuts. We include only *final goods*—goods ultimately bought and used by consumers. Households spend their incomes for these consumer goods, as is shown in the upper loop of Figure 21-1. Add together all the consumption dollars spent on these final goods, and you will arrive at this simplified economy's total GDP.

Thus, in our simple economy, you can easily calculate national income or product as the sum of the annual flow of *final* goods and services: (price of blue jeans × number of blue jeans) plus (price of apples × number of apples) and so forth for all other final goods. The gross domestic product is defined as the total money value of the flow of final products produced by the nation.

National accountants use market prices as weights in valuing different commodities because market prices reflect the relative economic value of diverse goods and services. That is, the relative prices of different goods reflect how much consumers value their last (or marginal) units of consumption of these goods.

Earnings or Cost Approach. The second and equivalent way to calculate GDP is the earnings or cost approach. Go to the lower loop in Figure 21-1. Through it flow all the costs of doing business; these costs include the wages paid to labor, the rents paid to land, the profits paid to capital, and so forth. But these business costs are also the earnings that households receive from firms. By measuring the annual flow of these earnings or incomes, statisticians will again arrive at the GDP.

Hence, a second way to calculate GDP is as the total of factor earnings (wages, interest, rents, and profits) that are the costs of producing society's final products.

Equivalence of the Two Approaches. Now we have calculated GDP by the upper-loop flow-of-product approach and by the lower-loop earnings-flow approach. Which is the better approach? The surprise is that *they are exactly the same.*

We can see why the product and earnings approaches are identical by examining a simple barbershop economy. Say the barbers have no expenses other than labor. If they sell 10 haircuts at $8 each, GDP is $80. But the barbers' earnings (in wages and profits) are also exactly $80. Hence, the GDP here is identical whether measured as flow of products ($80 of haircuts) or as cost and income ($80 of wages and profits).

In fact, the two approaches are identical because we have included "profit" in the lower loop along with other incomes. What exactly is profit? Profit is what remains from the sale of a product after you have paid the other factor costs—wages, interest, and rents. It is the residual that adjusts automatically to make the lower loop's costs or earnings exactly match the upper loop's value of goods.

To sum up:

GDP, or gross domestic product, can be measured in two different ways: (1) as the flow of final products, or (2) as the total costs or earnings of inputs producing output. Because profit is a residual, both approaches will yield exactly the same total GDP.

National Accounts Derived from Business Accounts

You might wonder where on earth economists find all the data for the national accounts. In practice, government economists draw on a wide array of sources, including surveys, income-tax returns, retail-sales statistics, and employment data.

The most important source of data is business accounts. An *account* for a firm or nation is a numerical record of all flows (outputs, costs, etc.) during a given period. We can show the relationship between business accounts and national accounts by constructing the accounts for an economy made up only of farms. The top half of Table 21-1 shows the results of a year's farming operations for a single, typical farm. We put sales of final products on the left-hand side and the various costs of production on the right. The bottom half of Table 21-1 shows how to construct the GDP accounts for our simple agrarian economy in which all final products are produced on

(a) Income Statement of Typical Farm			
Output in Farming		**Earnings**	
Sales of goods (corn, apples, etc.)	**$1,000**	Costs of production:	
		Wages	$ 800
		Rents	100
		Interest	25
		Profit (residual)	75
Total	$1,000	Total	$1,000

(b) National Product Account (millions of dollars)			
Upper-Loop Flow of Product		**Lower-Loop Flow of Earnings**	
Final output (10 × 1,000)	**$10,000**	Costs or earnings:	
		Wages (10 × 800)	$ 8,000
		Rents (10 × 100)	1,000
		Interest (10 × 25)	250
		Profit (10 × 75)	750
GDP total	$10,000	GDP total	$10,000

TABLE 21-1. **Construction of National Product Accounts from Business Accounts**

Part **(a)** shows the income statement of a typical farm. The left side shows the value of production, while the right side shows the farm's costs. Part **(b)** then adds up or aggregates the 10 million identical farms to obtain total GDP. Note that GDP from the product side exactly equals GDP from the earnings side.

10 million identical farms. The national accounts simply add together or *aggregate* the outputs and costs of the 10 million identical farms to get the two different measures of GDP.

The Problem of "Double Counting"

We defined GDP as the total production of final goods and services. A *final product* is one that is produced and sold for consumption or investment. GDP excludes *intermediate goods*—goods that are used up to produce other goods. GDP therefore includes bread but not wheat, and home computers but not computer chips.

For the flow-of-product calculation of GDP, excluding intermediate products poses no major complications. We simply include the bread and computers in GDP but avoid including the wheat and dough that went into the bread or the chips and plastic that went into the computers. If you look again at the upper loop in Figure 21-1, you will see that bread and computers appear in the flow of products, but you will not find any flour or computer chips.

What has happened to products like flour and computer chips? They are intermediate products and are simply cycling around inside the block marked "Producers." If they are not bought by consumers, they never show up as final products in GDP.

"Value Added" in the Lower Loop. A new statistician who is being trained to make GDP measurements might be puzzled, saying:

> I can see that, if you are careful, your upper-loop product approach to GDP will avoid including intermediate products. But aren't you in some trouble when you use the lower-loop cost or earnings approach?
>
> After all, when we gather income statements from the accounts of firms, won't we pick up what grain merchants pay to wheat farmers, what bakers pay to grain merchants, and what grocers pay to bakers? Won't this result in double counting or even triple counting of items going through several productive stages?

These are good questions, but there is an ingenious answer that resolves the problem. In making

Stage of production	Bread Receipts, Costs, and Value Added (cents per loaf)			
	(1) Sales receipts	(2) *Less:* Cost of intermediate products		(3) Value added (wages, profit, etc.) (3) = (1) − (2)
Wheat	23	0	=	23
Flour	53	23	=	30
Baked dough	110	53	=	57
Final product: bread	190	110	=	80
Total	376	186		190 (sum of value added)

TABLE 21-2. GDP Sums Up Value Added at Each Production Stage

To avoid double counting of intermediate products, we calculate value added at each stage of production. This involves subtracting all the costs of materials and intermediate products bought from other businesses from total sales. Note that every black intermediate-product item both appears in column (1) and is subtracted in the next stage of production in column (2). (How much would we overestimate GDP if we counted all receipts, not just value added? The overestimate would be 186 cents per loaf.)

lower-loop earnings measurements, statisticians are very careful to include in GDP only a firm's value added. **Value added** is the difference between a firm's sales and its purchases of materials and services from other firms.

In other words, in calculating the GDP earnings or value added by a firm, the statistician includes all costs except for payments made to other businesses. Hence business costs in the form of wages, salaries, interest payments, and dividends are included in value added, but purchases of wheat or steel or electricity are excluded from value added. Why are all the purchases from other firms excluded from value added to obtain GDP? Because those purchases will get properly counted in GDP in the values added by other firms.

Table 21-2 uses the stages of bread production to illustrate how careful adherence to the value-added approach enables us to subtract purchases of intermediate goods that show up in the income statements of farmers, millers, bakers, and grocers. The final calculation shows the desired equality between (1) final sales of bread and (2) total earnings, calculated as the sum of all values added in all the different stages of bread production.

Value-added approach: To avoid double counting, we take care to include only final goods in GDP and to exclude the intermediate goods that are used up

in making the final goods. By measuring the value added at each stage, taking care to subtract expenditures on the intermediate goods bought from other firms, the lower-loop earnings approach properly avoids all double counting and records wages, interest, rent, and profit exactly one time.

DETAILS OF THE NATIONAL ACCOUNTS

Now that we have an overview of the national income and product accounts, we will proceed, in the rest of this chapter, on a whirlwind tour of the various sectors. Before we start on the journey, look at Table 21-3 to get an idea of where we are going. This table shows a summary set of accounts for both the product and the income sides. If you know the structure of the table and the definitions of the terms in it, you will be well on your way to understanding GDP and its family of components.

Real vs. Nominal GDP: "Deflating" GDP by a Price Index

We define GDP as the dollar value of goods and services. In measuring the dollar value, we use the measuring rod of *market prices* for the different goods and services. But prices change over time, as

Product Approach	Earnings Approach
Components of gross domestic product:	**Earnings or costs as sources of gross domestic product:**
Consumption (*C*)	Compensation of labor (wages, salaries, and supplements)
+ Gross private domestic investment (*I*)	+ Corporate profits
+ Government purchases (*G*)	+ Other property income (rent, interest, proprietors' income)
+ Net exports (*X*)	+ Depreciation
	+ Production taxes
Equals: Gross domestic product	**Equals: Gross domestic product**

TABLE 21-3. Overview of the National Income and Product Accounts

This table presents the major components of the two sides of the national accounts. The left side shows the components of the product approach (or upper loop); the symbols *C, I, G,* and *X* are often used to represent these four items of GDP. The right side shows the components of the earnings or cost approach (or lower loop). Each approach will ultimately add up to exactly the same GDP.

inflation generally sends prices upward year after year. Who would want to measure things with a rubber yardstick—one that stretches in your hands from day to day—rather than a rigid and invariant yardstick?

The problem of changing prices is one of the problems economists have to solve when they use money as their measuring rod. Clearly, we want a measure of the nation's output and income that uses an invariant yardstick. Economists can replace the elastic yardstick with a reliable one by removing the price-increase component so as to create a real or quantity index of national output.

Here is the basic idea: We can measure the GDP for a particular year using the actual market prices of that year; this gives us the **nominal GDP,** or GDP at current prices. But we are usually more interested in determining what has happened to the **real GDP,** which is an index of the volume or quantity of goods and services produced. Real GDP is calculated by tracking the volume or quantity of production after removing the influence of changing prices or inflation. Hence, nominal GDP is calculated using changing prices, while real GDP represents the change in the volume of total output after price changes are removed.

The difference between the growth of nominal GDP and real GDP is the growth in the **price of GDP,** sometimes called the **GDP deflator.**

A simple example will illustrate the general idea. Say that a country produces 1000 bushels of corn in year 1 and 1010 bushels in year 2. The price of a bushel is $1 in year 1 and $2 in year 2. We can calculate nominal GDP (*PQ*) as $1 × 1000 = $1000 in year 1 and $2 × 1010 = $2020 in year 2. Nominal GDP therefore grew by 102 percent between the two years.

But the actual amount of output did not grow anywhere near that rapidly. To find real output, we need to consider what happened to prices. We use year 1 as the base year, or the year in which we measure prices. We set the price index, the GDP deflator, as $P_1 = 1$ in the first, or base, year. From the data in the previous paragraph, we see that the GDP deflator is $P_2 = \$2/\$1 = 2$ in year 2. Real GDP (*Q*) is equal to nominal GDP (*PQ*) divided by the GDP deflator (*P*). Hence real GDP was equal to $1000/1 = $1000 in year 1 and $2020/2 = $1010 in year 2. Thus the growth in real GDP, which corrects for the change in prices, is 1 percent and equals the growth in the output of corn, as it should.

A 1929–1933 comparison will illustrate the deflation process for an actual historical episode. Table 21-4 gives nominal GDP figures of $104 billion for 1929 and $56 billion for 1933. This represents a 46 percent drop in nominal GDP from 1929 to 1933. But the government estimates that prices on average dropped about 25 percent over this period. If we choose 1929 as our base year, with the GDP deflator of 1 in that year, this means that the 1933 price index was about 0.75. So our $56 billion 1933 GDP was really worth much more than half the $104 billion GDP of 1929. Table 21-4 shows that, in terms of 1929 prices, or dollars of 1929 purchasing power, real GDP fell to $76 billion. Hence, part of the near-halving shown by the

Date	(1) Nominal GDP (current $, billion)	(2) Index number of prices (GDP deflator, 1929 = 1)	(3) Real GDP ($, billion, 1929 prices) $3 = \dfrac{(1)}{(2)}$
1929	104	1.00	$\dfrac{104}{1.00} = 104$
1933	56	0.75	$\dfrac{56}{0.75} = 76$

TABLE 21-4. Real (or Inflation-Corrected) GDP Is Obtained by Dividing Nominal GDP by the GDP Deflator

Using the price index of column (2), we deflate column (1) to get real GDP, column (3). (Riddle: Can you show that 1929's real GDP was $77 billion in terms of 1933 prices? *Hint:* With 1933 as a base of 1, 1929's price index is 1.34.)

nominal GDP was due to the rapidly declining price level, or deflation, during the Great Depression.

The black line in Figure 21-2 shows the growth of nominal GDP since 2000, expressed in the actual dollars and prices that were current in each historical year. Then, for comparison, the real GDP, expressed in 2000 dollars, is shown in rust. Clearly, much of the increase in nominal GDP over the last half-century was due to inflation in the price units of our money yardstick.

Table 21-4 shows the simplest way of calculating real GDP and the GDP deflator. Sometimes these calculations give misleading results, particularly when the prices and quantities of important goods are changing rapidly. For example, over the last two decades, computer prices have been falling very sharply while the quantity of computers produced has risen rapidly (we return to this issue in our discussion of price indexes below).

When relative prices of different goods are changing very rapidly, using prices of a fixed year will give a misleading estimate of real GDP growth. To correct for this bias, statisticians use a procedure known as *chain weighting*. Instead of keeping the relative weights on each good fixed (say, by using weights for a given year, like 1990), the weights of the different goods and services change each year to reflect the changes in spending patterns in the economy. Today, the official U.S. government measures of GDP and the GDP price index rely upon chain weights. The technical names for these constructs are "real

GDP in chained dollars" and the "chain-type price index for GDP." As a shorthand, we generally refer to real GDP and the GDP price index.

Further Details on Chain Weights. The details of using chain weights are somewhat involved, but we can get the basic idea using a simple example. The calculation of chain weights involves linking the output or price series together by multiplying the growth rates from one period to another. An example for a haircut economy will show how this works. Say that the value of the haircuts was $300 in 1998. Further suppose that the quantity of haircuts increased by 1 percent from 1998 to 1999 and by 2 percent from 1999 to 2000. Then the value of real GDP (in chained 1998 dollars) would be $300 in 1998, $300 × 1.01 = $303 in 1999, and $303 × 1.02 = $309.06 in 2000. With many different goods and services, we would add together the growth rates of the different components of apples, bananas, catamarans, and so on, and weight the growth rates by the expenditure or output shares of the different goods.

To summarize:

Nominal GDP (PQ) represents the total money value of final goods and services produced in a given year, where the values are expressed in terms of the market prices of each year. Real GDP (Q) removes price changes from nominal GDP and calculates GDP in terms of the quantities of goods and services.

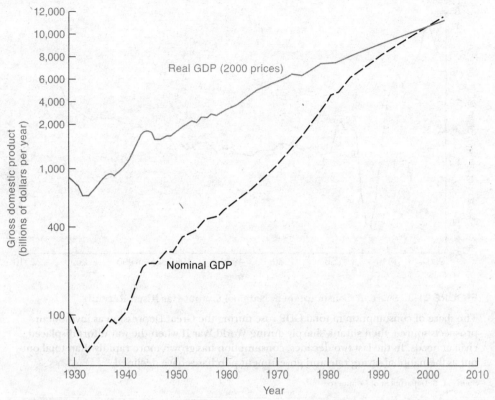

FIGURE 21-2. Nominal GDP Grows Faster than Real GDP because of Price Inflation

The rise in nominal GDP exaggerates the rise in output. Why? Because growth in nominal GDP includes increases in prices as well as growth in output. To obtain an accurate measure of real output, we must correct GDP for price changes.

Source: U.S. Department of Commerce.

The GDP price index (P) is the "price of GDP" and is approximately determined as follows:

$$Q = \text{real GDP} = \frac{\text{nominal GDP}}{\text{GDP price index}} = \frac{PQ}{P}$$

To correct for rapidly changing relative prices, the U.S. national accounts use chain weights to construct real GDP and price indexes.

Consumption

The first important part of GDP is consumption, or "personal consumption expenditures." Consumption is by far the largest component of GDP, equaling about two-thirds of the total in recent years. Figure 21-3 shows the fraction of GDP devoted to consumption over the last six decades. Consumption

expenditures are divided into three categories: durable goods such as automobiles, nondurable goods such as food, and services such as medical care. The most rapidly growing sector is services.

Investment and Capital Formation

So far, our analysis has banished all capital. In real life, however, nations devote part of their output to production of capital—durable goods that increase future production. Increasing capital requires the sacrifice of current consumption to increase future consumption. Instead of eating more pizza now, people build new pizza ovens to make it possible to produce more pizza for future consumption.

In the accounts, **investment** consists of the additions to the nation's capital stock of buildings,

FIGURE 21-3. Share of Consumption in National Output Has Risen Recently

The share of consumption in total GDP rose during the Great Depression as investment prospects soured, then shrank sharply during World War II when the war effort displaced civilian needs. In the last two decades, consumption has grown more rapidly than total output as the national saving rate and government purchases have declined.

Source: U.S. Department of Commerce.

equipment, software, and inventories during a year. The national accounts include mainly tangible capital (such as buildings and computers) but omit most intangible capital (such as research-and-development or educational expenses).

Real Investment Versus Financial Investment

Economists define "investment" (or sometimes *real investment*) as production of durable capital goods. In common usage, "investment" often denotes using money to buy General Motors stock or to open a savings account. For clarity, economists call this *financial investment*. Try not to confuse these two different uses of the word "investment."

If I take $1000 from my safe and buy some stocks, this is not what macroeconomists call investment. I have simply exchanged one financial asset for another. Investment takes place when a physical capital good is produced.

How does investment fit into the national accounts? If people are using part of society's production

possibilities for capital formation rather than for consumption, economic statisticians recognize that such outputs must be included in the upper-loop flow of GDP. Investments represent additions to the stock of durable capital goods that increase production possibilities in the future. So we must modify our original definition to read:

Gross domestic product is the sum of all final products. Along with consumption goods and services, we must also include gross investment.

Net vs. Gross Investment. Our revised definition includes "gross investment" along with consumption. What does the word "gross" mean in this context? It indicates that investment includes all investment goods produced. Gross investment is not adjusted for **depreciation,** which measures the amount of capital that has been used up in a year. Thus gross investment includes all the machines, factories, and houses built during a year—even though some were produced simply to replace some old capital goods that burned down or were thrown on the scrap heap.

If you want to get a measure of the increase in society's capital, gross investment is not a sensible measure. Because it excludes a necessary allowance for depreciation, it is too large—too gross.

An analogy to population will make clear the importance of considering depreciation. If you want to measure the increase in the size of the population, you cannot simply count the number of births, for this would clearly exaggerate the net change in population. To get population growth, you must also subtract the number of deaths.

The same point holds for capital. To find the net increase in capital, you must start with gross investment and subtract the deaths of capital in the form of depreciation, or the amount of capital used up.

Thus to estimate capital formation we measure *net investment*. Net investment is always births of capital (gross investment) less deaths of capital (capital depreciation):

Net investment equals gross investment minus depreciation.

Government

Up to now we have talked about consumers but ignored the biggest buyers of all—federal, state, and local governments. Somehow GDP must take into account the billions of dollars of product a nation *collectively* consumes or invests. How do we do this?

Measuring government's contribution to national output is complicated because most government services are not sold on the marketplace. Rather, government purchases both consumption-type goods (like food for the military) and investment-type items (such as computers or roads). In measuring government's contribution to GDP, we simply add all these government purchases to the flow of consumption, investment, and, as we will see later, net exports.

Hence, all the government payroll expenditures on its employees plus the costs of goods it buys from private industry (lasers, roads, and airplanes) are included in this third category of flow of products, called "government consumption expenditures and gross investment." This category equals the contribution of federal, state, and local governments to GDP.

Exclusion of Transfer Payments. Does this mean that every dollar of government expenditure is included in GDP? Definitely not. GDP includes only government purchases of goods and services; it excludes spending on transfer payments.

Government **transfer payments** are government payments to individuals that are not made in exchange for goods or services supplied. Examples of government transfers include unemployment insurance, veterans' benefits, and old-age or disability payments. These payments meet important social purposes, but, since they are not purchases of current goods or services, they are omitted from GDP.

Thus if you receive a wage from the government because you are a teacher, your wage is a factor payment and would be included in GDP. If you receive a welfare payment because you are poor, that payment is not in return for a service but is a transfer payment and would be excluded from GDP.

One peculiar government transfer payment is the interest on the government debt. Interest is treated as a payment for debt incurred to pay for past wars or government programs and is not considered to be a purchase of a current good or service. Government interest payments are considered transfers and are therefore omitted from GDP.

Finally, do not confuse the way the national accounts measure government spending on goods and services (G) with the official government budget. When the Treasury measures its expenditures, it includes purchases of goods and services (G) *plus* transfers.

Taxes. In using the flow-of-product approach to compute GDP, we need not worry about how the government finances its spending. It does not matter whether the government pays for its goods and services by taxing, by printing money, or by borrowing. Wherever the dollars come from, the statistician computes the governmental component of GDP as the actual cost to the government of the goods and services.

But while it is fine to ignore taxes in the flow-of-product approach, we must account for taxes in the earnings or cost approach to GDP. Consider wages, for example. Part of my wage is turned over to the government through personal income taxes. These direct taxes definitely do get included in the wage component of business expenses, and the same holds for direct taxes (personal or corporate) on interest, rent, and profit.

Or consider the sales tax and other indirect taxes that manufacturers and retailers have to pay on a loaf of bread (or on the wheat, flour, and dough stages). Suppose these indirect taxes total 10 cents per loaf, and suppose wages, profit, and other value-added items cost the bread industry 90 cents. What will the bread sell for in the product approach? For 90 cents? Surely not. The bread will sell for $1, equal to 90 cents of factor costs plus 10 cents of indirect taxes.

Thus the cost approach to GDP includes both indirect and direct taxes as elements of the cost of producing final output.

Net Exports

The United States is an open economy engaged in importing and exporting goods and services. The last component of GDP—and an increasingly important one in recent years—is **net exports,** the difference between exports and imports of goods and services.

How do we draw the line between our GDP and other countries' GDPs? The U.S. GDP represents all goods and services produced within the boundaries of the United States. Production differs from sales in the United States in two respects. First, some of our production (Iowa wheat and Boeing aircraft) is bought by foreigners and shipped abroad, and these items constitute our *exports*. Second, some of what we consume (Mexican oil and Japanese cars) is produced abroad and shipped to the United States, and such items are American *imports*.

A Numerical Example. We can use a simple farming economy to understand how the national accounts work. Suppose that Agrovia produces 100 bushels of corn and 7 bushels are imported. Of these, 87 bushels are consumed (in C), 10 go for government purchases to feed the army (as G), and 6 go into domestic investment as increases in inventories (I). In addition, 4 bushels are exported, so net exports (X) are $4 - 7$, or minus 3.

What, then, is the composition of the GDP of Agrovia? It is the following:

$$\text{GDP} = 87 \text{ of } C + 10 \text{ of } G + 6 \text{ of } I - 3 \text{ of } X$$

$$= 100 \text{ bushels}$$

Gross Domestic Product, Net Domestic Product, and Gross National Product

Although GDP is the most widely used measure of national output in the United States, two other concepts are frequently cited: net domestic product and gross national product.

Recall that GDP includes *gross* investment, which is net investment plus depreciation. A little thought suggests that including depreciation is rather like including wheat as well as bread. A better measure would include only *net* investment in total output. By subtracting depreciation from GDP we obtain **net domestic product** (NDP). If NDP is a sounder measure of a nation's output than GDP, why do national accountants focus on GDP? They do so because depreciation is somewhat difficult to estimate, whereas gross investment can be estimated fairly accurately.

An alternative measure of national output, widely used until recently, is **gross national product** (GNP). What is the difference between GNP and GDP? GNP is the total output produced with labor or capital *owned by U.S. residents*, while GDP is the output produced with labor and capital *located inside the United States*. For example, some of the U.S. GDP is produced in Honda plants that are owned by Japanese corporations. The profits from these plants are included in U.S. GDP but not in U.S. GNP because Honda is a Japanese company. Similarly, when an American economist flies to Japan to give a paid lecture on baseball economics, payment for that lecture would be included in Japanese GDP and in American GNP. For the United States, GDP is very close to GNP, but these may differ substantially for very open economies.

To summarize:

Net domestic product (NDP) equals the total final output produced within a nation during a year, where output includes net investment, or gross investment less depreciation:

$$\text{NDP} = \text{GDP} - \text{depreciation}$$

Gross national product (GNP) is the total final output produced with inputs owned by the residents of a country during a year.

Table 21-5 provides a comprehensive definition of important components of GDP.

GDP and NDP: A Look at Numbers

Armed with an understanding of the concepts, we can turn to look at the actual data in the important Table 21-6.

Flow-of-Product Approach. Look first at the left side of Table 21-6. It gives the upper-loop, flow-of-product approach to GDP. Each of the four major components

1. **GDP from the product side is the sum of four major components**:
    *   Personal consumption expenditure on goods and services (C)
    *   Gross private domestic investment (I)
    *   Government consumption expenditures and gross investment (G)
    *   Net exports of goods and services (X), or exports minus imports
2. **GDP from the cost side is the sum of the following major components:**
    *   Compensation (wages, salaries, and supplements)
    *   Property income (corporate profits, proprietors' incomes, interest, and rents)
    *   Production taxes and depreciation on capital
    (Remember to use the value-added technique to prevent double counting of intermediate goods bought from other firms.)
3. **The product and cost measures of GDP are identical** (by adherence to the rules of value-added bookkeeping and the definition of profit as a residual).
4. **Net domestic product (NDP) equals GDP minus depreciation.**

TABLE 21-5. Key Concepts of the National Income and Product Accounts

Gross Domestic Product, 2003 (billions of current dollars)				
Production Approach			**Earnings or Cost Approach**	
1. Personal consumption expenditures		7,752	1. Compensation of employees	6,186
Durable goods	942		2. Proprietors' income	846
Nondurable goods	2,208		3. Rental income	164
Services	4,602		4. Net interest	582
2. Gross private domestic investment		1,668	5. Corporate profits (with adjustments)	1,059
Fixed investment			6. Depreciation	1,308
Nonresidential	1,108		7. Production taxes	739
Residential	563		8. Statistical discrepancy and miscellaneous	100
Change in private inventories	−3			
3. Net exports of goods and services		−492		
Exports	1,048			
Imports	1,540			
4. Government consumption expenditures and gross investment		2,056		
Federal	757			
State and local	1,299			
Gross domestic product		**10,984**	**Gross domestic product**	**10,984**

TABLE 21-6. The Two Ways of Looking at the GDP Accounts, in Actual Numbers

The left side measures flow of products (at market prices). The right side measures flow of costs (factor earnings and depreciation).

Source: U.S. Department of Commerce.

appears there, along with the production in each component for 2003. Of these, *C* and *G* and their obvious subclassifications require little discussion.

Gross private domestic investment does require one comment. Its total ($1668 billion) includes all new business fixed investment, residential construction, and increase in inventory of goods. This gross total is the amount before a subtraction for depreciation of capital. After subtracting $1308 billion of depreciation from gross investment, we obtain $360 billion of net investment.

Finally, note the large negative entry for net exports, −$492 billion. This negative entry represents the fact that in 2003 the United States imported $492 billion more in goods and services than it exported.

Adding up the four components on the left gives the total GDP of $10,984 billion. This is the harvest we have been working for: the money measure of the American economy's overall performance for 2003.

Flow-of-Cost Approach. Now turn to the right-hand side of the table, which gives the lower-loop, flow-of-cost approach. Here we have all *costs of production* plus *taxes* and *depreciation.*

Compensation of employees represents wages, salaries, and other employee supplements. Net interest is a similar item. Remember that interest on government debt is not included as part of *G* or of GDP but is treated as a transfer.

Rent income of persons includes rents received by landlords. In addition, if you own your own home, you are treated as *paying rent to yourself.* This is one of many "imputations" (or derived data) in the national accounts. It makes sense if we really want to measure the housing services the American people are enjoying and do not want the estimate to change when people decide to own a home rather than rent one.

Production taxes are included as a separate item along with some small adjustments, including the inevitable "statistical discrepancy," which reflects the fact that the officials never have every bit of needed data.[1]

---

[1] Statisticians work with incomplete reports and fill in data gaps by estimation. Just as measurements in a chemistry lab differ from the ideal, so do errors creep into both upper- and lower-loop GDP estimates. These are balanced by an item called the "statistical discrepancy." Along with the civil servants who are heads of units called "Wages," "Interest," and so forth, there actually used to be someone with the title "Head of the Statistical Discrepancy." If data were perfect, that individual would have been out of a job.

Depreciation on capital goods that were used up must appear as an expense in GDP, just like other expenses.

Profit is a residual—what is left over after all other costs have been subtracted from total sales. There are two kinds of profits: profit of corporations and net earnings of unincorporated enterprises.

Income of unincorporated enterprises consists of earnings of partnerships and single-ownership businesses. This includes much farm and professional income.

Finally, corporate profits before taxes are shown. This entry's $1059 billion in Table 21-6 includes corporate-profit taxes, dividends, and undistributed corporate profits; the latter is what corporations leave or "plow back" into the business and is called *net corporate saving.*

On the right side, the flow-of-cost approach gives us the same $10,984 billion of GDP as does the flow-of-product approach. The right and left sides do agree.

From GDP to Disposable Income

The basic GDP accounts are of interest not only for themselves but also because of their importance for understanding how consumers and businesses behave. Some further distinctions will help illuminate the way the nation's books are kept.

National Income. To help us understand the division of total income among the different factors of production, we construct data on *national income (NI). NI* represents the total incomes received by labor, capital, and land. It is constructed by subtracting depreciation from GDP. National income equals total compensation of labor, rental income, net interest, income of proprietors, and corporate profits.

The relationship between GDP and national income is shown in the first two bars of Figure 21-4. The left-hand bar shows GDP, while the second bar shows the subtractions required to obtain *NI.*

Disposable Income. A second important concept asks, How many dollars per year do households actually have available to spend? The concept of disposable personal income (usually called **disposable income,** or *DI*) answers this question. To get disposable income, you calculate the market and transfer incomes received by households and subtract personal taxes.

From GDP to National Income to Disposable Income

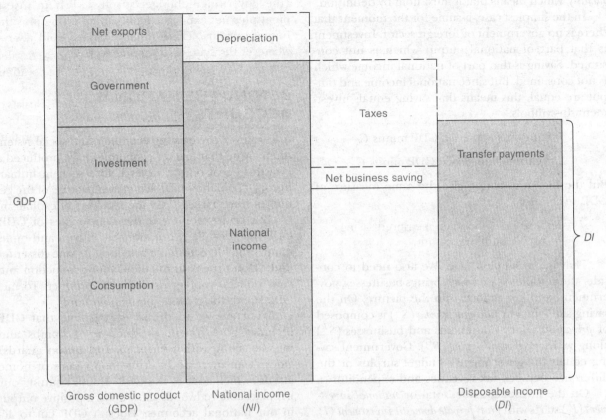

FIGURE 21-4. Starting with GDP, We Can Calculate National Income (*NI*) and Disposable Personal Income (*DI*)

Important income concepts are (1) GDP, which is total gross income to all factors; (2) national income, which is the sum of factor incomes and is obtained by subtracting depreciation from GDP; and (3) disposable personal income, which measures the total incomes, including transfer payments but minus taxes, of the household sector.

Figure 21-4 shows the calculation of *DI*. We begin with national income in the second bar. We then subtract all taxes and further subtract net business saving (Net business saving is profits after depreciation less dividends.) Finally, we add back the transfer payments that households receive from governments. This constitutes *DI*, shown as the right-hand bar in Figure 21-4. Disposable income is what actually gets into the hands of consumers to dispose of as they please. (This discussion omits some minor items such as the statistical discrepancy and net foreign factor incomes that are usually close to zero.)

As we will see in the next chapters, *DI* is what people divide between (1) consumption spending and (2) personal saving.

Saving and Investment

As we have seen, output can be either consumed or invested. Investment is an essential economic activity because it increases the capital stock available for future production. One of the most important points about national accounting is the identity between saving and investment. We will show that, under the accounting rules described above, *measured saving is exactly equal to measured investment.* This equality is an *identity*, which means that it must hold by definition.

In the simplest case, assume for the moment that there is no government or foreign sector. Investment is that part of national output which is not consumed. Saving is that part of national income which is not consumed. But since national income and output are equal, this means that saving equals investment. In symbols:

$$I = \text{product-approach GDP minus } C$$

$$S = \text{earnings-approach GDP minus } C$$

But the measures always give the same measure of GDP, so

$I = S$: the identity between measured saving and investment

That is the simplest case. We also need to consider the complete case which brings businesses, government, and net exports into the picture. On the saving side, total or *national saving* (S^T) is composed of *private saving* by households and businesses (S^P) along with *government saving* (S^G). Government saving equals the government's budget surplus or the difference between tax revenues and expenditures.

On the investment side, total or *national investment* (I^T) starts with *gross private domestic investment* (I) but also adds *net foreign investment*, which is approximately the same as net exports (X). Hence, the complete saving-investment identity is given by[2]

$$\frac{\text{National}}{\text{Investment}} = \frac{\text{private}}{\text{investment}} + \frac{\text{net}}{\text{exports}}$$

$$= \frac{\text{private}}{\text{saving}} + \frac{\text{government}}{\text{saving}} = \frac{\text{national}}{\text{saving}}$$

or

$$I^T = I + X = S^P + S^G = S^T$$

National saving equals national investment by definition. The components of investment are private domestic investment and foreign investment (or net exports). The sources of saving are private saving (by households and businesses) and government saving (the government budget surplus). Private investment plus net exports equals private saving plus the budget surplus. These identities must hold always, whatever the state of the business cycle.

BEYOND THE NATIONAL ACCOUNTS

Advocates of the existing economic and social system often argue that market economies have produced a growth in real output never before seen in human history. "Look how GDP has grown because of the genius of free markets," say the admirers of capitalism.

But critics point out the deficiencies of GDP. GDP includes many questionable entries and omits many valuable economic activities. As one dissenter said, "Don't speak to me of all your production and your dollars, your gross domestic product. To me, GDP stands for gross domestic pollution!"

What are we to think? Isn't it true that GDP includes government production of bombs and missiles along with salaries paid to prison guards? Doesn't an increase in crime boost sales of home alarms, which adds to the GDP? Doesn't cutting our irreplaceable redwoods show up as a positive output in our national accounts? Doesn't GDP fail to account for environmental degradation such as acid rain and global warming?

In recent years, economists have begun developing new measures to correct the major defects of the standard GDP numbers and better reflect the true satisfaction-producing outputs of our economy. The new approaches attempt to extend the boundaries of the traditional accounts by including important non-market activities as well as correcting for harmful activities that are included as part of national output. Let's consider some of the omitted pluses and minuses.

Omitted Nonmarket Activities. Recall that the standard accounts include primarily market activities. Much useful economic activity takes place outside the market. For example, college students are investing in human capital. The national accounts record the tuition, but they omit the opportunity costs of earnings forgone. Studies indicate that inclusion of nonmarket investments in education and other areas would more than double the national saving rate.

---

[2] For this discussion, we consider only private investment and therefore treat all government purchases as consumption. In most national accounts today, government purchases are divided between consumption and tangible investments. If we include government investment, then this amount will add to both national investment and the government surplus.

Similarly, many household activities produce valuable "near-market" goods and services such as meals, laundering, and child-care services. Recent estimates of the value of unpaid household work indicate that it might be almost 50 percent as large as total market consumption. Perhaps the largest omission from the market accounts is the value of leisure time. On average, Americans spend as much of their time on utility-producing leisure activities as they do on money-producing work activities. Yet the value of leisure time is excluded from our official national statistics.

You might wonder about the many activities in the underground economy, which covers a wide variety of market activities that are not reported to the government. These include activities like gambling, prostitution, drug dealing, work done by illegal immigrants, bartering of services, and smuggling. Actually, much underground activity is intentionally excluded because national output excludes illegal activities—these are by social consensus "bads" and not "goods." A swelling cocaine trade will not enter into GDP. For other, legal but unreported activities, like unreported tips, the Commerce Department makes estimates on the basis of surveys and audits by the Internal Revenue Service.

Omitted Environmental Damage. In addition to omitting activities, sometimes GDP omits some of the harmful side effects of economic activity. An important example is the omission of environmental damages. For example, suppose the residents of Suburbia buy 10 million kilowatt-hours of electricity to cool their houses, paying Utility Co. 10 cents per kilowatt-hour. That $1 million covers the labor costs, plant costs, and fuel costs. But suppose the company damages the neighborhood with pollution in the process of producing electricity. It incurs no monetary costs for this externality. Our measure of output should not only add in the value of the electricity (which GDP does) but also subtract the environmental damage caused by the pollution (which GDP does not).

Suppose that in addition to paying 10 cents of direct costs, the surrounding neighborhood suffers 1 cent per kilowatt-hour of environmental damage. This is the cost of pollution (to trees, trout, streams, and people) not paid by Utility Co. Then the total "external" cost is $100,000. To correct for this hidden cost in a set of augmented accounts, we must subtract $100,000 of "pollution bads" from the $1,000,000 flow of "electricity goods."

Augmented National Accounts

Considerable progress has been made in recent years in developing *augmented national accounts*, which are accounts designed to include both nonmarket and market activities. The general principle of augmented accounting is to include as much of economic activity as is feasible, whether or not that activity takes place in the market. Examples of augmented accounts include estimates of the value of nonmarket investments in human capital, the value of unpaid home production, the value of forests, and the value of leisure time.

In 1994, the U.S. Commerce Department unveiled its augmented national accounts with the introduction of *environmental accounts* (sometimes called "green accounts") designed to estimate the contribution of natural and environmental resources to the nation's income. The first step was the development of accounts to measure the contribution of subsoil assets like oil, gas, and coal.

Environmental critics have argued that America's wasteful ways are squandering our precious natural capital. Many were surprised by the results of this first assay into green accounting. The estimates take into account that discovery adds to our proven reserves while extraction subtracts from or depletes these reserves. In fact, these two activities just about canceled each other out: the net effect of both discoveries and depletion from 1958 to 1991 was between minus $2 billion and plus $1 billion, depending on the method, as compared to an average GDP over this period of $4200 billion (all these in 1992 prices).

There is much further work needed in this area before we have a full picture of nonmarket economic activity. Economists and environmentalists are watching this exciting new development carefully.

PRICE INDEXES AND INFLATION

We have concentrated in this chapter on the measurement of output. But people are also concerned with price trends, with movements in the overall price level, with inflation. What do these terms mean?

Let us begin with a careful definition:

A **price index** is a measure of the average level of prices. **Inflation** denotes a rise in the general level of prices. The **rate of inflation** is the rate of change of the general price level and is measured as follows:

Rate of inflation (year t)

$$= \frac{\begin{array}{c}\text{price level} \\ \text{(year } t\text{)}\end{array} - \begin{array}{c}\text{price level} \\ \text{(year } t-1\text{)}\end{array}}{\text{price level (year } t-1\text{)}} \times 100$$

But how do we measure the "price level" that is involved in the definition of inflation? The price level is a weighted average of the prices of the different goods and services in an economy. The government calculates the price level by constructing price indexes, which are averages of prices of goods and services.

The opposite of inflation is **deflation,** which occurs when the general level of prices is falling. Deflations were rare in the late twentieth century. In the United States, the last time consumer prices actually fell from one year to the next was 1955. Sustained deflations, in which prices fall steadily over a period of several years, are associated with depressions, such as those that occurred in the United States in the 1930s and the 1890s. More recently, Japan experienced a deflation in the late 1990s as its economy suffered a prolonged recession.

Price Indexes

When newspapers tell us "Inflation is rising," they are really reporting the movement of a price index. A price index is a weighted average of the prices of a number of goods and services. In constructing price indexes, economists weight individual prices by the economic importance of each good. The most important price indexes are the consumer price index, the GDP price index, and the producer price index.

The Consumer Price Index (CPI). The most widely used measure of inflation is the consumer price index, also known as the CPI, calculated by the U.S. Bureau of Labor Statistics (BLS). The CPI is a measure of the average change over time in the prices paid by urban consumers for a market basket of consumer goods and services. The market basket includes the prices of food, clothing, shelter, fuel, transportation, medical care, college tuition, and other goods and services purchased for day-to-day living. Prices on 364 separate classes of goods and services are collected from 23,000 establishments in 87 areas of the country.

How are the different prices weighted in constructing price indexes? It would clearly be silly merely to add up the different prices or to weight them by their mass or volume. Rather, a price index is constructed by *weighting each price according to the economic importance of the commodity in question.*

In the case of the traditional CPI, each item is assigned a fixed weight proportional to its relative importance in consumer expenditure budgets; the weights for each item are proportional to the total spending by consumers on that item as determined by a survey of consumer expenditures in the 1993–1995 period. As of December 1999, housing-related costs were the single biggest category in the CPI, taking up more than 41 percent of consumer spending budgets. By comparison, the cost of new cars and other motor vehicles accounts for only 5 percent of the CPI's consumer expenditure budgets.

Calculating the CPI

The formula for calculating changes in the CPI is the following:

CPI in period t = CPI in period $(t-1)$
    × weighted change in prices in period t

where

Weighted change in prices in period t
    = Σ [relative importance of good i in $(t-1)$]
    × [percentage increase of good i from $(t-1)$ to t]

To take a concrete example, the following table shows the actual price and relative-importance data for February 2003:

Category	Relative importance (%)	Change from February 2002 to February 2003 (% per year)
Food and beverages	15.6	1.4
Housing	40.9	2.6
Medical care	6.0	4.5
Other	37.5	3.9
Total	**100.0**	**3.0**

The rate of inflation over the period from February 2002 to February 2003 can be calculated to be 3.014 percent per year. (Question 9 at the end of this chapter provides another example for calculation.)

This example captures the essence of how the traditional CPI measures inflation. The only difference between this simplified calculation and the actual one is that the CPI in fact contains many more commodities and regions. Otherwise, the procedure is exactly the same.

GDP Price Index. Another widely used price index is the *GDP price index* (also sometimes referred to as the GDP deflator), which we met earlier in this chapter. The GDP price index is the price of all goods and services produced in the country (consumption, investment, government purchases, and net exports) rather than of a single component (such as consumption). This index also differs from the traditional CPI because it is a chain-weighted index that takes into account the changing shares of different goods (see the discussion of chain weights on page 430). In addition, there are price indexes for components of GDP, such as for investment goods, computers, personal consumption, and so forth, and these are sometimes used to supplement the CPI.

The Producer Price Index (PPI). This index, dating from 1890, is the oldest continuous statistical series published by the BLS. It measures the level of prices at the wholesale or producer stage. It is based on approximately 3400 commodity prices, including prices of foods, manufactured products, and mining products. The fixed weights used to calculate the PPI are the net sales of each commodity. Because of its great detail, this index is widely used by businesses.

Getting the Prices Right

Measuring prices accurately is one of the central issues of empirical economics. Price indexes affect not only obvious things like the inflation rate. They also are embedded in measures of real output and productivity. And through government policies, they affect monetary policy, taxes, government transfer programs like social security, and many private contracts.

The purpose of the consumer price index is to measure the cost of living. You might be surprised to learn that this is a difficult task. Some problems are intrinsic to price indexes. One issue is the *index-number problem*, which involves how the different prices are weighted or averaged. Recall that the traditional CPI uses a fixed weight for each good. As a result, the cost of living is overestimated compared to the situation where consumers substitute relatively inexpensive for relatively expensive goods.

The case of energy prices can illustrate the problem. When gasoline prices rose sharply in the 1970s, people tended to cut back on their purchases and buy smaller cars or travel less. Yet the CPI assumed that they bought the same quantity of gasoline even though gasoline prices tripled. The overall rise in the cost of living was thereby exaggerated. Statisticians have devised ways of minimizing such index-number problems by using different weighting approaches, such as chain weighting, discussed above, but government statisticians are just beginning to experiment with these newer approaches for the CPI.

A more important problem arises because of the difficulty of adjusting price indexes to capture the contribution of *new and improved goods and services.* An example will illustrate this problem. In recent years, consumers have benefited from compact fluorescent lightbulbs; these lightbulbs deliver light at approximately one-fourth the cost of the older, incandescent bulbs. Yet none of the price indexes incorporate the quality improvement. Similarly, as CDs replaced long-playing records, as cable TV with hundreds of channels replaced the older technology with a few fuzzy channels, as air travel replaced rail or road travel, and in thousands of other improved goods and services, the price indexes did not reflect the improved quality.

Recent studies indicate that if quality change had been properly incorporated into price indexes, the CPI would have risen less rapidly in recent years. This problem is especially acute for medical care. In this sector, reported prices have risen sharply in the last two decades. Yet we have no adequate measure of the quality of medical care, and the CPI completely ignores the introduction of new products, such as pharmaceuticals which replace intrusive and expensive surgery.

A panel of distinguished economists led by Stanford's Michael Boskin examined this issue and estimated that the upward bias in the CPI was slightly more than 1 percent per year. This is a small number with large implications. It indicates that our real-output numbers may have been *overdeflated* by the same amount. If the CPI bias carries through to the GDP deflator, then output per worker-hour in the United States has grown at 2 percent per year over the last two decades rather than the 1 percent per year as measured in the official national accounts.

This finding also implies that cost-of-living adjustments (which are used for social security benefits and in many labor agreements) have overcompensated people for movements in the cost of living. The Boskin panel estimated that if the government were to index transfer programs according to their bias estimate rather than using the current CPI, this would by 2008 reduce the government deficit by $180 billion and lower the U.S. national debt by more than $1 trillion over a decade. These findings indicate that the economics of accounting and of index numbers are no longer just abstruse concepts of interest only to a handful of technicians. Proper construction of price and output indexes affects our government budgets, our retirement programs, and even the way we assess our national economic performance.

In response to its own research and to its critics, the BLS has undertaken a major overhaul of the CPI. The most important innovation was the publication starting in 2002 of a "chained consumer price index" that augments the fixed-weight price index with a changing-weight system (like the chain weights used in the GDP accounts discussed on page 430 above) that accounts for consumer substitution. Over the first 3 years since it was published, people were surprised to learn that the chain CPI rose much more slowly—about 1 percent per year more slowly—than the traditional CPI. It appears that critics of the traditional CPI were correct that it overstates inflation.[3]

---

[3] See this chapter's Further Reading section for a symposium on CPI design.

ACCOUNTING ASSESSMENT

This chapter has examined the way economists measure national output and the overall price level. Having reviewed the measurement of national output and analyzed the shortcomings of the GDP, what should we conclude about the adequacy of our measures? Do they capture the major trends? Are they adequate measures of overall social welfare? The answer was aptly stated in a review by Arthur Okun:

> It should be no surprise that national prosperity does not guarantee a happy society, any more than personal prosperity ensures a happy family. No growth of GDP can counter the tensions arising from an unpopular and unsuccessful war, a long overdue self-confrontation with conscience on racial injustice, a volcanic eruption of sexual mores, and an unprecedented assertion of independence by the young. Still, prosperity . . . is a precondition for success in achieving many of our aspirations.[4]

---

[4] *The Political Economy of Prosperity* (Norton, New York, 1970), p. 124.

SUMMARY

1. The national income and product accounts contain the major measures of income and product for a country. The gross domestic product (GDP) is the most comprehensive measure of a nation's production of goods and services. It comprises the dollar value of consumption (C), gross private domestic investment (I), government purchases (G), and net exports (X) produced within a nation during a given year. Recall the formula:

$$GDP = C + I + G + X$$

This will sometimes be simplified by combining private domestic investment and net exports into total gross national investment ($I^T = I + X$):

$$GDP = C + I^T + G$$

2. Because of the way we define residual profit, we can match the upper-loop, flow-of-product measurement of GDP with the lower-loop, flow-of-cost measurement, as shown in Figure 21-1. The flow-of-cost approach uses factor earnings and carefully computes value added to eliminate double counting of intermediate

products. And after summing up all (before-tax) wage, interest, rent, depreciation, and profit income, it adds to this total all indirect tax costs of business. GDP does not include transfer items such as interest on government bonds or welfare payments.

3. By use of a price index, we can "deflate" nominal GDP (GDP in current dollars) to arrive at a more accurate measure of real GDP (GDP expressed in dollars of some base year's purchasing power). Use of such a price index corrects for the "rubber yardstick" implied by changing levels of prices.

4. Net investment is positive when the nation is producing more capital goods than are currently being used up in the form of depreciation. Since depreciation is hard to estimate accurately, statisticians have more confidence in their measures of gross investment than in those of net investment.

5. National income and disposable income are two additional official measurements. Disposable income (DI) is what people actually have left—after all tax payments, corporate saving of undistributed profits, and

transfer adjustments have been made—to spend on consumption or to save.

6. Using the rules of the national accounts, measured saving must exactly equal measured investment. This is easily seen in a hypothetical economy with nothing but households. In a complete economy, *private saving and government surplus equal domestic investment plus net foreign investment.* The identity between saving and investment is just that: saving must equal investment no matter whether the economy is in boom or recession, war or peace. It is a consequence of the definitions of national income accounting.

7. Gross domestic product and even net domestic product are imperfect measures of genuine economic welfare. In recent years, statisticians have started correcting for nonmarket measures such as unpaid work at home and environmental externalities.

8. Inflation occurs when the general level of prices is rising (and deflation occurs when it is falling). We measure the overall price level and rate of inflation using price indexes—weighted averages of the prices of thousands of individual products. The most important price index is the consumer price index (CPI), which traditionally measured the cost of a fixed market basket of consumer goods and services relative to the cost of that bundle during a particular base year. Recent studies indicate that the CPI trend has a major upward bias because of index-number problems and omission of new and improved goods, and the government has undertaken steps to correct some of this bias.

CONCEPTS FOR REVIEW

national income and product accounts (national accounts)
real and nominal GDP
GDP deflator
GDP = $C + I + G + X$
net investment =
   gross investment − depreciation

GDP in two equivalent views:
   product (upper loop)
   earnings (lower loop)
intermediate goods, value added
NDP = GDP − depreciation
government transfers
disposable income (*DI*)

investment-saving identity
$I = S$
$I^T = I + X = S^P + S^G = S^T$
inflation, deflation
price index:
   CPI
   GDP price index
   PPI

FURTHER READING AND INTERNET WEBSITES

Further Reading

A magnificent compilation of historical data on the United States is contained in *Historical Statistics of the United States,* 2 vols. (Government Printing Office, Washington, D.C., 1975). A review of the issues involving measuring the consumer price index is contained in "Symposium on the CPI," *Journal of Economic Perspectives,* Winter 1998.

Websites

The premium site for the U.S. national income and product accounts is maintained by the Bureau of Economic Analysis (BEA) at www.bea.gov. This site also contains recent issues of *The Survey of Current Business,* which discusses recent economic trends.

A comprehensive launching pad for government data in many sectors can be found at www.lib.umich.edu/govdocs/stats. The best single statistical source for data on the United States is *The Statistical Abstract of the United States,* published annually. It is available online at www.census.gov/statab/www/. Many important data sets can be found at www.economagic.com/.

A recent review of alternative approaches to augmented and environmental accounting is contained in a report by the National Academy of Sciences in William Nordhaus and Edward Kokkelenberg, eds., *Nature's Numbers: Expanding the National Accounts to Include the Environment* (National Academy Press, Washington, D.C., 1999), available at www.nap.edu. For price data, see the sites in the Chapter 32 Further Reading Section.

QUESTIONS FOR DISCUSSION

1. Define carefully the following and give an example of each:
   a. Consumption
   b. Gross private domestic investment
   c. Government consumption and investment purchase (in GDP)
   d. Government transfer payment (not in GDP)
   e. Exports

2. You sometimes hear, "You can't add apples and oranges." Show that we can and do add apples and oranges in the national accounts. Explain how.

3. Examine the data in the appendix to Chapter 20. Locate the figures for nominal and real GDP for 1999 and 1998. Calculate the GDP deflator. What were the rates of growth of nominal GDP and real GDP for 1999? What was the rate of inflation (as measured by the GDP deflator) for 1999?

4. Robinson Crusoe produces upper-loop product of $1000. He pays $750 in wages, $125 in interest, and $75 in rent. What must his profit be? If three-fourths of Crusoe's output is consumed and the rest invested, calculate Crusoeland's GDP with both the product and the income approaches and show that they must agree exactly.

5. Here are some brain teasers. Can you see why the following are not counted in U.S. GDP?
   a. The gourmet meals produced by a fine chef
   b. The purchase of a plot of land
   c. The purchase of an original Rembrandt painting
   d. The value I get in 2000 from playing a 1997 compact disc
   e. Damage to houses and crops from pollution emitted by electric utilities
   f. Profits earned by IBM on production in a British factory

6. Consider the country of Agrovia, whose GDP is discussed in "A Numerical Example" on page 434. Construct a set of national accounts like that in Table 21-6 assuming that wheat costs $5 per bushel, there is no depreciation, wages are three-fourths of national output, indirect business taxes are used to finance 100 percent of government spending, and the balance of income goes as rent income to farmers.

7. Review the discussion of bias in the CPI. Explain why failure to consider the quality improvement of a new good leads to an upward bias in the trend of the CPI. Pick a good you are familiar with. Explain how its quality has changed and why it might be difficult for a price index to capture the increase in quality.

8. In recent decades, women have worked more hours in paid jobs and fewer hours in unpaid housework.
   a. How would this increase in work hours affect GDP?
   b. Explain why this increase in measured GDP will overstate the true increase in output. Also explain how a set of augmented national accounts which includes home production would treat this change from nonmarket work to market work.
   c. Explain the paradox, "When a person marries his or her gardener, GDP goes down."

9. Examine the price data in Table 21-7. This shows actual data on the consumer price index for December 2000.
   a. Using the technique described in the box on page 440, calculate the percentage increase in the CPI from December 1999 to December 2000.
   b. The value of the CPI was 168.3 in December 1999 (based on 1983 = 100). What was the value of the CPI in December 2000?

Expenditure category	Relative importance, December 1999 (%)	Percentage change, December 1999 to December 2000
All items (1967 = 100)	100.00	?
Food and beverages	16.30	2.80
Housing	39.64	4.30
Apparel	4.68	−1.80
Transportation	17.45	4.10
Medical care	5.77	4.20
Recreation	6.01	1.70
Education and communication	5.42	1.30
Other goods and services	4.73	4.20

TABLE 21-7. Data for Consumer Price Index, December 2000

Source: Bureau of Labor Statistics at ftp://ftp.bls.gov/pub/news.release/History/cpi.01142000.news.

CHAPTER

22

Consumption and Investment

Micawber's equation:
Income 20 pound;
expenditure 19 pounds,
19 shillings and
sixpence = happiness.
Income 20 pound;
annual expenditure
20 pounds and
sixpence = misery.

Charles Dickens,
David Copperfield

Consumption, saving, and investment play a central role in a nation's economic performance. Nations that save and invest large fractions of their incomes tend to have rapid growth of output, income, and wages; this pattern characterized the United States in the nineteenth century, Japan in the twentieth century, and the "miracle" economies of East Asia in the last three decades. By contrast, nations which consume most of their incomes, like many poor countries in Africa and Latin America, invest little in new plant and equipment and show low rates of growth of productivity and wages. High consumption relative to income spells low investment and slow growth; high saving leads to high investment and rapid growth.

The interaction between spending and income plays quite a different role during business-cycle expansions and contractions. When economic conditions give rise to rapidly growing consumption and investment, this increases total spending or aggregate demand, raising output and employment in the short run. America's economic boom of the late 1990s was largely fueled by rapid growth in consumer spending. And when consumption falls because of higher taxes or loss of consumer confidence, as happened in Japan in the 1990s, this tends to reduce total spending and may produce a recession.

Because consumption and investment are so central to macroeconomics, we devote this chapter to them. Figure 22-1 shows how this chapter's analysis fits into the overall structure of the economy.

A. CONSUMPTION AND SAVING

This section considers consumption and saving behavior, beginning with individual spending patterns and then looking at aggregate consumption behavior. Recall from Chapter 21 that *consumption* (or, more precisely, personal consumption expenditures) is expenditures by households on final goods and services. *Saving* is that part of personal disposable income that is not consumed.

Consumption is the largest single component of GDP, constituting 66 percent of total spending over the last decade. What are the major elements of consumption? Among the most important categories are housing, motor vehicles, food, and medical care. Table 22-1 displays the major elements, broken down into the three categories of durable goods, nondurable goods, and services. The items themselves are familiar, but their relative importance,

445

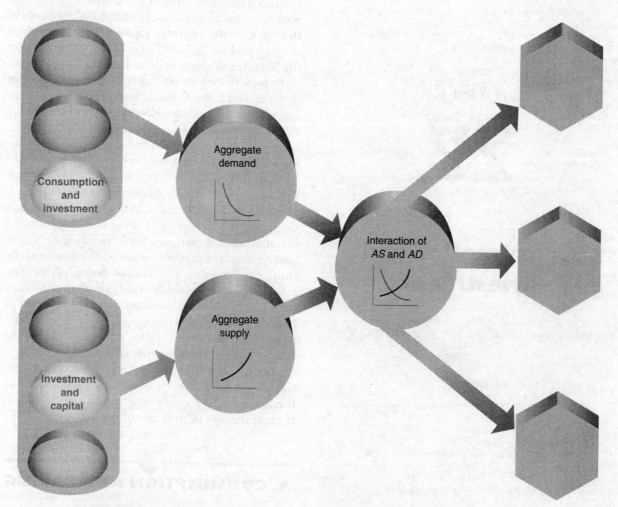

FIGURE 22-1. What Are the Major Forces Affecting Consumption and Investment?

This chapter analyzes two major components of GDP: consumption and investment. In later chapters, we will see that they affect both aggregate supply and aggregate demand.

particularly the increasing importance of services, is worth a moment's study.

Budgetary Expenditure Patterns

How do the patterns of consumption spending differ across different households in the United States? No two families spend their disposable incomes in exactly the same way. Yet statistics show that there is a predictable regularity in the way people allocate their expenditures among food, clothing, and other major items. The thousands of budgetary investigations of household spending patterns show remarkable agreement on the general, qualitative patterns of

behavior.[1] Figure 22-2 on page 448 tells the story. Poor families must spend their incomes largely on the necessities of life: food and shelter. As income increases, expenditure on many food items goes up. People eat more and eat better. There are, however, limits to the extra money people will spend on food when their incomes rise. Consequently, the proportion of total

---

[1] The spending patterns shown in Fig. 22-2 are called "Engel's Laws," after the nineteenth-century Prussian statistician Ernst Engel. The average behavior of consumption expenditure does change fairly regularly with income. But averages do not tell the whole story. Within each income class, there is a considerable spread of consumption around the average.

Category of consumption	Value of category, 2002 ($, billion)	Percent of total
Durable goods	872	11.9
Motor vehicles and parts	376.1	
Furniture and household equipment	318.7	
Other	177.1	
Nondurable goods	2,115	29.0
Food	1,029.4	
Clothing and shoes	324.3	
Energy goods	173.5	
Other	587.8	
Services	4,317	59.1
Housing	1,071.5	
Household operation	405.2	
Transportation	275.8	
Medical care	1,148.5	
Recreation	285.1	
Other	1,130.7	
Total personal consumption expenditures	7,304	100.0

TABLE 22-1. The Major Components of Consumption

We divide consumption into three categories: durable goods, nondurable goods, and services. The service sector is growing in importance as basic needs for food are met and as health, recreation, and education claim a larger part of family budgets.

Source: U.S. Department of Commerce, available at www.bea.gov.

spending devoted to food declines as income increases.

Expenditure on clothing, recreation, and automobiles increases more than proportionately to after-tax income, until high incomes are reached. Spending on luxury items increases in greater proportion than income. Finally, as we look across families, note that saving rises very rapidly as income increases. Saving is the greatest luxury of all.

The Evolution of Consumption in the Twentieth Century

Continual changes in technology, incomes, and social forces have led to dramatic changes in U.S. consumption patterns over time. In 1918, American households on average spent 41 percent of their incomes on food and drink. By comparison, households now spend only about 19 percent on these items. What lies behind this striking decline? The major factor is

that spending on food tends to grow more slowly than incomes. Similarly, spending on apparel has fallen from 18 percent of household income at the beginning of the twentieth century to only 6 percent today.

What are the "luxury goods" that Americans are spending more on? One big item is transportation. In 1918, Americans spent only 1 percent of their incomes on vehicles—but of course Henry Ford didn't sell his first Model T until 1908. Today, there are 1.3 cars for every household, so it is not surprising that 23 percent of spending goes for vehicle-related transportation expenses. What about recreation and entertainment? Households now lay out large sums for televisions, cellular phones, and VCRs, items that didn't exist 75 years ago. These new inventions have lifted entertainment expenses to 6 percent of household budgets, up from 3 percent. Housing services, too, take a bigger share of income—20 percent compared to 14 percent in the earlier period. That reflects, in part, the success of the American Dream:

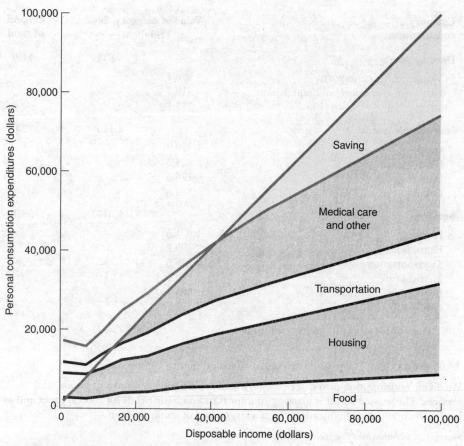

FIGURE 22-2. Family Budget Expenditures Show Regular Patterns

Surveys verify the importance of disposable income as a determinant of consumption expenditures. Notice the drop in food as a percentage of income as incomes rise. Note also that saving is negative at low incomes but rises substantially at high incomes.

Source: U.S. Department of Labor, *Consumer Expenditure Surveys, 1998*, available on the Internet at www.bls.gov/csxstnd.htm.

owning a big house in the suburbs is more expensive than renting a small apartment in the city.

Over the last decade, the biggest increase in consumption spending has been for health care, as both consumer payments for medical care and employer and government contributions for health care have soared. Surprisingly, consumers' out-of-pocket expenses for health care take about the same share of the *household* budget as they did in the early part of the twentieth century. The major increase has come as governments have taken over ever-larger fractions of health-care spending, contributing to the growth in government spending in the United States and other high-income countries.

CONSUMPTION, INCOME, AND SAVING

Income, consumption, and saving are all closely linked. More precisely, **personal saving** is that part of disposable income that is not consumed; saving equals income minus consumption. The relationship between income, consumption, and saving for the United States in 2002 is shown in Table 22-2. Begin with personal income (composed, as Chapter 21 showed, of wages, interest, rents, dividends, transfer payments, and so forth). In 2002, some $1114 billion of personal income, or 12.5 percent, went to personal taxes. This left $7816 billion of personal disposable income.

Household outlays for consumption (including interest) amounted to 96.3 percent of disposable income, or $7525 billion, leaving $291 billion as personal saving. The last item in the table shows the important **personal saving rate.** This is equal to personal saving as a percent of disposable income (3.7 percent in 2002).

Economic studies have shown that income is the primary determinant of consumption and saving. Rich people save more than poor people, both absolutely and as a percent of income. The very poor are unable to save at all. Instead, as long as they can borrow or draw down their wealth, they tend to dissave. That is, they tend to spend more than they earn, reducing their accumulated savings or going deeper into debt.

Table 22-3 contains illustrative data on disposable income, saving, and consumption drawn from budget studies on American households. The first column shows seven different levels of disposable income. Column (2) indicates saving at each level of income, and the third column indicates consumption spending at each level of income.

The *break-even point*—where the representative household neither saves nor dissaves but consumes all its income—comes at $25,000. Below the break-even point, say, at $24,000, the household actually consumes more than its income; it dissaves (see the −$200 item). Above $25,000 it begins to show positive saving [see the +$200 and other positive items in column (2)].

Column (3) shows the consumption spending for each income level. Since each dollar of income is divided between the part consumed and the remaining

Item	Amount, 2002 ($, billion)
Personal income	**8,929**
Less: Personal taxes	1,114
Equals: Disposable personal income	**7,816**
Less: Personal outlays (consumption and interest)	7,525
Equals: Personal saving	**291**
Memo: Personal saving as percent of disposable personal income	3.7

TABLE 22-2. Saving Equals Disposable Income Less Consumption

Source: U.S. Department of Commerce, available at www.bea.gov.

	(1) Disposable income ($)	(2) Net saving (+) or dissaving (−) ($)	(3) Consumption ($)
A	24,000	−200	24,200
B	25,000	0	25,000
C	26,000	200	25,800
D	27,000	400	26,600
E	28,000	600	27,400
F	29,000	800	28,200
G	30,000	1,000	29,000

TABLE 22-3. Consumption and Saving Are Primarily Determined by Income

Consumption and saving rise with disposable income. The break-even point at which people have zero saving is shown here at $25,000. How much of each extra dollar do people devote to extra consumption at this income level? How much to extra saving? (Answer: 80 cents and 20 cents, respectively, when we compare row B and row C.)

part saved, columns (3) and (2) are not independent; they must always exactly add up to column (1).

To understand the way consumption affects national output, we need to introduce some new tools. We need to understand how many extra dollars of consumption and saving are induced by each extra dollar of income. This relationship is shown by:

- The consumption function, relating consumption and income
- Its twin, the saving function, relating saving and income

The Consumption Function

One of the most important relationships in all macroeconomics is the **consumption function.** The consumption function shows the relationship between the level of consumption expenditures and the level of disposable personal income. This concept, introduced by Keynes, is based on the hypothesis that there is a stable empirical relationship between consumption and income.

We can see the consumption function most vividly in the form of a graph. Figure 22-3 below plots the seven levels of income listed in Table 22-3. Disposable income [column (1) of Table 22-3] is placed on the horizontal axis, and consumption [column (3)] is on the vertical axis. Each of the income-consumption combinations is represented by a single point, and the points are then connected by a smooth curve.

The relation between consumption and income shown in Figure 22-3 is called the consumption function.

The "Break-Even" Point.

To understand the figure, it is helpful to look at the 45° line drawn northeast from the origin. Because the vertical and horizontal axes have exactly the same scale, the 45° line has a very special property. At any point on the 45° line, the distance up from the horizontal axis (consumption) exactly equals the distance across from the vertical axis (disposable income). You can use your eyes or a ruler to verify this fact.

The 45° line tells us immediately whether consumption spending is equal to, greater than, or less than the level of disposable income. The **break-even point** on the consumption schedule that intersects the 45° line represents the level of disposable income at which households just break even.

This break-even point is at B in Figure 22-3. Here, consumption expenditure is exactly equal to disposable income: the household is neither a borrower nor a saver. To the right of point B, the consumption function lies below the 45° line. The relationship between income and consumption can be seen by examining the thin black line from E' to E in Figure 22-3. At an income of \$28,000 the level of consumption is \$27,400 (see Table 22-3). We can see that consumption is less than income by the fact that the consumption function lies below the 45° line at point E.

What a household is not spending, it must be saving. The 45° line enables us to find how much the household is saving. Net saving is measured by the vertical distance from the consumption function up to the 45° line, as shown by the EE'' saving arrow in rust.

The 45° line tells us that to the left of point B the household is spending more than its income. The excess of consumption over income is "dissaving" and is measured by the vertical distance between the consumption function and the 45° line.

To review:

At any point on the 45° line, consumption exactly equals income and the household has zero saving. When the consumption function lies above the 45° line, the household is dissaving. When the consumption function lies below the 45° line, the household has positive saving. The amount of dissaving or saving is always measured by the vertical distance between the consumption function and the 45° line.

The Saving Function

The **saving function** shows the relationship between the level of saving and income. This is shown graphically in Figure 22-4. Again we show disposable income on the horizontal axis; but now saving, whether negative or positive in amount, is on the vertical axis.

This saving function comes directly from Figure 22-3. It is the vertical distance between the 45° line and the consumption function. For example, at point A in Figure 22-3, we see that the household's saving is negative because the consumption function lies above the 45° line. Figure 22-4 shows this dissaving directly—the saving function is below the zero-saving line at point A. Similarly, positive saving occurs to the right of point B because the saving function is above the zero-saving line.

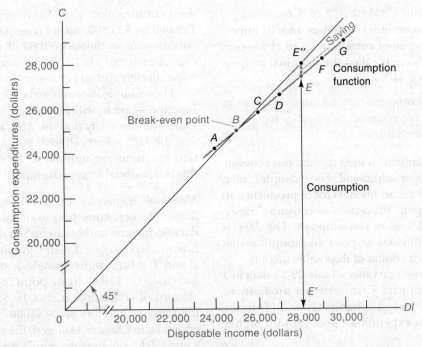

FIGURE 22-3. A Plot of the Consumption Function

The curve through $A, B, C, \ldots, G$ is the consumption function. The horizontal axis depicts the level of disposable income (DI). For each level of DI, the consumption function shows the dollar level of consumption (C) for the household. Note that consumption rises with increases in DI. The 45° line helps locate the break-even point and helps our eye measure net saving.

Source: Table 22-3.

FIGURE 22-4. The Saving Function Is the Mirror Image of the Consumption Function

This saving schedule is derived by subtracting consumption from income. Graphically, the saving function is obtained by subtracting vertically the consumption function from the 45° line in Fig. 22-3. Note that the break-even point B is at the same $25,000 income level as in Fig. 22-3.

The Marginal Propensity to Consume

Modern macroeconomics attaches much importance to the response of consumption to changes in income. This concept is called the marginal propensity to consume, or *MPC*.

The **marginal propensity to consume** is the extra amount that people consume when they receive an extra dollar of disposable income.

The word "marginal" is used throughout economics to mean extra or additional. For example, "marginal cost" means the additional cost of producing an extra unit of output. "Propensity to consume" designates the desired level of consumption. The *MPC* is therefore the additional or extra consumption that results from an extra dollar of disposable income.

Table 22-4 above rearranges Table 22-3's data in a more convenient form. First, verify its similarity to Table 22-3. Then, look at columns (1) and (2) to see how consumption expenditure goes up with higher levels of income.

Column (3) shows how we compute the marginal propensity to consume. From B to C, income rises by $1000, going from $25,000 to $26,000. How much

does consumption rise? Consumption grows from $25,000 to $25,800, an increase of $800. The extra consumption is therefore 0.80 of the extra income. Out of each extra dollar of income, 80 cents goes to consumption and 20 cents goes to saving.

The example shown here is a linear consumption function—one in which the *MPC* and *MPS* are constant. You can verify that the *MPC* is everywhere 0.80 and the *MPS* is everywhere 0.20. In reality, consumption functions are unlikely to be exactly linear, but this is a reasonable approximation for our purposes.

Marginal Propensity to Consume as Geometrical Slope. We now know how to calculate the *MPC* from data on income and consumption. Figure 22-5 shows how we can calculate the *MPC* graphically. Near points *B* and *C* a little right triangle is drawn. As income increases by $1000 from point *B* to point *C*, the amount of consumption rises by $800. The *MPC* in this range is therefore $800/$1000 = 0.80. But, as the appendix to Chapter 1 showed, the numerical slope of a line is "the rise over the run."[2] We can therefore see

---

[2] For curved lines, we calculate the slope as the slope of the tangent line at a point.

	(1) Disposable income (after taxes) ($)	(2) Consumption expenditure ($)	(3) Marginal propensity to consume *MPC*	(4) Net saving ($) (4) = (1) − (2)	(5) Marginal propensity to save *MPS*
A	24,000	24,200		−200	
			800/1,000 = 0.80		200/1,000 = 0.20
B	25,000	25,000		0	
			800/1,000 = 0.80		200/1,000 = 0.20
C	26,000	25,800		200	
			800/1,000 = 0.80		200/1,000 = 0.20
D	27,000	26,600		400	
			800/1,000 = 0.80		200/1,000 = 0.20
E	28,000	27,400		600	
			800/1,000 = 0.80		200/1,000 = 0.20
F	29,000	28,200		800	
			800/1,000 = 0.80		200/1,000 = 0.20
G	30,000	29,000		1,000	

TABLE 22-4. The Marginal Propensities to Consume and to Save

Each dollar of disposable income not consumed is saved. Each extra dollar of disposable income goes either into extra consumption or into extra saving. Combining these facts allows us to calculate the marginal propensity to consume (*MPC*) and the marginal propensity to save (*MPS*).

FIGURE 22-5. The Slope of the Consumption Function Is Its _MPC_

To calculate the marginal propensity to consume (_MPC_), we measure the slope of the consumption function by forming a right triangle and relating height to base. From point _B_ to point _C_, the increase in consumption is $800 while the change in disposable income is $1000. The slope, equal to the change in _C_ divided by the change in _DI_, gives the _MPC_. If the consumption function is everywhere upward-sloping, what does this imply about the _MPC_? If the line is a straight line, with a constant slope, what does this imply about the _MPC_?

that the slope of the consumption function is the same as the marginal propensity to consume.

The slope of the consumption function, which measures the change in consumption per dollar change in disposable income, is the marginal propensity to consume.

The Marginal Propensity to Save

Along with the marginal propensity to consume goes its mirror image, the marginal propensity to save, or _MPS_. The **marginal propensity to save** is defined as the fraction of an extra dollar of disposable income that goes to extra saving.

Why are _MPC_ and _MPS_ related like mirror images? Recall that disposable income equals consumption plus saving. This implies that each extra dollar of disposable income must be divided between extra consumption and extra saving. Thus if _MPC_ is 0.80, then _MPS_ must be 0.20. (What would _MPS_ be if _MPC_

were 0.6? Or 0.99?) Comparing columns (3) and (5) of Table 22-4 confirms that at any income level, _MPC_ and _MPS_ must always add up to exactly 1, no more and no less. _MPS_ + _MPC_ = 1, always and everywhere.

Brief Review of Definitions

Let's review briefly the main definitions we have learned:

1. The _consumption function_ relates the level of consumption to the level of disposable income.
2. The _saving function_ relates saving to disposable income. Because what is saved equals what is not consumed, saving and consumption schedules are mirror images.
3. The _marginal propensity to consume_ (_MPC_) is the amount of extra consumption generated by an extra dollar of disposable income. Graphically, it is given by the slope of the consumption function.

4. The *marginal propensity to save* (*MPS*) is the extra saving generated by an extra dollar of disposable income. Graphically, this is the slope of the saving schedule.
5. Because the part of each dollar of disposable income that is not consumed is necessarily saved, $MPS \equiv 1 - MPC$.

NATIONAL CONSUMPTION BEHAVIOR

Up to now we have examined the budget patterns and consumption behavior of typical families at different incomes. Let's now consider consumption for the entire nation. This transition from household behavior to national trends exemplifies the methodology of macroeconomics: We begin by examining economic activity on the individual level and then add up or aggregate the totality of individuals to study the way the overall economy operates.

Why are we interested in national consumption trends? Consumption behavior is crucial for understanding both short-term business cycles and long-term economic growth. In the short run, consumption is a major component of aggregate spending. When consumption changes sharply, the change is likely to affect output and employment through its impact on aggregate demand. This mechanism will be described in the chapters on Keynesian macroeconomics.

Additionally, consumption behavior is crucial because what is not consumed—that is, what is saved—is available to the nation for investment in new capital goods; capital serves as a driving force behind long-term economic growth. *Consumption and saving behavior are key to understanding economic growth and business cycles.*

Determinants of Consumption

We begin by analyzing the major forces that affect consumer spending. What factors in a nation's life and livelihood set the pace of its consumption outlays?

Current Disposable Income. Figure 22-6 shows how closely consumption followed current disposable income over the period 1929–1999. The only period when income and consumption did not move in tandem was during World War II, when goods were scarce and rationed and people were urged to save to help the war effort.

Both observation and statistical studies show that the current level of disposable income is the central factor determining a nation's consumption.

Permanent Income and the Life-Cycle Model of Consumption. The simplest theory of consumption uses only the current year's income to predict consumption expenditures. Consider the following examples, which suggest otherwise:

If bad weather destroys a crop, farmers will draw upon their previous saving.
Similarly, law-school students borrow for consumption purposes while in school because they believe that their postgraduate incomes will be much higher than their meager student earnings.

In both these circumstances, people are in effect asking, "Given my current and future income, how much can I consume today without incurring excessive debts?"

Careful studies show that consumers generally choose their consumption levels with an eye to both current income and long-run income prospects. In order to understand how consumption depends on long-term income trends, economists have developed the permanent-income theory and the life-cycle hypothesis.[3]

Permanent income is the trend level of income—that is, income after removing temporary or transient influences due to the weather or windfall gains or losses. According to the permanent-income theory, consumption responds primarily to permanent income. This approach implies that consumers do not respond equally to all income shocks. If a change in income appears permanent (such as being promoted to a secure and high-paying job), people are likely to consume a large fraction of the increase in income. On the other hand, if the income change is clearly transitory (for example, if it arises from a one-time bonus or a good harvest), a significant fraction of the additional income may be saved.

---

[3] The pathbreaking studies on longer-term influences were by Milton Friedman (on the permanent-income hypothesis) and Franco Modigliani (for the life-cycle model). Both received the Nobel Prize in economics for their accomplishments in these and other areas.

FIGURE 22-6. Consumption and Disposable Income, 1929–2003

U.S. consumption spending has closely tracked the level of personal disposable income over the last seven decades. Macroeconomists can forecast consumption accurately based on the historical consumption function.

Source: U.S. Department of Commerce. Real disposable income is deflated using the price index for personal consumption expenditures.

The *life-cycle hypothesis* assumes that people save in order to smooth their consumption over their lifetime. One important objective is to have an adequate retirement income. Hence, people tend to save while working so as to build up a nest egg for retirement and then spend out of their accumulated savings in their twilight years. One implication of the life-cycle hypothesis is that a program like social security, which provides a generous income supplement for retirement, will reduce saving by middle-aged workers since they no longer need to save as much for retirement.

Wealth and Other Influences. A further important determinant of the amount of consumption is wealth. Consider two consumers, both earning $50,000 per year. One has $200,000 in the bank, while the other has no savings at all. The first person may consume part of wealth, while the second has no wealth to draw down. The fact that higher wealth leads to higher consumption is called the *wealth effect*.

Wealth usually changes slowly from year to year. However, when wealth grows or declines rapidly, this can cause sharp movements in consumption. One important historical case was the stock market crash after 1929, when fortunes collapsed and paper-rich capitalists became paupers overnight. Economic historians believe that the sharp decline in wealth after the 1929 stock market crash reduced consumption spending and contributed to the depth of the Great Depression.

The opposite case occurred during the great stock market boom of the 1990s. Because of the sharp increase in asset prices, household net worth increased from $28 trillion to $42 trillion from 1995 to 2000. This increased consumption and lowered measured saving. Then, as the stock market fell sharply after 2000, consumers tightened their belts.

The National Consumption Function

Having reviewed the determinants of consumption, we may conclude that the level of disposable income is the primary determinant of the level of national consumption. Armed with this result, we can plot recent annual data on consumption and disposable income in Figure 22-7. The scatter diagram shows data for the period 1970–1999, with each point representing the level of consumption and disposable income for a given year.

In addition, you might draw a line in Figure 22-7 through the scatter points and label it "Fitted consumption function." This fitted consumption function shows how closely consumption has followed disposable income over the last quarter-century. In fact, economic historians have found that a close relationship between disposable income and consumption holds back to the nineteenth century.

The Declining Saving Rate

Although consumption behavior tends to be stable over time, the personal saving rate dropped sharply in the United States over the last two decades. The personal saving rate as measured in the national accounts averaged around 8 percent of personal disposable income over most of the twentieth century. Starting about 1980, however, it began to decline and has been barely positive over the last few years. (See Figure 22-8.)

This drop alarmed many economists because, over the long run, the growth in a nation's capital stock is largely determined by its national saving rate. National saving is composed of private and government saving. A high-saving nation has a rapidly growing capital stock and enjoys a rapid growth in its potential output.

FIGURE 22-7. A Consumption Function for the United States, 1970–1999

Draw a straight line through the scatter of data points. Can you verify that the *MPC* slope of the fitted line is close to 0.95? How can you see that the average saving rate has declined in the last two decades?

Source: U.S. Department of Commerce.

When a nation's saving rate is low, its equipment and factories become obsolete and its infrastructure begins to rot away.

What were the reasons for the sharp decline in the personal saving rate? This is a highly controversial question today, but economists point to the following potential causes:

- *Social security system.* Some economists argued that the social security system has removed some of the need for private saving. In earlier times, as the life-cycle model of consumption suggests, a household would save during working years to build up a nest egg for retirement. When the government collects social security taxes and pays out social security benefits, people have less need to save for retirement. Other income-support systems have a similar effect, reducing the need to save for a rainy day: crop insurance for farmers, unemployment insurance for workers, and medical care for the poor and elderly all alleviate the precautionary motive for people to save.

- *Capital markets.* Until recently, capital markets had numerous imperfections. People found it hard to borrow funds for worthwhile purposes, whether for buying a house, financing an education, or starting a business. As capital markets developed, often with the help of government, new loan instruments allowed people to borrow more easily. One example is the proliferation of credit cards, which encourage people to borrow (even though the interest rates are quite high). A generation ago, it would be difficult to borrow more than $1000 unless a person had substantial assets. Today, credit-card solicitations arrive daily in the mail. It is not unusual to receive multiple promotions offering credit lines of $10,000 or more in a single week! Some believe that the availability of easy credit reduces saving among those who have little in liquid assets.

- *The rapid growth in wealth.* Part of the decline in personal saving in the 1990s was surely caused by the rapid increase in personal wealth, primarily due to the exploding stock market. From 1995 to 1999, for example, the value of stocks rose by about $5 trillion. If households spent 3 percent of this gain each year (a figure consistent with past experience), the wealth effect would lower the personal saving rate by about 3 percentage points.

FIGURE 22-8. Personal Saving Rate Has Declined

After rising slowly over the postwar period, the personal saving rate took a sharp nosedive after 1980.

Source: U.S. Department of Commerce.

Alternative Measures of Saving

You might at this point ask, "If people are saving so little, why are there so many rich people?" This question raises an important point about measuring personal saving. Saving looks different to the household than to the nation as a whole. This is so because saving as measured in the national income and product accounts is not the same as that measured by accountants or in balance sheets. The *national-accounts measure of saving* is the difference between disposable income (excluding capital gains) and consumption. The *balance sheet measure of saving* calculates the change in real net worth (that is, assets less liabilities, corrected for inflation) from one year to the next; this measure includes real capital gains.

The different perspectives of the national accounts and household balance sheets are shown in Figure 22-9. When the major increase in the value of assets (particularly stocks) is included, the saving rate in the 1990s was a healthy 33 percent as compared to the 6 percent measured in the national accounts. Many economists believe that the wealth effect can go a long way toward explaining the decline in saving as measured in the national income accounts.

Does this alternative view mean that we can breathe a sigh of relief? Probably not. The reason is that the high saving during the 1990s was largely in

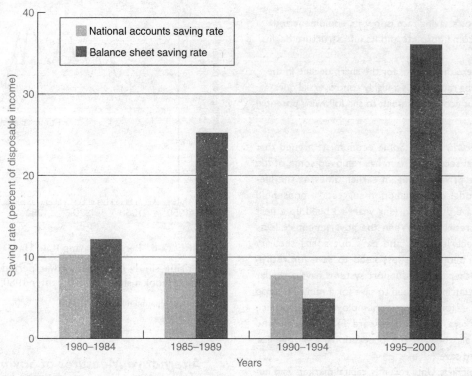

FIGURE 22-9. Two Measures of the Personal Saving Rate

According to the standard national accounts, the saving rate has fallen sharply in the last two decades. The usual measure differs considerably from saving as measured in household balance sheets, which is the change in real net worth (including capital gains on assets) divided by real disposable income. Because of the sharp increase in stock prices in the late 1990s, the balance sheet personal saving rate was high even as the national-accounts personal saving rate dropped sharply.

Source: Maria G. Perozek and Marshall B. Reinsdorf, "Alternative Measures of Personal Saving," *Survey of Current Business,* April 2002, pp. 13–24, available at www.bea.gov.

"paper wealth." But a rise in stock market valuations on existing assets may not reflect the productivity or "real wealth" of the economy. Although people feel richer when asset prices rise in a speculative bubble, the economy cannot produce more cars, computers, food, or housing. Moreover, if all stockholders decided to cash in their stocks, they would find that prices would fall and they could not convert their paper wealth into consumption.

Hence, economists are justified in worrying about the decline in the national-accounts saving rate. While consumers may *feel* richer because of the booming stock market, an economy is *actually* richer only when its productive tangible and intangible assets increase.

B. INVESTMENT

The second major component of private spending is investment. Investment plays two roles in macroeconomics. First, because it is a large and volatile component of spending, investment often leads to changes in aggregate demand and affects the business cycle. In addition, investment leads to capital accumulation. Adding to the stock of buildings and equipment increases the nation's potential output and promotes economic growth in the long run.

Thus investment plays a dual role, affecting short-run output through its impact on aggregate demand and influencing long-run output growth through the impact of capital formation on potential output and aggregate supply.

> ### The Meaning of "Investment" in Economics
>
> Remember that macroeconomists use the term "investment" or "real investment" to mean additions to the stock of productive assets or capital goods like computers or trucks. When Amazon.com builds a new warehouse or when the Smiths build a new house, these activities represent investment.
>
> Many people speak of "investing" when buying a piece of land, an old security, or any title to property. In economics, these purchases are really financial transactions or "financial investments," because what one person is buying, someone else is selling. There is investment only when real capital is produced.

DETERMINANTS OF INVESTMENT

In this discussion, we focus on *gross private domestic investment,* or *I.* This is the domestic component of national investment. Recall, however, that *I* is but one component of total social investment, which also includes foreign investment, government investment, and intangible investments in human capital and improved knowledge.

The major types of gross private domestic investment are the building of residential structures; investment in business fixed equipment, software, and structures; and additions to inventory. Of the total, about one-quarter is residential housing, one-twentieth is normally change in inventories, and the rest—averaging 70 percent of total investment in recent years—is investment in business plant, equipment, and software.

Why do businesses invest? Ultimately, businesses buy capital goods when they expect that this action will earn them a profit—that is, will bring them revenues greater than the costs of the investment. This simple statement contains the three elements essential to understanding investment: revenues, costs, and expectations.

Revenues

An investment will bring the firm additional revenue if it helps the firm sell more product. This suggests that the overall level of output (or GDP) will be an important determinant of investment. When factories are lying idle, firms have relatively little need for new factories, so investment is low. More generally, investment depends upon the revenues that will be generated by the state of overall economic activity. Most studies find that investment is very sensitive to the business cycle. A recent example of a large output effect was seen during the business downturn of 1979–1982, when output fell sharply and investment declined by 15 percent.

Costs

A second important determinant of the level of investment is the costs of investing. Because investment goods last many years, reckoning the costs of investment is somewhat more complicated than doing so for other commodities like coal or wheat. For durable goods, the cost of capital includes not only the price of the capital good but also the interest rate that borrowers pay to finance the capital as well as the taxes that firms pay on their incomes.

To understand this point, note that investors often raise the funds for buying capital goods by borrowing (say, through a mortgage or in the bond market). What is the cost of borrowing? It is the *interest rate* on borrowed funds. Recall that the interest rate is the price paid for borrowing money for a period of time; for example, you might have to pay 8 percent to borrow $1000 for a year. In the case of a family buying a house, the interest rate is the mortgage interest rate.

Additionally, taxes can have a major effect on investment. One important tax is the federal corporation income tax. This tax takes up to 34 cents of the last dollar of corporate profits, thereby discouraging investment in the corporate sector. Sometimes, the government gives tax breaks to particular activities or sectors. For example, the government encourages home ownership by allowing homeowners to deduct real-estate taxes and mortgage interest from their taxable income.

Expectations

The third element in the determination of investment is profit expectations and business confidence. Investment is, above all, a gamble on the future, a bet that the revenue from an investment will exceed its costs. If businesses are concerned that political conditions in Russia are unstable, they will be reluctant to invest there. Conversely, because businesses believe (rightly or wrongly) that Internet commerce will be an important feature of the distribution network, they are investing heavily in that sector.

Thus investment decisions hang by a thread on expectations and forecasts. But, as one wit said, forecasting is hazardous, especially about the future. Businesses spend much energy analyzing investments and trying to narrow the uncertainties about their investments.

We can sum up our review of the forces lying behind investment decisions as follows:

Businesses invest to earn profits. Because capital goods last many years, investment decisions depend on (1) the demand for the output produced by the new investment, (2) the interest rates and taxes that influence the costs of the investment, and (3) business expectations about the state of the economy.

THE INVESTMENT DEMAND CURVE

In analyzing the determinants of investment, we focus particularly on the relationship between interest rates and investment. This linkage is crucial because interest rates (influenced by central banks) are the major instrument by which governments influence investment. To show the relationship between interest rates and investment, economists use a schedule called the **investment demand curve.**

Consider a simplified economy where firms can invest in different projects: A, B, C, and so forth, up to H. These investments are so durable (like power plants or buildings) that we can ignore the need for replacement. Further, they yield a constant stream of net income each year, and there is no inflation. Table 22-5 shows the financial data on each of the investment projects.

Consider project A. This project costs $1 million. It has a very high return—$1500 per year of revenues per $1000 invested (this is a rate of return of 150 percent

(1)	(2)	(3)	(4)	(5)	(6)	(7)
			Cost per $1,000 of Project at Annual Interest Rate of:		Annual Net Profit per $1,000 Invested at Annual Interest Rate of:	
	Total investment in project ($, million)	Annual revenues per $1,000 invested ($)	10% ($)	5% ($)	10% ($) (6) = (3) − (4)	5% ($) (7) = (3) − (5)
Project						
A	1	1,500	100	50	1,400	1,450
B	4	220	100	50	120	170
C	10	160	100	50	60	110
D	10	130	100	50	30	80
E	5	110	100	50	10	60
F	15	90	100	50	−10	40
G	10	60	100	50	−40	10
H	20	40	100	50	−60	−10

TABLE 22-5. The Profitability of Investment Depends on the Interest Rate

The economy has eight investment projects, ranked in order of return. Column (2) shows the investment in each project. Column (3) calculates the perpetual return each year per $1000 invested. Columns (4) and (5) then show the cost of the project, assuming all funds are borrowed, at interest rates of 10 and 5 percent; this is shown per $1000 of the project.

The last two columns calculate the annual net profit per $1000 invested in the project. If net profit is positive, profit-maximizing firms will undertake the investment; if negative, the investment project will be rejected.

Note how the cutoff between profitable and unprofitable investments moves as the interest rate rises. (Where would the cutoff be if the interest rate rose to 15 percent per year?)

per year). Columns (4) and (5) show the cost of investment. For simplicity, assume that the investment is financed purely by borrowing at the market interest rate, here taken alternatively as 10 percent per year in column (4) and 5 percent in column (5).

Thus at a 10 percent annual interest rate, the cost of borrowing $1000 is $100 a year, as is shown in all entries of column (4); at a 5 percent interest rate, the borrowing cost is $50 per $1000 borrowed per year.

Finally, the last two columns show the *annual net profit* from each investment. For lucrative project A, the net annual profit is $1400 a year per $1000 invested at a 10 percent interest rate. Project H loses money.

To review our findings: In choosing among investment projects, firms compare the annual revenues from an investment with the annual cost of capital, which depends upon the interest rate. The difference between annual revenue and annual cost is the annual net profit. When annual net profit is positive, the investment makes money, while a negative net profit denotes that the investment loses money.[4]

Look again at Table 22-5 and examine the last column, showing annual net profit at a 5 percent interest rate. Note that at this interest rate, investment projects A through G would be profitable. We would thus expect profit-maximizing firms to invest in all seven projects, which [from column (2)] total up to $55 million in investment. Thus at a 5 percent interest rate, investment demand would be $55 million.

However, suppose that the interest rate rises to 10 percent. Then the cost of financing these investments would double. We see from column (6) that investment projects F and G become unprofitable at an interest rate of 10 percent; investment demand would fall to $30 million.

We show the results of this analysis in Figure 22-10. This figure shows the *demand-for-investment schedule,* which is here a downward-sloping step function of the interest rate. This schedule shows the amount of investment that would be undertaken at each

FIGURE 22-10. Investment Depends upon Interest Rate

The downward-stepping demand-for-investment schedule plots the amount that businesses would invest at each interest rate, as calculated from the data in Table 22-5. Each step represents a lump of investment: project A has such a high rate that it is off the figure; the highest visible step is project B, shown at the upper left. At each interest rate, all investments that have positive net profit will be undertaken.

interest rate; it is obtained by adding up all the investments that would be profitable at each level of the interest rate.

Hence, if the market interest rate is 5 percent, the desired level of investment will occur at point *M,* which shows investment of $55 million. At this interest rate, projects A through G are undertaken. If interest rates were to rise to 10 percent, projects F and G would be squeezed out; in this situation, investment demand would lie at point *M′* in Figure 22-10, with total investment of $30 million.[5]

Shifts in the Investment Demand Curve

We have seen how interest rates affect the level of investment. Investment is affected by other forces as well. For example, an increase in the GDP will shift the investment demand curve out, as shown in Figure 22-11(*a*) on the next page.

---

[4] This example greatly simplifies the calculations businesses must make in actual investment decisions. Usually, investments involve an uneven stream of returns, depreciation of capital, inflation, taxes, and multiple interest rates on borrowed funds. Discussion of the economics of discounting and present values is found in books on money and finance. See the Further Reading section at the end of this chapter.

---

[5] We will later see that when prices are changing, it is appropriate to use a real interest rate, which represents the nominal or money interest rate corrected for inflation.

FIGURE 22-11. Shifts in Investment Demand Function

In the demand-for-investment (*DI*) schedule, the arrows show the impact of **(a)** a higher level of GDP, **(b)** higher taxes on capital income, and **(c)** a burst of business euphoria induced by enthusiasm about prospects for the Internet.

An increase in business taxation would depress investment. Say that the government taxes away half the net yield in column (3) of Table 22-5, with interest costs in columns (4) and (5) not being deductible. The net profits in columns (6) and (7) would therefore decline. [Verify that at a 10 percent interest rate, a 50 percent tax on column (3) would raise the cutoff to between projects B and C, and the demand for investment would decline to $5 million.] The case of a tax increase on investment income is shown in Figure 22-11(*b*).

Finally, note the importance of expectations. In the late 1990s, investors became infatuated with the "new economy." They projected unrealistically rapid growth rates for companies like AOL–Time Warner and Yahoo! and NetZero, setting aside traditional precepts that business schools teach about investment. As a result, the demand for investment in software for Internet companies increased sharply until the bottom fell out of the market in 2000. Figure 22-11(c) displays how a bout of business optimism would shift out the investment demand schedule. The opposite case, of pessimism about profits in corrupt Russia, would explain why Western firms have invested warily in that economy. These are but two examples of how expectations can have powerful effects on investment.

After learning about the factors affecting investment, you will not be surprised to discover that investment is the most volatile component of spending. Investment behaves unpredictably because it depends on such uncertain factors as the success or failure of new and untried products, changes in tax rates and interest rates, political attitudes and approaches to stabilizing the economy, and similar changeable events of economic life. *In virtually every business cycle, investment fluctuations have been the driving force behind boom or bust.*

ON TO THE THEORY OF AGGREGATE DEMAND

We have now completed our introduction to the basic concepts of macroeconomics. We have examined the determinants of consumption and investment and seen how they can fluctuate from year to year, sometimes quite sharply.

At this point, macroeconomics branches into one of two major themes—business cycles and economic growth. In the chapters that follow, we begin our survey of business cycles, or the behavior of the economy in the short run. This approach, known as Keynesian economics, shows how changes in investment, government spending and taxation, foreign trade, and the money supply can be transmitted to the rest of the economy. We will see that actual GDP can diverge from its full-employment potential. We will also see how government fiscal and monetary policies can combat recessions and booms. At the heart of the analysis is the movement of consumption and investment that we explored in this chapter.

SUMMARY

A. Consumption and Saving

1. Disposable income is an important determinant of consumption and saving. The consumption function is the schedule relating total consumption to total disposable income. Because each dollar of disposable income is either saved or consumed, the saving function is the other side or mirror image of the consumption function.

2. Recall the major features of consumption and saving functions:
   a. The consumption (or saving) function relates the level of consumption (or saving) to the level of disposable income.
   b. The marginal propensity to consume (*MPC*) is the amount of extra consumption generated by an extra dollar of disposable income.
   c. The marginal propensity to save (*MPS*) is the extra saving generated by an extra dollar of disposable income.
   d. Graphically, the *MPC* and the *MPS* are the slopes of the consumption and saving schedules, respectively.
   e. $MPS \equiv 1 - MPC$.

3. Adding together individual consumption functions gives us the national consumption function. In simplest form, it shows total consumption expenditures as a function of disposable income. Other variables, such as permanent income or the life-cycle effect, wealth, and age also have a significant impact on consumption patterns.

4. The personal saving rate has declined sharply in the last two decades. To explain this decline, economists point to social security and government health programs, changes in capital markets, and the rapid rise in personal wealth due to the stock market boom of the 1990s. Declining saving hurts the economy because personal saving is a major component of national saving and investment. While people feel richer because of the booming stock market, the nation's true wealth increases only when its productive tangible and intangible assets increase.

B. Investment

5. The second major component of spending is gross private domestic investment in housing, plant, software, and equipment. Firms invest to earn profits. The major economic forces that determine investment are therefore the revenues produced by investment (primarily influenced by the state of the business cycle), the cost of investment (determined by interest rates and tax policy), and the state of expecatations about the future. Because the determinants of investment depend on highly unpredictable future events, investment is the most volatile component of aggregate spending.

6. An important relationship is the investment demand schedule, which connects the level of investment spending to the interest rate. Because the profitability of investment varies inversely with the interest rate, which affects the cost of capital, we can derive a downward-sloping investment demand curve. As the interest rate declines, more investment projects become profitable, showing why the investment demand schedule slopes downward.

CONCEPTS FOR REVIEW

Consumption and Saving

disposable income, consumption, saving

consumption and saving functions

personal saving rates

marginal propensity to consume (*MPC*)

marginal propensity to save (*MPS*)

$MPC + MPS \equiv 1$

break-even point

45° line

determinants of consumption:

    current disposable income

    permanent income

    wealth

    life-cycle effect

Investment

determinants of investment:

    revenues

    costs

    expectations

role of interest rates in *I*

investment demand function

FURTHER READING AND INTERNET WEBSITES

Further Reading

Economists have studied consumer expenditure patterns in order to improve predictions and help improve economic policy. One of the most influential studies is Milton Friedman, *The Theory of the Consumption Function* (University of Chicago Press, 1957). A historical overview by an economic historian is Stanley Lebergott, *Pursuing Happiness: American Consumers in the Twentieth Century* (Princeton University Press, Princeton, N.J., 1993).

Firms devote much management time to deciding about investment strategies. A good survey can be found in Richard A. Brealey and Stewart C. Myers, *Principles of Corporate Finance,* 6th ed. (McGraw-Hill, New York, 2000).

Websites

Data on total personal consumption expenditures for the United States are provided at the website of the Bureau of Economic Analysis, www.bea.gov.

Data on family budgets are contained in Bureau of Labor Statistics, "Consumer Expenditures," available at www.bls.gov.

Data and analysis of investment for the U.S. economy are provided by the Bureau of Economic Analysis at www.bea.gov.

Milton Friedman and Franco Modigliani made major contributions to our understanding of the consumption function. Visit the Nobel website at www.nobel.se/laureates to read about the importance of their contributions for macroeconomics.

QUESTIONS FOR DISCUSSION

1. Summarize the budget patterns for food, clothing, luxuries and saving.

2. In working with the consumption function and the investment demand schedule, we need to distinguish between shifts of and movements along these schedules.
    a. Define carefully for both curves changes that would lead to shifts of and those that would produce movements along the schedules.
    b. For the following, explain verbally and show in a diagram whether they are shifts of or movements along the consumption function: increase in disposable income, decrease in wealth, fall in stock prices.
    c. For the following, explain in words and show in a diagram whether they are shifts of or movements along the investment demand curve: expectation of a decline in output next year, rise of interest rates, increase in taxes on profits.

3. Exactly how were the *MPC* and *MPS* in Table 22-4 computed? Illustrate by calculating *MPC* and *MPS* between points *A* and *B*. Explain why it must always be true that $MPC + MPS \equiv 1$.

4. I consume all my income at every level of income. Draw my consumption and saving functions. What are my *MPC* and *MPS*?

5. Estimate your income, consumption, and saving for last year. If you dissaved (consumed more than your income), how did you finance your dissaving? Estimate the composition of your consumption in terms of each of the major categories listed in Table 22-1.

6. "Along the consumption function, income changes more than consumption." What does this imply for the *MPC* and *MPS*?

7. "Changes in disposable income lead to movements along the consumption function; changes in wealth or other factors lead to a shift of the consumption function." Explain this statement with an illustration of each case.

8. What would be the effects of the following on the investment demand function illustrated in Table 22-5 and Figure 22-10?
   a. A doubling of the annual revenues per $1000 invested shown in column (3)
   b. A rise in interest rates to 15 percent per year
   c. The addition of a ninth project with data in the first three columns of (J, 10, 70)
   d. A 50 percent tax on net profits shown in columns (6) and (7)

9. Using the augmented investment demand schedule from question 8(c) and assuming that the interest rate is 10 percent, calculate the level of investment for cases **a** through **d** in question 8.

10. **Advanced problem:** According to the life-cycle model, people consume each year an amount that depends upon their *lifetime* income rather than upon their current income. Assume that you expect to receive future income (in constant dollars) according to the schedule in Table 22-6.
    a. Assume that there is no interest paid on savings. You have no initial savings. Further assume that you want to "smooth" your consumption (enjoying equal consumption each year) because of diminishing extra satisfaction from extra consumption. Derive your best consumption trajectory for the 5 years, and write the figures in column (3). Then calculate your saving and enter the amounts in column (4); put your end-of-period wealth, or cumulative saving, for each year into column (5). What is your average saving rate in the first 4 years?
    b. Next, assume that a government social security program taxes you $2000 in each of your working years and provides you with an $8000 pension in year 5. If you still desire to smooth consumption, calculate your revised saving plan. How has the social security program affected your consumption? What is the effect on your average saving rate in the first 4 years? Can you see why some economists claim that social security can lower saving?

(1) Year	(2) Income ($)	(3) Consumption ($)	(4) Saving ($)	(5) Cumulative saving (end of year) ($)
1	30,000	_____	_____	_____
2	30,000	_____	_____	_____
3	25,000	_____	_____	_____
4	15,000	_____	_____	_____
5*	0	_____	_____	0

*Retired.

TABLE 22-6.

CHAPTER

23

Business Fluctuations and the Theory of Aggregate Demand

The fault, dear Brutus, is not in our stars—but in ourselves.

William Shakespeare,
Julius Caesar

The history of American capitalism is one of recurrent periods of boom and bust, of recessions and expansions. Sometimes, jobs are hard to find, factories are idle, and profits are low. These downturns are usually short and mild, as was the case in the recession that began in March 2001 and ended in November 2001. Infrequently, as during the 1930s in the Great Depression, the contraction may persist for a decade and cause widespread economic hardships.

At other times, business conditions are healthy, with rapidly growing employment, factories working overtime, and robust profits. The "fabulous 1990s" was such a prosperous period for American consumers. The economy grew rapidly; labor and product markets were exceptionally tight; unemployment was low and capacity utilization was high. Yet, unlike the case in earlier long expansions, inflation remained low throughout the 1990s expansion. The stock market rose to levels never seen before anywhere. Was this a "new era" of American capitalism fueled by globalization and the information economy? Or was this the same old capitalism accompanied by "special circumstances" that led to rapid growth and low inflation?

The short-term variations in economic activity are known as business cycles, or business fluctuations, and are covered in the first part of this chapter. Understanding business cycles has proved to be one of the most durable problems in all of macroeconomics. What causes business fluctuations? How can government policies reduce their virulence? Economists were largely unable to answer these questions until the 1930s. At that point, the revolutionary macroeconomic theories of John Maynard Keynes pointed to the importance of the forces of aggregate demand in determining business cycles. The lesson of Keynesian economics is that *changes in aggregate demand can have a powerful impact on the overall level of output, employment, and prices in the short run.*

There have been many challenges, modifications, and elaborations to the basic Keynesian framework since its earliest days. Still, the theory of aggregate demand remains the best way to understand the business cycle. In the second part of this chapter, therefore, we describe the foundations of aggregate demand analysis and show the basic Keynesian approach to business cycles. This discussion paves the way for the next chapter's examination of the Keynesian multiplier model, which describes the simplest income-determination theory. Figure 23-1 provides a road map for the analysis.

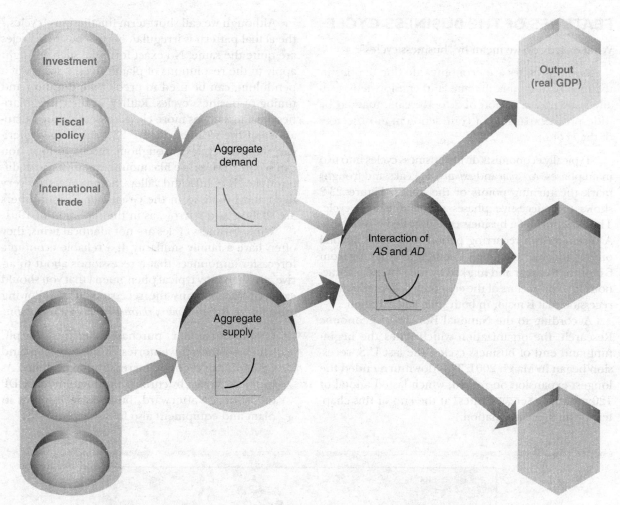

FIGURE 23-1. Business Fluctuations Have Been a Persistent Feature of Capitalism

The chapter begins with an analysis of the business cycle. It then develops the theory of aggregate demand to explain how demand shifts produce business fluctuations.

A. BUSINESS FLUCTUATIONS

Economic history shows that the economy never grows in a smooth and even pattern. A country may enjoy several years of exhilarating economic expansion and prosperity, as the United States did in the 1990s. This might be followed by a recession or even a financial crisis or, on rare occasions, a prolonged depression. Then national output falls, profits and real incomes decline, and the unemployment rate jumps to uncomfortably high levels as legions of workers lose their jobs.

Eventually the bottom is reached, and recovery begins. The recovery may be slow or fast. It may be incomplete, or it may be so strong as to lead to a new boom. Prosperity may mean a long, sustained period of brisk demand, plentiful jobs, and rising living standards. Or it may be marked by a quick, inflationary flaring up of prices and speculation, to be followed by another slump.

Upward and downward movements in output, inflation, interest rates, and employment form the business cycle that characterizes all market economies.

FEATURES OF THE BUSINESS CYCLE

What exactly do we mean by "business cycles"?

Business cycles are economywide fluctuations in total national output, income, and employment, usually lasting for a period of 2 to 10 years, marked by widespread expansion or contraction in most sectors of the economy.

Typically economists divide business cycles into two main phases, *recession* and *expansion*. Peaks and troughs mark the turning points of the cycles. Figure 23-2 shows the successive phases of the business cycle. The downturn of a business cycle is called a recession. A **recession** is a recurring period of decline in total output, income, and employment, usually lasting from 6 months to a year and marked by widespread contractions in many sectors of the economy. A **depression** is a recession that is major in both scale and duration.

According to the National Bureau of Economic Research, the organization which dates the beginning and end of business cycles, the last U.S. recession began in March 2001. This downturn ended the longest expansion on record, which lasted a total of 120 months. (See "Websites" at the end of this chapter for further information.)

Although we call short-term fluctuations "cycles," the actual pattern is irregular. No two business cycles are quite the same. No exact formula, such as might apply to the revolutions of planets or the swings of a pendulum, can be used to predict the duration and timing of business cycles. Rather, in their irregularities, business cycles more closely resemble the fluctuations of the weather. Figure 23-3 shows the American business cycles throughout recent history. You can see that cycles are like mountain ranges, with different levels of hills and valleys. Some valleys are very deep and broad, as in the Great Depression; others are shallow and narrow, as in the recession of 1991.

While business cycles are not identical twins, they often have a family similarity. If a reliable economic forecaster announces that a recession is about to arrive, are there any typical phenomena that you should expect to accompany the recession? The following are a few of the *customary characteristics* of a recession:

● Often, consumer purchases decline sharply, while business inventories of automobiles and other durable goods increase unexpectedly. As businesses react by curbing production, real GDP falls. Shortly afterward, business investment in plant and equipment also falls sharply.

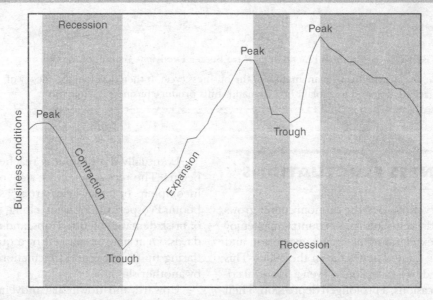

FIGURE 23-2. A Business Cycle, like the Year, Has Its Seasons

Business cycles are the irregular expansions and contractions in economic activity. (These are the actual monthly data on industrial production for a recent business-cycle period.)

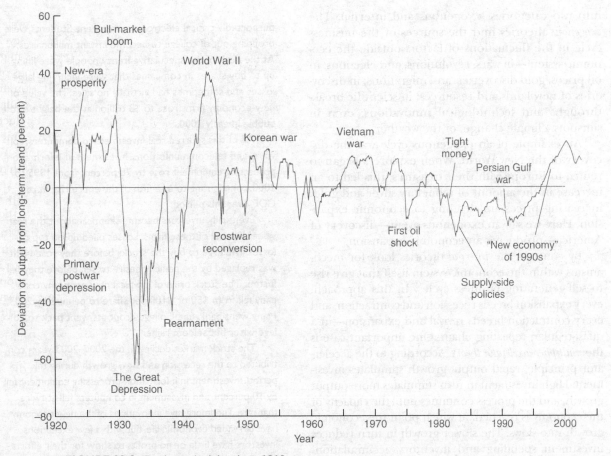

FIGURE 23-3. Business Activity since 1919

Industrial production has fluctuated irregularly around its long-run trend. Note how the long boom and information revolution of the 1990s has given a pronounced upward tilt to the business cycle. Can you detect a more stable economy in recent years?

Source: Federal Reserve Board, detrended by authors.

- The demand for labor falls—first seen in a drop in the average workweek, followed by layoffs and higher unemployment.
- As output falls, inflation slows. As demand for crude materials declines, their prices tumble. Wages and prices of services are unlikely to decline, but they tend to rise less rapidly in economic downturns.
- Business profits fall sharply in recessions. In anticipation of this, common-stock prices usually fall as investors sniff the scent of a business downturn. However, because the demand for credit falls, interest rates generally also fall in recessions.

Expansions are the mirror images of recessions, with each of the above factors operating in the opposite direction.

BUSINESS-CYCLE THEORIES

Exogenous vs. Internal Cycles. Over the years macroeconomics has been energized by vigorous debates about the sources of business cycles. Why do employment and output change directions so suddenly? Why should market economies blow hot and cold?

There is certainly no end of possible explanations, but it is useful to classify the different sources into two categories, exogenous and internal. The *exogenous* theories find the sources of the business cycle in the fluctuations of factors outside the economic system—in wars, revolutions, and elections; in oil prices, gold discoveries, and migrations; in discoveries of new lands and resources; in scientific breakthroughs and technological innovations; even in sunspots, climate change, or the weather.

An example of an exogenous cycle was the discovery of the New World. When explorers began to return to Europe with their treasures, this led to an increase in the amount of monetary silver and gold, increasing prices and leading to economic expansion. Here we saw an exogenous event—discovery of America—producing an economic expansion.

By contrast, the *internal* theories look for mechanisms within the economic system itself that give rise to self-generating business cycles. In this approach, every expansion breeds recession and contraction, and every contraction breeds revival and expansion—in a quasi-regular, repeating chain. One important case is the *multiplier-accelerator theory*. According to the accelerator principle, rapid output growth stimulates investment. High investment in turn stimulates more output growth, and the process continues until the capacity of the economy is reached, at which point the economic growth rate slows. The slower growth in turn reduces investment spending and inventory accumulation, which tends to send the economy into a recession. The process then works in reverse until the trough is reached, and the economy then stabilizes and turns up again. This internal theory of the business cycle shows a mechanism, like the motion of a pendulum, in which an exogenous shock tends to propagate itself throughout the economy in a cyclical fashion.

Speculative Boom and Bust

Another internal cycle is the speculative boom and bust that occurred in nineteenth-century capitalism and in the Great Depression and reappeared in the United States in the late 1990s and early 2000s. The phenomenal pattern of growth and innovation in the "new-economy" sectors—including computers, software, and the Internet—produced a speculative boom in new-economy stocks in the period from 1995 to 2000. Companies might be selling online dating services or grocery shopping, giving free Internet access or electronic birthday cards, or making some tiny but purportedly critical electronic component. Students were dropping out of college to become instant millionaires. At the peak of the speculative frenzy, people were lining up to buy shares in companies that were incurring large losses and sometimes had virtually no sales. The value of new-economy firms rose to $3 trillion at the height of the bubble in early 2000.

All of this spurred real investment in computers, software, and telecommunications. Investment in information-processing equipment rose by 70 percent from 1995 to 2000, contributing to one-fifth of the entire rise in real GDP over this period.

Eventually, investors became skeptical about the real value of many of these firms. Losses piled up on top of losses. The urge to buy the stocks before they rose higher was replaced by the panicky desire to sell before they fell further. The stock price of a typical new-economy company fell from $50 or $100 per share to pennies by 2003. Many went bankrupt. College dropouts went back to college wiser but seldom richer.

The stock market decline in the 2000–2003 years contributed to the recession and slow growth during this period. Investment in information-processing equipment fell by 10 percent, and investment in computers fell at twice that rate. The impressive innovations of the new economy have pervaded economic life, but with a few exceptions investors have little or no profits to show for their efforts.

Demand-Induced Cycles. One important source of business fluctuations is shocks to aggregate demand. A typical case is illustrated in Figure 23-4, which shows how a decline in aggregate demand lowers output. Say that the economy begins in short-run equilibrium at point *B*. Then, perhaps because of a decline in defense spending or tight money, the aggregate demand curve shifts leftward to *AD'*. If there is no change in aggregate supply, the economy will reach a new equilibrium at point *C*. Note that output declines from *Q* to *Q'*. In addition, prices are lower than they were at the previous equilibrium, and the rate of inflation falls.

The case of a boom is, naturally, just the opposite. Here, the *AD* curve shifts to the right, output approaches potential GDP or perhaps even overshoots it, and prices and inflation rise.

Business-cycle fluctuations in output, employment, and prices are often caused by shifts in aggregate demand. These occur as consumers, businesses, or governments change total spending relative to

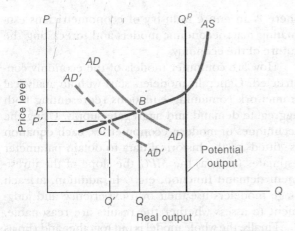

FIGURE 23-4. A Decline in Aggregate Demand Leads to an Economic Downturn

A downward shift in the *AD* curve along a relatively flat and unchanging *AS* curve leads to lower levels of output. Note that as a result of the downward shift in the *AD* curve, actual output declines relative to potential output in a recession.

the economy's productive capacity. When these shifts in aggregate demand lead to sharp business downturns, the economy suffers recessions or even depressions. A sharp upturn in economic activity can lead to inflation.

Thinking about Business Cycles

Economists have observed business cycles for almost two centuries. Here are some of the different approaches that have been proposed, along with their proponents:

1. *Monetary* theories attribute business fluctuations to the expansion and contraction of money and credit (M. Friedman). Under this approach, monetary factors are the primary source of fluctuations in aggregate demand. For example, the recession of 1981–1982 was triggered when the Federal Reserve raised nominal interest rates to 18 percent to fight inflation.
2. The *multiplier-accelerator model*, described above, proposes that exogenous shocks are propagated by the multiplier mechanism, which we examine in the next chapter, along with a theory of investment called the accelerator principle (P. Samuelson). This theory shows how the interaction of multiplier and accelerator can lead to regular cycles in aggregate demand; it is one of the few models that generates internal cycles.

3. *Political* theories of business cycles attribute fluctuations to politicians who manipulate economic policies in order to be reelected (W. Nordhaus, E. Tufte). Historically, presidential elections are sensitive to economic conditions in the year preceding the election. As a result, if they have a choice, most presidents would prefer to follow President Ronald Reagan's example. Although the U.S. economy went through a deep recession early in his term, by the time he was running for reelection in 1984, the economy was growing rapidly, which contributed to a reelection landslide.
4. *Equilibrium-business-cycle* theories claim that misperceptions about price and wage movements lead people to supply too much or too little labor, which leads to fluctuations of output and employment (R. Lucas, R. Barro, T. Sargent). In one version of these theories, unemployment rises in recessions because workers are holding out for wages that are too high.
5. *Real-business-cycle* proponents hold that innovations or productivity shocks in one sector can spread to the rest of the economy and cause recessions and booms (J. Schumpeter early in the twentieth century and E. Prescott, P. Long, C. Plosser in recent years). In this classical approach, cycles are caused primarily by shocks to aggregate supply, and not by changes in aggregate demand. Such an approach looks particularly attractive for explaining situations like the one in Russia, which made the transition from central planning to the market in the 1990s. That nation had rapid output declines largely due to disruption and confusion.
6. *Supply shocks* occur when business fluctuations are caused by shifts in aggregate supply (R. J. Gordon). The classic examples came during the oil crises of the 1970s, when sharp increases in oil prices contracted aggregate supply, increased inflation, and lowered output and employment. Many economists think that the low inflation and rapid growth of the American economy in the 1994–2000 period may be explained by favorable supply shocks. During this period, costs grew slowly because of declining oil and commodity prices, declining import prices, rapid productivity growth, and below-par increases in medical-care prices.

You might naturally wonder, Which of these theories best explains the facts of business cycles? Actually, each of the competing theories contains elements of truth, but none is universally valid. Indeed, a wise macroeconomist knows not only the different theories but also when and where to apply them.

FORECASTING BUSINESS CYCLES

Economists have developed forecasting tools to help them foresee changes in the economy. Like bright headlights on a car, a good forecast illuminates the economic terrain ahead and helps decision makers adapt their actions to economic conditions.

Econometric Modeling and Forecasting

In an earlier era, economists tried to peer into the future by looking at easily available data on items like money, boxcar loadings, and steel production. For example, a drop in steel production was a sign that businesses had reduced purchases and that the economy would soon slow down. Eventually this process was formalized by combining several different statistics into an "index of leading indicators." While it is not infallible, the index does give an early and mechanical warning on whether the economy is heading up or down.

For a more detailed look into the future, economists turn to computerized econometric forecasting models. An *econometric model* is a set of equations, representing the behavior of the economy, that has been estimated using historical data. Early pioneers in this area were Jan Tinbergen of the Netherlands and Lawrence Klein of the University of Pennsylvania—both winners of the Nobel Prize for their development of empirical macroeconomic models. Today,

there is an entire industry of econometricians estimating macroeconomic models and forecasting the future of the economy.

How are computer models of the economy constructed? Generally modelers start with an analytical framework containing equations representing both aggregate demand and aggregate supply. Using the techniques of modern econometrics, each equation is "fitted" to the historical data to obtain parameter estimates (such as the *MPC*, the slope of the investment demand function, etc.). In addition, at each stage modelers use their own experience and judgment to assess whether the results are reasonable.

Finally, the whole model is put together and run as a system of equations. In small models there are one or two dozen equations. Today, large systems forecast from a few hundred to 10,000 variables. Once the exogenous and policy variables are specified (population, government spending and tax rates, monetary policy, etc.), the system of equations can project important economic variables into the future.

Under ordinary circumstances, the forecasts do a fairly good job of illuminating the road ahead. At other times, particularly when there are major policy changes, forecasting is a hazardous profession. Figure 23-5 shows the results of a survey of forecasts of real GDP (or, earlier, real GNP) by the major forecasting groups in the United States. For

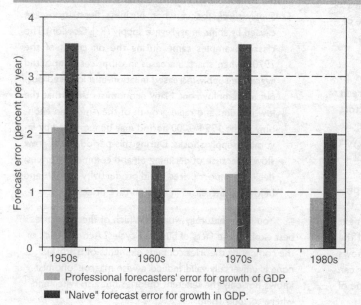

FIGURE 23-5. How Have Professional Forecasts Performed?

The record of professional forecasters is compared with that of "naive" forecasts. In every decade since systematic forecasting began, macroeconomic forecasts have improved upon guesswork, and the margin of improvement has grown slightly over time.

Source: Stephen McNees, *New England Economic Review*, July 1992. Figures are averages for each year of the decade.

■ Professional forecasters' error for growth of GDP.

■ "Naive" forecast error for growth in GDP.

comparison purposes, the study used as a benchmark a "naive forecast" in which the next year's forecasted output growth was simply equal to the current year's growth rate.

As the figure shows, professional forecasters systematically beat naive forecasts. In the first two decades, the average forecast error among professionals was more than half the error of naive forecasts, while in the 1970s and 1980s, professionals' errors dropped to less than half those of the naive approach. Another interesting feature shown in Figure 23-5 is that instability varies from period to period, with the 1950s and 1970s being relatively volatile while the 1960s and 1980s were tranquil periods. Clearly, forecasting is as much art as science in our uncertain world. Still, the strength of economic forecasting is that, year in and year out, professional forecasters provide more accurate forecasts than do those who use unsystematic or unscientific approaches.

B. FOUNDATIONS OF AGGREGATE DEMAND

The first half of this chapter described the short-term changes in output, employment, and prices that characterize business fluctuations in market economies. We showed how cyclical movements can occur when there are shifts in aggregate demand.

The time has come to explore in depth the foundations of aggregate demand. What are the major components of aggregate demand? How do they interact with aggregate supply to determine output and prices? What is the Keynesian theory of output determination, and how does it explain short-run fluctuations in GDP? We began to explore these questions in Chapter 20's introduction to macroeconomics. We now look at aggregate demand in more detail in order to get a better understanding of the forces which drive the economy. In the next chapter, we derive the simplest model of aggregate demand—the multiplier model.

Aggregate demand (or *AD*) is the total or aggregate quantity of output that is willingly bought at a given level of prices, other things held constant. *AD* is the desired spending in all product sectors: consumption, private domestic investment, government

purchases of goods and services, and net exports. It has four components:

1. *Consumption.* As we saw in the last chapter, consumption (*C*) is primarily determined by disposable income, which is personal income less taxes. Other factors affecting consumption are longer-term trends in income, household wealth, and the aggregate price level. Aggregate demand analysis focuses on the determinants of *real* consumption (that is, nominal or dollar consumption divided by the price index for consumption).

2. *Investment.* Investment (*I*) spending includes purchases of buildings, software, and equipment and accumulation of inventories. Our analysis in Chapter 22 showed that the major determinants of investment are the level of output, the cost of capital (as determined by tax policies along with interest rates and other financial conditions), and expectations about the future. The major channel by which economic policy can affect investment is monetary policy.

3. *Government purchases.* A third component of aggregate demand is government purchases of goods and services (*G*): purchases of goods like tanks or road-building equipment as well as the services of judges and public-school teachers. Unlike private consumption and investment, this component of aggregate demand is determined directly by the government's spending decisions; when the Pentagon buys a new fighter aircraft, this output directly adds to the GDP.

4. *Net exports.* A final component of aggregate demand is net exports (*X*), which equal the value of exports minus the value of imports. Imports are determined by domestic income and output, by the ratio of domestic to foreign prices, and by the foreign exchange rate of the dollar. Exports (which are imports of other countries) are the mirror image of imports, determined by foreign incomes and outputs, by relative prices, and by foreign exchange rates. Net exports, then, will be determined by domestic and foreign incomes, relative prices, and exchange rates.

Figure 23-6 on page 474 shows the *AD* curve and its four major components. At price level *P*, we can read the levels of consumption, investment, government purchases, and net exports, which sum to GDP, or *Q.* The sum of the four spending streams at this

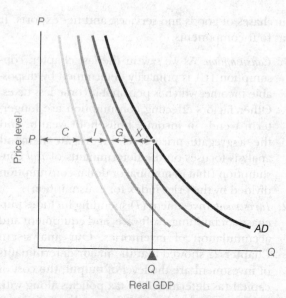

FIGURE 23-6. Components of Aggregate Demand

Aggregate demand (AD) consists of four components—consumption (C), domestic private investment (I), government spending on goods and services (G), and net exports (X).

Aggregate demand shifts when there are changes in macroeconomic policies (such as monetary-policy changes or changes in government expenditures or tax rates) or when exogenous events change spending (as would be the case with changes in foreign output, affecting X, or in business confidence, affecting I).

price level is aggregate spending, or aggregate demand, at that price level.

THE DOWNWARD-SLOPING AGGREGATE DEMAND CURVE

One important point you should notice is that the aggregate demand curve in Figure 23-6 slopes downward. This means that, holding other things constant, the level of real spending declines as the overall price level in the economy rises.

What is the reason for the downward slope? The basic reason is that there are some elements of income or wealth that do not rise when the price level rises. For example, some items of personal income might be set in nominal dollar terms—some government transfer payments, the minimum wage, and company pensions are examples. When the price level goes up,

therefore, real disposable income falls, leading to a decline in real consumption expenditures.

In addition, some elements of wealth may be fixed in nominal terms. Examples here would be holdings of money and bonds, which usually contain promises to pay a certain number of dollars in a given period. If the price level rises, therefore, the real value of wealth declines, and this would again lead to lower levels of real consumption.

One important route by which prices affect spending is through the money supply. Sometimes, the central bank keeps the money supply fixed in dollar terms (or growing at a given rate in nominal terms). So when prices rise, the real money supply (the nominal money supply corrected for changes in the price level) will fall. For example, suppose the nation's money supply is constant at $600 billion. Then, if the consumer price index doubles, the real money supply falls from $600 billion to $300 billion.

As the real money supply contracts, money becomes scarce or "tight." Interest rates and mortgage payments rise, and credit becomes harder to obtain. Tight money causes a decline in investment and consumption. In short, a rise in prices with a fixed money supply, holding other things constant, leads to tight money and produces a decline in total real spending. (We explore the monetary transmission mechanism in more detail in following chapters.)

As a result of all these effects of higher prices, the economy would move up and to the left *along* the downward-sloping AD curve.

We illustrate the impact of a lower money supply in Figure 23-7(a). Say that the economy is in equilibrium at point B, with a price level of 100, a real GDP of $3000 billion, and a money supply of $600 billion. Next assume that prices rise by 50 percent, so the price index P rises from 100 to 150. With a fixed nominal money supply, the real money supply declines from $600 billion to $400 billion. The smaller real money supply raises interest rates and lowers spending in interest-sensitive sectors like housing, plant and equipment, and automobiles. The effect is that total real spending declines to $2000 billion, shown as point C. We see here how higher prices have reduced real spending.

To summarize:

The AD curve slopes downward. This implies that real spending declines as the price level rises, other

(a) Movements along the Aggregate Demand Curve

(b) Shifts of Aggregate Demand

FIGURE 23-7. Movement along vs. Shifts of Aggregate Demand

In **(a)**, a higher price level with a fixed nominal money supply leads to tight money, higher interest rates, and declining spending on interest-sensitive investment and consumption. This illustrates a *movement along* the AD curve from B to C when other things are held constant.

In **(b)**, other things are no longer constant. Changes in variables underlying AD—such as the money supply, tax policy, or military spending—lead to changes in total spending at a given price level. This leads to a *shift of* the AD curve.

things held constant. Real spending declines with a higher price level because of the effect of higher prices on real incomes, real wealth, and the real money supply.

> **Microeconomic versus Macroeconomic Demand**
>
> We pause for an important reminder about the difference between macroeconomic and microeconomic demand curves. Recall from our study of supply and demand that the microeconomic demand curve has the price of an individual commodity on the vertical axis and production of that commodity on the horizontal axis, with all other prices and total consumer incomes held constant.
>
> In the aggregate demand curve, the general price level varies along the vertical axis, while total output and incomes vary along the horizontal axis. By contrast, incomes and output are held constant for the microeconomic demand curve.

> Finally, the negative slope of the microeconomic demand curve occurs because consumers substitute other goods for the good in question. If the meat price rises, the quantity demanded falls because consumers substitute bread and potatoes for meat, using more of the relatively inexpensive commodities and less of the relatively expensive one. The aggregate demand curve is downward-sloping for quite a different reason: Total spending falls when the overall price level rises primarily because a fixed dollar money supply must be rationed among those who need money by raising interest rates, tightening credit, and reducing total spending.
>
> Macroeconomic AD curves differ from their microeconomic cousins because aggregate demand relates prices and output for the entire economy while the micro curve analyzes the price and quantity for a single commodity. The AD curve slopes downward primarily because of the money-supply effect, while the micro demand curve slopes downward because consumers substitute other goods for the good whose price has risen.

Shifts in Aggregate Demand

We have seen that total spending in the economy tends to decline as the price level rises, holding other things constant. But those other things tend to change, and their influences produce changes in aggregate demand. What are the key variables that lead to shifts in aggregate demand?

We can separate the determinants of *AD* into two categories, as shown in Table 23-1 below. One set includes the macroeconomic *policy variables* under government control. These are monetary policy (steps by which the central bank can affect the supply of money and other financial conditions) and fiscal policy (taxes and government expenditures). Table 23-1 illustrates how these government policies can affect different components of aggregate demand.

The second category is *exogenous variables*, or variables that are determined outside the *AS-AD* framework. As Table 23-1 shows, some of these variables (such as wars or revolutions) are outside the scope of macroeconomic analysis proper, some (such as foreign economic activity) are outside the control of domestic policy, and others (such as the stock market) have significant independent movement.

What would be the effect of changes in the variables lying behind the *AD* curve? Consider the situation when the United States went to war in Iraq in 2003. The additional costs of the war included pay for the troops, purchases of ammunition and equipment, and costs of transportation. The effect of these purchases was an increase in *G*. Unless some other component of spending offset the increase in *G*, the total *AD* curve would shift out and to the right as *G* increased. Similarly, an increase in the money supply, a radical new innovation that increased the profitability of new investment, or an increase in the value of consumer wealth because of a stock-price increase would lead to an increase in aggregate demand and an outward shift of the *AD* curve.

Figure 23-7(*b*) on page 475 shows how the changes in the variables listed in Table 23-1 would affect the *AD* curve. To test your understanding, construct a similar table showing forces that would tend to decrease **aggregate demand** (see question 4 at the chapter's end).

Variable	Impact on aggregate demand
Policy variables	
Monetary policy	Increase in money supply lowers interest rates and relaxes credit conditions, inducing higher levels of investment and consumption of durable goods. In an open economy, monetary policy affects the exchange rate and net exports.
Fiscal policy	Increases in government purchases of goods and services directly increase spending; tax reductions or increases in transfers raise disposable income and induce higher consumption. Tax incentives like an investment tax credit can induce higher spending in a particular sector.
Exogenous variables	
Foreign output	Output growth abroad leads to an increase in net exports.
Asset values	Rise in stock market increases household wealth and thereby increases consumption; also, this leads to lower cost of capital and increases business investment.
Advances in technology	Technological advances can open up new opportunities for business investment. Important examples have been the railroad, the automobile, and computers.
Other	Political events, free-trade agreements, and the end of the cold war promote business and consumer confidence and increase spending on investment and consumer durables.

TABLE 23-1. Many Factors Can Increase Aggregate Demand and Shift Out the *AD* Curve

The aggregate demand curve relates total spending to the price level. But numerous other influences affect aggregate demand—some policy variables, others exogenous factors. The table lists changes that would tend to increase aggregate demand and shift out the *AD* curve.

RELATIVE IMPORTANCE OF FACTORS INFLUENCING DEMAND

While economists generally agree on the factors influencing demand, they differ in the emphasis they place on different forces. Some economists concentrate primarily on monetary forces in analyzing movements in aggregate demand, especially stressing the role of the money supply. According to these economists, who are often called *monetarists*, the supply of money is the primary determinant of the total dollar value of spending.

Other economists focus on exogenous factors instead. For example, some have argued that technological progress is one of the key determinants of booms and busts. For instance, railroads first became commercially practical in the 1850s. That innovation opened up two decades of massive investment in railroads all over the world and helped the industrial economies enjoy a sustained economic expansion. Economists looking at the 1990s have concluded that the fundamental technological changes in computer hardware, software, and communications have triggered rapid declines in prices in that sector and in the economy; have led to a significant increase in the overall potential growth of the economy; and have produced a remarkable increase in investment.

Mainstream macroeconomic thinking today is a synthesis of different approaches. In understanding business cycles, macroeconomists usually look to the insights of Keynesian economics, which emphasizes shocks to aggregate demand as the source of cyclical disturbances. These shocks might come from monetary or fiscal policy or from disturbances in the private sector. For example, fiscal policy was the leading determinant of aggregate demand changes during World War II, when military spending was absorbing almost half of GDP and monetary policy was passive. In the 1970s and 1980s, shocks from oil prices along with the reactions of monetary policy were the major factors causing cyclical patterns. In 1990 and again in 2001–2003, war and terrorism frightened consumers, reducing consumption spending and aggregate demand. Each period brings its own technological, political, and military shocks and leaves a unique cyclical impact in its wake.

We now have seen the major elements of the theory of aggregate demand. The next chapter explores the theory in greater depth by analyzing the simplest approach, the multiplier model.

Is the Business Cycle Avoidable?

The history of business cycles in the United States shows a remarkable trend toward greater stability over the last 150 years (look back at Figure 23-3). The period through 1940 witnessed numerous crises and depressions—prolonged, cumulative slumps like those of the 1870s, 1890s, and 1930s. Since 1945, business cycles have become less frequent and milder, and many Americans entered the millennium never having witnessed a major business downturn.

What has changed? Some believe that capitalism is inherently more stable now than it was in earlier times. Some of the stability comes from a larger and more predictable government sector. More important, in our view, is that a better understanding of macroeconomics now permits the government to conduct its monetary and fiscal policies to prevent shocks from turning into recessions and to keep recessions from snowballing into depressions.

During the 1990s, the American economy enjoyed the most stable period of its macroeconomic history. Some people wondered whether the business cycle was dead. Perhaps with wise management and free markets, they wrote, we have banished major recessions and inflations from the land. Is such a prognosis warranted? We believe that such pronouncements are premature. Business cycles may have been absent from North America, but they were actually *more prevalent* in other economies during the 1990s than in earlier decades. We take heed of the following prophetic words of one of the leading analysts of business cycles, Arthur Okun, written toward the end of the second-longest expansion in American history:

> Recessions are now generally considered to be fundamentally preventable, like airplane crashes and unlike hurricanes. But we have not banished air crashes from the land, and it is not clear that we have the wisdom or the ability to eliminate recessions. The danger has not disappeared. The forces that produce recurrent recessions are still in the wings, merely waiting for their cue.[1]

Shortly after Okun wrote these words, the United States entered the stormiest period of the postwar era.

---

[1] Arthur M. Okun, *The Political Economy of Prosperity* (Norton, New York, 1970), pp. 33 ff.

SUMMARY

A. Business Fluctuations

1. Business cycles or fluctuations are swings in total national output, income, and employment, marked by widespread expansion or contraction in many sectors of the economy. They occur in all advanced market economies. We distinguish the phases of expansion, peak, recession, and trough.

2. Many business cycles occur when shifts in aggregate demand cause sharp changes in output, employment, and prices. Aggregate demand shifts when changes in spending by consumers, businesses, or governments change total spending relative to the economy's productive capacity. A decline in aggregate demand leads to recessions or depressions. An upturn in economic activity can lead to inflation.

3. Business-cycle theories differ in their emphasis on exogenous and internal factors. Importance is often attached to fluctuations in such exogenous factors as technology, elections, wars, exchange-rate movements, or oil-price shocks. Most theories emphasize that these exogenous shocks interact with internal mechanisms, such as the multiplier and investment-demand shifts, to produce cyclical behavior. Just as people suffer from different diseases, so do business-cycle ailments vary in different times and countries.

B. Foundations of Aggregate Demand

4. Ancient societies suffered when harvest failures produced famines. The modern market economy can suffer from poverty amidst plenty when insufficient aggregate demand leads to deteriorating business conditions and soaring unemployment. At other times, excessive reliance on the monetary printing press leads to runaway inflation. Understanding the forces that affect aggregate demand, including government fiscal and monetary policies, can help economists and policymakers design steps to smooth out the cycle of boom and bust.

5. Aggregate demand represents the total quantity of output willingly bought at a given price level, other things held constant. Components of spending include (*a*) consumption, which depends primarily upon disposable income; (*b*) investment, which depends upon present and expected future output and upon interest rates and taxes; (*c*) government purchases of goods and services; and (*d*) net exports, which depend upon foreign and domestic outputs and prices and upon foreign exchange rates.

6. Aggregate demand curves differ from demand curves used in microeconomic analysis. The *AD* curves relate overall spending on all components of output to the overall price level, with policy and exogenous variables held constant. The aggregate demand curve is downward-sloping primarily because of the money-supply effect, which occurs when a rise in the price level, with the nominal money supply constant, reduces the real money supply. A lower real money supply raises interest rates, tightens credit, and reduces total real spending. This represents a movement along an unchanged *AD* curve.

7. Factors that change aggregate demand include (*a*) macroeconomic policies, such as monetary and fiscal policies, and (*b*) exogenous variables, such as foreign economic activity, technological advances, and shifts in asset markets. When these variables change, they shift the *AD* curve.

CONCEPTS FOR REVIEW

Business Fluctuations or Cycles

business cycle or business fluctuation
business-cycle phases:
   peak
   trough
   expansion
   contraction
recession

aggregate demand shifts and business
   fluctuations
exogenous and internal cycle theories
macroeconomic models

Aggregate Demand

real variable = nominal
   variable/price level

aggregate demand, *AD* curve
major components of aggregate
   demand: *C, I, G, X*
downward-sloping *AD* curve through
   money-supply effect
factors underlying and shifting the
   AD curve

FURTHER READING AND INTERNET WEBSITES

Further Reading

The classic study of business cycles by leading scholars at the National Bureau of Economic Research (NBER) is Arthur F. Burns and Wesley Clair Mitchell, *Measuring Business Cycles* (Columbia University Press, New York, 1946). A discussion of the NBER approach is contained in Geoffrey H. Moore, *Business Cycles, Inflation and Forecasting,* 2d ed. (Ballinger, Cambridge, Mass., 1983).

One of the major critics of Keynesian business-cycle theory is Robert E. Lucas. See his *Studies in Business-Cycle Theory* (MIT Press, Cambridge, Mass., 1981).

Websites

A consortium of macroeconomists participates in the NBER program on economic fluctuations and growth. You can sample the writings and data at www.nber.org/programs/efg/efg.html. The NBER also dates business cycles for the United States. You can see the recessions and expansions at www.nber.org/cycles.html.

Business-cycle data and discussion can be found at the site of the Bureau of Economic Analysis www.bea.gov. The first few pages of the *Survey of Current Business,* available at www.bea.gov/bea/pubs.htm, has a discussion of recent business-cycle developments.

QUESTIONS FOR DISCUSSION

1. Define carefully the difference between movements along the *AD* curve and shifts of the *AD* curve. Explain why an increase in potential output would shift out the *AS* curve and lead to a movement along the *AD* curve. Explain why a tax cut would shift the *AD* curve outward (increase aggregate demand). What would be the effect of a decrease in the money supply (a monetary tightening) on aggregate demand?

2. Describe the different phases of the business cycle. In which phase is the U.S. economy now?

3. Some changes in aggregate output originate from the demand side, while others arise from supply shocks.

   a. Give examples of each. Using the *AS-AD* apparatus, explain how you can distinguish between a business downturn originating from the supply side and one from the demand side. (*Hint:* What happens to *P* in each case?)

   b. State whether each of the following would lead to a supply-side business cycle or a demand-side cycle, and illustrate the impact using an *AS-AD* diagram like Figure 23-4: a wartime increase in defense spending; devastation from wartime bombing of factories and power plants; a decrease in net exports from a deep recession in Europe; a sharp increase in innovation and productivity growth caused by increased computer use.

4. Construct a table parallel to Table 23-1, listing events that would lead to a *decrease* in aggregate demand.

   (Your table should provide different examples rather than simply changing the direction of the factors mentioned in Table 23-1.)

5. In recent years, a new theory of real business cycles (or RBCs) has been proposed (this approach is further analyzed in Chapter 33). RBC theory suggests that business fluctuations are caused by shocks to productivity which then propagate through the economy.

   a. Show the RBC theory in the *AS-AD* framework.

   b. Discuss whether the RBC theory can explain the customary characteristics of business fluctuations described on pages 468–469.

6. **Advanced problem:** Find two dice and use the following technique to see if you can generate something that looks like a business cycle: Record the numbers from 20 or more rolls of the dice. Take five-period moving averages of the successive numbers. Then plot these. They will look very much like movements in GDP, unemployment, or inflation.

   One sequence thus obtained was 7, 4, 10, 3, 7, 11, 7, 2, 9, 10. . . . The averages were $(7 + 4 + 10 + 3 + 7)/5 = 6.2$, $(4 + 10 + 3 + 7 + 11)/5 = 7$, and so forth.

   Why does this look like a business cycle? [*Hint:* The random numbers generated by the dice are like exogenous shocks of investment or wars. The moving average is like the economic system's (or a rocking chair's) internal multiplier or smoothing mechanism. Taken together, they produce what looks like a cycle.]

7. **Advanced problem:** An eminent macroeconomist, George Perry of Brookings, wrote the following after the Persian Gulf war of 1990–1991:

> Wars have usually been good for the U.S. economy. Traditionally they bring with them rising output, low unemployment, and full use of industrial capacity as military demands add to normal economic activity. This time, for the first time, war and recession occurred together. What does this anomaly tell us about the recession? (*Brookings Review*, Spring 1991.)

Use the Internet or go to the library and find data on the major determinants of aggregate demand during the 1990–1991 period as well as during earlier wars (World War II, Korean war, Vietnam war). Examine particularly government spending on goods and services (especially defense spending), taxes, investment, and interest rates. Can you explain the anomaly that Perry describes? (Locations of macroeconomic data on the Internet are listed in the Introduction and under "Websites" in Chapter 21's Further Reading section).

8. **Data problem:** Find annual data on real GDP for the United States for the period 1948–2003 (see the website of the Bureau of Economic Analysis, www.bea.gov).
   a. Define "recessions" as years in which real GDP declined. Which years were recessions? (Note that this is not the customary way to define recessions.)
   b. Calculate the average growth rate of real GDP for 1948–1973, 1973–1988, and 1988–2003. What were the changes in the average growth rate over this period? [Hint: You can calculate the average growth rate by solving the equation $(1 + g) = (GDP_{1973}/GDP_{1948})^{1/(1973-1948)}$, where g is the average growth rate per year.]
   c. Some macroeconomists prefer to identify growth recessions, which are periods when GDP growth was significantly slower than trend growth. For example, define a "growth recession" as one where real GDP growth was at least 2 percentage points below the average. Which years were growth recessions during this period?

The Multiplier Model

*The outstanding faults
of the economic society
in which we live are its
failure to provide for
full employment and
its arbitrary and
inequitable
distribution of wealth
and incomes.*

John Maynard Keynes
*The General Theory of
Employment, Interest and
Money* (1935)

The United States and other market-oriented economies are subject to frequent and unpredictable fluctuations in output, prices, and unemployment. In the past, these fluctuations, known as business cycles, generally occurred because of changes in spending on investment, consumer durables, or defense. As economists, we want to understand the *mechanism* by which changes in spending get translated into changes in output and employment. This chapter develops the simplest approach to understanding business cycles, the *Keynesian multiplier model.*

We will see in the first part of this chapter how an increase in investment raises the incomes of consumers and thereby leads to a cascading but ever-decreasing chain of further spending increases. Investment changes are therefore *multiplied* into larger output increases. The multiplier mechanism actually applies much more broadly than to investment alone, as we will see in the second half of this chapter. In fact, changes in government purchases, exports, or other exogenous spending streams will also be amplified into larger output changes. We show below how government purchases have a multiplied effect upon output in much the same way as does investment; this point led many macroeconomists to recommend using fiscal policy as a tool for stabilizing the economy.

The multiplier model is the first complete model of short-run output determination that we will develop. It is an oversimplified description of the economy, however, because it omits important elements such as financial markets and monetary policy, interactions with the rest of the world, and price and wage behavior. These further elaborations will come onto the stage in due time. For now, we focus primarily on the leading role of changes in investment and government spending in determining movements in national output.

A. THE BASIC MULTIPLIER MODEL

When economists attempt to understand why major increases in wartime military spending led to rapid increases in GDP, or why the tax cuts of the 1960s or 1980s ushered in long periods of business-cycle expansions, or why the investment boom of the late 1990s produced America's longest expansion, they often turn to the multiplier model for the simplest explanation.

What exactly is the **multiplier model?** It is a macroeconomic theory used to explain how output is determined in the short run. The name "multiplier" comes from the finding that each dollar change in exogenous expenditures (such as investment) leads to more than a dollar change (or a multiplied change) in GDP. The multiplier model explains how shocks to investment, foreign trade, and government tax and spending policies can affect output and employment in an economy. The key assumptions underlying the multiplier model are that wages and prices are fixed and that there are unemployed resources. In addition, we are suppressing the role of monetary policy and assuming that there are no financial-market reactions to changes in the economy.

OUTPUT DETERMINATION WITH SAVING AND INVESTMENT

We first show how investment and saving are equilibrated in the multiplier model for a highly simplified economy. Recall Chapter 22's picture of the national consumption and saving functions; these are redrawn in Figure 24-1.[1] Each point on the consumption function shows desired or planned consumption at that level of disposable income. Each point on the saving schedule shows desired or planned saving at that income level. The two schedules are closely related: Since $C + S$ always equals disposable income, the consumption and saving curves are mirror twins that will always add up to the 45° line. We also carry over the SS schedule into Figure 24-2 on page 483.

We have seen that saving and investment are dependent on quite different factors: saving depends primarily on disposable income, while investment depends on factors such as output, interest rates, tax policy, and business confidence. For simplicity here, we treat investment as an *exogenous* variable, one whose level is determined outside the model.

Say that investment opportunities are such that investment would be exactly $200 billion per year regardless of the level of GDP. This means that if we draw a schedule of investment against GDP, it will have to be a horizontal line. The case of exogenous

---

[1] Here we shall initially simplify the picture by leaving out taxes, undistributed corporate profits, foreign trade, depreciation, and government fiscal policy. For the time being, we will assume that disposable income equals GDP.

(a) Consumption Function

(b) Saving Function

FIGURE 24-1. National Output Determines the Levels of Consumption and Saving

Recall from Chapter 22 the consumption and saving functions, CC and SS. These are mirror-image curves, so the break-even point at B on the upper diagram is the zero-saving point on the lower diagram where SS intersects the horizontal axis. The two points in **(a)** marked "500" emphasize the important property of the 45° line: Any point on it depicts a vertical distance exactly equal to the horizontal distance. The gray band marked $Q^P Q^P$ shows the level of potential GDP.

---

investment is shown in Figure 24-2, where the investment schedule is labeled II to distinguish it from the SS saving schedule. (Note that II does not mean Roman numeral 2.)

The saving and investment schedules intersect at point E in Figure 24-2. This point corresponds to a

FIGURE 24-2. The Equilibrium Level of National Output Is Determined by Intersection of Saving and Investment Schedules

The horizontal *II* line indicates constant investment. *E* marks the spot where the investment and saving curves intersect. Equilibrium GDP comes at the intersection of the *SS* and *II* curves because this is the only level of GDP at which the desired saving of households exactly matches the desired investment of business.

level of GDP given at point *M* and represents the equilibrium level of output in the multiplier model.

This intersection of the saving and investment schedules is the equilibrium level of GDP toward which national output will gravitate.

> **Reminder on the Meaning of Equilibrium**
> We often look for a macroeconomic "equilibrium" when analyzing business cycles or economic growth. What exactly does this term mean here? An **equilibrium** is a situation where the different forces at work are in balance. For example, if you see a ball rolling down a hill, the ball is not in equilibrium because the forces at work are pushing the ball down (this is therefore a **disequilibrium**). When the ball comes to rest in a hole at the bottom of the hill, the forces operating on the ball are in balance and the ball is in equilibrium.
>
> Similarly, in macroeconomics, an equilibrium level of output is one where the different forces of spending and saving are in balance; in equilibrium, the level of output tends to persist until there are changes in the forces affecting the economy.

Looking now at Figure 24-2, we see that point *E* is an equilibrium. The reason is that at this level of output, the desired saving of households equals the desired investment of firms. When desired saving and desired investment are not equal, output will tend to adjust up or down.

The saving and investment schedules shown in Figure 24-2 represent *desired* (or *planned*) levels. Thus at output level *M*, businesses will want to invest an amount equal to the vertical distance *ME*. Also, at that income level, households desire to save the amount *ME*. But there is no logical necessity for actual saving to equal planned saving (or for actual investment to equal planned investment). People can make mistakes. Or they may forecast events incorrectly. When mistakes happen, saving or investment might deviate from planned levels.

To see how output adjusts until desired saving and desired investment are equated, we consider three cases. In the first case, the system is at *E*, where the schedule of what business firms want to invest intersects the saving schedule of what households want to save. When everyone's plans are satisfied, everyone will be content to go on doing just what he or she has been doing.

At equilibrium, firms will not find inventories piling up on their shelves, nor will their sales be so brisk as to force them to produce more goods. So production, employment, income, and spending will remain the same. In this case GDP stays at point *E*, and we can rightly call it an *equilibrium*.

The second case—of a disequilibrium—begins with a GDP higher than at *E*. Consider point *A*, where GDP is to the right of *M* at an income level where the saving schedule is higher than the investment schedule. This is not an equilibrium because at this income level households are saving more than business firms want to invest. Firms will have too few customers and larger inventories of unsold goods than they want. What can businesses do to correct this situation? They can cut back production and lay off workers. This response reduces GDP, moving output leftward in Figure 24-2. The economy returns to equilibrium when it gets back to *E* and has no further tendency to change.

At this point, you should be able to analyze the third case. Show that if GDP were *below* its equilibrium level, strong forces would be set up to move it eastward back to *E*.

All three cases lead to the same conclusion:

The equilibrium level of GDP occurs at point E, where planned saving equals planned investment. At any other output, the desired saving of households differs from the desired investment of businesses. This difference will cause businesses to change their production and employment levels, thereby returning the system to the equilibrium GDP.

OUTPUT DETERMINED BY TOTAL EXPENDITURES

A second approach, and one that students often find more intuitive, is the *total expenditure approach* to determining national output. This method is illustrated in Figure 24-3, which shows a curve of total expenditures graphed against total national output or income. The black *CC* line is the consumption function, showing the desired consumption corresponding to each level

FIGURE 24-3. In the Total Expenditure Approach, Equilibrium GDP Level Is Found at the Intersection of the $C + I = TE$ Schedule with the 45° Line

Adding *II* to *CC* gives the $C + I$ curve of total desired spending. At E, where this curve intersects the 45° line, we get the same equilibrium as in the saving-and-investment diagram. (Note the similarities between this figure and Fig. 24-2: the investment added to *CC* is the same as *II* of Fig. 24-2, and so must be the E intersection.)

of income. We then add desired investment (which is at fixed level I) to the consumption function. This yields the level of total desired expenditure, or *TE*, represented by the rust $C + I$ curve in Figure 24-3.

We next put in a 45° line to help us identify the equilibrium. At any point on the 45° line, total desired expenditure (measured vertically) exactly equals the total level of output (measured horizontally).

We can now calculate the equilibrium level of output in Figure 24-3. Where planned expenditure, represented by the *TE* curve, equals total output, the economy is in equilibrium.

The total expenditure curve (*TE*) shows the level of desired expenditure by consumers and businesses corresponding to each level of output. The economy is in equilibrium at the point where the $TE = C + I$ curve crosses the 45° line—at point E in Figure 24-3. At point E the economy is in equilibrium because at that level desired expenditure on consumption and investment exactly equals the level of total output.

The Adjustment Mechanism

We will pause to emphasize why point E is an equilibrium. *An economy is in equilibrium when planned expenditure (on C and I) equals planned output.* What would happen if the system were to deviate from equilibrium, say, at output level D in Figure 24-3? At this level of output, the $C + I$ spending line is above the 45° line, so planned $C + I$ spending would be greater than planned output. This means that consumers would be buying more goods than businesses were producing. Auto dealers would find their lots emptying, and the backlog for computers would be getting longer and longer.

In this disequilibrium situation, auto dealers and computer manufacturers would respond by increasing their orders. Automakers would recall workers from layoff and gear up their production lines, while computer makers would add additional shifts. *Therefore, a discrepancy between total planned expenditures and total output leads to an adjustment of output.*

By following this chain of reasoning, we see that only when firms are producing what households and firms plan to spend on C and I, precisely at point E, will the economy be in equilibrium. (You should also work through what happens when output is above equilibrium.)

Planned versus Actual Amounts

In this section, we repeatedly discuss "planned" or "desired" spending and output. These words call attention to the difference between (1) the amount of planned or desired consumption or investment given by the consumption function or by the investment demand schedule and (2) the actual amount of consumption or investment measured after the fact.

The following dialogue will help you remember this distinction:

Confusio: I thought you said that saving always equals investment.

Clario: That is correct. As measured in the national accounts, saving and investment will always be exactly equal, in recession or boom.

Confusio: But why do I have to worry about desires and plans if S and I are always equal?

Clario: The reason is that the economy is in equilibrium only when firms and consumers are spending and producing their desired amounts.

Confusio: What happens when planned and actual amounts are different?

Clario: In fact, actual investment often differs from planned investment. For example, General Motors may sell fewer cars than what it had planned. When this happens, GM finds its inventories of cars increasing. This *involuntary* increase in inventory investment would not be an equilibrium, so GM would reduce its production.

Confusio: Aha! I see the point: Only when the level of output is such that planned spending on C + I equals planned output will there be no tendency for output, income, or spending to change.

Clario: Exactly.

An Arithmetic Analysis

An arithmetic example may help show why the equilibrium level of output occurs where planned spending and planned output are equal.

Table 24-1 on page 486 shows a simple example of consumption and saving functions. The break-even level of income, where the nation is too poor to do any net saving on balance, is assumed to be $3000 billion ($3 trillion). Each change of income of $300 billion is assumed to lead to a $100 billion change in saving and a $200 billion change in consumption; in other words, for simplicity MPC is assumed to be constant and exactly equal to $\frac{2}{3}$. Therefore, $MPS = \frac{1}{3}$.

Again, we assume that investment is exogenous. Suppose that the only level of investment that will be sustained indefinitely is exactly $200 billion, as shown in column (4) of Table 24-1. That is, at each level of GDP, businesses desire to purchase $200 billion of investment goods, no more and no less.

Columns (5) and (6) are the crucial ones. Column (5) shows the total GDP—this is simply column (1) copied once again into column (5). The figures in column (6) represent what business firms would actually be selling year in and year out; this is the planned consumption spending plus planned investment. It is the $C + I$ schedule from Figure 24-3 in numbers.

When businesses as a whole are producing too high a level of total product (higher than the sum of what consumers and businesses want to purchase), they will be involuntarily piling up inventories of unsalable goods.

Reading the top row of Table 24-1, we see that if firms are temporarily producing $4200 billion of GDP, planned or desired spending [shown in column (6)] is only $4000 billion. In this situation, excess inventories will be accumulating. Firms will respond by contracting their operations, and GDP will fall. In the opposite case, represented by the bottom row of Table 24-1, total spending is $3000 billion and output is $2700 billion. Inventories are being depleted and firms will expand operations, raising output.

We see, then, that when business firms as a whole are temporarily producing more than they can profitably sell, they will contract their operations, and GDP will fall. When they are selling more than their current production, they will increase their output, and GDP will rise.

Only when the level of actual output in column (5) exactly equals planned expenditure (*TE*) in column (6) will the economy be in equilibrium. In equilibrium, and only in equilibrium, will businesses' sales be exactly sufficient to justify the current level of aggregate output. GDP will neither expand nor contract.

GDP Determination Where Output Equals Planned Spending (billions of dollars)								
(1)	(2)	(3)	(4)	(5)	(6)			(7)
Levels of GDP and *DI*	Planned consumption	Planned saving (3) = (1) − (2)	Planned investment	Level of GDP (5) = (1)	Total planned consumption and investment, *TE* (6) = (2) + (4)			Resulting tendency of output
4,200	3,800	400	200	4,200	>	4,000	↓	Contraction
3,900	3,600	300	200	3,900	>	3,800		Contraction
3,600	3,400	200	200	3,600	=	3,600		**Equilibrium**
3,300	3,200	100	200	3,300	<	3,400	↑	Expansion
3,000	3,000	0	200	3,000	<	3,200		Expansion
2,700	2,800	−100	200	2,700	<	3,000		Expansion

TABLE 24-1. Equilibrium Output Can Be Found Arithmetically at the Level Where Planned Spending Equals GDP

The darker rust row depicts the equilibrium GDP level, where the $3600 that is being produced is just matched by the $3600 that households plan to consume and that firms plan to invest. In upper rows, firms will be forced into unintended inventory investment and will respond by cutting back production until equilibrium GDP is reached. Interpret the lower rows' tendency toward expansion of GDP toward equilibrium.

THE MULTIPLIER

Where is the multiplier in all this? To answer this question, we need to examine how a change in exogenous investment spending affects GDP. It is logical that an increase in investment will raise the level of output and employment. But by how much? The multiplier model shows that an increase in investment will increase GDP by an amplified or multiplied amount—by an amount greater than itself.

The **multiplier** is the impact of a 1-dollar change in exogenous expenditures on total output. In the simple *C* + *I* model, the multiplier is the ratio of the change in total output to the change in investment.

Note that the definition of the multiplier speaks of the change in output per unit change in *exogenous expenditures*. This indicates that we are taking certain components of spending as given outside the model. In the case in hand, the exogenous component is investment. Later, we will see that the same approach can be used to determine the effect of changes in government expenditures, exports, and other items on total output.

For example, suppose investment increases by $100 billion. If this causes an increase in output of $300 billion, the multiplier is 3. If, instead, the resulting increase in output is $400 billion, the multiplier is 4.

Woodsheds and Carpenters. Why is it that the multiplier is greater than 1? Let's suppose that I hire unemployed resources to build a $1000 woodshed. My carpenters and lumber producers will get an extra $1000 of income. But that is not the end of the story. If they all have a marginal propensity to consume of ⅔, they will now spend $666.67 on new consumption goods. The producers of these goods will now have extra incomes of $666.67. If their *MPC* is also ⅔, they in turn will spend $444.44, or ⅔ of $666.67 (or ⅔ of ⅔ of $1000). The process will go on, with each new round of spending being ⅔ of the previous round.

Thus an endless chain of *secondary consumption spending* is set in motion by my *primary* investment of $1000. But, although an endless chain, it is an ever-diminishing one. Eventually it adds up to a finite amount.

Using straightforward arithmetic, we can find the total increase in spending in the following manner:

$$
\left.\begin{array}{r}
\$1000.00 \\
+ \\
666.67 \\
+ \\
444.44 \\
+ \\
296.30 \\
+ \\
197.53 \\
+ \\
\vdots \\
\hline
\$3000.00
\end{array}\right\}
=
\left\{\begin{array}{c}
1 \times \$1000 \\
+ \\
\tfrac{2}{3} \times \$1000 \\
+ \\
(\tfrac{2}{3})^2 \times \$1000 \\
+ \\
(\tfrac{2}{3})^3 \times \$1000 \\
+ \\
(\tfrac{2}{3})^4 \times \$1000 \\
+ \\
\vdots \\
\hline
\dfrac{1}{1 - \tfrac{2}{3}} \times \$1000, \text{ or } 3 \times \$1000
\end{array}\right.
$$

This shows that, with an *MPC* of ⅔, the multiplier is 3; it consists of the 1 of primary investment plus 2 extra of secondary consumption respending.

The same arithmetic would give a multiplier of 4 for an *MPC* of ¾, because $1 + \tfrac{3}{4} + (\tfrac{3}{4})^2 + (\tfrac{3}{4})^3 + \cdots$ eventually adds up to 4. For an *MPC* of ½, the multiplier would be 2.[2]

The size of the multiplier thus depends upon how large the *MPC* is. It can also be expressed in

---

[2] The formula for an infinite geometric progression is

$$1 + r + r^2 + r^3 + \cdots + r^n + \cdots = \frac{1}{1 - r}$$

as long as *MPC* (*r*) is less than 1 in absolute value.

terms of the twin concept, the *MPS*. For an *MPS* of ¼, the *MPC* is ¾ and the multiplier is 4. For an *MPS* of ⅓, the multiplier is 3. If the *MPS* were $1/x$, the multiplier would be *x*.

By this time it should be clear that the simple multiplier is always the inverse, or reciprocal, of the marginal propensity to save. It is thus equal to $1/(1 - MPC)$. Our simple multiplier formula is

$$
\begin{aligned}
\text{Change} \\
\text{in output}
\end{aligned}
= \frac{1}{MPS} \times \text{change in investment}
$$

$$
= \frac{1}{1 - MPC} \times \text{change in investment}
$$

Graphical Picture of the Multiplier

Our discussion of the multiplier has relied up to now largely on common sense and arithmetic. Can we get the same result using our graphical analysis of saving and investment? The answer is yes.

Suppose, as in Table 24-1, that the *MPS* is ⅓ and a burst of inventions gives rise to an extra $100 billion of continuing investment. What will be the new equilibrium GDP? If the multiplier is indeed 3, the answer is $3900 billion.

A look at Figure 24-4 can confirm this result. Our old investment schedule *II* is shifted upward by $100 billion to the new level *I'I'*. The new intersection point is *E'*; the increase in income is exactly 3 times the increase in investment. As the rust arrows show, the horizontal output distance is 3 times as great as

Gross domestic product (billions of dollars)

FIGURE 24-4. Each Dollar of Investment Is "Multiplied" into 3 Dollars of Output

New investment shifts *II* up to *I'I'*. *E'* gives the new equilibrium output, with output increasing by 3 for each 1 increase in investment. (*Note:* The broken horizontal rust arrow is 3 times the length of the vertical rust arrow of the investment shift and is broken to show 2 units of secondary consumption spending for each 1 unit of primary investment.)

the upward shift in the investment schedule. We know that desired saving must rise to equal the new and higher level of investment. The only way that saving can rise is for national income to rise. With an *MPS* of ⅓ and an increase in investment of $100 billion, income must rise by $300 billion to bring forth $100 billion of additional saving to match the new investment. Hence, at equilibrium, $100 billion of additional investment induces $300 billion of additional income, verifying our multiplier arithmetic.[3]

THE MULTIPLIER MODEL IN PERSPECTIVE

The simplest multiplier model has been enormously influential in business-cycle theory over the last half-century. But it gives an oversimplified picture of the economy. One of the most important omissions is the impact of financial markets and monetary policy on the economy. Changes in output tend to affect interest rates, which in turn come back and affect the economy. Additionally, the simplest multiplier model omits the interactions between the domestic economy and the rest of the world. Finally, the model omits the supply side of the economy as represented by the interaction of spending with aggregate supply and prices. All these shortcomings will be remedied in later chapters, and it is useful to keep in mind that this first model is really a stepping stone on the path to understanding the economy in all its fascinating complexity.

It will be useful to put all this in perspective and to see how the multiplier model fits into a broader view of the macroeconomy. We are trying to understand what determines the level of national output in a country. In the long run, a country's production and living standards are largely determined by its potential output. But in the short run, business conditions will push the economy above or below its long-term trend. It is this deviation of output and employment from trend that is addressed by the simplest multiplier model and by its more complex and complete cousins.

---

[3] Alter Table 24-1, on page 486, to verify this answer. In column (4), we now put $300 billion instead of $200 billion of investment. Show that the new equilibrium output shifts one row up from the old rust equilibrium row. Can you also show that the multiplier works downward?

While the relationships presented here have been simplified, their essence will remain valid even when extended to situations involving government fiscal policy, monetary policy, and foreign trade. The main point to retain is that the multiplier analysis holds when there are unemployed resources. With excess capacity, an increase in aggregate demand can raise output levels. By contrast, if an economy is producing at capacity, there is no room for expansion when aggregate demand increases. In conditions of full employment, then, demand increases lead to higher prices rather than to output increases.

When investment or other spending increases in an economy with excess capacity and unemployed workers, much of the extra spending will end up in extra real output, with only small increases in the price level. However, as the economy reaches its capacity, it is not possible to coax out more production at the going price level. Hence, at full employment, higher spending will result in higher price levels rather than higher real output or employment.

The Multiplier Model Compared with the AS-AD Model

As you study the multiplier model, you might begin to wonder how this model fits in with the *AS-AD* model of Chapter 20. These are not, in fact, different approaches. Rather, the multiplier model is a special case of the aggregate demand-and-supply model. It explains how *AD* is affected by consumption and investment spending under certain precise assumptions.

One of the key assumptions in the multiplier analysis is that prices and wages are fixed in the short run. This is an oversimplification, for many prices adjust quickly in the real world. But this assumption captures the point that if some wages and prices are sticky—which is most definitely the case—then some of the adjustment to *AD* shifts will come through output adjustments. We will return to this important point in later chapters.

We can show the relationship between the multiplier analysis and the *AS-AD* approach in Figure 24-5. Part (*b*) displays an *AS* curve that becomes completely vertical when output equals potential output. However, when there are unemployed resources—to the left of potential output in the graph—output will be determined primarily by the strength of aggregate

FIGURE 24-5. How the Multiplier Model Fits the *AS-AD* Approach

The multiplier model is a way of understanding the workings of the *AS-AD* equilibrium.

(a) The top panel shows the output-expenditure equilibrium in the multiplier model. At point *E*, the spending line just cuts the 45° line, leading to equilibrium output of *Q.*

(b) The equilibrium can also be seen in the bottom panel, where the *AD* curve cuts the *AS* curve at point *E*. In the simplest multiplier model, wages and prices are assumed to be fixed, so the *AS* curve is horizontal until full employment is reached. Both approaches lead to exactly the same equilibrium output, *Q.*

demand. As investment increases, this increases *AD*, and equilibrium output rises.

The same economy can be described by the multiplier diagram in the top panel of Figure 24-5. The multiplier equilibrium gives the same level of output as the *AS-AD* equilibrium—both lead to a real GDP of *Q.* They simply stress different features of output determination.

This discussion again points to a crucial feature of the multiplier model. While it may be a highly useful approach to describe depressions or even recessions, it cannot apply to periods of full employment. Once factories are operating at full capacity and all workers are employed, the economy simply cannot produce more output.

We have now completed our presentation of the simple multiplier model. We next move on to extend the analysis of aggregate demand by showing how government fiscal policy enters the picture.

B. FISCAL POLICY IN THE MULTIPLIER MODEL

For centuries, economists have understood the *allocational* role of fiscal policy (government tax and spending programs). It has long been known that fiscal programs are instrumental in deciding how the nation's output should be divided between collective and private consumption and how the burden of payment for collective goods should be divided among the population.

Only with the development of modern macroeconomic theory has a further surprising fact been uncovered: Government fiscal powers also have a major *macroeconomic* impact upon the short-run movements of output, employment, and prices. The knowledge that fiscal policy has powerful effects upon economic activity led to the *Keynesian approach to macroeconomic policy,* which is the active use of government action to moderate business cycles. The approach was described by the Nobel Prize–winning macroeconomist James Tobin as follows:

> Keynesian policies are, first, the explicit dedication of macroeconomic policy instruments to real economic goals, in particular full employment and real growth of national income. Second, Keynesian demand

management is activist. Third, Keynesians have wished to put both fiscal and monetary policies in consistent and coordinated harness in the pursuit of macroeconomic objectives.

In this section we use the multiplier model to show how government purchases affect output.

HOW GOVERNMENT FISCAL POLICIES AFFECT OUTPUT

To understand the role of government in economic activity, we need to look at government purchases and taxation, along with the effects of those activities on private-sector spending. We now modify our earlier analysis by adding G to $C + I$ to get a new total expenditure curve $TE = C + I + G$. This new schedule can describe the macroeconomic equilibrium

when government, with its spending and taxing, is in the picture.

It will simplify our task in the beginning if we analyze the effects of government purchases with total taxes collected held constant (taxes that do not change with income or other economic variables are called *lump-sum taxes*). But even with a fixed dollar value of taxes, we can no longer ignore the distinction between disposable income and gross domestic product. Under simplified conditions (including no foreign trade, transfers, or depreciation), we know from Chapter 21 that GDP equals disposable income plus taxes. But with tax revenues held constant, GDP and DI will always differ by the same amount; thus, after taking account of such taxes, we can still plot the CC consumption schedule against GDP rather than against DI.

Figure 24-6 shows how the consumption function changes when taxes are present. This figure draws

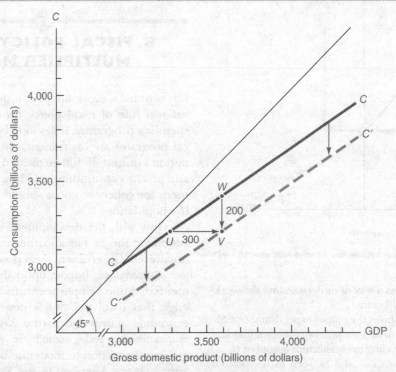

FIGURE 24-6. Taxes Reduce Disposable Income and Shift CC Schedule to the Right and Down

Each dollar of tax shifts the CC schedule to the right by the amount of the tax. A rightward CC shift also means a downward CC shift, but the downward CC shift is less than the rightward shift. Why? Because the downward shift is equal to the rightward shift times the MPC. Thus, if the MPC is ⅔, the downward shift is ⅔ times \$300 billion = \$200 billion. Verify that $WV = ⅔\ UV$.

the original no-tax consumption function as the black *CC* line. In this case, GDP equals disposable income. We use the same consumption function as in Table 24-1 on page 486. So consumption is 3000 when GDP (and *DI*) is 3000, and so forth.

Now introduce taxes of 300. At a *DI* of 3000, GDP must be equal to 3300 = 300 + 3000. Consumption is still 3000 when GDP is 3300 because *DI* is 3000. We can therefore plot consumption as a function of GDP by shifting the consumption function rightward to the rust *C'C'* curve. The amount of the rightward shift is *UV*, which is exactly equal to the amount of taxes, 300.

Alternatively, we can plot the new consumption function as a parallel *downward* shift by 200. As Figure 24-6 shows, 200 is the result of multiplying a decrease in income of 300 times the *MPC* of ⅔.

Turning next to the different components of aggregate demand, recall from Chapter 21 that GDP consists of four elements:

GDP = consumption expenditure
   + gross private domestic investment
   + government purchases of goods and services
   + net exports
  = C + I + G + X

For now, we consider a closed economy with no foreign trade, so our GDP consists of the first three components, C + I + G. (We add the final component of net exports when we consider open-economy macroeconomics.)

Figure 24-7 shows the effect of including government purchases. This diagram is very similar to the one

FIGURE 24-7. Government Purchases Add On Just like Investment to Determine Equilibrium GDP

We now add government purchases on top of consumption and investment spending. This gives us the new total planned expenditure schedule, *TE = C + I + G*. At *E*, where the *TE* schedule intersects the 45° line, we find the equilibrium level of GDP.

used earlier in this chapter (see Figure 24-3). Here, we have added a new expenditure stream, G, to the consumption and investment amounts. Diagrammatically, we place the new variable, G (government purchases of goods and services), on top of the consumption function and the fixed amount of investment. The vertical distance between the $C + I$ line and the new $TE = C + I + G$ line is just the quantity of G.

Why do we simply add G on the top? Because spending on government buildings (G) has the same macroeconomic impact as spending on private buildings (I); the collective expenditure involved in buying a government vehicle (G) has the same effect on jobs as private consumption expenditures on automobiles (C).

We end up with the three-layer cake of $TE = C + I + G$, calculating the amount of total spending forthcoming at each level of GDP. We now must go to its point of intersection with the 45° line to find the equilibrium level of GDP. At this equilibrium GDP level, denoted by point E in Figure 24-7, total planned spending exactly equals total planned output. Point E is thus the equilibrium level of output when we add government purchases to the multiplier model.

Impact of Taxation on Aggregate Demand

How does government taxation tend to reduce aggregate demand and the level of GDP? Extra taxes lower our disposable incomes, and lower disposable incomes tend to reduce our consumption spending. Clearly, if investment and government purchases remain the same, a reduction in consumption spending will then reduce GDP and employment. Thus, in the multiplier model, higher taxes without increases in government purchases will tend to reduce real GDP.[4]

A look back at Figure 24-6 confirms this reasoning. In this figure, the upper CC curve represents the level of the consumption function with no taxes. But the upper curve cannot be the consumption function because consumers definitely pay taxes on their incomes. Suppose that consumers pay $300 billion in taxes at every level of income; thus, DI is exactly $300 billion less than GDP at every level of output. As shown in Figure 24-6, this level of taxes can be

represented by a rightward shift in the consumption function of $300 billion. This rightward shift will also appear as a downward shift; if the MPC is ⅔, the rightward shift of $300 billion will be seen as a downward shift of $200 billion.

Without a doubt, taxes lower output in our multiplier model, and Figure 24-7 shows why. When taxes rise, $I + G$ does not change, but the increase in taxes will lower disposable income, thereby shifting the CC consumption schedule downward. Hence, the $C + I + G$ schedule shifts downward. You can pencil in a new, lower $C' + I + G$ schedule in Figure 24-7. Confirm that its new intersection with the 45° line must be at a lower equilibrium level of GDP.

Keep in mind that G is government purchases of goods and services. It excludes spending on transfers such as unemployment insurance or social security payments. These transfers are treated as negative taxes, so the taxes (T) considered here can best be thought of as taxes less transfers. Therefore, if direct and indirect taxes total $400 billion, while all transfer payments are $100 billion, then net taxes, T, are $400 − $100 = $300 billion. (Can you see why an increase in social security benefits lowers T, raises DI, shifts the $C + I + G$ curve upward, and raises equilibrium GDP?)

A Numerical Example

The points made up to now are illustrated in Table 24-2. This table is very similar to Table 24-1, which illustrated output determination in the simplest multiplier model. The first column shows a reference level of GDP, while the second shows a fixed level of taxes, $300 billion. Disposable income in column (3) is GDP less taxes. Planned consumption, taken as a function of DI, is shown in column (4). Column (5) shows the fixed level of planned investment, while column (6) exhibits the level of government purchases. To find total planned expenditures, TE, in column (7), we add together the C, I, and G in columns (4) through (6).

Finally, we compare total desired expenditures TE in column (7) with the initial level of GDP in column (1). If desired spending is above GDP, firms raise production to meet the level of spending, and output consequently rises; if desired spending is below GDP, output falls. This tendency, shown in the last column, assures us that output will tend toward equilibrium at $3600 billion.

---

[4] Strictly speaking, by "taxes" in this chapter we mean net taxes, or taxes minus transfer payments.

			Output Determination with Government (billions of dollars)				
(1) Initial level of GDP	(2) Taxes T	(3) Disposable income DI	(4) Planned consumption C	(5) Planned investment I	(6) Government expenditure G	(7) Total planned expenditure, TE (C + I + G)	(8) Resulting tendency of economy
4,200	300	3,900	3,600	200	200	4,000 ↓	Contraction
3,900	300	3,600	3,400	200	200	3,800 ↓	Contraction
3,600	**300**	**3,300**	**3,200**	**200**	**200**	**3,600**	**Equilibrium**
3,300	300	3,000	3,000	200	200	3,400 ↑	Expansion
3,000	300	2,700	2,800	200	200	3,200 ↑	Expansion

TABLE 24-2. Government Purchases, Taxes, and Investment Determine Equilibrium GDP

This table shows how output is determined when government purchases of goods and services are added to the multiplier model. In this example, taxes are "lump-sum" or independent of the level of income. Disposable income is thus GDP minus $300 billion. Total spending is $I + G +$ the consumption determined by the consumption function.

At levels of output less than $3600 billion, planned spending is greater than output, so output expands. Levels of output greater than $3600 are unsustainable and lead to contraction. Only at output of $3600 is output in equilibrium—that is, planned spending equals output.

FISCAL-POLICY MULTIPLIERS

The multiplier analysis shows that government fiscal policy is high-powered spending much like investment. The parallel suggests that fiscal policy should also have multiplier effects upon output. And this is exactly right.

The **government expenditure multiplier** is the increase in GDP resulting from an increase of $1 in government purchases of goods and services. An initial government purchase of a good or service will set in motion a chain of spending: if the government builds a road, the road-builders will spend some of their incomes on consumption goods, which in turn will generate additional incomes, some of which will be spent. In the simple model examined here, the ultimate effect on GDP of an extra dollar of G will be the same as the effect of an extra dollar of I: the multipliers are equal to $1/(1 - MPC)$. Figure 24-8 shows how a change in G will result in a higher level of GDP, with the increase being a multiple of the increase in government purchases.

To show the effects of an extra $100 billion of G, the $C + I + G$ curve in Figure 24-8 has been shifted

up by $100 billion. The ultimate increase in GDP is equal to the $100 billion of primary spending times the expenditure multiplier. In this case, because the MPC is ⅔, the multiplier is 3, so the equilibrium level of GDP rises by $300 billion.

This example, as well as common sense, tells us that the government expenditure multiplier is exactly the same number as the investment multiplier. They are both called **expenditure multipliers.**

Also, note that the multiplier horse can be ridden in both directions. If government purchases were to fall, with taxes and other influences held constant, GDP would decline by the change in G times the multiplier.

The effect of G on output can be seen as well in the numerical example of Table 24-2. You can pencil in a different level of G—say, $300 billion—and find the equilibrium level of GDP. It should give the same answer as Figure 24-8.

We can sum up:

Government purchases of goods and services (G) are an important force in determining output and employment. In the multiplier model, if G increases,

FIGURE 24-8. The Effect of Higher *G* on Output

Suppose that the government raises defense purchases by $100 billion in response to a threat to Mideast oil fields. This shifts upward the *C* + *I* + *G* line by $100 billion to *C* + *I* + *G'*.

The new equilibrium level of GDP is thus read off the 45° line at *E'* rather than at *E*. Because the *MPC* is ⅔, the new level of output is $300 billion higher. That is, the government expenditure multiplier is

$$3 = \frac{1}{1 - \frac{2}{3}}$$

(What would the government expenditure multiplier be if the *MPC* were ¾? ⁹⁄₁₀?)

output will rise by the increase in *G* times the expenditure multiplier. Government purchases therefore have the potential to stabilize or destabilize output over the business cycle.

Are Wars Necessary for Full Employment?

Historically, economic expansions were the constant companions of war. As can be seen in Table 24-3, major wars in the past were often accompanied by large increases in military spending. In World War II, for example, defense outlays rose by almost 10 percent of total GDP before Pearl Harbor

was bombed in December 1941. Indeed, many scholars believe that the United States emerged from the Great Depression largely because of the buildup for World War II. Similar but smaller military buildups accompanied economic expansions in the Korean and Vietnam wars.

By contrast, the Persian Gulf war of the early 1990s triggered a recession. The reason for this anomaly was that there was but a small increase in military spending and psychological factors triggered by the war more than offset the increase in *G*.

What were these psychological factors? After Iraq invaded Kuwait in August 1990, consumers and investors became frightened and reduced spending.

Economic Stimulus from Defense Spending			
War	Period of war or buildup	Increase in defense spending as percent of GDP	Real GDP growth over buildup period (%)
World War I	1916–1918	10.2	13.0
World War II			
Before Pearl Harbor	1939–1941	9.7	26.7
All years	1939–1944	41.4	69.1
Korean war	1950:3–1951:3	8.0	10.5
Vietnam war	1965:3–1967:1	1.9	9.7
Persian Gulf war	1990:3–1991:1	0.3	−1.3
Iraq war	2003:1–2003:2	0.1	0.5

TABLE 24-3. Economic Booms Accompany Large Increases in Military Spending

This table shows the period of the war or buildup, the size of the military buildup, and the resulting increase in real GDP. Major wars have produced sustained economic booms, but the smaller wars of the last two decades led to economic slowdowns because of adverse reactions in other sectors.

Source: Department of Commerce, National Income and Product Accounts, available at www.bea.gov, and estimates by authors.

Additionally, oil prices shot up, lowering real incomes. These factors then reversed after the rapid U.S. victory in February 1991.

What was the impact of the war in Iraq in early 2003? This war resembled the Persian Gulf war more than it did major wars. There was little increase in defense spending, while cautious consumers and businesses, along with high oil prices, produced a strong headwind that slowed the economy.

The role of wartime spending in economic expansions is one of the most direct and persuasive examples of the functioning of the multiplier model. Make sure you understand the underlying mechanism as well as why the sizes of the economic expansions shown in Table 24-3 are so different.

Impact of Taxes

Taxes also have an impact upon equilibrium GDP, although the size of tax multipliers is smaller than that of expenditure multipliers. Consider the following example: Suppose the economy is at its potential GDP and the nation raises defense spending by $200 billion. Such sudden increases have occurred at many points in the history of the United States—in the early 1940s for World War II, in 1951 for the Korean war, in the mid-1960s for the Vietnam war, and in the early 1980s during the Reagan administration's military buildup. Furthermore, say that economic planners wish to raise taxes just enough to offset the effect on GDP of the $200 billion increase in G. How much would taxes have to be raised?

We are in for a surprise. To offset the $200 billion increase in G, we need to increase tax collections by more than $200 billion. In our numerical example, we can find the exact size of the tax, or T, increase from Figure 24-6. That figure shows that a $300 billion increase in T reduces disposable income by just enough to produce a consumption decline of $200 billion when the MPC is ⅔. Put differently, a tax increase of $300 billion will shift the CC curve down by $200 billion. Hence, while a $1 billion increase in defense spending shifts up the C + I + G line by $1 billion, a $1 billion tax increase shifts down the C + I + G line by only $⅔ billion (when the MPC is ⅔). Thus offsetting an increase in government purchases requires an increase in T larger than the increase in G.

Tax changes are a powerful weapon in affecting output. But the tax multiplier is smaller than the expenditure multiplier by a factor equal to the *MPC*:

Tax multiplier = *MPC* × expenditure multiplier

The reason the tax multiplier is smaller than the expenditure multiplier is straightforward. When government spends $1 on *G*, that $1 gets spent directly on GDP. On the other hand, when government cuts taxes by a dollar, only part of that dollar is spent on *C*, while a fraction of that $1 tax cut is saved. The difference in the responses to a dollar of *G* and to a dollar of *T* is enough to lower the tax multiplier below the expenditure multiplier.[5]

Fiscal Policy in Practice

President John F. Kennedy adopted the principles of Keynesian economics in 1961, and fiscal policy became one of the nation's main weapons for fighting recession or inflation. He proposed substantial tax cuts to lift the economy out of a slump; after these were enacted, the economy grew rapidly. However, when the fiscal expansion from the Vietnam war buildup during 1965–1966 was added to the tax cuts, output rose above potential GDP and inflation began to heat up. To fight the rising inflation and offset the increased Vietnam war expenditures, Congress passed a temporary surtax on incomes in 1968.

The 1980s provided another dramatic demonstration of how fiscal policy works. In 1981, Congress passed President Ronald Reagan's "supply-side tax cuts" along with a large increase in defense spending. The fiscal expansion helped pull the American economy out of the deep recession of 1981–1982.

The mid-1980s ushered in a new fiscal era for the United States. The Reagan fiscal policy led to a sharp increase in the government's budget deficit (equal to the difference between spending and revenues). The government deficit and government debt rose sharply during the 1980s. The era of budget deficits put tight reins on the introduction of new government programs as Congress struggled to reduce the budget deficit.

Upon entering office in 1993, President William Clinton faced a painful set of fiscal dilemmas. The deficit remained stubbornly high, yet the economy was stagnating and the rate of joblessness was unacceptably high. Should the president tackle the deficit, increasing the level of *public saving* by raising taxes and lowering spending, so that the higher public saving might lead to an increase in *national saving and investment?* Or should the president worry that higher taxes and lower *G* might lower output as the fiscal contraction reduced *C* + *I* + *G* and choked off investment?

After wrestling with this dilemma, President Clinton decided that deficit reduction was the chief priority. The Budget Act of 1993 enacted fiscal measures that lowered the federal deficit by about $150 billion (or 2 percent of GDP) over the next 5 years. The combination of restrictions on spending, rising tax revenues, a booming economy, and high stock prices surprised all the experts by producing a budget surplus beginning in 1998.

The period of surpluses was short-lived, however. A series of unfavorable shocks—a stock market decline, recession, wars, and terrorism—led to a rapid deterioration in the government's fiscal position. In this environment, President George W. Bush persuaded Congress in 2001 to enact large across-the-board tax cuts and an abolition of the inheritance tax (although these were temporary rather than permanent). Another set of tax cuts in 2003 was designed to reduce the burden of taxes on capital by lowering taxes on dividends.

With the Bush administration's tax cuts, the nation has come full circle. No longer is fiscal policy seen as the primary weapon for fighting the business cycle. Rather, economists argue that tax changes

---

[5] For simplicity, we take the absolute value of the tax multiplier (since the multiplier is actually negative). The different multipliers can be seen using the device of the "expenditure rounds" shown on pages 486–487. Let the *MPC* be *r*. Then if *G* goes up by 1 unit, the total increase in spending is the sum of secondary respending rounds:

$$1 + r + r^2 + r^3 + \cdots = \frac{1}{1-r}$$

Now, if taxes are reduced by $1, consumers save $(1 - r)$ of the increased disposable income and spend *r* dollars on the first round. With the further rounds, the total spending is thus

$$r + r^2 + r^3 + \cdots = \frac{r}{1-r}$$

Thus the tax multiplier is *r* times the expenditure multiplier, where *r* is the *MPC*.

should primarily focus on national saving, investment, and innovation.

The Other Partner in Stabilization Policy

Our multiplier analysis has focused primarily on fiscal policy as a tool for stabilizing the economy. But Keynesian economists emphasize that fiscal policy is only one of the tools that can be used in business-cycle management. The government has another equally powerful weapon in monetary policy. Although monetary policy works quite differently, as we will see in the next two chapters, it has many advantages as a policy for combating unemployment and inflation.

Like two locomotives on a train—sometimes pulling in one direction and sometimes in different directions—monetary and fiscal policies are powerful engines for affecting output, employment, and prices in the short run.

MULTIPLIERS IN ACTION

A realistic understanding of the size of multipliers is a crucial part of diagnosis and prescription in economic policy. Just as a physician prescribing a painkiller must know the effect of different dosages, so an economist must know the quantitative magnitude of expenditure and tax multipliers. When the economy is growing too rapidly and a dose of fiscal austerity is prescribed, the economic doctor needs to know the actual size of multipliers before deciding how large a dose of tax increases or expenditure reductions to order.

Textbook models give a highly simplified picture of the structure of the macroeconomy. For a more realistic picture of the response of output to changes in government purchases, economists estimate large-scale econometric models (see the discussion of this in Chapter 23) and then perform numerical experiments on their models by calculating the impact of a change in government purchases on the economy. Such models can serve as the basis for policy recommendations. These large-scale models include not only the bare-bones factors that we have sketched up to now but also factors that we consider later such as a more realistic treatment of taxes, a complete monetary sector, and the behavior of wages and prices.

Including these additional factors tends to reduce the numerical size of multipliers.

A recent comprehensive survey of econometric models of the United States provides a representative sample of multiplier estimates. The models surveyed include equations to predict the behavior of all major sectors of the economy (including both monetary and financial sectors, along with investment demand schedules and consumption functions), and they incorporate a full set of links with the rest of the world. In the estimates, the level of real government purchases of goods and services is permanently increased by $1 billion. The models then calculate the impact on real GDP. The change in real GDP resulting from the increase in government purchases provides an estimate of the size of the government expenditure multiplier.

Figure 24-9 presents the results of this survey. The heavy rust line shows the average government expenditure multiplier estimated by eight models, while the light gray lines show the range of estimates of the individual models. The average multiplier for the first and second years is around 1.4, but after the second year the multiplier tends to decline slightly as monetary forces and international impacts come into play. (The monetary forces represent the impact of higher GDP on interest rates, which leads to a crowding out of investment, as we will explain in later chapters.)

One interesting feature of these estimates is that the different models (represented by the light gray lines in Figure 24-9) show considerable disagreement about the size of multipliers. Why do the estimates differ? To begin with, there is inherent uncertainty about the nature of economic relationships. Uncertainty about the structure of nature or society is of course what makes science so exciting; if everything were perfectly understood, scientists would be out of business. But understanding economic systems poses even greater challenges because economists cannot conduct controlled experiments in a laboratory. Even more vexing is the fact that the economy itself evolves over time, so the "correct" model for 1965 is different from the "correct" model for 2005.

In addition, economists have fundamental disagreements about the underlying nature of the macroeconomy. Some economists believe that a Keynesian approach best explains macroeconomic

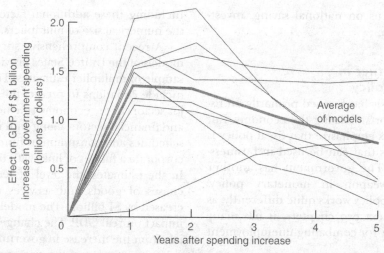

FIGURE 24-9. Expenditure Multipliers in Macroeconomic Models

A careful survey shows the estimated government expenditure multipliers in different macroeconomic models. These experiments show the estimated impact of a permanent $1 billion increase in the real value of government purchases of goods and services on real GDP at different intervals following the spending increase. That is, they show the impact of a $1 billion change in *G* on *Q*. The heavy rust line shows the average multiplier for the different models, while the gray lines represent the multipliers for each individual model.

Source: Ralph C. Bryant, Gerald Holtham, and Peter Hooper, "Consensus and Diversity in Model Simulations," in *Empirical Macroeconomics for Interdependent Economies* (Brookings Institution, Washington, D.C., 1988).

behavior, while others are convinced that a classical or real-business-cycle approach yields better insights. With all these uncertainties and differences in points of view, we can hardly be surprised that economists will provide different estimates of multipliers.

Beyond the Multiplier Model

We have completed our survey of the most important applications of the Keynesian multiplier model. This approach is an indispensable aid in understanding business fluctuations and the linkage between government fiscal policy and national output.

But it would be a mistake to believe you can turn a parrot into a macroeconomist by simply teaching it to say "*C + I + G*." Macroeconomic understanding requires understanding not just the models but also their strengths and weaknesses. Among the simplifications of the simplest multiplier model are the following:

- The multiplier model ignores the impact of money and credit upon consumption and investment.

- The simplest multiplier model ignores the way foreign trade affects output at home and abroad.
- Aggregate supply is left out of the story, so we have no way of analyzing how increases in spending are divided between prices and output.

These are not just trifling concerns—they are essential to understanding modern macroeconomics. In the next few chapters, we will incorporate these further realistic elements. Once we have incorporated the influence of money and interest rates, the behavior of wages and prices, and the impact of foreign trade, we will see that the impact of fiscal policy on the economy may be quite different from the simplest multiplier model.

We turn next to an analysis of one of the most fascinating parts of all economics: the study of money. Once we understand how the central bank determines the money supply, we will have a fuller appreciation of how governments can tame the business cycles that have run wild through much of the history of capitalism.

SUMMARY

A. The Basic Multiplier Model

1. The multiplier model provides a simple way to understand the impact of aggregate demand on the level of output. In the simplest approach, household consumption is a function of disposable income while investment is fixed. People's desire to consume and the willingness of businesses to invest are brought into balance by adjustments in output. The equilibrium level of national output must be at the intersection of the saving and investment schedules, *SS* and *II*. We can also see this using the expenditure-output approach, in which equilibrium output comes at the intersection of the total expenditure (*TE*) consumption-plus-investment schedule, *TE = C + I*, with the 45° line.

2. If output is temporarily above its equilibrium level, businesses find output higher than sales, with inventories piling up involuntarily and profits plummeting. Firms therefore cut production and employment back toward the equilibrium level. The only sustainable level of output comes when buyers voluntarily purchase exactly as much as businesses desire to produce.

3. Thus, for the simplified Keynesian multiplier model, investment calls the tune and consumption dances to the music. Investment determines output, while saving responds passively to income changes. Output rises or falls until planned saving has adjusted to the level of planned investment.

4. Investment has a *multiplied effect* on output. When investment changes, output will at first rise by an equal amount. But as the income receivers in the capital-goods industries get more income, they set in motion a whole chain of additional secondary consumption spending and employment.

   If people always spend *r* of each extra dollar of income on consumption, the total of the multiplier chain will be

$$1 + r + r^2 + \cdots = \frac{1}{1 - r} = \frac{1}{1 - MPC} = \frac{1}{MPS}$$

The simplest multiplier is numerically equal to the reciprocal of the *MPS* or, equivalently, to $1/(1 - MPC)$. The multiplier works in either direction, amplifying either increases or decreases in investment. This result occurs because it always takes more than a dollar of increased income to increase saving by a dollar.

5. Key points to remember are (*a*) the basic multiplier model emphasizes the importance of shifts in aggregate demand in affecting output and income and (*b*) it is primarily applicable for situations with unemployed resources.

B. Fiscal Policy in the Multiplier Model

6. The analysis of fiscal policy elaborates the Keynesian multiplier model. It shows that an increase in government purchases—taken by itself, with taxes and investment unchanged—has an expansionary effect on national output much like that of investment. The total expenditure *TE = C + I + G* schedule shifts upward to a higher equilibrium intersection with the 45° line.

7. A decrease in taxes—taken by itself, with investment and government purchases unchanged—raises the equilibrium level of national output. The *CC* schedule of consumption plotted against GDP is shifted upward and leftward by a tax cut. But since extra dollars of disposable income go partly into saving, the dollar increase in consumption will not be quite so great as the dollars of new disposable income. Therefore, the tax multiplier is smaller than the government expenditure multiplier.

8. Using statistical techniques and macroeconomic theory, economists have developed realistic models to estimate expenditure multipliers. For mainstream approaches, these tend to show multipliers of between 1 and 1½ for periods of up to 4 years.

CONCEPTS FOR REVIEW

The Basic Multiplier Model

$TE = C + I$ schedule

$TE = C + I + G$ schedule

two ways of viewing GDP determination:

  planned saving = planned investment

  planned C + planned I = planned GDP

investment equals saving: planned vs. actual levels

multiplier effect of investment

multiplier

$$= 1 + MPC + (MPC)^2 + \cdots$$

$$= \frac{1}{1 - MPC} = \frac{1}{MPS}$$

Government Purchases and Taxation

fiscal policy:

  G effect on equilibrium GDP

  T effect on CC and on GDP

multiplier effects of government purchases (G) and taxes (T)

$C + I + G$ curve

estimated multipliers in practice

FURTHER READING AND INTERNET WEBSITES

Further Reading

The multiplier model was developed by John Maynard Keynes in *The General Theory of Employment, Interest and Money* (Harcourt, New York, first published in 1935).

Advanced treatments can be found in the intermediate textbooks listed in the Further Reading section in Chapter 20.

Websites

Brad DeLong of the University of California at Berkeley has a Web page with many references to Keynes. See

www.j-bradford-delong.net/Index.html. One of Keynes's most influential books, *The Economic Consequences of the Peace* (1919), predicted with uncanny accuracy that the Treaty of Versailles would lead to disastrous consequences for Europe—it is available at www.socsci.mcmaster.ca/~econ/ugcm/3113/keynes/peace. Writings on Keynesian economics and many other current subjects can be found on Paul Krugman's website at www.wws.princeton.edu/~pkrugman/.

QUESTIONS FOR DISCUSSION

1. In the simple multiplier model, assume that investment is always zero. Show that equilibrium output in this special case would come at the break-even point of the consumption function. Why would equilibrium output come *above* the break-even point when investment is positive?

2. Define carefully what is meant by equilibrium in the multiplier model. For each of the following, state why the situation is *not* an equilibrium. Also describe how the economy would react to each of the situations to restore equilibrium.
   a. In Table 24-1, GDP is $3300 billion.
   b. In Figure 24-2, actual investment is zero.
   c. Car dealers find that their inventories of new cars are rising unexpectedly.

   d. In the simplest model of Section A, consumers plan to save $600 while businesses plan to invest $700.

3. Reconstruct Table 24-1 assuming that planned investment is equal to (*a*) $300 billion, (*b*) $400 billion. What is the resulting difference in GDP? Is this difference greater or smaller than the change in *I*? Why? When *I* drops from $200 billion to $100 billion, how much must GDP drop?

4. Give (*a*) the common sense, (*b*) the arithmetic, and (*c*) the geometry of the multiplier. What are the multipliers for *MPC* = 0.9? 0.8? 0.5? For *MPS* = 0.1? 0.8?

5. We have seen that investment responds to output through the accelerator principle (see Chapter 23). We might then define the *marginal propensity to invest,*

or *MPI*, as the change in investment per unit change in output. Suppose that investment is $I = \bar{I} + 1.2Q$ (which has an *MPI* of 1.2), while the *MPC* is 0.8. What is the marginal propensity to spend = *MPC* + *MPI*? Work out the explosive (!) chain of spending and respending when the marginal propensity to spend = 2. Try to explain the economics of the divergent infinite geometric series.

6. Explain in words and using the notion of expenditure rounds why the tax multiplier is smaller than the expenditure multiplier.

7. Explain why governments might use fiscal policy to stabilize the economy. Why would fiscal policy be effective in raising output in a Keynesian economy but not in an economy where aggregate supply is vertical?

8. "Even if the government spends billions on wasteful military armaments, this action can create jobs in a recession." Discuss.

9. The saving-and-investment diagram and the 45° line $C + I$ diagram are two different ways of showing how national output is determined in the multiplier model. Describe each. Show their equivalence.

10. **Advanced problem:** The growth of nations depends crucially on saving and investment. And from youth we are taught that thrift is important and that "a penny saved is a penny earned." But will higher saving necessarily benefit the economy? In a striking argument called *the paradox of thrift,* Keynes pointed out that when people attempt to save more, this will not necessarily result in more saving for the nation as a whole.

To see this point, assume that people decide to save more. Illustrate how this shifts up the *SS* curve in the multiplier model of Figure 24-4. Explain why this will *decrease output with no increase in saving!* Provide the intuition here that if people try to increase their saving and lower their consumption for a given level of business investment, sales will fall and businesses will cut back on production. Explain how far output will fall. Here then is the paradox of thrift: When the community desires to save more, the effect may actually be a lowering of income and output with no increase of saving.

Explain why this is a good example of the fallacy of composition. Further explain why the paradox might hold in an economy experiencing unemployment, whereas in a "classical" economy with full employment higher saving would indeed raise investment without a decline in output.

Financial Markets and the Special Case of Money

Over all history, money has oppressed people in one of two ways: either it has been abundant and very unreliable, or reliable and very scarce.

John Kenneth Galbraith,
The Age of Uncertainty
(1977)

One of the most important and innovative sectors of a modern economy is its financial system. This set of institutions and instruments forms the vital circulatory system through which the savings decisions of one group of individuals and nations are channeled to the investments of other businesses and nations. Because of its importance, we begin this chapter with a review of the workings of a modern financial system.

One unique financial asset, called money, plays a special role in the economy. It is the grease that facilitates transactions among the different players in the economy. The second section examines the nature of money and the reasons that people hold this asset. We then analyze the special role of banks, which create money from bank reserves. The last section of this chapter examines the fascinating behavior of stock prices.

All of these analyses will be necessary ingredients in the next chapter's analysis of how monetary policy plays a central place in managing the business cycle.

A. THE MODERN FINANCIAL SYSTEM

The Role of the Financial System

One sector of a modern economy, which is of growing importance, involves finance and the financial system. By **finance** we mean the process by which economic agents borrow from and lend to other agents in order to consume or invest. People may borrow or lend because their cash incomes sometimes do not match their desired spending. For example, students generally have spending needs for tuition and living expenses that exceed their current incomes. They often finance their excess spending with student loans. Similarly, working couples will generally save some of their current incomes for retirement, perhaps by buying stocks or bonds. They are thereby financing their retirement.

The activities involved in finance take place in the **financial system.** This encompasses the markets, firms, and other institutions which carry out the financial decisions of households, businesses, governments, at home and abroad. Important parts of the financial system include the money market (discussed later in this chapter), markets for fixed-interest assets like bonds or mortgages, stock markets for the ownership of firms, and foreign exchange markets which trade the monies of different countries. Most of the financial system in the United States is composed of for-profit entities, but government institutions such as the Federal Reserve System and other regulatory bodies are particularly important for ensuring an efficient and stable financial system.

Borrowing and lending take place in financial markets and through financial intermediaries. **Financial markets** are like other markets except that their products and services consist of financial instruments like stocks and bonds. Important financial markets are stock markets, bond markets, and foreign exchange markets.

Institutions which provide financial services and products are called **financial intermediaries.** Financial institutions differ from other businesses because their assets are largely financial, rather than real assets like plant and equipment. Many retail financial transactions (such as banking or purchase of insurance) take place through financial intermediaries rather than directly in financial markets.

The most important financial intermediaries are commercial banks, which take deposits of funds from households and other groups and lend these funds to businesses and those who need funds; banks also "create" the special product known as money. Other important financial intermediaries are insurance companies and pension funds, which provide specialized products, insurance policies, and investments held for retirement. Yet a third group of intermediaries "pool" and "subdivide" securities; these include mutual funds (which hold bonds and corporate stocks on behalf of small investors) and mortgage resellers (which buy mortgages from banks and repackage them for other investors).

All together, financial intermediaries have total liabilities of around $40 trillion, or around $400,000 per American household. Clearly, given the investments people have in this sector, a careful study here is important not only for good policy but for wise financial decisions by households.

The Functions of the Financial System
Because the financial system is such a critical part of a modern economy, let's consider its major functions:

- The financial system *transfers resources* across time, sectors, and regions. This function allows investments to be devoted to their most productive uses rather than being bottled up where they are least needed. We provided the example above of student loans and retirement saving. Another example is found in international finance. Japan, which has a high saving rate, transfers resources to China, which has robust investment opportunities; this transfer occurs through both loans and direct foreign investments in China.

- The financial system *manages risks* for the economy. In one sense, risk management is like resource transfer: it moves risks from those people or sectors that most need to reduce their risks and transfers or spreads the risks to others who are better able to weather them. For example, fire insurance on your house takes a risk that you may lose a $200,000 investment and spreads that risk among hundreds or thousands of stockholders of the insurance company.

- The financial system *pools and subdivides funds* depending upon the need of the individual saver or investor. As an investor, you might want to invest $10,000 in a diversified portfolio of common stocks. To buy efficiently a portfolio of 100 companies might require $10 million of funds. Here is where a stock mutual fund comes in: by having 1000 investors, it can buy the portfolio, subdivide it, and manage it for you. In return, a well-run mutual fund might charge $30 per year on your $10,000 portfolio. Additionally, a modern economy requires large-scale firms which have billions of dollars of invested plant and equipment. No single person is likely to be able to afford that—and if someone could, that person would not want all his or her eggs in one basket. Here is where the modern corporation comes in, with its ability to sell shares of stock to many people and pool these funds to make large and risky investments.

- The financial system performs an important *clearinghouse function*, which facilitates transactions between payers (purchasers) and payees (sellers). For example, when you write a check on your checking account to buy a new computer, a clearinghouse will debit your bank and credit the bank of the company selling the computer. This function allows rapid transfers of funds around the world.

Household purchases
government bond or
GM stock

Financial
markets

Firm floats bond issue
or has initial public
offering (IPO) of stock

Savers

Mutual fund
buys
diversified
portfolio of
stocks

Investors

Financial
intermediaries

Household deposits
monthly salary in
checking account

Small business borrows
from bank to invest
in pizza oven

FIGURE 25-1. The Flow of Funds Tracks Financial Flows in the Economy

Savers and investors transfer funds across time, space, and sectors through financial markets
and financial intermediaries. Some flows (such as buying 100 shares of XYZ) go directly
through financial markets, while others (such as purchasing shares of mutual funds or
depositing money in your checking account) go through financial intermediaries.

The Flow of Funds

We can illustrate a simplified account of financial
markets through a picture of the **flow of funds,**
shown in Figure 25-1. This shows two sets of economic agents—savers and investors—and representative examples of saving and investing through
financial markets and financial intermediaries. This
picture is highly simplified, for there are many different kinds of financial assets or instruments, as we
will see in the next section.

A MENU OF FINANCIAL ASSETS

Financial assets are monetary claims by one party
against another party. These consist primarily of
dollar-denominated assets (whose payments are fixed in
dollar terms) and *equities* (whose values represent the
value of claims on real assets).

Here are the major financial instruments or
assets:

- *Money* is a very special asset which will be defined
  carefully later in this chapter.
- *Savings accounts* are deposits with banks, usually
  guaranteed by governments, that have a fixed-
  dollar principal value and interest rates determined by short-term market interest rates.
- *Government securities* are bills and bonds of the
  federal, state, and local governments. They guarantee repayment of principal on maturity and
  pay interest along the way. Federal securities are
  considered the safest of all investments.
- *Equities* are ownership rights to companies. They
  yield dividends, which are payments drawn from
  the companies' net profits. Publicly traded equities, which are priced on stock markets, are
  discussed later in this chapter. Noncorporate

Financial Assets of Households				
	Percentage of Total Assets			
	1992	1995	1998	2001
Dollar denominated:				
Checking and savings accounts	17.5	13.9	11.4	11.5
Bonds and other nominal securities	17.5	13.2	9.3	8.4
Equities (stocks and mutual funds)	24.1	28.3	35.1	33.8
Retirement accounts and life insurance	31.6	35.3	34.0	33.7
Other	9.2	9.2	10.3	12.5
Total	100.0	100.0	100.0	100.0

TABLE 25-1. Financial Assets of U.S. Households, 1992–2001

Households own a wide variety of financial assets ranging from money to pension funds.

Source: Federal Reserve Board at www.federalreserve.gov/pubs/oss/oss2/2001/scf2001home.html.

equities are the values of partnerships, farms, and small businesses.

- *Financial derivatives* are new forms of financial instruments whose values are based on or derived from the values of other assets. One important example is a stock option, which is an instrument whose value depends upon the value of the stock to which it is benchmarked.
- *Pension funds* represent ownership in the assets that are held by companies or pension plans. Workers and companies contribute to these funds during working years, and the funds are then drawn down to pay pensions during retirement.

Note that these financial assets exclude the single most important assets owned by most people—their houses, which are tangible as opposed to financial assets. In addition, people have *implicit* assets in their future social security payments and government-provided medical care, but these have no ready market value.

Table 25-1 shows the major financial assets of households.

INTEREST RATES AND THE RETURN ON FINANCIAL ASSETS

When you borrow money or invest in different financial assets, you will naturally want to know what you will pay to borrow or earn on your investments.

These earnings are called the *return on investments;* in the special case of the return on fixed-interest securities they are call the *interest rate.* From an economic point of view, interest rates or other returns are the *price of borrowing or lending.* Let's focus on the important case of the interest rate.

The **interest rate** is the price paid for borrowing money. We usually calculate interest as percent per year on the amount of borrowed funds. There are many interest rates depending upon the maturity, risk, tax status, and other attributes of the borrower.

Some examples will illustrate how interest works:

- When you graduate from college, you have only $500. You decide to keep it in currency. If you spend none of your funds, at the end of a year you still have $500 because currency has a zero interest rate.
- A little later, you put $2000 in a savings account in your local bank, where the interest rate on savings accounts is 4 percent per year. At the end of 1 year, the bank will have paid $80 in interest into your account, so the account is now worth $2080.
- You start your first job and decide to buy a small house that costs $100,000. You go to your local bank and find that 30-year, fixed-interest-rate mortgages have an interest rate of 5 percent per year. Each month you make a mortgage payment of $790.79. Note that this payment is a little bit more

than the pro-rated monthly interest charge of $5/12$ percent per month. Why? Because it includes not only interest but also *amortization*. This is repayment of *principal*, the amount borrowed. By the time you have made your 360 monthly payments, you will have completely paid off the loan.

From these examples we see that interest rates are measured in percent per year. Interest is the price paid to borrow money, which allows the borrower to obtain real resources over the time of the loan.

Higher Interest Rates Tend to Lower Asset Prices

One important fact in financial markets is the inverse relationship between interest rates and asset prices. We can understand this using the concept of present value.

Suppose you own a mineral-water spring and decide to sell it. The market price will depend upon both the stream of future income and the interest rate. Putting these together yields the present value of the asset.

The **present value** of an asset is the dollar value today of the time stream of income generated by that asset. It is measured by calculating how much money invested today would be needed, at the going interest rate, to generate the asset's future stream of receipts.

Here are some examples:

- Begin with a 1-year bond. The bond returns $50 of interest plus the original principal of $1050 exactly 1 year from now. Furthermore, suppose the interest rate is 10 percent per year. How much should you pay for the bond today? Pay exactly $1000, because $1000 invested today at the market interest rate of 10 percent will be worth $1100 in 1 year. So the present value of the bond is $1000.
- A perpetual asset has a constant yield forever. Suppose your mineral spring is expected to yield $N of water each year forever. What is the present value (V) if the interest rate is i percent per year? The present value is simply $V = \$N/i$.
- Say there is a variable stream of income in the future. The general formula for present value evaluates the present value of each part of the stream of future receipts and then adds together all these separate present values. The summation in the following formula will give you the asset's present value:

$$V = \frac{N_1}{1 + i} + \frac{N_2}{(1 + i)^2} + \cdots + \frac{N_t}{(1 + i)^t} + \cdots$$

In this equation, i is the one-period market interest rate assumed to be constant. Further, N_1 is the net receipts (positive or negative) in period 1, N_2 the net receipts in period 2, N_t the net receipts in period t, and so forth.

We can now see that asset prices tend to move inversely with interest rates because the present value is reduced as the interest rate rises. For example, in the perpetuity case, a doubling of i in the denominator will halve the value of V. You can work through with a calculator the impact of a higher interest rate on the 1-year bond example. This is a general property of financial assets—that the value of stocks, bonds, real estate, and many other long-lived assets will decline as interest rates rise.

An Array of Interest Rates

Textbooks often speak of "*the* interest rate," but in fact today's complex financial system has a vast array of interest rates. Interest rates depend mainly on the characteristics of the loan or of the borrower. Let us review the major differences.

Loans differ in their *term* or *maturity*—the length of time until they must be paid off. The shortest loans are overnight. Short-term securities are for periods up to a year. Companies often issue bonds that have maturities of 10 to 30 years, and mortgages are up to 30 years in maturity. Longer-term securities generally command a higher interest rate than do short-term issues because lenders are willing to sacrifice quick access to their funds only if they can increase their yield.

Loans also vary in terms of *risk*. Some loans are virtually riskless, while others are highly speculative. Investors require that a premium be paid when they invest in risky ventures. The safest assets in the world are the securities of the U.S. government. These bonds and bills are backed by the full faith, credit, and taxing powers of the government. Intermediate in risk are borrowings of creditworthy corporations, states, and localities. Risky investments, which bear a significant chance of default or nonpayment, include those of companies close to bankruptcy, cities with shrinking tax bases, or countries like Argentina with large overseas debts and unstable political systems.

The U.S. government pays what is called the "riskless" interest rate; over the last two decades this has ranged from 3 to 15 percent per year for short-term loans. Riskier securities might pay 1, 2, or 5 percent per year more than the riskless rate; this premium reflects the amount necessary to compensate the lender for losses in case of default.

Assets vary in their liquidity. An asset is said to be *liquid* if it can be converted into cash quickly and with little loss in value. Most marketable securities, including common stocks and corporate and government bonds, can be turned into cash quickly for close to their current value. Illiquid assets include unique

assets for which no well-established market exists. For example, if you own the only Victorian mansion in a small town, you might find it difficult to sell the asset quickly or at a price near its realistic market value—your house is an illiquid asset. Because of the higher risk and the difficulty of realizing the asset values quickly, illiquid assets or loans require higher interest rates than do liquid, riskless ones.

When these three factors (along with other considerations such as tax status and administrative costs) are considered, it is not surprising that we see so many different financial instruments and so many different interest rates. Figure 25-2 and Table 25-2

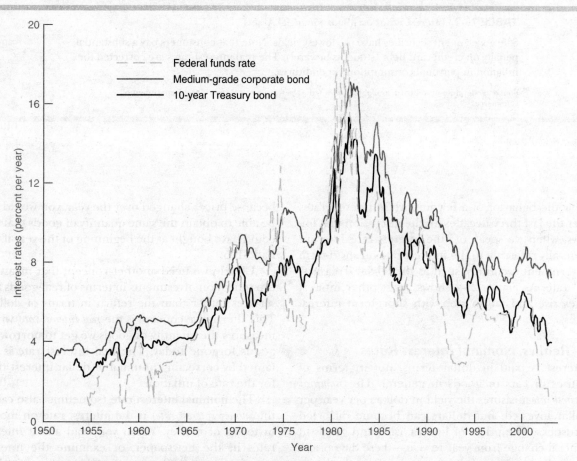

FIGURE 25-2. Most Interest Rates Move Together

This graph shows the major interest rates in the U.S. economy. The lowest rate is generally the federal funds rate, set by the Federal Reserve in its monetary policy. Longer-term and riskier interest rates are usually higher than safe and short-term rates.

Source: Federal Reserve System, available at www.federalreserve.gov/releases/.

Asset class	Period	Nominal rate of return (% per year)	Real rate of return (% per year)
Government securities:			
3 month	1947–2003	4.8	1.3
10 year	1947–2003	6.6	3.0
Corporate bonds:			
Safe (Aaa)	1947–2003	6.9	3.2
Risky (<Baa)	1947–2003	7.8	4.1
Corporate equities	1947–2003	10.1	6.4
Consumer loans:			
Mortgages (fixed rate)	1972–2003	9.6	5.0
Credit cards	1994–2003	15.2	13.1
New-car loans	1972–2003	10.9	6.3

TABLE 25-2. Interest Rates on Major Financial Assets

Safe government securities have the lowest yields. Note that consumers pay a substantial penalty on credit-card debt (students beware!). The real interest rates are corrected for inflation in personal consumption expenditures.

Source: Federal Reserve Board, available at www.federalreserve.gov/releases/, and Department of Commerce.

show the behavior of a few important interest rates over the last three decades. In the discussion that follows, when we speak of "the interest rate," we are generally referring to the interest rate on short-term government securities, such as the 90-day Treasury-bill rate. As Figure 25-2 shows, most other interest rates rise and fall in step with short-term interest rates.

Real vs. Nominal Interest Rates

Interest is paid in dollar terms, not in terms of houses or cars or goods in general. The *nominal interest rate* measures the yield in dollars per year per dollar invested. But dollars can become distorted yardsticks. The prices of houses, cars, and goods in general change from year to year—these days prices generally rise due to inflation. Put differently, the interest rate on dollars does not measure what a lender really earns in terms of goods and services. Let us say that you lend $100 today at 5 percent-per-year interest. You would get back $105 at the end of a year. But

because prices changed over the year, you would not be able to obtain the same quantity of goods that you could have bought at the beginning of the year if you had $105.

Clearly, we need another concept that measures the return on investments in terms of real goods and services rather than the return in terms of dollars. This alternative concept is the *real interest rate*, which measures the quantity of goods we get tomorrow for goods forgone today. The real interest rate is obtained by correcting nominal or dollar interest rates for the rate of inflation.

The **nominal interest rate** (sometimes also called the *money interest rate*) is the interest rate on money in terms of money. When you read about interest rates in the newspaper, or examine the interest rates in Figure 25-2, you are looking at nominal interest rates; they give the dollar return per dollar of investment.

In contrast, the **real interest rate** is corrected for inflation and is calculated as the nominal interest rate minus the rate of inflation. As an example, suppose the nominal interest rate is 8 percent per year and the inflation rate is 3 percent per year; we can calculate the real interest rate as $8 - 3 = 5$ percent per year.

To take a simple example, suppose that you live in an economy where the only product is bread. Further suppose that the price of bread in the first period is $1 per loaf and that bread inflation is 3 percent per year. If you lend $100 at 8 percent per year interest, you will have $108 at the end of the year. However, because of inflation, next year you will get back only 105 (and not 108) loaves of bread. The real (or bread) rate of interest is $8 - 3 = 5$ percent.[1]

During inflationary periods, we must use real interest rates, not nominal or money interest rates, to calculate the yield on investments in terms of goods earned per year on goods invested. The real interest rate is approximately equal to the nominal interest rate minus the rate of inflation.

The World's Safest Investment

U.S. Treasury bonds are generally considered a riskless investment. Their one shortcoming is that they pay a fixed-dollar interest rate. So if inflation heats up, as it did in the late 1970s, the real interest rate can easily turn negative.

In 1997, the U.S. government fixed this problem by introducing Treasury inflation-protected securities (TIPS). TIPS have their interest and principal tied to inflation, so they pay a constant real interest rate over their lifetime.

This is how they work: Each year the principal value is adjusted by the increase in the consumer price index (CPI). Let's take a specific example. In January 2000, the Treasury issued a $4\frac{1}{4}$ percent 10-year inflation-protected bond. Between January 2000 and June 2003, the CPI increased by 12 percent. Therefore, a $1000 bond would be valued at $1120 in June 2003. If the Treasury made an interest payment in June, it would be $4\frac{1}{4}$ percent of $1120, instead of $4\frac{1}{4}$ percent of $1000 for a standard bond. Let's further suppose that inflation averaged 3 percent per year from 2000 to 2010. Then the principal value on redemption would be $1343.92 [= $1000 $\times$ (1.03)^{10}], instead of $1000 for a conventional bond.

As long as people expect that there will be inflation in the coming years, the interest rate on TIPS would be less than that on standard Treasury bonds. For example, in May 2003, 10-year Treasury bonds had a yield of 3.57 percent while 10-year TIPS had a yield of 1.90 percent. This indicates that the marginal investor expected 10-year inflation to average $3.57 - 1.90 = 1.67$ percent per year.

The difference between nominal and real interest rates on long-term bonds is illustrated in Figure 25-3. The upper line shows the nominal interest rate, while the lower line shows a calculated real interest rate. In addition, the short rust line shows the real interest rate on TIPS. This figure shows that the rise in nominal interest rates from 1960 to 1980 was purely illusory, for nominal interest rates were just keeping up with inflation during those years. After 1980, however, real interest rates rose sharply and remained high for a decade. The data on TIPS show that the real interest rate declined sharply from 1997 through 2003.

Economists have been enthusiasts of indexed bonds for many years. Such bonds can be bought by pensioners who wish to guarantee that their retirement incomes will not be eroded by inflation. Similarly, parents who wish to save for their children's education can sock away some of their savings knowing that it will keep up with the general price level. Even monetary-policy makers find value in indexed bonds, for the difference between conventional bonds and TIPS gives an indication of what is happening to expected inflation. The main puzzle to many economists is why it took so long to introduce this important innovation.

---

[1] The exact algebra of real interest rates is as follows: Let π be the inflation rate, i the nominal interest rate, and r the real interest rate. If you invest $1 today, you get $(1 + i)$ back in 1 year. However, prices have risen, so you need $(1 + \pi)$ in 1 year to buy the same amount of goods that you could buy with $1 today. Instead of buying 1 unit of goods today, you can therefore buy $(1 + r)$ units tomorrow, where $(1 + r) = (1 + i)/(1 + \pi)$. For small values of i and π, $r = i - \pi$.

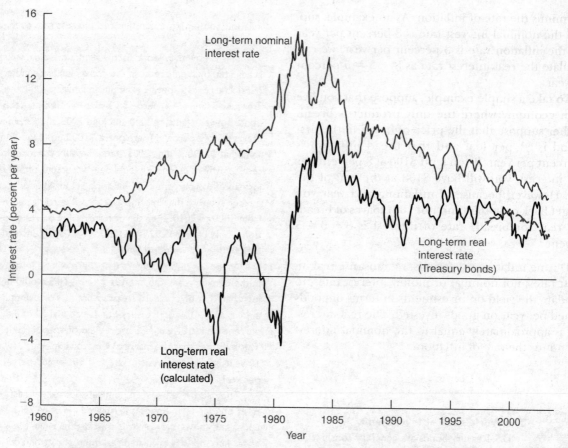

FIGURE 25-3. Real vs. Nominal Interest Rates

The rust line shows the nominal interest rate on long-term Treasury bonds. The black curve shows the "calculated" real interest rate, equal to the nominal or money rate less the realized inflation rate over the prior year. Note that real interest rates drifted downward until 1980. After 1980, however, real interest rates moved up sharply. The short rust line since 1997 shows the real interest rate on long-term inflation-indexed securities.

Source: Federal Reserve Bank of St. Louis, Federal Reserve Board, U.S. Department of Labor.

B. THE SPECIAL CASE OF MONEY

Let's now turn to the special case of money. If you think about it for a moment, you will realize that money is a strange thing. We study for years so that we can earn a good living, yet each dollar bill is just paper, with no intrinsic value. Money is useless until we get rid of it.

But money is anything but useless from a macroeconomic point of view. Monetary policy is today the most important tool that the government has to stabilize the business cycle. The central bank uses its control over the supply of money to stimulate the economy when unemployment begins to rise or to brake the economy when prices rise too quickly.

When money is well managed, as was the case for the United States in the 1990s, output grows smoothly with stable prices. But an unreliable monetary system, such as that seen in unstable Russia over the last decade, can lead to inflation or depression. Many of the world's most devastating macro-economic problems of the twentieth century can be traced to malfunctioning monetary systems.

We now turn to a careful analysis of the definition of and demand for money.

THE EVOLUTION OF MONEY

The History of Money

What is money? **Money** *is anything that serves as a commonly accepted medium of exchange.* Because money has a long and fascinating history, we will begin with a description of money's evolution.

Barter. In an early textbook on money, when Stanley Jevons wanted to illustrate the tremendous leap forward that occurred as societies introduced money, he used the following experience:

> Some years since, Mademoiselle Zélie, a singer of the Théâtre Lyrique at Paris, . . . gave a concert in the Society Islands. In exchange for an air from Norma and a few other songs, she was to receive a third part of the receipts.
>
> When counted, her share was found to consist of three pigs, twenty-three turkeys, forty-four chickens, five thousand cocoa-nuts, besides considerable quantities of bananas, lemons, and oranges. . . . [I]n Paris . . . this amount of live stock and vegetables might have brought four thousand francs, which would have been good remuneration for five songs. In the Society Islands, however, pieces of money were scarce; and as Mademoiselle could not consume any considerable portion of the receipts herself, it became necessary in the mean time to feed the pigs and poultry with the fruit.

This example describes **barter,** which consists of the exchange of goods for other goods. Exchange through barter contrasts with exchange through money because pigs, turkeys, and lemons are not generally acceptable monies that we or Mademoiselle Zélie can use for buying things. Although barter is better than no trade at all, it operates under grave disadvantages because an elaborate division of labor would be unthinkable without the introduction of the great social invention of money.

As economies develop, people no longer barter one good for another. Instead, they sell goods for money and then use money to buy other goods they wish to have. At first glance this seems to complicate rather than simplify matters, as it replaces one transaction with two. If you have apples and want nuts, would it not be simpler to trade one for the other rather than to sell the apples for money and then use the money to buy nuts?

Actually, the reverse is true: two monetary transactions are simpler than one barter transaction. For example, some people may want to buy apples, and some may want to sell nuts. But it would be a most unusual circumstance to find a person whose desires exactly complement your own—eager to sell nuts and buy apples. To use a classical economics phrase, instead of there being a "double coincidence of wants," there is likely to be a "want of coincidence." So, unless a hungry tailor happens to find an undraped farmer who has both food and a desire for a pair of pants, under barter neither can make a direct trade.

Societies that traded extensively simply could not overcome the overwhelming handicaps of barter. The use of a commonly accepted medium of exchange, money, permits the farmer to buy pants from the tailor, who buys shoes from the cobbler, who buys leather from the farmer.

Commodity Money. Money as a medium of exchange first came into human history in the form of commodities. A great variety of items have served as money at one time or another: cattle, olive oil, beer or wine, copper, iron, gold, silver, rings, diamonds, and cigarettes.

Each of the above has advantages and disadvantages. Cattle are not divisible into small change. Beer does not improve with keeping, although wine may. Olive oil provides a nice liquid currency that is as minutely divisible as one wishes, but it is a bit messy to handle. And so forth.

By the eighteenth century, commodity money was almost exclusively limited to metals like silver and gold. These forms of money had *intrinsic value,* meaning that they had use value in themselves. Because money had intrinsic value, there was no need for the government to guarantee its value, and the quantity of money was regulated by the market through the supply and demand for gold or silver. But metallic money has shortcomings because scarce resources are required to dig it out of the ground; moreover, it might become abundant simply because of accidental discoveries of ore deposits.

The advent of monetary control by central banks has led to a much more stable currency system. The intrinsic value of money is now the least important thing about it.

Modern Money. The age of commodity money gave way to the age of *paper money.* The essence of money is now laid bare. Money is wanted not for its own sake but for the things it will buy. We do not wish to consume money directly; rather, we use it by getting rid of it. Even when we choose to keep money, it is valuable only because we can spend it later on.

The use of paper currency has become widespread because it is a convenient medium of exchange. Currency is easily carried and stored. The value of money can be protected from counterfeiting by careful engraving. The fact that private individuals cannot legally create money keeps it scarce. Given this limitation on supply, currency has value. It can buy things. As long as people can pay their bills with currency, as long as it is accepted as a means of payment, it serves the function of money.

Most money today is *bank money*—checking deposits in a bank or other financial institution. Checks are accepted in place of cash payment for many goods and services.

In recent years, there has been rapid innovation in developing different ways of using money. Many financial institutions will now link a checking account to a savings account or even to a stock portfolio, allowing customers to write checks on the value of their stocks. With the rise of the Internet, people can pay their bills electronically and charge purchases over the Internet. The next horizon is electronic money, or e-money, which puts purchasing power on a card with an embedded computer chip.

Components of the Money Supply

Let us now look more carefully at the different kinds of money, focusing on the United States. The major *monetary aggregates* are the quantitative measures of the supply of money. They are known today as M_1 and M_2, and you can read about their week-to-week movements in the newspaper. Here we will provide the exact definitions as of 2003.

Narrow (Transactions) Money. One important and closely watched measure of money is *narrow,* or *transactions, money,* denoted by M_1, which consists of items that are actually used for transactions. The following are the components of M_1:

- *Coins.* M_1 includes coins not held by banks.
- *Paper currency.* More significant is paper currency. Most of us know little more about a $1 or $5 bill than that it is inscribed with the picture of an American statesman, that it bears some official signatures, and that each has a numeral showing its face value. Examine a $10 bill or some other paper bill. You will find that it says "Federal Reserve Note." But what "backs" our paper currency? Many years ago, paper money was backed by gold or silver. There is no such pretense today. Today, all U.S. coins and paper currency are *fiat money.* This term signifies something declared to be money by the government even if it has no value.

Paper currency and coins are *legal tender,* which must be accepted for all debts, public and private. Coins and paper currency (the sum known as *currency*) add up to almost one-half of total narrow money, M_1.

- *Checking accounts.* There is a third component of narrow money—checking deposits or bank money. These are funds, deposited in banks and other financial institutions, on which you can write checks. They are technically known as "demand deposits and other checkable deposits." If I have $1000 in my checking account at the Albuquerque National Bank, that deposit can be regarded as money. Why? For the simple reason that I can pay for purchases with checks drawn on it. The deposit is like any other medium of exchange.[2] Possessing the essential properties of money, bank checking-account deposits are counted as narrow money, as part of M_1.

Table 25-3 shows the dollar values of the different components of narrow money, M_1.

Broad Money. Although M_1 is, strictly speaking, the most appropriate measure of money as a means of payment, a second closely watched aggregate is *broad money,* or M_2. Sometimes called *near-money,* M_2 includes M_1 as well as other close substitutes for M_1. More precisely, the components of M_2 are:

---

[2] Students are often surprised to learn that credit cards are not money. The reason is that a credit card is actually an easy (but not cheap!) way to *borrow* money. When paying with a credit card, you are actually promising to pay the credit-card company—with money—at a later date.

Kinds of money	Billions of Dollars		
	1959	1973	2003
Currency (outside of financial institutions)	28.8	61.7	640.0
Demand deposits (excludes government deposits and certain foreign deposits)	110.8	209.3	305.7
Other checkable deposits	0.0	0.4	289.0
Total narrow (or transactions) money (M_1)	140.0	271.4	1,234.7
Savings accounts, small time deposits, and other	158.8	300.2	3,448.3
Total broad money (M_2)	298.8	571.6	4,683.0

TABLE 25-3. Components of the Money Supply of the United States

Two widely used definitions of the money supply are narrow money (M_1) and broad money (M_2). M_1 consists of currency and checking accounts. M_2 adds to these certain "near-monies" such as savings accounts and time deposits.

Source: Federal Reserve Board, available at www.federalreserve.gov/releases/.

- M_1
- Savings accounts and small time deposits
- Retail money market mutual funds

These are near-money because they are safe (some are guaranteed by the government) and can be quickly converted into M_1.

Why are these not narrow money? Because they cannot be used as means of exchange for all purchases. You cannot go into a store and pay with funds from your savings account.

There are many other technical definitions of money that are used by specialists in monetary economics. But for our purposes, we need master only the two major definitions of money.

Money is anything that serves as a commonly accepted medium of exchange. The most important concept is **narrow (transactions) money,** or M_1, which is the sum of coins and paper currency in circulation outside the banks, plus checkable deposits. Another important monetary aggregate is **broad money** (called M_2), which equals M_1 plus near-monies such as savings and time deposits and money market mutual funds.

THE DEMAND FOR MONEY

The demand for money is different from the demand for ice cream or movies. Money is not desired for its own sake; you cannot eat nickels, and we seldom hang $100 bills on the wall for the artistic quality of their engraving. Rather, we demand money because it serves us indirectly, as a lubricant to trade and exchange.

Money's Functions

Before we analyze the demand for money, let's note money's functions:

- The central function emphasized here is that money serves as a *medium of exchange.* Without money, we would be constantly roving around looking for someone to barter with. Money's value is often shown when the monetary system malfunctions. After Russia abandoned its central-planning system in the early 1990s, for example, people spent hours waiting in line for goods and tried to get dollars or other foreign currencies because the ruble had ceased to function as an acceptable means of exchange.
- Money is also used as the *unit of account,* the unit by which we measure the value of things. Just as we measure weight in kilograms, we measure value in money. The use of a common unit of account simplifies economic life enormously.
- Money is sometimes used as a *store of value.* In comparison with risky assets like stocks or real estate or gold, money is relatively riskless. In earlier days, people held currency as a safe form of wealth. Today, when people seek a safe haven for

their wealth, the vast preponderance of their wealth is held in non-monetary assets, such as savings accounts, stocks, bonds, and real estate.

The Costs of Holding Money

These three functions of money are extremely important to people, so important that individuals are willing to incur a cost to hold currency or low-yielding checking accounts. What is the *opportunity cost of holding money?* It is the sacrifice of interest that you must incur by holding money rather than another asset.

Say that you put $1000 in a savings account at the beginning of 2000; you would earn about 5 percent interest and would have $1050 at the end of 2000. This represents a 5 percent nominal interest rate. By contrast, suppose that you had left your $1000 in currency rather than in the savings account. You would end up with only $1000, for currency pays no interest. The opportunity cost of holding money as currency in this case would be $50.

The cost of holding money is the interest foregone from not holding other assets.

Two Sources of Money Demand

Transactions Demand for Money. People need money primarily because their incomes and expenditures do not come at the same time. For example, I might be paid on the last day of the month, but I buy food, newspapers, gasoline, and clothing throughout the month. The need to have money to pay for purchases, or transactions, of goods, services, and other items constitutes the *transactions demand for money.*

For example, suppose that a family that earns $3000 per month, keeps it in money, and spends it evenly during the month. Calculation will show that the family holds $1500 on average in money balances.

This example can help us see how the demand for money responds to different economic influences. If all prices and incomes double, the nominal demand for M doubles. Thus the transactions demand for money doubles if nominal GDP doubles with no change in real GDP or other real variables.

How does the demand for money vary with interest rates? As interest rates rise, the family might say, "Let's put only half of our money in the checking account at the beginning of the month and put the

other half in a savings account earning 8 percent per annum. Then on day 15, we'll take that $1500 out of the savings account and put it in our checking account to pay the next 2 weeks' bills."

This means that as interest rates rose and the family decided to put half its earnings in a savings account, the average money balance of our family fell from $1500 to $750. This shows how money holdings (or the demand for money) may be sensitive to interest rates: *other things equal, as interest rates rise, the quantity of money demanded declines.*

Asset Demand. In addition to its use for transactions needs, money is sometimes a store of value. The role of money as an investment is addressed by **financial economics,** which analyzes how investors should invest their funds to attain their objectives in the best possible manner.

In general, a well-constructed portfolio (or combination of assets) will contain low-risk investments as well as riskier ventures. But it is not generally advisable to hold M_1 (currency or checking deposits) as one of these nest eggs. The reason is that other assets (such as government securities) are just as safe as M_1 and have higher interest rates. In the language of finance, narrow money is a "dominated" asset because other assets are equally safe but have higher yields. However, it might be sensible to hold your assets in M_2 (say, in savings accounts) because these are high-yielding safe assets.

We summarize our findings on the demand for money as follows:

The major reason we own narrow money (M_1) is the transactions demand—that is, because we need a generally acceptable medium of exchange to buy goods and pay our bills. As our incomes rise the dollar value of the goods we buy goes up, and we therefore need more money for transactions, raising our demand for money.

The transactions demand for M will be sensitive to the cost of holding money. When interest rates on alternative assets rise relative to the interest rate on money, people and businesses tend to reduce their money holdings.

In addition, people sometimes hold money as an asset or store of value. But modern finance theory shows that narrow money (M_1) should generally not be part of a well-designed portfolio.

C. BANKING AND THE SUPPLY OF MONEY

We described the functions of financial intermediaries above. Of these intermediaries, the most important are commercial banks, which provide checking accounts to the public. Banks are fundamentally businesses that are organized to earn profits for their owners. A commercial bank is a relatively simple business concern. It provides certain services for customers and in return receives payments from them.

Table 25-4 shows the consolidated balance sheet of all U.S. commercial banks. A *balance sheet* is a statement of a firm's financial position at a point in time. It lists *assets* (items that a firm owns) and *liabilities* (items the firm owes). The difference between assets and liabilities is called *net worth*. Each entry in a balance sheet is valued at its actual market value or its historical cost.*

Except for minor rearrangements, a bank's balance sheet looks much like the balance sheet of any business. The unique feature of the bank balance sheet is an asset called **reserves.** These are cash on hand or funds deposited by the bank with the central bank. Some reserves are held for day-to-day business needs, but most serve to meet legal reserve requirements.

---

* Balance sheets, assets, and liabilities are extensively discussed in Chapter 7.

How Banks Developed from Goldsmith Establishments

Commercial banking began in England with the goldsmiths, who developed the practice of storing people's gold and valuables for safekeeping. At first, such establishments were simply like baggage checkrooms or warehouses. Depositors left gold for safekeeping and were given a receipt. Later they presented their receipt, paid a small fee for the safekeeping, and got back their gold.

What would the balance sheet of a typical goldsmith establishment look like? Perhaps like Table 25-5. We assume that First Goldsmith Bank no longer hammers gold bars but is occupied solely with storing people's money for safekeeping. A total of $1 million has been deposited in its vaults, and this whole sum is held as a cash asset (this is the item "Reserves" in the balance sheet). To balance this asset, there is a demand deposit of the same amount. Cash reserves are therefore 100 percent of deposits.

If the Goldsmith Bank were here today, its demand deposits would be part of the money supply; they would be "bank money." However, the bank money just offsets the amount of ordinary money (gold or currency) placed in the bank's safe and withdrawn from active circulation. No money creation has taken place. The process would be of no more interest than if the public decided to convert nickels into dimes. *A 100 percent reserve banking system has a neutral effect on money and the macroeconomy because it has no effect on the money supply.*

Balance Sheet of All Commercial Banking Institutions, 2003 (billions of dollars)			
Assets		**Liabilities**	
Reserves	41	Checking deposits	614
Loans	4,206	Savings and time deposits	3,964
Investments and securities	1,742		
Other assets	1,082	Other liabilities and net worth	2,493
Total	7,071	Total	7,071

TABLE 25-4. Reserves and Checking Deposits Are Major Balance Sheet Entries of Commercial Banks

Reserves and checking deposits are key to bank creation of money. Checking accounts are payable on demand and thus can be used quickly when customers write checks. Reserves are held primarily to meet legal requirements, not to provide against possible unexpected withdrawals.

Source: Federal Reserve Board, available at www.federalreserve.gov/releases/.

Goldsmith Balance Sheet			
Assets		**Liabilities**	
Reserves	+$1,000,000	Demand deposits	+$1,000,000
Total	+$1,000,000	Total	+$1,000,000

TABLE 25-5. First Goldsmith Bank Held 100 Percent Cash Reserves against Demand Deposits

In a primitive banking system, with 100 percent backing of deposits, no creation of money out of reserves is possible.

MODERN FRACTIONAL-RESERVE BANKING

Today's banks definitely do not keep 100 percent of deposits as reserves. Instead, in the United States, they are required by law and Federal Reserve regulation to keep a fixed fraction (today, 10 percent) of their checking deposits, or bank money, as reserves. We will discuss the exact details of these regulations in the next chapter. What is important for this chapter is to see how fractional-reserve banks can create money.

THE PROCESS OF DEPOSIT CREATION

In our simplified discussion of goldsmith banks, we suggested that banks turn reserves into bank money. There are, in fact, two steps in the process:

- The central bank determines the quantity of reserves of the banking system. The detailed process by which the central bank does this is discussed in the next chapter.
- Using those reserves as an input, the banking system transforms them into a much larger amount of bank money. The currency plus this bank money is the money supply, M_1. This process is called the *multiple expansion of bank deposits*.

How Deposits Are Created: First-Generation Banks

Let us consider what happens when new reserves are injected into the banking system. Assume that the Federal Reserve buys a $1000 government bond from Ms. Bondholder, and she deposits the $1000 in her checking account at Bank 1.

The change in the balance sheet of Bank 1, as far as the new demand deposit is concerned, is shown in Table 25-6(a).[3] When Ms. Bondholder made the deposit, $1000 of bank money, or checking deposits, was created. Now, if the bank were to keep 100 percent of deposits in reserves, as did the old goldsmiths, no extra money would be created from the new deposit of $1000. The depositor's $1000 checking deposit would just match the $1000 of reserves. But modern banks do not keep 100 percent reserves for their deposits. Because banks are assumed to keep a reserve requirement of 10 percent, Bank 1 must set aside as reserves $100 of the $1000 deposit.

---

[3] For simplicity, our tables will show only the *changes* in balance sheet items, and we use reserve ratios of 10 percent. Note that when bankers refer to their loans and investments, by "investments" they mean their holdings of bonds and other financial assets. They don't mean what economists mean by "investment," which is capital formation.

Assets		**Liabilities**	
Reserves	+$1,000	Deposits	+$1,000
Total	+$1,000	Total	+$1,000

TABLE 25-6(a). Bank 1 in Initial Position

Multiple-bank deposit creation is a story with many successive stages. At the start, $1000 of newly created reserves are deposited in the original, first-generation bank.

Assets		Liabilities	
Reserves	+$ 100	Deposits	+$1,000
Loans and investments	+ 900		
Total	+$1,000	Total	+$1,000

TABLE 25-6(b). Bank 1 in Final Position

A profit-maximizing bank will lend or invest any excess reserves. Thus Bank 1 has kept only $100 of the original cash deposit (as required reserves) and has lent or invested the other $900.

Assets		Liabilities	
Reserves	+$900	Deposits	+$900
Total	+$900	Total	+$900

TABLE 25-6(c). Second-Generation Banks in Initial Position

Assets		Liabilities	
Reserves	+$ 90	Deposits	+$900
Loans and investments	+ 810		
Total	+$900	Total	+$900

TABLE 25-6(d). Final Position of Second-Generation Banks

Next, the money lent out by Bank 1 soon goes to second-generation banks, which in turn lend out nine-tenths of it.

But Bank 1 now has $900 more in reserves than it needs to meet the reserve requirement. Because reserves earn no interest, our profit-minded bank will lend or invest the excess $900. The loan might be for a car, or the investment might be a purchase of a Treasury bond. Let's say the bank makes a loan. The person who borrows the money takes the $900 (in cash or check) and deposits it in her account in another bank. Very quickly, then, the $900 will be paid out by Bank 1.

After it has lent or invested $900, Bank 1's legal reserves are just enough to meet its legal reserve requirement. The balance sheet of Bank 1, after it has made all possible loans or investments (but still meets its reserve requirement), is shown in Table 25-6(b).

But if we calculate the amount of money, we are in for a big surprise. In addition to the original $1000 of deposits shown on the right of Table 25-6(b), there is $900 of demand deposits in another account (i.e., in the checking account of the person who got the $900). Hence, the total amount of M is now $1900. *Bank 1's activity has created $900 of new money.*

Chain Repercussions on Other Banks

After the $900 created by Bank 1 leaves the bank, it will soon be deposited in another bank, and at that point it starts up a chain of expansion whereby still more bank money is created.

To see what happens to the $900, let's call all the banks that receive the $900 *second-generation banks* (or Bank 2). Their combined balance sheets now appear as shown in Table 25-6(c). To these banks, the dollars deposited function just like our original $1000 deposit. These banks do not care that they are second in a chain of deposits. Their only concern is that they are holding too much nonearning cash, or excess reserves. Only one-tenth of $900, or $90, is legally needed against the $900 deposit. They will use the other nine-tenths to acquire $810 worth of loans and investments. Their balance sheets will soon reach the equilibrium in Table 25-6(d).

At this point, the original $1000 taken out of hand-to-hand circulation has produced a total of

$2710 (= $1900 + $810) of money. The total of M has increased, and the process continues.

The $810 spent by the second-generation banks in acquiring loans and investments will go to a new set of banks called *third-generation banks*. You can create the balance sheets (initial and final) for third-generation banks. Eventually, the third-generation banks will lend out their excess reserves and will thereby create $729 of new money. A fourth generation of banks will clearly end up with nine-tenths of $810 in deposits, or $729, and so on.

Final System Equilibrium

Now let's sum up all the money creation: $1000 + $900 + $810 + $729 + ⋯? Table 25-7 shows that the complete effect of the chain of money creation is $10,000. We can get the answer by arithmetic, by common sense, and by elementary algebra.

Common sense tells us that the process of deposit creation must come to an end only when every bank in the system has reserves equal to 10 percent of deposits. In all our examples, no cash reserves ever leaked out of the banking system; the money simply went from one set of banks to another set of banks. The banking system will reach equilibrium when the $1000 of new reserves is all used up as required reserves on new deposits. In other words, the final equilibrium of the banking system will be the point at which 10 percent of new deposits (D) equals the new reserves of $1000. What level of D satisfies this condition? The answer is $D = $10,000.

We can also see the answer intuitively by looking at a consolidated balance sheet for all the generations of banks together. This is shown in Table 25-8. If total new deposits were less than $10,000, the 10 percent reserve ratio would not yet have been

Position of bank	New deposits ($)	New loans and investments ($)	New reserves ($)
Original banks	1,000.00	900.00	100.00
2nd-generation banks	900.00	810.00	90.00
3rd-generation banks	810.00	729.00	81.00
4th-generation banks	729.00	656.10	72.90
5th-generation banks	656.10	590.49	65.61
6th-generation banks	590.49	531.44	59.05
7th-generation banks	531.44	478.30	53.14
8th-generation banks	478.30	430.47	47.83
9th-generation banks	430.47	387.42	43.05
10th-generation banks	387.42	348.68	38.74
Sum of first 10 generations of banks	6,513.22	5,861.90	651.32
⋮	⋮	⋮	⋮
Sum of remaining generations of banks	3,486.78	3,138.10	348.68
Total for banking system as a whole	10,000.00	9,000.00	1,000.00

TABLE 25-7. Finally, through This Long Chain, All Banks Create New Deposits of 10 Times New Reserves

The actions of all banks together produce the multiple expansion of reserves into M. The final equilibrium is reached when every dollar of original new reserves supports $10 of demand deposits. Note that in every generation each bank has "created" new money in the following sense: It ends up with a final bank deposit 10 times the reserve it finally retains. (Make sure you understand why the number is 10 times.)

Assets		Liabilities	
Reserves	+$ 1,000	Deposits	+$10,000
Loans and investment	+ 9,000		
Total	+$10,000	Total	+$10,000

TABLE 25-8. Consolidated Balance Sheet Showing Final Position of All Banks

All banks together ultimately increase deposits and M by a multiple of the original injection of reserves.

reached, and full equilibrium would not yet have been attained.[4]

Figure 25-4 gives a schematic overview of the process. It shows how $1 of new deposits or reserves, at the upper left, is transformed into $10 of total deposits, or bank money, on the right. Inside the rectangle, which represents the banking system as a whole, Bank 1 receives the initial new deposit. The rust arrows circulating around show how reserves are redistributed, while the black lines show new deposits. Though the chain has many links, each is a dwindling fraction and the whole effect does add up to the 10-to-1 total.

The Money-Supply Multiplier. We see that there is a new kind of multiplier operating on reserves. For every additional dollar in reserves provided to the banking system, banks eventually create $10 of additional deposits or bank money.

We described the expenditure multiplier as the ratio of the change in output to new investment or other spending. The money-supply multiplier is the ratio of the new money created to the change in reserves. Note that the arithmetic of M expansion is similar to that of the expenditure multiplier, *but don't confuse the two because they multiply different things.* The amplification here is from the stock of

reserves to the stock of total M; it has nothing to do with the extra output induced by investment or money.

The ratio of new checking deposits to the increase in reserves is called the money-supply multiplier. In the simple case analyzed here, the **money-supply multiplier** is defined as follows:

Money-supply multiplier

$$= \frac{\text{change of money}}{\text{change of reserves}}$$

$$= 10 = \frac{1}{0.1} = \frac{1}{\text{required reserve ratio}}$$

FIGURE 25-4. Multiple-Bank Expansion of Money

For each dollar of new reserves deposited in a bank, the system as a whole creates about $10 of bank money. The rust arrows in the box show that Bank 1 cannot do it alone. The money supply increases as reserves spread through the banking system.

---

[4] The algebraic solution can be shown as follows:

$$\$1000 + \$900 + \$810 + \cdots$$
$$= \$1000 \times [1 + \tfrac{9}{10} + (\tfrac{9}{10})^2 + (\tfrac{9}{10})^3 + \cdots]$$
$$= \$1000\left(\frac{1}{1 - \tfrac{9}{10}}\right) = \$1000 \times \frac{1}{0.1} = \$10,000$$

The money-supply multiplier summarizes the logic of how banks create money. The entire banking system can transform an initial increase in reserves into a multiplied amount of new deposits or bank money.

The process of deposit creation can also work in reverse when a drain in reserves reduces bank money. It is useful to reinforce your understanding of money creation by tracing in detail what happens when the Fed permanently destroys $2000 of reserves by selling a government bond to someone who withdraws cash from his checking account to pay for it. In the end, the withdrawal of $2000 of reserves from the banking system kills off $20,000 worth of deposits throughout the whole system.

The Contagion of Bank Panics

Fractional-reserve banking has great risks as well as great advantages. The fact that banks cover only a fraction of their deposits opens up the possibility of "bank panics" or "a run on the banks." Remember that under fractional-reserve banking, a bank has on hand only a small portion of the money that it owes to its depositors. Ordinarily, that is no problem, since only a small number of people will want to withdraw their money at any one time.

But what if too many people want their money at once? Then we can have the feeding frenzy known as a *bank run*. As soon as one depositor has trouble getting his or her money immediately, the other depositors get scared that their money is also gone. Driven by fear, depositors descend on the bank like a horde of hungry animals, demanding all of their money right away. Not even healthy banks can withstand this sort of mass demand for deposits. The United States was hit with major bank panics in 1857, 1895, and then in 1907. The bank panics of the 1930s, during the Great Depression, pushed more than 9000 banks into failure.

In the modern financial system, bank runs are rare and less dangerous, for two reasons. One reason is that the federal government ensures that all but the largest depositors will get their money back no matter what happens to the bank. Depositors therefore need not rush down to their bank at the first sign of trouble. In addition, the Federal Reserve takes an active role as the "lender of last resort," providing funds to healthy banks with temporary liquidity problems and making sure sick banks get liquidated in an orderly way.

Two Qualifications to Deposit Creation

The actual financial system is more complicated than our simple banking example. We have shown that $1000 of new reserves put into a bank will ultimately result in an increase of $10,000 of bank deposits. This example assumed that all the new money remained as checking deposits in the banking system and that no bank would have excess reserves. Let us see what would happen if some money leaked into circulation or if some banks had excess reserves.

Leakage into Hand-to-Hand Circulation. It is possible that, somewhere along the chain of deposit expansion, an individual who receives a check will not leave the proceeds in a bank checking account. He might put some cash in a cookie jar. Or some of the $1000 might be sent to a cousin in Mexico and used there instead of in the United States.

The effects of such withdrawals on our analysis are simple. When $1000 stayed in the banking system, $10,000 of new deposits was created. If $100 were to leak into circulation outside the banks and only $900 of new reserves were to remain in the banking system, the new checking deposits created would be $9000 ($900 × 10). Therefore, the 10-to-1 amplification would occur only if no reserves leaked from banks.

Possible Excess Reserves. Our analysis proceeded on the assumption that the commercial banks follow their legal reserve requirements to the letter. What would happen if the bank decided to keep rather than lend the new reserves? Then the whole process of multiple deposit creation would stop dead, with no expansion of deposits at all.

This decision would normally make no sense for the bank. Because the bank earns no interest on reserves, it would lose interest payments on the $900. So as long as the interest rate on investments is above the interest rate on reserves (set at zero), banks have a strong incentive to avoid holding any excess reserves.

In certain situations, it might be reasonable to have excess reserves. During the Great Depression, interest rates fell to 0.1 percent per year, so banks during this period often held significant excess reserves. In 1999, short-term interest rates were essentially zero in Japan, and banks had significant quantities of excess reserves. In late 2003, as short-term interest rates in the United States fell to the lowest levels since the Great Depression, excess reserves began to increase. In such pathological situations, central-bank control of the money supply becomes much more difficult.

D. THE STOCK MARKET

We close this chapter with a tour through one of the most exciting parts of a capitalist system—the stock market. A **stock market** is a place where the shares in publicly owned companies, the titles to business firms, are bought and sold. In 2003, the value of these titles was estimated at $12 trillion in the United States. Sales in a single year might total more than $10 trillion. The stock market is the hub of our corporate economy.

The New York Stock Exchange is America's main stock market, listing more than a thousand securities. Another important market is the NASDAQ, which had a meteoric rise and subsequent collapse in stock prices after 2000. Every large financial center has a stock exchange. Major ones are located in Tokyo, London, Frankfurt, Hong Kong, Toronto, Zurich, and, of course, New York.

Risk and Return on Different Assets

Before discussing major issues in stock market analysis, we need to introduce some elementary concepts in financial economics. We noted earlier in this chapter that assets have different characteristics. Two important characteristics are the rate of return and the risk.

The *rate of return* is the total dollar gain from a security (measured as a percent of the price at the beginning of the period). For savings accounts and short-term bonds, the return would be the interest rate. For most other assets, the return combines an income (like dividends) with a *capital gain* or *loss*, which represents the increase or decrease in the value of the asset.

We can illustrate the rate of return on stocks using data on stocks. (For this example, we ignore taxes and commissions.) Say that you bought a representative portfolio of $10,000 worth of stocks in U.S. companies in December 1997. During 1998, your fund paid dividends of $256. Moreover, because 1998 was an unusually good year for stocks, your fund rose in value to $13,500 at the end of the year, for a capital

gain of 35 percent. Your total return was therefore $(256 + 3500)/10,000 = 37.6$ percent for 1998.

But before you get too excited about these fantastic gains, be warned that in the period after 2000, those who invested in stocks had major losses. For example, if you decided to invest in a broad array of stocks in October 2001, you would have suffered a 27 percent *loss* over the next year.

The fact that some assets have predictable rates of return while others are quite risky leads to the next important characteristic of investments. **Risk** refers to the variability of the returns on an investment. If I buy a 1-year Treasury bond with a 6 percent return, the bond is a riskless investment because I am sure to get my dollar return. On the other hand, if I buy $10,000 of stocks, I am uncertain about their year-end value.

Economists often measure risk as the standard deviation of returns; this is a measure of dispersion whose range encompasses about two-thirds of the variation.[5] For example, from 1926 to 2003, common stocks had an annual standard deviation of return of 22 percent and an average annual return of 11 percent. This normally implies that the return was between −10 percent and +33 percent two-thirds of the time. The largest return was 54 percent in 1933, and the largest loss was −43 percent in 1931.

Individuals generally prefer higher return, but they also prefer lower risk because they are *risk-averse*. This means that they must be rewarded by higher returns to induce them to hold investments with higher risks. We would not be surprised, therefore, to learn that over the long run safe investments like bonds have lower average returns than risky investments like stocks.

Table 25-2 on page 508 showed the historical returns or interest rates on a number of important investments. We show the most important assets in the *risk-return diagram* in Figure 25-5 on the next page. This diagram shows the average real

---

[5] The standard deviation is a measure of variability that can be found in any elementary statistics text. It is roughly equal to the average deviation of a series from its mean. The precise definition of standard deviation is the square root of the squared deviations of a variable from its mean. As an example, if a variable takes the values of 1, 3, 1, 3, the mean or expected value is 2 while the standard deviation is 1.

FIGURE 25-5. Risk and Return on Major Investments, 1926–1998

Investments vary in their average returns and riskiness. Bonds tend to be safe, while stocks have much higher returns but face higher risks. This diagram shows the *historical* risk and return on different financial assets. Depending upon market sentiments, the *expected* risk and return may differ markedly from the historical experience.

Source: Ibbotson Associates, *Stocks, Bonds, Bills, and Inflation: 1999 Yearbook* (Ibbotson Associates, Chicago, 1999).

(or inflation-corrected) return on the vertical axis and the historical risk (measured as a standard deviation) on the horizontal axis. Note the positive relationship between risk and return.

Bubbles and Crashes

The history of finance is one of the most exciting parts of economics. Sometimes, sound judgments get put aside as markets engage in frenzies of speculation, often followed by moods of pessimism and falling prices.

Investors are sometimes divided into those who invest on firm foundations and those who try to outguess the market psychology. The firm-foundation approach holds that assets should be valued on the basis of their intrinsic value. For common stocks, the intrinsic value is the expected present value of the dividends. If a stock has a constant dividend of $2 per year and the appropriate interest rate with which to discount dividends is 5 percent per year, the intrinsic value would be $2/.05 = $40 per share. The firm-foundation approach is the slow but safe way of getting rich.

Impatient souls might share the view of Keynes, who argued that investors are more likely to worry about market psychology and to speculate on the future value of assets rather than wait patiently for stocks to prove their intrinsic value. He argued, "It is not sensible to pay 25 for an investment which is worth 30, if you also believe that the market will value it at 20 three months hence." The market psychologist tries to guess what the average investor thinks, which requires considering what the average investor thinks about the average investor, and so on, ad infinitum.

When a psychological frenzy seizes the market, it can result in speculative bubbles and crashes. A *speculative bubble* occurs when prices rise because people think they are going to rise in the future—it is the reverse of Keynes's just-cited dictum. A piece of land may be worth only $1000, but if you see a land-price boom driving prices up 50 percent each year, you might buy it for $2000 hoping you can sell it to someone else next year for $3000.

A speculative bubble fulfills its own promises for a while. If people buy because they think stocks will rise, their act of buying sends up the price of stocks. This causes other people to buy even more and sends the dizzy dance off on another round. But, unlike people who play cards or dice, no one apparently loses what the winners gain. Of course, the prizes are all on paper and would disappear if everyone tried to cash them in. But why should anyone want to sell such lucrative securities? Prices rise because of hopes and dreams, not because the profits and dividends of companies are soaring.

History is marked by bubbles in which speculative prices were driven up far beyond the intrinsic value of the asset. In seventeenth-century Holland, a tulip mania drove tulip prices to levels higher than the price of a house. In the eighteenth century, the stock of the South Sea Company rose to fantastic levels on empty promises that the firm would enrich its stockholders. In more recent times, similar bubbles have been found in biotechnology, Japanese land, "emerging markets," and a vacuum-cleaning company called ZZZZ Best, whose business was laundering money for the Mafia.

The most famous bubble of them all occurred in the American stock market in the 1920s. The "roaring twenties" saw a fabulous stock market boom, when everyone bought and sold stocks. Most purchases in this wild bull market were on margin. This means that a buyer of $10,000 worth of stocks put up only part of the price in cash and borrowed the difference, pledging the newly bought stocks as collateral for the purchase. What did it matter that you had to pay the broker 6, 10, or 15 percent per year on the borrowing when Auburn Motors or Bethlehem Steel might jump 10 percent in value overnight?

Speculative bubbles always produce crashes and sometimes lead to economic panics. The speculation of the 1920s was soon followed by the 1929 panic and crash. This event ushered in the long and painful Great Depression of the 1930s. By the trough of the Depression in 1933, the market had declined 85 percent.

Trends in the stock market are tracked using *stock-price indexes*, which are weighted averages of the prices of a basket of company stocks. Commonly followed averages include the Dow-Jones Industrial Average (DJIA) of 30 large companies and Standard and Poor's index of 500 companies (the "S&P 500"), which is a weighted average of the stock prices of the 500 largest American corporations.

Figure 25-6 on page 524 shows the history of the Standard and Poor's 500 price index over the last century. The lower curve shows the nominal stock-price average, which records the actual average during a particular month. The upper line shows the real price of stocks; this equals the nominal price divided by an index of consumer prices, where the curve is indexed to equal 100 in 2003. The straight lines (in logarithmic terms) show the average growth rates from 1900 to 2003. The average growth rate of stocks was 5 percent per year in dollar terms but only 1.8 percent per year after correcting for inflation.

The 1990s were yet another period of buoyant economic performance and booming stock prices. The major stock-price indexes rose by more than 350 percent over this period. Internet stocks became the darling of investors and sold at price-earnings ratios of more than 100 while traditional stocks sold for price-earning ratios of 20 or 30. Federal Reserve chairman Alan Greenspan cautioned against "irrational exuberance"; graybeards noted the parallel between the infatuation with the Internet and earlier disastrous investments in tulips or Florida real estate; Yale economist Robert Shiller published a best-selling book warning of an overvalued stock market pushed ever higher by unrealistic herdlike behavior. Yet investors ignored these financial Cassandras and plunged ahead.

But 20 percent annual growth rates could not go on forever. The Internet bubble came crashing down in early 2000. The NASDAQ index, which contains most of the speculative new-economy firms, lost 75 percent of its value in less than 2 years. The darlings of 1999 were the wallflowers 2 years later. The value of stocks declined by $7 trillion over a short period. For those who lost a fortune, it was little consolation that they had not enjoyed a fortune at the beginning of the speculative surge.

Where will it all end? Is there a crystal ball that will foretell the movement of stock prices? This is the subject of modern finance theory.

Efficient Markets and the Random Walk

Economists and finance professors have long studied prices in speculative markets such as the stock market or the foreign exchange market. One important hypothesis is that speculative markets tend to be "efficient." This finding has stirred great controversy in the economics profession and with financial analysts.

FIGURE 25-6. The Only Guarantee about Stock Prices Is That They Will Fluctuate

The Standard and Poor's index (the S&P 500) shown here tracks the value-weighted average of the stock prices of the 500 largest American companies. Stock prices in nominal terms are shown in the bottom line; these averaged a growth of 5 percent per year from 1900 to 2003.

The top line shows the "real" S&P 500, which is the S&P 500 corrected for movements in the consumer price index. This rose only 1.8 percent per year on average.

Source: Standard and Poor, Bureau of Labor Statistics.

What is the essence of the **efficient-market theory?** A summary statement is the following:

> Securities markets are extremely efficient in absorbing information about individual stocks and about the stock market as a whole. When new information arrives, the news is quickly incorporated into stock prices. Systems which attempt to forecast prices on the basis of the past or of fundamentals cannot produce higher returns greater than those that could be obtained by holding a randomly selected portfolio of individual stocks of comparable risk.[6]

A colorful story illustrates the basic message. A finance professor and a student are walking across the campus when they see what looks like a $100 bill lying on the ground. The professor tells the student, "Don't bother to pick it up. If it were really a $100 bill, it wouldn't be there." In other words, you can't get rich simply by bending down on a public thoroughfare!

This paradoxical view has been generally confirmed in hundreds of studies over the last half century. Their lesson is not that you will never become rich by following a rule or formula but that, on average, such rules do not outperform a diversified portfolio of stocks.

Rationale for the Efficient-Market View. Finance theorists have spent many years analyzing stock and bond

---

[6] This definition is adopted from Malkiel's 2003 article; see Further Readings. Note that "efficiency" is used differently in finance theory than in other parts of economics. Here, "efficiency" means that information is quickly absorbed, not that resources produce the maximal outputs.

markets in order to understand why well-functioning financial markets rule out persistent excess profits. The theory of efficient markets explains this.

An **efficient financial market** is one where all new information is quickly understood by market participants and becomes immediately incorporated into market prices. For example, say that Lazy-T Oil Company has just struck oil in the Gulf of Alaska. This event is announced at 11:30 A.M. on Tuesday. When will the price of Lazy-T's shares rise? The efficient-market theory holds that market participants will react at once, bidding the price of Lazy-T up by the correct amount. In short, at every point in time, markets have already digested and included in stock prices or corn prices or other speculative prices all the latest available information.

The theory of efficient markets holds that market prices contain all available information. It is not possible to make profits by acting on old information or at patterns of past price changes. Returns on stocks will be primarily determined by their riskiness relative to the market.

A Random Walk. The efficient-market view provides an important way of analyzing price movements in organized markets. Under this approach, the price movements of stocks should look highly erratic, like a random walk, when charted over a period of time.

A price follows a **random walk** when its movements over time are completely unpredictable. For example, toss a coin for heads or tails. Call a head "plus 1" and a tail "minus 1." Then keep track of the running score of 100 coin tosses. Draw it on graph paper. This curve is a random walk. Now, for comparison, also graph 100 days' movement of Microsoft stock and of Standard and Poor's 500 index. Note how similar all three figures appear.

Why do speculative prices resemble a random walk? Economists, on reflection, have arrived at the following truths: In an efficient market all predictable things have already been built into the price. It is the arrival of *new* information that affects stock or commodity prices. Moreover, the news must be random and unpredictable (or else it would be predictable and therefore not truly news).

To summarize:

The efficient-market theory explains why movements in stock prices look so erratic. Prices respond to news, to surprises. But surprises are unpredictable events—like the flip of a coin or next month's rainstorm—that may move in any direction. Because stock prices move in response to erratic events, stock prices themselves move erratically, like a random walk.

Qualifications to the Efficient-Market View. Although the efficient-market view has been the canon of finance in economics and business, many believe that it is oversimplified and misleading. Here are some of the reservations:

1. Researchers have uncovered many "anomalies" in stock-price movements that lead to some predictability. For example, stocks with high dividends or earnings relative to prices appear to perform better in subsequent periods. Similarly, sharp upward or downward movements tend to be followed by "reversals" in movements. To some, these anomalies are persuasive indicators of market inefficiencies; to others, they simply reflect the tendency of analysts to mine the data looking for patterns that are in fact spurious correlations.
2. Economists who look at the historical record ask whether it is plausible that sharp movements in stock prices could actually reflect new information. Consider the 30 percent drop in stock prices that occurred from October 15 to October 19, 1987. Efficient-market theories imply that this drop was caused by economic events that depressed the expected present value of future corporate earnings. Critics of the efficient-market view argue that there was no news that could make a 30 percent difference in the value of stock prices over those 4 days. Efficient-market theorists fall silent before this criticism.
3. Finally, the efficient-market view applies to individual stocks but not necessarily to the market as a whole. There is persuasive evidence of long, self-reversing swings in stock market prices. Perhaps these swings reflect changes in the general mood of the financial community. We saw periods of an exhilarated mood in the 1920s and 1990s, while the 1930s, 1970s, and early 2000s indicated a depressed market mentality. Let us say that we believed that the whole stock market showed an "irrational exuberance" and was overvalued. What could we do? Short sales are expensive and hard to execute for the most overpriced stocks. We could not individually buy or sell enough stocks to overcome the entire national mood. So,

from a macroeconomic perspective, speculative markets can exhibit waves of pessimism or optimism without powerful economic forces moving in to correct these mood swings.

PERSONAL FINANCIAL STRATEGIES

While taking a course in economics is no guarantee of great wealth, the principles of modern finance can definitely help you invest your nest egg wisely and avoid the worst financial blunders. What lessons does economics teach about personal investment decisions? We have culled the following five rules from the wisdom of the best brains on the street:

Lesson 1: Know thy investments. The absolute bedrock of a sound investment strategy is to be realistic and prudent in your investment decisions. For important investments, study the materials and get expert advice. Be skeptical of approaches that claim to have found the quick route to success. You can't get rich by listening to your barber or consulting the stars (although, unbelievably, some financial advisers push astrology to their clients). Hunches work out to nothing in the long run. Moreover, the best brains on Wall Street do not, on average, beat the averages (Dow-Jones, Standard and Poor's, etc.).

Lesson 2: Diversify, diversify—that is the law of the prophets of finance. One of the major lessons of finance is the advantage of diversifying your investments. "Don't put all your eggs in one basket" is one way of expressing this rule. By putting funds in a number of different investments, you can continue to average a high yield while reducing the risk. Calculations show that by diversifying their wealth among a broad array of investments—different common stocks, conventional and inflation-indexed bonds, real estate, domestic and foreign securities—people can attain a good return while minimizing the downside risk on their investments.

Lesson 3: Consider common-stock index funds. Investors who want to invest in the stock market can achieve a good return with the least possible risk by holding a broadly diversified portfolio of common stocks. A good vehicle for diversifying is an *index fund*. This is a portfolio of the stocks of many companies, weighting each company in proportion to its market value and often tracking a major stock index like the S&P 500. One major advantage of index funds is that they have low expenses and turnover-induced taxes.

Lesson 4: Minimize unnecessary expenses and taxes. People often find that a substantial amount of their investment earnings is nibbled away by taxes or expenses. For example, some mutual funds charge a high initial fee when you purchase the fund. Others might charge a management fee of 1 or even 2 percent of assets each year. Additionally, heavily "managed" funds have high turnover and may lead to large taxes on capital gains. Day traders may find great enjoyment in lightning movements in and out, and they may strike it rich, but they *definitely* will pay heavy brokerage and investment charges. By choosing your investments carefully, you can avoid these unnecessary drains on your investment income.

Lesson 5: Match your investments with your risk preference. You can increase your expected return by picking riskier investments (see Figure 25-6). But always consider how much risk you can afford—financially *and psychologically.* As one sage put it, investments are a tradeoff between eating well and sleeping well. If you get insomnia worrying about the ups and downs of the market, you can maximize your sleep by keeping your assets in inflation-indexed U.S. Treasury bonds. But in the long run, you might be snoozing soundly on a cot! If you want to eat well and can tolerate disappointments, you might invest more heavily in stocks, including ones in foreign countries and emerging markets, and incorporate more volatile small companies into your portfolio—rather than concentrating on short-term bonds and bank deposits.

Such are the lessons of history and economics. If, after reading all this, you still want to try your hand in the stock market, do not be daunted. But take to heart the caution of one of America's great financiers, Bernard Baruch:

If you are ready to give up everything else—to study the whole history and background of the market and all the principal companies whose stocks are on the board as carefully as a medical student studies anatomy—if you can do all that, and, in addition, you have the cool nerves of a great gambler, the sixth sense of a kind of clairvoyant, and the courage of a lion, you have a ghost of a chance.

SUMMARY

A. The Modern Financial System

1. Financial systems in a modern economy transfer resources over space, time, and sectors. The flow of funds in financial systems occurs through financial markets and financial intermediaries. The purpose of an efficient financial system is to ensure that savings are most efficiently invested. The major functions of a financial system are to transfer resources, manage risk, subdivide and pool funds, and clear transactions.

2. Interest rates are the prices paid for borrowing funds; they are measured in dollars per year paid back per dollar borrowed or in percent per year. People willingly pay interest because borrowed funds allow them to buy goods and services to satisfy consumption needs or make profitable investments.

3. We observe a wide variety of interest rates. These rates vary because of many factors such as the term or maturity of loans, the risk and liquidity of investments, and the tax treatment of the interest.

4. Nominal or money interest rates generally rise during inflationary periods, reflecting the fact that the purchasing power of money declines as prices rise. To calculate the interest yield in terms of real goods and services, we use the real interest rate, which equals the nominal or money interest rate minus the rate of inflation.

B. The Special Case of Money

5. Money is anything that serves as a commonly accepted medium of exchange or means of payment. Money also functions as a unit of account and a store of value. Unlike other economic goods, money is valued because of social convention. We value money indirectly for what it buys, not for its direct utility.

6. Two definitions of money are commonly used today. The first is narrow (or transactions) money (M_1)—made up of currency and checking deposits. The second important concept is broad money (M_2), which includes M_1 plus highly liquid near-monies like savings accounts.

7. The demand for money differs from that for other commodities. Money is held for its indirect rather than its direct value. But money holdings are limited because keeping funds in money rather than in other assets has an opportunity cost: we sacrifice interest earnings when we hold money.

8. People hold money primarily because they need it to pay bills or buy goods. Such transactions needs are met by M_1 and are chiefly related to the value of transactions or to nominal GDP. Economic theory predicts,

and empirical studies confirm, that the demand for money is sensitive to interest rates; higher interest rates lead to a lower demand for M.

C. Banking and the Supply of Money

9. Banks are commercial enterprises that seek to earn profits for their owners. One major function of banks is to provide checking accounts to customers. Banks are legally required to keep reserves on their checking deposits. These can be in the form of cash on hand or of non-interest-bearing deposits at the Federal Reserve. For illustrative purposes, we examined a required reserve ratio of 10 percent. In this case, the banking system as a whole—together with public or private borrowers and the depositing public—creates bank money 10 to 1 for each new dollar of reserves created by the Fed and deposited somewhere in the banking system.

10. Each small bank is limited in its ability to expand its loans and investments. It cannot lend or invest more than it has received from depositors; it can lend only about nine-tenths as much. Although no bank alone can expand its reserves 10 to 1, the banking system as a whole can. Each bank receiving $1000 of new deposits lends nine-tenths of its newly acquired cash on loans and investments. If we follow through the successive groups of banks in the dwindling, never-ending chain, we find for the system as a whole new deposits of

$$\$1000 + \$900 + \$810 + \$729 + \cdots$$
$$= \$1000 \times [1 + \tfrac{9}{10} + (\tfrac{9}{10})^2 + (\tfrac{9}{10})^3 + \cdots]$$
$$= \$1000\left(\frac{1}{1 - \tfrac{9}{10}}\right) = \$1000\left(\frac{1}{0.1}\right)$$
$$= \$10,000$$

More generally:

$$\text{Money-supply multiplier} = \frac{\text{change in bank money}}{\text{change in reserves}}$$
$$= \frac{1}{\text{required reserve ratio}}$$

11. There may be some leakage of new cash reserves of the banking system into circulation outside the banks or as excess reserves of banks. Such leakages reduce the 10-to-1 formula given by the money-supply multiplier.

D. The Stock Market

12. Assets have different characteristics, the most important being the rate of return and the risk. The rate of return is the total dollar gain from a security. Risk

refers to the variability of the returns on an investment. Because people are risk-averse, they require higher returns to induce them to buy riskier assets.

13. Stock markets, of which the New York Stock Exchange is the most important, are places where titles of ownership to the largest companies are bought and sold. The history of stock prices is filled with violent gyrations, such as the Great Crash of 1929. Trends are tracked by the use of stock-price indexes, such as the Standard and Poor's 500 and the familiar Dow-Jones Industrial Average.

14. Modern economic theories of stock prices generally focus on the role of efficient markets. An efficient market is one in which all information is quickly absorbed

by speculators and is immediately built into market prices. In efficient markets, there are no easy profits; looking at yesterday's news or past patterns of prices or elections or business cycles will not help predict future price movements. Thus, in efficient markets, prices respond to surprises. Because surprises are inherently random, stock prices and other speculative prices move erratically, as in a random walk.

15. Plant the five rules of personal finance firmly in your long-term memory: (*a*) Know thy investments. (*b*) Diversify, diversify—that is the law of the prophets of finance. (*c*) Consider common-stock index funds. (*d*) Minimize unnecessary expenses and taxes. (*e*) Match your investments with your risk preference.

CONCEPTS FOR REVIEW

The Modern Financial System

financial system, financial markets, financial intermediaries
functions of financial system
major financial assets or instruments
interest rate, real and nominal
interest-rate premiums due to:
   maturity
   risk
   illiquidity
interest as opportunity cost of
   holding money
inflation-indexed bonds

The Special Case of Money

money, narrow money (M_1), broad money (M_2)
commodity M, paper M, bank M
motives for money demand:
   transactions demand
   asset demand

Banking and Money Supply

bank reserves (vault cash and deposits with the Fed)
fractional-reserve banking
money-supply multiplier

The Stock Market

common stocks (corporate equities)
efficient market, random walk of stock prices
index fund
five rules for personal investing

FURTHER READING AND WEBSITES

Further Reading

There are many entertaining histories of money. A good one is John Kenneth Galbraith, *Money, Whence It Came, Where It Went* (Houghton, Boston, 1975). You can pursue advanced topics in monetary theory in an intermediate textbook, such as Lawrence S. Ritter, William L. Silber, and Gregory F. Udell, *Principles of Money, Banking, and Financial Markets*, 10th ed. (Addison Wesley Longman, New York, 1999). The standard reference on U.S. monetary history is Milton Friedman and Anna Jacobson Schwartz, *Monetary History of the United States 1867–1960* (Princeton University Press, Princeton, N.J., 1963).

Modern capital and finance theory are very popular subjects, often covered in the macroeconomics part of an introductory course or in special courses. Good books on the subject are Burton Malkiel, *A Random Walk down Wall Street* (Norton, New York, 2000). A recent book surveying financial history and theory and arguing that the stock market was extraordinarily overvalued in the bull market of 1981–2000 is Robert Shiller, *Irrational Exuberance* (Princeton University Press, Princeton, N.J., 2000). A recent summary of evidence on the efficient-market theory by Burton Malkiel and Robert Shiller is found in *Journal of Economic Perspectives*, Winter 2003.

Websites

Basic data on money, interest rates, and monetary policy can be found at the website of the Federal Reserve, www.federalreserve.gov. Interesting articles on monetary policy can be found in the *Federal Reserve Bulletin* at www.federalreserve.gov/publications.htm. The Federal Reserve also collects survey data on wealth, available in the January 2000 issue of *Federal Reserve Bulletin* at the same site.

A good source for data on financial markets is finance.yahoo.com. If you are interested in the latest buzz on Internet stocks and hot topics in technology, go to www.techstocks.com or the Motley Fool at www.fool.com.

QUESTIONS FOR DISCUSSION

1. Define M_1 and M_2. What is included in M_1? What is in M_2 but not M_1? Relate each of the components of M_2 to the factors behind the demand for money.

2. Suppose that all banks kept 100 percent reserves. Construct new versions of Tables 25-6(a) and 25-7 to reflect $1000 of reserves added to a banking system that keeps 100 percent reserves. What is the net effect of a reserve addition to the money supply in this case? Do banks "create" money?

3. Suppose that banks hold 20 percent of deposits as reserves and that $200 of reserves is subtracted from the banking system. Redo Tables 25-6(a) through 25-8. What is the money-supply multiplier in this case?

4. What would be the effect on the demand for money (M_1) of each of the following (with other things held equal)?
   a. An increase in real GDP
   b. An increase in the price level
   c. A rise in the interest rate on savings accounts and Treasury securities
   d. A doubling of all prices, wages, and incomes (Can you calculate exactly the effect on the demand for money?)

5. The opportunity cost of holding money is equal to the yield on safe short-term assets (such as Treasury bills) minus the interest rate on money. What is the impact of the following on the opportunity cost of holding money in checking deposits?
   a. Before 1980 (when checking deposits had zero yield) market interest rates increased from 8 to 9 percent.
   b. In 1984 (when checking accounts had a maximum yield of 5 percent) interest rates increased (1) from 3 to 4 percent and (2) from 8 to 9 percent.
   c. In 1991 (when the interest rates on certain checking accounts were deregulated), market interest rates increased (1) from 3 to 4 percent and (2) from 8 to 9 percent.
   d. How would you expect the demand for money to respond to the change in market interest rates in each of the above cases if the elasticity of demand for money with respect to the opportunity cost of money is 0.2?

6. Interest-rate problems (which may require a calculator):
   a. You invest $2000 at 13.5 percent per year. What is your total balance after 6 months?
   b. Interest is said to be "compounded" when you earn interest on whatever interest has already been paid; most interest rates quoted today are compounded. If you invest $10,000 for 3 years at a compound annual interest rate of 10 percent, what is the total investment at the end of each year?
   c. Consider the following data: The consumer price index in 1977 was 60.6, and in 1981 it was 90.9. Interest rates on government securities in 1978 through 1981 (in percent per year) were 7.2, 10.0, 11.5, and 14.0. Calculate the average nominal and real interest rates for the 4-year period 1978–1981.
   d. Treasury bills (T-bills) are usually sold on a discounted basis; that is, a 90-day T-bill for $10,000 would sell today at a price such that collecting $10,000 at maturity would produce the market interest rate. If the market interest rate is 6.6 percent per year, what would be the price on a 90-day $10,000 T-bill?

7. Present-value questions:
   a. Consider the 1-year bond in the discussion of present value. Calculate the present value of the bond if the interest rate is 1, 5, and 20 percent.
   b. What is the value of a perpetuity yielding $16 per year at interest rates of 1, 5, 10, and 20 percent per year?
   c. Compare the answers to **a** and **b**. Which asset is more sensitive to interest-rate changes? Quantify the difference.

8. Explain whether you think that each of the following should be counted as part of the narrow money supply (M_1) for the United States: savings accounts, subway tokens, postage stamps, credit cards, and $20 bills used by Russians in Moscow.

9. According to the efficient-market theory, what effect would the following events have on the price of GM's stock?

   a. A surprise announcement that the government is going to lower business taxes next July 1

   b. A decrease in business taxes on July 1, which is 6 months after Congress passed the legislation

   c. An announcement, unexpected by experts, that the United States is imposing quotas on imports of Japanese cars for the coming year

   d. Implementation of **c** by issuing regulations on December 31

10. Suppose reserve requirements were abolished. What would determine the level of reserves in the banking system? What would happen to the money-supply multiplier in this situation?

11. Suppose that one giant bank, Humongous Bank of America, held all the checking deposits of all the people, subject to a 10 percent legal reserve requirement. If there were an injection of reserves into the economy, could Humongous Bank lend out more than 90 percent of the deposit addition, knowing that the new deposit must come back to it? Would this change the ultimate money-supply multiplier?

12. **Advanced problem:** An option is the right to buy or sell a stock or other security for a specified price on or before a specific date. A "call option" is the right to buy the stock, while a "put option" is the right to sell the stock. Suppose you have a call option to buy 100 shares in a highly volatile stock, Fantasia.com, any time in the next 3 months at $10 per share. Fantasia currently sells at $9 per share.

    a. Explain why the value of the option is more than $1 per share.

    b. Suppose the option were to expire tomorrow and had an even chance of rising $5 or falling $5 before then. What would be the value of the option?

13. Flip a coin 100 times. Count a head as "plus 1" and a tail as "minus 1." Keep a running score of the total. Plot it on graph paper. This is a random walk. (Those with access to a computer can do this using a computer program, a random-number generator, and a plotter.)

    Next, keep track of the closing price of the stock of your favorite company for a few weeks (or get it from past issues of the newspaper). Plot the price against time. Can you see any difference in the pattern of changes? Do both look like random walks?

CHAPTER

26

Central Banking and Monetary Policy

There have been three great inventions since the beginning of time: fire, the wheel, and central banking.

Will Rogers

Where would you look to find the most important macroeconomic policymakers today? In the White House? Or in Congress? Perhaps in the United Nations or the World Bank? Surprisingly, the answer is that you would look in an obscure marble building in Washington that houses the Federal Reserve System. It is here that the Federal Reserve (or "Fed") determines the level of short-term interest rates, thereby profoundly affecting financial markets, wealth, output, employment, and prices. Indeed, the Fed's influence spreads not only throughout the 50 states but even, through financial and trade linkages, to virtually every corner of the world.

The Federal Reserve's central goal is low and stable inflation. It also seeks to promote steady growth in national output, low unemployment, and orderly financial markets. If output is growing rapidly and inflation is rising, the Federal Reserve Board is likely to raise interest rates, as this puts a brake on the economy and reduces price pressures. If the economy is sluggish and business is languishing, the Fed may consider lowering interest rates, a move which will give a boost to aggregate demand, increase output, and reduce unemployment. Every major country has a central bank that is responsible for managing its monetary affairs. This chapter will help you understand the Federal Reserve's central role in the U.S. economy.

Figure 26-1 shows the role of central banking in the economy and depicts its relationship to the banks, financial markets, and interest rates. Section A surveys how the Fed uses its instruments—bank reserves, the discount rate, and other tools—to determine the money supply and affect interest rates. Section B then analyzes the impact of monetary policy on the macroeconomy.

A. CENTRAL BANKING AND THE FEDERAL RESERVE SYSTEM

THE FEDERAL RESERVE SYSTEM

Structure of the Federal Reserve

History and Purpose. During the nineteenth century, the United States was plagued by banking panics. These occurred when people suddenly attempted to turn their bank deposits into currency (review the example on bank panics in the last chapter). When they arrived at the banks, they found that the banks had an inadequate supply of currency because the

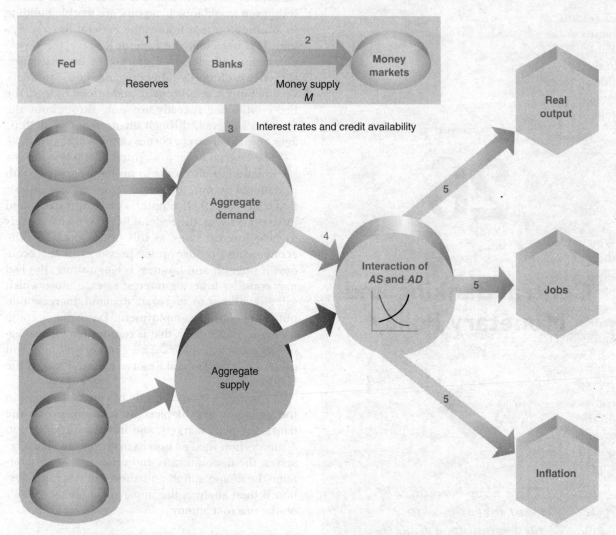

FIGURE 26-1. A Bird's-Eye View of How Monetary Policy Affects Output and Inflation

This diagram shows graphically the steps by which Fed policy affects economic activity. (1) is a change in reserves; leading to a change in M in (2); leading to (3), changes in interest rates and credit conditions. In (4), AD is changed by a response of investment and other interest-sensitive spending. In (5), changes in output, employment, and inflation follow. Remember that fiscal policy also feeds into the aggregate demand circle.

supply of currency was fixed and smaller than the amount of bank deposits. Bank failures and economic downturns ensued. After the severe panic of 1907, agitation and discussion led to the Federal Reserve Act of 1913 which was to "provide for the establishment of Federal reserve banks [and] to furnish an elastic currency."

As currently constituted, the **Federal Reserve System** consists of 12 regional Federal Reserve Banks, located in New York, Chicago, Richmond, Dallas, San Francisco, and other major cities. The regional structure was originally designed in the populist age to ensure that different areas would have a voice in banking matters and to avoid too great a concentration of central-banking powers in Washington or in the hands of the eastern bankers. Each Federal Reserve Bank today distributes coins and currency, supervises and regulates banks in its districts, and is part of a nationwide payments system.

The major purposes of the Federal Reserve are as follows:

Today the Federal Reserve's duties fall into four general areas: (1) conducting the nation's monetary policy; (2) supervising and regulating banking institutions; (3) maintaining the stability of the financial system; and (4) providing certain financial services to the government and the public.

Who's in Charge? The core of the Federal Reserve is the *Board of Governors* of the Federal Reserve System, which consists of seven members nominated by the president and confirmed by the Senate to serve overlapping terms of 14 years. Members of the Board are generally bankers or economists who work full time at the job.

The key decision-making body in the Federal Reserve System is the *Federal Open Market Committee* (FOMC). The 12 voting members of the FOMC include the seven governors plus five of the presidents of the regional Federal Reserve Banks. This key group controls the single most important and frequently used tool of modern monetary policy—the supply of bank reserves.

At the pinnacle of the entire system is the *Chairman of the Board of Governors,* who chairs the Board of Governors and the FOMC, acts as public spokesman for the Fed, and exercises enormous power over monetary policy. The most recent chairman has been Alan Greenspan, an economist, who is sometimes called the "second most powerful individual in America." Because of his long tenure (first appointed as Fed chairman in 1987) and successful management of the economy, Greenspan influences the entire economy through his impact on monetary policy and is often listened to on other economic issues as well.

In spite of the formally dispersed structure of the Fed, close observers think that power is quite centralized. The Federal Reserve Board, joined at meetings by the presidents of the 12 regional Federal Reserve Banks, operates under the Fed chairman to formulate and carry out monetary policy. The structure of the Federal Reserve System is shown in Figure 26-2.

FIGURE 26-2. The Major Players in Monetary Policy

Two important committees are at the center of monetary policy. The seven-member Board of Governors approves changes in discount rates and sets reserve requirements. The FOMC directs the setting of bank reserves. The chairman of the Board of Governors heads both committees. The size of each box indicates that person's or group's relative power; note the size of the chairman's box.

Is the Fed Too Independent?

On examining the structure of the Fed, one might ask, "In which of the three branches of government does the Fed lie?" The answer is, "None. Legally, the 12 regional banks are private. In reality, the Fed as a whole behaves as an independent government agency."

Although nominally a corporation owned by the commercial banks that are members of the Federal Reserve System, the Federal Reserve is in practice a public agency. It is directly responsible to Congress; it listens carefully to the advice of the president; and whenever any conflict arises between its making a profit and promoting the public interest, it acts unswervingly in the public interest.

Above all, the Federal Reserve is an *independent* agency. While it listens carefully to Congress and the president, and even to the election returns, in the end the Fed decides monetary policy according to its views about the nation's economic interests. As a result, the Fed sometimes comes into conflict with the executive branch. Almost every president has advice on Fed policy. When

Fed policies clash with administration goals, presidents occasionally use harsh words. The Fed listens politely but generally chooses the path it thinks best for the country, for its decisions do not have to be approved by anybody.

From time to time, critics argue that the Fed is too independent—that it is undemocratic for a small group of unelected people to govern the nation's financial markets. This is a sobering thought, for unelected bodies sometimes lose touch with social and economic realities. Defenders of independence respond that an independent central bank is the guardian of a nation's currency and the best protector against rampant inflation. Moreover, independence ensures that monetary policy is not subverted for partisan political objectives, as sometimes happens in countries where the executive branch controls the central bank. Historical studies show that countries with independent central banks have generally been more successful in keeping down inflation than those whose central banks are under the thumbs of elected officials.

Policy Objectives. What are the goals of the Federal Reserve System? This is how the Fed sees its role:

> The [Federal Reserve's] objectives include economic growth in line with the economy's potential to expand; a high level of employment; stable prices

(that is, stability in the purchasing power of the dollar); and moderate long-term interest rates.[1]

While it is not always easy to understand the exact reasoning that led to a particular monetary-policy step, historians who sift through the decisions usually find that the Fed is ultimately concerned with preserving the integrity of our financial institutions, combating inflation, defending the exchange rate of the dollar, and preventing excessive unemployment.

To summarize:

The Federal Reserve Board in Washington, together with the 12 Federal Reserve Banks, constitutes our American central bank. Every modern country has a central bank. Its primary mission is to control the nation's money supply and credit conditions.

Overview of the Fed's Operations

Figure 26-3 shows the various stages of Federal Reserve operations as seen by the Fed. The Federal Reserve has at its disposal a number of policy instruments. These can affect certain intermediate targets (such as reserves, the money supply, and interest rates). These instruments are intended to help achieve

---

[1] See *The Federal Reserve System: Purposes and Functions*, p. 2, under "Websites" in this chapter's Further Reading section.

The World as Seen from the Fed

FIGURE 26-3. While the Fed Ultimately Pursues Objectives like Stable Prices, Its Short-Term Operations Focus on the Intermediate Targets

In determining monetary policy, the Fed directly manipulates the instruments or policy variables under its control—open-market operations, the discount rate, and reserve requirements. These help determine bank reserves, the money supply, and interest rates—the intermediate targets of monetary policy. Ultimately, monetary and fiscal policies are partners in pursuing the major objectives of rapid growth, low unemployment, and stable prices.

the ultimate objectives of a healthy economy—low inflation, rapid growth in output, and low unemployment. It is important to keep these different groups (policy instruments, intermediate targets, and ultimate objectives) clearly distinct in our analysis.

The three major instruments of monetary policy are:

- *Open-market operations*—buying or selling of U.S. government securities in the open market to influence the level of reserves
- *Discount-rate policy*—setting the interest rate, called the *discount rate*, at which commercial banks and other depository institutions can borrow reserves from a regional Federal Reserve Bank
- *Reserve-requirements policy*—setting and changing the legal reserve-ratio requirements on deposits with banks and other financial institutions

In managing money, the Federal Reserve must keep its eye on a set of variables known as *intermediate targets*. These are economic variables that are intermediate in the transmission mechanism between Fed instruments and ultimate policy goals. When the Fed wants to affect its ultimate objectives, it first changes one of its instruments, such as the discount rate. This change affects an intermediate variable like interest rates, credit conditions, or the money supply. Much as a doctor interested in the health of a patient will monitor pulse and blood pressure, so

the Federal Reserve keeps a careful watch on its intermediate targets.

Balance Sheet of the Federal Reserve Banks

In analyzing central banking, we need to describe the consolidated balance sheet of the Federal Reserve System, shown in Table 26-1 below. U.S. government securities (e.g., bonds) make up most of the Fed's assets. The small items, loans and acceptances, are primarily loans or advances to commercial banks. The interest rate the Fed charges banks for such loans, or "discounts," is called the discount rate, which is another of the Fed's tools.

There are two unique items among its liabilities: currency and reserves. Federal Reserve *currency* is the Fed's principal liability. This comprises the coins and paper bills we use every day. The other major liability is *bank reserves,* which are balances kept on deposit by commercial banks with the Federal Reserve Banks. Taken along with the banks' vault cash, these are the reserves we have been talking about. They provide the basis for multiple deposit creation by the nation's banking system.

By altering its holding of government securities, the Fed can change bank reserves and thereby trigger the sequence of events that ultimately determines the total supply of money.

Combined Balance Sheet of 12 Federal Reserve Banks, February 2003 (billions of dollars)			
Assets		**Liabilities and Net Worth**	
U.S. government securities	$674.00	Federal Reserve currency	$ 714.00
Loans and acceptances	0.05	Deposits:	
Miscellaneous other assets	112.55	Reserve balances	14.70
		U.S. Treasury deposits	5.20
		Miscellaneous liabilities	52.70
Total	$786.60	Total	$786.60

TABLE 26-1. Federal Reserve Notes and Deposits Underlie Our Money Supply

By controlling its earning assets (government securities and loans), the Fed controls its liabilities (bank deposits and Federal Reserve notes). Bank deposits with the Fed plus vault cash of banks are total reserves and can be used to meet reserve requirements. Through changing reserves, the Fed determines the economy's money supply (currency and demand deposits, M_1), and thereby affects GDP, unemployment, and inflation.

Source: Federal Reserve Board, at www.federalreserve.gov/releases/h41.

THE NUTS AND BOLTS OF MONETARY POLICY

Open-Market Operations

The Fed's most useful tool is "open-market operations."

By selling or buying government securities in the open market, the Fed can lower or raise bank reserves. These so-called **open-market operations** are a central bank's most important monetary-policy instrument.

In setting policy, the FOMC decides whether to pump more reserves into the banking system by buying government bonds or whether to tighten monetary policy by selling government securities.

To see how an open-market operation changes reserves, let us suppose that the Fed thinks the economic winds are blowing up a little inflation. The FOMC holds its meeting in Washington and hears presentations and projections from its staff of talented economists. The committee decides to tighten money and credit.

It then sends instructions to the Federal Reserve Bank of New York, which is the operating arm of the Fed, to sell $1 billion of securities. To whom are the bonds sold? *To the open market.* This includes dealers in government bonds, who then resell them to commercial banks, big corporations, other financial institutions, and individuals.

The purchasers usually buy the bonds by writing checks to the Fed, drawn from an account in a commercial bank. Suppose that the Fed sells some bonds to XYZ Investments, which writes a check on Coyote Bank of Las Vegas. The Fed presents the check at Coyote Bank. When Coyote Bank pays the check, it will reduce its balance with the Fed by $10,000. When all the sales are completed, the entire commercial banking system will have lost $1 billion in reserves at the Federal Reserve System.

Table 26-2(*a*) shows the effect of a $1 billion open-market sale on the Federal Reserve balance sheet. The black entries show the Fed balance sheet before the open-market operation. The rust entry shows the effect of the open-market sale on the Federal Reserve balance sheet. The net effect is a reduction of both assets and liabilities by $1 billion: the Fed has sold $1 billion of government bonds, and its liabilities have declined by exactly the same amount, $1 billion of bank reserves.

Now let's focus on the impact on commercial banks, whose consolidated balance sheet is shown in Table 26-2(*b*). We will assume that banks hold 10 percent of their deposits as reserves with the central bank. After the open-market operation, banks see that they are short of reserves because they initially have lost $1 billion of reserves and $1 billion of deposits. The banks then sell some of their investments and call in some short-term loans. This sets off a multiple contraction of deposits. When the entire chain of impacts is finished, deposits are down by $10 billion, with the corresponding changes on the asset side of the banks' balance sheet (look carefully at the rust entries in Table 26-2(*b*)). In the end, the Fed's open-market sale has caused a $10 billion contraction in the money supply.

Later in this chapter, we will examine the complete monetary transmission mechanism—how monetary policy affects interest rates, aggregate demand, and output. At this point, it will be useful to look ahead at Figure 26-6(*a*) on page 544. This figure shows the impact of an open-market operation in the money market. The monetary tightening just described shifts the supply of money to the left, leading to a rise in interest rates and a decline in the quantity of money demanded. Indeed, it is exactly the rise in interest rates which has brought about the contraction in deposits shown in Table 26-2(*b*). As banks called in loans and investments, interest rates rose, and they continued to rise until the public moved $10 billion of its assets from zero-interest-rate demand deposits to other, higher-yielding assets.

Operating Procedures

The FOMC meets eight times a year to decide upon monetary policy and give operating instructions to the frontline troops at the Federal Reserve Bank of New York, which conducts open-market operations on a day-to-day basis. The operating procedures have changed over time. Sometimes they were vague instructions to "loosen credit a little."

Then in the 1970s, the Fed altered its operating procedures to pay closer attention to movements in the money supply. The most dramatic shift in policy came in 1979, when the Fed undertook its "monetarist experiment" to slow the rapid inflation. This involved targeting reserves and the money supply in a fashion recommended by monetarists. (We will review the monetarist experiment

Federal Reserve Balance Sheet (billions of dollars)			
Assets		**Liabilities**	
Securities	500 −1	Currency held by public	410
Loans	10	Bank reserves	100 −1
Total assets	**510 −1**	**Total liabilities**	**510 −1**

TABLE 26-2(a). Open-Market Sale by Fed Cuts Bank Reserves

Balance Sheet of Commercial Banks (billions of dollars)			
Assets		**Liabilities**	
Reserves	100 −1	Demand deposits	1,000 −10
Loans and investments	900 −9		
Total assets	**1,000 −10**	**Total liabilities**	**1,000 −10**

TABLE 26-2(b). Decline in Reserves Leads Banks to Reduce Loans and Investments until Money Supply Is Cut by 10-to-1 Ratio

The central bank decides to tighten money by draining some reserves from the banking system.

In **(a)**, the Fed sells $1 billion of securities. When banks write checks on their accounts with the Fed to pay for the securities, this operation reduces bank reserves by $1 billion. Bank reserves thus decline by $1 billion as a result of the open-market operation. The rust numbers indicate the effect of the open-market operation on the Fed's balance sheet.

Then, in **(b)**, we see the effect of the open-market operation on the balance sheet of banks. With a required reserve ratio of 10 percent of deposits, banks reduce loans and investments. The reserve contraction cascades through the banking system. Thus, demand deposits must fall by $10 billion for the banking system to be back in equilibrium. The rust entries show the effect of the open-market operation on the banking system and the money supply.

later in this chapter and in our discussion of monetarism in Chapter 33.)

Today, the Fed primarily operates by setting a short-term target for the **federal funds rate,** which is the interest rate that banks pay each other for the overnight use of bank reserves. Figure 26-4 on the next page shows the federal funds rate, which is under the control of the Fed, along with one short-term interest rate and an important long-term interest rate, the 10-year interest rate on Treasury bonds. While the Fed sets the general level and trend in interest rates, there are clearly many other factors at work in determining interest rates and financial conditions.

What is the objective of Fed policy today? Like many central banks around the world, the Fed is principally concerned with ensuring low and stable inflation while attempting to moderate swings in output and unemployment. There is no single variable that triggers monetary tightening or loosening. Rather, the Fed tends to look at a wide variety of indicators as well as at economic forecasts. It will track actual movements in wages and consumer and wholesale prices as well as movements in fiscal policy, exchange rates, and a multitude of economic indicators.

Discount-Rate Policy: A Second Instrument

When commercial banks are short of reserves, they are allowed to borrow from the Federal Reserve Banks. Their loans were included under the asset heading "Loans and acceptances" in the Fed balance sheet in Table 26-1. These loans are called *borrowed reserves*. When borrowed reserves are growing, the banks are borrowing from the Fed, thereby increasing total bank reserves (borrowed plus unborrowed reserves). Conversely, a drop in borrowed reserves promotes a contraction in total bank reserves.

In the early years, the Fed managed the money supply mainly by buying (or "discounting") commercial paper brought to it by banks or companies. This

FIGURE 26-4. Federal Reserve Determines Federal Funds Rate

The Fed sets a target for the federal funds rate, which is the interest rate charged by banks on overnight loans. This rate then affects all other interest rates, although the linkage is variable and is affected by expectations of future interest rates as well as overall financial conditions. Note the period from 1979 to 1982, when the Fed experimented with monetary targeting and produced much more volatile interest rates.

Source: Federal Reserve Board.

proved unsatisfactory because the Fed was in a passive position—waiting for people to come to the discount window. As the role of monetary policy became better understood, the Fed turned to open-market operations as the primary tool for adjusting the overall level of reserves. Today, the discount window is used primarily to buffer the day-to-day fluctuations in member-bank reserves, and (as you can see in Table 26-1) actual borrowings are typically extremely small.

Sometimes, the Fed may raise or lower the **discount rate,** which is the interest rate charged on bank borrowings from the 12 regional Federal Reserve Banks. For many years, the discount rate was the bellwether of monetary policy. For example, in 1965 when the Fed wanted to send a signal to markets that the Vietnam war boom threatened to become inflationary, it raised the discount rate. So powerful was this signal that Fed Chairman Martin was called to the LBJ ranch for a dressing-down by President Johnson, who was afraid the higher discount rate would slow the economy.

Today, the discount rate is a relatively minor instrument of monetary policy. Sometimes, a change in the discount rate is used to signal markets of a major policy change. But mostly, the discount rate simply follows market interest rates to prevent banks from making windfall profits by borrowing at a low discount rate and lending at a higher rate on the open market.

The Role of Reserve Requirements

The Nature of Reserves. In the last chapter, we showed how banks create money when reserves increase and they have fixed reserve requirements. Let's spend a moment considering why banks hold reserves.

In a free-market banking system, prudent bankers would always need to hold some reserves on hand. They would need to keep a small fraction of their deposits in cash or the equivalent to pay out to depositors who desired to convert their deposits to currency or who wrote checks on their accounts.

Many years ago, banks recognized that, although deposits are payable on demand, they are seldom all withdrawn together. Reserves equal to total deposits would be necessary if all depositors suddenly had to be paid off in full at the same time, but this never occurred. On a given day, some people made withdrawals while others made deposits. The two kinds of transactions generally balanced out.

The bankers did not need to keep 100 percent of deposits as sterile reserves; reserves earn no interest when they are sitting in a vault. So, early in banking history, banks hit upon the idea of using deposits to make investments. By putting most of the money deposited with them into earning assets and keeping only fractional cash reserves against deposits, banks maximize their profits.

The transformation into fractional-reserve banks—holding fractional rather than 100 percent reserves against deposits—was in fact revolutionary. It enabled banks to create money. That is, banks could turn each dollar of reserves into several dollars of deposits.

Legal Reserve Requirements. In the nineteenth century, banks sometimes had insufficient reserves to meet depositors' demands, and this occasionally spiraled into bank crises. Therefore, beginning at that time, and currently formalized under Federal Reserve regulations, banks are required to keep a certain fraction of their checkable deposits as reserves. Reserve requirements apply to all types of checking deposits, independent of the actual need for cash on hand. Bank reserves are held either as cash on hand ("vault cash") or as deposits with the Federal Reserve. Reserves have a zero yield because cash has no yield and the Fed pays no interest on bank deposits.

Under Federal Reserve regulations, banks are required to hold a fixed fraction of their checkable deposits as reserves. This fraction is called the **required reserve ratio.** Bank reserves take the form of vault cash (bank holdings of currency) and deposits by banks with the Federal Reserve System.

Table 26-3 shows current reserve requirements along with the Fed's discretionary power to change reserve requirements. The key concept is the level of required reserve ratios. They range from 10 percent against checkable deposits down to zero for personal

Type of deposit	Reserve ratio (%)	Range in which Fed can vary (%)
Checking (transactions) accounts:		
First $41 million	3	No change allowed
Above $41 million	10	8–14
Time and savings deposits:		
Personal	0	
Nonpersonal:		
Up to 1½ years' maturity	0	0–9
More than 1½ years' maturity	0	0–9

TABLE 26-3. Required Reserves for Financial Institutions

Reserve requirements are governed by law and regulation. The reserve-ratio column shows the percent of deposits in each category that must be held in non-interest-bearing deposits at the Fed or as cash on hand. Checking-type accounts in large banks face required reserves of 10 percent, while other major deposits have no reserve requirements. The Fed has power to alter the reserve ratio within a given range but does so only on the rare occasion when economic conditions warrant a sharp change in monetary policy.

Source: *Federal Reserve Bulletin,* February 2003.

savings accounts. For convenience in our numerical examples, we use 10 percent reserve ratios, with the understanding that the actual ratio may differ from 10 percent from time to time.

The level of required reserves is generally higher than what banks would voluntarily hold. A prudent banker today, concerned only with assuring customers that the bank has enough cash for daily transactions, might choose to keep only 5 percent of the bank's checking deposits in reserves.

Why would the Fed insist on such high reserve requirements? Bank reserves are kept above the prudent commercial level for an important reason: high reserve requirements enable the Federal Reserve to control the amount of checking deposits that banks can create. Legal reserve requirements are set high in order to allow the central bank to control the money supply. Reserve requirements help the Fed conduct its open-market operations by ensuring a stable relationship between open-market operations and deposits.

Put differently, high reserve requirements plus a zero return on reserves ensure that banks will want to hold just that legal minimum. The supply of bank money will then be determined by the supply of bank reserves (determined by the Fed through open-market operations) and by the money-supply multiplier (determined by the required reserve ratio). Because the Fed controls both bank reserves and the required reserve ratio, it has (within a small margin of error) firm control over the money supply.

Changes in Required Reserves. A final monetary instrument of the Fed is changes in reserve requirements. For instance, if the Fed wants to tighten money overnight, it can raise the required reserve ratio on checking accounts. It might even raise reserve requirements on time deposits.

Exactly how does an increase in required ratios operate to tighten credit? Suppose the required reserve ratio is 10 percent and banks had built up their reserves to meet this requirement. Now suppose the Fed raised the required reserve ratio to 20 percent. (This fantastic figure is for algebraic simplicity. The Fed cannot and would not take such a drastic step today.)

Even if the Fed does nothing else, banks now have to contract their loans and investment greatly—and their deposits as well. As the last chapter showed, bank deposits can now be only 5 times reserves, not 10 times reserves. So deposits will fall by half.

This painful cut will start to take place quickly. As soon as the new rule raising the requirement to 20 percent goes into effect, banks will find that they have insufficient reserves. They will have to sell some bonds and call in some loans. The bond buyers and borrowers will drain their checking accounts. The process ends only after banks have brought down their deposits to 5 rather than 10 times their reserves.

Such a huge change would lead to very high interest rates, credit rationing, large declines in investment, and massive reductions in output and employment. So this example warns that this powerful tool of changing reserve requirements has to be used with great caution. *Changes in reserve requirements are made extremely sparingly because they cause too large and abrupt a change in policy. Open-market operations can achieve the same results in a less disruptive way.*

Trends in Financial Regulation

The financial sector has historically been the source of economic disturbances and crises, and these led to pervasive regulation during the first half of the twentieth century. Widespread banking crises during the Great Depression led to controls on mergers and interest rates. Until the 1980s, interest rates paid by commercial banks were tightly controlled. Banks were not allowed to pay interest on checking accounts, and there were ceilings on interest rates on savings accounts and time deposits. As financial markets became more competitive, however, regulated interest rates could not long survive. Financial institutions devised new types of instruments which lured funds from low-yield deposits, and this trend accelerated in the high-interest-rate environment of the late 1970s and early 1980s. Eventually the regulatory edifice constructed during the Great Depression began to crumble.

Congress reacted with the Banking Acts of 1980 and 1982, which largely deregulated interest rates. The basis of the new approach was to separate transactions accounts from nontransactions accounts. The primary purpose of a *transactions account,* such as a checking account, is to serve as a means of payment. A *nontransactions account* contains assets whose primary purpose is for investment, not payment of bills (a savings account is an example of a nontransactions account).

Once this distinction had been made, the 1980 and 1982 Acts effectively deregulated nontransactions accounts. Today, nontransactions accounts earn market interest rates and are effectively outside the regulatory structure of the Federal Reserve. Transactions assets like checking accounts have with one major exception also been deregulated. The remaining and critical regulation is, as we see in Table 26-3, that these accounts are subject to substantial reserve requirements.

Although most interest-rate controls have been removed, the government continues its "fiduciary" regulation of banks. To instill confidence in the banking system and prevent "bank runs," the government inspects the books of banks and takes over insolvent banks. Additionally, the government guarantees up to $100,000 per deposit at banks that are members of the Federal Deposit Insurance Corporation (FDIC). The Fed and other regulatory agencies also inspect banking practices to ensure that the fraud and abuse of the 1980s savings and loan scandal does not recur.

The latest chapter came in 1999 when Congress repealed the 1933 Glass-Steagall Act. Glass-Steagall prohibited banks from selling other financial services, such as brokerage services or insurance, in order to reduce the riskiness of banks. The repeal removed the barriers among different financial institutions. Banks, insurance companies, and investment houses are now allowed to compete with one another and to offer one-stop financial shopping. Some economists worry that integrating heavily regulated banks, which enjoy the protection of deposit insurance, with competitive financial sectors may increase the overall riskiness of the financial sector in turbulent times.

Monetary Policy in the Open Economy

Central banks are particularly important in open economies, where they manage reserve flows and the exchange rate and monitor international financial developments.

Reserve Flows. The dollar is today used extensively both as a store of value and as a medium of international exchange by those who are involved in international trade and finance. Foreigners own hundreds of billions of dollars in U.S. dollar–denominated assets. Because narrow money has a zero or low interest rate, foreigners prefer to hold interest-bearing assets (bonds, stocks, etc.). However, foreigners do hold narrow money in U.S. dollar checking accounts because they need to buy and sell goods and assets. Additionally, many people in unstable or inflation-prone countries hold U.S. currency.

Why are we concerned about international money holdings at this point? The reason is that deposits by foreigners in the banking system increase the total amount of bank reserves in the same way that deposits by domestic residents do. Thus, changes in foreigners' dollar money holdings can set off a chain of expansion or contraction of the U.S. money supply.

For example, say the Japanese decide to deposit $1000 of U.S. currency in U.S. banks. What happens? There is a $1000 increase in reserves in the domestic banking system, as illustrated in Table 25-5(*a*) in the previous chapter. As a result, the banking system can expand deposits tenfold, in this case to $10,000.

Thus, the Fed's control of the nations's *M* is modified by international disturbances to bank reserves. But the Fed has the power to offset any change in reserves coming from abroad. It affects this by engaging in what is called sterilization. *Sterilization* refers to actions by a central bank that insulate the domestic money supply from international reserve flows. Sterilization usually is accomplished when the central bank implements an open-market operation that reverses the international reserve movement. In practice, the Fed routinely sterilizes international disturbances to reserves.

To summarize:

The central bank's control over bank reserves is subject to disturbances from abroad. These disturbances can, however, be offset if the central bank sterilizes the international flows.

The Role of the Exchange-Rate System.[2] One important element in a country's financial market is its exchange-rate system. As we will see in later chapters, international trade and finance involve the use of different national currencies, which are linked by relative prices called foreign exchange rates.

One important exchange-rate system is floating exchange rates, in which a country's foreign exchange rate is determined by market forces of supply and demand. The United States, Europe, and Japan today operate floating-exchange-rate systems. These three regions can pursue their monetary policies independently of other countries. This chapter's analysis concerns mainly the operation of monetary policy under floating exchange rates.

---

[2] This section contains materials that will be covered more extensively in Chapters 29 and 30 and should be reread after those chapters.

Some economies, such as Hong Kong as well as virtually all countries in earlier periods, maintain fixed exchange rates and "peg" their currencies to one or more external currencies. We will see shortly that *when a country has a fixed exchange rate, it must align its monetary policy with the country to which its currency is pegged.* For example, if Hong Kong has open capital markets and an exchange rate credibly fixed with the U.S. dollar, then Hong Kong must have the same interest rates as those in the United States . . . and it generally does.

We return to issues of open economies later. They are particularly crucial for understanding monetary policy outside the United States.

The Foreign Desk. The Federal Reserve acts as the government's operating arm in the international financial system. The Fed buys and sells different currencies on foreign exchange markets on behalf of the Treasury. While this task is generally routine, from time to time foreign exchange markets become disorderly, and the Fed, in cooperation with the Treasury, steps in. Sometimes, the Treasury decides that foreign-exchange-rate *intervention* is necessary—because the exchange rate of the dollar is either significantly higher or considerably lower than seems warranted by underlying fundamentals. The Fed is the agent of the Treasury in such intervention activities.

In addition, the Federal Reserve often takes the lead in working with foreign countries and with international agencies when international financial crises erupt. The Fed played an important role in the Mexican loan package in 1994–1995, worked with other countries to help calm markets during the East Asian crisis and global liquidity crisis in 1997 and 1998, and helped calm markets during the Argentine crisis of 2001–2002.

We have completed our analysis of the money supply. It can be summarized as follows:

The money supply is ultimately determined by the policies of the Fed. By setting reserve requirements and the discount rate, and especially by undertaking open-market operations, the Fed determines the level of reserves, the money supply, and short-term interest rates. Banks and the public are cooperating partners in this process. Banks create money by multiple expansion of reserves; the public agrees to hold money in depository institutions.

B. THE EFFECTS OF MONEY ON OUTPUT AND PRICES

THE MONETARY TRANSMISSION MECHANISM

Having examined the building blocks of monetary theory, we now describe the **monetary transmission mechanism,** the route by which changes in the supply of money are translated into changes in output, employment, prices, and inflation. For concreteness, assume that the Federal Reserve is concerned about inflation and has decided to slow down the economy. There are five steps in the process:

1. *To start the process, the Fed takes steps to reduce bank reserves.* As we saw in Section A of this chapter, the Fed reduces bank reserves primarily by selling government securities in the open market. This open-market operation changes the balance sheet of the banking system by reducing total bank reserves.

2. *Each dollar reduction in bank reserves produces a multiple contraction in checking deposits, thereby reducing the money supply.* This step was described in Chapter 25, where we saw that changes in reserves lead to a multiplied change in deposits. Since the money supply equals currency plus checking deposits, the reduction in checking deposits reduces the money supply.

3. *The reduction in the money supply increases interest rates and tightens credit conditions.* With an unchanged demand for money, a reduced supply of money will raise interest rates. In addition, the amount of credit (loans and borrowing) available to people will decline. Interest rates will rise for mortgage borrowers and for businesses that want to build factories, buy new equipment, or add to inventories. Higher interest rates tend to reduce asset prices (such as those of stocks, bonds, and houses) and therefore depress the values of people's assets.[3]

4. *With higher interest rates and lower wealth, interest-sensitive spending—especially investment—tends to fall.* The combination of higher interest rates, tighter

---

[3] To refresh your memory on the relationship between interest rates and asset prices, see the box "Higher interest rates tend to lower asset prices" on page 506 in Chapter 25.

credit, and lower wealth tends to reduce investment and consumption spending. Businesses will scale down their investment plans, as will state and local governments. For example, higher interest rates may lead airlines to stretch out their purchases of new aircraft. Similarly, consumers may decide to buy a smaller house, or to renovate their existing one, when rising mortgage interest rates increase monthly payments relative to monthly income. And in an economy increasingly open to international trade, higher interest rates may raise the foreign exchange rate of the dollar, depressing net exports. Hence, tight money will raise interest rates and reduce spending on interest-sensitive components of aggregate demand.

5. *Finally, the pressures of tight money, by reducing aggregate demand, will reduce income, output, jobs, and inflation.* The aggregate supply-and-demand (or, equivalently, the multiplier) analysis showed how such a drop in investment and other autonomous spending may depress output and employment sharply. Furthermore, as output and employment fall below the levels that would otherwise occur, prices tend to rise less rapidly or even to fall. Inflationary forces subside. If the Fed's diagnosis of inflationary conditions was correct, the drop in output and the rise in unemployment will help relieve inflationary forces.

We can summarize the steps as follows:

R down $\rightarrow M$ down $\rightarrow i$ up $\rightarrow I, C, X$ down $\rightarrow$
AD down $\rightarrow$ real GDP down and inflation down

This five-step sequence—from the Fed's changes in commercial-bank reserves, to a multiple change in total M, to changes in interest rates and credit availability, to changes in investment spending that shift aggregate demand, and finally to the response of output, employment, and inflation—is vital to the determination of output and prices. If you look back at Figure 26-1, you will see how each of the five steps fits into our thematic flowchart. We have already explained the first two steps; the balance of this chapter is devoted to analyzing steps 3 through 5.

THE MONEY MARKET

Step 3 in the transmission mechanism is the response of interest rates and credit conditions to changes in the supply of money. Recall from Chapter 25 that the

demand for money depends primarily on the need to undertake transactions. Households, businesses, and governments hold money so that they may buy goods, services, and other items. In addition, some part of the demand for M derives from the need for a supersafe and highly liquid asset.

The *supply of money* is jointly determined by the private banking system and the nation's central bank. The central bank, through open-market operations and other instruments, provides reserves to the banking system. Commercial banks then create deposits out of the central-bank reserves. By manipulating reserves, the central bank can determine the money supply within a narrow margin of error.

Supply of and Demand for Money

The supply of and demand for money jointly determine the market interest rates. Figure 26-5 shows the total quantity of money (M) on the horizontal axis and the nominal interest rate (i) on the vertical axis. The supply curve is drawn as a vertical line on the assumption that the Federal Reserve keeps the money supply constant at M^* in Figure 26-5.

In addition, we show the money demand schedule as a downward-sloping curve because the holdings of

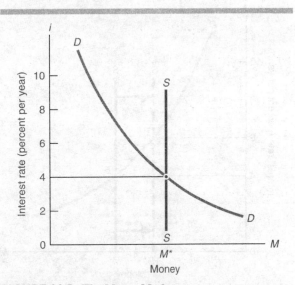

FIGURE 26-5. The Money Market

The interaction of the demand for and supply of money determines the interest rate. The Fed has a money target at M^*. The public has a downward-sloping money demand schedule. Here the money market is in equilibrium with a nominal interest rate of 4 percent per year.

money decline as interest rates rise. At higher interest rates, people and businesses shift more of their funds to higher-yield assets and away from low-yield or zero-yield money, as described in the previous chapter.

The intersection of the supply and demand schedules in Figure 26-5 determines the market interest rate. Recall that interest rates are the prices paid for the use of money. Interest rates are determined in **money markets,** which are the markets where short-term funds are lent and borrowed. Important interest rates include short-term rates such as the rates on 3-month Treasury bills and on short-term commercial paper (notes issued by large corporations). As noted above, the Federal Reserve operates primarily in the market for federal funds and affects the federal funds rate. Longer-term interest rates include 10-year or 20-year government and corporate bonds and mortgages on real estate. (See Figure 25-2 for a graph of recent trends in interest rates.)

In Figure 26-5, the equilibrium interest rate is 4 percent per year. Only at 4 percent is the level of

the money supply that the Fed has targeted consistent with the desired money holdings of the public. At a higher interest rate, there would be excessive money balances. People would get rid of their excessive money holdings by buying bonds and other financial instruments, thereby lowering market interest rates toward the equilibrium 4 percent rate. (What would happen at an interest rate of 2 percent?)

Money Market Shifts. To understand the monetary transmission mechanism, we need to see how changes in the money market affect interest rates. Suppose that the Federal Reserve becomes worried about inflation and tightens monetary policy by selling securities and reducing the money supply.

The impact of a monetary tightening is shown in Figure 26-6(*a*) below. The leftward shift of the money supply schedule means that market interest rates must rise to induce people to swap their money for bonds and other nonmonetary assets. The gap between *E* and *N* shows the extent of excess demand

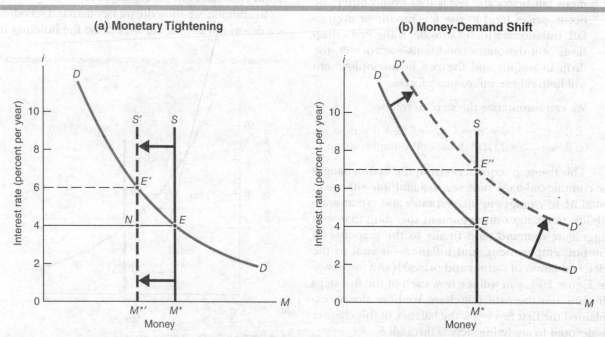

FIGURE 26-6. Changes in Monetary Policy or Prices Affect Interest Rates

In (**a**), the Federal Reserve contracts the money supply in response to fears of rising prices. The lower money supply produces an excess demand for money, shown by the gap *NE*. As the public adjusts its portfolio, interest rates rise to the new equilibrium at *E'*.

In (**b**), the demand for money increases as prices rise, other things held constant. The higher demand for money drives up market interest rates until the quantity of money demanded equals the money supply.

for money at the old interest rate. Interest rates rise until the new equilibrium is attained, shown in Figure 26-6(a) at point E', with a new and higher interest rate of 6 percent per year.

There are also frequent shocks to money demand. For example, suppose that an increase in oil or commodity prices raised the overall price level. With higher prices, the demand for money would increase, shifting the money demand curve to the right from DD to $D'D'$, as shown in Figure 26-6(b), and leading to an increase in equilibrium interest rates. (To check your understanding, make sure you can answer question 1 at the end of the chapter.)

To summarize our findings about the money market:

The money market is affected by a combination of (1) the public's desire to hold money (represented by the demand-for-money DD curve) and (2) the Fed's monetary policy (which is shown as a fixed money supply, SS). Their interaction determines the market interest rate, i. A restrictive monetary policy shifts the SS curve to the left, raising market interest rates. An increase in the nation's output or price level shifts the DD curve to the right and raises interest rates. An expansion of the money supply or a decline in money demand has the opposite effects.

THE MONETARY TRANSMISSION MECHANISM

We have seen how Fed policy can change interest rates. Let us now move on to examine how monetary policy affects the economy.

Graphical Analysis of Monetary Policy

Figure 26-7 on the next page illustrates the effects of a monetary expansion upon economic activity. Part (a), in the lower left, shows the money market; (b), in the lower right, shows the determination of investment; and (c), in the upper right, shows the determination of aggregate demand and GDP by the multiplier mechanism. We can think of the causality as moving counterclockwise from the money market through investment to the determination of aggregate demand and GDP as a whole.

Starting at the lower left, in Figure 26-7(a), we see the demand for and supply of money that were depicted in Figures 26-5 and 26-6. For purposes of the present discussion, assume that the money supply schedule was initially S_A and that the interest rate was 8 percent per year. If the Fed were concerned about a looming recession, it might increase the money supply by making open-market purchases, shifting the curve to S_B. In the case shown in Figure 26-7(a), market interest rates would thereby fall to 4 percent per year.

Figure 26-7(b) picks up the story to show how lower interest rates increase spending on interest-sensitive components of aggregate demand. We saw in Chapter 22 that a decline in interest rates would induce businesses to increase their spending on plant, equipment, and inventories. The effects of eased monetary policy are quickly seen in the housing market, where lower interest rates mean lower monthly mortgage payments on the typical house, encouraging households to increase housing purchases.

Additionally, asset prices tend to rise with lower interest rates. Consumption spending increases, both because lower interest rates generally increase the value of wealth—as stock, bond, and housing prices tend to rise—and because consumers tend to spend more on automobiles and other big-ticket consumer durables when interest rates are low and credit is plentiful. Moreover, as we will explore in a moment, lower interest rates tend to reduce the foreign exchange rate on the dollar, thereby increasing the level of net exports. We see, then, how lower interest rates lead to increased spending in many different areas of the economy.

These consequences are evident in Figure 26-7(b), where the drop in interest rates (caused by the increase in the money supply) leads to a rise in investment from A' to B'. In this case, we should construe "investment" in the very broad sense sketched a moment ago: it includes not only business investment but also consumer durables and residences, as well as net foreign investment in the form of net exports.

Finally, Figure 26-7(c) shows the impact of changes in investment in the multiplier model. This diagram is really Figure 24-2 turned on its side. Recall from Chapter 24 that, in the simplest multiplier model, equilibrium output is attained when desired saving equals desired investment. In Figure 26-7(c), we have shown this relationship by drawing the saving schedule as the SS schedule; this line represents the desired level of saving (measured along the horizontal axis) as a function of GDP on the vertical axis. Equilibrium GDP is attained at that level where the

FIGURE 26-7. Central Bank Determines the Money Supply, Changing Interest Rates and Investment, Thereby Affecting GDP

When the Fed raises the money supply, from S_A to S_B, interest rates fall as people increase their money balances, moving down the money demand schedule in (a).

    Lower interest rates reduce the cost of investment, thus encouraging business purchases of plant and equipment and consumer purchases of houses. The economy moves down the demand-for-investment schedule from A' to B' in (b).

    By the multiplier mechanism in (c), the higher investment raises aggregate demand and GDP from A'' to B''.

investment demand from panel (b) equals the desired saving from the SS schedule.

    The initial level of investment was 100, as read off at A' in panel (b), producing a level of GDP of 3000. After easier money has lowered the interest rate from 8 to 4 percent, investment rises to 200 at point B'. This higher level of investment raises aggregate

spending to the new equilibrium at B'' in panel (c) with a new equilibrium GDP of 3300.

    What has occurred? The rise in the money supply from S_A to S_B lowered the interest rate from A to B; this caused investment to rise from A' to B'; and this in turn, acting through the multiplier, led to a rise in GDP from A'' to B''.

Such is the route by which monetary policy acts through intermediate targets like the money supply and interest rates to affect its ultimate targets.

Economic Policy in the Recession of 1982

One of the most dramatic economic policies in the United States occurred when the Fed decided to reduce inflation in the 1979–1982 period. As a result of low unemployment and a major increase in oil prices, annual inflation in 1979 surged to 13 percent. The Federal Reserve in 1979 responded with its "monetarist experiment," concentrating on the growth of reserves and the money supply rather than on interest rates. It hoped that a clear and decisive strategy of targeting the monetary aggregates would help slow the unacceptable inflation.

The shift to targeting monetary aggregates in 1979 was highly controversial. The immediate result was a sharp reduction in the growth of the money supply and a consequent tightening of monetary policy. This led to an increase of market interest rates to levels not seen since the Civil War. As interest rates rose, investment and other interest-sensitive spending fell sharply, which led to the deepest recession since the 1930s. The policy was definitely successful in reducing inflation to 4 percent by 1982.

As the recession deepened, the Fed worried that its tight monetary policies had gone too far. Unemployment was over 10 percent, and Congress was up in arms. We can use this incident to see how the Fed conducts its monetary policies—tuning in as the Fed decided to relax its monetary policy.

Let's begin with the August 1982 directive. In the midst of the deepest recession of the postwar period, the FOMC began with its review of the economy:[4]

The information reviewed at this meeting suggests only a little further advance in real GDP in the current quarter, following a relatively small increase in the second quarter, while prices on the average are continuing to rise more slowly than in 1981.

What objectives did the Fed establish for monetary policy? It stated:

The Federal Open Market Committee seeks to foster monetary and financial conditions that will help to reduce inflation, promote a resumption of growth in output on a sustainable basis, and contribute to a sustainable pattern of international transactions.

The FOMC then gave the following operational directive to the New York Federal Reserve Bank in August 1982:

In the short run, the Committee continues to seek behavior of reserve aggregates consistent with growth of M_1 and M_2 from June to September [1982] at annual rates of about 5 percent and about 9 percent respectively.

How should we interpret these words? They are saying that, in light of the sharp recession of 1982, the Fed concluded that its monetary policy had become overly restrictive. Also, the definitions of the monetary aggregates became confused at this time because of the addition of a number of new assets (such as interest-bearing checking accounts) to M_1 and M_2. The ambiguity about the meaning of the M's meant that basing policy only on M movement was unwise.

The Fed therefore abandoned its strict monetary targeting in the fall of 1982. Interest rates fell sharply, with the 3-month Treasury-bill rate falling from 15 percent in the middle of 1981 to 8 percent at the end of 1982. As a result, real spending on housing almost doubled from 1982 to 1984, and the economy began to recover sharply in 1983.

Although the monetary policies of this period were extremely unpopular, in retrospect many economists believe that they were a good "investment in stable prices."

Monetary Policy in an Open Economy

The monetary transmission mechanism in the United States has evolved over the last two decades as the economy became more open and changes occurred in the exchange-rate system. The relationship between monetary policy and foreign trade has always been a major concern for smaller and more open economies like Canada and Britain. However, after the introduction of flexible exchange rates in 1973 and in the presence of increasing cross-border linkages, international trade and finance have come to play a new and central role in U.S. macroeconomic policy.

Let's review briefly the new route using the historical episode just analyzed. When the Federal Reserve tightened money in the 1979–1982 period, this process drove up interest rates on assets denominated in U.S. dollars. Attracted by higher dollar

---

[4] The FOMC quotations are from the *Federal Reserve Bulletin*, which contains monthly reports on Federal Reserve activities and other important financial developments.

interest rates, investors bought dollar securities, driving up the foreign exchange rate on the dollar. The higher exchange rate on the dollar encouraged imports into the United States and hurt U.S. exports. Net exports fell, reducing aggregate demand. This had the impact of both lowering real GDP and lowering the rate of inflation.

We will study the international aspects of macroeconomics in Chapters 29 and 30. For now, the main point to grasp is that foreign trade opens up another link in the monetary transmission mechanism. Monetary policy has the same impact on international trade as it has on domestic investment—tight money lowers foreign and domestic investment, thereby depressing output and prices. *The international-trade impact of monetary policy reinforces the domestic-economy impact.*

Monetary Policy in the AD-AS Framework

The three-part diagram in Figure 26-7 illustrates how an increase in the money supply would lead to an increase in aggregate demand. We can now show the effect on the overall macroeconomic equilibrium by using aggregate supply and demand curves.

The increase in aggregate demand produced by an increase in the supply of money causes a rightward shift of the *AD* curve as drawn in Figure 26-8 in the next column. This shift illustrates a monetary expansion in the presence of unemployed resources, with a relatively flat *AS* curve. The monetary expansion shifts aggregate demand from *AD* to *AD'*, shifting the equilibrium from *E* to *E'*. This example demonstrates how monetary expansion can increase aggregate demand and have a powerful impact on real output.

The sequence therefore runs as follows:

Monetary expansion bids down market interest rates. This stimulates interest-sensitive spending on business investment, housing, net exports, and the like. Aggregate demand increases via the multiplier mechanism, raising output and prices above the levels they would otherwise attain. Therefore, the basic sequence is

$$M \text{ up} \rightarrow i \text{ down} \rightarrow I, C, X \text{ up} \rightarrow AD \text{ up} \rightarrow$$
$$\text{GDP up and } P \text{ up}$$

But never forget the role of unemployed resources. The effect of an *AD* shift in a fully employed economy can be illustrated in Figure 26-8. Pencil in an *AD"* curve going through *E"* on the steep segment

Expansionary Monetary Policy

FIGURE 26-8. An Expansionary Monetary Policy Shifts *AD* Curve to the Right, Raising Output and Prices

Earlier discussion and Fig. 26-7 showed how an increase in the money supply would lead to an increase in investment and net exports and thereby to a multiplied increase in aggregate demand. This results in a rightward shift of the *AD* curve.

In the Keynesian region where the *AS* curve is relatively flat, a monetary expansion has its primary effect on real output, with only a small effect on prices. In a fully employed economy, the *AS* curve is near-vertical (shown at point *E"*), and a monetary expansion will primarily raise prices and nominal GDP with little effect on real GDP. Can you see why in the long run money may have little impact on real output?

of the *AS* curve; then pencil in a monetary expansion as a higher *AD"'*. Note how the monetary expansion would have little impact on real output. In a fully employed economy, the higher money stock would be chasing the same amount of output and would therefore mainly end up raising prices.

To clinch your understanding of this vital sequence, work through the opposite case of a monetary contraction. Say that the Federal Reserve decides, as it did in 1979–1982, to raise interest rates, slow the economy, and reduce inflation. You can trace this sequence in Figure 26-7 by reversing the direction of the monetary policy, thereby seeing how money, interest rates, investment, and aggregate demand interact when monetary policy is tightened. Then see how a leftward shift of the *AD* curve in Figure 26-8 would reduce both output and prices.

Monetary Effects in the Long Run

Many economists believe that changes in the supply of money in the long run will mainly affect the price level with little or no impact upon real output. We can understand this point by analyzing the effects of monetary changes in economies with different conditions of aggregate supply. As shown in Figure 26-8, monetary changes will affect aggregate demand and will tend to change real GDP in the short run when there are unemployed resources and the *AS* curve is relatively flat.

In our analysis of aggregate supply in the following chapters, we will see that the *AS* curve tends to be vertical or near-vertical in the long run as wages and prices adjust. Because of the price-wage adjustments and near-vertical *AS* curve, the output effects of *AD* shifts will diminish, and the price effects will tend to dominate in the long run. *This means that as prices and wages become more flexible in the long run, money-supply changes tend to have a larger impact on prices and a smaller impact on output.*

What is the intuition behind this difference between the short run and the long run? We can construct a highly simplified example to see the difference. Suppose we start out as in Figure 26-7, with a nominal GDP of 3000 and stable prices; then a monetary expansion that increases the money supply by 10 percent might increase nominal GDP by 10 percent to 3300. Studies by Robert J. Gordon and others indicate that, in the short run, "nominal GDP changes have been divided consistently, with two-thirds taking the form of output change and the remaining one-third the form of price change." Consequently, in the first year, the money-supply expansion might increase real GDP around 7 percent and increase prices around 3 percent. (Or, as is illustrated in Figure 26-8, with a gently sloping *AS* curve we see a large *Q* response and a small *P* response to the *AD* shift.)

As time passes, however, wages and prices begin to adjust more completely to the higher price and output levels. Higher demand in both labor and product markets raises wages and prices; wages are adjusted to reflect the higher cost of living; cost-of-living provisions in contracts raise wages and prices even

further. After a second year, prices might rise another 1 or 2 percent, with output then being only 5 or 6 percent above its original level. In the third year, prices might rise again while output falls somewhat. Where would it end? This process might continue until prices rise by fully 10 percent and output is back to the original level. Thus, the monetary policy would raise prices and wages by about 10 percent and real output would be unchanged.

If all adjustments eventually come in prices, all nominal variables are increased by 10 percent while all real variables are unchanged. In other words, nominal variables like the GDP deflator, the CPI, nominal GDP, wages, the money supply, dollar consumption, dollar imports, the dollar value of wealth, and so forth, are 10 percent higher. But real GDP, real consumption, real wages, real incomes, and the real value of wealth are all unchanged by the monetary policy. In such a case, then, we say that *money is neutral*, meaning that changes in the money supply have no effect on real variables.

A word of caution is in order: The scenario that money changes lead to proportionate changes in all nominal variables but no changes in real variables is intuitively plausible and supported by certain empirical evidence. But it is not a universal law. The long run may be a period of many decades; intervening events may throw the economy off the idealized long-run trajectory; and interest-rate changes along the path might have irreversible impacts upon the economy because of bankruptcies, trade changes, and other impacts. The long-run neutrality of money is therefore only a tendency and not a universal law.

This discussion of monetary policy has taken place without reference to fiscal policy. In reality, whatever the philosophical predilections of the government, every advanced economy simultaneously conducts both fiscal and monetary policies. Each policy has strengths and weaknesses. In the chapters that follow, we return to an integrated consideration of the roles of monetary and fiscal policies both in combating the business cycle and in promoting economic growth.

From Aggregate Demand to Aggregate Supply

We have completed our introductory analysis of the determinants of aggregate demand. We examined the foundations of aggregate demand and saw that *AD* is determined by exogenous factors, such as investment and net exports, along with government policies, such as monetary and fiscal policies. In the short run, changes in these factors lead to changes in spending and to changes in both output and prices.

In today's volatile world, economies are exposed to shocks from both inside and outside their borders. Wars, revolutions, financial and currency crises, oil shocks, defaults, and government miscalculations have led to periods of high inflation or high unemployment or both. No market mechanism provides an automatic pilot that can quickly eliminate macroeconomic fluctuations, and governments therefore take responsibility for moderating the swings of the business cycle.

While the United States experienced mild recessions in 1990 and 2001, it was fortunate over the last quarter-century to have avoided deep and prolonged downturns. Other countries were not so lucky. Japan, much of Europe, Latin America, and East Asian countries all have occasionally been caught in the turbulent storms of rapid inflation, high unemployment, currency crises, or sharp declines in living standards. These events are a reminder that there is no universal cure for unemployment and inflation in the face of all the shocks to which an economy is exposed.

We have now concluded our introductory chapters on short-run macroeconomics. The next part turns to issues of economic growth, the open economy, and economic policy.

SUMMARY

A. Central Banking and the Federal Reserve System

1. The Federal Reserve System is a central bank, a bank for bankers. Its objectives are to allow sustainable economic growth, maintain a high level of employment, ensure orderly financial markets, and above all preserve reasonable price stability.

2. The Federal Reserve System (or "Fed") was created in 1913 to control the nation's money and credit and to act as the "lender of last resort." It is run by the Board of Governors and the Federal Open Market Committee (FOMC). The Fed acts as an independent government agency and has great discretion in determining monetary policy.

3. The Fed has three major policy instruments: (a) open-market operations, (b) the discount rate on bank borrowing, and (c) legal reserve requirements on depository institutions. Using these instruments, the Fed affects intermediate targets, such as the level of bank reserves, market interest rates, and the money supply. All these operations aim to improve the economy's performance with respect to the ultimate objectives of monetary policy: achieving the best combination of low inflation, low unemployment, rapid GDP growth, and orderly financial markets. In addition, the Fed along with other federal agencies must backstop the domestic and international financial system in times of crisis.

4. The most important instrument of monetary policy is the Fed's open-market operations. Sales by the Fed of government securities in the open market reduce the Fed's assets and liabilities and thereby reduce the reserves of banks. The effect is a decrease in banks' reserve base for deposits. People end up with less M and more government bonds. Open-market purchases do the opposite, ultimately expanding M by increasing bank reserves.

5. Outflows of international reserves can reduce reserves and M unless offset by sterilization through open-market purchases of bonds. Inflows have the opposite effects unless offset. In recent years, the Fed has routinely sterilized international reserve movements. In open economies with fixed exchange rates, monetary policies must be closely aligned with those in other countries.

B. The Effects of Money on Output and Prices

6. If the Fed desires to slow the growth of output, the five-step sequence goes thus:
   a. The Fed reduces bank reserves through open-market operations.
   b. Each dollar reduction of bank reserves produces a multiple contraction of bank money and the money supply.
   c. In the money market, a reduction in the money supply moves along an unchanged money demand schedule, raising interest rates, restricting the amount and terms of credit, and tightening money.
   d. Tight money reduces investment and other interest-sensitive items of spending like consumer durables or net exports.
   e. The reduction in investment and other spending reduces aggregate demand by the familiar multiplier

mechanism. The lower level of aggregate demand lowers output and the price level or inflation. The sequence is summarized by

$$R \text{ down} \rightarrow M \text{ down} \rightarrow i \text{ up} \rightarrow I, C, X \text{ down} \rightarrow$$
$$AD \text{ down} \rightarrow \text{real GDP down and inflation down}$$

7. Although the monetary mechanism is often explained in terms of money affecting "investment," in fact the monetary mechanism is an extremely rich and complex process whereby changes in interest rates and asset prices influence a wide variety of elements of spending. These sectors include housing, affected by changing mortgage interest rates and housing prices; business investment, affected by changing interest rates and stock prices; spending on consumer durables, influenced by interest rates and credit availability; state and local capital spending, affected by interest rates; and net exports, determined by the effects of interest rates upon foreign exchange rates.

8. In an open economy, the international-trade linkage reinforces the domestic impacts of monetary policy. In a regime of flexible exchange rates, changes in monetary policy affect the exchange rate and net exports, adding yet another facet to the monetary mechanism. The trade link tends to reinforce the impact of monetary policy, operating in the same direction on net exports as it does on domestic investment.

9. Monetary policy may have different effects in the short run and the long run. In the short run, with a relatively flat AS curve, most of the change in AD will affect output and only a small part will affect prices. In the longer run, as the AS curve becomes more nearly vertical, monetary shifts lead predominantly to changes in the price level and much less to output changes. In the polar case where money-supply changes affect only nominal variables and have no effects on real variables, we say that money is neutral. Most real-world monetary shifts have left real economic effects in their wake.

CONCEPTS FOR REVIEW

Central Banking

bank reserves
Federal Reserve balance sheet
open-market purchases and sales
discount rate, borrowings from Fed
legal reserve requirements
FOMC, Board of Governors
policy instruments, intermediate
     targets, ultimate objectives

The Monetary Transmission Mechanism

demand for and supply of money
five-step monetary transmission
     mechanism:
     reserve change
     reserves to money
     money to interest rates
     interest rates to investment
     investment to GDP

interest-sensitive components of
     spending
monetary policy in the AS-AD
     framework
$R \text{ down} \rightarrow M \text{ down} \rightarrow i \text{ up} \rightarrow I \text{ down}$
     $\rightarrow AD \text{ down} \rightarrow \text{GDP down and}$
     $P \text{ down}$
monetary policy in the short run and
     the long run
"neutrality" of money

FURTHER READING AND INTERNET WEBSITES

Further Reading

The *Federal Reserve Bulletin* contains monthly reports on Federal Reserve activities and other important financial developments. (The *Bulletin* is available on the Internet at www.federalreserve.gov/pubs/bulletin/default.htm.)

Websites

The Federal Reserve System: Purposes and Functions (Board of Governors of the Federal Reserve System, Washington, D.C., 1994), available online at www.federalreserve.gov/pf/pf.htm, provides a useful description of the operations of the Fed. Also see the Further Reading and Websites section in Chapter 25 for a more detailed list of sites on monetary policy.

If you want to know which Reserve Bank region you live in, see www.federalreserve.gov/otherfrb.htm. Why are the eastern regions so small?

Biographies of the members of the Board of Governors can be found at www.federalreserve.gov/bios/. Particularly interesting are the transcripts and minutes of Fed meetings, at www.federalreserve.gov/fomc/.

QUESTIONS FOR DISCUSSION

1. Using Figure 26-6, work through each of the following:
   a. The Federal Reserve has decided that unemployment is rising too sharply and wants to reverse this trend by expanding the money supply. What steps must the Fed take to expand money? What will be the impact on the money supply curve? What is the reaction in money markets?
   b. As a result of a rapid economic expansion abroad, exports rise and real GDP increases. What happens to the demand for money? What is the impact upon the market interest rate?
   c. With the spread of automated teller machines (ATMs), people find they need lower "precautionary" balances of currency. The amount of money demanded at each level of interest rate and GDP falls. The Fed is uncertain about the significance of this behavior and therefore keeps the money supply constant. What will be the impact of the asset switch on money supply and demand? On market interest rates?

2. Suppose you are the chairperson of the Fed's Board of Governors at a time when the economy is beginning to overheat and you are called to testify before a congressional committee. Write an explanation for an interrogating senator outlining how you would proceed to maintain stable prices.

3. Consider the balance sheet of the Fed in Table 26-1. Construct a corresponding balance sheet for banks (like the one in Table 25-3 in the previous chapter) assuming that reserve requirements are 10 percent on checking accounts and zero on everything else.
   a. Construct a new set of balance sheets, assuming the Fed sells $1 billion in government securities by open-market operations.
   b. Construct another set of balance sheets to show what happens when the Fed increases reserve requirements to 20 percent.
   c. Assume banks borrow $1 billion of reserves from the Fed. How will this action change the balance sheets?

4. Assume that commercial banks have $100 billion of checkable deposits and $4 billion of vault cash.

Further assume that reserve requirements are 10 percent of checkable deposits. Assume that the public holds $200 billion of currency which is always fixed. Central-bank assets are entirely government securities.
   a. Construct the balance sheets for the central bank and the banking system. Make sure you include bank deposits with the central bank.
   b. Now assume that the central bank decides to engage in an open-market operation, selling $1 billion of government securities to the public. Show the new balance sheets. What has happened to M_1?
   c. Finally, using the graphical apparatus of the monetary transmission mechanism, show qualitatively the impact of the policy on equilibrium money supply, interest rates, investment, and output.

5. Using Figure 26-7, explain how the tight-money policies after 1979 lowered GDP. Also, explain each of the steps in words.

6. "A government deficit is bad because it leads to rapid monetary growth." Explain why this statement is wrong.

7. In Japan in 1998 and 1999, prices were falling at 2 percent per year while the short-term interest rate was 0.1 percent per year.
   a. What was the real interest rate?
   b. "In 1998 and 1999, Japan was caught in a *liquidity trap*, where the central bank could not lower real interest rates and was therefore unable to stimulate the economy." Explain this statement.

8. After the reunification of Germany in 1990, payments to rebuild the east led to a major expansion of aggregate demand in Germany. The German central bank responded by slowing money growth and driving German real interest rates extremely high. Trace through why this German monetary tightening would be expected to lead to a depreciation of the dollar. Explain why the depreciation would stimulate economic activity in the United States. Also, explain why European countries that had pegged their currencies to the German mark would find themselves plunged into deep recessions as German interest rates rose and pulled other European rates up with them.

Growth, Development, and the Global Economy

27

The Process of Economic Growth

The Industrial Revolution was not an episode with a beginning and an end. . . . It is still going on.

E. J. Hobsbawm
The Age of Revolution (1962)

The daily press is dominated by business-cycle developments. However important, these concerns are but small ripples on the larger wave of economic growth, in which advanced economies such as the United States accumulate larger quantities of capital equipment, push out the frontiers of technological knowledge, and become steadily more productive. Over the long run of decades and generations, living standards as measured by output per capita or consumption per household are primarily determined by aggregate supply and the level of productivity of a country.

This chapter begins with a survey of the theory of economic growth and then reviews the historical trends in economic activity with particular application to wealthy countries like the United States. The next chapter looks at the other end of the income spectrum by examining the plight of the developing countries, struggling to reach the level of affluence enjoyed in the West. The two chapters that follow examine the role of international trade and finance in macroeconomics. Figure 27-1 presents an overview of the growth chapters, using our familiar flowchart.

The Long-Term Significance of Growth

Look at the inside front cover of this book, where you will see the advance of real output over the twentieth century. You can see that real GDP has grown *by a factor of 30 since 1900.* This is perhaps the central economic fact of the century. Continuing rapid economic growth enables advanced industrial countries to provide more of everything to their citizens—better food and bigger homes, more resources for medical care and pollution control, universal education for children, more resources for the military, and public pensions for retirees.

The recent war in Iraq was an illustration of how the United States' economic power translates into military power. Because of its rapid economic growth, the United States produces about one-quarter of world output. Even though the United States spends only 4 percent of its GDP on the military, that is equal to the combined military spending of the rest of the world. Iraq, which devoted almost half of its output to the military, was outspent and outgunned by a factor of 50 or more.

Because economic growth is so important for living standards, it is a central objective of policy. Countries that run fastest in the economic-growth race, such as Britain in the nineteenth century and the United States in the twentieth century, serve as role models for other countries seeking the path to affluence. At the other extreme, countries in economic

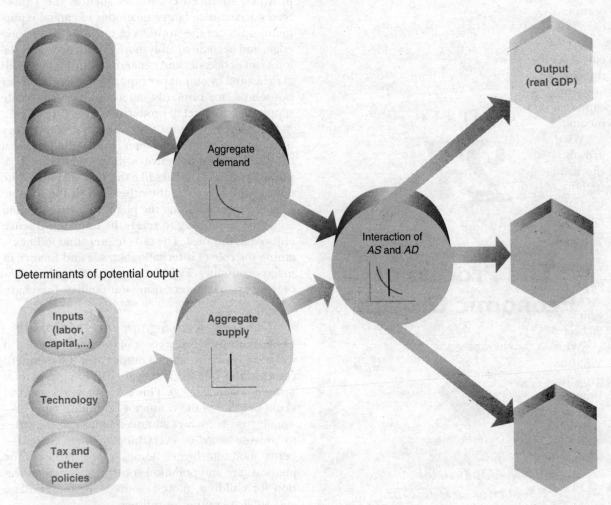

Determinants of potential output

FIGURE 27-1. Economic Growth Is Key to Long-Term Living Standards

In the long run, a nation's economic fortunes depend upon the growth of its potential output. This chapter examines the long-term growth trends along with the theories that explain the basic trends.

decline often experience political and social turmoil. The revolutions in Eastern Europe and the Soviet Union in 1989–1991 were sparked when those nations' residents compared their economic stagnation under socialism with the rapid growth experienced by their Western, market-oriented neighbors. Economic growth is the single most important factor in the success of nations in the long run.

A. THEORIES OF ECONOMIC GROWTH

Let's begin with a careful definition of exactly what we mean by economic growth: **Economic growth** represents the expansion of a country's potential GDP or national output. Put differently, economic growth occurs when a nation's production-possibility frontier (*PPF*) shifts outward.

A closely related concept is the growth rate of *output per person*. This determines the rate at which the country's living standards are rising. Countries are primarily concerned with the growth in per capita output because this leads to rising average incomes.

What are the long-term patterns of economic growth in high-income countries? Table 27-1 shows the history of economic growth since 1870 for 16 high-income countries including the major countries of North America and Western Europe, Japan, and Australia. We see the steady growth of output over this period. Even more important for living standards is the growth in output per hour worked, which moves closely with the increase in living standards. Over the entire period, output per worker grew by an average rate of 2.3 percent annually, which compounds to a growth factor of almost 20 over the 130-year period.

What were the major forces behind this growth? What can nations do to speed up their economic growth rate? And what are the prospects for the twenty-first century, given the slowdown in productivity growth of the last three decades along with the possibility of tighter environmental constraints? These are the issues that must be confronted by economic-growth analysis.

Economic growth involves the growth of potential output over the long run. The growth in output per capita is an important objective of government because it is associated with rising average real incomes and living standards.

THE FOUR WHEELS OF GROWTH

What is the recipe for economic growth? To begin with, many roads lead to Rome. There are many successful strategies on the road to self-sustained economic growth. Britain, for example, became the world economic leader in the 1800s by pioneering the Industrial Revolution, inventing steam engines and railroads, and emphasizing free trade. Japan, by contrast, came to the economic-growth race later. It made its mark by first imitating foreign technologies and protecting domestic industries from imports and then developing tremendous expertise in manufacturing and electronics.

Even though their individual paths may differ, all rapidly growing countries share certain common traits. The same fundamental process of economic growth and development that helped shape Britain and Japan is at work today in developing countries like China and India. Indeed, economists who have studied growth have found that the engine of economic progress must ride on the same four wheels, no matter how rich or poor the country.

Period	GDP	Average Annual Growth Rate in:		
		GDP per hour worked	Total hours worked	Labor force
1870–1913	2.5	1.6	0.9	1.2
1913–1950	1.9	1.8	0.1	0.8
1950–1973	4.8	4.5	0.3	1.0
1973–2000	2.7	2.2	0.5	1.1
Total period	**2.8**	**2.3**	**0.5**	**1.0**

TABLE 27-1. Patterns of Growth in 16 Industrial Countries

Over the last century, major high-income countries like the United States, Germany, France, and Japan have grown rapidly. Output has grown faster than inputs of labor, reflecting increases in capital and technological advance.

Source: Angus Maddison, *Phases of Capitalist Development* (Oxford, 1982), updated by authors from data from Maddison, the World Bank, and other publications.

These four wheels, or factors of growth, are:

- Human resources (labor supply, education, discipline, motivation)
- Natural resources (land, minerals, fuels, environmental quality)
- Capital formation (machines, factories, roads)
- Technology (science, engineering, management, entrepreneurship)

Often, economists write the relationship in terms of an *aggregate production function* (or *APF*), which relates total national output to inputs and technology. Algebraically, the *APF* is

$$Q = AF(K, L, R)$$

where Q = output, K = productive services of capital, L = labor inputs, R = natural-resource inputs, A represents the level of technology in the economy, and F is the production function. As the inputs of capital, labor, or resources rise, we would expect that output would increase, although output will probably show diminishing returns to additional inputs of production factors. We can think of the role of technology as augmenting the productivity of inputs. **Productivity** denotes the ratio of output to a weighted average of inputs. As technology (A) improves through new inventions or the adoption of technologies from abroad, this advance allows a country to produce more output with the same level of inputs.

Let's now see how each of the four factors contributes to growth.

Human Resources

Labor inputs consist of quantities of workers and of the skills of the workforce. Many economists believe that the quality of labor inputs—the skills, knowledge, and discipline of the labor force—is the single most important element in economic growth. A country might buy fast computers, modern telecommunications devices, sophisticated electricity-generating equipment, and hypersonic fighter aircraft. However, these capital goods can be effectively used and maintained only by skilled and trained workers. Improvements in literacy, health, and discipline, and most recently the ability to use computers, add greatly to the productivity of labor.

Natural Resources

The second classic factor of production is natural resources. The important resources here are arable land, oil and gas, forests, water, and mineral resources. Some high-income countries like Canada and Norway have grown primarily on the basis of their ample resource base, with large output in agriculture, fisheries, and forestry. Similarly, the United States, with its fertile farmlands, is the world's largest producer and exporter of grains.

But the possession of natural resources is not necessary for economic success in the modern world. New York City prospers primarily on its high-density service industries. Many countries, such as Japan, had virtually no natural resources but thrived by concentrating on sectors that depend more on labor and capital than on indigenous resources. Indeed, tiny Hong Kong, with but a minute fraction of the land area of resource-rich Russia, actually has a larger volume of international trade than does that giant country.

Capital Formation

Recall that tangible capital includes structures like roads and power plants, equipment like trucks and computers, and stocks of inventories. The most dramatic stories in economic history often involve the accumulation of capital. In the nineteenth century, the transcontinental railroads of North America brought commerce to the American heartland, which had been living in isolation. In the last century, waves of investment in automobiles, roads, and power plants increased productivity and provided the infrastructure which created entire new industries. Many believe that computers and the information superhighway will do for the twenty-first century what railroads and highways did in earlier times.

Accumulating capital, as we have seen, requires a sacrifice of current consumption over many years. Countries that grow rapidly tend to invest heavily in new capital goods; in the most rapidly growing countries, 10 to 20 percent of output may go into net capital formation. The United States today is a signal contrast. In 2003, the net national saving rate in the United States fell to zero from an average of around 7 percent during most of the period since World War II. The low saving rate was the result of low personal saving and large government fiscal deficits. The low saving was seen primarily in the large external (trade) deficit. Economists worry that the low saving rate will retard investment and economic growth in the decades to come and that the large foreign indebtedness may require major adverse changes in exchange rates and real wages.

When we think of capital, we must not concentrate only on computers and factories. Many investments will be undertaken only by governments and lay the framework for a thriving private sector. These investments are called **social overhead capital** and consist of the large-scale projects that precede trade and commerce. Roads, irrigation and water projects, and public-health measures are important examples. All these involve large investments that tend to be "indivisible," or lumpy, and sometimes have increasing returns to scale. These projects generally involve external economies, or spillovers that private firms cannot capture, so the government must step in to ensure that these social overhead or infrastructure investments are effectively undertaken. Some investments, such as transportation and communication systems, involve "network" externalities in which productivity depends upon the density of the using population.

Technological Change and Innovation

In addition to the three classic factors discussed above, technological advance has been a vital fourth ingredient in the rapid growth of living standards. Historically, growth has definitely not been a process of simple replication, adding rows of steel mills or power plants next to each other. Rather, a never-ending stream of inventions and technological advances led to a vast improvement in the production possibilities of Europe, North America, and Japan.

We are today witnessing an explosion of new technologies, particularly in computation, communication (such as the Internet), and the life sciences. But this is not the first time that American society has been shaken by fundamental inventions. Electricity, radio, the automobile, and television also diffused rapidly through the American economy in an earlier age. Figure 27-2 shows the diffusion of major inventions of the twentieth century. This S-shaped pattern is typical of the diffusion of new technologies.

Technological change denotes changes in the processes of production or introduction of new products or services. Process inventions that have greatly increased productivity were the steam engine, the generation of electricity, antibiotics, the internal-combustion engine, the wide-body jet, the microprocessor, and the fax machine. Fundamental

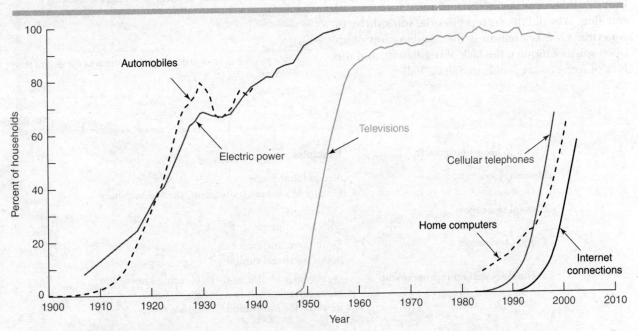

FIGURE 27-2. Diffusion of Major Technologies

Today's information technologies such as cellular telephones, computers, and the Internet are spreading rapidly through American society. Similar diffusion patterns were seen with other fundamental inventions in the past.

Source: *Economic Report of the President, 2000*, updated by authors.

product inventions include the telephone, the radio, the airplane, the phonograph, the television, the computer and the VCR.

The most dramatic developments of the modern era are occurring in information technology. Here, tiny notebook computers can outperform the fastest computer of the 1960s, while fiber-optic lines can carry 10,000 simultaneous conversations that required 10,000 paired copper-wire lines in an earlier period. These inventions provide the most spectacular examples of technological change. Nonetheless, technological advance is in fact a continuous process of small and large improvements, as witnessed by the fact that the United States issues over 100,000 new patents annually and that millions of other small refinements are routine progress in a modern economy.

Because of its importance in raising living standards, economists have long pondered how to encourage technological progress. Increasingly, it is becoming clear that technological change is not a mechanical procedure of simply finding better products and processes. Instead, rapid innovation requires the fostering of an entrepreneurial spirit. Consider the thriving Internet industry today—an industry that is reshaping the face of commerce and retailing. Why did the entrepreneurial spirit thrive in America? One key reason is the combination of an open spirit of inquiry, the lack of regulation, and the lure of free-market profits in Silicon Valley.

Table 27-2 summarizes the four wheels of economic growth.

Institutions, Incentives, and Innovation

In the very long run, the growth in the world's output and wealth has come primarily because of improvements in knowledge. Yet institutions to promote the creation and spread of knowledge, along with incentives to devote our human effort to that task, were developed late in human history—slowly in Western Europe over the last 500 years. This point was eloquently argued by William Baumol:

> The museum at Alexandria was the center of technological innovation in the Roman Empire. By the first century B.C., that city knew of virtually every form of machine gearing that is used today, including a working steam engine. But these seemed to be used only to make what amounted to elaborate toys. The steam engine was used to open and close the doors of a temple.[1]

Baumol and economic historian Joel Mokyr argue that innovation depends crucially on the development of incentives and institutions. They particularly point to the role of private ownership, the patent system, and a rule-based system of adjudicating disputes as devices for fostering innovation.

---

[1] See Baumol in the Further Reading section at the end of this chapter.

Factor in economic growth	Examples
Human resources	Size of labor force Quality of workers (education, skills, discipline)
Natural resources	Oil and gas Soils and climate
Capital formation	Equipment and factories Social overhead capital
Technology and entrepreneurship	Quality of scientific and engineering knowledge Managerial know-how Rewards for innovation

TABLE 27-2. The Four Wheels of Progress

Economic growth inevitably rides on the four wheels of labor, natural resources, capital, and technology. But the wheels may differ greatly among countries, and some countries combine them more effectively than others.

THEORIES OF ECONOMIC GROWTH

Virtually everyone is in favor of economic growth. But there are strong disagreements about the best way to accomplish this goal. Some economists and policymakers stress the need to increase capital investment. Others advocate measures to stimulate research and development and technological change. Still a third group emphasizes the role of a better-educated workforce. Some believe that economic protectionism is useful.

Economists have long studied the question of the relative importance of different factors in determining growth. In the discussion below, we look at the theories of economic growth, which offer some clues about the driving forces behind growth. Then, in the final part of this section, we see what can be learned about growth from its historical patterns over the last century.

The Classical Dynamics of Smith and Malthus

Early economists like Adam Smith and T. R. Malthus stressed the critical role of land in economic growth. In *The Wealth of Nations* (1776), Adam Smith provided a handbook of economic development. He began with a hypothetical idyllic age: "that original state of things, which precedes both the appropriation of land and the accumulation of [capital] stock." This was a time when land was freely available to all, and before capital accumulation had begun to matter.

What would be the dynamics of economic growth in such a "golden age"? Because land is freely available, people would simply spread out onto more acres as the population increases, just as the settlers did in the American west. Because there is no capital, national output would exactly double as population doubles. What about real wages? The entire national income would go to wages because there is no subtraction for land rent or interest on capital. Output expands in step with population, so the real wage rate per worker would be constant over time.

But this golden age cannot continue forever. Eventually, as population growth continues, all the land will be occupied. Once the frontier disappears, balanced growth of land, labor, and output is no longer possible. New laborers begin to crowd onto already-worked soils. Land becomes scarce, and rents rise to ration it among different uses.

Population still grows, and so does the national product. But output must grow more slowly than does population. Why? With new laborers added to fixed land, each worker now has less land to work with, and the law of diminishing returns comes into operation. The increasing labor-land ratio leads to a declining marginal product of labor and hence to declining real wage rates.[2]

How bad could things get? The dour Reverend T. R. Malthus thought that population pressures would drive the economy to a point where workers were at the minimum level of subsistence. Malthus reasoned that whenever wages were above the subsistence level, population would expand; below-subsistence wages would lead to high mortality and population decline. Only at subsistence wages could there be a stable equilibrium of population. He believed the working classes were destined to a life that is brutish, nasty, and short. This gloomy picture led Thomas Carlyle to criticize economics as "the dismal science."

Figure 27-3(*a*) shows the process of economic growth in Smith's golden age. Here, as population doubles, the production-possibility frontier (*PPF*) shifts out by a factor of 2 in each direction, showing that there are no constraints on growth from land or resources. Figure 27-3(*b*) shows the pessimistic Malthusian case, where a doubling of population leads to a less-than-doubling of food and clothing, lowering per capita output, as more people crowd onto limited land and diminishing returns drive down output per person.

---

[2] The theory in this chapter relies on an important finding from microeconomics. In analysis of the determination of wages under simplified conditions, including perfect competition, it is shown that the wage rate of labor will be equal to the extra or marginal product of the last worker hired. For example, if the last worker contributes goods worth $12.50 per hour to the firm's output, then under competitive conditions the firm will be willing to pay up to $12.50 per hour in wages to that worker. Similarly, the rent on land is the marginal product of the last unit of land, and the real interest rate will be determined by the marginal product of the least productive piece of capital.

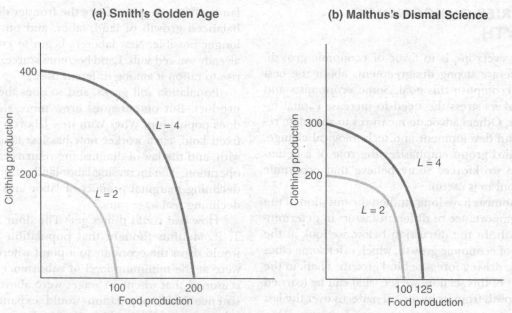

(a) Smith's Golden Age

(b) Malthus's Dismal Science

FIGURE 27-3. The Classical Dynamics of Smith and Malthus

In **(a)**, unlimited land on the frontier means that when population doubles, labor can simply spread out and produce twice the quantity of any food and clothing combination. In **(b)**, limited land means that increasing population from 2 million to 4 million triggers diminishing returns. Note that potential food production rises by only 25 percent with a doubling of labor inputs.

Are There Limits to Growth?

Often, earlier ideas reemerge in light of new social trends or scientific findings. In the last two decades, Malthusian ideas have surfaced as many antigrowth advocates and environmentalists have argued that economic growth is limited due to the finiteness of our natural resources and because of environmental constraints.

Economic growth involves a rapid increase in the use of land and mineral resources and (if not controlled) in the emissions of air and water pollution. For example, U.S. energy consumption from fuels totaled 220 trillion Btu (British thermal units) in 1850. By 1900, the total reached 7600 trillion Btu, and in 1995 energy use was 66,000 trillion Btu. At the same time, the emissions of sulfur dioxide grew from around 0.2 million tons annually in 1850, peaked at 31 million tons in 1970, and declined to 20 million tons in 1997. This important example shows why people are concerned that rapid economic growth may lead to resource exhaustion and environmental degradation.

Worries about the viability of growth surfaced prominently with a series of studies in the early 1970s by an ominous-sounding group called the "Club of Rome." Growth critics found a receptive audience because of mounting alarm about rapid population growth in developing countries and, after 1973, the upward spiral in oil prices and the sharp decline in the growth of productivity and living standards in the major industrial countries. This first wave of anxiety subsided with declines in natural-resource prices after 1980 and slowing population growth in developing countries.

A second wave of growth pessimism emerged over the last decade. It involves not the depletion of mineral resources like oil and gas but the presence of environmental constraints on long-term economic growth. The possibility of global environmental problems arises because of mounting scientific evidence that industrial activity is significantly changing the earth's climate and ecosystems. Among today's concerns are global warming, in which use of fossil fuels is warming the climate;

widespread evidence of acid rain; the appearance of the Antarctic "ozone hole" along with ozone depletion in temperate regions; deforestation, especially of the tropical rain forests, which may upset the global ecological balance; soil erosion, which threatens the long-term viability of agriculture; and species extinction, which threatens to limit potential future medical and other technologies.

Global environmental constraints are closely linked to the Malthusian constraints of an earlier age. Whereas Malthus held that production would be limited by finite land, today's growth pessimists argue that growth will be limited by the finite absorptive capacity of our environment. We can, some say, burn only a limited amount of fossil fuel before we face the threat of dangerous climate change. The need to reduce the use of fossil fuels might well slow our long-term economic growth.

What is the empirical evidence on the effect of resource exhaustion and environmental limits on economic growth? There is evidence that the quality of land and mineral resources has deteriorated over the last century and that we are required to drill deeper for oil, use more marginal lands, and mine lower-grade mineral ores. But until now technological advance has largely outweighed these trends, so the prices of oil, gas, most minerals, and land have actually declined relative to the price of labor. Moreover, new environmentally friendly technologies have become increasingly important, and many of the worst environmental abuses have been alleviated in the last two decades. Nonetheless, regulations to curb pollution impose costs on the economy. In 1999, pollution-control abatement expenditures were $18 billion. There is some evidence that environmental regulations have slowed productivity growth by a small amount over the last three decades.

Economic Growth with Capital Accumulation: The Neoclassical Growth Model

Malthus's forecast was dramatically wide of the mark because he did not recognize that technological innovation and capital investment could overcome the law of diminishing returns. Land did not become the limiting factor in production. Instead, the first Industrial Revolution brought forth power-driven machinery that increased production, factories that gathered teams of workers into giant firms, railroads and steamships that linked together the far

points of the world, and iron and steel that made possible stronger machines and faster locomotives. As market economies entered the twentieth century, a second Industrial Revolution grew up around the telephone, automobile, and electricity industries. Capital accumulation and new technologies became the dominant forces affecting economic development. Moreover, if the growth pessimists of today prove wrong, it will be largely because new environmentally friendly and resource-saving capital replaces today's resource-intensive, polluting technologies.

To understand how capital accumulation and technological change affect the economy, we must understand the **neoclassical model of economic growth.** This approach was pioneered by Robert Solow of MIT, who was awarded the 1987 Nobel Prize for this and other contributions to economic-growth theory. The neoclassical growth model serves as the basic tool for understanding the growth process in advanced countries and has been applied in empirical studies of the sources of economic growth.

Apostle of Economic Growth

Robert M. Solow was born in Brooklyn and educated at Harvard and then moved to the MIT Economics Department in 1950. Over the next few years he developed the neoclassical growth model and applied it in the growth-accounting framework discussed later in this chapter.

One of Solow's major studies was "A Contribution to the Theory of Economic Growth" in 1956. This was a mathematical version of the neoclassical growth model surveyed in this chapter. The importance of this study was highlighted as follows in Solow's Nobel Prize citation:

Solow's theoretical model had an enormous impact on economic analysis. From simply being a tool for the analysis of the growth process, the model has been generalized in several different directions. It has been extended by the introduction of other types of production factors and it has been reformulated to include stochastic features. The design of dynamic links in certain "numerical" models employed in general equilibrium analysis has also been based on Solow's model. But, above all, Solow's growth model constitutes a framework within which modern macroeconomic theory can be structured.

The increased interest of government to expand education and research and development was inspired by these studies. Every long-term report ... for any country has used a Solow-type analysis.[3]

Solow has also contributed to empirical studies of economic growth, to natural-resource economics, and to the development of capital theory. In addition, Solow served as a macroeconomic adviser for the Kennedy administration.

Solow is known for his enthusiasm for economics as well as for his humor. He worries that the hunger for publicity has led some economists to exaggerate their knowledge. He criticized economists for "an apparently irresistible urge to push their science further than it will go, to answer questions more delicate than our limited understanding of a complicated question will allow. Nobody likes to say 'I don't know.'"

A lively writer, Solow worries that economics is terrifically difficult to explain to the public. At his news conference after winning the Nobel Prize, Solow quipped, "The attention span of the people you write for is shorter than the length of one true sentence." Nonetheless, Solow continues to labor for his brand of economics, and the world increasingly listens to the apostle of economic growth from MIT.

Basic Assumptions. The neoclassical growth model describes an economy in which a single homogeneous output is produced by two types of inputs—capital and labor. In contrast to the Malthusian analysis, labor growth is assumed to be a given. In addition, we assume that the economy is competitive and always operates at full employment, so we can analyze the growth of potential output.

The major new ingredients in the neoclassical growth model are capital and technological change. For the moment, assume that technology remains constant. Capital consists of durable produced goods that are used to make other goods. Capital goods include structures like factories and houses, equipment like computers and machine tools, and inventories of finished goods and goods in process.

For convenience, we will assume that there is a single kind of capital good (call it K). We then measure the aggregate stock of capital as the total quantity of capital goods. In our real-world calculations, we approximate the universal capital good as the total dollar value of capital goods (i.e., the constant-dollar value of equipment, structures, and inventories). If L is the number of workers, then (K/L) is equal to the quantity of capital per worker, or the *capital-labor ratio*. We can write our aggregate production function for the neoclassical growth model without technological change as $Q = F(K, L)$.

Turning now to the economic-growth process, economists stress the need for **capital deepening,** which is the process by which the quantity of capital per worker increases over time. Examples of capital deepening include the multiplication of farm machinery and irrigation systems in farming, of railroads and highways in transportation, and of the increasing use of computers in banking. These are all examples of how the economy invests in capital goods, increasing the amount of capital per worker. As a result, the output per worker has grown enormously in farming, transportation, and banking.

What happens to the return on capital in the process of capital deepening? For a given state of technology, a rapid rate of investment in plant and equipment tends to depress the rate of return on capital.[4] This occurs because the most worthwhile investment projects get undertaken first, after which later investments become less and less valuable. Once a full railroad network or telephone system has been constructed, new investments will branch into more sparsely populated regions or duplicate existing lines. The rates of return on these later investments will be lower than the high returns on the first lines between densely populated regions.

In addition, the wage rate paid to workers will tend to rise as capital deepening takes place. Why? Each worker has more capital to work with and his or her marginal product therefore rises. As a result, the competitive wage rate rises along with the marginal product of labor.

---

[3] The citations of the committees for the Nobel Prizes in economics can be found on the Internet at www.nobel.se/laureates.

[4] Under perfect competition and without risk, taxes, or inflation, the rate of return on capital is equal to the real interest rate on bonds and other financial assets.

We can summarize the impact of capital deepening in the neoclassical growth model as follows:

Capital deepening occurs when the stock of capital grows more rapidly than the labor force. In the absence of technological change, capital deepening will produce a growth of output per worker, of the marginal product of labor, and of real wages; it also will lead to diminishing returns on capital and therefore to a decline in the rate of return on capital.

Geometrical Analysis of the Neoclassical Model

We can analyze the effects of capital accumulation by using Figure 27-4. This figure shows the aggregate production function graphically by depicting output per worker on the vertical axis and capital per worker on the horizontal axis. In the background, *and held constant for the moment*, are all the other variables that were discussed at the start of this section—the amount of land, the endowment of natural resources, and, most important of all, the technology used by the economy.

What happens as the society accumulates capital? As each worker has more and more capital to work with, the economy moves up and to the right on the aggregate production function. Say that the capital-labor ratio increases, from $(K/L)_0$ to $(K/L)_1$. Then the amount of output per worker increases, from $(Q/L)_0$ to $(Q/L)_1$.

What happens to the factor prices of labor and capital? As capital deepens, diminishing returns to capital set in, so the rate of return on capital and the real interest rate fall. (The slope of the curve in Figure 27-4 is the marginal product of capital, which is seen to fall as capital deepening occurs.) Also, because each worker can work with more capital, workers' marginal productivities rise and the real wage rate consequently also rises. The reverse would happen if the amount of capital per worker were to fall for some reason. For example, wars tend to reduce much of a nation's capital to rubble and lower the capital-labor ratio; after wars, therefore, we see a scarcity of capital and high returns on capital. Hence, our earlier verbal summary of the impact of capital deepening is verified by the analysis in Figure 27-4.

Long-Run Steady State. What is the long-run equilibrium in the neoclassical growth model without technological change? Eventually, the capital-labor ratio will stop rising. *In the long-run, the economy will enter a steady state in which capital deepening ceases, real wages stop growing, and capital returns and real interest rates are constant.*

We can show how the economy moves toward the steady state in Figure 27-4. As capital continues to accumulate, the capital-labor ratio increases as shown by the arrows from E' to E'' to E''' until finally the capital-labor ratio stops growing at V. At that point, output per worker (Q/L) is constant, and real wages stop growing.

Without technological change, output per worker and the wage rate stagnate. This is certainly a far better outcome than the world of subsistence wages predicted by Malthus. But the long-run equilibrium of the neoclassical growth model makes it clear that if economic growth consists only of accumulating capital through replicating factories with existing methods of production, then the standard of living will eventually stop rising.

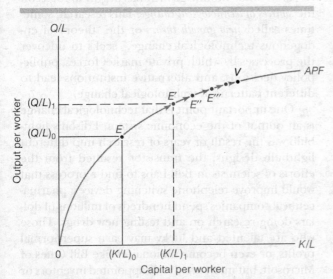

FIGURE 27-4. Economic Growth through Capital Deepening

As the amount of capital per worker increases, output per worker also increases. This graph shows the importance of "capital deepening," or increasing the amount of capital each worker has on hand. Remember, however, that other factors are held constant, such as technology, quality of the labor force, and natural resources.

The Importance of Technological Change

While the capital-accumulation model is a good first step down the road to understanding economic growth, it leaves some major questions unanswered. To begin with, the model with an unchanging technology predicts that real wages will gradually stagnate. But real wages have certainly not stagnated in the twentieth century. Additionally, it cannot explain the tremendous growth in productivity over time, nor does it account for the tremendous differences in per capita income among countries.

What is missing is technological change. We can depict technological change in our growth diagram as an upward shift in the aggregate production function, as illustrated in Figure 27-5. In this diagram, we show the aggregate production function for both 1950 and 2000. Because of technological change, the aggregate production function has shifted upward from APF_{1950} to APF_{2000}. This upward shift shows the advances in productivity that are generated by the vast array of new processes and products like

FIGURE 27-5. Technological Advance Shifts Up the Production Function

As a result of improvements in technology, the aggregate production function shifts *upward over time*. Hence improvements in technology combine with capital deepening to raise output per worker and real wages.

electronics, computers, advances in metallurgy, improved service technologies, and so forth.

Therefore, in addition to considering the capital deepening described above, we must also take into account advances in technology. The sum of capital deepening and technological change is the arrow in Figure 27-5, which produces an increase in output per worker from $(Q/L)_{1950}$ to $(Q/L)_{2000}$. Instead of settling into a steady state, the economy enjoys rising output per worker, rising wages, and increasing living standards.

Of particular interest is the impact of changing technologies on rates of profits and real interest rates. As a result of technological progress, the real interest rate need not fall. Invention increases the productivity of capital and offsets the tendency for a falling rate of profit.

Technological Change as an Economic Output

Up to now we have treated technological change as something that floats mysteriously down from scientists and inventors like manna from heaven. Recent research on economic growth has begun to focus on the *sources of technological change*. This research, sometimes called *new growth theory* or the "theory of endogenous technological change," seeks to uncover the processes by which private market forces, public-policy decisions, and alternative institutions lead to different patterns of technological change.

One important point is that technological change is an output of the economic system. Edison's lightbulb was the result of years of research into different lightbulb designs; the transistor resulted from the efforts of scientists in Bell Labs to find a process that would improve telephone switching devices; pharmaceutical companies spend hundreds of millions of dollars doing research on and testing new drugs. Those who are talented and lucky may earn supernormal profits, or even become billionaires like Bill Gates of Microsoft, but many are the disappointed inventors or companies that end up with empty pockets.

The other unusual feature of technologies is that they are public goods, or "nonrival" goods in technical language. This means that they can be used by many people at the same time without being used up. A new piece of software, a new miracle drug, a design for a new steelmaking process—I can use each of these without reducing its productivity for you and the British and the Japanese and everyone else. In addition, inventions are expensive to produce but inexpensive to reproduce. These features of technological change can produce severe market failures—they mean that inventors sometimes have great difficulty profiting from their inventions because other people can copy them. The market failures are largest for the most basic and fundamental forms of research. Therefore, governments must be careful to ensure that inventors have adequate incentives to engage in research and development. Governments increasingly pay attention to *intellectual property rights*, such as patents and copyrights, to provide adequate market rewards for creative activities.

What is the major contribution of new growth theory? It has changed the way we think about the growth process and public policies. If technological differences are the major reason for differences in living standards among nations, and if technology is a produced factor, then economic-growth policy will have to focus much more sharply on how nations can improve their technological performance. This is just the lesson drawn by Stanford's Paul Romer, one of the leaders of new growth theory:

> Economists can once again make progress toward a complete understanding of the determinants of long-run economic success. Ultimately, this will put us in position to offer policymakers something more insightful than the standard neoclassical prescription—more saving and more schooling. We will be able to rejoin the ongoing policy debates about tax subsidies for private research, antitrust exemptions for research joint ventures, the activities of multinational firms, the effects of government procurement, the feedback between trade policy and innovation, the scope of protection for intellectual property rights, the links between private firms and universities, the mechanisms for selecting the research areas that receive public support, and the costs and benefits of an explicit government-led technology policy.[5]

To summarize:

Technological change—which increases output produced for a given bundle of inputs—is a crucial ingredient in the growth of nations. The new growth theory seeks to uncover the processes which generate technological change. This approach emphasizes that technological change is an output that is subject to severe market failures because technology is a public good that is expensive to produce but cheap to reproduce. Governments increasingly seek to provide strong intellectual property rights for those who develop new technologies.

B. THE PATTERNS OF GROWTH IN THE UNITED STATES

The Facts of Economic Growth

The first part of this chapter described the basic theories of economic growth. But economists have not been content to rest with theory. A major research area all around the world has been measuring the different components of the economic-growth process and applying them to the important theories. An understanding of the patterns of economic growth will help sort out the reasons that some nations prosper while others decline.

Figure 27-6 depicts the key trends of economic development for the United States since the start of the twentieth century. Similar patterns have been found in most of the major industrial countries.

Figure 27-6(a) shows the trends in real GDP, the capital stock, and population. Population and employment have more than tripled since 1900. At the same time, the stock of physical capital has risen by a factor of 14. Thus, the amount of capital per worker (the K/L ratio) has increased by a factor of more than 4. Clearly, capital deepening has been an important feature of twentieth- and early-twenty-first-century American capitalism.

What about the growth in output? In a world without technological change, output growth would be somewhere between labor growth and capital growth. In fact, the output curve in Figure 27-6(a) is not in between the two factor curves, but actually lies above both curves. This indicates that technological progress must have increased the productivity of capital and labor.

For most people, an economy's performance is measured by earnings, shown in Figure 27-6(c) in

---

[5] See Paul Romer in this chapter's Further Reading section.

(a) Output, Labor, Capital

(b) Capital-Output Ratio

(c) Real Compensation and Output per Worker-Hour

(d) Real Interest Rate

FIGURE 27-6. Economic Growth Displays Striking Regularities

(a) The capital stock has grown faster than population and labor supply. Nonetheless, total output has grown even more rapidly than capital. (b) The capital-output ratio declined sharply during the first half of the twentieth century, but it has remained steady since then. (c) Real average hourly earnings have grown steadily and at the same rate as average product per worker-hour over the entire period. (d) The real interest rate has been trendless since 1900, suggesting that technological change has offset diminishing returns to capital accumulation.

Source: U.S. Departments of Commerce and Labor, Federal Reserve Board, U.S. Bureau of the Census, and historical studies by John Kendrick.

terms of real average hourly earnings (or money earnings corrected for inflation). Hourly earnings have grown impressively for most of the post-1900 period, as we would expect from the growth in the capital-labor ratio and from steady technological advance.

The real interest rate (i.e., the money interest rate minus the rate of inflation) is shown in Figure 27-6(d). Interest rates and profit rates fluctuated greatly in business cycles and wars but have displayed no strong trend upward or downward over the whole period. Either by coincidence or because of an economic mechanism inducing this pattern, technological change has largely offset diminishing returns to capital.

Output per worker-hour is the solid black curve in Figure 27-6(c). As could be expected from the deepening of capital and from technological advance, output per worker has risen steadily.

The fact that wages rise at the same rate as output per worker does not mean that labor has captured all the fruits of productivity advance. Rather, it means that labor has kept about the same share of total product, with capital also earning about the same relative share throughout the period. A close look at Figure 27-6(c) shows that real wages have grown at about the same rate as output per person since 1900. More precisely, the average growth rate of real wages was 2.1 percent per year, while that of output per person was 2.2 percent per year. These figures imply that labor's share of national income (and therefore also property's share) have changed very little over the course of the last 100 years.

Seven Basic Trends of Economic Growth

Economists studying the economic history of the advanced nations have found that the following trends apply in most countries:

1. The capital stock has grown more rapidly than population and employment, resulting in capital deepening.

2. For most of the period since 1900, there has been a strong upward trend in real average hourly earnings.

3. The share of labor compensation in national income has been remarkably stable over the last 100 years.

4. There were major oscillations in real interest rates and the rate of profit, particularly during business cycles, but there has been no strong upward or downward trend over the post-1900 period.

5. Instead of steadily rising, which would be predicted by the law of diminishing returns with unchanging technology, the capital-output ratio has actually declined since the start of the twentieth century.

6. For most of the period since 1900, the ratios of national saving and of investment to GDP were stable. Since 1980, the national saving rate has declined sharply in the United States.

7. After effects of the business cycle are removed, national product has grown at an average rate of close to 3 percent per year. Output growth has been much higher than a weighted average of the growth of capital, labor, and resource inputs, suggesting that technological innovation must be playing a key role in economic growth.

Relationship of the Seven Trends to Economic-Growth Theories

While the seven trends of economic history are not like the immutable laws of physics, they do portray fundamental facts about growth in the modern era. How do they fit into our economic-growth theories?

Trends 2 and 1—higher wage rates when capital deepens—fit nicely into our neoclassical growth model shown in Figure 27-4. Trend 3—that the wage share has been remarkably stable—is an interesting coincidence that is consistent with a wide variety of production functions relating Q to L and K.

Trends 4 and 5, however, warn us that technological change must be playing a role here, so Figure 27-5, with its picture of advancing technology, is more realistic than the steady state depicted in Figure 27-4. A steady profit rate and a declining, or steady, capital-output ratio cannot hold if the K/L ratio rises in a world with unchanging technology; taken together, they contradict the basic law of diminishing returns under deepening of capital. We must therefore recognize the key role of technological progress in explaining the seven trends of modern economic growth. Our models confirm what our intuition suggests.

The Sources of Economic Growth

We have seen that advanced market economies grow through increases in labor and capital and by technological change as well. But what are the relative contributions of labor, capital, and technology? To answer this question, we turn to an analysis of the quantitative aspects of growth and of the useful approach known as growth accounting. This approach is the first step in the quantitative analysis of economic growth for any country.

The Growth-Accounting Approach. Detailed studies of economic growth rely on what is called **growth accounting.** This technique is not a balance sheet or national product account of the kind we met in earlier chapters. Rather, it is a way of separating out the contributions of the different ingredients driving observed growth trends.

Growth accounting usually begins with the aggregate production function we met earlier in this chapter, $Q = AF(K, L, R)$. Often resources are omitted because land is constant. Using elementary calculus and some simplifying assumptions, we can express the growth of output in terms of the growth of the inputs plus the contribution of technological change. Growth in output (Q) can be decomposed into three separate terms: growth in labor (L) times its weight, growth in capital (K) times its weight, and technological innovation itself (T.C.).

Momentarily ignoring technological change, an assumption of constant returns to scale means that a 1 percent growth in L together with a 1 percent growth in K will lead to a 1 percent growth in output. But suppose L grows at 1 percent and K at 5 percent. It is tempting, but wrong, to guess that Q will then grow at 3 percent, the simple average of 1 and 5. Why wrong? Because the two factors do not necessarily contribute equally to output. Rather, the fact that three-fourths of national income goes to labor while only one-fourth goes to capital suggests that labor growth will contribute more to output than will capital growth.

If labor's growth rate gets 3 times the weight of K's, we can calculate the answer as follows: Q will grow at 2 percent per year ($= \frac{3}{4}$ of 1 percent $+ \frac{1}{4}$ of 5 percent). To growth of inputs, we add technological change and thereby obtain all the sources of growth.

Hence, output growth per year follows the *fundamental equation of growth accounting:*

$$\% \, Q \text{ growth} \tag{1}$$
$$= \tfrac{3}{4}(\% \, L \text{ growth}) + \tfrac{1}{4}(\% \, K \text{ growth}) + \text{T.C.}$$

where "T.C." represents technological change (or total factor productivity) that raises productivity and

where $\frac{3}{4}$ and $\frac{1}{4}$ are the relative contributions of each input to economic growth. Under conditions of perfect competition, these fractions are equal to the shares of national income of the two factors; naturally, these fractions would be replaced by new fractions if the relative shares of the factors were to change or if other factors were added.

To explain per capita growth, we can eliminate L as a separate growth source. Now, using the fact that capital gets one-fourth of output, we have from equation (1)

$$\% \, \frac{Q}{L} \text{ growth} = \% \, Q \text{ growth} - \% \, L \text{ growth}$$
$$= \tfrac{1}{4}\left(\% \, \frac{K}{L} \text{ growth}\right) + \text{T.C.} \tag{2}$$

This relation shows clearly how capital deepening would affect per capita output if technological advance were zero. Output per worker would grow only one-fourth as fast as capital per worker, reflecting diminishing returns.

One final point remains: We can measure Q growth, K growth, and L growth, as well as the shares of K and L. But how can we measure T.C. (technological change)? We cannot. Rather, we must *infer* T.C. as the residual or leftover after the other components of output and inputs are calculated. Thus if we examine the equation above, T.C. is calculated by subtraction from equation (1) as

$$\text{T.C.} = \% \, Q \text{ growth} - \tfrac{3}{4}(\% \, L \text{ growth})$$
$$- \tfrac{1}{4}(\% \, K \text{ growth}) \tag{3}$$

This equation allows us to answer critically important questions about economic growth. What part of per capita output growth is due to capital deepening, and what part is due to technological advance? Does society progress chiefly by dint of thrift and the forgoing of current consumption? Or is our rising living standard the reward for the ingenuity of inventors and the daring of innovator-entrepreneurs?

Numerical Example. To determine the contributions of labor, capital, and other factors to output growth, we substitute representative numbers for the period 1900–2003 into equation (2) for the growth of Q/L. Since 1900, worker-hours have grown 1.4 percent per year, and K has grown 2.6 percent per year, while Q has grown 3.4 percent per year. Thus, by arithmetic, we find that

$$\% \frac{Q}{L} \text{ growth} = \frac{1}{4}\left(\% \frac{K}{L} \text{ growth}\right) + \text{T.C.}$$

becomes

$$2.0 = \frac{1}{4}(1.2) + \text{T.C.} = 0.3 + 1.7$$

Thus of the 2 percent–per-year increase in output per worker, about 0.3 percentage point is due to capital deepening, while the largest portion, 1.7 percent per year, stems from T.C. (technological change).

Detailed Studies. More thorough studies refine the simple calculation but show quite similar conclusions. Table 27-3 presents the results of studies by the Department of Labor for the 1948–2001 period. During this time, output (measured as gross output of the private business sector) grew at an average rate of 3.6 percent per year, while input growth (of capital, labor, and land) contributed 2.2 percentage points per year. Hence **total factor productivity**—the growth of output less the growth of the weighted sum of all inputs, or what we have called T.C—averaged 1.3 percent annually.

Somewhat less than two-thirds of the growth in output in the United States can be accounted for by the growth in labor and capital. The remaining third is a residual factor that can be attributed to education, research and development, innovation, economies of scale, advances in knowledge, and other factors.

Other countries show different patterns of growth. For example, scholars have used growth accounting to study the Soviet Union, which grew rapidly during the period from 1930 until the mid-1960s. It appears, however, that the high growth rate came primarily from forced-draft increases in capital and labor inputs. For the last few years of the U.S.S.R.'s existence, productivity actually *declined* as the central-planning apparatus became more dysfunctional, as corruption deepened, and as incentives worsened. On the whole, the estimated pace of growth in total factor productivity for the Soviet Union over the half-century before its collapse was slower than that for the United States and other major market economies. Only the ability of the central government forcibly to divert output into investment (and away from consumption) offset the system's inefficiency.

	In percent per year	As percent of total
Contribution of Different Elements to Growth in Real GDP, United States, 1948–2001		
Real GDP growth (private business sector)	3.56	100
Contribution of inputs	2.22	63
Capital	1.13	32
Labor	1.09	31
Total factor productivity growth (research and development, education, advances in knowledge, and other sources)	1.34	37

TABLE 27-3. Advances in Knowledge Outweigh Capital in Contributing to Economic Growth

Studies using the techniques of growth accounting break down the growth of GDP in the private business sector into contributing factors. Recent comprehensive studies find that capital growth accounted for 32 percent of output growth. Education, research and development, and other advances in knowledge made up 37 percent of total output growth and about half of the growth of output per worker.

Source: U.S. Department of Labor, at www.bls.gov/bls/productivity.htm.

RECENT TRENDS IN PRODUCTIVITY

A careful look at productivity trends indicates that there are sharp movements from year to year as well as long swings. The growth of labor productivity is shown in Figure 27-7. Productivity grew briskly from World War II until the late 1960s.

Then, beginning around 1973, there were several years of poor performance, and even decline. Surveys of this period indicate that the poor productivity record stemmed from the sharp increases in oil prices, increasing stringency of regulations, and impacts of price and wage controls and pervasive controls in the energy industries, as well as a slowdown in research and development spending.

Economists worry about productivity because of its close association with growth in real wages and living standards. Figure 27-6(c) showed how growth in real wages has tracked productivity per person since 1900. This point is presented quantitatively in Table 27-4. Some elementary arithmetic shows that if labor's

share of national income is constant, this implies that real wages will grow at the rate of growth of labor productivity.[6]

The Productivity Rebound

Economists have been waiting for an upturn in productivity growth, hoping that the revolution in information technology would spur rapid growth throughout the economy. Indeed, innovations in information technology (computer hardware, software, and communications) have produced astonishing improvements in every corner of the economy. The prices of computers have fallen more than a

---

[6] To see this relationship, write labor's share as $W \times L = s \times P \times Q$, where s = labor's share, W = money wage rate, L = hours of work, P = price index, and Q = output. Dividing both sides by L and P yields $(W/P) = s \times (Q/L)$, which signifies that the real wage equals labor's share times labor productivity. Hence, if the share of labor of national income is constant, real wages will grow at the same rate as labor productivity.

FIGURE 27-7. Labor Productivity Growth in U.S. Business, 1948–2002

The trend in labor productivity declined gradually to a low in the late 1970s and early 1980s. Bolstered by impressive gains in information technology, especially computers, productivity growth has rebounded since the late 1990s.

Source: Bureau of Labor Statistics, at www.bls.gov/lpc/home.htm.

Productivity and Real Wages		
	Average Annual Percentage Growth in:	
Period	Labor productivity	Real wages
1948–1973	3.1	2.9
1973–2000	1.0	1.5

TABLE 27-4. Real Wages Mirror Productivity Growth

Over the long run, real wages tend to move with trends in labor productivity. After the productivity slowdown in 1973, real wage growth slowed sharply.

Source: U.S. Department of Labor. Productivity is for the U.S. business sector; nominal compensation is deflated using the consumer price index.

thousandfold in the last three decades. Electronic mail and the Internet are changing the face of retailing. Computers are the nerve system of business—running airline pricing and reservation systems, scanning price and quantity data in stores, dispatching electricity, clearing checks, dunning taxpayers, and sending students their tuition bills. Some economists think that computers are like a new fourth factor of production.

Until recently, experts were puzzled, in the words of Robert Solow, that "computers can be found everywhere except in the productivity statistics." Even as computers invaded every aspect of economic life, productivity growth showed little response. But this changed in about 1995, when productivity began growing rapidly. Having grown at 3.1 percent per year from 1948 to 1973, productivity growth slowed to 0.8 percent per year in the 1973–1995 period; productivity then surged ahead at 2.6 percent per year from 1995 to 2002. Real wages also picked up from a slow pace of improvement of 1.2 percent annually in 1973–1995 to 2.5 percent annually in 1995–2002.

Enthusiasts spoke of a "new era" and a "brave new world of American capitalism." Even Fed chairman Alan Greenspan, known primarily for his Delphic understatements, joined technological enthusiasts, arguing, "A perceptible quickening in the pace at which technological innovations are applied argues for the hypothesis that the recent acceleration in labor productivity is not just a cyclical phenomenon or a statistical aberration, but reflects, at least in part, a more deep-seated, still developing, shift in our economic landscape."

Economists who have looked at the numbers under a microscope have uncovered some interesting facts about the productivity rebound. Among the important factors in the productivity acceleration have been the following:

- *Productivity explosion in computers.* The productivity explosion (and consequent price decline) in computers has been extraordinary. From 1972 to 1995, the relative price of computers fell at about 18 percent per year, and in the 1995–2002 period the decline amounted to around 30 percent per year.
- *Capital deepening.* There has been a very sharp increase of investment since 1995. Companies invested heavily in computers and software to take advantage of their falling prices and the increasing power of new software.
- *Unmeasured outputs.* Many of the advances of the new economy have not been captured by the productivity statistics. The phenomenal advances of the Internet, e-mail, and cellular phones are largely missed in the productivity statistics. Some economists have found that productivity is significantly underestimated for software and communications equipment (see the discussion of price measurement in Chapter 21). Alternatively, consider the time that consumers save by shopping on the Internet, the saving of time and postage from the switch from snail-mail to e-mail, or the convenience of cellular telephones—none of these shows up in measured productivity. Others think the true gains from computers lie in the future. Stanford economic historian Paul David, who has studied past inventions like the electric motor, believes that it takes decades for the economy to reap the full benefits of fundamental inventions.

Whether or not the more rapid productivity growth is a permanent feature of our economy, it is clear that computers are shaping our economy and our lives in surprising ways.

This concludes our introduction to the principles of economic growth. The next chapter applies these principles to the struggle of poor countries to improve their living standards. In the remaining chapters in this part, we open our inquiry to international trade and finance.

SUMMARY

A. Theories of Economic Growth

1. The analysis of economic growth examines the factors that lead to the growth of potential output over the long run. The growth in output per capita is an important objective of government because it is associated with rising average real incomes and living standards.

2. Reviewing the experience of nations over space and time, we see that the economy rides on the four wheels of economic growth: (*a*) the quantity and quality of its labor force; (*b*) the abundance of its land and other natural resources; (*c*) the stock of accumulated capital; and, perhaps most important, (*d*) the technological change and innovation that allow greater output to be produced with the same inputs. There is no unique combination of these four ingredients, however; the United States, Europe, and Asian countries have followed different paths to economic success.

3. The classical models of Smith and Malthus describe economic development in terms of land and population. In the absence of technological change, increasing population ultimately exhausts the supply of free land. The resulting increase in population density triggers the law of diminishing returns, so growth produces higher land rents with lower competitive wages. The Malthusian equilibrium is attained when the wage rate has fallen to the subsistence level, below which population cannot sustain itself. In reality, however, technological change has kept economic development progressing in industrial countries by continually shifting the productivity curve of labor upward.

4. Concerns about limitations of natural resources and increasing environmental spillovers from economic activity have led many to question whether economic growth at present rates can long continue. One set of worries based on limited supplies of land, energy, and mineral resources has receded with continuing new discoveries and resource-saving technological change. Global environmental constraints may lead to costly environmental damages or the need for expensive preventive measures.

5. Capital accumulation with complementary labor forms the core of modern growth theory in the neoclassical growth model. This approach uses a tool known as the aggregate production function, which relates inputs and technology to total potential GDP. In the absence of technological change and innovation, an increase in capital per worker (capital deepening) would not be matched by a proportional increase in output per worker because of diminishing returns to capital. Hence, capital deepening would lower the rate of return on capital (equal to the real interest rate under risk-free competition) while raising real wages.

6. Technological change increases the output producible with a given bundle of inputs. This pushes upward the aggregate production function, making more output available with the same inputs of labor and capital. Recent analysis in the "new growth theory" seeks to uncover the processes which generate technological change. This approach emphasizes (*a*) that technological change is an output of the economic system, (*b*) that technology is a public or nonrival good that can be used simultaneously by many people, and (*c*) that new inventions are expensive to produce but inexpensive to reproduce. These features mean that governments must pay careful attention to ensuring that inventors have adequate incentives, through strong intellectual property rights, to engage in research and development.

B. The Patterns of Growth in the United States

7. Numerous trends of economic growth are seen in data for the twentieth and early twenty-first centuries. Among the key findings are that real wages and output per hour worked have risen steadily; that the real interest rate has shown no major trend; and that the capital-output ratio has declined. The major trends are consistent with the neoclassical growth model augmented by technological advance. Thus economic theory confirms what economic history tells us—that technological advance increases the productivity of inputs and improves wages and living standards.

8. The last trend, continual growth in potential output since 1900, raises the important question of the sources of economic growth. Applying quantitative techniques, economists have used growth accounting to determine that "residual" sources—such as technological change and education—outweigh capital deepening in their impact on GDP growth or labor productivity.

9. After 1970, productivity growth slowed under the weight of energy-price increases, increasing environmental regulation, and other structural changes. In the late 1990s, however, the explosion of productivity and the investment in computers and other information technologies have led to a sharp upturn in measured productivity growth.

CONCEPTS FOR REVIEW

four wheels of growth:
  labor
  resources
  capital
  technology
aggregate production function
Smith's golden age
capital-labor ratio
Malthus's limited land

modern Malthusianism: limited
  resources and environmental
  constraints
neoclassical growth model
K/L rise as capital deepens
new growth theory
technology as a produced good
seven trends of economic growth

growth accounting:
% Q growth = ¾ (% L growth)
  + 1/4 (% K growth)
  + T.C.
% Q/L growth = ¼ (% K/L
  growth) + T.C.

FURTHER READING AND INTERNET WEBSITES

Further Reading

One of the best surveys of economic growth is Robert Solow, *Economic Growth* (Oxford University Press, Oxford, U.K., 1970). See his pathbreaking article, "A Contribution to the Theory of Economic Growth," *Quarterly Journal of Economics*, 1956. The text reference is William Baumol, "Entreprenuership: Productive, Unproductive, and Destructive," *Journal of Political Economy*, October 1990, pp. 893–921.

Two excellent recent books on growth economics are Charles Jones, *Introduction to Economic Growth*, 2d ed. (Norton, New York, 2001), and the more technical monograph by Robert Barro and Xavier Sala-i-Martin, *Economic Growth* (McGraw-Hill, New York, 1995). A good survey of the role of technological change in growth theory is Paul Romer, "The Origins of Endogenous Growth," *Journal of Economic Perspectives*, Winter 1994, pp. 3–22.

Websites

A website devoted to economic growth is maintained by Jonathan Temple of Oxford www.bris.ac.uk/Depts/Economics/Growth/ and contains many references and links. The articles by Solow and Baumol are available at www.jstor.org. One of the most entertaining Web pages among economists is maintained by growth theorist Xavier Sala-i-Martin at www.columbia.edu/~xs23.

Data sets on economic growth can be found at www.nuff.ox.ac.uk/Economics/Growth/datasets.htm. Technological change is often associated with particular inventions. The lives and patents of great inventors can be found at www.invent.org/hall_of_fame/1_0_0_hall_of_fame.asp.

For those who wish to pursue the issue of productivity in the new economy, see *Economic Report of the President, 2000* at w3.access.gpo.gov/eop, chap. 3.

QUESTIONS FOR DISCUSSION

1. According to economic data, the living standards of a family in 2003 were about 9 times those of a family in 1900. What does this mean in terms of actual consumption patterns? Discuss with your parents or older relatives how your living standards today compare with those of their parents; make a comparison of the difference.

2. "If the government strengthens intellectual property rights, subsidizes basic science, and controls business cycles, we will see economic growth that would astound

the classical economists." Explain what the writer meant by this statement.

3. "With zero population growth and no technological change, persistent capital accumulation would ultimately destroy the capitalist class." Explain why such a scenario might lead to a zero real interest rate and to a disappearance of profits.

4. Recall the growth-accounting equation [equation (1) on page 570]. Calculate the growth of output if labor grows at 1 percent per year, capital grows at 4 percent

per year, and technological change is 1½ percent per year.

How would your answer change if:

a. Labor growth slowed to 0 percent per year?

b. Capital growth increased to 5 percent per year?

c. Labor and capital had equal shares in GDP?

Also, calculate for each of these conditions the rate of growth of output per worker.

5. Use the *PPF* to illustrate the Malthusian prediction and why it is flawed. Put per capita food production on one axis and per capita manufactures on the other. Assume that there are diminishing returns to labor in food production but that manufactures have constant returns to labor.

6. Critics of growth point to factors that will limit genuine growth in standards of living in the next century. Consider the following possible scenarios (which may or may not be realistic):

a. Global warming leads to warming and drying of the world's grain belt, lowering yields of important crops.

b. Increased terrorism forces governments, firms, and households to counteract threats by investing in defensive measures, such as increased defense spending and higher security investments.

c. Research and development is increasingly spent on military and space technologies.

d. Technological change leads to higher structural unemployment as the education and training of the population lag behind the skill requirements of increasingly demanding computer-intensive jobs. For each of these, discuss the impact on the growth of per capita consumption. Consider both market and nonmarket consumption. Use the growth-accounting approach to illustrate your argument where possible.

7. **Advanced problem:** Many fear that computers will do to humans what tractors and cars did to horses—the horse population declined precipitously early in this century after technological change made horses obsolete. If we treat computers as a particularly productive kind of *K*, what would their introduction do to the capital-labor ratio in Figure 27-4? Can total output go down with a fixed labor force? Under what conditions would the real wage decline? Can you see why the horse analogy might not apply?

CHAPTER
28

The Challenge of Economic Development

I believe in materialism. I believe in all the proceeds of a healthy materialism— good cooking, dry houses, dry feet, sewers, drain pipes, hot water, baths, electric lights, automobiles, good roads, bright streets, long vacations away from the village pump, new ideas, fast horses, swift conversation, theaters, operas, orchestras, bands—I believe in them all for everybody. The man who dies without knowing these things may be as exquisite as a saint, and as rich as a poet; but it is in spite of, not because of, his deprivation.

Francis Hackett

Planet Earth today contains people at vastly different living standards. At one end are the affluent of North America and Western Europe, where the richest 1 percent of the people enjoy about 20 percent of world income and consumption. At the other extreme are the destitute of Africa and Asia, around 1 billion people living in absolute poverty, with few comforts and seldom knowing where the next meal will come from.

What causes the great differences in the wealth of nations? Can the world peacefully survive with poverty in the midst of plenty, with much conspicuous consumption and agricultural surpluses in America alongside starvation and environmental degradation in Africa? What steps can poorer nations take to improve their living standards? What are the responsibilities of affluent countries?

These questions, concerning the obstacles facing developing countries, are among the greatest challenges facing modern economics. It is here that the tools of economics can make the greatest difference to people's daily lives. It is here that economics can literally make the difference between life and death. We begin by describing the characteristics of developing countries and reviewing some of the key ingredients in the process of economic development. The second part of this chapter examines alternative approaches to economic growth in developing countries, particularly the more successful models in Asia along with the failed communist experiment in Russia.

A. ECONOMIC GROWTH IN POOR COUNTRIES

ASPECTS OF A DEVELOPING COUNTRY

What is meant by a **developing country?** The most important characteristic of a developing country is that it has low per capita income. In addition, people in developing countries usually have poor health, low levels of literacy, extensive malnutrition, and little capital to work with.

Table 28-1 is a key source of data for understanding the major players in the world economy, as well as important indicators of underdevelopment. Countries are grouped into six major regions of the world.

A number of interesting features emerge from the table. Clearly, low-income countries are much poorer than advanced countries like the United States. People in countries with the lowest average incomes earn

	Population			Per capita GDP*		Education	Technology
Region	Number, 2001 (millions)	Growth rate, 1980–2001 (%)	Life expectancy at birth (years)	Dollars	Growth, 1980–2000 (% per year)	Youth illiteracy rate (% ages 15–24)	Personal computers (per 1,000 persons)
East Asia and Pacific (China, Indonesia, . . .)	1,823	1.4	69	3,790	6.2	3	19
Eastern Europe and Central Asia (Russia, Poland, . . .)	475	0.5	69	6,320	−0.8	1	52
Latin America and Caribbean (Brazil, Mexico, . . .)	524	1.8	71	6,900	0.7	5	59
Middle East and North Africa (Egypt, Iran, . . .)	301	2.6	68	5,430	−0.1	20	32
South Asia (India, Pakistan, . . .)	1,378	2.0	63	2,570	3.6	33	5
Sub-Saharan Africa (Nigeria, Ethiopia, . . .)	674	2.7	46	1,750	−0.7	23	10

*Data on per capita incomes use purchasing-power-parity valuation of incomes to reflect what incomes in the countries can actually buy.

TABLE 28-1. Important Indicators for Different Country Groups

The World Bank groups developing countries into six regions. For each, a number of important indicators of economic development are shown. Note that low-income countries tend to have high illiteracy and few computers. Some low-income countries have life expectancies close to those of rich countries.

Source: World Bank, *World Development Report,* and data at www.worldbank.org.

only about one-twentieth as much as people in high-income countries. For the table's data, *purchasing-power-parity* (PPP) calculations were used to measure relative incomes. Market exchange rates tend to understate the incomes of low-wage countries. (The use of purchasing-power-parity exchange rates to evaluate living standards is discussed in Chapter 29.)

In addition, many social and health indicators show the effects of poverty in low-income nations. Life expectancy is lower than in high-income countries, and educational attainment and literacy are often minimal.

There is a great diversity among developing countries. Some remain at the ragged edge of starvation—these are the poorest countries like Congo, Ethiopia, and Liberia. Other countries that were in that category two or three decades ago have graduated to the rank of middle-income countries. The more successful ones—Hong Kong, Singapore, and South Korea—have graduated from the developing group, and the most successful of these have per capita incomes that have reached the ranks of high-income countries. Yesterday's successful developing countries will be tomorrow's high-income countries.

Life in Low-Income Countries

To bring out the contrasts between advanced and developing economies, imagine that you are a typical 21-year-old in a low-income country such as Mali, India, or Bangladesh. You are poor. Even after making allowance for the goods that you produce and consume, your annual income barely averages $1000. Your counterpart in North America might have more than $30,000 in average earnings. Perhaps you can find cold comfort in the thought that only 1 person in 4 in the world averages more than $3000 in annual income.

For each of your fellow citizens who can read, there is one like you who is illiterate. Your life expectancy is four-fifths that of the average person in an advanced country; already two of your brothers and sisters have died before reaching adulthood. Birth rates are high, particularly for families where women receive no education, but mortality rates are also much higher here than in countries with good health-care systems.

Most people in your country work on farms. Few can be spared from food production to work in factories. You work with but one-sixtieth the horsepower of a prosperous North American worker. You know little about science, but much about your village traditions.

You and your fellow citizens in the 40 poorest countries constitute 55 percent of the world population but must divide among yourselves only 4 percent of world income. You are often hungry, and the food you eat is mainly roughage or rice. While you were among those who got some primary schooling, like most of your friends you did not go on to high school, and only the wealthiest go to a university. You work long hours in the fields without the benefit of machinery. At night you sleep on a mat. You have little household furniture, perhaps a table and a radio. Your only mode of transportation is an old pair of boots.

Human Development

This review of life in the poorest countries of the world reminds us of the importance of adequate incomes in meeting basic needs as well as the fact that life involves more than market incomes. Thoughtful economists such as Nobel Prize recipient Amartya Sen and Yale's Gustav Ranis emphasize that other factors should be considered in appraising a country's progress: Factors such as health and life expectancy, school enrollment, adult literacy, and independence of women are important goals along with increasing per capita market consumption.

Figure 28-1 shows a plot of life expectancy and per capita GDP. The correlation is strong, but there are exceptions to the general positive relationship. Some countries, such as Botswana, Equatorial Guinea, and South Africa, have low life expectancies relative to income because of the scourge of AIDS. No poor countries have high life expectancies, but countries like Greece and Costa Rica have life expectancies as high as or higher than those in the United States because of the poorly designed healthcare system in the United States.

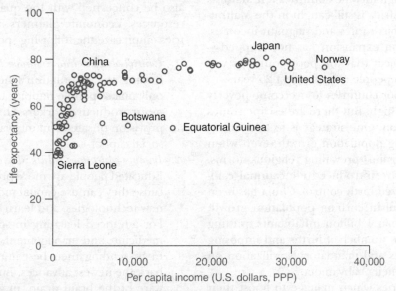

FIGURE 28-1. Life Expectancy and Incomes, 2000

Life expectancies are highly correlated with per capita incomes. Higher incomes allow greater investments in health care, but a healthier population is also more productive. Note that some middle-income African countries have been hard hit by the AIDS epidemic, threatening both health and economic development.

Source: Human Development Report, 2002.

THE FOUR ELEMENTS IN DEVELOPMENT

Having seen what it means to be a developing country, we now turn to an analysis of the process by which low-income countries improve their living standards. We saw in Chapter 27 that economic growth in the United States—growth in its potential output—rides on four wheels. These are (1) human resources, (2) natural resources, (3) capital formation, and (4) technology. These four wheels operate in rich and poor countries, although the mix and strategy for combining them will differ depending on the state of development. Let's see how each of the four wheels operates in developing countries and consider how public policy can steer the growth process in favorable directions.

Human Resources

Population Explosion: The Legacy of Malthus. Many poor countries are forever running hard just to stay in place. Even as a poor nation's GDP rises, so does its population. Recall our discussion in Chapter 27 of the Malthusian population trap, where population grows so rapidly that incomes remain at subsistence levels. While the high-income countries left Malthus behind long ago, Africa is still caught in the Malthusian bind of high birth rates and stagnant incomes. And the population expansion has not stopped—demographers project that the poor countries will add about 1 billion people over the next 25 years.

It's hard for poor countries to overcome poverty with birth rates so high. But there are escape routes from overpopulation. One strategy is to take an active role in curbing population growth, even when such actions run against prevailing religious norms. Many countries have introduced educational campaigns and subsidized birth control. China has been particularly forceful in curbing population growth among its more than 1 billion inhabitants, putting tight quotas on the number of births and imposing economic penalties and mandatory sterilization on those who violate their "baby quota."

And for countries which manage to boost their per capita incomes, there is the prospect of making the *demographic transition*, which occurs when a population stabilizes with low birth rates and low death rates. Once countries get rich enough, and infant mortality drops, people voluntarily reduce their birth rates. When women are educated and emerge from subservience, they usually decide to spend less of their lives in childbearing. Families substitute quality for quantity—devoting time and incomes to a better education for fewer children. Mexico, Korea, and Taiwan have all seen their birth rates drop sharply as their incomes have risen and their populations have received more education.

Slowly the results of economic development and birth control are being felt. The birth rate in poor countries has declined from 42 per 1000 in 1965 to 28 per 1000 in 1995, but that's still far higher than the birth rate of 12 per 1000 in the high-income countries. The struggle against poverty induced by excessive population growth continues.

However, the demographic transition has not been reached in every corner of the world. Fertility continues at a rapid pace in much of tropical Africa even as the AIDS epidemic rages through the population and lowers life expectancies in a way not experienced since the great plagues of earlier centuries. The specter of Malthus hangs over much of central Africa.

Human Capital. In addition to dealing with excessive population growth, developing countries must also be concerned with the quality of their human resources. Economic planners in developing countries emphasize the following specific programs:

1. *Control disease and improve health and nutrition.* Raising the population's health standards not only makes people happier but also makes them more productive workers. Health-care clinics and provision of safe drinking water are vitally useful social capital.

2. *Improve education, reduce illiteracy, and train workers.* Educated people are more productive workers because they can use capital more effectively, adopt new technologies, and learn from their mistakes. For advanced learning in science, engineering, medicine, and management, countries will benefit by sending their best minds abroad to bring back the newest advances. But countries must beware of the brain drain, in which the most able people get drawn off to high-wage countries.

3. *Above all, do not underestimate the importance of human resources.* Most other factors can be bought in the international marketplace. Most labor is home-grown, although labor can sometimes be

augmented through immigration. The crucial role of skilled labor has been shown again and again when sophisticated mining, defense, or manufacturing machinery fell into disrepair and disuse because the labor force of developing countries had not acquired the necessary skills for its operation and maintenance.

Natural Resources

Some poor countries of Africa and Asia have meager endowments of natural resources, and such land and minerals as they do possess must be divided among dense populations. Perhaps the most valuable natural resource of developing countries is arable land. Much of the labor force in developing countries is employed in farming. Hence, the productive use of land—with appropriate conservation, fertilizers, and tillage—will go far in increasing a poor nation's output.

Moreover, land ownership patterns are a key to providing farmers with strong incentives to invest in capital and technologies that will increase their land's yield. When farmers own their own land, they have better incentives to make improvements, such as in irrigation systems, and undertake appropriate conservation practices.

Some economists believe that natural wealth from oil or minerals is not an unalloyed blessing. Countries like the United States, Canada, and Norway have used their natural wealth to form the solid base of industrial expansion. In other countries, the wealth has been subject to plunder and *rent seeking* by corrupt leaders and military cliques. Countries like Nigeria and Congo (formerly Zaire), which are fabulously wealthy in terms of mineral resources, failed to convert their underground assets into productive human or tangible capital because of venal rulers who drained that wealth into their own bank accounts and conspicuous consumption.

Capital Formation

A modern economy requires a vast array of capital goods. Countries must abstain from current consumption to engage in fruitful roundabout production. But there's the rub, for the poorest countries are near a subsistence standard of living. When you are poor to begin with, reducing current consumption to provide for future consumption seems impossible.

The leaders in the growth race invest at least 20 percent of output in capital formation. By contrast, the poorest agrarian countries are often able to save only 5 percent of national income. Moreover, much of the low level of saving goes to provide the growing population with housing and simple tools. Little is left over for development.

But let's say a country has succeeded in hiking up its rate of saving. Even so, it takes many decades to accumulate the highways, telecommunications systems, computers, electricity-generating plants, and other capital goods that underpin a productive economic structure.

Even before acquiring the most sophisticated computers, however, developing countries must first build up their *infrastructure,* or social overhead capital, which consists of the large-scale projects upon which a market economy depends. For example, a regional agricultural adviser helps farmers in an area learn of new seeds or crops; a road system links up the different markets; a public-health program inoculates people against typhoid or diphtheria and protects the population beyond those inoculated. In each of these cases it would be impossible for an enterprising firm to capture the social benefits involved, because the firm cannot collect fees from the thousands or even millions of beneficiaries. Because of the large indivisibilities and external effects of infrastructure, the government must step in to make or ensure the necessary investments.

In many developing countries, the single most pressing problem is too little saving. Particularly in the poorest regions, urgent current consumption competes with investment for scarce resources. The result is too little investment in the productive capital so indispensable for rapid economic progress.

> **Foreign Borrowing and Emerging-Market Crisis**
>
> If there are so many obstacles to finding domestic saving for capital formation, why not borrow abroad? Economic theory tells us that a rich country, which has tapped its own high-yield investment projects, can benefit both itself and the recipient by investing in high-yield projects abroad.
>
> The trend in financial flows to developing countries is shown in Figure 28-2. This illustrates how both portfolio

FIGURE 28-2. **Investment in Developing Countries**

Investments in developing countries have grown rapidly. These include both direct investment (which involves purchasing tangible assets) and portfolio investment (which involves
purchasing stocks, bonds, and other financial instruments). This trend shows one of the
leading indicators of "globalization."

Source: Council of Economic Advisers.

and direct investments in developing countries have
grown in recent years and shows one of the major indicators of globalization of financial markets.

But risks are the necessary companion of reward in
foreign lending. The history of lending from rich to poor
regions shows a cycle of opportunity, lending, profits,
overexpansion, speculation, crisis, and drying-up of funds,
followed by a new round of lending by yet another group
of starry-eyed investors. No sooner has one crisis been
forgotten than another erupts.

It is instructive to review the saga of *emerging
markets,* which is the name often given to rapidly growing
low- and middle-income countries that are promising areas for foreign investment. In the 1990s, investors in
wealthy countries sent their funds abroad in search of
higher returns; poor countries, hungry for funds, welcomed this flow of foreign funds. From Thailand to South
Africa, both loans and equity investments grew rapidly
during the 1990s.

As long as the growth in emerging markets continued,
all was quiet and returns were solid. But a slowdown in
growth combined with a series of banking crises led to
massive outflows of short-term funds from Thailand,
Indonesia, and South Korea. Bankers who had invested

heavily called in their loans. This led to a sharp increase in
the supply of the currencies of these countries. Most countries were on fixed-exchange-rate systems, and the selling
overwhelmed the countries' foreign exchange reserves.
One after another, the currencies of the East Asian countries depreciated sharply. Many called upon the IMF to provide short-term funds, but the IMF required contractionary
monetary and fiscal policies. All these factors together produced sharp business recessions throughout East Asia.

Within 3 years, most of these countries had recovered from the crisis after a period of *adjustment*—slow
output growth, declining real wages, debt reschedulings,
and trade surpluses. Economic growth had resumed. The
world had survived another financial crisis. Nevertheless,
the international-financial virus is always lying dormant,
waiting to infect the next herd of exuberant speculators.

Technological Change and Innovations

The final and most important wheel is technological advance. Here developing countries have one
major advantage: They can hope to benefit by relying on the technological progress of more advanced
nations.

Imitating Technology. Poor countries need not find modern Newtons to discover the law of gravity; they can read about it in any physics book. They don't have to repeat the slow, meandering route to the Industrial Revolution; they can buy tractors, computers, and power looms undreamed of by the great merchants of the past.

Japan and the United States clearly illustrate this in their historical developments. The United States provides a hopeful example to the rest of the world. The key inventions involved in the automobile originated almost exclusively abroad. Nevertheless, Ford and General Motors applied foreign inventions and rapidly became the world leaders in the automotive industry.

Japan joined the industrial race late, and only at the end of the nineteenth century did it send students abroad to study Western technology. The Japanese government took an active role in stimulating the pace of development and in building railroads and utilities. By adopting productive foreign technologies, Japan moved into its position today as the world's second-largest industrial economy. The examples of the United States and Japan show how countries can thrive by adapting foreign science and technology to local market conditions.

Entrepreneurship and Innovation. From the histories of the United States and Japan, it might appear that adaptation of foreign technology is an easy recipe for development. You might say: "Just go abroad; copy more efficient methods; put them into effect at home; then sit back and wait for the extra output to roll in."

Alas, implementing technological change is not that simple. You can send a textbook on chemical engineering to Poorovia, but without skilled scientists, engineers, entrepreneurs, and adequate capital, Poorovia couldn't even think about building a working petrochemical plant. The advanced technology was itself developed to meet the special conditions of the advanced countries—including ample skilled engineers and workers, reliable electrical service, and quickly available spare parts and repair services. These conditions do not prevail in poor countries.

One of the key tasks of economic development is promoting an entrepreneurial spirit. A country cannot thrive without a group of owners or managers willing to undertake risks, open new businesses, adopt new technologies, and import new ways of doing business. At the most fundamental level, innovation and entrepreneurship thrives when property rights are clear and complete and taxes and other drains on profits (such as corruption) are low and predictable. Government can also foster entrepreneurship through specific investments: by setting up extension services for farmers, by educating and training the workforce, and by establishing management schools.

Vicious Cycles to Virtuous Circles

We have emphasized that poor countries face great obstacles in combining the four elements of progress—labor, capital, resources, and innovation. In addition, countries find that the difficulties reinforce each other in a *vicious cycle of poverty*.

Figure 28-3 illustrates how one hurdle raises yet other hurdles. Low incomes lead to low saving; low saving retards the growth of capital; inadequate capital prevents introduction of new machinery and rapid growth in productivity; low productivity leads to low incomes. Other elements in poverty are also self-reinforcing. Poverty is accompanied by low levels of education, literacy, and skill; these in turn prevent the adoption of new and improved technologies and lead to rapid population growth, which eats away at improvements in output and food production.

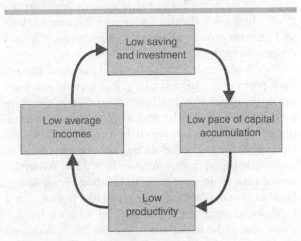

FIGURE 28-3. The Vicious Cycle of Poverty

Many obstacles to development are self-reinforcing. Low levels of income prevent saving, retard capital growth, hinder productivity growth, and keep income low. Successful development may require taking steps to break the chain at many points.

Overcoming the barriers of poverty often requires a concerted effort on many fronts, and some development economists recommend a "big push" forward to break the vicious cycle. If a country is fortunate, simultaneous steps to invest more, improve health and education, develop skills, and curb population growth can break the vicious cycle of poverty and stimulate a virtuous circle of rapid economic development.

STRATEGIES OF ECONOMIC DEVELOPMENT

We see how countries must combine labor, resources, capital, and technology in order to grow rapidly. But this is no real formula; it is the equivalent of saying that an Olympic sprinter must run like the wind. Why do some countries succeed in running faster than others? How do poor countries ever get started down the road of economic development?

Historians and social scientists have long been fascinated by the differences in the pace of economic growth among nations. Some early theories stressed climate, noting that all advanced countries lie in the earth's temperate zone. Others have pointed to custom, culture, or religion as a key factor. Max Weber emphasized the "Protestant ethic" as a driving force behind capitalism. More recently, Mancur Olson has argued that nations begin to decline when their decision structure becomes brittle and interest groups or oligarchies prevent social and economic change.

No doubt each of these theories has some validity for a particular time and place. But they do not hold up as universal explanations of economic development. Weber's theory leaves unexplained why the cradle of civilization appeared in the Near East and Greece while the later-dominant Europeans lived in caves, worshiped trolls, and wore bearskins. Where do we find the Protestant ethic in bustling Hong Kong? How can we explain that a country like Japan, with a rigid social structure and powerful lobbies, has become one of the world's most productive economies?

Even in the modern era, people become attached to simple, holistic explanations of economic development. Two decades ago, people considered import substitution (the replacement of imports with domestically produced goods) to be the most secure development strategy. Then, in the 1970s, reliance on labor-intensive techniques was thought advantageous. Today, as we will see, economists tend to emphasize reliance on market forces with an outward orientation. This history should serve as a warning to be wary of oversimplified approaches to complex processes.

Nonetheless, historians and development economists have learned much from the study of the varieties of economic growth. What are some of the lessons? The following account represents a montage of important ideas developed in recent years. Each approach describes how countries might break out of the vicious cycle of poverty and begin to mobilize the four wheels of economic development.

The Backwardness Hypothesis

One view emphasizes the international context of development. We saw above that poorer countries have important advantages that the first pioneers along the path of industrialization did not. Developing nations can now draw upon the capital, skills, and technology of more advanced countries. A hypothesis advanced by Alexander Gerschenkron of Harvard suggests that *relative backwardness* itself may aid development. Countries can buy modern textile machinery, efficient pumps, miracle seeds, chemical fertilizers, and medical supplies. Because they can lean on the technologies of advanced countries, today's developing countries can grow more rapidly than did Britain or Western Europe in the period 1780–1850. As low-income countries draw upon the more productive technologies of the leaders, we would expect to see *convergence* of countries toward the technological frontier. Convergence occurs when those countries or regions that have initially low incomes tend to grow more rapidly than ones with high incomes.

Industrialization vs. Agriculture

In most countries, incomes in urban areas are almost double those in agriculture. And in affluent nations, much of the economy is in industry and services. Hence, many nations jump to the conclusion that industrialization is the cause rather than the effect of affluence.

We must be wary of such inferences, which confuse the association of two characteristics with causality. Some people say, "Rich people drive BMWs, but driving a BMW will not make you a rich person." Similarly, there is no economic justification for a poor country to insist upon having its own national airline and large steel mill. These are not the fundamental necessities of economic growth.

The lesson of decades of attempts to accelerate industrialization at the expense of agriculture has led many analysts to rethink the role of farming. Industrialization is capital-intensive, attracts workers into crowded cities, and often produces high levels of unemployment. Raising productivity on farms may require less capital, while providing productive employment for surplus labor. Indeed, if Bangladesh could increase the productivity of its farming by 20 percent, that advance would do more to release resources for the production of comforts than would trying to construct a domestic steel industry to displace imports.

State vs. Market

The cultures of many developing countries are hostile to the operation of markets. Often, competition among firms or profit-seeking behavior is contrary to traditional practices, religious beliefs, or vested interests. Yet decades of experience suggest that extensive reliance on markets provides the most effective way of managing an economy and promoting rapid economic growth.

What are the important elements of a market-oriented policy? The important elements include the predominance of private property and ownership, an outward orientation in trade policy, low tariffs and few quantitative trade restrictions, the promotion of small business, and the fostering of competition. Moreover, markets work best in a stable macroeconomic environment—one in which taxes are predictable and inflation is low.

Growth and Outward Orientation

A fundamental issue of economic development concerns a country's stance toward international trade. Should developing countries attempt to be self-sufficient, to replace most imports with domestic production? (This is known as a strategy of *import substitution*.) Or should a country strive to pay for the imports it needs by improving efficiency and competitiveness, developing foreign markets, and keeping trade barriers low? (This is called a strategy of *outward orientation* or *openness*.)

Policies of import substitution were often popular in Latin America until the 1980s. The policy most frequently used toward this end was to build high tariff walls around manufacturing industries so that local firms could produce and sell goods that would otherwise be imported.

A policy of openness keeps trade barriers as low as practical, relying primarily on tariffs rather than quotas and other nontariff barriers. It minimizes the interference with financial flows and allows supply and demand to operate in financial markets. It avoids a state monopoly on exports and imports. It keeps government regulation to the minimum necessary for an orderly market economy. Above all, it relies primarily on a private market system of profits and losses to guide production, rather than depending on public ownership and control or the commands of a government planning system.

The success of outward-expansion policies is best illustrated by the successful East Asian countries. A generation ago, countries like Taiwan, South Korea, and Singapore had per capita incomes one-quarter to one-third of those in the wealthiest Latin American countries. Yet, by saving large fractions of their national incomes and channeling these to high-return export industries, the East Asian countries overtook every Latin American country by the late 1980s. The secret to success was not a doctrinaire laissez-faire policy, for the governments in fact engaged in selective planning and intervention. Rather, the openness and outward orientation allowed the countries to reap economies of scale and the benefits of international specialization and thus to increase employment, use domestic resources effectively, enjoy rapid productivity growth, and provide enormous gains in living standards.

While openness provides many benefits, excessive openness, particularly to short-term financial flows, is an invitation to speculative attack. What investors lendeth, investors can taketh back. This syndrome can cause financial and banking crises, as we noted for the East Asian economies in our discussion earlier in this chapter.

The fruits of openness were demonstrated in a recent study by Jeffrey Sachs and Andrew Warner.[1] They examined the relationship between openness and economic growth. An *open economy* is defined as one characterized by low trade barriers, open financial

---

[1] See this chapter's Further Reading section.

markets, and private markets. A *closed economy* is the opposite.

They find that openness is strongly associated with rapid economic growth. The basic story is shown in Figure 28-4. The left panel shows the performance of closed economies. The closed economies had an average growth rate of per capita income of only 0.9 percent annually over the 1970–1989 period. There was no convergence of these countries—many with low incomes—toward the high-income countries. Figure 28-4(*b*) shows the growth of open economies. These grew at an average rate of 4.5 percent annually over the same period; moreover, low-income open economies showed strong convergence toward rich countries. The importance of openness could hardly be more emphatically shown than by these trends.

Summary Judgment

Decades of experience in dozens of countries have led many development economists to the following summary view of the way government can best promote rapid economic development:

The government has a vital role in establishing and maintaining a healthy economic environment. It must ensure respect for the rule of law, enforce contracts, and orient its regulations toward competition and innovation. Government often plays a leading role in investment in human capital through education, health, and transportation, but it should look to the private sector where it has no comparative advantage. Government should focus its efforts on areas where there are clear signs of market failures and

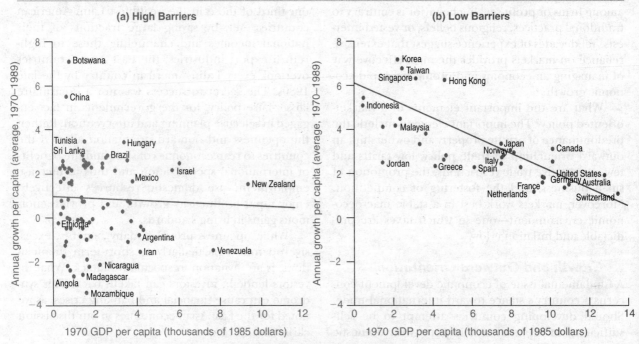

FIGURE 28-4. Openness and Economic Growth, 1970–1989

What is the impact of outward orientation on economic growth? Panel **(a)** shows that economies with high barriers grew slowly and did not converge to high-income countries. Panel **(b)** shows the low-barrier economies—market economies with relatively low barriers to trade and financial flows. They grew much more rapidly and tended to converge to the highest-income regions.

Source: Jeffrey Sachs and Andrew Warner, "Economic Reform and the Process of Global Integration," *Brookings Papers on Economic Activity*, no. 1, 1995, pp. 42–43.

should dismantle regulatory impediments to the private sector in areas where government has comparative disadvantage.

B. ALTERNATIVE MODELS FOR DEVELOPMENT

A BOUQUET OF "ISMS"

People continually look for ways to improve their living standards. Economic betterment is particularly compelling for poor countries seeking a path to the riches they see around them. This textbook has surveyed in depth the mixed market economy of the United States, which combines fundamentally free markets with a sizable government sector. What other alternatives are available?

At one extreme is *free-market absolutism,* which holds that the best government is the least government. At the other extreme is complete communism, with the government operating a collectivized economic order in which the first-person singular hardly exists. Between the extremes of laissez-faire and communism lie mixed capitalism, managed markets, socialism, and many combinations of these models. In this section, we describe briefly some of the influential alternative strategies for growth and development:

1. *The Asian managed-market approach.* South Korea, Taiwan, Singapore, and other countries of East Asia have devised their own brands of economics that combine strong government oversight with powerful market forces.
2. *Socialism.* Socialist thinking encompasses a wide variety of different approaches. In Western Europe after World War II, socialist governments operating in a democratic framework expanded the welfare state, nationalized industries, and planned their economies. In recent years, however, these countries moved back toward a free-market framework with extensive deregulation and privatization.
3. *Soviet-style communism.* For many years, the clearest alternative to the market economy existed in the Soviet Union. Under the Soviet model, the state owned all the land and most of the capital, set wages and most prices, and directed the microeconomic operation of the economy.

The Central Dilemma: Market vs. Command

A survey of alternative economic systems may seem like a bewildering array of economic "isms." And indeed, there is a great variety in the way countries organize their economies.

These are the issues that run through all the debates about alternative economic systems: Should economic decisions be taken primarily in the private market or by government command? Should private ownership and decisions guide the economy, or should government take the commanding heights?

At one end of the spectrum is the *market economy.* In a market system, people act voluntarily and primarily for financial gain or personal satisfaction. Firms buy factors and produce outputs, selecting inputs and outputs in a way that will maximize their profits. Consumers supply factors and buy consumer goods to maximize their satisfactions. Agreements on production and consumption are made voluntarily and with the use of money, at prices determined in free markets, and on the basis of arrangements between buyers and sellers. Although individuals differ greatly in terms of economic power, the relations between individuals and firms are horizontal in nature, essentially voluntary, and nonhierarchical.

At the other end of the spectrum is the *command economy,* where decisions are made by government bureaucracy. In this approach, people are linked by a vertical relationship, and control is exercised by a multilevel hierarchy. The planning bureaucracy determines *what* goods are produced, *how* they are produced, and *for whom* output is produced. The highest level of the pyramid makes the major decisions and develops the elements of the plan for the economy. The plan is subdivided and transmitted down the bureaucratic ladder, with the lower levels of the hierarchy executing the plan with increasing attention to detail. Individuals are motivated by coercion and legal sanctions; organizations compel individuals to accept orders from above. Transactions and commands may or may not use money; trades may or may not take place at established prices.

In between are the socialist and the managed-market economies. In both cases government plays an important role in guiding and directing the economy, though much less so than in a command economy. The tension between markets and command runs through all discussions about alternative economic systems. Let us look in more detail at some of the alternatives to the mixed market economies.

THE ASIAN MODELS

Dragons and Laggards

The East Asian *crisis* has captured most of the headlines over the last few years, but the really impressive fact of that region is the East Asian *miracle* of rapid economic growth over the last half-century in South Korea, Singapore, Hong Kong, and Taiwan. Table 28-2 compares the performance of the "Asian dragons" to that of the "Latin laggards" and the stagnant economies of sub-Saharan Africa. Even with the crisis of the late 1990s, the East Asian countries show an outstanding growth record.

A recent World Bank study analyzed the economic policies of different regions to see whether any patterns emerged.[2] The results confirmed common views but also found a few surprises. Here are the high points:

- *Investment rates.* The Asian dragons followed the classic recipe of high investment rates to ensure

---

[2] See this chapter's Further Reading section for the World Bank study on the East Asian miracle.

that their economies benefited from the latest technology and could build up the necessary infrastructure. As Table 28-2 shows, investment rates among the Asian dragons were almost 20 percentage points higher than those of other regions.
- *Macroeconomic fundamentals.* Successful countries had a steady hand on macroeconomic policies, keeping inflation low and saving rates high. They invested heavily in human capital as well as in physical capital and did more to promote education than any other developing region. The financial systems were managed to ensure monetary stability and a sound currency.
- *Outward orientation.* The Asian dragons were outward-oriented, often keeping their exchange rates undervalued to promote exports, encouraging exports with fiscal incentives, and pursuing technological advance by adopting best-practice techniques of high-income countries.

The crisis of the late 1990s revealed certain flaws in the development strategies of some of these countries—reminding us of J. K. Galbraith's remark that depression reveals what the auditors missed. The strategy of "managed" capitalism, involving subsidies and directed loans, has significant potential for corruption, sometimes called "crony capitalism." This can lead to overinvestment in privileged sectors and to low returns to capital. This syndrome was particularly prominent in Indonesia and South Korea, while other countries such as Singapore managed to avoid the misallocations associated with rampant corruption.

Regions	Average growth of per capita GDP, 1965–1998	Investment as percent of GDP, 1990
East Asia and Pacific	5.7	35
South Asia	2.7	19
Latin America and Caribbean	1.3	17
Sub-Saharan Africa	−0.3	9

TABLE 28-2. Attention to Fundamentals Spurred Growth for the Asian Dragons

Source: World Bank, *The East Asia Miracle: Economic Growth and Government Policies* (1993) and *World Development Indicators* (2000).

The Perils of Corruption

What is corruption, and why is it so debilitating? The following discussion by economic development specialist Robert Klitgaard explains how corruption influences the economy:

At the broadest level, corruption is the misuse of office for unofficial ends. The catalogue of corrupt acts includes bribery, extortion, influence-peddling, nepotism, fraud, speed money, embezzlement, and more. Although we tend to think of corruption as a sin of government, of course it also exists in the private sector. Indeed, the private sector is involved in most government corruption.

Different varieties of corruption are not equally harmful. Corruption that undercuts the rules of the game—for example, the justice system or property rights or banking and credit—devastates economic and political development. Corruption that allows polluters to foul rivers or hospitals to extort patients can be environmentally and socially corrosive. In comparison, some speed money for public services and mild corruption in campaign financing are less damaging. Of course the extent of corruption matters, too. Most systems can stand some corruption, and it is possible that some truly awful systems can be improved by it. But when corruption becomes the norm, its effects are crippling. So, although every country has corruption, the varieties and extent differ. The killer is systematic corruption that destroys the rules of the game. It is one of the principal reasons why the most underdeveloped parts of our planet stay that way.[3]

Battling corruption is particularly difficult because the state, which is the instrument of justice, is often itself corrupt.

The Chinese Giant: Market Leninism

One of the major surprises in economic development during the last decade was the rapid growth in the Chinese economy. After the Chinese revolution of 1949, China initially adopted a Soviet-style central-planning system. The high-water mark of centralization came with the Cultural Revolution of 1966–1969, which led to an economic slowdown in China. After the death of the revolutionary leader Mao Tse-tung, a new generation concluded that economic reform was necessary if the Communist party was to survive. Under Deng Xiaoping (1977–1997), China decentralized a great deal of economic power

and allowed competition. Economic reform was, however, not accompanied by political reform; the democracy movement was ruthlessly repressed in Tiananmen Square in 1989, and the Communist party has continued to monopolize the political process.

To spur economic growth, the Chinese leadership has taken dramatic steps such as setting up "special economic zones" and allowing alternative forms of ownership. The most rapidly growing parts of China have been the coastal regions, such as the southern region near Hong Kong. This area has become closely integrated with countries outside China and has attracted considerable foreign investment. In addition, China has allowed collective, private, and foreign firms, free from central planning or control, to operate alongside state-owned firms. These more innovative forms of ownership have grown rapidly and by the late 1990s were producing more than half of China's GDP.

The robust performance of the Chinese economy has surprised observers almost as much as did the collapse of the Soviet economy. According to the World Bank, China's real GDP growth averaged 9 percent per year for the period 1977–2001. Exports grew over 16 percent per year during that period. The share of the labor force in agriculture fell from 30 percent in 1977 to 18 percent in 2000. By 2003, China had exports of $550 billion and had accumulated $300 billion in foreign exchange reserves. This remarkable economic progress was made while political reforms and freedoms were sharply curbed. Many countries are watching carefully to see if China can stay on its fast-growth track.

SOCIALISM

As a doctrine, socialism developed from the ideas of Marx and other radical thinkers of the nineteenth century. Socialism is a middle ground between laissez-faire capitalism and the central-planning model, which we discuss in the next subsection. A few common elements characterize most socialist philosophies:

- *Government ownership of productive resources.* Socialists traditionally believed that the role of private property should be reduced. Key industries such as railroads and banking should be nationalized (that is, owned and operated by the state). In

---

[3] See the reference under "Websites" in the Further Reading section at the end of the chapter.

recent years, because of the poor performance of many state-owned enterprises, enthusiasm for nationalization has ebbed in most advanced democracies.

- *Planning.* Socialists are suspicious of the "chaos" of the marketplace and question the allocational efficiency of the invisible hand. They insist that a planning mechanism is needed to coordinate different sectors. In recent years, planners have emphasized subsidies to promote the rapid development of high-technology industries, such as microelectronics, aircraft manufacture, and biotechnology; these policies are sometimes called "industrial policies."

- *Redistribution of income.* Inherited wealth and the highest incomes are to be reduced by the militant use of government taxing powers; in some West European countries, marginal tax rates have reached 98 percent. Government social security benefits, free medical care, and cradle-to-grave welfare services paid for with progressive taxes increase the well-being of the less privileged and guarantee minimum standards of living.

- *Peaceful and democratic evolution.* Socialists often advocate the peaceful and gradual extension of government ownership—evolution by ballot rather than revolution by bullet.

Socialist approaches fell out of favor with the collapse of communism, the stagnation in Europe, and the success of market-oriented economies. Thoughtful socialists are combing through the wreckage to find a future role for this branch of economic thought.

THE FAILED MODEL: SOVIET COMMUNISM

For many years, developing countries looked to the Soviet Union and other communist countries as role models on how to industrialize. Communism offered both a theoretical critique of Western capitalism and a seemingly workable strategy for economic development. We begin by reviewing the theoretical underpinnings of Marxism and communism and then examine how the Soviet-style command economy worked in practice. Finally, we will look at the problems that the ex-communist countries are experiencing in making the transition to a market-based economy.

Karl Marx: Economist as Revolutionary

On the surface, Karl Marx (1818–1883) lived an uneventful life, studiously poring through books in the British Museum, writing newspaper articles, and working on his scholarly studies of capitalism. Although originally attracted to German universities, his atheism, pro-constitutionalism, and radical ideas led him to journalism. He was eventually exiled to Paris and London, where he wrote his massive critique of capitalism, *Capital* (1867, 1885, 1894).

The centerpiece of Marx's work is an incisive analysis of the strengths and weaknesses of capitalism. Marx argued that all commodity value is determined by labor content—both the direct labor and the indirect labor embodied in capital equipment. For example, the value of a shirt comes from the efforts of the textile workers who put it together, plus the efforts of the workers who made the looms. By imputing all the value of output to labor, Marx attempted to show that profits—the part of output that is produced by workers but received by capitalists—amount to "unearned income."

In Marx's view, the injustice of capitalists' receiving unearned income justifies transferring the ownership of factories and other means of production from capitalists to workers. He trumpeted his message in *The Communist Manifesto* (1848): "Let the ruling classes tremble at a Communist revolution. The proletarians have nothing to lose but their chains." And the ruling capitalist classes did tremble at Marxism for more than a century!

Like many great economists, but with more passion than most, Marx was deeply moved by the struggle of working people and hoped to improve their lives. He penned the words that appear on his gravestone: "Up 'til now philosophers have only interpreted the world in various ways. The point, though, is to change it!" Our epitaph for Marx might echo the appraisal of the distinguished intellectual historian, Sir Isaiah Berlin: "No thinker in the nineteenth century has had so direct, deliberate, and powerful an influence on mankind as Karl Marx."

Baleful Prophesies

Marx saw capitalism as inevitably leading to socialism. In Marx's world, technological advances enable capitalists to replace workers with machinery as a means of earning greater profits. But this increasing accumulation of capital has two contradictory consequences. As the supply of available capital increases, the rate of profit on capital falls. At the same time, with fewer jobs, the unemployment rate rises and wages fall. In Marx's terms, the "reserve army of the unemployed" would grow, and the working class would become increasingly "immiserized"—by which he meant that working conditions would deteriorate and workers would grow progressively alienated from their jobs.

As profits decline and investment opportunities at home become exhausted, the ruling capitalist classes resort to imperialism. Capital tends to seek higher rates of profit abroad. And, according to this theory (particularly as later expanded by Lenin), the foreign policies of imperialist nations increasingly attempt to win colonies and then mercilessly milk surplus value from them.

Marx believed that the capitalist system could not continue this unbalanced growth forever. Marx predicted increasing inequality under capitalism, along with a gradual emergence of class consciousness among the downtrodden proletariat. Business cycles would become ever more violent as mass poverty resulted in macroeconomic underconsumption. Finally, a cataclysmic depression would sound the death knell of capitalism. Like feudalism before it, capitalism would contain the seeds of its own destruction.

The *economic interpretation of history* is one of Marx's lasting contributions to Western thought. Marx argued that economic interests lie behind and determine our values. Why do business executives vote for conservative candidates, while labor leaders support those who advocate raising the minimum wage or increasing unemployment benefits? The reason, Marx held, is that people's beliefs and ideologies reflect the material interests of their social and economic class. In fact, Marx's approach is hardly foreign to mainstream economics. It generalizes Adam Smith's analysis of self-interest from the dollar votes of the marketplace to the ballot votes of elections and the bullet votes of the barricades.

From Textbooks to Tactics: Soviet-Style Command Economy

Marx wrote extensively about the faults of capitalism, but he left no design for the promised socialist land. His arguments suggested that communism would arise in the most highly developed industrial countries. Instead, it was feudal Russia that adopted the Marxist vision. Let's examine this fascinating and horrifying chapter of economic history.

Historical Roots. An analysis of Soviet communism is of the utmost importance for economics because the Soviet Union served as a laboratory for theories about the functioning of a command economy. Some economists claimed that socialism simply could not work; the Soviet experience proved them wrong. Its advocates argued that communism would overtake capitalism; Soviet history also refutes this thesis.

Although czarist Russia grew rapidly from 1880 to 1914, it was considerably less developed than industrialized countries like the United States or Britain. World War I brought great hardship to Russia and allowed the communists to seize power. From 1917 to 1933, the Soviet Union experimented with different socialist models before settling on central planning. But dissatisfaction with the pace of industrialization led Stalin to undertake a radical new venture around 1928—collectivization of agriculture, forced-draft industrialization, and central planning of the economy.[4]

Under the collectivization of Soviet agriculture between 1929 and 1935, 94 percent of Soviet peasants were forced to join collective farms. In the process, many wealthy peasants were deported, and conditions deteriorated so much that millions perished. The other part of the Soviet "great leap forward" came through the introduction of economic planning for rapid industrialization. The planners created the first 5-year plan to cover the period 1928–1933. The first plan established the priorities of Soviet planning: heavy industry was to be favored over light industry, and consumer goods were to be the residual sector after all the other priorities had been met. Although there were many reforms and changes in emphasis, the Stalinist model of a command economy applied in the Soviet Union, and after World War II in Eastern Europe, until the fall of Soviet communism at the end of the 1980s.

How the Command Economy Functioned. In the Soviet-style command economy, the broad categories of output were determined by political decisions. Military spending in the Soviet Union was always allocated a substantial part of output and scientific

---

[4] See this chapter's Further Reading section for studies of Soviet economic history.

resources, while the other major priority was investment. Consumption claimed the residual output after the quotas of higher-priority sectors were filled.

In large part, decisions about how goods were to be produced were made by the planning authorities. Planners first decided on the quantities of final outputs (the *what*). Then they worked backward from outputs to the required inputs and the flows among different firms. Investment decisions were specified in great detail by the planners, while firms had considerable flexibility in deciding upon their mix of labor inputs.

Clearly no planning system could specify all the activities of all the firms—this would have required trillions of commands every year. Many details were left to the managers of individual factories. It was here, in what is called the *principal-agent problem*, that the command economy ran into its deepest difficulties.

The principal-agent problem arises because the person at the top of a hierarchy (the "principal") wants to provide appropriate incentives for the people making the decisions down the hierarchy (the "agents") to behave according to the principal's wishes. In a market economy, profits and prices serve as the mechanism for coordinating consumers and producers. A command economy is plagued by an inability to find an efficient substitute for profits and prices as a way of motivating the agents.

A useful example of the failure to solve the principal-agent problem is found in Soviet book publication. In a market economy, commercial decisions about books are made primarily on the basis of profit and loss. In the Soviet Union, because profits were taboo, planners instead used quantitative targets. A first approach was to reward firms according to the number of books produced, so publishers printed thousands of thin unread volumes. Faced with a clear incentive problem, the center (principal) changed the system so that the producers (agents) were rewarded on the basis of the number of pages printed, and the result was fat books with onion-skin paper and large type. The planners then changed the criterion to the number of words—to which the publishers responded by printing huge volumes with tiny type. None of these mechanisms was capable of signaling consumer wants effectively.

The principal-agent problem crops up in organizations in all countries, but the Soviet model had few mechanisms (like bankruptcy in markets and

elections for public goods) to provide an ultimate check on waste.

Comparative Economic Performance. From World War II until the mid-1980s, the United States and the Soviet Union engaged in a superpower competition for public opinion, military superiority, and economic dominance. How well did the command economies perform in the economic growth race? Any attempt at answering this question is bedeviled by the absence of reliable statistics. Most economists believed until recently that the Soviet Union grew rapidly from 1928 until the mid-1960s, with growth rates perhaps surpassing those in North America and Western Europe. After the mid-1960s, growth in the Soviet Union stagnated and output actually began to decline. Estimates of living standards today are treacherous, but per capita income in Russia in the early 1990s appears to be less than one-quarter of that in the United States.

A revealing comparison of the performance of market and command economies can be made by contrasting the experiences of East Germany and West Germany. These countries started out with roughly equal levels of productivity and similar industrial structures at the end of World War II. After four decades of capitalism in the West and Soviet-style socialism in the East, productivity in East Germany had fallen to a level estimated between one-fourth and one-third of that in West Germany. Moreover, the East German growth tended to emphasize production of intermediate goods and commodities of little value to consumers. Quantity, not quality, was the goal.

Finally, what of the scourges of capitalism—unemployment and inflation? Unemployment was traditionally low in Soviet-style economies because labor was generally in short supply as a result of the ambitious economic plans. Furthermore, controlled prices tended to be quite stable, so measured inflation was absent. In the late 1980s and early 1990s, however, open inflation erupted. In addition, prices were well below market-clearing levels, and acute shortages arose in what is called *repressed inflation*.

Balance Sheet. Is there a final balance sheet on the experience with Soviet central planning? The Soviet model demonstrated that a command economy can work—it is capable of mobilizing capital and labor and producing both guns and butter. But the Soviet economy, with borders closed to trade, technologies, and people, became increasingly obsolete over time. Innovation withered because of poor incentives. In competition with the open-market economies, particularly as the world turned to increasingly high-quality goods and services, Russia could export virtually nothing except raw materials.

Growth slowed, and per capita income declined in the latest period of central planning. Its leaders finally abandoned Soviet central planning as it was seen to be morally, politically, and economically bankrupt.

From Marx to Market

Beginning in 1989, the countries of Eastern Europe and the former Soviet Union rejected the communist experiment and introduced market economies. A cruel joke heard in Eastern Europe is "Question: What is communism? Answer: The longest road from capitalism to capitalism." Having decided to take the road back to a market economy, a command economy has an arduous path to follow. Among the major obstacles on the road to reform are the following:

- *Price reform and free-market pricing.* Prices of both inputs and outputs were often far below market-clearing levels. Food, housing, and energy were generally heavily subsidized, while automobiles and consumer durables sold at levels far above the world price levels. The first step in most countries was to allow supply and demand to set prices.
- *Hard budget constraints.* Enterprises in command economies operated with "soft budget constraints." This term means that operating losses are covered by subsidies and do not lead to bankruptcy. In a market economy, firms must be fiscally responsible—enterprises know that unprofitability ultimately means economic bankruptcy for the firm and economic ruin for the managers.
- *Privatization.* In market economies, output is primarily produced in private firms; in the United States, for example, only 3 percent of GDP is produced by the federal government. In Soviet-style communist countries, by contrast, between 80 and 90 percent of output was produced by the state. Moving to the market required that the actual decisions about buying, selling, pricing,

producing, borrowing, and lending be made by private agents.
- *Other reforms.* Transition to the market required setting up the legal framework for a market, establishing a modern banking system, breaking up the pervasive monopolies, tightening monetary and fiscal policy in order to prevent runaway inflation, and opening up the economy to international competition.
- *Sequencing of the transition.* The most difficult issue in moving to the market was where to begin. The reform debate divided between a radical (or "shock-therapy") approach and a gradual (or "step-by-step") approach. One influential adviser was Harvard's Jeffrey Sachs, a brilliant young economist who has nursed many ailing countries back to health. He persuaded the Polish government to adopt the shock-therapy approach in January 1990. This was the model that Russia followed in 1991–1992 under President Yeltsin and a government led by economist Yegor Gaidar. The radical Russian reformers freed prices and international trade, dismantled the planning apparatus, and attempted to keep money tight. The next few years saw pitched battle between the reformers, bureaucrats from the old regime, and wistful romantics who yearned for the "good old days" under communism. "Two steps forward and one step backward" has characterized the reform movement in Russia and many formerly socialist countries.

This checklist of reforms applies also to other countries that have traveled some distance down the road to a centrally planned economy and want a more market-oriented economy.

Reform's Progress

Reforms in centrally planned countries have been through a decade of transition, and the initial returns are sobering. First, virtually all countries suffered deep depressions as they shucked off their socialist structures. The sources of the decline in output are varied, but a major reason is undoubtedly that the delicate web of buyer-seller relationships was completely disrupted by the transition. Second, many countries experienced rapid inflation, and some (like Ukraine) suffered from hyperinflation. The major impetus of the rapid price rises came when the freeing of prices and wages triggered an initial inflation, and this was followed by a classic wage-price spiral. An additional shock to inflation came in those countries where a weak government was unable to contain the budget deficit and government consequently relied upon the monetary printing press to finance its expenditures.

Figure 28-5 shows the growth trajectories of the major transition economies over the 1990s. What were the characteristics of countries with the most successful transitions? These countries had relatively short histories of central planning, had deeper traditions of civil society and greater "social capital," made more rapid transitions to the market, were closer to the rich core countries of Western Europe, and moved more quickly to integrate themselves into the larger world economy. Poland and Slovenia exemplified successful transitions. Most of the former communist countries of Eastern Europe cast their lots with the unified market of Western Europe, and eight of them joined the European Union in 2003.

The greatest difficulties came in the eastern and Asian remnants of the former Soviet Union, particularly in those countries like Ukraine and Russia where the transition was slow and reluctant. Russia was torn by corruption, great inequality, budget deficits, inflation, civil war, and political instability during much of the 1990s.

With President Boris Yeltsin's resignation in 1999 and under the new president, Alexander Putin, Russia's rocky transition to a market democracy took another turn. Putin began a firm orientation to the West and attempted to bring order to a chaotic economy, and Russia appeared to have turned the corner and be showing positive economic growth. The struggles between the old autocratic elements and the new market-oriented "oligarchs" reemerged in 2003 with the arrest of Russia's richest businessman, raising again troubling questions about the depth of that country's commitment to market reforms and democratic freedoms.

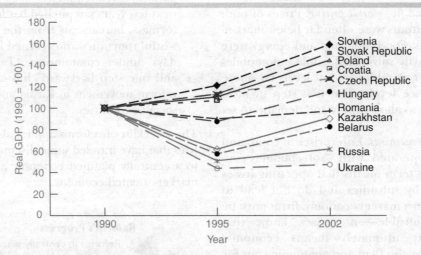

FIGURE 28-5. The Transition to the Market Has Been a Mixed Success

Most transition countries had a steep output drop after they shucked off their central-planning systems. Those countries like Poland and Slovenia with strong market traditions, decisive economic reforms, and close links to Western Europe recovered relatively quickly. Others, like Russia and Ukraine, introduced reforms in a more halting way, had weaker market-economy traditions, and had inconsistent macroeconomic policies with high inflation—they consequently experienced sharp economic declines after the transition and are still not back to 1990 levels of GDP.

Source: International Monetary Fund, World Economic Outlook (WEO) Database, available at www.imf.org/external/pubs/ft/weo/2003/01/index.htm.

A CAUTIONARY FINAL NOTE

This chapter has described the problems and prospects of poor countries struggling to be rich and free—to provide the dry houses, education, electric lights, fast horses, automobiles, and long vacations of the excerpt that opened this chapter. What are the prospects of attaining these goals? We close with a hopeful note and sober warning from Sachs and Warner:

> The world economy at the end of the twentieth century looks much like the world economy at the end of the nineteenth century. A global capitalist system is taking shape, drawing almost all regions of the world into arrangements of open trade and harmonized economic institutions. As in the nineteenth century, this new round of globalization promises to lead to economic convergence for the countries that join the system. . . .
>
> And yet there are also profound risks for the consolidation of market reforms in Russia, China, and Africa, as well as for the maintenance of international agreements among the leading countries. . . . The spread of capitalism in the [last] twenty-five years is an historic event of great promise and significance, but whether we will be celebrating the consolidation of a democratic and market-based world system [twenty-five years hence] will depend on our own foresight and good judgments in the years to come.[5]

------

[5] See the reference in the Further Reading section at the end of the chapter.

SUMMARY

A. Economic Growth in Poor Countries

1. Most of the world's population live in developing countries, which have relatively low per capita incomes. Such countries often exhibit rapid population growth, a low level of literacy, poor health, and a high proportion of their population living and working on farms.

2. The key to development lies in four fundamental factors: human resources, natural resources, capital formation, and technology. Explosive population causes problems as the Malthusian prediction of diminishing returns haunts the poorest countries. On the constructive agenda, improving the population's health, education, and technical training has high priority.

3. Investment and saving rates in poor countries are low because incomes are so depressed that little can be saved for the future. International financing of investment in poor countries has witnessed many crises over the last two centuries. The most recent cycle came in 1997–1998 when many East Asian countries borrowed heavily and were unable to repay their loans.

4. Technological change is often associated with investment and new machinery. It offers much hope to the developing nations because they can adopt the more productive technologies of advanced nations. This requires entrepreneurship. One task of development is to spur internal growth of the scarce entrepreneurial spirit.

5. Numerous theories of economic development help explain why the four fundamental factors are present or absent at a particular time. Geography and climate, custom, religious and business attitudes, class conflicts and political systems—each affects economic development. But none does so in a simple and invariable way. Development economists today emphasize the growth advantage of relative backwardness, the need to respect the role of agriculture, and the art of finding the proper boundary between state and market. The most recent consensus is on the advantages of openness.

B. Alternative Models for Development

6. Other approaches have competed with the mixed market economy as models for economic development. Alternative strategies include the managed-market approach of the East Asian countries, socialism, and the Soviet-style command economy.

7. The managed-market approach of Japan and the Asian dragons, such as South Korea, Hong Kong, Taiwan, and Singapore, has proved remarkably successful over the last quarter-century. Among the key ingredients are macroeconomic stability, high investment rates, a sound financial system, rapid improvements in education, and an outward orientation in trade and technology policies.

8. Socialism is a middle ground between capitalism and communism, stressing government ownership of the

means of production, planning by the state, income redistribution, and peaceful transition to a more egalitarian world.

9. Historically, Marxism took its deepest roots in semifeudal Russia. A study of resource allocation in the Soviet-style command economy shows great central planning of broad elements of resource allocation, particularly the emphasis on heavy industry. The Soviet economy grew rapidly in its early decades, but stagnation and collapse have today put Russia and other formerly communist countries at income levels far below those of North America, Japan, and Western Europe.

10. Faced with slowing economic growth and the desire for economic reform, Russia and other formerly communist countries are making the difficult transition to market economies. Transition raises many obstacles, such as soft budget constraints, frozen and distorted prices, and an inadequate legal framework. Two major transition strategies are the shock-therapy approach of multiple simultaneous measures and the more cautious step-by-step approach, in which reforms are sequenced to prevent disruption. The lessons of the transition are broadly applicable to countries hoping to cast off government controls for a market-oriented system.

CONCEPTS FOR REVIEW

Economic Development

developing country
indicators of development
four elements in development
vicious cycles, virtuous circles

backwardness hypothesis
openness and convergence

Alternative Models for Development

the central dilemma of markets vs.
command

socialism, communism
the principal-agent problem
Soviet-style command economy
transition to the market

FURTHER READING AND INTERNET WEBSITES

Further Reading

The influential study on the East Asian miracle is contained in World Bank, *The East Asia Miracle: Economic Growth and Government Policies* (World Bank, Washington, D.C., 1993). The data in Figure 28-4 are from the fascinating paper by Jeffrey Sachs and Andrew Warner, "Economic Reform and the Process of Global Integration," *Brookings Papers on Economic Activity,* no. 1, 1995, pp. 42–43, while the quote at the end of the chapter is on pp. 63–64.

A highly readable account of developments in Soviet economic history is contained in Alec Nove, *An Economic History of the U.S.S.R.,* 3d ed. (Penguin, Baltimore, 1990). A careful study of the Soviet economic system is provided by Paul R. Gregory and Robert C. Stuart, *Russian and Soviet Economic Performance and Structure,* 6th ed. (Harper & Row, New York, 1997).

Websites

The World Bank has information on its programs and publications at its site, www.worldbank.org; the International

Monetary Fund (IMF) provides similar information at www.imf.org. The United Nations website has links to most international institutions and their databases at www.unsystem.org. A good source of information about high-income countries is the Organisation for Economic Cooperation and Development (OECD) website, www.oecd.org. U.S. trade data are available at www.census.gov. You can find information on many countries through their statistical offices. A compendium of national agencies is available at www.census.gov/main/.

One of the best sources for studies of developing countries is the World Bank, especially the annual *World Development Review* at www.worldbank.org.

The quote from Klitgaard was published in *Finance and Development,* March 1998, and can be found at www.gwdg.de/~uwww/icr.htm.

QUESTIONS FOR DISCUSSION

1. Do you agree with the celebration of material well-being expressed in the chapter's opening quotation? What would you add to the list of the benefits of economic development?

2. Delineate each of the four important factors driving economic development. With respect to these, how was it that the high-income oil-exporting countries became rich? What hope is there for a country like Mali, which has very low per capita resources of capital, land, and technology?

3. Some fear the "vicious cycle of underdevelopment." In a poor country, rapid population growth eats into whatever improvements in technology occur and lowers living standards. With a low per capita income, the country cannot save and invest and mainly engages in subsistence farming. With most of the population on the farm, there is little hope for education, decline in fertility, or industrialization. If you were to advise such a country, how would you break through the vicious cycle?

4. Compare the situation a developing country faces today with the one it might have faced (at an equivalent level of per capita income) 200 years ago. Considering the four wheels of economic development, explain the advantages and disadvantages that today's developing country might experience.

5. Some economists today question whether it is wise to allow complete openness on both financial and current accounts. They argue that allowing free flow of short-term financial movements increases vulnerability to speculative attacks. Give the pros and cons of limiting short-term financial movements. Might you want to use a tax on short-term flows rather than quantitative restrictions?

6. Analyze the way that *what*, *how*, and *for whom* are solved in a Soviet-style command economy, and compare your analysis with the solution of the three central questions in a market economy.

7. **Advanced problem** (relying upon the growth accounting of Chapter 27): We can extend our growth-accounting equation to include three factors and write the following equation:

$$g_Q = s_L g_L + s_K g_K + s_R g_R + \text{T.C.}$$

where g_Q = the growth rate of output, g_i = the growth rate of inputs (i = inputs to production: L for labor, K for capital, and R for land and other natural resources), and s_i = the contribution of each input to output growth as measured by its share of national income $(0 \le s_i \le 1$ and $s_L + s_K + s_R = 1)$. T.C. measures technological change.

a. In the poorest developing countries, the share of capital is close to zero, the main resource is agricultural land (which is constant), and there is little technological change. Can you use this to explain the Malthusian hypothesis in which per capita output is likely to be stagnant or even to decline (i.e., $g_Q < g_L$)?

b. In advanced industrial economies, the share of land resources drops to virtually zero. Why does this lead to the growth-accounting equation studied in the last chapter? Can you use this to explain how countries can avoid the Malthusian trap of stagnant incomes?

c. According to economists who are pessimistic about future prospects (including a group of *neo-Malthusians* from the Club of Rome, which was discussed in the previous chapter), T.C. is close to zero, the available supply of natural resources is declining, and the share of resources is large and rising. Does this explain why the future of industrial societies might be bleak? What assumptions of the neo-Malthusians might you question?

*The benefit of
international trade—a
more efficient
employment of the
productive forces of
the world.*

John Stuart Mill

INTERNATIONAL LINKAGES

The twentieth century divides into two distinct periods. The period from 1914 to 1945 was characterized by destructive competition, shrinking international trade, growing financial isolation, hot and cold military and trade wars, despotism, and depression. After World War II, most of the world enjoyed growing economic cooperation, widening trade linkages, increasingly integrated financial markets, an expansion of democracy, and rapid economic growth.

The stark contrast between the first and second halves of the twentieth century is a reminder of the high stakes in the wise management of our national and global economies. Economically, no nation is an island unto itself. When the bell tolls depression or financial crisis, the sounds reverberate around the world.

What are the economic links among nations? The important economic concepts involve international trade and finance. International trade in goods and services allows nations to raise their standards of living by specializing in areas of comparative advantage in production, exporting goods and services in which they are relatively efficient and importing those in which they are relatively inefficient. In a modern economy, trade takes place using different currencies. The international financial system plays an important role for it is the lubricant that facilitates exchange through the buying and selling of commodities for dollars, Euros, and other currencies and the exchanging of one currency for another.

International trade often seems a zero-sum, Darwinian conflict for market shares, profits, and vital resources. A closer look reveals, however, that nations in the second half of the twentieth century evolved beyond the red-in-tooth-and-claw struggle— they built institutions that serve the common cause of growth and fairness in the international arena.

But economic integration is not without its perils. The last decade saw a rapid succession of financial crises—a crisis of confidence in the exchange-rate regime in Europe in 1991–1992, a collapse of the currency in Mexico in 1994–1995, a series of banking and currency crises in East Asia in 1997, a default on Russian debt and a global liquidity crisis in 1998, and a series of currency crises in Latin America, culminating in the collapse of Argentina's currency and economy in early 2002. Each of these required that policymakers in the countries involved and in other countries consider the need for intervention and policy adjustments, but in the end none led to widespread economic collapse.

This chapter and the next one survey international macroeconomics. This topic includes the principles governing the international monetary system, which is the major focus of the present chapter, as well as the impact of foreign trade on output, employment, and prices, which is covered in the next chapter.

International macroeconomics involves many of the most controversial questions of the day: Does foreign trade raise or lower our output and employment? What is the link between domestic saving, domestic investment, and the trade balance? What are the causes of the occasional financial crises that spread contagiously from country to country? What will be the effect of the European Monetary Union on Europe's macroeconomic performance? And why has the United States become the world's largest debtor country in the last decade? The economic stakes are high in finding wise answers to these questions.

TRENDS IN FOREIGN TRADE

An economy that engages in international trade is called an **open economy.** A useful measure of openness is the ratio of a country's exports or imports to its GDP. Figure 29-1 shows the trend in the shares of

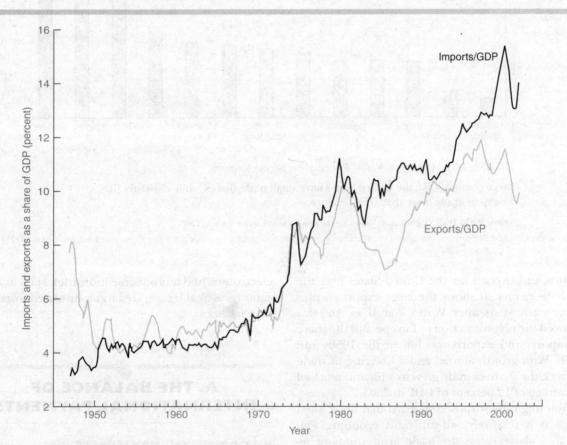

FIGURE 29-1. Growing U.S. Openness

Like all major market economies, the United States has increasingly opened its borders to foreign trade over the last half-century. The result is a growing share of output and consumption involved in international trade. Since the 1980s, imports have far outdistanced exports, causing the United States to become the world's largest debtor nation.

Source: U.S. Department of Commerce.

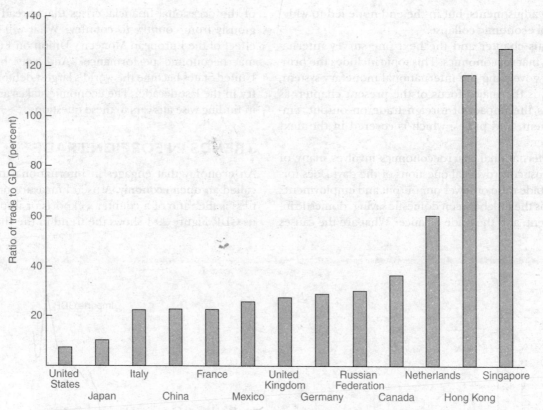

FIGURE 29-2. Openness Varies Enormously across Regions

Large countries like the United States have small trade shares, while city-states like Singapore trade more than they produce.

Source: World Trade Organization. Shares are the ratio of merchandise trade to GDP.

imports and exports for the United States over the last half-century. It shows the large export surplus in the early years after World War II as America financed the reconstruction of Europe. But the share of imports and exports was low in the 1950s and 1960s. With growth abroad and a lowering of trade barriers, the share of trade grew steadily and reached an average of 12 percent of GDP in 2003.

You might be surprised to learn that the United States is a relatively self-sufficient economy. Figure 29-2 above shows the trade proportions of selected countries. Small countries and those in highly integrated regions like Western Europe are more open than the United States. Moreover, the degree of openness is much higher in many U.S. industries than in the overall economy, particularly in manufacturing industries like steel, textiles, consumer

electronics, and autos. Some industries, such as education and health care, are largely insulated from foreign trade.

A. THE BALANCE OF INTERNATIONAL PAYMENTS

BALANCE-OF-PAYMENTS ACCOUNTS

We begin this chapter with a review of the way nations keep their international accounts. Economists keep score by looking at income statements and balance sheets. In the area of international economics, the key accounts are a nation's balance of payments. A country's **balance of international payments** is a systematic statement of all economic transactions between that country and the rest of the world. Its major components are the current account and the financial account. The basic structure of the balance of payments is shown in Table 29-1, and each element is discussed below.

Debits and Credits

Like other accounts, the balance of payments records each transaction as either a plus or a minus. The general rule in balance-of-payments accounting is the following:

If a transaction earns foreign currency for the nation, it is called a *credit* and is recorded as a plus item. If a transaction involves spending foreign currency, it is a *debit* and is recorded as a negative item. In general, exports are credits and imports are debits.

Exports earn foreign currency, so they are credits. Imports require spending foreign currency, so they are debits. How is the U.S. import of a Japanese camera recorded? Since we ultimately pay for it in Japanese yen, it is clearly a debit. How shall we treat interest and dividend income on investments

received by Americans from abroad? Clearly, they are credit items like exports because they provide us with foreign currencies.

Details of the Balance of Payments

Balance on Current Account. The totality of items under section I in Table 29-1 is the **balance on current account.** This includes all items of income and outlay—imports and exports of goods and services, investment income, and transfer payments. The current-account balance is akin to the net income of a nation. It is conceptually similar to net exports in the national output accounts.

In the past, many writers concentrated on the **trade balance,** which consists of merchandise imports or exports. The composition of merchandise imports and exports consists mainly of primary commodities (like food and fuels) and manufactured goods. In an earlier era, the mercantilists strove for a trade surplus (an excess of exports over imports), calling this a "favorable balance of trade." They hoped to avoid an "unfavorable trade balance," by which they meant a trade deficit (an excess of imports over exports). Even today, we find traces of mercantilism when many nations seek to maintain trade surpluses.

Today, economists avoid this language because a trade deficit is not necessarily harmful. As we will see, the trade deficit is really a reflection of the imbalance between domestic investment and domestic saving. Often, a nation has a trade deficit because its domestic capital is highly profitable and it is beneficial to borrow abroad to invest at home and raise domestic incomes.

In addition, *services* are increasingly important in international trade. Services consist of such items as shipping, financial services, and foreign travel. A third item in the current account is *investment income*, which includes the earnings on foreign investments (such as earnings on U.S. assets abroad). One of the major developments of the last two decades has been the growth in services and investment income. A final element is transfers, which represent payments not in return for goods and services.

Table 29-2 presents a summary of the U.S. balance of international payments for 2002. Note its two main divisions: current account and financial account. Each item is listed by name in column (a). Credits are listed in column (b), while column (c) shows the debits. Column (d) then lists the net credits or debits; it shows a credit if on balance the item added to our stock of

I. Current account
 Merchandise (or "trade balance")
 Services
 Investment income
 Unilateral transfers

II. Financial account
 Private
 Government
 Official reserve changes
 Other

TABLE 29-1. Basic Elements of the Balance of Payments

The balance of payments has two fundamental parts. The *current account* represents the spending and receipts on goods and services along with transfers. The *financial account* includes purchases and sales of financial assets and liabilities. An important principle is that the two must always sum to zero:

Current account + financial account − I + II = 0

(a) Items	(b) Credits (+)	(c) Debits (−)	(d) Net credits (+) or debits (−)
U.S. Balance of Payments, 2002 **(billions of dollars)**			
I. Current account			−503
a. Merchandise trade balance	683	−1,167	−484
b. Services	289	−240	49
c. Investment income	245	−257	−12
d. Unilateral transfers			−56
II. Financial account [lending (−) or borrowing (+)]			503
a. Private borrowing or lending	534	−152	381
b. Government			
Official U.S. reserve assets, changes			−4
Foreign official assets in the U.S., changes			97
c. Statistical discrepancy			29
III. Sum of Current and Financial Accounts			0

TABLE 29-2. Basic Elements of Balance of Payments, 2002

Source: U.S. Department of Commerce, website, April 2003.

foreign currencies or a debit if the total subtracted from our foreign-currency supply.

In 2002 our merchandise exports gave us credits of $683 billion. But our merchandise imports gave us debits of $1167 billion. The *net* difference between credits and debits was a debit of $484 billion. This trade deficit is listed in column (d), in the second row. (Be sure you know why the algebraic sign is shown as − rather than as +.) From the table we see that services provided a surplus, while net investment income was slightly negative. Our current-account deficit was thus $503 billion for 2002.

Financial Account.[1] We have now completed our analysis of the current account. But how did the United States "finance" its $503 billion current-account deficit

in 2002? It must have either borrowed or reduced its foreign assets, for by definition, when you buy something, you must either pay for it or borrow for it. This identity means that *the balance of international payments as a whole must by definition show a final zero balance.*

Financial-account transactions are asset transactions between Americans and foreigners. They occur, for example, when a Japanese pension fund buys U.S. government securities or when an American buys stock in a German firm.

Credits and debits are somewhat more complicated in the financial accounts. The general rule, which is drawn from double-entry business accounting, is this: Increases in a country's assets and decreases in its liabilities are entered as debits; conversely, decreases in a country's assets and increases in its liabilities are entered as credits. A debit entry is represented by a negative (−) sign and a credit entry by a positive (+) sign.

You can usually get the right answer more easily if you remember this simplified rule: Think of the United States as exporting and importing stocks, bonds, or other securities—that is, exporting and importing IOUs in return for foreign currencies. Then you can treat these exports and imports of securities

---

[1] In 1999, the United States revised its international accounts to conform to new guidelines. What was formerly called the "capital account" became the "financial account." A newly defined capital account consists of capital transfers and the acquisition and disposal of nonproduced nonfinancial assets. This new terminology is helpful because it emphasizes that the financial account involves flows of financial assets and liabilities rather than aircraft and factories. The newly defined capital account is extremely small and has been omitted from the discussion in this chapter.

like other exports and imports. When we borrow abroad to finance a current-account deficit, we are sending IOUs (in the form of Treasury bills) abroad and getting foreign currencies. Is this a credit or a debit? Clearly, this is a credit because it brought foreign currencies into the United States.

Similarly, if U.S. banks lend abroad to finance a computer assembly plant in Mexico, the U.S. banks are importing IOUs from the Mexicans and the United States is losing foreign currencies; this is clearly a debit item in the U.S. balance of payments.

Line II shows that in 2002 the United States was a net *borrower:* we borrowed abroad more than we lent to foreigners. The United States was a net exporter of IOUs (a net borrower) in the amount of \$503 billion.[2]

The Life Cycle of the Balance of Payments

The balance of payments of industrial countries often have similar life cycles as the nations grow from young debtors to mature creditors. This sequence is found, with variations related to their particular histories, in the advanced economies of North America, Europe, and Southeast Asia. We can illustrate the stages by recounting briefly the history of the balance of payments of the United States:

1. *Young and growing debtor nation.* From the Revolutionary War until the Civil War, the United States imported on current account more than it exported. Europe lent the difference, which allowed the country to build up its capital stock. The United States was a typical young and growing debtor nation.

2. *Mature debtor nation.* From about 1873 to 1914, the U.S. balance of trade moved into surplus. But growth of the dividends and interest that were owed abroad on past borrowing kept the current account more or less in balance. Financial flows were also nearly in balance as lending just offset borrowing.

3. *New creditor nation.* During World War I, the United States expanded its exports tremendously. America

lent money to allies England and France for war equipment and postwar relief needs. The United States emerged from the war a creditor nation.

4. *Mature creditor nation.* In the fourth stage, earnings on foreign investments provided a large surplus that was matched by a deficit on merchandise trade. This pattern was followed by the United States until the early 1980s. Countries like Japan today play the role of mature creditor nation as they enjoy large current-account surpluses which they in turn invest abroad.

The United States has entered an interesting new position over the last two decades. *Even though it was a rich country and the world's economic superpower, the United States borrowed heavily from abroad to finance its domestic investment.* In part, the foreign borrowing was caused by low U.S. domestic saving relative to its investment. While Americans were saving relatively little, financial flows came to the United States because of the country's political stability, low inflation, booming stock market, and robust technological innovation. The counterpart of American dissaving was that other countries, particularly Japan, were saving more than they were investing and were running a current-account surplus.

Is this new stage of the U.S. balance of payments a temporary aberration? Or does it mark the beginning of many more years of structural current-account deficits? Many economists worry that the large deficit is not sustainable and that it will lead to a major decline in the exchange rate of the dollar. Even if the U.S. current account swings back toward balance, however, the country will still have a large foreign debt to service. At some point, the United States will once again be a mature debtor nation, going back to stage 2, above.

B. THE DETERMINATION OF FOREIGN EXCHANGE RATES

FOREIGN EXCHANGE RATES

We are all familiar with domestic trade. When I buy Florida oranges or California computers, I naturally want to pay in dollars. Luckily, the orange grower and the computer manufacturer want payment in U.S. currency, so all trade can be carried out in

---

[2] As with all economic statistics, the balance-of-payments accounts necessarily contain statistical errors (called the "statistical discrepancy"). These reflect the fact that many flows of goods and finance (from small currency transactions to the drug trade) are not recorded. We include the statistical discrepancy in line II(c) of Table 29-2.

dollars. Economic transactions within a country are relatively simple.

But suppose I am in the business of selling Japanese bicycles. Here, the transaction becomes more complicated. The bicycle manufacturer wants to be paid in Japanese currency rather than in U.S. dollars. Therefore, in order to import the Japanese bicycles, I must first buy Japanese yen (¥) and use those yen to pay the Japanese manufacturer. Similarly, if the Japanese want to buy U.S. merchandise, they must first obtain U.S. dollars. This new complication involves foreign exchange.

Foreign trade involves the use of different national currencies. The **foreign exchange rate** is the price of one currency in terms of another currency. The foreign exchange rate is determined in the foreign exchange market, which is the market where different currencies are traded.

That little paragraph contains much information that will be explained in this section. We begin with the fact that most major countries have their own currencies—the U.S. dollar, the Japanese yen, the Mexican peso, and so forth. (European countries are an exception in that they have a common currency, the Euro.) *We follow the convention of measuring exchange rates as the amount of foreign currency that can be bought with 1 unit of the domestic currency.* For example, the foreign exchange rate of the dollar might be 100 yen per U.S. dollar (¥100/$).

When we want to exchange one nation's money for another's, we do so at a foreign exchange rate. For example, if you traveled to Canada in early 2004, you would get about 1.3 Canadian dollars for 1 U.S. dollar. There is a foreign exchange rate between U.S. dollars and the currency of every other country. In fall 2000, the foreign exchange rate per U.S. dollar was 0.80 Euro, 0.55 British pound, 106 Japanese yen, and 11 Mexican pesos.

With foreign exchange, it is possible for me to buy a Japanese bicycle. Suppose its quoted price is 20,000 yen. I can look in the newspaper for the foreign exchange rate for yen. Suppose the rate is ¥100/$. I could go to the bank to convert my $200 into ¥20,000. With my Japanese money, I then can pay the exporter for my bicycle in the currency it wants.

You should be able to show what Japanese importers of American trucks have to do if they want to buy, say, a $36,000 truck from an American exporter.

Here yen must be converted into dollars. You will see that, when the foreign exchange rate is 100 yen per dollar, the truck shipment costs them ¥3,600,000. [3]

Businesses and tourists do not have to know anything more than this for their import or export transactions. But the economics of foreign exchange rates cannot be grasped until we analyze the forces underlying the supply and demand for foreign currencies and the functioning of the foreign exchange market.

THE FOREIGN EXCHANGE MARKET

Like most other prices, foreign exchange rates vary from week to week and month to month according to the forces of supply and demand. The **foreign exchange market** is the market in which currencies of different countries are traded and foreign exchange rates are determined. Foreign currencies are traded at the retail level in many banks and firms specializing in that business. Organized markets in New York, Tokyo, London, and Zurich trade hundreds of billions of dollars worth of currencies each day.

We can use our familiar supply and demand curves to illustrate how markets determine the price of foreign currencies. Figure 29-3 shows the supply and demand for U.S. dollars that arise in dealings with Japan.[4] The *supply* of U.S. dollars comes from people in the United States who need yen to purchase Japanese goods, services, or financial assets. The *demand* for dollars comes from people in Japan who buy U.S. goods, services, or investments and who, accordingly, need dollars to pay for these items. The price of foreign exchange—the foreign exchange rate—settles at that price where supply and demand are in balance.

Let us first consider the supply side. The supply of U.S. dollars to the foreign exchange market originates when Americans need yen to buy Japanese automobiles, cameras, and other commodities, to vacation in Tokyo, and so forth. In addition, foreign exchange is required if Americans want to purchase

---

[3] These examples ignore transactions costs and the spread between buying price and selling price (the "bid-ask spread"). These costs can be substantial, particularly for small transactions. One of the advantages of a common currency among regions with substantial trade is that it reduces transactions costs and thereby improves efficiency.

[4] This is a simplified example in which we consider only the bilateral trade between Japan and the United States.

FIGURE 29-3. Exchange-Rate Determination

Behind the supplies and demands for foreign exchange lie purchases of goods, services, and financial assets. Behind the demand for dollars is the Japanese desire for American goods and investments. The supply of dollars comes from Americans desiring Japanese goods and assets. Equilibrium comes at E. If the foreign exchange rate were above E, there would be an excess supply of dollars. Unless the government bought this excess supply with official reserves, market forces would push the foreign exchange rate back down to balance supply and demand at E.

Japanese assets, such as shares in Japanese companies. In short, *Americans supply dollars when they purchase foreign goods, services, and assets.*

In Figure 29-3, the vertical axis is the crucial foreign exchange rate (e), measured in units of foreign currency per unit of domestic currency—that is, in yen per dollar, in Mexican pesos per dollar, and so forth. Make sure you understand the units here. The horizontal axis shows the quantity of dollars bought and sold in the foreign exchange market.

The supply of U.S. dollars is represented by the upward-sloping *SS* curve. The upward slope indicates that as the foreign exchange rate rises, the number of yen that can be bought per dollar increases. This means, with other things held constant, that the prices of Japanese goods fall relative to those of

American goods. Hence, Americans will tend to buy more Japanese goods, and the supply of U.S. dollars therefore increases. This shows why the supply curve slopes upward. Let's take the example of bicycles. If the foreign exchange rate were to rise from ¥100/$ to ¥200/$, the bicycle which cost ¥20,000 would fall in price from $200 to $100. If other things are constant, Japanese bicycles would be more attractive, and Americans would sell more dollars in the foreign exchange market to buy more bicycles. Hence, the quantity supplied of dollars would be higher at a higher exchange rate.

What lies behind the demand for dollars (represented in Figure 29-3 by the *DD* demand curve for dollar foreign exchange)? Foreigners demand U.S. dollars when they buy American goods, services, and assets. For example, suppose a Japanese student buys an American economics textbook or takes a trip to the United States. She will require U.S. dollars to pay for these items. Or when Japan Airlines buys a Boeing 767 for its fleet, this transaction increases the demand for U.S. dollars. If Japanese pension funds invest in U.S. stocks, this would require a purchase of dollars. *Foreigners demand U.S. dollars to pay for their purchases of American goods, services, and assets.*

The demand curve in Figure 29-3 slopes downward to indicate that as the dollar's value falls (and the yen therefore becomes more expensive), Japanese residents will want to buy more foreign goods, services, and investments. They will therefore demand more U.S. dollars in the foreign exchange market. Consider what happens when the foreign exchange rate on the dollar falls from ¥100/$ to ¥50/$. American computers, which had sold at $2000 × (¥100/$) = ¥200,000 now sell for only $2000 × (¥50/$) = ¥100,000. Japanese purchasers will therefore tend to buy more American computers, and the quantity demanded of U.S. foreign exchange will increase.

Market forces move the foreign exchange rate up or down to balance the supply and demand. The price will settle at the *equilibrium foreign exchange rate*, which is the rate at which the dollars willingly bought just equal the dollars willingly sold.

The balance of supply and demand for foreign exchange determines the foreign exchange rate of a currency. At the market exchange rate of 100 yen per dollar shown at point E in Figure 29-3, the exchange rate is in equilibrium and has no tendency to rise or fall.

We have discussed the foreign exchange market in terms of the supply and demand for dollars. But in this market, there are two currencies involved, so we could just as easily analyze the supply and demand for Japanese yen. To see this, you should sketch a supply-and-demand diagram with yen foreign exchange on the horizontal axis and the yen rate ($ per ¥) on the vertical axis. If ¥100/$ is the equilibrium looking from the point of view of the dollar, then $0.01/¥ is the *reciprocal exchange rate*. As an exercise, go through the analysis in this section for the reciprocal market. You will see that in this simple bilateral world, for every dollar statement there is an exact yen counterpart: supply of dollars is demand for yen; demand for dollars is supply of yen.

There is just one further extension necessary to get to actual foreign exchange markets. In reality, there are many different currencies. We therefore need to find the supplies and demands for each and every currency. And in a world of many nations, it is the many-sided exchange and trade, with demands and supplies coming from all parts of the globe, that determine the entire array of foreign exchange rates.

> ### Terminology for Exchange-Rate Changes
> Foreign exchange markets have a special vocabulary. By definition, a fall in the price of one currency in terms of one or all others is called a *depreciation*. A rise in the price of a currency in terms of another currency is called an *appreciation*. In our example above, when the price of the dollar rose from ¥100/$ to ¥200/$, the dollar appreciated. We also know that the yen depreciated.
>
> In the supply-and-demand diagram for U.S. dollars, a fall in the foreign exchange rate (e) is a depreciation of the U.S. dollar, and a rise in e represents an appreciation.
>
> The term "devaluation" is often confused with the term "depreciation." Devaluation is confined to situations in which a country has officially fixed or "pegged" its exchange rate relative to one or more other currencies. In this case, a *devaluation* occurs when the pegged or fixed exchange rate is changed by lowering the price of the currency. A *revaluation* occurs when the official price is raised.
>
> For example, in December 1994 Mexico devalued its currency when it lowered the official price at which it was defending the peso from 3.5 pesos per dollar to 3.8 pesos per dollar. Mexico soon found it could not defend the

new parity and "floated" its exchange rate. At that point, the peso fell, or depreciated, even further.

When a country's currency falls in value relative to that of another country, we say that the domestic currency has undergone a **depreciation** while the foreign currency has undergone an **appreciation**.

When a country's official foreign exchange rate is lowered, we say that the currency has undergone a **devaluation**. An increase in the official foreign exchange rate is called a **revaluation**.

Effects of Changes in Trade

What would happen if there were changes in demand? For example, if Japan has a recession, its demand for imports declines. As a result, the demand for American dollars would decrease. The result is shown in Figure 29-4. The decline in purchases of American goods, services, and investments decreases

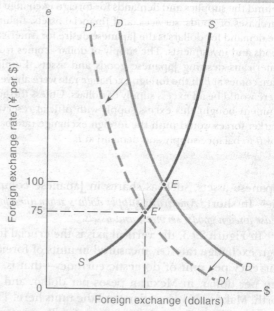

FIGURE 29-4. A Decrease in Demand for Dollars Leads to Dollar Depreciation

Suppose that a recession or deflation in Japan reduces the Japanese demand for dollars. This would shift the demand for dollars to the left from *DD* to *D'D'*. The exchange rate of the dollar depreciates, while the yen appreciates. Why would the new exchange rate discourage American purchases of Japanese goods?

the demand for dollars in the market. This change is represented by a leftward shift in the demand curve. The result will be a lower foreign exchange rate—that is, the dollar will depreciate and the yen will appreciate. At the lower exchange rate, the quantity of dollars supplied by Americans to the market will decrease because Japanese goods are now more expensive. Moreover, the quantity of dollars demanded by the Japanese will decline because of the recession. How much will exchange rates change? Just enough so that the supply and demand are again in balance. In the example shown in Figure 29-4, the dollar has depreciated from ¥100/$ to ¥75/$.

Let's take a case involving the financial account. Suppose, as happened in 2000, that the Federal Reserve tightens U.S. monetary policy because inflationary pressures have been increasing. This would make U.S. dollar assets more attractive than foreign assets as dollar interest rates rise relative to interest rates on Japanese or European securities. As a result, the demand for dollars increases and the dollar appreciates. This sequence is shown in Figure 29-5.

Exchange Rates and the Balance of Payments

What is the connection between exchange rates and adjustments in the balance of payments? In the simplest case, assume that exchange rates are determined by private supply and demand with no government intervention. Consider what happened in 1990 after German unification when the German central bank decided to raise interest rates to curb inflation. After the monetary tightening, foreigners moved some of their assets into German marks to benefit from high German interest rates. This produced an excess demand for the German mark at the old exchange rate. In other words, at the old foreign exchange rate, people were, on balance, buying German marks and selling other currencies. (You can redraw Figure 29-5 to show this situation.)

Here is where the exchange rate plays its role as equilibrator. As the demand for German marks increased, it led to an appreciation of the German mark and a depreciation of other currencies, such as the U.S. dollar. The movement in the exchange rate continued until the financial and current accounts were back in balance. The equilibration for the current account is easiest to understand. Here, the appreciation

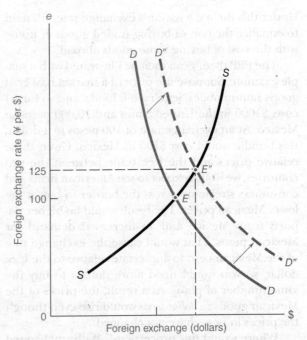

FIGURE 29-5. Monetary Tightening Increases Demand for Dollars and Produces Dollar Appreciation

Monetary policy can affect the exchange rate through the financial account. If the central bank raises dollar interest rates, this induces investors into dollar securities and raises the demand for dollar foreign exchange. The result is an appreciation of the dollar. (Explain why this leads to depreciation of the Japanese yen or the Euro.)

of the mark made German goods more expensive and led to a decline in German exports and an increase in German imports. Both of these factors tended to reduce the German current-account surplus.

Exchange-rate movements serve as a balance wheel to remove disequilibria in the balance of payments.

Purchasing-Power Parity and Exchange Rates

In the short run, market-determined exchange rates are highly volatile in response to monetary policy, political events, and changes in expectations. But over the longer run, exchange rates are determined primarily by the relative prices of goods in different countries. An important implication is the *purchasing-power-parity (PPP) theory of exchange rates.*

Under this theory, a nation's exchange rate will tend to equalize the cost of buying traded goods at home with the cost of buying those goods abroad.

The PPP theory can then be illustrated with a simple example. Suppose the price of a market basket of goods (automobiles, jewelry, oil, foods, and so forth) costs $1000 in the United States and 10,000 pesos in Mexico. At an exchange rate of 100 pesos to a dollar, this bundle would cost $100 in Mexico. Given these relative prices and the free trade between the two countries, we would expect to see American firms and consumers streaming across the border to buy at the lower Mexican prices. The result would be higher imports from Mexico and an increased demand for Mexican pesos. That would cause the exchange rate of the Mexican peso to appreciate relative to the U.S. dollar, so you would need more dollars to buy the same number of pesos. As a result, the prices of the Mexican goods *in dollar terms* would rise even though the prices in pesos have not changed.

Where would this process end? With unchanged domestic prices in the two countries, the peso's exchange rate must fall to 10 pesos to the dollar. Only at this exchange rate would the price of the market basket of goods be equal in the two markets. At 10 pesos to the dollar, we say that the currencies have equal purchasing power in terms of the traded goods. (You can firm up your understanding of this discussion by calculating the price of the market basket in both Mexican pesos and U.S. dollars before and after the appreciation of the peso.)

The PPP doctrine also holds that countries with high inflation rates will tend to have depreciating currencies. For example, if Country A's inflation rate is 10 percent while inflation in Country B is 2 percent, the currency of Country A will tend to depreciate relative to that of Country B by the difference in the inflation rates, that is, 8 percent annually. Alternatively, let's say that runaway inflation leads to a hundred fold rise of prices in Russia over the course of a year, while prices in the United States are unchanged. According to the PPP theory, the Russian ruble should depreciate by 99 percent in order to bring the prices of American and Russian goods back into equilibrium.

We should caution that the PPP theory is only an approximation and cannot predict the precise movement of exchange rates. The leeway in the PPP theory is seen in the relationship between the U.S. dollar and the Japanese yen over the last decade; this exchange rate has been as high as 168 yen to a dollar and as low as 85 yen to a dollar, even though most economists calculate the PPP level as being around 120 yen to a dollar. Trade barriers, transportation costs, and the presence of nontraded services allow prices to diverge significantly across countries. In addition, financial flows can overwhelm trade flows in the short run. So while the PPP theory is a useful guide to exchange rates in the long run, exchange rates can diverge from their PPP level for many years.

PPP and the Size of Nations

By any measure, the United States still has the largest economy in the world. But which country has the second largest? Is it Japan, Germany, Russia, or some other country? You would think this would be an easy question to answer, like measuring height or weight. The problem, however, is that Japan totes up its national output in yen, while Russia's national output is given in rubles, and America's is in dollars. To be compared, they all need to be converted into the same currency.

The customary approach is to use the market exchange rate to convert each currency into dollars, and by that yardstick Japan has the second-largest economy. However, there are two difficulties with using the market rate. First, because market rates can rise and fall sharply, the "size" of countries might change by 10 or 20 percent overnight. Moreover, using market exchange rates, many poor countries appear to have a very small national output.

Today, economists generally prefer to use PPP exchange rates to compare the living standards in different countries. The difference can be dramatic, as Figure 29-6 shows. When market exchange rates are used, the outputs of low-income countries like China and India tend to be understated. This understatement occurs because a substantial part of their output comes in labor-intensive services, which are usually extremely inexpensive in low-wage countries. Hence, when we calculate PPP exchange rates including the prices of nontraded goods, the GDPs of low-income countries rise relative to those of high-wage countries. For example, when PPP exchange rates are used, China's GDP is 5 times the level calculated with market exchange rates. Furthermore, on the basis of PPP exchange rates, China leaps ahead of Japan to become the second-largest economy in the world.

FIGURE 29-6. PPP Calculations Change the Relative Size of Nations, 1998

Using PPP exchange rates changes the economic ranking of nations. After correcting for the purchasing power of incomes, China moves from a middle-ranking country to an economic superpower. Note that points along the 45° line are ones for which GDPs using the two exchange rates are equal. Points above the line, such as China, are ones for which the PPP estimate of GDP is above the standard calculation. Japan is below the line because relative prices in Japan are high due to high rents and trade barriers.

Source: World Bank. Note that outputs are shown on a ratio scale.

C. THE INTERNATIONAL MONETARY SYSTEM

While the simple supply-and-demand diagrams for the foreign exchange market explain the major determinants, they do not capture the drama and central importance of the international monetary system. The 1990s witnessed crisis after crisis in international finance—in Europe in 1991–1992, in Mexico and Latin America in 1994–1995, in East Asia and Russia in 1997–1998, and then back to Latin America in 1998–2002. Although the United States avoided most of the fallout from these crises, this period underlined the importance of a well-functioning international monetary system.

What is the **international monetary system?** This term denotes the institutions under which payments are made for transactions that cross national boundaries. In particular, the international monetary system determines how foreign exchange rates are set and how governments can affect exchange rates.

The importance of the international monetary system was well described by economist Robert Solomon:

> Like the traffic lights in a city, the international monetary system is taken for granted until it begins to malfunction and to disrupt people's lives. . . . A well-functioning monetary system will facilitate international trade and investment and smooth adaptation to change. A monetary system that functions poorly may not only discourage the development of trade and investment among nations but subject their economies to disruptive shocks when necessary adjustments to change are prevented or delayed.[5]

---

[5] See this chapter's Further Reading section for the citation.

The central element of the international monetary system involves the arrangements by which exchange rates are set. In recent years, nations have used one of three major exchange-rate systems:

- A system of fixed exchange rates
- A system of flexible or floating exchange rates, where exchange rates are determined by market forces
- Managed exchange rates, in which nations intervene to smooth exchange-rate fluctuations or to move their currency toward a target zone.

FIXED EXCHANGE RATES: THE CLASSICAL GOLD STANDARD

At one extreme is a system of **fixed exchange rates,** where governments specify the exact rate at which dollars will be converted into pesos, yen, and other currencies. Historically, the most important fixed-exchange-rate system was the **gold standard,** which was used off and on from 1717 until 1933. In this system, each country defined the value of its currency in terms of a fixed amount of gold, thereby establishing fixed exchange rates among the countries on the gold standard.[6]

The functioning of the gold standard can be seen easily in a simplified example. Suppose people everywhere insisted on being paid in bits of pure gold metal. Then buying a bicycle in Britain would merely require payment in gold at a price expressed in ounces of gold. By definition there would be no foreign-exchange-rate problem. Gold would be the common world currency.

This example captures the essence of the gold standard. Once gold became the medium of exchange or money, foreign trade was no different from domestic trade; everything could be paid for in gold. The only difference between countries was that they could choose different *units* for their gold coins. Thus, Queen Victoria chose to make British coins about ¼ ounce of gold (the pound) and President

McKinley chose to make the U.S. unit ½₀ ounce of gold (the dollar). In that case, the British pound, being 5 times as heavy as the dollar, had an exchange rate of $5/£1.

This was the essence of the gold standard. In practice, countries tended to use their own coins. But anyone was free to melt down coins and sell them at the going price of gold. So exchange rates were fixed for all countries on the gold standard. The exchange rates (also called "par values" or "parities") for different currencies were determined by the gold content of their monetary units.

Hume's Adjustment Mechanism

The purpose of an exchange-rate system is to promote international trade and finance while facilitating adjustment to shocks. How exactly does the *international adjustment mechanism* function? What happens if a country's wages and prices rise so sharply that its goods are no longer competitive in the world market? Under flexible exchange rates, the country's exchange rate could depreciate to offset the domestic inflation. But under fixed exchange rates, equilibrium must be restored by deflation at home or inflation abroad.

Let's examine the international adjustment mechanism under a fixed-exchange-rate system with two countries, America and Britain. Suppose that American inflation has made American goods uncompetitive. Consequently, America's imports rise and its exports fall. It therefore runs a trade deficit with Britain. To pay for its deficit, America would have to ship gold to Britain. Eventually—if there were no adjustments in either America or Britain—America would run out of gold.

In fact, an automatic adjustment mechanism does exist, as was demonstrated by the British philosopher David Hume in 1752. He showed that the outflow of gold was part of a mechanism that tended to keep international payments in balance. His argument, though nearly 250 years old, offers important insights for understanding how trade flows get balanced in today's economy.

Hume's explanation rested in part upon the quantity theory of prices, which is a theory of the overall price level that is analyzed in macroeconomics. This doctrine holds that the overall price level in an economy is proportional to the supply of money. Under the gold standard, gold was an important part of the money supply—either directly, in the form of

---

[6] Why was gold used as the standard of exchange and means of payment, rather than some other commodity? Certainly other materials could have been used, but gold had the advantages of being in limited supply, being relatively indestructible, and having few industrial uses. Can you see why wine, wheat, or cattle would not be a useful means of payment among countries?

gold coins, or indirectly, when governments used gold as backing for paper money.

What would be the impact of a country's losing gold? First, the country's money supply would decline either because gold coins would be exported or because some of the gold backing for the currency would leave the country. Putting both these consequences together, a loss of gold leads to a reduction in the money supply. According to the quantity theory, the next step is that prices and costs would change proportionally to the change in the money supply. If the United States loses 10 percent of its gold to pay for a trade deficit, the quantity theory predicts that U.S. prices, costs, and incomes would fall 10 percent. In other words, the economy would experience a deflation. If gold discoveries in California increase America's gold supplies, we would expect to see a major increase in the price level in the United States.

The Four-Pronged Mechanism. Now consider Hume's theory of international payments equilibrium. Suppose that America runs a large trade deficit and begins to lose gold. According to the quantity theory of prices, this loss of gold reduces America's money supply, driving down America's prices and costs. As a result, (1) America decreases its imports of British and other foreign goods, which have become relatively expensive; and (2) because America's domestically produced goods have become relatively inexpensive on world markets, America's exports increase.

The opposite effect occurs in Britain and other foreign countries. Because Britain's exports are growing rapidly, it receives gold in return. Britain's money supply therefore increases, driving up British prices and costs according to the quantity theory. At this point, two more prongs of the Hume mechanism come into play: (3) British and other foreign exports have become more expensive, so the volume of goods exported to America and elsewhere declines; and (4) British citizens, faced with a higher domestic price level, now import more of America's low-priced goods.

Figure 29-7 illustrates the logic in Hume's mechanism. Make sure you can follow the logical chain from the original deficit at the top through the adjustment to the new equilibrium at the bottom.

The result of Hume's four-pronged gold-flow mechanism is an improvement in the balance of payments of the country losing gold and a worsening in

that of the country gaining the gold. In the end, an equilibrium of international trade and finance is reestablished at new relative prices, which keep trade and international lending in balance with no net gold flow. This equilibrium is a stable one and requires no tariffs or other government intervention.

Adjustment with Fixed Exchange Rates. Understanding the gold standard is important not only because of its historical role but also because it is a pure example of a fixed-exchange-rate system. The same analysis applies to all fixed-exchange-rate systems: If exchange rates are not free to move when the prices or incomes among countries get out of line, *domestic* prices and incomes must adjust to restore equilibrium. Now that Europe has adopted a common currency, any imbalance in output or employment among the European nations must be made through changes in domestic price levels rather than changes in exchange rates.

In Hume's mechanism, it is gold flows that move prices and wages and ensure equilibrium. In modern macroeconomic thinking, prices and wages adjust through movements in output and employment.

When a country adopts a fixed exchange rate, it faces an inescapable fact: Real output and employment must adjust to ensure that its relative prices are aligned with those of its trading partners.

INTERNATIONAL MONETARY INSTITUTIONS AFTER WORLD WAR II

In the early part of the twentieth century, even nations which were ostensibly at peace engaged in debilitating trade wars and competitive devaluations. After World War II, international institutions were developed to foster economic cooperation among nations. These institutions continue to be the means by which nations coordinate their economic policies and seek solutions to common problems.

The United States emerged from World War II with its economy intact—able and willing to help rebuild the countries of friends and foes alike. The postwar international political system responded to the needs of war-torn nations by establishing durable institutions that facilitated the quick recovery

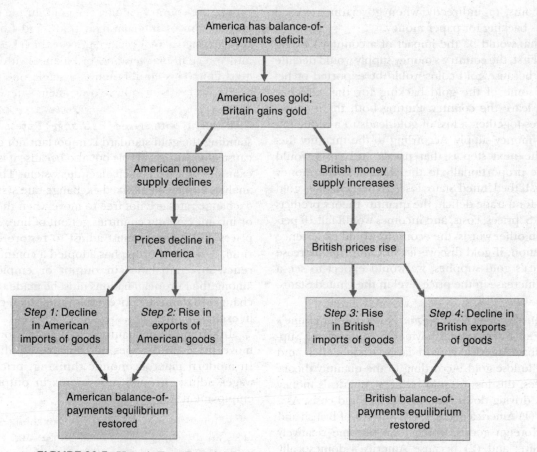

FIGURE 29-7. Hume's Four-Pronged International Adjustment Mechanism

Hume explained how a balance-of-payments disequilibrium would automatically produce equilibrating adjustments under a gold standard. Trace the lines from the original disequilibrium at the top through the changes in prices to the restored equilibrium at the bottom. This mechanism works in modified form under any fixed-exchange-rate system. Modern economics augments the mechanism in the fourth row of boxes by replacing the fourth row with "Prices, output, and employment decline in America" and "Prices, output, and employment rise in Britain."

of the international economy. The major international economic institutions of the postwar period were the General Agreement on Tariffs and Trade (rechartered as the World Trade Organization in 1995), the Bretton Woods exchange-rate system, the International Monetary Fund, and the World Bank. These four institutions helped the industrial democracies rebuild themselves and grow rapidly after the devastation of World War II, and they continue to be the major international institutions today.

The International Monetary Fund

An integral part of the Bretton Woods system was the establishment of the International Monetary Fund (or IMF), which still administers the international monetary system and operates as a central bank for central banks. Member nations subscribe by lending their currencies to the IMF; the IMF then relends these funds to help countries in balance-of-payments difficulties. The main function of the IMF is to make temporary loans to countries which have balance-of-payments problems or are under speculative attack in financial markets.

The World Bank

Another international financial institution created after World War II was the World Bank. The Bank is capitalized by high-income nations that subscribe in proportion to their economic importance in terms of GDP and other factors. The Bank makes long-term low-interest loans to countries for projects which are economically sound but which cannot get private-sector financing. As a result of such long-term loans, goods and services flow from advanced nations to developing countries.

The Bretton Woods System

Economists of the 1930s and 1940s, particularly John Maynard Keynes, were greatly influenced by the economic crisis of the prewar period. They were determined to avoid the economic chaos and competitive devaluations that had occurred during the Great Depression. They believed that the gold standard was too inflexible and served to deepen and lengthen business cycles.

To replace the gold standard, the **Bretton Woods system** established a parity for each currency in terms of both the U.S. dollar and gold. The revolutionary innovation of the Bretton Woods system was that exchange rates were *fixed but adjustable*. When one currency got too far out of line with its appropriate or "fundamental" value, the parity could be adjusted. The ability to adjust exchange rates when fundamental disequilibrium arose was the central distinction between the Bretton Woods system and the gold standard.

The Bretton Woods system functioned effectively for the quarter-century after World War II. The system eventually broke down when the dollar became overvalued and the U.S. refused to take the necessary contractionary steps to regain international competitiveness. In 1971–1973, the United States abandoned the Bretton Woods system, and the world moved into the modern era.

How to Ensure a Credibly Fixed Exchange Rate through the "Hard Fix"

Although the collapse of the Bretton Woods system marked the end of a predominantly fixed exchange-rate system, many countries continue to opt for fixed exchange rates. A recurrent problem with fixed-exchange-rate systems is that they are prey to speculative attacks when the country runs low on foreign exchange reserves. (We will return to this problem in the next chapter.) How can countries improve the credibility of their fixed-exchange-rate systems? Are there "hard" fixed-exchange-rate systems that will better withstand speculative attacks?

Specialists in this area emphasize the importance of establishing credibility. In this instance, credibility may be enhanced by creating a system that would actually make it *hard* for the country to change its exchange rate. This approach is similar to a military strategy of burning the bridges behind the army so that there is no retreat and the soldiers will have to fight to the death. Indeed, Argentina's president tried to instill credibility in Argentina's system by proclaiming that he would choose "death before devaluation."

One solution is to create **currency boards.** A currency board is a monetary institution that issues only currency that is fully backed by foreign assets in a key foreign currency, usually the U.S. dollar. A currency board defends an exchange rate that is fixed by law rather than just by policy, and the currency board is usually independent, and sometimes even private. Under currency boards, a payments deficit will generally trigger Hume's automatic adjustment mechanism. That is, a balance-of-payments deficit will reduce the money supply, leading to an economic contraction and eventually reducing domestic prices and restoring adjustment. A currency board system has worked effectively in Hong Kong, but the system in Argentina was unable to withstand economic and political turmoil and collapsed in 2002.

An even harder fixed exchange rate is established when countries adopt a **common currency** through monetary union. The United States has had a common currency since 1776. The most important recent example of a monetary union occurred when eleven European countries adopted the "Euro" as their common currency in 1999. This is the hardest fix of all because the currencies of the different countries are defined to be the same. (We will return to a further analysis of the Euro in the next chapter.) A variant of the common currency comes when a country adopts a key currency for its own money. This approach was followed when Ecuador adopted the U.S. dollar as its currency in 2000.

Will these new systems help prevent the financial disruptions that plagued countries with soft fixed-exchange-rate systems in the 1990s? This is one of the key unresolved questions of modern macroeconomic policy.

Intervention

When a government fixes its exchange rate, it must "intervene" in foreign exchange markets to maintain the rate. Government exchange-rate **intervention** occurs when the government buys or sells foreign exchange to affect exchange rates. For example, the Japanese government on a given day might buy $1 billion worth of Japanese yen with U.S. dollars. This would cause a rise in value, or an appreciation, of the yen.

Figure 29-8 illustrates the operation of a fixed-exchange-rate system. In 1991, Argentina established a currency board which fixed the exchange rate at 1 U.S. dollar per peso. The initial equilibrium is shown as point A in Figure 29-8. At an exchange rate of $1 per peso, the quantities of pesos supplied and demanded are equal.

Suppose that the demand for pesos falls—perhaps because inflation in Argentina is higher than that in the United States or because Brazil, an important trading partner, has a recession or a depreciation. This produces a downward shift in the demand for pesos from D to D'. In a world of flexible exchange rates, the peso would depreciate and reach a new equilibrium, say, at B in Figure 29-8.

Recall that Argentina is committed to maintaining the parity of $1 per peso. What can it do?

- One approach is to intervene by *buying the depreciating currency (pesos) and selling the appreciating currency (dollars)*. In this example, if Argentina's central bank buys the amount shown by the segment *CA*, this will increase the demand for pesos and maintain the official parity.
- An alternative would be to use monetary policy. Argentina could *induce the private sector to increase its demand for pesos* by raising interest rates. Say that Argentinian interest rates rise relative to U.S. rates; this would lead investors to move funds into pesos and increase the private demand for pesos, in effect moving the private demand curve back toward the original *D* demand curve.

These two operations are not really as different as they sound. In effect, both involve monetary policies in Argentina. In fact, one of the complications of managing the open economy, as we will see shortly, is that the need to use monetary policies to manage the exchange rate can collide with the need to use monetary policy to stabilize the domestic business cycle.

FLEXIBLE EXCHANGE RATES

Fixed exchange rates are one of the cornerstones of today's international monetary system—the other important system is flexible exchange rates. A country has **flexible exchange rates** when exchange rates move purely under the influence of supply and demand. In such a system, the government neither announces an exchange rate nor takes steps to enforce one. Another term often used is **floating exchange rates,** which means the same thing.

Today, flexible exchange rates are used by the three major economic regions—the United States, the countries of Euroland, and Japan. For these three regions, the movements of exchange rates are determined almost entirely by private supply and demand for goods, services, and investments.

Many middle-size countries also rely upon flexible rates. Let us see how exchange rates are determined under flexible rates. In 1994, the peso was under attack in foreign exchange markets, and the

FIGURE 29-8. Governments Intervene to Defend Fixed Exchange Rate

Say that Argentina establishes a currency board with a fixed exchange rate of 1 U.S. dollar per peso. Initial equilibrium is at *A*. Deteriorating economic conditions—perhaps inflation or concerns over recession in Brazil—lead to a decline in the demand for pesos. In a flexible-exchange-rate system, the new equilibrium would be at *B*, with an exchange rate of 0.5 dollar to the peso (or 2 pesos to the dollar). Argentina can reestablish official parity by buying *CA* worth of pesos, in effect shifting the demand back to the original demand curve, *D*. Alternatively, by raising Argentina's interest rates, the government can induce private investors to increase their demand for pesos by *CA*.

Mexicans allowed the peso to float. At the original exchange rate of approximately 4 pesos per U.S. dollar, there was an excess supply of pesos. This meant that at that exchange rate, the supply of pesos by Mexicans who wanted to buy American and other foreign goods and assets outweighed the demand for pesos by Americans and others who wanted to purchase Mexican goods and assets.

What was the outcome? As a result of the excess supply, the peso depreciated relative to the dollar. How far did the exchange rates move? Just far enough so that—at the depreciated exchange rate of about 6 pesos to the dollar—the quantities supplied and demanded were balanced.

What is behind the equilibration of supply and demand? Two main forces are involved: (1) With the dollar more expensive, it costs more for Mexicans to buy American goods, services, and investments, causing the supply of pesos to fall off in the usual fashion. (2) With the depreciation of the peso, Mexican goods and assets become less expensive for foreigners. This increases the demand for pesos in the marketplace. (Note that this simplified discussion assumes that all transactions occur only between the two countries; a more complete discussion would involve the demands and supplies of currencies from all countries.)

Where is the government? In a freely flexible exchange-rate system, the government is on the sidelines. It allows the foreign exchange market to determine the value of the dollar, just as it allows markets to determine the value of lettuce, machinery, GM stock, or copper. Consequently, it is possible to get enormous swings in flexible exchange rates over relatively short periods.

MANAGED EXCHANGE RATES

In between the two extremes of rigidly fixed and completely flexible is the middle ground of **managed exchange rates.** Here, exchange rates are basically determined by market forces but governments buy or sell currencies or change their money supplies to affect their exchange rates. Sometimes governments lean against the winds of private markets. At other times governments have "target zones" which guide their policy actions. This system is becoming less important as countries are increasingly gravitating toward fixed- or flexible-exchange-rate systems.

TODAY'S HYBRID SYSTEM

Unlike the earlier uniform system under either the gold standard or Bretton Woods, today's exchange-rate system fits into no tidy mold. Without anyone's having planned it, the world has moved to a hybrid exchange-rate system. The major features are as follows:

- A few countries allow their currencies to *float freely*. In this approach, a country allows markets to determine its currency's value and it rarely intervenes. The United States has fit this pattern for most of the last two decades. While the Euro is just an infant as a common currency, Europe appears to be leaning toward the freely floating group.
- Some major countries have *managed but flexible* exchange rates. Today, this group includes Canada, Japan, and many developing countries. Under this system, a country will buy or sell its currency to reduce the day-to-day volatility of currency fluctuations. In addition, a country will sometimes engage in systematic intervention to move its currency toward what it believes to be a more appropriate level.
- Many countries, particularly small ones, peg their currencies to a major currency or to a "basket" of currencies in a *fixed exchange rate*. Sometimes, the peg is allowed to glide smoothly upward or downward in a system known as a gliding or crawling peg. A few countries have the hard fix of a currency board.
- In addition, almost all countries tend to intervene either when markets become "disorderly" or when exchange rates seem far out of line with the "fundamentals"—that is, when they are inappropriate for existing price levels and trade flows.

To summarize:

A *freely flexible* exchange rate is one determined purely by supply and demand without any government intervention. A *fixed-exchange-rate* system is one where governments state official exchange rates, which they defend through intervention and monetary policies. A *managed-exchange-rate* system is a hybrid of fixed and flexible rates in which governments attempt to affect their exchange rates *directly* by buying or selling foreign currencies or *indirectly*, through monetary policy, by raising or lowering interest rates.

SUMMARY

A. The Balance of International Payments

1. The balance of international payments is the set of accounts that measures all the economic transactions between a nation and the rest of the world. It includes exports and imports of goods, services, and financial instruments. Exports are credit items, while imports are debits. More generally, a country's credit items are transactions that make foreign currencies available to it; debit items are ones that reduce its holdings of foreign currencies.

2. The major components of the balance of payments are:
   I. Current account (merchandise trade, services, investment income, transfers)
   II. Financial account (private, government, and official-reserve changes)
   The fundamental rule of balance-of-payments accounting is that the sum of all items must equal zero: $I + II = 0$.

3. Historically, countries tend to go through stages of the balance of payments: from the young debtor borrowing for economic development, through mature debtor and young creditor, to mature creditor nation living off earnings from past investments. In the 1980s, the United States moved to a different stage where low domestic saving and attractive investment opportunities again led it to borrow heavily abroad and become a debtor nation.

B. The Determination of Foreign Exchange Rates

4. International trade involves the new element of different national currencies, which are linked by relative prices called foreign exchange rates. When Americans import Japanese goods, they ultimately need to pay in Japanese yen. In the foreign exchange market, Japanese yen might trade at ¥100/$ (or, reciprocally, ¥1 would trade for $0.01). This price is called the foreign exchange rate.

5. In a foreign exchange market involving only two countries, the supply of U.S. dollars comes from Americans who want to purchase goods, services, and investments from Japan; the demand for U.S. dollars comes from Japanese who want to import commodities or financial assets from America. The interaction of these supplies and demands determines the foreign exchange rate. More generally, foreign exchange rates are determined by the complex interplay of many countries buying and selling among themselves. When trade or financial flows change, supply and demand shift and the equilibrium exchange rate changes.

6. A fall in the market price of a currency is a depreciation; a rise in a currency's value is called an appreciation. In a system where governments announce official foreign exchange rates, a decrease in the official exchange rate is called a devaluation, while an increase is a revaluation.

7. According to the purchasing-power-parity (PPP) theory of exchange rates, exchange rates tend to move with changes in relative price levels of different countries. The PPP theory applies better to the long run than the short run. When this theory is applied to measure the purchasing power of incomes in different countries, it raises the per capita outputs of low-income countries.

C. The International Monetary System

8. A well-functioning international economy requires a smoothly operating exchange-rate system, which denotes the institutions that govern financial transactions among nations. Three important exchange-rate systems are (*a*) flexible exchange rates, in which a country's foreign exchange rate is determined by market forces of supply and demand; (*b*) fixed exchange rates, such as the gold standard or the Bretton Woods system, in which countries set and defend a given structure of exchange rates; and (*c*) managed exchange rates, in which government interventions and market forces interact to determine the level of exchange rates.

9. Classical economists like David Hume explained international adjustments to trade imbalances by the gold-flow mechanism. Under this process, gold movements would change the money supply and the price level. For example, a trade deficit would lead to a gold outflow and a decline in domestic prices that would (*a*) raise exports and (*b*) curb imports of the gold-losing country while (*c*) reducing exports and (*d*) raising imports of the gold-gaining country. This mechanism shows that under fixed exchange rates, countries which have balance-of-payments problems must adjust through changes in domestic price and output levels.

10. After World War II, countries created a group of international economic institutions to organize international trade and finance. Under the Bretton Woods system, countries "pegged" their currencies to the dollar and to gold, providing fixed but adjustable exchange rates. After the Bretton Woods system collapsed in 1973, it was replaced by today's hybrid system. Today, the major economic regions (the United States, Euroland, and Japan) have currencies that float relative to each other. Most small countries peg their currencies to the dollar or to other currencies.

CONCEPTS FOR REVIEW

Balance of Payments

balance of payments
   I. current account
   II. financial account
balance-of-payments identity:
   I + II = 0
official-reserve changes
debits and credits
stages of balance of payments

Foreign Exchange Rates

foreign exchange rate, foreign
   exchange market
supply of and demand for foreign
   exchange
exchange-rate terminology:
   appreciation and depreciation
   revaluation and devaluation

International Monetary System

exchange-rate systems:
   flexible
   fixed rates (gold standard, Bretton
     Woods, currency board)
   managed
   common currency
international adjustment mechanism
Hume's four-pronged gold-flow
   mechanism

FURTHER READING AND INTERNET WEBSITES

Further Reading

A fascinating collection of essays on international macroeconomics is Paul Krugman, *Pop International* (MIT Press, Cambridge, Mass., 1997). The quotation on the international monetary system is from Robert Solomon, *The International Monetary System, 1945–1981: An Insider's View* (Harper & Row, New York, 1982), pp. 1, 7.

Websites

Data on trade and finance for different countries can be found in the websites listed for Chapter 28. An extensive page on the Euro is maintained by Giancarlo Corsetti at www.econ.yale.edu/~corsetti/euro/. Data on exchange rates can be found at finance.yahoo.com/m3?u.

Some of the best popular writing on international economics is found in *The Economist,* which is also available at www.economist.com. One of the best sources for policy writing on international economics is www.iie.com/homepage.htm, the website of the Institute for International Economics. One of the leading scholar-journalists of today is Paul Krugman of Princeton. His Web page at www.wws.princeton.edu/~pkrugman/ contains many interesting readings on international economics.

QUESTIONS FOR DISCUSSION

1. Table 29-3 shows some foreign exchange rates (in units of foreign currency per dollar) as of early 2004. Fill in the last column of the table with the reciprocal price of the dollar in terms of each foreign currency, being especially careful to write down the relevant units in the parentheses.

2. Figure 29-3 shows the demand and supply for U.S. dollars in an example in which Japan and the United States trade only with each other.
   a. Describe and draw the reciprocal supply and demand schedules for Japanese yen. Explain why the supply of yen is equivalent to the demand for

   dollars. Also explain and draw the schedule that corresponds to the supply of dollars. Find the equilibrium price of yen in this new diagram and relate it to the equilibrium in Figure 29-3.
   b. Assume that Americans develop a taste for Japanese goods. Show what would happen to the supply and demand for yen. Would the yen appreciate or depreciate relative to the dollar? Explain.

3. Draw up a list of items that belong on the credit side of the balance of international payments and another list of items that belong on the debit side. What is meant by a trade surplus? By the balance on current account?

Currency	Price	
	Units of foreign currency per dollar	**Dollars per unit of foreign currency**
Zloty (Poland)	3.76	_____ ($/zloty)
Real (Brazil)	2.91	_____ (_____)
Yuan (China)	8.28	_____ (_____)
Peso (Mexico)	10.98	_____ (_____)
Ruble (Russia)	28.49	_____ (_____)
Euro	0.80	_____ (_____)

TABLE 29-3.

4. Construct hypothetical balance-of-payments accounts for a young debtor country, a mature debtor country, a new creditor country, and a mature creditor country.

5. Consider the situation for Germany described on page 607. Using a figure like Figure 29-3, show the supply and demand for German marks before and after the shock. Identify on your figure the excess demand for marks *before* the appreciation of the mark. Then show how an appreciation of the mark would wipe out the excess demand.

6. A Middle East nation suddenly discovers huge oil resources. Show how its balance of trade and current account suddenly turn to surplus. Show how it can acquire assets in New York as a financial-account offset. Later, when it uses the assets for internal development, show how its current and financial items reverse their roles.

7. Consider the following quotation from the 1984 *Economic Report of the President:*

   In the long run, the exchange rate tends to follow the differential trend in the domestic and foreign price level. If one country's price level gets too far out of line with prices in other countries, there will eventually be a fall in demand for its goods, which will lead to a real depreciation of its currency.

   Explain how the first sentence relates to the PPP theory of exchange rates. Explain the reasoning behind the PPP theory. In addition, using a supply-and-demand diagram like that of Figure 29-3, explain the sequence of events, described in the second sentence of the quotation, whereby a country whose price level is relatively high will find that its exchange rate depreciates.

8. A nation records the following data for 2000: exports of automobiles ($100) and corn ($150); imports of oil ($150) and steel ($75); tourist expenditures abroad ($25); private lending to foreign countries ($50); private borrowing from foreign countries ($40); official-reserve changes ($30 of foreign exchange bought by domestic central bank). Calculate the statistical discrepancy and include it in private lending to foreign countries. Create a balance-of-payments table like Table 29-2.

9. Consider the following three exchange-rate systems: the classical gold standard, freely flexible exchange rates, and the Bretton Woods system. Compare and contrast the three systems with respect to the following characteristics:
   a. Role of government vs. that of market in determining exchange rates
   b. Degree of exchange-rate volatility
   c. Method of adjustment of relative prices across countries
   d. Need for international cooperation and consultation in determining exchange rates
   e. Potential for establishment and maintenance of severe exchange-rate misalignment

10. Consider the European monetary union. List the pros and cons. How do you come down on the question of the advisability of monetary union? Would your answer change if the question concerned the United States?

CHAPTER

30

Open-Economy Macroeconomics

Before I built a wall
I'd ask to know
What I was walling in
or walling out . . .

Robert Frost

The international business cycle exerts a powerful effect on every nation of the globe. American monetary policy can produce depressions, poverty, and revolutions in South America. Political disturbances in the Middle East can set off a spiral in oil prices that triggers a global recession. Revolutions or defaults or wars can rock stock markets and shake business confidence around the world. To ignore international trade is to miss half the economic ball game.

The last chapter surveyed the major concepts of international macroeconomics—the balance of payments, the determination of exchange rates, and the international monetary system. The present chapter continues the story by showing how macroeconomic shocks in one country have ripple effects on the output and employment of other countries and examining the linkage between domestic saving and investment and the trade balance. The chapter concludes with a review of some of the key international issues of today.

A. FOREIGN TRADE AND ECONOMIC ACTIVITY

Net Exports and Output in the Open Economy

Open-economy macroeconomics is the study of how economies behave when the trade and financial linkages among nations are considered. The previous chapter described the basic concepts of the balance of payments. We can restate those here in terms of the national income and product accounts.

Foreign trade involves imports and exports. Although the United States produces most of what it consumes, it nonetheless has a large quantity of **imports,** which are goods and services produced abroad and consumed domestically. **Exports** are goods and services produced domestically and purchased by foreigners.

Net exports are defined as exports of goods and services minus imports of goods and services. For 2002, net exports for the United States were minus $424 billion, derived from $1015 billion of exports minus $1439 billion of imports. When a country has positive net exports, it is accumulating foreign assets. The counterpart of net exports is **net foreign investment,** which denotes net U.S. savings abroad and is approximately equal to the value of net exports.

Because the U.S. had negative net exports, its net foreign investment was negative, implying that the U.S. foreign indebtedness was growing.

In 2000, the United States had negative net exports, which signifies that the U.S. was borrowing from abroad and therefore had negative net foreign investment. In other words, *foreigners were making a significant contribution to U.S. investment.* Why is it that rich America borrowed so much from abroad? This puzzling phenomenon is explained by a relatively low U.S. saving rate and a high domestic investment rate driven by the long economic boom and the technological dynamism of the United States.

In an open economy, a nation's expenditures may differ from its production. Total domestic *expenditures* (sometimes called *domestic demand*) are equal to consumption plus domestic investment plus government purchases. This measure differs from total *domestic product* (or GDP) for two reasons. First, some part of domestic expenditures will be on goods produced abroad, these items being imports (denoted by *Im*) like Mexican oil and Japanese automobiles. In addition, some part of America's domestic production will be sold abroad as exports (denoted by *Ex*)—items like wheat and Boeing aircraft. The difference between national output and domestic expenditures is exports minus imports equals net exports, or $Ex - Im = X$.

To calculate the *total production* of American goods and services, we need to add trade to domestic demand. That is, we need to know the total production for American residents as well as the net production for foreigners. This total includes domestic expenditures $(C + I + G)$ plus sales to foreigners (Ex) less domestic purchases from foreigners (Im). Total output, or GDP, equals consumption plus domestic investment plus government purchases plus net exports:

$$\text{Total domestic output} = \text{GDP}$$
$$= C + I + G + X$$

Determinants of Trade and Net Exports

What determines the levels of exports and imports and therefore of net exports? It is best to think of the import and export components of net exports separately.

Imports into the United States are positively related to U.S. income and output. When U.S. GDP rises, imports into the U.S. increase (1) because some of the increased $C + I + G$ purchases (such as cars and shoes) come from foreign production and also (2) because America uses foreign-made inputs (like oil or steel) in producing its own goods. The demand for imports depends upon the relative price of foreign and domestic goods. If the price of domestic cars rises relative to the price of Japanese cars, say, because the dollar's exchange rate appreciates, Americans will buy more Japanese cars and fewer American ones. Hence *the volume and value of imports will be affected by domestic output and the relative prices of domestic and foreign goods.*

Exports are the mirror image of imports: U.S. exports are other countries' imports. American exports therefore depend primarily upon foreign output as well as upon the prices of U.S. exports relative to foreign goods. As foreign output rises, or as the exchange rate of the dollar depreciates, the volume and value of American exports tend to grow.

Figure 30-1 shows the ratio of net exports to GDP. For most of the period after World War II, the U.S. external accounts were in surplus or balance. Starting in the early 1980s, a decline in national saving, fueled by large federal budget deficits, led to a sharp appreciation of the dollar. Foreign economies grew less rapidly than the U.S. economy, depressing exports. The net effect was a large trade deficit and growing foreign indebtedness. Was it a good thing or a bad thing? The following discussion in 2000 by the president's Council of Economic Advisers puts the U.S. trade deficit in an economic context:

> By themselves, external trade and current account deficits are neither inherently good nor inherently bad. What matters are the reasons for the deficits. The main reason for the deficits today appears to be the strength of the U.S. economic expansion relative to the slow or negative growth in many other countries. . . . These deficits are essentially a macroeconomic phenomenon, reflecting a higher rate of domestic investment than of national saving. The deficit's growth . . . reflects rising investment rather than falling saving.[1]

---

[1] See *Economic Report of the President, 2000,* pp. 231–235, in this chapter's Further Reading section.

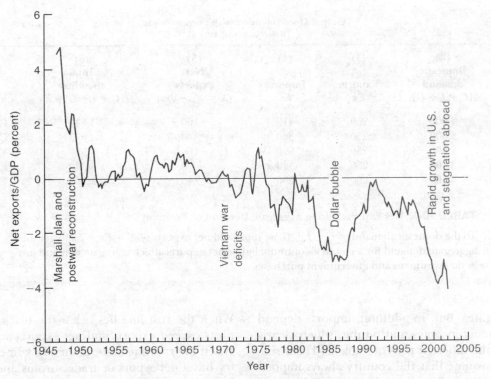

FIGURE 30-1. U.S. Net Exports Turned Sharply Negative in 1980s

The United States had a large surplus after World War II as it helped rebuild Europe. Note how net exports turned sharply negative in the early 1980s as domestic saving declined sharply and the dollar appreciated. In the late 1990s, net exports again turned negative with strong economic growth at home and recessions abroad.

SHORT-RUN IMPACT OF TRADE ON GDP

How do changes in a nation's trade flows affect its GDP and employment? We first analyze this question in the context of our short-run model of output determination, the multiplier model of Chapter 25. The multiplier model shows how, in the short run when there are unemployed resources, changes in trade will affect aggregate demand, output, and employment.

There are two major new macroeconomic elements in the presence of international trade: First, we have a fourth component of spending, net exports, which adds to aggregate demand. Second, an open economy has different multipliers for private investment and government domestic spending because some spending leaks out to the rest of the world.

Table 30-1 on the next page shows how introducing net exports affects output determination. This table begins with the same components as those for a closed economy. (Look back to Table 25-2 to refresh your memory about the major components and the way they sum to total spending.) Total domestic demand in column (2) is composed of the consumption, investment, and government purchases we analyzed earlier. Column (3) then adds the exports of goods and services. As described above, these depend upon foreign incomes and outputs and upon prices and exchange rates, all of which are also taken as given for this analysis. Exports are assumed to be a constant level of $250 billion of foreign spending on domestic goods and services.

The interesting new element arises from imports, shown in column (4). Like exports, imports depend upon exogenous variables such as prices and

Output Determination with Foreign Trade (billions of dollars)						
(1) Initial level of GDP	(2) Domestic demand (C + I + G)	(3) Exports Ex	(4) Imports Im	(5) Net exports (X = Ex − Im)	(6) Total spending (C + I + G + X)	(7) Resulting tendency of economy
4,100	4,000	250	410	−160	3,840 ↓	Contraction
3,800	3,800	250	380	−130	3,670 ↓	Contraction
3,500	3,600	250	350	−100	3,500	Equilibrium
3,200	3,400	250	320	−70	3,330 ↑	Expansion
2,900	3,200	250	290	−40	3,160 ↑	Expansion

TABLE 30-1. Net Exports Add to Aggregate Demand of Economy

To the domestic demand of $C + I + G$, we must add net exports of $X = Ex − Im$ to get total aggregate demand for a country's output. Higher net exports affect aggregate demand just as do investment and government purchases.

exchange rates. But, in addition, imports depend upon domestic incomes and output, which clearly change in the different rows of Table 30-1. For simplicity, we assume that the country always imports 10 percent of its total output, so imports in column (4) are 10 percent of column (1).

Subtracting column (4) from column (3) gives net exports in column (5). Net exports are a negative number when imports exceed exports and a positive number when exports are greater than imports. Net exports in column (5) are the net addition to the spending stream contributed by foreign trade. Total spending on domestic output in column (6) equals domestic demand in column (2) plus net exports in column (5). Equilibrium output in an open economy occurs where total net domestic and foreign spending in column (6) exactly equals total domestic output in column (1). In this case, equilibrium comes with net exports of −100, indicating that the country is importing more than it is exporting. At this equilibrium, note as well that domestic demand is greater than output. (Make sure that you can explain why the economy is not in equilibrium when spending does not equal output.)

Figure 30-2 shows the open-economy equilibrium graphically. The upward-sloping black line marked $C + I + G$ is the same curve used in Figure 25-7. To this line we must add the level of net exports that is forthcoming at each level of GDP. Net exports from column (5) of Table 30-1 are added to get the rust line of total aggregate demand or total spending.

When the rust line lies below the black curve, imports exceed exports and net exports are negative. When the rust line is above the black line, the country has a net-export or trade surplus and output is greater than domestic demand.

Equilibrium GDP occurs where the rust line of total spending intersects the 45° line. This intersection comes at exactly the same point, at $3500 billion, that is shown as equilibrium GDP in Table 30-1. Only at $3500 billion does GDP exactly equal what consumers, businesses, governments, and foreigners want to spend on goods and services produced in the United States.

The Marginal Propensity to Import and the Spending Line

Note that the aggregate demand curve, the rust $C + I + G + X$ curve in Figure 30-2, has a slightly smaller slope than the black curve of domestic demand. The explanation of this is that *there is an additional leakage from spending into imports*. This new leakage arises from our assumption that 10 cents of every dollar of income is spent on imports. To handle this requires introducing a new term, the **marginal propensity to import**. The marginal propensity to import, which we will denote MPm, is the increase in the dollar value of imports for each $1 increase in GDP.

The marginal propensity to import is closely related to the marginal propensity to save (MPS). Recall that the MPS tells us what fraction of an additional

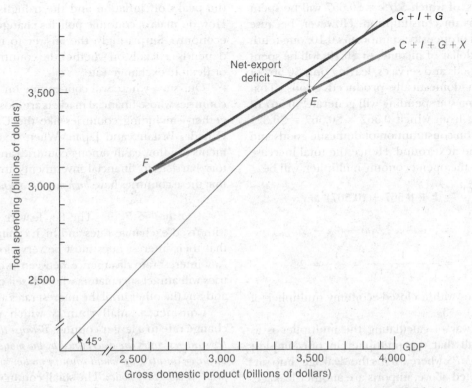

FIGURE 30-2. Adding Net Exports to Domestic Demand Gives Equilibrium GDP in the Open Economy

The black line represents domestic demand ($C + I + G$), purchases by domestic consumers, businesses, and governments. To this must be added net foreign spending. Net exports plus domestic demand give the rust line of total spending. Equilibrium comes at point E, where total GDP equals total spending on goods and services produced in the United States. Note that the slope of the rust total demand curve is less than that of domestic demand to reflect the leakage from spending into imports.

dollar of income is not spent but leaks into saving. The marginal propensity to import tells how much of additional output and income leaks into imports. In our example, the MPm is 0.10 because every $300 billion of increased income leads to $30 billion of increased imports. (What is the marginal propensity to import in an economy with no foreign trade? Zero.)

Now examine the slope of the total spending line in Figure 30-2—that line shows total spending on $C + I + G + X$. Note that the slope of the total spending line is less than the slope of the domestic demand line of $C + I + G$. As GDP and total incomes rise by $300, spending on consumption rises by the income change times the MPC (assumed to be two-thirds), or by $200. At the same time, spending on imports, or foreign goods, also rises by $30.

Hence spending on domestic goods rises by only $170 ($200 − $30), and the slope of the total spending line falls from 0.667 in our closed economy to $170/$300 = 0.567 in our open economy.

The Open-Economy Multiplier

Surprisingly, opening up an economy lowers the multiplier.

One way of understanding the expenditure multiplier in an open economy is to calculate the rounds of spending and responding generated by an additional dollar of government spending, investment, or exports. Suppose that Germany needs to buy American computers to modernize antiquated facilities in what used to be East Germany. Each extra dollar of U.S. computers will generate $1 of income in the

United States, of which $2/3 = 0.667 will be spent by Americans on consumption. However, because the marginal propensity to import is 0.10, one-tenth of the extra dollar of income, or $0.10, will be spent on foreign goods and services, leaving only $0.567 of spending on domestically produced goods. That $0.567 of domestic spending will generate $0.567 of U.S. income, from which $0.567 \times $0.567 = 0.321 will be spent on consumption of domestic goods and services in the next round. Hence the total increase in output, or the open-economy multiplier, will be

$$\begin{matrix}\text{Open-economy}\\ \text{multiplier}\end{matrix} = 1 + 0.567 + (0.567)^2 + \cdots$$

$$= 1 + (\tfrac{2}{3} - \tfrac{1}{10}) + (\tfrac{2}{3} - \tfrac{1}{10})^2 + \cdots$$

$$= \frac{1}{1 - \tfrac{2}{3} + \tfrac{1}{10}} = \frac{1}{\tfrac{13}{30}} = 2.3$$

This compares with a closed-economy multiplier of $1/(1 - 0.667) = 3$.

Another way of calculating the multiplier is as follows: Recall that the multiplier in our simplest model was $1/MPS$, where MPS is the "leakage" into saving. As we noted above, imports are another leakage. The total leakage is the dollars leaking into saving (the MPS) plus the dollars leaking into imports (the MPm). Hence, the open-economy multiplier should be $1/(MPS + MPm) = 1/(0.333 + 0.1) = 1/0.433 = 2.3$. Note that both the leakage analysis and the rounds analysis provide exactly the same answer.

To summarize:

Because a fraction of any income increase leaks into imports in an open economy, the **open-economy multiplier** is smaller than that of a closed economy. The exact relationship is

$$\text{Open-economy multiplier} = \frac{1}{MPS + MPm}$$

where MPS = marginal propensity to save and MPm = marginal propensity to import.

MACROECONOMIC POLICY AND THE EXCHANGE-RATE SYSTEM

Our analysis of business cycles and economic growth has generally focused on policies in a closed economy. We analyzed the way that monetary and fiscal policies can help stabilize the business cycle, shaving the peaks off inflation and the troughs off output. How do macroeconomic policies change in an open economy? Surprisingly, the answer to this question depends crucially on whether the country has a fixed or flexible exchange rate.

Our survey here will concentrate on high-income countries whose financial markets are closely linked together—including countries like the United States, Canada, Britain, and Japan. When financial investments can flow easily among countries and the regulatory barriers to financial investments are low, we say that these countries have *high mobility of financial capital*.

Fixed Exchange Rates. The key feature of countries with fixed exchange rates and high capital mobility is that their interest rates must be very closely aligned. Any interest-rate divergence between two such countries will attract speculators who will sell one currency and buy the other until the interest rates are equalized.

Consider a small country which pegs its exchange rate to a larger country. *Because the small country's interest rates are determined by the monetary policy of the large country, the small country no longer has an independent monetary policy.* The small country's monetary policy must be devoted to ensuring that its interest rates are aligned with its partner's.

Macroeconomic policy in such a situation is therefore exactly the case described in our multiplier model above. From the small country's point of view, investment is exogenous, because it is determined by world interest rates. Fiscal policy will be highly effective because there will be no monetary reaction to changes in G or T.

Flexible Exchange Rates. One important insight in this area is that macroeconomic policy with flexible exchange rates operates in quite a different way from the fixed-exchange-rate case. Monetary policy becomes highly effective with a flexible exchange rate.

Let's consider the case of the United States. The monetary transmission mechanism in the United States has changed significantly in recent decades as a result of increased openness and a switch to a flexible exchange rate. In the modern era, international trade and finance have come to play an increasingly important role in U.S. macroeconomic policy.

One of the best examples of the operation of macroeconomic policy with flexible exchange rates occurred when the Federal Reserve tightened money in the 1979–1982 period. The monetary tightening raised U.S. interest rates, which attracted funds from abroad into dollar securities. This increase in demand for dollars drove up the foreign exchange rate on the dollar. (Review the previous chapter's Figure 29-5.) At this point, the multiplier mechanism swung into action. The high dollar exchange rate reduced net exports and contributed to the deep U.S. recession of 1981–1983 in the way we described earlier. The net effect was a reduction in real GDP.

Foreign trade produces a new and powerful link in the monetary transmission mechanism when a country has flexible exchange rates. When monetary policy changes interest rates, this affects exchange rates and net exports as well as domestic

investment. Monetary tightening leads to exchange-rate appreciation and a decline in net exports (and monetary easing does the opposite). The interest-rate impact on net exports reinforces the impact on domestic investment: tight money lowers output and prices.

TRADE AND ECONOMIC ACTIVITY, 1980–2003

In a world where nations are increasingly linked by trade and finance, foreign trade can have a major impact on domestic output and employment. Figure 30-3 shows two major troughs in U.S. net exports—in the early 1980s and in the 1995–2001

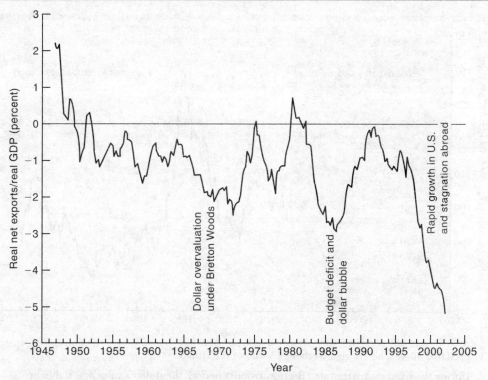

FIGURE 30-3. Net Exports Can Help or Hurt Depending upon Domestic Demand

With a strong rise of the dollar and weak economic growth abroad, U.S. real net exports turned sharply negative in the early 1980s. The shift produced a massive drag on aggregate spending in the $C + I + G + X$ equation and helped produce the deepest recession of the last half-century. The growing trade deficit after 1995 coincided with strong growth in domestic demand, which moderated output and price growth.

Source: U.S. Department of Commerce.

period. Describing each of these periods will help us understand the role of international trade in domestic performance.

The Overvalued Dollar of the 1980s. The decade of the 1980s witnessed a dramatic cycle of dollar appreciation and depreciation. The rise of the dollar began in 1980 after tight monetary policy and loose fiscal policy in the United States drove interest rates up sharply. High interest rates at home and economic turmoil abroad attracted funds into the dollar. Figure 30-4 shows that during the period from 1979 to early 1985 the exchange rate on the dollar rose 80 percent. In 1985, many economists believed the dollar was overvalued—an *overvalued currency* is one whose value is high relative to its long-run or sustainable level.

As the dollar rose, American export prices increased and the prices of goods imported into the United States fell. From 1980 to 1985, the prices of imported goods and services fell by 6 percent, while the prices of our exports in foreign currencies rose over 80 percent. In response, the volume of imports rose 51 percent while export volumes rose only 2 percent.

Figure 30-5 illustrates the dramatic effect of the appreciating dollar on trade flows. From the peak in 1980 to the trough in 1986, real net exports declined by $158 billion—this amounted to 3 percent of 1983 GDP.

By itself, this sharp decline in net exports would be contractionary. Unfortunately, the trade impact reinforced a decline in domestic demand induced by tight monetary policy. The result was the deepest recession in 50 years.

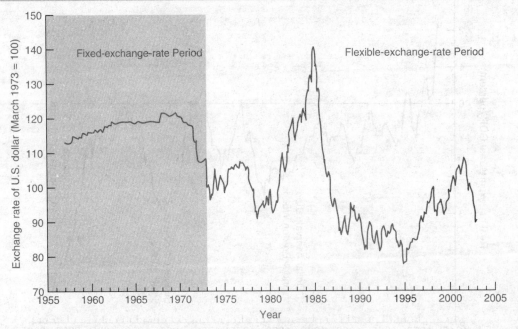

FIGURE 30-4. The Foreign Exchange Value of the Dollar

During the fixed-exchange-rate (Bretton Woods) period, the dollar's value was stable in exchange markets. After the United States moved to flexible exchange rates in 1973, the dollar's value became more volatile. When the United States pursued its tight-money policies in the early 1980s, the high interest rates pulled up the dollar. In the late 1990s and early 2000s, high interest rates in the United States along with stagnation in Japan and Europe led to appreciation of the dollar and a mini-bubble that burst in 2003.

Source: Federal Reserve System, at www.federalreserve.gov/releases/h10/summary/.

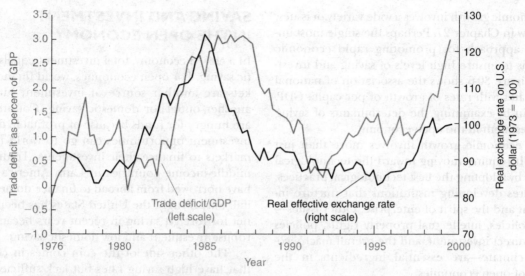

FIGURE 30-5. Trade and Exchange Rates

Trade flows respond to exchange-rate changes, but with a time lag. The real appreciation of the dollar during the early 1980s increased U.S. export prices and reduced prices of goods imported into the United States. As a result, the trade deficit rose sharply. When the dollar depreciated after 1985, the trade deficit began to shrink. The recent increase in the current-account deficit has resulted from dollar appreciation and slow growth outside the United States.

Source: Council of Economic Advisers, *Economic Report of the President,* 2000.

Countercyclical Trade in the 1995–2001 Period. The late 1990s were the opposite—and a happier—story. After 1995, the combination of low real interest rates and a booming stock market led to rapid growth in domestic demand in the United States, particularly private investment. Unemployment fell sharply. A rapid increase in foreign demand for U.S. assets led to a sharp appreciation of the dollar.

In this period, the macroeconomic impact of the dollar appreciation was appropriate. As the American economy approached full employment, import prices and net exports declined and the foreign sector exercised a slight drag on the economy. Had the dollar depreciated rather than appreciated, the foreign sector would have been expansionary, the American economy would have experienced rising inflation, and the Fed would have found it necessary to tighten money to choke off the boom. In the late 1990s, therefore, a dollar appreciation and declining net exports were just what the macroeconomic doctor ordered.

B. INTERDEPENDENCE IN THE GLOBAL ECONOMY

ECONOMIC GROWTH IN THE OPEN ECONOMY

The first section described the short-run impact of international trade and policy changes in the open economy. These issues are crucial for open economies combating unemployment and inflation. But countries must also keep their eye on the implications of their policies for long-run economic growth. Particularly for small countries, the concerns about economic-growth policies are paramount. Sometimes, it is useful to think of an individual region within the United States (such as a state or metropolitan area) as a small open economy with a fixed exchange rate.

Economic growth involves a wide variety of issues, as we saw in Chapter 27. Perhaps the single most important approach for promoting rapid economic growth is to ensure high levels of saving and investment. Figure 30-6 shows the association of national saving rates with rates of growth of per capita GDP. We begin by examining the determinants of saving and investment in the open economy.

But economic growth involves more than just capital. It requires moving toward the technological frontier by adopting the best technological practices. It requires developing institutions that nurture investment and the spirit of enterprise. Other issues—trade policies, intellectual property rights, policies toward direct investment, and the overall macroeconomic climate—are essential ingredients in the growth of open economies.

SAVING AND INVESTMENT IN THE OPEN ECONOMY

In a closed economy, total investment equals domestic saving. For open economies, world financial markets are another source of investment funds and another outlet for domestic saving. Countries that are hungry for funds because of profitable domestic investment opportunities can go to world financial markets to finance their investments. Traditionally, middle-income countries in Latin America or Asia have borrowed from abroad to finance domestic capital. Surprisingly, the United States has been a magnet for foreign saving in recent years because of its robust investment and low domestic saving.

The other side of the coin comes in countries that have high saving rates but lack sufficient high-yield domestic investment opportunities. Countries like England in the last century or Japan in recent years have provided substantial funds to capital-short countries. We first review the investment-saving relationship and then examine the mechanisms for allocating saving among countries.

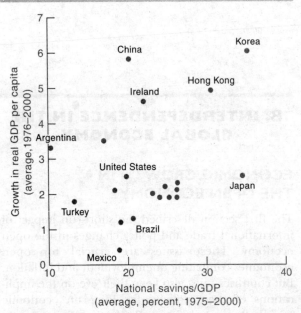

FIGURE 30-6. National Investment and Economic Growth

Countries that have high saving and investment rates also have above-average rates of per capita economic growth. In the long run, promoting high saving and investment is one of the most secure routes to increasing growth.

Source: World-Penn tables.

The Saving-Investment Relation in an Open Economy

Let's pause to recall our saving-investment identities from Chapter 21:

$$I_T = I + X = S + (T - G)$$

This states that total national investment (I_T) consists of investment in domestic capital (I) plus net foreign investment or net exports (X). This must equal total private saving (S) by households and businesses plus total public saving, which is given by the government surplus ($T - G$).

We can rewrite the identity as follows to emphasize the components of net exports:

$$X = S + (T - G) - I$$

or

Net exports = private saving
            + government saving
            − domestic investment

This important equation shows that net exports are the difference between domestic saving and domestic investment. The components of total U.S. national investment for recent decades are shown in Table 30-2.

Saving and Investment as Percentage of NNP			
	1959–1981	1982–1997	1998–2002
Net national saving	**10.7**	**5.6**	**5.3**
Net private saving	10.7	9.2	4.6
Net government saving	0.0	−3.5	0.6
Net national investment	**10.0**	**5.1**	**6.3**
Net private investment	8.9	6.4	7.1
Net government investment	2.1	1.4	1.3
Net foreign investment	0.4	−1.7	−4.1
Statistical discrepancy	0.7	0.5	−1.0

TABLE 30-2. Trade Balance and Net Foreign Investment Are Part of National Saving and Investment

After large budget deficits began in 1982, national saving and investment were squeezed. About half the squeeze resulted in lower domestic investment, while the rest came through a trade and net-export deficit. The budget turnaround after 1997 was matched by a sharp decline in private saving and led to little change in net national investment.

Source: Bureau of Economic Analysis.

Determination of Saving and Investment at Full Employment

We need to go beyond the identities to understand the mechanism by which saving and investment are equalized in the open economy. The equilibration of saving and investment in the short run is just the mirror image of the multiplier mechanism shown in Figure 30-2.

It is useful to consider how saving and investment are allocated in the long run in a "classical" economy with full employment and flexible prices. We consider the simplest case where there is no inflation or uncertainty. We begin with a closed economy and then extend the analysis to an open economy.

Closed Economy. In a closed economy, we know that investment must equal private saving plus the government surplus. We simplify by assuming that taxes, government spending, and private saving are independent of interest rates. Hence, total domestic saving (public and private) is a given amount at full employment.

By contrast, as we learned in Chapter 22, investment is very sensitive to the interest rate. Higher interest rates reduce spending on housing and business plant and equipment. We therefore write our investment schedule as $I(r)$ to indicate that investment depends upon the real interest rate, r.

Figure 30-7 shows how national saving and investment are equilibrated in a full-employment closed economy. The saving and investment schedules determine an interest rate at r^* with healthy levels of saving and investment.

Now suppose that the government increases its purchases, increasing the government deficit or reducing the surplus. This will shift the saving schedule to the left to $S + T - G'$. As a result, the real interest rate increases to equilibrate saving and investment, and the level of investment falls. The major point is that *a higher government deficit lowers investment in the full-employment closed economy.*

Open-Economy Saving. An open economy has alternative sources of investment and alternative outlets for saving. We show this situation in Figure 30-8 for a small open economy with a high degree of mobility of financial capital. A small open economy must equate its domestic interest rate with the world real interest rate, r^W. It is too small to affect the world interest rate, and because capital mobility is high, financial capital will move to equilibrate interest rates at home and abroad.

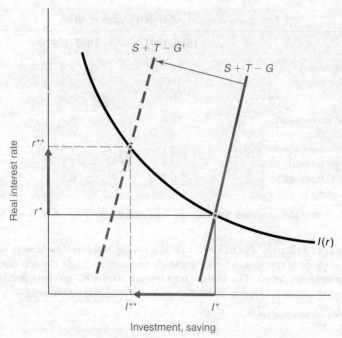

FIGURE 30-7. Saving and Investment in the Closed Economy

Investment is inversely related to the real interest rate, while private saving and public saving are relatively unresponsive to the interest rate. Equilibrium saving and investment comes at r^*. Suppose that government purchases increase. This increases the government deficit and therefore reduces public saving. The result is a shift in the national saving curve to the left to $S + T - G'$, raising the market interest rate to r^{**} and reducing national saving and investment to I^{**}.

Figure 30-8 helps explain the determination of saving, investment, and net exports in the open economy. At the prevailing world interest rate, domestic investment is shown at point A, which is the intersection of the investment schedule and the interest rate. Total national saving is given at point B on the total saving schedule, $S + T - G$. The difference between them—given by the line segment AB—is net exports. (This equality is shown by the saving-investment identity in the box on page 628.)

Hence net exports are determined by the balance between national saving and investment as determined by domestic factors plus the world interest rate.

This discussion pushes into the background the mechanism by which a country adjusts its trade, saving, and investment. It is here that the exchange rate plays the crucial equilibrating role. *Changes in exchange rates are the mechanism by which saving and investment adjust.* That is, exchange rates move to ensure that the level of net exports balances the difference between domestic saving and investment.[2]

This analysis can help explain the trends in saving, investment, and trade patterns in major countries in recent years. Figure 30-8 describes well

---

[2] More generally, the adjustment occurs through changes in the relative prices of domestic and foreign goods. The relative price of domestic to foreign goods is determined by both the foreign exchange rate and the domestic and foreign price levels. Under a flexible exchange rate, the adjustment would occur quickly through changes in the exchange rate itself. With a fixed exchange rate, the price levels of the two countries would do the adjustment. The required end result—a change in the relative prices—is the same in either case.

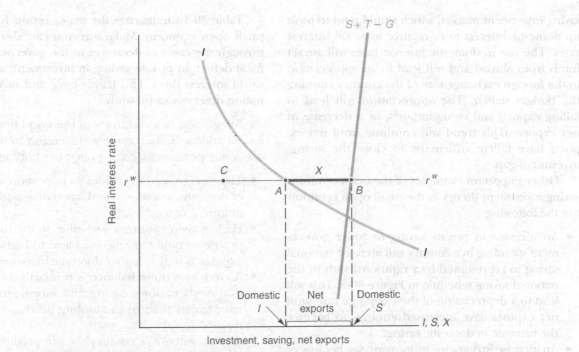

FIGURE 30-8. Saving and Investment in a Small Open Economy

Domestic investment and domestic saving are determined by income, interest rates, and government fiscal policy, as in Fig. 30-7. But the small open economy with mobile financial capital has its real interest rates determined in world financial markets. At the relatively high real interest rate at r^W, domestic saving exceeds domestic investment and the excess saving flows to more lucrative investment opportunities abroad. The difference is net exports and net foreign investment, X, which is the difference between national saving and domestic investment at the prevailing interest rate. A trade surplus such as has been seen in Japan and Germany for most of the last two decades is caused by the interaction of high domestic saving and depleted domestic investment.

the role of Japan in the world economy. Japan has traditionally had a high domestic saving rate. Yet in recent years—because of high production costs at home and competitive conditions in neighboring newly industrialized countries—the return on Japanese capital has been depressed. Japanese saving therefore seeks outlets abroad, with the consequence that Japan has had a large trade surplus and high net exports. Similar trends were seen in high-saving and low-investment Germany until German reunification in 1990.

The United States has seen an interesting twist in its saving and investment position, as was shown in Table 30-2. Until 1980, the United States had a modestly positive net-export position. But in the early

1980s the U.S. government's fiscal position shifted sharply toward deficit. You can depict this by drawing a new $S + T' - G'$ line in Figure 30-8 that intersects the real-interest-rate line at point C. You can see that total national saving would decline with a larger government deficit. Domestic investment would be unchanged. Net exports would turn negative and be given by the line segment CA.

We can also use this analysis to explain the mechanism by which net exports adjust to provide the necessary investment when the government runs a budget deficit. Consider a country with a net-export surplus as shown in Figure 30-8. Suppose that the government suddenly begins to run a large budget deficit. This change will lead to an imbalance in the saving-investment market, which would tend to push up domestic interest rates relative to world interest rates. The rise in domestic interest rates will attract funds from abroad and will lead to an appreciation in the foreign exchange rate of the country running the budget deficit. The appreciation will lead to falling exports and rising imports, or a decrease in net exports. This trend will continue until net exports have fallen sufficiently to close the saving-investment gap.

Other important examples of the open-economy saving-investment theory in the small open economy are the following:

- An increase in private saving or lower government spending in a country will increase national saving as represented by a rightward shift in the national saving schedule in Figure 30-8. This will lead to a depreciation of the exchange rate until net exports have increased enough to balance the increase in domestic saving.
- An increase in domestic investment, say, because of an improved business climate or a burst of innovations, will lead to a shift in the investment schedule. This will lead to an appreciation of the exchange rate until net exports decline enough to balance saving and investment. In this case, domestic investment crowds out foreign investment.
- An increase in world interest rates will reduce the level of investment. This will lead to an increase in the difference between saving and investment, to a depreciation in the foreign exchange rate, and to an increase in net exports and foreign investment. (This would be a shift along the investment schedule.)

Table 30-3 summarizes the major results for the small open economy. Make sure you can also work through the cases of decreases in the government's fiscal deficit, in private saving, in investment, and in world interest rates. This handy table and its explanation deserve careful study.[3]

Integration of a country into the world financial system adds an important new dimension to macroeconomic performance and policy. Key findings are:

- The foreign sector provides an important source of domestic investment and a potential outlet for domestic saving.
- Higher saving at home—whether in the form of private or public saving—will lead to higher net exports as well as higher domestic investment.
- A country's trade balance is primarily a reflection of its national saving and investment balance rather than of its absolute productivity or wealth.
- Adjustments in a country's trade accounts require a change in domestic saving or investment.
- In the long run, adjustments in trade accounts will be brought about by movements in the country's relative prices, often through exchange-rate changes.

---

[3] This discussion covers "small" open economies that cannot affect the world interest rate. For "large" open economies like the United States, the impact would be somewhere between the small-economy and the closed-economy cases. This more complex case is covered in intermediate textbooks (see the Further Reading section in Chapter 20).

Change in policy or exogenous variable	Change in exchange rate	Change in investment	Change in net exports
Increase in G or decrease in T	$e\uparrow$	0	$X\downarrow$
Increase in private S	$e\downarrow$	0	$X\uparrow$
Increase in investment demand	$e\uparrow$	$I\uparrow$	$X\downarrow$
Increase in world interest rates	$e\downarrow$	$I\downarrow$	$X\uparrow$

TABLE 30-3. Major Conclusions of Saving-Investment Model in Small Open Economy

Make sure you understand the mechanism by which each of these occurs.

PROMOTING GROWTH IN THE OPEN ECONOMY

Increasing the growth of output in open economies involves more than just waving a magic wand that will attract investors or savers. The saving and investing climate involves a wide array of policies, including a stable macroeconomic environment, secure property rights, and, above all, a predictable and attractive climate for investment. We review in this section some of the ways that open economies can improve their growth rates by using the global marketplace to their best advantage.

Over the long run, the single most important way of increasing per capita output and living standards is to ensure that the country *adopts best-practice techniques* in its production processes. It does little good to have a high investment rate if the investments are in the wrong technology. This point was abundantly shown in the last years of Soviet central planning (discussed in Chapter 28), when the investment rate was extremely high but much investment was poorly designed, left unfinished, or put in unproductive sectors. Moreover, individual small countries do not need to start from scratch in designing their own turbines, machinery, computers, and management systems. Often, reaching the technological frontier will involve engaging in joint ventures with foreign firms, which in turn requires that the institutional framework be hospitable to foreign capital.

Another important set of policies is *trade policies.* Evidence suggests that an open trading system promotes competitiveness and adoption of best-practice technologies. By keeping tariffs and other barriers to trade low, countries can ensure that domestic firms feel the spur of competition and that foreign firms are permitted to enter domestic markets when domestic producers sell at inefficiently high prices or monopolize particular sectors.

When countries consider their saving and investment, they must not concentrate entirely on physical capital. *Intangible capital* is just as important. Studies show that countries that invest in human capital through education tend to perform well and be resilient in the face of shocks. Many countries have valuable stocks of natural resources—forests, minerals, oil and gas, fisheries, and arable land—that must

be managed carefully to ensure that they provide the highest yield for the country.

One of the most complex factors in a country's growth involves *immigration* and *emigration.* Historically, the United States has attracted large flows of immigrants that not only have increased the size of its labor forces but also have enhanced the quality of its culture and scientific research. More recently, however, the immigrants have possessed less education and lower skills than the domestic labor force. As a result, according to some studies, immigration has depressed the relative wages of low-wage workers in the United States. Countries that "export" workers, such as Mexico, often have a steady stream of earnings that are sent home by citizens to their relatives, and this can provide a nice supplement to export earnings.

One of the most important and subtle influences concerns the *institutions of the market.* The most successful open economies—like the Netherlands and Luxembourg in Europe or Taiwan and Hong Kong in Asia—have provided a secure environment for investment and entrepreneurship. This involved establishing a secure set of property rights, guided by the rule of law. Increasingly important is the development of intellectual property rights so that inventors and creative artists are assured that they will be able to profit from their activities. Countries must fight corruption, which is a kind of private taxation system that preys on the most profitable enterprises, creates uncertainty about property rights, raises costs, and has a chilling effect on investment.

A *stable macroeconomic climate* means that taxes are reasonable and predictable and that inflation is low, so lenders need not worry about inflation confiscating their investments. It is crucial that exchange rates be relatively stable, with a convertibility that allows easy and inexpensive entry into and exit out of the domestic currency. Countries that provide a favorable institutional structure attract large flows of foreign financial capital, while countries that have unstable institutions, like Russia or Sudan, attract relatively little foreign funds and suffer "capital flight," in which local residents move their funds abroad to avoid taxes, expropriation, or loss of value.

Figure 30-9 illustrates the impact of the investment climate on national investment. The left-hand panel depicts a country that has a favorable investment

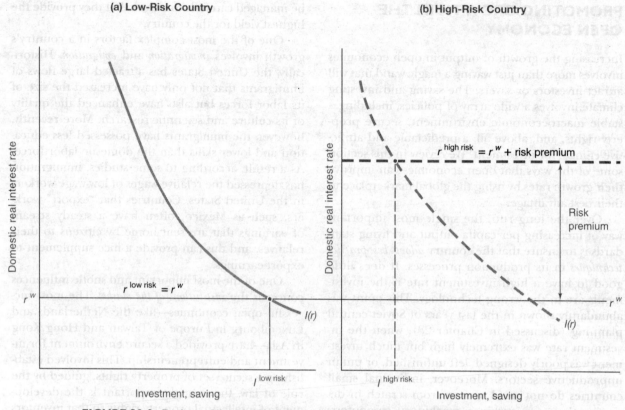

FIGURE 30-9. Business Climate Affects Interest Rate and Investment Level

In the low-risk country in **(a)**, a stable economic climate leads to a low domestic interest rate at r^W and a high level of investment at $I^{\text{low risk}}$. In the high-risk country, racked by political turmoil, corruption, and economic uncertainty, investors require a large risk premium on their investments, so the domestic interest rate is far above the world interest rate. The result is a depressed level of investment as foreign investors seek safer terrain.

climate, so the domestic interest rate is equal to the world interest rate. The overall level of investment there is high, and the country can attract foreign funds to finance domestic investment. Panel (*b*) shows a high-risk country—plagued by revolution, high inflation, unpredictable taxes, nationalizations, corruption, an unstable foreign exchange rate, and so on. In the high-risk country, domestic interest rates have a high "risk premium" over world interest rates, so the real cost of capital might be 10 or 20 or 30 percent per year compared to 5 percent in the low-risk country. The risky country will have trouble attracting domestic *and* foreign investment, and the resulting level of investment will be low.

Promoting economic growth in an open economy involves ensuring that business is attractive for foreign and domestic investors who have a wide array of investment opportunities in the world economy. The ultimate goals of policy are to have high rates of saving and investment in productive channels and to ensure that businesses use best-practice techniques. Achieving these goals involves setting a stable macroeconomic climate, guaranteeing dependable property rights for both tangible investments and intellectual property, providing exchange-rate convertibility that allows investors to take home their profits, and maintaining confidence in the political and economic stability of the country.

C. INTERNATIONAL ECONOMIC ISSUES AT CENTURY'S START

In this final section, we apply the tools of international economics to examine two of the central issues that have concerned nations in recent years. In the first part, we examine the issue of the difference between competitiveness and productivity. In the final part, we will turn to one of the durable issues of the global economy—the choice between fixed and flexible exchange rates.

COMPETITIVENESS AND PRODUCTIVITY

"The Deindustrialization of America"

Often, when unemployment rises sharply in the presence of trade deficits, people raise alarms about a nation's productivity and competitiveness. Just such a situation occurred in the United States in the 1980s, and a review of this history is a helpful reminder about the determinants of trade flows.

The overvalued dollar in the 1980s produced severe economic hardships in many U.S. sectors exposed to international trade. Industries like automobiles, steel, textiles, and agriculture found the demand for their products shrinking as exchange-rate appreciation led to a rise in their prices relative to the prices of foreign competitors. Unemployment in America's manufacturing heartland increased sharply, factories were closed, and the midwest became known as the "rust belt."

Many noneconomists interpreted U.S. trade problems as indicative of "America in decline." They fretted that America's technological leadership was eroding because of excessive regulation, declining innovation, and managerial sloth. Some advocated economic protection against Japan and Western Europe, while others argued for "industrial policies" for beleaguered industries to help stem the "deindustrialization of America." America was pictured as a land condemned to serving potato chips while others were manufacturing our computer chips.

Economists saw a different syndrome at work— the classic disease of an overvalued exchange rate. To understand the fundamentals, we must distinguish a nation's competitiveness from its productivity.

Competitiveness refers to the extent to which a nation's goods can compete in the marketplace; this depends primarily upon the relative prices of domestic and foreign products. Competitiveness must be distinguished from *productivity,* which is measured by the output per unit of input. Productivity is fundamental to the growth in living standards in a nation: to a first approximation, a nation's real income grows in step with its productivity growth.

It is true that U.S. competitiveness fell sharply during the 1980s. But this fall was not caused by a deterioration in productivity growth. Rather, deteriorating competitiveness during the 1980s arose because the decline in national saving in the United States led to an appreciation of the dollar and raised American prices relative to those of its trading partners. In fact, productivity growth grew slightly more rapidly during that period than in the prior decade.

Fundamental source of competitiveness: As the theory of comparative advantage demonstrates, nations are not inherently uncompetitive. Rather, they become uncompetitive when their prices move out of line with those of their trading partners.

Trends in Productivity

The real story about U.S. real income is not about competitiveness but about productivity. Recall that productivity measures the output per worker or per bundle of inputs. Real incomes in the United States stagnated until the early 1990s because productivity growth slowed and not because America became uncompetitive in the global marketplace.

Competitiveness is important for trade but has no intrinsic relationship to the level or growth of real incomes. China enjoyed a massive trade surplus in the 1990s at the same time that the United States ran a large trade deficit. But surely that does not mean that Americans would trade their living standards for those in China. Loss of competitiveness in international markets results from a nation's *prices* being out of line from those of its trading partners; it has no necessary connection with how a nation's *productivity* compares with other countries' productivity.

A particularly revealing study by the McKinsey Global Institute found that in 1990 manufacturing productivity in Japan was 17 percent below that in the United States while German productivity was

21 percent below U.S. levels.[4] Furthermore, the United States maintained a productivity lead in four of the nine manufacturing industries studied: computers, soaps and detergents, beer, and food. Japanese workers had higher productivity than U.S. workers in automobiles, auto parts, metalworking, steel, and consumer electronics production. In none of the industries surveyed were German workers the most productive, and indeed German productivity had declined relative to that in the United States during the 1980s.

The McKinsey study investigated the sources of productivity differences among the major countries in the nine industries studied. What emerged was surprising:

- Economies of scale and manufacturing technologies played a small role in some industries.
- Surprisingly, workers' skill levels and education were of little importance, being essentially the same in all three nations.
- Large differences in productivity exist within firms in the same industry. Managers could significantly improve productivity in *all* industries by adopting best-practice technologies.

Studies of productivity differences among countries emphasize the importance of *competition* and *outward orientation*. An essential aspect of policy is to force domestic industries to compete with the leading technologies and firms in a particular industry. Foreign direct investment by the most productive country (such as the Japanese auto transplants on American soil) has contributed to dramatic productivity improvements both through introducing leading-edge technologies and in stimulating competition.

The surest route to high productivity and therefore to high living standards is to expose domestic industries to world markets and to allow vigorous competition with companies that have adopted the most advanced technologies.

THE EUROPEAN MONETARY UNION

An ideal exchange-rate system is one that allows high levels of predictability of relative prices while stabilizing the economy in the face of economic shocks. In a

well-functioning system, people can trade and invest in other countries without worrying that exchange rates will suddenly change and make their ventures unprofitable. This ideal seemed to be attained during most of the Bretton Woods era, when exchange-rate changes were infrequent yet output and trade grew rapidly.

From the early 1990s, however, fixed-exchange-rate systems were often *destabilizing* rather than stabilizing. Time and again, fixed-exchange-rate systems were the subject of intense speculative attack that spread to other countries through contagion. This was seen in Europe in 1991–1992, Mexico in 1994–1995, Russia and East Asia in 1997–1998, and Latin America from 1998 to 2002.

Nowhere was criticism of the flexible-exchange-rate system more persistent and profound than in Western Europe. As a result, the countries of the European Union opted for a system of fixed exchange rates and then took the giant step of linking their economic fortunes through the European Monetary Union, which forged a common currency, the Euro.

European Monetary System: Europe's Bretton Woods System

After the demise of the Bretton Woods system in 1973, several countries of Western Europe joined to form a fixed-exchange-rate system known as the European Monetary System (or EMS). One of the implications of fixed exchange rates and open borders is that countries must give up control over domestic interest rates. If France has an exchange rate that is tightly tied to Germany, free-market French interest rates cannot diverge significantly from those in Germany.

The loss of control over monetary policy would not be fatal during normal times. But in times of crisis, a common interest rate might lead to such divergent inflation and unemployment rates that countries in recession may be tempted to devalue their exchange rates. That is exactly what happened in 1989–1993, and the result almost destroyed the European Monetary System and eventually led to monetary union.

The first key factor in the crisis of the EMS was the reunification of Germany in 1990. Following reunification, Germany's fiscal policy turned sharply expansionary as the nation poured money into rebuilding eastern Germany. The expansion in western Germany led to a rise in the German

---

[4] See the Further Reading section at the end of this chapter.

inflation rate. The German central bank responded by raising German interest rates to dampen domestic demand. In this situation, German monetary policy was being used for *domestic* macroeconomic management, and the *international* effects of the measures on Germany's trading partners were subordinated to domestic economic concerns.

Faced with rising German interest rates, other nations in the EMS had to raise their interest rates to prevent their currencies from depreciating against the German mark. Many countries found themselves with overvalued exchange rates. These interest-rate increases, along with a worldwide recession and a sharp decline in output from the collapsing communist bloc, pushed Europe, outside of Germany, into a deep recession.

The Fundamental Contradiction of Fixed Exchange Rates

"You can't have it all" is one of the central tenets of economics. This was driven home in macroeconomic affairs on several occasions during the 1990s. As countries on fixed exchange rates liberalized their financial markets, they encountered a *fundamental contradiction of fixed exchange rates: A country cannot simultaneously have (a) a fixed but adjustable exchange rate, (b) free capital and financial movements, and (c) an independent domestic monetary policy.*

This contradiction among the three objectives was explained by Paul Krugman as follows:

The point is that you can't have it all: A country must pick two out of three. It can fix its exchange rate without emasculating its central bank, but only by maintaining controls on capital flows (like China today); it can leave capital movement free and retain monetary autonomy, but only by letting the exchange rate fluctuate (like Britain—or Canada); or it can choose to leave capital free and stabilize the currency, but only by abandoning any ability to adjust interest rates to fight inflation or recession (like Argentina today, or for that matter most of Europe).[5]

Speculative Attack! European countries ran into the fundamental contradiction in the early 1990s. Their exchange rates were attacked by speculators who

---

[5] See "Websites" in this chapter's Further Reading section.

---

believed that countries would not long tolerate overvalued exchange rates and the consequent high interest rates and high unemployment. One by one, currencies came under attack—the Finnish mark, the Swedish crown, the Italian lira, the British pound, the Spanish peseta. In the end, only the inner sanctum of France and Germany withstood the speculative attacks.

This episode shows a corollary of the fundamental contradiction: *A fixed-exchange-rate system is prone to devastating speculative attack if financial capital flows freely among countries.* Why is this? A fixed but adjustable exchange rate is susceptible to attack when speculators believe that changes in the exchange rate are imminent. If a currency is likely to be devalued, speculators will quickly start selling that currency. The supply of the currency increases while demand drops.

At this point, central banks step in to defend the currency (recall the graphical description of intervention in Figure 29-8 on page 614). But given the private resources available for speculative attacks—easily tens of billions of dollars in a few hours—the defender of a weak currency quickly runs out of reserves. Unless "hard-currency" countries are willing to provide unlimited lines of credit, the defending central bank will eventually surrender and either devalue or allow the currency to float.

Toward a Common Currency: The Euro

Since World War II, the democratic countries of Western Europe have pursued ever-closer economic integration, primarily to promote political stability after two devastating wars. Peace and trade go hand in hand, according to many political scientists. Beginning in 1957 with a free-trade agreement, Western Europeans gradually removed all barriers to trade in goods, services, and finance. The final step in economic integration was to adopt a common currency. This would not only foster closer economic ties but also resolve the problem of unstable currencies that plagued the earlier fixed-exchange-rate systems.

European experts believed that it would be necessary for countries to meet a minimal set of *convergence criteria* before they were allowed in the monetary club. These criteria included inflation and interest rates close to the lowest among the countries, along with stringent limitations on government deficits and government debts. Eleven European countries met the convergence criteria and joined the European Monetary Union (EMU) on January 1, 1999. These countries, sometimes called Euroland, adopted the "Euro" as the new money of Western Europe.

The monetary structure under the European Monetary Union resembles that of the United States. Monetary policy is lodged in the *European Central Bank (ECB)*, which conducts monetary policy for countries in the accord. The ECB undertakes open-market operations and thereby determines interest rates for the Euro.

One of the major questions for monetary policy involves the objectives of the central bank. The ECB is directed under its charter to pursue "price stability" as its primary objective, although it can pursue other communitywide goals as long as these do not compromise price stability. The ECB defines price stability as an increase in Euroland consumer prices of below 2 percent per year over the medium term. As we will see in our discussion of monetary policy in Chapter 34, this emphasis on inflation targeting has been widely adopted by central banks outside the United States.

Costs and Benefits of Monetary Union

What are the costs and benefits of European monetary union? Advocates of monetary union see important *benefits*. Under a common currency, exchange-rate volatility within Europe will be reduced to zero, so trade and finance will no longer have to contend with the uncertainties about prices induced by changing exchange rates. The primary result will be a reduction in transactions costs among countries. To the extent that national financial markets are segmented, moving to a common currency may allow a more efficient allocation of capital across countries. Some believe that firm macroeconomic discipline will be preserved by having an independent European central bank committed to strict inflation targets. Perhaps the most important benefit may be political integration and stability of Western Europe—a region that has been at peace for half a century after being at war with itself for most of its recorded history.

Some economists are skeptical about the wisdom of monetary union in Europe and point to significant *costs* of such union. The dominant concern is that the individual countries will lose the use of both monetary policy and exchange rates as tools for macroeconomic adjustment. This question concerns the optimal currency area, a concept first proposed by Columbia's Robert Mundell, who won the 1999 Nobel Prize for his contributions in this field. An **optimal currency area** is one whose regions have high labor mobility or have common and synchronous aggregate supply or demand shocks. In an optimal currency area, significant changes in exchange rates are not necessary to ensure rapid macroeconomic adjustment.

Most economists believe that the United States is an optimal currency area. When the United States is faced with a shock that affects the different regions asymmetrically, labor migration tends to restore balance. For example, workers left the hard-hit northern states and migrated to the oil-rich southwestern states after the oil shocks of the 1970s.

Is Europe an optimal currency area? Some economists think it is not because of the rigidity of its wage structures and the low degree of labor mobility among the different countries. When a shock has occurred—for example, after the 1990 reunification of Germany—inflexible wages and prices led to rising inflation in the regions with a demand increase and rising unemployment in depressed regions. Monetary union might therefore condemn unfortunate regions to persistent low growth and high unemployment.

Notwithstanding these dilemmas, Europeans resolved to move ahead with monetary union. The first step was to begin transactions in Euros. The trickiest step came on January 1, 2002, when the countries of Euroland replaced their local currencies with Euro coins and notes. The Euro was launched smoothly and is now taking its place among the world's major currencies.

What is the initial balance sheet on the European Monetary Union? The creation of the Euro has removed one of the major sources of instability in the European economy—intra-European exchange-rate movements. In addition, it has led to a convergence of interest rates and inflation rates among different countries. On the other hand, Europe has continued to experience high unemployment rates since the Euro's introduction. Moreover, Europe has yet to face a major economic crisis, and that will be the ultimate test of this revolutionary new institution.

The European Monetary Union is one of history's great economic experiments. Never before has such a large and powerful group of countries turned its economic fortunes over to a multinational body like the European Central Bank. Never before has a central bank been charged with the macroeconomic fortunes of a large group of nations with 300 million people producing $7 trillion of goods and services. While optimists point to the microeconomic benefits of a larger market and lower transactions costs, pessimists worry that monetary union threatens stagnation and unemployment because of the lack of price and wage flexibility and insufficient labor mobility among countries. To date, the Euro and the European Central Bank have functioned in a satisfactory manner.

FINAL ASSESSMENT

This survey of international economics must acknowledge a mixed picture, with some successes and some failures. Nonetheless, if we step back from the details, an impartial jury of historians would surely rate the last half-century as one of unparalleled success for the countries of North America and Western Europe:

- *Robust economic performance.* The period has seen the most rapid and sustained economic growth in recorded history. It is the only half-century since the Industrial Revolution that has avoided a deep depression, and none of the major industrial countries have suffered from the cancer of hyperinflation.
- *The emerging monetary system.* The international monetary system continues to be a source of turmoil, with frequent crises as countries encounter balance-of-payments or currency crises. Nonetheless, we can see an emerging system in which the major economic regions—the United States, Europe, and Japan—conduct independent monetary policies with flexible exchange rates, while smaller countries either float or have "hard" fixed exchange rates tied to one of the major blocks. One of the major tests in the coming years will be to see whether Euroland can withstand major macroeconomic shocks.
- *The reemergence of free markets.* You often hear that imitation is the sincerest from of flattery. In economics, imitation occurs when a nation adopts another nation's economic structure in the hope that it will produce growth and stability. In the last 15 years, country after country threw off the shackles of communism and stifling central planning—not because the textbooks convinced them to do so but primarily because they could see how the market-oriented countries of the West prospered while the command economies of the East collapsed. *For the first time, an empire collapsed simply because it could not produce sufficient butter along with its guns.*

SUMMARY

A. Foreign Trade and Economic Activity

1. An open economy is one that engages in international exchange of goods, services, and investments. Exports are goods and services sold to buyers outside the country, while imports are those purchased from foreigners. The difference between exports and imports of goods and services is called net exports.

2. When foreign trade is introduced, domestic demand can differ from national output. Domestic demand comprises consumption, investment, and government purchases ($C + I + G$). To obtain GDP, exports (Ex) must be added and imports (Im) subtracted, so

$$GDP = C + I + G + X$$

where X = net exports = $Ex - Im$. Imports are determined by domestic income and output along with the prices of domestic goods relative to those of foreign goods; exports are the mirror image, determined by foreign income and output along with relative prices. The dollar increase of imports for each dollar increase in GDP is called the marginal propensity to import (MPm).

3. Foreign trade has an effect on GDP similar to that of investment or government purchases. As net exports rise, there is an increase in aggregate demand for domestic output. Net exports hence have a multiplier effect on output. But the expenditure multiplier in an open economy will be smaller than that in a closed

economy because of leakages from spending into imports. The multiplier is

$$\text{Open-economy multiplier} = \frac{1}{MPS + MPm}$$

Clearly, other things equal, the open-economy multiplier is smaller than the closed-economy multiplier, where $MPm = 0$.

4. The operation of monetary policy has new implications in an open economy. An important example involves the operation of monetary policy in a small open economy that has a high degree of capital mobility. Such a country must align its interest rates with those in the countries to whom it pegs its exchange rate. This means that countries operating on a fixed exchange rate essentially lose monetary policy as an independent instrument of macroeconomic policy. Fiscal policy, by contrast, becomes a powerful instrument because fiscal stimulus is not offset by changes in interest rates.

5. An open economy operating with flexible exchange rates can use monetary policy for macroeconomic stabilization which operates independently of other countries. In this case, the international link adds another powerful channel to the domestic monetary mechanism. A monetary tightening leads to higher interest rates, attracting foreign financial capital and leading to a rise (or appreciation) of the exchange rate. The exchange-rate appreciation tends to depress net exports, so this impact reinforces the contractionary impact of higher interest rates on domestic investment.

6. The international monetary mechanism was an important factor in changing the U.S. investment pattern in the 1980s. Loose fiscal policy and tight money reduced net exports and shifted the composition of GDP away from tradeable goods to nontradeable goods.

B. Interdependence in the Global Economy

7. In the longer run, operating in the global marketplace provides new constraints and opportunities for countries to improve their economic growth. Perhaps the most important element concerns saving and investment, which are highly mobile and respond to incentives and the investment climate in different countries.

8. The foreign sector provides another source for saving and another outlet for investment. Higher domestic saving—whether through private saving or government fiscal surpluses—will increase the sum of domestic investment and net exports. Recall the identity:

$$X = S + (T - G) - I$$

or

$$\begin{aligned}\text{Net exports} = \ &\text{private saving}\\ &+ \text{government saving}\\ &- \text{domestic Investment}\end{aligned}$$

In the long run, a country's trade position primarily reflects its national saving and investment rates. Reducing a trade deficit requires changing domestic saving and investment. One important mechanism for bringing trade flows in line with domestic saving and investment is the exchange rate.

9. Besides promoting high saving and investment, countries increase their growth through a wide array of policies and institutions. Important considerations are a stable macroeconomic climate, strong property rights for both tangible investments and intellectual property, a convertible currency with few restrictions on financial flows, and political and economic stability.

C. International Economic Issues at Century's Start

10. Popular analysis looks at large trade deficits and sees "deindustrialization." But this analysis overlooks the important distinction between productivity and competitiveness. Competitiveness refers to how well a nation's goods can compete in the global marketplace and is determined primarily by relative prices. Productivity denotes the level of output per unit of input. Real incomes and living standards depend primarily upon productivity, whereas the trade and current-account positions depend upon competitiveness. There is no close linkage between competitiveness and productivity.

11. Fixed exchange rates are a source of instability in a world of highly mobile financial capital. Recall the fundamental contradiction of fixed exchange rates: A country cannot simultaneously have a fixed but adjustable exchange rate, free capital and financial movements, and an independent domestic monetary policy.

12. European countries chose to move to the "superhard" fixed exchange rates in a common currency and a unitary central bank. A common currency is appropriate when a region forms an optimal currency area. Advocates of European monetary union point to the improved predictability, lower transactions costs, and potential for better capital allocation. Skeptics worry that a common currency—like any irrevocably fixed exchange-rate system—will require flexible wages and prices to promote adjustment to macroeconomic shocks.

CONCEPTS FOR REVIEW

$C + I + G + X$ curve for open economy

net exports $= X = Ex - Im$

domestic demand vs. spending on GDP

marginal propensity to import (MPm)

multiplier:
in closed economy $= 1/MPS$
in open economy $= 1/(MPS + MPm)$
impact of trade flows and exchange rates on GDP

saving-investment identity in open economies: $X = S + (T - G) - I$

equilibration in saving-investment market in closed and open economies

growth policies in the open economy

competitiveness vs. productivity

FURTHER READING AND INTERNET WEBSITES

Further Reading

The quotation from the *Economic Report of the President, 2000* (Government Printing Office, Washington, D.C., 2000), can also be found at w3.access.gpo.gov/eop. The McKinsey study is from McKinsey Global Institute, *Manufacturing Productivity* (Washington, D.C., 1993).

Websites

Data on trade and finance for different countries can be found in the websites for Chapter 28.

Robert Mundell won the Nobel Prize in 1999 for his contribution to international macroeconomics. Visit www.nobel.se/laureates to read about his contribution. The quotation from Krugman is from his article in *Slate*, at slate.msn.com/Dismal/99-10-18/Dismal.asp, describing Mundell's accomplishments.

The website of the European Central Bank at www.ecb.int explains some of the issues involved in the management of the Euro. Also see the sites listed for Chapter 28.

QUESTIONS FOR DISCUSSION

1. Assume that an expansionary monetary policy leads to a decline or depreciation of the U.S. dollar relative to the currencies of America's trading partners in the short run with unemployed resources. Explain the mechanism by which this will produce an economic expansion in the United States. Explain how the trade impact reinforces the impact on domestic investment.

2. Explain the short-run impact upon net exports and GDP of the following in the multiplier model, using Table 30-1 where possible:
   a. An increase in investment (I) of $100 billion
   b. A decrease in government purchases (G) of $50 billion
   c. An increase of foreign output which increased exports by $10 billion

   d. A depreciation of the exchange rate that raised exports by $30 billion and lowered imports by $20 billion at every level of GDP

3. What would the expenditure multiplier be in an economy without government spending or taxes where the MPC is 0.8 and the MPm is 0? Where the MPm is 0.1? Where the MPm is 0.9? Explain why the multiplier might even be less than 1.

4. Consider Table 30-3.
   a. Explain each of the entries in the table.
   b. Add another column with the heading "Change in interest rates" to Table 30-3. Then, on the basis of the graph in Figure 30-7, fill in the table for a closed economy.

5. An eminent macroeconomist recently wrote: "Moving toward a monetary union by adopting a common currency is not really about the currency. The most important factor is that countries in the union must agree on a single monetary policy for the entire region." Explain this statement. Why might adopting a single monetary policy cause troubles?

6. Consider the city of New Heaven, which is a very open economy. The city exports reliquaries and has no investment or taxes. The city's residents consume 50 percent of their disposable incomes, and 90 percent of all purchases are imports from the rest of the country. The mayor proposes levying a tax of $100 million to spend on a public-works program. Mayor Cains argues that output and incomes in the city will rise nicely because of something called "the multiplier." Estimate the impact of the public-works program on the incomes and output of New Heaven. Do you agree with the mayor's assessment?

7. Review the bulleted list of the three interactions of saving, investment, and trade on page 632. Make a graph like that of Figure 30-8 to illustrate each of the impacts. Make sure that you can explain the reverse cases mentioned in the paragraph that follows the bulleted list.

8. Politicians often decry the large trade deficit of the United States. Economists reply that to reduce the trade deficit would require a tax increase or a cut in government expenditures. Explain the economists' view using the analysis of the saving-investment balance in Figure 30-8. Also, explain the quotation from the *Economic Report 2000* on page 620.

9. Consider a country like Russia, which is trying to make a transition to the market. It has had high inflation, many changes in its tax treatment of foreign investment, political instability (including civil wars in Chechnya), and highly uncertain and variable property rights. Explain why each of these factors would reduce the attractiveness of investment in Russia, and use your discussion to explain the risk premium on investment in Figure 30-9.

10. Consider the example of small open economies like Belgium and the Netherlands that have highly mobile

financial capital and fixed exchange rates but also have high government budget deficits. Suppose that these countries find themselves in a depressed economic condition, with low output and high unemployment. Explain why they cannot use monetary policy to stimulate their economies. Why would fiscal expansion be effective if they could tolerate higher budget deficits? Why would a depreciation of the exchange rate produce both higher output and a lower government deficit?

11. **Advanced problem.** After the reunification of Germany, payments to rebuild the former East Germany led to a major expansion of aggregate demand in Germany. The German central bank responded by slowing money growth and driving up German real interest rates. These actions took place in the context of the European Monetary System, in which most countries had fixed exchange rates and where the German central bank was dominant in monetary policy.

   a. Explain why European countries having fixed exchange rates and following the lead of the German central bank would find their interest rates rising along with German interest rates. Explain why other European countries would thereby be plunged into deep recessions.

   b. Explain why countries would prefer the European Monetary Union to the earlier system.

   c. Trace through why this German monetary tightening would be expected to lead to a depreciation of the dollar. Explain why the depreciation would stimulate economic activity in the United States.

12. **Advanced problem.** Reread the definition of the fundamental contradiction as well as the discussion by Paul Krugman on page 637. Explain why the three elements cannot go together. Use this result to explain the European monetary crisis of 1989–1993. Why is there not a fundamental contradiction for the fixed-exchange-rate system between "California dollars" and "Texas dollars." Explain the arguments for and against each of the three "possible" choices in the contradiction described by Krugman.

Unemployment, Inflation, and Economic Policy

Unemployment and the Foundations of Aggregate Supply

Be nice to people on your way up because you'll meet them on your way down.

Wilson Mizner

Among the durable features of a market economy are the periodic recessions or depressions in which unemployment rises sharply and the expansions when unemployment melts away as the economy grows rapidly. The United States enjoyed an extraordinary decade of expansion and declining unemployment over the 1990s. From the trough of the recession in 1992 to the peak of the expansion in 2001, the U.S. economy added more than 35 million jobs. The next 2 years were ones of slow growth, with a period of employment decline.

This pattern is seen with multiple variations in other countries around the world. Europe and Japan were not as fortunate as the United States in the 1990s and experienced persistently high unemployment. Although better understanding of macroeconomics has allowed most countries to avoid the worst depressions, occasional bouts of high unemployment continue to plague many market economies.

In the present chapter, we first review the foundations of aggregate supply and see how unemployment is determined by the interaction of aggregate supply and demand. We then examine the major policy issues surrounding unemployment.

A. THE FOUNDATIONS OF AGGREGATE SUPPLY

Earlier chapters focused on aggregate demand and economic growth. This section describes the factors determining aggregate supply, which is critical for understanding the evolution of the economy. In the short run, the nature of the inflationary process and the effectiveness of government countercyclical policies depend on aggregate demand. In the long run of a decade or more, economic growth and rising living standards are closely linked with increases in aggregate supply.

This distinction between short-run and long-run aggregate supply is crucial to modern macroeconomics. In the short run, it is the interaction of aggregate supply and demand that determines business-cycle fluctuations, inflation, unemployment, recessions, and booms. But in the long run, it is the growth of potential output working through aggregate supply which explains the trend in output and living standards.

Let's start with a few definitions. Recall that **aggregate supply** describes the behavior of the production side of the economy. The **aggregate supply curve,** or *AS* curve, is the schedule showing the level of total national output that will be produced at each possible price level, other things being equal.

In analyzing aggregate supply, it is crucial to distinguish *AS* curves according to the period. The short run of up to a few years involves the **short-run aggregate supply schedule.** Aggregate supply in the short run is seen as an *upward-sloping AS* curve—one along which higher prices are associated with increases in the production of goods and services.

For the long run (several years or a decade or more), we look at the **long-run aggregate supply schedule.** This relationship is shown as a *vertical AS* schedule, one in which increases in the price level are not associated with an increase in total output supplied.

This section is devoted to explaining these central points.

DETERMINANTS OF AGGREGATE SUPPLY

Aggregate supply depends fundamentally upon two distinct sets of forces: potential output and input costs. Let us examine each of these influences.

Potential Output

The key concept for understanding aggregate supply is *potential output* or *potential GDP.* **Potential output** is the maximum sustainable output that can be produced without triggering rising inflationary pressures.

Over the long run, aggregate supply depends primarily upon potential output. Hence, long-run *AS* is determined by the same factors which influence long-run economic growth: the amount and quality of available labor, the quantity of machines and other capital goods used by workers, and the level of technology. The analysis of long-run growth trends therefore concerns both the growth of potential output and the determination of aggregate supply.

For quantitative purposes, macroeconomists generally use the following definition of potential output:

Potential GDP is the highest sustainable level of national output. We measure potential GDP as the output that would be produced at a benchmark level of the unemployment rate called the *nonaccelerating inflation rate of unemployment* (or the *NAIRU*). Current estimates of the NAIRU for the United States are in the range of 5 to 6 percent of the labor force.

Potential output is a growing target. As the economy grows, potential output increases as well, and the aggregate supply curve shifts to the right. Table 31-1 shows the key determinants of aggregate supply, broken down into factors affecting potential output and production costs. From our analysis of economic growth, we know that the prime factors determining the growth in potential output are the growth in inputs and technological progress.

> ### Potential Output Is Not Maximum Output
>
> We must emphasize a subtle point about potential output: Potential output is the maximum sustainable output but not the absolute maximum output that an economy can produce. The economy can operate with output levels above potential output for a short time, and indeed this was the situation during the long economic expansion of the late 1990s. Factories and workers can work overtime for a while, but production above potential is not indefinitely sustainable. If the economy produces more than its potential output for long, price inflation tends to rise as unemployment falls, factories are worked intensively, and workers and businesses try to extract higher wages and profits.
>
> A useful analogy is someone running a marathon. Think of potential output as the maximum speed that a marathoner can run without becoming "overheated" and dropping out from exhaustion. Clearly, the runner can run faster than the sustainable pace for a while, just as the U.S. economy grew faster than its potential growth rate during the 1990s. But over the entire course, the economy, like the marathoner, can produce only at a maximum sustainable "speed," and this sustainable output speed is what we call potential output.

Variable	Impact on aggregate supply
Potential output	
Inputs	Supplies of capital, labor, and land are the important inputs. Potential output comes when unemployment of labor and other resources is at noninflationary levels. Growth of inputs increases potential output and aggregate supply.
Technology and efficiency	Innovation, technological improvement, and increased efficiency increase the level of potential output and raise aggregate supply.
Production costs	
Wages	Lower wages lead to lower production costs; lower costs mean that quantity supplied will be higher at every price level for a given potential output.
Import prices	A decline in foreign prices or an appreciation in the exchange rate reduces import prices. This leads to lower production costs and raises aggregate supply.
Other input costs	Lower oil prices or less burdensome environmental regulation lowers production costs and thereby raises aggregate supply.

TABLE 31-1. Aggregate Supply Depends upon Potential Output and Production Costs

Aggregate supply relates total output supplied to the price level. Behind the *AS* curve lie fundamental factors of productivity as represented by potential output as well as production costs. Listed factors would increase aggregate supply, shifting the *AS* curve down or to the right.

Input Costs

The aggregate supply curve is affected not only by potential output but also by changes in the costs of production. As production costs rise, businesses are willing to supply a given level of output only at a higher price. For example, if input costs rose so much that production costs exactly doubled, the price at which businesses would supply each level of output would also double. The *AS* curve would shift upward so that each output *AS* pair (P, Q) would be replaced by $(2P, Q)$.

Table 31-1 above shows some of the cost factors affecting aggregate supply. By far the most important cost is labor earnings, which constitute about three-quarters of the overall cost of production for a country like the United States. For the small open economies like the Netherlands or Hong Kong, import costs play an even greater role than wages in determining aggregate supply.

How can we graph the relationship between potential output, costs, and aggregate supply? Figure 31-1 on page 648 illustrates the effect of changes in potential output and in costs on aggregate supply. The left-hand panel shows that an increase in potential output with no change in production costs would shift the aggregate supply curve outward from *AS* to *AS'*. If production costs were to increase with no change in potential output, the curve would shift straight up from *AS* to *AS''*, as shown in Figure 31-1(*b*).

The real-world shifting of *AS* is displayed in Figure 31-2. The curves are realistic empirical estimates for two different years, 1982 and 2000. The vertical lines, marked Q^p and $Q^{p'}$, indicate the levels of potential output in the two years. According to studies, real potential output grew about 67 percent over this period.

The figure shows how the *AS* curve shifted outward and upward over the period. The *outward* shift was caused by the increase in potential output that came from growth in the labor force and capital as well as from improvements in technology. The *upward* shift was caused by increases in the cost of production, as wages, import prices, and other production costs rose. Putting together the cost increases and the potential-output growth gives the aggregate supply shift shown in Figure 31-2.

(a) Increase in Potential Output

(b) Increase in Costs

FIGURE 31-1. How Do Growth in Potential Output and Cost Increases Affect Aggregate Supply?

In **(a)**, growth in potential output with unchanged production costs shifts the *AS* curve rightward from *AS* to *AS'*. When production costs increase, say, because of higher wages or import costs, but with unchanged potential output, the *AS* curve shifts vertically upward, as from *AS* to *AS''* in **(b)**.

Aggregate Supply and Potential Output

FIGURE 31-2. In Reality, Aggregate Supply Shifts Combine Cost Increases and Increased Potential Output

Between 1982 and 2000, potential output grew due to increases in capital and labor inputs along with technological improvements. At the same time, increases in wages and other costs meant that the price level at which businesses would produce the economy's potential output increased.

AGGREGATE SUPPLY IN THE SHORT RUN AND LONG RUN

How do shifts in aggregate demand affect output and employment? This question engages one of the major controversies about modern macroeconomics—the determination of aggregate supply.

The major bone of contention is how aggregate supply responds to changes in demand. Economists of the **Keynesian school** believe that changes in aggregate demand have a significant and lasting effect on output. Hence, if aggregate demand falls because of a monetary tightening or a falloff in consumer spending, Keynesians hold that this will in the short run lead to falling output and employment. In terms of our curves, this means that the *AS* curve is relatively flat in the short run; a decline in *AD* will therefore lead to a small decline in prices but a relatively large decrease in output.

A contrary view is represented by the **classical approach** to macroeconomics. This school emphasizes that the price mechanism contains powerful equilibrating forces that will keep the economy near full employment without any government actions; consequently, there is little involuntary unemployment. In terms of the *AS* function, the classical approach holds that the *AS* curve is very steep or even vertical; changes in aggregate demand therefore have little effect on output.

Which view is correct? Actually, each view has merit in certain circumstances, as is illustrated in Figure 31-3. The key difference is the time period of the analysis. The short-run *AS* curve on the left is upward-sloping or Keynesian. It indicates that firms are willing to increase their output levels in response to changes in aggregate demand, particularly when there is slack in the economy. But the expansion of output cannot go on forever. As output increases, labor shortages appear and factories operate close to capacity. Wages and prices begin to rise more rapidly. A larger fraction of the response to aggregate demand increase comes in the form of price increases and a smaller fraction comes in output increases.

Figure 31-3(*b*) shows what happens in the long run—after wages and prices have had time to react. When all adjustments have taken place, the long-run *AS* curve becomes vertical or classical. In the long-run and classical case, the level of output supplied is independent of aggregate demand.

FIGURE 31-3. *AS* Is Relatively Flat in the Short Run but Turns Vertical in the Long Run

The short-run *AS* curve in (**a**) slopes upward because many costs are inflexible in the short run. But inflexible prices and wages become unstuck as time passes, so the long-run *AS* curve in (**b**) is vertical and output is determined by potential output. Can you see why a Keynesian economist in (**a**) might desire to stabilize the economy through demand-management policies while a classical economist in (**b**) would concentrate primarily on increasing potential output?

Why Do Short-Run AS and Long-Run AS Differ?

Why does aggregate supply behave differently in the long and short runs? Why do firms raise both prices and output in the short run as aggregate demand increases? Why, by contrast, do increases in demand lead to price changes with little output change in the long run?

The key to these puzzles lies in the behavior of wages and prices in a modern market economy. Some elements of business costs are *inflexible* or *sticky* in the short run. As a result of this inflexibility, businesses can profit from higher levels of aggregate demand by producing more output.

Suppose that concerns over national security lead to an increase in defense spending. Firms know that in the short run many of their production costs are fixed in dollar terms—workers are paid $15 per hour, rent is $1500 per month, and so forth. In response to the higher demand, firms will generally raise their output prices and increase production. This positive association between prices and output is seen in the upward-sloping AS curve in Figure 31-3(*a*).

We have spoken repeatedly of "sticky" or "inflexible" costs. What are some examples? The most significant is wages. For a variety of reasons, wages adjust slowly when economic conditions change. Take unionized workers as an example. They are usually paid according to a long-term union contract which specifies a dollar wage rate. For the life of the labor agreement, the wage rate faced by the firm will be largely fixed in dollar terms. It is quite rare for wages to be raised more than once a year even for nonunion workers. It is even more uncommon for money wages or salaries actually to be cut, except when a company is visibly facing the threat of bankruptcy.[1]

Other prices and costs are similarly sticky in the short run. When a firm rents a building, the lease will often last for a year or more and the rental is generally set in dollar terms. In addition, firms often sign contracts with their suppliers specifying the prices to be paid for materials or components. Some prices are fixed by government regulation, particularly those for utilities like electricity, water, and local telephone service.

Putting all these cases together, you can see how a certain short-run stickiness of wages and prices exists in a modern market economy.

What happens in the long run? Eventually, the inflexible or sticky elements of cost—wage contracts, rent agreements, regulated prices, and so forth—become unstuck and negotiable. Firms cannot take advantage of fixed-money wage rates in their labor agreements forever; labor will soon recognize that prices have risen and insist on compensating increases in wages. Ultimately, all costs will adjust to the higher output prices. If the general price level rises by *x* percent because of the higher demand, then money wages, rents, regulated prices, and other costs will in the end respond by moving up around *x* percent as well.

Once costs have adjusted upward as much as prices, firms will be unable to profit from the higher level of aggregate demand. In the long run, after all elements of cost have fully adjusted, firms will face the same ratio of price to costs as they did before the change in demand. There will be no incentive for firms to increase their output. The long-run AS curve therefore tends to be vertical, which means that output supplied is independent of the level of prices and costs.

The aggregate supply for an economy will differ from potential output in the short run because of inflexible elements of costs. In the short run, firms will respond to higher demand by raising both production and prices. In the longer run, as costs respond to the higher level of prices, most or all of the response to increased demand takes the form of higher prices and little or none the form of higher output. Whereas the short-run AS curve is upward-sloping, the long-run AS curve is vertical because, given sufficient time, all costs adjust.

B. UNEMPLOYMENT

In the early 2000s, in the wake of the stock market decline, terrorist attacks, accounting scandals, and war, the number of unemployed in the United States rose by 2½ million persons. Most of these were "job losers," people who lost their jobs involuntarily. In earlier periods, such as the Great Depression or the early 1980s, the unemployment rate rose much more, reaching an all-time high of 25 percent in 1933.

---

[1] See the study by Bewley in this chapter's Further Reading section for a discussion of why wages are sticky.

The presence of involuntary unemployment in a market economy raises troubling questions: How can millions of people be unemployed when there is so much work to be done? What flaw in a modern mixed economy forces so many who want work to remain idle? To what extent is high unemployment primarily due to flawed government programs (such as unemployment insurance) that reduce the incentive to work? Or is the cause rooted in wage and price dynamics? The balance of this chapter provides a tour of the meaning of unemployment and some answers to these important questions.

MEASURING UNEMPLOYMENT

Changes in the unemployment rate make monthly headlines. Look back to Figure 20-3 on page 411 to refresh your memory about the long-term trend. You can also look forward to Figure 32-10 on page 682 to compare the unemployment rate with the NAIRU. What lies behind the numbers?[2] Statistics on unemployment and the labor force are among the most carefully designed and comprehensive economic data the nation collects. The data are gathered monthly in a procedure known as *random sampling* of the population.[3] Each month about 60,000 households are interviewed about their recent work history.

The survey divides the population of those 16 years and older into four groups:[4]

---

[2] For data on and methods for estimating employment and unemployment, see the website listings in this chapter's Further Reading section.

[3] Random sampling is an essential technique for estimating the behavior or characteristics of an entire population. It consists of choosing a subgroup of the population at random (say, by selecting telephone digits through a computer-generated series of random numbers) and then surveying the selected group. Random sampling is used in many social sciences, as well as in market research.

[4] The following classifications from the Bureau of Labor Statistics give the complete definitions for the United States: People are classified as *employed* if they did any work at all as paid employees during the reference week; worked in their own business or profession or on their own farm; or worked without pay at least 15 hours in a family business or farm. People are also counted as employed if they were temporarily absent from their jobs because of illness, bad weather, vacation, labor-management disputes, or personal reasons.

People are classified as *unemployed* if they meet all of the following criteria: They had no employment during the reference week; they were available for work at that time; and they made specific efforts to find employment sometime during the 4-week period ending with the reference week. Persons laid off from a job and expecting recall are counted as unemployed.

- **Employed.** These are people who perform any paid work, as well as those who have jobs but are absent from work because of illness, strikes, or vacations.
- **Unemployed.** This group includes people who are not employed but are actively looking for work or waiting to return to work. To be counted as unemployed, a person must do more than simply think about work. A person must report specific efforts to find a job (such as having a job interview or sending out resumes).
- **Not in the labor force.** This includes the 34 percent of the adult population that is keeping house, retired, too ill to work, or simply not looking for work.
- **Labor force.** This includes all those who are either employed or unemployed.

Figure 31-4 shows how the male and female populations in the United States are divided among the categories of employed, unemployed, and not in the labor force. (The status of students is examined in question 6 at the end of this chapter.)

The definition of labor-force status used by the government is the following:

People with jobs are employed; people without jobs but looking for work are unemployed; people without jobs who are not looking for work are outside the labor force. The **unemployment rate** is the number of unemployed divided by the total labor force.

IMPACT OF UNEMPLOYMENT

High unemployment is both an economic and a social problem. Unemployment is an economic problem because it represents waste of a valuable resource. Unemployment is a major social problem because it causes enormous suffering as unemployed workers struggle with reduced incomes. During periods of high unemployment, economic distress spills over to affect people's emotions and family lives.

Economic Impact

When the unemployment rate goes up, the economy is in effect throwing away the goods and services that the unemployed workers could have produced. During recessions, it is as if vast quantities of automobiles, housing, clothing, and other commodities were simply dumped into the ocean.

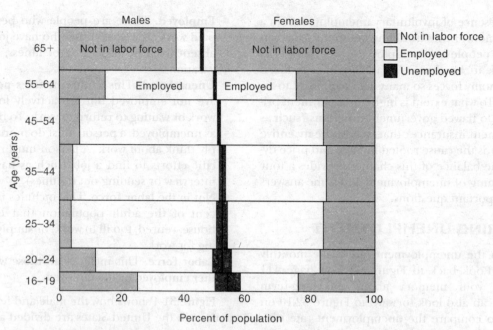

FIGURE 31-4. Labor-Force Status of the Population, 2003

How do Americans spend their time? This figure shows how males and females of different ages are divided among employed, unemployed, and not in the labor force. The size of each block indicates the relative proportion of the population in the designated category. Note the continuing difference in labor-force behavior of men and women.

Source: U.S. Department of Labor, *Employment and Earnings*.

How much waste results from high unemployment? What is the opportunity cost of recessions? Table 31-2 provides a calculation of how far output fell short of potential GDP during the major periods of high unemployment over the last half-century. The largest economic loss occurred during the Great Depression, but the oil and inflation crises of the 1970s and 1980s also generated more than a trillion dollars of lost output. Since 1992, the U.S. economy has grown rapidly, with a very mild slowdown following the stock market decline, terrorist attacks, and heightened concerns about security.

The economic losses during periods of high unemployment are the greatest documented wastes in a modern economy. They are many times larger than the estimated inefficiencies from microeconomic waste due to monopoly or from the waste induced by tariffs and quotas.

Social Impact

The economic cost of unemployment is certainly large, but no dollar figure can adequately convey the human and psychological toll of long periods of persistent involuntary unemployment. The personal tragedy of unemployment has been proved again and again. We can read of the futility of a job search in San Francisco during the Great Depression:

> I'd get up at five in the morning and head for the waterfront. Outside the Spreckles Sugar Refinery, outside the gates, there would be a thousand men. You know dang well there's only three or four jobs. The guy would come out with two little Pinkerton cops: "I need two guys for the bull gang. Two guys to go into the hole." A thousand men would fight like a pack of Alaskan dogs to get through. Only four of us would get through.[5]

Or we can listen to the recollection of an unemployed construction worker:

> I called the roofing outfits and they didn't need me because they already had men that had been working for them five or six years. There wasn't that many

---

[5] Studs Terkel, *Hard Times: An Oral History of the Great Depression in America* (Pantheon, New York, 1970).

	Average unemployment rate (%)	Lost Output	
		GDP loss ($, billion, 2003 prices)	As percentage of GDP during the period
Great Depression (1930–1939)	18.2	2,560	27.6
Oil and inflation crises (1975–1984)	7.7	1,570	3.0
Post-new-economy slump (2001–2003)	5.5	220	0.2

TABLE 31-2. Economic Costs from Periods of High Unemployment

The two major periods of high unemployment since 1929 occurred during the Great Depression and during the oil shocks and high inflation from 1975 to 1984. The lost output is calculated as the cumulative difference between potential GDP and actual GDP. Note that during the Great Depression losses relative to GDP were almost 10 times greater than losses in the oil-inflation slump. The slowdown in the early 2000s was mild by comparison to earlier downturns.

Source: Authors' estimates on the basis of official GDP and unemployment data.

openings. You had to have a college education for most of them. And I was looking for anything, from car wash to anything else.

So what do you do all day? You go home and you sit. And you begin to get frustrated sitting home. Everybody in the household starts getting on edge. They start arguing with each other over stupid things 'cause they're all cramped in that space all the time. The whole family kind of got crushed by it.[6]

It would be surprising if such experiences did not leave scars. Psychological studies indicate that being fired from a job is generally as traumatic as the death of a close friend or failure in school. Nevertheless, unemployment is not limited to the unskilled, as many well-paid managers, professionals, and white-collar workers learned in the corporate downsizings of the last two decades. Listen to the story of one middle-aged corporate manager who lost his job in 1988 and was still without permanent work in 1992:

I have lost the fight to stay ahead in today's economy. . . . I was determined to find work, but as the months and years wore on, depression set in. You can only be rejected so many times; then you start questioning your self-worth.[7]

---

[6] Harry Maurer, *Not Working: An Oral History of the Unemployed* (Holt, New York, 1979).

[7] *Business Week*, Mar. 23, 1992.

OKUN'S LAW

The most distressing consequence of any recession is a rise in the unemployment rate. As output falls, firms need fewer labor inputs, so new workers are not hired and current workers are laid off. The impact can be dramatic: By the end of the recession of 1981–1982, about 1 out of every 10 American workers was unemployed. It turns out that unemployment usually moves inversely with output over the business cycle. This co-movement, first identified by Arthur Okun, is known as Okun's Law.

Okun's Law states that for every 2 percent that GDP falls relative to potential GDP, the unemployment rate rises about 1 percentage point.

This means that if GDP begins at 100 percent of its potential and falls to 98 percent of potential, the unemployment rate rises by 1 percentage point, say, from 6 to 7 percent. Figure 31-5 shows how output and unemployment have moved together over time.

We can illustrate Okun's Law by examining output and unemployment trends in the 1990s. During the recession of 1991, the unemployment rate rose to 6.9 percent. At that point, actual GDP was estimated to be 2.5 percent below potential output. Then, over the next 9 years, output grew 5.8 percent faster than potential output, so that in 1999 actual GDP was estimated to be 3.3 percent above potential output.

FIGURE 31-5. Okun's Law Illustrated, 1955–2002

According to Okun's Law, whenever output grows 2 percent faster than potential GDP, the unemployment rate declines 1 percentage point. This graph shows that unemployment changes are well predicted by the rate of GDP growth. What output growth would lead to no change in unemployment according to the line?

Source: U.S. Departments of Commerce and Labor.

According to Okun's Law, the unemployment rate should have fallen by 2.9 percentage points (5.8/2) to 4.0 percent (6.9 − 2.9). In fact, the unemployment rate for 1999 was 4.2 percent—a remarkably accurate prediction. This shows how Okun's Law can be used to relate changes in the unemployment rate to the growth in output.

One important consequence of Okun's Law is that actual GDP must grow as rapidly as potential GDP just to keep the unemployment rate from rising. In a sense, GDP has to keep running just to keep unemployment in the same place. Moreover, if you want to bring the unemployment rate down, actual GDP must be growing faster than potential GDP.

Okun's Law provides the vital link between the output market and the labor market. It describes the association between short-run movements in real GDP and changes in unemployment.

Unemployment and Politics
Unemployment is one of the most important issues to voters. When unemployment is high during election years, incumbent politicians are often thrown out of office. During depressions and recessions, as in 1932, 1960, 1980, and 1992, incumbent parties lost the White House. By contrast, in boom years with low unemployment (like 1964, 1972, 1984, and 1996), incumbents were reelected.

Suppose you are the economic adviser to President Mary James, who has just been elected. Here is the dialogue:

PRESIDENT JAMES: Unemployment is too high. I would like fiscal and monetary policy to get the unemployment rate down from 7 percent to 5 percent by the time we are running for reelection. How fast must the economy grow over the next 4 years to meet my target?

CHIEF ECONOMIST: We can figure that out from Okun's Law. The economy must grow at the growth rate of potential GDP (about 3 percent annually for the United States today), *plus* enough to reduce the unemployment rate about ½ percentage point each year. The average annual growth rate for GDP must then be 3 percent for trend plus 1 percent to reduce unemployment. Therefore, we must target a growth rate of real GDP of 4 percent per year until the election.

Make sure that you can explain the reasoning of the chief economist.

ECONOMIC INTERPRETATION OF UNEMPLOYMENT

Let's turn now to the economic analysis of unemployment. Some of the important questions we address are: What are the reasons for being unemployed? What is the distinction between "voluntary" and "involuntary" unemployment? What is the relationship between different kinds of unemployment and the business cycle?

Three Kinds of Unemployment

In sorting out the structure of labor markets, economists identify three different kinds of unemployment: frictional, structural, and cyclical.

Frictional unemployment arises because of the incessant movement of people between regions and jobs or through different stages of the life cycle. Even if an economy were at full employment, there would always be some turnover as students search for jobs when they graduate from school or parents reenter the labor force after having children. Because frictionally unemployed workers are often moving between jobs, or looking for better jobs, it is often thought that they are *voluntarily unemployed*.

Structural unemployment signifies a mismatch between the supply of and the demand for workers. Mismatches can occur because the demand for one kind of labor is rising while the demand for another kind is falling and supplies do not quickly adjust. We often see structural imbalances across occupations or regions as certain sectors grow while others decline. For example, an acute shortage of nurses arose in the mid-1980s as the number of nurses grew slowly while the demand for nursing care grew rapidly because of an aging population and other forces. Not until nurses' salaries rose rapidly and the supply adjusted did the structural shortage of nurses decline. By contrast, the demand for coal miners has been depressed for decades because of the lack of geographic mobility of labor and capital; unemployment rates in coal-mining communities remain high today. In European countries, high real wages, welfare benefits, and taxes have created high levels of structural unemployment for entire economies over the last decade.

Cyclical unemployment exists when the overall demand for labor is low. As total spending and output fall, unemployment rises virtually everywhere. In the recession year 1982, the unemployment rate rose in 48 of the 50 states. This simultaneous rise in unemployment in many markets signaled that the increased unemployment was largely cyclical. Similarly, from the recession's trough in 1991 to the boom year of 2000, the unemployment rate fell in every state in the United States.

The distinction between cyclical, frictional, and structural unemployment helps economists diagnose the general health of the labor market. High levels of frictional or structural unemployment can occur even though the overall labor market is in balance, for example, when turnover is high or when high minimum wages price certain groups out of the labor force. Cyclical unemployment occurs during recessions, when employment falls as a result of an imbalance between aggregate supply and demand.

Microeconomic Foundations

On the face of it, the cause of unemployment seems clear: too many workers chasing too few jobs. Yet this simple phenomenon has presented a tremendous puzzle for economists for 60 years. Experience shows that prices rise or fall to clear competitive markets. At the market-clearing price, buyers willingly buy what sellers willingly sell. But something is gumming up the workings of the labor market when many hospitals are searching for nurses but cannot find them while thousands of coal miners want to work at the going wage but cannot find a job. Similar symptoms of labor market failures are found in all market economies.

Economists look to the microeconomics of labor markets to help understand the existence of unemployment. Although no universally accepted theory has emerged, many analysts believe that unemployment arises because wages are not flexible enough to clear markets. We explore below why wages are inflexible and why inflexible wages lead to involuntary unemployment.

Voluntary and Involuntary Unemployment

Let us first start by examining the causes of *voluntary unemployment* in a typical labor market. A group of workers has a labor supply schedule shown as *SS* in Figure 31-6 on page 656. The supply curve becomes completely inelastic at labor quantity L^* when wage levels are high. We will call L^* the labor force.

The left-hand panel of Figure 31-6 shows the usual picture of competitive supply and demand, with a market equilibrium at point *E* and a wage of W^*. At the competitive, market-clearing equilibrium, firms willingly hire all qualified workers who desire to work at the market wage. The number of employed is represented by the line from *A* to *E*. Some members of the labor force would like to work, but only at a higher wage rate. These unemployed workers, represented by the segment *EF*, are voluntarily unemployed in the sense that they choose not to work at the market wage rate.

The existence of voluntary unemployment implies an often misunderstood point: *Unemployment may be an efficient outcome in a situation where heterogeneous workers are searching for and testing different kinds of jobs.* The voluntarily unemployed workers might prefer leisure or other activities to jobs at the going wage rate. Or they may be frictionally unemployed, perhaps searching for their first job. Or they might be low-productivity workers who prefer retirement or unemployment insurance to low-paid work. There are countless reasons

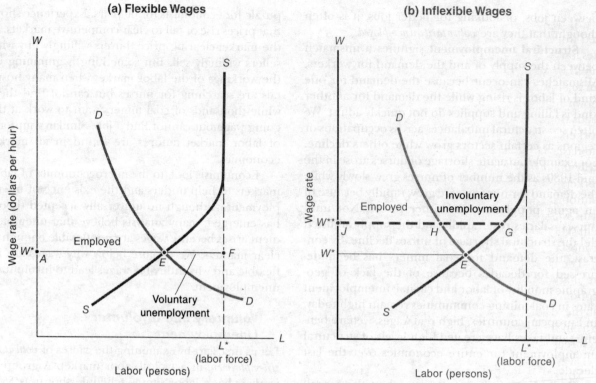

FIGURE 31-6. **Inflexible Wages Can Lead to Involuntary Unemployment**

We can depict different kinds of unemployment by using the microeconomic supply-and-demand framework. In **(a)**, wages move to W^* to clear the labor market. All unemployment is voluntary. Part **(b)** shows what happens if wages do not adjust to clear the labor market. At the too high wage at W^{**}, JH workers are employed, but HG workers are involuntarily unemployed. Many believe that **(a)** resembles the flexible labor market of the United States while **(b)** shows the impact of high labor taxes, comprehensive minimum wages, and generous social-welfare legislation in Europe.

why people might voluntarily choose not to work at the going wage rate, and yet these people might be counted as unemployed in the official statistics.

But now go back to reread the quotations from unemployed workers on pages 652–653. Who would seriously argue that these workers are voluntarily unemployed? They surely do not sound like people carefully balancing the value of work against the value of leisure. Nor do they resemble people choosing unemployment as they search for a better job. We simply cannot reconcile the experience of many unemployed workers with an elegant classical theory of voluntary unemployment. One of Keynes's great breakthroughs was to let the facts oust this beautiful but irrelevant theory. He explained why we see occasional bouts of involuntary

unemployment, periods in which qualified workers are unable to get jobs at the going wage rates.

The key to his approach was to note that wages do not adjust to clear labor markets. Instead, wages tend to respond sluggishly to economic shocks. If wages do not move to clear markets, a mismatch between job seekers and job vacancies can arise. This mismatch may lead to the patterns of unemployment that we see today.

We can understand how inflexible wages lead to involuntary unemployment with an analysis of a *non-clearing labor market*, shown in Figure 31-6(*b*). Here, an economic disturbance leaves the labor market with too high a wage rate. Labor's wage is at W^{**} rather than at the equilibrium or market-clearing wage of W^*.

At the too high wage rate, there are more qualified workers looking for work than there are vacancies looking for workers. The number of workers willing to work at wage W^{**} is at point G on the supply curve, but firms want to hire only H workers, as shown by the demand curve. Because the wage exceeds the market-clearing level, there is a surplus of workers. The unemployed workers represented by the dashed line segment HG are said to be **involuntarily unemployed,** signifying that they are qualified workers who want to work at the prevailing wage but cannot find jobs. When there is a surplus of workers, firms will ration out the jobs by setting more stringent skill requirements and hiring the most qualified or most experienced workers.

The opposite case occurs when the wage is below the market-clearing rate. Here, in a labor-shortage economy, employers cannot find enough workers to fill the existing vacancies. Firms put help-wanted signs in their windows, advertise in newspapers, and even recruit people from other towns.

Sources of Wage Inflexibility

The theory of involuntary unemployment assumes that wages are inflexible. But this raises a further question: Why do wages not move up or down to clear markets? Why are labor markets not like the auction markets for grain, corn, and common stocks?

These questions are among the deepest unresolved mysteries of modern economics. Few economists today would argue that wages move quickly to erase labor shortages and surpluses. Yet no one completely understands the reasons for the sluggish behavior of wages and salaries. We can therefore provide no more than a tentative assessment of the sources of wage inflexibility.

A helpful distinction is that between auction markets and administered markets. An *auction market* is a highly organized and competitive market where the price floats up or down to balance supply and demand. At the Chicago Board of Trade, for example, the price of "number 2 hard red wheat delivered in Kansas City" or "dressed 'A' broiler chickens delivered in New York" changes every minute to reflect market conditions—market conditions that are seen in frantic buy and sell orders of farmers, millers, packers, merchants, and speculators.

Most goods and all labor are sold in administered markets and not in competitive auction markets. Nobody grades labor into "grade B Web page developer" or "class AAA assistant professor of economics." No specialist burns the midnight oil trying to make sure that the wages of computer programmers or professors are set at just the market-clearing level where all qualified workers are placed into jobs.

Rather, most firms *administer* their wages and salaries, setting pay scales and hiring people at an entry-level wage or salary. These wage scales are generally fixed for a year or so, and when they are adjusted, the pay goes up for all categories. For example, a bank might have 15 different categories of staff: three grades of secretaries, two grades of tellers, and so forth. Each year, the bank managers will decide how much to increase wages and salaries—say, 3 percent in 2003 on average. Sometimes, the compensation in each category will move up by that percentage; sometimes, the firm might decide to move one category up or down more than the average. Given the procedure by which wages and salaries are determined, there is little room for major adjustments when the firm finds shortages or gluts in a particular area. Except in extreme cases, the firm will tend to adjust the minimum qualifications required for a job rather than its wages when it finds labor market disequilibrium.[8]

For unionized labor markets, the wage patterns are even more rigid. Wage scales are typically set for a 3-year contract period; during that period, wages are not adjusted for excess supply or demand in particular areas. Moreover, unionized workers seldom accept wage cuts even when many of the union's workers are unemployed.

To summarize:

Most wages in America and other market economies are administered by firms or contracts. Wages and salaries are set infrequently and adjust to meet shortages or surpluses only over an extended period of time.

---

[8] The example of college admissions illustrates the kind of adjustment that takes place when shortages or gluts occur. Many colleges found that applications for places soared in the last few years. How did they react? Did they raise their tuition enough to choke off the excess demand? No. Instead, they raised their admission standards, requiring better grades in high school and higher average SAT scores. Upgrading the requirements rather than changing wages and prices is exactly what happens in the short run when firms experience excess supply of labor.

Let's go a step further and ask, What is the economic reason for the sluggishness of wages and salaries? Many economists believe that the inflexibility arises because of the costs of administering compensation (such costs are called "menu costs"). To take the example of union wages, negotiating a contract is a long process that requires much worker and management time and produces no output. It is because collective bargaining is so costly that such agreements are generally negotiated only once every 3 years.

Setting compensation for nonunion workers is less costly, but it nevertheless requires scarce management time and has important effects on worker morale. Every time wages or salaries are set, every time fringe benefits are changed, earlier compensation agreements are changed as well. Some workers will feel the changes are unfair, others will complain about unjust procedures, and grievances may be triggered.

Personnel managers therefore prefer a system in which wages are adjusted infrequently and most workers in a firm get the same pay increase, regardless of the market conditions for different skills or categories. This system may appear inefficient to economists, because it does not allow for a perfect adjustment of wages to reflect market supply and demand. But it does economize on scarce managerial time and helps promote a sense of fair play and equity in the firm. In the end, it may be cheaper to recruit workers more actively or to change the required qualifications than to upset the entire wage structure of a firm simply to hire a few new workers.

The theory of sticky wages and involuntary unemployment holds that the slow adjustment of wages produces surpluses and shortages in individual labor markets. Labor markets are nonclearing markets in the short run. But labor markets do eventually respond to market conditions as wages of high-demand occupations move up relative to those of low-demand occupations. In the long run, major pockets of unemployment and job vacancies tend to disappear as wages and employment adjust to market conditions. But the long run may be many years, and periods of unemployment can therefore persist for many years.

LABOR MARKET ISSUES

Having analyzed the causes of unemployment, we turn next to major labor market issues for today. Which groups are most likely to be unemployed? How long are they unemployed? Why has unemployment in Europe skyrocketed in the last decade?

Who Are the Unemployed?

We can diagnose labor market conditions by comparing years in which output is above its potential (of which 1999–2000 was a recent period) with those of deep recessions (such as was seen in 1982). Differences between these years show how business cycles affect the amount, sources, duration, and distribution of unemployment.

Table 31-3 shows unemployment statistics for peak and trough years. The first two columns of numbers are the unemployment rates by age, race, and sex. These data show that the unemployment rate of every group tends to rise during recession. The last two columns show how the total pool of unemployment is distributed among different groups; observe that the distribution of unemployment across groups changes relatively little throughout the business cycle.

Note also that nonwhite workers tend to experience unemployment rates more than twice those of whites in both trough and peak periods. Until the 1980s, women tended to have higher unemployment rates than men, but in the last two decades unemployment rates differed little by gender. Teenagers, with high frictional unemployment, have generally had unemployment rates much higher than adults.

Duration of Unemployment

Another key question concerns duration. How much of the unemployment experience is long-term and of major social concern, and how much is short-term as people move quickly between jobs?

Figure 31-7 shows the duration of unemployment in 2003. A surprising feature of American labor markets is that a very large fraction of unemployment is of short duration. In 2003, one-third of unemployed workers were jobless for less than 5 weeks, and long-term unemployment was relatively rare.

In Europe, with lower mobility and greater legal obstacles to economic change, long-term unemployment in the mid-1990s reached 50 percent of the unemployed. Long-term unemployment poses a serious social problem because the resources that families have available—their savings, unemployment insurance, and goodwill toward one another—begin to run out after a few months.

Labor market group	Unemployment Rate of Different Groups (% of labor force)		Distribution of Total Unemployment across Different Groups (% of total unemployed)	
	Trough (1982)	Peak (March 2000)	Trough (1982)	Peak (March 2000)
By age:				
16–19	23.2	13.3	18.5	20.2
20 years and older	8.6	3.3	81.5	80.0
By race:				
White	8.6	3.6	77.2	77.6
Black and other	17.3	7.3	22.8	22.4
By sex (adults only):				
Male	8.8	3.8	58.5	50.5
Female	8.3	4.3	41.5	49.5
All workers	9.7	4.1	100.0	100.0

TABLE 31-3. Unemployment by Demographic Group

This table shows how unemployment varies across different demographic groups in peak and trough years. The first set of figures shows the unemployment rate for each group in 1982 and during the peak period of 2000. The last two columns show the percent of the total pool of unemployed that is in each group.

Source: U.S. Department of Labor, *Employment and Earnings*.

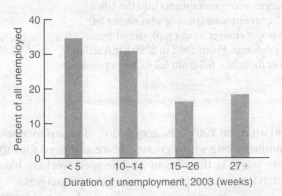

FIGURE 31-7. Most Unemployment in the United States Is Short-Term

What is the average duration of unemployment? In early 2003, shortly after a recession and during a period of slow growth, only 18 percent of the unemployed were unemployed for more than 26 weeks, while 35 percent were unemployed for less than 5 weeks. In recessions, the duration of unemployment increases. European countries with stagnant labor markets find that more than half of their unemployed have been without jobs for more than a year.

Source: Bureau of Labor Statistics, *Employment Situation Summary*, February 2003, at www.bls.gov/cps/home.htm#news.

Sources of Joblessness

Why are people unemployed? Figure 31-8 shows how people responded when asked the source of their unemployment, looking at the recession year of 1982 and the full-employment year of 2000.

There is always some frictional unemployment that results from changes in people's residence or from the life cycle—moving, entering the labor force for the first time, and so forth. The major changes in the unemployment rate over the business cycle arise from the increase in job losers. This source swells enormously in a recession for two reasons: First, the number of people who lose their jobs increases, and then it takes longer to find a new job.

Unemployment by Age

How does unemployment vary over the life cycle? Teenagers generally have the highest unemployment rate of any demographic group, and nonwhite teenagers in recent years have experienced unemployment rates between 30 and 50 percent. Is this unemployment frictional, structural, or cyclical?

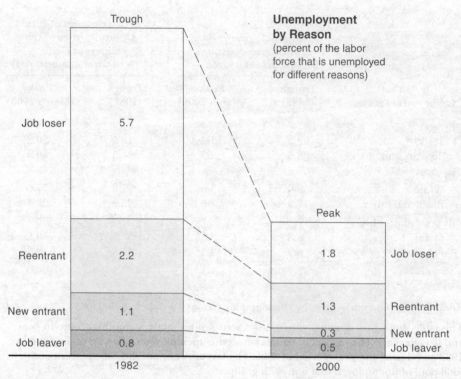

FIGURE 31-8. Distribution of Unemployment by Reason, 1982 and 2000

Why do people become unemployed? Very few were unemployed in the full-employment year of 2000 because they left their jobs, and almost 2 percent were new entrants into the labor force (say, because they just graduated from college) or reentrants (people who earlier left the labor force and are back looking for a job). The major change in unemployment from peak to trough, however, is found in the number of job losers. From 1982 to 2000 the fraction of workers who became unemployed because they lost their jobs fell from 5.7 to 1.8 percent.

Source: Bureau of Labor Statistics, at www.bls.gov/data.

Recent evidence indicates that, particularly for whites, teenage unemployment has a large frictional component. Teenagers move in and out of the labor force very frequently. They get jobs quickly and change jobs often. The average duration of teenage unemployment is only half that of adult unemployment; by contrast, the average length of a typical job is 12 times greater for adults than teenagers. In most years, half the unemployed teenagers are "new entrants" who have never had a paying job before. All these factors suggest that teenage unemployment is largely frictional; that is, it represents the job search and turnover necessary for young people to discover their personal skills and to learn what working is all about.

But teenagers do eventually learn the skills and work habits of experienced workers. Table 31-4 shows the unemployment rates at different ages for blacks and whites in 2001. The acquisition of experience and training, along with a greater desire and need for full-time work, is the reason middle-aged workers have much lower unemployment rates than teenagers.

Teenage Unemployment of Minority Groups. While most evidence suggests that unemployment is largely frictional for white teenagers, the labor market for young African-American workers has behaved quite differently. For the first decade after World War II, the labor-force participation rates and unemployment rates of black and white teenagers were virtually identical. After that time, however, unemployment rates for black teenagers rose sharply relative to those of other groups while their labor-force participation rates have fallen. By 2001, 25 percent of black teenagers (16 to 19 years of age) were employed, **compared to 42 percent**

	Unemployment Rate (% of labor force)	
Age	White	Black
16–17	15.2	31.1
18–19	11.1	27.8
20–24	6.9	16.2
25–34	4.1	8.1
35–44	3.2	6.4
45–54	2.8	4.8
55–64	2.9	3.9
65–69	2.9	4.8
70–74	2.8	3.1
Over 75	2.8	3.3

TABLE 31-4. Unemployment Rates at Different Ages, 2001

As workers search for jobs and gain training, they settle on a particular occupation; they tend to stay in the labor force; and they find a preferred employer. As a result, the unemployment rates of older people fall to a fraction of those of teenagers.

Source: U.S. Department of Labor, *Employment and Earnings,* January 2003.

of white teenagers. Figure 31-9 below compares the unemployment rates of black teenagers, white teenagers, and all male white workers.

What accounts for this extraordinary divergence in the experience of minority teenagers from that of other groups? One explanation might be that labor market forces (such as the composition or location of jobs) have worked against black workers in general. This explanation does not tell the whole story. While adult black workers have always suffered higher unemployment rates than adult white workers—because of lower education attainment, fewer contacts with people who can provide jobs, less on-the-job training, and racial discrimination—the ratio of black to white adult unemployment rates has not increased since World War II.

Numerous studies of the sources of the rising black teenage unemployment rate have turned up no clear explanations for the trend. One possible source is discrimination, but a rise in the black-white unemployment differential would require an increase in

FIGURE 31-9. Unemployment Rates of Different Groups

Unemployment rates of teenagers, especially black teenagers, have been higher than those of adult workers. The long expansion of the 1990s cut into black teenage unemployment, but the recession and slow growth of the early 2000s increased joblessness.

Source: U.S. Department of Labor, at www.bls.gov/cps/cpsatabs.htm.

racial discrimination—even in the face of increased legal protection for minority workers.

Another theory holds that a high minimum wage along with rising costs of fringe benefits tends to drive low-productivity black teenagers into unemployment. The change in the relation of the minimum wage to average wages allows a test of this hypothesis. From 1981 to 1989, the ratio of the minimum wage to average wages in nonfarm establishments fell from 46 to 34 percent, yet no improvement in the relative unemployment situation of black teenagers occurred. That no improvement took place casts doubt on the minimum wage as the prime suspect. Some conservative critics of the modern welfare state blame high unemployment of blacks on the culture of dependency that is nurtured by government aid to the poor, although there is little firm data to support this proposition.

Does high teenage unemployment lead to long-lasting labor market damage, with permanently lower levels of skills and wage rates? This question is a topic of intensive ongoing research, and the tentative answer is yes, particularly for minority teenagers. It appears that when youths are unable to develop on-the-job skills and work attitudes, they earn lower wages and experience higher unemployment when they are older. This finding suggests that public policy has an important stake in devising programs to reduce teenage unemployment among minority groups.

Unemployment: High in Europe, Low in America

While American unemployment rates fell to unusually low levels over the 1990s, European unemployment rose sharply over the last three decades. European powerhouse economies like Germany and France were unable to reduce their unemployment rates below 8 percent in the last decade. Figure 31-10 on the bottom of this page shows the unemployment history in the two regions.

How can we explain the divergent labor markets of these two regions? Part of the reason probably lies in differences in macroeconomic policies. The United States has a single central bank, the Federal Reserve, that keeps careful watch over the American economy. When unemployment

FIGURE 31-10. Unemployment in the United States and Europe

While unemployment has cycled without a marked trend in the United States, European unemployment has risen sharply over the last three decades. Some of the increase in European unemployment stems from the demand side, but the general trend stems from European labor market rigidities and social-welfare legislation.

Source: U.S. Department of Labor and OECD.

begins to rise, as it did in 1982 and again in 1991, the Fed loosened monetary policy to stimulate aggregate demand, increase output, and stem the unemployment increase.

Central banking in Europe was fragmented until very recently. Until 1999, Europe was a confederation of countries whose monetary policies were dominated by the German central bank, the Bundesbank. The Bundesbank was fiercely independent and aimed primarily at maintaining price stability *in Germany*. When unemployment rose in the rest of Europe and inflation rose in Germany—as happened after the reunification of Germany in 1990—the Bundesbank increased interest rates. This tended to depress output and raise unemployment in countries whose monetary policies were tied to Germany's. You can see this syndrome in the rise in unemployment in Europe after 1990.

A second feature of European unemployment relates to rising structural unemployment. Europe was the birthplace of the welfare state, and countries like Germany, France, and Sweden legislated generous welfare benefits, unemployment insurance, minimum wages, and job protection for workers. These policies tend to increase real wages because workers possess greater bargaining power and have more attractive alternative uses for their time. Persons who are collecting welfare or unemployment benefits might be voluntarily unemployed, but they are generally counted as unemployed in the actual statistics. The United States has been less generous in its unemployment and welfare benefits, and recent changes in

welfare laws will make welfare even less attractive relative to work in the coming years.

We can understand the divergent economies in terms of our labor market supply-and-demand diagrams in Figure 31-6. American labor market institutions resemble the flexible-wage economy shown in part (*a*). A decline in the demand for labor will lead to an equilibrium at *E*. By contrast, the more rigid labor market institutions in Europe resemble Figure 31-6(*b*). In Europe, real wages have not declined as much as in the United States, but the number of the employed has grown slowly while unemployment has grown sharply.

What is the remedy for the high level of unemployment in Europe? Some economists believe that the new European Central Bank may maintain a better balance of aggregate supply and demand in that region. (Recall our discussion of the European Monetary Union in Chapter 30.) Demand-management policies will do little to cure Europe's structural unemployment, however. Many experts believe that it will be necessary to improve European labor market institutions by reducing the generosity of welfare and unemployment insurance and removing restrictions on hiring and firing practices of firms.

Slowly and painfully, reforms have been introduced in many countries. These reforms, along with monetary easing, a depreciating Euro, and the pull of the American economic locomotive, have begun to reduce the high unemployment in the European economy.

SUMMARY

A. The Foundations of Aggregate Supply

1. Aggregate supply describes the relationship between the output that businesses willingly produce and the overall price level, other things being constant. The factors underlying aggregate supply are (*a*) potential output, determined by the inputs of labor, capital, and natural resources available to an economy, along with the technology or efficiency with which these inputs are used, and (*b*) input costs, such as wages, energy prices, and import prices. Changes in these underlying factors will shift the *AS* curve.

2. Two major approaches to output determination are the classical and Keynesian views. The classical view holds that prices and wages are flexible; any excess supply or

demand is quickly extinguished and full employment is established after *AD* or *AS* shocks. The classical view is represented by a vertical *AS* curve. The Keynesian view holds that prices and wages are sticky in the short run due to contractual rigidities such as labor-union agreements. In this kind of economy, output responds positively to higher levels of aggregate demand because the *AS* curve is relatively flat, particularly at low levels of output. In a Keynesian variant, the economy can experience long periods of persistent unemployment because wages and prices adjust slowly to shocks and equilibration toward full employment is slow.

3. A synthesis of classical and Keynesian views distinguishes the long run from the short run. In the short

term, because wages and prices do not have time to adjust fully, the *AS* curve is upward-sloping, showing that businesses will supply more output at a higher price level. By contrast, in the long run, wages and prices have time to adjust fully to shocks, so we treat the long-run *AS* curve as vertical or classical. Hence, in the long run, output will be determined by a nation's potential output, and the evolution of aggregate demand will affect prices rather than output.

B. Unemployment

4. The government gathers monthly statistics on unemployment, employment, and the labor force in a sample survey of the population. People with jobs are categorized as employed; people without jobs who are looking for work are said to be unemployed; people without jobs who are not looking for work are considered outside the labor force. Over the last decade, 66 percent of the population over 16 was in the labor force, while 6 percent of the labor force was unemployed.

5. There is a clear connection between movements in output and the unemployment rate over the business cycle. According to Okun's Law, for every 2 percent that actual GDP declines relative to potential GDP, the unemployment rate rises 1 percentage point. This rule is useful in translating cyclical movements of GDP into their effects on unemployment.

6. Recessions and the associated high unemployment are extremely costly to the economy. Major periods of slack like the 1970s and early 1980s cost the nation hundreds of billions of dollars and have great social costs as well. Yet, even though unemployment has plagued capitalism since the Industrial Revolution, understanding its causes and costs has been possible only with the rise of modern macroeconomic theory.

7. Economists divide unemployment into three groups: (*a*) frictional unemployment, in which workers are between jobs or moving in and out of the labor force; (*b*) structural unemployment, consisting of workers who are in regions or industries that are in a persistent slump because of labor market imbalances or high real wages; and (*c*) cyclical unemployment, pertaining to workers laid off when the overall economy suffers a downturn.

8. Understanding the causes of unemployment has proved to be one of the major challenges of modern macroeconomics. Some unemployment (often called voluntary) would occur in a flexible-wage, perfectly competitive economy when qualified people chose not to work at the going wage rate. Voluntary unemployment might be the efficient outcome of competitive markets.

9. The theory of sticky wages and involuntary unemployment holds that the slow adjustment of wages produces surpluses and shortages in individual labor markets. This theory holds that cyclical unemployment occurs because wages are inflexible, failing to adjust quickly to labor surpluses or shortages. If wages are above market-clearing levels, some workers are employed but other qualified workers cannot find jobs. Such unemployment is involuntary and also inefficient in that both workers and firms could benefit from an appropriate use of monetary and fiscal policies.

10. Labor markets fail to clear partly because of costs involved in administering the compensation system. Frequent adjustment of compensation for market conditions would command too large a share of management time, would upset workers' perceptions of fairness, and would undermine worker morale and productivity. In the long run, wages tend to adjust and remove abnormal levels of unemployment or job vacancies. But the slow pace of wage adjustment means that societies may suffer prolonged periods of unemployment.

11. A careful look at the unemployment statistics reveals several regularities:

    a. Recessions hit all groups in roughly proportional fashion—that is, all groups see their unemployment rates go up and down in proportion to the overall unemployment rate.

    b. A very substantial part of U.S. unemployment is short-term. In low-unemployment years (such as 1999) about 85 percent of unemployed workers are unemployed less than 26 weeks. The average duration of unemployment rises sharply in deep and prolonged recessions.

    c. In most years, a substantial amount of unemployment is due to simple turnover, or frictional causes, as people enter the labor force for the first time or reenter it. Only during recessions is the pool of unemployed composed primarily of job losers.

    d. The persistent unemployment in Europe appears to arise from a combination of weak aggregate demand and inflexible labor market institutions.

CONCEPTS FOR REVIEW

Foundations of Aggregate Supply

aggregate supply, *AS* curve
factors underlying and shifting
    aggregate supply
aggregate supply: role of potential
    output and production costs
short-run vs. long-run *AS*
classical vs. Keynesian views of
    aggregate supply
flexible vs. sticky wages and prices

Unemployment

population status:
    unemployed
    employed
    labor force
    not in labor force
unemployment rate
frictional, structural, and cyclical
    unemployment

Okun's Law

flexible-wage (market-clearing)
    unemployment vs. inflexible-wage
    (non-market-clearing)
    unemployment
voluntary vs. involuntary
    unemployment

FURTHER READING AND INTERNET WEBSITES

Further Reading

A recent study surveying many businesses about their employment practices to help understand cyclical wage behavior is Truman F. Bewley, *Why Wages Don't Fall during a Recession* (Harvard University Press, Cambridge, Mass., 2000).

Websites

Analysis of employment and unemployment for the United States comes from the Bureau of Labor Statistics, at www.bls.gov. Statistics on unemployment in Europe and other OECD countries can be found at www.oecd.org. The BLS site also has an online version of *The Monthly Labor Review* at www.bls.gov/opub/mlr/mlrhome.htm, which is an excellent source for studies about employment, labor issues, and compensation. It contains articles on everything from "Baseball negotiations" (www.bls.gov/opub/mlr/2002/12/contents.htm) to an economic analysis of women entering the legal profession (www.bls.gov/opub/mlr/2002/08/contents.htm).

QUESTIONS FOR DISCUSSION

1. Explain carefully what is meant by the aggregate supply curve. Distinguish between movements along the curve and shifts of the curve. What might increase output by moving along the *AS* curve? What could increase output by shifting the *AS* curve?
2. Construct a table parallel to Table 31-1, illustrating events that would lead to a decrease in aggregate supply. (Be imaginative rather than simply using the same examples.)
3. What, if anything, would be the effect of each of the following on the *AS* curve in both the short run and the long run, other things being constant?
   a. Potential output increases by 25 percent.
   b. The threat of war leads the government to raise defense spending, and the central bank offsets the expansionary impact of this through tight money.
   c. Successful collusion among OPEC countries leads to a tripling of world oil prices.
   d. Environmentalists persuade governments to impose costly regulations on all new investments and energy use and to curb output in natural-resource sectors.
4. Assume that the unemployment rate is 7 percent and GDP is $4000 billion. What is a rough estimate of potential GDP if the NAIRU is 5 percent? Assume that potential GDP is growing at 3 percent annually. What will potential GDP be in 2 years? How fast will GDP have to grow to reach potential GDP in 2 years?
5. What is the labor-force status of each of the following?
   a. A teenager who sends out résumés in searching for a first job
   b. An autoworker who has been laid off and would like to work but has given up hope of finding work or being recalled

c. A retired person who moved to Florida and answers advertisements for part-time positions

d. A parent who works part-time, wants a full-time job, but doesn't have time to look

e. A teacher who has a job but is too ill to work

6. In explaining its procedures, the Department of Labor gives the following examples:

a. "Joan Howard told the interviewer that she has filed applications with three companies for summer jobs. However, it is only April and she doesn't wish to start work until at least June 15, because she is attending school. Although she has taken specific steps to find a job, Joan is classified as not in the labor force because she is not currently available for work."

b. "James Kelly and Elyse Martin attend Jefferson High School. James works after school at the North Star Café, and Elyse is seeking a part-time job at the same establishment (also after school). James' job takes precedence over his non-labor force activity of going to school, as does Elyse's search for work; therefore, James is counted as employed and Elyse is counted as unemployed."

Explain each of these examples. Take a survey of your classmates. Using the examples above, have people classify themselves in terms of their labor-force status as employed, unemployed, or not in the labor force.

7. Assume that Congress is considering a law that would set the minimum wage above the market-clearing wage for teenagers but below that for adult workers. Using supply-and-demand diagrams, show the impact of the minimum wage on the employment, unemployment, and incomes of both sets of workers. Is the unemployment voluntary or involuntary? What would you recommend to Congress if you were called to testify about the wisdom of this measure?

8. Do you think that the economic costs and personal stress of a teenager unemployed for 1 month of the summer might be less or more than those of a head-of-household unemployed for 1 year? Do you think that this suggests that public policy should have a different stance with respect to these two groups?

9. Make a list of reasons why unemployment looks so different in the United States as compared to Europe. Using the framework in Figure 31-6, show how a decrease in the demand for labor would lead to unchanged unemployment but lower wages in flexible-wage America, shown in (a), but to lower employment, higher unemployment, and unchanged wages in rigid-wage Europe, in (b).

Ensuring Price Stability

Lenin is said to have declared that the best way to destroy the capitalist system was to debauch the currency. By a continuing process of inflation, governments can confiscate, secretly and unobserved, an important part of the wealth of their citizens.

J. M. Keynes

The United States recently experienced low and stable inflation that was unprecedented in the nation's history and unique among high-income countries. This experience was primarily due to the success of monetary policy in keeping output in a narrow corridor between inflationary excesses and depressionary downturns. In part, the low inflation was found in the restrained wage growth due to a decline in labor-union membership, a graying workforce, and greater worker docility in the face of aggressive management cost containment.

Additionally, inflation was restrained because of phenomenal price declines in computers and other new-economy products as well as relative quiet in oil and commodity markets.

One new factor in the inflation equation was the growing "globalization" of production. As the United States became more integrated in world markets, domestic firms found that their prices were constrained by the prices of international competitors. Even when domestic sales of automobiles were booming, domestic automakers could not raise their prices too much for fear of losing market share to Japanese and other foreign producers.

These were the forces at work in the American economy that kept inflation in check over the last two decades. Other countries were not so lucky, however. The present chapter will examine the meaning and determinants of inflation and describe the important public-policy issues that arise in this area. Figure 32-1 provides an overview of this chapter.

A. DEFINITION AND IMPACT OF INFLATION

WHAT IS INFLATION?

We described the major price indexes and defined inflation in Chapter 21, but it will be useful to reiterate the basic definitions here:

Inflation occurs when the general level of prices is rising. Today, we calculate inflation by using price indexes—weighted averages of the prices of thousands of individual products. The consumer price index (CPI) measures the cost of a market basket of consumer goods and services relative to the cost of that bundle during a particular base year. The GDP deflator is the price of GDP.

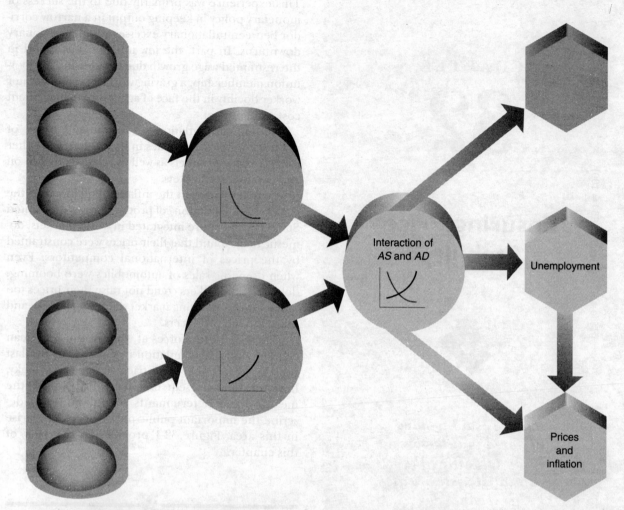

FIGURE 32-1. Inflation Is a Fundamental Constraint on Economic Policy

What are inflation's economic impacts? What forces lead to persistent inflation? How can governments slow inflation? These questions are central to macroeconomic theory and policy today.

The rate of inflation is the percentage change in the price level:

Rate of inflation (year t)

$$= \frac{\begin{array}{c} \text{price level} \\ (\text{year } t) \end{array} - \begin{array}{c} \text{price level} \\ (\text{year } t - 1) \end{array}}{\text{price level (year } t - 1)} \times 100$$

If you are unclear on the definitions, refresh your memory by reviewing Chapter 21.

The History of Inflation

Inflation is as old as market economies. Figure 32-2 depicts the history of prices in England since the thirteenth century. Over the long haul, prices have generally risen, as the rust line reveals. But examine also the black line, which plots the path of *real wages* (the wage rate divided by consumer prices). Real wages meandered along until the Industrial Revolution. Comparing the two lines shows that inflation is not necessarily accompanied by a decline in real income.

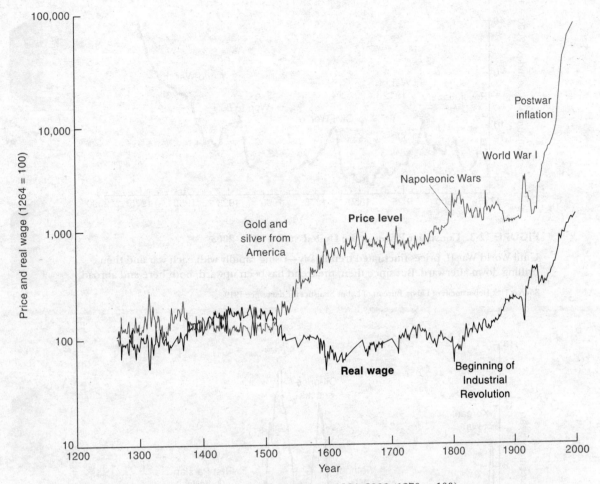

FIGURE 32-2. English Price Level and Real Wage, 1264–2002 (1270 = 100)

The graph shows England's history of prices and real wages since the Middle Ages. In early years, price increases were associated with increases in the money supply, such as from discoveries of New World treasure and the printing of money during the Napoleonic Wars. Note the meandering of the real wage prior to the Industrial Revolution. Since then, real wages have risen sharply and steadily.

Source: E. H. Phelps Brown and S. V. Hopkins, *Economica*, 1956, updated by the authors.

You can see, too, that real wages have climbed steadily since around 1800, rising more than tenfold.

Figure 32-3 on page 670 focuses on the behavior of consumer prices in the United States since the Revolutionary War. Until World War II, the United States was generally on a combination of gold and silver standards, and the pattern of price changes was regular: prices would soar during wartime and then fall back during the postwar slump. But the pattern changed dramatically after World War II. Prices and wages now travel on a one-way street that goes only upward. They rise rapidly in periods of economic expansion and slow down in periods of slack.

Figure 32-4 on page 670 shows CPI inflation over the last half-century. You can see that the last few years, with low and stable inflation, were an unusually tranquil period.

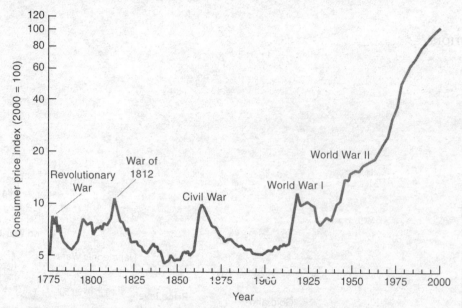

FIGURE 32-3. Consumer Prices in the United States, 1776–2003

Until World War II, prices fluctuated trendlessly—rising rapidly with each war and then drifting down afterward. But since then, the trend has been upward, both here and abroad.

Source: U.S. Department of Labor, Bureau of Labor Statistics for data since 1919.

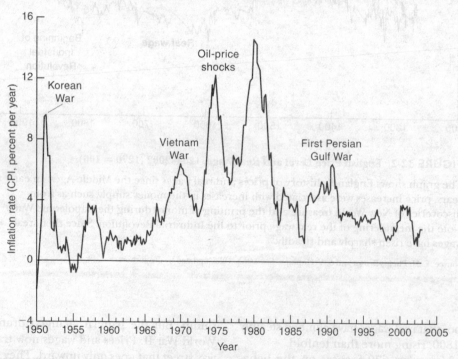

FIGURE 32-4. Inflation Has Remained Low and Stable in Recent Years

Historically, inflation in the United States was variable, and it reached unacceptably high rates in the early 1980s. In the last decade, skillful monetary management by the Federal Reserve along with favorable supply shocks led to low and stable inflation.

Source: Bureau of Labor Statistics, www.bls.gov. This graph shows inflation of the consumer price index.

Three Strains of Inflation

Like diseases, inflations exhibit different levels of severity. It is useful to classify them into three categories: low inflation, galloping inflation, and hyperinflation.

Low Inflation. Low inflation is characterized by prices that rise slowly and predictably. We might define this as single-digit annual inflation rates. When prices are relatively stable, *people trust money* because it retains its value from month to month and year to year. People are willing to write long-term contracts in money terms because they are confident that the relative prices of goods they buy and sell will not get too far out of line. Most industrial countries have experienced low inflation over the last decade.

Galloping Inflation. Inflation in the double-digit or triple-digit range of 20, 100, or 200 percent a year is called **galloping inflation** or "very high inflation." Galloping inflation is relatively common, particularly in countries suffering from weak governments, war, or revolution. Many Latin American countries, such as Argentina, Chile, and Brazil, had inflation rates of 50 to 700 percent per year in the 1970s and 1980s.

Once galloping inflation becomes entrenched, serious economic distortions arise. Generally, most contracts get indexed to a price index or to a foreign currency like the dollar. In these conditions, money loses its value very quickly, so people hold only the bare-minimum amount of money needed for daily transactions. Financial markets wither away, as capital flees abroad. People hoard goods, buy houses, and never, never lend money at low nominal interest rates.

Hyperinflation. While economies seem to survive under galloping inflation, a third and deadly strain takes hold when the cancer of **hyperinflation** strikes. Nothing good can be said about a market economy in which prices are rising a million or even a trillion percent per year.

Hyperinflations are particularly interesting to students of inflation because they highlight its disastrous impacts. Consider this description of hyperinflation in the Confederacy during the Civil War:

> We used to go to the stores with money in our pockets and come back with food in our baskets. Now we go with money in baskets and return with food in our

pockets. Everything is scarce except money! Prices are chaotic and production disorganized. A meal that used to cost the same amount as an opera ticket now costs twenty times as much. Everybody tends to hoard "things" and to try to get rid of the "bad" paper money, which drives the "good" metal money out of circulation. A partial return to barter inconvenience is the result.

The most thoroughly documented case of hyperinflation took place in the Weimar Republic of Germany in the 1920s. Figure 32-5 shows how the government unleashed the monetary printing presses, driving both money and prices to astronomical levels. From January 1922 to November 1923, the price index rose from 1 to 10,000,000,000. If a person had owned 300 million marks worth of German bonds in early 1922, this amount would not have bought a piece of candy 2 years later.

Studies have found several common features in hyperinflations. First, the real money stock (measured by the money stock divided by the price level)

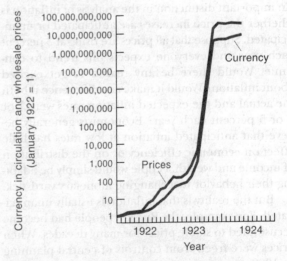

The German Hyperinflation

FIGURE 32-5. Money and Hyperinflation in Germany, 1922–1924

In the early 1920s, Germany could not raise enough taxes, so it used the monetary printing press to pay the government's bills. The stock of currency rose astronomically from early 1922 to December 1923, and prices spiraled upward as people frantically tried to spend their money before it lost all value.

falls drastically. By the end of the German hyper-inflation, real money demand was only one-thirtieth of its level 2 years earlier. People are in effect rushing around, dumping their money like hot potatoes before they get burned by money's loss of value. Second, relative prices become highly unstable. Under normal conditions, a person's real wages move only a percent or less from month to month. During 1923, German real wages changed on average one-third (up or down) each month. This huge variation in relative prices and real wages—and the inequities and distortions caused by these fluctuations—took an enormous toll on workers and businesses, highlighting one of the major costs of inflation.

The impact of inflation was beautifully expressed by J. M. Keynes:

> As inflation proceeds and the real value of the currency fluctuates wildly from month to month, all permanent relations between debtors and creditors, which form the ultimate foundation of capitalism, become so utterly disordered as to be almost meaningless; and the process of wealth-getting degenerates into a game and a lottery.

Anticipated vs. Unanticipated Inflation

An important distinction in the analysis of inflation is whether the price increases are anticipated or unanticipated. Suppose that all prices are rising at 3 percent each year and everyone expects this trend to continue. Would there be any reason to get excited about inflation? Would it make any difference if both the actual and the expected inflation rates were 1 or 3 or 5 percent each year? Economists generally believe that anticipated inflation at low rates has little effect on economic efficiency or on the distribution of income and wealth. People would simply be adapting their behavior to a changing monetary yardstick.

But the reality is that inflation is usually unanticipated. For example, the Russian people had become accustomed to stable prices for many decades. When prices were freed from controls of central planning in 1992, no one, not even the professional economists, guessed that prices would rise by 400,000 percent over the next 5 years. People who were unlucky enough to hold their wealth in ruble assets saw their savings become worthless.

In more stable countries like the United States, the impact of unanticipated inflation is less dramatic, but the same general point applies. An unexpected jump in prices will impoverish some and enrich others. How costly is this redistribution? Perhaps "cost" does not describe the problem. The effects may be more social than economic. An epidemic of burglaries may not lower GDP, but it causes great distress. Similarly, randomly redistributing wealth by inflation is like forcing people to play a lottery they would prefer to avoid.

The Quagmire of Deflation

If inflation is so bad, should societies instead strive for *deflation*—a situation where prices are actually falling rather than rising?

Historical experience and macroeconomic analysis suggest that deflation combined with low interest rates can produce serious macroeconomic difficulties.

A gentle deflation by itself is not particularly harmful. Rather, deflations generally trigger economic problems because they may lead to a situation where monetary policy becomes impotent.

Normally, if prices begin to fall because of a recession, the central bank can stimulate the economy by increasing bank reserves and lowering interest rates. But if prices are falling rapidly, then real interest rates may be relatively high. For example, if the nominal interest rate is $1/4$ percent and prices are falling at $3\frac{3}{4}$ percent per year, then the real interest rate is 4 percent per year. At such a high real interest rate, investment may be choked off, with recessionary consequences.

The central bank may decide to lower interest rates. *But the lower limit on nominal interest rates is zero.* Why so? Because when interest rates are zero, then bonds are essentially money, and people will hardly want to hold a bond paying negative interest when money has a zero interest rate. Now, when the central bank has lowered interest rates to zero, in our example, real interest rates would still be $3\frac{3}{4}$ percent per year, which might still be too high to stimulate the economy. The central bank is trapped in a quagmire—a quagmire called the *liquidity trap*—in which it can lower short-term interest rates no further. The central bank has run out of ammunition.

Deflation was frequently observed in the nineteenth and early twentieth centuries but largely disappeared in the late twentieth century. However, at the end of the 1990s, Japan entered a period of sustained deflation. This was in part caused by a tremendous fall in asset prices, particularly land and stocks, but also by a long recession. Short-term interest rates were essentially zero after 2000. For example, the yield on 1 year bank deposits was 0.032 percent per year in mid-2003. The Bank of Japan appeared helpless in the face of deflation and zero interest rates.

The United States also had a brief skirmish with deflation and the liquidity trap in late 2002 and early 2003, as short-term interest rates fell to their lowest point in half a century.

Are there any remedies for deflation and the liquidity trap? One clear solution is to use fiscal policy. A fiscal stimulus will increase aggregate demand, and it will do so without any crowding out from higher interest rates. Some monetary specialists argue that the central bank could buy long-term bonds, inflation-protected bonds, or even stocks—for these are not in a liquidity trap. But most economists believe that the best defense is a good offense: make sure that the economy stays safely away from deflation by maintaining full employment and a gradually rising price level.

THE ECONOMIC IMPACTS OF INFLATION

Central bankers are united in their determination to contain inflation. During periods of high inflation, opinion polls often find that inflation is economic enemy number one. What is so dangerous and costly about inflation? We noted above that during periods of inflation all prices and wages do not move at the same rate; that is, changes in *relative prices* occur. As a result of the diverging relative prices, two definite effects of inflation are:

- A *redistribution* of income and wealth among different groups
- *Distortions* in the relative prices and outputs of different goods, or sometimes in output and employment for the economy as a whole

Impacts on Income and Wealth Distribution

Inflation affects the distribution of income and wealth primarily because of differences in the assets and liabilities that people hold.[1] When people owe money, a sharp rise in prices is a windfall gain for them. Suppose you borrow $100,000 to buy a house and your annual fixed-interest-rate mortgage payments are $10,000. Suddenly, a great inflation

doubles all wages and incomes. Your *nominal* mortgage payment is still $10,000 per year, but its real cost is halved. You will need to work only half as long as before to make your mortgage payment. The great inflation has increased your wealth by cutting in half the real value of your mortgage debt.

If you are a lender and have assets in fixed-interest-rate mortgages or long-term bonds, the shoe is on the other foot. An unexpected rise in prices will leave you the poorer because the dollars repaid to you are worth much less than the dollars you lent.

If an inflation persists for a long time, people come to anticipate it and markets begin to adapt. An allowance for inflation will gradually be built into the market interest rate. Say the economy starts out with interest rates of 3 percent and stable prices. Once people expect prices to rise at 9 percent per year, bonds and mortgages will tend to pay 12 percent rather than 3 percent. The 12 percent nominal interest rate reflects a 3 percent real interest rate plus a 9 percent inflation premium. There are no further major redistributions of income and wealth once interest rates have adapted to the new inflation rate. The adjustment of interest rates to chronic inflation has been observed in all countries with a long history of rising prices.[2]

Because of institutional changes, some old myths no longer apply. It used to be thought that common stocks were a good inflation hedge, but stocks generally move inversely with inflation today. A common saying was that inflation hurts widows and orphans; today, they are insulated from inflation because social security benefits are indexed to consumer prices. Also, unanticipated inflation benefits debtors and hurts lenders less than before because many kinds of debt (like "floating-rate" mortgages) have interest rates that move up and down with market interest rates.

The major redistributive impact of inflation comes through its effect on the real value of people's wealth. In general, unanticipated inflation redistributes wealth from creditors to debtors, helping borrowers and hurting lenders. An unanticipated decline in inflation has the opposite effect. But inflation mostly churns income and assets, randomly redistributing wealth among the population with little significant impact on any single group.

---

[1] The important elements of balance sheets were described in Chapters 7 and 25.

[2] Fig. 25-3 shows movements in nominal and real interest rates for the United States in recent years.

Impacts on Economic Efficiency

In addition to redistributing incomes, inflation affects the real economy in two specific areas: It can harm economic efficiency, and it can affect total output. We begin with the efficiency impacts.

Inflation impairs economic efficiency because it *distorts prices and price signals.* In a low-inflation economy, if the market price of a good rises, both buyers and sellers know that there has been an actual change in the supply and/or demand conditions for that good, and they can react appropriately. For example, if the neighborhood supermarkets all boost their beef prices by 50 percent, perceptive consumers know that it's time to start eating more chicken. Similarly, if the prices of new computers fall by 90 percent, you may decide it's time to turn in your old model.

By contrast, in a high-inflation economy it's much harder to distinguish between changes in relative prices and changes in the overall price level. If inflation is running at 20 or 30 percent per month, price changes are so frequent that changes in relative prices get missed in the confusion.

Inflation also *distorts the use of money.* Currency is money that bears a zero nominal interest rate. If the inflation rate rises from 0 to 10 percent annually, the real interest rate on currency falls from 0 to −10 percent per year. There is no way to correct this distortion.

As a result of the negative real interest rate on money, people devote real resources to reducing their money holdings during inflationary times. They go to the bank more often—using up "shoe leather" and valuable time. Corporations set up elaborate cash-management schemes. Real resources are thereby consumed simply to adapt to a changing monetary yardstick rather than to make productive investments.

Many economists point to the *distortion of inflation on taxes.* Certain parts of the tax code are written in dollar terms. When prices rise, the real value of those provisions tends to decline. For example, you might be able to subtract a fixed-dollar "standard deduction" from your income in calculating your taxable income. With inflation, the real value of that standard deduction would decline and the real value of your taxes would rise. Such "taxation without legislation" has led many countries to index their tax laws to prevent inflation-induced tax increases. Parts of the U.S. tax code were indexed during the 1980s.

Indexing of tax brackets alone will not purge the tax system of the impacts of inflation because inflation distorts measures of income. For example, if you earned an interest rate of 6 percent on your funds in 2003, half of this return simply replaced your loss in the purchasing power of your funds from a 3 percent inflation rate. Yet the tax code does not distinguish between real return and the interest that just compensates for inflation. Many similar distortions of income and taxes are present in the tax code today.

But these are not the only costs; some economists point to *menu costs* of inflation. The idea is that when prices are changed, firms must spend real resources adjusting their prices. For instance, restaurants reprint their menus, mail-order firms reprint their catalogs, taxi companies remeter their cabs, cities adjust parking meters, and stores change the price tags of goods. Sometimes, the costs are intangible, such as those involved in gathering people to make new pricing decisions.

Macroeconomic Impacts

What are the macroeconomic effects of inflation? This question is addressed in the next section, so we merely highlight the major points here. Until the 1970s, high inflation in the United States usually went hand in hand with economic expansions; inflation tended to increase when investment was brisk and jobs were plentiful. Periods of deflation or declining inflation—the 1890s, the 1930s, some of the 1950s—were times of high unemployment of labor and capital.

But a more careful examination of the historical record reveals an interesting fact: The positive association between output and inflation appears to be only a temporary relationship. Over the longer run, there seems to be an inverse-U-shaped relationship between inflation and output growth. Table 32-1 shows the results of a recent multicountry study of the association between inflation and growth. It indicates that economic growth is strongest in countries with low inflation, while countries with high inflation or deflation tend to grow more slowly. (But beware the *ex post* fallacy here, as explored in question 7 at the end of the chapter.)

What Is the Optimal Rate of Inflation?

Most nations seek rapid economic growth, full employment, and price stability. But just what is meant

Inflation rate (% per year)	Growth of per capita GDP (% per year)
−20–0	0.7
0–10	2.4
10–20	1.8
20–40	0.4
100–200	−1.7
1,000+	−6.5

TABLE 32-1. Inflation and Economic Growth

The pooled experience of 127 countries shows that the most rapid growth is associated with low inflation rates. Deflation and moderate inflation accompany slow growth, while hyperinflations are associated with sharp downturns.

Source: Michael Bruno and William Easterly, "Inflation Crises and Long-Run Growth," World Bank Policy Research Working Paper 1517, September 1995.

by "price stability"? Exactly zero inflation? Over what period? Or is it perhaps low inflation?

One school of thought holds that policy should aim for absolutely stable prices or zero inflation. If we are confident that the price level in 20 years will be very close to the price level today, we can make better long-term investment and saving decisions.

Many macroeconomists believe, however, that, while a zero-inflation target might be sensible in an ideal economy, we do not live in a frictionless system. Perhaps the most important friction is the resistance of workers to declines in money wages. If the average wage level were stable, this would be the average of some wages that are rising and some that are falling. But workers and firms are extremely reluctant to cut money wages. Evidence for the downward rigidity of wages is found in a comprehensive government survey of wage changes in manufacturing over the period 1958–1978. During this period, on average less than 0.1 percent of workers received wage cuts, even in years when inflation was extremely low.

From a macroeconomic point of view, this suggests that zero inflation would be associated with a higher sustainable level of unemployment and a lower level of output than would be the case at an inflation rate of 2 to 4 percent. A recent study estimates that targeting stable prices would cost the

United States between 1 and 3 percent lower output and employment *permanently* as compared with an inflation target of around 3 percent. The authors conclude:

> Downward rigidity [of wages] interferes with the ability of some firms to make adjustments in real wages, leading to inefficient reductions in employment. . . . The main implication for policymakers is that targeting zero inflation will lead to a large inefficiency in the allocation of resources, as reflected in an unemployment rate that is unnecessarily high.[3]

We can summarize our discussion in the following way:

> While economists may disagree on the exact target for inflation, most agree that a predictable and gently rising price level provides the best climate for healthy economic growth. A careful sifting of the evidence suggests that low inflation like that seen recently in the United States has little impact on productivity or real output. By contrast, galloping inflation or hyperinflation can cause serious harm to productivity and to individuals through the redistribution of income and wealth.

B. MODERN INFLATION THEORY

Can market economies simultaneously enjoy the blessings of full employment and price stability? Is there no way to control inflation other than by economic slowdowns that keep unemployment undesirably high? If recessions are too high a price to pay for the control of inflation, do we need "incomes policies" that can lower inflation without raising unemployment?

Questions, questions, questions. Yet answers to these are critical to the economic health of modern mixed economies. In the balance of this chapter we explore modern inflation theory and analyze the costs of lowering inflation.

---

[3] See the reference to Akerlof, Dickens, and Perry in this chapter's Further Reading section.

PRICES IN THE *AS-AD* FRAMEWORK

There is no single source of inflation. Like illnesses, inflations occur for many reasons. Some inflations come from the demand side; others, from the supply side. But one key fact about modern inflations is that they develop an internal momentum and are costly to stop once under way.

Inertial Inflation

In modern industrial economies like the United States, inflation has great momentum and tends to persist at the same rate. Inertial inflation is like a lazy old dog. If the dog is not "shocked" by the push of a foot or the pull of a cat, it will stay put. Once disturbed, the dog may chase the cat, but then it eventually lies down in a new spot where it stays until the next shock.

During the 1990s, prices in the United States rose steadily at around 3 percent annually, and most people came to expect that inflation rate. This expected rate of inflation was built into the economy's institutions. Wage agreements between labor and management were designed around a 3 percent inflation rate; government monetary and fiscal plans assumed a 3 percent rate. During this period, the *inertial rate of inflation* was 3 percent per year. Other names sometimes heard for this concept are the *core, underlying,* or *expected* inflation rate.

While inflation can persist at the same rate for a while, history shows that shocks to the economy tend to push inflation up or down. The economy is constantly subject to changes in aggregate demand, sharp oil- and commodity-price changes, poor harvests, movements in the foreign exchange rate, productivity changes, and countless other economic events that push inflation away from its inertial rate.

The economy has an ongoing **inertial rate of inflation** to which people's expectations have adapted. This built-in inertial inflation rate tends to persist until a shock causes it to move up or down.

Demand-Pull Inflation

One of the major shocks to inflation is a change in aggregate demand. In earlier chapters we saw that changes in investment, government spending, or net exports can change aggregate demand and propel output beyond its potential. We also saw how a nation's central bank can affect economic activity. Whatever the reason, **demand-pull inflation** occurs when aggregate demand rises more rapidly than the

economy's productive potential, pulling prices up to equilibrate aggregate supply and demand. In effect, demand dollars are competing for the limited supply of commodities and bid up their prices. As unemployment falls and workers become scarce, wages are bid up and the inflationary process accelerates.

One important factor behind demand inflation is rapid *money-supply growth.* Increases in the money supply increase aggregate demand, which in turn increases the price level. Thus, when the German central bank printed billions and billions of paper marks in 1922–1923 and they came into the marketplace in search of bread or housing, it was no wonder that the German price level rose a billionfold. This was demand-pull inflation with a vengeance. This scene was replayed when the Russian government financed its budget deficit by printing rubles in the early 1990s. The result was an inflation rate that averaged 25 percent *per month* [or $100 \times (1.25^{12} - 1) = 1355$ percent per year].[4]

Figure 32-6 illustrates the process of demand-pull inflation in terms of aggregate supply and demand. Starting from an initial equilibrium at point E,

---

[4] The next chapter's review of alternative approaches to macroeconomics examines "monetarist" theories, which hold that price changes depend principally on changes in the money supply.

FIGURE 32-6. Demand-Pull Inflation Occurs When Too Much Spending Chases Too Few Goods

When aggregate demand increases, the rising spending is competing for limited goods. Prices rise from P to P' in demand-pull inflation. How would cost-push inflation be analyzed in this framework?

suppose there is an expansion of spending that pushes the *AD* curve up and to the right. The economy's equilibrium moves from *E* to *E'*. At this higher level of demand, prices have risen from *P* to *P'*. Demand-pull inflation has taken place.

Cost-Push Inflation

The rudiments of demand-pull inflation were understood by the classical economists and used by them to explain historical price movements. But a strange thing happened during the last half-century—the inflation process changed. Look back at the history of prices on page 670 and note that prices today travel a one-way street—up in recessions, up faster in booms. What differentiates modern inflation from the simple demand-pull variety is that prices and wages rise even in recessions when 30 percent of factory capacity lies idle and 10 percent of the labor force is unemployed. This phenomenon is known as *cost-push* or *supply-shock* inflation.

Inflation resulting from rising costs during periods of high unemployment and slack resource utilization is called **cost-push inflation.**

In looking for explanations of cost-push inflation, economists often start with wages. In 1982, for example, when the unemployment rate was almost 10 percent, wages rose 5 percent. Wages tend to rise even in recession because they are administered prices and because of the strong resistance to wage cuts.

Sometimes, cost-push shocks lead to an upward push to inflation. In 1973, in 1978, and again in late 1999 and early 2000, countries were minding their own macroeconomic business when severe shortages in oil markets occurred. Oil prices rose sharply, business costs of production increased, and a sharp burst of cost-push inflation followed. Sometimes, cost shocks are favorable. For example, during the 1990s, the United States enjoyed downward pressure on aggregate supply because of rapid productivity growth; falling energy, import, and commodity prices; and favorable trends in health costs.

Expectations and Inertial Inflation

Why, you might ask, does inflation have such strong inertia or momentum? The answer is that most prices and wages are set with an eye to future economic conditions. When prices and wages are rising rapidly and are expected to continue doing so, businesses and workers tend to build the rapid rate of inflation into their price and wage decisions. High or low inflation expectations tend to be self-fulfilling prophecies.

We can use a hypothetical example to illustrate the role of expectations in inertial inflation. Say that in 2004, Brass Mills Inc., a nonunionized light-manufacturing firm, was contemplating its annual wage and salary decisions for 2005. Its sales were growing well, and it was experiencing no major supply or demand shocks. Brass Mills' chief economist reported that no major inflationary or deflationary shocks were foreseen, and the major forecasting services were expecting national wage growth of 4 percent in 2005. Brass Mills had conducted a survey of local companies and found that most employers were planning on increases in compensation of 3 to 5 percent during the next year. All the signals, then, pointed to wage increases of around 4 percent for 2005 over 2004.

In examining its own internal labor market, Brass Mills determined that its wages were in line with the local labor market. Because the managers did not want to fall behind local wages, Brass Mills decided that it would try to match local wage increases. It therefore set wage increases at the expected market increase, an average 4 percent wage increase for 2005.

The process of setting wages and salaries with an eye to expected future economic conditions can be extended to virtually all employers. This kind of reasoning also applies to many product prices—such as college tuitions, automobile-model prices, and long-distance telephone rates—that cannot be easily changed after they have been set. Because of the length of time involved in modifying inflation expectations and in adjusting most wages and many prices, inertial inflation will yield only to major shocks or changes in economic policy.

Figure 32-7 illustrates the process of inertial inflation. Suppose that potential output is constant and that there are no supply or demand shocks. If everyone expects average costs and prices to rise at 3 percent each year, the *AS* curve will shift upward at 3 percent per year. If there are no demand shocks, the *AD* curve will also shift up at that rate. The intersection of the *AD* and *AS* curves will be 3 percent higher each year. Hence, the macroeconomic equilibrium moves from *E* to *E'* to *E''*. Prices are rising 3 percent from one year to the next: inertial inflation has set in at 3 percent.

FIGURE 32-7. An Upward Spiral of Prices and Wages Occurs When Aggregate Supply and Demand Shift Up Together.

Suppose that production costs and *AD* rise by 3 percent each year. *AS* and *AD* curves would shift up 3 percent each year. As the equilibrium moves from *E* to *E′* to *E″*, prices march up steadily because of inertial inflation.

Inertial inflation occurs when the *AS* and *AD* curves are moving steadily upward at the same rate.

Price Levels vs. Inflation

Using Figure 32-7 above, we can make the useful distinction between movements in the price level and movements in inflation. In general, an increase in aggregate demand will raise prices, other things being equal. Similarly, an upward shift in the *AS* curve resulting from an increase in wages and other costs will raise prices, other things being equal.

But of course other things always change; in particular, *AD* and *AS* curves never sit still! Figure 32-7 shows, for example, the *AS* and *AD* curves marching up together.

What if there were an unexpected shift in the *AS* or *AD* curve during the third period? How would prices and inflation be affected? Suppose, for example, that the third period's *AD″* curve shifted to the left to *AD‴* because of a monetary contraction. This

might cause a recession, with a new equilibrium at *E‴* on the *AS″* curve. At this point, output would have fallen below potential; prices and the inflation rate would be lower than at *E″*, but the economy would still be experiencing inflation because the price level at *E‴* is still above the previous period's equilibrium *E′* with price *P′*.

This example is a reminder that supply or demand shocks may reduce the price level below the level it would otherwise have attained. Nonetheless, because of inflation's momentum, the economy may continue to experience inflation.

THE PHILLIPS CURVE

A useful way of understanding inflation is the **Phillips curve.** This curve shows the relationship between unemployment and inflation. The basic idea is that when output is high and unemployment is low, wages and prices tend to rise more rapidly. This occurs because workers and unions press more strongly for wage increases when jobs are plentiful, and firms can more easily raise prices when sales are brisk. The converse also holds—high unemployment tends to slow inflation.

Short-Run Phillips Curve

Macroeconomists distinguish between the short-run Phillips curve and the long-run Phillips curve. A typical short-run Phillips curve is shown in Figure 32-8. On the diagram's horizontal axis is the unemployment rate. On the black left-hand vertical scale is the annual rate of price inflation. The rust right-hand vertical scale shows the rate of money-wage inflation. As you move leftward on the Phillips curve by reducing unemployment, the rate of price and wage increase indicated by the curve becomes higher.

An important piece of inflation arithmetic underlies this curve. Say that labor productivity (output per worker) rises at a steady rate of 1 percent each year. Further, assume that firms set prices on the basis of average labor costs, so prices always change just as much as average labor costs per unit of output. If wages are rising at 4 percent, and productivity is rising at 1 percent, then average labor costs will rise

at 3 percent. Consequently, prices will also rise at 3 percent.

Using this inflation arithmetic, we can see the relation between wage and price increases in Figure 32-8. These two scales in the figure differ only by the assumed rate of productivity growth (so the price change of 4 percent per year would correspond to a wage change of 5 percent per year if productivity grew by 1 percent per year and if prices always rose as fast as average labor costs).

FIGURE 32-8. The Short-Run Phillips Curve Depicts the Tradeoff between Inflation and Unemployment

A short-run Phillips curve shows the inverse relationship between inflation and unemployment. The rust wage-change scale on the right-hand vertical axis is higher than the black left-hand inflation scale by the assumed 1 percent rate of growth of average labor productivity.

The Logic of Wage-Price Arithmetic

This relationship between prices, wages, and productivity can be formalized as follows: The fact that prices are based on average labor costs per unit of output implies that P is always proportional to WL/Q, where P is the price level, W is the wage rate, L is labor-hours, and Q is output. Assume that average labor productivity (Q/L) is growing smoothly at 1 percent per year. Hence, if wages are growing at 4 percent annually, prices will grow at 3 percent annually (= 4 percent growth in wages − 1 percent growth in productivity). More generally,

$$\text{Rate of} \atop \text{inflation} = {\text{rate of} \atop \text{wage growth}} - {\text{rate of} \atop \text{productivity growth}}$$

This shows the relationship between price inflation and wage inflation.

We can illustrate how closely this relationship holds with actual numbers for a high-inflation period and for a low-inflation period. The following table shows the major long-run determinants of inflation to be wage growth and productivity change. From the first to the second period, inflation rose because wage growth increased slightly while productivity fell sharply. In the last 2 years, inflation was very low because wage growth was restrained while productivity growth rebounded.

	Rate of CPI inflation (%)	Rate of wage growth (%)	Rate of productivity growth (%)
1959–1973	3.1	5.8	3.2
1974–1997	6.0	6.3	1.5
1998–1999	2.4	3.9	2.5

Source: Bureau of Labor Statistics data on the business sector, at www.bls.gov.

The Nonaccelerating Inflation Rate of Unemployment

Economists who looked carefully at inflationary periods noticed that the Phillips curve drawn in Figure 32-8 was quite unstable. Based on theoretical work of Edmund Phelps and Milton Friedman, along with statistical tests of the actual history, macroeconomists developed the modern theory of inflation, which distinguishes between the long run and the short run. The downward-sloping Phillips curve of Figure 32-8 holds only in the short run. In the long run, the Phillips curve is *vertical*, not downward-sloping. This approach implies that in the long-run there is a minimum unemployment rate that is consistent with steady inflation. This is the *nonaccelerating inflation rate of unemployment* or *NAIRU* (pronounced "nay-rew").[5]

The **nonaccelerating inflation rate of unemployment** (or **NAIRU**) is that unemployment rate consistent with a constant inflation rate. At the NAIRU, upward and downward forces on price and wage inflation are in balance, so there is no tendency for inflation to change. The NAIRU is the lowest unemployment rate that can be sustained without upward pressure on inflation.

The idea behind the NAIRU is that the state of the economy can be divided into three situations:

- *Excess demand.* When markets are extremely tight, with low unemployment and high utilization of capacity, then prices and wages will be subject to demand-pull inflation and rising inflation.
- *Excess supply.* In recessionary situations, with high unemployment and idled factories, firms tend to sell at discounts and workers push less aggressively for wage increases. Wage and price inflation tend to moderate.
- *Neutral pressures.* Sometimes the economy is operating "in neutral." The upward wage pressures from job vacancies just match the downward wage pressures from unemployment. There are no supply shocks from oil or other exogenous sources. Here, the economy is at the NAIRU, and inflation neither rises nor falls.

---

[5] Other terms will sometimes be encountered. The original name for the NAIRU was the "natural rate of unemployment." This term is unsatisfactory because there is nothing natural about the NAIRU.

From Short Run to Long Run

How does the economy move from the short run to the long run? The basic idea is that when price changes are unanticipated, the short-run Phillips curve tends to shift up or down. This point is illustrated by a series of steps in a "boom cycle" here and in Figure 32-9:

- *Period 1.* In the first period, unemployment is at the NAIRU. There are no demand or supply surprises, and the economy is at point *A* on the lower short-run Phillips curve (*SRPC*) in Figure 32-9.
- *Period 2.* Next, suppose there is an economic expansion which lowers the unemployment rate. As unemployment declines, firms recruit workers more vigorously, giving larger wage increases than formerly. As output approaches capacity, price markups rise. Wages and prices begin to accelerate. In terms of our Phillips curve, the economy moves up and to the left to point *B* on its short-run Phillips curve (along *SRPC* in Figure 32-9). As shown in the figure, inflation expectations have not yet changed, so the economy stays on the original Phillips curve, on *SRPC*. The lower unemployment rate raises inflation during the second period.
- *Period 3.* Because inflation has risen, firms and workers are surprised, and they revise upward their inflationary expectations. They begin to incorporate the higher expected inflation into their wage and price decisions. The result is a *shift in the short-run Phillips curve.* We can see the new curve as *SRPC'* in Figure 32-9. The new short-run Phillips curve lies above the original Phillips curve, reflecting the higher expected rate of inflation. We have drawn the curve so that the new expected inflation rate for period 3 equals the actual inflation rate in period 2. If a slowdown in economic activity brings the unemployment rate back to the NAIRU in period 3, the economy moves to point *C*. Even though the unemployment rate is the same as it was in period 1, actual inflation will be higher, reflecting the upward shift in the short-run Phillips curve.

Note the surprising outcome. Because the expected inflation rate has increased, the rate of inflation is higher in period 3 than during period 1 even though the unemployment rate is the same. The economy in period 3 will have the same *real* GDP and unemployment rate as it did in period 1, even though

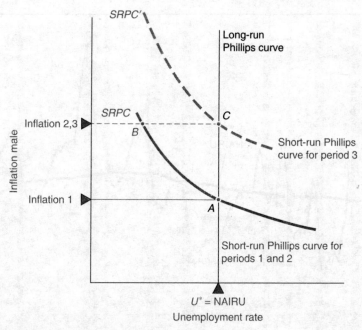

FIGURE 32-9. The Shifting Phillips Curve

This figure shows how economic expansion leads to an inflationary surprise and an upward shift in the short-run Phillips curve. The steps in the shift are explained by the bullets in the text. Note that if you connect points *A*, *B*, and *C*, the shifting curve produces a clockwise loop.

the *nominal* magnitudes (prices and nominal GDP) are now growing more rapidly than they did before the expansion raised the expected rate of inflation.

We can also track a "recession cycle" that occurs when unemployment rises and the actual inflation rate falls below its expected rate. The expected rate of inflation declines in recessions, and the economy enjoys a lower inflation rate when it returns to the NAIRU. This painful cycle of austerity occurred during the Carter-Volcker-Reagan wars against inflation during 1979–1984.

The Vertical Long-Run Phillips Curve
When the unemployment rate departs from the NAIRU, the inflation rate will tend to change. What happens if the gap between the actual unemployment rate and the NAIRU persists? For example, say that the NAIRU is 5 percent while the actual unemployment rate is 3 percent. Because of the gap, inflation will tend to rise from year to year. Inflation might be 3 percent in the first year, 4 percent in the second year, 5 percent in the third year—and might

continue to move upward thereafter. When would this upward spiral stop? It stops only when unemployment moves back to the NAIRU. Put differently, as long as unemployment is below the NAIRU, wage inflation will tend to increase.

The opposite behavior will be seen at high unemployment. In that case, inflation will tend to fall as long as unemployment is above the NAIRU.

Only when unemployment is *at* the NAIRU will inflation stabilize; only then will the shifts of supply and demand in different labor markets be in balance; only then will inflation—at whatever is its inertial rate—tend neither to increase nor to decrease.

The modern theory of inflation has important implications for economic policy. It implies that there is a minimum level of unemployment that an economy can enjoy in the long run. If the economy is pushed to very high levels of output and employment, this will ignite an upward spiral of wage and price inflation. This theory also provides a formula for curbing inflation. When the inflation rate is too high, a country can tighten money, trigger a recession,

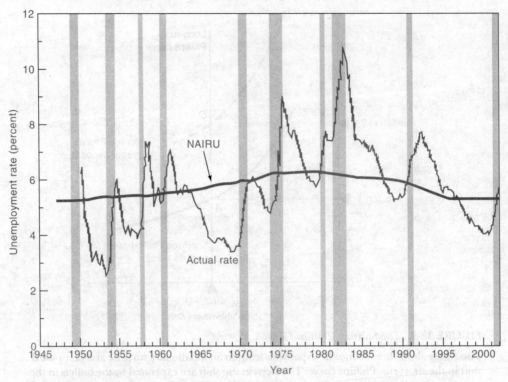

FIGURE 32-10. Actual Unemployment Rate and NAIRU

The NAIRU is the unemployment rate at which upward and downward forces acting on inflation are in balance.

Source: Actual unemployment rate from Bureau of Labor Statistics; NAIRU from estimates of the Congressional Budget Office.

raise the unemployment rate above the NAIRU, and thereby reduce inflation.

The NAIRU defines the neutral zone between excessive tightness/rising inflation and high unemployment/falling inflation. In the short run, inflation can be reduced by raising unemployment above the NAIRU, but in the long run, the NAIRU is the lowest sustainable rate of unemployment.

Quantitative Estimates

Although the NAIRU is a crucial macroeconomic concept, precise numerical estimates of the NAIRU have proved elusive. Many macroeconomists have used advanced techniques to estimate the NAIRU. For this text, we have adopted the estimates prepared by the Congressional Budget Office (CBO). According to the CBO, the NAIRU rose gradually from the 1950s, peaked at 6.3 percent of the labor force around 1980, and declined to 5.2 percent by 2002. CBO

estimates, along with the actual unemployment rate through the end of 1999, are shown in Figure 32-10.

The Inflation Puzzle of the 1990s

The United States experienced a period of unusual macroeconomic stability and prosperity in the late 1990s. Output grew rapidly, unemployment fell sharply, and inflation was at its lowest rate for three decades.

While most Americans were satisfied with the robust economic growth, macroeconomists were puzzled about the unusual behavior of wages and prices. Economic studies from earlier periods suggested that wage and price inflation would begin to rise when unemployment fell below the NAIRU, which was generally thought to be around 5½ percent of the labor force. Unemployment fell below 5 percent for 3 years running, starting in 1997. Yet inflation fell over this period.

The puzzle for inflation theorists is shown in Figure 32-11. The line marked "Actual" shows the actual inflation rate for the period 1995–1999. The line marked "Predicted" shows the predicted inflation rate based on the historical relationship between inflation and unemployment and assuming a NAIRU of 5½ percent. Standard Phillips-curve theories would predict an inflation rate of over 4 percent for 1999, while the actual inflation rate was closer to 2 percent.

Many classical and supply-side economists see the 1990s as yet another nail in the Phillips-curve coffin. Others look to special factors as an explanation. What might have led to the restrained inflation in the 1990s? Here is the view of Fed chairman Alan Greenspan:

> The increasing availability of labor-displacing equipment and software, at declining prices and improving delivery lead times, is arguably at the root of the loss of business pricing

power in recent years. To be sure, other inflation-suppressing forces have been at work as well. Marked increases in available global capacity were engendered as a number of countries that were previously members of the autarchic Soviet bloc opened to the West, and as many emerging-market economies blossomed. Reductions in Cold War spending in the United States and around the world also released resources to more productive private purposes. In addition, deregulation that removed bottlenecks and hence increased supply response in many economies, especially ours, has been a formidable force suppressing price increases as well. Finally, the global economic crisis of 1997 and 1998 reduced the prices of energy and other key inputs into production and consumption, helping to hold down inflation for several years.[6]

---

[6] See this chapter's Further Reading section for a reference to Greenspan's speech as well as for articles by Lawrence Katz, Alan Krueger, and Robert Gordon that discuss the inflation puzzle of the 1990s.

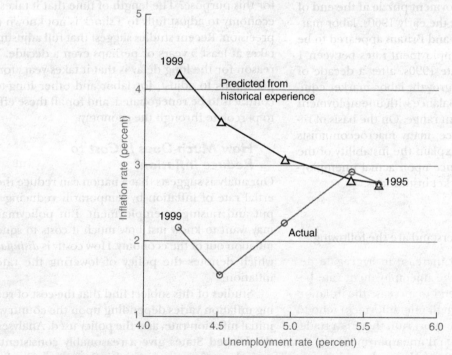

FIGURE 32-11. Actual and Predicted Inflation, 1995–1999

The late 1990s saw unusually moderate inflation for a period of rapid growth and low unemployment. This figure shows actual inflation for the late 1990s along with that predicted by a standard equation. Did this signal a "new era" in the American economy—or simply a coincidence of favorable price and wage surprises?

Source: Actual CPI and unemployment rate from Bureau of Labor Statistics. Predicted inflation assumes a NAIRU of 5.5 percent.

Doubts about the NAIRU

The concept of the nonaccelerating inflation rate of unemployment, along with its output twin of potential GDP, is crucial for understanding inflation and the connection between the short run and the long run in macroeconomics. But the mainstream view remains controversial.

Critics wonder whether the NAIRU is a stable and reliable concept. The inflation experience of the United States has undermined faith about a stable NAIRU for that country. Another question is whether an extended period of high unemployment will lead to a deterioration of job skills, to loss of on-the-job training and experience, and thereby to a higher NAIRU. Might not slow growth of real GDP reduce investment and leave the country with a diminished capital stock? Might not that capacity shortage produce rising inflation even with unemployment rates above the NAIRU?

Experience in Europe over the last two decades confirms some of these worries (recall our discussion of the European unemployment puzzle at the end of the previous chapter). In the early 1960s, labor markets in Germany, France, and Britain appeared to be in equilibrium with unemployment rates between 1 and 2 percent. By the late 1990s, after a decade of stagnation and slow job growth, labor market equilibrium seemed to be in balance with unemployment rates in the 6 to 12 percent range. On the basis of recent European experience, many macroeconomists are looking for ways to explain the instability of the NAIRU and its dependence upon actual unemployment as well as labor market institutions.

Review

The major points to understand are the following:

- In the short run, an increase in aggregate demand which lowers the unemployment rate below the NAIRU will tend to increase the inflation rate. Recessions and high unemployment tend to lower inflation. In the short run, there is a trade-off between inflation and unemployment.
- When inflation is higher or lower than what people expect, inflation expectations adjust. The changed inflation expectations will generally shift the short-run Phillips curve up or down.
- The long-run Phillips curve is vertical at the nonaccelerating inflation rate of unemployment (NAIRU). Unemployment above (below) the NAIRU will tend to lower (increase) the rate of inflation.
- Phillips curves are unstable across countries and time.

C. DILEMMAS OF ANTI-INFLATION POLICY

The economy evolves in response to political forces and technological change. Our economic theories, designed to explain issues like inflation and unemployment, must also adapt. In this final section on inflation theory, we discuss the pressing issues that arise in combating inflation.

How Long Is the Long Run?

The NAIRU theory holds that the Phillips curve is vertical in the long run. Just how long is the long run for this purpose? The length of time that it takes the economy to adjust fully to a shock is not known with precision. Recent studies suggest that full adjustment takes at least 5 years or perhaps even a decade. The reason for the long delay is that it takes years for expectations to adjust, for labor and other long-term contracts to be renegotiated, and for all these effects to percolate through the economy.

How Much Does It Cost to Reduce Inflation?

Our analysis suggests that a nation can reduce the inertial rate of inflation by temporarily reducing output and raising unemployment. But policymakers may want to know just how much it costs to squeeze inflation out of the economy. How costly is *disinflation*, which denotes the policy of lowering the rate of inflation?

Studies of this subject find that the cost of reducing inflation varies depending upon the country, the initial inflation rate, and the policy used. Analyses for the United States give a reasonably consistent answer: Lowering the inertial inflation rate by 1 percentage point costs the nation about 4 percent of 1 year's GDP. In terms of the current level of GDP, this amounts to an output loss of about $400 billion (in 2003 prices) to reduce the inflation rate by 1 percentage point.

To understand the cost of disinflation, consider the Phillips curve. If the Phillips curve is relatively flat, reducing inflation will require much unemployment and loss in output; if the Phillips curve is steep, a small rise in unemployment will bring down inflation quickly and relatively painlessly. Statistical analyses indicate that when the unemployment rate rises 1 percentage point above the NAIRU for 1 year and then returns to the NAIRU, the inflation rate will decline about ½ percentage point. Therefore, to reduce inflation by 1 full percentage point, unemployment must be held 2 percentage points above the NAIRU for 1 year.

Recall that Okun's Law (discussed in Chapter 31) holds that when the unemployment rate is 2 percentage points above the NAIRU, actual GDP is 4 percent below potential GDP. In 2003 terms, with a potential GDP (in 1999 prices) of $10,000 billion, reducing inflation by 1 percentage point would require about a 2-percentage-point increase in the unemployment rate (U) for 1 year. In dollars, then, a disinflation of 1 percentage point would cost 2 U points $\times$ 2 percent of GDP per U point $\times$ $10,000 billion of GDP = $400 billion. There is uncertainty here, however, and estimates of the cost range from $200 to $550 billion per point of inflation reduction.

This statistical estimate of the cost of reducing inflation can be compared to the American experience during the deep recession in the early 1980s. Table 32-2 shows a calculation of the estimated output loss from the recession (compared to producing at potential output), along with the estimated decline in the inertial inflation rate. This calculation indicates that the disinflation of the 1980–1984 period cost the nation approximately $275 billion of lost output (in 2003 prices) per percentage-point reduction in inflation. This episode corroborates statistical estimates of the cost of disinflation.

Credibility and Inflation

One of the most important questions in anti-inflation policy concerns the role of credibility of policy. Many economists argue that the Phillips-curve approach is too pessimistic. The dissenters hold that credible and

---

The Cost of Disinflation, 1980–1984	
Inertial rate of inflation:	
1979	9%
1984	4%
Change:	−5 percentage points
Difference between potential and actual GDP (2003 prices):	
1980	$150 billion
1981	170
1982	440
1983	425
1984	190
Total: $1,375 billion	

Cost of disinflation = $1,375 billion/5 percentage points
= $275 billion per percentage point
= 24 percent of GDP
= 4.8 percent of GDP per point of inflation

TABLE 32-2. The Cost of Disinflation, 1980–1984

What was the cost of reducing inflation in the 1980–1984 period? Tight monetary policy led to a deep recession during which the economy produced $1375 billion less than its potential GDP. As a result, the inflation rate declined by 5 percentage points. Dividing these two figures provides an estimate of $275 billion of output lost per percentage-point reduction in inflation.

Source: Authors' estimates based on CBO estimates of the NAIRU.

publicly announced policies—for example, adopting fixed monetary rules or targeting nominal GDP—would allow anti-inflation policies to reduce inflation with lower output and unemployment costs.

The idea relies on the fact that inflation is an inertial process that depends on people's expectations of future inflation. A credible monetary policy—such as one that relentlessly targets a fixed, low inflation rate—might lead people to expect that inflation would be lower in the future, and this belief might in some measure be a self-fulfilling prophecy. Those emphasizing credibility backed their theories by citing "regime changes," such as monetary and fiscal reforms that ended Austrian and Bolivian hyperinflations at relatively low cost in terms of unemployment or lost GDP.

Many economists were skeptical about claims that credibility would significantly lower the output costs of disinflation. While such policies might work in countries torn by hyperinflation, war, or revolution, Draconian anti-inflation policies would be less credible in the United States. Congress and the president often lose heart when unemployment rises sharply to fight inflation, and farmers or construction workers storm the Capitol and circle the White House.

The bold U.S. experiment of 1980–1984 provided a good laboratory to test the credibility critique. During this period, monetary policy was tightened in a clear and forceful manner. Yet the price tag was still high, as Table 32-2 shows. Using tough, preannounced policies to enhance credibility does not appear to have lowered the cost of disinflation in the United States.

Because the United States has such a high degree of stability of its political and economic institutions, its experience may be unusual. Economists have examined anti-inflation policies in other countries and have determined that anti-inflation policies can sometimes be *expansionary*. A recent study by Stanley Fischer, Ratna Sahay, and Carlos A. Végh concluded as follows:

> Periods of high inflation are associated with bad macroeconomic performance. In particular, high inflation is bad for growth. The evidence is based on a sample of 18 countries which have experienced very high inflation episodes. During such periods, real GDP per capita fell on average by 1.6 percent per annum (compared to positive growth of 1.4 percent

in low inflation years). . . . Exchange rate–based stabilizations appear to lead to an initial expansion in real GDP and real private consumption.[7]

How Can We Lower the NAIRU?

Given the costs of high unemployment, we might ask: Is the NAIRU the optimal level of unemployment? If not, what can we do to lower it toward a more desirable level? Economists of a classical persuasion often argue that the NAIRU (or what they call the "natural rate") represents the economy's efficient unemployment level. They hold that it is the outcome of supply and demand grinding out an efficient pattern of jobs, job vacancies, and job search. It would make no more sense to lower the NAIRU than to lower the vacancy rate for apartments or the number of spare tires we carry in our cars.

Other economists strongly disagree, holding that the NAIRU is likely to be above the optimal unemployment rate or the unemployment rate at which an economy's net economic welfare is maximized. This group argues that there are many spillovers or externalities in the labor market. For example, workers who have been laid off suffer from a variety of social and economic hardships. Yet employers do not pay the costs of unemployment; most of the costs (unemployment insurance, health costs, family distress, etc.) spill over as external costs and are absorbed by the worker or by the government. To the extent that unemployment has "external" costs, the NAIRU is likely to be higher than the optimal rate. Lowering the unemployment rate would raise the nation's net economic welfare.

An enormous social dividend, therefore, would reward the society that discovers how to reduce the NAIRU significantly. What measures might lower the NAIRU?

- *Improve labor market services.* Some unemployment occurs because job vacancies are not matched up with unemployed workers. Through better information, such as computerized job lists, the amount of frictional and structural unemployment can be reduced.
- *Bolster training programs.* If you read the help-wanted section of your Sunday newspaper, you will find that most of the job vacancies call for

---

[7] See the reference to Fischer et al. in this chapter's Further Reading section.

skills held by few people. Conversely, most of the unemployed are unskilled or semiskilled workers or find themselves in the wrong job or in a depressed industry. Many believe that government or private training programs can help unemployed workers retool for better jobs in growing sectors. If successful, such programs provide the double bonus of allowing people to lead productive lives and of reducing the burden on government transfer programs.

- *Remove government obstacles.* We noted above that in protecting people from the hardships of unemployment and poverty, the government has at the same time removed the sting of unemployment and reduced incentives to seek work. Some economists call for reforming the unemployment-insurance system and for reducing the disincentives for work in health, disability, and social security programs. The United States has significantly reduced the generosity of its income-support programs in the last two decades, including a radical restructuring of welfare in 1996. While welfare reform is likely

to increase the labor-force participation of low-income households, the impact on the NAIRU is unclear. If welfare cuts bring into the workforce unskilled and inexperienced workers who tend to have higher unemployment rates, these measures may well raise the NAIRU.

* * *

Having surveyed the history and theory of unemployment and inflation, we conclude with the following cautious summary:

Critics believe that the high unemployment that often prevails in North America and Europe is a central flaw in modern capitalism. Indeed, unemployment must sometimes be kept above its socially optimal level to ensure price stability, and the tension between price stability and low unemployment is one of the cruelest dilemmas of modern society. While the United States has avoided high unemployment and high inflation in the last decade, other countries have not been so fortunate.

SUMMARY

A. Definition and Impact of Inflation

1. Recall that inflation occurs when the general level of prices is rising. The rate of inflation is the percentage change in a price index from one period to the next. The major price indexes are the consumer price index (CPI) and the GDP deflator.

2. Like diseases, inflations come in different strains. We generally see low inflation in the United States (a few percentage points annually). Sometimes, galloping inflation produces price rises of 50 or 100 or 200 percent each year. Hyperinflation takes over when the printing presses spew out currency and prices start rising many times each month. Historically, hyperinflations have almost always been associated with war and revolution.

3. Inflation affects the economy by redistributing income and wealth and by impairing efficiency. Unanticipated inflation usually favors debtors, profit seekers, and risk-taking speculators. It hurts creditors, fixed-income classes, and timid investors. Inflation leads to distortions in relative prices, tax rates, and real interest rates. People take more trips to the bank, taxes may creep

up, and measured income may become distorted. And when central banks take steps to lower inflation, the real costs of such steps in terms of lower output and employment can be painful.

B. Modern Inflation Theory

4. At any time, an economy has a given inertial or expected inflation rate. This is the rate that people have come to anticipate and that is built into labor contracts and other agreements. The inertial rate of inflation is a short-run equilibrium and persists until the economy is shocked.

5. In reality, the economy receives incessant price shocks. The major kinds of shocks that propel inflation away from its inertial rate are demand-pull and cost-push. Demand-pull inflation results from too much spending chasing too few goods, causing the aggregate demand curve to shift up and to the right. Wages and prices are then bid up in markets. Cost-push inflation is a new phenomenon of modern industrial economies and occurs when the costs of production rise even in periods of high unemployment and idle capacity.

6. The Phillips curve shows the relationship between inflation and unemployment. In the short run, lowering one rate means raising the other. But the short-run Phillips curve tends to shift over time as expected inflation and other factors change. If policymakers attempt to hold unemployment below the NAIRU for long periods, inflation will tend to spiral upward.

7. Modern inflation theory relies on the concept of the nonaccelerating inflation rate of unemployment, or NAIRU, which is the lowest sustainable unemployment rate that the nation can enjoy without risking an upward spiral of inflation. It represents the level of unemployment of resources at which labor and product markets are in inflationary balance. Under the NAIRU theory, there is no permanent tradeoff between unemployment and inflation, and the long-run Phillips curve is vertical.

C. Dilemmas of Anti-inflation Policy

8. A central concern for policymakers is the cost of reducing inertial inflation. Current estimates indicate that a substantial recession is necessary to slow inertial inflation.

9. Economists have put forth many proposals for lowering the NAIRU; notable proposals include improving labor market information, improving education and training programs, and refashioning government programs so that workers have greater incentives to work.

CONCEPTS FOR REVIEW

History and Theories of Inflation

$$\text{Inflation}(t) = \frac{P(t) - P(t-1)}{P(t-1)} \times 100$$

strains of inflation:
  low
  galloping
  hyperinflation
impacts of inflation (redistributive, on output and employment)

anticipated and unanticipated inflation
costs of inflation:
  "shoe leather"
  menu costs
  income and tax distortions
  loss of information
inertial, demand-pull, and cost-push inflation

short-run and long-run Phillips curves
nonaccelerating inflation rate of unemployment (NAIRU) and the long-run Phillips curve

Anti-inflation Policy

costs of disinflation
measures to lower the NAIRU

FURTHER READING AND INTERNET WEBSITES

Further Reading

The source of the quote on low inflation is George A. Akerlof, William T. Dickens, and George L. Perry, "The Macroeconomics of Low Inflation," *Brookings Papers on Economic Activity*, no. 1, 1996, pp. 1–59. The quotation from Stanley Fischer, Ratna Sahay, and Carlos A. Végh is from their article, "Modern Hyper- and High Inflations," *Journal of Economic Literature*, September 2002, pp. 837–880.

Interesting analyses of the inflation puzzle of the 1990s can be found in Lawrence F. Katz and Alan B. Krueger, "The High-Pressure U.S. Labor Market of the 1990s," *Brookings Papers on Economic Activity*, no. 1, 1999, and Robert J. Gordon, "Foundations of the Goldilocks Economy," *Brookings Papers on Economic Activity*, no. 2, 1998.

A discussion of factors influencing the NAIRU can be found in Congressional Budget Office, *The Effect of Changes in Labor Markets on the Natural Rate of Unemployment*, April 2002, available at www.cbo.gov or www.cbo.gov/byclasscat. cfm?cat=32.

Websites

The quotes from Alan Greenspan are from a speech before the Economic Club of New York, January 13, 2000, which is available at the Federal Reserve Web page at www.bog. frb.fed.us/boarddocs/speeches/2000.

Analysis of the consumer price data for the United States comes from the Bureau of Labor Statistics, at www.bls.gov.

QUESTIONS FOR DISCUSSION

1. Consider the following impacts of inflation: tax distortions, income and wealth redistribution, shoe-leather costs, menu costs. For each, define the cost and provide an example.

2. "During periods of inflation, people use real resources to reduce their holdings of fiat money. Such activities produce a private benefit with no corresponding social gain, which illustrates the social cost of inflation." Explain this quotation and give an example.

3. Unanticipated deflation also produces serious social costs. For each of the following, describe the deflation and analyze the associated costs:
   a. During the Great Depression, prices of major crops fell along with the prices of other commodities. What would happen to farmers who had large mortgages?
   b. Japan experienced a mild deflation in the 1990s. Assume that Japanese students each borrowed 2,000,000 yen (about $20,000) to pay for their education, hoping that inflation would allow them to pay off their loans in inflated yen. What would happen to these students if wages and prices began to *fall* at 5 percent per year?

4. The data in Table 32-3 describe inflation and unemployment in the United States from 1979 to 1987. Note that the economy started out near the NAIRU in 1979 and ended near the NAIRU in 1987. Can you explain the decline of inflation over the intervening years? Do so by drawing the short-run and long-run Phillips curves for each of the years from 1979 to 1987.

5. Many economists argue as follows: "Because there is no long-run tradeoff between unemployment and inflation, there is no point in trying to shave the peaks and troughs from the business cycle." This view suggests that we should not care whether the economy is stable or fluctuating widely as long as the average level of unemployment is the same. Discuss critically.

6. A leading economist has written: "If you think of the social costs of inflation, at least of moderate inflation, it is hard to avoid coming away with the impression that they are minor compared with the costs of

unemployment and depressed production." Write a short essay describing your views on this issue.

7. Consider the data on annual inflation rates and growth of per capita GDP shown in Table 32-1. Can you see that low inflation is associated with the highest growth rates? What are the economic reasons that growth might be lower for deflation and for hyperinflation. Explain why the *ex post* fallacy might apply here (see the discussion in Chapter 1).

8. The following policies and phenomena affected labor markets over the last two decades. Explain the likely effect of each on the NAIRU:
   a. Unemployment insurance became subject to taxation.
   b. Funds for training programs for unemployed workers were cut sharply by the federal government.
   c. The fraction of the workforce in labor unions fell sharply.
   d. The welfare-reform act of 1996 sharply reduced payments to low-income families and required them to work if they were to receive government payments.

Year	Unemployment rate (%)	Inflation rate, CPI (% per year)
1979	5.8	11.3
1980	7.1	13.5
1981	7.6	10.3
1982	9.7	6.2
1983	9.6	3.2
1984	7.5	4.4
1985	7.2	3.6
1986	7.0	1.9
1987	6.2	3.6

TABLE 32-3. Unemployment and Inflation Data for the United States, 1979–1987

Source: *Economic Report of the President, 2000.*

33

The Warring Schools of Macroeconomics

If you lay all the economists end to end, they still won't reach a conclusion.

George Bernard Shaw

If you listen to debates about the federal deficit, tax policy, or social security, you will hear spirited arguments on almost everything except the definition of GDP. Some economists propose reducing the government deficit, while others argue for lower taxes to spur long-term growth. Some want the government to take a more active role in managing the economy, while others believe that the government should remain as small and unobtrusive as possible. It's easy to agree with Shaw's little quip at the beginning of this chapter.

We are convinced, however, that a careful study of economics will allow you to look behind the heated debates to see that there are a few recurring issues that separate the different schools. One theme stems from different views about how aggregate demand is determined; another concerns the role of price flexibility; yet another revolves around how people form their expectations and make decisions.

Our philosophy in this textbook is to consider all the important schools of thought. We tend to emphasize the modern mainstream Keynesian approach as the best way to explain the business cycle in market economies. But the forces behind long-run economic growth are best understood by using the neoclassical model. And to these basic tools we must increasingly add the open-economy issues discussed in Chapters 29 and 30.

While our key task has been to present mainstream thinking, experience shows how important it is to keep our minds open to alternative points of view. Time and again in science, the orthodoxies of one period are overturned by new discoveries. Schools, like people, are subject to hardening of the arteries. Students learn the embalmed truth from their teachers and sacred textbooks, and the imperfections in the orthodox doctrines are ignored as unimportant. For example, John Stuart Mill, one of the greatest economists and philosophers of all time, wrote in his 1848 classic, *Principles of Political Economy:* "Happily, there is nothing in the laws of Value which remains for the present and any future writer to clear up." And this was written before supply-and-demand analysis was even discovered!

Historians of science observe that the progress of science is discontinuous. New schools of thought rise, spread their influence, and convince skeptics. Perhaps somewhere in the warring schools of macroeconomics that we review in this chapter lie the seeds of the new theory that will resolve the painful dilemmas of the mixed market economy.

A. CLASSICAL STIRRINGS AND KEYNESIAN REVOLUTION

THE CLASSICAL TRADITION

Since the dawn of economics two centuries ago, economists have wondered whether or not a market economy has a tendency to move spontaneously toward a long-run, full-employment equilibrium without the need for government intervention. Using modern language, we label as **classical** those approaches that emphasize the self-correcting forces in an economy. The classical approach holds that prices and wages are flexible and the economy is stable, so the economy moves automatically and quickly to its full-employment equilibrium. Our discussion uses the aggregate supply-and-demand framework to explain the scientific foundations and the policy implications of the classical approach to macroeconomics.

Say's Law of Markets

Before Keynes developed his macroeconomic theories, the major economic thinkers generally adhered to the classical view of the economy, at least in good times. Early economists were fascinated by the Industrial Revolution, with its division of labor, accumulation of capital, and growing international trade. These economists knew about business cycles, but they viewed them as temporary and self-correcting aberrations.

Classical analysis revolved around **Say's Law of Markets.** This theory, propounded in 1803 by the French economist J. B. Say, states that overproduction is impossible by its very nature. This is sometimes expressed as "supply creates its own demand." What is the rationale for Say's Law? It rests on a view that there is no essential difference between a monetary economy and a barter economy—that whatever factories can produce, workers can afford to buy.

A long line of the most distinguished economists, including David Ricardo (1817), John Stuart Mill (1848), and Alfred Marshall (1890), subscribed to the classical macroeconomic view that overproduction is impossible. The classical view was stated clearly by the leading British economist A. C. Pigou, writing during the Great Depression:

With perfectly free competition there will always be a strong tendency toward full employment. Such unemployment as exists at any time is due wholly to the frictional resistances [that] prevent the appropriate wage and price adjustments being made instantaneously.[1]

The classical theory holds that wages and prices are flexible so that markets will very quickly "clear," or return to equilibrium. As a result, the economy operates at full employment.

The durable and valid core of Say's Law and of the classical approach is shown in Figure 33-1. This shows an economy where prices and real wages are determined in competitive markets, moving flexibly up and down to eliminate any excess demand or supply. In terms of our *AS-AD* analysis, it can be described by a standard, downward-sloping aggregate demand curve along with a vertical aggregate supply curve.

---

[1] See Pigou in the Further Reading section at the end of this chapter.

FIGURE 33-1. According to Say's Law, Supply Creates Its Own Demand as Prices Move to Balance Demand with Aggregate Supply

Classical economists thought that persistent periods of glut could not occur. If *AS* or *AD* shifted, prices would react flexibly to ensure that full-employment output was sold. Here we see how flexible prices move down enough to match real expenditures with full-employment output after a decline in aggregate demand.

Suppose that aggregate demand falls due to tight money, falling exports, or other exogenous forces. As a result, the *AD* curve shifts leftward to *AD'* in Figure 33-1. At the original price level of *P*, total spending would fall to point *B*. As a result of the excess supply, the overall price level falls from *P* to *P'*. As the price level falls, full employment is reestablished at point *C*.

The classical view of the economy is that changes in the money supply, fiscal policy, or other spending have no lasting impact upon output or employment. Prices and wages move flexibly to maintain full employment.

Policy Consequences

The classical view has two conclusions that are vitally important for economic policy. To begin with, under the classical view the economy has only brief and temporary lapses from full employment and full utilization of capacity. There will be no long and sustained recessions or depressions, and qualified workers can quickly find work at the going market wage.

None of this implies that the classical economy is a nirvana of frictionless perfect competition. We may see frictional unemployment of people moving between jobs or structural unemployment of unionized workers who have bargained for above-equilibrium wage rates. Market power may produce *microeconomic* waste, distortions, and inefficiencies. But in the classical view, an economy has no pervasive and persistent *macroeconomic* waste in the sense of underutilized resources due to insufficient aggregate demand.

The second surprising element of the classical view is that aggregate demand policies cannot influence the level of unemployment and real output. Rather, monetary and fiscal policies can affect only the economy's price level, along with the composition of real GDP. This second classical proposition is easily seen in Figure 33-1. Consider an economy in equilibrium at point *A*. Suppose that the central bank decides to contract the money supply to reduce inflation. For a brief instant, at the initial price level *P*, there is excess supply. However, as prices and wages quickly begin to fall under the pressure of excess supply, the economy moves to the new equilibrium at point *C*. The contractionary economic policy has reduced the overall price level. But output

and employment are essentially unchanged because price and wage flexibility has ensured a smooth transition between the old equilibrium and the new one.

At the heart of the classical view is the belief that prices and wages are flexible and that wage-price flexibility provides a self-correcting mechanism that quickly restores full employment. This approach is very much alive in the writings of today's new classical school, which we review later in this chapter. New classical economists move beyond the simplest classical approaches by allowing for imperfect information, the existence of technological shocks, and frictions from shifts of resources among industries. Although dressed in modern clothing, their policy conclusions are closely linked to those of the classical economists of an earlier age.

THE KEYNESIAN REVOLUTION

While classical economists were preaching the impossibility of persistent unemployment, economists of the 1930s could hardly ignore the vast army of unemployed workers begging for work and selling pencils on street corners. How could economics explain such massive and persistent idleness?

Keynes's *The General Theory of Employment, Interest and Money* (1936) offered an alternative macroeconomic theory, a new set of theoretical spectacles for looking at the impact of economic policies as well as external shocks. In fact, the Keynesian revolution combined two different elements. First, Keynes presented the concept of aggregate demand that was explored in depth in earlier chapters. A second and equally revolutionary feature was the Keynesian theory of aggregate supply. Whereas the classical approach assumed flexible prices and wages with the implication of a vertical classical *AS* curve, the Keynesian approach insisted on price and wage inflexibility and the flat or upward-sloping *AS* curve. In Keynes's approach, supply definitely does not create its own demand; demand can have a life of its own.

The Surprising Consequences

By combining these two new elements, Keynes brought a veritable revolution to macroeconomics. The essence of Keynes's argument is shown in Figure 33-2 on the next page. This now-familiar diagram combines an aggregate demand curve with a Keynesian, upward-sloping aggregate supply curve.

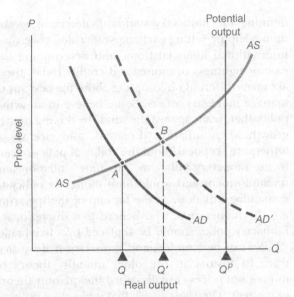

FIGURE 33-2. Aggregate Demand Helps Determine Output in the Keynesian Approach.

Keynesian aggregate supply slopes upward, implying that output will increase with higher aggregate demand as long as there are unused resources. With depressed demand, output will be in equilibrium at point *A*, with high unemployment.

If aggregate demand increases from *AD* to *AD'*, real output increases from *Q* to *Q'*. Keynesians emphasize that stimulating aggregate demand can succeed in increasing output and employment.

The first observation is that a modern market economy can get trapped in an underemployment equilibrium—a balance of aggregate supply and demand in which output is far below potential and a substantial fraction of the workforce is involuntarily unemployed. For example, if aggregate demand is depressed (shown as point *A* in Figure 33-2), the economy may get stuck in a high-unemployment equilibrium for a decade. A nation could remain in its low-output, high-misery condition for a long time because there is no self-correcting mechanism or invisible hand to guide the economy back to full employment.

Keynes's second observation follows from the first. Through monetary and fiscal policies, the government can stimulate the economy and help maintain high levels of output and employment. For example, if the government were to increase its purchases, aggregate demand would increase, say, from *AD* to *AD'* in Figure 33-2. The impact would be an increase in output from *Q* to *Q'*, which reduces the gap between actual GDP and potential GDP.

Keynes's analysis created a revolution in macroeconomics, particularly among young economists who were living through the Great Depression of the 1930s and sensed something was terribly wrong with the classical model. Of course, the Great Depression was not the first event to reveal the flaws in the classical synthesis. Anyone with common sense could see the massive involuntary unemployment during depressions. But for the first time, the classical approach was confronted by a competing analysis. The Keynesian approach presented a new synthesis that swept through economics and fundamentally changed the way that economists and governments think about business cycles and economic policy.

THEORIES AND POLICY

In economics, what people see depends upon the theoretical spectacles they wear. Does a president, senator, or macroeconomist lean toward a classical or a Keynesian view? The answer to this question will often explain that person's view on many of the major economic-policy debates of the day.

Examples are legion. Economists who tend toward the classical view will often be skeptical about the need for government to stabilize business cycles. They argue that a government policy designed to increase aggregate demand will instead lead to escalating inflation. Even worse, Keynesian remedies will, in their view, slow long-run economic growth. Classical-type economists tend to worry about the long-run consequences of government actions on investment and economic growth. For example, in the classical view, government deficits may crowd out private investment. More public spending on health care or welfare will divert resources from private investment in factories and machinery.

Keynesian economists take a different tack. They think that the macroeconomy is prone to business cycles, with alternating periods of high unemployment followed by speculation and inflation. If the classical economist sees the economy as a temperate fellow who has the requisite glass of mineral water and vitamins every day, the Keynesian might picture the economy as a manic-depressive who periodically has a binge of irrational exuberance and shortly thereafter falls into a depressed hangover. Indeed, as one Fed chairman put it, the role of the Federal Reserve is to take the punch bowl away just when the party is getting lively.

Keynesians believe that the government can affect real economic activity by taking monetary or fiscal steps to change aggregate demand. A modern Keynesian economist would approve of steps to reduce aggregate demand when inflation is rising or to increase aggregate demand in recessions. Such economists in the United States increasingly lean toward using monetary policy to stabilize business cycles. But they also maintain the importance of fiscal automatic stabilizers that reduce the multiplier effect of unforeseen shocks, and they argue vehemently against policies, such as a constitutional amendment requiring a balanced budget, that would have fiscal policy exacerbate business fluctuations.

The debate between Keynesian and classical economists revolves fundamentally around whether the economy has strong self-correcting forces in flexible wages and prices that help maintain full employment. Classical approaches generally emphasize long-run economic growth and forgo business-cycle stabilization policies. Keynesian economists desire to supplement growth policies with appropriate monetary and fiscal policies to curb business-cycle excesses.

B. THE MONETARIST APPROACH

Inflation is always and everywhere a monetary phenomenon in the sense that it is and can be produced only by a more rapid increase in the quantity of money than in output.

Milton Friedman, *The New Palgrave Dictionary of Economics* (1987)

Financial and monetary systems cannot manage themselves. The government, including the central bank, must make fundamental decisions about defining the monetary standard, determining the money supply, setting exchange-rate rules, governing international financial flows, and determining the ease or tightness of money and credit. Today, there are many different philosophies about the best way to manage monetary affairs. Some believe in an active policy that "leans against the wind" by slowing money growth when inflation threatens, and vice versa. Others are skeptical about the ability of policymakers to use monetary policy to "fine-tune" inflation and unemployment and would limit monetary policy to containing inflation. At the far end of the spectrum are the monetarists, who believe that discretionary monetary policy should be replaced by a fixed rule.

We can best understand monetarism if we first trace its history in the older quantity theory of money and prices (usually called the quantity theory of money). Then we can see that it has close linkages to both classical and Keynesian approaches.

THE ROOTS OF MONETARISM

Monetarism holds that the money supply is the primary determinant of short-run movements in nominal GDP and of long-run movements in prices. Of course, Keynesian macroeconomics also recognizes the key role of money in determining aggregate demand. The main difference between monetarists and Keynesians lies in the different approaches to the determination of aggregate demand. While Keynesian theories hold that many forces other than money affect aggregate demand, monetarists argue that changes in the money supply are the primary factor that determines output and price movements.

In order to understand monetarism, we need to introduce a new equation (the *equation of exchange*), a new concept (the *velocity of money*), and a new relationship (the *quantity theory of money*).

The Equation of Exchange and the Velocity of Money

Sometimes money turns over very slowly; it sits under the mattress or in bank accounts for long periods between transactions. At other times, particularly during rapid inflation, people get rid of money quickly and money circulates rapidly from hand to hand. The speed of turnover of money is described by the concept of the velocity of money, introduced at the turn of this century by Cambridge University's

Alfred Marshall and Yale's Irving Fisher. It measures the number of times per year that the average dollar in the money supply is spent for goods and services. When the quantity of money is large relative to the flow of expenditures, the velocity of circulation is low; when money turns over rapidly, money's velocity is high.

The concept of velocity is formally introduced in the **equation of exchange.** This equation states:

$$MV \equiv PQ \equiv (p_1 q_1 + p_2 q_2 + \cdots)$$

where M is the money supply, V is the velocity of money, P is the price level, and Q is real output. This can be restated as the *definition of the velocity of money* by dividing by M:

$$V \equiv \frac{PQ}{M}$$

We generally measure PQ as total income or output, GDP, and the associated velocity concept is the *income velocity of money.*

Velocity is the rate at which money circulates through the economy. The **income velocity of money** is measured as the ratio of nominal GDP to the stock of money.[2]

We can think of the income velocity of money intuitively as the speed at which money changes hands in the economy. As a simple example, assume that the economy produces only bread and that GDP consists of 48 million loaves of bread, each selling at a price of \$1, so GDP = PQ = \$48 million per year. If the money supply is \$4 million, then by definition V = \$48/\$4 = 12 per year. This means that money turns over once a month as earnings are used to buy monthly bread.[3]

Figure 33-3 shows the history of the income velocity of transactions money (M_1) and broad money (M_2). The velocity of M_2 has been surprisingly stable over the last century and a half, while that of M_1 has risen sharply in the last five decades. The question of the stability and predictability of the velocity is central to macroeconomic policy.

The Quantity Theory of Prices

Having defined an interesting new variable called velocity, we now describe how early monetary specialists used the concept of velocity to explain movements in the overall price level. The key assumption is that *the velocity of money is relatively stable and predictable.* The reason for stability, according to monetarists, is that velocity mainly reflects underlying patterns in the timing of income and spending. If people get paid once a month and tend to spend all their incomes evenly over the course of the month, income velocity will be 12 per year. Incomes could double, prices might rise 20 percent, and total GDP may be up many times—yet with unchanged spending patterns the income velocity of money would remain unchanged. Only as people or businesses modify their spending patterns or the way they pay their bills does the velocity of income change.

On the basis of this insight about the relative stability of velocity, some early writers used velocity to explain changes in the price level. This approach, called the **quantity theory of money and prices**, rewrites the definition of velocity as follows:

$$P \equiv \frac{MV}{Q} \equiv \left(\frac{V}{Q}\right)M \equiv kM$$

This equation is obtained from the earlier definition of velocity by substituting the variable k as a shorthand for V/Q and solving for P. We write the equation this way because many classical economists believed that if transactions patterns were stable, k would be constant or relatively stable. In addition, they generally assumed full employment, which meant real output would grow smoothly and would equal potential GDP. Putting these two assumptions together, $k (= V/Q)$ would be near-constant in the short run and a smoothly growing trend in the long run.

What are the implications of the quantity theory? As we can see from the equation, if k were constant, the price level would then move proportionally with the supply of money. A stable money supply would produce stable prices; if the money supply grew rapidly, so would prices. Similarly, if the money supply

---

[2] The definitional equations have been written with the three-bar identity symbol rather than with the more common two-bar equality symbol. This usage emphasizes that they are "identities"—statements which tell us nothing about reality but which hold true by definition even if the United States experienced a hyperinflation or were in a deep depression.

[3] The velocity of money is closely related to the demand for money. If we rewrite the equation of exchange, we have $M/(PQ) = 1/V$. The left-hand side is the demand for money per unit of GDP. Our earlier discussion of money demand applies equally well to an analysis of velocity.

FIGURE 33-3. Trends in Velocity

Income velocity of M_1 is the ratio of nominal GDP to M_1, and similarly income velocity of M_2 is the ratio of nominal GDP to M_2. One of the tenets of monetarism is that V is relatively stable and predictable. How stable does V appear? Can you think of some reasons why V has grown over time? *Hint:* How do interest rates affect velocity?

Source: V_1 and V_2 constructed by the authors from data from the Federal Reserve Board, U.S. Department of Commerce, Milton Friedman and Anna Schwartz, and private scholars.

was multiplied by 10 or 100, the economy would experience galloping inflation or hyperinflation. Indeed, the most vivid demonstrations of the quantity theory of money can be seen in hyperinflations. Turning back to Figure 32-5 (page 671), note how prices rose a billionfold in Weimar Germany after the central bank unleashed the monetary printing presses. This is the quantity theory with a vengeance.

To understand the quantity theory of money, it is essential to recall that money differs fundamentally from ordinary goods like bread or cars. We want bread to eat and cars to drive. But we want money only because it buys us bread and cars. If prices in Russia today are 1000 times what they were a few years ago, it is natural that people will need about 1000 times as much money to buy things as they did before. Here lies the core of the quantity theory of money: the demand for money rises proportionally with the price level.

The quantity theory of money and prices holds that prices move proportionally with the supply of money. Although the quantity theory of money and prices is only a rough approximation, it does help explain why countries with low money growth have moderate inflation while others with rapid money growth find their prices galloping along.

MODERN MONETARISM

Modern monetary economics was developed after World War II by Chicago's Milton Friedman and his numerous colleagues and followers. (You may want to reread the biography of Friedman in Chapter 2.) Under Friedman's leadership, monetarists challenged the Keynesian approach to macroeconomics and emphasized the importance of monetary policy in macroeconomic stabilization. About two decades ago, the monetarist approach branched. One fork continued the older tradition, which we will now describe. The younger offshoot became the influential new classical school, which is analyzed later in this chapter.

The monetarist approach postulates that the growth of money determines nominal GDP in the short run and prices in the long run. This analysis operates in the framework of the quantity theory of money and prices and relies on the analysis of trends in velocity. Monetarists argue that the velocity of money is stable (or, in extreme cases, constant). If correct, this is an important insight, for the quantity equation shows that if V is constant, movements in M will affect PQ (or nominal GDP) proportionally.

The Essence of Monetarism

Like all serious schools of thought, monetarism has differing emphases and degrees. The following points are central to monetarist thinking:

1. *Money-supply growth is the prime systematic determinant of nominal GDP growth.* Monetarism holds that nominal aggregate demand is affected primarily by changes in the money supply. Fiscal policy has no impact upon aggregate demand. This is put neatly in the following oversimplified way: "Only money matters."

   Two propositions are central to monetarist theories. First, as Friedman has stated, "There is an extraordinary empirical stability and regularity to such magnitudes as income velocity that cannot but impress anyone who works extensively with monetary data." Second, many monetarists used to argue that the demand for money is completely insensitive to interest rates.[4]

   From the equation of exchange, if velocity V is stable, M will determine nominal GDP. Fiscal policy has no impact because, if V is stable, the only factor that can affect PQ is M. With constant V, there is simply no door by which taxes or government expenditures can enter the stage.

2. *Prices and wages are relatively flexible.* Recall that one of the precepts of Keynesian economics is that prices and wages are "sticky." While generally accepting the view that there is some inertia in wage-price setting, monetarists argue that the Phillips curve is relatively steep even in the short run and insist that the long-run Phillips curve is vertical. In the *AS-AD* framework, monetarists hold that the short-run *AS* curve is quite steep.

The monetarists put points 1 and 2 together. Because (1) money is the prime determinant of nominal GDP and (2) prices and wages are fairly flexible around potential output, the implication is that money-supply changes have only small and temporary effects on real output. M mainly affects P.

Accordingly, money can affect both output and prices in the short run. But within a few years, because the economy tends to operate near full employment, money's main impact is on the price level. Fiscal policy affects output and prices negligibly in both the short run and the long run. This is the essence of monetarist doctrine.

3. *The private sector is stable.* Finally, monetarists believe that the private economy, left to its own devices, is not prone to instability. Instead, most fluctuations in nominal GDP result from government action—in particular, changes in the money supply, which depend on the policies followed by the central bank.

Comparison of Monetarist and Keynesian Approaches

How do monetarist views compare with modern Keynesian approaches? In fact, there has been considerable convergence in views between these schools over the last three decades, and the disputes today are ones of emphasis rather than of fundamental beliefs.

We depict the major differences between monetarists and modern Keynesians in Figure 33-4. This figure shows both views in terms of the behavior of aggregate supply and demand. Two major differences stand out.

First, the two schools disagree about the forces that operate on aggregate demand. Monetarists believe that aggregate demand is affected solely (or primarily) by the money supply and that the impact of money on aggregate demand is stable and reliable. They also believe that fiscal policy or autonomous changes in spending, unless accompanied by monetary changes, will have negligible effects upon output and prices.[5]

---

[4] If velocity is constant, then it is invariant to the interest rate. On the other hand, if velocity responds to the interest rate, this allows fiscal policy and other nonmonetary forces to affect output by changing velocity. The proposition that the demand for money is insensitive to the interest rate has fallen out of favor in recent years.

[5] Note as well that the *AD* curve is drawn as a "rectangular hyperbola" under the monetarist assumptions. Recall that an equation $xy = constant$ describes a rectangular hyperbola in a graph of x and y. For given M and V, the aggregate demand curve is described by $PQ = constant$, so the *AD* curve is a rectangular hyperbola.

FIGURE 33-4. Comparison of Monetarist and Keynesian Views

In essence, monetarists say, "Only money matters for aggregate demand." Mainstream macroeconomists reply, "Money matters, but so does fiscal policy." A second difference revolves around aggregate supply, where Keynesian economists stress that the *AS* curve is relatively flat. If prices and wages are relatively flexible, as monetarists believe, then output will generally be close to its potential.

Keynesian economists, by contrast, hold that the world is more complex. While agreeing that money has an important effect upon aggregate demand, output, and prices, they argue that other factors also matter. Moreover, Keynesians point to conclusive evidence that *V* rises systematically with interest rates, so keeping *M* constant is not enough to keep nominal or real GDP constant. In one of the most remarkable examples of convergence, both monetarists and Keynesians today tend to believe that stabilization policy in the United States should be conducted primarily through monetary policy.

The second major difference between monetarist and Keynesian economists concerns the behavior of aggregate supply. Keynesian economists emphasize the inertia in prices and wages. Monetarists think that Keynesian economists exaggerate the economy's wage-price stickiness and that the short-run *AS* curve is quite steep—not vertical, perhaps, but much steeper than a Keynesian economist would allow.

Because they hold differing views about the slope of the *AS* curve, Keynesian economists and monetarists disagree on the short-run impact of changes in aggregate demand. Keynesian economists believe that a change in (nominal) demand will significantly change output with little effect on prices in the short run. Monetarists hold that a shift in demand will primarily end up changing prices rather than quantities.

The essence of monetarism in macroeconomic thinking centers on the importance of money in determining aggregate demand and on the relative flexibility of wages and prices.

The Monetarist Platform: Constant Money Growth

Over the last four decades, monetarism has played a significant role in shaping economic policy. Monetarist economists often espouse free markets and laissez-faire microeconomic policies. But the foremost contribution to macroeconomic policy has been their advocacy of fixed monetary rules in preference to discretionary fiscal and monetary policies.

In principle, a monetarist might recommend using monetary policy to fine-tune the economy. But monetarists have taken a different tack, arguing that the private economy is stable and that the government tends to destabilize the economy. Moreover, monetarists believe that money affects output only after long and variable lags, so the design of effective stabilization policies is a formidable task.

Thus a cardinal part of the monetarist economic philosophy is a **monetary rule:** Optimal monetary policy sets the growth of the money supply at a fixed rate and holds to that rate through all economic conditions.

What is the rationale for this view? Monetarists believe that a fixed growth rate of money (at 3 to 5 percent annually) would eliminate the major source of instability in a modern economy—the capricious and unreliable shifts of monetary policy. If we replaced the Federal Reserve with a computer program that always produces a fixed M-growth rate, there would be no bursts in M growth. With stable velocity, nominal GDP would grow at a stable rate. And if M grew at about the growth rate of potential GDP, the economy would soon attain price stability.

The Monetarist Experiment

Monetarist views gained widespread influence in the late 1970s. In the United States, many thought that Keynesian stabilization policies had failed to contain inflation. When inflation moved up into the double-digit range in 1979, many economists and policy-makers believed that monetary policy was the only hope for an effective anti-inflation policy.

In October 1979, the new chairman of the Federal Reserve, Paul Volcker, launched a fierce counterattack against inflation in what has been called a *monetarist experiment.* In a dramatic change of its operating procedures, the Fed decided to stop focusing on interest rates and instead endeavored to keep bank reserves and the money supply on predetermined growth paths.[6]

The Fed hoped that a strict quantitative approach to monetary management would accomplish

two things. First, it would allow interest rates to rise sharply enough to reduce aggregate demand, raise unemployment, and slow wage and price growth through the Phillips-curve mechanism. In addition, some believed that a tough and credible monetary policy would deflate inflationary expectations, particularly in labor contracts, and demonstrate that the high-inflation period was over. Once people's expectations were deflated, the economy could experience a relatively painless reduction in the underlying rate of inflation.

The experiment was successful in slowing the growth of nominal GDP and in reducing inflation. With tight money and high interest rates, nominal GDP growth slowed from 13 percent in 1978 to 4 percent in 1982. The unemployment rate rose from 6 to 10 percent over the same period. Inflation fell sharply. Any lingering doubts about the effectiveness of monetary policy were killed by the monetarist experiment. Money works. Money matters. Tight money can wring inflation out of the economy.

The Decline of Monetarism

Paradoxically, just as the monetarist experiment succeeded in rooting inflation out of the American economy—indeed, perhaps *because* of the success—changes in financial markets led to shifts in behavior that undermined the monetarist approach. During and after the monetarist experiment, the behavior of velocity changed sharply. Recall that monetarists hold that velocity is relatively stable and predictable. Given stable velocity, changes in the money supply would get smoothly translated into changes in nominal GDP.

But just as the monetarist doctrine was adopted, velocity became extremely unstable. Figure 33-5 shows the rate of change in velocity over the period 1960–1999. It shows how M_1 velocity was relatively stable in the 1960–1980 period as monetarism became influential. Velocity became much more unstable after 1980, however, as the high interest rates of the 1979–1982 period spurred financial innovations and the spread of interest-bearing checking accounts. Some believe that the instability in velocity was actually produced by the heavy reliance on targeting monetary aggregates during this period.

As the velocity of money became increasingly unstable, the Federal Reserve gradually stopped using it as a guide for monetary policy. By the early 1990s,

---

[6] Recall the discussion of the monetarist experiment in Chapter 26.

FIGURE 33-5. Rate of Change of Income Velocity of M_1

Monetarists rely upon stable velocity of money to argue for a constant rate of growth of the money supply. Velocity of money was relatively constant until the early 1980s. After that time, an active monetary policy, more volatile interest rates, and financial innovations led to extreme instability of velocity.

Source: Velocity defined as the ratio of GDP to M_1; money supply from the Federal Reserve Board and GDP from the Commerce Department, 2-year difference.

the Fed had turned primarily to trends in output, inflation, employment, and unemployment for its key indicators of the state of the economy. Indeed, in 1999, the minutes of the Federal Open Market Committee contain not a single mention of the term "velocity" to describe the state of the economy or to explain the reasons for the committee's short-run policy actions.

None of these developments diminishes the importance of money in the conduct of macroeconomic policy. Indeed, monetary policy is currently the major macroeconomic policy tool used for business-cycle management in the United States and Europe.

Although monetarism is no longer in fashion, monetary policy is the central tool of stabilization policy in large market economies today.

C. NEW APPROACHES TO MACROECONOMICS

Existing Keynesian macroeconomic models cannot provide reliable guidance in the formulation of monetary, fiscal, or other types of policy. . . . [T]here is no hope that minor or even major modifications of these models will lead to significant improvements in their reliability.

Robert E. Lucas Jr. and Thomas J. Sargent, "After Keynesian Macroeconomics"

Although most macroeconomists agree that monetary policy can affect unemployment and output, at least in the short run, a new branch of the classical school challenges the standard approach. This theory, called **new classical macroeconomics,** was developed by Robert Lucas (Chicago), Thomas Sargent (Chicago and Stanford), and Robert Barro (Harvard). This approach is much in the spirit of the classical approach, discussed above, in emphasizing the role of flexible wages and prices, but it adds a new feature, called rational expectations, to explain observations such as the Phillips curve. For his contributions to developing the new classical approach, and particularly the modern view of rational expectations, Robert Lucas was awarded the Nobel Prize in economics in 1996.

FOUNDATIONS

New classical macroeconomics holds that (1) prices and wages are flexible and (2) people use all available information in making decisions. These two postulates are the essence of the new classical approach to macroeconomics.

The first part of the new classical approach draws on the classical assumption of price and wage flexibility. This familiar assumption simply means that prices and wages adjust rapidly to balance supply and demand.

The second and new assumption draws upon modern developments in areas such as statistics and behavior under uncertainty. This hypothesis holds that people form their expectations on the basis of all available information. Under this assumption, the government cannot "fool" the people, for people are well informed and have access to the same information as the government.

We discussed the significance of price and wage flexibility for macroeconomics earlier in this chapter. We now turn to the rational-expectations hypothesis.

Rational Expectations

Expectations are important in economic life. They influence how much investors will spend on investment goods and whether consumers spend or save for the future. But what is a sensible way to treat expectations in economics? New classical macroeconomists answer this question with the **rational-expectations hypothesis.** According to rational

expectations, forecasts are unbiased and are based on all available information.[7]

What does all this mean? To begin with, the rational-expectations hypothesis holds that people make unbiased forecasts.[8] A more controversial assumption is that people use all available information and economic theory in making decisions. This implies that people understand how the economy works and what the government is doing. Thus, suppose that the government always boosts spending in election years. Rational-expectations theory assumes that people will anticipate this kind of behavior and act accordingly.

The key new assumption in new classical macroeconomics is that because of rational expectations the government cannot fool the people with systematic economic policies.

IMPLICATIONS FOR MACROECONOMICS

The insights of the new classical macroeconomics and related approaches will be illustrated with a number of important applications.

The Misperceptions Business Cycle

In our discussion in Chapter 31, we defined involuntary unemployment as a situation where qualified workers are unable to find jobs at the going wage. New classical economists think that most unemployment is voluntary. In their view, labor markets adjust quickly after economic disturbances as wages adjust to equilibrate supply and demand. Unemployment increases primarily because people quit to hunt for better jobs, not because they cannot find jobs.

This led to one early approach, developed by Robert Lucas, which held that misperceptions are

---

[7] Rational expectations is closely related to the efficient-market hypothesis concerning stock and other asset prices described in Chapter 25.

[8] A forecast is "unbiased" if it contains no systematic forecasting errors. Clearly a forecast cannot always be perfectly accurate—you cannot foresee how a coin flip will come up on a single toss. But you should not commit the statistical sin of *bias* by predicting that a fair coin would come up tails 10 or 90 percent of the time. You would be making an unbiased forecast if you predicted that the coin would come up tails 50 percent of the time or that one of the numbers on a die would, on average, come up one-sixth of the time.

the key to business cycles. Under this approach, high unemployment arises because workers are confused about economic conditions—workers voluntarily quit their jobs in a recession in the hope of getting better ones but are surprised to find that there are no job vacancies. In the expansion phase of the business cycle, high output and low unemployment occur when people are fooled into working harder because they overestimate real wages.

The misperceptions theory caused a stir of excitement because it could explain business cycles without such inelegant assumptions as inflexible wages and prices. It has gone out of fashion, however, because it had trouble explaining many cyclical phenomena, such as why workers tend to quit more (rather than less) in expansions and tend to lose jobs (rather than quit) in recessions.

Real Business Cycles

A closely related approach that has increasingly attracted classical macroeconomists, also relying on rational expectations and competitive markets but emphasizing different mechanisms, is **real-business-cycle (RBC) theory.** This approach holds that business cycles are primarily due to changes in technology and does not invoke any monetary or demand-side forces.

In the RBC approach, shocks to technology, investment, or labor supply change the potential output of the economy. In other words, they shift a *vertical AS* curve. These supply shocks are transmitted into actual output by the fluctuations of aggregate supply and are completely independent of *AD*. Similarly, movements in the unemployment rate are the result of movements in the nonaccelerating inflation rate of unemployment (NAIRU) due to microeconomic forces such as the intensity of sectoral shocks or to tax and regulatory policies.

The Ricardian View of Fiscal Policy

One of the most influential criticisms of Keynesian macroeconomics was a new view of the role of fiscal policy. This view, known as the **Ricardian view of fiscal policy** and developed by Harvard's Robert Barro, argues that changes in tax rates have no impact upon consumption spending.

The idea is a logical extension of the life-cycle model of consumption introduced in Chapter 22. Under the Ricardian view, individuals are farsighted

and form part of a succession of family members, like a dynasty. Parents care not only about their own consumption but also about the well-being of their children; the children, in turn, care about the well-being of their children; and so on. This structure, called "dynastic preferences," implies that the current generation's horizon stretches into the indefinite future through the overlapping concern of each generation about its offspring.

Here is where the surprising result comes: If the government cuts my taxes but leaves expenditures unchanged, this necessarily requires increased borrowing. But, with unchanged expenditures, the government will have to raise taxes to pay the interest on its new borrowing at some point in the future. In the Ricardian view, consumers have rational expectations about future policy, so when a tax cut occurs, they know they must plan for a future tax increase. They therefore will increase their saving by the amount of the tax cut, and consumption will remain unchanged. Moreover, even if the future tax increase comes after their lifetimes, people take into account the well-being of their children; they therefore cut current consumption so that they can increase their bequests to their children to pay the extra taxes.

The net result is that *in the Ricardian view tax changes have no impact upon consumption.* Moreover, government debt is not net debt from the point of view of households because they offset these assets in their mental calculations with the present value of taxes that must be paid to service the debt.

The Ricardian view of debt and deficits has stirred much controversy among macroeconomists. Critics point out that it requires that households be extremely farsighted, planning to give bequests to their children and constantly weighing their own interests against those of their descendants. The chain would be broken were there no children, no bequests, no concern for children, or poor foresight. The empirical evidence to date has not been kind to the Ricardian view, but it is a useful reminder of the logical limitations on fiscal policy.

Efficiency Wages

Another important recent development, fusing elements of both classical and Keynesian economics, is called **efficiency-wage theory.** This approach was developed by Columbia's Edmund Phelps, Joseph Stiglitz (chair of President Clinton's Council of

Economic Advisers in 1995–1997), and Janet Yellen (a governor of the Fed and chair of the Clinton Council of Economic Advisers from 1997 to 1999). It explains the rigidity of real wages and the existence of involuntary unemployment in terms of firms' attempts to keep wages above the market-clearing level to increase productivity. According to this theory, higher wages lead to higher productivity because workers are healthier (particularly in poor countries), because workers will have higher morale or be less likely to goof off, because good workers are then less likely to quit and look for new jobs, or because higher wages may attract better workers.

As firms raise their wages to increase productivity, job seekers may be willing to stand in line for these high-paying jobs, thereby producing involuntary wait unemployment. *The startling feature of this theory is that the involuntary unemployment is an equilibrium feature and will not disappear over time.*

Supply-Side Economics
In the early 1980s, another loosely organized school joined the debate. This school, known as **supply-side economics,** emphasized incentives and tax cuts as a means of increasing economic growth. Supply-side economics was espoused forcefully by President Reagan in the United States (1981–1989) and by Prime Minister Thatcher in Great Britain (1979–1990).

A first theme of supply-side economics was the key role played by incentives, particularly adequate returns to working, saving, and entrepreneurship. Supply siders pointed to the miracles performed by unfettered free markets and sought to avoid the disincentives due to high tax rates; moreover, they argued that Keynesians, in their excessive concern with demand management, had ignored the impact of tax rates and incentives on aggregate supply.

The other strand of supply-side thinking was its advocacy of large tax cuts. We saw in our analysis of the multiplier model how taxes could affect aggregate demand and output. Supply-side economists argued that the demand-side impacts were overemphasized. Instead, in their view, high taxes lead people to reduce their labor and capital supply. Indeed, some supply-side economists, particularly Arthur Laffer, have suggested that high tax rates might actually lower tax revenues. This *Laffer-curve* proposition holds that high tax rates shrink the tax base because they reduce economic activity. Mainstream

economists across the political spectrum, and even some supply-side economists, scoffed at the Laffer proposition that cutting tax rates would increase tax revenues.

To fix what they view as a defective tax system, supply-side economists proposed a radical restructuring of the tax system, through an approach sometimes called "supply-side tax cuts." The philosophy underlying supply-side tax cuts was that the reforms should improve incentives by lowering tax rates on the last dollar of income (or marginal tax rates); that the tax system should be less progressive (that is, it should lower the tax burden on high-income individuals); and that the system should be designed to encourage productivity and supply rather than to manipulate aggregate demand.

After occupying center stage during the 1980s, the supply-side approach to economics faded away after Ronald Reagan left office. In studying this period, economists generally have found that many of the supply-side assertions were not supported by economic experience. The legacies of the supply-side policies were high budget deficits and growing government debt. The deficits were not reversed by lower tax rates but by a period of expenditure reductions and tax increases.

Many of the supply-side policies were proposed again in 2001, when President George W. Bush successfully negotiated another round of income-tax cuts. These cuts were not rationalized by the argument that they would raise revenues, however. Instead, the economic rationale was that they would improve the efficiency of the tax system and raise the long-run rate of economic growth.

POLICY IMPLICATIONS
Policy Ineffectiveness
The new non-Keynesian approaches have several important implications for macroeconomic policy. One of the most important contentions, coming from the new classical approach, is the *ineffectiveness of systematic fiscal and monetary policies in reducing unemployment.* The basic idea is that a predictable attempt to stimulate the economy would be known in advance and would have no effect on the economy.

For example, suppose that the government always stimulated the economy whenever elections approached. After a couple of episodes of politically motivated fiscal policy, people would rationally come to expect that behavior. They might say to themselves,

> Elections are coming. However, from experience I know that the government always pumps up the economy before elections. I will get an election-year tax cut, but that will be followed by a stealth tax increase next year. They can't fool me into consuming more or working harder.

This is the **policy-ineffectiveness theorem** of classical macroeconomics. With rational expectations and flexible prices and wages, anticipated government policy cannot affect real output or unemployment.

The Desirability of Fixed Rules

Earlier, we described the monetarist case for fixed rules. New classical macroeconomics puts this argument on a much firmer footing. An economic policy can be divided into two parts, a predictable part (the "rule") and an unpredictable part ("discretion").

New classical macroeconomists argue that discretion is a snare and a delusion. Policymakers, they contend, cannot forecast the economy any better than the private sector can. Therefore, by the time policymakers act on the news, flexibly moving prices in markets populated by well-informed buyers and sellers have already adapted to the news and reached their efficient supply-and-demand equilibria. There are no further *discretionary* steps the government can take to improve the outcome or prevent the unemployment that is caused by transient misperceptions or real-business-cycle shocks.

Although they cannot make things better, government policies can definitely make things worse. They can generate unpredictable discretionary policies that give misleading economic signals, confuse people, distort their economic behavior, and cause waste. According to new classical macroeconomists, governments should avoid any discretionary macroeconomic policies rather than risk such confusing "noise."

Monetarist Rules and the Lucas Critique

Although the new classical school has shown some pitfalls that face policy-making, it has also levied a devastating argument against a key monetarist assumption. Monetarists believe that the velocity of money has shown a remarkable stability. Thus, they conclude, we can stabilize $MV \equiv PQ \equiv$ nominal GDP by imposing a fixed-money rule.

But the *Lucas critique*, named after Chicago's Robert Lucas, argues that people may change their behavior when policy changes. Just as the apparent short-run Phillips curve might shift when Keynesian governments attempt to manipulate it, so might the apparently constant velocity change if the central bank adopts a fixed-money-growth rule.

This insight was borne out in the period from 1979 to 1982, when the United States conducted the monetarist experiment described in the previous section. Velocity became extremely unstable, and eventually the Fed downplayed the use of monetary aggregates in managing monetary policy. (Recall Figure 33-5 and the discussion of unstable velocity above.)

The Lucas critique is a stern warning that economic behavior can change when policymakers rely too heavily upon past regularities.

STATE OF THE DEBATE

The new classical macroeconomics remains at the center of macroeconomic controversies. In one sense, the debate is a replay of the earlier arguments between Keynes and the classical economists. As in earlier debates, one of the key issues revolves around the extent of price and wage flexibility. Keynesian economists point to much evidence suggesting that prices and particularly wages move slowly in response to shocks, and few economists believe that labor markets are in constant supply-demand equilibrium. When the assumption of perfectly flexible wages and prices is abandoned, policy will regain its power to affect the real economy in the short run.

Additionally, critics point to some of the counterfactual implications of new classical macroeconomics. The theory holds that business-cycle fluctuations are "equilibrium" situations where firms and workers are confused by price or money shocks. But can misperceptions about wages and prices really explain deep depressions and persistent bouts of unemployment? Did it really take people a full decade to learn how hard times were in the Great Depression? And can Europeans be unaware of the depressed job markets that have persisted in their countries since 1990?

Finally, how can we reconcile the theoretical prediction that cyclical unemployment is produced when workers quit to look for better jobs with the evidence showing that the fraction of job losers rises sharply in recessions (see Figure 31-8, page 660)? Because most classical theories have similar implications, many mainstream economists are skeptical of the usefulness of new classical approaches for understanding business-cycle movements in output, employment, and goods prices.

A New Synthesis?

After two decades of digesting the new classical approach to macroeconomics, elements of a synthesis of old and new theories are beginning to appear. Economists now realize they must pay careful attention to expectations. A useful distinction is between the adaptive (or "backward-looking") approach and the rational (or "forward-looking") approach. The adaptive assumption holds that people form their expectations simply and mechanically on the basis of past information; the forward-looking or rational approach was described above. The importance of forward-looking expectations is crucial to understanding behavior, particularly in competitive auction markets like those in the financial sector.

Some macroeconomists have begun to fuse the new classical view of expectations with the Keynesian view of product and labor markets. This synthesis is embodied in macroeconomic models that assume (1) labor and goods markets display inflexible wages and prices, (2) the prices and quantities in financial auction markets adjust rapidly to economic shocks and expectations, and (3) the expectations in auction markets are formed in a forward-looking way.

One important prediction of new approaches is that forward-looking models tend to have large "jumps" or discontinuous changes in interest rates, stock prices, exchange rates, and oil prices in reaction to major news. Sharp reactions are often seen after elections or when wars break out. For example, when the United States invaded Iraq in March 2003, oil prices declined by 35 percent and stock prices rose by 10 percent *in a single week*. The new classical prediction of "jumpy" prices replicates one realistic feature of auction markets and thus suggests where forward-looking expectations might be important in the real world.

Figure 33-6 compares another difference, the expenditure multipliers of four forward-looking models and of seven adaptive-expectations models. Note that the multipliers of the forward-looking models are significantly smaller than those of the adaptive models.

The smaller multipliers in the forward-looking models arise because of faster reactions in financial markets. One reason is that, after a fiscal expansion, interest rates generally rise more rapidly in forward-

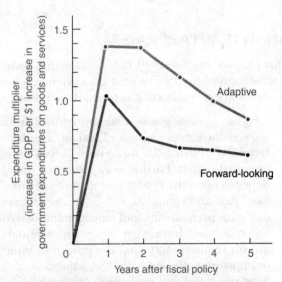

FIGURE 33-6. Comparison of Multipliers in Forward-Looking and Adaptive Models

What is the difference in the expenditure multipliers of models that are adaptive (backward-looking) and forward-looking (rational)? Because interest rates crowd out domestic investment and exchange rates affect net exports, adjustment takes place more rapidly in forward-looking models. Forward-looking expenditure multipliers are considerably smaller than those in adaptive models.

Source: Ralph C. Bryant, Gerald Holtham, and Peter Hooper, "Consensus and Diversity in the Model Simulations," in Ralph C. Bryant et al., eds., *Empirical Macroeconomics for Interdependent Economies* (Brookings Institution, Washington, D.C., 1988), Fig. 3-33.

looking models because forward-looking market participants predict a future expansion of output after an increase in government spending. This higher expected future output tends to increase interest rates today, and investment therefore tends to decline rapidly in forward-looking models. In addition, as interest rates rise quickly in response to a fiscal stimulus in forward-looking models, the flexible and forward-looking exchange rate of the dollar tends to jump upward. A rise in the exchange rate of the dollar leads to a reduction in net exports and tends to reduce the size of the fiscal stimulus.

The new classical approach to macroeconomics has brought many fruitful insights. Most important, it reminds us that the economy is populated by intelligent information processors who react to and often anticipate policy. This reaction and counterreaction can actually change the way the economy behaves.

* * *

AN INTERIM APPRAISAL

This chapter has surveyed the debates that divide macroeconomists. After hearing the evidence, a jury of impartial economists might conclude as follows:

1. *Long-run economic growth.* The trend growth in living standards, real wages, and real incomes is determined primarily by the growth in per capita potential output. Furthermore, potential output depends upon the quality and quantity of inputs like labor and capital as well as on the technology, entrepreneurship, and management skills of an economy. Improving long-run economic growth requires increasing the growth of inputs or improving efficiency and technology.
2. *Short-run output and employment.* Output and employment in the short run are determined by the interaction of aggregate supply and demand. At least for a few years, changes in aggregate demand (whether influenced by fiscal and monetary policies or by exogenous factors) can definitely influence output and employment. Monetary and fiscal policies have the potential to stabilize business cycles. Central banks are well placed to take the lead in stabilization policy.
3. *Unemployment and inflation.* Inflation has a great deal of inertia. However, when the economy is operating at high levels of utilization of capital and labor, inflation tends to rise. Conversely, recessions and high unemployment tend to reduce inflation. The NAIRU is that neutral zone for the unemployment rate where inflation is stable. But the inflation-unemployment tradeoff is unstable over time and space, so managing inflation is a complicated process. Moreover, countries cannot buy permanently lower unemployment by allowing high inflation to persist.

SUMMARY

A. Classical Stirrings and Keynesian Revolution

1. Classical economists relied upon Say's Law of Markets, which holds that "supply creates its own demand." In modern language, the classical approach means that flexible wages and prices quickly erase any excess supply or demand and quickly reestablish full employment and full utilization of capacity. In a classical system, macroeconomic policy has no role to play in stabilizing the real economy, although it will still determine the path of prices.
2. The Keynesian revolution postulated inflexibility of prices and wages, so output and unemployment are determined by the interaction of supply and demand forces. The Keynesian *AS* curve is upward-sloping rather than classically vertical, and monetary or fiscal policies therefore affect both prices and real output. There is no automatic self-correcting price mechanism, and the economy can therefore experience prolonged periods of depression or inflation.
3. In the modern Keynesian view, monetary and fiscal policies can substitute for flexible wages and prices, stimulating the economy during recessions and slowing aggregate demand during booms to forestall inflationary tendencies.

B. The Monetarist Approach

4. Monetarism holds that the money supply is the primary determinant of short-run movements in both real and nominal GDP as well as of long-run movements in nominal GDP.
5. Monetarism relies upon the analysis of trends in the velocity of money to understand the impact of money on the economy. The income velocity of circulation of money (V) is defined as the ratio of the dollar GDP flow to the stock of M:

$$V \equiv \frac{PQ}{M} \equiv \frac{GDP}{M}$$

While V is definitely not a constant—if only because it rises with interest rates—monetarists count on its movements being regular and predictable.
6. From velocity's definition comes the quantity theory of prices:

$$P \equiv kM \text{ where } k \equiv \frac{V}{Q}$$

The quantity theory of prices regards P as almost strictly proportional to M. This view is useful for understanding hyperinflations and certain long-term trends, but it should not be taken literally.

7. The monetarist school holds to three major propositions: (*a*) The growth of the money supply is the major systematic determinant of nominal GDP growth; (*b*) prices and wages are relatively flexible; and (*c*) the private economy is stable. These propositions suggest that macroeconomic fluctuations arise primarily from erratic money-supply growth.

8. Monetarists often propose that the money supply grow at a fixed rate of 3 to 5 percent annually. Some monetarists believe that this will produce steady growth with stable prices in the long run.

9. The Federal Reserve conducted a full-scale monetarist experiment from 1979 to 1982. The experience during this period convinced remaining skeptics that money is a powerful determinant of aggregate demand and that most of the short-run effects of money changes are on output rather than on prices. However, as suggested by

the Lucas critique, velocity may become quite unstable when a monetarist approach is followed.

C. New Approaches to Macroeconomics

10. New classical macroeconomics holds that expectations are rational, prices and wages are flexible, and unemployment is largely voluntary. The policy-ineffectiveness theorem holds that predictable government policies cannot affect real output and unemployment. If economic policymakers systematically attempt to increase output and decrease unemployment, people will quickly understand and anticipate the policy. Fixed policy rules will produce better economic outcomes. The theory of the real business cycle points to supply-side technological disturbances and labor market shifts as the clue to business-cycle fluctuations.

11. Review the interim appraisal for the current mainstream synthesis of the warring schools of macroeconomics.

CONCEPTS FOR REVIEW

Classical Economists vs. Keynes

flexible vs. sticky wages and prices
Say's Law of Markets
alternative views of aggregate supply

Velocity and Monetarism

equation of exchange: $MV \equiv PQ$
velocity of circulation of money:
$\quad V \equiv PQ/M$

quantity theory of money and
$\quad$ prices: $P \equiv kM$
1979–1982 monetarist experiment

New Approaches to Macroeconomics

rational (forward-looking)
$\quad$ expectations, adaptive (backward-looking) expectations
policy-ineffectiveness theorem

real business cycle, efficiency wages
tenets of supply-side economics
key assumptions: rational
$\quad$ expectations and flexible prices
$\quad$ and wages
Lucas critique
Ricardian view of fiscal policy

FURTHER READING AND INTERNET WEBSITES

Further Reading

The quote from Alfred Pigou is from *The Theory of Unemployment* (Macmillan, London, 1933). The classic monetary history of the United States by Milton Friedman and Anna Jacobson Schwartz describes a monetarist interpretation of history. See their *Monetary History of the United States 1867–1960* (Princeton University Press, Princeton, N.J., 1963).

Many of the foundations of new classical economics were developed by Robert Lucas and republished in *Studies in Business-Cycle Theory* (MIT Press, Cambridge, Mass., 1990). Modern efficiency-wage theory is presented in Edmund Phelps, *Structural Slumps: The Modern Equilibrium Theory of*

Unemployment, Interest, and Assets (Harvard University Press, Cambridge, Mass., 1994).

A nontechnical review of the troops of the warring schools is given by Paul Krugman, *Peddling Prosperity: Economic Sense and Nonsense in the Age of Diminished Expectations* (Norton, New York, 1994).

Websites

Real-business-cycle theory has its own website at ideas. uqam.ca/QMRBC/index.html.

The Nobel Prize citations of Milton Friedman and Robert Lucas (one of the major pioneers of the new classical macroeconomics) can be found at www.nobel.se/laureates.

QUESTIONS FOR DISCUSSION

1. Monetarists say, "Only money matters." Keynesians answer, "Money matters, but other things, like fiscal policy, matter too." Explain and evaluate each position. Could you disagree with monetarists and still believe that monetary policy should be used to counter recessions? Explain.

2. Assume that nominal GDP was $1000 billion in year 0 while the GDP deflator was 1 in year 0. Furthermore, the money supply in years 0, 1, 2, 3 and 4 was (in billions) $50, $52, $55, $58 and $60.
   a. Give the level of nominal output in years 1, 2, 3, and 4 according to the strict quantity theory of money.
   b. If there was no growth in potential output and the level of the money supply was following a preannounced path, what would the level of real GDP be according to new classical macroeconomics?

3. If, in boom times, we printed and spent $100 trillion in new greenbacks, what would happen to prices? Is there some truth, then, to the quantity theory? What might happen to prices if M were increased 1 percent in a depression? Compare the two cases.

4. A Keynesian economist might recommend a tax cut to revive the economy. What would be the effect on the AD curve, on price, and on real output? Relate your answer to the monetarist theory. (*Hint:* What happens to velocity?)

5. Define income velocity (V). For the data in Table 33-1, calculate the annual growth rate of the money supply and the level and rate of change of velocity. Also draw or plot on a computer graphs of the variables.

6. What would monetarists, Keynesians, and new classical macroeconomists predict to be the impacts of each of the following on the course of prices, output, and employment (in each case, hold tax rates and the money supply constant unless specifically mentioned):
   a. A large tax cut
   b. A large increase in the money supply
   c. A wave of innovations that increase potential output by 10 percent
   d. A burst of exports

7. In the discussion of the demand for money, and in the demand-for-money schedule in Figure 26-4, it was shown that the demand for money would be sensitive to interest rates. What would be the impact of higher interest rates on velocity for a given level of nominal GDP? What are the implications of interest-sensitive demand for money on monetarist arguments that rely upon constant velocity of money?

8. State and explain Say's Law of Markets. Starting from a macroeconomic equilibrium, assume that potential output increases but aggregate demand is unchanged. Using a graphical extension of Figure 33-1, show how supply creates its own demand. Describe the process in words.

9. **Advanced problem** (on rational expectations): Consider the effect of rational expectations on consumption behavior.
   a. Say the government proposes a temporary tax cut of $20 billion, lasting for a year. Consumers with adaptive expectations might assume that their disposable incomes would be $20 billion higher every year. What would be the impact on consumption spending and GDP in the simple multiplier model of Chapter 24?
   b. Next suppose that consumers have rational expectations. They rationally forecast that the tax cut is for only 1 year. Being "life-cycle" consumers, they recognize that their average lifetime incomes will increase (say) only $2 billion per year, not $20 billion per year. What would be the reaction of such consumers? Analyze, then, the impact of rational expectations on the effectiveness of temporary tax cuts.
   c. Finally, assume that consumers behave according to the Ricardian view. What would be the impact of the tax cut on saving and consumption. Explain the difference between the different models.

Year	Nominal GDP ($, billion)	Money supply, M_1 ($, billion, lagged 12 months)
1981	3,131.4	408.9
1982	3,259.2	436.5
1983	3,535.0	474.5
1984	3,932.8	521.2
1985	4,213.0	522.1
1986	4,452.9	620.1
1987	4,742.5	724.7
1988	5,108.3	750.4
1989	5,489.1	787.5
1990	5,803.3	794.8

TABLE 33-1.

*The task of economic stabilization
requires keeping the economy from
straying too far above or below the
path of steady high employment. One
way lies inflation, and the other lies
recession. Flexible and vigilant fiscal
and monetary policy will allow us to
hold the narrow middle course.*

President John F. Kennedy
(1962)

*Productivity isn't everything, but in
the long run it is almost everything.*

Paul Krugman (1990)

The U.S. economy has changed enormously over the last 50 years. Farmers are an endangered part of the population. Factory work has declined, and manufacturing involves more people at computers than on production lines. Taxes are higher, and government has become a permanent part of the economic landscape. Technology has revolutionized daily life. Advanced telecommunications systems enable businesses to control their operations across the country and around the world, and ever-more-powerful computers have eliminated many of the repetitive tasks which used to employ so many people. Goods and money flow easily across national boundaries.

Yet, after a half-century of change, the central goals of macroeconomic policy remain the same: good jobs, low unemployment, rising productivity and real incomes, and low and stable inflation. The challenge is to find a set of policies which can achieve these objectives as we begin the new millennium.

This chapter uses the tools of macroeconomics to examine some of today's major policy issues. We begin with an assessment of the consequences of government deficits and debt on economic activity and discuss the surprising turn toward surplus in the United States.

We then analyze controversies involving short-run economic stabilization, including current questions on the roles of monetary policy and fiscal policy. Should the government stop trying to smooth out business cycles and, instead, rely on fixed rules rather than discretion? We conclude with an analysis of the nagging worries posed by the slowdown in productivity and real wage growth over the last two decades and inquire into the policies that countries can pursue to improve their productivity and growth performance.

A. THE ECONOMIC CONSEQUENCES OF THE GOVERNMENT DEBT

As the United States entered the twenty-first century, its fiscal policies were stable and the federal government was running a budget surplus. Then, like a monster rising from the deep, the budget deficit rose to swallow up the nation's fiscal resources and terrify the populace. Because of a recession, terrorism, tax cuts, and a war in Iraq, the nation went from a surplus of $240 billion in 2000 to a deficit of $460 billion in 2003, with deficits as far as the eye of forecasters could see.

How did the budget deficit get so high? What should the government do about it? These important questions will be addressed in the present section. We will see that the popular concern with deficits has a firm economic foundation. A high deficit and government debt during periods of full employment carry serious consequences, including reduced national saving and investment and slower long-run economic growth.

Governments use budgets to plan and control their fiscal affairs. A **budget** shows, for a given year, the planned expenditures of government programs and the expected revenues from tax systems. The budget typically contains a list of specific programs (education, welfare, defense, etc.), as well as tax sources (individual income tax, social-insurance taxes, etc.).

A **budget surplus** occurs when all taxes and other revenues exceed government expenditures for a year. A **budget deficit** is incurred when expenditures exceed taxes. When revenues and expenditures are equal during a given period—a rare event on the federal level—the government has a **balanced budget.**

When the government incurs a budget deficit, it must borrow from the public to pay its bills. To borrow, the government issues bonds, which are IOUs that promise to pay money in the future. The **government debt** (sometimes called the *public debt*) consists of the total or accumulated borrowings by the government; it is the total dollar value of government bonds.

It is useful to distinguish between the total debt and the net debt. The *net debt,* also called the *debt held by the public,* excludes debt held by the government itself. Net debt is owned by households, banks, businesses, foreigners, and other nonfederal entities. The *gross debt* equals the net debt plus bonds owned by the government, primarily by the social security trust fund. The social security trust fund is running a large surplus, so the difference between these two concepts is growing rapidly today.

Debt versus Deficit

People often confuse the debt with the deficit. You can remember the difference as follows: Debt is water in the tub, while a deficit is water flowing into the tub. The government debt is the *stock* of liabilities of the government. The deficit is a *flow* of new debt incurred when the government spends more than it raises in taxes. For example, when the government ran a deficit of $460 billion during 2003, it added that amount to the stock of government debt. By contrast, when the government enjoyed a surplus of $240 billion in 2000, this reduced the government debt by that amount.

FISCAL HISTORY

Like Sisyphus, federal policymakers toil endlessly to push the stone of fiscal balance up the hill only to have it roll down to crush them again. The government passed law after law in the 1980s and 1990s to stop the rising deficit. No sooner was the deficit vanquished than it reappeared and grew rapidly after 2001. Was this typical, or was it a new feature of the American economy?

Deficits were not new to the American economy, but large deficits during peacetime are a unique feature of recent economic history. For the first two centuries after the American Revolution, the federal government of the United States generally balanced its budget. Heavy military spending during wartime was financed by borrowing, so the government debt soared in wartime. In peacetime, the government would pay off some of its debt, and the debt burden would shrink.

Then, starting in 1940, the fiscal affairs of state began to change rapidly. Table 34-1 illuminates the major trends. This table lists the major federal budget categories and their shares in GDP for the period from 1940 to 2004. The key features were the following:

- The share of federal spending and taxes grew sharply from 1940 to 1960 primarily because of the expansion of military and civilian spending. This growth was financed by a significant increase in individual and corporate taxation.
- The period from 1960 to 1980 marked the "New Society" programs for health, income security, and expanded social security. As a result, the expenditure share grew sharply. The share of federal revenues in GDP stabilized over this period.
- The period from 1980 to 2000 was a time in which both major political parties began to run against "big government." The supply-side tax cuts of the early 1980s produced a string of deficits. Public concern over the high deficits led to deficit-reduction measures, the most important being the 1990 and 1993 budget acts of the first Bush and Clinton administrations. These put tight caps on expenditure growth and raised taxes. Although health spending grew sharply, most other expenditure categories declined as a share of GDP.
- The early 2000s witnessed the sharpest deterioration in the U.S. fiscal condition since World War II. The sharp stock market decline reduced tax revenues; recession and slow recovery increased the deficit; two major tax cuts further reduced

Federal Budget Component	Percent of GDP				
	1940	1960	1980	2000	2004
Revenues	**6.4%**	**17.6%**	**18.5%**	**20.6%**	**16.3%**
Individual income taxes	0.9%	7.7%	8.8%	10.2%	7.2%
Corporation income taxes	1.2%	4.1%	2.3%	2.1%	1.4%
Social insurance and retirement receipts	1.8%	2.8%	5.7%	6.7%	6.5%
Other	2.7%	3.0%	1.8%	1.6%	1.2%
Expenditures					
Total	**9.4%**	**17.5%**	**21.2%**	**18.2%**	**18.9%**
National defense and international affairs	1.8%	9.7%	5.3%	3.2%	3.5%
Health	0.1%	0.2%	2.0%	3.6%	4.3%
Income security	1.5%	1.4%	3.1%	2.6%	2.8%
Social security	0.0%	2.2%	4.2%	4.2%	4.2%
Net interest	0.9%	1.3%	1.9%	2.3%	1.5%
Other	5.2%	2.7%	4.7%	2.4%	2.6%
Surplus or deficit (−) (on-budget and off-budget)	−2.9%	0.1%	−2.6%	2.4%	−2.6%

TABLE 34-1. Federal Budget Trends, 1940–2004

The federal share of the economy grew sharply from 1940 to 1960 as the United States took an active military role in world affairs during hot and cold wars. After 1960, the federal share stabilized, but the composition of spending moved from military to health and other social spending. The federal government deficit grew sharply in the early 2000s as revenues declined sharply.

Source: Data are for fiscal years and come from the Department of the Treasury, Office of Management and Budget, and Department of Commerce.

revenues; and increased spending for homeland security, the military, and the war in Iraq led to large increases in expenditures. This period was a reminder that trouble seldom comes alone but arrives in twos and threes.

GOVERNMENT BUDGET POLICY

The government budget serves two major economic functions. First, it is a device by which the government can set national priorities, allocating national output among private and public consumption and investment and providing incentives to increase or reduce output in particular sectors. From a macroeconomic point of view, it is through fiscal policy that the budget affects the key macroeconomic goals. More precisely, by **fiscal policy** we mean the setting of taxes and public expenditures to help dampen the swings of the business cycle and contribute to the maintenance of a growing, high-employment economy, free from high or volatile inflation.

Some early enthusiasts of the Keynesian approach believed that fiscal policy was like a knob they could turn to control or "fine-tune" the pace of the economy. A bigger budget deficit meant more stimulus for aggregate demand, which could lower unemployment and pull the economy out of recession. A budget surplus could slow down an overheated economy and dampen the threat of inflation.

Today, few believe that the business cycle can be quite so easily eliminated. Some 70 years after Keynes, recessions and inflations are still with us, and fiscal policy works better in theory than in practice. Moreover, monetary policy has become the preferred tool for moderating business-cycle swings. Still, whenever unemployment rises, there is usually strong public pressure for the government to boost spending. In this section, we will review the major ways in which government can employ fiscal policy, and we will examine the practical shortcomings that have become apparent.

Actual, Structural, and Cyclical Budgets

Modern public finance distinguishes between structural and cyclical deficits. The idea is simple. The *structural* part of the budget is active—determined by discretionary policies such as those covering tax rates, public-works or education spending, or the size of defense purchases. In contrast, the *cyclical* part of the budget is determined passively by the state of the business cycle, that is, by the extent to which national income and output are high or low. The precise definitions follow:

The **actual budget** records the actual dollar expenditures, revenues, and deficits in a given period.

The **structural budget** calculates what government revenues, expenditures, and deficits would be if the economy were operating at potential output.

The **cyclical budget** is the difference between the actual budget and the structural budget. It measures the impact of the business cycle on the budget, taking into account the effect of the cycle on revenues, expenditures, and the deficit.

The actual, structural, and cyclical budget deficits as a share of GDP are shown in Figure 34-1. The distinction between the actual and the structural budgets is important for policymakers who want to distinguish between long-term or trend budget

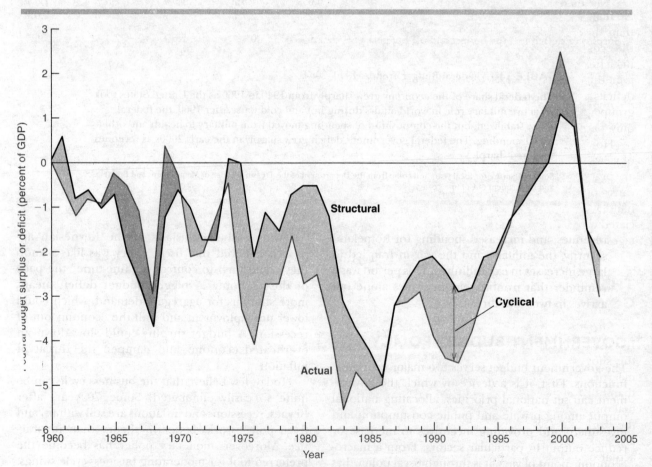

FIGURE 34-1. Actual, Structural, and Cyclical Budget Deficits

The rust line shows the actual budget deficit or surplus (as a percentage of potential GDP). The black curve depicts the structural component. The difference between the actual and the structural deficits or surpluses is the cyclical deficit or surplus.

Source: Congressional Budget Office, at www.cbo.gov.

changes and short-term changes that are primarily driven by the business cycle. Structural spending and revenues consist of the discretionary programs enacted by the legislature; cyclical spending and deficits consist of the taxes and spending that react automatically to the state of the economy.

The nation's saving and investment balance is primarily affected by the structural budget. Efforts to change government saving should focus on the structural budget because no durable change comes simply from increased taxes due to an economic boom.

THE ECONOMICS OF THE DEBT AND DEFICITS

No macroeconomic issue is more controversial today than the impact of large government deficits upon the economy. Some argue that large deficits are placing a heavy burden on future generations. Others rejoin that there is little evidence of an impact of deficits on interest rates or investment. Yet a third group argues that deficits are favorable for the economy, particularly in recessionary times.

How can we sort through the conflicting points of view? At one extreme, we must avoid the customary practice of assuming that a public debt is bad because private debtors are punished. On the other hand, we must recognize the genuine problems associated with large government deficits and the advantages that come from a lower government debt.

THE SHORT-RUN IMPACT OF GOVERNMENT DEFICITS

Short Run vs. Long Run

It is useful to separate the impact of fiscal policy into the short run and the long run. The *short run* in macroeconomics considers situations where less than full employment may prevail—that is, where actual output may differ from potential output. This is the world of the Keynesian multiplier model. The *long run* refers to a full-employment situation, where actual output equals potential output. This is the world of our economic-growth analysis.

We have already discussed the role of fiscal policy in the short run, so that needs only a brief review in this section. The impact in the long run is more novel and will be presented in the next section.

Fiscal Policy and the Multiplier Model

We discussed in earlier chapters the way that fiscal policy affects the economy in the short run—that is, in an economy with less than full employment.

Suppose that the government purchases computers for its schools or missiles for its army. Our multiplier model says that in the short run, with no change in interest or exchange rates, GDP will rise by a multiple (perhaps $1\frac{1}{2}$ or 2) times the increase in G. The same argument applies (with a smaller multiplier) to reductions in taxes, T. At the same time, the government deficit will rise because the deficit equals $T - G$ and thus rises with T cuts or G increases.

This then is the basic result for the short run: With less than full employment, increases in the structural deficit arising from discretionary T cuts or G increases will tend to produce higher output and lower unemployment, and perhaps higher inflation.

We must, however, qualify the simplest multiplier analysis because it should account for the reaction of financial markets. As output and inflation rise, interest rates are likely to rise and the foreign exchange rate is likely to appreciate (if the country has a floating exchange rate). The rising interest rates and appreciated currency will tend to choke off or "crowd out" domestic and foreign investment.[1]

Might it be that the crowding out will actually offset the entire fiscal stimulus? This depends upon many factors, such as the size of the economy and the policies of the central bank. The general view of macroeconomists is that the net impact of fiscal stimulus (after including any crowding-out effects) will definitely be positive for at least 1 or 2 years.

Fiscal policy tends to expand the economy in the short run—that is, under conditions of less than full employment. Higher spending and lower taxes tend to increase aggregate demand, output, employment, and inflation. Because of the financial reaction of interest rates and exchange rates, the expansionary impact is reduced and may eventually disappear.

---

[1] *Warning:* Crowding out applies only to structural deficits. If the deficit rises because of a recession, the logic of crowding out simply does not apply. A recession causes a *decline* in the demand for money and leads to *lower* interest rates; the monetary authority tends to *loosen* monetary policy in a recession. The fact that crowding out does not apply in recessions is a reminder that there is no automatic link between deficits and investment.

GOVERNMENT DEBT AND ECONOMIC GROWTH

We turn now from the short run to the long run—to the impact of fiscal policy, and particularly a large government debt, on investment and economic growth. The analysis here deals with the costs of servicing a large external debt, the inefficiencies of levying taxes to pay interest on the debt, and the impact of the debt on capital accumulation.

Historical Trends

Before we begin our analysis of government debt, it is useful to review historical trends. Long-run data for the United States appear in the figure on the front endpaper of this text, which shows the ratio of net federal debt to GDP since 1789. Notice how wars drove up the ratio of debt to GDP, while rapid output growth with generally balanced budgets in peacetime reduced the ratio of debt to GDP. Then, with growing deficits after 1980, the U.S. saw its debt-GDP ratio rising in peacetime.

Most industrialized countries today find themselves with rapidly growing government debt. Table 34-2 compares the United States with seven other large industrial countries. Japan's debt-GDP ratio has climbed sharply over the last decade because of aggressive fiscal policy and a prolonged recession. Japan's debt rating has been downgraded, and many economists worry that Japan is caught in a vicious cycle of high debt leading to high debt service, which in turn increases the growth of the debt.

External vs. Internal Debt

The first distinction to be made is between an internal debt and an external debt. *Internal government debt* is owed by a nation to its own residents. Many argue that an internal debt poses no burden because "we owe it all to ourselves." While this statement is oversimplified, it does represent a genuine insight. If each citizen owned $10,000 of government bonds and were liable for the taxes to service just that debt, it would make no sense to think of debt as a heavy load of rocks that each citizen must carry. People simply owe the debt to themselves.

An external debt is quite a different situation. An *external debt* occurs when foreigners own a fraction of the assets of a country. For example, because of its large current-account deficits, the United States owed the rest of the world $3 trillion at the end of 2003. What this means is that U.S. residents will eventually have to export that much in goods and services or sell that much of the nation's assets to foreigners. Suppose that the real interest rate on that debt is 5 percent per year. Then, each year, U.S. residents would need to ship abroad $150 billion (about $500 per capita) to "service" the external debt.

So an external debt definitely does involve a net subtraction from the resources available for consumption in the debtor nation. This lesson has been learned time and again by developing countries—particularly when their creditors wanted their debts paid back quickly.

| | Ratio of Gross Government Debt to GDP (%)* | | | |
	1980	1990	2000	2003
Japan	52	65	124	158
Italy	58	97	111	106
France	30	40	65	67
United States	33	56	58	64
Germany	30	42	61	63
United Kingdom	60	44	52	51
Russian Federation	n.a.	n.a.	59	39
Mexico	n.a.	48	21	25

*Figures are gross debt and include holdings of government trust funds.

TABLE 34-2. Government Debt in Major Industrial Countries

Slow growth and rising entitlement programs led to rising deficits and growing public debts in most industrial countries in the last two decades. Japan's debt-GDP ratio led to a downgrading of its debt ratings even though it is the second-largest economy in the world.

Source: Economist Intelligence Unit.

Efficiency Losses from Taxation

An internal debt requires payments of interest to bondholders, and taxes must be levied for this purpose. But even if the same people were taxed to pay the same amounts they receive in interest, there would still be the *distorting effects on incentives* that are inescapably present in the case of any taxes. Taxing Paula's interest income or wages to pay Paula interest would introduce microeconomic distortions. Paula might work less and save less; either of these outcomes must be reckoned as a distortion of efficiency and well-being.

Displacement of Capital

Perhaps the most serious consequence of a large public debt is that it displaces capital from the nation's stock of private wealth. As a result, the pace of economic growth slows and future living standards will decline.

What is the mechanism by which debt affects capital? Recall from our earlier discussion that people accumulate wealth for a variety of purposes, such as retirement, education, and housing. We can separate the assets people hold into two groups: (1) government debt and (2) capital like houses and financial assets like corporate stocks that represent ownership of private capital.

The effect of government debt is that people will accumulate government debt instead of private capital, and the nation's private capital stock will be displaced by public debt.

To illustrate this point, suppose that people desire to hold exactly 1000 units of wealth for retirement and other purposes. As the government debt increases, people's holdings of other assets will be reduced dollar for dollar. This occurs because as the government sells its bonds, other assets must be reduced, since total desired wealth holdings are fixed. But these other assets ultimately represent the stock of private capital; stocks, bonds, and mortgages are the counterparts of factories, equipment, and houses. In this example, if the government debt goes up 100 units, we would see that people's holdings of capital and other private assets fall by 100 units. This is the case of 100 percent displacement (which is the long-run analog of 100 percent crowding out).

Full displacement is unlikely to hold in practice. The higher debt may increase interest rates and stimulate domestic saving. In addition, the country may borrow abroad rather than reduce its domestic capital stock (as America did in the 1980s). The exact amount of capital displacement will depend on the conditions of production and on the saving behavior of domestic households and foreigners.

A Geometric Analysis. The process by which the stock of capital is displaced in the long run is illustrated in Figure 34-2 on page 716. The left panel shows the supply and demand for capital as a function of the real interest rate or return on capital. As interest rates rise, firms demand less capital while individuals may want to supply more. The equilibrium shown is for a capital stock of 4000 units with a real interest rate of 4 percent

Now say that the government debt rises from 0 to 1000—because of war, recession, supply-side fiscal policies, or some other reason. The impact of the increase in debt can be seen in the right-hand diagram of Figure 34-2. This figure shows the 1000-unit increase in debt as a shift in the supply-of-capital (or SS) curve. As depicted, the households' supply-of-capital schedule shifts 1000 units to the left, to S'S'.

We represent an increase in government debt as a leftward shift in the households' supply-of-capital schedule. Note that, because the SS curve represents the amount of private capital that people willingly hold at each interest rate, the capital holdings are equal to the total wealth holdings minus the holdings of government debt. Since the amount of government debt (or assets other than capital) rises by 1000, the amount of private capital that people can buy after they own the 1000 units of government debt is 1000 less than total wealth at each interest rate. Therefore, if SS represents the total wealth held by people, S'S' (equal to SS less 1000) represents the total amount of capital held by people. In short, after 1000 units of government debt are sold, the new supply-of-capital schedule is S'S'.

As the supply of capital dries up—with national saving going into government bonds rather than into housing or into companies' stocks and bonds—the market equilibrium moves northwest along the demand-for-K curve. Interest rates rise. Firms slow their purchases of new factories, trucks, and computers.

In the illustrative new long-run equilibrium, the capital stock falls from 4000 to 3500. Thus, in this example, 1000 units of government debt have displaced 500 units of private capital. Such a reduction has significant economic effects, of course. With less capital, potential output, wages, and the nation's income are lower than they would otherwise be.

The diagrams in Figure 34-2 are illustrative. Economists do not have a firm estimate of the magnitude of the displacement effect. Looking at historical trends, the best evidence suggests that domestic capital is

FIGURE 34-2. Government Debt Displaces Private Capital

Firms demand capital, while households supply capital by saving in private and public
assets. The demand curve is the downward-sloping business demand for *K*, while the supply
curve is the upward-sloping household supply of wealth.

Before-debt case in **(a)** shows the equilibrium without government debt: *K* is 4000 and
the real interest rate is 4 percent.

After-debt case in **(b)** shows the impact of 1000 units of government debt. Debt shifts the
net supply of *K* to the left by the 1000 units of the government debt. The new equilibrium
arises northwest along the demand-for-*K* curve, moving from point *A* to point *B*. The interest
rate is higher, firms are discouraged from holding *K*, and the capital stock falls.

partially displaced by government debt but that some
of the impact comes in higher foreign debt.

Debt and Growth

Considering all the effects of government debt on
the economy, a large public debt is likely to reduce
long-run economic growth. Figure 34-3 illustrates
this connection. Say that an economy were to operate over time with no debt. According to the principles of economic growth outlined in Chapter 27, the
capital stock and potential output would follow the
hypothetical paths indicated by the solid black lines
in Figure 34-3.

Next consider a situation with a growing national
debt. As the debt accumulates over time, more and

more capital is displaced, as shown by the dashed
rust line for the capital stock in the bottom of Figure 34-3. As taxes are raised to pay interest on the
debt, inefficiencies further lower output. Also, an increase in external debt lowers national income and
raises the fraction of national output that has to be
set aside for servicing the external debt. Taking all
the effects together, output and consumption will
grow more slowly than they would have had there
been no large government debt and deficit, as can be
seen by comparing the top lines in Figure 34-3.

What is the impact of a budget surplus and a *declining* government debt? Here, the argument works
in the other direction. A lower national debt means
that more of national wealth is put into capital rather

FIGURE 34-3. Impact of Government Debt on Economic Growth

The solid lines show the paths of capital and output if the government balances its books and has no debt. When the government incurs a debt, private capital is reduced. The dashed lines illustrate the impact on capital and output of the higher government debt.

than government bonds. A higher capital stock increases the growth of output and increases wages and consumption per person.

This is the major point about the long-run impact of a large government debt on economic growth: A large government debt tends to reduce the growth in potential output because it displaces private capital, increases the inefficiency from taxation, and forces a nation to reduce consumption to service its foreign borrowing.

Deficit Confusions Unraveled

Having completed our analysis of the economic impacts of deficits and debt, we can summarize the key points by unraveling some of the major confusions in this area.

The impact of fiscal policy on the economy is one of the most misunderstood facets of macroeconomics. The confusion arises because fiscal policy operates differently depending upon the time period:

- *In the short run, higher spending and lower tax rates tend to increase aggregate demand and thereby to raise output and lower unemployment.* This is the Keynesian impact of fiscal policy, which operates by raising actual output relative to potential output. We would expect that the expansionary impact of fiscal policy—the increase in capacity utilization—would last at most for a few years. It might be offset by a monetary tightening, especially if the central bank thought the economy was operating near the inflation danger zone of the NAIRU. There may be some crowding out of investment if the monetary reaction is strong.

- *In the long run, higher spending and lower tax rates tend to depress the growth rate of the economy.* This is the growth impact of fiscal policy. The growth impact concerns the impact of government deficits on the national saving and investment balance in a full-employment economy. If taxes are lower, this will decrease public saving and, because private saving is unlikely to rise as much as public saving falls, total national saving and investment will decline. The investment decline will lead to slower growth in the capital stock and therefore in potential output.

These two impacts of fiscal policy can easily confuse people and are the source of many debates about fiscal policy. Consider the following debate between Senators Hawk and Dove:

Senator Dove: The economy is tipping into recession. We cannot afford to sit around while millions of people lose their jobs. Now is the time for a major tax cut, focused on middle-income people who will quickly spend the extra take-home pay. Recessions are not the time for old-fashioned dogmas about deficits.

Senator Hawk: A tax cut today would be the height of fiscal irresponsibility. With lower taxes, the deficit will grow even larger, interest rates will rise, and businesses will reduce their spending on new plant, equipment, and information technology. With all the critical needs facing the nation, we can ill-afford slower economic growth over the next decade.

Make sure that you understand the implicit theories underlying the positions of the two distinguished senators. They are both right . . . and both wrong.

B. STABILIZING THE ECONOMY

While the United States has enjoyed a period of economic growth along with low unemployment and inflation that are the envy of the world, other nations have not been so fortunate. Europe and Japan were mired in a decade-long slump with high unemployment rates. East Asian economies saw their miracle turn temporarily to debacle by financial market turmoil. While inflation has been stilled in most countries, few can forget the runaway price increases of the 1970s and early 1980s. No one can predict where or when a virulent business cycle will next strike.

It is therefore still critical to find policies which strike the proper balance between too high unemployment and unacceptable inflation. We have seen that the path of output and prices is determined by the interaction of aggregate supply and demand. *But policies to stabilize the business cycle must operate primarily through their impact on aggregate demand.* In other words, the primary way that government can counter recessions or slow inflation is by using its monetary and fiscal levers to affect the growth in aggregate demand.

These observations leave open two crucial questions: What is the best division of labor between monetary and fiscal policies for stabilizing the economy? Is it possible that monetary- and fiscal-policymakers do more harm than good by actively trying to stabilize the economy?

THE INTERACTION OF MONETARY AND FISCAL POLICIES

For large economies like the United States or Euroland, the best combination of monetary and fiscal policies will depend upon two factors: the need for demand management and the desired fiscal-monetary mix.

Demand Management

The top consideration in business-cycle management is the overall state of the economy and the need to adjust aggregate demand. When the economy is stagnating, fiscal and monetary policies can be used to stimulate the economy and promote economic recovery. When inflation threatens, monetary and fiscal policies can help slow the economy and dampen inflationary fires. These are examples of *demand management*, which refers to the active use of monetary and fiscal policies to affect the level of aggregate demand.

Suppose, for example, that the economy is entering a severe recession. Output is low relative to its potential. What can the government do to revive the lagging economy? It can increase aggregate demand by raising money growth or by boosting government spending or both. After the economy has responded to the monetary and fiscal stimulus, output growth and employment will increase and unemployment will fall. (What steps could the government take during inflationary periods?)

Let's review the relative strengths and weaknesses of monetary policy and fiscal policy.

Does Fiscal Policy Matter? Over the last three decades, fiscal policy has lost much of its attractiveness to policymakers and macroeconomists as a stabilization tool. In the early stages of the Keynesian revolution, macroeconomists emphasized fiscal policy as the most powerful and balanced remedy for demand management. Gradually, shortcomings of fiscal policy became apparent. The shortcomings stem from timing, politics, and macroeconomic theory.

One concern is that the time span between cyclical shock and effective response is long and growing longer. To begin with, it takes time before economists can recognize that a cyclical turning point has been reached. Then, in addition to the recognition lag, there is a response lag while the president decides what to do and Congress debates and passes the measure. Finally, even when taxation or spending is changed, there is an effectiveness lag before the economy responds.

While recognition, response, and effectiveness lags are present for both monetary policy and fiscal policy, the response lag for fiscal policy can be so long that it becomes useless for stabilization. The response lag in the United States has increased over the last few years as congressional budget procedures have become more complex, with almost a year's delay between presidential recommendations and final congressional action.

Another problem with fiscal policy is that it is easier to cut taxes than to raise them, and easier to raise spending than to cut it. During the 1960s, Congress was enthusiastic about passing the Kennedy-Johnson tax cuts. Two years later, when the Vietnam war expansion ignited inflationary pressures, contractionary policies were called for.

The history of taxes in the 1981–2001 period shows again the asymmetrical nature of tax cuts and tax increases. When President Ronald Reagan proposed a tax cut, it was enacted in 6 months. After the deficit emerged, the federal government struggled mightily to raise revenues and curb spending, but attaining a surplus required 17 years. Presidents love to have tax-cutting planks in their platform, but no one wants to run on a program of "raise taxes to reduce the deficit." The last candidate to be openly pro-tax-increase was Walter Mondale in 1984, and he was beaten in a landslide.

In addition, even when put into action speedily, fiscal policy may not work as well as macroeconomists once thought. For example, many economists used to advocate temporary tax cuts during recessions and temporary tax increases when the economy becomes overheated and inflation looms. However, studies indicate that consumers realize that the tax changes are temporary and thus they do not change their spending patterns very much, since the temporary tax changes have little effect upon their permanent or lifetime incomes.

Effectiveness of Monetary Policy. Compared to fiscal policy, monetary policy operates much more indirectly on the economy. Whereas an expansive fiscal policy actually buys goods and services or puts income into the hands of consumers and businesses, monetary policy affects spending by altering interest rates, credit conditions, exchange rates, and asset prices. In the early years of the Keynesian revolution, some macroeconomists were skeptical about the effectiveness of monetary policy—some said, "Monetary policy was like pushing on a string." Over the last two decades, however, these concerns have been put to rest as the Federal Reserve has shown itself quite capable of slowing down, or speeding up, the economy.

The Federal Reserve is much better placed to conduct stabilization policy than are the fiscal-policy makers. Its staff of professional economists can recognize cyclical movements as well as anyone. And it can move quickly when the need arises. For example, on January 28, 1994, the Commerce Department announced that the economy was growing surprisingly rapidly at year-end 1993; only 1 week later, the Fed moved to slow down the economy by raising interest rates for the first time in half a decade. This episode stands in stark comparison to the 2-year tightening of fiscal policy during the Vietnam war.

A key ingredient in Fed policy is its independence, and the Fed has proved that it can stand the heat of making politically unpopular decisions when they are necessary to slow inflation. Most important, as we noted above, is that from the point of view of demand management, monetary policy can do, or undo, anything that fiscal policy can accomplish.

Of course, to stabilize the economy, the central bank has to apply the right amount of monetary stimulus or restraint. Recent estimates of the quantitative impacts of monetary policy on the economy in different macroeconomic models are shown in Table 34-3. This study estimated the impact on the U.S. economy of increasing the money supply by 4 percent above the money supply of a baseline projection, with the money supply remaining 4 percent higher than the baseline for the indefinite future.

The results show a substantial initial response of real GDP to an increase in the money supply. By contrast, the increase in the price level builds up slowly over time, with less than one-fifth of the increase in nominal GDP in year 1 coming in prices. At the end of 5 years, according to the model simulations, most of the increase in nominal GDP shows up in prices rather than in real output. The models confirm the Keynesian prediction of a sluggish reaction of wages and prices to changes in the money supply but also indicate that the economy behaves increasingly like a classical economy in the long run.

How might the monetary authorities use these statistical results? Suppose, for example, that the Federal Reserve forecasts that real GDP will grow by 4 percent in the coming year; further, the Fed believes that a growth rate of 3 percent is the most that the economy can sustain without the risk of an unacceptable inflation. What change in the money supply would be needed to slow the rate of growth of real GDP by 1 percentage point? The answer is that the money-supply growth would have to be slowed by somewhat more than 4 percent to produce a 1-percentage-point decrease in real GDP.

Of course, the usefulness of such calculations depends on whether the statistical correlations which held in the past will still be true in the future. Monetary economists stress that the impacts of monetary policy are uncertain and may change over time as the economy evolves. For example, as the economy becomes increasingly exposed to foreign trade, the impact of monetary policy on net exports becomes more important at the same time that the impact

Money, Output, and Prices					
	Response of Affected Variable to 4% Change in Money Supply (% change in affected variable from baseline path)				
Affected variable	Year 1	Year 2	Year 3	Year 4	Year 5
Real GDP	0.9	1.1	1.2	1.1	0.8
Consumer prices	0.2	0.7	1.1	1.5	1.8
Nominal GDP	1.1	1.8	2.3	2.5	2.7

TABLE 34-3. Estimated Effect of Monetary Policy on Output and Prices

A survey of eight econometric models examined the impact of monetary policy. In each case, a baseline run of the model was "shocked" by adding 4 percent to the money supply in year 1 and holding the money supply 4 percent above the baseline in all years thereafter. Estimates in the table show the average calculated response of the models.

Note the strong initial response of real output to a monetary-policy shift, with the peak response coming in year 3. The impact upon the price level builds up gradually because of the inertial response of price and wage behavior. Note that the impact on nominal GDP is less than proportional to the money growth even after 5 years.

Source: Ralph C. Bryant, Peter Hooper, and Gerald Holtham, "Consensus and Diversity in the Model Simulations," in Ralph Bryant et al., eds., *Empirical Macroeconomics for Interdependent Economies* (Brookings Institution, Washington, D.C., 1988).

upon housing and other domestic sectors is mitigated by financial deregulation.

We can summarize the current state of fiscal and monetary policy as follows:

Because of their political independence and rapid decision making, central banks are well placed to be the front line of defense in stabilizing the economy against business-cycle shocks. Discretionary fiscal policy is sometimes used, but economists doubt its countercyclical effectiveness because of asymmetric attitudes toward tax changes and because of political obstacles to rapid enactment.

The Fiscal-Monetary Mix

The second factor affecting fiscal and monetary policy is the desired **fiscal-monetary mix,** which refers to the relative strength of fiscal and monetary policies and their effect on different sectors of the economy. A *change in the fiscal-monetary mix* is an approach which tightens one policy while easing the other in such a way that aggregate demand and therefore total output remain constant. The basic idea is that fiscal policy and monetary policy are substitutes in demand management. But while alternative combinations of

monetary and fiscal policies can be used to stabilize the economy, they have different impacts upon the *composition* of output. By varying the mix of taxes, government spending, and monetary policy, the government can change the fraction of GDP devoted to business investment, consumption, net exports, and government purchases of goods and services.

Effect of Changing the Mix of Monetary and Fiscal Policies. To understand the impact of changing the fiscal-monetary mix, let's examine a specific set of policies. Suppose that the federal government reduces the federal budget deficit by $100 billion and that higher monetary growth exactly offsets the contractionary impact of the fiscal steps. This package is similar to the deficit-reduction measures enacted in 1993 along with a monetary policy that offset the drag from higher taxes and lower government spending.

We can estimate the impact using a quantitative economic model, such as the sophisticated DRI long-term model of the United States. Table 34-4 shows the results of this experiment. Two interesting features emerge: First, the simulation indicates that a change in the fiscal-monetary mix would indeed change the composition of real GDP. While the

Sector		Change in output ($, billion, 2003 prices)
Investment sectors		**132**
Gross private domestic investment		48
Housing	18	
Business fixed investment	30	
Net exports		83
Consumption sectors		**−106**
Government purchases of goods and services		−68
Personal consumption expenditures		−38
Memoranda:		
Change in real GDP		26
Change in federal deficit		−100

TABLE 34-4. Changing the Fiscal-Monetary Mix

What would be the impact of a change in the fiscal-monetary mix for the United States? This simulation assumes that the federal deficit is cut by $100 billion through higher personal taxes and lower federal nondefense expenditures while the Federal Reserve uses monetary policy to keep unemployment on an unchanged trajectory. The simulation takes the average of the changes from the baseline path over the period 2000–2009.

Source: Simulation using the DRI model of the U.S. economy.

deficit declines by $100 billion, business investment goes up by $30 billion. Investment in housing, too, increases as interest rates fall. At the same time, personal consumption declines, freeing up resources for investment. This simulation shows how a change in the fiscal-monetary mix might change the composition of output.

The simulation contains one particularly interesting result: Net exports rise far more than either housing or business fixed investment. This occurs because of the strong depreciation of the dollar which results from the lower interest rates. While this result is clearly sensitive to the reaction of financial markets and exchange rates to the deficit-reduction package, it suggests that some of the popular analyses of the impact of such a package may be misleading. Many analysts have argued that a deficit-reduction package would have a significant impact upon domestic business investment and upon productivity. However, to the extent that lower deficits mainly help net exports and housing, the nation is likely to experience relatively little increase in productivity growth. According to the DRI model, cutting the budget deficit by $100 billion will raise the growth rate of potential

output from 2.3 percent per year to 2.6 percent per year over a 10-year period. Perhaps the small size of the payoff explains why it is so hard to muster the political will to cut the deficit.

Alternative Mixes in Practice

The fiscal-monetary mix has been sharply debated in American economic policy. Here are two major alternatives:

• *Loose fiscal–tight monetary policy.* Assume that the economy begins in an initial situation with low inflation and output at its potential. A new president decides that it is necessary to increase defense spending sharply without raising taxes. By itself, this would increase the government deficit and increase aggregate demand. In this situation, the Federal Reserve would be inclined to tighten monetary policy to prevent the economy from overheating. The result would be higher real interest rates and an appreciation of the dollar exchange rate. The higher interest rates would squeeze investment, while the appreciated dollar would reduce net exports. The net effect therefore would be that the higher defense spending would crowd out domestic investment and net exports. This policy was the one followed by the United States in the early 1980s and again in the early 2000s.

- *Tight fiscal–loose monetary policy.* Suppose that a country becomes concerned about a low national saving rate and desires to raise investment so as to increase the capital stock and boost the growth rate of potential output. To implement this approach, the country could raise consumption taxes and squeeze transfer payments so as to reduce disposable income and thereby lower consumption (tight fiscal policy). This would be accompanied by an expansionary monetary policy to lower interest rates and raise investment, lower the exchange rate, and expand net exports. This course would encourage private investment by increasing public saving. This was the economic philosophy of President Clinton which was embodied in the 1993 Budget Act and led to the budget surplus at decade's end.

RULES VS. DISCRETION

We have seen that fiscal and monetary policy can *in principle* stabilize the economy. Many economists believe that countries should *in practice* take steps to shave the peaks and troughs off the business cycle. Other economists are skeptical of our ability to forecast cycles and take the right steps at the right time for the right reasons; this second group concludes that government cannot be trusted to make good economic policy, so its freedom to act should be strictly limited.

For example, fiscal conservatives worry that it's easier for Congress to increase spending and cut taxes than to do the reverse. That means it's easy to increase the budget deficit during recessions but much harder to turn around and shrink the deficit again during booms, as a countercyclical fiscal policy would require. For that reason, conservatives have made several attempts to limit the ability of Congress to appropriate new funds or increase the deficit.

At the same time, monetary conservatives would like to tie the hands of central banks and force them to target money growth or inflation. This is designed to eliminate the uncertainty about policy and enhance the credibility of the central bank as an inflation fighter.

At the most general level, the debate about "rules versus discretion" boils down to whether the advantages of flexibility in decision making are outweighed by the uncertainties and potential abuse in unconstrained decisions. Those who believe that the economy is inherently unstable and complex and that governments generally make wise decisions are comfortable with giving policymakers wide discretion to react aggressively to stabilize the economy. Those who believe that the government is the major destabilizing force in the economy and that policymakers are prone to selfishness and misjudgments favor tying the hands of the fiscal and monetary authorities.

Budget Constraints on Legislatures?

As deficits began to grow during the 1980s, many people argued that Congress lacks the self-control to curb excessive spending and a burgeoning government debt. One proposal put forth by conservatives was a *constitutional amendment requiring a balanced budget.* Such an amendment was criticized by economists because it would make it difficult to use fiscal policy to fight recessions. To date, none of the proposed constitutional amendments has passed Congress.

Instead, Congress legislated a series of *budgetary rules to limit spending and tax reductions.* The first attempt was the Gramm-Rudman Act in 1985, which required that the deficit be reduced by a specified dollar amount each year and that the budget be balanced by 1991. If Congress was unable to meet the quantitative Gramm-Rudman target, expenditures would be automatically cut across the board.

The results fell far short of the congressional mandate. The Gramm-Rudman bill went into effect in late 1985, but the ambitious deficit targets were not met. The bill was amended in 1987, but the controls on the deficits proved unworkable and ineffective. In 1990 the targets were replaced by a set of spending limitations. These limitations were incorporated in the 1993 Budget Act and imposed stringent restrictions on the growth of discretionary programs (which include defense and nonentitlement civilian programs like education, science, and general government). The 1993 and 1997 Budget Acts required that discretionary programs decline by almost one-quarter in real terms over the 1993–1998 period.

The other important change introduced in the 1990 amendments and included in the 1993 and 1997 acts is a *pay-as-you-go budget rule.* This requires that Congress find the revenues to pay for any new spending program. The pay-as-you-go provision imposes a budget constraint on Congress, requiring that the costs of new programs be explicitly recognized through either higher taxes or lower expenditures in other areas.

What has been the impact of the budget constraints on Congress? The budget rules produced significant fiscal discipline, helped reduce the deficit over the 1990s, and eventually produced the surplus after 1998. However, when the deficit changed to surplus and the urgency of deficit reduction disappeared, policymakers began to evade the earlier budget caps with gimmicks like "emergency spending" for predictable items like the decennial census. Finally, in 2002, the budget caps were allowed to expire. It is an open question whether they will be revived as the deficit reemerges in the years ahead.

Monetary Rules for the Fed?

In our discussion of monetarism in Chapter 33, we laid out the case for fixed policy rules. The traditional argument for fixed rules is that the private economy is relatively stable and active policy-making is likely to destabilize rather than stabilize the economy. Moreover, to the extent that a central bank under the thumb of the government may be tempted to expand the economy before elections and to create a political business cycle, fixed rules will tie its hands. In addition, modern macroeconomists point to the value of being able to commit to action in advance. If the central bank can commit to follow a noninflationary rule, people's expectations will adapt to this rule and inflationary expectations may be dampened.

Until recently, advocates of fixed monetary rules (particularly monetarists) recommended a fixed nominal growth of, say, 4 percent per year in the money supply. With a constant velocity and output growing at 3 percent a year, this would lead to steady annual inflation of 1 percent. But as the data on velocity show (see particularly Figure 33-3 in the previous chapter), velocity was never terribly stable and it has become increasingly unstable in the last two decades. Given the apparent instability of velocity, it would be hard to claim that a fixed monetary rule could have actually stabilized output during this period.

Targeting Inflation. Central banks have adopted many different approaches to monetary policy in recent decades. These range from highly discretionary approaches which coordinate monetary and fiscal policies under the direction of the government to highly mechanized approaches with fixed targets for the money supply or bank reserves.

One of the most important new developments in the last decade has been the trend toward inflation targeting in many countries. **Inflation targeting** is the announcement of official target ranges for the inflation rate along with an explicit statement that low and stable inflation is the overriding goal of monetary policy. Inflation targeting in hard or soft varieties has been adopted in recent years by many industrialized countries, including Canada, Britain, Australia, and New Zealand. Moreover, the treaty authorizing the new European Central Bank mandates that price stability be the ECB's primary objective, although it is not formally required to target inflation.[2] A number of economists and legislators are advocating this approach for the United States as well.

Inflation targeting involves the following:

- The government or central bank announces that monetary policy will strive to keep inflation near a numerically specified target.
- The target usually involves a range, such as 1 to 3 percent per year, rather than literal price stability. Generally, the government targets an inertial or core inflation rate such as the CPI excluding volatile food and energy prices and excluding price-raising taxes.
- Inflation is the primary or overriding target of policy in the medium run and long run. However, countries always make room for short-run stabilization objectives, particularly with respect to output, unemployment, financial stability, and the foreign exchange rate. These short-run objectives recognize that supply shocks can affect output and unemployment and that it may be desirable to have temporary departures from the inflation target to avoid excessive unemployment or output losses.

Proponents of inflation targeting point to many advantages. If there is no long-run tradeoff between unemployment and inflation, a sensible inflation target is that rate which maximizes the efficiency of the price system. Our analysis of inflation in Chapter 32 suggested that a low and stable rate of inflation would promote efficiency and minimize unnecessary redistribution of income and wealth. In addition, some economists believe that a strong and credible commitment to low and stable inflation will improve the short-run inflation-unemployment tradeoff. Finally,

---

[2] European monetary union was discussed in Chapter 30.

an explicit inflation target would increase the transparency of monetary policy.

Inflation targeting is a compromise between rule-based approaches and purely discretionary policies. The main disadvantage would come if the central bank began to rely too rigidly on the inflation rule and thereby allowed excessive unemployment in periods of severe supply shocks. Critics recall how the rigid rules of the 1979–1982 monetarist experiment led to highly volatile interest rates and a deep recession. Skeptics worry that the economy is too complex to be governed by fixed rules. Arguing by analogy, they ask whether one would advocate a fixed speed limit for cars or an automatic pilot for aircraft in all kinds of weather and emergencies.

The Federal Reserve has not been saddled with rigid targets or rules. Fortunately, under Paul Volcker (chairman of the Federal Reserve, 1979–1987) and Alan Greenspan (chairman, 1987–), monetary policy was managed with exceptional skill in a period of great structural change and turbulence. The success of this monetary policy in this period testifies to the wisdom of disinterested discretionary policies aimed at clearly articulated goals.

The debate over rules versus discretion is one of the oldest debates of political economy. There is no single best approach for all times and places. Indeed, the dilemma reflects the difficulty that democratic societies have in making tradeoffs between short-run policies intended to attract political support and long-run policies designed to enhance the general welfare.

C. ECONOMIC PROSPECTS IN THE NEW CENTURY

THE HIGH STAKES IN ECONOMIC GROWTH

As we begin the twenty-first century, it is good to recall the striking words of MIT's Paul Krugman:

> Productivity isn't everything, but in the long run it is almost everything. A country's ability to improve its living standards over time depends almost entirely on its ability to raise its output per worker.[3]

---

[3] See this chapter's Further Reading section.

Promoting a high and growing standard of living for the nation's residents is one of the fundamental goals of macroeconomic policy. Because the current *level* of real income reflects the history of the *growth* of productivity, we can measure the relative success of past growth by examining the per capita GDPs of different countries. A brief list is presented in Table 34-5. This table compares incomes by using *purchasing-power-parity* exchange rates that measure the purchasing power of (or quantity of goods and services that can be bought by) different national currencies. Evidently, the United States has been successful in its past growth performance. Perhaps the most worrisome issue in recent years is that the growth in living standards has not been widely shared among the population.

In discussing growth rates, the numbers often seem tiny. A successful policy might increase a country's growth rate by only 1 percentage point per year (recall the estimated impact of the deficit-reduction package in the last section). But over long periods, this makes a big difference. Table 34-6 shows how tiny acorns grow into mighty oaks as small growth-rate differences cumulate and compound over time. A 4 percent-per-year growth difference leads to a 50-fold difference in income levels over a century.

Country	Per capita GDP, 2003*
United States	37,470
Japan	27,840
Italy	27,670
Germany	27,660
France	27,370
United Kingdom	27,010
Mexico	9,290
Russian Federation	6,250
China	5,070
India	2,770
Iraq	2,720
Nigeria	987

*Data adjusted using purchasing-power-parity exchange rates.

TABLE 34-5. Current Incomes Represent Effects of Past Growth

Those countries that have grown most rapidly in the past have reached the highest levels of per capita GDP.

Source: World Bank and Economist Intelligence Unit.

Growth rate (% per year)	Real Income per Capita (constant prices)		
	2000	2050	2100
0	$24,000	$ 24,000	$ 24,000
1	24,000	39,471	64,916
2	24,000	64,598	173,872
4	24,000	170,560	1,212,118

TABLE 34-6. Small Differences in Growth Rates Compound into Large Income Differentials over the Decades

How can public policy boost economic growth? As we emphasized in our chapters on economic growth, the growth of output per worker and of living standards depends upon a country's saving rate and upon its technological advance. Issues involving saving were discussed earlier in this chapter. Technological change includes not only new products and processes but also improvements in management as well as entrepreneurship and the spirit of enterprise—and we close our discussion with this topic.

THE SPIRIT OF ENTERPRISE

Although investment is a central factor in economic growth, technological advance is perhaps even more important. If we took the workers in 1900 and doubled or tripled their capital in mules, saddles, picks, and cow paths, their productivity still could not come close to that of today's workers using huge tractors, superhighways, and supercomputers.

Fostering Technological Advance

While it is easy to see how technological advance promotes growth in productivity and living standards, governments cannot simply command people to think longer or be smarter. Centrally planned socialist countries used "sticks" to promote science, technology, and innovation, but their efforts failed because neither the institutions nor the "carrots" were present to encourage both innovation and introduction of new technologies. Governments often promote rapid technological change best when they set a sound economic and legal framework with strong intellectual property rights and then allow great economic freedom within that framework. *Free markets in labor, capital, products, and ideas have proved to be the most fertile soil for innovation and technological change.*

Within the framework of free markets, governments can foster rapid technological change both by encouraging new ideas and by ensuring that technologies are effectively used. Policies can focus on both the supply side and the demand side.

Promoting Demand for Better Technologies. The world is full of superior technologies that have not been adopted; otherwise, how could we explain the vast differences in productivity shown in Table 34-5? Before considering how to supply new technologies, therefore, governments must help ensure that firms and industries are at the *technological frontier,* which is the best-practice technology anywhere.

The major lesson here is that "necessity is the mother of invention." In other words, vigorous competition among firms and industries is the ultimate discipline that ensures innovation. Just as athletes perform better when they are trying to outrun their competitors, so are firms spurred to improve their products and processes when the victors are given fame and fortune while the laggards may go bankrupt.

Vigorous competition involves both domestic and foreign competitors. For large countries on the technological frontier, domestic competition is necessary to promote innovation. The movement to deregulation over the last two decades has brought competition to airlines, energy, telecommunications, and finance, and the positive impact on innovation has been dramatic. For small or technologically backward countries, import competition is crucial to adopting advanced technologies and ensuring product market competition.

Promoting Supply of New Technologies. Rapid economic growth requires pushing out the technological frontier by increasing the supply of inventions as well as ensuring that there is adequate demand for existing advanced technologies. There are three ways by which governments can encourage the supply of new technologies.

First, governments can ensure that the basic science, engineering, and technology are appropriately supported. In this respect, the world leader in the last half-century has been the United States, which combines company support for applied research with top-notch university basic research generously supported by government funding. Particularly outstanding have been the impressive improvements in biomedical technology in the form of new drugs and equipment that benefit consumers directly in daily life. The government's role in supporting for-profit research is accomplished by a strong patent system, predictable and cost-effective regulations, and fiscal incentives such as the current R&D tax credit.

Second, governments can advance technologies at home through encouraging investment by foreign firms. As foreign countries reach and pass the American technological frontier, they can also contribute to American know-how by establishing operations in the United States. The last decade has brought a number of Japanese automakers to the United States, and Japanese-owned plants have introduced new technologies and managerial practices to the benefit of both the profits of Japanese shareholders and the productivity of American workers.

Third, governments can promote new technologies by pursuing sound macroeconomic policies. These include low and stable taxes on capital income and a low cost of capital to firms. Indeed, the importance of the cost of capital brings us back full circle to the issue of the low saving rate and high real interest rate. American firms are sometimes accused of being myopic and being unwilling to invest for the long run. At least part of this myopia comes from being faced with high real interest rates—high real interest rates *force* rational American firms to look for quick payoffs in their investments. A change in economic policy that lowered real interest rates would change the "economic spectacles" through which firms look

when considering their technological policies. If real interest rates were lower, firms would view long-term, high-risk projects such as investments in technology more favorably, and the increased investment in knowledge would lead to more rapid improvements in technology and productivity.

Valediction on Economic Growth

Following the Keynesian revolution, the capitalist democracies believed that they could flourish and grow rapidly while moderating the extremes of unemployment and inflation, poverty and wealth, privilege and deprivation. Many of these goals were met as the market economies experienced a period of output expansion and employment growth never before seen, and the last 15 years have been a period of unprecedented stability and low inflation in the United States. All the time, Marxists carped that capitalism was doomed to crash in a cataclysmic depression; ecologists fretted that market economies would choke on their own fumes; and libertarians worried that government planning was leading us down the road to serfdom. But the pessimists overlooked the spirit of enterprise, which was nurtured by an open society and free markets and which led to a continuous stream of technological improvements.

A valediction from John Maynard Keynes, as timely today as it was in an earlier age, provides a fitting summary of our review of economic policy:

> It is Enterprise which builds and improves the world's possessions. If Enterprise is afoot, wealth accumulates whatever happens to Thrift; and if Enterprise is asleep, wealth decays whatever Thrift may be doing.

ECONOMIC PROGRESS AND POLITICAL FREEDOMS

One of the remarkable features of the twentieth and early-twenty-first centuries is the close association between economic progress and political freedoms. Philosophers of an earlier age believed that great wealth was the mark of aristocracies and monarchies. Yet a look at the world today reveals a striking fact: *While not every country with a market economy is democratic, every country with a democratic political system has a market economy. Moreover, virtually every high-income country is both a market economy and a political democracy.* The freedom of the marketplace goes hand in hand with political freedoms such as free and fair elections, the presence of a significant opposition, and self-determination for major minority groups; these go hand in hand with civil liberties such as freedom of expression and association, a free press, rule of law, and respect for human rights.

Why is a democratic political system hospitable to economic development? The link is described by Yale political scientist Robert Dahl as follows:

> Democratic systems foster the education of their people; and an educated workforce is helpful to innovation and economic growth. In addition, the rule of law is usually sustained more strongly in democratic countries; courts are more independent; property

rights are more secure; contractual agreements are more effectively enforced; and arbitrary intervention in economic life by government and politicians is less likely. Finally, modern economies depend on communication, and in democratic countries the barriers to communication are much lower.[4]

Figure 34-4 shows how the march of freedoms generally goes alongside the growth of average incomes. The association between the two is clear, with the highest freedoms enjoyed by the richest countries

[4] See Dahl in the Further Reading section at the end of this chapter.

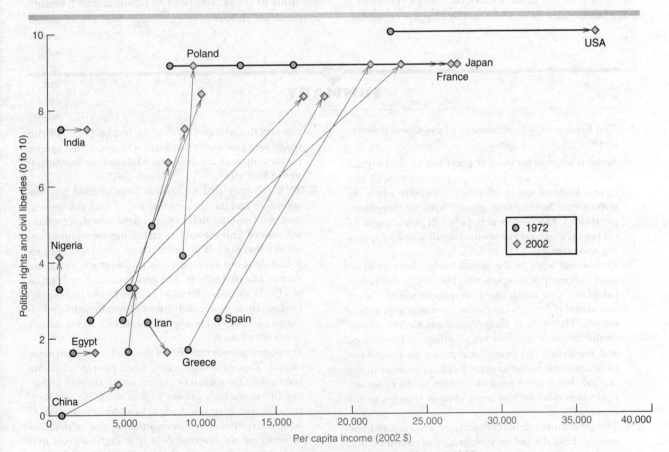

FIGURE 34-4. Economic Progress and Political Freedom, 1972 and 2002

High-income countries generally have the most political freedoms and civil liberties. As countries succeed in raising incomes, political freedoms often, but not always, go hand in hand. You can see how freedoms have generally increased over the last three decades.

Source: Freedom House for data on political rights and civil liberties. The index takes 0 to be the lowest and 10 to be the highest. Per capita incomes for 2002 come from the World Bank and the Economist Intelligence Unit and correct for purchasing-power parities.

while many poor countries suffer under the yoke of repression and curbs on speech, assembly, and the press. There are important exceptions, however, for a market economy is neither necessary nor sufficient for democracy. Some countries making the transition from traditional societies to advanced capitalism pass through a period of authoritarian rule—this was seen in the East Asian societies of Taiwan and South Korea and in much of Latin America during the last century. And during difficult economic times, countries sometimes experience democracy "fatigue" and allow strong leaders to overturn democratic institutions.

Additionally, we must not misinterpret the economic side of the coin. A modern market economy is not a laissez-faire society of anarchy plus the constable.

The businesses in a free-enterprise system must pay taxes, meet health, safety and environmental standards, and obey the society's speed limits.

So, as we close our survey of economics, perhaps we can relax and speculate on what can never be proved scientifically. Our cautiously optimistic reading of history is this: A modern democracy, proceeding carefully and applying the best of accumulated wisdom, can have the best of both worlds. It can repair the worst flaws of a market economy, promoting efficiency and fairness without excessive costs to either.

But at the same time it can preserve those precious things that can never be captured in our GDP: freedom to speak, freedom to change, and freedom to live as we choose.

SUMMARY

A. The Economic Consequences of the Government Debt

1. Budgets are systems used by governments and organizations to plan and control expenditures and revenues. Budgets are in surplus (or deficit) when the government has revenues greater (or less) than its expenditures. Macroeconomic policy depends upon fiscal policy, which comprises the overall stance of spending and taxes.

2. Economists separate the actual budget into its structural and cyclical components. The structural budget calculates how much the government would collect and spend if the economy were operating at potential output. The cyclical budget accounts for the impact of the business cycle on tax revenues, expenditures, and the deficit. To assess fiscal policy, we should pay close attention to the structural deficit; changes in the cyclical deficit are a *result* of changes in the economy, while structural deficits are a *cause* of changes in the economy.

3. The government debt represents the accumulated borrowings from the public. It is the sum of past deficits. A useful measure of the size of the debt is the debt-GDP ratio, which for the United States has tended to rise during wartime and fall during peacetime. The 1980s were an exception, for the debt-GDP ratio rose sharply during this period.

4. In understanding the impact of government deficits and debt, it is crucial to distinguish between the short run and the long run. Review the box on page 717 and make sure you understand why a larger deficit can increase output in the short run while decreasing output in the long run.

5. To the degree that we borrow from abroad for consumption and pledge posterity to pay back the interest and principal on such external debt, our descendants will indeed find themselves sacrificing consumption to service this debt. If we leave future generations an internal debt but no change in capital stock, there are various internal effects. The process of taxing Peter to pay Paula, or taxing Paula to pay Paula, can involve various microeconomic distortions of productivity and efficiency but should not be confused with owing money to another country.

6. Economic growth may slow if the public debt displaces capital. This syndrome occurs when people substitute public debt for capital or private assets, thereby reducing the economy's private capital stock. In the long run, a larger government debt may slow the growth of potential output and consumption because of the costs of servicing an external debt, the inefficiencies that arise from taxing to pay the interest on the debt, and the diminished capital accumulation that comes from capital displacement.

B. Stabilizing the Economy

7. Nations face two considerations in setting monetary and fiscal policies: the appropriate level of aggregate

demand and the best monetary-fiscal mix. The mix of fiscal and monetary policies helps determine the composition of GDP. A high-investment strategy would call for a budget surplus along with low real interest rates.

8. After the Keynesian revolution, many economists had high hopes for countercyclical stabilization policy. In practice, fiscal policy has proved a cumbersome policy, particularly because of the difficulty of raising taxes and cutting expenditures during inflationary periods. Consequently, the United States today relies almost entirely upon monetary policy to stabilize the economy.

9. Should governments follow fixed rules or discretion? The answer involves both positive economics and normative values. Conservatives often espouse rules, while liberals often advocate active fine-tuning to attain economic goals. More basic is the question of whether active and discretionary policies stabilize or destabilize the economy. Economists often stress the need for *credible*

policies, whether credibility is generated by rigid rules or by wise leadership. A recent trend among countries is inflation targeting for monetary policy, which is a flexible rule-based system that sets a medium-term inflation target while allowing short-run flexibility when economic shocks make attaining a rigid inflation target too costly.

C. Economic Prospects in the New Century

10. Remember the dictum: "Productivity isn't everything, but in the long run it is almost everything." A country's ability to improve its living standards over time depends almost entirely on its ability to improve the technologies and capital used by the workforce.

11. Promoting economic growth entails advancing technology. The major role of government is to ensure free markets, protect strong intellectual property rights, promote vigorous competition, and support basic science and technology.

CONCEPTS FOR REVIEW

The Economics of Debt and Deficits

government budget
budget deficit, surplus, and balance
budget:
    actual
    structural
    cyclical
short-run impact of G and T on
    output

long-run impacts on economic
    growth:
    internal vs. external debt
    distortions from taxation
    displacement of capital

Stabilization

demand management
fiscal-monetary mix

fixed rules vs. discretion
inflation targeting

Long-Run Growth and Productivity

reaching the technological frontier
    vs. moving it outward
the spirit of enterprise

FURTHER READING AND INTERNET WEBSITES

Further Reading

The Krugman quotation is from Paul Krugman, *The Age of Diminished Expectations* (MIT Press, Cambridge, Mass., 1990), p. 9. The source for Table 34-3 is Ralph C. Bryant, Peter Hooper, and Gerald Holtham, "Consensus and Diversity in the Model Simulations," in Ralph Bryant et al., eds., *Empirical Macroeconomics for Interdependent Economies* (Brookings Institution, Washington, D.C., 1988). The quote from Robert Dahl is from *On Democracy* (Yale University Press, New Haven, Conn., 1998), p. 59.

Websites

Economic issues and data on fiscal policy, budgets, and the debt are regularly provided by the nonpartisan Congressional Budget Office, which is staffed by professional economists. Recent documents are available at www.cbo.gov. The data on freedoms come from Freedom House's website at www.freedomhouse.org.

A survey of monetary discipline can be found in a January 2000 speech, "Inflation Targeting," by Federal Reserve governor Edward Gramlich at www.federalreserve.gov/boarddocs/speeches/2000.

QUESTIONS FOR DISCUSSION

1. A common confusion is that between the debt and the deficit. Explain each of the following:
   a. A budget deficit leads to a growing government debt.
   b. Reducing the deficit does not reduce the government debt.
   c. Reducing the government debt requires running a budget surplus.
   d. Even though the government deficit was reduced to zero in the 1993–1998 period, the government debt still rose significantly in these years.

2. Is it possible that government *promises* might have a displacement effect along with government debt? Thus, if the government were to promise large future social security benefits to workers, would workers feel richer? Might they reduce saving as a result? Could the capital stock end up smaller? Illustrate using Figure 34-2.

3. Trace the impact upon the government debt, the nation's capital stock, and real output of a government program that borrows abroad and spends the money on the following:
   a. Capital to drill for oil, which is exported (as did Mexico in the 1970s)
   b. Grain to feed its population (as did the Soviet Union in the 1980s)

4. Construct a graph like that in Figure 34-3 showing:
   a. The path of consumption and net exports with and without a large government debt
   b. The paths of consumption with a balanced budget and with a government fiscal surplus

5. Review the debate between the senators on page 717. Explain which senator would be correct in the following situations:
   a. The government increased military spending during the Great Depression.
   b. The government reduced tax rates during a period of full employment in the early 1960s.
   c. The government refused to raise taxes during the full-employment period of the Vietnam war.

6. What are the various arguments for and against rigid inflation targeting in which the inflation target is required each year? Specifically, consider the difficulties of attaining a rigid inflation target after a sharp supply shock which shifted the Phillips curve up. Compare a rigid inflation target with a flexible inflation target in which the target would be attained on average over a 5-year period.

7. Political candidates have proposed the policies listed below to speed economic growth in recent years. For each, explain qualitatively the impact upon the growth of potential output and of per capita potential output. If possible, give a quantitative estimate of the increase in the growth of potential output and per capita potential output over the next decade.
   a. Cut the federal budget deficit (or raise the surplus) by 2 percent of GDP, increasing the ratio of investment to GDP by the same amount.
   b. Increase the federal subsidy to R&D by ¼ percent of GDP, assuming that this subsidy will increase private R&D by the same amount and that R&D has a social rate of return that is 4 times that of private investment.
   c. Decrease defense spending by 1 percent of GDP, with a multiplier of 2.
   d. Decrease the number of immigrants so that the labor force declines by 5 percent.
   e. Increase investments in human capital (or education and on-the-job training) by 1 percent of GDP.

8. J. M. Keynes wrote, "If the Treasury were to fill old bottles with banknotes, bury them in disused coal mines, and leave it to private enterprise to dig the notes up again, there need be no more unemployment and the real income of the community would probably become a good deal greater than it actually is" (*The General Theory*, p. 129). Explain why Keynes's analysis of the utility of a discretionary public-works program might be correct during a depression. How could well-designed fiscal or monetary policies have the same impact on employment while producing a larger quantity of useful goods and services?

Glossary of Terms[1]

A

Ability-to-pay principle (of taxation). The principle that one's tax burden should depend upon the ability to pay as measured by income or wealth. This principle does not specify *how much* more those who are better off should pay.

Absolute advantage (in international trade). The ability of Country A to produce a commodity more efficiently (i.e., with greater output per unit of input) than Country B. Possession of such an absolute advantage does not necessarily mean that A can export this commodity to B successfully. Country B may still have the comparative advantage.

Actual, cyclical, and structural budget. The *actual budget* deficit or surplus is the amount recorded in a given year. This is composed of the *structural budget,* which calculates what government revenues, expenditures, and deficits would be if the economy were operating at potential output, and the *cyclical budget,* which measures the effect of the business cycle on the budget.

Adaptive expectations. See **expectations.**

Adverse selection. A type of market failure in which those people with the highest risk are the most likely to buy insurance. More broadly, adverse selection encompasses situations in which sellers and buyers have different information about a product, such as in the market for used cars.

Aggregate demand. Total planned or desired spending in the economy during a given period. It is determined by the aggregate price level and influenced by domestic investment, net exports, government spending, the consumption function, and the money supply.

Aggregate demand (*AD*) curve. The curve showing the relationship between the quantity of goods and services that people are willing to buy and the aggregate price level, other things equal. As with any demand curve, important variables lie behind the aggregate demand curve, e.g., government spending, exports, and the money supply.

Aggregate supply. The total value of goods and services that firms would willingly produce in a given time period. Aggregate supply is a function of available inputs, technology, and the price level.

Aggregate supply (*A S*) curve. The curve showing the relationship between the output firms would willingly supply and the aggregate price level, other things equal. The *AS* curve tends to be vertical at potential output in the very long run but may be relatively flat in the short run.

Allocative efficiency. A situation in which no reorganization or trade could raise the utility or satisfaction of one individual without lowering the utility or satisfaction of another individual. Under certain limited conditions, perfect competition leads to allocative efficiency. Also called *Pareto efficiency.*

Appreciation (of a currency). See **depreciation** (of a currency).

Appropriable. Term applied to resources for which the owner can capture the full economic value. In a well-functioning competitive market, appropriable resources are usually priced and allocated efficiently. Also refer to **inappropriable.**

Arbitrage. The purchase of a good or asset in one market for immediate resale in another market in order to profit from a price discrepancy. Arbitrage is an important force in eliminating price discrepancies, thereby making markets function more efficiently.

Asset. A physical property or intangible right that has economic value. Important examples are plant, equipment, land, patents, copyrights, and financial instruments such as money or bonds.

Automatic (or **built-in**) **stabilizers.** The property of a government tax and spending system that cushions income changes in the private sector. Examples include unemployment compensation and progressive income taxes.

Average cost. Refer to **cost, average.**

Average cost curve, long-run (*LRAC,* or *LAC*). The graph of the minimum average cost of producing a commodity for each level of output, assuming that technology and input prices are given but that the producer is free to choose the optimal size of plants.

Average cost curve, short-run (*SRAC,* or *SAC*). The graph of the minimum average cost of producing a commodity for each level of output, using the given state of technology, input prices, and existing plant.

Average fixed cost. Refer to **cost, average fixed.**

Average product. Total product or output divided by the quantity of

---

[1] Words in bold type within definitions appear as separate entries in the glossary. For a more detailed discussion of particular terms, the text will provide a useful starting point. More complete discussions are contained in Douglas Greenwald, ed., *The McGraw-Hill Encyclopedia of Economics* (McGraw-Hill, New York, 1994); David W. Pearce, *Macmillan Dictionary of Modern Economics,* rev. ed. (Macmillan, London, 1992); and John Eatwell, Murray Milgate, and Peter Newman, *The New Palgrave: A Dictionary of Economics,* 4 vols. (Macmillan, London, 1987).

one of the inputs. Hence, the average product of labor is defined as total product divided by the amount of labor input, and similarly for other inputs.

Average revenue. Total revenue divided by total number of units sold—i.e., revenue per unit. Average revenue is generally equal to price.

Average tax rate. Total taxes divided by total income; also known as *effective tax rate*.

Average variable cost. Refer to **cost, average variable.**

B

Balance of international payments. A statement showing all of a nation's transactions with the rest of the world for a given period. It includes purchases and sales of goods and services, gifts, government transactions, and capital movements.

Balance of trade. The part of a nation's balance of payments that deals with merchandise (or visible) imports or exports, including such items as foodstuffs, capital goods, and automobiles. When services and other current items are included, this measures the *balance on current account*. In balance-of-payments accounting, the current account is financed by the *financial account*.

Balance on current account. See **balance of trade.**

Balance sheet. A statement of a firm's financial position as of a given date, listing **assets** in one column and **liabilities** plus **net worth** in the other. Each item is listed at its actual or estimated money value. Totals of the two columns must balance because net worth is defined as assets minus liabilities.

Balanced budget. Refer to **budget, balanced.**

Bank, commercial. A financial intermediary whose prime distinguishing feature until recently was that it accepts checkable deposits. All financial institutions that hold savings and checkable deposits are called depository institutions.

Bank money. Money created by banks, particularly the checking accounts (part of M_1) that are generated by a multiple expansion of bank reserves.

Bank reserves. Refer to **reserves, bank.**

Barriers to entry. Factors that impede entry into a market and thereby reduce the amount of competition or the number of producers in an industry. Important examples are legal barriers, regulation, and product differentiation.

Barter. The direct exchange of one good for another without using anything as money or as a medium of exchange.

Benefit principle (of taxation). The principle that people should be taxed in proportion to the benefits they receive from government programs.

Bond. An interest-bearing certificate issued by a government or corporation, promising to repay a sum of money (the principal) plus interest at a specified date in the future.

Break-even point (in macroeconomics). For an individual, family, or community, that level of income at which 100 percent is spent on consumption (i.e., the point where there is neither saving nor dissaving). Positive saving begins at higher income levels.

Broad money (M_2). A measure of the **money supply** that includes transactions money (or M_1) as well as savings accounts in banks and similar assets that are very close substitutes for transactions money.

Budget. An account, usually for a year, of planned expenditures and expected receipts. For a government, the receipts are tax revenues. See also **actual, cyclical, and structural budget.**

Budget, balanced. A budget in which total expenditures just equal total receipts (excluding any receipts from borrowing).

Budget constraint. See **budget line.**

Budget deficit. For a government, the excess of total expenditures over total receipts, with borrowing not included among receipts. This difference (the deficit) is ordinarily financed by borrowing.

Budget line. A line indicating the combination of commodities that a consumer can buy with a given income at a given set of prices. Also sometimes called the *budget constraint*.

Budget surplus. Excess of government revenues over government spending; the opposite of budget deficit.

Business cycles. Fluctuations in total national output, income, and employment, usually lasting for a period of 2 to 10 years, marked by widespread and simultaneous expansion or contraction in many sectors of the economy.

C

$C + I$, $C + I + G$, or $C + I + G + X$ **schedule.** A schedule showing the planned or desired levels of aggregate demand for each level of GDP, or the graph on which this schedule is depicted. The schedule includes consumption (C), investment (I), government spending on goods and services (G), and net exports (X).

Capital (capital goods, capital equipment). (1) In economic theory, one of the triad of productive inputs (land, labor, and capital). Capital consists of durable produced goods that are in turn used in production. (2) In accounting and finance, "capital" means the total amount of money subscribed by the shareholder-owners of a corporation, in return for which they receive shares of the company's stock.

Capital consumption allowance. See **depreciation** (of an asset).

Capital deepening. In economic-growth theory, an increase in the capital-labor ratio. (Contrast with **capital widening.**)

Capital gains. The rise in value of a capital asset, such as land or common stocks, the gain being the difference between the sales price and the purchase price of the asset.

Capital markets. Markets in which financial resources (money, bonds, stocks) are traded. These, along with **financial intermediaries,** are institutions through which saving in the economy is transferred to investors.

Capital-output ratio. In economic-growth theory, the ratio of the total capital stock to annual GDP.

Capital widening. A rate of growth in real capital stock just equal to the growth of the labor force (or of the population), so the ratio between total capital and total labor remains unchanged. (Contrast with **capital deepening.**)

Capitalism. An economic system in which most property (land and capital) is privately owned. In such an economy, private markets are the primary vehicles used to allocate resources and generate incomes.

Cardinal utility. See **ordinal utility.**

Cartel. An organization of independent firms producing similar products that work together to raise prices and restrict output. Cartels are illegal under U.S. antitrust laws.

Central bank. A government-established agency (in the United States, the Federal Reserve System) responsible for controlling the nation's money supply and credit conditions and for supervising the financial system, especially commercial banks and other depository institutions.

Change in demand vs. change in quantity demanded. A change in the quantity buyers want to purchase, prompted by any reason other than a change in price (e.g., increase in income, change in tastes), is a *change in demand*. In graphical terms, it is a shift of the demand curve. If, in contrast, the decision to buy more or less is prompted by a change in the good's price, then it is a *change in quantity demanded*. In graphical terms, a change in quantity demanded is a movement along an unchanging demand curve.

Change in supply vs. change in quantity supplied. This distinction for supply is the same as that for demand, so see **change in demand vs. change in quantity demanded.**

Checking accounts (or bank money). A deposit in a commercial bank or other financial intermediary upon which checks can be written and which is therefore transactions money (or M_1); also called *checkable deposits*. Checkable deposits are the largest component of M_1.

Chicago School of Economics. A group of economists (among whom Henry Simons, F. A. von Hayek, and Milton Friedman have been the most prominent) who believe that competitive markets free of government intervention will lead to the most efficient operation of the economy.

Classical approach. See **classical economics.**

Classical economics. The predominant school of economic thought prior to the appearance of Keynes's work; founded by Adam Smith in 1776. Other major figures who followed Smith include David Ricardo, Thomas Malthus, and John Stuart Mill. By and large, this school believed that economic laws (particularly individual self-interest and competition) determine prices and factor rewards and that the price system is the best possible device for resource allocation.

Classical theories (in macroeconomics). Theories emphasizing the self-correcting forces in the economy. In the classical approach, there is generally full employment, and policies to stimulate aggregate demand have no impact upon output.

Clearing market. A market in which prices are sufficiently flexible to equilibrate supply and demand very quickly. In markets that clear, there is no rationing, unemployed resources, or excess demand or supply. In practice, this is thought to apply to many commodity and financial markets but not to labor or many product markets.

Closed economy. See **open economy.**

Collective bargaining. The process of negotiations between a group of workers (usually a union) and their employer. Such bargaining leads to an agreement about wages, fringe benefits, and working conditions.

Collusion. An agreement between different firms to cooperate by raising prices, dividing markets, or otherwise restraining competition.

Collusive oligopoly. A market structure in which a small number of firms (i.e., a few oligopolists) collude and jointly make their decisions. When they succeed in maximizing their joint profits, the price and quantity in the market closely approach those prevailing under monopoly.

Command economy. A mode of economic organization in which the key economic functions—*what, how,* and *for whom*—are principally determined by government directive. Sometimes called a *centrally planned economy.*

Commodity money. Money with **intrinsic value;** also, the use of some commodity (cattle, beads, etc.) as money.

Common currency. A situation where several countries form a monetary union with a single currency and a unified central bank; e.g., the European Monetary Union (EMU), which introduced the Euro in 1999.

Common stock. The financial instrument representing ownership and, generally, voting rights in a corporation. A certain share of a company's stock gives the owner title to that fraction of the votes, net earnings, and assets of the corporation.

Communism. A communist economic system (also called *Soviet-style central planning*) is one in which the state owns and controls the means of production, particularly industrial capital. Such economies are also characterized by extensive central planning, with the state setting many prices, output levels, and other important economic variables.

Comparative advantage (in international trade). The law of comparative advantage says that a nation should specialize in producing and exporting those commodities which it can produce at *relatively* lower cost and that it should import those goods for which it is a *relatively* high-cost producer. Thus it is a comparative advantage, not an absolute advantage, that should dictate trade patterns.

Compensating differentials. Differences in wage rates among jobs that serve to offset or compensate for the nonmonetary differences of the jobs. For example, unpleasant jobs that require isolation for many months in Alaska pay wages much higher than those for similar jobs nearer to civilization.

Competition, imperfect. Term applied to markets in which perfect competition does not hold because at least one seller (or buyer) is large enough to affect the market price and therefore faces a downward-sloping demand (or supply) curve. Imperfect competition refers to any kind of market imperfection—pure monopoly, oligopoly, or **monopolistic competition.**

Competition, perfect. Term applied to markets in which no firm or consumer is large enough to affect the market price. This situation arises where (1) the number of sellers and buyers is very large and (2) the products offered by sellers are homogeneous (or indistinguishable). Under such conditions, each firm faces a horizontal (or perfectly elastic) demand curve.

Competitive equilibrium. The balancing of supply and demand in a market or economy characterized by **perfect competition.** Because perfectly competitive sellers and buyers individually have no power to influence the market, price will move to the point at which it equals both marginal cost and marginal utility.

Competitive market. See **competition, perfect.**

Complements. Two goods which "go together" in the eyes of consumers (e.g., left shoes and right shoes). Goods are *substitutes* when they compete with each other (as do gloves and mittens).

Compound interest. Interest computed on the accrued total of interest and principal. For example, suppose $100 (the principal) is deposited in an account earning 10 percent interest compounded annually. At the end of year 1, interest of $10 is earned. At the end of year 2, the interest payment is $11, $10 on the original principal and $1 on the interest—and so on in future years.

Concentration ratio. The percentage of an industry's total output accounted for by the largest firms. A typical measure is the *four-firm concentration ratio,* which is the fraction of output accounted for by the four largest firms.

Conglomerate. A large corporation producing and selling a variety of unrelated goods (e.g., some cigarette companies have expanded into such unrelated areas as liquor, car rental, and movie production).

Constant returns to scale. See **returns to scale.**

Consumer price index (CPI). A price index that measures the cost of a fixed basket of consumer goods in which the weight assigned to each commodity is the share of expenditures on that commodity by urban consumers in 1982–1984.

Consumer surplus. The difference between the amount that a consumer would be willing to pay for a commodity and the amount actually paid. This difference arises because the marginal utilities (in dollar terms) of all but the last unit exceed the price. Under certain conditions, the money value of consumer surplus can be measured (using a demand-curve diagram) as the area under the demand curve but above the price line.

Consumption. In macroeconomics, the total spending, by individuals or a nation, on consumer goods during a given period. Strictly speaking, consumption should apply only to those goods totally used, enjoyed, or "eaten up" within that period. In practice, consumption expenditures include all consumer goods bought, many of which last well beyond the period in question—e.g., furniture, clothing, and automobiles.

Consumption function. A schedule relating total consumption to personal **disposable income** (*DI*). Total wealth and other variables are also frequently assumed to influence consumption.

Consumption-possibility line. See **budget line.**

Cooperative equilibrium. In game theory, an outcome in which the parties act in unison to find strategies that will optimize their joint payoffs.

Corporate income tax. A tax levied on the annual net income of a corporation.

Corporation. The dominant form of business organization in modern capitalist economies. A corporation is a firm owned by individuals or other corporations. It has the same rights to buy, sell, and make contracts as a person would have. It is legally separate from those who own it and has **limited liability.**

Correlation. The degree to which two variables are systematically associated with each other.

Cost, average. Total cost (refer to **cost, total**) divided by the number of units produced.

Cost, average fixed. Fixed cost (refer to **cost, fixed**) divided by the number of units produced.

Cost, average variable. Variable cost (refer to **cost, variable**) divided by the number of units produced.

Cost, fixed. The cost a firm would incur even if its output for the period in question were zero. Total fixed cost is made up of such individual contractual costs as interest payments, mortgage payments, and directors' fees.

Cost, marginal. The extra cost (or the increase in total cost) required to produce 1 extra unit of output (or the reduction in total cost from producing 1 unit less).

Cost, minimum. The lowest attainable cost per unit (whether average, variable, or marginal). Every point on an average cost curve is a minimum in the sense that it is the best the firm can do with respect to cost for the output which that point represents. Minimum average cost is the lowest point, or points, on that curve.

Cost, total. The minimum attainable total cost, given a particular level of technology and set of input prices. *Short-run total cost* takes existing plant and other fixed costs as given. *Long-run total cost* is the cost that would be incurred if

the firm had complete flexibility with respect to all inputs and decisions.

Cost, variable. A cost that varies with the level of output, such as raw-material, labor, and fuel costs. Variable costs equal total cost minus fixed cost.

Cost-push inflation. Inflation originating on the supply side of markets from a sharp increase in costs. In the aggregate supply-and-demand framework, cost-push is illustrated as an upward shift of the *AS* curve. Also called **supply-shock** inflation.

Credit. (1) In monetary theory, the use of someone else's funds in exchange for a promise to pay (usually with interest) at a later date. The major examples are short-term loans from a bank, credit extended by suppliers, and commercial paper. (2) In balance-of-payments accounting, an item such as exports that earns a country foreign currency.

Cross elasticity of demand. A measure of the influence of a change in one good's price on the demand for another good. More precisely, the cross elasticity of demand equals the percentage change in demand for good A when the price of good B changes by 1 percent, assuming other variables are held constant.

Currency. Coins and paper money.

Currency appreciation (or depreciation). See **depreciation** (of a currency).

Currency board. A monetary institution operating like a central bank for a country that only issues currency that is fully backed by assets denominated in a key foreign currency, often the U.S. dollar.

Current account. See **balance of trade.**

Cyclical budget. See **actual, cyclical, and structural budget.**

Cyclical unemployment. See **frictional unemployment.**

D

Deadweight loss. The loss in real income or consumer and producer surplus that arises because of monopoly, tariffs and quotas, taxes, or other distortions. For example, when a monopolist raises its price, the loss in consumer satisfaction is more than the gain in the monopolist's revenue—the difference being the deadweight loss to society due to monopoly.

Debit. (1) An accounting term signifying an increase in assets or decrease in liabilities. (2) In balance-of-payments accounting, a debit is an item such as imports that reduces a country's stock of foreign currencies.

Decreasing returns to scale. See **returns to scale.**

Deficit spending. Government's expenditures on goods and services and transfer payments in excess of its receipts from taxation and other revenue sources. The difference must be financed by borrowing from the public.

Deflating (of economic data). The process of converting "nominal" or current-dollar variables into "real" terms. This is accomplished by dividing current-dollar variables by a **price index.**

Deflation. A fall in the general level of prices.

Demand curve (or demand schedule). A schedule or curve showing the quantity of a good that buyers would purchase at each price, other things equal. Normally a demand curve has price on the vertical or *Y* axis and quantity demanded on the horizontal or *X* axis. Also see **change in demand vs. change in quantity demanded.**

Demand for money. A summary term used by economists to explain why individuals and businesses hold money balances. The major motivations for holding money are (1) *transactions demand,* signifying that people need money to purchase things, and (2) *asset demand,* relating to the desire to hold a very liquid, risk-free asset.

Demand-pull inflation. Price inflation caused by an excess demand for goods in general, caused, e.g., by a major increase in aggregate demand. Often contrasted with **cost-push inflation.**

Demography. The study of the behavior of a population.

Depreciation (of an asset). A decline in the value of an asset. In both business and national accounts, depreciation is the dollar estimate of the extent to which capital has been "used up" or worn out over the period in question. Also termed *capital consumption allowance* in national-income accounting.

Depreciation (of a currency). A nation's currency is said to depreciate when it declines relative to other currencies. For example, if the foreign exchange rate of the dollar falls from 6 to 4 French francs per U.S. dollar, the dollar's value has fallen, and the dollar has undergone a depreciation. The opposite of a depreciation is an *appreciation,* which occurs when the foreign exchange rate of a currency rises.

Depression. A prolonged period characterized by high unemployment, low output and investment, depressed business confidence, falling prices, and widespread business failures. A milder form of business downturn is a **recession,** which has many of the features of a depression to a lesser extent.

Derived demand. The demand for a factor of production that results (is "derived") from the demand for the final good to which it contributes. Thus the demand for tires is derived from the demand for automobile transportation.

Devaluation. A decrease in the official price of a nation's currency, as expressed in the currencies of other nations or in terms of gold.

Thus, when the official price of the dollar was lowered with respect to gold in 1971, the dollar was devalued. The opposite of devaluation is *revaluation,* which occurs when a nation raises its official foreign exchange rate relative to gold or other currencies.

Developing country. Same as **less-developed country.**

Differentiated products. Products which compete with each other and are close substitutes but are not identical. Differences may be manifest in the product's function, appearance, location, quality, or other attributes.

Diminishing marginal utility, law of. The law which says that as more and more of any one commodity is consumed, its marginal utility declines.

Diminishing returns, law of. A law stating that the additional output from successive increases of one input will eventually diminish when other inputs are held constant. Technically, the law is equivalent to saying that the marginal product of the varying input declines after a point.

Direct taxes. Taxes levied directly on individuals or firms, including taxes on income, labor earnings, and profits. Direct taxes contrast with *indirect taxes,* which are levied on goods and services and thus only indirectly on people, such as sales taxes and taxes on property, alcohol, imports, and gasoline.

Discount rate. (1) The interest rate charged by a Federal Reserve Bank (the central bank) on a loan that it makes to a commercial bank. (2) The rate used to calculate the present value of some asset.

Discounting (of future income). The process of converting future income into an equivalent present value. This process takes a future dollar amount and reduces it by a discount factor that reflects the appropriate interest rate. For ex-

ample, if someone promises you $121 in 2 years, and the appropriate interest rate or discount rate is 10 percent per year, then we can calculate the present value by discounting the $121 by a discount factor of $(1.10)^2$. The rate at which future incomes are discounted is called the **discount rate.**

Discrimination. Differences in earnings that arise because of personal characteristics that are unrelated to job performance, especially those related to gender, race, ethnicity, sexual orientation, or religion.

Disequilibrium. The state in which an economy is not in **equilibrium.** This may arise when shocks (to income or prices) have shifted demand or supply schedules but the market price (or quantity) has not yet adjusted fully. In macroeconomics, unemployment is often thought to stem from market disequilibria.

Disinflation. The process of reducing a high inflation rate. For example, the deep recession of 1980–1983 led to a sharp disinflation over that period.

Disposable income (*DI*). Roughly, take-home pay, or that part of the total national income that is available to households for consumption or saving. More precisely, it is equal to GDP less all taxes, business saving, and depreciation plus government and other transfer payments and government interest payments.

Disposable personal income. Same as **disposable income.**

Dissaving. Negative saving; spending more on consumption goods during a period than the disposable income available for that period (the difference being financed by borrowing or drawing on past savings).

Distribution. In economics, the manner in which total output and income is distributed among individuals or factors (e.g., the distribution of income between labor and capital).

Distribution theory. See **theory of income distribution.**

Division of labor. A method of organizing production whereby each worker specializes in part of the productive process. Specialization of labor yields higher total output because labor can become more skilled at a particular task and because specialized machinery can be introduced to perform more carefully defined subtasks.

Dominant equilibrium. See **dominant strategy.**

Dominant strategy. In game theory, a situation where one player has a best strategy no matter what strategy the other player follows. When all players have a dominant strategy, we say that the outcome is a *dominant equilibrium.*

Downward-sloping demand, law of. The rule which says that when the price of some commodity falls, consumers will purchase more of that good, other things held equal.

Duopoly. A market structure in which there are only two sellers. (Compare with **oligopoly.**)

Duopoly price game. A situation in game theory where the market is supplied by two firms that are deciding whether to engage in economic warfare by undercutting each others' prices.

E

Econometrics. The branch of economics that uses the methods of statistics to measure and estimate quantitative economic relationships.

Economic good. A good that is scarce relative to the total amount of it that is desired. It must therefore be rationed, usually by charging a positive price.

Economic growth. An increase in the total output of a nation over time. Economic growth is usually measured as the annual rate of increase in a nation's real GDP (or real potential GDP).

Economic regulation. See **regulation.**

Economic rent. Refer to **rent, economic.**

Economic surplus. A term denoting the excess in total satisfaction or utility over the costs of production; equals the sum of consumer surplus (the excess of consumer satisfaction over total value of purchases) and producer surplus (the excess of producer revenues over costs).

Economics. The study of how societies use scarce resources to produce valuable commodities and distribute them among different people.

Economics of information. Analysis of economic situations that involve information as a commodity. Because information is costly to produce but cheap to reproduce, market failures are common in markets for informational goods and services such as invention, publishing, and software.

Economies of scale. Increases in productivity, or decreases in average cost of production, that arise from increasing all the factors of production in the same proportion.

Economies of scope. Economies of producing multiple goods or services. Thus economies of scope exist if it is cheaper to produce good X and good Y together rather than separately.

Effective tax rate. Total taxes paid as a percentage of the total income or other tax base; also known as *average tax rate.*

Efficiency. Absence of waste, or the use of economic resources that produces the maximum level of satisfaction possible with the given inputs and technology. A shorthand expression for **allocative efficiency.**

Efficiency-wage theory. According to this theory, higher wages lead to higher productivity. This occurs because with higher wages workers are healthier, have higher morale, and have lower turnover.

Efficient financial market. A financial market displaying the characteristics of an **efficient market.**

Efficient market (also efficient-market theory). A market or theory in which all new information is quickly understood by market participants and becomes immediately incorporated into market prices. In economics, efficient-market theory holds that all currently available information is already incorporated into the price of common stocks (or other assets).

Elasticity. A term widely used in economics to denote the responsiveness of one variable to changes in another. Thus the elasticity of X with respect to Y means the percentage change in X for every 1 percent change in Y. For especially important examples, see **price elasticity of demand** and **price elasticity of supply.**

Employed. According to official U.S. definitions, persons are employed if they perform any paid work or if they hold jobs but are absent because of illness, strike, or vacations.

Equal-cost line. A line in a graph showing the various possible combinations of factor inputs that can be purchased with a given quantity of money.

Equal-product curve (or isoquant). A line in a graph showing the various possible combinations of factor inputs which will yield a given quantity of output.

Equation of exchange. A definitional equation which states that $MV \equiv PQ$, or the money stock times velocity of money equals the price level times output. This equation forms the core of **monetarism.**

Equilibrium. The state in which an economic entity is at rest or in which the forces operating on the entity are in balance so that there is no tendency for change.

Equilibrium (for a business firm). That position or level of output in which the firm is maximizing its profit, subject to any constraints it may face, and therefore has no incentive to change its output or price level. In the standard theory of the firm, this means that the firm has chosen an output at which marginal revenue is just equal to marginal cost.

Equilibrium (for the individual consumer). That position in which the consumer is maximizing utility, i.e., has chosen the bundle of goods which, given income and prices, best satisfies the consumer's wants.

Equilibrium, competitive. Refer to **competitive equilibrium.**

Equilibrium, general. Refer to **general-equilibrium analysis.**

Equilibrium, macroeconomic. A GDP level at which intended aggregate demand equals intended aggregate supply. At the equilibrium, desired consumption (C), government expenditures (G), investment (I), and net exports (X) just equal the quantity that businesses wish to sell at the going price level.

Equimarginal principle. A principle for deciding the allocation of income among different consumption goods. Under this principle, a consumer's utility is maximized by choosing the consumption bundle such that the marginal utility per dollar spent is equal for all goods.

Exchange rate. See **foreign exchange rate.**

Exchange-rate system. The set of rules, arrangements, and institutions under which payments are made among nations. Historically, the most important exchange-rate systems have been the gold exchange standard, the Bretton Woods system, and today's flexible-exchange-rate system.

Excise tax vs. sales tax. An excise tax is one levied on the purchase of a specific commodity or group of commodities (e.g., alcohol or tobacco). A *sales tax* is one levied on

all commodities with only a few specific exclusions (e.g., all purchases except food).

Exclusion principle. A criterion by which public goods are distinguished from private goods. When a producer sells a commodity to person A and can easily exclude B, C, D, etc., from enjoying the benefits of the commodity, the exclusion principle holds and the good is a private good. If, as in public health or national defense, people cannot easily be excluded from enjoying the benefits of the good's production, then the good has public-good characteristics.

Exogenous vs. induced variables. Exogenous variables are those determined by conditions outside the economy. They are contrasted with *induced variables,* which are determined by the internal workings of the economic system. Changes in the weather are exogenous; changes in consumption are often induced by changes in income.

Expectations. Views or beliefs about uncertain variables (such as future interest rates, prices, or tax rates). Expectations are said to be *rational* if they are not systematically wrong (or "biased") and use all available information. Expectations are said to be *adaptive* if people form their expectations on the basis of past behavior.

Expenditure multiplier. See **multiplier.**

Exports. Goods or services that are produced in the home country and sold to another country. These include merchandise trade (like cars), services (like transportation), and interest on loans and investments. *Imports* are simply flows in the opposite direction—into the home country from another country.

External diseconomies. Situations in which production or consumption imposes uncompensated costs on other parties. Steel facto-

ries that emit smoke and sulfurous fumes harm local property and public health, yet the injured parties are not paid for the damage. The pollution is an external diseconomy.

External economies. Situations in which production or consumption yields positive benefits to others without those others paying. A firm that hires a security guard scares thieves from the neighborhood, thus providing external security services. Together with external diseconomies, these are often referred to as **externalities.**

External variables. Same as **exogenous variables.**

Externalities. Activities that affect others for better or worse, without those others paying or being compensated for the activity. Externalities exist when private costs or benefits do not equal social costs or benefits. The two major species are **external economies** and **external diseconomies.**

F

Factors of production. Productive inputs, such as labor, land, and capital; the resources needed to produce goods and services. Also called *inputs.*

Fallacy of composition. The fallacy of assuming that what holds for individuals also holds for the group or the entire system.

Federal funds rate. The interest rate that banks pay each other for the overnight use of bank reserves.

Federal Reserve System. The **central bank** of the United States; consists of the Board of Governors and 12 regional Federal Reserve Banks.

Fiat money. Money, like today's paper currency, without **intrinsic value** but decreed (by fiat) to be legal tender by the government. Fiat money is accepted only as long as people have confidence that it will be accepted.

Final good. A good that is produced for final use and not for resale or further manufacture. (Compare with **intermediate goods.**)

Finance. The process by which economic agents borrow from and lend to other agents in order to save and spend.

Financial account. See **balance of trade.**

Financial assets. Monetary claims or obligations by one party against another party. Examples are bonds, mortgages, bank loans, and equities.

Financial economics. That branch of economics which analyzes how rational investors should invest their funds to attain their objectives in the best possible manner.

Financial intermediaries. Institutions which provide financial services and products. These include depository institutions (such as commercial or savings banks) and nondepository institutions (such as money market mutual funds, brokerage houses, insurance companies, or pension funds).

Financial markets. Markets whose products and services consist of financial instruments like stocks and bonds.

Financial system. The markets, firms, and other institutions which carry out the financial decisions of households, businesses, governments, and the rest of the world. Important parts of the financial system include the money market, markets for fixed-interest assets like bonds or mortgages, stock markets for the ownership of firms, and foreign exchange markets which trade the monies of different countries.

Firm (business firm). The basic, private producing unit in an economy. It hires labor, rents or owns capital and land, and buys other inputs in order to make and sell goods and services.

Fiscal-monetary mix. The combination of fiscal and monetary policies used to influence macroeconomic activity. A tight-monetary–loose-fiscal policy will tend to encourage consumption and retard investment, while an easy-monetary–tight-fiscal policy will have the opposite effect.

Fiscal policy. A government's program with respect to (1) the purchase of goods and services and spending on transfer payments and (2) the amount and type of taxes.

Fixed cost. Refer to **cost, fixed.**

Fixed exchange rate. See **foreign exchange rate.**

Flexible exchange rates. A system of foreign exchange rates among countries wherein the exchange rates are predominantly determined by private market forces (i.e., by supply and demand) without governments' setting and maintaining a particular pattern of exchange rates; also sometimes called *floating exchange rates.* When the government refrains from any intervention in exchange markets, the system is called a pure flexible-exchange-rate system.

Floating exchange rates. See **flexible exchange rates.**

Flow of funds. The account which traces how money and other financial instruments flow through the economy.

Flow vs. stock. A *flow* variable is one that has a time dimension or flows over time (like the flow through a stream). A *stock* variable is one that measures a quantity at a point of time (like the water in a lake). Income represents dollars per year and is thus a flow. Wealth as of December 2005 is a stock.

Foreign exchange. Currency (or other financial instruments) of different countries that allow one country to settle amounts owed to other countries.

Foreign exchange market. The market in which currencies of different countries are traded.

Foreign exchange rate. The rate, or price, at which one country's currency is exchanged for the currency of another country. For example, if you can buy 1.9 German marks for 1 U.S. dollar, then the exchange rate for the mark is 1.9. A country has a *fixed exchange rate* if it pegs its currency at a given exchange rate and stands ready to defend that rate. Exchange rates which are determined by market supply and demand are called **flexible exchange rates.**

Four-firm concentration ratio. See **concentration ratio.**

Fractional-reserve banking. A regulation in modern banking systems whereby financial institutions are legally required to keep a specified fraction of their deposits in the form of deposits with the central bank (or in vault cash).

Free goods. Those goods that are not **economic goods.** Like air or seawater, they exist in such large quantities that they need not be rationed out among those wishing to use them. Thus, their market price is zero.

Free trade. A policy whereby the government does not intervene in trading between nations by tariffs, quotas, or other means.

Frictional unemployment. Temporary unemployment caused by changes in individual markets. It takes time, for example, for new workers to search among different job possibilities; even experienced workers often spend a minimum period of unemployed time moving from one job to another. Frictional is thus distinct from *cyclical unemployment,* which results from a low level of aggregate demand in the context of sticky wages and prices.

Full employment. A term that is used in many senses. Historically, it was taken to be that level of employment at which no (or minimal) involuntary unemployment exists. Today, economists rely upon the concept of the **nonaccelerating inflation rate of unemployment** (*NAIRU*) to indicate the highest sustainable level of employment over the long run.

G

Gains from trade.   The aggregate increase in welfare accruing from voluntary exchange; equal to the sum of consumer surplus and gains in producer profits.

Galloping inflation.   See **inflation.**

Game theory.   An analysis of situations involving two or more decision makers with at least partially conflicting interests. It can be applied to the interaction of oligopolistic markets as well as to bargaining situations such as strikes or to conflicts such as games and war.

GDP deflator.   The "price" of GDP, i.e., the price index that measures the average price of the components in GDP relative to a base year.

General-equilibrium analysis.   Analysis of the equilibrium state for the economy as a whole in which the markets for all goods and services are simultaneously in equilibrium. By contrast, **partial-equilibrium analysis** concerns the equilibrium in a single market.

GNP.   See **gross national product.**

Gold standard.   A system under which a nation (1) declares its currency unit to be equivalent to some fixed weight of gold, (2) holds gold reserves against its money, and (3) will buy or sell gold freely at the price so proclaimed, with no restrictions on the export or import of gold.

Government debt.   The total of government obligations in the form of bonds and shorter-term borrowings. Government debt held by the public excludes bonds held by quasi-governmental agencies such as the central bank.

Government expenditure multiplier.   The increase in GDP resulting from an increase of $1 in government purchases.

Gross domestic product, nominal (or nominal GDP).   The value, at current market prices, of the total final output produced inside a country during a given year.

Gross domestic product, real (or real GDP).   The quantity of goods and services produced in a nation during a year. Real GDP takes nominal GDP and corrects for price increases.

Gross national product, real (or real GNP).   Nominal GNP corrected for inflation, i.e., real GNP equals nominal GNP divided by the GNP deflator.

Growth accounting.   A technique for estimating the contribution of different factors to economic growth. Using marginal productivity theory, growth accounting decomposes the growth of output into the growth in labor, land, capital, education, technical knowledge, and other miscellaneous sources.

H

Hedging.   A technique for avoiding a risk by making a counteracting transaction. For example, if a farmer produces wheat that will be harvested in the fall, the risk of price fluctuations can be offset, or hedged, by selling in the spring or summer the quantity of wheat that will be produced.

Herfindahl-Hirschman Index (HHI).   A measure of market power often used in analysis of market structure. It is calculated by summing the squares of the percentage market shares of all participants in a market. Perfect competition would have an HHI of near zero, while complete monopoly has an HHI of 10,000.

High-powered money.   Same as **monetary base.**

Horizontal equity vs. vertical equity.   *Horizontal equity* refers to the fairness or equity in treatment of persons in similar situations; the principle of horizontal equity states that those who are essentially equal should receive equal treatment. *Vertical equity* refers to the equitable treatment of those who are in different circumstances.

Horizontal integration.   See **integration, vertical vs. horizontal.**

Horizontal merger.   See **merger.**

Human capital.   The stock of technical knowledge and skill embodied in a nation's workforce, resulting from investments in formal education and on-the-job training.

Hyperinflation.   See **inflation.**

I

Imperfect competition.   Refer to **competition, imperfect.**

Imperfect competitor.   Any firm that buys or sells a good in large enough quantities to be able to affect the price of that good.

Implicit-cost elements.   Costs that do not show up as explicit money costs but nevertheless should be counted as such (such as the labor cost of the owner of a small store). Sometimes called **opportunity cost,** although "opportunity cost" has a broader meaning.

Imports.   See **exports.**

Inappropriability.   See **inappropriable.**

Inappropriable.   Term applied to resources for which the individual cost of use is free or less than the full social costs. These resources are characterized by the presence of externalities, and thus markets will allocate their use inefficiently from a social point of view.

Incidence (or tax incidence).   The ultimate economic effect of a tax on the real incomes of producers or consumers (as opposed to the legal requirement for payment). Thus a sales tax may be paid by a retailer, but it is likely that the incidence falls upon the consumer. The exact incidence of a tax depends on the price elasticities of supply and demand.

Income. The flow of wages, interest payments, dividends, and other receipts accruing to an individual or nation during a period of time (usually a year).

Income effect (of a price change). Change in the quantity demanded of a commodity because the change in its price has the effect of changing a consumer's real income. Thus it supplements the **substitution effect** of a price change.

Income elasticity of demand. The demand for any given good is influenced not only by the good's price but by buyers' incomes. Income elasticity measures this responsiveness. Its precise definition is percentage change in quantity demanded divided by percentage change in income. (Compare with **price elasticity of demand.**)

Income statement. A company's statement, covering a specified time period (usually a year), showing sales or revenue earned during that period, all costs properly charged against the goods sold, and the profit (net income) remaining after deduction of such costs. Also called a *profit-and-loss statement.*

Income tax, personal. Tax levied on the income received by individuals in the form of either wages and salaries or income from property, such as rents, dividends, or interest. In the United States, personal income tax is **progressive,** meaning that people with higher incomes pay taxes at a higher average rate than people with lower incomes.

Income velocity of money. See **velocity of money.**

Incomes policy. A government policy—often used in wartime—that attempts directly to restrict wage and price changes in an effort to slow inflation. Such policies range from voluntary wage-price guidelines to outright legal control over wages, salaries, and prices.

Increasing returns to scale. See **returns to scale.**

Independent goods. Goods whose demands are relatively separate from each other. More precisely, goods A and B are independent when a change in the price of good A has no effect on the quantity demanded of good B, other things equal.

Indexing (or indexation). A mechanism by which wages, prices, and contracts are partially or wholly adjusted to compensate for changes in the general price level.

Indifference curve. A curve drawn on a graph whose two axes measure amounts of different goods consumed. Each point on one curve (indicating different combinations of the two goods) yields exactly the same level of satisfaction for a given consumer.

Indifference map. A graph showing a family of indifference curves for a consumer. In general, curves that lie farther northeast from the graph's origin represent higher levels of satisfaction.

Indirect taxes. See **direct taxes.**

Induced variables. See **exogenous vs. induced variables.**

Industry. A group of firms producing similar or identical products.

Inertial rate of inflation. A process of steady inflation that occurs when inflation is expected to persist and the ongoing rate of inflation is built into contracts and people's expectations.

Infant industry. In foreign-trade theory, an industry that has not had sufficient time to develop the experience or expertise to exploit the economies of scale needed to compete successfully with more mature industries producing the same commodity in other countries. Infant industries are often thought to need tariffs or quotas to protect them while they develop.

Inferior good. A good whose consumption goes down as income rises.

Inflation (or inflation rate). The inflation rate is the percentage of annual increase in a general price level. *Hyperinflation* is inflation at extremely high rates (say, 1000, 1 million, or even 1 billion percent a year). *Galloping inflation* is a rate of 50 or 100 or 200 percent annually. *Moderate inflation* is a price-level rise that does not distort relative prices or incomes severely.

Inflation targeting. The announcement of official target ranges for the inflation rate along with an explicit statement that low and stable inflation is the overriding goal of monetary policy. Inflation targeting in hard or soft varieties has been adopted in recent years by many industrial countries.

Innovation. A term particularly associated with Joseph Schumpeter, who meant by it (1) the bringing to market of a new and significantly different product, (2) the introduction of a new production technique, or (3) the opening up of a new market. (Contrast with **invention.**)

Inputs. Commodities or services used by firms in their production processes; also called *factors of production.*

Insurance. A system by which individuals can reduce their exposure to risk of large losses by spreading the risks among a large number of persons.

Integration, vertical vs. horizontal. The production process is one of stages—e.g., iron ore into steel ingots, steel ingots into rolled steel sheets, rolled steel sheets into an automobile body. *Vertical integration* is the combination in a single firm of two or more different stages of this process (e.g., iron ore with steel ingots). *Horizontal integration* is the combination in a single firm of different units that operate at the same stage of production.

Intellectual property rights. Laws governing patents, copyrights, trade secrets, electronic media, and other commodities comprised primarily of information. These laws generally provide the original creator the right to control and be compensated for reproduction of the work.

Interest. The return paid to those who lend money.

Interest rate. The price paid for borrowing money for a period of time, usually expressed as a percentage of the principal per year. Thus, if the interest rate is 10 percent per year, then $100 would be paid for a loan of $1000 for 1 year.

Intermediate goods. Goods that have undergone some manufacturing or processing but have not yet reached the stage of becoming final products. For example, steel and cotton yarn are intermediate goods.

International monetary system (also international financial system). The institutions under which payments are made for transactions that reach across national boundaries. A central policy issue concerns the arrangement for determining how foreign exchange rates are set and how governments can affect exchange rates.

Intervention. An activity in which a government buys or sells its currency in the foreign exchange market in order to affect its currency's exchange rate.

Intrinsic value (of money). The commodity value of a piece of money (e.g., the market value of the weight of copper in a copper coin).

Invention. The creation of a new product or discovery of a new production technique. (Distinguish from **innovation**.)

Investment. (1) Economic activity that forgoes consumption today with an eye to increasing output in the future. It includes tangible capital such as houses and intangible investments such as education.

Net investment is the value of total investment after an allowance has been made for depreciation. *Gross investment* is investment without allowance for depreciation. (2) In finance terms, "investment" has an altogether different meaning and denotes the purchase of a security, such as a stock or a bond.

Investment demand (or investment demand curve). The schedule showing the relationship between the level of investment and the cost of capital (or, more specifically, the real interest rate); also, the graph of that relationship.

Invisible hand. A concept introduced by Adam Smith in 1776 to describe the paradox of a laissez-faire market economy. The invisible-hand doctrine holds that, with each participant pursuing his or her own private interest, a market system nevertheless works to the benefit of all as though a benevolent invisible hand were directing the whole process.

Involuntarily unemployed. See **unemployment.**

Isoquant. See **equal-product curve.**

K

Keynesian economics. The body of thought developed by John Maynard Keynes holding that a capitalist system does not automatically tend toward a full-employment equilibrium. According to Keynes, the resulting underemployment equilibrium could be cured by fiscal or monetary policies to raise aggregate demand.

Keynesian school. See **Keynesian economics.**

L

Labor force. In official U.S. statistics, that group of people 16 years of age and older who are either employed or unemployed.

Labor-force participation rate. The ratio of those in the labor force to the entire population 16 years of age or older.

Labor productivity. See **productivity.**

Labor supply. The number of workers (or, more generally, the number of labor-hours) available to an economy. The principal determinants of labor supply are population, real wages, and social traditions.

Labor theory of value. The view, often associated with Karl Marx, that every commodity should be valued solely according to the quantity of labor required for its production.

Laissez-faire ("Leave us alone"). The view that government should interfere as little as possible in economic activity and leave decisions to the marketplace. As expressed by classical economists like Adam Smith, this view held that the role of government should be limited to maintenance of law and order, national defense, and provision of certain public goods that private business would not undertake (e.g., public health and sanitation).

Land. In classical and neoclassical economics, one of the three basic factors of production (along with labor and capital). More generally, land is taken to include land used for agricultural or industrial purposes as well as natural resources taken from above or below the soil.

Law of diminishing marginal utility. See **diminishing marginal utility, law of.**

Law of diminishing returns. See **diminishing returns, law of.**

Law of downward-sloping demand. The nearly universal observation that when the price of a commodity is raised (and other things are held constant), buyers buy less of the commodity. Similarly, when the price is lowered, other things being constant, quantity demanded increases.

Least-cost rule (of production). The rule that the cost of producing a specific level of output is minimized when the ratio of the marginal revenue product of each input to the price of that input is the same for all inputs.

Legal tender. Money that by law must be accepted as payment for debts. All U.S. coins and currency are legal tender, but checks are not.

Less-developed country (LDC). A country with a per capita income far below that of "developed" nations (the latter usually includes most nations of North America and Western Europe).

Liabilities. In accounting, debts or financial obligations owed to other firms or persons.

Libertarianism. An economic philosophy that emphasizes the importance of personal freedom in economic and political affairs; also sometimes called "liberalism." Libertarian writers (including Adam Smith in an earlier age and Milton Friedman and James Buchanan today) hold that people should be able to follow their own interests and desires and that government activities should be limited to guaranteeing contracts and to providing police and national defense, thereby allowing maximum personal freedom.

Limited liability. The restriction of an owner's loss in a business to the amount of capital that the owner has contributed to the company. Limited liability was an important factor in the rise of large corporations. By contrast, owners in partnerships and individual proprietorships generally have *unlimited liability* for the debts of those firms.

Long run. A term used to denote a period over which full adjustment to changes can take place. In microeconomics, it denotes the time over which firms can enter or leave an industry and the capital stock can be replaced. In **macro**-economics, it is often used to mean the period over which all prices, wage contracts, tax rates, and expectations can fully adjust.

Long-run aggregate supply schedule. A schedule showing the relationship between output and the price level after all price and wage adjustments have taken place, and the AS curve is therefore vertical.

Lorenz curve. A graph used to show the extent of inequality of income or wealth.

M

M_1, M_2. See **money supply.**

Macroeconomic equilibrium. Refer to **equilibrium, macroeconomic.**

Macroeconomics. Analysis dealing with the behavior of the economy as a whole with respect to output, income, the price level, foreign trade, unemployment, and other aggregate economic variables. (Contrast with **microeconomics.**)

Malthusian theory of population growth. The hypothesis, first expressed by Thomas Malthus, that the "natural" tendency of population is to grow more rapidly than the food supply. Per capita food production would thus decline over time, thereby putting a check on population. In general, a view that population tends to grow more rapidly as incomes or living standards of the population rise.

Managed exchange rate. The most prevalent exchange-rate system today. In this system, a country occasionally intervenes to stabilize its currency but there is no fixed or announced parity.

Marginal cost. Refer to **cost, marginal.**

Marginal principle. The fundamental notion that people will maximize their income or profits when the marginal costs and marginal benefits of their actions are equal.

Marginal product (*MP*). The extra output resulting from 1 extra unit of a specified input when all other inputs are held constant. Sometimes called *marginal physical product.*

Marginal product theory of distribution. A theory of the distribution of income proposed by John B. Clark, according to which each productive input is paid according to its **marginal product.**

Marginal propensity to consume (*MPC*). The extra amount that people consume when they receive an extra dollar of disposable income. To be distinguished from the *average propensity to consume,* which is the ratio of total consumption to total disposable income.

Marginal propensity to import (*MPm*). In macroeconomics, the increase in the dollar value of imports resulting from each dollar increase in the value of GDP.

Marginal propensity to save (*MPS*). That fraction of an additional dollar of disposable income that is saved. Note that, by definition, $MPC + MPS = 1$.

Marginal revenue (*MR*). The additional revenue a firm would earn if it sold 1 extra unit of output. In perfect competition, *MR* equals price. Under imperfect competition, *MR* is less than price because, in order to sell the extra unit, the price must be reduced on all prior units sold.

Marginal revenue product (*MRP*) (of an input). Marginal revenue multiplied by marginal product. It is the extra revenue that would be brought in if a firm were to buy 1 extra unit of an input, put it to work, and sell the extra product it produced.

Marginal tax rate. For an income tax, the percentage of the last dollar of income paid in taxes. If a tax system is progressive, the marginal tax rate is higher than the average tax rate.

Marginal utility (*MU*). The additional or extra satisfaction yielded from consuming 1 additional unit of a commodity, with amounts of all other goods consumed held constant.

Market. An arrangement whereby buyers and sellers interact to determine the prices and quantities of a commodity. Some markets (such as the stock market or a flea market) take place in physical locations; other markets are conducted over the telephone or are organized by computers, and some markets now are organized on the Internet.

Market-clearing price. The price in a supply-and-demand equilibrium. This denotes that all supply and demand orders are filled at that price, so that the books are "cleared" of orders.

Market economy. An economy in which the *what, how,* and *for whom* questions concerning resource allocation are primarily determined by supply and demand in markets. In this form of economic organization, firms, motivated by the desire to maximize profits, buy inputs and produce and sell outputs. Households, armed with their factor incomes, go to markets and determine the demand for commodities. The interaction of firms' supply and households' demand then determines the prices and quantities of goods.

Market equilibrium. Same as **competitive equilibrium.**

Market failure. An imperfection in a price system that prevents an efficient allocation of resources. Important examples are **externalities** and **imperfect competition.**

Market power. The degree of control that a firm or group of firms has over the price and production decisions in an industry. In a monopoly, the firm has a high degree of market power; firms in perfectly competitive industries have no market power. **Concentration ratios** are the most widely used measures of market power.

Market share. That fraction of an industry's output accounted for by an individual firm or group of firms.

Markup pricing. The pricing method used by many firms in situations of imperfect competition; under this method they estimate average cost and then add some fixed percentage to that cost in order to reach the price they charge.

Marxism. The set of social, political, and economic doctrines developed by Karl Marx in the nineteenth century. As an economic theory, Marxism predicted that capitalism would collapse as a result of its own internal contradictions, especially its tendency to exploit the working classes. The conviction that workers would inevitably be oppressed under capitalism was based on the **iron law of wages,** which holds that wages would decline to subsistence levels.

Mean. In statistics, the same thing as "average." Thus for the numbers 1, 3, 6, 10, 20, the mean is 8.

Median. In statistics, the figure exactly in the middle of a series of numbers ordered or ranked from lowest to highest (e.g., incomes or examination grades). Thus for the numbers 1, 3, 6, 10, 20, the median is 6.

Mercantilism. A political doctrine emphasizing the importance of balance-of-payments surpluses as a device to accumulate gold. Proponents therefore advocated tight government control of economic policies, believing that laissez-faire policies might lead to a loss of gold.

Merchandise trade balance. See **balance of trade.**

Merger. The acquisition of one corporation by another, which usually occurs when one firm buys the stock of another. Important examples are (1) *vertical mergers,* which occur when the two firms are at different stages of a production process (e.g., iron ore and steel), (2) *horizontal mergers,* which occur when the two firms produce in the same market (e.g., two automobile manufacturers), and (3) *conglomerate mergers,* which occur when the two firms operate in unrelated markets (e.g., shoelaces and oil refining).

Microeconomics. Analysis dealing with the behavior of individual elements in an economy—such as the determination of the price of a single product or the behavior of a single consumer or business firm. (Contrast with **macroeconomics.**)

Minimum cost. Refer to **cost, minimum.**

Mixed economy. The dominant form of economic organization in noncommunist countries. Mixed economies rely primarily on the price system for their economic organization but use a variety of government interventions (such as taxes, spending, and regulation) to handle macroeconomic instability and market failures.

Model. A formal framework for representing the basic features of a complex system by a few central relationships. Models take the form of graphs, mathematical equations, and computer programs.

Momentary run. A period of time that is so short that production is fixed.

Monetarism. A school of thought holding that changes in the money supply are the major cause of macroeconomic fluctuations. For the short run, this view holds that changes in the money supply are the primary determinant of changes in both real output and the price level. For the longer run, it holds that prices tend to move proportionally with the money supply. Monetarists often conclude that the best macroeconomic policy is one with stable growth in the money supply.

Monetary base. The net monetary liabilities of the government that are held by the public. In the United States, the monetary base is equal to currency and bank reserves. Sometimes called *high-powered money.*

Monetary economy. An economy in which the trade takes place through a commonly accepted medium of exchange.

Monetary policy. The objectives of the central bank in exercising its control over money, interest rates, and credit conditions. The instruments of monetary policy are primarily open-market operations, reserve requirements, and the discount rate.

Monetary rule. The cardinal tenet of monetarist economic philosophy is the monetary rule which asserts that optimal monetary policy sets the growth of the money supply at a fixed rate and holds to that rate through thick and thin.

Monetary transmission mechanism. In macroeconomics, the route by which changes in the supply of money are translated into changes in output, employment, prices, and inflation.

Monetary union. An arrangement by which several nations adopt a common currency as a unit of account and medium of exchange. The European Monetary Union adopted the Euro as the common currency in 1999.

Money. The means of payment or medium of exchange. For the items constituting money, see **money supply.**

Money demand schedule. The relationship between holdings of money and interest rates. As interest rates rise, bonds and other securities become more attractive, lowering the quantity of money demanded. See also **demand for money.**

Money funds. Shorthand expression for very liquid short-term financial instruments whose interest rates are not regulated. The major examples are money market mutual funds and commercial-bank money market deposit accounts.

Money market. A term denoting the set of institutions that handle the purchase or sale of short-term credit instruments like Treasury bills and commercial paper.

Money supply. The narrowly defined money supply (narrow money, or M_1) consists of coins, paper currency, and all demand or checking deposits; this is transactions money. The broadly defined supply (broad money, or M_2) includes all items in M_1 plus certain liquid assets or near-monies—savings deposits, money market funds, and the like.

Money-supply effect. The relationship whereby a price rise operating on a fixed nominal money supply produces tight money and lowers aggregate spending.

Money-supply multiplier. The ratio of the increase in the money supply (or in deposits) to the increase in bank reserves. Generally, the money-supply multiplier is equal to the inverse of the required reserve ratio. For example, if the required reserve ratio is 0.125, then the money-supply multiplier is 8.

Money, velocity of. Refer to **velocity of money.**

Monopolistic competition. A market structure in which there are many sellers supplying goods that are close, but not perfect, substitutes. In such a market, each firm can exercise some effect on its product's price.

Monopoly. A market structure in which a commodity is supplied by a single firm. Also see **natural monopoly.**

Monopsony. The mirror image of monopoly: a market in which there is a single buyer; a "buyer's monopoly."

Moral hazard. A type of market failure in which the presence of insurance against an insured risk increases the likelihood that the risky event will occur. For example, a car owner insured 100 percent against auto theft may be careless about locking the car because the presence of insurance reduces the incentive to prevent the theft.

MPC. See **marginal propensity to consume.**

MPS. See **marginal propensity to save.**

Multiplier. A term in macroeconomics denoting the change in an induced variable (such as GDP or money supply) per unit of change in an external variable (such as government spending or bank reserves). The *expenditure multiplier* denotes the increase in GDP that would result from a $1 increase in expenditure (say, on investment).

Multiplier model. In macroeconomics, a theory developed by J. M. Keynes that emphasizes the importance of changes in autonomous expenditures (especially investment, government spending, and net exports) in determining changes in output and employment. Also see **multiplier.**

N

NAIRU. See **nonaccelerating inflation rate of unemployment.**

Narrow money (M_1). A measure of the **money supply** that includes coins, paper currency, and all demand or checking deposits; also called *transactions money.*

Nash equilibrium. In game theory, a set of strategies for the players where no player can improve his or her payoff given the other player's strategy. That is, given player A's strategy, player B can do no better, and given B's strategy, A can do no better. The Nash equilibrium is also sometimes called the *noncooperative equilibrium.*

National debt. Same as **government debt.**

National income and product accounts (NIPA). A set of accounts that measures the spending, income, and output of the entire nation for a quarter or a year.

National saving rate. Total saving, private and public, divided by net domestic product.

Natural monopoly. A firm or industry whose average cost per unit of production falls sharply over the entire range of its output, as, e.g., in local electricity distribution. Thus a single firm, a monopoly, can supply the industry output more efficiently than can multiple firms.

"Near-money." Financial assets that are risk-free and so readily convertible into money that they are close to actually being money. Examples are money funds and Treasury bills.

Neoclassical model of growth. A theory or model used to explain long-term trends in the economic growth of industrial economies. This model emphasizes the importance of capital deepening (i.e., a growing capital-labor ratio) and technological change in explaining the growth of potential real GDP.

Net domestic product (NDP). GDP less an allowance for depreciation of capital goods.

Net economic welfare (NEW). A measure of national output that corrects several limitations of the GDP measure.

Net exports. In the national product accounts, the value of exports of goods and services minus the value of imports of goods and services.

Net foreign investment. Net saving by a country abroad; approximately equal to net exports.

Net investment. Gross investment minus depreciation of capital goods.

Net worth. In accounting, total assets minus total liabilities.

New classical macroeconomics. A theory which holds that (1) prices and wages are flexible and (2) people make forecasts in accordance with the rational-expectations hypothesis. The main implication of this theory is the policy-ineffectiveness theorem.

Nominal GDP. See gross domestic product, nominal.

Nominal (or money) interest rate. The interest rate paid on different assets. This represents a dollar return per year per dollar invested. Compare with the real interest rate, which represents the return per year in goods per unit of goods invested.

Nonaccelerating inflation rate of unemployment (NAIRU). An unemployment rate that is consistent with a constant inflation rate. At the NAIRU, upward and downward forces on price and wage inflation are in balance, so there is no tendency for inflation to change. The NAIRU is the lowest unemployment rate that can be sustained without upward pressure on inflation. The NAIRU is the unemployment rate at which the long-run Phillips curve is vertical.

Noncooperative equilibrium. See Nash equilibrium.

Nonrenewable resources. Those natural resources, like oil and gas, that are essentially fixed in supply and whose regeneration is not quick enough to be economically relevant.

Normative vs. positive economics. Normative economics considers "what ought to be"—value judgments, or goals, of public policy. Positive economics, by contrast, is the analysis of facts and behavior in an economy, or "the way things are."

Not in the labor force. That part of the adult population that is neither working nor looking for work.

O

Okun's Law. The empirical relationship, discovered by Arthur Okun, between cyclical movements in GDP and unemployment. The law states that when actual GDP declines 2 percent relative to potential GDP, the unemployment rate increases by about 1 percentage point. (Earlier estimates placed the ratio at 3 to 1.)

Oligopoly. A situation of imperfect competition in which an industry is dominated by a small number of suppliers.

Open economy. An economy that engages in international trade (i.e., imports and exports) of goods and capital with other countries. A closed economy is one that has no imports or exports.

Open-economy multiplier. In an open economy, changes in income leak into imports as well as into saving. Therefore, the open-economy multiplier for investment or government expenditure is given by the formula:

Open-economy multiplier
$$= 1/(MPS + MPm),$$

where MPS = marginal propensity to save and MPm = marginal propensity to import.

Open-market operations. The activity of a central bank in buying or selling government bonds to influence bank reserves, the money supply, and interest rates. If securities are bought, the money paid out by the central bank increases commercial-bank reserves, and the money supply increases. If securities are sold, the money supply contracts.

Opportunity cost. The value of the next-best use (or opportunity) for an economic good, or the value of the sacrificed alternative. Thus, say that the best alternative use of the inputs employed to mine a ton of coal was to grow 10 bushels of wheat. The opportunity cost of a ton of coal is thus the 10 bushels of wheat that *could* have been produced but were not. Opportunity cost is particularly useful for valuing nonmarketed goods such as environmental health or safety.

Optimal currency area. A grouping of regions or countries which have high labor mobility or have common and synchronous aggregate supply or demand shocks. Under such conditions, significant changes in exchange rates are not necessary to ensure rapid macroeconomic adjustment, and the countries can have fixed exchange rates or a common currency.

Ordinal utility. A dimensionless utility measure used in demand theory. Ordinal utility enables one to state that A is preferred to B, but we cannot say by how much. That is, any two bundles of goods can be ranked relative to each other, but the absolute difference between bundles cannot be measured. This contrasts with *cardinal utility*, or dimensional utility, which is sometimes used in the analysis of behavior toward risk. An example of a cardinal measure comes when we say that a substance at 100 K (kelvin) is twice as hot as one at 50 K.

Other things constant. A phrase (sometimes stated "*ceteris paribus*") which signifies that a factor under consideration is changed while all other factors are held constant or unchanged. For example, a downward-sloping demand curve shows that the quantity demanded will decline as the price rises, as long as other things (such as incomes) are held constant.

Outputs. The various useful goods or services that are either consumed or used in further production.

P

Paradox of thrift. The principle, first proposed by John Maynard Keynes, that an attempt by a society to increase its saving may result in a reduction in the amount which it actually saves.

Paradox of value. The paradox that many necessities of life (e.g., water) have a low "market" value while many luxuries (e.g., diamonds) with little "use" value have a high market price. It is explained by the fact that a price reflects not the total utility of a commodity but its marginal utility.

Pareto efficiency (or Pareto optimality). See **allocative efficiency.**

Partial-equilibrium analysis. Analysis concentrating on the effect of changes in an individual market, holding other things equal (e.g., disregarding changes in income).

Partnership. An association of two or more persons to conduct a business which is not in corporate form and does not enjoy limited liability.

Patent. An exclusive right granted to an inventor to control the use of an invention for, in the United States, a period of 20 years. Patents create temporary monopolies as a way of rewarding inventive activity and, like other intellectual property rights, are a tool for promoting invention among individuals or small firms.

Payoff table. In game theory, a table used to describe the strategies and payoffs of a game with two or more players. The profits or utilities of the different players are the *payoffs*.

Payoffs. See **payoff table.**

Perfect competition. Refer to **competition, perfect.**

Personal income. A measure of income before taxes have been deducted. More precisely, it equals disposable personal income plus net taxes.

Personal saving. That part of income which is not consumed; in other words, the difference between disposable income and consumption.

Personal saving rate. The ratio of personal saving to personal disposable income, in percent.

Phillips curve. A graph, first devised by A. W. Phillips, showing the trade-off between unemployment and inflation. In modern mainstream macroeconomics, the downward-sloping "tradeoff" Phillips curve is generally held to be valid only in the short run; in the long run, the Phillips curve is usually thought to be vertical at the nonaccelerating inflation rate of unemployment (NAIRU).

Policy-ineffectiveness theorem. A theorem which asserts that, with rational expectations and flexible prices and wages, anticipated government monetary or fiscal policy cannot affect real output or unemployment.

Portfolio theory. An economic theory that describes how rational investors allocate their wealth among different financial assets—that is, how they put their wealth into a "portfolio."

Positive economics. See **normative vs. positive economics.**

Post hoc fallacy. From the Latin, *post hoc, ergo propter hoc,* which translates as "after this, therefore because of this." This fallacy arises when it is assumed that because event A precedes event B, it follows that A *causes* B.

Potential GDP. High-employment GDP; more precisely, the maximum level of GDP that can be sustained with a given state of technology and population size without accelerating inflation. Today, it is generally taken to be equivalent to the level of output corresponding to the **nonaccelerating inflation rate of unemployment (NAIRU).** Potential output is not necessarily maximum output.

Potential output. Same as **potential GDP.**

Poverty. Today, the U.S. government defines the "poverty line" to be the minimum adequate standard of living.

PPF. See **production-possibility frontier.**

Present value (of an asset). Today's value for an asset that yields a stream of income over time. Valuation of such time streams of returns requires calculating the present worth of each component of the income, which is done by applying a discount rate (or interest rate) to future incomes.

Price. The money cost of a good, service, or asset. Price is measured in monetary units per unit of the good (as in 3 dollars per 1 hamburger).

Price discrimination. A situation where the same product is sold to different consumers for different prices.

Price-elastic demand (or **elastic demand**). The situation in which price elasticity of demand exceeds 1 in absolute value. This signifies that the percentage change in quantity demanded is greater than the percentage change in price. In addition, elastic demand implies that total revenue (price times quantity) rises when price falls because the increase in quantity demanded is so large. (Contrast with **price-inelastic demand.**)

Price elasticity of demand. A measure of the extent to which quantity demanded responds to a price change. The elasticity coefficient (price elasticity of demand E_p) is the percentage change in quantity demanded divided by percentage change in price. In figuring percentages, use the averages of old and new quantities in the numerator and of old and new prices in the denominator; disregard the minus sign. Refer also to **price-elastic demand, price-inelastic demand,** and **unit-elastic demand.**

Price elasticity of supply. Conceptually similar to **price elasticity of demand,** except that it measures the supply responsiveness to a price change. More precisely, the price elasticity of supply measures the percentage change in quantity supplied divided by the percentage change in price. Supply elasticities are most useful in perfect competition.

Price flexibility. Price behavior in "auction" markets (e.g., for many raw commodities or the stock market), in which prices immediately respond to changes in demand or in supply.

Price index. An index number that shows how the average price of a bundle of goods changes over time. In computing the average, the prices of the different goods are generally weighted by their economic importance (e.g., by each commodity's share of total consumer expenditures in the **consumer price index**).

Price-inelastic demand (or **inelastic demand**). The situation in which price elasticity of demand is below 1 in absolute value. In this case, when price declines, total revenue declines, and when price is increased, total revenue goes up. Perfectly inelastic demand means that there is no change at all in quantity demanded when price goes up or down. (Contrast with **price-elastic demand** and **unit-elastic demand.**)

Price of GDP. See **GDP deflator.**

Prisoner's dilemma. A famous game in which the noncooperative equilibrium is inefficient.

Private good. See **public good.**

Producer price index. The price index of goods sold at the wholesale level (such as steel, wheat, oil).

Producer surplus. The difference between the producer sales revenue and the producer cost. The producer surplus is generally measured as the area above the supply curve but under the price line up to the amount sold.

Product, average. Refer to **average product.**

Product, marginal. Refer to **marginal product.**

Product differentiation. The existence of characteristics that make similar goods less-than-perfect substitutes. Thus locational differences make similar types of gasoline sold at separate points imperfect substitutes. Firms enjoying product differentiation face a downward-sloping demand curve instead of the horizontal demand curve of the perfect competitor.

Production function. A relation (or mathematical function) specifying the maximum output that can be produced with given inputs for a given level of technology; applies to a firm or, as an aggregate production function, to the economy as a whole.

Production-possibility frontier (*PPF*). A graph showing the menu of goods that can be produced by an economy. In a frequently cited case, the choice is reduced to two goods, guns and butter. Points outside the *PPF* (to the northeast of it) are unattainable. Points inside it are inefficient since resources are not being fully employed, resources are not being used properly, or outdated production techniques are being utilized.

Productive efficiency. A situation in which an economy cannot produce more of one good without producing less of another good; this implies that the economy is on its production-possibility frontier.

Productivity. A term referring to the ratio of output to inputs (total output divided by labor inputs is *labor productivity*). Productivity increases if the same quantity of inputs produces more output. Labor productivity increases because of improved technology, improvements in labor skills, or capital deepening.

Productivity growth. The rate of increase in **productivity** from one period to another. For example, if an index of labor productivity is 100 in 2004 and 101.7 in 2005, the rate of productivity growth is 1.7 percent per year for 2005 over 2004.

Productivity of capital, net. See **rate of return on capital.**

Profit. (1) In accounting terms, total revenue minus costs properly chargeable against the goods sold (see **income statement**). (2) In economic theory, the difference between sales revenue and the full opportunity cost of resources involved in producing the goods.

Profit-and-loss statement. See **income statement.**

Progressive, proportional, and regressive taxes. A progressive tax weighs more heavily upon the rich; a regressive tax does the opposite. More precisely, a tax is *progressive* if the average tax rate (i.e., taxes divided by income) is higher for those with higher incomes; it is a *regressive* tax if the average tax rate declines with higher incomes; it is a *proportional* tax if the average tax rate is equal at all income levels.

Property rights. Rights that define the ability of individuals or firms to own, buy, sell, and use the capital goods and other property in a market economy.

Proportional tax. See **progressive, proportional, and regressive taxes.**

Proprietorship, individual. A business firm owned and operated by one person.

Protectionism. Any policy adopted by a country to protect domestic industries against competition from imports (most commonly, a tariff or quota imposed on such imports).

Public choice (also **public-choice theory**). Branch of economics and political science dealing with the way that governments make choices and direct the economy. This theory differs from the theory of markets in emphasizing the influence of vote maximizing for politicians, which contrasts to profit maximizing by firms.

Public debt. See **government debt.**

Public good. A commodity whose benefits are indivisibly spread among the entire community, whether or not particular individuals desire to consume the public good. For example, a public-health measure that eradicates polio protects all, not just those paying for the vaccinations. To be contrasted with *private goods,* such as bread, which, if consumed by one person, cannot be consumed by another person.

Pure economic rent. See **rent, economic.**

Q

Quantity demanded. See **change in demand vs. change in quantity demanded.**

Quantity equation of exchange. A tautology, $MV \equiv PQ$, where M is the money supply, V is the income velocity of money, and PQ (price times quantity) is the money value of total output (nominal GDP). The equation must always hold exactly since V is defined as PQ/M.

Quantity supplied. See **change in supply vs. change in quantity supplied.**

Quantity theory of money and prices. A theory of the determination of output and the overall price level holding that prices move proportionately with the money supply. A more cautious approach put forth by monetarists holds that the money supply is the most important determinant of changes in nominal GDP (see **monetarism**).

Quota. A form of import protectionism in which the total quantity of imports of a particular commodity (e.g., sugar or cars) during a given period is limited.

R

Random-walk theory (of stock market prices). See **efficient market.**

Rate of inflation. See **inflation.**

Rate of return (or **return**) **on capital.** The yield on an investment or on a capital good. Thus, an investment costing $100 and yielding $12 annually has a rate of return of 12 percent per year.

Rational expectations. See **expectations.**

Rational-expectations hypothesis. A hypothesis which holds that people make unbiased forecasts and, further, that people use all available information and economic theory to make these forecasts.

Rational-expectations macroeconomics. A school, led by Robert Lucas, Robert Barro, and Thomas Sargent, holding that markets clear quickly and that expectations are rational. Under these and other conditions it can be shown that predictable macroeconomic policies have no effect on real output or unemployment. Sometimes called **new classical macroeconomics.**

Real-business-cycle theory. A theory that explains business cycles purely as shifts in aggregate supply, primarily due to technological disturbances, without any reference to monetary or other demand-side forces.

Real GDP. See **gross domestic product, real.**

Real interest rate. The interest rate measured in terms of goods rather than money. It is thus equal to the money (or nominal) interest rate less the rate of inflation.

Real wages. The purchasing power of a worker's wages in terms of goods and services. It is measured by the ratio of the money wage rate to the consumer price index.

Recession. A period of significant decline in total output, income, and employment, usually lasting from 6 months to a year and marked by widespread contractions in many sectors of the economy. See also **depression.**

Regressive tax.   See **progressive, proportional, and regressive taxes.**

Regulation.   Government laws or rules designed to control the behavior of firms. The major kinds are *economic regulation* (which affects the prices, entry, or service of a single industry, such as telephone service) and *social regulation* (which attempts to correct externalities that prevail across a number of industries, such as air or water pollution).

Renewable resources.   Natural resources (like agricultural land) whose services replenish regularly and which, if properly managed, can yield useful services indefinitely.

Rent, economic (or pure economic rent).   Term applied to income earned from land. The total supply of land available is (with minor qualifications) fixed, and the return paid to the landowner is rent. The term is often extended to the return paid to any factor in fixed supply—i.e., to any input having a perfectly inelastic or vertical supply curve.

Required reserve ratio.   See **reserves, bank.**

Reserves, bank.   That portion of deposits that a bank sets aside in the form of vault cash or non-interest-earning deposits with Federal Reserve Banks. In the United States, banks are required to hold 10 percent of checking deposits (or transactions accounts) in the form of reserves.

Reserves, international.   International money held by a nation to stabilize or "peg" its foreign exchange rate or provide financing when the nation faces balance-of-payments difficulties. Under the gold standard, this money was gold. Today, the bulk of reserves are U.S. dollars, with Euros and Japanese yen the other major reserve currencies. If a nation were prepared to allow its exchange rate to float freely, it would need minimal reserves.

Resource allocation.   The manner in which an economy distributes its resources (its factors of production) among the potential uses so as to produce a particular set of final goods.

Returns to scale.   The rate at which output increases when all inputs are increased proportionately. For example, if all the inputs double and output is exactly doubled, that process is said to exhibit *constant returns to scale.* If, however, output grows by less than 100 percent when all inputs are doubled, the process shows *decreasing returns to scale;* if output more than doubles, the process demonstrates *increasing returns to scale.*

Revaluation.   An increase in the official foreign exchange rate of a currency. See also **devaluation.**

Ricardian view of fiscal policy.   A theory developed by Harvard's Robert Barro which holds that changes in tax rates have no impact upon consumption spending because households foresee, say, that tax cuts today will require tax increases tomorrow to finance the government's financing requirements.

Risk.   In financial economics, refers to the variability of the returns on an investment.

Risk averse.   A person is risk-averse when, faced with an uncertain situation, the displeasure from losing a given amount of income is greater than the pleasure from gaining the same amount of income.

Risk spreading.   The process of taking large risks and spreading them around so that they are but small risks for a large number of people. The major form of risk spreading is **insurance,** which is a kind of gambling in reverse.

Rule of 70.   A useful shortcut for approximating compound interest. A quantity that grows at r percent per year will double in about $70/r$ years.

S

Sales tax.   See **excise tax vs. sales tax.**

Saving function.   The schedule showing the amount of saving that households or a nation will undertake at each level of income.

Say's Law of Markets.   The theory that "supply creates its own demand." J. B. Say argued in 1803 that, because total purchasing power is exactly equal to total incomes and outputs, excess demand or supply is impossible. Keynes attacked Say's Law, pointing out that an extra dollar of income need not be spent entirely (i.e., the marginal propensity to spend is not necessarily unity).

Scarcity.   The distinguishing characteristic of an economic good. That an economic good is scarce means not that it is rare but only that it is not freely available for the taking. To obtain such a good, one must either produce it or offer other economic goods in exchange.

Scarcity, law of.   The principle that most things that people want are available only in limited supply (the exception being **free goods**). Thus goods are generally scarce and must somehow be rationed, whether by price or some other means.

Schedule (demand, supply, aggregate demand, aggregate supply).   Term used interchangeably with "curve," as in demand curve, supply curve, etc.

Securities.   A term used to designate a wide variety of financial assets, such as stocks, bonds, options, and notes; more precisely, the documents used to establish ownership of these assets.

Short run.   A period in which not all factors can adjust fully. In microeconomics, the capital stock and other "fixed" inputs cannot be adjusted and entry is not free in the short run. In macroeconomics, prices, wage contracts, tax rates, and expectations may not fully adjust in the short run.

Short-run aggregate supply schedule. The schedule showing the relationship between output and prices in the short run wherein changes in aggregate demand can affect output; represented by an upward-sloping or horizontal *AS* curve.

Shutdown price (or point or rule). In the theory of the firm, the shutdown point comes at that point where the market price is just sufficient to cover average variable cost and no more. Hence, the firm's losses per period just equal its fixed costs; it might as well shut down.

Single-tax movement. A nineteenth-century movement, originated by Henry George, holding that continued poverty in the midst of steady economic progress was attributable to the scarcity of land and the large rents flowing to landowners. The "single tax" was to be a tax on economic rent earned from landownership.

Slope. In a graph, the change in the variable on the vertical axis per unit of change in the variable on the horizontal axis. Upward-sloping lines have positive slopes, downward-sloping curves (like demand curves) have negative slopes, and horizontal lines have slopes of zero.

Social insurance. Mandatory insurance provided by government to improve social welfare by preventing the losses created by market failures such as moral hazard or adverse selection.

Social overhead capital. The essential investments on which economic development depends, particularly for sanitation and drinking water, transportation, and communications; sometimes called *infrastructure.*

Social regulation. See **regulation.**

Socialism. A political theory which holds that all (or almost all) the means of production, other than labor, should be owned by the community. This allows the return on capital to be shared more equally than under capitalism.

Speculator. Someone engaged in speculation, i.e., someone who buys (or sells) a commodity or financial asset with the aim of profiting from later selling (or buying) the item at a higher (or lower) price.

Spillovers. Same as **externalities.**

Stagflation. A term, coined in the early 1970s, describing the coexistence of high unemployment, or *stag*nation, with persistent in*flation.* Its explanation lies primarily in the inertial nature of the inflationary process.

Statistical discrimination. Treatment of individuals on the basis of the average behavior or characteristics of members of the group to which they belong. Statistical discrimination can be self-fulfilling by reducing incentives for individuals to overcome the stereotype.

Stock, common. Refer to **common stock.**

Stock market. An organized marketplace in which common stocks are traded. In the United States, the largest stock market is the New York Stock Exchange, on which are traded the stocks of the largest U.S. companies.

Stock vs. flow. See **flow vs. stock.**

Strategic interaction. A situation in oligopolistic markets in which each firm's business strategies depend upon its rival's plans. A formal analysis of strategic interaction is given in **game theory.**

Structural budget. See **actual, cyclical, and structural budget.**

Structural unemployment. Unemployment resulting because the regional or occupational pattern of job vacancies does not match the pattern of worker availability. There may be jobs available, but unemployed workers may not have the required skill, or the jobs may be in different regions from where the unemployed workers live.

Subsidy. A payment by a government to a firm or household that provides or consumes a commodity. For example, governments often subsidize food by paying for part of the food expenditures of low-income households.

Substitutes. Goods that compete with each other (as do gloves and mittens). By contrast, goods that go together in the eyes of consumers (such as left shoes and right shoes) are *complements.*

Substitution effect (of a price change). The tendency of consumers to consume more of a good when its relative price falls (to "substitute" in favor of that good) and to consume less of the good when its relative price increases (to "substitute" away from that good). This substitution effect of a price change leads to a downward-sloping demand curve. (Compare with **income effect.**)

Substitution rule. A rule which asserts that if the price of one factor falls while all other factor prices remain the same, firms will profit by substituting the now-cheaper factor for all the other factors. The rule is a corollary of the **least-cost rule.**

Supply curve (or supply schedule). A schedule showing the quantity of a good that suppliers in a given market desire to sell at each price, holding other things equal.

Supply shock. In macroeconomics, a sudden change in production costs or productivity that has a large and unexpected impact upon aggregate supply. As a result of a supply shock, real GDP and the price level change unexpectedly.

Supply-side economics. A view emphasizing policy measures to affect aggregate supply or potential output. This approach holds that high marginal tax rates on labor and capital incomes reduce work effort and saving.

T

Tangible assets.   Those assets, such as land or capital goods like computers, buildings, and automobiles, that are used to produce further goods and services.

Tariff.   A levy or tax imposed upon each unit of a commodity imported into a country.

Tax incidence.   See incidence.

Technological change.   A change in the process of production or an introduction of a new product such that more or improved output can be obtained from the same bundle of inputs. It results in an outward shift in the production-possibility curve. Often called technological progress.

Technological progress.   See technological change.

Terms of trade (in international trade).   The "real" terms at which a nation sells its export products and buys its import products. This measure equals the ratio of an index of export prices to an index of import prices.

Theory of income distribution.   A theory explaining the manner in which personal income and wealth are distributed in a society.

Time deposit.   Funds, held in a bank, that have a minimum "time of withdrawal"; included in broad money (M_2) but not in M_1 because they are not accepted as a means of payment.

Token money.   Money with little or no intrinsic value.

Total cost.   Refer to cost, total.

Total factor productivity.   An index of productivity that measures total output per unit of total input. The numerator of the index is total output (say, GDP), while the denominator is a weighted average of inputs of capital, labor, and re-

sources. The growth of total factor productivity is often taken as an index of the rate of technological progress. Also sometimes called multifactor productivity.

Total product (or output).   The total amount of a commodity produced, measured in physical units such as bushels of wheat, tons of steel, or number of haircuts.

Total revenue.   Price times quantity, or total sales.

Trade balance or merchandise trade balance.   See balance of trade.

Trade barrier.   Any of a number of protectionist devices by which nations discourage imports. Tariffs and quotas are the most visible barriers, but in recent years nontariff barriers (or NTBs), such as burdensome regulatory proceedings, have replaced more traditional measures.

Transactions demand for money.   See demand for money.

Transactions money (M_1).   A measure of the money supply which consists of items that are actually for transactions, namely, currency and checking accounts; also called narrow money.

Transfer payments, government.   Payments made by a government to individuals, for which the individual performs no current service in return. Examples are social security payments and unemployment insurance.

Treasury bills (T-bills).   Short-term bonds or securities issued by the federal government.

U

Underground economy.   Unreported economic activity. The underground economy includes otherwise legal activities not reported to the taxing authorities (such as garage sales or services "bartered" among friends) and illegal activities (such as the drug trade, gambling, and prostitution).

Unemployed.   People who are not employed but are actively looking for work or waiting to return to work.

Unemployment.   (1) In economic terms, involuntary unemployment occurs when there are qualified workers who are willing to work at prevailing wages but cannot find jobs. (2) In the official (U.S. Bureau of Labor Statistics) definition, a worker is unemployed if he or she (a) is not working and (b) either is waiting for recall from layoff or has actively looked for work in the last 4 weeks. See also frictional unemployment and structural unemployment.

Unemployment rate.   The percentage of the labor force that is unemployed.

Unit-elastic demand.   The situation, between price-elastic demand and price-inelastic demand, in which price elasticity is just equal to 1 in absolute value. See also price elasticity of demand.

Unlimited liability.   See limited liability.

Usury.   The charging of an interest rate above a legal maximum on borrowed money.

Utility (also total utility).   The total satisfaction derived from the consumption of goods or services. To be contrasted with marginal utility, which is the additional utility arising from consumption of an additional unit of the commodity.

V

Value, paradox of.   Refer to paradox of value.

Value added.   The difference between the value of goods produced and the cost of materials and supplies used in producing them. In a \$1 loaf of bread embodying \$0.60 worth of wheat and other materials, the value added is \$0.40. Value added consists of the wages, interest, and profit components added to the output by a firm or industry.

Value-added tax (VAT). A tax levied upon a firm as a percentage of its value added.

Variable. A magnitude of interest that can be defined and measured. Important variables in economics include prices, quantities, interest rates, exchange rates, dollars of wealth, and so forth.

Variable cost. Refer to **cost, variable.**

Velocity of money. In serving its function as a medium of exchange, money moves from buyer to seller to new buyer and so on. Its "velocity" refers to the speed of this movement. The *income velocity of money* is defined as nominal GDP divided by the total money supply $V \equiv P \times Q/M \equiv \text{GDP}/M$.

Vertical equity. See **horizontal equity vs. vertical equity.**

Vertical integration. See **integration, vertical vs. horizontal.**

Vertical merger. See **merger.**

Voluntarily unemployed. Term applied to individuals who are unemployed because they perceive the value of wages to be less than the opportunity use of time, say, in leisure.

W

Wealth. The net value of tangible and financial items owned by a nation or person at a point in time. It equals all assets less all liabilities.

Welfare economics. The normative analysis of economic systems, i.e., the study of what is "wrong" or "right" about the economy's functioning.

Welfare state. A concept of the mixed economy arising in Europe in the late nineteenth century and introduced in the United States in the 1930s. In the modern conception of the welfare state, markets direct the detailed activities of day-to-day economic life while governments regulate social conditions and provide pensions, health care, and other aspects of the social safety net.

What, how, and *for whom.* The three fundamental problems of economic organization. *What* is the problem of how much of each possible good and service will be produced with the society's limited stock of resources or inputs.

How is the choice of the particular technique by which each good shall be produced. *For whom* refers to the distribution of consumption goods among the members of that society.

Winner-take-all games. Situations in which payoffs are determined by merit relative to other competitors/players rather than by absolute merit. These contests generally are characterized by rewards heavily or entirely concentrated among the very best competitors.

Y

Yield. Same as the **interest rate** or **rate of return** on an asset.

Z

Zero-profit point. For a business firm, that level of price at which the firm breaks even, covering all costs but earning zero profit.

Note: Page references in **boldface** indicates Glossary terms; page numbers followed by n indicate footnotes.

Index